# WHERE TO SKI AND Snowboard 2005

The 1,000 Best Winter Sports Resorts in Europe and North America

**GET THE COST OF THIS BOOK REFUNDED WHEN YOU BOOK YOUR NEXT HOLIDAY!**
If you book your next winter sports holiday through the specialist travel agency Ski Solutions, you can get the cost of this book knocked off the bill.

There's no catch. Ski Solutions sells the complete range of package holidays offered by UK bonded tour operators. And if that choice isn't enough, they can tailor-make a holiday just for you.

When you make your booking, fill in the two forms at the back of the book. Ski Solutions will knock £16.99 off your bill. That's all there is to it.

Ski Solutions are on 020 7471 7700.

**GET THE NEXT EDITION FREE! BY SENDING US RESORT REPORTS**
We are keen to get feedback on the resorts our readers visit. The 100 best reports earn a free copy of the new edition, in advance of publication. What's more, regular book winners may be invited to become 'resort observers', getting free lift passes in exchange for specially detailed reports.

On page 10 there's guidance on what feedback we need. Send e-mails to:
**reports@snow-zone.co.uk**
or write to:
**Where to Ski and Snowboard**
**FREEPOST SN815**
**The Old Forge**
**Norton St Philip**
**Bath BA2 7ZZ**

# WHERE *to* SKI AND Snowboard 2005

The 1,000 Best Winter Sports Resorts in Europe and North America

Edited by
**Chris Gill**
and
**Dave Watts**

NortonWood

Published in Great Britain by
NortonWood Publishing
The Old Forge
Norton St Philip
Bath BA2 7LW
United Kingdom

tel 01373 835208
e-mail w9@snow-zone.co.uk

*Editors* Chris Gill and Dave Watts
*Assistant editors* Mandy Crook, Catherine Weakley, Emma Morris, Leigh Thompson, Robin Campbell, Henry Druce, Wendy-Jane King, Sheila Reid
*Australia/NZ editor* Bronwen Gora
*Contributors* Chris Allan, Alan Coulson, Nicky Holford, James Hooke, Eric Jackson, Tim Perry, Adam Ruck, Helena Wiesner, Ian Porter

*Advertising manager* Sam Palmer

Design by Val Fox
Production by Guide Editors
Contents photos generally by Snowpix.com / Chris Gill
*Production manager* Ian Stratford
*Production assistant* Alex Gill
*Proof-reader* Sally Vince
Printed and bound in Italy by Officine Grafiche Calderini SpA

10 9 8 7 6 5 4 3 2 1

ISBN 0 9536371 6 6

A CIP catalogue entry for this book is available from the British Library.

Book trade sales are handled by
Portfolio Books Ltd
Unit 5, Perivale Industrial Park
Horsenden Lane South
Greenford UB6 7RL

tel 020 8997 9000
fax 020 8997 9097
e-mail sales@portfoliobooks.com

Individual copies of the book can be bought by phoning: **01373 835208**

This edition published 2004

# Contents

# Resort chapters

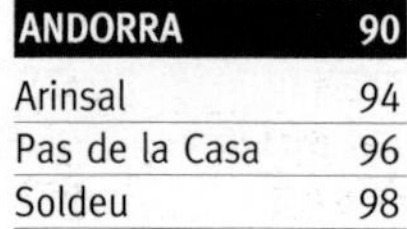

# About this book

***It's simply the best***

In the first edition of *Where to Ski,* in 1994, we said that we believed it was the best guide to winter sports resorts that you could buy. Ten years on, the gap between this and rival guides is wider than ever. Here's why:

- With every new edition we try to take a step forward in the way we cover the world of skiing and boarding. This year, we've introduced a new style of short chapter so that we can **cover more resorts in detail**. These Short Turns entries are gathered together at the end of each country section (or state/region section in North America). Over the years, we have expanded the book from 512 to 704 pages, increasing the number of resorts covered in detail from 250 to over 400 and the total number covered from 500 to over 1,000.
- By making the most of technology we are able to go to press later every year, and get the late-breaking news that makes the book **up to date for the 2004/05 season ahead**. (When we started, we went to press in June; three years ago it was mid-July; this year, it's 8 August.) To see what we mean, check out our 'What's new?' chapter, crammed with new resort developments.
- We work hard to make our information **reader-friendly**, with clearly structured text, comparative ratings and no-nonsense verdicts for the main aspects of each resort.
- We don't hesitate to express **critical views**. We learned our craft at Consumers' Association, where Chris became editor of *Holiday Which?* magazine and Dave became editor of *Which?* itself – so a consumerist attitude comes naturally to us.
- Our resort chapters give an **unrivalled level of detail** – including scale plans of each major resort and all the facts you need about them.
- We benefit enormously from the **reports that hundreds of readers send in on the resorts they visit**. The 100 best reports are rewarded by a free copy of the book, and many of our best regular reporters get a free week's lift pass. (Prove your worth by sending us useful reports, and you too could ski for free.)
- We use **colour printing** fully – this year more than ever. We include not only piste maps for every major resort but also scores of photographs, chosen not just to add colour but to allow you to see for yourself what the resorts are like.

Our ability to keep on improving *Where to Ski and Snowboard* is largely due to the support of our advertisers – many of whom have been with us since the first edition in 1994. We are grateful for that support, and hope our readers will in turn support our advertisers.

We are uncompromising in our commitment to helping you, our readers, to make an informed choice; we're confident that you'll find this edition the best yet. Enjoy your skiing and riding this season.

Chris Gill and Dave Watts
Norton St Philip, 8 August 2004

# WHERE *to* SKI AND SNOWBOARD 2006

# Get next year's edition **free!**

## by reporting on your holiday

**There are too many resorts for us to visit them all every year, and too many hotels, bars and mountain restaurants for us to see. So we are very keen to encourage more readers to send in reports on their holiday experiences. As usual, we'll be giving 100 copies of the next edition to the writers of the best reports.**

There are five main kinds of feedback we need:

- what you particularly **liked and disliked** about the resort
- what aspects of the resort came as a **surprise** to you
- your other suggestions for **changes to our evaluation** of the resort – changes we should make to the ratings, verdicts, descriptions etc
- your experience of **queues** and other weaknesses in the lift system, and the **ski school** and associated childcare arrangements
- your feedback on **individual facilities** in the resort – the hotels, bars, restaurants (including mountain restaurants), nightspots, equipment shops, sports facilities etc.

You can send your reports to us in three ways. In order of preference, they are:

- by e-mail to: reports@snow-zone.co.uk (don't forget to give us your postal address)
- word-processed and printed on paper
- handwritten on a form that we can provide.

Consistently helpful reporters are invited to become 'resort observers', which means that when possible we'll arrange free lift-passes in your holiday resorts, in exchange for detailed reports on those resorts.

**Our postal address is:**

Where to Ski and Snowboard, FREEPOST SN815,
The Old Forge, Norton St Philip, Bath BA2 7ZZ

# Ten years on

***A lot has changed since this book was first published***

*Where to Ski and Snowboard* is 10 years old with this edition. We published our first hard-hitting reviews of ski resorts way back in 1994. Looking back, there have been some big changes since then.

**FRANCE FLYING HIGH**

In the early 1990s Austria was the most popular country for British skiers. According to the Crystal Ski Industry report, Austria then attracted around 33% of UK skiers, with France in second place with 29%. Now France is the destination of choice for over 36% of us, with only 20% going to Austria. Italy is not far behind, doubling its market share over the decade to attract 16% of UK skiers. North America has grown from a mere 2% to 6% over the period. The main losers have been Switzerland and Bulgaria, whose shares have fallen from 10% to 5% and 8% to 2% respectively. For those of you busily totalling these shares and finding they don't add up to 100%, last season almost all the missing 15% of UK skiers went to Andorra; Crystal's report doesn't have a comparable figure for ten years ago because it lumped Andorra in with 'other destinations'. All these percentages are of a rising number of ski and snowboard holidays being taken – up from 750,000 in 1994 to over a million in 2004.

Looking at the number of reports we receive from readers, a lot of the top resorts from ten years ago are still firm favourites. Over the last two seasons the top resorts (in order, most popular first) have been: Courchevel, Zermatt, Tignes, Banff, Méribel, Val-d'Isère, Serre-Chevalier, Cervinia, St Anton, Monterosa, Ischgl, Chamonix, La Plagne, Kitzbühel and Megève. Notable newcomers to this list, compared with ten years ago, are Banff – the only North American resort to break into the otherwise Alpine-dominated list – and a clutch of up and coming resorts that used to have very low profiles on the British market: Serre-Chevalier, Monterosa and Ischgl. Resorts that have dropped out include Les Arcs (which is, in our view, likely to see a revival now that the Vanoise Express and Arc 1950 are in place), Verbier, Alpe-d'Huez, Val-Thorens and Obergurgl.



**THE BIRTH OF BUDGET AIRLINES**

Ten years ago, budget flights to the Alps did not exist. EasyJet did not start flying to Geneva until the 1997/98 season. We were reliant on the high-priced national carriers such as British Airways and Swissair. But now budget flights have mushroomed; last season there were over 900,000 seats available to ski destination airports such as Geneva, Zürich, Salzburg and Turin. This has made arranging independent ski holidays much cheaper and easier.

**SNOWBOARDING AND TERRAIN-PARKS BECOME MAINSTREAM**

Ten years ago snowboarding was in its infancy and predominantly a teens and early-20s craze, with its own culture, disdain for 'two plankers' and a music-based après-ski scene. But now it has become mainstream and we are delighted to say that our appeal in last year's edition for more reports from snowboarders, to help make the book as useful as possible for boarders, resulted in a significant increase in snowboarder reports. So please keep those reports flowing in. This year, we are reserving ten of our hundred free books for the best reports on the snowboarding aspects of resorts.

Terrain-parks and half-pipes were rare in 1994, but now virtually every self-respecting resort (outside Italy, at least) has a park and many (especially in North America) have two or three, suitable for different standards of users. Whistler in Canada has four terrain-parks plus a half-pipe and a super-pipe.

## SKIING IS NOW EASIER, FASTER AND MORE FUN

Ten years ago most of us were still skiing around on what now seem old-fashioned 'skinny skis', and Ali Ross was pretty much the only well-known instructor around preaching the gospel of 'carving' – exploiting the waisted shape of the ski to produce a smooth turn, with no skidding. Now pretty much all skis have hour-glass shapes to provide vastly improved carving power and quicker turns. And they are shorter and wider to make skiing easier and more fun; the extra width on free-ride skis has made powder and off-piste much easier to ski and accessible to those of us who would have floundered around on skinny skis. Twin-tip skis have lured a lot of younger skiers who converted to snowboarding back to skiing – and terrain-parks now seem to be as popular with skiers as with boarders.

## BRITISH-RUN SKI SCHOOLS TAKE OFF

After a long battle with the ESF, British-trained ski instructors with the top BASI 1 qualification at last won the right to work in the French Alps without having to pass a further French test. Ten years ago there were only a few British-run ski schools in the Alps – notably Masterclass (now Supreme) in Courchevel and the British Alpine Ski School (BASS) in Morzine and Les Gets. Now schools run by dynamic young British instructors are mushrooming. BASS now operates in several other resorts including Val-d'Isère, Tignes, Courchevel and Verbier. New Generation started up in Courchevel in 1998/99 and now operates in Méribel, Les Arcs and Val-d'Isère as well. Eureka in Serre-Chevalier and The Development Centre in Val-d'Isère are both owned and run by Brits. We normally get very positive reports about these new schools and they have brought a much-needed dose of competition to the ski school market and the complacency and protectionism of the ESF.

## GOODBYE TO QUEUES, HELLO TO CROWDS

Most of the serious lift queues that we complained about bitterly in the first edition have been eliminated. Who remembers these highlights of your holidays a decade back?

- the Hahnenkaam cable–car – the main way out of Kitzbühel – which shifted just 380 people an hour and created queues measured in hours. It has now been replaced by a gondola carrying six or seven times as many people an hour.
- the rickety old gondola at Tortin in Verbier where queues of over an hour to get back to Chassoure were not unusual
- the decrepit old funicular at Davos, which made many people take up cross-country rather than wait hours to get up to the Parsenn – this relic was not replaced until a couple of years ago.

But surprisingly some long-standing queues still exist, notably the top cable-car at the Grand Montets above Argentière in Chamonix, the Penken gondola in Mayrhofen and the gondola and train out of Grindelwald.

Austria.
You've arrived!
www.austria.info/uk

Pinguin-Design © anaplus

These days, crowded pistes are more of a problem than lift queues. Most Alpine resorts have ignored the fact that eliminating queues by building faster, higher-capacity lifts put more people on their pistes. As well as crowds, irresponsible skiing and riding add to the dangers. The blue Couloir run at Alpe-d'Huez has featured in these pages before as an example of the worst crowding – a 2004 reporter said of it: 'I witnessed more collisions in one week than I do in a year working as a traffic police officer on one of Britain's busiest motorways.' And another said of Verbier: 'I have never seen so many wipeouts, instances of ski rage and people ploughing into each other. My husband saw one guy fly over the piste on to a table in the restaurant. I saw people doing jumps about 20 yards away from a chair-lift with a huge queue. I have never been anywhere like it, with people showing such a complete lack of respect for others.'

In North America, these problems are much less of an issue because resorts plan new runs when they plan increased lift capacity – and they put resources into policing the trails (and the 'Slow Skiing' zones in particular), taking away the lift passes of people judged to be behaving irresponsibly. Quite right, too. Yob culture on the slopes ruins them for everyone else, and it's time the Alpine resort authorities tackled the problem.





### HAVE WINTER SPORTS GOT CHEAPER?

We had a vague idea that the costs of winter holidays had fallen in real terms over our decade of existence, and thought it would be interesting to quantify the change. After burrowing around in our archives for a few hours, what we found was a complicated picture.

Retail prices in the UK have gone up by 28% in the last ten years. Package holidays in major resorts – using the same hotels, with the same operators – have gone up appreciably more. The ten examples we looked at, across a range of countries, had gone up typically by 40% to 60%. But lift pass prices, in the Alps at least, have gone up less than prices in Britain. A rise of 15% to 20% is typical in major resorts, but there are some spectacular exceptions: weekly passes in Verbier and St Anton have risen hardly at all. In North America, though, it's a different picture altogether. In dollars, lift passes in major resorts cost almost twice their 1994 price; it's only because of the current strength of the pound against the US and Canadian dollars that the increase in £££ is more modest – around 50%. The difference between American and European lift pass prices is now huge – basically, they are twice the Alpine price. If you are crossing the pond, make sure you investigate advance purchase deals through tour operators, which can bring these prices down to Alpine levels.

### NOT IN COURCHEVEL, THEY HAVEN'T

This year, though, we've had reports of sky-high prices in Courchevel 1850 in particular, fuelled at least in part by a huge influx of affluent Russian visitors. Roman Abramovich and friends effectively take the place over in early January (the Russian Christmas holidays), with one local claiming there were over 18,000 Russian visitors there from 2 to 12 January 2004, making up 95% of resort visitors. We've had reports of a bottle of wine on sale in a mountain restaurant at 9,500 euros (over £6,000) and four small beers in a bar in town costing £45, Another reporter told us that when Russians arrived in a restaurant where he was about to eat, he was 'moved to a terrible table right by the kitchen – abysmal service'.

**AND THE NEXT TEN YEARS?**
Since it's our birthday, we think we're entitled to a birthday wish or two. In the next ten years, as well as a clamp-down on yob culture on the pistes of the Alps, noted above, we'd like to see:
• Safer off-piste slopes in Europe. Some resorts, such as Avoriaz and Zermatt, are adopting the US-style approach of having areas of ungroomed slopes which they control for avalanches, opening and closing them according to the conditions. Let's see more.
• Standardised piste grading. There are just as many seriously undergraded and overgraded pistes in Europe as there always have been. What we need is a standardised grading system for pistes that applies throughout the skiing world – or at least Europe.

**AND FINALLY ...**
*Where to Ski and Snowboard* wouldn't be Britain's leading ski resort guide without the support of two groups of people. First, our thanks to those who take the trouble to send us invaluable reports on the resorts they visit. We reward the best with a free book, and a select band of readers have earned a free book every year since 1994 when the book started; so special thanks to David Holmes, Allen Joslin, Alan Shepherd, Sally Robson, Alison Biden and Maureen Grenville.

Thanks also to our advertisers. Quite a few have been with us since the second edition, but there is a smaller band who had the faith to support us from the very first edition and have stuck with us ever since: Le Ski, Flexiski, Ski Independence, Snow Fun, Ski Beat, Skiworld, Ski Solutions, Ski Weekend and Esprit Ski. To all of them special thanks, and best wishes for the decade ahead.

# LIVE IN AUSTRIA'S LARGEST SK

## FIVE REGIONS, 25 LOCATIONS, 860 KM SLOPE

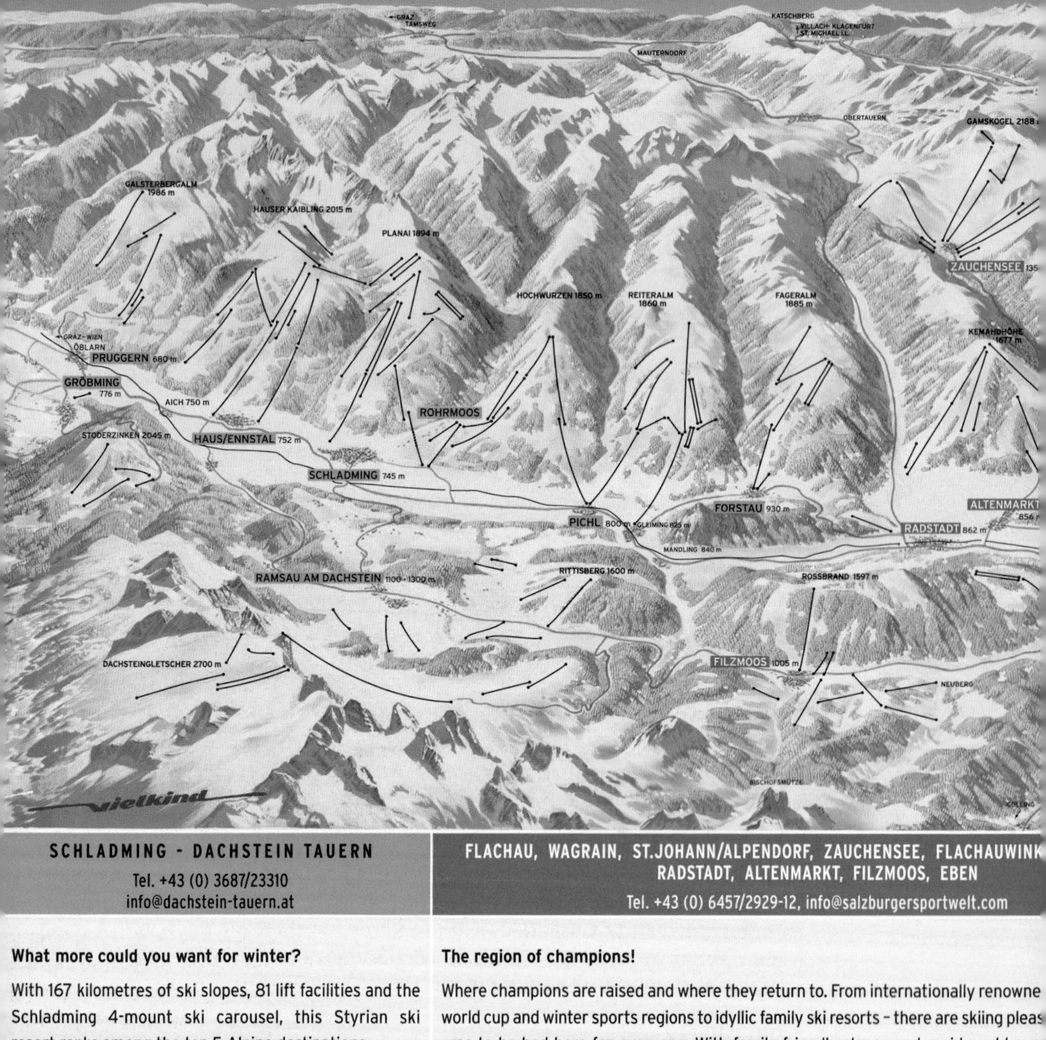

GRAZ
TAMSWEG
KATSCHBERG
VILLACH- KLAGENFURT
ST. MICHAEL I.L.
MAUTERNDORF
OBERTAUERN
GAMSKOGEL 2188
GALSTERBERGALM 1986 m
HAUSER KAIBLING 2015 m
PLANAI 1894 m
HOCHWURZEN 1850 m
REITERALM 1860 m
FAGERALM 1885 m
ZAUCHENSEE
KEMAHDHÖHE 1677 m
GRAZ-WIEN
ÖBLARN
PRUGGERN 680 m
GRÖBMING 776 m
AICH 750 m
ROHRMOOS
STODERZINKEN 2045 m
HAUS/ENNSTAL 752 m
SCHLADMING 745 m
FORSTAU 930 m
ALTENMARKT 856
PICHL 800 m
GLEIMING 825 m
RADSTADT 862 m
MANDLING 840 m
RAMSAU AM DACHSTEIN 1100 - 1300 m
RITTISBERG 1600 m
ROSSBRAND 1597 m
DACHSTEINGLETSCHER 2700 m
FILZMOOS 1005 m
NEUBERG
BISCHOFSMÜTZE
SOLLING
vielkind

**SCHLADMING - DACHSTEIN TAUERN**
Tel. +43 (0) 3687/23310
info@dachstein-tauern.at

**FLACHAU, WAGRAIN, ST.JOHANN/ALPENDORF, ZAUCHENSEE, FLACHAUWINK**
**RADSTADT, ALTENMARKT, FILZMOOS, EBEN**
Tel. +43 (0) 6457/2929-12, info@salzburgersportwelt.com

**What more could you want for winter?**

With 167 kilometres of ski slopes, 81 lift facilities and the Schladming 4-mount ski carousel, this Styrian ski resort ranks among the top 5 Alpine destinations.

**The region of champions!**

Where champions are raised and where they return to. From internationally renowne world cup and winter sports regions to idyllic family ski resorts – there are skiing pleas ures to be had here for everyone. With family friendly slopes and rapid world cup

## Click on this...

Live cams..."snow and slope info"...last minute deals...bookable offers...information regarding vacant rooms in hotels, pensions etc...can be found under **www.skiamade.com**

# Ski amadé

KREUZKOGEL 2686 m · SPORTGASTEIN 1590 m · GRAUKOGEL 2492 m · STUBNERKOGEL 2276 m · BAD GASTEIN 1002 m · HÜTTSCHLAG 1030 m · KREUZKOGEL 2027 m · SKIZENTRUM ANGERTAL 1176 m · SCHLOSSALM 2050 m · MOOSKOPF 1980 m · FULLSECK 2033 m · FLACHAUWINKL 1000 m · KLEINARL 1014 m · BAD HOFGASTEIN 860 m · SONNTAGSKOGEL 1849 m · GRIESSENKARECK 2000 m · GROSSARL 920 m · RAURIS · DORFGASTEIN 830 m · BRUCK a. G. · LEND · TAXENBACH · ALPENDORF 800 m · SCHWARZACH · WAGRAIN 850 m · ST. VEIT · GOLDEGG · SCHNEEBERG 1921 m · ZELL A. SEE · MAYERDÖRFL 941 m · FLACHAU 920 m · ST. JOHANN i. P. 600 m · ABERG LANGECK 2000 m · WASTLHÖHE 1730 m · MÜHLBACH 920 m · HOCHKEIL 1783 m · EBEN i. PONGAU 855 m · HÜTTAU · GABÜHEL 1634 m · BISCHOFSHOFEN 552 m · HINTERMOOS 1000 m · HINTERREIT 1000 m · DIENTEN 1071 m · WERFENWENG · NATRUN 1200 m · HINTERTHAL 1001 m · HOCHKÖNIG 2941 m · MARIA ALM 805 · SAALFELDEN · TENNENGEBIRGE · WERFEN · AUTOBAHN MÜNCHEN WIEN

| LEINARL, | GROSSARLTAL | HOCHKÖNIGS WINTERREICH | GASTEIN |
|---|---|---|---|
| | Tel. +43 (0) 6414/28112<br>amade@grossarltal.info | Tel. +43 (0) 6216/2020 2727-0<br>region@hochkoenig.at | Tel. +43 (0) 6432/3393-101<br>amade@gastein.com |
| | **A poem ...** | **Skiing in a majestic setting** | **Slopes to revel on and thermal baths to revel in!** |
| arving-, freestyle-, snowboard-, as well as floodlit runs. | Where things are still as they should be and the ski carousel takes you to "cloud nine". | Fairy-tale skiing enjoyment, authentic character and a cosy atmosphere. | Slopes and wellness fun at their best, with ski mountains up to 2,700 m in height and the world famous Gastein thermal baths. |

Further information can be found under:

**www.skiamade.com**

# What's new?

***New lifts and other major developments in top resorts***

## Andorra

**Arinsal/Pal** The gondola from the valley town of La Massana up to Pal is to open for the 2004/05 season. For 2003/04 the Cortal drag-lift in the beginners' area at Arinsal was replaced by a chair.

**Grand Valira** This is the new name for the linked slopes of Soldeu and Pas de la Casa. A joint lift pass was offered last season, and we understand this will be the only weekly pass available this season.

**Pas de la Casa** The Coma Blanca 1 drag is being replaced by a six-pack. A joint lift pass is now sold covering Soldeu (see above).

**Soldeu** For 2004/05 the chair from El Tarter to Riba Escorxada is to be replaced by an eight-seat gondola. A joint lift pass is now sold covering Pas de la Casa (see above).

## Austria

**Bad Gastein** A fast quad has replaced the triple chair from the Angertal up to Stubnerkogel.

**Ellmau** For 2004/05 a drag-lift serving the slopes between Hartkaiser and Astberg above Going will be replaced with a quad chair.

**Hintertux/Tux Valley** For 2004/05 the Eggalm Nord double chair-lift, which links the end of the red run from Rastkogel to the Eggalm slopes, is to be replaced by a fast six-seater chair with covers.



**Innsbruck** For 2003/04 an eight-person gondola opened on the Stubaier Gletscher, from the Eisgrat restaurant to the highest slopes on the Schaufelspitze. The Mutters ski area will stay closed for 2004/05.

**Ischgl** For 2003/04 a six-pack replaced the T-bar between Bodenalp and Höllenkar. Another six-pack was installed at Alp Trida and a further one is planned above it for 2004/05.

**Kitzbühel** For 2004/05 a new 30-person gondola is to link the main Hahnenkaam-Pengelstein and Jochberg-Pass Thurn areas, eliminating the need to ski down to the valley or catch a bus. The first lift after the new gondola, heading to Pass Thurn, is being upgraded from a T-bar to a six-pack. 2003/04 saw a new eight-person gondola from Skirast towards Pengelstein and a new fast quad on Gaisberg. The Bichlalm area was given over entirely to off-piste, with a snowcat replacing the top lift.

**Lech** For 2003/04 a fast eight-seater chair replaced the Steinmähder chair towards Zuger Hochlicht; one six-pack replaced the Hasensprung and another now connects Lech and Zürs. A new T-bar at Rüfikopf gives easier access to two good ski routes.

**Mayrhofen** For 2004/05 a fast six-pack is due ti replace a T-bar in the Horberg sector. For 2003/04 the Tappenalm double chair became a fast eight-seater, the Knorren double chair a six-pack and the Finkenberg 2 double chair an eight-seater gondola. Austria's steepest piste (gradient of up to 78%) opened beneath the new Knorren chair.

**Montafon** For 2004/05 Golm will get a new quad chair-lift with covers. The Aussergolmbahn will replace a T-bar and extend up to Grüneck, where a new ski-tunnel, built for 2003/04, links the slopes of Aussergolm with the main Golm slopes. The Zamangbahn gondola was upgraded for 2003/04.

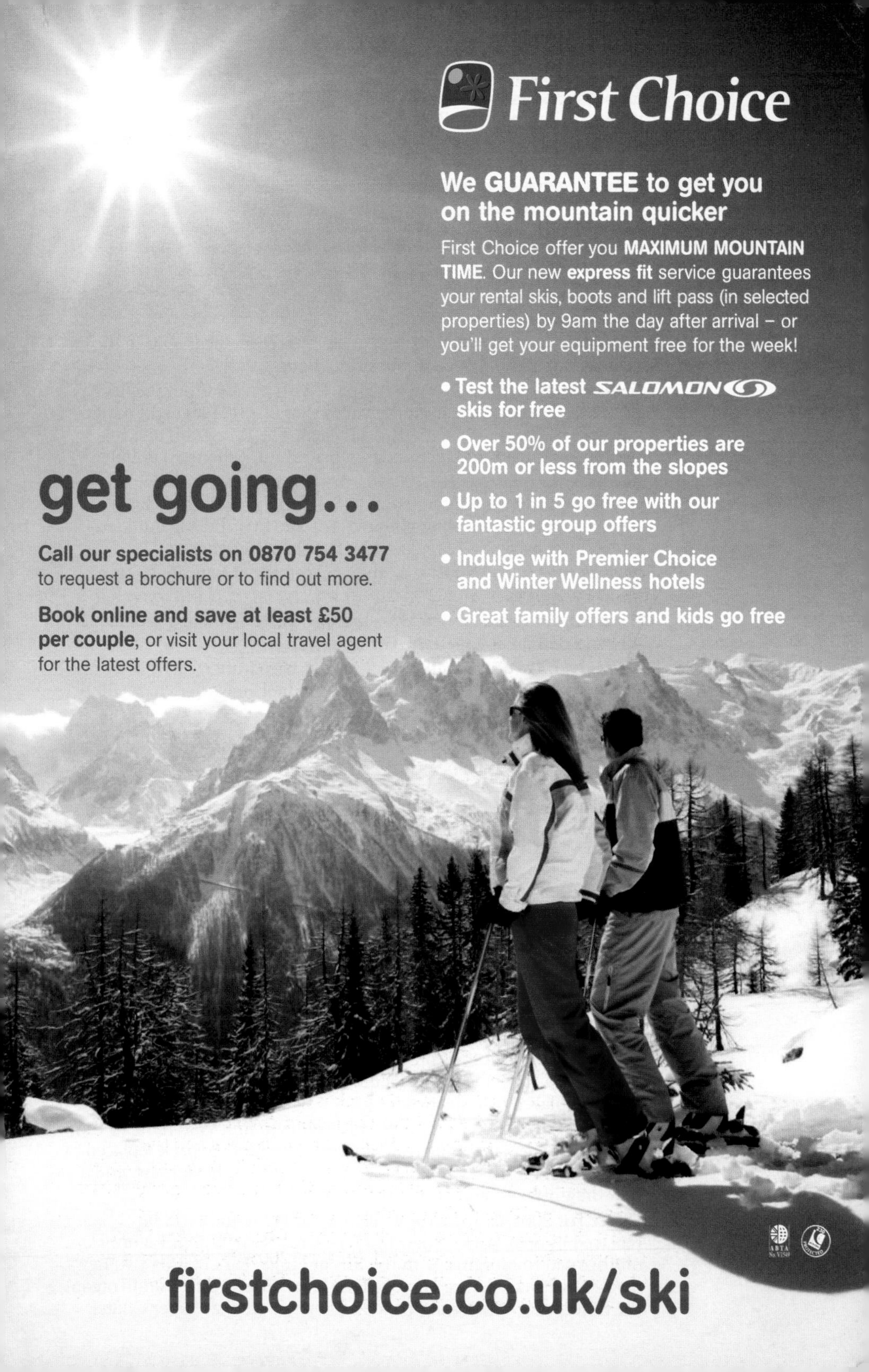
First Choice
We GUARANTEE to get you on the mountain quicker
First Choice offer you MAXIMUM MOUNTAIN TIME. Our new express fit service guarantees your rental skis, boots and lift pass (in selected properties) by 9am the day after arrival – or you'll get your equipment free for the week!
• Test the latest SALOMON skis for free
• Over 50% of our properties are 200m or less from the slopes
• Up to 1 in 5 go free with our fantastic group offers
• Indulge with Premier Choice and Winter Wellness hotels
• Great family offers and kids go free
get going...
Call our specialists on 0870 754 3477 to request a brochure or to find out more.
Book online and save at least £50 per couple, or visit your local travel agent for the latest offers.
firstchoice.co.uk/ski

**Obergurgl** For 2004/05 a six-seat chair with covers will replace the Schermerbahn double chair out of Hochgurgl.

**Obertauern** For 2004/05 a new six-pack with covers should replace the Gamsleiten double from the valley. For 2003/04 an eight-seater gondola replaced the Zehnerkar cable-car. The Kringsalm quad became a six-pack and a fast quad replaced the Achenrain double.

**Saalbach-Hinterglemm** For 2004/05 the two successive Westgipfel double chairs from Hinterglemm to Schattberg West are to be replaced by an eight-seater gondola. For 2003/04 the Asitzmulden and Zehner T-bars were replaced by fast six-seater chairs.

**Schladming** For 2003/04 a six-pack replaced two T-bars above Haus.

**Sölden** For 2004/05 the Seiterkar lift is to be upgraded to a six-seat chair with covers. The new two-stage Schwarze Schneid gondola has also speeded up access to the two glaciers.

**Söll** For 2004/05 a new quad will replace the Grundried T-bar serving the black run below Hohe Salve. The Hopfgartenchair will be replaced by an eight-person gondola.

**St Anton** In 2003/04 a fast six-seat chair replaced the Arlenmähder T-bar above the Arlberg Pass, running to a new, higher top station. Another six-pack replaced the T-bar to Gampberg, on Rendl.

**Westendorf** In 2003/04 a new quad chair, the Schneeberglift, replaced the T-bar on the nursery slopes near the centre.

## France

**Alpe-d'Huez** For 2004/05 a Funitel jumbo gondola, the Marmottes III, will go from the top of the Marmottes II gondola to the Sarenne glacier. For 2003/04 the Lac Blanc chair-lift was upgraded to a quad.

**Les Arcs** For 2003/04 the Vanoise Express cable-car linked Les Arcs to La Plagne. The mini-resort of Arc 1950 opened, and an open-topped gondola connects it to Arc 2000. In this area, the Bois de L'Ours chair towards 1800 and the Marmottes drag were replaced by six-packs.

**Avoriaz** In 2003/04 the Zore chair-lift above the gondola from Morzine was upgraded to a fast quad. For 2004/05 the Fornet chair will be replaced by a six-pack.

**Chamonix** For 2004/05 a new gondola is due to link Vallorcine to the Le Tour-Col de Balme ski area. For 2003/04 a new six-pack replaced the Herse chair from Croix de Lognan at the Grands Montets, and a new drag-lift was built at the top of Flégère.

**Châtel** For 2004/05 the two-seater chair at Pré-la-Joux will be replaced by a six-pack. A new piste, Le Gros Nant, will link Vonnes, on the road to Morgins, with the lifts at Linga. For 2003/04 two new drags were installed. One improved the link between Châtel and Torgon, the other serves the terrain-park and boarder-cross at Super-Châtel.

**La Clusaz/Le Grand-Bornand** The Beauregard cable-car at La Clusaz was replaced for 2003/04, tripling capacity. Le Grand-Bornand replaced the Maroly drag-lift with a six-person chair.

**Courchevel** For 2004/05 a new six-pack is due to replace the Les Tovets drag from 1550 to 1850 and the Dou du Midi chair here will be removed. The centre of 1850 is being rebuilt.

**Les Deux-Alpes** The La Toura chair-lift at mid-mountain has been replaced by a fixed-grip quad with moving carpet.

**Flaine** A new eight-seat gondola linked Samoëns directly to Samoëns 1600 for 2003/04. A new quad chair replaced the Damoiseaux drag-lift at Samoëns 1600. The snowmaking system is being revamped.

**Les Gets** The Perrières six-pack opened up a new way to La Rosta and Ranfolly. The Chavannes and Charniaz chairs were replaced.

**Megève** For 2004/05 the Le Jaillet and La Giettaz slopes will be linked by three new runs and two drag-lifts.

**Les Menuires** For 2004/05 a six-pack with covers to Roc des 3 Marches is planned to replace two drag-lifts. For 2003/04 more snowmaking was installed, and a six-pack replaced two drags above Les Menuires.

**Méribel** For 2004/05 a new fast chair is planned to replace the slow Plan de l'Homme chair from Méribel to halfway up Tougnète.

**Montgenèvre** For 2003/04 the Tremplin drag was replaced by a chair and a new red slope was added.

**Morzine** For 2004/05, the Fornet chair is to be replaced by a six-pack.

**La Plagne** For 2004/05 access from Montchavin to L'Arpette will be improved by six-packs replacing the Bijolin chair and the two Salla drags. In 2003/04 the Vanoise Express cable-car linked La Plagne with Les Arcs, to form Paradiski.

SNOWPIX.COM / CHRIS GILL

Not before time, Les Sybelles is getting some fast chairs this winter ↓

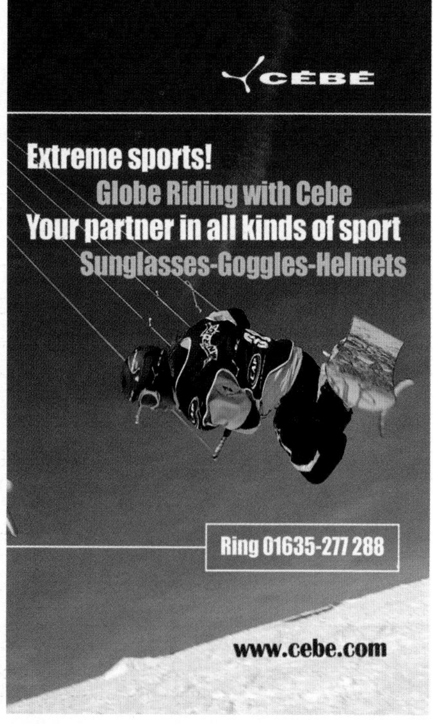

**Risoul** A new boarder-cross park was built off Peyrefolle for 2003/04. It includes a half-pipe, handrail and big air.

**La Rosière** For 2004/05 two six-packs are planned to replace the main Roches Noires chair out of the resort and the Les Eucherts drag-lift.

**Serre-Chevalier** For 2003/04 the Bletonet triple chair at the bottom of Chantemerle was replaced by a fast six-pack, doubling capacity.

**St-Martin-de-Belleville** For 2004/05 there will be long-promised improvements to the drag-lift from the church up to the main slope. A six-pack with covers to Roc des 3 Marches above St-Martin is planned to replace two drag-lifts.

**Les Sybelles** For 2004/05 two successive six-packs will go from the lift base at St-Sorlin-d'Arves to Les Perrons and the link to the rest of Les Sybelles. In La Toussuire, the chair to Grande Verdette will be replaced by a six-pack, meeting another new six-pack to Tête de Ballard and the link to the rest of Les Sybelles.

**Tignes** For 2004/05 the Merle Blanc and Grattalu chairs are to be replaced by fast chairs. For 2003/4 the terrain-park was moved from Le Lac to Val Claret. A new gondola from Les Boisses to the top of the Chaudannes chair above Le Lac is due at the end of 2005.

**Val-d'Isère** For 2003/04 a six-pack replaced the double chair linking Solaise and Col de l'Iseran. The Plan chair on Solaise was removed, allowing Piste M to be remodelled.

**Val-Thorens** For 2003/04 a gondola replaced the Bouquetin chair towards Méribel.

## Italy

**Bormio** For 2004/05 two new chair-lifts will access Cima Bianca from mid-mountain. For 2003/04 the queue-prone cable-car from the base to Bormio 2000 was replaced by a gondola.

**Cervinia** For 2003/04 a tunnel was built under the road so you can ski down to the gondola station in Valtournenche.

**Cortina d'Ampezzo** For 2004/05 the Pian di Ra Bigontina chair-lift at Faloria will be replaced by a fast quad. New cross-country tracks will be opened at Passo Tre Croci.

**Courmayeur** For the 2003/04 season a new boarder-cross run was created by the Plan de la Gabba chair.

**Livigno** For 2003/04 a six-pack replaced a drag in the Federia sector.

**Madonna di Campiglio** For 2004/05 a new six-pack is planned for the top Groste slopes, replacing the two parallel chairs Groste I and II. In 2003/04 a fast quad with covers replaced two chair-lifts serving the slopes between Monte Vigo and Pradalago.

**Monterosa Ski** From 2004/05 Alagna should finally be linked to and from Gressoney by a piste and a new 100-person cable-car.

**Sauze d'Oulx** For 2004/05 there is to be a new gondola up from Cesana and a new lift on M Fraiteve. For 2003/04 the Soleil Boeuf chair was replaced by the fast Ski Lodge quad.

**Selva/Sella Ronda** For 2004/05 a new underground funicular will link Ciampinoi and Col Raiser/Seceda. The Floralpina drag is to be replaced by a fast quad. In Alta Badia, the Piz chair out of San Cassiano is to be replaced by an eight-seat gondola. On Marmolada it is hoped the cable-car to the glacier will be upgraded.

**Sestriere** For 2004/05 the Clos dell'Acqua drag is to be replaced. For 2003/04 the Garnel drag was replaced by a quad chair and the Trebials chair from Borgata by a fast quad.

## SWITZERLAND

**CHAMPÉRY** For 2004/05 a National Ice Sports Centre will open.

**CRANS-MONTANA** For 2004/05 the Toula chair-lift is being upgraded to a six-pack. A new black run is being created off it.

**DAVOS** For 2003/04 a new toboggan run opened on Madrisa. On the Jakobshorn snowmaking was installed on the Gämpen piste down to Bolgen. The Klosters bypass road is due for completion in 2005.

**GRINDELWALD** The railway from Grindelwald to the Kleine Scheidegg is to get new rolling stock and a 'more sophisticated' timetable for 2004/05. For 2003/04 the Läger double chair-lift on Männlichen was replaced by a fast quad with covers, doubling capacity.

**VERBIER** New marked trails for snow-shoeing are planned for 2004/05. Two pistes solely for slower skiers are planned – one on Savoleyres and one at La Chaux. For 2003/04 a new snow bridge was built at Col Brunet to avoid congestion and collisions.

**VILLARS** For 2003/04 a new terrain-park was made on the top of Chaux Ronde with three difficulty levels.

**WENGEN** For 2004/05 the double chair from Innerwengen to Allmend is to be replaced by a fast quad. For 2003/04 the slow Läger double chair on Männlichen was replaced by a fast quad.

**ZERMATT** For 2003/04 two new six-packs were built, one from Trockener Steg to Furggsattel, the other from Riffelberg to Gifthittli, below Gornergrat. For 2004/05 more snowmaking is planned.

## UNITED STATES

### CALIFORNIA

**HEAVENLY** For 2004/05 the Powderbowl and Waterfall chairs will be replaced by a fast six-pack.

**MAMMOTH** For 2004/05 a fast quad will replace the triple Chair 17 above Canyon Lodge. The first phase of the Village at Mammoth was opened in 2003/04, with a gondola up to the Canyon Lodge lift base.

### COLORADO

**ASPEN** For 2004/05 a fast quad will replace the Buttermilk West chair. On Aspen Mountain the oldest chair in the resort – the F.I.S. – is due to be replaced by a new two-seater.

**BEAVER CREEK** For 2004/05 a new base area will be created close to the valley town of Avon. Two fast quads will link to the main slopes at the top of Strawberry Park via Bachelor Gulch.

**KEYSTONE** Keystone will expand its terrain by 860 acres this season by operating snowcats to access Erickson Bowl and Little Bowl.

**STEAMBOAT** For 2004/05 a new triple chair will replace the Burgess Creek double.

**VAIL** For 2004/05 a yurt will be built at Two Elk. Snowmaking will be improved on eastern areas of Golden Peak.

**WINTER PARK** For 2004/05 Intrawest plans to invest $4 million to improve the learning zone in Sorensen Park.

### REST OF THE WEST

**ALTA** For 2004/05 a fast quad will replace the Collins and Germania chairs. The start of the Wildcat chair will be moved.

**BIG SKY** For 2004/05, a fast quad chair is due to replace the triple Southern Comfort on Andesite Mountain.

**THE CANYONS** For 2003/04, the terrain-park was moved to a higher location by the Snow Canyon lift.

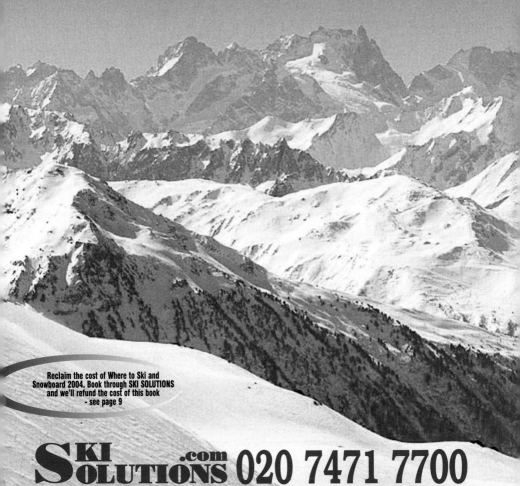

**Deer Valley** For 2004/05 a fast quad to the top of Flagstaff and a short triple linking Flagstaff to Bald Mountain are planned.

**Park City** For 2003/04 a fourth terrain-park was created and 'fast lanes' introduced on four lifts.

**Snowbird** For 2004/05 there is to be a new super-pipe next to the intermediate Big Emma terrain-park.

**Smugglers' Notch** 2004/05 will see more snowmaking on Morse Mountain and further gladed areas opened up on Sterling Mountain.

## Canada

### Western Canada

**Banff** In Sunshine Village a new fast quad has replaced the chair up to Mount Standish and the terrain has been increased with four new expert runs on Goat's Eye Mountain. The Wild West area, also on Goat's Eye, is due to open for 2004/05.

**Big White** For 2004/05 a two-person chair-lift will serve the steep Cliff area. A new terrain-park is being built above the village, served by a two-person chair and by Big White's first snowmaking.

**Fernie** For 2004/05 there will be more glading to thin out the trees. Better access is planned from Currie Bowl to the fast Great Bear chair.

**Panorama** For 2003/04 the Champagne Express fast quad replaced the two-person Horizon chair and the T-bar above it. The Summit T-bar to the top was replaced by a fixed-grip quad.

**Sun Peaks** For 2003/04 there were two new black runs on Mt Morrisey, a new blue on Sundance and a new floodlit tubing park.

**Whistler** For 2004/05 another 1,100 acres of terrain is due to open on Whistler Mountain. Four new runs from the Peak down to Whistler Creekside will open, as will 700 acres in Flute Bowl.

## Spain

At Sierra Nevada a new triple chair from Borreguiles and a new quad on Loma de Dîlar were installed for 2003/04.

**Baqueira-Beret** 2003/04 saw the first phase of an expansion in the Bonaigua area. Three new chairs, including two fast quads, opened, along with three new runs and two itineraries. For 2004/05 a new fast quad is planned, which will access Beret from Baqueira.

## Bulgaria

In Pamporovo, a new triple and a quad chair and three new runs are planned for 2004/05. In Borovets two new fast quads are planned to replace a single chair and a drag.

## Finland

For 2004/05 in Levi the Himmeriikki lift is being moved to the southern side of the mountain.

## Norway

**Hemsedal** For 2004/05 a new eight-seat chair is planned to replace the Holvinheisen lift from the base to the mid-mountain.

## Scotland

At the Lecht, the new day lodge is due to open for 2004/05. At Cairngorm there are plans to move two button lifts to the Ptarmigan Bowl to improve access for novices.

# Buying property

***Fancy a chalet or apartment on the slopes?***

*by* **Dave Watts**

**Buying your own place in a ski resort has been many people's ambition for years. And now more and more of us are doing just that – the numbers of Britons buying in the Alps has at least doubled in the last five years and, according to some sources it has tripled. And we are buying places in North America too. So where should you look, what can you expect to pay and what are the pitfalls to beware of?**

Most people see the idea of a place in the snow as a mixture of pleasure and investment. They hope to use their place themselves for a few weeks a year and let it out for the rest of the winter (and perhaps for part of the summer too).

Jon Wyatt bought one of the first of a new development of chalets to be built in Ste-Foy-Tarentaise and completed at Christmas 2001. For £300,000 he and his partner bought a chalet with a main four-bedroomed two-storey unit and a separate two-bedroomed apartment beneath. Since they bought, a lot more development has gone on and the surrounding area was a building site for the first season or two. But prices have soared and new four-bedroomed chalets being built now are priced at around £550,000.

'Initially, I was looking at better-known resorts but prices were too high so I decided to look at smaller resorts,' said Jon. 'We bought it mainly because of our love of skiing and snowboarding and had originally planned to spend a few weeks there each year. But because of work commitments that hasn't worked out as we had hoped; last year we spent a week there in January and a few days in August. But we have been able to rent it out pretty much non-stop all through the winter right from the start and even for a few weeks in the summer. The apartment is getting more difficult now though, because competition from other owners has increased as more apartments have been built. That is putting a damper on the rent that we can get.'



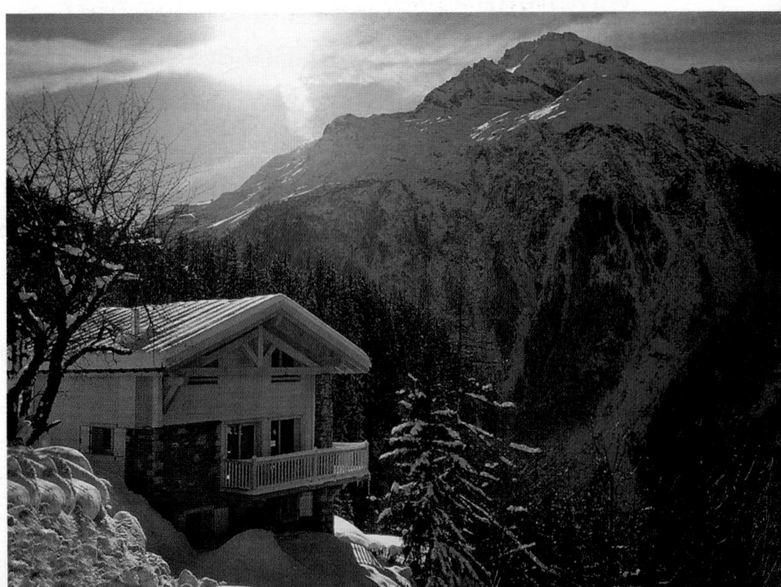

JON WYATT / WWW.SKYSCAPES.CO.UK

Jon Wyatt's chalet in Ste-Foy-Tarentaise (see www.ste-foy-chalet.co.uk). He is delighted with it but wishes he could spend more time there →

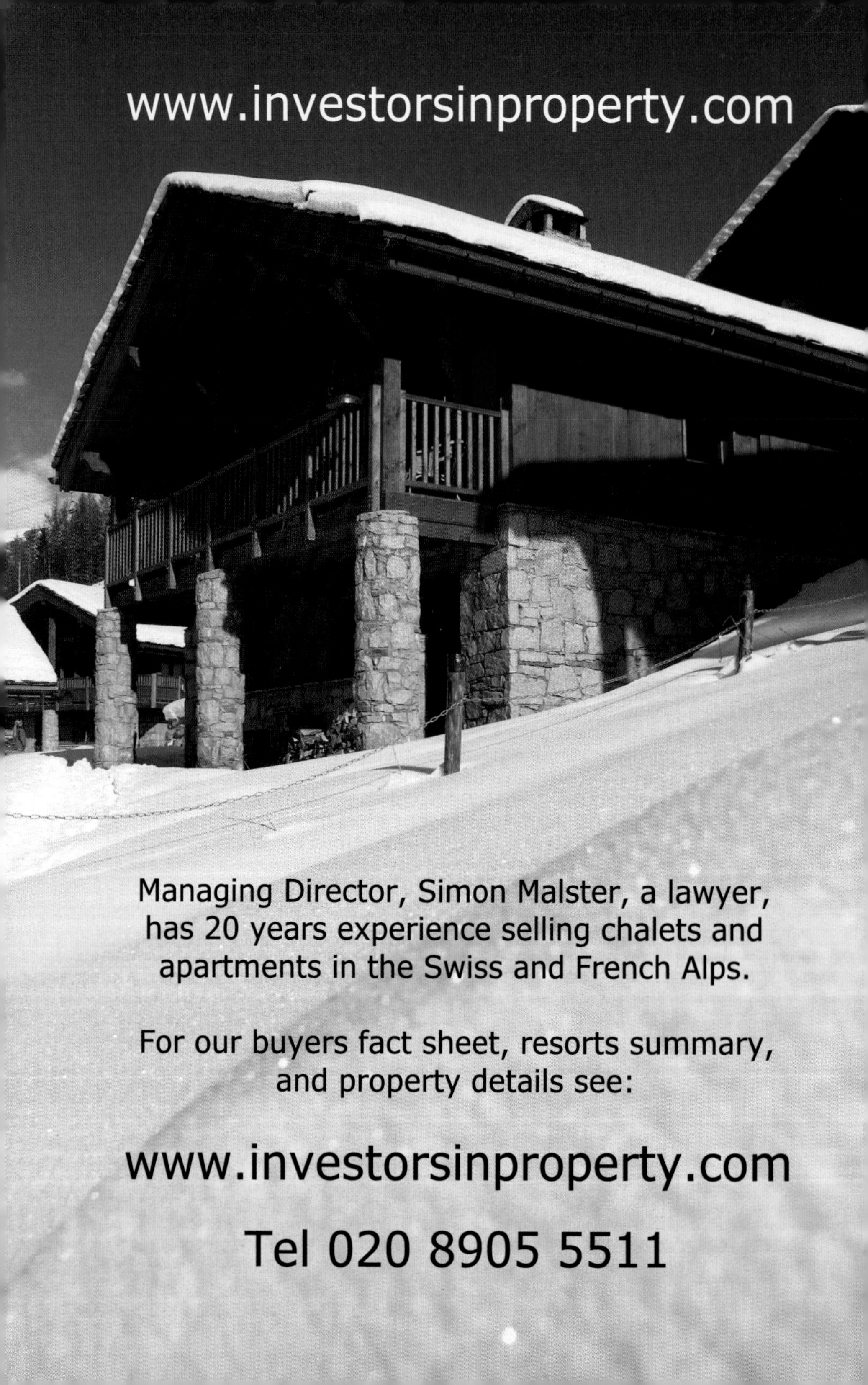
www.investorsinproperty.com
Managing Director, Simon Malster, a lawyer, has 20 years experience selling chalets and apartments in the Swiss and French Alps.
For our buyers fact sheet, resorts summary, and property details see:
www.investorsinproperty.com
Tel 020 8905 5511

Jon reckons the rent doesn't even cover the mortgage, let alone the other costs such as local taxes, utility bills, logs for the fire, cleaning and changeover costs etc. He decided to finance the purchase through a euro mortgage rather than a UK one because the interest rate was lower and the monthly payments fixed for 20 years. 'But the rate is variable and has fallen, so whereas I expected to have around 16 years left on the mortgage now, there's currently only 13.'

**WHAT TO LOOK FOR**

Simon Malster of Investors in Property has been selling properties in the Alps for around 20 years. He says the key things to look for if you want a place primarily for the skiing are:

- to choose a resort which is high and snow-sure, charming and attractive and has a nice ambience

- to choose a property which has good views, is within walking distance of the centre of the resort and is either ski-in, ski-out or within walking distance of a lift.

Resorts with property available that fulfil these criteria include Arc 1950 in France and Saas-Fee in Switzerland, says Malster. If you are looking for more dual season use, he thinks you should consider places such as Megève (though this is very expensive) and Morzine in France, and Villars and Wengen in Switzerland.

Zigi Davenport of Alpine Apartments Agency says that there is a huge demand for properties in the Chamonix area, partly because it is so close to Geneva airport, which is served by a large number of cheap flights from the UK these days.

Although France is by far the most popular country to buy in, Malster recommends you look at Switzerland too. But he says, 'Foreigners are not allowed to buy all over Switzerland – only in certain communes. So, for example, you are allowed to buy in Saas-Fee but not in neighbouring Zermatt.' He reckons that Swiss property is more spacious and cheaper per square metre than in France. In general you can expect to pay the same in Swiss francs (2.2 to the pound at the time we went to press) as in euros (1.5 to the pound) for the same amount of space, which makes Switzerland 30 per cent cheaper.

For example, says Malster, you can expect to pay around £320,000 for 60 square metres in Arc 1950 in France, or £275,000 for 75 square metres in Wengen or Saas-Fee in Switzerland.

Erna Low began working with the Canadian company, Intrawest, as their UK PR and sales representative when they developed their first resort in Europe, Arc 1950. Joanna Yellowlees-Bound, chief executive of Erna Low, said, 'I started looking at the apartments from a point of view of renting for our tour operator business but I was so impressed that we ended up buying a three-bedroomed apartment there of our own. It became quickly apparent that the strategic alliance between Intrawest and Erna Low was very strong, with many Erna Low clients looking to invest in ski properties – mainly in Europe, but also now in North America where Intrawest have properties, including in resorts such as Tremblant in Québec, which is a friendly year-round resort, and Whistler in British Columbia. So, as well as tour operating and resort representation, we have now branched out into property sales. We are also hoping to soon have properties in Colorado, USA, as well – in Aspen's Snowmass area and in Keystone's River Run area.'

## NEW OR RESALES

There has been a lot of building going on in recent years, especially in the French Alps and North America. Many new French and North American properties are offered on a sale-and-leaseback arrangement where you buy the property but lease it back to the management company after reserving a certain number of weeks for yourself. The management company puts your property along with others into a 'rental pool' and shares the rental out (after deducting the management charges) between the owners at the end of each year. One advantage of this in France is that you can then claim back the 19.6% VAT that is charged on newly built property (some developers do this for you so you never have to pay the VAT out). The leaseback period has to be for at least nine years and the rental yield is 'likely to be around 3% in the early years rising to, say, 7% in the later years', says Joanna Yellowlees-Bound.

Around half the properties that Investors in Property sells are resales and half new. 'But in France in particular, some of the older buildings are not nearly so attractive as the newer ones – they tend to be much more cramped,' says Simon Malster. But Zigi Davenport pointed out that building was now slowing down in France. 'Since July 2002 the Savoie region has said that there can be no more new building in open spaces. They will allow infilling in a village if land adjoins a main road, but elsewhere it has put a stop to much that was planned. In the centre of Méribel, for example, there has been virtually no new building in the last two years and any older building now has greater potential for renovation.'

## BUYING COSTS, TAX AND OTHER FINANCIAL CONSIDERATIONS

Each country has its own legal system and tax laws, which can complicate things. For example, in Switzerland buying costs depend on where the property is and could amount to up to 5 per cent. The annual tax also varies but can be over 1 per cent. But Switzerland charges no income tax on rental income (though it will be taxable in the UK). There may be restrictions about when you will be able to resell it.

In France, expect the notary's legal fees to be 2 to 3 per cent for properties less than five years old; and there are additional purchase taxes of almost 5 per cent if you are buying a property more than five years old. Rental income has to be declared to the French tax authorities but you should be able to reclaim any French tax you pay against your UK liability. French inheritance laws regarding property are complicated and need to be taken account of. And there may be capital gains tax issues.

Some people buy their properties through companies they set up to get round various legal and tax issues. But this issue has been clouded by a recent suggestion that occupation of a company-owned home could be classed as a 'benefit in kind' and be taxed. On the other hand, the Chancellor of the Exchequer has announced that 'buy to let' properties will be able to be included in self-administered personal pension plans soon, bringing tax advantages.

You may find it pays to have an expert in foreign property and tax laws to advise you on the best way to structure any purchase and to deal with the tax implications.

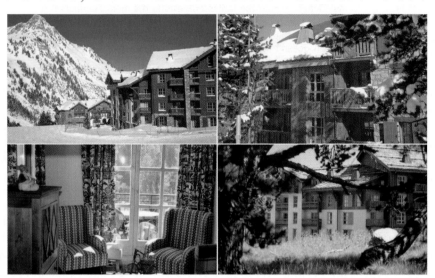

# New gear for 2005

***The latest kit means more fun for less effort***

*by* **Dave Watts**

TOP FREERIDE SKIS:
**Rossignol Bandit B2**
**Salomon Scream 10 Hot**

**Skis just keep on getting shorter, wider and more fun. Boots are becoming comfier and more responsive to help get the best performance out of the radical sidecuts of the latest skis. On the snowboard front, boots are at last getting more stylish and colourful, step-in bindings are all but dead and 'step-outs' are all the rage. And with both skis and snowboards high-performance women-specific models are being developed to help the ladies outperform the men. The market for helmets and protective gear is on the up and there's good news for those who can't stand being without their sound systems on the slopes (which doesn't include us, I hasten to add).**

↑ Two top free-ride skis: Volkl 724 Pro Head Monster IM 75

Skis have changed beyond recognition in the last 10 years, the changes being ushered in by the carving revolution which started in the early 1990s. The upshot of this is that we are now skiing on skis which are 20cm or more shorter than they were in the old days, and which provide more stability, performance and confidence in return for less effort. Skis are not just shorter but also wider, meaning more surface area, and they have hourglass shapes to provide vastly improved carving power and quicker turns. The major benefits of these new skis are better edge grip and more flotation – making off-piste attainable for a wider range of people – and skiing is now a lot less tiring. Last March I went on a week-long test of all the new skis for the 2005 season, organised by the Snowsports Industries of Great Britain (a trade body of UK equipment distributors and retailers). Out of over 400 skis from 14 different manufacturers in the test, there wasn't a poor ski to be seen.



### FREERIDE REVOLUTION CONTINUES

More and more people are now buying freeride skis to allow them to ski off-piste more easily and confidently. Because of their width they quite literally float through powder and crud alike, allowing you to ski for longer without getting tired and to tackle terrain that you would have floundered around in on a pair of narrower, traditional skis. The best of the latest generation of freeride skis work just as well on the piste as they do off, carving great turns at both low and high speed. My favourite in this category – and indeed in the whole test – was the Rossignol Bandit B2, now in its second year in the shops. Other models to look out for include the K2 Apache Recon, Head Monster IM 75, Salomon Scream 10 Hot, Stockli Stormrider XL (a Swiss ski relatively new to the UK market) and the Volkl 724 Pro. More high-performance skis made specially for women are now being made and the Rossignol Bandit B2 Women is a classic example.

If you want a ski specifically designed for those wanting to stick to the pistes, you are spoiled for choice, as not only are there on-piste

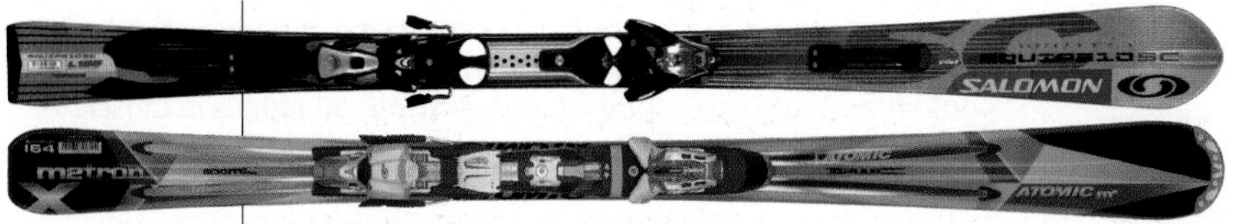


↑ Two new on-piste skis: Salomon Streetracer 10 Atomic Metron M10

skis but also a huge range marketed as skiercross skis. Skiercross is the newest type of ski race – instead of racing one at a time against the clock, in skiercross four or more skiers start at the same time. They then fly as fast as possible down a course that has bends, banks and jumps, and the only rule is that whoever crosses the finish line first wins. Collisions and falls are the norm and add to the fun.

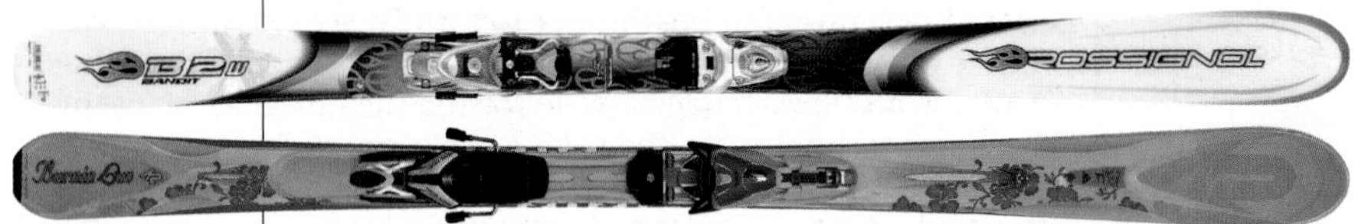


↑ Two high-performance women's skis: Rossignol Bandit B2 Women K2 Burnin' Luv

Of the new on-piste skis the top performers give fabulous edge grip and carving power. These include the Salomon Streetracer and Atomic Metron ranges – the latter being somewhat wider under the boot and so having rather more of an all-mountain personality – and the Rossignol Zenith range. Of the women-specific skis the K2 Burnin' Luv is a great performer. The top skiercross skis are derived from race GS skis but have a more radical sidecut and give awesome on-piste performance when skied hard and fast. Detuned versions of these are more suited to the majority of skiers but still have the bright graphics that give skiercross skis their young and aggressive image. Atomic, Head and Volkl lead the field in the skiercross group.

Virtually all ski brands now have their own system of integrated bindings, where the bindings are mounted on special rails or plates on the ski or into the sides through specially drilled holes, rather than being screwed to the top surface. This allows the ski to flex naturally and give better edge grip and transmission of power from boot to ski – ever more important as skis have become shorter.

So what length of ski should you go for? This depends on your skiing style and ability, your height and weight and the type of ski you are buying. Take advice from the shop, but if in doubt, opt for a shorter rather than longer length – it will be easier to ski. Commonly recommended lengths vary from chin height to eye level for many on-piste skis, to head height or maybe more for many freeride skis.

**SNOW + ROCK TIP**

TOP SKIS FOR:
WOMEN
**Rossignol Bandit B2 Women**
**K2 Burnin' Luv**
SKIERCROSS
**Head XRC 1100 RD**
**Volkl Supersport 5 Star**
ON-PISTE FOR EXPERTS
**Volkl P60 Custom**
**Atomic Metron M10**
ON-PISTE RED RUN SKIERS
**Head IC 170**
**Volkl Supersport 4 Star**

**BOOTS: YOUR MOST IMPORTANT PIECE OF EQUIPMENT**

Ski boots are your most important purchase. Invest some time and get a pair that fit properly. They will enhance your skiing pleasure and performance as well as comfort. Snow+Rock offers the largest range in Europe: 59 models from six manufacturers in UK adult size 1 to 15, and starting at children's size 7, so they should have the right boot for you no matter what size or shape your foot. Always

**SNOW + ROCK TIP**

TOP BOOTS FOR:
RED RUN SKIERS:
**Salomon X-Wave 8.0**
**Rossignol Elite Bandit 2**
EXPERTS:
**Salomon X-Wave 10.0**
**Tecnica Diablo Fire Hotform**

↑ Two new boots: Salomon Course Spaceframe, with its hexagonal cut-outs Lange CRL 80 W, one of its women's boots, with a luxurious goose down liner

↑ Giro Bad Lieutenant

have custom-built footbeds made to the shape of your particular feet. These will support your foot and distribute pressure evenly under the whole foot, improving comfort and control and reducing muscle cramps and foot fatigue. Remember to wear technical ski socks when you are trying out different boots (and, of course, when you are out on the mountain). With modern, shaped skis, ski boots no longer need to be so stiff in forward flex; they need to have a progressive flex, and to get the best out of shaped skis they need to have plenty of lateral and rearward stiffness to transmit your foot and leg movements to the skis' edges and use the skis' shape to the full. Almost all boots today have heat-mouldable liners to mirror your foot for comfort and performance; but for the ultimate performance try a personalised custom-fit liner from Conform'able or Zipfit.

Some of the innovations in boots this year include the launch of Salomon's first Spaceframe boot (following the introduction of the Spaceframe technology to their skis last season) in their top-of-the-range models such as the Course Spaceframe and Pro Model Spaceframe. These incorporate 'asymmetrical softening' of the shell, where the outer side is softened with the aid of hexagonal cut-outs and the inner side remains hard – the design directs power to the inside edge as the outside of the boot flexes more. Some women's boots are being given extra comfort and warmth by adding luxurious linings such as goose down in some of the Lange range. Another trend is easier-closing systems and buckles.

Other boots to check out this year include: Salomon X-Wave 8, Rossignol Bandit B2, Atomic T9, and Tecnica Diablo Flame. There are men's and women's versions of all these boots.

### SAFER CRASH LANDINGS

With the speed (and crowds) on the piste increasing and the new freeride skis opening up steeper off-piste terrain to more people, helmets and protective body gear are becoming very popular. The choice of helmets is now very wide (Snow+Rock stock 18 different models, for example, to suit a range of head sizes and shapes as well as your outfit). They expect the Giro 9.9, which is very light with good ventilation, to be a big seller. Giro also make a trendy retro-looking Bad Lieutenant helmet. Also popular are helmets designed with removable ear pads to allow substitute ones with a built-in sound system to be inserted. As for body protection, Dainese offers state-of-the-art gear from head to toe.

New on the UK market last winter were Snowskins. These are compression leggings and long-sleeved tops developed in Australia to enhance blood circulation and reduce muscle fatigue from lactic acid build-up. They work in a similar way to compression stockings sold to help prevent deep vein thrombosis on long-haul flights. They enable you to ski longer and harder, reduce muscle pain and tiredness, reduce the risk of injury, wick away perspiration and keep you warm. If worn after skiing as well, they will help your muscles recover faster (why not splash out on two pairs?).

## EXTRAS WORTH HAVING

Motorola walkie-talkies, which can cost as little as £99 for a pair, enable you to stay in touch with your mates on a different part of the mountain or back in the resort, without the expense of using your mobile phone. Goggles are an essential item in bad weather. Over the years I've tried lots of different pairs with and without my spectacles underneath. Having now given up with the bother of contact lenses I find the best solution to the perennial problem of fogging-up is to use a pair of Smith Turbo goggles which have a built-in two-speed fan to clear any mist on either the spectacle or goggle lens; it works with a pair of AAA batteries. Hydration packs mean you can keep hydrated without carrying bottles around with you – some come built into backpacks, others slip in to a pocket designed for them. Be sure to get one that has insulation for the tube – to prevent the water freezing in it – and it's a safe precaution to blow excess water back into the pack after drinking anyway. Anyone who intends to do a lot of off-piste skiing or boarding should kit themselves out with the essential safety gear of avalanche transceiver, shovel and probe; it's also a good idea to have Recco reflectors so that rescue teams who have Recco detectors can easily locate you (some clothing brands such as Tenson have Reccos built-in and you can buy reflectors which attach to your boots).

↑ Snowskins
Smith Turbo Goggles
Motorola T5522
Zipfit liner

TOP SNOWBOARD BOOTS:
**Vans BFB**
**Salomon F22**
TOP SNOWBOARD BOOTS FOR WOMEN:
**Burton Sable**
**Vans Tara Dakides**

## GET ON BOARD

Anybody looking to buy new snowboard equipment this winter will find that most manufacturers have frozen their prices from last year whilst still offering technological advances over last year's kit.

For the past couple of years boots have generally been available in any colour as long as it's black. Thankfully, those days are gone. For women this year there are boots like the Burton Emerald with its Gucci styling and the Vans Tara Dakides pro model with its take on the Burberry check. For those who prefer a little more subtlety there is still the legendary Vans Omni, which has a Boa lacing system that uses wire and a tensioning system to give a comfortable, precise fit.

For the guys who want to stand out, there is Salomon's new F Ltd. This strictly limited edition is an evolution of the F concept (where there is no sole to the liner, which is attached directly on to the sole of the outer, allowing a shorter shell and a greater 'feel' for what's going on underneath you). Burton has launched a new lace system on its Ion boots with toggles on the left and right cuffs: you pull the left to tighten the lower half of the lacing and the right to tighten the top half. A simple but effective way to the best fit and performance.

On the binding front, the step-in market has all but died. In practice, two-strap bindings can be put on just as quickly as stepping in, and the comfort now afforded by a conventional binding and boot combination far outweighs the convenience of step-in.

Both K2 and Burton have launched a new type of binding which the industry is referring to as 'step-out'. They look like normal two strap bindings, but on the K2 Cinche hi-back there is a lever which

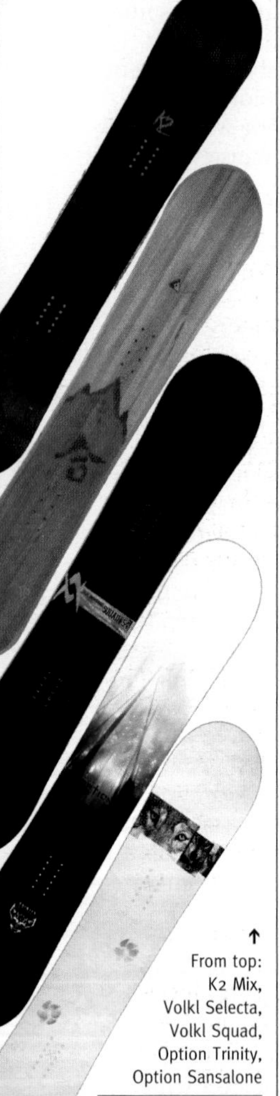

↑ From top: K2 Mix, Volkl Selecta, Volkl Squad, Option Trinity, Option Sansalone

lets the hi-back drop down (similar to the Flow system) and you can then 'step-out'. The binding looks like any other and you can use it as a two-strap if you wish. Burton's Fusion binding looks the same as much of their range but has a small lever on the side of the base plate. When this is activated you step out of the binding, taking the straps with you by way of a small plate that runs underneath the boot. To get back in, it's like putting your foot into a shoe (toes first and then push down with your heel). There is an automatic ratchet system that allows up to 14mm of snow to be caught under the heel. As this is compacted down whilst riding, the ratchet automatically tightens itself. Both these systems show real innovation and it's only a matter of time before the rest of the industry follows.

Up until this season, the choice of top-end women's boards (circa £400) was very limited. Women would end up buying a unisex model that might not be totally suitable (often the board wouldn't be narrow enough). That has all changed now, with the development of boards such as the Burton Feelgood ES and Option Trinity. Both are aimed at the advanced female rider and are definitely not for the faint hearted. Intermediate female riders will be spoilt for choice as there are no fewer than six models available for around the £350 mark, including the K2 Mix, which features real lace embedded in the top sheet, and Option's now iconic Bella. Snow+Rock's selection of 11 women-specific boards is set to be the largest in the country.

Volkl have come up with what is arguably the lightest board on the market: the Squad Flex 3 features an air core that makes it so light and snappy to ride that learning to jump and spin will be grasped in no time. For freeriders, the new Selecta has a form of swallowtail that takes away all the back leg burn normally associated with powder days. There is a real 'soul-surfer' feel about it: it's very easy to ride, the tail is filled with a soft p-tex-like material and it is surprisingly good on piste as well as off it. It's not just for advanced riders and we have even seen 5'4" women riding the 175cm.

In keeping with the whole retro theme at the moment, riders are starting to use shorter boards again. After riding at full tilt for a couple of years, many people seem to be trying to slow themselves down a little to concentrate on the freestyle aspect of snowboarding. It's not about how fast you can get down the hill; it's about how many tricks you can perform on the way that counts. The younger ones among us will be reaching for boards like Ride's Kink and the legendary Burton Dominant for rail slides and skate style riding.

Snow+Rock's board range covers 51 different models, including a new Burton youth package aimed at the little rippers that have progressed passed junior kit, but aren't quite heavy enough for the full-size adult version. This is a sector that is growing really quickly in the UK with so many kids going to dry-slope snowboard nights; these youngsters could become the pro riders of tomorrow.

New technology is now creeping into snowboard clothing. For example, Burton has teamed up with Apple and released a jacket that has a special pocket for an iPod and a socket in the collar to plug

↑ Bright new boots (from left):
Burton Emerald
Vans Tara Dakides
Salomon F Ltd

↑ Two new 'step-out' bindings:
Burton Fusion
K2 Cinche

your headphones into (all the wiring is hidden in the stitching). And there is a set of 'soft touch' buttons on the sleeve so you don't need to open pockets etc to adjust the volume or change tracks. Complementing the jacket is the new Burton Headphone Beany, with a pair of flat headphones built in to the hat. They are easily removable for washing, and provide great quality sound but let in enough outside noise to hear what's going on around you.

Nike's new flagship jacket, the 3L Commwear is state of the art in hands-free communication. It features a Motorola walkie-talkie that plugs into a microphone and speaker that is built into the collar. The PTT (push to talk) button on the chest activates the microphone so you can stay in touch with your friends when you're on the move without even having to take your gloves off.

**WHY BUY IN THE UK?**

Prices in the UK are competitive with Europe and the range of choice available in the UK is far better. Shops in the mountains often tend to stock mainly local brands (eg French brands in France, Austrian or German in Austria). What's more, if you do find the product cheaper elsewhere in Europe, Snow+Rock offers a price pledge on all products to give you the confidence to buy in the UK. It also offers a number of other exclusive guarantees to give you peace of mind to purchase in England – such as a comfort guarantee on all ski boots and a ski suitability and breakage guarantee.

If you visit any ski shop participating in a special 'Everyone's a Winner' Snowlife promotion between 20 September 2004 and mid-January 2005 you'll be able to enter a free prize draw. Three lucky winners will each win a brand new Volvo V50 Sportswagon. And everyone who spends over £50 in a participating shop will receive a book of discount vouchers with potential savings worth £500.

# Family holidays

***How can you improve the chance of success?***

*by* **Chris Gill**

**Regular readers of my annual bulletins from the child-rearing front may recall that in last year's edition I appealed to readers to help with this year's effort. Write down the five most valuable lessons you have learned about taking the family skiing, I said, and I'll aim to produce a distillation for the benefit of those about to take the plunge.**

**Well, here's the result. I heard from over 30 parents; grateful thanks to all of them, and free copies of this edition to the 10 most helpful. With the benefit of the digest that follows, I'm sure you will find the process hassle-free. I've tried to give the findings some structure, but you'll find lots of the sections are linked or even overlapping. Good luck!**

## HOW TO TRAVEL

Not a lot to report here, and most of it's pretty obvious. Between two and three hours seems to be the maximum length of airport transfer you should attempt. If you have a fairly long transfer to the resort, 'try to travel in daylight so that the kids have something to look at out the window', suggests Fraser Ralston. Bear in mind that transfers at peak periods can take much longer than the published times; Phil Morris, having suffered an eight-hour transfer to Les Deux-Alpes, recommends taking reserves of snacks and soft drinks; and sleeping pills, I would add.



## TAKING AND MAKING FRIENDS

Several parents stressed the value of ensuring companionship for your kids – either by taking friends of similar age or by making it easy to make friends in the resort. The natural way to do the first is to go with another family with compatible children. 'It's quite amazing how much more the children enjoy the holiday and how much easier they are to deal with,' notes Mark Hunt. And the key to the latter may be travelling with a specialist family operator who will provide suitable chums – 'there will be lots of other children on the flight and bus, which is what your children want,' says David Weaver. See 'Childcare in the resort'.

## CHILDCARE IN THE RESORT

If you are taking young children who need to be looked after either full-time or part-time, there are of course several ways to arrange things. Broadly speaking, our correspondents fell into two camps – those who recommend taking your own nanny/granny (or whatever) with you, and those who have happily relied on the services of specialist UK tour operators. Not much support for resort nurseries.

David Walton points out that taking your own childcare with you works well if you're driving in a large car to a large apartment: 'Get a friend's teenage daughter to join you, pay for their lift pass and food, and get them to babysit for a few hours a day in return.'

Going with another family and simply sharing the burdens is another formula that works for some. 'We did this about four years ago and wished we had tried it many years earlier,' said Eddie Baines. Of course, going with another family also has a clear bearing on the business of companionship – see 'Taking and making friends'.

The tour operator supporters delivered enthusiastic reports on

Family Ski Co, Simply Ski, Ski Peak, Snowbizz and Snowline. The only critical report was on Esprit, but this was outweighed by several positive ones. The last word on this business, though, goes to Julie Taylor: 'Mark Warner are fab! We have travelled with them for the last eight seasons since our first son was nine months old.'

Travelling with a specialist operator has benefits other than the services of the nannies, of course – see 'Taking and making friends'.

'Book early if you want to use these companies. By the time the brochure hits the doormat, it's too late,' notes Martin Law. This is, of course, particularly true of half-term week.

**WHERE TO GO**

A popular issue, this, with pointers coming from about half of our correspondents. They ranged across a number of issues. Not surprisingly, among the most common was the need to choose a mountain with suitably gentle runs – long, top-to-bottom runs, as well as nursery slopes.

Other mountain-related suggestions included: avoid drag-lifts for as long as possible; avoid chilly north-facing slopes; avoid resorts with fragmented slope areas, and uphill walks between them; look for self-contained lift/piste loops, where children can pretty much be left to their own devices. One suggestion that struck a particular chord with me came from Helen Gallop: look for places where you can 'ski below the tree line, where there are plenty of dips, bumps and tracks to play in'. Straying off the piste to play in the fringes of the forest was definitely a highlight of a family holiday we had a couple of years back, in Les Arcs.

But what about the village? Here we got conflicting advice again.

'Choose a small resort with accommodation close to the lift, such as Champoussin or Valmorel,' says Martin Nicholas. Others stressed the need for a range of non-skiing activities, which may point you in the opposite direction. 'Some small resorts do not really offer anything substantial, whereas larger resorts generally do,' said Fraser Ralston. Obviously, if you have non-skiers in the party, their needs have to be met, as well as those of storm-bound children. Andrew Osborne points out that areas like the Jungfrau region, with its countless mountain railways, are especially attractive for grandparents lumbered with babysitting duties (see 'Childcare in the resort').

**ACTIVITIES OFF THE SLOPES**

Choice of resort links with the whole question of what the kids will do in the evenings (and perhaps the afternoons if skiing all day doesn't appeal). Swimming pools and games rooms get the thumbs up, of course. Not all parents are convinced that the dangers of sledging are outweighed by its rewards but for most who offered a view, sledges are a key aid to holiday happiness. 'Hire or buy a toboggan,' says Sally Newton. ' Daisy and a friend she met stayed out until dark nearly every night.' Ski-in, ski-out accommodation is a related key ingredient, of course (see 'Where to stay').

**HOW SHOULD THEY LEARN?**
This is the big one. We got advice on this crucial question from practically everyone who took part in our little survey.

Lesson One, which to be honest I wish I had learned some years ago, is not to talk at all about learning, lessons and school, but somehow to turn ski school into an adventure. 'Make sure your child knows that by going with the school [oops!] they'll be taken places you wouldn't take them,' says Paula Wid, 'and that they'll be better than you very soon.'

When it comes to choosing a school, the advice is clear: avoid the ESF – 'draconian and insensitive', says Jen Warren – and go instead for a British-run school staffed by native English-speakers and limiting class sizes to modest numbers. The downsides are that prices are higher and that you absolutely must book ahead in high season.

Several people raised the idea of hiring a private instructor. 'If all at the same level, having private family lessons works out just as cheap,' says Rachel Swinscoe.

And what about dry-slope lessons before you go? Emphatically a good idea, say the few families who express a view. Even one lesson 'gave the children a little bit of extra confidence', says Jeremy Wartnaby. 'Have lessons over the summer months,' says Lynne Wallis, 'often cheaper, and often have fewer people in the group.'

**KITTING OUT THE KIDS**
Three main messages here, and all easy to convey: don't skimp on quality of equipment or clothing, and particularly gloves; do what you can to prevent loss of gloves, but take a spare pair anyway; and insist on the wearing of helmets. In principle, one should be wary of the last message – after all, most parents are not in a position to evaluate thoroughly the case for wearing helmets. But my view is that the advice is supported by the available evidence. I even wear a helmet myself, at least in wooded terrain.

A more unusual and therefore interesting bit of advice is to buy, not hire, your kids' equipment. 'Buy in the end-of-season sales here,' says Helen Melvin, 'and avoid the bedlam of the resort ski hire shop.' The larger the family, she points out, the more economical buying can be, because boots and skis can cascade down the family. Well, she's certainly right about the bedlam.

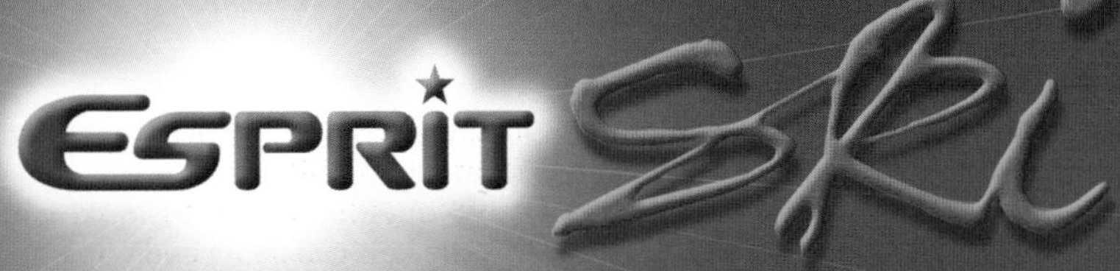
ESPRIT Ski

**WHERE TO STAY?**

A popular topic, and no doubt about the most widely supported piece of advice: 'If you can afford it, book ski-in, ski-out accommodation.' It isn't simply a question of getting to ski school in the morning, either – it means 'the kids can come and go as they please, in safety,' observes Helen Gallop. 'If you can persuade the kids to have a rest around lunch time you can also save the cost of lunch on the mountain,' notes Andrew Clark.

And what sort of accommodation? Some people enthuse about 'child-friendly hotels', but on looking more closely I realised that they are mainly enthusing about such things as swimming pools, which are by no means limited to hotels. Mark Hunt also noted that 'some hotels which say they are family-friendly are not', and advocates checking on facilities directly with the hotel before you book. On the other hand, a sizeable group of readers reckoned that 'apartments are much easier than hotels', to quote Dave Walton. Flexibility over meals seems to be the key factor here. 'Whether it's cooking your child's favourite meals in the apartment, or finding a restaurant that suits the whole family, an apartment brings a great deal of flexibility to the holiday,' said Clive Murgatroyd.

**AND FINALLY ...**

One of the main messages to emerge was the crucial need to adjust your expectations of your holiday – to focus on enjoying the holiday as a whole, and not just the skiing/boarding. 'Recognise that a holiday with kids will be different from one without them,' says Sally Newton. 'Enjoy the whole mountain experience,' says Nigel Birch. 'It's not all about skiing, it's about having a good time as a family.'

# Luxury chalets

## *The ultimate ski holiday?*

*by* **Chris Gill**

**In the beginning, the catered chalet business – explained in the box later in this chapter, for the benefit of those not familiar with the concept – didn't do luxury. It was only in the late 1980s that one or two companies realised that there might be a market for indulgent holidays without the fleets of bellboys and room-service waiters that hotels are obliged to lay on. All you had to do was provide comfortable and stylish accommodation, good food and wine, and a little bit of personal service – just enough to make the customer feel the staff are there to do something other than have a good time. The new formula worked, probably better than anyone would have expected.**

You can find isolated luxury chalets in all sorts of places, from Austria to Aspen, but the breed in general is still not widespread: most are concentrated in the more upmarket French mega-resorts.

The greatest concentration is found in Méribel, particularly in the hands of long-time local specialist Meriski. This company, more than any other, illustrates the transformation of the chalet business. In the 1980s it was a run-of-the-mill chalet operation, but then it successfully repositioned itself upmarket, and now has a wide range of impressively comfortable chalets.

Descent International now has an enviable portfolio of properties in the secluded Brames area of the resort. The famously luxurious chalet Brames is the grandest property I have visited in Méribel, with a two-storey living room and some beautiful bedrooms, and a glorious view up the valley towards Mont Vallon. To this the company has added the equally desirable 10-bed chalets Aurore and Boréale, nearby, which share an outdoor heated pool – and more recently the beautifully furnished chalet Génépi at Belvedere.

VIP has six impressive chalets, including Indiana Lodge – right on the slopes with great views over town and an outdoor hot-tub – and Kublai Lodge – with Indonesian decor, steam room, gym and cinema. Belvedere Chalets has four properties. Scott Dunn Ski has three – in terms of luxury, towards the lower end of this company's increasingly impressive range of properties.

If you like the idea of luxury but want to keep the cost down, consider staying with Bonne Neige down in the old village of Les Allues. Les Allodis is a converted barn that makes a real change from the modern properties that dominate in Méribel – all beams and antique furniture, but with mod cons including outdoor hot-tub.

Courchevel is well established as the smartest resort in France, and now has quite a few smart chalets on the UK package market. Flexiski has a beautiful, rustic 10-bed chalet off the Bellecôte piste – Anemone, one of Courchevel's originals. But this is now rather eclipsed by the recently added pair of chalets Chinchilla and Hermine. Scott Dunn Ski has several properties in Courchevel, of which the undoubted gem is the swanky Aurea, costing twice as much as some of the company's more modest offerings. A favourite of mine – though far from the swankiest on the UK market – is Lotus Supertravel's 10-bed chalet Founets, which has a lovely high-ceilinged sitting/dining room and a great position. The company's Plein Sud and Aiguille de Fruit look impressive, too.

Next-door La Tania has developed quite a range of comfortable chalet properties, including the best of the Ski Amis range, the 14-bed Balkiss. Le Ski and Snowline have several properties here, too.

Val-d'Isère is the other great chalet resort in France. Scott Dunn's already impressive portfolio here has really grown with the acquisition of The Ski Company Ltd's grand enclave of four modern chalets at the southern extremity of the resort, with splendid views from their picture windows – Bergerie, Mistral, Lafitenia, all 10-bed, and the 18-bed Chardon. But even these properties are put in the shade by the 12-bed Eagle's Nest – an extraordinary place, complete with an indoor jet-stream pool, and all four floors linked by lift.

YSE's ancient Mountain Lodges are old favourites, offering no picture windows but splendidly atmospheric and comfortable living rooms, with stone walls and ample leather sofas. This Val specialist also has some very attractive modern properties. VIP now has 20 very smart places, 12 of which are spacious, stylish chalet-apartments in their newly built Aspen Lodge on the main street, with a reception desk, lounge area with coffee bar, and open fireplace. Their 200-year-old Farmhouse, by the church, has been beautifully converted. Lotus Supertravel has one luxury contender in the form of chalet Renard.

Chamonix isn't particularly known for luxury chalets, but locally based Collineige has secured an enviable range of highly individual

### THE CHALET HOLIDAY IN ITS ORIGINAL FORM

*The catered chalet holiday is a uniquely British idea. Tour operators install their own cooks and housekeepers in private chalets which they take over for the season. They package them with travel from the UK, normally offering half-board. Dinner is a no-choice affair at a communal table, including wine unlimited in quantity (often highly limited in quality). You can either book a whole chalet (the smallest typically sleep around six or eight) or book space in a larger chalet that you share with whoever else turns up.*

*In the early days of the chalet, in the 1960s and 70s, taking a chalet holiday meant roughing it in creaky old buildings, putting up with spartan furniture and paper-thin walls, and with six or more people sharing a bathroom. And the chalet girl – always a girl, back then – was often straight out of college or finishing school, and more intent on having a fun season on the slopes than preparing gourmet meals. Happily, things have changed.*

SKI AMIS
Ski in the French Alps
Quality catered and self catered ski holidays
see our website for full details or call us
www.skiamis.com
info@skiamis.com
020 7692 0850

bonne-neige-ski.com
Meribel
QUALITY CATERED CHALETS
Allodis & St Joseph
◆10 years of quality service◆
◆Superb Food and Wine◆
◆En-suite rooms & Family Suites◆
◆Personal, Professional Team◆
◆Ski Hosting, 3 full days a week◆
◆Saunas and Hot-tubs◆
+44(0)1270 256966
ukoffice@bonne-neige-ski.com

Val d'Isère & Méribel
The ultimate collection of luxury ski chalets
■ Modern, stylish yet traditional chalets
■ Many chalets with hot tub or sauna
■ Personal service from reservation to resort
ATOL 3356 AITO
08701 123 119
www.vip-chalets.com
VIP

MERISKI
Luxury chalets in Méribel
01285 648518
www.meriski.co.uk
AITO
ATOL

properties, ranging from characterful old houses through rustic retreats to modern architect-designed chalets – Valhalla is particularly striking, with its double-height living room. Flexiski's wood-built eight-bed chalet Bornian looks wonderful, too.

Morzine is known mainly for cheap-and-cheerful properties, but Snowline's new Nebraska and Dakota Lodges sound exceptional – and in the nearby backwater of Essert-Romand is the deeply comfortable Chalet Gueret, rebuilt with all mod cons a few years back after the all-wood original burned down.

In Switzerland, Verbier is the chalet capital. Chalet Goodwood is much the best I have visited here – fabulously comfortable and stylish, in a central position. It is now run by Descent International, whose equally swanky Septième Ciel could scarcely be in a more different location – high on the Savoleyres side of Verbier, a drive from the Place Centrale. Ski Verbier's portfolio includes several glorious properties. At the top of the range are the recently built Attelas and Sorojasa, but a double-height living room makes chalet Danny equally compelling. Flexiski's Bouvreuil is a tastefully furnished apartment.

In Zermatt, Scott Dunn has long been the main source, and has gone up a gear recently with the acquisition of two central, spacious and stylish 10-bed apartments that were briefly offered by the Ski Company. Total's range here includes the Génépy, stylishly created within a lovely old wooden building.

In Austria, luxury chalets are curiously rare, but in St Anton Lotus Supertravel has the Chiara and Flexiski the Amalien Haus.

# All-inclusive holidays

***Come home on-budget***

*by* **Chris Gill**

**For anyone who wants to keep control of their holiday spending, there's nothing to beat an all-inclusive holiday. Perhaps surprisingly, no one sells winter sports packages that include absolutely everything. But there are a couple of companies that come close.**

Club Med is the big name in this game, with huge hotels (called 'villages') in around 20 resorts in the Alps. The great majority are in France (it's a French company), but Club Med has taken over a handful of old hotels in Swiss resorts and also has places elsewhere.

Holidays are available with or without flights and transfers. They all include insurance. But the key feature of the package is that it includes all meals, including beer and wine. Because this is a French operation, lunch is a serious meal. Usually, it's taken back at the village; most are in high resorts, where this is not difficult, but returning to base half-way through the day doesn't appeal to everyone. In a very few resorts Club Med has taken over a mountain restaurant, which is a better arrangement.

Generally, Club Med prices include your lift pass and tuition. Some do only half-day tuition, but most do a full day. Skiing or boarding equipment costs extra, but is usually available on-site.

Most villages have childcare facilities, and for many Club Med regulars these are at the heart of the formula – though how well they will work for English-speaking kids must be open to doubt.





Equity Ski's pricing is a lot simpler, as well as different. They don't include lunch, and they include drinks with dinner only in the case of catered chalet holidays. But all their holiday prices include your equipment hire, as well as lift pass, insurance and either tuition or guiding around the slopes (it depends on where you are staying).

The Equity programme falls roughly into two halves. They offer a moderate number of Austrian and French resorts, in which they generally run their own catered chalets or hotels, and sometimes offer other hotels too. Then, in a larger number of Italian resorts, they offer two or three standard hotels that may be shared with other companies' clients, in the conventional way.

Equity's resorts are a mix of established big names – Val-Thorens, Mayrhofen, Sauze d'Oulx – and smaller, less well-known places such as St Michael and Le Corbier (part of Les Sybelles). It includes one or two useful 'back-door' resorts attached to major ski areas – St-Martin-de-Belleville for the Trois Vallées, Folgarida for Madonna di Campiglio.

# Corporate ski trips

***A great way to motivate your staff and clients***

*by* **Chris Gill**

**There are all kinds of reasons why companies find it valuable to get staff or clients together for a bit of a treat outside the usual business environment. Common ones include team building, rewarding performance, bonding with clients and holding conferences in exotic locations. And there are all kinds of places you can go and all kinds of activities you can lay on. But few can rival ski resorts and skiing for sheer impact. If your sales force would benefit from some quality time together, if you want to bond more closely with the half-dozen customers who give you half your business, or if the managers of your various European offices really need to be introduced to your head office hymn sheet, read on.**



First, for those who already know how corporate trips work, we invited Amin Momen of Momentum Travel to bring us up to date on the corporate market. 'It's clear that the City is booking its events earlier this year,' he says, 'to get the most convenient flights through Geneva (where there's a lack of capacity). More companies are also asking us to organise ski races as part of their events, the most popular discipline being giant slalom. Great news for City-based and Canary Wharf-based groups is that Swiss International are again operating flights to Geneva from City airport. And the hot new favourite resort seems to be Engelberg.' Happily, Engelberg is covered this year in one of our new Short Turns entries – see page 502.



## WHAT'S THE ATTRACTION?

The mountain/skiing/boarding environment is one that has lots of advantages for corporate events. The clear fresh air, sun and snowy, dramatic mountain scenery have a huge and immediate impact on people arriving from the European lowlands and their dreary winters. There is a great sense of fun and liberation and people are happy to cast inhibitions aside and let their hair down. And a winter sports break need not appeal just to skiers. Helena Kania went on a team building weekend to Morzine organised by her company Cable & Wireless and told us, 'I didn't set foot on skis or board but just loved the fresh air, sunshine, views and meeting up with the others in

Filippo Guerrini-Maraldi of Lloyds ↘
Einar Johansen of Goldman Sachs ↓

mountain restaurants. And we all got on much better when we got back to work after sharing a great experience.' The best resorts have a range of activities available, including ones that will fit naturally into the evening timetable. There are excellent and capacious hotels, many with conference facilities. The flights to the Alps from northern Europe are short. And the perceived status of ski resorts is high – whoever you invite will be in no doubt that they are being given a treat (as will their friends and business colleagues).

**WHAT'S THE COST?**

The obvious answer is that it depends. Perhaps a more useful one is that it may be less than you'd think, and indeed less than some of the alternatives. Chris Scudds of Alpine Events reckons that 'a two-night ski trip including flight and ski hire could cost the same as a two-night stay in the UK' because UK hotel and restaurant costs are relatively high.

**WHAT SORT OF CORPORATE EVENT WILL WORK?**

More or less any event that is better done away from the office will work in the Alps. Examples of events that have been successfully held in ski resorts include those with these objectives:

- communication to middle managers of a new business strategy
- concentrated attempt to crack a crucial business problem
- staff morale boost after recent business difficulties
- new product launches to sales staff or key customers
- gathering together of staff from geographically spread sites
- team-building by giving groups shared objectives
- sales incentive 'prizes'
- client 'reward' to build business loyalty
- Christmas parties with a different feel to them.

**HOW LONG A TRIP?**

Corporate trips of a few days are the norm – Thursday to Sunday, say. But you can have two full, action-packed days in the Alps by leaving on Friday after work and returning late on Sunday night – arriving back at work on Monday morning refreshed, invigorated and remotivated. Some companies take over a cluster of chalets for a week or two and have different groups moving in and out, staying for a variety of durations. Others hire helicopters for airport transfers and just go for one night.

**HOW BIG A GROUP?**

In principle, your group can be any size you like. A lot of groups are 30 to 50. But they can be smaller, or much larger. When we were in Whistler a couple of years back, the whole of the 550-room Fairmont Chateau Whistler had been taken over by a medical conference. Someone with plenty of experience of handling large groups is Amin Momen of Momentum Travel, who for the last few years has organised the Swiss International City Ski Championships in Courmayeur, involving around 200 racers, plus lots of hangers-on. 'Such a large group is quite a challenge,' says Amin, 'but it helps enormously that we have such good local contacts in the resort. If strings need to be pulled to solve a problem, we know exactly which strings.' With really small groups, be aware that the social success is going to depend on how the individuals mesh.

**WHERE TO GO?**

How easy it is to settle on a resort for a corporate trip depends hugely on the nature of your project. If it's a dozen people travelling out together for a relaxed couple of days, you're really organising nothing more than a short holiday and a swanky chalet might be good. If you are getting a large group together from all corners of the globe and need serious conference facilities, you're playing a different ball game. Finding the right accommodation, meeting rooms and support services can be a real headache, and it's in dealing with this sort of challenge that the services of a tour operator or event management company will really pay off.

Because corporate trips tend to be short, you'll want to keep the travel time to the minimum, so that it doesn't dominate the proceedings. Transfer times from airports to resorts generally range from one to four hours, and you'll probably want to operate at the lower end of that range if you can.

You may want to have a particular range of activities available. Or you may want your choice of resort to carry a message to your 'delegates'. Choosing Courchevel or St Moritz is effectively saying 'No expense spared – nothing but the best for you.' Whatever you do, choose a resort with a good snow record and/or extensive snowmaking. You don't want to invite people on a skiing break to find that there's no snow. Avoid early season for the same reason. A March trip to a high resort will mean good snow and it should mean strong sunshine, too. Don't get hung up on size – with only a couple of days to spend on the slopes, almost any resort has plenty of terrain, especially with good local guides to help you make the most of it.

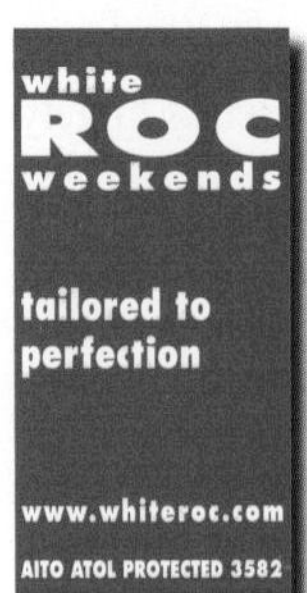




**WHERE TO STAY?**

Large groups really have no option: you'll need a large hotel (or two). Obviously, you and/or your event organiser will want to consider lots of angles to identify a place with the right blend of qualities. But for smaller groups there is the alternative of staying in one or more catered chalets – Alpine houses run by UK-based or at least UK-oriented companies, usually with native English-speaking staff. Some of these properties are very swanky and expensive, others less so. You can get some idea of what is on offer by checking out our chapter on luxury chalets, starting on page 45.

**ORGANISING THE SKIING**

A typical corporate group will naturally contain a mixture of experienced skiers and non-skiers. You'll need to make sure everyone is equipped with suitable clothing, equipment and lift passes. You'll also want to organise tuition or guiding – preferably just for your group rather than stuffing your guests in ski school classes. Make sure you have enough instructors/guides so that you can form groups of equal ability.

Lunch in a mountain restaurant can be an opportunity to get your group together, but for a large and disparate group it can present some challenges. Another possibility, in good weather, is a swanky picnic, with plenty of champagne buried in the snow.

You might want to think about a race for delegates, though bear in mind that this won't appeal to the complete beginners in the group. Other forms of competition, such as on-snow treasure hunts, could be used to include non-skiers too.

**SWISS INTERNATIONAL CITY SKI CHAMPIONSHIPS**

*The City Ski Championships have been organised by weekend skiing specialist Momentum Ski and held annually in Courmayeur in Italy's Aosta valley since 2000. Among its attractions is the array of former skiing stars who turn up to set the pace. Former Olympic gold medallist Tommy Moe of the USA and Britain's downhill star of the 1980s Konrad Bartelski are regulars, and in 2005 they'll be joined by the great Franz Klammer. Around 200 skiers from 40 City firms take part in the event. In 2004, the fastest genuine amateur was Filippo Guerrini-Maraldi of Lloyds, with ex-pro racer Einar Johansen of Goldman Sachs as usual pushing hard at the heels of the fastest on the course, Tommy Moe.*

*The race is only part of the attraction of the weekend. There's a welcome drinks party on the Friday evening, dinner at various restaurants, late night drinks in the Bar Roma, a race-side buffet on the piste, champagne reception courtesy of Veuve Clicquot, followed by gala presentation dinner in the evening and then ... clubbing at Poppie's till dawn.*

*The 2005 event is later than usual, from 17 to 20 March and promises to be even better than ever. Konrad Bartelski will again be running the Snow+Rock pre-race ski clinics, which are really popular with the competitors, and Graham Bell and Matt Chilton from the BBC will be doing the commentary.For more details contact Momentum on 020 7371 9111 or see www.cityskichampionships.com.*

## WHAT OTHER ACTIVITIES?

Because it's likely that not everyone will want to go skiing or boarding, you'll need to be able to offer some other activities with a broad appeal. This may influence your choice of resort. Typical activities to consider would include dog-sledding, snowmobiling, skating, curling, tobogganing, ballooning, swimming, flights in planes or helicopters. Bear in mind that activities like these tend to occupy relatively short, defined periods of time – in contrast to skiing and boarding which, of course, soak up any number of days. So you may need quite a range of activities to keep people busy all day. Walking and snow-shoeing can also fill whole days, but they do require an energetic approach.

Then there are the evenings to consider. They are a time when all the group can be brought together, so it's important to think about how you're going to use those opportunities to best effect. You can organise activities with more of a team emphasis, and you can create social events that reinforce your message – perhaps taking over a whole bar or a mountain restaurant, for example. In the right resort, dinner in a mountain restaurant could be followed by dangerous descents on skis or toboggans.

## MANAGEMENT ISSUES

Like any business project, a skiing trip brings its own administrative burdens. As well as making it all happen smoothly – which means managing the delegates as tightly as the suppliers of all the components making up the trip – someone has to control expenditure, and provide clear, always up-to-date information. This is a key area to sort out with your organising company.

# Weekend breaks

***Why a quick fix of the white stuff is addictive***





**A weekend away with just one day off work can give you three great days on the slopes, leaving you with the feeling of having been away for ages and returning to work feeling really refreshed. And it does not need to cost you an arm and a leg.**

Short break ski trips have become much more popular in the last few years, partly because of the growth of budget airlines. I was very sceptical of them before I tried them myself several years ago. But now I am addicted to them. A quick fix of the white stuff really does seem almost as good as a week. I have had successful weekends all over the place. My first was to the classic weekend destination of Chamonix, which has local areas suitable for all types of weather and snow conditions. Next came Zell am See in Austria, with skiing on the glacier at Kaprun. Then a weekend in Val-d'Isère at the time of the Premier Neige race – great fun. Other great pre-Xmas weekends have been in Courchevel and Saas-Fee. A January weekend in Courmayeur, a February one in Aosta (skiing Cervinia, Monterosa and Pila on successive days) and a March one in Engelberg have all been great.

And I've met many other weekend addicts, including people who rent apartments for the season and go out every other weekend and others who book up 12 or so weekend flights well in advance and decide where to go when they know where the best snow is.

## ARRANGING THE WEEKEND

The key to making the most of your time is to catch late flights each way – so it helps if you live near a suitable airport. Swiss has well-timed flights to Zürich from Heathrow and London City, and BA (with Swiss on a code share) flies to Geneva from Heathrow (but book early as these late flights are very popular). EasyJet has suitable flights from both Gatwick and Luton to Geneva, from Luton to Zürich and Nice, and from Liverpool to Geneva. Alitalia has flights to Milan from Heathrow, and Ryanair has flights to Salzburg, Turin and Verona from Stansted.

We don't recommend flying to Munich if you are travelling out on a Friday or back on a Sunday – the queues on the motorway can be horrendous, as the whole of Munich seems to go weekend skiing and the airport is on the far side of the city from the Alps. Similarly, allow plenty of time if you are driving back to Lyon airport on a Sunday evening – we encountered very heavy traffic after leaving Courchevel in what we had thought was good time.

Booking a rental car or taxi in advance is usually cheaper than arranging one after you arrive. Several tour operators can arrange the rental as part of a complete weekend package. Taxis can be ridiculously expensive compared with the cost of renting a car. For example, you would expect to pay over £200 each way between Geneva airport and Courchevel by taxi if you book locally – but renting a small car for the weekend would be much less than the one-way taxi price. In our experience train and bus times between airports and resorts are more suitable for week-long visitors than for weekenders looking for maximum time on the slopes.

Using a weekend specialist, such as one of those advertising in this

chapter, makes sense if you don't want the hassle of making your own arrangements. They know the best resorts to go to, can arrange transfers by their own staff or through local companies, and have special deals with hotels that do them good room rates or that might not otherwise take weekend bookings. Some arrange special weekend courses (eg with off-piste guides or even heli-skiing) and can arrange groups of similar standard for you to ski with if you are travelling alone. And local tour operator reps and contacts can save you valuable time arranging lift passes (beware of big weekend queues on Saturday and Sunday mornings) and equipment hire, and advise on local restaurants and other facilities.

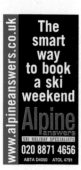

## CHOOSING A RESORT

As for choosing a resort, there are various considerations. Many people think they should go for a resort within a short drive of their arrival airport. But by definition, resorts close to major airports are close to large numbers of people poised to hit the slopes on fine weekends, which can mean queues for the lifts, crowds on the slopes and competition for hotel beds. These days, most resorts are within striking distance of a major airport and an hour's extra transfer time is not really that much if it gets you to quieter slopes.

Resorts close to Geneva include Chamonix, St-Gervais, Megève and Les Contamines (all in the Mont Blanc area and sharing an area lift pass), Flaine and La Clusaz in France, and Villars and Les Diablerets in Switzerland. All these are within an hour or so of Geneva by car. Verbier and Crans-Montana in Switzerland are a bit further, as are the Three Valleys and other Tarentaise resorts – Val-d'Isère can be reached in under three hours now – and Morzine and the Portes du Soleil resorts in France. EasyJet's Nice flight puts Isola 2000 within a 90km/56 mile drive.

Flying to Zürich opens up lots of other possibilities. Flims, Davos and Klosters are the nearest big resorts, and the less well-known resorts of Engelberg and Andermatt are within easy reach. St Anton and Lech in Austria are within striking distance, as are the resorts of the Montafon valley. Ryanair's Salzburg flights make most of the eastern Austrian resorts a short drive away.

In Italy, Courmayeur is a popular weekend destination and is easily accessible from Geneva through the Mont Blanc tunnel. Resorts such as Champoluc, Sauze d'Oulx and Sestriere are easily accessible from Milan or Turin. Ryanair's Verona flights put you very near the Sella Ronda resorts and Cortina d'Ampezzo.

Unless you are booking at short notice when you know the snow is good, we'd be tempted to avoid low resorts such as Megève and Villars – unless you have transport to get you to more snow-sure slopes. And because you don't want your whole weekend ruined by a white-out if it snows all the time, we'd also be tempted to avoid very high resorts where the skiing is entirely above the tree line – this rules out places such as Tignes and Val-Thorens in France, Obergurgl in Austria and Cervinia in Italy. Another consideration is that hotels in big, popular winter resorts such as St Anton, Verbier and Val-

*by* **Dave Watts**

d'Isère now often refuse to take weekend bookings except in very low season (eg early January or late March) because they can get more profitable week-long bookings. But many of the more summer-oriented resorts, which generally have accommodation spare in winter, are well worth considering – places such as Chamonix, Morzine, Engelberg, Villars and Mürren.

## WHAT ABOUT PRICE?

The cost can vary enormously. The flight and transfer or car hire are the expensive fixed costs and obviously make a weekend proportionately more expensive than a full week. But as we said before, you do get three days' skiing (half a full week) for only one day off work, and the three days makes a substantial break. A four-night break is, of course, even better – it only costs two days off work and means you can travel out and back on Thursday and Monday evenings (quieter than Fridays and Sundays).

In general, through a good specialist tour operator you can expect to pay from around £350 a head for flights, car hire and a double room in a 3-star hotel for three nights, assuming two people sharing. With lift passes and meals you could be looking at around £500. For a 4-star hotel add another £100 or so.



## MIDWEEK BREAKS

If you can get away midweek, there are many potential advantages. Flights (especially on the budget airlines) should be cheaper, and accommodation may be, too. And resorts that get busy at weekends, such as Morzine, Verbier, Courmayeur and Champoluc, can be very quiet midweek in low season.

# Flying to the snow

## *Competition means good deals for consumers*

*by* **Dave Watts**

**Since EasyJet started the first cheap scheduled flights to the Alps in the mid-1990s, budget flights have mushroomed. In 1997/98 there were 72,000 seats on budget airlines available to major ski gateway airports. Last season there were over 900,000. And this coming season sees a new budget airline called Zoom flying to Canada from Gatwick and Glasgow. EasyJet still has by far the biggest range of flights to the key Alpine destination airport of Geneva. Ryanair has a lot of flights to a number of other convenient airports, but is in danger of alienating skiers with its mean baggage allowance and high charges for carrying skis and boards. Most other budget airlines except EasyJet and Zoom also charge for ski and board carriage and some don't even guarantee to get them on the aircraft at all. The explosion of budget flights has also stimulated the established airlines to offer some competitive deals.**

I have used budget flights a lot over the last few seasons. Nearly all flights have been pretty much on time, and their no-frills service and pay-as-you-eat food is all you need on a short flight of 90 minutes or less. They are particularly convenient for me because I live only 20 minutes from Stansted and 40 minutes from Luton, the airports they mainly operate from. From Heathrow, Swiss and BA have well-timed flights for weekend or short-break trips and often offer competitive fares; check their web sites.

Budget airline prices vary according to demand, and in general the cheapest flights are for midweek early or late in the day, booked months in advance. As a flight fills up, the prices go up. But you may also get a bargain by booking at the last minute if the flight is not full. At their lowest, prices can be £40 return or less; at their peak they can be well over £200 return. Watch out for extra charges though, such as a fee (with Ryanair £1.75 per passenger for each leg of a return fight) for paying by credit card.



In general, flights have got more flexible. Although the budget airlines won't normally give you a refund if you decide not to travel, most will now allow you to change the flight time or route and the name of the passenger – but at a cost of perhaps £15 each way for each change. But check when you book because the rules change.

Budget airline policies on carrying skis and boards and on excess and hand baggage vary. EasyJet has a 20kg baggage allowance plus 10kg of sports equipment such as skis or board. Ryanair has a measly baggage allowance of only 15kg and charges £17 each way for skis or board and won't guarantee to carry them unless they are pre-booked. Flybe and bmibaby both have 20kg baggage allowances and charge £15 and £10 each way for skis respectively. Excess baggage is generally charged at £4/kg each way and can add up quickly. We have been told by some check-in staff that they have been instructed to enforce the baggage limits strictly as the airlines see this as a way of making money even if the fare is cheap. A war had recently broken out on hand luggage as we went to press. Ryanair announced it was to increase its hand luggage allowance to 10kg as the start of a long-term move to discourage all hold luggage (can you imagine going skiing for a week without hold luggage?). EasyJet retaliated by removing all weight limits on hand luggage, so long as you have

**AIRLINE CONTACT DETAILS**

Phone numbers and web sites for the major airlines are listed on page 670.

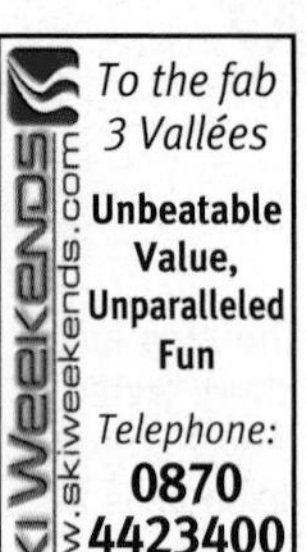


only one piece which measures 55 x 40 x 20cm maximum.

Key airports for skiers include Geneva (for most French resorts and some Swiss and Italian), Zürich (for eastern Swiss and western Austrian resorts), Lyon (for many French resorts), Milan (for most Italian resorts except the Dolomites), Munich (for most Austrian resorts) and Barcelona (for Andorra and the Pyrenees), plus some smaller airports that we mention below.

EasyJet flies from Luton, Gatwick, East Midlands, Liverpool, Newcastle and Bristol to Geneva, Barcelona and Nice (only 90km/56 miles from Isola 2000), from Luton to Zürich and from Gatwick and Stansted to Milan. It also flies from Stansted to Lyon, Munich, Barcelona and Nice and from Stansted and some other airports to Venice (for the Dolomites) and Malaga (for Sierra Nevada).

Ryanair flies from Stansted to Milan, Turin (nearer than Milan for western Italian resorts), Venice and Verona (for the Dolomites), Salzburg (for most Austrian resorts), Friedrichshafen (just over the German border but handy for western Austrian resorts), Klagenfurt (for the Carinthia region of Austria), Carcassonne and Perpignan (both for Andorra and the Pyrenees) and Girona (for Andorra).

Flybe has flights from Southampton to Geneva, Chambéry, Salzburg and Toulouse and from some regional airports to Salzburg and Toulouse. And bmibaby has flights from Cardiff, Teesside and East Midlands to Geneva and some other relevant airports.

Swiss International Air Lines operates several direct flights a day from Heathrow, London City, Birmingham and Manchester to Zürich and code-shares British Airways flights from Heathrow to Geneva. There is also a Saturday flight between Heathrow and Sion, less than half an hour's transfer to Crans-Montana, and a bit further to Saas-Fee, Zermatt and Verbier. Swiss carries skis or snowboard free on top of your 20kg baggage allowance. Check its web site for the lowest fares.

Alitalia goes from Heathrow to Milan, which gives access to many Italian resorts. British Airways goes to Geneva, Zürich, Munich, Milan, Venice and Verona from a variety of UK airports. They both allow 23kg baggage including skis or board.

Zoom will be a new budget airline flying to Canada this winter with direct flights from Gatwick and Glasgow to Vancouver and from Gatwick to Montreal, with economy and premium economy cabins. They allow 20kg of baggage plus skis or board. Lots of airlines serve the USA but the only non-stop direct flight to Denver, Colorado, remains British Airways. Getting to Utah, Wyoming and Montana resorts means a change of plane and going through customs on the way. For California, you can fly straight to San Francisco or LA with BA, United or Virgin. Most transatlantic airlines allow two pieces of hold luggage, each up to 32kg; skis or board count as one, so pack your boots in one of your bags.

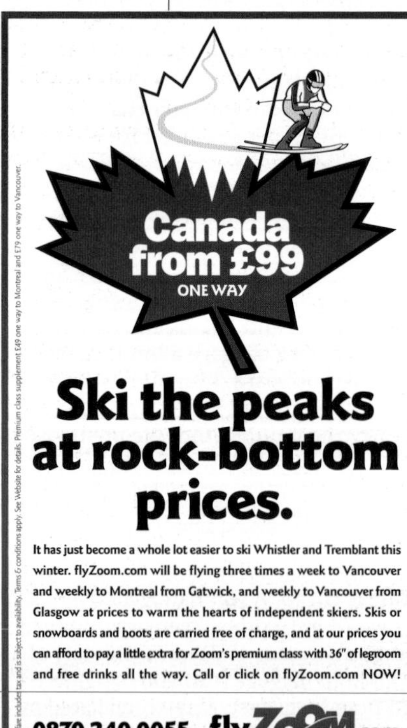

# Drive to the Alps

***And ski where you please***

*by* **Chris Allan**

**More and more people from Britain are doing what the French, the Germans and the Dutch have done for years, and driving to their Alpine resorts. It has various advantages. For many people, it's just less hassle than checking in at dawn for a flight from Gatwick, and less tedious than sitting around waiting for a delayed charter plane that's stuck in Majorca. For families (especially those going self-catering), it simplifies the job of moving half the contents of your house to the Alps. If there are four or five people in your party, the cost can be lower than travelling by air. And for a few adventurous people, taking a car opens up the exciting possibility of touring around several resorts in one trip.**

**Cross-Channel ferries are faster and more pleasant than ever, with the possibility of a seriously good lunch on P&O's short crossings as an alternative to the quicker shuttle-trains through the tunnel. And the motorway networks in northern France and on the approaches to the Alps have improved immensely in the last decade. You can now get to most resorts easily in a day, if you're based in south-east England.**

For us, the freedom factor is the key. If the snow's bad in your resort, if the lift queues are horrendous, or if the resort you've plumped for turns out to be a let-down, you don't have to grin and bear it – if you have a car, you can try somewhere else.

Another plus-point is that you can extend the standard six-day holiday by two days by taking only one extra day off work – crossing the Channel early on a Friday morning and returning nine days later on the Sunday evening. On the outward journey, we often spend a day in a different resort before moving on to our final destination late on the Saturday. After a full day on the slopes on the final Saturday, driving for a few hours before stopping for the night means you won't find Sunday's journey too demanding, and you may even have time for a traditional French Sunday lunch.





### AS YOU LIKE IT

If you fancy visiting several resorts, you can use one as a base and make day trips to others when it suits you. This way, you can still take advantage of package holiday prices.

The key to turning this kind of holiday into a success is to go for a base that offers easy road access to other resorts. Our suggestions for France are in a separate chapter. A good choice in Austria is the Tirol: the resorts east of Innsbruck offer many options. Söll is a convenient base for exploring resorts such as Alpbach and Kitzbühel. Further east in Salzburgerland there are lots of possibilities – and the Ski Amadé lift pass described in our Austrian introduction means you can exploit them conveniently and economically. Western Austria is not ideal for this sort of holiday, but from St Anton you could make day trips to Zürs, Ischgl and Serfaus.



### AROUND THE ALPS IN SEVEN DAYS

If you want to see as much of the Alps as possible, consider making a Grand Tour by car, moving every day or two to a different resort and enjoying the complete freedom of going where you want, when you

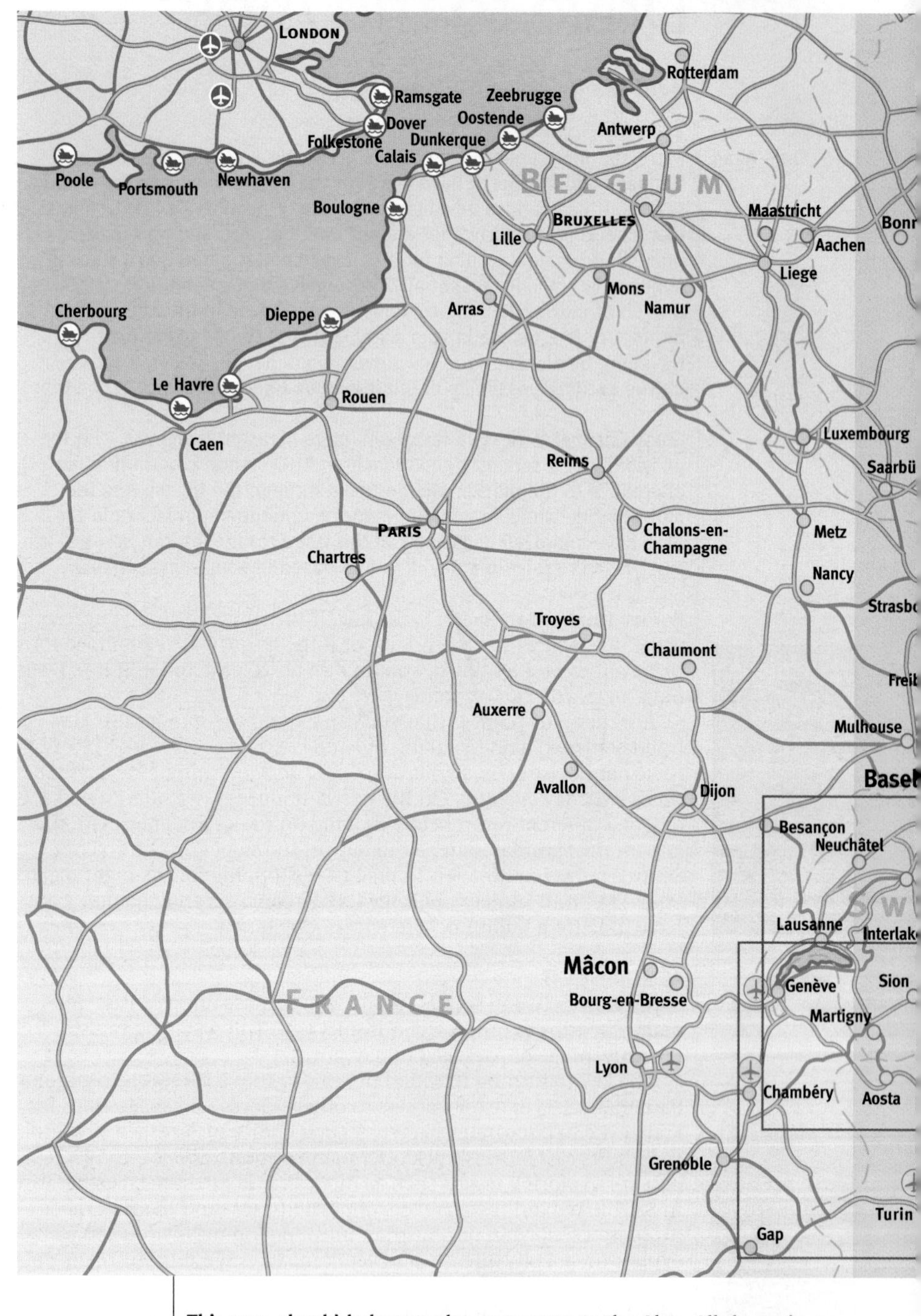


This map should help you plan your route to the Alps. All the main routes from the Channel and all the routes up into the mountains funnel through (or close to) three 'gateways', picked out on the map in larger type – Mâcon, Basel and Ulm. Decide which gateway suits your destination, and pick a route to it. Occasionally, using different Channel ports will lead you to use different gateways.

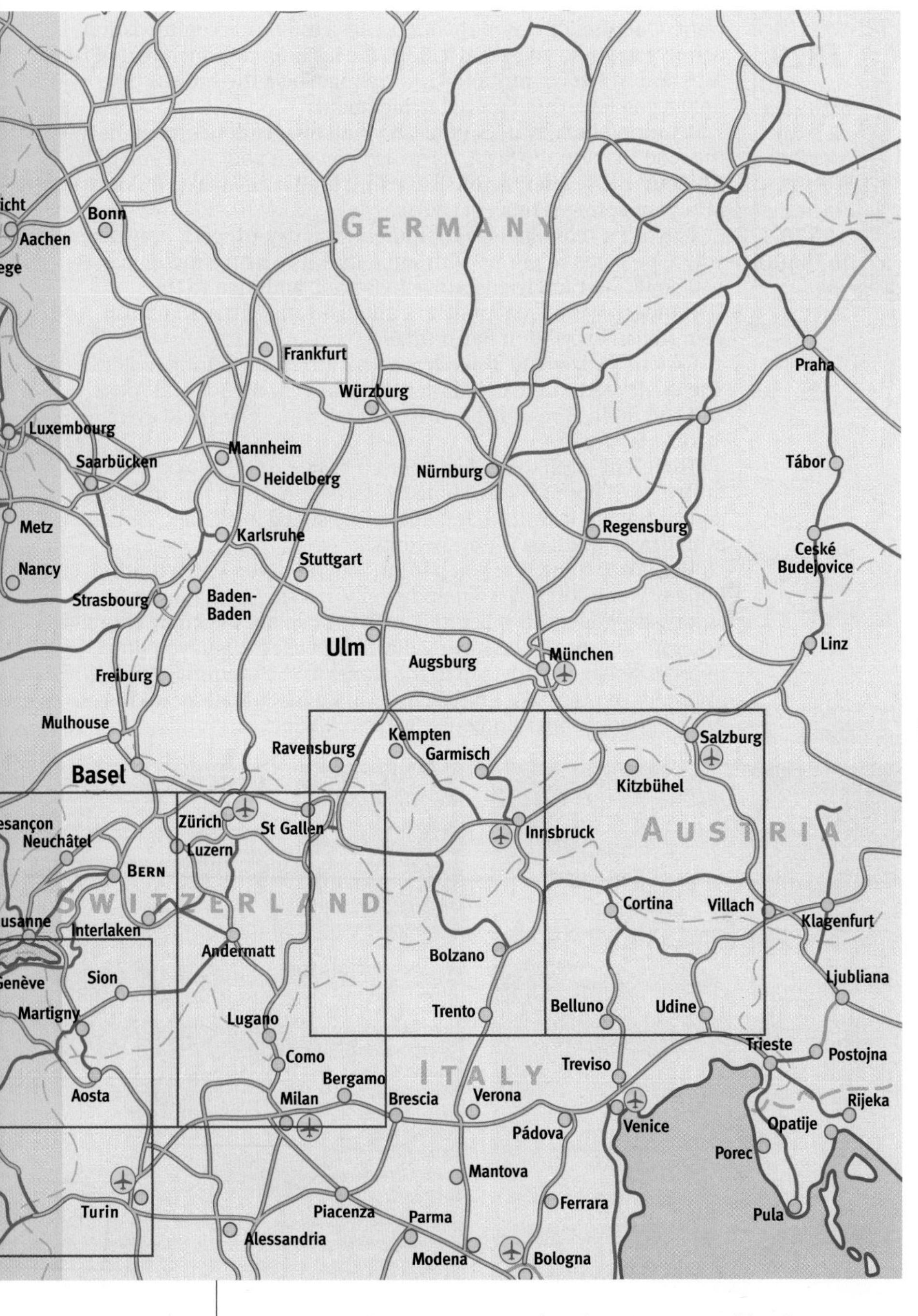


**The boxes on the map correspond to the areas covered by the more detailed maps at the start of the main country sections of the book:**
**Austria page 106**
**France page 200**
**Italy page 380**
**Switzerland page 436**

want. Out of high season there's no need to book accommodation before you go, so you can decide at the last minute which part of the Alps and which countries to visit – going where the snow is best, unless you have other special requirements.

A touring holiday doesn't mean you'll be spending more time on the road than on the piste – provided you plan your route carefully. An hour's drive after the lifts have shut is all it need take. It does eat into your après-ski time, of course.

Italy is far more suitable for tourers than day-trippers, provided you're prepared to put up with some slow drives on winding passes. You could start in Livigno, drive to Bormio and then to the Dolomites, visiting Madonna di Campiglio and Selva, and finish your Italian expedition in Cortina.

Eastern Switzerland also offers a very attractive touring holiday. You could start in Davos/ Klosters, take in Lenzerheide and Arosa and end up in Flims. With a little extra driving, you could even include St Moritz.

There's no need to confine yourself to one country. You could imitate the famous Haute-Route by starting in Argentière in France and ending up in Switzerland's Saas-Fee, taking in Verbier, Zermatt – even Crans-Montana if time permits.

The major thing that you have to watch out for with a touring holiday is the cost of accommodation. Checking into a resort hotel as an independent traveller for a night or two doesn't come cheap. You can save money by staying down the valley – and you don't necessarily have to drive up to the slopes in the morning. For example, you can take a funicular from Bourg-St-Maurice up to Les Arcs; a gondola links Brides-les-Bains to Méribel.

**TYRES / CHAINS**

For several seasons now we have used winter tyres made by a specialist Dutch company, Vredestein. The editorial Audi Allroad is shown here wearing Wintrac 'V'-rated tyres, apparently good for 149mph. We've found these (like the company's Snowtracs) excellent both on-snow and off. We leave them on year-round – they are no noiser than standard tyres.

So effective is the combination of 4WD and Vredestein Wintracs that we still haven't had a chance to evaluate Spikes Spiders. We keep taking them to the Alps, but never have to bring them into action. These are clever Swiss gadgets that you use instead of chains on cars (like the Audi) with wide wheels that can't take chains. You can hire or buy from the UK agents.

www.vredestein.com
t 01933 677770
www.spikesspider.com
t 01706 819365

# Drive to the French Alps

## *To make the most of them*

*by* **Chris Gill**

**If you've read the preceding chapter, you'll have gathered that we are keen on driving to the Alps. But we're particularly keen on driving to the French Alps. The drive is a relatively short one, whereas many of the transfers to major French resorts from Geneva airport are relatively long. And the route from the Channel is through France rather than Germany, which for Francophiles like us means it's a pleasant prospect rather than a grim one.**



### TRAVEL TIME

The French Alps are the number-one destination for British car-borne skiers. The journey time is surprisingly short. From Calais, for example, you can comfortably cover the 900km/560 miles to Chamonix in about nine hours plus stops – with the exception of the final few miles, the whole journey is on motorways. And except on peak weekends the traffic is relatively light, especially if you steer clear of Paris. Look back at the map of Europe in the previous chapter to see what's involved.

With some southern exceptions, all the resorts of the French Alps are within a day's driving range, provided you cross the Channel early in the day (or overnight). Weekend traffic jams used to make the journey from Albertville to the Tarentaise resorts (from the Trois Vallées to Val-d'Isère) a nightmare for drivers and coach passengers alike; thanks to road improvements these are largely a thing of the past, but on peak-season Saturdays you can still encounter serious queues around Moutiers, where there is a traffic management scheme involving traffic lights placed well away from the town, to minimise pollution.





### DAY-TRIP BASES

Most people driving to the French Alps do it simply because they find it a more relaxing way to get themselves, their kit and perhaps their kids to their chosen resort. But, as we have explained in the previous chapter, having a car opens up different kinds of holiday for the more adventurous. Day-tripping, for example.

In the southern French Alps, Serre-Chevalier and Montgenèvre are ideal bases for day-tripping. They are within easy reach of one another, and Montgenèvre is at one end of the Milky Way lift network, which includes Sauze d'Oulx and Sestriere in Italy – you can drive on to these resorts, or reach them by lift and piste. On the French side of the border, a few miles south, Puy-St-Vincent is an underrated resort that is well worth a visit for a day – as is Risoul, a little further south. The major resorts of Alpe-d'Huez and Les Deux-Alpes are also within range, as is the cult off-piste resort of La Grave. Getting to them involves crossing a high pass, but it's a major route linking Grenoble to Briançon and all points south, and is kept open pretty reliably.

The Chamonix valley is an ideal destination for day-trippers. The Mont-Blanc lift pass covers Chamonix, Les Contamines, Megève and others. Flaine and its satellites are fairly accessible – and so are Verbier in Switzerland, if the intervening passes are open, and Courmayeur in Italy, now that the Mont Blanc tunnel is open once again. You could stay in a valley town such as Cluses, to escape resort prices altogether, or base yourself in a relatively cheap resort such as St-Gervais.

## MOVING ON

A look at the map in this chapter shows that a different approach will pay dividends in the Tarentaise region of France. Practically all the resorts here – from Valmorel to Val-d'Isère – are found at the end of long winding roads up from the main valley. You could visit them all from a base such as Aime, but it would be hard work. If instead you stayed in a different resort each night, moving on from one to the next in the early evening, you could have the trip of a lifetime. Imagine a week in which you could explore the Three Valleys, the Paradiski area (La Plagne/Les Arcs) and Val-d'Isère/Tignes.

## GETTING THERE

The map in our Driving to the Alps chapter, ahead of this one, shows the main routes across France to the Alps. Whatever route you prefer across the Channel, the gateway to the French Alps is Mâcon – though if you're taking a short crossing to Calais, this may be only roughly true. Your route south is via Reims, Troyes and Dijon; but if you are heading for Geneva, to get to the northern French Alps, you no longer have to tangle with the busy A6 from Paris via Beaune to Mâcon and Lyon. The relatively new A39 autoroute south from Dijon means that you can head for Bourg-en-Bresse, staying well east of Mâcon. If you need an overnight stop north of Dijon, there are plenty of characterful towns to consider – Arras, St-Quentin, Laon, Troyes. Reims makes a particularly neat stopover – the autoroute passes close to the centre, with its impressive Gothic cathedral.

From the more westerly Channel ports of Le Havre or Caen your route to Mâcon sounds dead simple: the A13 to Paris then the A6 south. But you have to get through or around Paris in the process.

The most direct way around the city is the notorious périphérique – a hectic, multi-lane urban motorway close to the centre, with exits every few hundred yards and traffic that is either worryingly fast-moving or jammed solid. If the périphérique is jammed it takes ages. The more reliable alternative is to take a series of motorways and dual carriageways through the south-west fringes of Greater Paris. One such route is signed fairly clearly, but with the aid of a detailed map (such as that in the Michelin road atlas) you can take a more direct route from Versailles to the A6 near Orly.

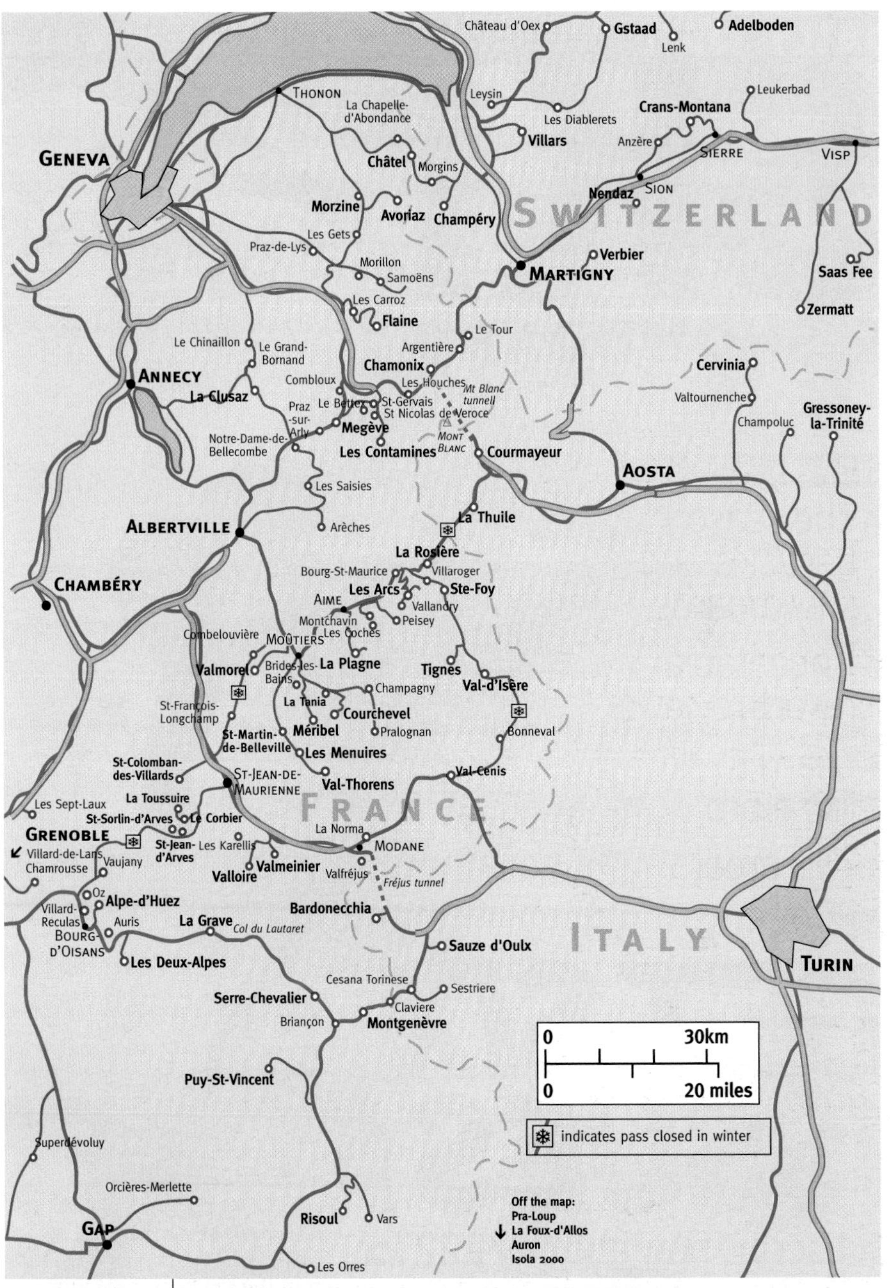


## Getting around the French Alps

Pick the right gateway – Geneva, Chambéry or Grenoble – and you can hardly go wrong. The approach to Serre-Chevalier and Montgenèvre involves the 2058m/6,750ft Col du Lauteret; but the road is a major one and kept clear of snow or reopened quickly after a fall. Crossing the French-Swiss border between Chamonix and Verbier involves two closure-prone passes – the Montets and the Forclaz. When necessary, one-way traffic runs beside the tracks through the rail tunnel beneath the passes.

# Travelling by rail

***Let the train take the strain***

*by* **Dave Watts**

**Taking the train to the Alps can be a great way to get more time on the slopes without taking more time off work. You can leave on Friday night, arriving in your resort on Saturday morning, and return on the following Saturday night, arriving back home on the Sunday – eight days' skiing for five days out of the office. Even if you opt for a different service that doesn't deliver the eight-day week, travelling by train is one of the most restful ways to get to the Alps.**

**The most popular train destination, with several different direct and indirect services, is the Tarentaise valley in France. You can step off the train in Bourg-St-Maurice and on to a funicular straight up to Arc 1600, and there are quick bus transfers to the other famous mega-resorts of this region – Val-d'Isère, Tignes, La Plagne, Courchevel and Méribel, with slightly longer transfers to Les Menuires and Val-Thorens.**

**But you can travel by train to many other resorts. And many traditional resorts, especially in Switzerland, are on the rail network and therefore reachable without resorting to buses. How many times you'll have to change trains is another matter. You can also put your car on a motorail service (but no longer from Calais).**

## DIRECT TRAIN SERVICES TO THE FRENCH ALPS

Since 1997, Eurostar has offered a truly direct service to the Alps – you board the train at London Waterloo or Ashford in Kent and disembark at Moûtiers or Bourg-St-Maurice in the Tarentaise valley, without changing trains en route. The special winter services will run from 19 December through to end-March. Standard return tickets cost from £179 (£269 for first class, which includes meals on board). Seats can also be booked as part of a package holiday. There's an overnight service which, for most of the season, allows you two extra days' skiing or boarding – it leaves on Friday night, arriving early on Saturday morning, and returns late Saturday evening, arriving back on Sunday morning. The service uses standard Eurostar carriages with no special sleeping arrangements – you just doze (or not) in your seat. The daytime service gives you no more than the standard six days on the slopes: both outward and return services leave on Saturday morning, arriving late afternoon. The outbound service also stops at Ashford, in Kent, and Aime (between Moûtiers and Bourg-St-Maurice). The return service doesn't stop at Aime (because of passport control issues). As Christmas Day and New Year's Day fall on Saturdays this season, the first three overnight departures (on 19 and 26 Dec and 2 Jan) will be on Sundays, returning the following Sunday (arriving back Monday am). The first three daytime services (20 and 27 December and 3 January) will run Monday to Monday.

All the other train services to the Alps involve a change somewhere along the line, but they can still be fairly convenient and also allow for extra time on the slopes. Unlike Eurostar, many of the other services are equipped with sleeping compartments.

The Snowtrain is another weekly overnight service to the Tarentaise giving an eight-day week on the slopes, but it starts from Calais. It runs from 26 December until 25 March, normally leaving Calais on Friday night and arriving in the Alps the following morning. For the return journey you leave the Alps on Saturday evening arriving back Sunday morning. You cross the Channel by ferry from Dover. The train works on a charter basis and can be booked through UK tour operators – they have allocated spaces on each service. Overnight amenities include on-board couchettes (six drop-down berths to a compartment) and a disco/bar. Beware, it can get very noisy and crowded. It is possible to book a compartment for the exclusive use of four or five people on both legs of the journey. Booking independently costs £149 return for most of the season.

There is a similar Friday night sleeper service to the Tarentaise starting from Paris. It runs from 19 December until 1 April. You take the Eurostar to Paris from London Waterloo and change trains at Paris Gare du Nord for an overnight service to the Alps. The return journey leaves the Alps on Saturday evening, arriving in Paris early on Sunday morning. It costs £209 return including couchettes for most of the season. As with Eurostar, both the Dover and the Paris sleeper services will run Sunday to Sunday (or Monday) over Christmas and New Year this season.

There are a number of indirect services available on the French railway throughout the week, but most mean crossing Paris from the Gare du Nord to the Gare de Lyon or Gare d'Austerlitz – the change of station is not difficult, though, with a direct metro, regular buses and plenty of taxis at your disposal. Indirect services to many Alpine destinations via Brussels or Lille also run every day of the week and involve only a change of platform. This can be easier than going via Paris, and the timing of the slower overnight services via Brussels may suit you better; the services tend to be less frequent and are often more expensive, but are worth considering at peak dates.

Motorail is another option, getting your car to the Alps without having to drive it all the way. The French services have been cut back and the main option left is Paris to Lyon. An alternative is using a German DB AutoZug service from Dusseldorf, Hamburg or Cologne. Destinations include Salzburg, Innsbruck and Villach in Austria, Bolzano and Verona (for the Dolomites), Lindau (near the Austrian and Swiss borders at Lake Constance), Lörach (near the Swiss border at Basel), Narbonne (for Andorra and the Pyrenees) and Munich.

For more details of French rail services contact Rail Europe on 08701 244 646 for overnight ski trains or 08705 848 848 for Eurostar trains. Or visit www.raileurope.co.uk.

# Choosing your resort

## *Get it right first time*

**Most people get to go skiing or boarding only once or twice a year – and then only for a week at a time. So choosing the right resort is crucially important. This book is designed to help you get it right first time. Here is some advice on how to use our information to best effect – particularly for the benefit of readers with relatively narrow experience of different resorts. Chamonix, Châtel and Courchevel are all French resorts, but they are as similar as chalk and Camembert. Start to consider resorts in other countries – Alpbach in Austria, say, or Zermatt in Switzerland – and the differences become even more pronounced. And once you admit resorts in North America as well as those in Europe, the range of variation becomes extremely wide.**

Lots of factors need to be taken into account. The weight you attach to each of them depends on your own personal preferences, and on the make-up of the group you are going on holiday with. Starting on page 85 you'll find 20 shortlists of resorts which we rate as outstanding in various key respects.

Each resort chapter is organised in the same way, to help you choose the right resort. This short introduction takes you through the structure and what you will find under each heading we use.

**WHICH RESORT?**

We start each chapter with a one-line verdict, in which we aim to sum up the resort in a few words. If you like the sound of it, you might want to go next to our Costs rating, in the margin. These ratings, ranging from ①②③④⑤⑥ to ①②③④⑤⑥, reflect the total cost of a week's holiday from Britain, including a typical package of flights plus half-board accommodation, a lift pass and meals and drinks on the spot. As you might expect with a six-point scale, three means on the low side of average, four means on the high side. Further on, in the margin text, we give the cost of lift passes in local currency; these are for the 2003/04 season. Below the Costs rating, in the Ratings section, we rate each resort from 11 points of view – the more stars the better. (All these star ratings are brought together in one chart, which follows this chapter.) Still looking at the information in the margin, in most chapters we have a News section; this is likely to be of most use and interest in resorts you already know from past visits.

For major resorts, the next things to look at are our lists of the main good and bad points about the resort and its slopes, picked out with + and –. These lists are followed by a summary in **bold type**, in which we've aimed to weigh up the pros and cons, coming off the fence and giving our view of who might like the resort. These sections should give you a good idea of whether the resort is likely to suit *you*, and whether you should read our detailed analysis of it.

You'll know by now whether this is, for example, a high, hideous, convenient, purpose-built resort with superb, snow-sure slopes for all standards of skier or boarder but absolutely no nightlife, or whether it's a pretty, traditional village with gentle wooded skiing, ideal for beginners if only there was some snow. We then look at each aspect in more detail.

## THE RESORT

Resorts vary enormously in character and charm. At the extremes of the range are the handful of really hideous modern apartment-block resorts thrown up in France in the 1960s – step forward Les Menuires and Flaine – and the captivating old traffic-free mountain villages of which Switzerland has an unfair number. But it isn't simply a question of old versus new. Some purpose-built places (such as Valmorel) can have a much friendlier feel than some traditional resorts with big blocky buildings (eg Davos). And some places can be remarkably strung out (eg Vail) whereas others are surprisingly compact (eg Wengen).

The landscape can have an important impact – whether the resort is at the bottom of a narrow, shady valley (eg Ischgl) or on a sunny shelf with panoramic views (eg Crans-Montana). Some places are working towns as well as ski resorts (eg Bormio). Some are full of bars, discos and shops (eg St Anton). Others are peaceful backwaters (eg Arabba). Traffic may choke the streets (eg Sölden). Or the village may be traffic-free (eg Mürren).

In this first section of each chapter, we try to sort out the character of the place for you. Later, in the Staying there section, we tell you more about the hotels, restaurants, bars and so on.

## THE MOUNTAINS

**The slopes** Some mountains and lift networks are vast and complex, while others are much smaller and lacking variation. The description here tells you how the area divides up into different sectors and how the links between them work.

**Terrain-parks** We summarise here the specially prepared fun-parks and other terrain features most resorts now arrange for freestylers.

**Snow reliability** This is a crucial factor for many people, and one that varies enormously. In some resorts you don't have to worry at all about a lack of snow, while others (including some very big names) are notorious for treating their paying guests to ice, mud and slush. Whether a resort is likely to have decent snow on its slopes normally depends on the height, the direction most of the slopes face (north good, south bad), its snow record and how much snowmaking it has. But bear in mind that in the Alps high resorts tend to have rocky terrain where the runs will need more snow than those on the pasture land of lower resorts. Many resorts have increased their snowmaking capacity in recent years and we list the latest amount they claim to have in the Key facts section and comment on it in the snow reliability text. Bear in mind that snowmaking can operate only if temperatures are low enough (typically –2°C or less), so it's much more useful in midwinter than in spring.

**For experts, intermediates, beginners** Most (though not all) resorts have something to offer beginners, but relatively few will keep an expert happy for a week's holiday. As for intermediates, whether a resort will suit you really depends on your standard and inclinations. Places such as Cervinia and Obergurgl are ideal for those who want easy cruising runs, but have little to offer intermediates looking for more challenge. Others, such as Sölden and Val-d'Isère, may intimidate the less confident intermediate who doesn't know the area well. Some, such as the Trois Vallées and Portes du Soleil, have vast amounts of terrain so that you can cover different ground each day. But some other well-known names, such as Alpbach and Courmayeur, and many North American resorts, have surprisingly small areas.

**For cross-country** We don't pretend that this is a guide for avid cross-country skiers. But if you or one of your group wants to try it, our summary here will help you gauge whether the resort is worth considering or whether it is a washout. It looks not just at the amount of cross-country available but also at its scenic beauty and whether or not the tracks are likely to have decent snow (many are at low altitude).

**Queues** Another key factor. Most resorts have improved their lift systems enormously in the last 10 years, and monster queues are largely a thing of the past. Crowding on the pistes is more of a worry in many resorts, and we mention problems of this kind here. On our piste maps, note that we mark with a chair symbol only fast chairs; these offer short ride times, and also shift large numbers of people per hour. Lifts not marked with a symbol are slow chairs or drag-lifts.

**Mountain restaurants** Here's a subject that divides people clearly into two opposing camps. To some, having a decent lunch in civilised surroundings – either in the sun, contemplating amazing scenery, or in a cosy hut, sheltered from the elements – makes or breaks their holiday. Others regard a prolonged midday stop as a waste of valuable skiing time, as well as valuable spending money. We are firmly in the former camp. We get very disheartened by places with miserable restaurants and miserable food (eg many resorts in America); and there are some resorts that we go to regularly partly because of the cosy huts and excellent cuisine (eg Zermatt).

**Schools and guides** This is an area where we rely heavily on readers' reports of their own or their friends' experiences. The only way to judge a ski school is by trying it. Reports on schools are always extremely valuable and frequently record disappointment.

**Facilities for children** If you need nursery facilities, don't go to Italy. In other countries, facilities for looking after and teaching children can vary enormously between resorts. We say what is available in each resort, including what childcare arrangements are on offer from UK tour operators – often the most attractive option for Brits. But, again, to be of real help we need first-hand reports from people whose children have actually used the facilities.

## SNOWBOARDING

The Mountains section applies to both skiers and snowboarders. But because certain things are important to snowboarding that aren't relevant (or aren't as relevant) to skiing, we also include a special assessment for snowboarders, picked out in a separate box. This covers issues such as whether the slopes present special attractions or problems (eg flat sections that snowboarders have to 'scoot' along), how much you can expect to have to use drag-lifts and whether you'll find specialist schools and shops in the resort.

## STAYING THERE

**How to go** The basic choice is between catered chalets, hotels and self-catering accommodation. The catered chalet holiday remains a peculiarly British phenomenon. A tour operator takes over a chalet (or a hotel in some cases), staffs it with young Brits (or Antipodeans), fills it with British guests, provides half-board and free wine, and lets you drink your duty-free booze without hassle. You can take over a complete chalet, or share one with other groups. It is a relatively economical way of visiting the expensive top resorts.

Hotels, of course, can vary a lot but, especially in France and Switzerland, can work out very expensive. In North America, watch out for supplements: rooms are often capable of sleeping four, and UK tour operators are inclined to base their standard brochure prices on the assumption that you fill all available bed spaces.

Apartments can be very economical but most French ones, in particular, tend to be very small. It's not unusual for brochure prices to be based on four people sleeping in a one-room studio, for example – to be comfortable, pay extra for under-occupancy. But some recently built French apartments are more spacious and comfortable – where we know of these we name them.

We also look at what's available for independent travellers who want to fix their own hotels or self-catering accommodation. With hotels we've given each a price rating from ① to ⑥ – the more coins, the more expensive the hotel.

**Eating out** The range of restaurants varies widely. Even some big resorts, such as Les Arcs, may have little choice because most of the visitors stay in their apartments or chalets. Others, such as Val-d'Isère, have a huge range available, including national and regional cuisine, pizzas, fondues and international fare. American resorts generally have an excellent range of restaurants – most people eat out. This is an area where we rely a lot on reporters recommending restaurants that were good last season – and we are often able to recommend some out-of-the-way restaurants that you might not otherwise find.

**Après-ski** Tastes and styles vary enormously. Most resorts have pleasant places in which to have an immediate post-skiing beer or hot chocolate. Some then go dead. Others have noisy bars and discos until the early hours. And, especially in Austrian resorts, there may be a lot of events such as tobogganing and bowling that are organised by British tour operator reps. For this section we are largely dependent on hearing from reporters who are keen après-skiers; sadly our readership doesn't seem to include many.

**Off the slopes** This is largely aimed at assessing how suitable a resort is for someone who doesn't intend to use the slopes – a non-skiing spouse or elderly relative or friend, for example. In some resorts, such as most French purpose-built places, there is really nothing to amuse them. In others, such as Seefeld in Austria, there are more people walking, skating and swimming than there are people skiing or boarding. Excursion possibilities vary widely. And there are great variations in the practicality of meeting skiers and boarders for lunch up the mountain.

**Staying up the mountain/down the valley** If there are interesting options for staying on the slopes above the resort village or in valley towns below it, we've picked them out. The former is often good for avoiding early-morning scrums for the lifts, the latter for cutting costs considerably.

# Resort ratings at a glance

| | ANDORRA | | | AUSTRIA | | | | |
|---|---|---|---|---|---|---|---|---|
| | ARINSAL | PAS DE LA CASA | SOLDEU | ALPBACH | BAD GASTEIN | ELLMAU | HINTERTUX | ISCHGL |
| Page | 94 | 96 | 98 | 109 | 111 | 114 | 117 | 126 |
| Snow | **** | **** | **** | ** | *** | ** | ***** | **** |
| Extent | * | *** | ** | * | **** | **** | ** | **** |
| Experts | * | * | * | * | *** | * | *** | *** |
| Intermediates | ** | *** | *** | ** | **** | **** | *** | **** |
| Beginners | *** | **** | **** | **** | ** | **** | ** | ** |
| Convenience | *** | **** | *** | ** | ** | *** | ** | *** |
| Queues | *** | *** | *** | *** | *** | **** | *** | **** |
| Restaurants* | ** | *** | * | *** | **** | ** | ** | **** |
| Scenery | *** | *** | *** | *** | *** | *** | *** | *** |
| Resort charm | * | * | * | ***** | *** | *** | *** | **** |
| Off-slope | * | * | * | *** | **** | *** | * | *** |
| | KITZBÜHEL | LECH | MAYRHOFEN | OBERGURGL | OBERTAUERN | SAALBACH-HINTERGLEMM | SCHLADMING | SÖLDEN |
| Page | 132 | 138 | 145 | 153 | 158 | 160 | 166 | 170 |
| Snow | ** | **** | *** | ***** | **** | *** | **** | ***** |
| Extent | *** | **** | *** | ** | ** | *** | *** | *** |
| Experts | *** | **** | * | ** | *** | ** | ** | *** |
| Intermediates | **** | **** | *** | *** | **** | **** | **** | **** |
| Beginners | ** | **** | ** | **** | **** | *** | **** | ** |
| Convenience | ** | *** | * | **** | **** | **** | *** | ** |
| Queues | ** | **** | * | ***** | **** | *** | **** | *** |
| Restaurants* | **** | ** | **** | ** | *** | **** | **** | *** |
| Scenery | *** | *** | *** | *** | *** | *** | *** | *** |
| Resort charm | **** | **** | *** | **** | ** | **** | **** | ** |
| Off-slope | ***** | *** | **** | ** | ** | ** | **** | ** |
| | SÖLL | ST ANTON | ST JOHANN IN TIROL | WESTENDORF | ZELL AM SEE | | | |
| Page | 172 | 178 | 186 | 188 | 190 | | | |
| Snow | ** | **** | ** | ** | ** | | | |
| Extent | **** | **** | ** | * | ** | | | |
| Experts | * | ***** | * | * | ** | | | |
| Intermediates | **** | *** | *** | ** | *** | | | |
| Beginners | *** | * | **** | *** | *** | | | |
| Convenience | ** | *** | *** | *** | ** | | | |
| Queues | *** | ** | *** | **** | ** | | | |
| Restaurants* | ** | *** | **** | *** | *** | | | |
| Scenery | *** | *** | *** | *** | *** | | | |
| Resort charm | *** | **** | *** | **** | *** | | | |
| Off-slope | ** | *** | *** | ** | **** | | | |

* Refers to mountain restaurants only

# FRANCE

| | ALPE-D'HUEZ | LES ARCS | AVORIAZ | CHAMONIX | CHÂTEL | LA CLUSAZ | LES CONTAMINES | COURCHEVEL |
|---|---|---|---|---|---|---|---|---|
| Page | 204 | 213 | 223 | 227 | 235 | 240 | 246 | 248 |
| Snow | **** | **** | *** | **** | ** | ** | **** | **** |
| Extent | **** | *** | ***** | *** | ***** | *** | ** | ***** |
| Experts | **** | **** | *** | ***** | *** | *** | ** | **** |
| Intermediates | **** | **** | **** | ** | **** | **** | *** | ***** |
| Beginners | ***** | **** | **** | * | *** | **** | ** | **** |
| Convenience | **** | **** | **** | * | ** | *** | ** | **** |
| Queues | **** | *** | *** | ** | *** | *** | *** | **** |
| Restaurants* | **** | ** | **** | ** | *** | **** | **** | **** |
| Scenery | **** | *** | *** | ***** | **** | *** | **** | *** |
| Resort charm | * | * | ** | **** | *** | **** | **** | ** |
| Off-slope | *** | * | * | ***** | ** | *** | ** | *** |

| | LES DEUX-ALPES | FLAINE | LES GETS | LA GRAVE | MEGÈVE | LES MENUIRES | MÉRIBEL | MONTGENÈVRE |
|---|---|---|---|---|---|---|---|---|
| Page | 257 | 263 | 270 | 272 | 274 | 280 | 282 | 292 |
| Snow | **** | **** | ** | *** | ** | **** | *** | **** |
| Extent | *** | **** | *** | * | ***** | ***** | ***** | **** |
| Experts | **** | **** | *** | ***** | ** | **** | **** | ** |
| Intermediates | ** | ***** | **** | * | **** | ***** | ***** | **** |
| Beginners | *** | ***** | **** | * | *** | *** | **** | ***** |
| Convenience | *** | ***** | *** | *** | ** | ***** | *** | **** |
| Queues | ** | *** | *** | **** | **** | **** | **** | **** |
| Restaurants* | ** | ** | *** | ** | **** | *** | *** | ** |
| Scenery | **** | **** | *** | **** | ***** | *** | *** | *** |
| Resort charm | ** | * | *** | *** | **** | * | *** | *** |
| Off-slope | ** | * | *** | * | **** | * | *** | * |

| | MORZINE | LA PLAGNE | PUY-ST-VINCENT | RISOUL | LA ROSIÈRE | SERRE-CHEVALIER | STE-FOY | ST-MARTIN-DE-BELLEVILLE |
|---|---|---|---|---|---|---|---|---|
| Page | 296 | 305 | 315 | 317 | 320 | 322 | 329 | 333 |
| Snow | ** | **** | *** | *** | *** | *** | *** | *** |
| Extent | ***** | **** | ** | *** | *** | **** | * | ***** |
| Experts | *** | *** | *** | ** | ** | *** | **** | **** |
| Intermediates | **** | ***** | *** | **** | *** | **** | *** | ***** |
| Beginners | *** | **** | *** | **** | ***** | **** | ** | *** |
| Convenience | ** | ***** | ***** | **** | *** | *** | *** | *** |
| Queues | *** | *** | *** | **** | *** | *** | ***** | **** |
| Restaurants* | *** | *** | *** | *** | * | *** | ** | **** |
| Scenery | *** | **** | *** | *** | *** | *** | *** | *** |
| Resort charm | *** | * | ** | ** | *** | *** | *** | **** |
| Off-slope | *** | * | * | * | * | ** | * | * |

| | LES SYBELLES | LA TANIA | TIGNES | VAL-D'ISÈRE | VALMOREL | VAL-THORENS | | |
|---|---|---|---|---|---|---|---|---|
| Page | 335 | 340 | 343 | 354 | 364 | 366 | | |
| Snow | *** | *** | ***** | ***** | *** | ***** | | |
| Extent | ***** | ***** | ***** | ***** | *** | ***** | | |
| Experts | ** | **** | ***** | ***** | ** | **** | | |
| Intermediates | *** | ***** | ***** | ***** | **** | ***** | | |
| Beginners | **** | ** | ** | *** | ***** | **** | | |
| Convenience | *** | **** | **** | *** | ***** | ***** | | |
| Queues | **** | **** | **** | **** | **** | *** | | |
| Restaurants* | ** | **** | *** | ** | ** | **** | | |
| Scenery | *** | *** | *** | *** | *** | *** | | |
| Resort charm | */**** | *** | ** | *** | **** | ** | | |
| Off-slope | * | * | * | ** | ** | ** | | |

| | BORMIO | CERVINIA | CORTINA D'AMPEZZO | COURMAYEUR | LIVIGNO | MADONNA DI CAMPIGLIO | MONTEROSA SKI | SAUZE D'OULX |
|---|---|---|---|---|---|---|---|---|
| Page | 383 | 385 | 390 | 395 | 400 | 404 | 406 | 410 |
| Snow | *** | ***** | *** | **** | **** | *** | *** | ** |
| Extent | ** | *** | *** | ** | ** | *** | **** | **** |
| Experts | * | * | ** | *** | ** | ** | *** | ** |
| Intermediates | *** | **** | *** | **** | *** | **** | **** | **** |
| Beginners | ** | ***** | ***** | ** | **** | **** | ** | ** |
| Convenience | *** | *** | * | * | ** | *** | **** | ** |
| Queues | *** | *** | **** | *** | **** | **** | **** | *** |
| Restaurants* | **** | *** | **** | **** | *** | *** | ** | *** |
| Scenery | *** | **** | ***** | **** | *** | **** | **** | *** |
| Resort charm | **** | ** | **** | **** | *** | *** | *** | ** |
| Off-slope | **** | * | ***** | *** | ** | *** | * | * |

| | SELVA | SESTRIERE | LA THUILE | | | | | |
|---|---|---|---|---|---|---|---|---|
| Page | 415 | 423 | 425 | | | | | |
| Snow | **** | *** | **** | | | | | |
| Extent | ***** | **** | *** | | | | | |
| Experts | *** | *** | ** | | | | | |
| Intermediates | ***** | **** | **** | | | | | |
| Beginners | **** | *** | **** | | | | | |
| Convenience | *** | **** | *** | | | | | |
| Queues | *** | *** | **** | | | | | |
| Restaurants* | **** | ** | * | | | | | |
| Scenery | ***** | *** | *** | | | | | |
| Resort charm | *** | * | *** | | | | | |
| Off-slope | *** | * | ** | | | | | |

* Refers to mountain restaurants only

| | ANDERMATT | AROSA | CHAMPÉRY | CRANS-MONTANA | DAVOS | FLIMS | GRIN'WALD | MÜRREN |
|---|---|---|---|---|---|---|---|---|
| Page | 439 | 441 | 443 | 445 | 447 | 454 | 456 | 460 |
| Snow | **** | *** | ** | ** | **** | *** | ** | *** |
| Extent | * | ** | ***** | *** | ***** | **** | *** | * |
| Experts | **** | * | *** | ** | **** | *** | ** | *** |
| Intermediates | ** | *** | **** | **** | ***** | ***** | **** | *** |
| Beginners | * | **** | ** | *** | ** | **** | *** | ** |
| Convenience | *** | *** | * | ** | ** | *** | ** | *** |
| Queues | ** | **** | **** | *** | ** | *** | ** | *** |
| Restaurants* | * | **** | *** | *** | *** | *** | *** | ** |
| Scenery | *** | *** | **** | **** | **** | *** | ***** | ***** |
| Resort charm | **** | ** | **** | ** | ** | *** | **** | ***** |
| Off-slope | ** | **** | *** | **** | ***** | *** | **** | *** |

| | SAAS-FEE | ST MORITZ | VERBIER | VILLARS | WENGEN | ZERMATT | | |
|---|---|---|---|---|---|---|---|---|
| Page | 464 | 469 | 475 | 485 | 488 | 493 | | |
| Snow | ***** | **** | *** | ** | ** | **** | | |
| Extent | ** | ***** | ***** | *** | *** | **** | | |
| Experts | *** | **** | ***** | ** | ** | ***** | | |
| Intermediates | **** | **** | *** | *** | **** | **** | | |
| Beginners | ***** | ** | ** | **** | *** | * | | |
| Convenience | *** | ** | ** | *** | *** | * | | |
| Queues | *** | ** | *** | *** | *** | *** | | |
| Restaurants* | *** | **** | *** | *** | **** | ***** | | |
| Scenery | **** | **** | **** | *** | ***** | ***** | | |
| Resort charm | ***** | * | *** | **** | ***** | ***** | | |
| Off-slope | **** | ***** | *** | **** | **** | **** | | |

| | CALIFORNIA HEAVENLY | MAMMOTH | | COLORADO ASPEN | BEAVER CR'K | BRECK'RIDGE | COPPER MOUNTAIN | KEYSTONE |
|---|---|---|---|---|---|---|---|---|
| Page | 510 | 515 | | 523 | 529 | 531 | 536 | 538 |
| Snow | **** | **** | | ***** | ***** | ***** | ***** | ***** |
| Extent | *** | *** | | **** | ** | ** | ** | ** |
| Experts | *** | **** | | ***** | **** | **** | **** | *** |
| Intermediates | **** | **** | | ***** | **** | **** | **** | **** |
| Beginners | **** | **** | | ***** | ***** | **** | **** | **** |
| Convenience | * | ** | | ** | **** | *** | **** | ** |
| Queues | **** | **** | | **** | ***** | **** | **** | **** |
| Restaurants* | * | * | | *** | ** | ** | * | *** |
| Scenery | **** | *** | | *** | *** | *** | *** | *** |
| Resort charm | * | ** | | **** | ** | *** | ** | ** |
| Off-slope | ** | * | | **** | *** | *** | * | ** |

# USA

| | SNOWMASS | STEAMBOAT | TELLURIDE | VAIL | WINTER PARK | | | |
|---|---|---|---|---|---|---|---|---|
| Page | 540 | 542 | 544 | 546 | 552 | | | |
| Snow | ***** | **** | **** | ***** | ***** | | | |
| Extent | **** | *** | ** | **** | *** | | | |
| Experts | ***** | *** | **** | **** | **** | | | |
| Intermediates | ***** | **** | *** | ***** | **** | | | |
| Beginners | ***** | ***** | ***** | *** | ***** | | | |
| Convenience | **** | *** | **** | *** | *** | | | |
| Queues | **** | **** | ***** | ** | **** | | | |
| Restaurants* | *** | *** | * | ** | *** | | | |
| Scenery | *** | *** | **** | *** | *** | | | |
| Resort charm | ** | ** | **** | *** | ** | | | |
| Off-slope | *** | ** | ** | *** | * | | | |
| | REST OF THE WEST ALTA | BIG SKY | THE CANYONS | DEER VALLEY | JACKSON HOLE | PARK CITY | SNOWBIRD | |
| Page | 559 | 561 | 563 | 565 | 567 | 572 | 577 | |
| Snow | ***** | **** | **** | **** | **** | **** | ***** | |
| Extent | *** | *** | *** | ** | *** | *** | *** | |
| Experts | ***** | **** | *** | *** | ***** | **** | ***** | |
| Intermediates | *** | **** | *** | **** | ** | **** | *** | |
| Beginners | *** | **** | *** | **** | *** | **** | ** | |
| Convenience | **** | **** | **** | **** | *** | *** | ***** | |
| Queues | *** | ***** | **** | **** | *** | **** | ** | |
| Restaurants* | ** | * | *** | **** | * | ** | * | |
| Scenery | *** | *** | *** | *** | *** | *** | *** | |
| Resort charm | ** | ** | ** | *** | *** | *** | * | |
| Off-slope | * | ** | ** | ** | *** | *** | * | |
| | NEW ENGLAND KILLINGTON | SMUGGLERS' NOTCH | STOWE | | | | | |
| Page | 584 | 588 | 590 | | | | | |
| Snow | *** | *** | *** | | | | | |
| Extent | ** | * | * | | | | | |
| Experts | *** | *** | *** | | | | | |
| Intermediates | *** | *** | **** | | | | | |
| Beginners | **** | **** | **** | | | | | |
| Convenience | * | ***** | * | | | | | |
| Queues | **** | **** | **** | | | | | |
| Restaurants* | * | * | ** | | | | | |
| Scenery | *** | *** | *** | | | | | |
| Resort charm | * | ** | **** | | | | | |
| Off-slope | * | * | * | | | | | |

* Refers to mountain restaurants only

| | WESTERN CANADA BANFF | BIG WHITE | FERNIE | KICKING HORSE | LAKE LOUISE | PANORAMA | SUN PEAKS | WHISTLER |
|---|---|---|---|---|---|---|---|---|
| Page | 596 | 602 | 604 | 609 | 611 | 616 | 619 | 621 |
| Snow | **** | ***** | ***** | **** | *** | *** | **** | **** |
| Extent | **** | *** | *** | *** | **** | ** | *** | **** |
| Experts | **** | *** | ***** | **** | **** | **** | *** | ***** |
| Intermediates | **** | **** | ** | *** | **** | *** | **** | ***** |
| Beginners | *** | **** | **** | *** | *** | **** | **** | *** |
| Convenience | * | **** | **** | * | * | **** | **** | **** |
| Queues | **** | ***** | **** | ***** | **** | **** | ***** | *** |
| Restaurants* | *** | * | * | ** | ** | * | * | ** |
| Scenery | **** | *** | *** | *** | ***** | *** | *** | *** |
| Resort charm | *** | ** | ** | * | *** | ** | *** | *** |
| Off-slope | ***** | ** | ** | * | **** | * | ** | ** |

| | EASTERN CANADA TREMBLANT |
|---|---|
| Page | 633 |
| Snow | **** |
| Extent | * |
| Experts | ** |
| Intermediates | *** |
| Beginners | **** |
| Convenience | **** |
| Queues | *** |
| Restaurants* | ** |
| Scenery | *** |
| Resort charm | **** |
| Off-slope | *** |

| | SPAIN BAQUEIRA | NORWAY HEMSEDAL | SWEDEN ÅRE | NEW ZEALAND QUEENST'WN |
|---|---|---|---|---|
| Page | 636 | 647 | 650 | 658 |
| Snow | *** | **** | *** | ** |
| Extent | ** | * | ** | * |
| Experts | *** | ** | ** | *** |
| Intermediates | **** | **** | **** | *** |
| Beginners | ** | *** | **** | *** |
| Convenience | *** | ** | *** | * |
| Queues | *** | **** | **** | *** |
| Restaurants* | ** | * | *** | * |
| Scenery | *** | ** | *** | **** |
| Resort charm | ** | ** | *** | ** |
| Off-slope | * | * | *** | ***** |

* Refers to mountain restaurants only

# Resort shortlists

***To help you spot resorts that will suit you***

**To streamline the job of spotting the ideal resort for your own holiday, here are lists of the best ten or so resorts for 20 different categories. Some lists embrace European and North American resorts, but most we've confined to Europe, because America has too many qualifying resorts (eg for beginners) or because America does things differently, making comparisons invalid (eg for off-piste).**

**SOMETHING FOR EVERYONE**
***Resorts with everything from reassuring nursery slopes to real challenges for experts***
Alpe-d'Huez, France p204
Les Arcs, France p213
Aspen, Colorado p523
Courchevel, France p248
Flaine, France p263
Mammoth, California p515
Vail, Colorado p546
Val-d'Isère, France p354
Whistler, Canada p621
Winter Park, Colorado p552

**INTERNATIONAL OVERSIGHTS**
***Resorts that deserve as much attention as the ones we go back to every year, but don't seem to get it***
Alta, Utah p559
Andermatt, Switzerland p439
Bad Gastein, Austria p111
Big Sky, Montana p561
Les Contamines, France p246
Copper Mountain, Colorado p536
Flims-Laax, Switzerland p454
Monterosa Ski, Italy p406
Risoul, France p317
Telluride, Colorado p544

**RELIABLE SNOW IN THE ALPS**
***Alpine resorts with good snow records or lots of snowmaking, and high or north-facing slopes***
Argentière/Chamonix, France p227
Cervinia, Italy p385
Courchevel, France p248
Hintertux, Austria p117
Lech/Zürs, Austria p138
Obergurgl, Austria p153
Saas-Fee, Switzerland p464
Val-d'Isère/Tignes, France pp354/343
Val-Thorens, France p366
Zermatt, Switzerland p493

**OFF-PISTE WONDERS**
***Alpine resorts where, with the right guidance and equipment, you can have the time of your life***
Alpe-d'Huez, France p204
Andermatt, Switzerland p439
Argentière/Chamonix, France p227
Davos/Klosters, Switzerland p447
La Grave, France p272
Lech/Zürs, Austria p138
Monterosa Ski, Italy p406
St Anton, Austria p178
Val-d'Isère/Tignes, France pp354/343
Verbier, Switzerland p475

SNOWPIX.COM / CHRIS GILL

Les Arcs doesn't get on the shortlist for village charm (this is Arc 2000, with Arc 1950 taking shape in the background) but it does get listed for convenience and one or two other things →

**POWDER PARADISES**
***Resorts with the snow, the terrain and (ideally) the lack of crowds that make for powder perfection***
Alta/Snowbird, Utah pp559/577
Andermatt, Switzerland p439
Big Sky, Montana p561
Big White, Canada p602
Brighton/Solitude, Utah p579
Fernie, Canada p604
Grand Targhee, Wyoming p567
La Grave, France p272
Jackson Hole, Wyoming p567
Kicking Horse, Canada p609
Kirkwood, California, p520
Monterosa Ski, Italy p406
Red Mountain, Canada p630
Snowbasin, Utah p579
Ste-Foy, France p329

**BLACK RUNS**
***Resorts with steep, mogully, lift-served slopes within the safety of the piste network***
Alta/Snowbird, Utah pp559/577
Andermatt, Switzerland p439
Argentière/Chamonix, France p227
Aspen, Colorado p523
Beaver Creek, Colorado p529
Courchevel, France p248
Jackson Hole, Wyoming p567
Whistler, Canada p621
Winter Park, Colorado p552
Zermatt, Switzerland p493

**CHOPAHOLICS**
***Resorts where you can quit the conventional lift network and have a day riding helicopters or cats***
Aspen, Colorado p523
Crested Butte, Colorado p557
Fernie, Canada p604
Grand Targhee, Wyoming p567
Lech/Zürs, Austria p138
Monterosa Ski, Italy p406
Panorama, Canada p616
Verbier, Switzerland p475
Whistler, Canada p621
Zermatt, Switzerland p493

**WEATHERPROOF SLOPES**
***Alpine resorts with snow-sure slopes if the sun shines, and trees in case it doesn't***
Les Arcs, France p213
Courchevel, France p248
Courmayeur, Italy p395
Flims, Switzerland p454
Schladming, Austria p166
Selva, Italy p415
Serre-Chevalier, France p322
Sestriere, Italy p423
La Thuile, Italy p425

**HIGH-MILEAGE PISTE-BASHING**
***Extensive intermediate slopes with big lift networks***
Alpe-d'Huez, France p204
Davos/Klosters, Switzerland p447
Flims/Laax, Switzerland p454
Milky Way: Sauze d'Oulx (Italy), Montgenèvre (France) pp410/292
Paradiski, France, p302
Portes du Soleil, France/Switz p313
Selva/Sella Ronda, Italy p415
Les Sybelles, France p335
Trois Vallées, France p352
Val-d'Isère/Tignes, France pp354/343
Whistler, Canada p621

**MOTORWAY CRUISING**
***Long, gentle, super-smooth pistes to bolster the frail confidence of those not long off the nursery slope***
Les Arcs, France p213
Breckenridge, Colorado p531
Cervinia, Italy p385
Cortina, Italy p390
Courchevel, France p248
Megève, France p274
La Plagne, France p305
Snowmass, Colorado p540
La Thuile, Italy p425
Vail, Colorado p546

**RESORTS FOR BEGINNERS**
***European resorts with gentle, snow-sure nursery slopes and easy, longer runs to progress to***
Alpe-d'Huez, France p204
Les Arcs, France p213
Cervinia, Italy p385
Courchevel, France p248
Flaine, France p263
Montgenèvre, France p292
Pamporovo, Bulgaria p638
La Plagne, France p305
Saas-Fee, Switzerland p464
Soldeu, Andorra p98

**MODERN CONVENIENCE**
***Alpine resorts where there's plenty of slope-side accommodation to make life easy***
Les Arcs, France p213
Avoriaz, France p223
Courchevel, France p248
Flaine, France p263
Les Menuires, France p280
Obertauern, Austria p158
La Plagne, France p305
Puy-St-Vincent, France, p315
La Tania, France, p340
Tignes, France, p343
Valmorel, France p364
Val-Thorens, France p366

**BACK-DOOR RESORTS**
***Cute little Alpine villages linked to big, bold ski areas, giving you the best of two different worlds***
Les Brévières (Tignes), France p343
Champagny (La Plagne), France p305
Leogang (Saalbach), Austria p160
Montchavin (La Plagne), France p305
Peisey (Les Arcs), France p213
Le Pré (Les Arcs), France p213
Samoëns (Flaine), France, p263
St-Martin (Three Valleys), France p333
Stuben (St Anton), Austria, covered in Lech chapter p138
Vaujany (Alpe-d'Huez), France p204

**SNOW-SURE BUT SIMPATICO**
***Alpine resorts with high-rise slopes, but low-rise, traditional-style buildings***
Andermatt, Switzerland p439
Arabba, Italy p415
Argentière, France p227
Les Contamines, France p246
Ischgl, Austria p126
Lech/Zürs, Austria p138
Monterosa Ski, Italy p406
Obergurgl, Austria p153
Saas-Fee, Switzerland p464
Zermatt, Switzerland p493

**SPECIALLY FOR FAMILIES**
***Alpine resorts where you can easily find accommodation surrounded by snow, not by traffic and fumes***
Les Arcs, France p213
Avoriaz, France p223
Flaine, France p263
Lech, Austria p138
Montchavin (La Plagne), France p305
Mürren, Switzerland p460
Puy-St-Vincent, France p315
Risoul, France p317
Saas-Fee, Switzerland p464
Les Sybelles, France p335
Valmorel, France p364
Wengen, Switzerland p488

**SPECIAL MOUNTAIN RESTAURANTS**
***Alpine resorts where the mountain restaurants can really add an extra dimension to your holiday***
Alpe-d'Huez, France p204
La Clusaz, France p240
Courmayeur, Italy p395
Kitzbühel, Austria p132
Megève, France p274
St Johann in Tirol, Austria p186
St Moritz, Switzerland p469
Selva, Italy p415
Söll, Austria p172
Zermatt, Switzerland p493

**DRAMATIC SCENERY**
***Resorts where the mountains are not just high and snowy, but spectacularly scenic too***
Chamonix, France p227
Cortina, Italy p390
Courmayeur, Italy p395
Heavenly, California p510
Jungfrau resorts (Grindelwald, Mürren, Wengen), Switzerland pp456/460/488
Lake Louise, Canada p611
Megève, France, p274
Saas-Fee, Switzerland p464
St Moritz, Switzerland p469
Selva, Italy p415
Zermatt, Switzerland p493

**VILLAGE CHARM**
***Resorts with traditional character that enriches your holiday – from mountain villages to mining towns***
Alpbach, Austria p109
Champéry, Switzerland p443
Courmayeur, Italy p395
Crested Butte, Colorado p557
Lech, Austria p138
Mürren, Switzerland p460
Saas-Fee, Switzerland p464
Telluride, Colorado p544
Wengen, Switzerland p488
Zermatt, Switzerland p493

**LIVELY NIGHTLIFE**
***European resorts where you'll have no difficulty finding somewhere to boogy, and someone to do it with***
Chamonix, France p227
Ischgl, Austria p126
Kitzbühel, Austria p132
Saalbach, Austria p160
St Anton, Austria p178
Sauze d'Oulx, Italy p410
Sölden, Austria p170
Pas de la Casa, Andorra p96
Val-d'Isère, France p354
Verbier, Switzerland p475

**OTHER AMUSEMENTS**
***Alpine resorts where those not interested in skiing or boarding can still find plenty to do***
Bad Gastein, Austria p111
Chamonix, France p227
Cortina, Italy p390
Davos, Switzerland p447
Gstaad, Switzerland p503
Innsbruck, Austria p122
Kitzbühel, Austria p132
Megève, France p274
St Moritz, Switzerland p469
Zell am See, Austria p190

# Our resort chapters

## *How to get the best out of them*



**FINDING A RESORT**

The bulk of the book consists of chapters devoted to individual major resorts, plus minor resorts that share the same lift system. These chapters are grouped by country – first, the five major European destination countries in alphabetical order; then the US and Canada (where resorts are grouped by states or regions); then minor European countries; then Australasia. Within each group, resorts are ordered alphabetically – except that each country/state/region section now ends with Short Turns: a handful of short chapters covering resorts that don't merit full treatment.

There's a **chapter-by-chapter listing** on the facing page, as well as in the Contents section at the start of the book.

Short cuts to the resorts that might suit you are provided by a table of comparative **star ratings** and a series of **shortlists** of resorts with particular merits. To find these, just turn back a few pages towards the front of the book.

At the back of the book is an **index** to the resort chapters, combined with a **directory** giving basic information on hundreds of other minor resorts. Where the resort you are looking up is covered in a chapter devoted to a bigger resort, the page reference will take you to the start of that chapter, not to the exact page on which the minor resort is described.

There's further guidance on using our information in the chapter on Choosing your resort – designed to be helpful particularly to people with narrow experience of resorts, who may not appreciate how big the differences between one resort and another can be (ie like chalk and cheese).

**READING A CHAPTER**

The **cost** of visiting each resort is rated on a scale of one to six – ①②③④⑤⑥ to ①②③④⑤⑥ – reflecting the typical cost of a one-week trip based on a half-board package from the UK, plus a lift pass and an allowance for lunch in mountain restaurants. We assume two people sharing a room – even in the US, where package prices are often based on four people sharing.

**Star ratings** summarise our view of the resort in 11 respects, including how well it suits different standards of skier/boarder. The more stars, the better, on a five-point scale.

We give phone numbers and internet addresses of the **tourist office** and phone numbers for recommended **hotels.**

The UK tour operators offering **package holidays** in each resort are listed in the index at the back of the book, not in the main chapters.

Our **mountain maps** show the resorts' own classification of runs – so those for the US and Canada show green, blue and black runs, and no red ones (unlike Europe). On some maps we also follow the North American convention of using black diamonds to indicate open expert terrain where the runs are not defined. We do not distinguish single-diamond terrain from the steeper double-diamond.

We show all the lifts on the mountain, including any definitely planned for construction for the coming season. We use the following symbols to identify **fast or high-capacity lifts**:

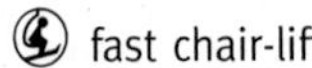
fast chair-lift

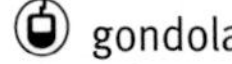
gondola

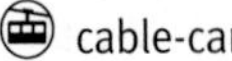
cable-car

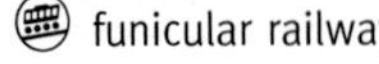
funicular railway

## THE WORLD'S BEST WINTER SPORTS RESORTS

**To find a minor resort – or a major resort, if you don't know what country it's in – go to the index/directory at the back of the book**

**More Brits now go to Andorra for winter holidays than to Switzerland, Canada and the USA combined – Andorra is neck and neck with Italy as the third most popular country to visit. Despite a continuing building boom, it is still often difficult to find a bed, even in low season. It's also difficult to get away from fellow Brits. And from traffic and construction sites – Andorra has lots of both.**

**Andorra used to be seen primarily as a cheap and cheerful holiday destination, aimed mainly at younger singles and couples looking for a good time in the duty-free bars and clubs as well as learning to ski or snowboard. And most of the resorts are still excellent for that market. Tour operator-organised pub crawls of 100+ guests are common. But there's more to it than that. The ski schools have always been excellent, with lots of native English-speaking instructors. In recent years, some more upmarket hotels have been built (though they often resemble Spanish summer package hotels and have self-service buffet meals). And lots of money has been pumped in to developing powerful lift systems and piste-grooming fleets that many well-known Alpine resorts would be proud of; this makes the slopes much more attractive to intermediates as well as beginners. Andorra no longer competes with eastern Europe for the budget market; it costs more, and what it delivers is in a different league – the Alpine league.**

**There are big differences in the characters of the resorts. Soldeu is the one that has tried hardest to move upmarket; chapters on Soldeu and the other two major resorts of Arinsal and Pas de la Casa follow.**



**This introduction includes some comments on the valley towns that are also marketed as ski resorts by some tour operators, and on the excellent out-of-the-way day skiing area of Arcalis.**

Andorra has a relatively reliable snow record. Its situation close to both the Atlantic and the Mediterranean oceans, together with the high altitude of its resorts, means it usually gets substantial natural snowfalls. It has also invested heavily in snowmaking. This combination means you can book Andorra months in advance with some confidence. And an early reservation is necessary: late bookers can have difficulty finding an Andorra package.

Both package holiday prices and prices for drinks and extras such as instruction and equipment rental are generally lower than in the Alps. But some reporters have found duty-free luxury goods prices not the super-bargains they had expected.

Duty-free spirits prices and large, unmeasured helpings mean that nightlife can be very lively. If you want to spend your nights in the company of drunken young Brits, you will have no trouble finding places where you can. But in our recent experience you will equally have no trouble avoiding such scenes, and finding more civilised places in which to relax. As one of our 'more mature' reporters said: 'Great potential as a Geriatric Paradise ... with quality spirits at £3.50 a litre I was so impressed that I intend to organise a group in future years when most of my friends can travel in low season and can wax their zimmers and drink the duty-free booze until their hearts are content! Saga louts on tour – BEWARE!'

The sight of cranes is still common, as hotels and apartments are

SKI ANDORRA / IGOR NATXITUBE

← None of Andorra's main resorts could be called a pretty sight, but Pas de la Casa is the least pretty of the lot; it also has rather bleak local slopes

built to keep up with demand. It is no longer true to say that the resorts resemble giant construction sites, but they all have construction sites within them (or on the edge of them as they expand in sprawling fashion along the roadside). And don't be surprised if a 'new' hotel you visit still has building work going on within it to finish it off.

Adjacent resorts have linked their slopes together, meaning bigger ski areas and a bit more variety. Arinsal and Pal were linked by a cable-car for the 2000/01 season. The big news this year is that, at last, the long-standing feud between the communities of Pas de La Casa and Soldeu has been put aside to allow them to move in to the big league and market themselves together as the ski domain of Grand Valira, with one lift pass available to cover the whole area. The resorts' slopes have been physically linked by lift and piste for a few seasons and form an impressive area that is comparable with big-name resorts such as Kitzbühel and Les Deux-Alpes.

## STAYING DOWN THE VALLEY

Several valley towns can be used as bases, either to use the slopes of one resort or to explore several resorts in the course of a week.

One obviously strong candidate here is **Encamp**, which has a powerful 18-seater gondola giving a quick way into the whole of the Grand Valira ski area. Encamp seemed to us the least attractive of the valley towns (not least because of its situation on the traffic-choked main road), but we can't claim to have examined it closely and a couple of reporters this year recommend it. It is certainly cheap.

**La Massana** is a more appealing town, and has the attraction of being quite well placed for access to Arcalis – an excellent but




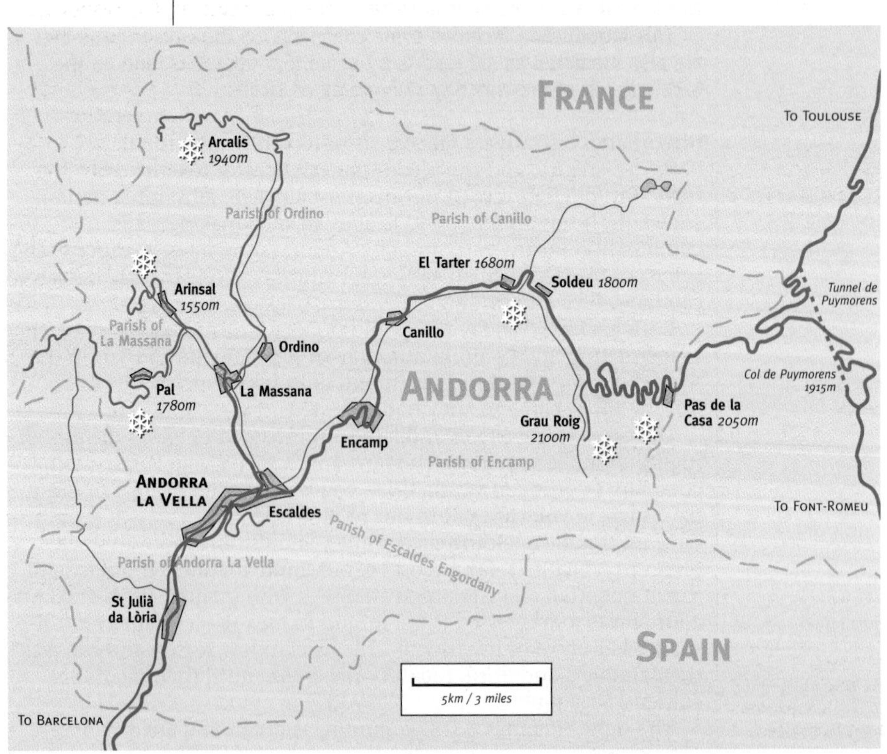

accommodation-free ski area directly to the north (see below). La Massana is more often used as a base for Pal and Arinsal, which are much closer, and this season should see completion of the long-awaited gondola from here up to the Pal slopes. This will make La Massana an attractive place to stay. **Ordino** is slightly nearer Arcalis, and pleasantly rustic.

The capital of **Andorra la Vella** is not far down the valley from Encamp but is a more attractive base for someone wanting a more rounded holiday (though still choked by traffic and 'appalling' resultant fumes). The duty-free shopping could fill a page, but probably the most interesting feature is the Caldea spa 'probably the best off-slope activity in Andorra', according to a reporter. The interior is laid out in a 'Hanging Gardens of Babylon' style, and the facilities are very impressive – indoor and outdoor pools, with fountains and waterfalls, saunas, hot-tubs, Turkish baths, sunbeds, hydrotherapy, massage ... even a grapefruit bath! There are plenty of high-quality, if relatively expensive, hotels. Andorra la Vella is not a big place, and most hotels are within easy walking distance of the centre. There is plenty of choice when it comes to dining out and plenty of bars and nightclubs that stay open until 4am. However, the clientele is generally a more sophisticated bunch, mainly Andorrans and Spaniards, and the 'drink-until-you-drop' attitude of the mountain resorts is rare.

**LIFT PASSES**

**Ski Andorra**
The Ski Andorra pass covers all Andorran areas and allows skiing at any single one of them each day for five out of six consecutive days: €144 (under 12: €116).

**Phone numbers**
From abroad use the prefix +376.

**TOURIST OFFICE**

**t** 864389
skiandorra@skiandorra.ad
www.skiandorra.ad

## SKIING AND BOARDING AWAY FROM THE MAIN RESORTS

**Arcalis** is the most remote area of slopes in Andorra, tucked away at the head of a long valley, and most British visitors to Andorra never hear about it. But it makes a very worthwhile day trip – the variety of the terrain is greater than in most of the main resorts, the slopes are usually deserted except at weekends (when locals pour in) and the snow is usually the best you will find. It provides excellent intermediate and beginner terrain, but of all Andorra's resorts it has the most to offer experts, including lots of off-piste between the marked runs. There is no accommodation at the mountain, just a day lodge and a lot of car parking, but buildings are now springing up along the Vall d'Ordino leading up to it.

SKI ANDORRA / IGOR NATXITUBE

The slopes of Arcalis are interestingly varied, and well worth a day-trip visit →

# Arinsal

*Much improved by the recent cable-car link with Pal*

## COSTS

①②③④⑤⑥

## RATINGS

**The slopes**

| | |
|---|---|
| Snow | **** |
| Extent | * |
| Expert | * |
| Intermediate | ** |
| Beginner | *** |
| Convenience | *** |
| Queues | *** |
| Mountain restaurants | ** |

**The rest**

| | |
|---|---|
| Scenery | *** |
| Resort charm | * |
| Off-slope | * |

## NEWS

The long-awaited gondola from La Massana to Pal is expected to open for the 2004/05 season, greatly increasing the attractions of the valley town as a holiday base.

Last winter the Cortal drag-lift in the beginners' area at Arinsal was replaced by a chair.

Snowmaking has been extended in the Séturia sector, on the Posalletes piste.



## REPORTS WANTED

Recently we have had few reports on this resort. If you go there, please do send us a report.

The best reports earn a copy of the next edition, and can lead to free lift passes in future.

See page 10.

- + Lively bars
- + Ski school geared to British needs
- + Cable-car link with Pal is very good news for non-beginners
- + Pretty, tree-lined slopes in Pal

- − Very confined and bleak local slopes
- − Runs to village need good snow to be open, and don't lead to centre
- − Long, linear and rather dour village, with no focus
- − Obtrusive construction sites

**Arinsal is the most British-dominated resort in Andorra, despite the fact that the village is the least attractive. This may be partly because the Spanish and French set their sights higher; but it is also because British tour operators offer packages here at tempting prices.**

**The resort attracts mainly first-time skiers and riders who come here for the cheap alcohol-fuelled nightlife as much as the experience on the slopes. But the village doesn't have many other attractions.**

## THE RESORT

Arinsal is a long, narrow village of grey, stone-clad buildings, near the head of a steep-sided valley north of Andorra la Vella. Development in recent years has been rapid.

The gondola from the village centre is the main way to the slopes; for most guests, the alternative chair-lift 1km/0.5 miles out of town is irrelevant – though you can stay next to it and ski to the door in good conditions. Or you can drive to the top of the gondola. There is some accommodation at Pal, but it is a bus-ride from the lift base. Staying in Arinsal (preferably close to the gondola station) and accessing the Pal slopes via the recent cable-car link makes better sense for most visitors. But there is also attractive accommodation in the lower town of La Massana (see introduction to Andorra). A gondola link from here to Pal's slopes is due to open for this season and will make this a good place to stay.

## THE MOUNTAINS

The small local area above Arinsal's gondola is a narrow, east-facing bowl of open slopes. Pal's slopes, in contrast, are the most densely wooded of the Andorran resorts, calling to mind American resorts. They mainly face east; those down to the link with Arinsal face north.

**Slopes** Arinsal's slopes consist essentially of a single, long, narrow, rather bleak bowl above the upper gondola station at Comallempla, with runs leading straight back towards that point served by a network of chairs and drags. Almost at the top is the cable-car link to and from Pal. Pal's slopes are widely spread around the mountain, with four main lift bases, all reachable by road. The main one, La Caubella, at the opposite extreme from the Arinsal link, is the arrival point of the new gondola from La Massana.

**Terrain-parks** Arinsal's big freestyle area claims to be the most radical in Europe. It includes a huge half-pipe, big jump, terrain-park with spines, fun boxes, rails and quarter-pipes, boarder- and ski-cross run and a chill-out area.

**Snow reliability** With most runs above 1950m/6,400ft, north-easterly orientation and an impressive 370 snow-guns, snow is relatively assured.

**Experts** These aren't great mountains for experts, but there are short, sharp black slopes at Arinsal – one now deliberately ungroomed – and quite long and challenging reds (and one black) at Pal. There are also off-piste free-ride areas marked on the map in both Arinsal and Pal – the latter offering some great tree-skiing.

**Intermediates** Arinsal offers a reasonable range of difficulty, but any confident intermediate is going to want to explore the much more interesting, varied and extensive Pal slopes.

**Beginners** Around half the guests here are beginners. Arinsal and Pal both have gentle nursery slopes set apart from the main runs; they can get very

## KEY FACTS

| | |
|---|---|
| Resort | 1470m<br>4,820ft |
| Slopes | 1550-2560m<br>5,090-8,400ft |
| Lifts | 29 |
| Pistes | 63km<br>39 miles |
| Green | 10% |
| Blue | 39% |
| Red | 39% |
| Black | 12% |
| Snowmaking | 19km<br>12 miles |

**Phone numbers**
From abroad use the prefix +376.

## TOURIST OFFICES

**Arinsal**
t 737020
palarinsal@palarinsal.com
www.palarinsal.com

**Pal**
t 737000



crowded at peak times. There are long easy runs to progress to, as well.
**Snowboarding** It's a good place to learn. But over half the lifts are drags, and some of them are vicious. And there are some tedious flat sections in Pal too. We're told crash helmets are compulsory in the terrain-park.
**Cross-country** There isn't any.
**Queues** Although its capacity was boosted in 2002, Arinsal's gondola builds queues to return to the village at peak times. The cable-car link can close if the wind is high.
**Mountain restaurants** Mainly self-service, crowded, with snack food. The restaurant at Comallempla is said to run a barbie if the weather permits.
**Schools and guides** Arinsal's ski school is its pride and joy, and is geared to the British market – over half the instructors are native English-speakers. The reports we have are all positive. Class sizes can, however, be very large in peak season. English speaking is not so widespread in the Pal school.
**Facilities for children** There is a ski kindergarten for four to eight-year-olds and a nursery for younger children.

## STAYING THERE

**How to go** There is a wide choice of hotel and self-catering packages.
**Hotels** Rooms in the hotel Arinsal (835640) are not large, but it is well run, ideally placed and has a pleasant bar. The Princesa Parc (736500) is a big glossy 4-star place close to the gondola, with a swanky spa. The Xalet Verdu (737140) is a smooth little 4-star. The St Gotthard (836005) is big but popular, except for its position a long way down the hill from the gondola. The Micolau (835052) is a characterful stone house, close to the centre, with simple rooms and a jolly, beamed restaurant. If there is snow to the valley, you can ski to the Crest (835866) at the old chair-lift station.
**Self-catering** There is a reasonable choice of places. Aparthotel Sant Andreu is simple but comfortable, with a relaxed bar-restaurant on site.
**Eating out** The Surf disco-pub does grills. Cisco's is a Tex-Mex place in a lovely wood and stone building. The Rocky Mountain is popular for steaks. The Micolau does good food. Borda Callisa does Indian.
**Après-ski** Arinsal has plenty of lively bars and discos, such as Quo Vadis, El Cau, Surf, Rocky Mountain and Cisco's, (a major snowboarder hangout). El Derbi is heaving on karaoke night. If, like us, you prefer something quieter, head for Borda Callisa – out of the way and pleasantly relaxed – or the bar of the hotel Arinsal.
**Off the slopes** There are lots of activities. Or go shopping in Andorra la Vella, half an hour away by infrequent bus or inexpensive taxi.



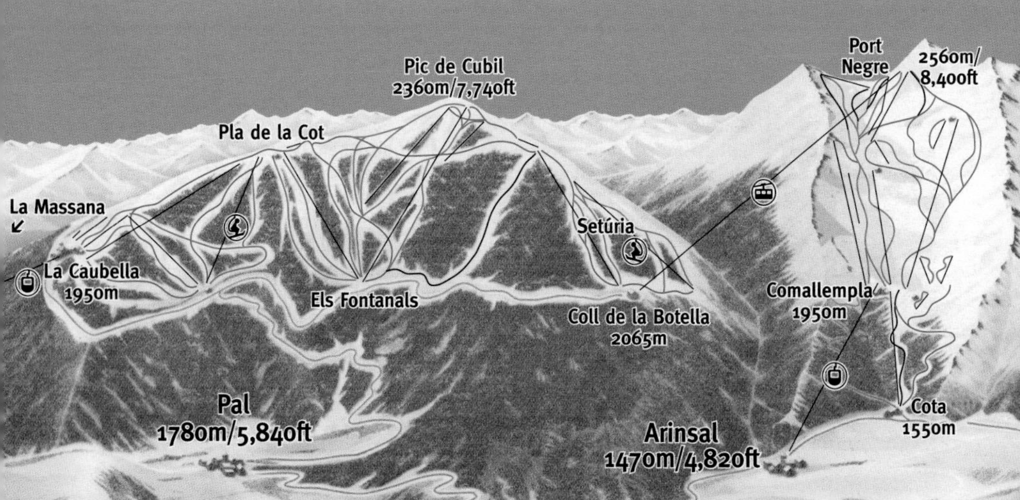

# Pas de la Casa

*Andorra's biggest area and liveliest resort – now with access to Soldeu*

## COSTS

①②③④⑤⑥

## RATINGS

**The slopes**

| | |
|---|---|
| Snow | **** |
| Extent | *** |
| Expert | * |
| Intermediate | *** |
| Beginner | **** |
| Convenience | **** |
| Queues | *** |
| Mountain restaurants | *** |

**The rest**

| | |
|---|---|
| Scenery | *** |
| Resort charm | * |
| Off-slope | * |

## NEWS

The ancient feud with Soldeu – linked to Pas de la Casa for several years – has at last ended, and a single pass is now available for what is one of Europe's largest ski domains – Grand Valira

The Coma Blanca 1 drag is being replaced by a six-pack, helping to deal with weekend crowds at Grau Roig.

## REPORTS WANTED

**Recently we have had few reports on this resort. If you go there, please do send us a report.**

**The best reports earn a copy of the next edition, and can lead to free lift passes in future.**

**See page 10.**



- + New joint lift-pass with Soldeu means these resorts now rival many major resorts in the Alps
- + Good proportion of fast lifts
- + Andorra's liveliest nightlife
- + Attractive accommodation at Grau Roig, cheap places at Encamp

- − Pas is an eyesore and the centre suffers from traffic (and fumes)
- − Weekend crowds from France
- − Very few woodland slopes, and none directly above the village – unpleasant in bad weather

**The tour op brochures (and the readers' reports we get) all say that Pas is Andorra's wildest party resort, and we don't doubt it. Having driven through it and skied down to it, we are quite happy to stay over the hill in Soldeu – or, for ideal access to the Pas slopes, secluded Grau Roig.**

## THE RESORT

Sited right on the border between Andorra and France, Pas de la Casa owes its development as much to duty-free sales to the French as to skiing. It is a sizeable collection of concrete-box-style apartment blocks and hotels, a product of the late 1960s and early 1970s. As one reporter put it: 'The resort reminded us of Playa de las Americas in Tenerife – ugly, characterless with loads of restaurants with plastic-covered faded photos to show the discerning eater what a whopper cheeseburger and chips actually looks like.' Most accommodation is conveniently placed near the lift base and slopes. The town centre boasts plenty of cheap shops and bars, as well as a sports centre. Reporters complain that that the heavy traffic generates fumes.

The resort attracts a lot of French visitors (so beware the February school holidays) and Spanish families, with only a smattering of Brits.

The lift system spreads from Pas over three adjacent valleys. The valley furthest from Pas has nothing but a lift station, but in the attractively wooded middle one is Grau Roig ('Rosh'). This is a mini-resort that acts as the access point for day visitors arriving by road, but it also makes a good base.

The road through from France goes on over the Port d'Envalira towards Soldeu and central Andorra but in 2003 a toll tunnel opened which avoids the pass and takes you to near Grau Roig. There is accommodation at the pass, which we suggest you avoid.

## THE MOUNTAINS

The area now shared by Pas and Soldeu almost scrapes into Europe's top 20 for size. With the exception of a couple of attractively wooded slopes in the central valley, the slopes above Pas are all open, and vulnerable to bad weather. Soldeu is more sheltered.

**Slopes** The treeless local slopes, facing north-east, descend from a high, north–south ridge; lifts go up to it at four points. Runs on the far side of the ridge converge on Grau Roig, where there is some wooded terrain at the head of the valley. And a single lift goes on further west to the bowl of Llac del Cubill, where the Pas area adjoins the Soldeu one. On the far side of this bowl is the arrival station of the 6km/4 mile gondola up from Encamp.

**Terrain-parks** There is a boarder-cross course and a half-pipe.

**Snow reliability** The combination of height and lots of snowmaking means good snow reliability and a season that often reaches late April. But on both our recent visits the snow has been better in Soldeu – maybe the grooming is better there.

**Experts** There are few challenges on-piste – the black runs are rarely of serious steepness, and moguls are rare. But there seem to be plenty of off-piste slopes inviting exploration – a reader recommends the bowls above Grau Roig, in particular.

**Intermediates** The slopes cater for confident intermediates far better, with plenty of top-to-bottom reds and blues on the main ridge, though they do rather lack variety.

The Rifugi dels Llacs dels Pessons takes a bit of finding, but it's worth it for a serious sit-down lunch →

SKI ANDORRA / IGOR NATXITUBE

## KEY FACTS

| Resort | 2100m<br>6,890ft |
|---|---|
| GrandValira (Soldeu/El Tarter/Pas/Grau Roig) | |
| Slopes | 1710-2560m<br>5,610-8,400ft |
| Lifts | 63 |
| Pistes | 192km<br>119 miles |
| Green | 15% |
| Blue | 30% |
| Red | 35% |
| Black | 20% |
| Snowmaking | 62km<br>39 miles |

**Phone numbers**
From abroad use the prefix +376.

**Central reservations phone number**
For all resort accommodation call 801060.

## TOURIST OFFICE

t 801060
info@pasgrau.com
www.pasgrau.com



**Beginners** There are beginner slopes in both Pas and Grau Roig. The Pas area is a short but inconvenient bus-ride out of town. Progression to longer runs is easier in Grau Roig, too.
**Snowboarding** Boarding is popular with the young crowd the resort attracts. Drags are usually avoidable.
**Cross-country** There are loops totalling 12km/7 miles below Grau Roig.
**Queues** Queues are rarely serious during the week. But at weekends and French school holidays some can develop, especially at Grau Roig.
**Mountain restaurants** There are routine places at the ridge above Pas and the top of the gondola from Encamp. The Rifugi dels Llacs dels Pessons at the head of the Grau Roig bowl is by far the best place – a cosy, beamed table-service restaurant with excellent food.
**Schools and guides** The ski school has a high reputation – good English.
**Facilities for children** There are ski kindergartens at Pas and Grau Roig, and a non-ski one at the latter.

## STAYING THERE

**How to go** There are lots of apartments and hotels and a few chalets.
**Hotels** Himalaia-Pas is close to the slopes, has a pool and is 'comfortable and recommendable', says a reporter. The Grau Roig hotel is in a league of its own for comfort and seclusion (note that some tour operators list it under Soldeu). Beware of hotels catering to the 18-30 crowd – one reader in the Camelot reported vibrations from the basement disco until 5.30am.
**Eating out** It's not a resort for gourmets – though one reporter had 'good charcuterie and paella at the restaurant next to the Burger King'.
**Après-ski** Après-ski is very lively. The Marseilles, Milwaukee and Safari bars are popular. The Billboard is 'by far the best club'.
**Off the slopes** Off-slope activity is limited to shopping, visiting the leisure centre or taking a trip to Andorra la Vella for more of the same.



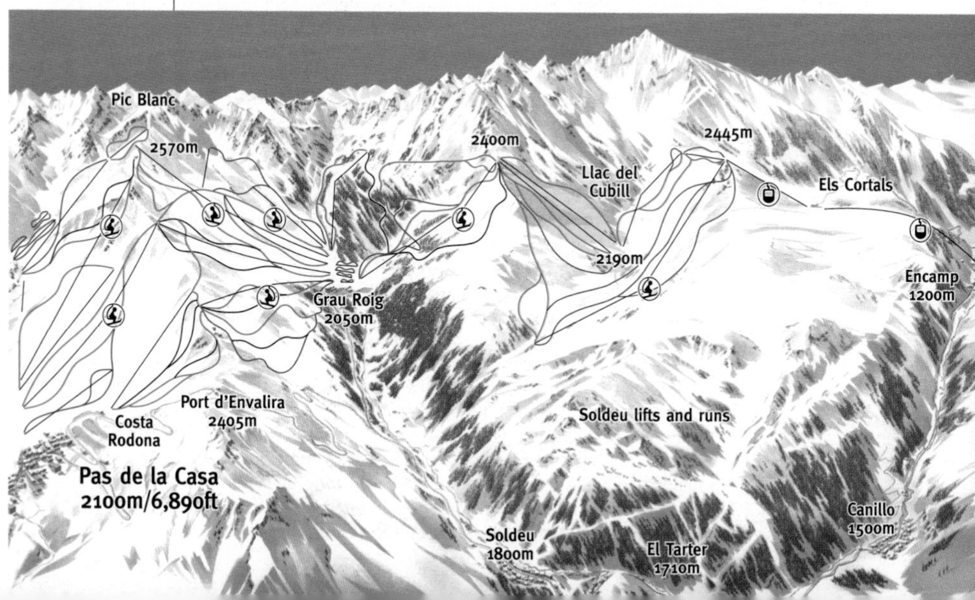

SNOWPIX.COM / CHRIS GILL

# Soldeu

*Ideal for beginners and improvers, but check where you're staying*

## COSTS

## RATINGS

**The slopes**

| | |
|---|---|
| Snow | **** |
| Extent | ** |
| Expert | * |
| Intermediate | *** |
| Beginner | **** |
| Convenience | *** |
| Queues | *** |
| Mountain restaurants | * |

**The rest**

| | |
|---|---|
| Scenery | *** |
| Resort charm | * |
| Off-slope | * |

## NEWS

For 2004/05 there are plans to replace the chair from El Tarter to Riba Escorxada with an eight-seat gondola and to upgrade the high-altitude link to Canillo from a drag-lift to a chair.

Snowmaking was increased last winter and the home run down to El Tarter was improved.



- + New joint lift-pass with Pas de la Casa means these resorts now rival many major resorts in the Alps
- + Impressively efficient lift system
- + Not as rowdy a resort as it once was
- + Ski school has excellent British-run section for English-speaking visitors

- – Slopes can get very crowded
- – Village is on the main road through Andorra and suffers heavy traffic
- – Some hotels are way out of town
- – Not much to do off the slopes

**If we were planning a holiday in Andorra, it would be in Soldeu (or the isolated hotel at Grau Roig, up the road – covered in the Pas de la Casa chapter). Despite the traffic, it is the least unattractive village, and its slopes are the most interestingly varied (though crowded). The alternative bases of El Tarter and Canillo, and accommodation being built along the busy main road that links them all, are often sold as Soldeu; they are much quieter, but also much cheaper.**

**For many people the trickier question is whether to go to Andorra or to go somewhere completely different. Soldeu no longer competes on package holiday prices with the bargain basements of eastern Europe, so the alternatives are more likely to be in Austria or Italy. It's easy to find villages there that are a lot prettier than Soldeu, scenery that is more impressive, and off-slope diversions that are more, well, diverting. But you would often have to settle for less extensive and interesting slopes, less reliable snow, less carefully organised ski lessons – and higher prices for lift passes, lessons and booze.**

## THE RESORT

The village is an ever-growing ribbon of modern buildings – not pretty, but mainly with traditional stone cladding – on a steep hillside, lining the busy road that runs through Andorra from France to Spain. Most are hotels, apartments or bars, with the occasional shop; for serious shopping – or any other off-slope diversions – you have to head down to Canillo (see end of this chapter) or Andorra la Vella.

The steep hillside leads down to the river, and the slopes are on the opposite side. A gondola takes you from the heart of Soldeu to the heart of the slopes at Espiolets, and a wide bridge across the river forms the end of the piste home, with elevators to take you up to the gondola.

El Tarter, a few miles by road and 200m/660ft vertical down the valley, and Canillo, another 200m/660ft lower, offer alternative lifts into the slopes. Between all three resorts, hotels and apartments are being built along the main road and sold under the Soldeu banner – so check carefully where your proposed accommodation is. If you are staying a bus-ride from Soldeu, you can leave skis, boards and boots (for a fee) at the bottom or top (cheaper says a reporter) of the gondola.

## THE MOUNTAINS

The main local slopes are on open mountainsides above the woods, though there are runs in the woods back to all of the resort lift bases. At the eastern end, the slopes and lifts link with those of Pas de la Casa, but there's no joint lift pass. Keen skiers and riders will want to explore the Pas area, and will tailor their pass buying accordingly. There is easy access at Grau Roig, a few miles up the valley.

### THE SLOPES
***Pleasantly varied but crowded***

The gondola rises over wooded, north-facing slopes to Espiolets, a broad shelf that is virtually a mini-resort – the ski school is based here, and there are extensive nursery slopes. A gentle run to the east takes you to an area of long, easy runs served by one of Soldeu's four six-packs and a quad. And beyond that is an extensive area

**KEY FACTS**

| | |
|---|---|
| **Resort** | 1800m<br>5,910ft |
| GrandValira (Soldeu/El Tarter/Pas/Grau Roig) | |
| **Slopes** | 1710-2560m<br>5,610-8,400ft |
| **Lifts** | 63 |
| **Pistes** | 192km<br>119 miles |
| **Green** | 15% |
| **Blue** | 30% |
| **Red** | 35% |
| **Black** | 20% |
| **Snowmaking** | 62km<br>39 miles |

of more varied slopes, served by a quad and another six-pack, that overlaps with the Pas de la Casa area. Going west from Espiolets takes you to the open bowl of Riba Escorxada and the arrival point of the lift up from El Tarter. From here, a third six-pack serves sunny slopes on Tosa dels Espiolets and a fourth goes to the high-point of Tossal de la Llosada and the link with the slopes above Canillo. One problem is that, apart from the Canillo sector, many of the blue runs can get unpleasantly crowded.

**TERRAIN-PARKS**

***A good one sponsored by Nike***

The terrain-park above Riba Escorxada was expanded and redesigned for 2002/03. As well as jumps, rails and a half-pipe there's a boarder-cross run and a bumps area. Some lessons and free demonstrations are arranged for adults and children over six.

**SNOW RELIABILITY**

***Much better than people expect***

Despite its name (Soldeu means Sun God) the slopes enjoy reliable snow. Most slopes are north-facing, with a good natural snow record and snowmaking on over a third of the pistes. The excellent grooming helps maintain good snow too.

**FOR EXPERTS**

***Hope for good off-piste***

It's a limited area for experts, at least on-piste. The Avet black run down to Soldeu deserves its grading, but most of the others would be no more than reds (or even blues) in many resorts. The blacks on Tosa dels Espiolets, for example, are indistinguishable from the neighbouring (and more direct) red and blue. But there is plenty of off-piste potential – notably in the bowl above Riba Escorxada, in the area where Soldeu meets Pas (we had a great time there in fresh powder on our 2003 visit), and above El Forn. And the off-piste remains untouched for days because most visitors are beginners and early intermediates. When conditions permit at weekends, a snowcat takes people up to Pic d'Encampadana whence a range of off-piste routes (dotted on our map) descend to Riba Escorxada.

**FOR INTERMEDIATES**

***Explore Grand Valira***

There is plenty to amuse all but the very keenest intermediates. The area east of Espiolets is splendid for building confidence, while those who already have it will be able to explore the whole mountain. Riba Escorxada is a fine section for mixed ability groups.

**boarding**

*The excellent school and gentle beginner slopes make this a good place to learn. Intermediates may find the flattish areas of slopes irritating to scoot along but will welcome the many chair-lifts and few drags. Competent free-riders should enjoy the off-piste and weekend snowcat service when it's running (see Experts).*

**LIFT PASSES**

**GrandValira**
Covers all lifts in Soldeu, El Tarter, Canillo, Grau Roig and Pas de la Casa.

**Main pass**
1 day €35
6 days €168

**Children**
Under 12: 6 days €129
Under 6: free pass

**Notes**
Local day and half-day passes available.

**Alternative pass**
The Ski Andorra pass covers all Andorran areas and allows skiing at any single one of them each day for five out of six consecutive days for €144 (under 12: €117).

**SCHOOLS**

**Soldeu**
t 890591

**El Tarter**
t 890541

**Canillo**
t 890691

**Classes**
15hr: €92.50

**Private lessons**
€31.50 for 1hr for 1 or 2 people.

**CHILDREN**

**Nurseries at Espiolets, Riba Escorxada and El Forn**
Ages 2 or 3 to 10

**Snow gardens run by ski schools**
From age 3; 15hr €88

**Ski schools**
Ages 6 to 11; 6 days €141





The relatively new Canillo/El Forn sector has an easy, little-used blue run along the ridge with excellent views all the way to Pal and Arinsal and an easy black in the valley. Many of the blues and reds have short steeper sections, preceded by a 'slow' sign and netting in the middle of the piste to slow you down.

### FOR BEGINNERS
***One of the best***

This is an excellent place to start. The Espiolets nursery area is huge, and served by moving carpet lifts (though one reader reckons the slope above El Tarter is even better. It is relatively snow-sure, and there are numerous easy pistes to move on to (though the crowds can be off-putting). And the ski school is top-notch.

### FOR CROSS-COUNTRY
***Er, what cross-country?***

There is no cross country in Soldeu. There is some not far away at Grau Roig (see Pas de la Casa chapter), but Andorra's serious cross-country resort is La Rabassa, in the south-west corner of the country – 15km/9 miles of loops at an altitude of 2000m/6,560ft.

### QUEUES
***Crowds more of a problem***

The lift system is on the whole impressively new and powerful – including four six-packs – and seems to be able to cope. But there are queues at the morning peak for both the gondola out of Soldeu and the chair from El Tarter; start early or late to avoid them. However, 2004 visitors were most impressed by the control and organisation of the gondola queue. More of a problem can be late afternoon crowds on the blue slopes – the reds and blacks are much quieter. The final bend on the Esquirol run to El Tarter was named 'carnage corner' by a visitor last year, who recommends a return by chair for the inexperienced. El Tarter is very busy with local skiers at the weekend.

### MOUNTAIN RESTAURANTS
***Not a highlight***

The mountain restaurants are crowded and the food generally dull. There is a choice of places at Espiolets, including table-service at crowded refectory-style tables. The Roc de les Bruixes at El Forn claims to be 'gastronomic' but we lack reports on it. Reporters favour descending to El Tarter, particularly to the snack bar in the Hotel del Clos.

### SCHOOLS AND GUIDES
***One of the best for Brits***

The scale of the teaching operation here is very impressive. The ski school is effectively run as two units. One deals with English-speaking clients, is led by an Englishman and has mostly native-English-speaking instructors. 40% of the pupils are beginners, and the school has devised a special 'team teaching' scheme to cope with this number of beginners. The school maintains its excellent reputation for teaching and friendliness. 2002/03 saw new Ski Workshop and Check-Up Clinics with small class sizes.

### FACILITIES FOR CHILDREN
***With altitude***

Children are looked after at the mid-mountain stations.There are nurseries and snow playgrounds at Espiolets, Riba Escorxada and El Forn for children from two or three to ten years old.

SKI ANDORRA / IGOR NATXITUBE

There are some excellent terrain features →

## GETTING THERE

**Air** Toulouse 192km/119 miles (3½hr).

**Rail** L'Hospitalet-Près-L'Andorre (25km/16 miles); buses and taxis to Soldeu

## ACTIVITIES

**Indoor** Ice skating, swimming, gym, squash, tennis

**Outdoor** Thermal spas, snowmobiling, dog-sledding, snow-shoeing, tobogganing, paintballing, helicopter rides

**Phone numbers**
From abroad use the prefix +376.

**Central reservations phone number**
Call 890501.

## TOURIST OFFICE

**t** 890500
soldeu@soldeu.ad
www.soldeu.ad

## STAYING THERE

### HOW TO GO

***Be careful where you stay***

A wide range of UK tour operators offer packages here, mainly in hotels but with some apartments and chalets. Location is important – many places are a bus-ride from town.

**Hotels** The best hotels are far removed from the standards of a decade ago.

((((4 **Sport Hotel Village** (870500) By far the best in town, with style and space in the public areas – comfortable chairs and sofas, high ceilings, beams and picture windows. Built over the gondola station by the family that sold the land to the lift company.

(((3 **Sport** (870600) Comfortable, good lounge areas, lively bar and a popular basement disco-bar. But dull buffet-style food. No ski room.

(((3 **Piolets** (871787) Pleasant enough, with a pool. Central.

((2 **Himalaia** (878515) Recently refurbished, central.

**Self-catering** The Edelweiss apartments are spacious, pleasant and well placed opposite the Sport hotel.

### EATING OUT

***Some gourmand delights***

We enjoyed excellent, satisfying meals at three cute rustic restaurants. Borda del Rector (Andorran run and authentic Andorran cuisine), nearer to El Tarter than Soldeu, was our favourite. The other two were both British-run: Snails and Quails, 3km/2 miles up the road in Bordes d'Envalira, and Fat Albert's in downtown Soldeu. L'Esquirol (Indian) and Pussycat have had good reports.

### APRES-SKI

***Lively***

Après-ski is lively 'but not loutish' – mainly bars and rep-organised events (such as pub crawls with maybe 100 participants). The bar at Fat Albert's has videos shot on the mountain and often a live band. The Pussycat is a good late-night place, with changing party themes. The Piccadilly, under the Sport hotel, is popular. The Aspen and the nearby Avalanche attract a younger crowd. We liked the Villager. The Naudi has a quieter locals' bar. Expect noise from late-night revellers.

### OFF THE SLOPES

***Head downhill***

There is little to amuse non-skiers in Soldeu itself. Down in Canillo is the smart Palau de Gel, and in Andorra la Vella the impressive Caldea spa, and some very serious shopping opportunities. Some of the bigger hotels have excellent sports facilities.

## El Tarter 1710m/5,610ft

El Tarter has grown over recent years and is rather sprawling, with no real centre. Reporters recommend the hotels del Clos ('good food but up a steep hill') and del Tarter and the local ski school – and we have a rave review this year of the big new four-star Euro Esqui half-way to Soldeu ('very friendly staff, spacious rooms', with efficient minibus shuttle to El Tarter lifts). But they complain that the resort is 'dull at night'. The Mosquit is a recommended pizzeria; a British-run bar, Peanuts, beneath it seems set to monopolise the British custom.

## Canillo 1500m/4,920ft

If you like the idea of deserted local slopes and don't mind riding a gondola down at the end of the day, consider Canillo, which looked an acceptably pleasant spot as we repeatedly drove through it. It has the impressive Palau de Gel – an Olympic ice rink plus swimming pool, gym and other amenities.

Saalbach Zentrum
Skibrücke
Skibus

# Austria

**Austria's holiday recipe is quite distinctive. It doesn't suit everybody, but for many people nothing else will do; in particular, France won't do. Austria is the land of cute little villages clustered around onion-domed churches – there are no monstrous, purpose-built, apartment-block resorts of the kind that are so common in France. It's the land of friendly wooded mountains, reassuring to beginners and timid intermediates in a way that bleak snowfields and craggy peaks will never be. It's the land of friendly, welcoming people who don't find it demeaning to speak their guests' language (if it's English, at least). And it's the land of jolly, alcohol-fuelled après-ski action – in many resorts, starting in mid-afternoon with dancing in mountain restaurants and going on as long as you have the legs for it. For many visitors to Austrian resorts the partying is as important as the skiing or riding. Of course, there are exceptions to all these norms.**

**In general – and we should note here that Austria has some of the world's best glacier areas – Austria isn't the first place you'll want to consider if reliable snow is at the top of your priorities. Most of the resorts are relatively low, and conditions are more likely to be problematic here than in higher resorts. But Austrian resorts have made great strides in their attempts to catch up with their rivals – most have radically increased their snowmaking capacity in recent years. In midwinter, especially, lack of snow generally goes hand in hand with low night-time temperatures, even at low altitudes, and snowmaking comes into its own. And recent seasons have been bumper snow years for much of Austria.**



It's the après-ski that strikes most first-time visitors as being Austria's unique selling point. The few French resorts that have lively après-ski are dominated by British or Scandinavian holidaymakers (and resort workers); the French themselves are noticeable by their absence, and you could be in London or Stockholm rather than France.

But Austrian après-ski remains very Austrian – or perhaps German. Huge quantities of beer and schnapps are drunk, German is the predominant language and German drinking songs are common. So is incredibly loud Europop music. People pack into mountain restaurants at the end of the day and dance in their ski boots on the dance floor, on the tables, on the bar, on the roof beams – wherever there's room. There are open-air ice bars on the mountain, umbrella bars and countless transparent 'igloo' bars in which to shelter from bad weather. In many resorts the bands don't stop playing and the DJs don't stop working until darkness falls, when the happy punters slide off in the general direction of the village to find another watering hole lower down. After dinner the drinking and dancing starts again – for those who take time out for dinner, that is. Of course, not all Austrian resorts conform to this image. But lots of big-name ones with the best and most extensive slopes do. St Anton, Saalbach-Hinterglemm, Ischgl, Sölden and Zell am See, for example, fit this bill.

One thing that all Austrian resorts have in common is reliably comfortable accommodation – whether it's in 4-star hotels with

SAALBACH-HINTERGLEMM TOURIST OFFICE

← The classic Austrian formula: gentle wooded slopes leading down to a traditional-style village with an onion-domed church at its heart, and with darkness falling there will be at least one bar in the place where people are dancing on the tables in their ski-boots – this is Saalbach

pools, saunas and spas, or in great-value, family-run guest houses, of which Austria has thousands. The accommodation scene is very much dominated by hotels and guest houses; catered chalets and self-catering apartments are in general much less widely available (though there are one or two resorts, such as St Anton and Kitzbühel, where catered chalets are more easily come by).

One thing to beware of is Austria's strange aversion to credit cards. Reporter after reporter complains that many establishments do not accept cards – even quite upmarket hotels and restaurants, as well as many ski lift companies. So check if they are accepted well in advance, and have access to plenty of cash in case you need it.

Most Austrian resorts are real, friendly villages on valley floors, with skiing and boarding on the wooded slopes above them. They have expanded enormously since the war, but practically all the development has been in traditional chalet style, and the villages generally look good even without the snow that is the saving grace of many French and even some Swiss resorts. Unlike Courchevel and Verbier, many Tirolean resorts are as busy in August as in February.

Outside the big-name resorts, the skiing is often quite limited. There are many Austrian resorts that a keen skier could explore fully in half a day. Those who start their skiing careers in such resorts may not be worried by this; those who have tried the bigger areas of France and developed a taste for them may find the list of acceptable Austrian resorts quite a short one.

Unfortunately, several of the resorts on that shortlist bring you up against another problem – low altitude, and therefore poor snow conditions. Kitzbühel is at 760m/2,490ft and Söll at 700m/2,300ft, for example. The top heights of Austrian resorts are relatively low, too – typically 1800m to 2000m (5,910ft to 6,560ft); as we have noted above, snowmaking is becoming more widespread, but it works only when the conditions are right. The resorts of the Arlberg, at the western end of the Tirol – St Anton, Lech and Zürs – stand apart from these concerns, with excellent snow records and extensive skiing. And there are other resorts where you can be fairly confident of good snow, such as Obergurgl, Obertauern and Ischgl, not to mention the year-round slopes on glaciers such as those at Hintertux, Neustift, Kaprun and Sölden. But for many other resorts our advice is to book late, when you know what the snow conditions are like.

There are some extensive areas of slopes that are little known in the UK and well worth considering. Bad Gastein, Schladming, Ischgl, Sölden and Lech spring to mind.

Snowboarders don't need big areas; and snowboarding in slushy snow is not as unpleasant as skiing in it. So it's not surprising that boarding in Austria is booming.

Nightlife is not limited to drinking and dancing. There are lots of floodlit toboggan runs, and UK tour operator reps organise Tirolean, bowling, fondue, karaoke and other evenings. And not all resorts are raucous. Lech and Zürs, for example, are full of rich, cool, 'beautiful' people enjoying the comfort of 4-star sophisticated hotels. And resorts such as Niederau in the Wildschönau and Westendorf and Alpbach in the Tirol are pretty, quiet, family resorts.

Austrian resorts are now easier to get to independently using cheap flights. The standard arrival airports are Munich and Salzburg, and for western resorts Zürich. But don't overlook less well-known airports such as Klagenfurt in Carinthia and Friedrichshafen, just over the German border and handy for resorts in western Austria.

SkiWelt
Wilder Kaiser
Brixental

GOING
ELLMAU
SCHEFFAU
SÖLL
ITTER
HOPFGARTEN
BRIXEN I.THALE
WESTENDORF

## GETTING AROUND THE AUSTRIAN ALPS

Austria presents few problems for the car-borne visitor, because practically all the resorts are valley villages which involve neither steep approach roads nor high altitude.

The dominant feature of Austria for the ski driver is the thoroughfare of the Inn valley, which runs through the Tirol from Landeck via Innsbruck to Kufstein. The motorway along it extends, with one or two breaks, westwards to the Arlberg pass and on to Switzerland. This artery is relatively reliable except in exceptionally bad conditions – the altitude is low, and the road is a vital transport link which is kept open in virtually any conditions.

The Arlberg – which divides Tirol from Vorarlberg, but which is also the watershed between Austria and Switzerland – is one of the

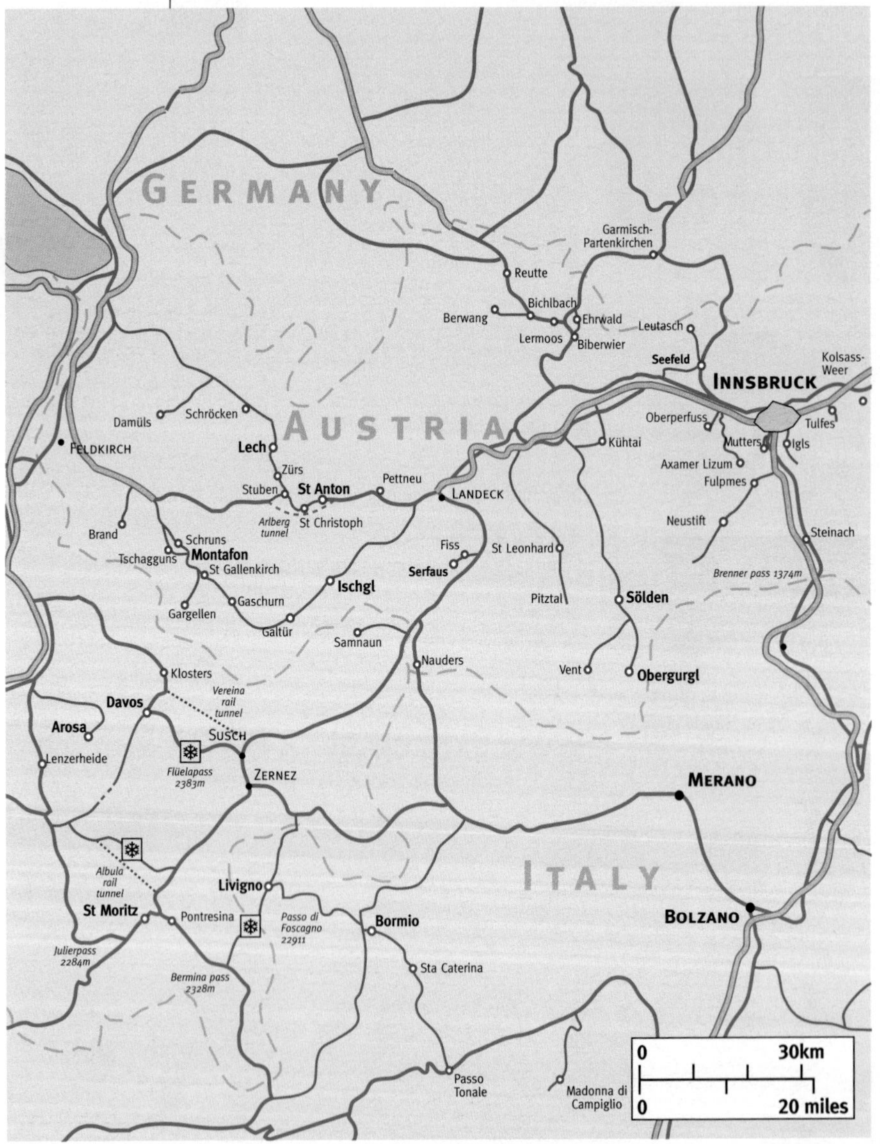

few areas where driving plans are likely to be seriously affected by snow. The east–west Arlberg pass itself has a long tunnel underneath it; this isn't cheap, and you may want to take the high road when it's clear, through Stuben, St Christoph and St Anton. The Flexen pass road to Zürs and Lech (which may be closed by avalanche risk even when the Arlberg pass is open) branches off just to the west of the Arlberg summit.

At the eastern end of the Tirol, the Gerlos pass road from Zell am Ziller over into Salzburg province can be closed. Resorts in Carinthia, such as Bad Kleinkirchheim, are usually reached by motorway, thanks to the Tauern and Katschberg tunnels. The alternative is to drive over the Radstädter Tauern pass through Obertauern, or use the car-carrying rail service from Böckstein to Mallnitz.

## SKI AMADÉ – ONE PASS, TWO DOZEN RESORTS, 270 LIFTS, 865km OF PISTES

*There are more extensive lift passes in the Alps than Salzburgerland's Ski Amadé, but they are very few. What's more, with a car you really could aim to get around most of the resorts it covers – they are clustered close together, no high passes are involved in getting from one resort to another, and many areas are geared to people arriving by car, with out-of-town lifts and serious car parks. (They are also conveniently close to Salzburg airport – we got an early cheap flight there last winter, and were on the slopes in Flachau before lunch time.)*

*Some of the major components of the consortium are covered in their own chapters in the Austria section. In the Schladming chapter we also cover the smaller linked resorts of Haus in Ennstal and Pichl, as well as Schladming's elevated outpost of Rohrmoos. Also close to Schladming is Ramsau in Dachstein, which has slopes at village level but also a lift up to the lip of the Dachstein glacier. In the Bad Gastein chapter we cover not only the resorts in the Gastein valley, but also the next-door valley of Grossarl, which is linked over the hill to Dorfgastein.*

*This year we have given one of our new half-page chapters (grouped at the end of each country section) to Wagrain, which is one of the main resorts in the biggest sub-region, the Salzburger Sportwelt. As well as the extensive three-valley system linking Wagrain to Flachau and Alpendorf/St Johann im Pongau, this area embraces a similarly extensive lift network linking Zauchensee, Flachauwinkl and Kleinarl, plus more modest lift systems at Filzmoos, Radstadt-Altenmarkt, Eben and Goldegg.*

*High on our agenda for investigation next winter is the one major area we have not so far covered – Hochkönig's Winterreich, with 150km/93 miles of runs linking Muhlbach, Dienten and Maria Alm. Hochkönig is a high and craggy peak nearby which gives this sector more visual drama than is usual in this region of predominantly low, rounded, wooded mountains.*

*Considering the extent of the lift networks it covers (and the generally impressive efficiency of the lifts) the Ski Amadé pass is not expensive – last year, around 155 euros depending on the season. This is less than you'll pay for anything vaguely similar in France or Italy. Prices on the spot are not bad either – readers report prices in the mountain restaurants (which are very numerous) lower than in areas with a bigger international reputation.*

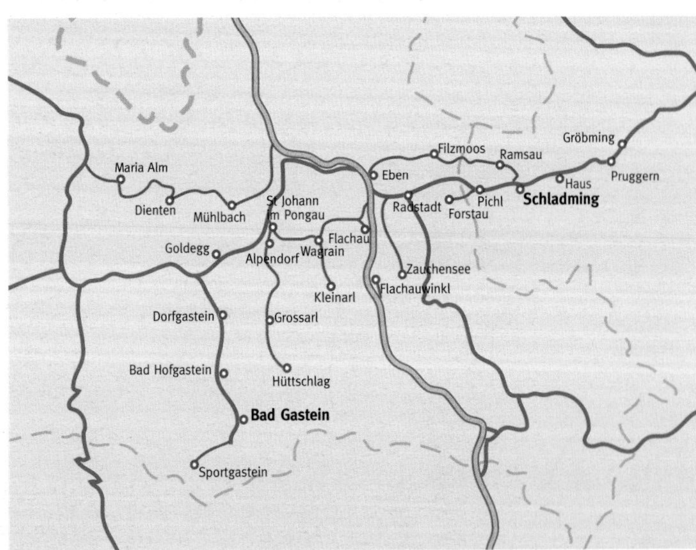

ALPBACH TOURIST OFFICE

# Alpbach

*Traditional charm for those who like familiar slopes*

## COSTS

(1)(2)(3)(4)(5)(6)

## RATINGS

| **The slopes** | |
|---|---|
| Snow | ** |
| Extent | * |
| Expert | * |
| Intermediate | ** |
| Beginner | **** |
| Convenience | ** |
| Queues | *** |
| Mountain restaurants | *** |
| **The rest** | |
| Scenery | *** |
| Charm | ***** |
| Off-slope | *** |

## NEWS

The snowmaking capacity, which has improved the main slopes down to the valley in recent years, was further extended last season to cover a total of 43km/27 miles.

In 2002/03 a quad chair replaced one of the Muldenlift drags behind Gmahkopf.

## REPORTS WANTED

**Recently we have had few reports on this resort. If you go there, please do send us a report.**

**The best reports earn a copy of the next edition, and can lead to free lift passes in future.**

**See page 10.**

+ Charming traditional village with a relaxed atmosphere – great for young children
+ Handy, central nursery slopes
+ Several other worthwhile resorts within day-trip distance
+ Good, varied, intermediate terrain, not without challenges; but ...

− Slopes limited in extent and variety
− Main slopes are a shuttle-bus-ride away from the centre
− Few long easy runs for beginners to progress to
− Low altitude means lower slopes can suffer from poor snow – though a north-facing aspect and increased snowmaking help

**Alpbach is an old British favourite – there is even a British ski club, the Alpbach Visitors. It is exceptionally pretty and friendly, and inspires great loyalty in the visitors who take to it – a regular reporter who has been going for 20 years claims only junior status.**

## THE RESORT

Alpbach is near the head of a valley, looking south across it towards the Wiedersbergerhorn, where most of the slopes are to be found. It's an exceptionally pretty, captivating place; traditional chalets crowd around the pretty church (the graves are lit by candles at night), and the nursery slopes are only a few steps away.

Alpbach is small, but it's not necessarily convenient. The main village is the place to stay for atmosphere and après-ski, but involves using a free shuttle-bus to and from Achenwirt, a mile away, where the main gondola goes up to Hornboden. The backwater hamlet of Inneralpbach is much more convenient for the slopes, with its own lifts up to the heart of the slopes.

The Inn valley is a few miles north, and trips east to Kitzbühel or west to Innsbruck are possible. The Hintertux and Stubaier glaciers are within reach.

## THE MOUNTAIN

Alpbach's slopes, on two flanks of the Wiedersbergerhorn, are small and simple. Piste grooming is excellent.

**Slopes** Chair-lifts and drags serve the open, north-facing slopes above the tree line, with black runs following the lift lines and reds (and a single blue) taking less direct routes. The runs are mostly of 200m to 400m (650ft to 1,300ft) vertical, but you can get 500m/1,650ft down the second stage

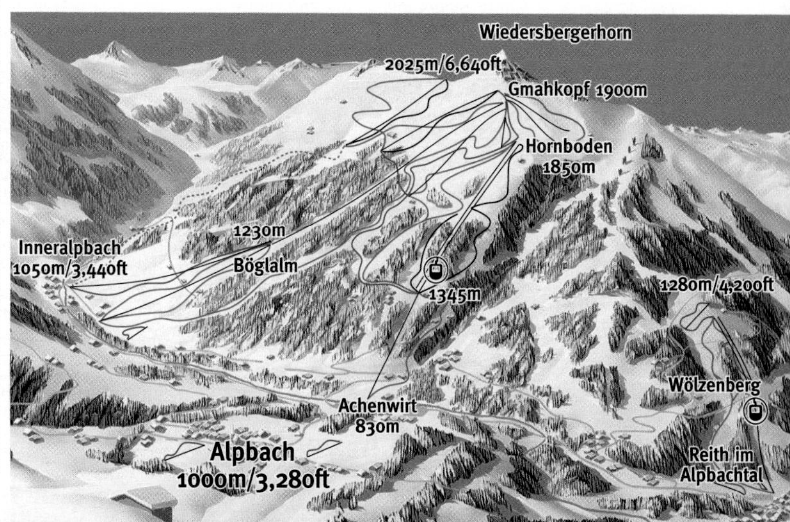

## KEY FACTS

| | |
|---|---|
| Resort | 1000m<br>3,280ft |
| Slopes | 670-2025m<br>2,200-6,640ft |
| Lifts | 20 |
| Pistes | 45km<br>28 miles |
| Blue | 15% |
| Red | 70% |
| Black | 15% |
| Snowmaking | 25km<br>16 miles |



**Phone numbers**
From elsewhere in Austria add the prefix 05336.
From abroad use the prefix +43 5336.



## TOURIST OFFICE

t 6000
info@alpbach.at
www.alpbach.at

ALPBACH TOURIST OFFICE

The village and nursery slopes occupy a sunny shelf, a bus-ride from the main mountain ↓

of the gondola, and 1000m/3,300ft when snow is good down to valley level. Behind Gmahkopf is a short west-facing slope where a quad chair-lift replaced one of the Muldenlift drags in 2002/03. The tiny area at Reith (about 3km/2 miles down the valley from Achenwirt) is on the lift pass and amazingly is accessed by an eight-seat gondola.

**Terrain-parks** There's a small terrain-park with half-pipe at the top of the main gondola.

**Snow reliability** Alpbach cannot claim great snow reliability, but at least most of the Wiedersbergerhorn faces north. The home runs down to the base stations – and the sunny village nursery slope – have snowmaking.

**Experts** Alpbach isn't ideal, but the reds and the three blacks are not without challenge, and runs of 1000m/3,300ft vertical are not to be sniffed at. There are a number of off-piste routes to the valley, short tours are offered, and the schools apparently take the top classes off-piste.

**Intermediates** There is fine intermediate terrain; the problem is that it's limited. This resort is for practising technique on familiar slopes, not high mileage.

**Beginners** Beginners love the sunny nursery slopes beside the village. But the main slopes are not ideal for confidence-building: most are classified red (there are only a couple of blues).

**Snowboarding** There's some good free-riding terrain, and the schools offer a range of options.

**Cross-country** 22km/14 miles of pretty cross-country trails rise up beyond Inneralpbach; the most challenging is about 8km/5 miles long and climbs 300m/1,000ft.

**Queues** Serious queues are rare, thanks to the efficient gondola and the chair-lift upgrades. At busy times, the Inneralpbach chair-lift is quieter than the Achenwirt gondola.

**Mountain restaurants** The small area has squeezed in six mountain restaurants – each worth a visit.

**Schools and guides** Alpbach and Alpbach Aktiv are the two main ski schools. We have had excellent reports on both in the past, but the Alpbach school has recently enjoyed better support.

**Facilities for children** Reporters find the village very child-friendly, and babysitters can be arranged by the tourist office.

## STAYING THERE

**How to go** Hotels and pensions dominate in UK packages.

**Hotels** Of the smart 4-star places, the Alpbacherhof (5237) and ancient Böglerhof (5227) get most votes. But simpler Haus Thomas (5944) – 'very clean ... you feel like part of the family' – Haus Angelika (5339) and Haus Theresia (5386) are recommended by visitors. The Alphof (5371) is 'excellent' – and its noisy disco has been replaced by additional health facilities. Pension Edelweiss (5268) is close to the nursery slopes and is reported to offer B&B and 'clean, spacious apartments and excellent value'.

**Self-catering** There is quite a bit to choose from now, easily bookable through the tourist office web site.

**Eating out** The popular Post and Alphof both provide 'excellent food' according to our most recent report, which also favoured the 'superb' Jakober and its non-smoking room. The Wiedersbergerhorn in Inneralpbach is highly recommended for 'the absolutely delicious spit-roasted chicken'. The Rossmoos Inn is also recommended for its lively Tirolean evenings and 'superb' food.

**Après-ski** At peak times this is typically Tirolean, with lots of noisy tea-time beer-swilling in the bars of central hotels such as the Jakober and the Post. In the evening the Waschkuchl Bar is good for a drink. We understand there is no longer a disco to be found.

**Off the slopes** There are pretty walks and trips to Innsbruck and Salzburg. There's also an indoor swimming pool and an outdoor ice rink.

# Bad Gastein

*Spa-town resort with extensive slopes and few British visitors*

**COSTS**

①②③④⑤⑥

**RATINGS**

**The slopes**

| | |
|---|---|
| Snow | *** |
| Extent | **** |
| Expert | *** |
| Intermediate | **** |
| Beginner | ** |
| Convenience | ** |
| Queues | *** |
| Mountain restaurants | **** |

**The rest**

| | |
|---|---|
| Scenery | *** |
| Resort charm | *** |
| Off-slope | **** |

**NEWS**

The Bad Hofgastein spa underwent a major revamp last winter and now includes six 'adventure and vitality worlds' including a 'multimedia adventure dome' and a rooftop bar with 360-degree views of the mountains.

A fast quad recently replaced the slow triple chair from the Angertal up to Stubnerkogel, greatly improving the link from Schlossalm. There are plans for a major new base station in the Angertal, with lots of facilities designed to meet the needs of people with cars.

+ Extensive, varied slopes above and below the tree line
+ Excellent, testing long runs for confident intermediates, and some under-used off-piste
+ More reliable snow than in most low-altitude Austrian resorts
+ Lots of good, atmospheric, traditional mountain restaurants
+ Ski Alliance Amadé lift pass covers wide range of nearby resorts
+ Excellent thermal spas, but ...

− Main resorts are spa towns, without the usual Austrian resort ambience
− Bad Gastein itself has a weird, steep, confined setting, with narrow streets congested by local traffic
− Valley slopes are split into five areas, and bus services are inadequate – unless you take a car, budget for a lot of taxi rides
− Timid intermediates will find most sectors too challenging – and beginners are better off elsewhere

**The Gastein valley is beginning to attract more Brits, to judge by our readers' reports. Rightly so – the slopes form one of Austria's bigger and more varied areas, and snow is more reliable than average. Steeply tiered Bad Gastein itself is a difficult place to like; we much prefer rustic Dorfgastein or spacious Bad Hofgastein – described at the end of this chapter. The valley needs a top-notch public transport system, and it doesn't have one.**

## THE RESORT

Bad Gastein sits near the head of the Gastein valley. It is an old spa that has now spread widely, but still has a compact core. A bizarre combination of buildings is laid out in a cramped horseshoe, set in what is virtually a gorge. The central area is no pleasure at all to explore, and impossible for those with impediments (such as small children). Up the hill, above the centre of the town, is a modern suburb with more of a ski-resort feel and immediate access to the gondola up to the major sector, Stubnerkogel, which links via Angertal with Bad Hofgastein's Schlossalm sector. Across town, the double chair up Graukogel is a taxi-ride from the centre. A 25-minute bus-ride away, at the head of the valley, is Sportgastein, served by a gondola, with little other development.

A confusing range of ski-bus routes (covered by the lift pass) connects the villages and lift stations. There are trains, too. The ski-bus service is not super-efficient, and a car is a distinct asset here. It also allows exploitation of the Ski Alliance Amadé lift pass, which covers over 30 resorts in the region. Also worth visiting but not on the lift pass are snow-sure Obertauern and glacial Kaprun.

## THE MOUNTAIN

Most of the runs are on the open slopes above the tree line, though there are some woodland runs.

**Slopes** Stubnerkogel has runs in all directions from the peak giving about 500m/1,640ft vertical on the open slopes above the tree line and rather more below it. There is night skiing once a week on the nursery slope. The much smaller Graukogel is unjustly neglected; its wooded runs are a great asset in bad weather, and quiet at other times. The high slopes of Sportgastein, in contrast, are more exposed both to wind and sun.

We cover the slopes above Bad Hofgastein and Dorfgastein below.

**Terrain-parks** See Dorfgastein.

**Snow reliability** The area is higher than many Austrian rivals, and there is snowmaking on crucial sections.

**Experts** The few black runs are not severe, but many reds are long and satisfying. Graukogel has some of the most testing slopes and is a great place to go in a blizzard. The other sectors have plenty of opportunities to go off-piste. Sportgastein is also worth the trip, not least for the shady 8km/5-mile Nord skiroute – no longer shown on the piste map, but still there (and popular) last winter.

## KEY FACTS

| | |
|---|---|
| **Resort** | 1080m<br>3,540ft |
| For the Gastein valley and Grossarl areas | |
| **Slopes** | 840-2685m<br>2,760-8,810ft |
| **Lifts** | 48 |
| **Pistes** | 200km<br>124 miles |
| **Blue** | 29% |
| **Red** | 59% |
| **Black** | 12% |
| **Snowmaking** | 93km<br>58 miles |
| For Bad Gastein and Bad Hofgastein only | |
| **Slopes** | 860-2685m<br>2,820-8,810ft |
| **Lifts** | 31 |
| **Pistes** | 131km<br>81 miles |

**Intermediates** Good for the confident, who will find long, leg-sapping runs in all the sectors in the valley. The timid are better off sticking to Schlossalm (see Bad Hofgastein, below).

**Beginners** Nursery slopes are scattered and none is ideal. The main slope at Bad Gastein is simply too steep. And progression is tricky – the genuinely easy blue runs are often boring paths.

**Snowboarding** The valley hosts snowboard events, but doesn't seem to cater particularly well for holiday boarders. There's still a fairly high proportion of drag-lifts.

**Cross-country** There are 90km/56 miles of trails, but they are all low down.

**Queues** There are few problems outside the peak season.

**Mountain restaurants** Atmospheric, traditional huts abound – at least one reporter is pressing for a 5-star rating. The Jungerstube's 'excellent service and hospitality', Bergstadl and the cosy Stubneralm have been recommended.

**Schools and guides** We lack recent reports.

**Facilities for children** There are facilities for all-day care and there's a 'Fun Centre' for kids at the top of the Stubnerkogel gondola. There's also a snow adventure park at Angertal. Parents last year found the facilities 'excellent', and the care of children, in small groups, 'attentive'.

## STAYING THERE

**How to go** Although apartments make up nearly 15% of the total beds available, British tour operators sell mainly hotel-based packages.

**Hotels** There are lots of smart 4-star and 3-star hotels with good spa facilities. The Wildbad (37610), nearer the main lift, was rated 'wonderful' by a recent reporter. The atmosphere of the central Salzburgerhof (62300) was enjoyed by a reporter last year who also found it 'excellent value'. The Grüner Baum (25160), occupying an entire hamlet, is a lovely retreat, but wildly inconvenient except for langlauf.

**Eating out** There is a fair range of restaurants. The central Wirtshaus Jägerhäusl does excellent food in a warm, traditional atmosphere (especially upstairs). The Vier Jahreszeiten, a short drive away in Böckstein, offers big portions, 'very good value and friendly service' according to a 2004 visitor.

**Après-ski** The town feels generally subdued, but there are numerous popular bars and several discos to be found – plus a casino and (allegedly) a lap-dancing club. Highlights from a wide-ranging report this year include the 'boisterous' Bergfex, the 'cosy, friendly, wood-panelled' Hexenhäusl, the 'vibrant, Wild-West-style' Silver Bullet, the 'friendlier' Eden and the

Weinfassl for 'dancing and drinking games'. Places for a quiet late drink include the smart Bellini bar, or maybe the relaxing Ritz cocktail bar.
**Off the slopes** You can enjoy the naturally warm spas without testing the regenerative effect of radon gas. There are plenty of other things to do, including coach trips.

# Bad Hofgastein

## 860m/2,820ft

Bad Hofgastein is a sizeable, quiet spa village set spaciously in a broad section of the valley.

### THE RESORT

Although sprawling, the village has a pleasant pedestrianised centre. The slopes of Schlossalm are reached by a funicular to Kitzsteinalm starting across the valley, a long walk or short shuttle-bus-ride away.

### THE MOUNTAINS

Schlossalm is a broad, open bowl, with runs through patchy woods both to Bad Hofgastein and Angertal.
**The slopes** Schlossalm is the valley's gentlest area, with sunny open slopes graded blue and red. But the top lifts lead to some challenging terrain, and the Kleine Scharte cable-car serves a serious 750m/2,460ft vertical. A key feature is the splendid long red run from Hohe Scharte, ending at Kitzsteinalm or the valley floor.
**Terrain-parks** See Dorfgastein.
**Snow reliability** Snowmaking is now fairly extensive, but snow-cover down to the bottom is unreliable, especially on the sunny Angertal slopes.
**Experts** There are no real challenges on the local pistes but there is ample opportunity to go off-piste.
**Intermediates** All intermediates will enjoy the Schlossalm slopes – and the more confident can go further afield.
**Beginners** You have to catch a bus to the limited nursery area at Angertal.
**Snowboarding** Pleasantly varied terrain, but no special facilities except at Grossarl (see Dorfgastein). Drag-lifts are dotted around every sector.
**Cross-country** Bad Hofgastein makes a fine base for cross-country when its lengthy valley-floor trails have snow.
**Queues** Crowds are not generally a problem, but the access funicular can generate big queues at peak times.
**Mountain restaurants** Well up to the high local standard. Kleine Scharte, Aeroplanstadl and Hamburger Skihütte have been recommended. Après-ski starts early at Aeroplanstadl.
**Schools and guides** We lack recent reports.
**Facilities for children** At Angertal: see Bad Gastein.

### STAYING THERE

**How to go** This is essentially a hotel resort.
**Hotels** A reporter found the 'impressive' facilities and half-board at the 4-star St Georg (61000) to be excellent value. The 3-star Rauscher (64120) is handy for the shuttle-bus and provides 'clean, spacious rooms and good food'.
**Self-catering** Accommodation can be organised through the tourist office.
**Eating out** There is a good range of restaurants. Piccola Italia and Osteria Di Vino are 'well worth a visit'. The Wintergarten is an intimate restaurant, the Maier one of the better informal places. The Bertahof, on the way to Bad Gastein in Vorderscheeberg, has a high reputation. In the hamlet of Wieden is the Schmaranzgut – a splendidly rustic micro-brewery with cooking on an open fire.
**Après-ski** It is quiet by Austrian standards. At close of play the central Piccolo ice bar is popular; there are several good places for cakes, among them Café Weitmoser, an historic little castle. Later on, the Glocknerkeller and the Gasteiner Discostadl are among the bars playing disco music.
**Off the slopes** The Alpen Therme Gastein spa is 'huge', with several pools, and a 'river' as well as saunas, steam baths and restaurants. Other amenities include ice skating.

# Dorfgastein 830m/2,720ft

Dorfgastein is a rustic village further down the valley. It has its own extensive slopes, accessed by a two-stage gondola or chair-lifts starting 500m/1,640ft outside the village, linked with the slopes of Grossarl in the next valley. Runs are varied and long – from top to bottom, about 8km/5 miles to either village – with a good mix of open and wooded runs amid lovely scenery. The low-altitude nursery slopes can be cold and icy. Over in Grossarl is a boarders-only park with a half-pipe and two quarter-pipes, jumps and other challenges. There are a few shops and après-ski places.

**Phone numbers**
Bad Gastein
From elsewhere in Austria add the prefix 06434.
From abroad use the prefix +43 6434.

**Bad Hofgastein**
From elsewhere in Austria add the prefix 06432.
From abroad use the prefix +43 6432.

**Dorfgastein**
From elsewhere in Austria add the prefix 06433.
From abroad use the prefix +43 6433.

**TOURIST OFFICE**

For all resorts in the Gastein valley contact the Bad Hofgastein office
**t** 3393
info@gastein.com
www.gastein.com

ALBIN NIEDERSTRASSER

# Ellmau

*A quiet base for exploration of the extensive Ski Welt area*

**COSTS**

①②③④⑤⑥

**RATINGS**

| **The slopes** | |
|---|---|
| Snow | ** |
| Extent | **** |
| Expert | * |
| Intermediate | **** |
| Beginner | **** |
| Convenience | *** |
| Queues | **** |
| Mountain restaurants | ** |
| **The rest** | |
| Scenery | *** |
| Resort charm | *** |
| Off-slope | *** |

**NEWS**

Lift improvements continue around the Ski Welt region. For 2004/05 the Sonnschwendlift drag, serving the slopes between Hartkaiser and Astberg above Going, will be replaced with a new quad.

Snowmaking now covers 160km/99 miles of piste in the Ski Welt region (over half the total).

**KEY FACTS**

| | |
|---|---|
| **Resort** | 800m 2,620ft |
| For entire Ski Welt | |
| **Slopes** | 620-1890m 2,030-6,200ft |
| **Lifts** | 91 |
| **Pistes** | 250km 155 miles |
| **Blue** | 43% |
| **Red** | 48% |
| **Black** | 9% |
| **Snowmaking** | 160km 99 miles |



- + Part of Ski Welt, Austria's largest linked ski and snowboard area
- + Pretty, friendly slopes
- + Excellent nursery slopes (but snow reliability can be a problem)
- + Cheap by Austrian standards
- + Quiet, charming family resort – more appealing than neighbouring Söll
- + Massive recent investment in snowmaking has paid off, but ...

- – Ski Welt is at low altitude, and has a poor natural snow record
- – Main lift a bus-ride from village – though reachable via a drag-lift
- – Upper-mountain runs are mostly short, and offer little for experts or adventurous intermediates
- – Limited range of nightlife
- – Ski Welt slopes can get crowded at weekends and in high season

**If you like the sound of the large, undemanding Ski Welt circuit, Ellmau has a lot to recommend it as your base – quieter than Söll, but with more amenities than other neighbours such as Scheffau (covered in the Söll chapter). And Austria's largest snowmaking system makes the area less risky than it was.**

## THE RESORT

Ellmau sits at the north-eastern corner of the Ski Welt. Although sizeable and becoming more commercialised each year, it remains quiet, with traditional chalet-style buildings, welcoming bars and shops, and a pretty church.

Ellmau has a compact centre, but its accommodation is scattered – so the buses around the resort are important. Happily, reports this year suggest they are now better organised.

Make sure you get a guest card entitling you to various discounts, including entry to the leisure centre.

## THE MOUNTAIN

The Ski Welt is the largest mountain circuit in Austria. It links Going, Scheffau, Söll, Itter, Hopfgarten and Brixen. The piste map covering this huge area is, not surprisingly, difficult to comprehend. Most runs are easy, and short – which means that getting around the area can take time, despite increasing numbers of fast lifts. Westendorf is covered by the Ski Welt pass, though its local slopes are not linked. Kitzbühel, Waidring, Fieberbrunn and St Johann are in easy reach for day trips and are covered by the Kitzbüheler Alpenskipass.

**Slopes** Ellmau is close to the best slopes in the area, above Scheffau. The funicular railway on the edge of the village takes you up to Hartkaiser, from where a fine long red (a favourite with reporters) leads down to Blaiken (Scheffau's lift base station). A choice of gondolas take you up to Brandstadl.

Immediately beyond Brandstadl, the slopes become rather bitty; an array of short runs and lifts link Brandstadl to Zinsberg. From Zinsberg, excellent, long, south-facing pistes lead down to Brixen. Then it's a short bus-ride to Westendorf's pleasant separate area. Part-way down to Brixen you can head towards Söll, and if you go up Hohe Salve you get access to a long, west-facing run to Hopfgarten.

Ellmau and Going share a pleasant little area of slopes on Astberg, slightly apart from the rest of the area, and well suited to the unadventurous and families. One piste leads to the funicular for access to the rest of Ski Welt. The main Astberg chair is rather inconveniently positioned, midway between Ellmau and Going.

**Terrain-parks** None locally, but there's a good park at Westendorf.

**Snow reliability** With a low average height, and important links that get a lot of sun, the snowmaking that the Ski Welt has installed is essential. And the Ellmau-Going sector now claims almost all its slopes are covered by snowmaking. This can, of course, only be used when it is cold enough and it cannot prevent slush and icy patches forming. Recent reporters experienced slushy, spring-like conditions as early as late January. The north-facing Eiberg

## LIFT PASSES

**Ski Welt Wilder Kaiser-Brixental**
Covers all lifts in the Wilder Kaiser-Brixental area from Going to Westendorf, and the ski-bus.

**Beginners**
Points tickets.

**Main pass**
1 day €31
6 days €153

**Children**
Under 16: 6 days €92
Under 7: free pass

**Notes**
Single ascent and part-day passes available.

**Alternative passes**
Kitzbüheler Alpen-skipass covers five large ski areas: Schneewinkel (St Johann), Kitzbühel, Ski Welt, Wildschönau and Alpbachtal.

## ON YOUR OWN?

You can team up with other skiers/ boarders by turning up at 10am or 1pm at one of seven designated points in the Ski Welt; there are stickers to identify participants, and even a web site forum for making prior arrangements.

area above Scheffau holds its snow well. And grooming is reported to be of a 'very high standard'.

**Experts** There's are steep plunges off the Hohe Salve summit, and a little mogul field between Brandstadl and Neualm, but the area isn't really suitable unless you seek out off-piste opportunities. The ski route from Brandstadl down to Scheffau is a highlight, 'a long challenging mogul field', and you can go off-piste with a guide from Brandstadl to Söll.

**Intermediates** With good snow, the Ski Welt is a paradise for those who love easy cruising. There are lots of blue runs and many of the reds deserve a blue grading. It is a big area and you get a feeling of travelling around. The main challenge is when the snow isn't perfect – ice and slush can make even gentle lower slopes seem tricky. For timid intermediates the easy slopes of Astberg are handy for Ellmau guests.

**Beginners** Ellmau has an array of good nursery slopes, now covered by snowmaking. The main ones are at the Going end, but there are some by the road to the funicular. The Astberg chair opens up a more snow-sure plateau at altitude. The Brandstadl-Hartkaiser area has a section of short, easy runs, and a nice long piste running the length of the funicular, which even near-beginners can manage.

**Snowboarding** Ellmau is a good place to try boarding as the local slopes are easy. Freaks on the Snow is a recommended hire shop – a reporter found staff 'enthusiastic' and helpful when kitting out her nine-year-old.

**Cross-country** When there is snow, there are long, quite challenging trails, but trails at altitude are lacking.

**Queues** Continued lift upgrades have greatly improved this once queue-prone area. With the exception of peak times, reporters comment on quiet and crowd-free slopes with 'few queues'.

**Mountain restaurants** The smaller places are fairly consistent in providing good-value food in pleasant surroundings. The Rübezahl above Ellmau is our favourite in the whole Ski Welt, but can be 'smokey and busy' according to a 2004 reporter. The Aualm, just below Brandstadl, is favoured especially for its cakes and glühwein but a reporter this year felt 'disappointed' with the new layout and change of staff. The Jagerhütte (below Hartkaiser) is good for 'home-made strudel' later in the day before enjoying the 'quiet and pleasant' home-run. The Hausleitenstube is also worth a visit. The hut at Neualm, halfway down to Scheffau, has been recommended. The larger self-service restaurants are functional (the Jochstube at Eiberg is a pleasant exception) and suffer queues.

**Schools and guides** The three schools have good reputations – except that classes can be very large. Tops is highly rated for children's lessons – a 2004 reporter writes that her son 'made good progress' with private snowboard instruction. Another felt her children 'improved a lot and had fun'





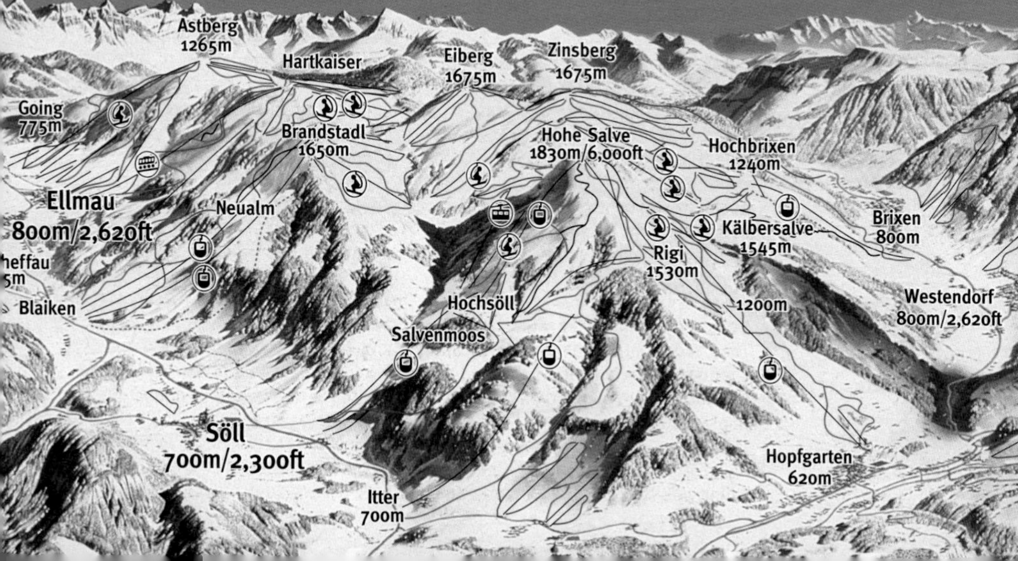

↑ Across the valley from the ski slopes, Wilder Kaiser forms a dramatic backdrop

SNOWPIX.COM / CHRIS GILL





**Phone numbers**
From elsewhere in Austria add the prefix 05358.
From abroad use the prefix +43 5358.

**TOURIST OFFICES**

**Ellmau**
t 2301
info@ellmau.at
www.ellmau.at

**Going**
t 2438
info@going.at
www.going.at

with good English-speaking instructors. As well as the main schools there are mountaineering schools that organise tours in the Wilder Kaiser and the Kitzbühel mountains.
**Facilities for children** Ellmau is an attractive resort for families, described by a regular visitor as 'so child-friendly'. Tops ski school is recommended (see Schools). Kindergarten facilities seem to be satisfactory and include fun ideas such as a mini train to the lifts. Kinderland has its own fun-park and play areas. We have had no recent reports, however.

## STAYING THERE

**How to go** Ellmau is essentially a hotel and pension resort, though there are apartments that can be booked locally.
**Hotels** The Bär (2395) is an elegant, relaxed Relais & Châteaux chalet, but twice the price of any other hotel. 'Luxury without pretensions,' said a reporter who found the weekly gala dinner 'outstanding'; 'wonderful food', 'worth every penny' wrote another. The Hochfilzer (2501) is central, well equipped (with outdoor hot-tub) and popular with reporters (as is the simpler Pension Claudia, which it owns – use of hotel facilities allowed).
**Self-catering** There is a wide variety. The Landhof apartments continue to impress – 'spacious, immaculately clean and well-equipped' – and offer pool, sauna and steam room. Our regular reporter on these matters rates the village supermarket 'excellent'.
**Eating out** The jolly Gasthof Lobewein is a splendid central chalet, with cheerful service in countless rooms and excellent food. Hotel Hochfilzer has a reputation for good food. The Ellmauer Tenne has live music 'most nights'.
**Après-ski** Cafes Käiserstuberl and Bettina are good for coffee and cakes. There are several busy bars. Memory (which has internet facilities) is the early-evening riotous party pub. Pub 66 and Ötzy have regular events such as karaoke and 'erotic dancers'. Rep-organised events include bowling, sleigh rides, Tirolean folklore and tubing. There's an Instructors' Ball and ski displays with 'a party atmosphere' each week, and the toboggan run from the Astberg lift is recommended.
**Off the slopes** The Kaiserbad leisure centre is good. There are many excursions available, including Salzburg and Vitipeno. Valley walks are spoiled by the busy main road. Heading up to Hartkaiser to relax on the terrace 'was a highlight for our non-skiers,' writes a reporter.

# Going 775m/2,540ft

Going is a tiny, attractively rustic village, ideal for families looking for a quiet time. It is well placed for the limited but quiet slopes of the Astberg and for the vast area of nursery slopes between here and Ellmau. Prices are low, but it's not an ideal base for covering the whole of the Ski Welt on the cheap unless you have a car for quick access to Scheffau and Söll. The Lanzenhof (2428) is a cosy central pension doing excellent traditional food in its woody dining rooms.

# Hintertux/Tux valley

*Powerful lifts, excellent snow, varied slopes and villages*

**COSTS**

①②③④⑤⑥

**RATINGS**

**The slopes**

| | |
|---|---|
| Snow | ***** |
| Extent | ** |
| Expert | *** |
| Intermediate | *** |
| Beginner | ** |
| Convenience | ** |
| Queues | *** |
| Mountain restaurants | ** |

**The rest**

| | |
|---|---|
| Scenery | *** |
| Resort charm | *** |
| Off-slope | * |

**NEWS**

The slow Eggalm Nord double chair-lift which links the end of the red run from Rastkogel to the Eggalm slopes is due to be replaced for the 2004/05 season by a fast six-seater chair with covers. It will start lower than the old lift, cutting out the short climb to reach it and it will end 100m/330ft higher, giving a choice of runs down.

- + Hintertux has one of the best glaciers in the world, open summer as well as winter, with some great runs for intermediates and experts on guaranteed good snow
- + Massive investment in new lifts has linked Lanersbach to Mayrhofen and speeded up access to the glacier
- + Some excellent off-piste opportunities
- + A choice of quiet, unspoiled, traditional villages to stay in

- − Lanersbach and Hintertux are a 15-minute bus-ride apart
- − Not for those who want a huge choice of shops and throbbing nightlife on their doorstep
- − Not ideal for beginners or timid intermediates, with few easy runs to valley level
- − Glacier can be cold and bleak in midwinter, and there are lots of T-bars and slow chairs

**The Tux valley has always had its attractions, chief among them the Hintertux glacier, which arguably has the most challenging and interesting runs of any lift-served Alpine glacier. For guaranteed good snow, Hintertux is simply one of the best places to go. But the valley now has much broader appeal. Since 2001 the quieter, friendlier, lower slopes above Lanersbach and its nearby twin, Vorderlanersbach, have been linked by fast new lifts with those above Mayrhofen and Finkenberg, down in the Zillertal, to form a fair-sized circuit. With the glacier only 20 minutes away by bus, these quiet, unspoiled, traditional villages are more attractive bases for many people than either Hintertux or Mayrhofen (covered in its own chapter).**



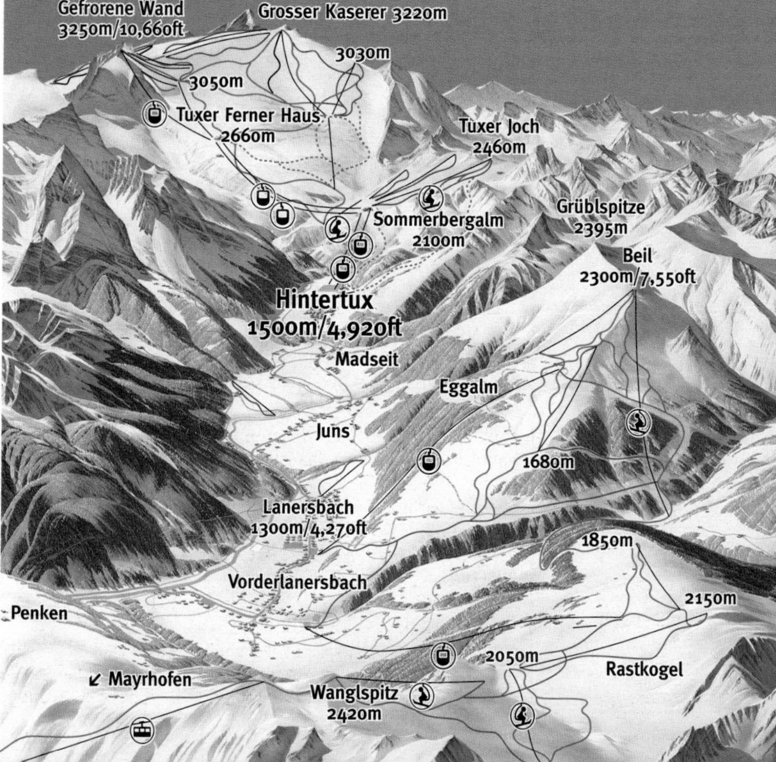

## KEY FACTS

| | |
|---|---|
| **Resort** | 1500m 4,920ft |
| For Ski and Glacier World Zillertal 3000 | |
| **Slopes** | 630-3250m 2,070-10,660ft |
| **Lifts** | 67 |
| **Pistes** | 233km 145 miles |
| **Blue** | 27% |
| **Red** | 58% |
| **Black** | 15% |
| **Snowmaking** | 86km 53 miles |
| For Hintertux only | |
| **Slopes** | 1500-3250m 4,920-10,660ft |
| **Lifts** | 21 |
| **Pistes** | 86km 53 miles |
| For Ziller valley | |
| **Slopes** | 630-3250m 2,070-10,660ft |
| **Lifts** | 175 |
| **Pistes** | 589km 366 miles |





## LIFT PASSES

**Ski and Glacier World Zillertal**
1-, 2- or 3-day passes cover Hintertux glacier, Eggalm, Rastkogel and Penken areas; 4-day and over passes include all Ziller valley lifts, ski-bus and railway.

**Main pass**
1 day €34.50
6 days €163

**Children**
Under 19: 6 days €130
Under 15: 6 days €98
Under 6: free pass

**Notes**
Part-day passes available.

**Alternative passes**
Zillertaler ski pass also available without Hintertux glacier.

The Tux valley has a variety of small villages to stay in, linked by regular free ski-buses. A free night-bus also runs until 2am. Vorderlanersbach is the first village you come to as you enter the valley and Lanersbach is just beyond it. Both are small, traditional villages with attractive old buildings and small roads and paths, and their centres are bypassed by the main road so they remain peaceful and quiet.

Both have gondola links into the local slopes; that from Vorderlanersbach leads to the links with the Penken-Horberg slopes above Mayrhofen – see separate chapter. Hintertux is at the head of the valley, a couple of minutes from the glacier lifts and 15 minutes by bus beyond Lanersbach. On the way up there you pass through two other villages, Juns and Madseit.

There are some good rustic restaurants and bars and a few places along the valley with discos or live music. But nightlife tends to be quieter than in many bigger Austrian resorts.

The Tux valley and Mayrhofen lifts now form what is called the Ski and Glacier World Zillertal 3000. Lift passes for four days or more also cover the countless resorts in the rest of the Ziller valley.

# Hintertux 1500m/4,920ft

### THE RESORT

Tiny Hintertux is bleakly set at the end of the Tux valley. It is little more than a small collection of hotels and guest houses; there is another, smaller group of hotels near the lifts, which lie a 15-minute walk away from the village, across a car park that fills with day-visitors' cars and coaches, especially when snow is poor in lower resorts.

### THE MOUNTAINS

Hintertux's slopes are fairly extensive and, for a glacier, surprisingly challenging. The glacier is one of the best in the world, with varied terrain that attracts national ski teams for summer training. In winter it provides guaranteed good snow even when lower resorts are suffering badly.

**Slopes** A series of three speedy gondolas takes you up from the base to the top of the glacier (vertical rise 1750m/5,740ft) in under 20 minutes. The first stage is an eight-seater up to Sommerbergalm, while the second and third stages (linked by a short slope at Tuxer Ferner Haus) have 24-person cabins. On the two lower stages there is a parallel smaller gondola which is pressed into service to meet demand at peak times. From Sommerbergalm, a fast quad chair serves the slopes below Tuxer Joch; from the top of this sector, an excellent secluded off-piste run goes down to the base station. Between the top of the glacier and Tuxer Ferner Haus there are further chairs and drag-lifts to play on and links across to another 1000m/3,300ft-vertical chain of lifts below Grosser Kaserer on the west. Behind Gefrorene Wand is the area's one sunny piste, served by a triple chair. Descent to the valley involves a short ascent to Sommerbergalm on the way, now achieved by a six-seater chair-lift.

**Terrain-parks** Europe's highest World Cup half-pipe is on the glacier (a popular hang-out throughout the summer), and there is a terrain-park.

**Snow reliability** Snow does not come more reliable than this. Even off the glacier, the other slopes are high and face north, making for very reliable snow-cover. The runs from Tuxer Ferner Haus down to Sommerbergalm have snowmaking as well.

**Experts** There is more to amuse experts here than on any other glacier, with a couple of serious black runs at glacier level and steep slopes and ungroomed ski routes beneath. A lot of the off-piste is little used and one reporter said, 'We found untracked snow not far from the lifts two weeks after the last snowfall.'

**Intermediates** The area particularly suits good or aggressive intermediates. The long runs down from Gefrorene Wand and Kaserer are fun. And there is a pleasant, tree-lined ski route to the valley from Sommerbergalm and another from Tuxer Joch. Moderate intermediates will love the glacier.

**Beginners** There is a nursery slope at valley level, but the glacier isn't the ideal place to progress to.

**Snowboarding** There are some great off-piste opportunities, but boarders complain about the number of T-bars.

**Cross-country** See the Lanersbach information later in the chapter.

**Queues** There used to be huge queues at Hintertux when snow was poor elsewhere. Improved lifts have largely solved this problem. But the main runs can get crowded, and then it is best to head over to the quieter Kaserer lifts and runs.

100%
SNOW GUARANTEE
picture: marcotoniolo.com

↑ The tiny village of Hintertux is in a bleak, snowy setting, at the foot of one of the world's best lift-served glaciers

TVB TUX / JP FANKHAUSER



## SCHOOLS

**Hintertux/Madseit**
t 87755
info@skischule-hintertux.at

**Happy Skiing**
t 87240
info@skischule-lanersbach.at

**Luggis**
t 86808
info@luggis-schischule.at

**Tux 3000**
t 87747
info@tux-3000.at

**Classes**
(Hintertux prices)
5 days (2hr am and pm) €119

**Private lessons**
€48 for 1hr; each additional person €15

**Mountain restaurants** The mountain restaurants tend to get very crowded and the big self-service places lack charm – 'rather soulless except for Tuxerjochhaus,' as one visitor said. The 90-year-old Spannagelhaus is another exception, and there are great views from Gletscherhütte, at the top.
**Schools and guides** There are now four schools, which serve all the resorts in Tux, but we lack reports on them. The newest, Tux 3000, has special guiding, touring and race training programmes.
**Facilities for children** Most of the ski schools run classes for children aged 4 to 14 and lunch is provided.

### STAYING THERE

**How to go** Most hotels are large and comfortable and have spa facilities, but there are also more modest pensions.
**Hotels** Close to the lifts are the 4-star Vierjahreszeiten (8525) and Neuhintertux (8580) – a 2004 reporter says of the latter, 'Less than a minute from the lift, not expensive given the quality, with a relatively new spa including an open-air pool.' We have enjoyed staying in the 3-star Hintertuxerhof (85300) a short walk away; good food, sauna and steam room. Pensions Kössler (87490) and Willeiter (87492) are in the heart of the village.
**Self-catering** There are plenty of apartments.
**Eating out** Restaurants are mainly hotel-based. The Vierjahreszeiten is pleasant and informal.
**Après-ski** There can be a lively après-ski scene both at mid-mountain (Sommerbergalm) and at the bottom of the lifts as they shut; the newish but woody Hohenhaus Tenne has several different bars, the Rindererhof has a popular tea dance, and there are a couple of local bars. The free night-bus gets you to and from the other villages until 2am, but Hintertux is not the place for keen clubbers.
**Off the slopes** The spa facilities are excellent, including a thermal indoor pool, but there are many more options in Mayrhofen.

## Lanersbach 1300m/4,270ft

Lanersbach and neighbouring Vorderlanersbach have long been attractive bases for anyone planning to explore the multiple resorts of the Zillertal and the higher Tuxertal. With the construction of direct links, via Rastkogel, with Mayrhofen's slopes their attractions are now greatly reinforced.

## CHILDREN

**Guest kindergarten**
(in Tux Tourist Association building, Lanersbach)
**t** 872402
Ages 1 to 3

**Ski school**
All three ski schools run children's classes where lunch is provided. Hintertux school takes children from 10am to 3pm (5 days including lunch €169).

## GETTING THERE

**Air** Salzburg 200km/124 miles (3½hr); Munich 176km/109 miles (3hr); Innsbruck 88km/55 miles (1½hr).

**Rail** Local line to Mayrhofen; regular buses from station.

## ACTIVITIES

**Indoor** Bowling, swimming, tennis, squash, saunas and fitness rooms in hotels open to public

**Outdoor** Ice rink, curling, winter hiking trails, paragliding, tobogganing, snow-shoe tours, cave trekking, snow climbing

**Phone numbers**
From elsewhere in Austria add the prefix 05287.
From abroad use the prefix +43 5287.

## TOURIST OFFICE

**Tux**
**t** 8506
info@tux.at
www.tux.at

## THE RESORT

Lanersbach is an attractive, spacious, traditional village largely unspoiled by the busy road up to Hintertux that passes the main lift. Happily, the quiet centre near the pretty church is bypassed by the road, yet is within walking distance of the gondola up to Eggalm. The village is small and delightfully uncommercialised, but it has all you need in a resort. And prices are relatively low. Vorderlanersbach is even smaller, with a gondola up to the Rastkogel area.

## THE MOUNTAINS

**Slopes** The slopes of Eggalm, accessed by the gondola from Lanersbach, offer a small network of pleasantly varied, intermediate pistes, usually delightfully quiet. You can descend on red or blue runs back to the village or to Vorderlanersbach, where a gondola goes up to the higher, open Rastkogel slopes; here, two fast chair-lifts – the latest a covered eight-seater – serve some very enjoyable long red and blue runs and link with Mayrhofen's slopes. But beware: the linking run is classified red but is very tricky and many people opt to walk up the steep slope to the top of the 150-person cable-car link from Mayrhofen and ride down (see copy in margin in Mayrhofen chapter). To get back from Rastkogel to Eggalm you have to take a red run which can suffer from poor snow and is shown on some local piste maps as a ski-route – a strange flaw in the system – or ride the gondola down to Vorderlanersbach (there are no pistes back to Vorderlanersbach) and catch the bus to Lanersbach.
**Terrain-parks** The Mayrhofen and Hintertux pipes and parks are easily accessed.
**Snow reliability** Snow conditions are usually good, at least in early season; by Austrian standards, these are high slopes and there is some snowmaking on Eggalm. But Rastkogel is basically south-facing, and the low links with Eggalm, in particular, are not reliable.
**Experts** There are no pistes to challenge experts, but there is a fine off-piste route starting a short walk from Beil and finishing at the village.
**Intermediates** The slopes suit intermediates best – especially now that they are linked in to Mayrhofen's Penken slopes.
**Beginners** Both areas have nursery slopes (as do Madseit and Juns) but there are few ideal progression slopes – most of the easy runs are on the higher lifts of the Rastkogel sector.
**Snowboarding** The area isn't great for novices – there are drag-lifts dotted around the mountains, some in key places.
**Cross-country** There are 14km/9 miles of cross-country trails, alongside the Tux creek, between Madseit and Vorderlanersbach, and a 6km/4-mile skating track in Juns/Madseit.
**Queues** We have no reports of any problems. Indeed, Eggalm can be delightfully quiet.
**Mountain restaurants** There's no shortage but most, though fairly rustic, are self-service with simple food; the small Lattenalm on Eggalm is a table-service exception with a terrace that has splendid views of the Tux glacier.
**Schools and guides** There are four schools in the valley, but we lack recent reports on them.
**Facilities for children** The non-ski nursery takes children aged from one to three, and most of the schools take children from four years upwards.

## STAYING THERE

**How to go** Lanersbach and Vorderlanersbach are essentially hotel-based resorts.
**Hotels** The Lanersbacherof (87256) is a good 4-star with pool, sauna, steam and hot-tub close to the lifts, but it is also on the main road. The cheaper 3-star Pinzger (87541) and Alpengruss (87293) are similarly situated. In Vorderlanersbach the 3-star Kirchlerhof (8560) is 'really friendly, with comfortable rooms and excellent food', says a regular visitor.
**Self-catering** Quite a lot of apartments are available.
**Eating out** Restaurants are mainly hotel-based, busy, and geared to serving dinner early.
**Après-ski** Nightlife is generally quiet by Austrian standards, which suits us. We enjoyed the jolly Hühnerstall in Lanersbach (an old wooden building with traditional Austrian music) and the ancient wine bar in Vorderlanersbach. There is a disco or two.
**Off the slopes** Off-slope facilities are fairly good considering the size of the resorts. Some hotels have pools, hot-tubs and fitness rooms open to non-residents. There is a tennis centre in Vorderlanersbach which also has squash and bowling. Innsbruck and Salzburg are possible excursions.

INNSBRUCK TOURISMUS

# Innsbruck

*A cultured city base for a range of little ski resorts – and a big glacier*

## COSTS

(1)(2)(3)(4)(5)(6)

## KEY FACTS

| | |
|---|---|
| **Resort** | 575m<br>1,890ft |
| **Slopes** | 800-3210m<br>2,620-10,530ft |
| **Lifts** | 75 |
| **Pistes** | 217km<br>135 miles |
| **Blue** | 39% |
| **Red** | 50% |
| **Black** | 11% |
| **Snowmaking** | 39km<br>24 miles |

## NEWS

Last season a new eight-person gondola opened on the Stubaier Gletscher, running from the Eisgrat restaurant at 2900m/9,510ft to the highest slopes on the Schaufelspitze.

In Igls there is a new artificial ice rink.

It seems certain that the Mutters ski area will stay closed for the 2004/05 season, as new lifts planned for it have been further delayed.



**Innsbruck is not a ski resort in the usual sense. It is an historic university city of 130,000 inhabitants, with a vibrant cultural life, and is a major tourist destination in summer. Its local slopes are mainly of local interest. But the city has twice hosted the Olympic Winter Games, and is surrounded by little resorts that share a lift pass and are accessible by efficient bus services. Among them is a glacier that is one of best in the world – the Stubaier Gletscher. This year the portfolio is expanded by the addition of little Oberperfuss and the more distant Kühtai – at 2020m/6,630ft, one of Austria's highest resorts. Meanwhile, lower down, the slopes above Mutters remain closed, awaiting agreement on their redevelopment. Seefeld, host of the Olympic cross-country events, is no longer covered by the Innsbruck lift pass, so is no longer dealt with here.**

The Inn valley is a broad, flat-bottomed trench hereabouts, but Innsbruck manages to fill it from side to side. It is a sizeable city and, as you would expect from its Olympic background, it has an excellent range of winter sports facilities, as well as a captivating car-free medieval core. It has smart, modern, shopping areas, trendy bars and restaurants, museums (including, of course, one devoted to the Olympics), concert halls, theatres, a zoo and other attractions that you might seek out on a summer holiday, but normally wouldn't expect to find when going skiing.

Winter diversions off the slopes include over 300km/186 miles of cross-country trails, some at valley level but others appreciably above it; curling and skating at the Olympic centre; several toboggan runs totalling 60km/37 miles, the longest (above Birgitz) an impressive 11km/7 miles and 1060m/3,480ft vertical; and rides on a four-man bob at Igls.

INNSBRUCK TOURISMUS

A handsome city in a fine setting ↓

Not the least of the attractions of staying in such a place is that you don't pay ski resort prices for anything.

There are hotels, inns and B&Bs of every standard and style, with 3-star and 4-star hotels forming the nucleus. Among the more distinctive hotels are the grand 5-star Europa Tyrol (59310), the ancient 4-star Goldener Adler (571111) and the 3-star Weisses Kreuz (59479) in the central pedestrian zone, and the 4-star art nouveau Best Western Neue Post (59476).

As well as traditional Austrian restaurants there are several Italians, plus a smattering of more exotic alternatives from Mexican to Japanese.

There is an impressive 1400m/4,600ft vertical of slopes on the south-facing slopes of **Seegrube-Nordkette**. The focus of the slopes at Seegrube is reached by cable-car rising 1050m/3,450ft from Hungerburg on the outskirts of the city (with buses and a funicular up to the cable-car departure station). Although there are red runs to the valley, the snow is not reliable. You go up here expecting to ski the red runs of 370m/1,210ft vertical below Seegrube, served by a chair-lift. A further stage of the cable-car rises 350m/1,150ft vertical to access the Karinne ski route, which is said to be fearsomely steep (up to 70% gradient). You can ski it with a guide and collect a T-shirt and certificate to prove it.

But for visitors, if not for residents, skiing usually means heading for the opposite side of the Inn trench.

The standard Innsbruck lift pass covers the lifts in all the resorts dealt with here. Free ski-bus services run to and from all the lift-pass-covered areas, but only at the beginning and

↑ Igls is very close to Innsbruck, but still a separate village

INNSBRUCK TOURISMUS

## LIFT PASSES

**Innsbruck Gletscher Skipass**
Covers all resorts in this chapter.

**Main pass**
6 days €150

**Senior citizens**
Over 60: 6 days €120

**Children**
Under 19: 6 days €120
Under 15: 6 days €90
Under 7: free

**Other passes**
Super-Skipass also covers days in the Arlberg (St Anton) and Kitzbühel.

end of the day. A car makes life more convenient, especially if you are staying outside downtown Innsbruck.

There are terrain-parks at Seegrube, Axamer Lizum, Schlick 2000 and the Stubaier Gletscher.

A major road runs southwards from Innsbruck over the Brenner pass to Italy – opening up the possibility of excursions to resorts in the Dolomites.

### TULFES 920m/3,020ft

**Tulfes gets rather overshadowed by the Olympic resorts of Igls and Axamer Lizum, but it has some worthwhile runs.**

The runs are on the north-facing slopes of Glungezer. A chair-lift from above the village serves red and blue runs of 600m/1,970ft vertical. This leads to a drag up to the tree line serving a red run of 500m/1,640ft vertical. And this in turn leads to a drag and a chair-lift serving open red runs from the top at 2305m/7,560ft – almost 1400m/4,600ft above the village.

Like Igls, the village sits on the shelf on the side of the Inn valley. There are a dozen hotels and gasthofs.

### IGLS 900m/2,950ft

**Igls seems almost a suburb of Innsbruck – the city trams run out to the village – but it is a small resort in its own right. Its famous downhill race course is an excellent piste.**

The village of Igls is small and quiet, with not much in the way of diversions apart from the beautiful walks, an artificial ice rink, the Olympic bob run and the tea shops. You can stay in Igls, and a couple of UK operators sell packages there. Most hotels are small and in the centre of the village, a bit of a walk from the cable-car station. An exception is the family-run 5-star Sporthotel (377241), which occupies the prime site, centrally placed between the tram and the cable-car stations: 'Excellent facilities, good food and nice bar,' says a reporter.

The skiing on Patscherkofel is very limited and revolves around the excellent, varied, long red run that formed the men's downhill course in 1976, when Franz Klammer took ski racing (and the Olympic gold medal) by storm. There is a blue-run variation on this run (with a five-minute hike to reach the start, says a reporter), but no other pistes. A cable-car rises 1050m/3,450ft from the village (and you can take it down if the lower runs are poor or shut). At the top, a chair rises a further 275m/900ft to the summit offering wonderful views over Innsbruck and ski routes back down. A fast quad and a couple of drags serve slopes below the cable-car station. There is a short beginner lift at village level, and another a short bus-ride up





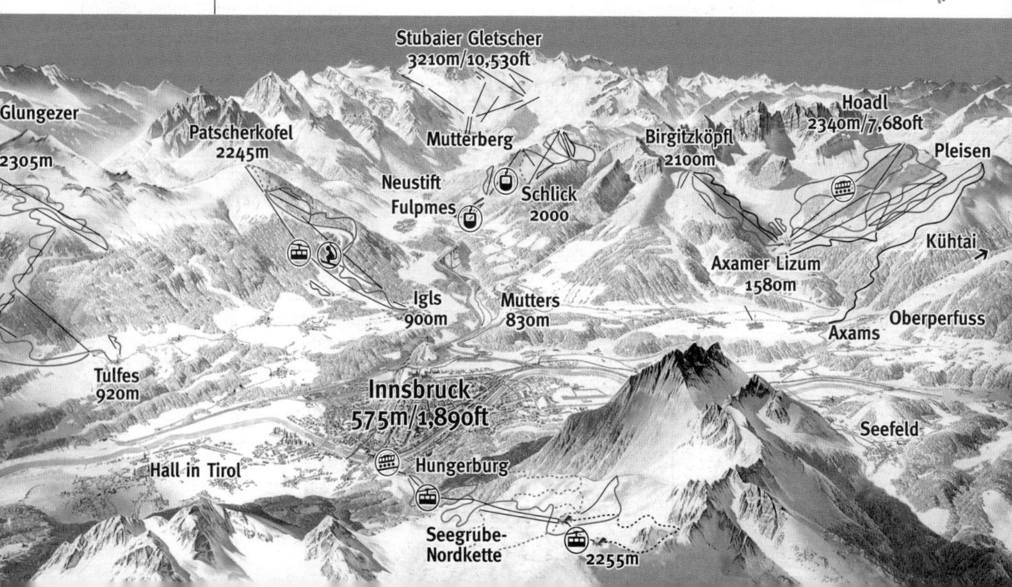

↑ The Stubai glacier is one of the world's best for skiing and boarding
TVB NEUSTIFT





**TOURIST OFFICES**

**Innsbruck**
t 59850
info@innsbruck.tvb.co.at
www.ski-innsbruck.at

**Tulfes**
t 78324
info@tulfes.at
www.tulfes.at

**Igls**
t 377101
igls@innsbruck.tvb.co.at
www.tiscover.com/igls

**Fulpmes**
t 62235
info@stubai.at
www.tiscover.com/fulpmes

**Neustift**
t 2228
tv.neustift@neustift.at
www.neustift.com

**Axamer Lizum**
t 68178
axams@innsbruck.tvb.co.at
www.tiscover.com/axams

**Oberperfuss**
t 81489
oberperfuss@innsbruck.info
www.tiscover.co.at/oberperfuss

**Kühtai**
t 5229
info@kuehtai.co.at
www.kuehtai.co.at

the hill. We have received mixed reports on the grooming of the trails.

Après-ski is quiet. The resort suits families but others might prefer to stay in Innsbruck.

**FULPMES** 935m/3,070ft

**Fulpmes is a sizeable village between Innsbruck and Neustift, on the way to the Stubaier Gletscher, with a fair-sized ski area of its own called Schlick 2000.**
A two-stage gondola leads to a series of chair- and drag-lifts serving a few mainly short blue and red runs on the Sennjoch. There are also two ski routes and a terrain-park.

**STUBAIER GLETSCHER** 1750m/5,740ft

**The Stubaier Gletscher is one of the best glacier ski and snowboard areas in the world; it is open in summer as well as in winter. The nearest place to stay is picturesque Neustift, 20km/12 miles away and served by regular buses.**
The glacier is accessed by two alternative two-stage gondolas from the huge car park at Mutterberg. Last winter another gondola right to the top of the slopes was added – so you can now get to the top by riding three successive gondolas.

On the glacier a variety of chair- and drag-lifts (including three six-person chairs) allow fabulous high altitude cruising on blue and red runs, which normally have excellent snow on slopes between 3200m and 2300m (10,500ft and 7,550ft). A lovely 10km/6 mile ungroomed ski route through a deserted bowl takes you down to the valley – or, if you start at the top, a descent of about 14km/9 miles and 1450m/4,760ft vertical is possible. There is also good off-piste on the glacier to be explored with a guide.

There is a terrain-park and half-pipe, a fun area for kids at Gamsgarten and a 20m/66ft ice tower.

A 2004 reporter confirms that improvements to the lifts have virtually eliminated what used to be enormous queues. On a busy weekend there were only short delays mid-morning at the gondola middle station and occasionally at the Eisjoch six-pack.

Neustift is an attractive Tirolean village halfway along the Stubai valley, with the main road bypassing the village centre. It has a small area of local slopes, but what you go for is the glacier proximity to the glacier. There are lots of 4- and 3-star hotels in the village – the Sonnhof (2224) and the Hoferwirt (25600) have been recommended by reporters. Most of the restaurants are hotel-based – reporters recommend Bellafonte's pizzas and the Hoferwirt.



**AXAMER LIZUM** 1580m/5,180ft

**The mountain outpost of the Inn-side village of Axams is a simple ski station and nothing more, but it does have some good slopes and reliable snow conditions – and, as a reporter says, 'You feel as if you are in a wilderness.'**
Axamer Lizum could scarcely offer a sharper contrast to Igls. It offers much more varied slopes and a network of lifts, with the base station at a much

↑ There's not much more to the 'resort' of Axamer Lizum than this – though the slopes are quite extensive by local standards

INNSBRUCK TOURISMUS

higher altitude. The slopes here hosted all the Olympic Alpine events in 1976 except the men's downhill, and this is the standard local venue for weekends – hence the huge car park, which is the most prominent feature of the 'resort'.

The main slopes on Hoadl and Pleisen are blues and reds, almost entirely above the trees but otherwise nicely varied, and there is scope to 'play in gullies and bumps, as well as true off-piste,' says our reporter. The vertical of the main east-facing slopes above the main lift station is 'only' 700m/2,300ft, but for good skiers at least there is the possibility (given good snow conditions) of a 1300m/4,260ft descent at the end of the day from Pleisen to the outskirts of Axams – an easy 6.5km/4 mile black. On the opposite side of the valley, a chair-lift serves a fairly easy black slope. Beyond it are the slopes of Mutters, closed since 2001 and unlikely to re-open for a further year or two at least.

Snowmaking now covers 70% of the slopes and there is a new large restaurant with panoramic views on Hoadl.

There are two good nursery lifts, and two ski schools.

You can stay up here – there is a 4-star hotel at the lift base, the Lizumerhof (68244) – 'Nice rooms and decent modern Austrian cuisine,' says a reporter – and there are a couple of 3-stars, too. But there's little in the way of après-ski apart from a couple of bars – the Alm bar is the most atmospheric – and you have to eat in your hotel or go to Axams.

There is also accommodation not far away at lower altitude in Axams – including four 3-star hotels – and in other nearby villages such as Götzens (one 4-star hotel, two 3-star gasthofs) and Birgitz (two 3-star hotels).

**Phone numbers**
**Calling long-distance**
Add the prefix given below for each resort. When calling from abroad use the country code 43 and omit the initial 0.

**Innsbruck and Igls**
0512

**Tulfes**
05223

**Fulpmes**
05225

**Neustift**
05226

**Axamer Lizum**
05234

**Oberperfuss**
05232

**Kühtai**
05239

## OBERPERFUSS 815m/2,675ft

**No, we hadn't heard of it, either – until the lifts on its local hill, Rangger Köpfl, were brought into the fold of the Innsbruck area lift pass.**

The hill is a very limited one, with five lifts in a largely linear arrangement serving 17km/11 miles of easy-intermediate slopes – but an impressive vertical of 1200m/3,940ft. The village is small but self-sufficient, with one of most things you need (pharmacy, bakery) including a big 3-star hotel, the Krone (81465). It is prettily rustic, and targets the family market with the aid of a moving carpet lift on the nursery slopes.

## KÜHTAI 2020m/6,630ft

**A collection of comfortable hotels spread along a high road pass 25km/16 miles west of Innsbruck – higher than equally snow-sure Obergurgl or Obertauern, but cheaper than either.**

Glaciers apart, Kühtai's altitude means it must be one of Austria's most snow-sure resorts. That is its main attraction, given the limited nature of the village.

Half a dozen drags and three fast quad chairs serve red cruisers of 400m/1,300ft to 500m/1,650ft vertical on either side of the road, plus some token blue and black runs (which may be easier than the reds because they get less traffic). There is a good nursery slope, but no easy blues to graduate to. The resort attracts families during school holidays (notably carnival) and crowds of day-trippers on fine weekends – especially if lower resorts are short of snow – but is otherwise crowd-free. There are now three mountain restaurants. There are two ski schools.

The village is quiet in the evening, but for its size has 'a reasonable selection of bars and restaurants', says a report – practically all in hotels. The 4-star hotels include the Jagdschloss (5201) – a much-developed old hunting lodge. The 3-star hotel Elisabeth (5240) is recommended – 'very friendly, excellent food'. From one or two other hotels we have reports of English emphatically not spoken – and there is little resort information in English, either on paper or on the resort web site.

There are several free postbuses from Innsbruck morning and afternoon, but the journey takes over an hour.

ISCHGL TOURIST OFFICE

# Ischgl

*One of Austria's best – and at last finding a place on the British market*

## COSTS

①②③④⑤⑥

## RATINGS

**The slopes**

| | |
|---|---|
| Snow | **** |
| Extent | **** |
| Expert | *** |
| Intermediate | **** |
| Beginner | ** |
| Convenience | *** |
| Queues | **** |
| Mountain restaurants | **** |

**The rest**

| | |
|---|---|
| Scenery | *** |
| Resort charm | **** |
| Off-slope | *** |

## NEWS

For 2003/04 a six-seat chair with covers, the Paznauner Thaya, replaced an old T-bar between Bodenalp and Höllenkar. Another six-pack, the Viderjochbahn, was installed at Alp Trida – and for 2004/05 another six-pack is to be built above that, improving access from the Swiss side to the slopes below the Greitspitz and to the Austrian side.

Three new ski routes were laid out for 2003/04 (Höllspitz–Höllkar; below Zeblas; Flimjoch–Idalp) and snow-guns were added on four runs.



- + Charming old Tirolean village, expanded in sympathetic fashion
- + High slopes with reliable snow
- + Lots of good intermediate runs
- + Superb modern lift system
- + Wide range of accommodation from luxury hotels to simple B&Bs
- + Very lively après-ski

- − Not ideal for beginners or timid intermediates, for various reasons
- − English less widely spoken than is usual in Austria
- − Few seriously steep runs
- − Very little wooded terrain to give shelter in bad weather
- − EuroTrash-style après-ski – e.g. table-dancing in plush 4-star hotels – and a lot of heavy drinking

**For years we've been saying that Ischgl is unjustly neglected in Britain, mainly because of a shortage of package holidays to the resort. That's now changing, with three major operators going there this season – and last season we got a flood of reports from readers. With one clear exception ('the place is full of maniacs') most enthusiastically endorse our view that this is one of Austria's best. Unless cost is an obstacle, put it on your Austrian short-list.**

**Samnaun, over the Swiss border, is tour-op-free, and likely to remain so. But for independent travellers it has attractions – it's a charming, relaxed village, and for a party including some novices makes a better base than Ischgl.**

## THE RESORT

Ischgl is a quite compact village tucked away in the long, narrow Paznaun valley, south of St Anton on the Swiss border (the skiing is shared with Swiss Samnaun). It's set where a stream (the Fimbabach) joins the river Trisanna, and part of the village is built on high ground between the converging rivers.

The narrow main street plus a couple of side streets are traffic-free – the village is bypassed by the valley road up to Galtür – and at the west end of the pedestrian zone is the main access lift, the 24-person Silvrettabahn, up to the main mid-mountain focus of Idalp. Two other gondolas – one to Idalp, the other to the higher point of Pardatschgrat – start close together on the eastern fringe of the village, beside the Fimbabach. Because of the high ground in between, getting to these lifts from the middle of the village used to be hard work; but now an underground moving carpet connects them to the heart of the village.

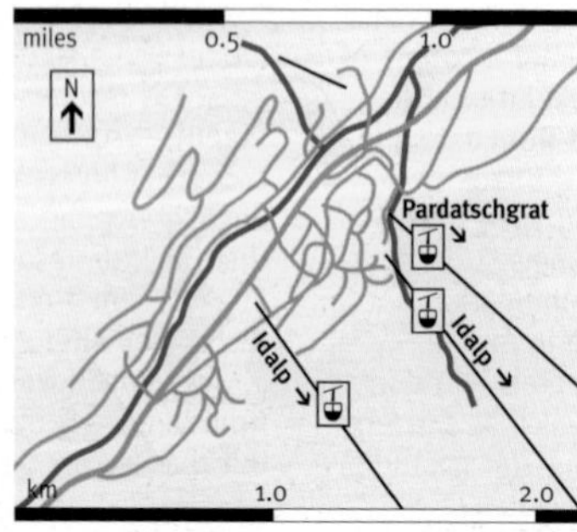


The buildings are practically all in traditional chalet style, and the place has a neat, prosperous air. The wooded flanks of the valley rise steeply from the village, which as a result gets almost no sun in early season. There's a selection of lively bars and an excellent sports centre; shops are mainly confined to winter-sports. There is a lot of heavy drinking, but it rarely constitutes a nuisance.

Choice of location is much less important since the construction of the underground walkway, but the best spot, all things considered, is on or near the main street. Beware of accommodation across the bypass road, a long way from the lifts.

There are frequent buses down the valley to Kappl and up it to Galtür (covered by the regional ski pass), which are described at the end of this chapter. A car makes trips to St Anton viable. It's a very long taxi-ride from Samnaun, should you get stuck there.

## KEY FACTS

| | |
|---|---|
| **Resort** | 1400m<br>4,590ft |
| **Slopes** | 1400-2870m<br>4,590-9,420ft |
| **Lifts** | 42 |
| **Pistes** | 200km<br>124 miles |
| **Blue** | 18% |
| **Red** | 61% |
| **Black** | 21% |
| **Snowmaking** | 75km<br>47 miles |



## THE MOUNTAINS

Ischgl is a fair-sized, relatively high, snow-sure area. Practically all the slopes are above the tree line, and bleak in bad weather, the main exception being the steep lower slopes above the village and a couple of short runs low down in the Fimbatal. The slopes are shared with duty-free Samnaun in Switzerland.

There are increasing numbers of ski routes on the piste map – some (regrettably) replacing pistes. These routes are unpatrolled, and avalanche-controlled only 'in the immediate area of avalanche warning signs'.

Some reporters complain about the closure of lifts at about 4pm, even in late season. This is common in Austria.

### THE SLOPES

***Cross-border cruising***

The sunny **Idalp** plateau, reached by two of the village gondolas, is the hub of the slopes. It can be very crowded, especially at ski school meeting time, lunchtime (lock up your skis!) and the end of the day. Pardatschgrat, reached by the third gondola, is about 300m/ 1,000ft higher. From here it's an easy run down to Idalp, where lifts radiate to a wide variety of mainly north-west- and west-facing runs. The red runs back to Ischgl itself provoke regular complaints; neither is easy, conditions can be tricky, and beer-lubricated crowds don't help. Quite a few people ride the gondolas down instead. If in a group, the wide, quiet ski route down the pretty Velilltal is the way to go.

A short piste brings you from Idalp to the lifts serving the **Höllenkar** bowl, leading up to the area's south-western extremity and high-point at Palinkopf. There are further lifts beyond here, on the west-facing flanks of the **Fimbatal**.

On the Swiss side the hub of activity is **Alp Trida**, surrounded by south- and east-facing runs with great views and 'glorious, gentle cruises'. From here a quiet, scenic red run goes down to Compatsch, from where there are buses to Ravaisch – for the cable-car back – and Samnaun-Dorf. From Palinkopf there is a beautiful long run down an unspoiled valley to Samnaun-Dorf. It is not difficult, but it is excessively sunny in parts and prone to closure because of avalanche risk. There is a long, flat stretch at the end.

### TERRAIN-PARKS

***One of Europe's best***

Between Idjoch and Idalp is a championship half-pipe and an excellent terrain-park, 'Boarder's Paradise', with jumps, a quarter-pipe, rails, a boarder-cross course and a timed race course. It is reported to be very quiet. There's a separate kids' snowboard area.

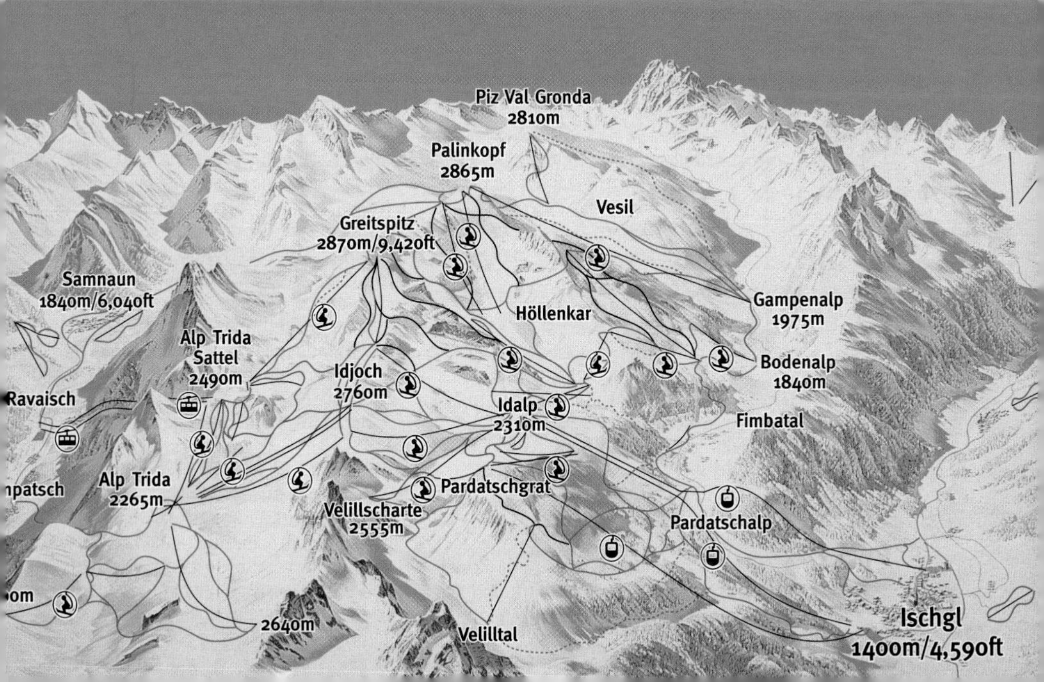

LIFT PASSES

**Two-Country VIP Skipass**
Covers all lifts in Ischgl and Samnaun and local buses.

**Main pass**
1 day €38.50
6 days €168.50

**Senior citizens**
Over 60: 6 days €142.50

**Children**
Under 16: 6 days €101
Under 7: free pass

**Notes**
Half-day pass available. Passes for two days and over available only to those staying in Ischgl, Samnaun or Mathon on presenting a guest card. Note that the lift pass office does not take credit cards.

**Alternative passes**
Regional (Silvretta) ski pass covers Ischgl, Samnaun, Galtür, Kappl and See.

SCHOOLS

**Ischgl**
t 5257/5404
schischule@ischgl.at

**Classes**
5 days (2hr am and pm) €148

**Private lessons**
€108 for 2hr; each additional person €15





## boarding

*Ischgl was one of the first resorts to wholeheartedly welcome boarders. It has one of the best terrain-parks in Europe and is constantly improving it. The use of speed boards and the carving courses are very popular. The lifts are generally boarder-friendly. The area is well-suited to beginners and intermediates; experts will love Ischgl after fresh snow, even if the gradients are less impressive than in St Anton. Silvretta Sports and Intersport Mathoy are recommended snowboard shops.*

### SNOW RELIABILITY
***Very good***

All the slopes, except the runs back to the resort, are above 2000m/6,560ft and many of those on the Ischgl side are north-west-facing. So snow conditions are generally reliable (which can lead to crowds when bus-loads of visitors arrive from lower resorts). There is snowmaking on various runs including several above Idalp, the two main descents to Ischgl and some key slopes on the Samnaun side.

### FOR EXPERTS
***Not much on-piste challenge***

Ischgl can't compare with nearby St Anton for exciting slopes, and some of the runs marked black on the piste map would be red elsewhere. But there is plenty of beautiful off-piste to be found with a guide (Alp Trida is popular) – and, because there are few experts around, it doesn't get tracked out quickly. The best areas to head for are Greitspitz and Palinkopf – the wooded lower slopes of the Fimbatal are delightful in a snowstorm. Ski route 39 is recommended to leave you 'suitably exhausted' after the testing 1000m/3,280ft descent. The best steep piste is 4, from Pardatschgrat towards Ischgl. You can do the top half of this repeatedly by catching the gondola at the mid-station. The variant 4a, into Velilltal, is now a ski route. Black 14a, from the Greitspitz, is the newest run in the area and is steeper than most.

### FOR INTERMEDIATES
***Something for everyone***

Most of the slopes are wide, forgiving and ideal for intermediates.

At the tough end of the spectrum our favourite runs are those from Palinkopf down to Gampenalp and on along the valley to the secluded restaurant at Bodenalp.

There are also interesting and challenging black runs down the Höllspitz chair, and from both the top and bottom of the drag-lift from Idjoch up to Greitspitz. The reds from Pardatschgrat and Velillscharte down the beautiful valley to Velilltal and the red from Greitspitz into Switzerland are great for quiet, high-speed cruising.

For easier motorway cruising, there is lots of choice, including the Swiss side, where the runs from the border down to Alp Trida should prove ideal.

### FOR BEGINNERS
***Not ideal***

Beginners go up the mountain to Idalp, where there are good, sunny, snow-sure nursery slopes and a short beginners' drag-lift. The blue runs on the east side of the bowl offer pleasant progression for fast learners. Over at Alp Trida there are further easy expanses – you can return by lift.

### FOR CROSS-COUNTRY
***Plenty in the valley***

There are 48km/30 miles of cross-country track in the Paznaun valley between Ischgl, Galtür and Wirl. This tends to be pretty sunless, especially in early season, and is away from the main slopes, which makes meeting downhillers for lunch inconvenient.

### QUEUES
***An amazing transformation***

Visitors these days are mightily impressed by the number of fast chairs on the mountain, but there are some flaws in the system. Queues can form in the village – a reporter had a 30-minute wait at the Pardatschgratbahn, but the nearby Fimbabahn gets few queues. Up the mountain – the Flimsattelbahn return from Alp Trida is particularly noted as a problem by reporters, with one waiting '40 minutes on two occasions'. Some may look serious, but most shift quickly.

### MOUNTAIN RESTAURANTS
***Much improved***

Mountain restaurants tend to be very crowded but quite good quality, with over half now offering table-service. The Paznauner Taja, above Bodenalp, is an attractive, rustic chalet with 'great

## CHILDREN

**Kindergarten**
(run by ski school at Idalp)
**t** 5257/5404
For non-skiing children (no small infants); 10am to 4pm; €33 per day, inc lunch

**Ski kindergarten**
(run by ski school at Idalp)
**t** 5257/5404
Ages 3 to 5; €41 per day; lunch available

**Ski school**
Takes children from the age of 5 (5 full days €133)

## GETTING THERE

**Air** Innsbruck 100km/62 miles (1½hr); Zürich 300km/186 miles (3hr); Munich 300km/186 miles (3hr).

**Rail** Landeck (30km/19 miles); frequent buses from station.

ISCHGL TOURISMUS

Lots of glorious intermediate slopes above the tree line ↓

spit-roasted chickens', but gets very crowded. There is table service upstairs and often a band playing on the terrace, or throbbing disco music. Down in Fimbatal is the Bodenalpe, a quieter, rustic table-service restaurant.

At Idalp there is a busy, big self-service cafeteria, and a good table-service alternative (splendid views from the terrace). The self-service up at Pardatschgrat tends to be quieter. The Schwarze Wand pizzeria at the top of Höllenkar is recommended by reporters. From Gampenalp you can be towed by snowmobile to the remote Heidelberger hütte. The 5km/3 mile tow is 'tough on the knees but exhilarating'. Enjoy lunch then make your own way back to Gampenalp – 'there is a lot of poling involved, some uphill climbs and a few gentle schusses' (not, therefore, recommended to snowboarders), but it is well worth the effort.

The restaurants on the Swiss side at Alp Trida are pleasant, quieter and generally receive the best recommendations from reporters. The Alp Bella (table- or self-service) has been recommended for a quiet time, 'good views and local specialities'. Also highly rated are the Skihaus AlpTrida – 'best goulash soup ever' – and the Panorama Sattel (top of the Samnaun cable-car) – 'excellent food', 'splendid views'. Above the big Alp Trida self-service is the upmarket Marmotte, with table-service indoors and out (reservations needed).

Recommended by several reporters is the Schmuggler Alm down in Samnaun – the first house you get to if you take the long red from Palinkopf: 'Table service, great food, good value – and they take euros.' But a recent visitor complains of 'rude DJs, brash barmen and Eurotrash music'.

### SCHOOLS AND GUIDES
***Good despite language problems***

The school meets up at Idalp and starts very late (10.30 to 12.30 and 1.30 to 3.30) – perhaps to allow people to get over their hangovers. In the past we've had rave reports of both adult and children's classes, but recent reporters said class sizes were large at around 12 people and their instructor spoke limited English. But another found hiring an instructor for an afternoon was 'helpful'. One reporter observed small classes using coloured tubes instead of poles to 'help with correct hand position and posture'. As well as normal lessons the school organises off-piste tours – this is a great touring area.

### FACILITIES FOR CHILDREN
***High-altitude options***

The childcare facilities are all up at Idalp – there's an enclosed learning zone and adventure garden with cartoon characters, where children can safely enjoy their classes, but we have no first-hand reports of the service they provide.





## STAYING THERE

### HOW TO GO
***Increasing choice of packages***

Very few British tour operators have offered Ischgl in the past, but the number is growing fast.

**Hotels** There is a good selection from luxurious and expensive to basic B&Bs. Beware: some don't take credit cards.

((((5) **Trofana Royal** (600) One of Austria's most luxurious hotels, with prices to match. A celebrity chef runs the kitchen. Sumptuous spa facilities.

((((5) **Madlein** (5226) Convenient, 'hip', modern hotel. Pool, sauna, steam room. Nightclub and disco.

((((5) **Elisabeth** (5411) Right by the Pardatsch gondola with lively après-ski. Pool, sauna and steam room.

((((5) **Solaria** (5205) Near the Madlein and just as luxurious, but with a 'friendly family atmosphere'.

((((5) **Brigitte (5646)** Highly recommended by a reporter. 'Central, but quiet', 'fantastic food'. Pool.

((((4) **Piz Tasna** (5277) Up hill behind church: 'Quiet location, friendly, lovely views over village, excellent food.'

((((4) **Goldener Adler (5217)** Recommended by two reporters this year. Convenient, modern hotel, with 'outstanding food'. Sauna and whirlpool.

It's not surprising that the home runs are narrow, given the terrain ➔

ISCHGL TOURISMUS





## ACTIVITIES

**Indoor** Silvretta Centre (bowling, billiards, swimming pool, sauna, solarium, massage), tennis, museums

**Outdoor** Skating, sleigh rides, hiking tours, 7km/4 miles floodlit toboggan run

((((4) **Sonne** (5302) Highly rated by reporters. In the centre of the village. Lively stube. Sauna, hot-tub, solarium.
(((3) **Olympia (5432)** 'Well-appointed, family-run' with 'good-sized rooms'. Bar and restaurant.
(((3) **Jägerhof** (5206) 'Jewel of a hotel,' said a reporter. Friendly, good food, large rooms. Sauna and steam.
(((3) **Christine** (5346) Probably the best B&B in town. 'Huge rooms, nice views, good position near the lifts.'
((2) **Dorfschmeide** (5769) Small, central B&B recommended by a reporter.
Other recommendations by reporters include the Albona (5500), the Sylvia (5690) and the newish Ida (50005).
**Self-catering** Some attractive apartments are available – the Golfais are conveniently placed by the Pardatschgratbahn gondola and are recommended.

### EATING OUT
***Plenty of choice***

Most of our reporters eat in their hotels. For a lighter meal such as pizza try the Nona, the Schatzi or the Trofana Alm, which is as much a bar as a restaurant, and for fondue or ribs the Kitzloch, with its galleries over the dance floor. The Allegra and Salz & Pfeffer 'pasta and pizza' have been recommended (best to book). The Grillalm and Salnerhof are popular, 'traditional Austrian fare, huge portions'. A reporter pronounces The Nudel Himmel (above the Hollboda bar) his favourite – local dishes at reasonable prices. The Nevada Alm is also recommended, 'friendly staff, but little English is spoken'.

### APRES-SKI
***Very lively***

Ischgl is one of the liveliest resorts in the Alps, from early afternoon on. Lots of people are still in ski boots late in the evening. At close of play head for Trofana Alm near the Silvrettabahn or the Schatzi bar of the hotel Elisabeth by the Pardatschgratbahn – indoor and outdoor bars and scantily clad dancing girls; 'great fun' writes a 2004 reporter. Niki's Stadl across the road is a great place to sing along to live Austrian hits. The Kitzloch 'rocks', with dancing on the tables in ski-boots. The Sunn-Alm at the hotel Sonne gets crowded and has live music. The Kuhstahl under the Sporthotel Silvretta and Fire & Ice (expensive drinks) over the road are both lively all evening. The Hollboda bar is recommended for live music. Guxa, 'a cigars and cocktails type of place', and Allegra liven up after dinner, and the Golden Eagle is 'good for live bands'. The Coyote Ugly at the hotel Madlein – 'a lap dancing bar that just manages to avoid seediness' – has been recommended. There's now a branch of the famous Pacha nightclubs, also in Ibiza and London (a bit 'tacky' says a recent visitor). The Living Room (hotel Grillalm) is allegedly 'more hands-on' than table dancing. And the club under the hotel Post has an ancient Roman theme. The Post also has a casino.

### OFF THE SLOPES
***No sun but a nice pool***

The village gets little sun in the middle of winter, and the resort is best suited to those keen to hit the slopes. But

**Phone numbers**
**Calling long-distance**
Add the prefix given below for each resort. When calling from abroad use the country code 43 and omit the initial 0.

**Ischgl**
05444
**Galtür**
05443
**Kappl**
05445

**Samnaun (Switzerland)**
From elsewhere in Switzerland add the prefix 081.
From abroad use the prefix +41 81.

**TOURIST OFFICES**

**Ischgl**
t 5266
info@ischgl.com
www.ischgl.com
**Galtür**
t 8521
info@galtuer.com
www.galtuer.com
**Kappl**
t 6243
info@kappl.at
www.kappl.at
**Samnaun**
(Switzerland)
t 868 5858
info@samnaun.ch
www.samnaun.ch

there's no shortage of off-slope activities. There are 24km/15 miles of marked walks, a 7km/4 mile floodlit toboggan run and a splendid sports centre. And you can browse upmarket shops, which sell Versace and Bogner.

It's easy to get around the valley by bus, and there are restaurants that pedestrians can get to by gondolas. Ischgl has one of the most accessible lift-systems to non-skiers and hikers. The 'excellent' Smuggler's Pass (25 euros) for pedestrians enables them to explore the lifts for a day and lunch with skiing friends. It covers specially selected lifts in the area.

## Samnaun 1840m/6,040ft

Samnaun is a small, quiet duty-free community in a corner of Switzerland more easily reached from Austria. A recent reporter saw no other Brits there all week.

There are four small components, roughly 1km/0.5 miles apart: Samnaun-Dorf, prettily set at the head of the valley is the main focus, with some swanky hotels and duty-free shops; Ravaisch, where the cable-car goes up; tiny Plan; and the hamlets of Laret and Compatsch, at the end of the main run down from the slopes (where there are several choices of lunchtime eateries). We've stayed happily on the edge of Dorf in the Waldpark B&B (8618310), and have eaten well at La Pasta. A reporter recommends the Hotel Post (8619200) and the Stammerspitze Café. There's a smart AlpenQuell spa-pool-fitness centre.

The Schmuggler Alm (see Mountain restaurants) is a popular après-ski spot.

## Kappl 1260m/4,135ft

A couple of reporters recommend visiting Kappl, a 15-minute bus-ride down the valley. It is included on the area pass and has its own 40km/25 miles of piste. The slopes – served by an access gondola from the road and fast quads above it – offer plenty of variety, with several tough reds, including the 8km/5 mile Lattenabfarht down a deserted valley from the top of the area. Most of the slopes are open, but there are some woodland runs for bad-weather days. The village offers a couple of dozen hotels and guest-houses. It is very family-oriented, with the new Sunny Mountain development offering lots of attractions.

## Galtür 1585m/5,200ft

Galtür hit the headlines when it was struck by a devastating avalanche in 1999, but the village centre has since been rebuilt and fortified and is now home to the Alpinarium, which opened for 2003/04, featuring an exhibition centre, climbing wall, internet and archive room, all built within the new avalanche-protection structures.

Galtür is a charming, peaceful, traditional village clustered around a pretty little church, amid impressive mountain scenery. Quieter, sunnier and cheaper than Ischgl, it is a good base for a quiet family holiday and mixed-ability groups. There are good 3-and 4-star hotels – the Almhof (8253), Flüchthorn (8202), 'quiet and friendly' Alpenrose (8201) and Ballunspitze (8214) have been recommended. There are a couple of jolly bars – Tommy's Garage is recommended – 'good music and reasonably priced'.

Galtür's own slopes, above a lift base at Wirl, outside the village, are not very challenging and can be bleak in poor weather, but its black runs are ideal for intermediates and there are fine nursery slopes plus good 'graduation' pistes for improvers. There is a small terrain-park at the top of the Soppalift drag but 'nobody seemed to use it'. The school has a high reputation and offers small classes. Children are well catered for – Kinderland has its own tow, carousel and magic carpet and the lifts have child-only lanes. Galtür has 60km/37 miles of cross-country loops, some quite testing.

Of the three mountain restaurants, the lively Wieberhimml oozes character and is recommended by a reporter this year. Or you could return to Wirl or the village.

Off-slope facilities are limited, but there's a natural ice rink and a sports centre with pool, tennis and squash. Night skiing and sledding are available every Wednesday evening on floodlit slopes and a popular local event is the Barrel Stave race – competitors strap wooden barrel pieces to their feet and race downhill.

While the bus service to Ischgl is reasonably frequent during the day, it finishes early in the evening (last bus leaves Ischgl at 7.30pm). Taxis are very good value (20 euros one way), especially for groups, and are easily arranged.

KITZBÜHEL TOURIST OFFICE

# Kitzbühel

*Wonderful old town and extensive slopes, but unreliable snow*

## COSTS

①②③④⑤⑥

## RATINGS

**The slopes**

| | |
|---|---|
| Snow | ** |
| Extent | *** |
| Expert | *** |
| Intermediate | **** |
| Beginner | ** |
| Convenience | ** |
| Queues | ** |
| Mountain restaurants | **** |

**The rest**

| | |
|---|---|
| Scenery | *** |
| Resort charm | **** |
| Off-slope | ***** |

## NEWS

The big news for 2004/05 is that a new 30-person jumbo-gondola is due to link Pengelstein to Wurzhöhe over the Saukaser valley, so eliminating the need to ski down to the valley on the 'ski safari' route to Pass Thurn and the need to catch a bus back. The first lift after the new gondola, heading to Pass Thurn, is being upgraded from a T-bar to a six-pack. These two lifts will make the journey to Pass Thurn much faster.

2003/04 saw a new eight-person gondola from Skirast towards Pengelstein, making the blue runs down to Skirast useable without having to catch a bus at the end. And a new high-speed quad opened on Gaisberg, along with night skiing and a toboggan run.

The Bichlalm area was made entirely off-piste, with the top drag replaced by a snowcat.



- + Large, attractive, varied slopes offering a sensation of travel
- + Beautiful medieval town centre
- + Vibrant nightlife
- + Plenty of off-slope amenities, both for the sporty and not-so-sporty
- + A surprisingly large amount of cheap and cheerful accommodation
- + Jolly mountain restaurants

- − Often poor snow, especially on lower slopes (though there's a decent amount of snowmaking, and getting to the best snow above Pass Thurn will be easier from 2004/05)
- − Surprisingly little challenging terrain – though plenty of off-piste
- − Disappointing nursery area
- − Some crowded pistes

**Kitzbühel's Hahnenkamm downhill course is the most spectacular on the World Cup circuit and there is a lot to like about the resort and the mountains around it. A new gondola planned for 2004/05 will at last form a proper link between the two main areas of slopes, Hahnenkamm-Pengelstein and Jochberg-Pass Thurn. The big drawback is the ski area's low altitude, which means the snow quality on the lower slopes is unreliable – on our 2004 visit we were blessed with superb powder right down to the village, but that was the first time on countless visits. Serious money has been invested in snowmaking but our advice is to wait until you know the conditions are good, and book at the last minute.**

**The resort has a beautiful, traffic-free, old centre complete with cobbled streets and lovely buildings, including expensive, elegant hotels. But this is no Gstaad: there is also a huge amount of inexpensive accommodation which attracts low-budget visitors, many of whom are young and like to party in its famous après-ski haunts.**

## THE RESORT

Set at a junction of broad, pretty valleys, Kitzbühel is a large, animated town, with separate areas of local slopes on each side. The beautiful walled medieval centre – with quaint church, cobbled streets and attractively painted buildings – is traffic-free and a compelling place to stay.

But the resort spreads widely, and busy roads surround the old town, reducing the charm factor somewhat. Visitors used to peaceful little Austrian villages are likely to be disappointed by its urban nature. But many visitors love the sophisticated, glitzy, towny ambience and swanky shops and cafes.

The bus service around town is 'seriously busy at peak times', says a 2004 visitor, who ended up walking instead. Having a car is useful for visiting lots of other resorts covered by the Kitzbüheler Alpenskipass.

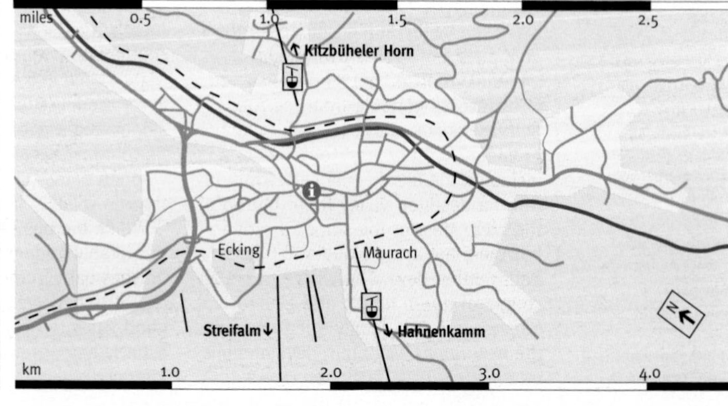

When there's this much fresh snow Kitzbühel is a fabulous intermediate playground ➔

KITZBUHEL TOURIST OFFICE / ALBIN NIEDERSTRASSER

## KEY FACTS

| | |
|---|---|
| **Resort** | 760m 2,490ft |
| **Slopes** | 800-2000m 2,620-6,560ft |
| **Lifts** | 53 |
| **Pistes** | 163km 101 miles |
| **Blue** | 37% |
| **Red** | 40% |
| **Black** | 23% |
| **Snowmaking** | 65km 40 miles |

## LIFT PASSES

**Kitzbühel**
Covers all lifts in Kitzbühel, Kirchberg, Jochberg, Pass Thurn, Bichlalm and Aschau, linking buses, and reduction for swimming pool.

**Main pass**
1 day €34
6 days €160

**Children**
Under 19: 6 days €128
Under 16: 6 days €88
Under 7: free pass

**Notes**
Single ascent tickets for the major lifts and area day passes. Graded prices for late-start day passes.

**Alternative passes**
Kitzbüheler Alpen-skipass covers five large ski areas – Kitzbühel, Schneewinkel (St Johann), Wilder Kaiser, Alpbach and Wildschönau. Salzburg Super Ski Card covers 15 ski areas in the Salzburg province.

The size of Kitz makes choice of location important. Many visitors prefer to be close to the Hahnenkamm gondola, south-west of the centre. Beginners should bear in mind that the Hahnenkamm nursery slopes are often lacking in snow, and then novices are taken up the Horn.

## THE MOUNTAINS

Kitzbühel's extensive slopes – shared with Kirchberg – offer a very attractive mixture of entirely open runs higher up and patchy forest lower down. Most face north-east or north-west.

### THE SLOPES
#### *Big but bitty*

The slopes are divided into five areas, the two biggest of which should at last be linked by a new 30-person gondola for the 2004/05 season.

The **Hahnenkamm-Pengelstein** sector is by far the largest. After the Hahnenkamm gondola from the edge of the town, followed by a tedious walk along a flat piste, you descend into the bowl of Ehrenbachgraben, where several chair-lifts fan out. One goes up to Ehrenbachhöhe, the arrival point of lifts from Kirchberg. Another takes you to the gentle peak of Steinbergkogel, the high point of the sector. Beyond is the slightly lower peak of Pengelstein, whence several long runs lead down to the west and the new gondola up from Skirast and shuttle-buses back from Aschau.

Pengelstein is also the start of the new gondola for 2004/05 over the valley to Wurzhöhe and the **Jochberg-Pass Thurn** sector. This will make the link much quicker than using the old routes down to the valley and bus-ride back. Pass Thurn is well worth the excursion, for better snow and fewer crowds, though the new gondola may mean more people make the journey. Runs are short, but a few fast chairs are starting to replace T-bars, making the area more appealing.

The **Kitzbüheler Horn** is accessed by a gondola starting close to the railway station, some way from the centre. The second stage leads to the sunny Trattalm bowl, but the alternative cable-car takes you up to the summit of the Horn, from where a fine, solitary piste leads down into the Raintal on the east side. There are blue, red and black runs back towards town.

The small and sunny **Bichlalm** area is now an entirely off-piste sector – no grooming, a few marked ski routes – accessed by an ancient single-person chair with a snowcat to take you almost 300m/980ft higher.

There's floodlit skiing on Thursday and Friday on **Gaisberg**, a small area of slopes at Kirchberg, on the other side of the road from the main ski area.

## boarding

*Kitzbühel was slow off the mark with boarding, keeping to its image of World Cup downhill venue/skier party town. However, things have changed, and now there is a boarder-cross course (as well as a half-pipe and terrain-park) on the Kitzbüheler Horn, an area with few drag-lifts. The Kasereck and Silberstuben runs on the Hahnenkamm are said to be a natural fun terrain-park. Many lifts in the main area are drags, but all major lifts are gondolas and chair-lifts – the area suits beginners and intermediates well.*

The piste map has been greatly improved by the addition of altitudes and mountain restaurants but reporters still complain of confusion and poor piste signage around Pengelstein.

**TERRAIN-PARKS**
***Take the Hornbahn***

There is a half-pipe, with a music system, a terrain-park and a boarder-cross course on the Kitzbüheler Horn.

**SNOW RELIABILITY**
***More snowmaking now***

Last season was exceptionally good for snow, but even then some reporters complained of worn patches, ice and slush on the lower slopes. In a normal year, the lower slopes can be very tricky or bare at times (though the snow at the top is often OK). The problem is that Kitzbühel's slopes have one of the lowest average heights in the Alps. To make matters worse, the Horn is also sunny. The expansion of snowmaking in recent years has improved matters when it's cold enough to make snow – major runs right down to Kitzbühel, Kirchberg, Klausen and Jochberg are covered. But many slopes still remain unprotected. If snow is poor, head for Pass Thurn.

**FOR EXPERTS**
***Plan to go off-piste***

Steep slopes – pistes and off-piste terrain – are mostly concentrated around the bowl of Ehrenbachgraben. The most direct of these are challenging mogul fields. Nearby is the Streif red, the basis for the famous Hahnenkamm Downhill race – see the feature panel. When conditions allow, there is plenty of gentler off-piste potential elsewhere – some of it safely close to pistes, some requiring a guide. We had a wonderful morning in fresh powder on the ski routes of the off-piste-only Bichlalm area in January 2004 and saw only eight other people plus a few ski tourers all morning. The ancient single-person chair and small (maximum 14 people) snowcat make it feel like you are in a time-warp and the views over the valley to the main ski area are stunning.

**FOR INTERMEDIATES**
***Lots of alternatives***

The Hahnenkamm area is prime intermediate terrain. Good intermediates will want to do the World Cup downhill run, of course (see feature panel). And the long blues of around 1000m/3,300ft vertical to

## SCHOOLS

**Rote Teufel (Red Devil)**
t 62500
info@rote-teufel.at

**Hahnenkamm Egger**
t 63177
office@schischule-hahnenkamm.at

**Kitzbüheler Horn**
t 64454
sebastianzwicknagl@utanet.at

**Total**
t 72011
hinterseer@skischule-total.at

**Reith**
t 65496
josef-dagn@schischule-reith.at

**Aurach**
t 65804
skinoichl@tirol.com

**Classes**
(Rote Teufel prices)
6 days (2hr am and pm) €135

**Private lessons**
€180 for 1 day

Klausen from Ehrenbachhöhe and to Skirast from Steinbergkogel or Pengelstein are also satisfying. The east-facing Raintal run on the Horn is excellent for good intermediates.

The runs above Jochberg are particularly good for mixed abilities and the short, high runs at the top of the Pass Thurn area are ideal if you are more timid. There are also easy reds down to both Pass Thurn and Jochberg. Much of the Horn is good cruising.

### FOR BEGINNERS
***Not ideal***

The Hahnenkamm nursery slopes are no more than adequate, and prone to poor snow conditions. The Horn has a high, sunny, nursery-like section, and precocious learners will soon be cruising home from there on the long Hagstein piste. There are some easy runs to progress to if the snow is OK. But there are many more conveniently arranged places to start.

### FOR CROSS-COUNTRY
***Plentiful but low***

There are nearly 40km/25 miles of trails scattered around, but all are at valley level and prone to lack of snow.

### QUEUES
***Still some problems***

Replacing the old Hahnenkamm cable-car with a speedy six-person gondola has vastly reduced morning queues. However, once up the mountain there are bottlenecks at slow old chairs and drags, including the key Steinbergkogel lift from Ehrenbachgraben, on the way to Pengelstein. The Maierl chairs out of Kirchberg can also be tiresome – a right turn to the gondola at Klausen is the alternative. But we have had reports of queue-free weeks and maximum queues of ten minutes at half-term. Both the Horn and the Hahnenkamm can have crowded pistes – it will be interesting to see if these and the quieter pistes of Pass Thurn become more evenly balanced once the new gondola link opens (send us reports please!).

### MOUNTAIN RESTAURANTS
***A highlight***

There are many restaurants, now thankfully marked on the piste map. 'One of the reasons we keep going back,' says one of our Kitz regulars. On the Horn, Hornköpflhütte's good food and sunny terraces still get praised despite a slight climb to reach it.

### THE HAHNENKAMM DOWNHILL

*Kitzbühel's Hahnenkamm Downhill race, held in mid-January each year, is the toughest as well as one of the most famous on the World Cup circuit. On the race weekend the town is packed and there is a real carnival atmosphere, with bands, people in traditional costumes and huge (and loud) cowbells everywhere.*

*The race itself starts with a steep icy section before you hit the famous Mausfalle and Steilhang, where even Franz Klammer used to get worried. The course (now thankfully served by snow-guns) starts near the top of the Hahnenkamm gondola and drops 860m/2,820ft to finish amid the noise and celebrations right on the edge of town. Ordinary mortals can now try most of the course after the race weekend, whenever the snow is good enough – it's an unpisted red ski route mostly. We found it steep and tricky in parts, even when going slowly – it must be terrifying at race speeds of 80mph or more. The course is normally closed from the start of the season until after the race.*

↑Kitzbühel's car-free medieval centre is one of the most pleasant in the Alps to stroll around

SNOWPIX.COM / CHRIS GILL



### GETTING THERE

**Air** Salzburg 80km/50 miles (1½hr); Munich 160km/99 miles (2hr); Innsbruck 95km/59 miles (1½hr).

**Rail** Mainline station in resort. Postbus every 15min from station.

### CHILDREN

There is no non-ski nursery, but babysitters and nannies can be hired

**Ski school**

Most schools cater for small children, offering lunchtime supervision as well as lessons – generally from the age of 3 or 4 (6 days approx €145)

Alpenhaus 'does excellent self-service meals for great prices' but can get crowded, the Gipfelhaus is quieter with 'super views and a sheltered terrace'. Gasthof Hagstein is an attractive farmhouse. At Jochberg-Pass Thurn the Jägerwurzhütte and Trattenbachalm are recommended, Hanglalm has 'the best Kaiserschmarrn' and Panoramaalm great views. In the Hahnenkamm sector we loved the rustic Seidlalm right by the lower part of the downhill course and had a jolly meal at Berghaus Tyrol below Ehrenbachhöhe. Melkalm 'is worth the effort of finding'. The Hochbrunn has 'very friendly' staff and 'good strudel'. The Kasereckhütte on the main run to Jochberg is 'brilliant'. The expensive table-service restaurant at the top of the gondola has good food, but service has been criticised.

### SCHOOLS AND GUIDES
***Mixed reviews***

We get conflicting reports on the original school, Rudi Sailer's 200-strong Red Devils, though this year a 15-year-old boarder reported good progress and had fun. The other five schools emphasise their small scale and personal nature. The Total school is the best established of these and includes video analysis. A reporter said: 'Never seen so many British instructors. Very good.' But a couple said, 'Our child's instructor was so cautious that they had virtually no fun.'

### FACILITIES FOR CHILDREN
***Not an ideal choice***

There is no non-ski nursery, but provided your children can take classes, you can deposit them at any of the schools. The Total school has supervision until 5pm.

## STAYING THERE

### HOW TO GO
***Mainly hotels and pensions***

Kitz is essentially a hotel resort.
**Chalets** A few tour operators run chalet-hotels here. A reporter this year praised the 'ski to door' convenience of First Choice's chalet Karlberger.
**Hotels** There is an enormous choice, especially of 4-star and 3-star hotels.
((((5 **Tennerhof** (63181) Luxurious former farmhouse, with renowned restaurant. Beautiful panelled rooms.
((((5 **Schloss Lebenberg** (6901) Modernised 'castle' with smart pool; inconvenient location but free shuttle-bus. Free nursery for kids aged 3-plus.
(((4 **Weisses Rössl** (625410) Smartly traditional exclusive 5-star aparthotel.
(((4 **Goldener Greif** (64311) Historic inn, elegantly renovated; vaulted lobby-sitting area, panelled bar, casino.
(((4 **Jägerwirt** (6981) Modern chalet with 'helpful staff and wonderful food'. Not ideally placed.
(((4 **Schwarzer Adler** (6911) Traditional hotel, near centre, highly praised by a reporter again this year: 'Great food and lovely leisure centre in basement.'
(((4 **Schweizerhof** (62735) Comfortable chalet right by Hahnenkamm gondola.
((3 **Hahnenhof** (62582) Small and traditional, with rustic charm.
((3 **Strasshofer** (62285) A favourite with a regular reporter – 'central, family-run, friendly, good food, good with children, quiet rooms at back'.
(2 **Mühlbergerhof** (62835) Small, friendly pension in good position.
**Self-catering** Many of the best (and best-positioned) are attached to hotels.

### EATING OUT
***Something for everyone***

There is a wide range of restaurants to suit all pockets, including pizzerias and fast-food outlets (even McDonald's). The Neuwirt in the Schwarzer Adler hotel is regarded as the best in town and wins awards in food guides. The Unterberger Stuben ('excellent but expensive,' says a reporter) and Schwedenkapelle are also highly rated. Good, cheaper places include the traditional Huberbräu-Stüberl, Chizzo, Eggerwirt and, a little out of town with great views, Hagstein which serves big pans of communal food for groups. Goldene Gams has a wide-ranging menu and both traditional and modern dining rooms. The Casino does a

## ACTIVITIES

**Indoor** Aquarena Centre (pools, slides, sauna, solarium, mud baths, aerated baths, underwater massage) – discounted entry with lift pass; indoor tennis hall, fitness centre, beauty centre, bridge, indoor riding school, bowling, museums, casino, cinema

**Outdoor** Ice rink (curling and skating), sleigh rides, toboggan run, ballooning, wildlife park, 40km/25 miles of cleared walking paths (free guided tours), copper mine tours

**Phone numbers**
**Kitzbühel**
From elsewhere in Austria add the prefix 05356.
From abroad use the prefix +43 5356.

**Kirchberg**
From elsewhere in Austria add the prefix 05357.
From abroad use the prefix +43 5357.

## TOURIST OFFICES

**Kitzbühel**
**t** 621550
info@kitzbuehel.com
www.kitzbuehel.com

**Kirchberg**
**t** 2309
info@kirchberg.at
www.kirchberg.at

combined dinner/entry package. On Fridays and Saturdays you can dine at the top of the Hahnenkamm gondola.

### APRES-SKI
***A main attraction***

Nightlife is a great selling point of Kitz. There's something for all tastes, from throbbing bars full of teenagers to quiet little places, nice cafes and smart spots for fur-coat flaunting.

Immediately after the slopes close, the town is jolly without being much livelier than many other Tirolean resorts. The new Streifalm bar at the foot of the slopes is popular, with 'white pine and slate, open fire, widescreen TV and europop music', as is the Sportbar Hölz. Cafes Praxmair, Kortschak, Langer and Rupprechter are among the most atmospheric tea-time places for cakes and pastries. Stamperl is a very lively bar. Later the American-style Highways bar and s'Lichtl (with thousands of lights hanging from the ceiling) get packed. Seppi's Pub is recommended for sport on TV, pizzas and the eccentric owner. Olympia and Take 5 are the main discos. The Londoner Pub is a famous drinking place, well summarised by a report last year: 'Very crowded, very noisy and great fun, but the bar staff were mostly rude and arrogant.' The Casino is 'worth a visit', says a 2004 reporter, 'compact, casual, staff keen to explain how to lose/save money, expensive drinks from a space-age bar but tourists can get special deals with a free glass of bubbly and gaming chips'.

### OFF THE SLOPES
***Plenty to do***

The lift pass gives a 50% reduction for the pools in the impressive Aquarena leisure centre. There's a museum and concerts are organised. The railway makes excursions easy (eg to Salzburg and Innsbruck).

## Kirchberg 850m/2,790ft

### THE RESORT

Kirchberg is a large, spread out, lively village. There are three ways into the slopes, all a bus-ride from the village.

### THE MOUNTAIN

**Slopes** The Maierl chair-lifts and the gondola from Klausen take you to Ehrenbachhöhe, at the heart of the Kitzbühel slopes. The gondola from Skirast meets chairs to Pengelstein and the new gondola towards Pass Thurn. The separate small Gaisberg ski area is on the other side of the valley.
**Snow reliability** Kirchberg suffers from the same unreliable snow as Kitzbühel.
**Experts** Few challenging slopes.
**Intermediates** The main slopes back are easy cruises when snow is good.
**Beginners** There's a beginner lift and area at the foot of the Gaisberg slopes.
**Snowboarding** Kitzbühel has the edge, with the terrain-park on the Horn.
**Cross-country** There are plenty of trails – but they can suffer from lack of snow.
**Queues** There are some bottlenecks.
**Mountain restaurants** There are some good local huts.
**Schools and guides** We lack recent reports on the three schools.
**Facilities for children** There are non-ski and ski kindergartens.

### STAYING THERE

**How to go** There's a wide choice of chalet-style hotels and pensions.
**Hotels** The 4-star Klausen (2128), close to the main gondola, and the Sporthotel Tyrol (2787), a bit out of the centre, have been recommended.
**Self-catering** There is some available.
**Eating out** Mostly in hotels, but there's a pizzeria and a steak house too.
**Après-ski** There's a toboggan run on Gaisberg. Nightlife is very lively.
**Off the slopes** Some hotels have swimming pools, saunas and so on.

LECH TOURIST OFFICE

# Lech

*Captivating blend of reliable snow, extensive slopes and village charm*



## COSTS

(1)(2)(3)(4)(5)(6)

## RATINGS

**The slopes**

| | |
|---|---|
| Snow | **** |
| Extent | **** |
| Expert | **** |
| Intermediate | **** |
| Beginner | **** |
| Convenience | *** |
| Queues | **** |
| Mountain restaurants | ** |

**The rest**

| | |
|---|---|
| Scenery | *** |
| Resort charm | **** |
| Off-slope | *** |

## NEWS

For 2003/04 three more high-speed chairs with covers were installed: an eight-seater replacing the Steinmähder chair towards Zuger Hochlicht, a six-pack replacing the Hasensprung chair which feeds the Steinmähder and a six-pack instead of the Trittalp chair connecting Lech and Zürs. A new T-bar, Schafalplift, at Rüfikopf gives easier access to two good ski routes, and there is new snowmaking on the Zürs nursery slopes. A new mountain restaurant, the Rud-Alpe, opened and the Kriegeralpe started opening in winter. An indoor ice rink was built.

- + Picturesque Alpine village
- + Sunny and usually uncrowded slopes with excellent snow record and extensive snowmaking
- + Fair-sized, largely intermediate piste network with some recently updated lifts, plus good, extensive off-piste
- + Easy access to the tougher slopes of St Anton and other Arlberg resorts
- + Lively après-ski scene
- + Some very smart hotels

- − Surprising shortage of compelling village shops for window-shopping
- − Local traffic intrudes on main street of Lech (and spoils Zürs entirely)
- − Very few tough pistes, so the adventurous must go off-piste and on ski routes
- − Blue runs back to the village are rather steep for nervous novices
- − Generally expensive
- − Still a few slow, old lifts

**Lech and its higher, linked neighbour Zürs are the most fashionable resorts in Austria, each able to point to a string of rich and vaguely royal visitors. But, like all such 'exclusive' resorts, they aren't actually exclusive in any real sense. A holiday here is unlikely to be cheap, but it doesn't have to cost any more than in countless other international resorts in the Alps. We don't feel out of place here, and neither would you. We often see Lech described as 'a very chic resort' – but it has none of the flash shops of St Moritz or Cortina, for example.**

**The real point about these resorts is that their combination of impressive snowfall, traditional Alpine atmosphere (in Lech, if not in Zürs) and excellent hotels offering a truly personal service from their family owners is a rare and attractive thing. One of the few other Austrian resorts to offer it is St Anton, over the hill, covered by the same lift pass, and easily visited by bus.**

## THE RESORT

Lech is an old farming village set in a high valley that spent long periods of winter cut off from the outside world until the Flexen Pass road through Zürs was constructed at the end of the 19th century. (Even now, the road can be closed for days on end after an exceptional snowfall; a road tunnel is planned, but is not imminent.)

The village is attractive, with its upmarket hotels built in traditional chalet style, its gurgling river plus bridges, its adequately impressive scenery and the high incidence of snow on the streets. But its appeal is dimmed slightly by traffic on the main street that forms its spine: although the pavements have been widened and parking is controlled, it can still get very busy, especially at weekends.

The clientele is largely up-market Germans and Austrians, with very few Brits. The fur coat count is one of the highest in the Alps.

The heart of the village is a short stretch of the main street beside the river; most of the main hotels are clustered here. Right on this street is the base station of the Rüfikopf cable-car, departure point for exploration of the Zürs slopes. A short walk away, across the river, are the Schlegelkopf chair-lifts, leading up into Lech's main area of slopes. Chalets, apartments and pensions are dotted around the valley, and the village spreads along the main street for 2km/1.5 miles. Some of the cheaper accommodation is quite a walk from the lifts.

Not far from the centre is the cable-car up to Oberlech – a small, traffic-free collection of 4-star hotels and chalets set on the mountainside above

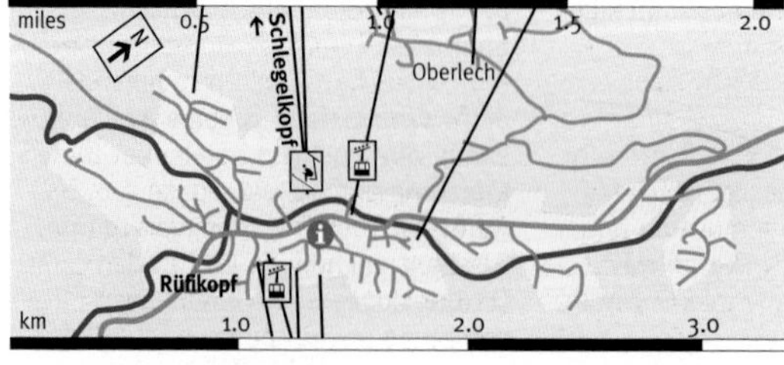

The area gets a lot of snow and off-piste is the main attraction for experts, especially when you can cruise down into tiny Zug in virgin powder like this →

LECH TOURIST OFFICE

**KEY FACTS**

| | |
|---|---|
| **Resort** | 1450m<br>4,760ft |
| For Arlberg region | |
| **Slopes** | 1305-2650m<br>4,280-8,690ft |
| **Lifts** | 82 |
| **Pistes** | 260km<br>162 miles |
| **Blue** | 35% |
| **Red** | 43% |
| **Black** | 22% |
| **Snowmaking** | 65km<br>40 miles |
| For Lech-Zürs only | |
| **Slopes** | 1450-2450m<br>4,760-8,040ft |
| **Lifts** | 32 |
| **Pistes** | 110km<br>68 miles |



Lech; the cable-car works until 1am, allowing access to Lech's much livelier nightlife and shopping. If you miss that, you can still get the night bus or a taxi to drop you within walking distance. If you stay there, luggage is delivered to your hotel from the cable-car via underground tunnels, leaving you unburdened for the short, snowy walk.

Zug is a hamlet, 3km/2 miles from Lech, with a lift into the Lech-Oberlech area. The limited accommodation here is mostly bed and breakfast with one 4-star hotel. From Lech, Zug makes a good night out: you can take a horse-drawn sleigh for a fondue at the Rote Wand, Klösterle or Auerhahn, followed by a visit to the Rote Wand disco.

As well as Lech and Zürs, the Arlberg lift pass covers St Anton, St Christoph and Stuben, all reachable by car, by free but busy ski-bus, or by less crowded, but not free, post-bus. The little-used Sonnenkopf area at Klösterle, linked by free ski-bus from Stuben, is also covered.

## THE MOUNTAINS

Most of the slopes are treeless, the main exception being the lower runs below Oberlech.

The toughest runs here are classed as unpatrolled 'ski routes' (as at St Anton – read that chapter for more on this), or 'high-alpine touring runs', which are not protected against avalanche and should be skied only with a guide. We don't have much of a problem with the latter category – in other resorts, these off-piste runs would simply not appear on the piste map at all. But the ski route concept is bad news, reducing the resort's responsibility for runs that are a key part of the area, and that should be patrolled pistes. The only ways down to Zug, for example, are ski routes; the only way to complete the Lech-Zürs-Lech circuit (the Madloch-Lech run) is a ski route; and of the eight identified runs from the Kriegerhorn, six are ski routes. We understand that, in practice, these routes are often closed if avalanche conditions are dangerous and most people ski them (often into a piste-like state) without a guide or instructor.

The piste map attempts to cover the whole of the Arlberg region in one view, and as a result is unclear in places – particularly around Oberlech.

### THE SLOPES
***One-way traffic***

The main slopes centre on **Oberlech**, 250m/820ft above Lech (just below the tree line), and can be reached from the village by chair-lifts as well as the cable-car. The wide, open pistes above Oberlech are perfect for intermediates and there is also lots of off-piste. Zuger Hochlicht, the high point of this sector, gives stunning views.

The **Rüfikopf** cable-car takes Lech residents to the west-facing slopes of Zürs. This mountainside, with its high point at **Trittkopf**, is a mix of quite challenging intermediate slopes and flat/uphill bits. On the other side of Zürs the east-facing mountainside is of a more uniform gradient. Chairs go up to **Seekopf** with intermediate runs back down. There's a chair up to **Muggengrat** (the highest point of the Zürs area) from below Zürsersee. This has a good blue run back under it and accesses a lovely long red with lots of nearby off-piste options away from all

**LIFT PASSES**

**Arlberg Ski pass**
Covers all St Anton, St Christoph, Lech, Zürs and Stuben lifts, and linking bus between Rauz and Zürs.

**Main pass**
1 day €38.50
6 days €179

**Senior citizens**
Over 65 (60 for women): 6 days €155

**Children**
Under 16: 6 days €107
Under 20: 6 days €155

**Notes**
Single ascent, half-day and afternoon 'taster' tickets available. Pass also covers Sonnenkopf (10 lifts) at Klösterle, 7km/4 miles west of Stuben (free bus link from Stuben).





the lifts back down to Zürs. The long, scenic ski route back to Lech is accessed via the Madloch chair – which is slow and vulnerable to closure by wind. You can peel off part-way down and head for Zug and the slow chair-lift up to the Kriegerhorn above Oberlech, or continue to Lech – it comes out at the opposite end of town to the Oberlech cable-car, a walk from the centre. There are no lifts back towards Lech from Zürs, so the circuit is clockwise only. Those wanting to avoid the ski route can always get the bus from Zürs to Lech.

### TERRAIN-PARKS
***In Lech only***
There's a good terrain-park above Lech at the Schlegelkopf, with jumps, a boarder-cross and a half-pipe. It was extended and reshaped for last season.

### SNOW RELIABILITY
***One of Austria's best***
Lech and Zürs both get a lot of snow, but Austrian weather station records show a big difference between them despite their proximity. Lech gets an average of almost 8m/26ft of snow between December and March, almost twice as much as St Anton and three times as much as Kitzbühel; but Zürs gets 50% more than Lech. The altitude is high by Austrian resort standards and there is excellent snowmaking on Lech's sunny lower slopes.

This combination, together with excellent grooming, means that the Lech-Zürs area normally has good coverage from early December until late April. And the snow is frequently better here than on St Anton's predominantly south-facing slopes.

### FOR EXPERTS
***Off-piste is main attraction***
There is only one black piste on the map, and there is no denying that for the competent skier who prefers to stick to patrolled runs the area is very limited. There are the two types of off-piste route referred to above. The piste map recommends that ski routes, of which there are lots, should be used only 'by skiers with alpine experience or accompanied by a ski instructor' – the vast majority of people don't bother with an instructor. But experts will get a lot more out of the area if they do have a guide, as there is plenty of excellent off-piste other than

## boarding

*Lech's upper-crust image has not stood in the way of its snowboarding development, and it continues to improve its facilities. Chairs and cable-cars, with hardly any drags, and perfectly manicured pistes make the area ideal for beginner and intermediate boarders although the west facing slopes at Zürs have many flat/uphill sections. Lessons are with the local ski school. More confident boarders should hire a guide and track some powder.*

the marked ski routes, much of it accessed by long traverses. Especially in fresh snow, it can be wonderful.

Many of the best runs start from the top of the Steinmähder chair (a new fast eight-seater from 2003/04), which finishes just below Zuger Hochlicht. Some routes involve a short climb to access bowls of untracked powder. From the Kriegerhorn there are shorter off-piste runs down towards Lech and a very scenic long ski route down to Zug (followed by a slow chair and a rope tow to pull you along a flat area to the pistes). Most runs, however, are south- or west-facing and can suffer from sun.

At the end of the season, when the snow is deep and settled, the off-piste off the shoulder of the Wöstertäli from the top of the Rüfikopf cable-car down to Lech can be superb. There are also good runs from the top of the Trittkopf cable-car in the Zürs sector, including a tricky one down to Stuben.

Experts will also enjoy cruising some of the steeper red runs and will want to visit St Anton during the week, where there are more challenging pistes as well as more off-piste.

Heli-lifts are available to a couple of remote spots, at least on weekdays.



### FOR INTERMEDIATES
***Flattering variety for all***

The pistes in the Oberlech area are nearly all immaculately groomed blue runs, the upper ones above the trees, the lower ones in wide swathes cut through them. It is ideal territory for leisurely cruisers not wanting surprises. And even early intermediates will be able to take on the circuit to Zürs and back, the only significant red involved being the beautiful long ski route back to Lech from the top of the Madloch chair in Zürs. It shouldn't be difficult but, since as a ski route it is groomed only occasionally, several readers have found it unpleasantly mogulled. 'They should make it a proper pisted run,' complained one. We couldn't agree more.

It's worth noting that the final blue-run descents to Lech (as opposed to Oberlech) are uncomfortably steep for nervous novices.

More adventurous intermediates should take the fast Steinmähder chair to just below Zuger Hochlicht and from there take the scenic red run all the way to Zug (the latter part on a ski route rather than a piste). And if you feel ready to have a stab at some off-piste, Lech is a good place to try it.

Zürs has many more interesting red runs, on both sides of the village. We particularly like the west-facing reds from Trittkopf and the usually quiet east-facing Muggengrat Täli, which starts in a steep bowl – you can take the plunge, or skirt it on a catwalk.

## SCHOOLS

**Lech**
t 2355
skischule-lech@aon.at

**Oberlech**
t 2007
skischule-oberlech@aon.at

**Zürs**
t 2611
ernst.haas@skischule-zuers.at

**Classes**
(Lech prices)
6 days (2hr am and 2hr pm) €160

**Private lessons**
€195 for 1 day; each additional person €16

## CHILDREN

NB All mini-clubs run 9am to 4.30, Sun to Fri

**Miniclub Lech**
t 21610
Ages from 3 – must be potty trained

**Little Zürs**
t 245252
Ages from 3

**Kinderland Oberlech**
t 2007
Ages from 2½

**Babysitting list**
held by tourist office

**Ski school**
From 4½ to 14:
6 days €148

### FOR BEGINNERS
***Easy slopes in all areas***

The main nursery slopes are in Oberlech, but there is also a nice isolated area in the village dedicated purely to beginners. There are good, easy runs to progress to, both above and below Oberlech.

### FOR CROSS-COUNTRY
***Picturesque valley trail***

A 25km/16 miles trail starts from the centre of Lech and leads through the beautiful Zug valley, following the Lech river to Zug and back. In Zürs there is a 4km/2.5 mile mile track to the Flexen Pass and back.

### QUEUES
***A few complaints***

The resort proudly boasts that it limits numbers on the slopes to 14,000 for a more enjoyable experience. Most reporters also stress how much quieter Lech's slopes are than St Anton's. There have been significant lift improvements in the last few years, but there are still one or two bottlenecks – the Schlegelkopf fast quad out of Lech gets very busy first thing and the crucial Madloch double chair at the top of the Zürs area generates peak-time queues on the Lech-Zürs-Lech circuit. Some readers mention the Rüfikopf cable-car to Zürs as generating queues.

### MOUNTAIN RESTAURANTS
***On the up***

The Rud-Alpe on the lower slopes above Lech is a rustic place, newly built using the timbers of an old hut. 'Excellent decor, food and service,' says one reporter. The Kriegeralpe, higher up, has been extended so it can open in winter as well as in summer. Rustic and charming, it was too busy to sit down in when we called by. One reader commented that it has a 'limited menu, but is good for drinks'.

At Oberlech, there are several big sunny terraces set prettily around the piste. Quite often you'll find a live band playing outside one. The Ilga Stube is reported to have 'good food, rustic atmosphere, friendly staff and reasonable prices'. The Alter Goldener Berg is a lovely old building, 'We had an excellent lunch on the terrace, enhanced by a jazz band,' says a reporter. The Mohnenfluh, at the top of the nursery lift, does 'excellent' food.

The self-service Seekopf restaurant does decent food and has a good sun terrace – but you may have to queue to even get into the food serving area. Also popular is the cosy Palmenalpe above Zug, but it too gets crowded. The Schröfli Alm, just above the base of the Seekopf lift, is a pleasant chalet.

### SCHOOLS AND GUIDES
***Excellent in parts***

The ski schools of Lech, Oberlech and Zürs all have good reputations and the instructors speak good English. Group lessons are divided into no fewer than 10 ability levels. One past visitor enjoyed 'the best lessons I have ever had'. In peak periods, however, you should book both instructors and guides well in advance, as many are booked regularly every year by an exclusive clientele.

### FACILITIES FOR CHILDREN
***Oberlech's fine, but expensive***

Oberlech makes an excellent choice for families who can afford it, particularly as it's so convenient for the slopes. The Sonnenburg and the Goldener Berg have in-house kindergartens. Children of visitors staying in Oberlech have free access to the kindergarten there, Kinderland. Reporters tell us the Oberlech school is great for children, with small classes, good English spoken and lunch offered.

Snowy Lech, set among pretty scenery, is the end of the road in winter ↑

LECH TOURIST OFFICE

## GETTING THERE

**Air** Zürich 200km/124 miles (1½hr); Innsbruck 110km/68 miles (1½hr). Friedrichshafen 120km/75 miles (1½hr).

**Rail** Langen (15km/9 miles); 9 buses daily from station, buses connect with international trains.

## ACTIVITIES

**Indoor** Tennis, hotel swimming pools and saunas, squash, museum, ice rink

**Outdoor** Cleared walking paths, toboggan run (from Oberlech), snow-shoeing, horse-drawn sleigh rides

**Phone numbers**
**Lech and Zürs**
From elsewhere in Austria add the prefix 05583.
From abroad use the prefix +43 5583.

**Stuben**
From elsewhere in Austria add the prefix 05582.
From abroad use the prefix +43 5582.

## STAYING THERE

### HOW TO GO
***Surprising variety***

There is quite a variety of accommodation from luxury hotels through to simple but spotless B&Bs.

**Hotels** There are three 5-star hotels, over 30 4-star and countless more modest places.

(((((5) **Arlberg** (2134-0) Patronised by royalty and celebrities (Princess Diana used to stay here). Elegantly rustic chalet, centrally placed. Pool.

(((((5) **Post** (2206-0) Lovely old Relais & Chateaux place on main street with pool, sauna. 'Absolutely first class,' says a 2004 reporter.

((((4) **Krone** (2551) One of the oldest buildings, in a prime spot by the river.

((((4) **Tannbergerhof** (2202-0) Splendidly atmospheric inn on main street, with outdoor bar and popular disco (tea time as well as later). Pool.

((((4) **Haldenhof** (2444-0) Friendly and well run, with antiques and a fine collection of prints and paintings.

((((4) **Burg Vital** (Oberlech) (2291-930) 'Excellent – no criticism,' said a reporter of this plush luxury hotel with pool, sauna and squash.

((((4) **Burg** (Oberlech) (2291-0) Sister hotel of Burg Vital – same facilities and with famous outdoor umbrella bar.

((((4) **Sonnenburg** (Oberlech) (2147) Luxury on-piste chalet (popular for lunch). Good children's facilities. Pool.

((((4) **Monzabon** (2104) 'Characterful, with friendly staff,' says a reporter. Pool and, new last season, an indoor ice rink.

(((3) **Pension Angerhof** (2418) Beautiful ancient pension, with wood panels and quaint little windows.

(((3) **Pension Fernsicht** (2432) Pension with spa facilities.

**Self-catering** There is lots available to independent bookers.

**Chalets** There are a couple run by British tour operators, including Total's chalet-hotel with pool and sauna.

### EATING OUT
***Mainly hotel-based***

There are over 50 restaurants in Lech, nearly all of them in hotels. Reporter recommendations include the Krone, Ambrosius (above a shopping arcade), and the Post, which serves Austrian nouvelle-type food. The Madlochblick has a typically Austrian restaurant, very cosy with good solid food. Hûs Nr 8 is one of the best non-hotel restaurants and does good fondue, but you need to book (one 2004 reporter could not get in even four days ahead in late January). Schneggarei does good pizza. Bistro Casarole is a small casual place with a short menu of excellent grills. The Fux does 'excellent modern/Asian food, utterly un-Austrian'. In Oberlech hotel Montana was highly recommended by a 2003 reporter and there is a good fondue at the Alter Goldener Berg, a tavern built in 1432. In Zug the Rote Wand is excellent for fondues, kaiserschmarren (a delicious chopped pancake and fruit dessert) and a good night out. A reporter recommends Gasthaus Älpele near Zug – 3km/2 miles from the road, up the valley on the cross-country route – for its atmosphere and good food. Transport is provided in covered wagons attached to a snowcat.

### APRES-SKI
***Good but expensive***

At Oberlech, the umbrella bar of the Burg hotel is popular immediately after the slopes close, as is the champagne bar in Hotel Montana. Down in Lech the outdoor bars of hotels Krone (in a lovely setting by the river) and Tannbergerhof (where there's an afternoon disco inside) are popular. Later on, discos in the hotels Kristberg, Arlberg, Almhof-Schneider and Krone liven up too. The latter's Side Step specialises in 60s and 70s music. S'Pfefferkörndl is a good place for a drink, and you can get a steak or pizza there until late. Schneggarei's music (rap to funky house) makes a change from Austrian drinking songs, early and late. The smart, modern Fux bar and restaurant has live music, pop art in the toilets and a huge wine list. Archiv, in the Ambrosius shopping centre is good for cocktails and attracts a younger crowd until 2am. The Rote Wand in Zug has a disco.

After 7.30pm the free resort bus becomes a pay-for bus called James, which runs until 4am.

**OFF THE SLOPES**

***At ease***

Many visitors to Lech don't indulge in sports and the main street often presents a parade of fur-clad strollers. The range of shopping is surprisingly limited, with Strolz's plush emporium (including a champagne bar) right in the centre the main attraction.

It's easy for pedestrians to get to Oberlech or Zug to meet friends for lunch. The village outdoor bars make ideal posing positions. There are various sporting activities and 29km/18 miles of walking paths – the one along the river to Zug is especially beautiful, and recommended by several readers.

There is a floodlit sledging run from Oberlech to town: 'Loved by kids and not to be missed,' says a reporter.

## Zürs 1720m/5,640ft

Ten minutes' drive towards St Anton from Lech, Zürs is almost on the Flexen Pass, with good snow virtually guaranteed. Austria's first recognisable ski lift was built here in 1937.

The village is even more upmarket than Lech, with no hotels of less than 3-star standing, and a dozen 4-star and 5-star hotels around which life revolves. We stayed at the 5-star Zürserhof (25130) for a couple of nights and found it excellent – great service, food and spa facilities. But apart from the excellent hotels, we find Zürs a difficult place to like. It has nothing resembling a centre, few shops and the traffic doesn't so much intrude as ruin the place. Mathie's-Stüble has been recommended for lunch and strudel. Nightlife is quiet. Vernissage, at the Skiclub Alpenrose (22710), is reported to be the best nightspot in town. There's a disco in the Edelweiss hotel (26620) and a piano bar in the Alpenhof (21910). Kaminstüble and Mathie's-Stüble are worth trying. Serious dining means the Zürserhof and the Lorünser (22540). All phone numbers given are for 4- or 5-star hotels.

Many of the local Zürs instructors are booked for the entire season by regular clients, and more than 80% of them are booked privately.

## Stuben 1405m/4,610ft

Stuben is linked by lifts and pistes to St Anton, but is on the Vorarlberg side of the Arlberg pass (St Anton is in the Tirol). There are infrequent but timetabled buses between the village and Lech and Zürs, and more frequent ones from Rauz, reachable on skis.

Dating back to the 13th century, Stuben is a small, unspoiled village, where the only concessions to the new era are a few unobtrusive hotels, a school, two or three bars, a couple of banks and a few little shops. The old church and traditional buildings, usually snow-covered, make Stuben a really charming Alpine village.

The Albona mountain above Stuben has north-facing slopes that hold powder well and some wonderful, deserted off-piste descents including beautifully long runs down to Langen and to St Anton. These are, however, 'high-alpine touring runs' and should be taken seriously. A regular reporter recommends small Rasthaus Ferwall for lunch (ask your guide to book) at the end of a 'very easy off-piste run'. The slow village chair can be a cold ride. A quicker and warmer way to get to St Anton in the morning, if you have a car, is to drive up the road to Rauz. Stuben has sunny nursery slopes separate from the main slopes, but lack of progression runs make it unsuitable for beginners.

Evenings are quiet, but several places have a pleasant atmosphere. The charming old Post (7610) is a very comfortable 4-star with a fine restaurant.

**TOURIST OFFICES**

**Lech**
t 21610
info@lech-zuers.at
www.lech-zuers.at

**Zürs**
t 2245
zuersinfo@lech-zuers.at
www.lech-zuers.at

**Stuben**
t 3990
info@stuben.at
www.stuben.com

STUBEN TOURIST OFFICE

That's it folks – not much to Stuben; but it's a charming, quiet place to stay ↓

TVB MAYRHOFEN / A DÄHLING

# Mayrhofen

*Traditional British favourite with recently expanded area of slopes*



## COSTS

(1)(2)(3)(4)(5)(6)

## RATINGS

**The slopes**

| | |
|---|---|
| Snow | *** |
| Extent | *** |
| Experts | * |
| Intermediates | *** |
| Beginners | ** |
| Convenience | * |
| Queues | * |
| Mountain restaurants | **** |

**The rest**

| | |
|---|---|
| Scenery | *** |
| Resort charm | *** |
| Off-slope | **** |

## NEWS

For 2004/05 a fast six-pack is due to replace the Gerent T-bar in the Horberg sector. A shuttle-bus link between the bottom and just below the top of the Horberg gondola is planned to ease the queues (down as much as up).

For 2003/04 the Tappenalm double chair in the Horberg sector became a fast eight-seater, the Knorren double chair from the centre of the ski area to the Penken ridge above Finkenberg a six-pack, and the Finkenberg 2 double chair from the top of the Finkenberg gondola to the Penken ridge was replaced by an eight-seater gondola. Austria's steepest piste with a gradient of up to 78% opened beneath the new Knorren chair.

- + The local terrain expanded by 40% three seasons ago and the area is now well served by high-speed lifts
- + Snow-sure by Tirol standards, and you have the snow guarantee of the Hintertux glacier nearby
- + Various nearby areas on the same lift pass, and reached by free bus
- + Lively après-ski – though it's easily avoided if you prefer peace
- + Excellent children's amenities
- + Wide range of off-slope facilities

- − No runs back to the village from Penken – the main area of slopes
- − Smaller Ahorn area – the best bet for novices – is completely separate
- − Often long queues for gondola out of town – which is inconveniently sited for many visitors
- − Slopes can be crowded
- − Many short runs, though newly linked slopes are longer
- − Few steep pistes, but the run back from the new slopes is one of them

**Mayrhofen has long been a British favourite. Many visitors like it for its lively nightlife, but it's also an excellent family resort, with highly regarded ski schools and kindergartens and a fun pool with special children's area. The liveliest of the nightlife is confined to a few places, easily avoided by families. And there are quieter alternative bases, including Finkenberg (covered in this chapter) and Lanersbach (covered in the Hintertux chapter).**

**Mayrhofen's main Penken-Horberg slopes are entirely above the tree line, with no pistes down to valley level. The upside is better-than-average snow, for the Tirol; the downside, shorter-than-average runs (typically around 350m/1,150ft vertical). The recently built link with Lanersbach opens up some welcome longer runs, as well as adding around 40% to the accessible slopes, but the run back is one of the area's most challenging.**

## THE RESORT

Mayrhofen is a fairly large resort sitting in the flat-bottomed Zillertal. Most shops, bars and restaurants are on the one main, long, largely pedestrianised street, with hotels and pensions spread over a wider area. As the village has grown, architecture has been kept traditional.

Despite its reputation for lively après-ski, Mayrhofen is not dominated by lager louts. They exist, but tend to gather in a few easily avoided bars. The central hotels are mainly slightly upmarket, and overall the resort feels pleasantly civilised (though we have had a few complaints about traffic).

The main lift to Penken is set towards one end of the main street, while the cable-car to the much smaller and increasingly neglected Ahorn sector is out in the suburbs, about 1km/0.5 miles from the centre. The free bus service can be crowded and it finishes early (5pm), so location is important. The original centre, around

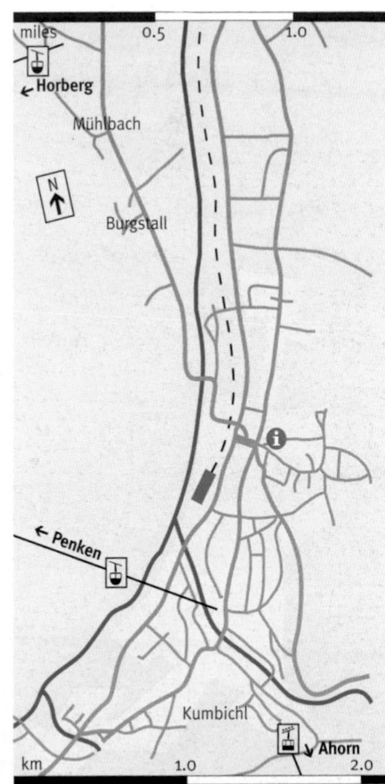

## KEY FACTS

| | |
|---|---|
| **Resort** | 630m 2,070ft |
| For Ski and Glacier World Zillertal 3000 | |
| **Slopes** | 630-3250m 2,070-10,660ft |
| **Lifts** | 67 |
| **Pistes** | 233km 145 miles |
| **Blue** | 27% |
| **Red** | 58% |
| **Black** | 15% |
| **Snowmaking** | 86km 53 miles |
| For Mayrhofen-Lanersbach only (ie excluding Hintertux glacier) | |
| **Slopes** | 630-2500m 2,070-8,200ft |
| **Lifts** | 45 |
| **Pistes** | 147km 91 miles |
| For Ziller valley | |
| **Slopes** | 630-3250m 2,070-10,660ft |
| **Lifts** | 175 |
| **Pistes** | 589km 366 miles |





the market, tourist office and bus/railway stations, is now on the edge of things. The most convenient area is on the main street, close to the Penken gondola station.

Free buses mean you can have an enjoyably varied week visiting different areas on the Ziller valley lift pass, including the extensive Arena slopes linking Zell to Königsleiten and the excellent glacier up at Hintertux. But if you plan to split your time between the Lanersbach-Mayrhofen slopes and the glacier, consider staying in Lanersbach (see Hintertux chapter).

The buses get packed at peak times, so it's worth planning your outings carefully ('Get the 8am bus and you'll be in Hintertux just as the lifts open,' recommends a reporter).

## THE MOUNTAINS

Practically all Mayrhofen's slopes are above the tree line, and of moderate difficulty. When you buy a lift pass, make sure it covers the Hintertux glacier, unless you are absolutely confident that you won't want to try it.

### THE SLOPES
***Rather inconvenient***

Lifts to the two main sectors are a longish walk or a bus-ride apart.

The larger area is **Penken-Horberg,** accessed by the main jumbo gondola from one end of town. It is also accessible via gondolas at Hippach and Finkenberg, both a bus-ride away. You cannot get back to Mayrhofen on snow – you either catch the main gondola down or, if cover is good, you can descend to either Finkenberg or Hippach on unpisted ski-routes. But the buses back from Finkenberg run only at hourly intervals.

A jumbo cable-car now links the Penken area with the **Rastkogel** slopes above Vorderlanersbach, which is in turn linked to **Eggalm** above Lanersbach – see the Hintertux chapter. These new links are a great step forward, but getting to Eggalm depends on good snow on a low, sunny run, and getting back from Rastkogel means braving a very tricky red run or walking up a steep slope to ride the cable-car down – see panel in margin opposite.

The smaller, gentler **Ahorn** area seems to be going into decline. A reader who learned to ski there returned a couple of seasons ago to find the place deserted at 4pm. We hear there are tentative plans to revive it by building a new access gondola and extending the railway line to the bottom of it.

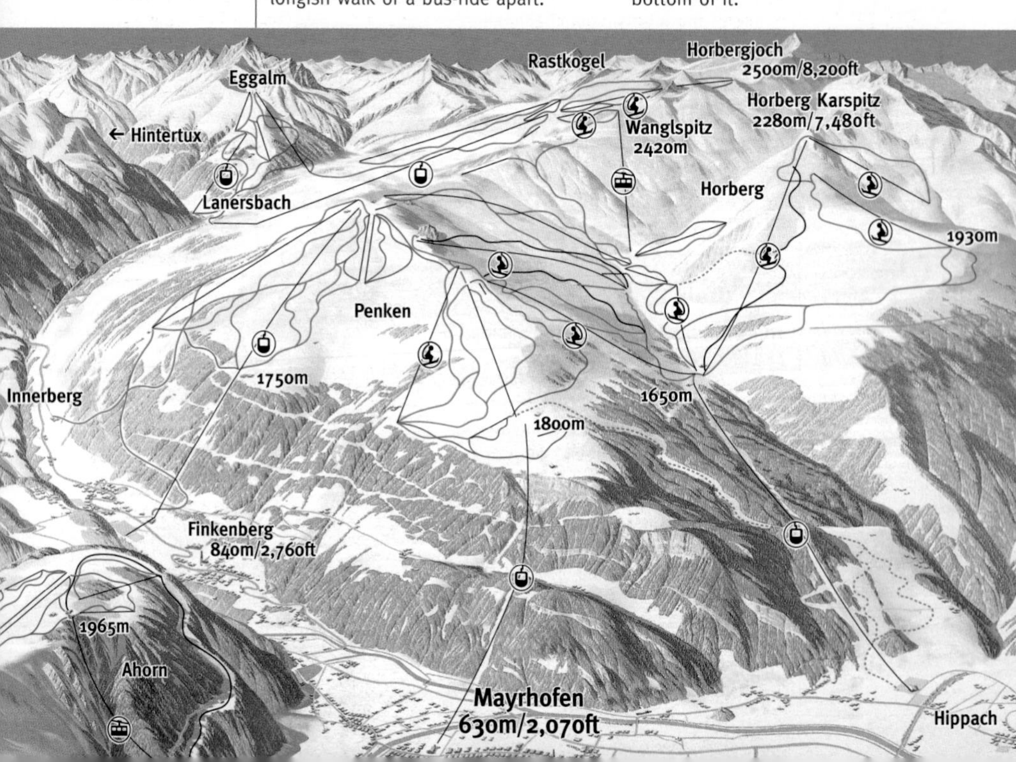

## LIFT PASSES

**Ski and Glacier World Zillertal**
1-, 2- or 3-day passes cover Penken, Eggalm, Rastkogel and Hintertux glacier areas; 4-day and over passes include all Ziller valley lifts, ski-bus and railway.

**Main pass**
1 day €34.50
6 days €163

**Children**
Under 19: 6-days €130
Under 15: 6-days €98
Under 6: free pass

**Notes**
Part-day passes available.

**Alternative passes**
Zillertaler ski pass also available without Hintertux glacier.

## LANERSBACH LINK

Most reporters say that the red piste back from Rastkogel is too difficult for timid intermediates. We agree; when we did it at the end of the day in good snow conditions, it was a long, tricky mogul field, more a black than a red, with tired intermediates struggling and falling. Reporters talk about parts of it being sheet ice at times. Many visitors opt instead to walk up the steep slope (perhaps 150m/490ft) to the top of the cable-car and ride down. The lift company really should make the piste easier or build a drag-lift up to the cable-car (or both). Currently, the way home spoils a good day out.

SNOWPIX.COM / CHRIS GILL

What a choice! To get from Rastkogel to Mayrhofen you can walk up to the cable-car (left) or tackle the long, tricky red run (right) →

## boarding

*Mayrhofen is not ideal for learning to snowboard – the nursery slopes are inconvenient and the lifts are mainly drags. For intermediates, the Penken slopes are good and the lifts are mainly gondolas and chairs. The terrain-park is popular and the British Snowboard Championships used to be held here. More advanced riders will enjoy the Hintertux glacier, further up the valley – see separate chapter.*

### TERRAIN-PARKS
***Honoured by the Brits***

There is a good terrain-park, extended for last winter and with novice, intermediate and expert lines, rails and a half-pipe beneath the Sun-Jet chair-lift on Penken.

### SNOW RELIABILITY
***Good by Austrian standards***

Although the lifts go no higher than 2500m/8,200ft, the area is reasonably good for snow-cover because practically all of Mayrhofen's slopes are above 1500m/4,900ft. Snowmaking covers nearly all the main slopes in the Penken-Horberg area. And there is one of the best glaciers in the Alps at Hintertux. As mentioned above, poor snow on the run linking to Eggalm can be a problem.

### FOR EXPERTS
***Commit Harakiri***

Austria's steepest piste, with a gradient of 78% and called Harakiri, was opened last season under the Knorren chair. Always willing to put our lives at risk to inform our readers, both the editors of this guide tried it in January 2004, one of us twice! It is steep and it was hard and icy in the centre; but it is fairly short, we found the snow reasonably grippy near the edges and it was delightfully deserted(!). It does offer a worthwhile challenge for the brave but did not seem as steep as, for example, Mont Fort in Verbier or Stockhorn in Zermatt.

The black run under the Schneekar chair on Horberg is a good, fast cruise when groomed, but there are few other steepish pistes. The long unpisted trail to Hippach is quite challenging but rarely has good snow because of its low altitude. There is, however, some decent off-piste to be found, such as from the top of the Horbergjoch at the top of Rastkogel – we had a great time there in fresh powder – and under the cable-car linking to Lanersbach. You can also try the other resorts covered by the valley lift pass.

### FOR INTERMEDIATES
***On the tough side***

Most of Mayrhofen's slopes are on the steep side of the usual intermediate range – great for confident or competent intermediates. And the Lanersbach expansion made the area much more interesting for avid piste-bashers, with some good long runs on Rastkogel and delightfully quiet runs on Eggalm. But many of the runs in the main Penken area are quite short. And (except on Ahorn) there are few really gentle blue runs, making the area less than ideal for nervous intermediates or near beginners (see the panel on the left as well). The overcrowding on many runs can add to the intimidation factor.

If you're willing to travel, each of the main mountains covered by the Ziller valley pass is large and varied enough for an interesting day out.

## SCHOOLS

**Die Roten Profis (Manfred Gager)**
t 63800
m.gager@tirol.com

**Total (Max Rahm)**
t 63939
smt@aon.at

**Mount Everest (Peter Habeler)**
t 62829
peter@habeler.com

**Mayrhofen 3000 (Michael Thanner)**
t 64015
skischule@mayrhofen3000.at

**Classes**
(Roten Profis prices)
6 half days (2½hr am or pm) €102

**Private lessons**
2½hr: €115 for 1 person

## CHILDREN

**Wuppy's Kinderland**
t 63612
Ages 3mnth to 7yr; 9am to 5pm, Mon-Fri

**Die Roten Profis**
t 63800
m.gager@tirol.com
Ages 3 upwards; 9.30-3.30

**Total**
t 63939
smt@aon.at
Ages 2 to 4, 9.30-3.30

**Ski school**
All run classes for children aged 4 or 5 to 14. Lunch can be provided (6 days including lunch €180)





### FOR BEGINNERS
***Overrated: big drawbacks***

Despite its reputation for teaching, Mayrhofen is not ideal for beginners. The Ahorn nursery slopes are excellent – high, extensive and sunny – but it's a rather tiresome journey to and from them and intermediate mates will want to be on Penken. The Penken nursery area is less satisfactory and there are very few easy blues to progress to.

### FOR CROSS-COUNTRY
***Go to Lanersbach***

There is a fine 20km/12 mile trail along the valley to Zell am Ziller, plus small loops close to the village. But snow here is not reliable. Vorderlanersbach has a much more snow-sure trail.

### QUEUES
***Still some problems***

The Penken jumbo-gondola is very oversubscribed at peak times. Reports of 45-minute queues unless you arrive before it opens at 9am or leave it until mid-morning are common – an alternative is to take the bus to Hippach. There are queues to get down at the end of the day, too – perhaps to be eased by a proposed new shuttle-bus (see News). The slopes can also get very crowded, causing queues for some lifts.

### MOUNTAIN RESTAURANTS
***Plenty of them***

Most of Penken's many mountain restaurants are attractive and serve good-value food but can get crowded. The newish Schneekar restaurant at the top of the Horberg section has been highly recommended ('table-service, traditional food, open fire, wooden beams, leather sofa, sometimes with a jazz pianist'). The Almstüberl at the mid-station of the Finkenberg gondola 'was usually quiet when others were packed'. Vronis remains a firm favourite with reporters ('fabulous steaks'). Schiestl's Sunnalm and Kressbrunnalm were also recommended by a 2004 visitor.

### SCHOOLS AND GUIDES
***Excellent reputation***

Mayrhofen's popularity is founded on its schools, and a high proportion of guests take lessons. We have received many positive reports over the years, but a few negative ones too, including a complete beginner in a class of 15 with an instructor who spoke no English – 'we got by on sign language'.

### FACILITIES FOR CHILDREN
***Good but inconvenient***

Mayrhofen majors on childcare and the facilities are excellent. But you may prefer resorts where children don't have to be bussed around and ferried up and down the mountain.

## STAYING THERE

### HOW TO GO
***Plenty of mainstream packages***

There is a wide choice of hotel holidays available from UK tour operators, but few catered chalets.

**Hotels** Most of the hotels packaged by UK tour operators are centrally located, a walk from the Penken gondola.

((((5 **Elisabeth** (6767) The resort's only 5-star – 'but deserves only 4,' says a reporter, who complains of tired decor and variable food. Casino.

(((4 **Manni's** (633010) Well-placed, smartly done out; pool.

(((4 **Kramerwirt** (6700) Lovely hotel, oozing character, 'friendly and helpful staff, good rooms, interesting food'.

((3 **Strass** (6705) Right by the Penken gondola. Lively bars, disco, fitness centre, pool; but very big and with a down-market feel ('Brits in football shirts') and rooms that lack style.

((3 **Neuhaus** (6703) 'First-class facilities,' says a reporter; good food but rooms above the bar are not ideal.

((3 **Rose** (62229) Well placed, near centre. Good food.

((3 **Neue Post** (62131) Convenient family-run 4-star on the main street – 'good food and nice big rooms'.

((3 **Waldheim** (62211) Smallish, cosy 3-star gasthof, near the gondola.

### EATING OUT
***Wide choice***

Manni's is good for pizzas ('but expensive, especially for wine'). Wirthaus zum Griena is a 'wonderful old wooden building offering traditional farmhouse cuisine'. We had good lamb and pepper steak at Tyroler Stuben. A favourite with tour op reps is the Mount Everest in the Andrea hotel. The 'lively' Rundum was recommended for its 'good service'.

### APRES-SKI
***Lively but not rowdy***

Après-ski is a great selling point. At close of play, the umbrella bar, at the top of the Penken gondola, the Ice Bar at the hotel Strass and Nicki's Schirmbar get packed out. Some of the

Finkenberg, looking down the valley to Mayrhofen (the tourist office took this photo carefully to avoid the busy main road being in it) →

TVB FINKENBERG

## GETTING THERE

**Air** Salzburg 175km/109 miles (3hr); Munich 190km/118 miles (2½hr); Innsbruck 75km/47 miles (1hr).

**Rail** Local line through to resort; regular buses from station.

## ACTIVITIES

**Indoor** Bowling, adventure pool, 2 hotel pools open to the public, massage, sauna, squash, fitness centre, indoor tennis centre, indoor riding-school, pool and billiards

**Outdoor** Ice rink, curling, horse sleigh rides, 45km/28 miles of cleared paths, hang-gliding, paragliding, ballooning, panoramic flights, tobogganing

**Phone numbers**
From elsewhere in Austria add the prefix 05285.
From abroad use the prefix +43 5285.

## TOURIST OFFICES

**Mayrhofen**
**t** 6760
info@mayrhofen.at
www.mayrhofen.com

**Finkenberg**
**t** 62673
info@finkenberg.at
www.finkenberg.at

other bars in the Strass are rocking places later on, including the new Speak Easy, with live music. However, the Sport's Arena disco is said to be 'for the kids'. Recent visitors have preferred the Apropos ('great music') and Schlüssel Alm ('still the best all-round late-night venue'). Mo's American theme bar and Scotland Yard remain popular with Brits, but the latter was reported to be 'dated, dirty and smoky'. Try Am Kamin or the small casino (both in the hotel Elisabeth) if you're after more Manhattan than Mayrhofen (though a 2004 reporter said the casino was 'usually deserted'). The Neue Post bar and the Passage are good for a quiet drink.

### OFF THE SLOPES
***Good for all***

Innsbruck is easily reached by train. There are also good walks and sports amenities, including the swimming pool complex – with saunas, solariums and lots of other fun features. Pedestrians have no trouble getting up the mountain to meet friends for lunch.

## Finkenberg 840m/2,760ft

Finkenberg is a much smaller, quieter village than Mayrhofen.

### THE RESORT

Finkenberg is no more than a collection of traditional-style hotels, bars, cafes and private homes spread along the busy, steep main road between Mayrhofen and Lanersbach. Some hotels are within walking distance of the gondola, and many of the more distant ones run minibuses.

### THE MOUNTAIN

Finkenberg shares Mayrhofen's main Penken slopes.

**Slopes** A two-stage gondola gives direct access to the Penken slopes – and in good conditions you can ski back to the village on a ski-route.

**Snow reliability** The local slopes are not as well-endowed with snowmaking as those on Mayrhofen's side.

**Experts** Not much challenge, except off-piste, the Harakiri piste and the run back from Lanersbach.

**Intermediates** The whole area opens up from the top of the gondola.

**Beginners** There's a village nursery slope, but it's a sunless spot, and good conditions are far from certain.

**Snowboarding** No special facilities.

**Cross-country** Cross-country skiers have to get a bus up to Lanersbach.

**Queues** The gondola gives queue-free access to the Penken.

**Mountain restaurants** See the recommendations given for Mayrhofen.

**Schools and guides** The Finkenberg School has a good reputation.

**Facilities for children** There's a non-ski nursery, and the ski nursery takes children from age four.

### STAYING THERE

**Hotels** There are quite a few. Sporthotel Stock (6775) has great spa facilities and is owned by the family of former downhill champion Leonard Stock.

**Eating out** A 2004 reporter recommends the Eberl and Neuwirt.

**Après-ski** The main après-ski spots are the Laterndl Pub (at the foot of the gondola) and Finkennest.

**Off the slopes** Curling, ice-skating, swimming and good local walks.

ALPENSZENE MONTAFON

# Montafon

*Extensive slopes, well off the beaten package path*

**COSTS**

(1)(2)(3)(4)(5)(6)

**NEWS**

For 2004/05 Golm will get a new quad chair-lift with covers. The Aussergolmbahn will replace an old T-bar and extend up to Grüneck, where a new ski-tunnel, built for 2003/04, links the slopes of Aussergolm with the main Golm slopes.

The Zamangbahn gondola, serving the Hochjoch slopes at Schruns, was upgraded from four- to six-seat cabins for 2003/04.

Further snowmaking improved the runs in the Silvretta Nova, Golm and Schafberg ski areas.



MONTAFON TOURISMUS

Most of the runs are on open slopes above the tree line ↓

**The 40km/25 mile-long Montafon valley contains no less than eleven resorts and five main lift systems. Packages from the UK are few (accommodation to suit tour operators is not easy to find), but for the independent traveller the valley is well worth a look – especially the Silvretta Nova area (linking Gaschurn and St Gallenkirch) and high, tiny, isolated Gargellen.**

The Montafon is neglected by the UK travel trade. Its location in Vorarlberg, west of the Arlberg pass, makes it a bit remote from the standard Austrian charter airport of Salzburg – and the valley lacks the large hotels that big operators apparently need.

The valley runs south-east from the medieval city of Bludenz – parallel with the nearby Swiss border. The first sizeable community you come to is Vandans, linked to its Golm ski area by gondola. Next are Schruns, at the foot of Hochjoch, and Tschagguns, across the valley at the foot of Grabs. Further on are St Gallenkirch and Gaschurn, at opposite ends of the biggest area, Silvretta Nova. Up a side valley to the south of St Gallenkirch is Gargellen, close to the Swiss border – a tiny village, but not unknown in Britain.

The valley road goes on up to Partenen, where it climbs steeply to Bielerhöhe and the Silvrettasee dam, at the foot of glaciers and Piz Buin (of sunscreen fame) – the highest peak in the Vorarlberg. In summer you can drive over the pass to Galtür and Ischgl. In winter Bielerhöhe is a great launch pad for ski-tours, and there are high, snow-sure cross-country trails totalling 26km/16 miles on and around the frozen lake. You get there by taking a cable-car from Partenen to Trominier, and then a mini-bus – free with the area lift pass.

There are more ordinary cross-country trails along the valley, and an 11km/7 mile woodland trail at Kristberg, above Silbertal – up a side valley to the east of Schruns. Trails total 100km/62 miles.

The shared valley lift pass covers the respectable post-bus service and the Bludenz-Schruns trains, as well as the 65 lifts – so exploration of the valley does not require a car.

The top heights hereabouts are no match for the nearby Arlberg resorts; but there is plenty of skiing above the mid-mountain lift stations at around 1500m/5,000ft, and most of the slopes are not excessively sunny, so snow reliability (aided by snowmaking on quite a big scale) is reasonable. Practically all the pistes are accurately classified blue or red, but there are plentiful off-piste opportunities (including 37km/23 miles of 'ski routes'). There are snowboard terrain-parks in most sectors, the newest being Lagoon1 at Silvretta Nova which also features a half-pipe.

There are 12 ski schools in the valley, operating in each of the different ski areas. And eight ski kindergartens take kids from age three.

Tobogganing is popular, and there are several runs on the different mountains – the Silvretta Nova's 6km/4 mile floodlit run down to St Gallenkirch being the most impressive.

**GARGELLEN** 1425m/4,680ft

**Gargellen is a real backwater – a tiny village tucked up a side valley, with a small but varied piste network on Schafberg that is blissfully quiet.**
The eight-person gondola from the

## KEY FACTS

| | |
|---|---|
| **Resorts** | 655-1425m<br>2,150-4,680ft |
| **Slopes** | 680-2395m<br>2,230-7,860ft |
| **Lifts** | 65 |
| **Pistes** | 209km<br>130 miles |
| **Blue** | 54% |
| **Red** | 32% |
| **Black** | 14% |
| **Snowmaking** | 81km<br>50 miles |

## TOURIST OFFICE

**Montafon**
**t** 722530
info@montafon.at
www.montafon.at

The tourist office is in Schruns, so from elsewhere in Austria add the prefix 05556, from abroad use the prefix +43 5556.

**Phone numbers**
**Gargellen**
From elsewhere in Austria add the prefix 05557.
From abroad use the prefix +43 5557.

village up to the Schafberg slopes seems rather out of place in this tiny collection of hotels and guest houses, huddled in a steep-sided, narrow valley. The runs it takes you to are gentle, with not much to choose between the blues and reds; but there is lots of off-piste terrain. There are four unpatrolled ski-routes. A special feature is the day-tour around the Madrisa – a small-scale off-piste adventure taking you over to Klosters in Switzerland. It involves a 300m/1,000ft climb, but is otherwise easy.

The altitude of the village (the highest in the Montafon) and north-east facing slopes make for reasonable snow reliability. And there is snowmaking on one of the several pistes to the valley, which include a couple of excellent away-from-the-lifts runs at the extremities of the area. With care you can ski to the door of the hotel Madrisa (6331) among others. Behind the hotel is a rather steep nursery slope. There are four pleasant mountain restaurants, including two rustic huts at the tree line – the Obwaldhütte and the Kessl-Hütte. The former holds a weekly après-ski party after the lifts close, followed by a torchlit descent. (Slide shows and bridge are more typical evening entertainments.) The Barga pizzeria at the foot of the Vergalden drag, can also be reached by walkers.

**SCHRUNS** 700m/2,300ft

**Schruns is the most rounded resort in the valley – a towny little place, with the shops in its car-free centre catering for locals and for summer tourists.**

A cable-car and gondola (which has just received a performance boost) go up from points outside the village into the Hochjoch slopes. Above the trees is a fair-sized area of easy blue runs, with the occasional red alternative, served by slow chairs and drags and the fast eight-seat Seebliga chair. There are restaurants at strategic points – the Wormser Hütte is a climbing refuge with 'stunning' views. Parents can leave their kids under supervision at the huge NTC Dreamland children's facility at the top of the cable-car, by the skier services building. The blue run from Kreuzjoch back to Schruns is exceptional: about 12km/7.5 miles long and over 1600m/5,250ft vertical. Snow-guns cover the lower half of this, plus the Seebliga area.

Easily accessible across the valley are the limited slopes of Grabs, above the rather formless village of Tschagguns, and the more extensive area of Golm, where a gondola goes from Vandans up to a handful of chairs and drags serving easy slopes above the trees, and offering a vertical descent of over 1400m/4,590ft. A six-pack now goes to the top of the area,

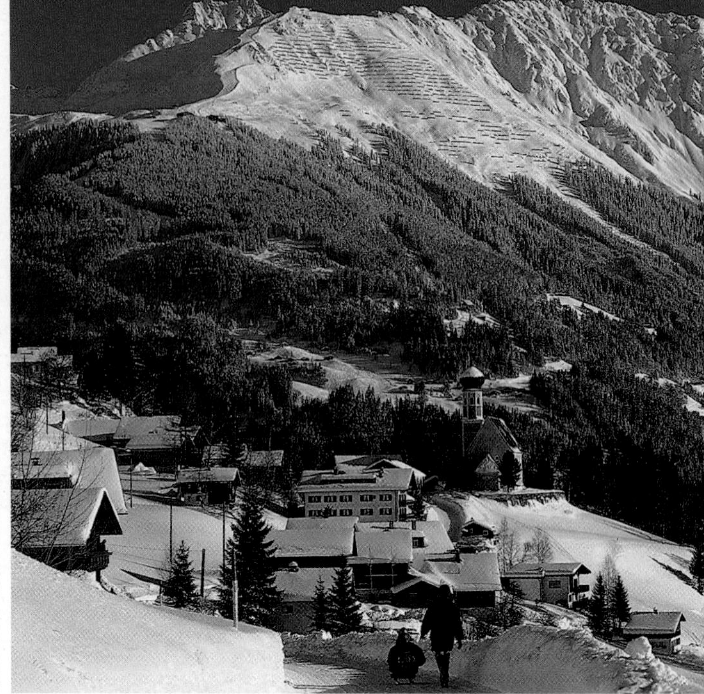

There are several charming towns and villages to choose from in the valley →

ALPENSZENE MONTAFON





**Phone numbers**
**Schruns**
From elsewhere in Austria add the prefix 05556.
From abroad use the prefix +43 5556.
**Gaschurn**
From elsewhere in Austria add the prefix 05558.
From abroad use the prefix +43 5558.

**TOURIST OFFICES**

**Gargellen**
t 6303
tourismus@gargellen.at
www.gargellen.at
**Schruns**
t 721660
info@schruns-tschagguns.at
www.schruns-tschagguns.at
**Gaschurn**
t 82010
info@gaschurn-partenen.com
www.gaschurn-partenen.com

and will be linked in 2004/05, via the ski tunnel, to a new quad on the Aussergolm slopes on the back of the hill. Snow-guns cover two major upper slopes, and the run to the valley.

As you are reminded at every opportunity, Ernest Hemingway ensconced himself in Schruns in 1925/26, and his favourite drinking table in the hotel Taube (72384) is still there to be admired. The Löwen (7141) and the Alpenhof Messmer (726640) are elegant, well-equipped 4-stars with big pools, the former a hub of the après-ski scene.

## GASCHURN / ST GALLENKIRCH

1000m/3,280ft / 900m/2,950ft

**Silvretta Nova is the biggest lift and piste network in the valley. As a result, German cars fill to overflowing the huge car parks at the valley lift stations. Gaschurn is an attractive place to stay.**

The two main resorts here are quite different. Whereas St Gallenkirch is strung along the main road and spoiled by traffic, Gaschurn is a pleasant village, bypassed by the valley traffic, with the wood-shingled Posthotel Rössle (83330) in the centre.

The lift network covers two parallel ridges running north-south, with most of the runs on their east- and west-facing flanks. The slopes are accessed from three points along the valley. A gondola from Gaschurn takes you up to the east ridge, while another gondola from St Gallenkirch goes up to Valisera on the west ridge. A chair-lift to Garfrescha gives access to the central valley from Gortipohl – on the road between the two resorts.

This is the most challenging area in the valley, with as many red as blue runs, and some nominal blacks. Most of the slopes are above the tree line, typically offering a modest 300m/1,000ft vertical. The Rinderhütte six-pack serves more red pistes from the top of the area. There is lots of off-piste potential, including steep (and quite dangerous) slopes down into the central valley. The map shows four 'ski routes'; outrageously, their status is not explained.

There are lots of mountain restaurants, many impressive in different ways. At the top of the east ridge is the state-of-the-art Nova Stoba, with seats for over 1,500 people in various rooms catering for different markets, including splendid panelled rooms with table-service. The big terrace bar gets seriously boisterous in the afternoons. At the top of the other ridge is the splendidly woody Valisera Hüsli. There is snowmaking on one-third of the slopes, with cover down to two of the valley stations.

# Obergurgl

*Chalet-style hotels on high, snow-sure slopes attract a loyal clientele*

## COSTS

①②③④⑤⑥

## RATINGS

| **The slopes** | |
|---|---|
| Snow | ***** |
| Extent | ** |
| Expert | ** |
| Intermediate | *** |
| Beginner | **** |
| Convenience | **** |
| Queues | ***** |
| Mountain restaurants | ** |
| **The rest** | |
| Scenery | *** |
| Resort charm | **** |
| Off-slope | ** |

## NEWS

The substantial investment in lift improvements of recent years is to be built on for 2005 with a six-seat chair with covers planned to replace the Schermerbahn double chair out of Hochgurgl.

- + Glaciers apart, one of the Alps' most reliable resorts for snow – especially good for a late-season holiday
- + Excellent area for beginners, timid intermediates and families
- + Mainly queue- and crowd-free
- + Traditional-style village with very little traffic
- + Jolly tea-time après-ski
- + Obergurgl and Hochgurgl slopes are now linked by gondola

- − Limited area of slopes, with no tough pistes and now no terrain-park or half-pipe
- − Exposed setting, with few sheltered slopes for bad weather
- − Few off-slope leisure amenities except in hotels
- − Disappointing mountain restaurants
- − Village is spread out and disjointed
- − For a small Austrian resort, rather expensive

**A loyal band of visitors go back every year to Obergurgl or higher Hochgurgl, booking a year in advance in recognition of the limited supply of beds. They love the high, snow-sure, easy intermediate slopes, the end-of-the-valley seclusion and the civilised atmosphere in the reassuringly expensive hotels.**

**We're unconvinced. If we're going to a bleak, high, snow-sure resort where there is not much to do but ski or board, we'd rather go somewhere with more skiing or boarding to do. But, of course, most such places aren't in Austria – important to some – and their hotels might be less reassuringly expensive.**

## THE RESORT

Obergurgl is based on a traditional old village, set in a remote spot, the dead end of a long road up past Sölden. It is the highest parish in Austria and is usually under a blanket of snow from November until May. The surrounding slopes are bleak, with an array of avalanche barriers giving them a forbidding appearance.

Obergurgl has no through traffic and few day visitors. The village centre is mainly traffic-free, and entirely so at night. Village atmosphere is relaxed during the day, jolly immediately after the slopes close, but rather subdued later at night; there are some nightspots, but most people stay in their hotels. The resort is popular with British families and well-heeled groups looking for a relaxing winter break.

Despite its small size, this is a village of parts. At the northern entrance to the resort is a cluster of hotels near the main Festkogl gondola, which takes you to all the local slopes. This area is good for getting to the slopes and for ease of access by car, but it's a long walk or a shuttle-bus from the village centre and the nursery slopes. The road then passes another group of hotels set on a little hill to the east, around the ice rink (beware steep, sometimes treacherous walks here). The village proper starts with an attractive little square with church, fountain, and the original village hotel (the Edelweiss und Gurgl). Just above are the Rosskar and Gaisberg chair-lifts to the local slopes. There is an underground car park in the centre of the village.

Hochgurgl, a gondola-ride away, is little more than a handful of hotels at the foot of its own slopes. It looks like it might be a convenience resort dedicated to skiing from the door, but it isn't: from nearly all the hotels you

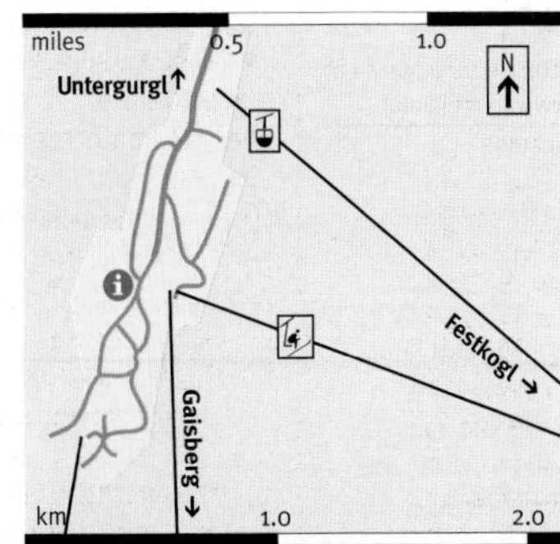

| KEY FACTS | |
|---|---|
| Resort | 1930m 6,330ft |
| Slopes | 1795-3080m 5,890-10,100ft |
| Lifts | 23 |
| Pistes | 110km 68 miles |
| Blue | 32% |
| Red | 50% |
| Black | 18% |
| Snowmaking | 22km 14 miles |







have to negotiate roads and/or stairs to get to or from the snow. Hochgurgl is even quieter than Obergurgl at night.

In the valley below Hochgurgl (and linked by gondola) is Untergurgl, linked to Obergurgl by regular ski-buses. For a budget base, it is worth considering. For a day out, it's a short bus or car trip to Sölden (see separate chapter), and a long car trip to Kühtai (a worthwhile high area near Innsbruck). Much closer is the tiny touring launch-pad of Vent.

## THE MOUNTAINS

The gondola between Obergurgl and Hochgurgl means that the two can now be thought of as forming a single area. Even so, the slopes are surprisingly limited, and lacking interest or challenge for keen intermediates or experts. You don't get the sense of travel, as you do in bigger Alpine resorts. Most of the slopes are very exposed – there are few woodland runs to head to in poor conditions. Wind and white-outs can shut the lifts and, especially in early season, severe cold can curtail enthusiasm.

The lift pass is quite expensive for the relatively small area. Piste grooming is very good, but reporters complain of poor signposting.

### THE SLOPES
***Limited cruising***

**Obergurgl** is the smaller of the two linked areas. It is in two sections, well linked by piste in one direction, more loosely in the other. The gondola and the Rosskar fast quad chair from the village go to the higher Festkogl area. This is served by two drags and a chair up to 3035m/9,960ft (you can join the Rosskar lift at its mid-station too). From here you can head back to the gondola base or over to Gaisberg, with its high point at Hohe Mut, reached by a long, slow chair. On the lightly wooded lower part of this area, two fast chair-lifts have replaced three drag-lifts. A double chair up from Obergurgl's village square provides the other link on to the Gaisberg slopes. There are two 'ski routes', one of them the only run from Hohe Mut. The piste map used to explain that these are unpatrolled, but no longer does so.

The slopes of **Hochgurgl** consist of two high, gentle bowls, either side of the Schermerspitze, served by the continuing gondola and chair-lifts, and open mountainsides either side of the 'village' served by drag-lifts. From the top stations there are spectacular views of the Dolomites. A single run leads down through the woods from Hochgurgl to Untergurgl.

### TERRAIN-PARKS
***Due for a revival?***

Obergurgl had a terrain-park, half-pipe and quarter-pipe; then it scrapped them; now it has realised that the market for boarders and trick skiers is worth developing, and is surveying teenagers to find out what they want.

### SNOW RELIABILITY
***Excellent***

Obergurgl has high slopes and is arguably the most snow-sure of Europe's non-glacier resorts – even

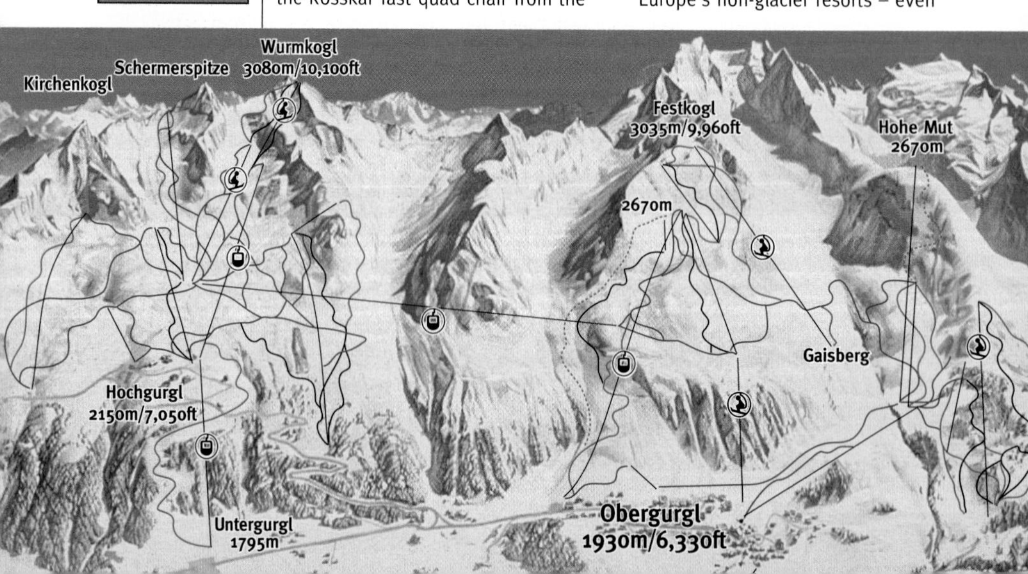

A great place to be the day after a snowstorm, but not during it ➔

OBERGURGL TOURIST OFFICE

**LIFT PASSES**

**Obergurgl ski pass**
Covers lifts in Obergurgl and Hochgurgl, and local ski-bus.

**Main pass**
1 day €37
6 days €183

**Senior citizens**
Over 60: 6 days €136

**Children**
Under 16: 6 days €107
Under 8: free pass

**Notes**
Half-day passes available.

without its snowmaking, which is now impressively extensive. It has a longer season than most Austrian resorts.

### FOR EXPERTS
***Not generally recommendable***

There are few challenges on-piste – most of the blacks could easily be red, and where they deserve the grading it's only for short stretches (for example, at the very top of Wurmkogl). But the Hohe Mut ski route can have big moguls, and there is a fair amount of enjoyable off-piste to be found with a guide – and the top school groups often go off-piste when conditions are right. This is a well-known area for ski touring, and we have reports of very challenging expeditions on the glaciers at the head of the valley.

### FOR INTERMEDIATES
***Good but limited***

There is some perfect intermediate terrain here, made even better by the normally flattering snow conditions. The problem is, there's not much of it. Keen piste-bashers will quickly tire of travelling the same runs and be itching to catch the bus to Sölden, down the valley – unfortunately, there is no pass-sharing arrangement.

Hochgurgl has the bigger area of easy runs, and these make good cruising. For more challenging intermediate runs, head to the Vorderer Wurmkogllift, on the right as you look at the mountain. Less confident intermediates may find the woodland piste down from Hochgurgl to the bus stop at Untergurgl tricky.

The Obergurgl area has more red than blue runs but most offer no great challenge to a confident intermediate. There is some easy cruising around mid-mountain on the Festkogl. The blue run from the top of the Festkogl gondola down to the village, via the Gaisberg sector, is one of the longest cruises in the area. And there's another long enjoyable run down the length of the gondola, with a scenic off-piste variant in the adjoining valley.

In the Gaisberg area, there are very easy runs in front of the Nederhütte and back towards the village.

### FOR BEGINNERS
***Fine for first-timers or improvers***

The inconveniently situated Mahdstuhl nursery slope above Obergurgl is adequate for complete beginners. And the gentle Gaisberg run – under the chair out of the village – is ideal to move on to as soon as a modicum of control has been achieved. The easy slopes served by the Bruggenboden chair are also suitable.

The Hochgurgl nursery slopes are an awkward walk from the hotels, but otherwise satisfactory. And there are good blue slopes to move on to.

## boarding

*Obergurgl is a traditional ski destination, attracting an affluent and (dare we say it?) 'older' clientele. But the resort is actually pretty good for snowboarding and there are signs that the resort now wants to attract younger visitors. Beginners will be pleased to find that most of the slopes can be reached without having to ride drag-lifts. And there's some good off-piste potential for more advanced riders.*

## CHILDREN

**Kindergarten in Obergurgl**
For non-skiing children from age 3

**Alpina, Austria and Hochfirst hotels**
Kindergartens in these hotels

**Bobo's ski kindergarten**
From age 3

**Ski schools**
Take children over the age of 5 (6 full days €170)

## SCHOOLS

**Obergurgl**
t 6305

**Hochgurgl**
t 626599

**Classes**
(Obergurgl prices)
6 days (2hr am and pm) €170

**Private lessons**
€112 for a half-day; each additional person €15

The quality of the snow and piste preparation make learning here easier than in most lower Austrian resorts.

### CROSS-COUNTRY
*Limited but snow-sure*

Three small loops, one each at Obergurgl, Untergurgl and Hochgurgl, give just 12km/7 miles of trail. All are relatively snow-sure and pleasantly situated. Lessons are available.

### QUEUES
*Few problems*

Major lift queues are rare. You can expect high-season queues for the village lifts at the start of ski school, but these tend to clear quickly. The resort is remote and has not attracted many day-trippers in the past, even when lower villages have been short of snow. Although quicker access from Untergurgl via the gondola (and increased parking) have encouraged day visitors, a 2004 peak season skier reports no serious queues.

### MOUNTAIN RESTAURANTS
*Little choice*

Compared with most Austrian resorts, mountain huts are neither numerous nor very special. However, the jolly Nederhütte at Gaisberg has a 'substantial menu', which more than satisfied a visiting vegetarian, with 'tasty and huge portions'. David's Skihütte is 'very friendly', cheerful and good value. The small hut at Hohe Mut serves 'good, tasty, local dishes' and has excellent views.

At Hochgurgl, Wurmkogelhütte – a big, but pleasantly woody and spacious self-service is the only place for a proper meal, serving 'fine, standard Austrian' fare. The tiny hut above it at Wurmkoglgipfel is in an exceptional position and does limited food. Many people return to one village or the other for lunch in the sun.

### SCHOOLS AND GUIDES
*Further good news*

We continue to receive positive reports of the Obergurgl school, with good English spoken and excellent lessons and organisation. A reporter tells us that the school worked hard to uphold a new promise of a maximum of nine to a class. Demand for private instruction appears to be increasing and it is advisable to book ahead during peak periods.

### FACILITIES FOR CHILDREN
*Check out your hotel*

Children's ski classes start at five years and children from age three can join Bobo's ski-kindergarten. There is also a non-skiing kindergarten, the Pingu Club, for kids aged three and up. There's lunchtime supervision for ski school and kindergarten children alike. Many hotels offer childcare of one sort or another, and the Alpina has been particularly recommended.

## STAYING THERE

### HOW TO GO
*Plenty of good hotels*

Most package accommodation is in hotels and pensions. Demand for rooms in these villages exceeds supply, and for once it is true that you should book early to avoid disappointment.

**Hotels** Accommodation is of high quality: most hotels are 4-stars, and none is less than a 3-star. Couples have been surprised to be asked to share tables even at 4-star hotels.

A cheaper option is to stay down the valley in Untergurgl, where the 4-star Jadghof (6431) is recommended. Some hotels don't accept credit cards.

((((4 **Edelweiss und Gurgl** (6223) The focal hotel – biggest, oldest, one of the most appealing; on the central square, near the main lifts. Pool and outdoor whirlpool.

((((4 **Alpina de Luxe** (600) Big, smart chalet with excellent children's facilities. Pool.

((((4 **Bergwelt** (6274) Recently recommended as 'very smart'. Beauty and spa facilities, including outdoor pool.

((((4 **Hochfirst** (63250) Good spa facilities, comfortable, four or five minutes from gondola. Ski bus stop right outside. Casino.

((((4 **Crystal** (6454) Near the Festkogl lift. If you don't mind the ocean-liner appearance, it's one of the best.

((((4 **Gamper** (6545) 'Excellent,' says a reporter – 'Good food, friendly staff.' Far end of town, past the square.

((((4 **Gotthard-Zeit** (6292) 'Elegant', spacious, comfortable, good food. Spa facilities. Small pool. Sun terrace. Recommended too for skiing convenience but a 'steep walk back from the village' if you are on foot.

((((4 **Jenewein** (6203) Recommended as 'most convenient', with 'attractive' spa facilities.

## GETTING THERE

**Air** Innsbruck 99km/62 miles (2hr); Salzburg 288km/179 miles (3hr); Munich 204km/127 miles (4hr).

**Rail** Train to Ötz; regular buses from station, transfer 1½hr.

## ACTIVITIES

**Indoor** Pools, saunas, whirlpools, steam baths and massage in hotels; bowling, billiards, squash, table tennis

**Outdoor** Natural ice rink, snow-shoe outings, winter hiking paths

**Phone numbers**
From elsewhere in Austria add the prefix 05256.
From abroad use the prefix +43 5256.

## TOURIST OFFICE

**t** 6466
info@obergurgl.com
www.obergurgl.com

(((3 **Wiesental** (6263) Comfortable, well situated, good value. Sun terrace popular for lunch and après-ski.
(((3 **Granat-Schlössl** (6363) Amusing pseudo-castle, surprisingly affordable.
((2 **Alpenblume** (6278) Good B&B hotel, well-placed for Festkogl lift.
((2 **Gurgl** (6533) B&B near Festkogl lift; friendly, pizzeria, same owners as Edelweiss und Gurgl.
((2 **Schönblick** (6251) B&B with downhill walk to main lifts, 'very clean, big rooms, hearty breakfast, friendly owner'.
**Hochgurgl** has equally good hotels.
(((((5 **Hochgurgl** (6265) The only 5-star in the area. Luxurious, with pool.
((((4 **Angerer Alm** (6241) 'Staff were really friendly and nothing was too much trouble,' says a recent reporter. Pool.
(((3 **Sporthotel Ideal** (6290) Well situated for access to the slopes. Pool.
(((3 **Laurin** (6227) Well equipped, traditional rooms, excellent food.
**Self-catering** The Lohmann is a high-standard large modern apartment block, well placed for the slopes, less so for the village centre below. The 3-star Pirchhütt has apartments close to the Festkogl gondola, and the Wiesental hotel has more central ones.

## EATING OUT

### *Wide choice, limited range*

Hotel dining rooms and à la carte restaurants dominate. A reporter recommends the independent and rustic Krumpn's Stadl (where staff dress in traditional clothing). The Hexenkuchl in the Jenewein received favourable reports again this year, serving 'good quality Austrian food, but not cheap'. The 'friendly' Deutschmann is said to serve up 'good, reasonably priced food'. The Romantika at the hotel Madeleine and the Belmonte are popular pizzerias. Hotel Alpina has a particularly good reputation for its food – though a report says the Gotthard-Zeit and Hochfirst are 'just as good'. The restaurant at the Gamper is pleasantly cosy. The two restaurants in the Edelweiss und Gurgl are reportedly 'superb', and food at the Josl 'excellent'. Nederhütte (which has a fondue evening with live music, which 'rocks', says a reporter) and David's Skihütte up the mountain are both open in the evenings and popular snowmobile destinations. The 5-star hotel Hochgurgl is recommended for a



'delicious' treat, 'reasonably priced for what we had'. Remember, credit cards are not widely accepted.

## APRES-SKI

### *Lively early, quiet later*

Obergurgl is more animated in the evening than you might expect. The Nederhütte mountain restaurant has lively tea dancing – you ski home afterwards though (or ride down on a snowmobile, says a reporter). All the bars at the base of the Rosskar and Gaisberg lifts are popular at close of play – the Umbrella Bar outside the Edelweiss hotel is particularly busy in good weather. The Hexenkuchl at the Jenewein is also popular and a reporter this year enjoyed the 'excellent' and 'popular sun terrace' at the Wiesental.

Later on, the crowded Krumpn's Stadl barn is the liveliest place in town with live music on alternate nights. The Josl, Jenewein and Edelweiss und Gurgl hotels have atmospheric bars. The Bajazzo is a more sophisticated late-night haunt. When we visited, the Austriakeller disco attracted an extraordinary age range – 6 to 60. There's a casino at the Hochfirst.

Hochgurgl is very quiet at night except for Toni's Almhütte bar in the Olymp Sporthotel – one of three places with live music. There's also the African Bar disco.

## OFF THE SLOPES

### *Very limited*

There isn't much to do during the day, with few shops and limited public facilities. Innsbruck is over two hours away by post-bus. Sölden (20 minutes away) has a leisure centre and shopping facilities. Pedestrians can walk to restaurants in the Gaisberg area to meet friends for lunch and there are 11km/7 miles of hiking paths. The health suite at the Hochfirst is said to be open to non-residents.

TVB OBERTAUERN

# Obertauern

*Small, varied area, with great snow record and lively après-ski scene*

## COSTS

(1)(2)(3)(4)(5)(6)

## RATINGS

| **The slopes** | |
|---|---|
| Snow | **** |
| Extent | ** |
| Expert | *** |
| Intermediate | **** |
| Beginner | **** |
| Convenience | **** |
| Queues | **** |
| Mountain restaurants | *** |
| **The rest** | |
| Scenery | *** |
| Resort charm | ** |
| Off-slope | ** |

## NEWS

Last season the Zehnerkar cable-car was replaced by an eight-seater gondola. The Kringsalm quad became a six-pack with covers and a high-speed quad replaced the Achenrain double.

For 2004/05 a new six-pack with covers should replace the Gamsleiten double from the valley.

- + Excellent snow record
- + Well-linked, user-friendly circuit
- + Slopes for all abilities
- + Good modern lift system
- + Good mountain restaurants
- + Lively but not intrusive après-ski
- + Compact resort centre – family-friendly if you pick your spot

- – Village lacks traditional charm
- – Slopes are of limited vertical
- – Lifts and snow can suffer from exposure to high winds

**If you like the après-ski jollity of Austria but have a hankering for the good snow of high French resorts, Obertauern could be just what you're looking for. The terrain is a bit limited by French standards, and the village is no Alpbach. But it's a lot prettier than Flaine – and if you've grown up on slush and ice in lower Austrian resorts, moving up in the world by 1000m/3,300ft or so will be something of a revelation.**

## THE RESORT

In the land of picture-postcard resorts grown out of rustic villages, Obertauern is different – a mainly modern development at the top of the Tauern pass road. Built in (high-rise) chalet style, it's not unattractive – but it lacks a central focus of shops and bars. Although the core is compact, there is accommodation spread widely along the road, and beginners in particular need to make sure their choice of accommodation, ski school and nursery slope will work together.

## THE MOUNTAIN

The slopes and lifts form a ring around the village. The Tauern pass road divides them into two unequal parts; that apart, the slopes are well linked to make a user-friendly circuit that can be travelled clockwise or anticlockwise in a couple of hours. Visitors used to big areas will soon start to feel they have seen it all. Vertical range is limited, and runs are short – most major lifts are in the 200m to 400m (650ft to 1,300ft) vertical range. There's now a clearer piste map but

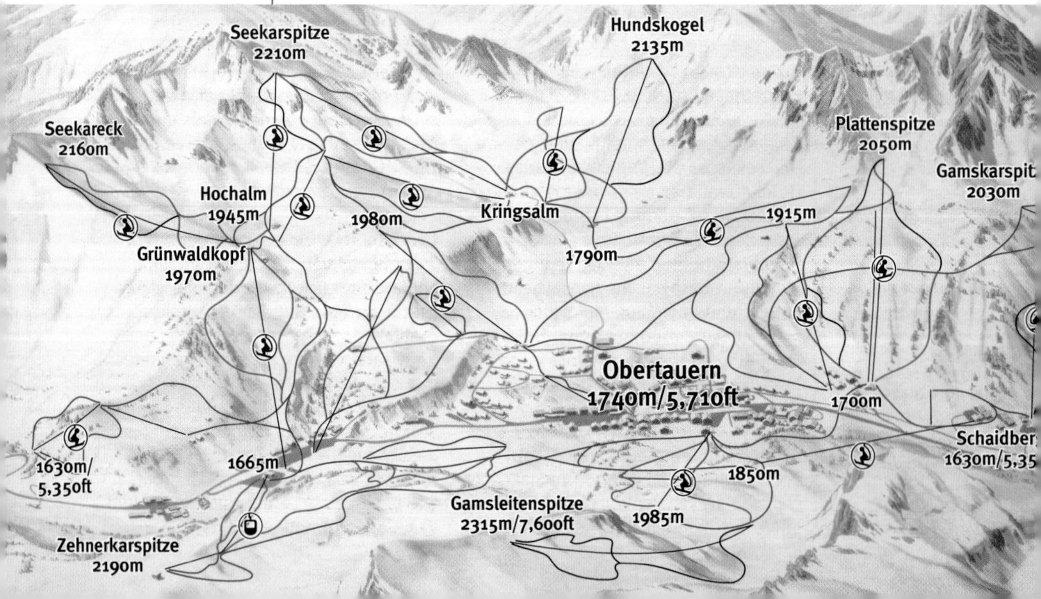

Seekarspitze 2210m
Hundskogel 2135m
Seekareck 2160m
Plattenspitze 2050m
Gamskarspit 2030m
Hochalm 1945m
Kringsalm
1980m
1915m
Grünwaldkopf 1970m
1790m
Obertauern 1740m/5,710ft
1700m
1630m/ 5,350ft
1665m
Schaidber 1630m/5,35
1850m
Gamsleitenspitze 2315m/7,600ft
1985m
Zehnerkarspitze 2190m

↑ Obertauern is one of the most snow-sure resorts in Austria – but it's a shame there isn't more vertical to play on
TVB OBERTAUERN

## KEY FACTS

| | |
|---|---|
| **Resort** | 1740m<br>5,710ft |
| **Slopes** | 1630-2315m<br>5,350-7,600ft |
| **Lifts** | 29 |
| **Pistes** | 120km<br>75 miles |
| **Blue** | 50% |
| **Red** | 35% |
| **Black** | 15% |
| **Snowmaking** | 85km<br>53 miles |

**Phone numbers**
From elsewhere in Austria add the prefix 06456.
From abroad use the prefix +43 6456.

## TOURIST OFFICE

t 7252
info@obertauern.com
www.obertauern.com

reporters complain that while pistes are numbered on the mountain, they are not on the map.
**Slopes** Most pistes are on the sunny slopes to the north of the road and village: a wide, many-faceted basin of mostly gentle runs, some combining steepish pitches with long schusses. The slopes on the other side of the road – on Gamsleitenspitze, to the south-west – are generally quieter and have some of Obertauern's most difficult runs. There is floodlit skiing from one chair-lift twice a week.
**Terrain-parks** There is one at Hochalm.
**Snow reliability** The resort has exceptional snow reliability because of its altitude. But lifts can be closed by wind (which may blow snow away too).
**Experts** There are genuinely steep black pistes from the top Gamsleiten chair, but it is prone to closure. Reporters recommend joining an off-piste guided group to explore the area.
**Intermediates** Most of Obertauern's circuit is of intermediate difficulty. Stay low for easier pistes, or try the tougher runs higher up; you can't complete the whole circuit without venturing on to reds. In the Hochalm area, the Seekareck and Panorama chairs take you to challenging runs. The chair to Hundskogel leads to a red and a black. And over at the Plattenkar quad there are splendid black/red runs.
**Beginners** Obertauern has very good nursery slopes, but they are spread around and beginners must choose accommodation carefully to avoid long walks – there are no ski buses. The Schaidberg chair leads to a drag-lift serving a high-altitude beginners' slope and there is an easy run back home.
**Snowboarding** Drag-lifts are optional and Blue Tomato is a specialist school.
**Cross-country** There are 17km/11 miles of trails in the heart of the resort.
**Queues** When nearby resorts have poor snow, non-residents arrive by the bus-load. However, the modern lift system is impressively efficient. The Sonnenlift double chair from the bottom end of the resort is a bottleneck at ski school start time.
**Mountain restaurants** Mountain restaurants are plentiful and good, but crowded. The Edelweisshütte 'has to be savoured at least once' for the afternoon sing-songs. The old Lürzer Alm at village level remains popular.
**Schools and guides** There are six schools. 'Bondi Bill', a previously commended instructor, is still with Skischule Krallinger. Frau Holle school has a 'caring attitude' and 'excellent English'. A 2004 visitor found Willi Grilltsch school 'very efficient' but would have preferred morning-only rather than the the all-day group lessons that were the only option.
**Facilities for children** Most of the schools take children.

## STAYING THERE

**How to go** Two major British tour operators offer packages here.
**Hotels** Practically all accommodation is in hotels (mostly 3-star and 4-star) and guest houses. The following have been recommended: Steiner (7306) – 'lavish spa facilities, magnificent food'; Kohlmayr (7272) – 'excellent, warm welcoming ambiance'; Enzian (72070) – 'very good facilities'; Schütz (72040) – pool and spa; Edelweiss (7245); Gamsleiten (72860) – 'definitely upmarket'; Alpina (7336).
**Eating out** The choices are mostly hotels and the busy après-ski bars at the foot of the lifts. The Hochalm at the top of the Grünwaldkopf quad sometimes serves early evening meals.
**Après-ski** There's a lively and varied après-ski scene. The Latsch'n Alm, with terrace and dancing, is good at tea time. Later, try the Lürzer Alm, with farmyard-style decor and a disco. The Taverne has various bars, a pizzeria, and a disco. The Rossenhimmel night-club and Römerbar are worth a look.
**Off the slopes** There's an excellent, large sports centre – fitness room, tennis, squash and badminton, sauna and steam bath, no pool. However, Salzburg is an easy trip.

For lunch with friends, non-skiers can ride the Zehnerkar gondola or Grünwaldkopf chair or work up an appetite walking to the Kringsalm hut.

# Saalbach-Hinterglemm

*Attractive villages, lively nightlife and good intermediate circuit*

## COSTS

①②③④⑤⑥

## RATINGS

| | |
|---|---|
| **The slopes** | |
| Snow | *** |
| Extent | *** |
| Expert | ** |
| Intermediate | **** |
| Beginner | *** |
| Convenience | **** |
| Queues | *** |
| Mountain restaurants | **** |
| **The rest** | |
| Scenery | *** |
| Resort charm | **** |
| Off-slope | ** |

## KEY FACTS

| | |
|---|---|
| **Resort** | 1000m 3,280ft |
| **Slopes** | 930-2095m 3,050ft-6,870ft |
| **Lifts** | 56 |
| **Pistes** | 200km 124 miles |
| **Blue** | 45% |
| **Red** | 48% |
| **Black** | 7% |
| **Snowmaking** | 70km 43 miles |



- ➕ Large, well-linked, intermediate circuit with impressive lift system
- ➕ Saalbach is a big but pleasant, affluent village, lively at night
- ➕ Village main streets largely traffic-free
- ➕ Atmospheric mountain restaurants dotted around the slopes
- ➕ Sunny slopes
- ➕ Large snowmaking installation and excellent piste maintenance

- ➖ Large number of low, south-facing slopes that suffer from the sun
- ➖ Limited steep terrain
- ➖ Nursery slopes in Saalbach are not ideal – sunny, and crowded in parts
- ➖ Saalbach spreads along the valley – some lodgings are far from central
- ➖ Hinterglemm sprawls along a long street with no clearly defined centre
- ➖ Saalbach can get rowdy at night

**Saalbach-Hinterglemm is one of Austria's major resorts, with a claimed 200km/124 miles of pistes. Compared with other big names nearby, it emerges well: it has better expert terrain and better mountain restaurants than the Ski Welt (Söll, Ellmau etc), more impressive lifts and snowmaking than Kitzbühel, and has the edge on both in terms of village altitude and skiing convenience.**

**If you cast the net wider, though, you become more aware of what a weakness it is to have most slopes facing south, especially when those slopes are mainly below the 1900m/6,230ft mark. There is a limit to what snowmaking can achieve, especially in February and March.**

## THE RESORT

Saalbach and Hinterglemm are separate villages, their centres 4km/2 miles apart, which have expanded along the floor of their dead-end valley. They haven't quite merged, but they have adopted a single shared marketing identity. This doesn't mean they offer a single kind of holiday.

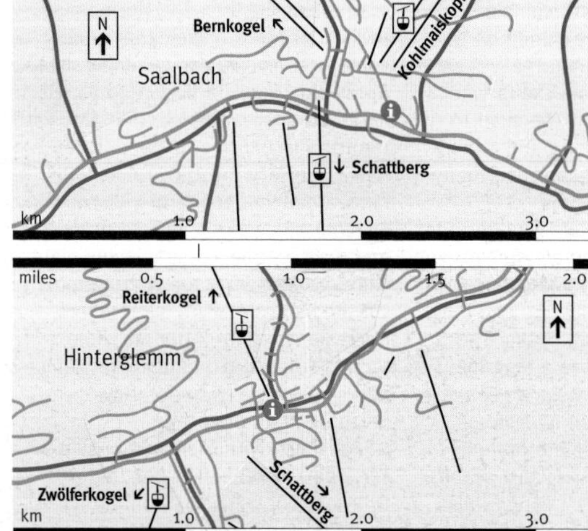


Saalbach is an attractive, typically Austrian village, with traditional-style (although mostly modern) buildings huddled together around a classic onion-domed church. But it is more convenient than most Austrian villages, with pistes coming right down to the traffic-free village centre; the result is close to an ideal blend of Austrian charm with French convenience.

Saalbach has a justified reputation as a party town – but those doing the partying seem to be a strangely mixed bunch. Big-spending BMW and Mercedes drivers, staying in the smart, expensive hotels that line the main street, share the bars with teenagers (including British school kids) spending more on alcohol than on their cheap and cheerful pensions out along the road to Hinterglemm. It can get very rowdy, with drunken revellers still in their ski boots long after dark.

Hinterglemm also has lifts and runs close to the centre, and offers quick access to some of the most interesting slopes. It is a more diffuse collection of hotels and holiday homes, where prices are lower and less cash is flashed. The main street, lined with bars and hotels, has been relieved of through traffic, which is not quite the

## NEWS

For the 2004/05 season the two successive Westgipfel double chairs from Hinterglemm up to Schattberg West are due to be replaced by an eight-seater gondola. This will bring the number of gondolas up to eight; in combination with 10 fast chairs, this amounts to an impressive system.

For the 2003/04 season the Asitzmulden (on the link to Leogang) and Zehner (behind Zwölferkogel) T-bars were replaced by high-speed six-seater chairs, with covers in the case of the Zehner.

More snowmaking was also added last season.

same as being traffic-free. It is lively without being rowdy, and for many people is the more attractive option.

In both villages, the amount of walking depends heavily on where you stay. There is an excellent valley bus service, but it isn't perfect: it finishes early, gets very busy at peak times and doesn't get you back to hotels in central Hinterglemm, or to hotels set away from the main road. Taxis are plentiful and not expensive.

Several resorts in Salzburg province are reachable by road – including Bad Hofgastein, Kaprun and Zell am See, the last a short bus-ride away.

## THE MOUNTAINS

The slopes form a 'circus' almost entirely composed of intermediate, lightly wooded slopes.

### THE SLOPES

### *User-friendly circuit*

Travelling anticlockwise, you can make a complete circuit of the valley on skis, crossing from one side to the other at Vorderglemm and Lengau. You have to tackle a red run from Schattberg West, but otherwise can stick to blues. Going clockwise, you have to truncate the circuit because there is no lift on the south side at Vorderglemm – and there is more red-run skiing to do (and a black if you want to do the full circuit).

On the south-facing side, five sectors can be identified – from west to east, **Hochalm**, **Reiterkogel**, **Bernkogel**, **Kohlmaiskopf** and **Wildenkarkogel**. The last connects via Seidl-Alm to Leogang – a small, high, open area, leading to a long, north-facing slope down to Leogang village. An eight-person gondola brings you most of the way back.

The links across these south-facing slopes work well: when traversing the whole hillside you need to descend to the valley floor only once – at Saalbach, where the main street separates Bernkogel from the slopes of Kohlmaiskopf.

The north-facing slopes are different in character – two distinct mountains, with long runs from each to the valley. An eight-seat gondola has replaced the old, queue-prone cable-car from Saalbach to **Schattberg**. The high, open, sunny slopes behind the peak are served by a fast quad.

From Schattberg, long runs go down





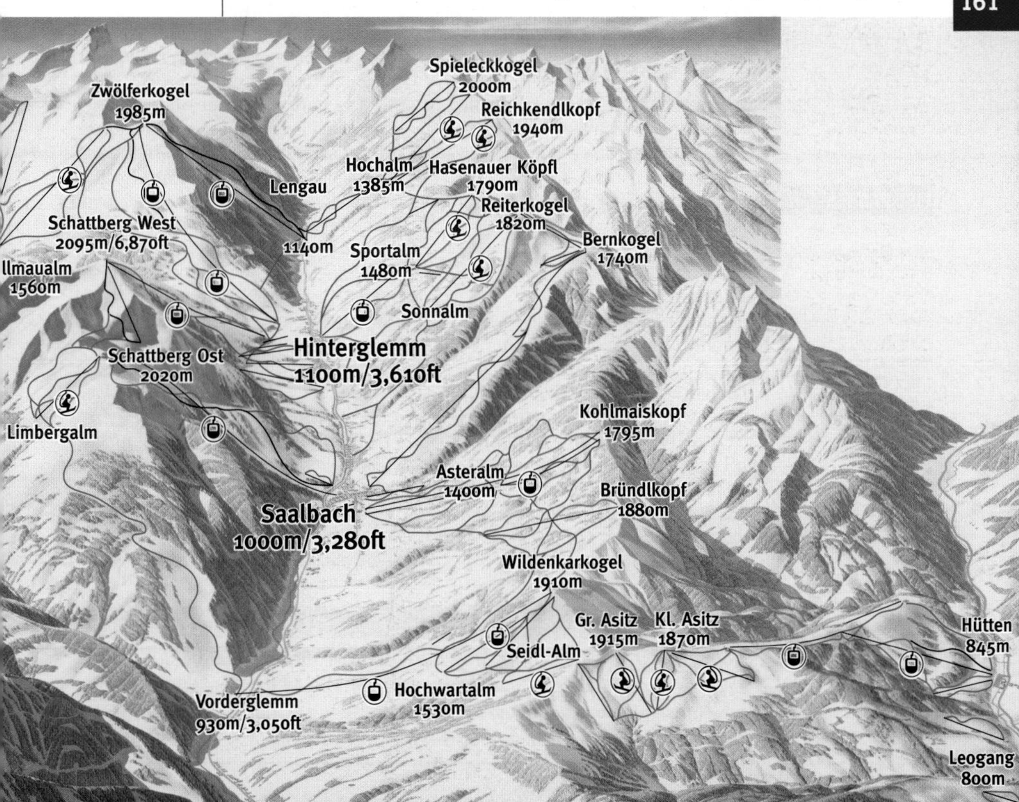

↑ Don't you just love jumps and rollers like these – they are so much easier to avoid than moguls

SAALBACH-HINTERGLEMM TOURIST OFFICE





## LIFT PASSES

**Skicircus Saalbach Hinterglemm Leogang**
Covers Saalbach, Hinterglemm and Leogang lifts, and the ski-bus.

**Main pass**
1 day €34.50
6 days €164

**Children**
Under 19: 6 days €147.50
Under 16: 6 days €82
Under 6: free pass

**Notes**
Part-day passes available.

**Alternative pass**
Salzburg Super Ski Card covers all lifts and pistes in Salzburgerland including Zell am See, Kaprun, Schladming and Bad Gastein.

to Saalbach, Vorderglemm and Hinterglemm. From the last, lifts go not only to Schattberg but also to the other north-facing hill, **Zwölferkogel**, served by a two-stage eight-seater gondola. A six-pack (new for last season) and drag-lift serve open slopes on the sunny side of the peak, and a gondola provides a link from Lengau and the south-facing Hochalm.

The Hinterglemm nursery slopes are well used, and floodlit every evening.

### TERRAIN-PARKS
***Excellent***

There's a large half-pipe on Bernkogel above Saalbach, another below Seidl-Alm and terrain-parks on the north-facing slopes just above Hinterglemm (floodlit) and below Kl. Asitz on the way to Leogang. (The Asitzmulden T-bar serving this one was replaced by a six-pack last season – a great improvement.) There are also dedicated 'carving' and 'mogul' zones on the pistes.

### SNOW RELIABILITY
***A tale of two sides***

The south-facing slopes are in the majority, and can suffer when the sun comes out. Most are above 1400m/4,600ft, which helps. The north-facing slopes keep their snow better but can get icy. The long north-facing run down to Leogang often has the best snow in the area. Piste maintenance is good, and snowmaking covers many top-to-bottom runs – but the low altitude is a problem that won't go away.

### FOR EXPERTS
***Little steep stuff***

There are few challenging slopes. Off-piste guides are available, but snow conditions and forest tend to limit the potential. The main attractions are the north-facing slopes. The long (4km/2.5 mile) Nordabfahrt run beneath the Schattberg gondola is a genuine black – a fine fast bash first thing in the morning if it has been groomed. The Zwölferkogel Nordabfahrt at Hinterglemm is less consistent, but its grading is justified by a few short, steeper pitches. The World Cup downhill run from Zwölferkogel is interesting, as is the 5km/3 mile Schattberg West-Hinterglemm red (and its scenic 'ski route' variant).

### FOR INTERMEDIATES
***Paradise***

This area is ideal for both the mileage-hungry piste-basher and the more leisurely cruiser. For those looking for more of a challenge, the most direct routes down from Hochalm, Reiterkogel, Kohlmaiskopf and Hochwartalm are good fun. Only the delightful blue from Bernkogel into Saalbach – 'the ultimate cruiser', to quote a recent visitor – gets really crowded at times. The alternative long ski route is very pleasant, taking you through forest and meadows.

The north-facing area has some more challenging runs, with excellent relentless reds from both Schattberg West and Zwölferkogel, and a section of relatively high, open slopes around Zwölferkogel. None of the black runs is beyond an adventurous intermediate. The long, pretty cruise to Vorderglemm gets you right away from lifts.

Our favourite intermediate run is the long, off-the-main-circuit cruise on north-facing snow down to Leogang.

### FOR BEGINNERS
***Best for improvers***

Saalbach's two nursery slopes are right next to the village centre. But they are south-facing and the upper one gets a lot of through-traffic. The lower one is very small but the lift is free.

## boarding

*Saalbach is great for boarding. Slopes are extensive, lifts are mainly chairs and gondolas (though there are some connecting drags), and there are pistes to appeal to beginners, intermediates and experts alike – with few flats to negotiate. For experienced boarders, there's off-piste terrain between the lifts.*

Pretty Saalbach with the splendid Nordabfahrt black run in the background ➔

SAALBACH-HINTERGLEMM TOURIST OFFICE

Alternatives are trips to the short, easy runs at Bernkogel and Schattberg.

Hinterglemm's spacious nursery area is separate from the main slopes. It is north-facing, so lacks sun in midwinter, but is more reliable for snow later on.

There are lots of easy blue runs to move on to, especially on the south-facing side of the valley.

**FOR CROSS-COUNTRY**
***Go to Zell am See***

Trails run beside the road along the valley floor from Saalbach to Vorderglemm and between Hinterglemm and the valley end at Lindlingalm. In mid-winter these 10km/6 miles of trails get very little sun, and are not very exciting. The countryside beyond nearby Zell am See offers more scope.

**QUEUES**
***Main bottleneck eliminated***

Queues are a problem only in high season, when the lifts from Saalbach up the south-facing slopes can cause waits of up to 15 minutes at peak times, which include the end as well as the start of the day. Replacement of the Schattberg cable-car by a gondola has eliminated the other regular queue, but it has increased pressure on the double chair to Schattberg West that you need to get to Hinterglemm. High-season queues can also arise for the chair to Hasenauer Köpfl and the drag to Bründlkopf. The new gondola due to replace the double chairs towards Schattberg from Hinterglemm should eliminate queues there at the end of the day.

**MOUNTAIN RESTAURANTS**
***Excellent quality and quantity***

The area is liberally scattered with around 40 attractive huts that serve good food. Many have pleasant rustic interiors and a lively ambience.

On the south-facing slopes, the Panoramaalm on the Kohlmaiskopf slope, Thurneralm close to Bründlkopf and Walleggalm on Hochalm serve particularly good food. Across in the Hinterglemm direction, the 'enterprising' Rosswaldhütte is recommended, not least for its 'excellent rösti'. The little Bernkogelhütte, overlooking Saalbach, has a great atmosphere. Reporters recommend the Bärnalm near the top of the Bernkogel chair – 'good food, good value'.

The Wildenkarkogel Hütte has a big terrace and possibly the loudest mountain-top music we've heard, with resident DJ from mid-morning. The Alte Schmiede at the top of the Leogang gondola, with rustic decor including water wheels, is recommended for its 'good food' including 'the best pizza in the area', although you may have to wait for it.

The Simalalm at the base of the Limbergalm quad chair is 'great for the sun and the views'. On the north-facing slopes, the Bergstadl halfway down the red run from Schattberg West has stunning views and good food. Ellmaualm, at the bottom of the Zehner lift has been praised, the toilets being an 'outstanding' feature. The 12er-Treff umbrella bar at the top of the Zwölferkogel gondola is good for lounging in the sun.

## SCHOOLS

**Saalbach**

**Fürstauer**
t 8444
fuerstauer@ skischule-saalbach.at

**Aamadall**
t 668256
aamadall@ aamadall.com

**Hinterholzer**
t 7607
info@schischule-hinterholzer.at

**Zink**
t 0664 162 3655
zink@aon.at

**Snowboard**
t 20047
school@board.at

**easy ski**
t 0699 111 80010
skischule@easyski.at

**Hinterglemm**

**Hinterglemmer**
t 63460
snow-fun@ saalbach.net

**Activ**
t 0676 517 1325
info@skischule-activ.at





**Classes**
(Fürstauer prices)
6 days (4hr) €164

**Private lessons**
€90 for 2hr, for 1 or 2 people; extra person €10

## CHILDREN

Several hotels have nurseries

**Ski schools**
Some take children in miniclubs from about age 3 and can provide lunchtime care. From about age 4½, children can join ski school (€139 for 6 days – Fürstauer prices)

## GETTING THERE

**Air** Salzburg 90km/56 miles (2hr); Munich 218km/135 miles (3½hr).

**Rail** Zell am See 19km/12 miles (40min); hourly buses.

### SCHOOLS AND GUIDES
***An excess of choice***

We're all in favour of competition but visitors to Saalbach-Hinterglemm may feel that they are faced with rather too much of this particular good thing, with no fewer than eight schools to choose from. We have had conflicting reports of the Fürstauer school. One visitor last year said it was 'terrific' and the instructors 'took great care of our children', who made excellent progress. But an adult beginner had some complaints. A Hinterglemm boarder had 'worthwhile' lessons with Hinterglemmer.

### FACILITIES FOR CHILDREN
***Hinterglemm tries harder***

Saalbach doesn't go out of its way to sell itself to families, although it does have a ski kindergarten. Hinterglemm has some good hotel-based nursery facilities – the one at the Theresia is reportedly excellent.

## STAYING THERE

### HOW TO GO
***Cheerful doesn't mean cheap***

**Chalets** We are aware of a few 'club hotels' but Saalbach isn't really a chalet resort.

**Hotels** There are a large number of hotels in both villages, mainly 3-star and above. Be aware that some central hotels are affected by disco noise.

**Saalbach**

((((4 **Alpenhotel** (6666) Luxurious, with open-fire lounge, disco, small pool.

((((4 **Berger's Sporthotel** (6577) Liveliest of the top hotels, with a daily tea dance, and disco. Good pool.

((((4 **Kendler** (62250) Position second to none, right next to the Bernkogel chair. Classy, expensive, good food.

((((4 **Saalbacher Hof** (71110) Retains a friendly feel despite its large size.

((((4 **Gartenhotel** (71440) 'Small, good quality with sophisticated, simple, low calorie food,' says a 2004 reporter.

(((3 **Haider** (6228) Best-positioned of the 3-stars, right next to the main lifts.

(((3 **Kristiana** (6253) Near enough to lifts but away from night-time noise. 'Excellent food.' Sauna, steam bath.

(((3 **König** (6384) Cheaper 3-star and more basic rooms.

**Hinterglemm**

((((4 **Theresia** (71140) Hinterglemm's top hotel, and one of the best for families. Out towards Saalbach, but nursery slopes nearby. Pool.



((((4 **Egger** (63220) 'I'll stay here next time, on the slopes,' says a reader.

(((3 **Wolf** (63460) Small but well-equipped 4-star. 'Especially good' food, excellent position. Pool.

(((3 **Sonnblick** (6408) Convenient 3-star in a 'quiet location' with 'friendly service' and 'the comfiest holiday beds I have slept in', says a guest.

((2 **Haus Ameshofer** (8119) Beside piste at Reiterkogel lift. 'Great value ski-in, ski-out B&B,' says a reporter.

**Self-catering** There's a big choice of apartments for independent travellers.

### EATING OUT
***Wide choice of hotel restaurants***

This is essentially a half-board resort, with few non-hotel restaurants. Peter's restaurant, at the top of Saalbach's main street, is atmospheric and serves excellent meat dishes cooked on hot stones. One reader enjoyed the excellent food, with 'an emphasis on the meatier, richer dishes', at the Hotel Neuhaus. The Wallner Pizzeria on the main street is good value. The Auwirt hotel on the outskirts of Saalbach has a good à la carte restaurant.

### APRES-SKI
***It rocks from early on***

Après-ski is very lively from mid-afternoon until the early hours and can get positively wild. In Saalbach the rustic Hinterhagalm at the top of the main nursery slope is packed by 3.30pm. When it closes around 6pm, the crowds slide down to Bauer's Ski-alm and try to get into the already heaving old cow shed to continue drinking and dancing. The tiny Zum Turn (next door to the church and cemetery) is a medieval jail that also gets packed from 4pm until late.

Castello's 'at the bottom of the main street' was the place to be, according to a visitor last year. The Neuhaus Taverne has live music and

↑ Tiny Leogang is attractive, but it's a bus-ride from the gondola into the main slopes

SAALFELDEN LEOGANG TOURISTIK GMBH

## ACTIVITIES

**Indoor** Swimming pools, sauna, massage, solarium, tennis

**Outdoor** Ice-rink, curling, tobogganing, snow-shoeing, sleigh rides, 40km/25 miles of cleared paths

**Phone numbers**

**Saalbach**
From elsewhere in Austria add the prefix 06541.
From abroad use the prefix +43 6541.

**Leogang**
From elsewhere in Austria add the prefix 06583.
From abroad use the prefix +43 6583.

## TOURIST OFFICES

**Saalbach**
**t** 680068
contact@saalbach.com
www.saalbach.com

**Leogang**
**t** 8234
office@sale-touristik.at
www.leogang-saalfelden.at

attracts a mature clientele. Bobby's Pub is cheap, often full of British school kids, has bowling and serves Guinness. King's Disco livens up after midnight. Classic Bar is recommended for its 'smart lap-dancing room'. Arena disco has go-go dancers and is very popular, as is Bergers Sporthotel Galerie. A reader recommends the Bergeralm: '3km up the toboggan track, marvellous atmosphere and reindeer steaks before a 1am descent.'

In Hinterglemm there are a number of ice bars, which are crowded immediately after the lifts close, including the Gute Stube of Hotel Dorfschmiede in the centre of town with loud music blasting out and people spilling into the street. A wider age group enjoys the live music later on at the smart, friendly Tanzhimmel – an open, glass-fronted bar with a dance floor. The Hexenhäusl gets packed and has an animated model of a witch revealing her undergarments. A similar fascination with moving models is demonstrated at the rustic Goasstall by the piste down from Sportalm, where a model goat is equally revealing (and where real goats graze behind glass near the men's toilet). Bla Bla is small, modern and smart, with reasonable prices. The Almbar has good music and some dancing.

Tour operator reps organise tobogganing, sleigh rides and bowling.

### OFF THE SLOPES

***Surprisingly little to do***

Saalbach is not very entertaining if you're not into winter sports. There are few shops other than supermarkets and ski shops. Walks tend to be restricted to the paths alongside the cold cross-country trails or along the Saalbach toboggan run to Spielberghs. But there are excursions to Kitzbühel and Salzburg.

## Leogang 800m/2,620ft

A much less expensive alternative to Saalbach-Hinterglemm.

### THE RESORT

Leogang is an attractive, although rather scattered, quiet, farming community-cum-mountain resort. It's best to stay at Hütten, near the lift.

### THE MOUNTAIN

The village is linked to the eastern end of the Saalbach-Hinterglemm circuit.

**Slopes** A gondola from Hütten takes you into the ski area. The local slopes tend to be delightfully quiet.

**Snow reliability** The local slopes have some of the best snow in the region, being north- and east-facing, with snowmaking on the run home.

**Experts** Not much challenge locally.

**Intermediates** Great long red run cruise home from the top of the gondola. Plus the circuit to explore.

**Beginners** Good nursery slopes by the village, and short runs to progress to.

**Snowboarding** The whole area is great for boarding and there's a terrain-park.

**Cross-country** The best in the area. There are 20km/12 miles of trails, plus a panoramic high-altitude trail.

**Queues** No local problems.

**Mountain restaurants** A couple of good local huts.

**Schools and guides** Leogang Altenberger school has a high reputation – 'excellent service and lessons; highly recommended'.

**Facilities for children** There is a non-ski nursery, and children can start school at four years old.

### STAYING THERE

**Hotels** The luxury Krallerhof (82460) has its own nursery lift, which can be used to get across to the main lift station. The 4-star Salzburgerhof (73100) is one of the best-placed hotels, within a two-minute walk of the gondola; sauna and steam.

**Self-catering** There are quiet apartments available.

**Eating out** Restaurants are hotel-based. The upscale Krallerhof has the excellent food you would expect. The much cheaper Gasthof Hüttwirt has a high reputation for home cooking.

**Après-ski** The rustic old chalet Kraller Alm is very much the focal tea-time and evening rendezvous.

**Off the slopes** Excursions to Salzburg are possible.

SCHLADMING TOURIST OFFICE

# Schladming

*Old and pretty town with extensive intermediate slopes*

## COSTS

①②③④⑤⑥

## RATINGS

**The slopes**

| | |
|---|---|
| Snow | **** |
| Extent | *** |
| Expert | ** |
| Intermediate | **** |
| Beginner | **** |
| Convenience | *** |
| Queues | **** |
| Mountain restaurants | **** |

**The rest**

| | |
|---|---|
| Scenery | *** |
| Resort charm | **** |
| Off-slope | **** |

## NEWS

For 2003/04 a new six-pack with covers replaced two T-bars on Hauser Kaibling. This is all part of the huge investment in the area and another piece in the plan to encourage people eastwards towards Hauser Kaibling and so relieve the pressure on Planai and Hochwurzen at peak times.



## REPORTS WANTED

**Recently we have had few reports on this resort. If you go there, please do send us a report.**

**The best reports earn a copy of the next edition, and can lead to free lift passes in future.**

**See page 10.**

- ⊞ Extensive slopes on four interlinked mountains
- ⊞ Excellent slopes for intermediates
- ⊞ Extensive snowmaking operation and good piste maintenance
- ⊞ Very sheltered slopes, among trees
- ⊞ Lots of good mountain restaurants
- ⊞ Charming town with friendly people and a life independent of tourism
- ⊞ Ski Alliance Amadé lift pass covers wide range of nearby resorts

- ⊟ Slopes lack variety
- ⊟ Very little to entertain experts, on- or off-piste
- ⊟ Most runs are north-facing, so can be shady and cold in early season
- ⊟ Nursery slopes (at Rohrmoos) are inconvenient unless you stay beside them – and beginners are expected to pay for a full lift pass

**Since its four previously separate mountains were linked by lifts and pistes, Schladming has been able to compete with major resorts that are better known internationally. A keen intermediate who wants to make the most of the links can get a real sense of travelling around on the snow. And as the list of plus-points suggests, we see many attractions in the place.**

**If you like your slopes to be reassuringly consistent, Schladming has a strong claim on your attention. If, on the other hand, you like the spice of variety and the thrill of a serious challenge, you might find it all rather tame.**

**The resort does not offer one of Austria's wildest après-ski scenes, but that doesn't seem to bother most of our reporters, who enjoy its established, valley-town ambience.**

## THE RESORT

The old town of Schladming has a long skiing tradition and has hosted World Cup races for many years. It sits at the foot of Planai, one of four mountains that are now linked by lifts and pistes to offer 115km/71 miles of runs. A gondola starting close to the centre goes most of the way up this home mountain. To the east is the small, rustic village of Haus, where a cable-car and gondola go up to the highest of the four linked mountains, Hauser Kaibling. From the western suburbs of Schladming there are chair-lifts back towards Planai and on towards the next mountain to the west, Hochwurzen. The latter chain of lifts passes through Rohrmoos, a quiet, scattered village set on what is effectively a giant nursery slope.

The town (it is definitely not a village) has a charming, traffic-free main square, prettily lit at night, around which you'll find most of the shops, restaurants and bars (and some appealing hotels). The busy main road

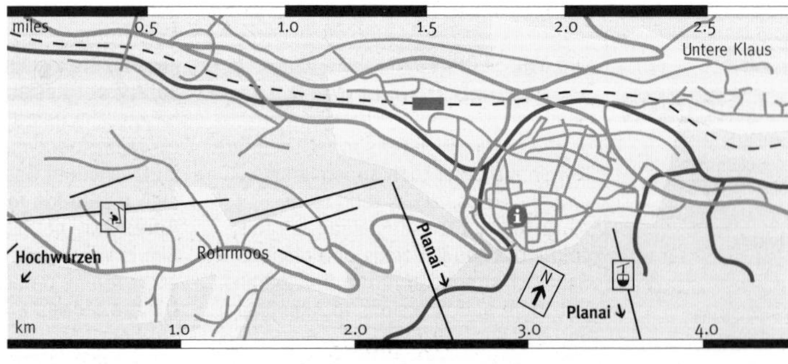

**KEY FACTS**

| Resort | 745m<br>2,440ft |
|---|---|
| For the Sportregion Schladming-Ramsau/ Dachstein area | |
| Slopes | 745-2015m<br>2,440-6,610ft |
| Lifts | 88 |
| Pistes | 167km<br>104 miles |
| Blue | 29% |
| Red | 61% |
| Black | 10% |
| Snowmaking | 100% |
| For Schladming only | |
| Slopes | 745-2015m<br>2,440-6,610ft |
| Lifts | 52 |
| Pistes | 115km<br>71 miles |

bypasses the town and is separated from it by a river. Much of the accommodation is close to the centre – just a few minutes' walk from the Planai gondola – but it can be noisy into the early hours because of nearby bars. The modern sports centre and tennis halls are five minutes' walk from the centre. Rohrmoos makes an excellent base for beginners who aren't looking for lively nightlife. Haus is preferable for those looking for more of a village atmosphere.

It can be quicker to get to a particular hill by car, taxi or bus rather than on skis or board – though you certainly don't need to and we've had mixed reports about the efficiency of the bus services. Reporters have been impressed with the free internet access at the top of the Planai gondola: 'We sent emails instead of postcards,' said one.

Apart from the main slopes we describe here, there are five or six other separate mountains. To the east, beyond Haus, is Galsterbergalm, above Pruggern. Fageralm is above Forstau, up a side valley to the west. North of the main valley, Ramsau has its own low slopes and access to the Dachstein glacier. And near Gröbming is the small area of Stoderzinken. The Ski Alliance Amadé lift pass also covers many other resorts in this part of Austria. Trips to Bad Gastein are feasible by rail but include at least one change. Drivers can also visit Wagrain/Flachau, Kleinarl and Maria Alm. Tour operators organise day trips to other resorts, too. Snow-sure Obertauern is not far away but is not included on the lift pass.

## THE MOUNTAINS

Most pistes are on the wooded north-facing slopes above the main valley, with some going into the side valleys higher up, and there are some open slopes above the trees. Again this year, we have had a complaint about the piste maps and discrepancies between different versions ('runs red on one, blue on the other; marked on one, not on the other'). But another reporter found signposting 'excellent' and liked the descriptions at the start of many runs.

### THE SLOPES
***Four linked sectors – and more***

Each of the linked sectors is quite a serious mountain with a variety of lifts and runs to play on. **Planai** and **Hauser Kaibling** are linked at altitude via the high, wooded bowl between them. In contrast, the links with **Hochwurzen** (where you can try night skiing or boarding; though it is not included on the lift pass) and the fourth linked mountain, **Reiteralm**, are at valley level. So although the links offer the ability to travel around, getting around the whole area can take time – and involves some uninteresting linking runs. The link between Planai and Hochwurzen involves riding a lift through a tunnel, whichever way you are travelling. Some people who want to spend time on Reiteralm prefer to get the bus, or a taxi, to the lift base at Pichl or Gleiming.

All the mountains have fairly similar heavily wooded terrain, with mainly red runs of much the same pitch.



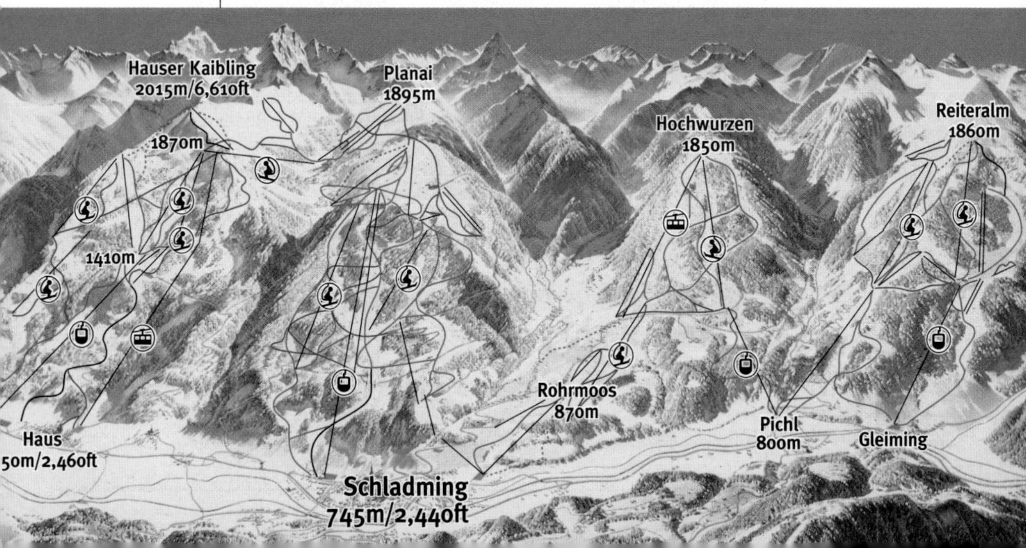

Goodness knows why they allowed this monstrosity to be built near the top of Hauser Kaibling. Apart from that it's a lovely view! ➔

TVB HAUS IM ENNSTAL

## LIFT PASSES

**Ski Alliance Amadé Ski Pass**
Covers over 270 lifts in more than 30 ski resorts in the Gastein valley and Grossarl; Salzburger Sportwelt; Hochkönigs Winterreich; also buses, trains and road tolls between the resorts.

**Main pass**
1 day €33.50
6 days €161

**Children**
Under 20: 6 days €148.50
Under 17: 6 days €80.50
Under 7: free pass

**Notes**
Part-day tickets are available.

**Alternative pass**
Salzburg Super Ski Card covers all lifts and pistes in Salzburgerland including Zell am See, Kaprun and Saalbach-Hinterglemm.

## SCHOOLS

**Tritscher**
t 22137
office@tritscher.at

**Blue Tomato (snowboarding)**
t 24223
info@blue-tomato.at

**Hopl**
t 61268
info@hopl.at

**Classes**
(Tritscher prices)
5 half-days (2½hr am) €110

**Private lessons**
Half day €90; each additional person €15





### TERRAIN-PARKS
***Three to try***
There are two terrain-parks and half-pipes on the main linked area, with a park on the Galsterbergalm.

### SNOW RELIABILITY
***Excellent in cold weather***
Schladming's impressive snowmaking operation makes it a particularly good choice for early holidays; and the northerly orientation of the slopes and good maintenance help keep the slopes in better shape than in some neighbouring resorts. Schladming claims 100% snowmaking, and certainly the main runs to the valley have full cover. Be wary of the steep bottom part of the World Cup downhill run back to town – it can get extremely icy. The best natural snow is usually found on Reiteralm and Hochwurzen.

### FOR EXPERTS
***Strictly intermediate stuff***
Schladming's status as a World Cup downhill venue doesn't make it macho. The steep black finish to the Men's Downhill course and the moderate mogul runs at the top of Planai and Hauser Kaibling are the only really challenging slopes. Hauser Kaibling's off-piste is good, although limited.

### FOR INTERMEDIATES
***Red runs rule***
The area is ideal for intermediate cruising. The majority of runs are red but it's often difficult to distinguish them from many of the blues.

The open sections at the top of Planai and Hauser Kaibling have some more challenging slopes. And the two World Cup pistes, and the red that runs parallel to the Haus downhill course, are ideal for fast intermediates.

Hauser Kaibling has a lovely meandering blue running from top to bottom for the less confident intermediates, and Reiteralm has some gentle blues with good snow. Runs are well groomed, so intermediates will find the slopes generally flattering.

### FOR BEGINNERS
***Good slopes but poorly sited***
Complete beginners generally start on the extensive but low-altitude Rohrmoos nursery area – fine if you are based there, a bus-ride away if you are not. Another novice area near the top of Planai is more convenient for most people and has better snow, but the runs are less gentle.

### FOR CROSS-COUNTRY
***Extensive network of trails***
Given sufficient snow-cover, there are 300km/186 miles of trails in the region, and the World Championships have been held at nearby Ramsau. There are local loops along the main valley floor and in the valleys between Planai and Hochwurzen.

### QUEUES
***Avoid peak periods***
The area (especially the Planai gondola first thing) can have queues at peak-season and weekends. The upgraded gondola at Haus has relieved pressure there, but the Reiteralm gondola is slow. Reporters recommend avoiding peak February dates and going to Fageralm on busy days. A 2004 reporter found no queues at all in mid-March.

## boarding

*Schladming is popular with boarders. Most lifts on the spread-out mountains are gondolas or chairs, with some short drags around. The area is ideal for beginners and intermediates, except when the lower slopes are icy, though there are few exciting challenges for expert boarders bar the off-piste tree runs. The Blue Tomato snowboard shop – reportedly 'well organised' – runs the specialist snowboard school.*

## ACTIVITIES

**Indoor** Swimming pool, sauna, bowling, indoor tennis court, squash, museum

**Outdoor** Ice skating, curling, tobogganing, sleigh rides, 30km/19 miles of cleared paths

## CHILDREN

**Kinderclub Rohrmoos**
Takes children from 18mnth.

**Ski schools**
Take children from age 4 (€190 for 5 days including lunch – Tritscher price).

## GETTING THERE

**Air** Salzburg 90km/ 56 miles (1½hr).

**Rail** Main line station in resort.

**Phone numbers**
**Schladming**
From elsewhere in Austria add the prefix 03687.
From abroad use the prefix +43 3687.

**Haus**
From elsewhere in Austria add the prefix 03686.
From abroad use the prefix +43 3686.

## TOURIST OFFICES

**Schladming**
**t** 22777
info@schladming-rohrmoos.com
www.schladming-rohrmoos.com

**Haus**
**t** 22340
info@haus.at
www.haus.at

### MOUNTAIN RESTAURANTS
***Plenty of nice places***

There are plenty of attractive rustic restaurants in all sectors, though Planai probably has the edge. A reporter returning to Austria after a decade skiing elsewhere, said, 'It was an absolute delight to be reminded of what I had been missing!' Onkel Willi's Hütte is popular for its live music, open fire, indoor nooks and crannies and large terrace, Mitterhausalm is good, and the Schladminger Hütte at the top of the Planai gondola has 'great food'. The Knapplhof at Hauser Kaibling is full of ski racing mementos.

### SCHOOLS AND GUIDES
***Generally okay reports***

We have generally had good reports in the past, but we lack recent ones.

### FACILITIES FOR CHILDREN
***Rohrmoos is the place***

The extensive gentle slopes of Rohrmoos are ideal for building up youngsters' confidence.

## STAYING THERE

### HOW TO GO
***Packages mean hotels***

Packaged accommodation is in hotels and pensions, but there are plenty of apartments for independent travellers.

**Hotels** Most of the accommodation is in modestly priced pensions but there are also a few more upmarket hotels.

((((4 **Sporthotel Royer** (200) Big, smart and comfortable, a few minutes' walk from the main Planai lift. Pool, sauna.

(((3 **Alte Post** (22571) Characterful old inn with great position on the main square. Good food, but some rooms small and a reporter complains of her bed being an uncomfortable sofa-bed.

(((3 **Zum Stadttor** (24525) Similarly priced, although less charming and well placed. 'Comfortable with excellent food,' says a reporter.

(((3 **Kirchenwirt** (22435) Just off the main square. 'Traditional atmosphere, wonderful food,' says a visitor.

(((3 **Neue Post** (22105) Large rooms, friendly, good food, central.

(((3 **Schladmingerhof** (23525) Bright, modern 'fairly basic' chalet in peaceful position, out in Untere Klaus.

(((3 **Zum Kaiserweg** (22038) Family run. Very near the Planai West Tunnel lift. 'Good value, excellent food.'

**Self-catering** Haus Girik (22663) is close to the gondola.

### EATING OUT
***Some good places***

We had a great meal at Fritzi's Gasthaus (which has a good reputation). Other recommendations include the Kirchenwirt hotel ('excellent home cooking'), Giovanni's (for pizza), Gasthof Brunner ('good value') and Talbachschenke ('good grills and atmosphere'). Hotels Neue and Alte Post are 'good but expensive'.

### APRES-SKI
***Explore the side streets***

Some of the mountain restaurants are lively at the end of the afternoon, but reporters agree that down in the town there's a disappointing lack of tea-time animation. Charly's Treff (with umbrella bar) opposite the Planai gondola is the main exception (and has great photos of local hero Arnold Schwarzenegger). The Siglu also rocks from 3pm.

There is, however, no lack of options later on – many of the central bars open later and stay open until dawn. The local Schladminger beer is worth a try. Popular spots include the local brewpub Schwalbenbräu. The Beisl is a smart, beautiful bar attracting a varied age group. Hanglbar has wooden decor and middle-of-the-road music and occasional karaoke. Maria's Mexican is 'relaxing' with chilled music and margueritas. The Porta gets very crowded and has live music. The Sonderbar is a disco with three bars.

### OFF THE SLOPES
***Good for all but walkers***

Non-skiers are fairly well catered for. Some mountain restaurants are easily reached on foot. The town shops and museum are worth a look. Train trips to Salzburg are easy (and recommended as worth a day off the slopes by several readers). Buses run to the old walled town of Radstadt. There's a public pool and ice rink.

## Haus 750m/2,460ft

Haus is a real village with a life of its own and its own ski schools and kindergartens. The user-friendly nursery slopes are between the village and the gondola. There's a railway station, so excursions are easy, but off-slope activities and nightlife are very limited. Hotel prices are generally lower than in Schladming. Hotel Gürtl (2383) has been recommended for 'good food and ambience'.

FRANK HEUER

# Sölden

*Dynamic, snow-sure, high-altitude area, with throbbing nightlife*

**COSTS**

①②③④⑤⑥

**RATINGS**

**The slopes**

| | |
|---|---|
| Snow | ***** |
| Extent | *** |
| Expert | *** |
| Intermediate | **** |
| Beginner | ** |
| Convenience | ** |
| Queues | *** |
| Mountain restaurants | *** |

**The rest**

| | |
|---|---|
| Scenery | *** |
| Resort charm | ** |
| Off-slope | ** |

**NEWS**

The new two-stage Schwarze Schneid gondola further speeds up access to the two glaciers. For 2004/05 the Seiterkar lift – the key lift back from the Tiefenbach glacier – is to be upgraded to a six-seat covered chair.



**REPORTS WANTED**

Recently we have had few reports on this resort. If you go there, please do send us a report.

The best reports earn a copy of the next edition, and can lead to free lift passes in future.

See page 10.

- ✚ Excellent snow reliability, with access to two glaciers
- ✚ Fairly extensive network of slopes suited to adventurous intermediates
- ✚ Impressive lift system, now linking with glacier slopes
- ✚ Very lively après-ski/nightlife

- ▬ Busy road through sprawling village
- ▬ Some central hotels are distant from the two main access lifts
- ▬ Inconvenient beginners' slopes
- ▬ Drink-fuelled nightlife too rowdy for many visitors
- ▬ Limited off-slope activities

**Sölden is virtually unknown on the UK package market, but deserves a serious look from keen intermediates. It has recently invested massively in new lifts to exploit the Rettenbach and Tiefenbach glaciers and link them to the lower slopes. There are some seriously long runs, as well as some seriously rowdy après-ski (which can be avoided by staying off the main street).**

## THE RESORT

Despite its traditional Tirolean-style buildings and tree-filled valley, Sölden is no beauty: it is a large, traffic-filled place that sprawls along both sides of a river and busy main road. The resort attracts a young, lively crowd – mostly Dutch and German – bent on partying.

Gondolas from opposite ends of town go up to Sölden's home slopes – the peak of Gaislachkogl and the lift junction of Giggijoch, above the satellite resort of Hochsölden. A free shuttle-bus serves both lift stations.

## THE MOUNTAIN

The two similar-sized home sectors are linked by chair-lifts out of the Rettenbachtal that separates them. The Rettenbach and Tiefenbach glaciers – 15km/9 miles away by road, and until quite recently closed in winter – are now connected by a series of fast lifts from Rotkogl. The piste from the Rettenbach glacier to the Tiefenbach glacier goes through a tunnel. The return trip is by chair-lift.

**Slopes** Practically all the slopes you spend your days on are above the trees. Both main sectors have red runs through trees to the village – but a reporter describes the one down from Hochsölden as 'a nightmare – mogulled, narrow and crowded'.

**Terrain-parks** Two in winter above Giggijoch: the BASE boarder park has a half-pipe, kickers and rails; the BASE Easycross area has a boarder-cross run with waves and jumps.

**Snow reliability** The slopes are high and north-east-facing; there is some snowmaking; and there are two extensive glaciers. What more could you ask for?

**Experts** None of the black pistes dotted around Sölden's map is particularly serious, but there are quite a few non-trivial reds. And there are extensive off-piste possibilities – particularly from Gaislachkogl to the mid-station. At the top of the valley is one of the Alps' premier touring areas.

**Intermediates** Most of Sölden's main slopes are red runs ideal for keen intermediates, and there are some serious verticals to be racked up; there is a drop of over 1800m/5,910ft from the top of the new Schwarze Schneid gondola to the village – though it does involve a ski-route. There are several easy blacks, and the long, quiet piste down to Gaislachalm is ideal for high-speed cruising. Giggijoch offers gentler gradients, but gets extremely crowded.

**Beginners** The beginners' slopes are situated inconveniently – just above the village at Innerwald – and are prone to poor snow. Near-beginners can use the blues at Giggijoch.

**Snowboarding** Sölden is not ideal for beginners but there's great free-riding for experienced boarders. And all drag-lifts can be avoided.

**Cross-country** There are a couple of uninspiring loops by the river, plus small areas at Zwieselstein and Vent.

**Queues** The main bottleneck – the Seiterkar triple chair back from the Tiefenbach glacier – should be eased for 2004/05 by a new six-pack.

## KEY FACTS

| | |
|---|---|
| Resort | 1380m<br>4,530ft |
| Slopes | 1380-3250m<br>4,530-10,660ft |
| Lifts | 34 |
| Pistes | 149km<br>93 miles |
| Blue | 32% |
| Red | 52% |
| Black | 16% |
| Snowmaking | 35 guns |



**Mountain restaurants** The self-service places around Giggijoch can get extremely crowded – try Schwarzkogl on run 24 instead, says a regular visitor. She also recommends Gampealm, towards the end of piste 11, an atmospheric old hut with 'good value food and substantial soups'. To escape the crowds try the cluster of places around Gaislachalm (Silbertal has 'good variety, large portions and 1 litre beers') – or head down the excellent red piste 7 to the calm, rustic s'Pfandl at Ausserwald.

**Schools and guides** The three schools all restrict class sizes to seven or eight people.

**Facilities for children** Children of three years and up can join the ski kindergarten. There are special family lift pass deals.

**Phone numbers**
From elsewhere in Austria add the prefix 05254.
From abroad use the prefix +43 5254.

## TOURIST OFFICE

**t** 5100
info@soelden.com
www.soelden.com

## STAYING THERE

**How to go** There are few UK packages.

**Hotels** Sölden has some good hotels. The 5-star Central (22600) is the best and one of the biggest in town. The 4-star Regina (2301), by the Gaislachkogl lift is heartily recommended by a reporter. The Haus Grüner Karl B&B (2477) above town on run 7 is highly praised by a regular visitor (with restaurants for dinner '2 to 10 minutes' walk'). Self-catering apartments at the Posthäusl (31380) are of good quality.

**Eating out** Reporter recommendations include the Tavola in the hotel Rosengarten, Cafe Hubertus, Nudeltopf and Corso for pizza; and s'Pfandl at Ausserwald for Tirolean stuff.

**Après-ski** Sölden's après-ski is famous. It starts up the mountain, notably at Giggijoch, and progresses via bars in the main street – notably the greenhouse-style Dominic Bla-Bla – to countless places with live bands and throbbing discos, and table dancing and striptease at Andy's Rodelhütte. Somewhat tamer are the nightly toboggan evenings, with drinking and dancing before an exciting 6km/4 mile floodlit run back to town from the Gaislachalm mountain restaurant.

**Off the slopes** There's a sports centre, swimming pool and an ice rink. Trips to Innsbruck are possible.

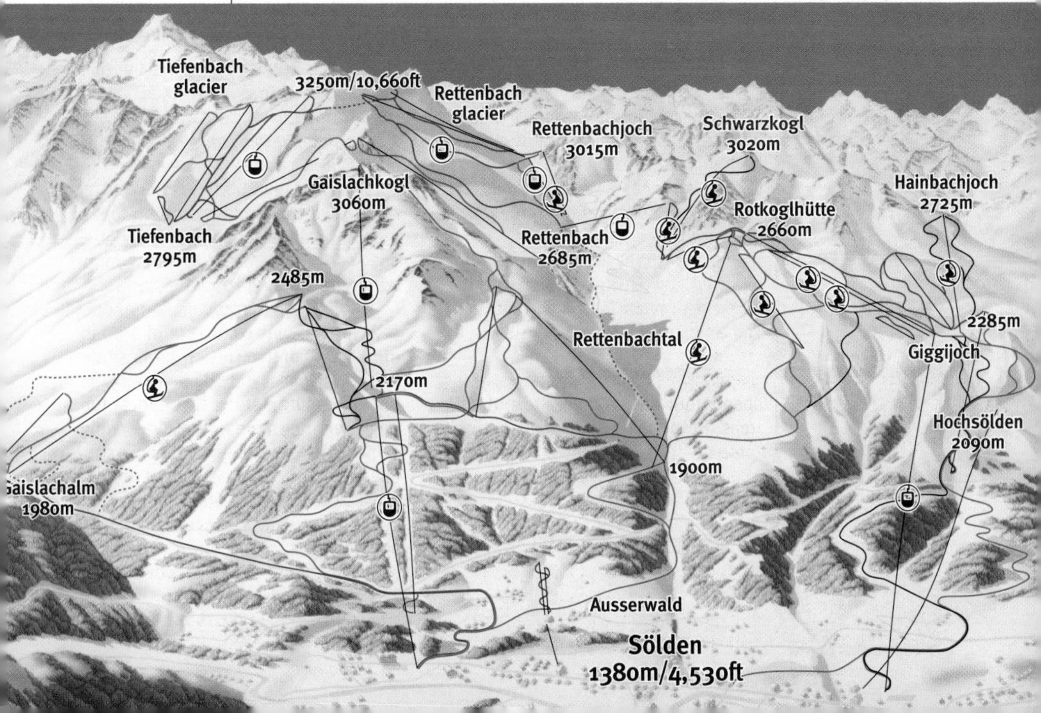

SOLL TOURIST OFFICE

# Söll

*Lively but inconvenient base for the extensive Ski Welt slopes*

## COSTS

(1)(2)(3)(4)(5)(6)

## RATINGS

| **The slopes** | |
|---|---|
| Snow | ** |
| Extent | **** |
| Expert | * |
| Intermediate | **** |
| Beginner | *** |
| Convenience | ** |
| Queues | *** |
| Mountain restaurants | ** |
| **The rest** | |
| Scenery | *** |
| Resort charm | *** |
| Off-slope | ** |

## NEWS

For 2003/04 50 new snow-guns have been added on the slopes of Brixen and Söll. Coverage in the Ski Welt now amounts to more than 160km/99 miles.

For 2004/05 a new quad will replace the Grundried T-bar which serves one of the few black runs in Söll, below Hohe Salve. And at Hopfgarten, the chair out of the village will finally be replaced by an eight-person gondola.



- + Part of Ski Welt, Austria's largest linked ski and snowboard area
- + Local slopes are the highest in the Ski Welt and north-facing, so they keep their snow relatively well
- + Plenty of cheap and cheerful pensions for those on a budget
- + Pretty village with lively après-ski
- + Massive recent investment in snowmaking has paid off, but ...

- − Ski Welt is at low altitude, and has a poor natural snow record
- − Long walk or infrequent buses from the village to the lifts
- − Little to amuse experts or to challenge good intermediates
- − Ski Welt slopes can get crowded at weekends and in high season – especially above Söll
- − Mostly short runs in local sector

**Söll has long been popular with groups of British beginners and intermediates, attracting a mixture of young singles looking for a fun time and families looking for a quiet time. In the 1980s it gained notoriety as prime lager-lout territory; it still has some loud bars but has calmed down a lot.**

**When the snow is good Söll can be a great place for a holiday – cruising the attractive and undemanding pistes of Austria's largest linked area. Its main real drawback has always been snow – or lack of it. Because of its low altitude and sunny slopes, pistes have often been slushy or bare, not just above Söll but also throughout the extensive Ski Welt circuit. But this problem has been tackled by a massive investment in snowmaking, and well over half of the Ski Welt's 250km/155 miles of piste are now covered by snowmaking – more than in any other Austrian ski area. This ensures the region's main pistes and links stay open, though it can't prevent slush and ice developing.**

**Many visitors are surprised by the small size of the village and the long distance between it and the slopes (and by the bus service).**

## THE RESORT

Söll is a small, pretty, friendly village – much smaller than you might expect from its reputation; you can explore it in a few minutes and there aren't many shops. New buildings are traditional in design and there's a huge church near the centre which, according to a reporter, is well worth a visit at dusk as the graveyard is lit with candles. The pretty scenery adds to Söll's charm, and it benefits from being off the main road through the Tirol.

The slopes are a bus- or taxi-ride or a 15-minute walk from the centre, the other side of a busy road with a pedestrian tunnel underneath. You can leave your equipment at the bottom of the gondola for a small charge. The bus service has been criticised by most reporters as being too infrequent.

There is some accommodation out near the lifts but most is in or around the village centre – a free ski-bus-ride from the slopes. Being on the edge of the village nearest the lifts is best for those who are prepared to walk to the slopes. The other side of town has the advantage that you can board the bus there before it gets too crowded. Be aware that some guest houses are literally miles from the centre and lifts, and that the ski-bus does not serve every nook and cranny of this sprawling community.

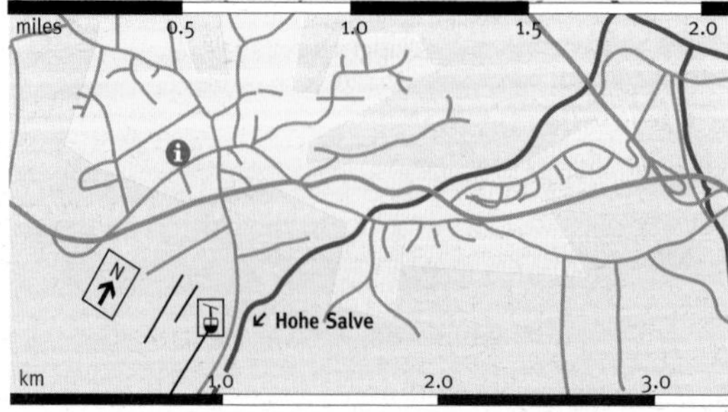

## KEY FACTS

| | |
|---|---|
| **Resort** | 700m<br>2,300ft |
| For entire Ski Welt | |
| **Slopes** | 620-1890m<br>2,030-6,200ft |
| **Lifts** | 91 |
| **Pistes** | 250km<br>155 miles |
| **Blue** | 43% |
| **Red** | 48% |
| **Black** | 9% |
| **Snowmaking** | 160km<br>99 miles |

## ON YOUR OWN?

You can team up with other skiers/ boarders by turning up at 10am or 1pm at one of seven designated points in the Ski Welt; there are stickers to identify participants, and even a web site forum for making prior arrangements.



## THE MOUNTAINS

The Ski Welt covers Hopfgarten, Brixen, Scheffau and Ellmau. It is the largest linked area in Austria, and will easily keep an early or average intermediate amused for a week. But that doesn't make it a Trois Vallées. It is basically a typically small, low, pastoral Austrian hill multiplied several times. One section is much like another, and most slopes best suit early to average intermediates. Runs are mostly short and scenery attractive rather than stunning – although the panoramic views from the Hohe Salve are impressive.

Westendorf is separate, but covered by the area pass. The Kitzbüheler Alpenskipass also covers many other resorts easily reached by car including Kitzbühel – an impressive total of 260 lifts and 680km/423 miles of pistes.

### THE SLOPES
***Short run network***

A gondola takes all but complete beginners up to the mid-mountain shelf of Hochsöll, where there are a couple of short lifts and connections in several directions.

These include an eight-person gondola to the high point of Hohe Salve. From here there are stunning views and runs down to Kälbersalve, Rigi and Hopfgarten. Rigi can also be reached by chairs and runs without going to Hohe Salve – to which it is itself linked by chairs. Rigi is also the start of runs down to Itter. From Kälbersalve you can head down south-facing runs to Brixen or up to Zinsberg and Eiberg and towards Ellmau.

A quicker way to Ellmau without taking as many south-facing slopes is by using a cable-car from Hochsöll.

We continue to receive criticism of the piste map, which is hopelessly over-ambitious in trying to show the whole area in a single view.

### TERRAIN-PARKS
***Not a major feature***

None locally but there's a popular park at Westendorf.

### SNOW RELIABILITY
***Artificial help saves the day***

With a very low average height, and important links that get a lot of sun, the snowmaking that the Ski Welt has installed in recent seasons is essential. At 160km/99 miles and covering over half the area's pistes, it is Austria's biggest snowmaking installation. We were there one January before any major snowfalls, and snowmaking was keeping the links open well. It did not, however, stop slush and ice forming.

### FOR EXPERTS
***Not a lot***

The two black runs from Hohe Salve towards Hochsöll and Kälbersalve and the black run alongside the Brixen gondola are the only challenging pistes. There are further blacks in Scheffau and Ellmau, but the main challenges are off-piste – from Brandstadl down to Söll, for example.

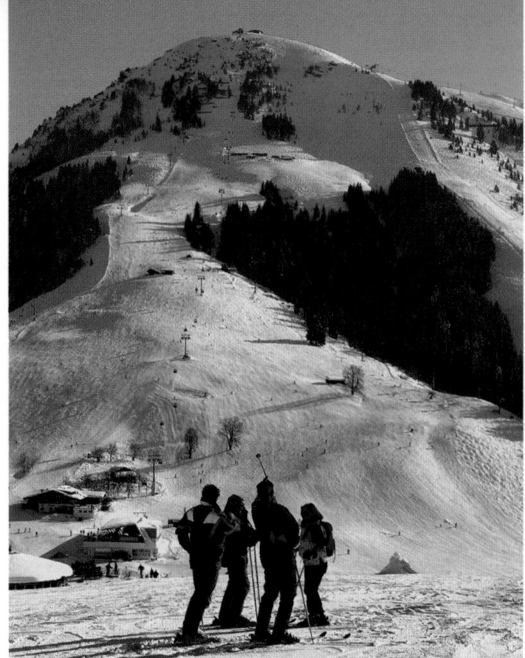

↑ By some way the most serious hill in the Ski Welt – Hohe Salve

SOLL TOURIST OFFICE





## LIFT PASSES

**Ski Welt Wilder Kaiser-Brixental**
Covers all lifts in the Wilder Kaiser-Brixental area from Going to Westendorf, and the ski-bus.

**Beginners**
Points tickets.

**Main pass**
1 day €31
6 days €153

**Children**
Under 16: 6 days €92
Under 7: free pass

**Notes**
Single ascent and part-day passes available.

**Alternative passes**
Kitzbüheler Alpenskipass covers five large areas: Schneewinkel (St Johann), Kitzbühel, Ski Welt, Wildschönau and Alpbach.

### FOR INTERMEDIATES
***Mainly easy runs***

When blessed with good snow – not something to bank on – the Ski Welt is a paradise for early intermediates and those who love easy cruising. There are lots of blue runs and many of the reds could be blue. It is a big area and you really get a feeling of travelling around. The main challenge you may find is when the snow isn't perfect – ice and slush can make even gentle slopes seem tricky. In general the most difficult slopes are those from the mid-stations to the valleys – to Blaiken, Brixen and Söll, for example.

### FOR BEGINNERS
***Excellent when snow is good***

The big area of nursery slopes between the main road and the gondola station is ideal when snow is abundant – gentle, spacious, uncrowded and free from good skiers whizzing past. But it can get icy or slushy. In poor snow the Hochsöll area is used. Near-beginners and fast learners can get home to the bottom station when the narrow blue from Hochsöll is not too icy.

### FOR CROSS-COUNTRY
***Neighbouring villages are better***

Söll has 30km/19 miles of local trails but they are less interesting than those between Hopfgarten and Kelchsau or the ones around and beyond Ellmau. Lack of snow-cover can be a problem.

### QUEUES
***Much improved***

Lift upgrades have greatly improved this once queue-prone area. The gondola at Scheffau-Blaiken has cut the weekend queues there. When snow is poor, the links between Zinsberg and Eiberg get crowded.

### MOUNTAIN RESTAURANTS
***Good, but crowded***

There are quite a few jolly little chalets scattered about, but we have had a few complaints of insufficient seating and long queues. The atmospheric Stöckalm (a converted cow shed), Kraftalm and Gründlalm are all near Hochsöll. The Hochsöll itself is reportedly 'excellent'. The highly rated Gasthof Hohe Salve (top of the gondola) offers a large, revolving terrace and 'stunning view', which is also accessible to non-skiers via a moving carpet. Above Brixen the Filzalm is a good place for a quick drink on the way back from the circuit or you could indulge in the 'excellent Kaiserschmarren' at the Almfried. Check out our Ellmau chapter for more recommendations in that sector.

### SCHOOLS AND GUIDES
***More reports, please***

The Söll-Hochsöll school has a fairly good reputation. But we lack recent reports.

### FACILITIES FOR CHILDREN
***Fast becoming a family resort***

Söll has fairly wide-ranging facilities – the Söll-Hochsöll ski kindergarten, a Mini Club, which looks after children aged three to five who don't want to spend all day on the slopes, and a special kids-only drag and slope on the opposite side of the village to the main lifts. Reports welcome.

## boarding

*Söll is a good place to try out boarding: slopes are gentle and there are plenty of gondolas and chairs. For competent boarders it's more limited – the slopes of the Ski Welt are tame. A reporter recommends the Scheffau school.*

## SCHOOLS

**Söll-Hochsöll**
t 5454
info@skischule-soell.com

**ProSöll**
t 0664 256 0184
info@proski-soell.com

**Classes**
(Söll-Hochsöll prices)
5 4-hr days: €120

**Private lessons**
€45 for 1hr; each additional person €15

## CHILDREN

**Mini-club**
t 5454
info@skischule-soell.com
9.45–4pm, Sat to Thu; ages 3 to 5

**Ski schools**
Söll-Hochsöll takes children from 5 to 14 for 4hr daily (5 days €120).
ProSöll takes ages 3½ to 14 for 4hr daily (5 days €115).

## GETTING THERE

**Air** Salzburg 94km/58 miles (2hr); Innsbruck 73km/45 miles (1½hr).

**Rail** Wörgl (13km/8 miles) or Kufstein (15km/9 miles); bus to resort.

## ACTIVITIES

**Indoor** Swimming, sauna, solarium, massage, bowling, squash

**Outdoor** Natural ice rink (skating, curling), sleigh rides, 3km/2 miles of floodlit ski and toboggan runs, walks, paragliding

## STAYING THERE

### HOW TO GO

***Mostly cheap, cheerful gasthofs***

The major mainstream tour operators offer packages here.

**Hotels** There is a wide choice of simple gasthofs, pensions and B&Bs, and an adequate amount of better-quality hotel accommodation – mainly 3-star.

(((3) **Greil** (5289) One of only two 4-star options – attractive, but out of the centre far from the lifts and pool.

(((3) **Postwirt** (5081) Attractive, central, traditional 4-star with built-in stube.

(((3) **Bergland** (5454) Small 3-star, well placed between the village and lifts.

(((3) **Panorama** (5309) 3-star far from lifts but with own bus stop; wonderful views; pleasant rooms; good cakes.

(((3) **Tulpe** (5223) Next to the lifts.

((2) **Feldwebel** (5224) Central 3-star.

((2) **Schirast** (5544) Next to the lifts.

((2) **Gasthof Tenne** (5282) B&B gasthof between centre and main road.

**Chalets** There are few catered chalets but a couple of big 'club hotels' run by British tour operators.

**Self-catering** The central Aparthotel Schindlhaus has nice accommodation, though the best apartments in town are attached to the Bergland hotel.

### EATING OUT

***A fair choice***

Some of the best restaurants are in hotels. The Greil and Postwirt are good, but the Schindlhaus is said to be the best. Giovanni does excellent pizzas, while other places worth a visit include the Dorfstub'n and the Venezia.

### APRES-SKI

***Still some very loud bars***

Söll is not as raucous as it used to be, but it's still very lively and a lot of places have live music. The Salvenstadl (Cow Shed) bar was recommended as 'the best with live music' by a recent

reporter. Pub 15 is a bit sleazy but lively. The Whisky Mühle is a large disco that can get a little rowdy, especially after other bars close. Buffalo's Pub-Bar is popular. There's a floodlit piste and separate toboggan run – both from top to bottom of the gondola.

### OFF THE SLOPES

***Not bad for a small village***

You could spend a happy day in the wonderfully equipped Panoramabad: taking a sauna, swimming, lounging about. The large baroque church would be the pride of many tourist towns. There are numerous coach excursions, including trips to Salzburg, Innsbruck and even Vipiteno over in Italy.

# Scheffau 745m/2,440ft

This is one of the most attractive of the Ski Welt villages.

### THE RESORT

Scheffau is a rustic little place complete with pretty white church. It is spacious yet not sprawling and has a definite centre, a kilometre off the busy main road, which increases its charm at the cost of convenience – you can ski to the Ski Welt lifts at Blaiken (where there are several hotels) but need a bus to get back.

SOLL TOURIST OFFICE

Walks and langlauf are alternatives to the slopes of Hohe Salve, in the background →

## THE MOUNTAIN

Scheffau is well placed for the Ski Welt's best (and most central and snow-sure) section of pistes.
**Slopes** Two gondolas (including an eight-seater) give rapid access directly to Brandstadl.
**Snow reliability** Nearby Eiberg is the place to go when snow is poor.
**Experts** The pistes above Blaiken are some of the longest and steepest in the Ski Welt.
**Intermediates** This is as good a base as any in the area.
**Beginners** The nursery slope is in the village, making Scheffau a poor choice for mixed-ability parties; but a reporter rates the easy blues at Brandstadl as 'excellent for beginner snowboarders'.
**Cross-country** See Söll and Ellmau.
**Queues** The second gondola has cut weekend queues at Blaiken.
**Mountain restaurants** See Söll, Ellmau.
**Schools and guides** The school is well regarded, but groups can be large. A reporter's private snowboarding lesson was 'the best I've ever had'.
**Facilities for children** Both the ski kindergarten and non-ski nursery have good reputations. The children's ski area and school 'Kinder-Kaiserland' is also reported to be 'very good'. And excellent progress was made by a four-year-old at Ski Esprit's nursery.

## STAYING THERE

**How to go** Major operators offer packages here.
**Hotels** The best hotels – both with pool, sauna and steam room – are the 4-star Kaiser (8000) and 3-star Alpin (85560) – 'excellent food, lots of choice, spacious rooms'. Pool ('a bit cold') and sauna. The Wilden Kaiser (8118), Blaiken (8126) and Waldhof (8122) are good value gasthofs near the gondolas. And the central Gasthof Weberbauer (8115) is said to be 'good value' and 'efficient'.
**Eating out** There aren't many village restaurants, and those staying in B&B places are advised to book tables.
**Après-ski** 'Non-existent,' says one happy reporter – but the bars in Blaiken are said to offer 'loud music'. The usual rep-organised events such as bowling and tobogganing are available.
**Off the slopes** Walking apart, there is little to do. Tour operators organise trips to Innsbruck and Salzburg.



# Hopfgarten 620m/2,030ft

Hopfgarten is an unspoiled, friendly and traditional resort tucked away from the busy Wörgl road.

## THE RESORT

The village is a good size: small enough to be intimate, large enough to have plenty of off-slope amenities. Most hotels are within five minutes' walk of the lift to Rigi.

## THE MOUNTAIN

Hopfgarten is at the western extremity of the Ski Welt.
**Slopes** Hopfgarten offers queue-free access to Rigi and Hohe Salve – the high point of the main Ski Welt circuit.
**Terrain-parks** None locally but it's a short bus-ride to Westendorf, where there is a park, or Kelchsau, where there is a half-pipe.
**Snow reliability** The resort's great weakness is the poor snow quality on the south-west-facing home slope.
**Experts** Experts should venture off-piste for excitement.
**Intermediates** When snow is good, the runs down to Hopfgarten and the nearby villages of Brixen and Itter are some of the best in the Ski Welt.
**Beginners** There is a beginners' slope in the village, but it is sunny as well as low; lack of snow-cover means paying for a lift pass to higher slopes.
**Snowboarding** The Ski Welt is best suited to free-riding the extensive intermediate slopes.
**Cross-country** Hopfgarten is one of the best cross-country bases in the area. There are fine trails to Kelchsau (11km/7 miles) and Niederau (15km/9 miles), and the Itter-Bocking loop (15km/9 miles) starts nearby. Westendorf's trails are close.
**Queues** Morning queues to leave the village should be a thing of the past if the promised gondola materialises.
**Mountain restaurants** See Söll.

**Phone numbers**
**Calling long-distance**
Add the prefix given below for each resort. When calling from abroad use the country code 43 and omit the initial 0.

**Söll**
05333
**Scheffau**
05358
**Hopfgarten**
05335
**Itter**
05335
**Brixen**
05334

**Schools and guides** Partly because Hopfgarten seems to attract large numbers of Australians, English is widely spoken in the two schools.
**Facilities for children** Hopfgarten is a family resort, with a nursery and ski kindergarten.

**STAYING THERE**
**How to go** Cheap and cheerful gasthofs, pensions and little private B&Bs are the norm here.
**Hotels** The exceptions to the rule are the comfortable 4-star hotels Hopfgarten (3920) with pool, and Sporthotel Fuchs (2420), both well placed for the main lift.
**Eating out** Most of the restaurants are hotel-based, but there are exceptions, including a Chinese and a pizzeria.
**Après-ski** Après-ski is generally quiet, though a lively holiday can usually be ensured if you go with Aussie-dominated Contiki Travel.
**Off the slopes** Off-slope amenities include swimming, riding, bowling, skating, tobogganing and paragliding. The railway makes trips to Salzburg, Innsbruck and Kitzbühel.

## Itter 700m/2,300ft

Itter is a tiny village halfway around the mountain between Söll and Hopfgarten, with nursery slopes close to hand and a gondola just outside the village into the Ski Welt, via Hochsöll.

There's a hotel and half a dozen gasthofs and B&Bs. The school has a rental shop, and when conditions are good this is a good beginners' resort.

## Brixen 800m/2,620ft

It may not be pretty, but Brixen has a queue-free, high-capacity gondola up to the main Ski Welt slopes.

**THE RESORT**
Brixen im Thale is a very scattered roadside village at the south-east edge of the Ski Welt, close to Westendorf. The main hotels are near the railway station, a bus-ride from the lifts.

**THE MOUNTAIN**
Brixen is on the south side of the main Ski Welt circuit, and a short bus-ride from separate Westendorf.
**Slopes** The gondola takes you to Hochbrixen, where lifts diverge for Hohe Salve and Söll, or Astberg and Ellmau. There's a small area of north-facing runs, including nursery slopes, on the other side of the village.
**Terrain-parks** None locally but there's a good park nearby at Westendorf.
**Snow reliability** A chain of snow-guns on the main south-facing piste helps to preserve the snow as long as possible and the area benefited from further snowmaking in 2003/04.
**Experts** The black run alongside the Brixen gondola is one of the few challenging pistes in the area.
**Intermediates** When snow is good, Brixen has some of the best slopes in the Ski Welt – including some challenging ones.
**Beginners** The nursery slopes are secluded and shady, but meeting up with friends for lunch is a hassle – the area is a bus-ride from the village.
**Snowboarding** See Söll.
**Cross-country** In addition to valley-floor trails, a 5km/3 mile loop up the mountain at Hochbrixen provides fine views and fairly reliable snow.
**Queues** Lift upgrades have improved the once queue-prone area.
**Mountain restaurants** The Filzalm above Brixen has been recommended.
**Schools and guides** The ski school runs the usual group classes, and mini-groups for five to seven people.
**Facilities for children** There is an all-day ski kindergarten.

**STAYING THERE**
**How to go** There are plenty of hotels and pensions.
**Hotels** The hotel Alpenhof (88320) and the Sporthotel (8191) are both 4-star hotels with pools.
**Eating out** Mainly hotel-based, but the restaurant opposite the gondola has been recommended.
**Après-ski** Après-ski is quiet, but livelier Westendorf is a short taxi-ride.
**Off the slopes** Activities include tennis, hotel-based spa facilities and days out to Salzburg, Innsbruck and Kitzbühel.

**TOURIST OFFICES**

**Söll**
t 5216
info@soell.com
www.soell.at

**Scheffau**
t 7373
scheffau@skiwelt.at
www.scheffau.com

**Hopfgarten**
t 2322
info@hopfgarten.tirol.at
www.hopfgarten.at

**Itter**
t 2670
itter@skiwelt.at
www.itter.at

**Brixen**
t 8433
brixen@skiwelt.at
www.brixenimthale.at

TVB ST ANTON AM ARLBERG

# St Anton

*Non-stop on- and off-slope action and pretty village base*

## COSTS

①②③④⑤⑥

## RATINGS

**The slopes**

| | |
|---|---|
| Snow | **** |
| Extent | **** |
| Expert | ***** |
| Intermediate | *** |
| Beginner | * |
| Convenience | *** |
| Queues | ** |
| Mountain restaurants | *** |

**The rest**

| | |
|---|---|
| Scenery | *** |
| Resort charm | **** |
| Off-slope | *** |

## NEWS

In 2003/04 there were two new high-speed, six-person chair-lifts. One replaced the Arlenmähder T-bar above the Arlberg Pass and runs to a new, higher top station, allowing access to the the runs to Rauz without going to the top (useful if the weather is bad or you want to avoid the steepest section of the Rauz run). There's also a new blue piste down to the Arlenmähder chair. The other new chair has replaced the T-bar to Gampberg on Rendl.

For 2002/03 two rope tows with a moving carpet in between were installed to take you from the roundabout on the edge of town near the Galzig cable-car to the Rendl gondola. So you no longer need to take the bus or walk – but you still need to on the way back as the new system works only one way.



- ⊞ Extensive, varied slopes for experts and adventurous intermediates, with more to explore in Lech-Zürs a bus-ride away
- ⊞ Heavy snowfalls, backed up by a fair amount of snowmaking
- ⊞ Very lively après-ski, from mid-afternoon onward
- ⊞ Despite expansion, the resort retains some traditional charm – and the animated village centre is mainly car-free
- ⊞ Improved lift system has made Nasserein a viable base and reduced queuing problems, but ...

- ⊟ Still some serious lift queues, at resort level and at mid-mountain
- ⊟ Slopes far from ideal for beginners or timid intermediates
- ⊟ Most of the tough stuff is off-piste – and the distinction between piste and off-piste is unhelpfully blurred
- ⊟ Pistes can get very crowded – some of them dangerously so
- ⊟ Main slopes get a lot of sun, quickly affecting the snow conditions
- ⊟ Resort spreads widely, with some long treks to key lifts and bars
- ⊟ Can get rowdy, with noisy drunks in the central streets in the early hours

**St Anton is undeniably a big-league resort. For competent skiers and riders with an appetite for non-stop action and the stamina to keep up with it, we'd rate it even higher: it is one of the great resorts, with an après-ski scene that can be as taxing as the splendid bowls below the Valluga. The combination draws ski bums from around the world, as well as lots of regular holiday visitors.**

**But it won't suit everyone, as our ⊟ points make clear. Many people who might be thinking of trying an Austrian change from Val-d'Isère, or of taking a step up from Kitzbühel, are liable be put off by this list, and rightly so. The St Anton formula works brilliantly for some people, but very badly for others.**

**The 2001 Alpine World Ski Championships have left a legacy that is worthwhile, but not quite the transformation that is advertised. The new leisure/conference centre looks as dreary as its name – Arlberg-well.com – sounds silly. Removal of the divisive railway line to the far side of the river has certainly simplified access to the lifts, but where the railway was there is now just a kind of gap that is meant to be a park. The improved lifts from village level to Gampen have eased the queues and given the suburb of Nasserein a huge boost. Further investment in lifts and pistes have taken place (see News) but the improvement that is most needed is a new piste or two back to the village from Galzig, to relieve pressure on the spectacularly overcrowded Steissbachtal and the home run below it. There are off-piste routes that could be developed, given the will.**

## THE RESORT

St Anton is at the foot of the road up to the Arlberg pass, at the eastern end of a lift network that spreads across to St Christoph and across the pass to Stuben. The resort is a long, sprawling mixture of traditional and modern buildings crammed into a narrow valley. It used to be sandwiched between a busy road and the mainline railway – but the railway was moved in 2000, and where there were tracks there is now a little area of parkland.

Although it is crowded and commercialised, St Anton is full of character, its traffic-free main street lined by traditional-style buildings. It is an attractively bustling place, day and night. Several reporters have observed that it has better-than-usual everyday shopping with a 'wonderful Spar'.

The main hub of the resort is around the base stations of the two-stage cable-car up via Galzig to Valluga Grat and the fast quad chair up to Gampen. The attractive, lively main street and its hotels are only a short

| KEY FACTS | |
|---|---|
| **Resort** | 1305m<br>4,280ft |
| For Arlberg region | |
| **Slopes** | 1305-2650m<br>4,280-8,690ft |
| **Lifts** | 82 |
| **Pistes** | 260km<br>162 miles |
| **Blue** | 36% |
| **Red** | 42% |
| **Black** | 22% |
| **Snowmaking** | 65km<br>40 miles |
| For St Anton, St Christoph and Stuben only | |
| **Slopes** | 1305-2650m<br>4,280-8,690ft |
| **Lifts** | 39 |
| **Pistes** | 120km<br>75 miles |

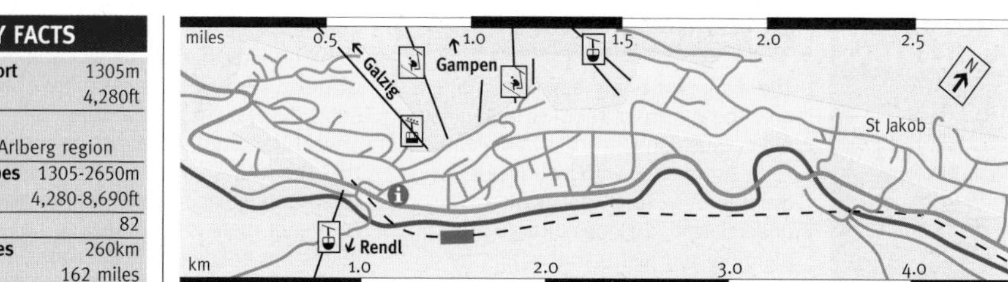


walk from these lifts, and for most purposes a location on or close to this main street is ideal.

The resort spreads down the valley, thinning out before broadening again to form the suburb of Nasserein. This backwater now has an eight-person gondola up to Gampen, and makes an appealing base for a quiet time. The nightlife action is a short bus-ride or 15-minute walk away. Staying between St Anton centre and Nasserein is also a more attractive idea since the Fang chair-lift, which gives access to the Nasserein gondola, was built.

On the other side of the main road a gondola goes up to the Rendl area. This is now linked one-way by rope tows and a moving carpet from the end of St Anton's main street (see News) – but the return journey still involves a bus-ride or short walk.

St Anton spreads up the hill to the west of the centre, towards the Arlberg pass – first to Oberdorf, then Gastig, 10 minutes' walk from the centre. Further up the hill are the suburbs of Dengert and Moos – a long way out, but quite close to the slopes.

Regular buses go to Stuben, Zürs and Lech (all described in the Lech chapter) and the much less well-known but worthwhile Sonnenkopf area above Klösterle. These buses can get crowded early and late in the day. Minibus-style taxis can be economic if widely shared.

Serfaus, Nauders, Ischgl and Sölden are also feasible outings by car.

## THE MOUNTAINS

The main slopes are essentially open: only the run from Rendl to the valley offers much shelter from bad weather.

St Anton vies with Val-d'Isère for the title of 'resort with most underclassified slopes'. There are plenty of red pistes that would be black in many other resorts, and plenty of blues that would be red.

Many of the most popular steep runs marked on the piste map are classified as 'ski routes'. These have widely spaced markers, they may be groomed occasionally in part, but they are not patrolled and are protected from avalanches only 'in the immediate vicinity of the markers'.

Clearly you should not ski such runs alone, and the piste map recommends them only for people with 'alpine experience or with a ski instructor'. In theory this puts these routes out of bounds for many holidaymakers, but in practice many tackle them without the services of an instructor. One reader sums up the problem with admirable clarity: 'It is entirely unreasonable to expect everyone to take guides on these routes, and it seems irresponsible to ignore the fact that people will go on them. On some of the ski routes there were snow-guns. This doesn't fit with the idea that you're on your own.' A 2004 reporter comments: 'Ski routes offer endless possibilities for competent skiers and yet the authorities seem to leave them open or tape them off with no apparent consistent logic. There seems to be no indication of snow conditions off-piste, leaving the possibility of a crisis developing from a little adventure.' Another reader points out that the routes vary from 'an easy red to a double-black-diamond nightmare'. On Rendl there is a lift serving no pistes but only a single ski route. The situation is, to quote another reader, 'absurd'.

Until 1999, the piste map also showed several 'high-alpine touring runs' not marked on the ground at all, and not protected against avalanche. These no longer appear on the map, though runs of that kind are still shown over in Lech and Stuben. Read the Lech chapter for more on these.

The Arlberg region piste map is poor, attempting to fit too many different mountain aspects into a single view. It's at its worst over in Lech, but it's also unsatisfactory on Galzig. Fortunately the on-mountain maps and signs are clearer. Reporters have complained of poor and limited piste grooming. The local cable TV, showing the state of some of the pistes and queues, can be very useful.

### THE SLOPES

#### *Large linked area*

St Anton's slopes fall into three main sectors, two of them linked.

The major sector is that beneath the local high-spot, the **Valluga**, accessed by cable-car via **Galzig**. The tiny top stage of the cable-car to the Valluga itself is mainly for sightseeing – you

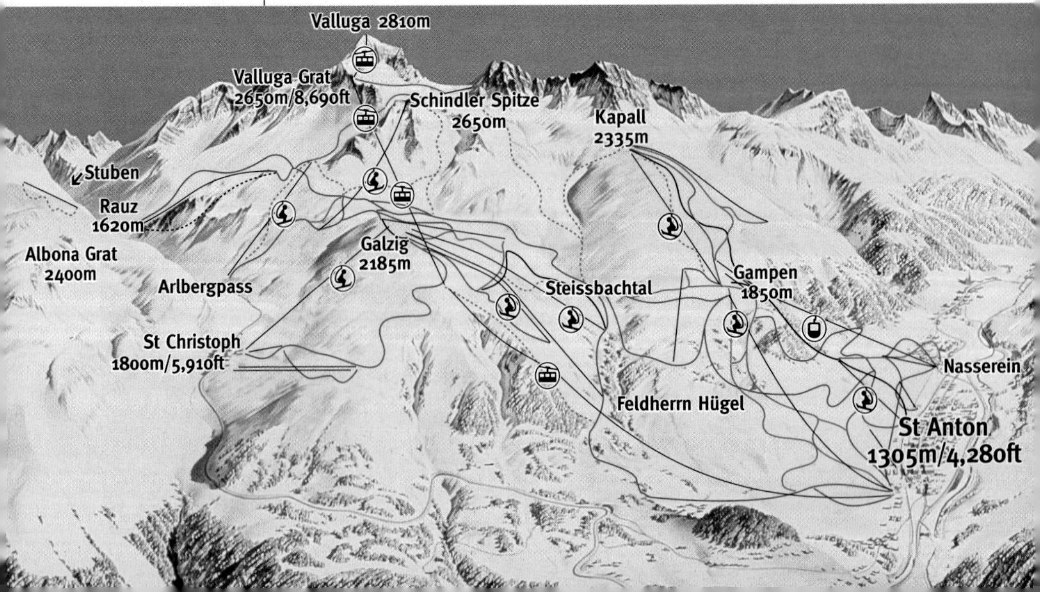

Valluga 2810m
Valluga Grat 2650m/8,690ft
Schindler Spitze 2650m
Kapall 2335m
Stuben
Rauz 1620m
Albona Grat 2400m
Arlbergpass
Galzig 2185m
Steissbachtal
Gampen 1850m
St Christoph 1800m/5,910ft
Nasserein
Feldherrn Hügel
St Anton 1305m/4,280ft

## LIFT PASSES

**Arlberg Ski Pass**
Covers all St Anton, St Christoph, Lech, Zürs and Stuben lifts, and linking bus between Rauz and Zürs.

**Beginners**
Limited pass covering beginners' lifts.

**Main pass**
1 day €38.50
6 days €179

**Senior citizens**
Over 65 for men and 60 for women: 6 days €155

**Children**
Under 20: 6 days €155
Under 16: 6 days €107
Under 6: free pass

**Notes**
Single ascent, half-day and afternoon 'taster' tickets available. Pass also covers Sonnenkopf (10 lifts) at Klösterle, 7km/4 miles west of Stuben (free bus link from Stuben).

## THE VALLUGA RUNS

*The off-piste runs in the huge bowl beneath the summit of the Valluga, reached by either the Schindlergrat chair or the Valluga I cable-car, are justifiably world-famous. In good snow, this whole area is an off-piste delight for experts.*

*Except immediately after a fresh snowfall, you can see tracks going all over the mountain. There are two main ski routes marked on the piste map – both long, steep descents that quickly get mogulled. The Schindlerkar is the first you come to and it divides into two – the Schindlerkar gully being the steeper option. For the second, wider and somewhat easier, Mattun run, you traverse further at the top. Both these feed down into the Steissbachtal gully where there are lifts back up to Galzig and Gampen. The Schweinströge – a high-alpine route no longer shown on the map – starts off in the same direction as the red run to Rauz, but you traverse the shoulder of the Schindler Spitze and down a narrow gully.*

can take skis or a board up only if you have a guide to lead you down the tricky off-piste run to Zürs. The slightly lower station of Valluga Grat gives access to St Anton's famous high, sunny bowls, and to the long, beautiful red/blue run to Rauz, at the western end of St Anton's own slopes. From here you can go on to explore the rather neglected slopes of Stuben.

All of these high runs can also be accessed by riding the Schindlergrat triple chair. Other runs from Galzig go south-west to St Christoph and east into the Steissbachtal. Most of the runs in this whole sector funnel into this 'Happy Valley', producing incredible congestion, especially late in the day.

Beyond this valley, with lift and piste links in both directions, is the **Gampen-Kapall** sector, reachable by chair-lift from central St Anton or gondola from Nasserein. From Gampen at mid-mountain, pistes lead back to St Anton and Nasserein. Or you can ride a six-pack on up to Kapall to ski the treeless upper mountain.

A handful of lifts serve the west-facing runs at the top of **Rendl**, with a single north-facing piste returning to the gondola bottom station.

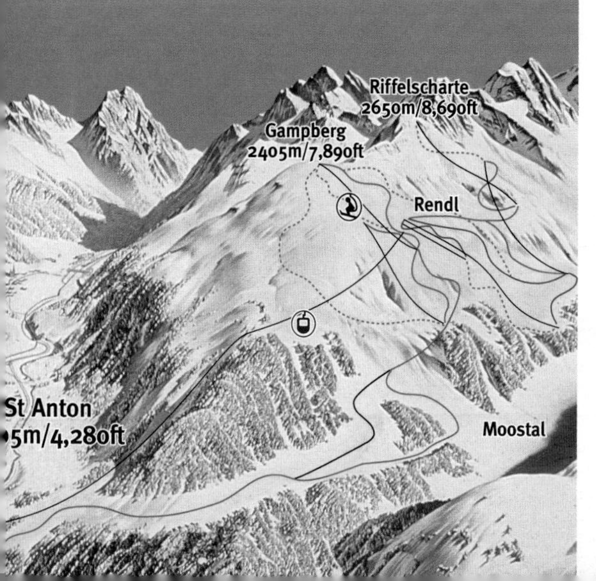


### TERRAIN-PARKS
***Head for Rendl***

On Rendl, just below the top of the gondola, is St Anton's only terrain-park. This includes a half-pipe, quarter pipe, jumps, rail slides and a washboard (several humps in a row).

### SNOW RELIABILITY
***Generally very good cover***

If the weather is coming from the west or north-west (as it often is), the Arlberg gets it first, and as a result St Anton and its neighbours get heavy falls of snow. They often have much better conditions than other resorts of a similar height, and we've had great fresh powder here as late as mid-April. But many of the slopes face south or south-east, causing icy or heavy conditions at times. It's vital to time descents of the steeper runs off the Valluga to get decent conditions.

The lower runs are now well equipped with snowmaking, which generally ensures the home runs remain open. As an April 2004 visitor said, 'Pistes were kept open while surrounded by green fields.'

### FOR EXPERTS
***One of the world's great areas***

St Anton vies with Chamonix, Val-d'Isère and a handful of other resorts for the affections of experts. There are countless opportunities for going off-piste and guidance is very desirable. It has some of the most consistently challenging and extensive slopes in the

world. The jewel in the crown is the off-piste terrain in the bowls beneath the Valluga – see feature panel. The ultimate challenge, perhaps, is to go with a guide off the back of the Valluga. The initial pitch is very, very steep (a fall can be fatal) but after that the run down to Zürs is very beautiful and usually deserted. Reporters who have tried it have loved it.

Lower down, there are challenging runs in many directions from both Galzig and Gampen-Kapall. These lower runs can be doubly tricky if the snow has been hit by the sun.

The Rendl area across the road has plenty of open space beneath the top lifts and there is some delightful fun to be had off the back of this ridge.

One of our reporters particularly liked the Sonnenkopf area down-valley from Stuben for its excellent off-piste route to Langen. See also the Stuben section at the end of the Lech chapter.

The few black pistes offer genuine challenges. These include the World Championship race courses – Kandahar from Kapall down to Gampen and the previously red Fang run from there down to the village.

On top of all this, bear in mind that many of the red runs on the piste map are long and challenging, too.

**FOR INTERMEDIATES**
***Some real challenges***

St Anton is well suited to good, adventurous intermediates. They will be able to try the Mattun run and the easier version of the Schindlerkar run from Valluga Grat (see feature panel). The run from Schindler Spitze to Rauz is very long (over 1000m/3,300ft vertical), varied and ideal for good (and fit) intermediates. Alternatively, turn off from this part way down and take the Steissbachtal to the lifts back to Galzig. The Kapall-Gampen section is also interesting, with sporty bumps among trees on the lower half. Good intermediates may enjoy the men's downhill run from the top to town.

Less adventurous intermediates will find St Anton less to their taste. There are few easy cruising pistes. The most obvious are the short blues on Galzig and the Steissbachtal (aka 'Happy Valley'). These are reasonably gentle but get uncomfortably crowded. As one reporter says, 'More timid skiers will not be happy with the crowded areas and the very fast skiers who will pass them.' The blue to St Christoph is generally quieter. The narrowish blues between Kapall and Gampen can have some challenging bumps. For the best easy cruising, take the bus to Lech.

In the Rendl area a variety of trails suitable for good and moderate intermediates criss-cross, including a lovely long tree-lined run (over 1000m/3,300ft vertical from the top) back to the valley gondola station. This is the best run in the whole area when visibility is poor, though it has some quite awkward sections.

**FOR BEGINNERS**
***Far from ideal***

St Anton has better nursery slopes now, near the Fang lift. But there are no easy, uncrowded runs for beginners to progress to. A mixed party of experts, intermediates and novices would be better off staying in Lech or Zürs; those who want to explore St Anton can get on the bus to Rauz.

**FOR CROSS-COUNTRY**
***Limited interest***

St Anton is not a great cross-country resort, but trails total around 35km/

**boarding**

*Though steeped in skiing tradition, St Anton is moving with the times and improving facilities for boarders. Although we don't really recommend it to beginners, for good boarders it is one of the best free-ride areas in the world, with lots of steep terrain and natural hits. There are still a few T-bars around but fast chair-lifts are now the main ways around the mountains. The Arlberg ski school has a special Snowboard Academy section.*

## SCHOOLS

**Arlberg**
t 3411
skischool.arlberg@st-anton.at

**St Anton**
t 3563
office@skistanton.com

**Piste to Powder**
t 0664 174 6282,
UK 01661 824318
graham@skimountaineering.com

**Classes**
(Arlberg prices)
6 days (2½hr am and 2hr pm) €196

**Private lessons**
€208 for full day; each additional person €17

SNOWPIX.COM / CHRIS GILL

What a shame they didn't build the new leisure and conference centre in traditional Tirolean style – this could be be in Flaine or La Plagne ↓

22 miles and snow conditions are usually good. There are a couple of uninspiring trails near town, another at St Jakob 3km/2 miles away, and a pretty trail through trees along the Ferwalltal to the foot of the Albona area. There is also a tiny loop at St Christoph.

### QUEUES
***Improved, but still a problem***

Queues are not the problem they once were, since the replacement of several lifts by fast chairs. But they can still be tiresome in peak season and at weekends. Recent reporters found long queues for the cable-car to Galzig and one hit 'massive' queues for the chair to Gampen, which attracts crowds when higher lifts are closed. At mid-mountain, queues for the Schindlergrat chair appear to have been eased by the new Arlenmähder chair allowing access to the run to Rauz without going to the top. The Zammermoos chair out of the Steissbachtal can generate queues. There are US-style 'singles lines' at some lifts; but, despite taped exhortations in several languages, the chairs are rarely filled.

Perhaps more of a worry than the lift queues are the crowded pistes. Clearly the worst is the Steissbachtal which can be uncomfortably crowded even in January and a nightmare on a March weekend. Run 1 home at the end of the day is also crowded and 'really dangerous,' according to one reporter staying this past New Year. Several reporters recommend going to Rendl or Stuben on busy days or heading down to Rauz or St Christoph and getting a bus back to town rather than tangling with the Steissbachtal. This long-standing problem is not going to go away until the resort creates an alternative easy piste from Galzig to the village.

### MOUNTAIN RESTAURANTS
***Plenty of choice***

We often end up lunching in St Christoph at the atmospheric Hospiz Alm, famed for its slide down to the toilets as well as its food. But some readers have met poor service, and it isn't cheap. The cosy Arlberg Taja St Christoph just above it, and Traxl's ice bar at the Maiensee Hotel, have been recommended by readers. Other recommendations include the self-service restaurant at Galzig for 'superb views and tasty food', Sennhütte on the Galzig home run and Rodelalm on Gampen: 'A real hut with good food at low prices and a lovely fire.' Slightly lower still on Galzig, the Mooserwirt serves typical Austrian food at what seem high prices, but 'the portions are absolutely massive'; the Krazy Kanguruh does burgers, pizzas and snacks; Taps Bar next door 'good goulash soup'.

Over on Rendl, the self-service Rendl restaurant offers 'excellent food and value' and 'great views' with zero queuing even when busy. Bifangalm, near the end of the run to the valley, is 'friendly and atmospheric'.

The restaurant at Kapall received a bad review from one of our reporters: 'A very limited menu and the atmosphere of a transport cafe.'

## GETTING THERE

**Air** Innsbruck 100km/62 miles (1½hr); Zürich 200km/124 miles (3hr); Friedrichshafen 120km/75 miles (1½hr).

**Rail** Mainline station in resort.

## CHILDREN

**The kindergarten at the Kinderwelt**
t 2526
From age 30mnth; must be toilet-trained; 10am to 4.30

**Ski schools**
Both Austrian schools take children aged from 5 (6 days including lunch €274 at Arlberg school)

## ACTIVITIES

**Indoor** Swimming pool (also hotel pools open to the public, with sauna and massage), fitness centre, tennis, squash, bowling, museum, cinema in Vallugasaal

**Outdoor** Swimming pool, cleared walking paths, natural ice rink (skating, curling), sleigh rides, tobogganing, paragliding

**Phone numbers**
From elsewhere in Austria add the prefix 05446.
From abroad use the prefix +43 5446.

### SCHOOLS AND GUIDES
***Mixed reports***

The St Anton school provides much-needed competition to the Arlberg school, which generates conflicting reports. One reporter commented, 'Not enough attention was paid to putting equal standards together and groups were big.' Another complained of old-fashioned technique: 'They need to turn the clock forward.' But some reporters were very happy: 'Children and parents were delighted.' We have skied with excellent off-piste guides and had good reports of Piste to Powder, an off-piste guiding outfit run by British guide Graham Austick. We also have reports of tour ops being stopped from supplying their own ski host to show guests around the pistes unless they hire an instructor too.

### FACILITIES FOR CHILDREN
***Getting better***

The youth centre attached to the Arlberg school is excellent, and the special slopes both for toddlers (at the bottom) and bigger children (at Gampen) are well done. At Nasserein there is a moving carpet lift on the baby slope, and a reporter rates this an 'absolutely ideal' place to stay with young kids.

## STAYING THERE

### HOW TO GO
***Austria's main chalet resort***

There's a wide range of places to stay, from quality hotels to cheap and cheerful pensions and apartments.

**Chalets** Plenty of catered chalets are offered by UK tour operators. With the new gondola, Nasserein now makes a convenient chalet base.

**Hotels** There is one 5-star hotel and lots of 4- and 3-stars and B&Bs.

((((5) **Raffl's St Antoner Hof** (2910) Best in town, but its position on the bypass is less than ideal. Pool.

(((4) **Schwarzer Adler** (22440) Centuries-old inn on main street. Widely varying bedrooms.

(((4) **Alte Post** (2553) Atmospheric place on main street with lively après-ski bar. Endorsed by a reporter.

(((4) **Post** (2213) Comfortable if uninspiring 4-star at the centre of affairs, close to both lifts and nightlife.

(((4) **Sporthotel** (3111) Central position, varied bedrooms, good food. Pool.

((3) **Grischuna** (2304) Welcoming and family-run in peaceful position up the hill west of town; close to the slopes.

((3) **Goldenes Kreuz** (22110) A comfortable B&B hotel halfway to Nasserein, ideal for cruising home.

**Self-catering** There are plenty of apartments available but package deals are few and far between. The Bachmann apartments near the Nasserein gondola were highly recommended by a 2003 reporter.

### EATING OUT
***Mostly informal***

Places such as the Trödlerstube and Reselhof serve big portions of traditional Austrian food. Fuhrmannstube is 'great value, with an excellent menu and cheery owner'. At the Museum, as well as learning about the history of the resort, you can enjoy upmarket food and wine in elegant panelled rooms. Similarly ambitious in culinary terms but quite different in style is Ben.venuto, in the Arlberg-well.com building: stark decor, eclectic menu and excellent cooking. Bobo's serves good, although expensive, Mexican. Scotty's and Pomodoro have been recommended for pizza. In Nasserein, the Tenne is noted for game dishes, while Alt St Anton is a cosy chalet doing a good range of excellent traditional dishes. If you do the floodlit toboggan run above Nasserein, don't miss the Rodelalm for traditional food, beer and schnapps – booking essential.

Building this gondola has made Nasserein a much more attractive base, especially for families ↗

ST ANTON TOURIST OFFICE

## TOURIST OFFICES

**St Anton**
**t** 22690
info@stantonamarlberg.com
www.stantonamarlberg.com

**St Christoph**
www.tiscover.com/st.christoph

### APRES-SKI
***Throbbing till late***

St Anton's bars rock from mid-afternoon until the early hours. Après-ski starts in a collection of bars on the slopes above the village. The Krazy Kanguruh is probably the most famous, but the Mooserwirt is now the 'in' place, filling up with revellers as soon as the lunch trade finishes – reputedly dispensing more beer than any other bar in Austria. By 4pm tables inside and out are being danced on. The Griabli opposite has live bands and is almost as popular. All this is followed by a slide down the piste in the dark. The bars in town are in full swing by 4pm, too. Most are lively, with loud music; sophisticates looking for a quieter time are less well provided for. The Underground has live music, but gets packed. Equally popular are the Hazienda, Piccadilly and, for late-night dancing, Stanton. Recent reporters have recommended Scotty's (in Mark Warner's chalet-hotel Rosanna, with extended happy hour), Jacksy's, Pub 37, Bobo's, Alibi and Funky Chicken. In Nasserein, Tom Dooley's is 'relaxed and welcoming'.



### OFF THE SLOPES
***Some improvement***

St Anton is a resort for keen skiers and riders. But the new fitness, swimming and skating facilities of Arlberg-well.com are impressive. The village is lively during the day, with a fair selection of shops. Getting by bus to the other Arlberg resorts is easy, as is visiting Innsbruck by train. Many of the best mountain huts are not readily accessible by lift for pedestrians.

### STAYING DOWN THE VALLEY
***Nice and quiet***

Beyond Nasserein is St Jakob. It can be reached on snow, but is dependent on the free shuttle-bus in the morning. Pettneu is a quiet village further down the valley, with slopes that suit beginners most. It's best for drivers.

## St Christoph 1800m/5,910ft

A small, exclusive collection of pricey hotels, restaurants and bars right by the Arlberg Pass, with drag-lifts for local slopes and a fast quad chair-lift to the heart of St Anton's slopes. It's quiet at night. The best hotel of all is the huge 5-star Arlberg-Hospiz (2611).

# St Johann in Tirol

*Relax on easy runs with plenty of pit stops and friendly locals*

## COSTS

①②③④⑤⑥

## HOW IT RATES

**The slopes**

| | |
|---|---|
| Snow | ** |
| Extent | ** |
| Expert | * |
| Intermediate | *** |
| Beginner | **** |
| Convenience | *** |
| Queues | *** |
| Mountain restaurants | **** |

**The rest**

| | |
|---|---|
| Scenery | *** |
| Resort charm | *** |
| Off-slope | *** |

## NEWS

St Johann's ski area is so small that not a lot changes.

A new eight-seater gondola replaced the old single-person chair from Oberndorf three seasons ago, and snowmaking now covers almost half the slopes.

A new ski school has opened, on which we've had a glowing report.



## REPORTS WANTED

Recently we have had few reports on this resort. If you go there, please do send us a report.

The best reports earn a copy of the next edition, and can lead to free lift passes in future.

See page 10.

- + Charming traffic-free centre
- + Lots of mountain restaurants
- + Plenty of off-slope activities
- + Easy to visit neighbouring resorts
- + Few Brits by Tirol standards
- + Ideal for beginners and intermediates
- + Relatively good snow record

- − Very small area, with little to interest experts or keen piste-bashing intermediates
- − Weekend crowds from Germany
- − Can be especially crowded when nearby resorts with less reliable snow are suffering

**This charming and friendly resort is an attractive place for beginners and leisurely part-timers who like to spend as much time having drinks and lunch as they do actually cruising the slopes. Keener and more proficient skiers and boarders will soon get bored unless they are prepared to visit surrounding resorts covered by the local pass or the Kitzbüheler Alpenskipass.**

## THE RESORT

St Johann is a sizeable valley town where life doesn't revolve entirely around skiing. Reporters emphasise the friendliness of the locals. The attractive traffic-free centre, where most of the hotels are found, is wedged between a railway track, main roads and rivers, and the five-to ten-minute walk to the main lift includes a level crossing and walking beside a busy road. But there is the alternative of staying in hotels near the lift base. There is also accommodation in the hamlet of Eichenhof to the east, with drag-lifts into the slopes.

The local pass covers several other resorts to the north and east; Fieberbrunn and Waidring's Steinplatte are particularly worth a visit. The Kitzbüheler Alpenskipass covers the whole region, and Kitzbühel itself is only 10 minutes by car or train.

## THE MOUNTAINS

St Johann's local slopes are on the north-facing side of the Kitzbüheler Horn – the 'back' side of Kitzbühel's 'second' and smaller mountain.

**Slopes** The main access lift from the village is a gondola to Harschbichl with a mid-station at Angereralm. From the top, a choice of north-facing pistes lead back through the trees towards town – mainly reds on the upper mountain, blues lower down. A sunnier sector of west-facing pistes lead down to the gondola at Oberndorf.

**Terrain-parks** St Johann has a terrain-park, a half-pipe and a carving course.

**Snow reliability** St Johann gets more snow than neighbouring Kitzbühel and the Ski Welt, and this, together with its largely north-facing slopes, means that it often has better conditions (as a 2004 reporter discovered last March). It also has substantial snowmaking.

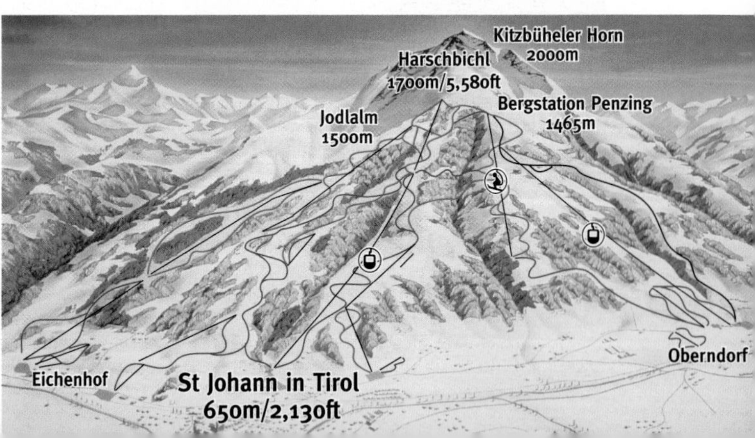

The centre of town is attractive and traffic-free →

TVB ST JOHANN IN TIROL

## KEY FACTS

| | |
|---|---|
| **Resort** | 650m<br>2,130ft |
| **Slopes** | 670-1700m<br>2,200-5,580ft |
| **Lifts** | 17 |
| **Pistes** | 60km<br>37 miles |
| **Blue** | 41% |
| **Red** | 47% |
| **Black** | 12% |
| **Snowmaking** | 28km<br>17 miles |

**Phone numbers**
From elsewhere in Austria add the prefix 05352.
From abroad use the prefix +43 5352.

## TOURIST OFFICE

**t** 63335
info@st.johann.tirol.at
www.st.johann.tirol.at

**Experts** There is nothing here to challenge an expert. The long black run on the piste map is really a moderate red – and the snow suffers from the strong afternoon sun.

**Intermediates** The slopes are varied. But keen piste-bashers will ski them all in a day and are likely to want to go on to explore nearby resorts. Decent intermediates have a fairly direct-running piste between Harschbichl and town and the black mentioned above. There are some easier red runs on the top part of the mountain, but the best (3a and 4b) are served by long drags or a slow, old chair. The Penzing piste is served by a high-speed quad. The less adventurous can get off the village gondola at the mid-station and take gentle pistes down from there.

**Beginners** The main nursery slopes are excellent. The slopes served by the first stage of the village gondola make good runs to progress to – though the last part just above the village is a bit steep for some. 'Superb. I could not have picked a better place to learn to ski,' said one past reporter.

**Snowboarding** It's drag-lifts or nothing on the nursery slopes.

**Cross-country** Given good snow, St Johann is one of the best cross-country resorts in Austria. The wide variety of trails totals 75km/47 miles.

**Queues** Rare except at peak times.

**Mountain restaurants** With 14 restaurants spread over just 60km/37 miles of piste, St Johann must have the densest array of huts of any sizeable resort in Europe. All those tried by one reporter had 'excellent food, especially the Hochfeld'. Harschbichlhütte is also recommended for 'excellent food'. Our favourite is the Angerer Alm, just above the gondola mid-station, with good local food and the most amazing wine cellar. Besgeigeralm is a rustic restaurant on the Oberndorf side.

**Schools and guides** We have had glowing reports in the past of the St Johann and Eichenhof schools. And a 2004 visitor reports 'exceptional instruction by the new Wilder Kaiser school in small groups of six or so'. So you'll be spoiled for choice.

**Facilities for children** The village nursery, geared to the needs of workers rather than visitors, offers exceptionally long hours.

## STAYING THERE

**How to go** British tour operators concentrate on hotels, but there are numerous apartments available.

**Hotels** All hotels are 3- or 4-star. There are dozens of B&B pensions.
The 4-star Sporthotel Austria (62507) is near the lift, with pool, sauna and steam. The Post (62230) is a 13th-century inn on the main street – 'By far the nicest,' says a regular. Fischer (62332) is central, 'very comfortable' with 'friendly staff and good food'.

**Self-catering** There are plenty of apartments to rent.

**Eating out** The restaurants stick mostly to good old-fashioned Austrian cooking. The Rustico was recommended by a 2004 reporter. The Huber-Bräu is a working brewery, which serves good food but closes early. The Bären specialises in Tirolean dishes. For a special meal, locals recommend the Ambiente. The Rialto does good pizza.

**Après-ski** Ice bars and tea dancing greet you as you come off the slopes – Max's Pub is at the bottom of the main piste. In town there are lots of bars that reporters have enjoyed. Tour reps organise outings and the resort itself puts on an event most evenings.

**Off the slopes** There's a public pool with sauna, steam-room and solarium, indoor tennis, ice rink, curling and 40km/25 miles of cleared walks. The railway makes for easy outings to Salzburg or Innsbruck.

TVB WESTENDORF

# Westendorf

*Charming Ski Welt resort with its own small but testing area of slopes*

## COSTS

(1)(2)(3)(4)(5)(6)

## RATINGS

**The slopes**

| | |
|---|---|
| Snow | ** |
| Extent | * |
| Expert | * |
| Intermediate | ** |
| Beginner | *** |
| Convenience | *** |
| Queues | **** |
| Mountain restaurants | *** |

**The rest**

| | |
|---|---|
| Scenery | *** |
| Resort charm | **** |
| Off-slope | ** |

## NEWS

In 2003/04 a new quad chair, the Schneeberglift, replaced the T-bar on the nursery slopes near the centre, improving access for beginners.

The 3-star hotel Holzhamerhof was upgraded to a 4-star and became the Residence 4 Jahreszeiten.



- ➕ Charming traditional village
- ➕ Access to the extensive Ski Welt circuit via nearby Brixen
- ➕ Good local beginners' slopes
- ➕ Jolly if rather limited après-ski scene

- ➖ Local slopes are limited in extent, and mainly of genuine red gradient – so they suit neither keen intermediates nor novices
- ➖ Poor natural snow record, though now extensive snowmaking

**Westendorf is on the Ski Welt lift pass, and its serious red slopes are worth visiting from Söll or Ellmau. As a base, we find it difficult to recommend. Keen intermediates will want quicker access to the main Ski Welt circuit, while novices and timid intermediates may find the local slopes challenging.**

## THE RESORT

Westendorf is a small village with a charming main street and attractive onion-domed church (it was once declared 'Europe's most beautiful village' in a floral competition). The centre is close to the nursery slopes but a five-minute walk from the main gondola outside the village.

## THE MOUNTAIN

The local slopes are small, but you can get into the Ski Welt circuit easily via a bus to Brixen and then a gondola.

**Slopes** A two-stage gondola takes you to Talkaser, from where one main north-west-facing red run goes back to the resort (with blue options on the lower half). Short west- and east-facing pistes at the top run below the peaks of Choralpe, Fleiding and Gampen. A couple of red runs from Fleiding go down past the lifts to hamlets served by buses. A 2004 reporter particularly enjoyed these.

**Terrain-parks** There's a good terrain-park with jumps, boxes, rails and a half-pipe, with something for all levels of ability.

**Snow reliability** Westendorf's snow reliability is a bit better than some other Ski Welt resorts and half its pistes now have snowmaking.

**Experts** The slopes are among the most testing in the Ski Welt area, and we guess it's possible to have a lot of fun with a guide.

**Intermediates** Nearly all the local terrain is genuinely red in gradient. The main Ski Welt area has mile after mile of easier intermediate runs.

**Beginners** Extensive village nursery slopes are Westendorf's pride and joy. There are a couple of blues to progress to, but the reds are real reds.

**Snowboarding** The new chair on the nursery slopes will make life easier for beginners. There are some tedious catwalks at altitude.

**Cross-country** There are 30km/19 miles of local cross-country trails along the valley but snow-cover is erratic.

**Queues** Given good conditions, queues are rare, and far less of a problem than in the main Ski Welt area. If poor weather closes the upper lifts, queues can become long.

**Mountain restaurants** Alpenrosenhütte is woody and warm, with good food; recent visitors enjoyed the quiet, 'very pleasant' Brechhornhaus; the Choralp (top of gondola) gets busy but is 'reasonably priced'; the Gassnerwirt is good but you have to catch a bus back to town.

TVB WESTENDORF

The red slopes are genuine reds – this is on the back of Fleiding →

Great nursery slopes, given decent snow. Beyond the village, Hohe Salve and the main Ski Welt circuit →

TVB WESTENDORF

## KEY FACTS

| | |
|---|---|
| **Resort** | 800m 2,620ft |
| For Westendorf only | |
| **Slopes** | 800-1890m 2,620-6,200ft |
| **Lifts** | 13 |
| **Pistes** | 45km 28 miles |
| **Blue** | 49% |
| **Red** | 40% |
| **Black** | 11% |
| **Snowmaking** | 40km 25 miles |
| For Ski Welt | |
| **Slopes** | 620-1890m 2,030-6,200ft |
| **Lifts** | 91 |
| **Pistes** | 250km 155 miles |
| **Blue** | 43% |
| **Red** | 48% |
| **Black** | 9% |
| **Snowmaking** | 160km 99 miles |

## ON YOUR OWN?

You can team up with other skiers/ boarders by turning up at 10am or 1pm at one of seven designated points in the Ski Welt; there are stickers to identify participants, and even a web site forum for making prior arrangements.

**Phone numbers**
From elsewhere in Austria add the prefix 05334.
From abroad use the prefix +43 5334.

## TOURIST OFFICE

**t** 6230
info@westendorf.com
www.westendorf.com

**Schools and guides** The three ski schools have quite good reputations, though classes can be large. One reporter tells of her teenage son's 'excellent' private lesson with the Top school: 'He's been skiing since he was three, but this was a revelation.' Others praise the Westendorf school: 'teachers very good, good value, great prize-giving in town hall' and 'excellent instructor, good English, really improved my skiing'.

**Facilities for children** Westendorf sells itself as a family resort. Both the nursery and the ski kindergarten are open all day.

## STAYING THERE

**How to go** A couple of mainstream operators offer packages here.

**Hotels** There are central 4-star hotels – the Jakobwirt (6245) and the 'excellent' Schermer (6268) – and a dozen 3-star ones. The 3-star Post (6202) is 'good value, right in the centre, few facilities except rooms, dining room and bar'. Among more modest guest houses, Haus Wetti (6348) is popular, and away from the church bells. Pension Ingeborg (6577) has been highly recommended and is next to the gondola station.

**Self-catering** The Schermerhof apartments are of good quality.

**Eating out** Most of the best restaurants are in hotels – the Schermer, Mesnerwirt, Post and Jakobwirt are good. The Wastlhof and Klingler have also been recommended. Get a taxi to Berggasthof Stimlach for a good evening out.

**Après-ski** Nightlife is quite lively, but it's a small place with limited options. The One for the Road Bar and Liftstüberl, at the bottom of the gondola, are packed at the end of the day. The Moskito Bar has live music and theme nights but is said by a (grown-up) reporter to be 'a bit of a dive'. The Village Pub, next to the hotel Post, is very popular and sells draught Guinness.

**Off the slopes** There are excursions by rail or bus to Innsbruck and Salzburg. Walks and sleigh rides are very pretty. In February, the Jump and Freeze night is recommended viewing – 'all good fun' in a party atmosphere.

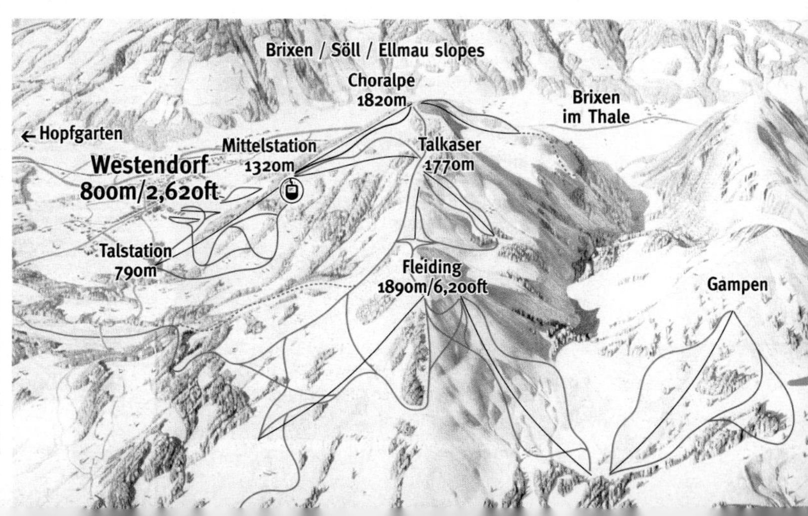

ZELL AM SEE TOURIST OFFICE

# Zell am See

*Charming lakeside town, varied slopes and glacier option at Kaprun*

## COSTS

①②③④⑤⑥

## RATINGS

| **The slopes** | |
|---|---|
| Snow | ** |
| Extent | ** |
| Expert | ** |
| Intermediate | *** |
| Beginner | *** |
| Convenience | ** |
| Queues | ** |
| Mountain restaurants | *** |
| **The rest** | |
| Scenery | *** |
| Resort charm | *** |
| Off-slope | **** |

## NEWS

For 2003/04 the main gondola out of Zell am See was fitted with new cabins and upgraded, giving a 25% quicker journey, and renamed City Xpress.



- ➕ Pretty, tree-lined slopes with great views down to the lake
- ➕ Lively, but not rowdy, nightlife
- ➕ Charming old town centre with beautiful lakeside setting
- ➕ Lots to do off the slopes
- ➕ Huge range of cross-country trails
- ➕ Kaprun glacier nearby
- ➕ Varied terrain including a couple of steep black runs

- ➖ Sunny, low slopes often have poor conditions despite snowmaking, which makes the area more limited
- ➖ Trek to lifts from much of the accommodation, and sometimes crowded buses
- ➖ Less suitable for beginners than most small Austrian resorts
- ➖ The Kaprun glacier gets lengthy queues when it is most needed

**Zell am See is not a rustic village like most of its Austrian rivals, but a lakeside summer resort town with a charming old centre. For a small area, Zell's slopes have a lot of variety and challenging terrain, but not enough to keep a keen intermediate or expert happy for long – only 75km/47 miles of piste, if you ignore Kaprun's Kitzsteinhorn glacier. Zell is close to Kaprun, but if snow is in short supply Zell visitors have no special claim: you have to queue for access along with visitors coming from Saalbach, Kitzbühel and other low resorts.**

## THE RESORT

Zell am See is a long-established, year-round resort town set between a large lake and a mountain. Its charming, traffic-free medieval centre is on a flat promontory, and the resort has grown up around this attractive core. A gondola at the edge of town (served by ski-buses) goes up one arm of the horseshoe-shaped mountain, and there are hotels around here, too. 2km/1 mile away in the Schmittental, in the centre of the horseshoe, are two cable-cars; there is some accommodation, too.

A more radical alternative is to stay in Schüttdorf, 3km/2 miles away, where there is another gondola. But it is a characterless dormitory with little else going for it. Though closer to Kaprun, this is, perversely, a drawback unless you have a car. Trying to get on a glacier bus is tough, as they tend to be full when they leave Zell. Cross-country skiers and families wishing to use the Areitalm nursery stand to gain most from staying in Schüttdorf.

Kaprun's snow-sure glacier slopes are only a few minutes by crowded buses (best to get on at the bus station says a 2004 reporter); Saalbach is easily reached by bus and Bad Hofgastein by train. At a push, Wagrain, Schladming and Obertauern are car trips.

## THE MOUNTAINS

Zell's mountain is horseshoe-shaped. The easiest runs are along the open ridges, with steeper pistes descending through woods to the Schmittental.

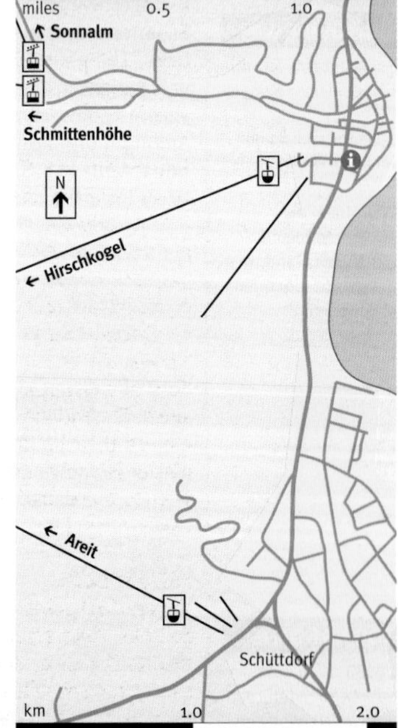

This is where the crowds go to find the best snow, the Kitzsteinhorn glacier →

ZELL AM SEE TOURIST OFFICE

**KEY FACTS**

| | |
|---|---|
| **Resort** | 755m<br>2,480ft |
| For Zell and Kaprun | |
| **Slopes** | 755-3030m<br>2,480-9,940ft |
| **Lifts** | 57 |
| **Pistes** | 130km<br>81 miles |
| **Blue** | 43% |
| **Red** | 38% |
| **Black** | 19% |
| **Snowmaking** | 61.5km<br>38 miles |
| For Zell only | |
| **Slopes** | 755-2000m<br>2,480-6,560ft |
| **Lifts** | 28 |
| **Pistes** | 75km<br>47 miles |
| **Snowmaking** | 50km<br>31 miles |
| For Kaprun only | |
| **Slopes** | 785-3030m<br>2,580-9,940ft |
| **Lifts** | 29 |
| **Pistes** | 55km<br>34 miles |
| **Snowmaking** | 5.5km<br>3 miles |

**THE SLOPES**
***Varied but limited***

The new town gondola (now called City Xpress) takes you to Mittelstation and is said to be 'very efficient'. From there it's either an easy or a steep run to the cable-car station in the Schmittental. Or you can take a fast chair up to Hirschkogel to meet the gondola up from Schüttdorf – you can ride this up further or take an alternative chair to Schmittenhöhe. This is also where the main Schmittental cable-car brings you. A gentle cruise and a single short drag-lift moves you to Sonnkogel. Here several routes lead down to Sonnalm mid-station – where another cable-car from the Schmittental arrives. A black piste runs from here to the valley floor. At the end of the day you can take a gentle piste back to town or ride one of the lifts down.

**TERRAIN-PARKS**
***Man-made and 'natural'***

There's a half-pipe on Schmittenhöhe and a terrain-park on the Kitzsteinhorn glacier.

**SNOW RELIABILITY**
***Good snowmaking, but lots of sun***

Zell am See's slopes get so much sun the snow can suffer as a result. Lots of slopes are now well covered by snow-guns, including the sunny home run to Schüttdorf and 70% of the lower slopes. But though reporters have seen 'lots of snowmaking in evidence', slush, ice and closed runs have still marred their holidays. The Kaprun glacier is snow-sure, but expect long queues there (and for buses there and back) when snow is short elsewhere.

**FOR EXPERTS**
***Several blacks, but still limited***

Zell has more steep slopes than most resorts this size, but can't entertain an expert for a week. When we were last there it was fabulous speeding down the immaculately groomed black runs 13 and 14 – they were deserted first thing in the morning. However, as a reporter points out, 'they are more like French reds'. Off-piste opportunities are limited.

**FOR INTERMEDIATES**
***Bits and pieces for most grades***

Good intermediates have a choice of fine, long runs, but this is not a place for mileage. All blacks are usually well groomed and within a brave intermediate's capability, and there's a lovely cruising run between Areit and Schüttdorf when conditions are good. Some Sonnkogel pistes are also suitable. The timid can cruise the ridge all day on quiet, attractive runs, or head past Mittelstation to Zell's cable-cars on an easy blue.

Kaprun's high, snow-sure glacier runs are also ideal for intermediates not looking for too great a challenge.

**FOR BEGINNERS**
***Two low nursery areas***

There are small nursery slopes at the cable-car area and at Schüttdorf, both covered by snow-guns. Near-beginners and fast learners have plenty of short, easy runs at Schmittenhöhe, Breiteck and Areit. Some are used by complete beginners when snow conditions are poor lower down, but it means buying a lift pass.

**FOR CROSS-COUNTRY**
***Excellent if snow allows***

The valley floor has extensive areas, including a superb area on the Kaprun golf course. At altitude there are just two short loops, one at the top of the Kaprun glacier, and the other at the top of the Zell gondola.

**QUEUES**
***Not normally a problem***

Zell am See doesn't have many problems except at peak times, when

## LIFT PASSES

**Europa–Sportregion Kaprun–Zell am See**
Covers all lifts in Zell and Kaprun, and buses between them.

**Main pass**
1 day €34.50
6 days €164

**Children**
Under 19: 6 days €147.50
Under 16: 6 days €82
Under 6: free pass

**Notes**
One-day pass price is for Schmittenhöhe (Zell) only. Kitzsteinhorn-only and Maiskogel-only day passes also available.

**Alternative passes**
Salzburg Super Ski Card covers huge area round Salzburg province from Abtenau to Zell and is available for three days or more.





## boarding

*Zell is well suited to boarders and most lifts are chairs, gondolas and cable-cars. You'll also find plenty of life in the evenings. The Kaprun glacier has powder in its wide, open bowl. But it also has a high proportion of drag-lifts – a day of this and the 'small walk' to enter the terrain-park exhausted some reporters who said 'a chair-lift would be most welcome'. Snowboard Academy is a specialist school.*

the cable-cars are generally the worst hit. One reporter recommends getting to Schmittenhöhe via the Sonnalm cable-car as a quieter route. When snow is poor there are few daytime queues at Zell – many people are away queueing at Kaprun – but getting down by lift at the end of the day can involve delays. The queue for the bus back from Kaprun was said by a 2004 reporter to be 'chaotic – a heaving mass, all scrambling and fighting to get on the one small bus provided'.

### MOUNTAIN RESTAURANTS
***Plenty of little refuges***

There are plenty of cosy, atmospheric huts dotted around the Zell slopes, helpfully named on the piste map. Among the best are Glocknerhaus, Kettingalm, Areitalm, Breiteckalm and Blaickner's Sonnalm ('the best strudel' says a 2004 reporter). Pinzgauer Hütte, in the woods at the back of Schmittenhöhe, is also recommended by reporters. The Berghotel at Schmittenhöhe is good, but expensive. Its bar with loud music is lively in the afternoons (see Après-ski). The Panorama-Pfiff gets crowded, but 'has wonderful views and quite good food'.

### SCHOOLS AND GUIDES
***A wide choice***

There is a choice of schools in both Zell am See and Kaprun. We get few reports, but a recent one said boarding lessons from the main Zell school were 'well organised', though classes were a bit large and English not always spoken fluently. There are also specialist cross-country centres at Schüttdorf and at Kaprun.

### FACILITIES FOR CHILDREN
***Schüttdorf's the place***

We have no recent reports on the childcare provisions, but staying in Schüttdorf has the advantage of direct gondola access to the Areitalm snow-kindergarten. There's a children's adventure park on the mountain.

↑ The top of Zell's slopes at Schmittenhöhe, complete with the Berghotel and Schnapps Hans ice bar

ZELL AM SEE TOURIST OFFICE



## CHILDREN

**Kinderskiwelt Areit**
t 56020
Ages from 2; with ski lessons for children over 3

**Babysitter list**
At the tourist office

**Ski schools**
Take children from age 4 (5 days including lunch €190)

## SCHOOLS

**Zell am See**
t 56020
skischule@zellamsee.at

**Sport Alpin**
t 0664 453 1417
info@sport-alpin.at

**Snowboard Academy**
t 0664 253 0381
office@fot.at

**Classes**
(Zell prices)
5 days (2hr am and pm) €135

**Private lessons**
€50 for 1 hr

## GETTING THERE

**Air** Salzburg 87km/54 miles (2hr); Munich 180km/112 miles (3hr).

**Rail** Station in resort.

## STAYING THERE

### HOW TO GO
*Choose charm or convenience*

Lots of hotels, pensions and apartments.
**Hotels** A broad range of hotels (more 4- than 3-stars) and guest houses.
((((4) **Salzburgerhof** (7650) Best in town – the only 5-star. It is nearer the lake than the gondola, but has courtesy bus and pool.
((((4) **Tirolerhof** (7720) Excellent 4-star in old town. 'Greatly improved' pool, hot-tub and steam room. 'Very comfortable, very friendly and efficient staff,' says a reporter.
((((4) **Eichenhof** (47201) On outskirts of town, but popular and with a minibus service, great food and lake views.
((((4) **Alpin** (7690) Modern 4-star chalet next to the Zell gondola.
((((4) **Zum Hirschen** (7740) Comfortable 4-star, easy walk to gondola. Sauna, steam, splash pool, popular bar.
((((4) **Schwebebahn** (724610) Attractive 4-star in secluded setting in the Schmittental, by the cable-cars.
((((4) **Metzgerwirt** (72520) 4-star close lake and centre. 'Very good, really wild decor, friendly,' says a visitor.
((2) **Margarete** (72724) B&B in the Schmittental, by the cable-cars.
**Self-catering** Lots of options. Apartment Hofer (80480) is mid-range and close to the Ebenberg lift (linking to the gondola); no boarders. More comfortable are the 3-star Diana (72436) and Seilergasse (68787), both in the centre.

### STAYING UP THE MOUNTAIN
*Three options*

As well as the Berghotel (72489) at the top of the Schmittenhöhe cable-car, the Breiteckalm (73419) and Sonnalm (73262) restaurants have rooms.

### EATING OUT
*Plenty of choice*

Zell has more non-hotel places than is usual in a small Austrian resort. The Ampere is quiet and sophisticated; Giuseppe's is a popular Italian with excellent food; and Kupferkessel and Traubenstüberl both do wholesome regional dishes. There are Chinese restaurants in Zell and Schüttdorf. Car drivers can try the excellent Erlhof.

### APRES-SKI
*Plenty for all tastes*

Après-ski is lively and varied, with tea dances and high-calorie cafes, plus bars and discos aplenty. 'Even as a 55-year-old I had a great time pubbing,' says a reporter. When it's sunny, Schnapps Hans ice bar outside the Berghotel, up the mountain at Schmittenhöhe, really buzzes, with 'great music, a crazy DJ and dancing on tables and on the bar. All ages loved it.' The Diele disco bar rocks; Crazy Daisy on the main road has two crowded bars (one now called Irish Daisy) and 'the group loved it' says one reporter; 'good Guinness' says another. Classic has a live band and 60s and 70s music. The Viva disco allows no under 18s; one reader proclaimed it 'excellent'. Or try the smart Hirschenkeller, the cave-like Lebzelter Keller and the Sportstüberl, with nostalgic ski photos adorning the walls. Lupo's has 'the cheapest beer in town and satellite TV, but is scruffy'.

### OFF THE SLOPES
*Lots of choices*

There is plenty to do in this year-round resort. The train trip to Salzburg is a must, Kitzbühel is also well worth a visit and Innsbruck is within reach.

You can often walk across the frozen lake to Thumersbach, plus there are good sports facilities, a motor museum, sleigh rides and alpine flights.

## ACTIVITIES

**Indoor** Swimming, sauna, solarium, fitness centre, spa, tennis, squash, bowling, art gallery, museum, riding hall, cinema, library, massage

**Outdoor** Ice rink, curling, tobogganing, plane flights, sleigh rides, shooting range, paragliding, hang gliding

**Phone numbers**
**Zell am See**
From elsewhere in Austria add the prefix 06542.
From abroad use the prefix +43 6542.

**Kaprun**
From elsewhere in Austria add the prefix 06547.
From abroad use the prefix +43 6547.

## TOURIST OFFICE

**Zell am See/Kaprun**
**t** 7700
welcome@europasportregion.info
www.europasportregion.info

# Kaprun 785m/2,580ft

### THE RESORT

Kaprun is a spacious, charming and quite lively village. The main road to the glacier bypasses it, leaving the centre pleasantly quiet.

### THE MOUNTAIN

There is a small area of slopes on the outskirts of the village at Maiskogel, served by a cable-car and drag-lifts and best suited to early intermediates. There is also a separate nursery area. But most people will want to spend most of their time on the slopes of the nearby Kitzsteinhorn glacier or on Zell am See's slopes. Buses to and from both are often crowded. The lift pass covers only one ascent of the Kitzsteinhorn access gondola per day.

**Slopes** A 15-person, two-stage gondola has replaced the funicular, which suffered a tragic fire in autumn 2000. The first-stage runs parallel with an older eight-person gondola, ending in the same mid-mountain area. The second stage, up to the Alpincenter and main slopes, runs parallel to a fast quad chair. The main slopes are in a big bowl above the Alpincenter served by a cable-car, lots of T-bars and three chairs. The area above the top of the Alpincenter is open in summer and is particularly good for an early pre-Christmas or late post-Easter break.

**Snow reliability** Snow is nearly always good because of the glacier. And there's snowmaking too.

**Queues** Queues have always been a problem here. Our 2004 reports tell of 15-minute waits for the access gondola (down as well as up) and up to 10 minutes for the upper lifts. See Zell am See for comments on the buses home.

**Mountain restaurants** There are three decent mountain restaurants – the Gletschermühle and Krefelderhütte near the Alpincenter, and the Häusalm near the new gondola mid-station. All these get busy. Bella Vista at the top of the mountain has good views.

**Experts** There's little to challenge experts except for some good off-piste; the one slightly tough piste starts at the very top.

**Intermediates** Pistes are mainly gentle blues and reds and make for great easy cruising on usually good snow. From Alpincenter there is an entertaining red run down to the new gondola mid-station. This is our favourite run on the mountain, though it does get crowded. There's also a good unpisted ski route.

**Beginners** There are a couple of nursery slopes in the village and some gentle blues on the glacier to progress to.

**Snowboarding** There's a terrain-park on the glacier and some excellent natural half-pipes.

**Cross-country** The Kaprun golf course is superb, but at altitude there is just one short loop – at the top of the glacier.

**Schools and guides** There are several ski schools.

**Facilities for children** All of the schools offer children's classes and there's a kindergarten in the village.

### STAYING THERE

**How to go** There are some catered chalets and chalet-hotels.

**Hotels** The Orgler (82050), 'spacious' Mitteregger (8207 ) and Tauernhof (8235) are among the best hotels.

**Après-ski** Nightlife is quiet, but the Baum bar is lively.

**Eating out** Good restaurants include the Dorfstadl, Hilberger's Beisl and Schlemmerstube.

**Off the slopes** Off-slope activities are good, and include a fine sports centre with outdoor rapids.

TVB BAD KLEINKIRCHHEIM

# Bad Kleinkirchheim

**BKK attracts surprisingly few British visitors and is tucked away in the province of Carinthia, in the far south-east of Austria near the Italian and Slovenian borders. The slopes aren't easy but suit good intermediates well.**

### KEY FACTS

| | |
|---|---|
| Resort | 1090m<br>3,580ft |
| Slopes | 1100-2055m<br>3,610-6,740ft |
| Lifts | 26 |
| Pistes | 90km<br>56 miles |
| Blue | 17% |
| Red | 72% |
| Black | 11% |
| Snowmaking | 75km<br>47 miles |

## THE RESORT

BKK, as the locals call it, is home to Austrian super-hero, 1976 Olympic downhill champion Franz Klammer. He was born nearby, learned to ski here, and recently celebrated his 50th birthday here. This old spa town has mainly chalet-style buildings and is very spread out along the valley; the most convenient place to stay is near one of the main lifts out. There are three 5-stars and 17 4-star hotels, as well as cheaper options. Not surprisingly, there are superb spa facilities, but nightlife is rather quiet compared with many Austrian resorts.

## THE MOUNTAINS

BKK's main home slopes are reached by gondola or a high-speed quad from different parts of the village. They link in with St Oswald's slopes further along the valley, served by two gondolas. Despite Franz Klammer's endorsement, BKK has little to keep experts interested for a week. There are a few short black runs, including one that turns into the red Franz Klammer Downhill to the bottom of the gondola. Virtually all the slopes are ideal for intermediates. Over 70% are graded red and are long, wide and flattering. Having the two separate but linked areas adds a bit of variety. The lift pass also covers all other resorts in Carinthia.

There are nursery slopes and drag-lifts for beginners at both BKK and St Oswald – the St Oswald ones are much warmer and sunnier in mid-winter. Once off the nursery slopes, there is an easy blue run at the top of the Nockalm gondola and a long blue all the way from the top to the bottom.

### TOURIST OFFICE

**t** 04240 8212
info@badkleinkirchheim.at
www.bkk.at

TVB SEEFELD

# Seefeld

**Seefeld is a smart, all-round winter holiday resort in a pretty setting, with superb cross-country trails and off-slope activities, and a couple of small, separate areas of downhill slopes. Innsbruck is not far away.**

### KEY FACTS

| | |
|---|---|
| Resort | 1200m<br>3,940ft |
| Slopes | 1200-2100m<br>3,940-6,890ft |
| Lifts | 32 |
| Pistes | 45km<br>28 miles |
| Blue | 70% |
| Red | 30% |
| Black | 0% |
| Snowmaking | 15km<br>9 miles |

## THE RESORT

A classic post-war Tirolean tourist development, Seefeld is well designed in traditional Tirolean style, with a large, pedestrian-only centre. Lots of people come here for the curling, skating and swimming rather than skiing. The upmarket nature of the resort is reflected in the hotels – there are four 5-stars and almost 30 4-stars. The village is on a main railway line.

## THE MOUNTAINS

The slopes are in two main sectors – Gschwandtkopf and Rosshütte. Both are on the outskirts, served by a regular free shuttle-bus. The nursery slopes in the centre of the village are broad and gentle, with snowmaking.

Gschwandtkopf is a rounded hill with 300m/980ft of intermediate vertical down two main slopes, while Rosshütte is more extensive and has a terrain-park and half-pipe. The top of Rosshütte can be reached by a funicular – 'very efficient' says a reader – and then a cable-car. From the valley two six-seater chairs go to the shoulder of Härmelekopf – an improvement on the cable-car from Rosshütte – allowing repeated runs of the lower half as well as the long run from the top.

Rosshütte has some seriously steep off-piste challenges for experts and will offer intermediates an interesting day out from Innsbruck – but the terrain is of no interest for a week's stay.

Seefeld's 285km/177 miles of excellent cross-country trails are some of the best in the Alps – one reason why nearby Innsbruck has been able to hold the Winter Olympics twice (and the Nordic World Ski Championships).

### TOURIST OFFICE

**t** 05212 2313
info@seefeld.at
www.seefeld.at

TVB SERFAUS

## KEY FACTS

| | |
|---|---|
| **Resort** | 1430m<br>4,690ft |
| **Slopes** | 1200-2700m<br>3,940-8,860ft |
| **Lifts** | 53 |
| **Pistes** | 160km<br>99 miles |
| **Blue** | 20% |
| **Red** | 70% |
| **Black** | 10% |
| **Snowmaking** | 75km<br>47 miles |

## TOURIST OFFICE

**t** 05476 6239
info@serfaus.com
www.serfaus-fiss-ladis.com
www.serfaus.com

# Serfaus

**Serfaus offers the charm and nightlife of a typical Austrian village but with extensive slopes (shared with Fiss and Ladis), fairly reliable snow and the huge benefit of being largely traffic-free.**

## THE RESORT

Serfaus is attractive and friendly, with chalet-style buildings set on a sunny shelf. It is largely traffic-free, with an underground railway running from a car park at one end to the lifts at the other, with two stops en route. Most accommodation is in comfortable, chalet-style hotels.

Most visitors are well-heeled Germans, many of them family groups. There are few British visitors. There are several après-ski bars, but evenings are not riotous. There is a 10km/6 mile toboggan run to the village.

## THE MOUNTAINS

Three gondolas radiate from the village, including one to the mid-mountain focus of Komperdell (1980m/6,500ft). There's a broad area of intermediate slopes above here, with some good long runs down to the village. There are a few black runs, lots of ski routes, and plenty of little-used off-piste. A chain of lifts and runs extends west, ending an extraordinary 11km/7 miles from the village. Many of the drags here are due to be replaced by fast lifts in the next year or two.

One of the village gondolas leads to the slopes of Fiss (1435m/4,710ft), where there are extensive sunny slopes served by a long gondola to Schönjoch and shorter shady runs beyond.

Most of the slopes in both sectors are above the tree line (ie above 1800m/5,910ft), and there is extensive snowmaking – so the area is reasonably snow-sure despite the sun. Queues are not a problem.

Both the village and mid-station nursery slopes are good, and there is ample opportunity for progression.

SNOWPIX.COM / CHRIS GILL

## KEY FACTS

| | |
|---|---|
| **Resort** | 850m<br>2,790ft |
| **Slopes** | 850-2190m<br>2,790-7,190ft |
| **Lifts** | 64 |
| **Pistes** | 200km<br>124 miles |
| **Blue** | 20% |
| **Red** | 75% |
| **Black** | 5% |

## TOURIST OFFICE

**t** 06413 8448
info@wagrain.info
www.wagrain.info
www.sportwelt-amade.com

# Wagrain

**Wagrain is a towny little resort at the centre of a lift system that is typical of many in Salzburger Land – spreading widely across several low, partly wooded ridges. Flachau and Alpendorf/St Johann are at its extremities.**

## THE RESORT

Wagrain is an unremarkable valley village where life does not revolve entirely around skiing. The lift stations are on the fringes of the village and served by ski-buses – one up at the elevated suburb of Kirchboden, along with the nursery slopes and the excellent Wasserwelt pool complex.

## THE MOUNTAINS

It's an impressive lift system, with eight six-packs and countless quad chairs. To the south-west of Wagrain, a gondola to Grafenberg leads to an area of short lifts and runs and so to Hirschkogel above Alpendorf, a satellite of St Johann im Pongau. To the east, from Kirchboden, another gondola goes to Griessenkareck, at the top of the slopes down to Flachau. It's a big area – 15km/9 miles from end to end – with some good, long, although easy runs. The slopes are practically all graded red, with a few blues dotted around. The reds are generally not very testing, but they are genuine reds, and none of the home runs is really easy. The few stretches of black are for purely decorative purposes. Despite the altitude, most of the upper slopes are fairly open. Some get too much sun for comfort, and snow reliability is not a strong point. There are lots of attractive mountain restaurants.

The Salzburger Sportwelt lift pass area includes another similar lift system (tantalisingly close but connected only by buses) to the south, linking Zauchensee, Flachauwinkl and Kleinarl – more easily accessed from Wagrain or Flachau than Alpendorf/St Johann. There are also smaller areas at Filzmoos and Radstadt/ Altenmarkt.

TVB WILDSCHÖNAU

# Wildschönau

**Wildschönau is the dramatic-sounding name adopted by a group of small resorts in the Tirol – Niederau, Oberau and Auffach. The slopes are limited, but the resorts are popular with beginners and families.**

## KEY FACTS

| | |
|---|---|
| Resort | 830m<br>2,720ft |
| Slopes | 830-1905m<br>2,720-6,250ft |
| Lifts | 28 |
| Pistes | 64km<br>40 miles |
| Blue | 34% |
| Red | 50% |
| Black | 16% |
| Snowmaking | 15km<br>9 miles |

## TOURIST OFFICE

**t** 05339 82550
info@wildschoenau.tirol.at
www.wildschoenau.com

## THE RESORT

Niederau is the main resort; it's a spread-out little place, with a small cluster of restaurants and shops around the gondola station forming the nearest thing to a focal point. The 4-star Sonnschein (05339 8353) is reportedly the best hotel, and there's a lively but not rowdy après-ski scene. Auffach, a bus-ride away, is a much smaller village, and Oberau, between the two, is the valley's administrative and cultural centre. The villages have traditional chalet-style buildings.

## THE MOUNTAINS

Niederau's slopes are spread over a wooded mountainside that rises no higher than 1600m/5,250ft, so snow reliability is not great. The slopes at Auffach continue above the tree line.

For experts the mountains have little to offer. At Niederau there are a couple of unpisted routes and a black run that is almost of blue gradient.

Most of the slopes suit intermediates well, and the red runs generally deserve their grading. But the run out to the base of the main lifts (a gondola and a slow chair) is wide and flat. And the slopes are very limited – we skied virtually all the runs there in a couple of hours. Auffach has a top-to-bottom gondola serving a 1000m/3,280ft vertical red run, plus a few short, above-the-tree-line runs served by a few drags and a fast chair.

Niederau attracts beginners, and there are excellent nursery slopes at the top and bottom. But there's really only one gentle blue to progress to. There are much better places to learn.

The ski schools have good reputations but classes can be large.

# France

**Over one-third of British skiers and snowboarders choose France for their holidays each year, almost double the number who go to Austria, the next most popular country. It's not difficult to see what attracts us to France. The country has the biggest lift-and-piste networks in the world; for those who like to cover as many miles in a day as possible, these are unrivalled. Most of these big areas are also at high altitude, ensuring high-quality snow for a long season. And French mountains offer a mixture of some of the toughest, wildest slopes in the Alps, and some of the longest, gentlest and most convenient beginner runs.**

**French resort villages can't be quite so uniformly recommended; but, equally, they don't all conform to the standard image of soulless, purpose-built service stations, thrown up without concern for appearance during the boom of the 1960s and 1970s. Many resorts are based on more traditional villages, or offer these as an option. Another advantage of smaller villages and less well-known resorts is that they tend to be cheaper. Some of the big-name resorts can now be very expensive – no more so than Courchevel 1850 where we have heard of staggering prices from reporters who visited last season.**

**Towards the front of the book there is a special chapter on driving to the French Alps – still very popular, especially with people going self-catering, despite the growth of the budget airlines. The French Alps are easy to get to by car, and comfortable apartments are becoming more common as the French continue their retreat from the short-sighted ways of the 1960s.**



## ANY STYLE OF RESORT YOU LIKE

The main drawback to France, hinted at above, is the monstrous architecture of some of the purpose-built resorts. But not all French resorts are hideous. Certainly, France has its fair share of Alpine eyesores, chief among them central Les Menuires, central La Plagne, Flaine, Tignes, Isola 2000 and Les Arcs. But all these places have learned from past mistakes, and newer developments there are being built in a much more attractive, traditional chalet style. The later generation of purpose-built resorts, such as Valmorel, La Rosière and La Tania, have been built in much more sympathetic style than their predecessors. The big advantages of the high, purpose-built resorts are the splendid quality and extent of the slopes they serve, the reliability and quality of the snow, and the amazing slope-side convenience of most of the accommodation.

If you prefer, there are genuinely old mountain villages to stay in, linked directly to the big lift networks. These are not usually as convenient for the slopes, but they give you a feel of being in France rather than in a winter-holiday factory. Examples include Montchavin or Champagny for La Plagne, Vaujany for Alpe-d'Huez, St-Martin-de-Belleville, Les Allues or Brides-les-Bains for the Trois Vallées and Les Carroz, Morillon or Samoëns (now with a gondola to the slopes) for Flaine. There are also old villages with their own slopes that have developed as resorts while retaining some or all of their rustic ambience – such as Serre-Chevalier and La Clusaz.

SNOWPIX.COM / CHRIS GILL

← Purpose-built high in the mountains, and surrounded by lifts and pistes: La Plagne is a typical French post-war resort – pictured here are two of the most visually attractive parts of what is a highly fragmented resort: Belle-Plagne and Plagne-Villages

## Getting around the French Alps

Pick the right gateway – Geneva, Chambéry or Grenoble – and you can hardly go wrong. The approach to Serre-Chevalier and Montgenèvre involves the 2060m/6,760ft Col du Lauteret; but the road is a major one and kept clear of snow or re-opened quickly after a fall. Crossing the French-Swiss border between Chamonix and Verbier involves two closure-prone passes – the Montets and the Forclaz. When necessary, one-way traffic runs beside the tracks through the rail tunnel beneath the passes.

Megève deserves a special mention – an exceptionally charming little town combining rustic style with luxury and sophistication; shame about the traffic.

And France has Alpine centres with a long mountaineering and skiing history. Chief among these is Chamonix, which sits in the shadow of Mont Blanc, Europe's highest peak, and is the centre of the most radical off-piste terrain in the Alps. Chamonix is a big, bustling town, where skiing and boarding go on alongside tourism in general. At the opposite end of the vacation spectrum is tiny La Grave, at the foot of mountains that are almost as impressive – the highest within France – but with only a few simple hotels.

## IMPROVING APARTMENTS

One of the most welcome developments on the French resort scene in recent years has been the availability of genuinely comfortable and stylish apartments, in contrast to the cramped and, frankly, primitive places that have dominated the market since the 1960s. Central to this shift has been a company called MGM, which has developed apartments (and some chalets) in several resorts; most of these have their own pool and spa, as well as rooms of normal size. We have also been very impressed by the Montagnettes apartments we've stayed in – they are spacious and well furnished. Other top-of-the range apartments include the Soderev and Chalet de Neige ranges.

And now Intrawest – a Canadian company that specialises in building attractive ski resorts that blend in with their surroundings and that has developed Whistler and other pace-setting resorts in North America – has taken its first step into Alpine property

Many French purpose-built resorts are meant to be traffic-free, but Avoriaz really is ➔

OT AVORIAZ / PASCAL VALETTE

development. The first phase of Arc 1950 – a brand new village it is developing – opened for last winter, offering an ambience and style rarely seen on a large scale in French resorts. See the Les Arcs chapter for more on this development.

Tour operator Erna Low offers an especially good range of comfortable apartments in its brochure and covers all the developers mentioned above.

## PLAT DU JOUR

France has advantages over most rival destinations in the gastronomic stakes. While many of its mountain restaurants serve fast food, most also do at least a plat du jour that is in a different league from what you'll find in Austria or the US. It is generally possible to find somewhere to get a half-decent lunch and to have it served at your table, rather than queuing repeatedly for every element of your meal. In the evening, most resorts have restaurants serving good, traditional French food as well as regional specialities. And the wine is decent and affordable.

Many French resorts (though not all) have suffered from a lack of nightlife, but things have changed in recent years. In resorts dominated by apartments with few international visitors, there may still be very little going on after dinner, but places such as Méribel are now distinctly lively in the evening. (It should also be said that nightlife isn't important to many British holidaymakers. Quite a few of our reporting readers say they can't recommend nightspots because all they want to do after dinner is to fall into bed.)

France is unusual among European countries in using four grades of piste (instead of the usual three) – a system of which we heartily approve. The very easiest runs are classified green; except in Val-d'Isère, they are reliably gentle. Since it's relative novices who care most about choosing just the right sort of terrain to build confidence, this is a genuinely helpful system, and one that ought to be adopted internationally.

## AVOID THE CROWDS

French school holidays mean crowded slopes, so they are worth avoiding if possible. The country is divided into three zones, with three fortnight holidays staggered over a four-week period – this season, 5 February to 7 March; from 19 to 28 February the Paris holidays overlap with the other zones – so you can expect that period to be particularly busy.

Always be first on the slopes
...prebook your skis at
skiset.co.uk
SKISET
280 SKI SHOPS IN FRANCE & SWITZERLAND
skiset.co.uk
access code : wheretoski

OT ALPE-D'HUEZ / AGENCE NUTS

# Alpe-d'Huez

*An impressive and sunny all-rounder with alternative bases to stay*

**COSTS**

①②③④⑤6

**RATINGS**

| **The slopes** | |
|---|---|
| Snow | **** |
| Extent | **** |
| Expert | **** |
| Intermediate | **** |
| Beginner | ***** |
| Convenience | **** |
| Queues | **** |
| Mountain restaurants | **** |
| **The rest** | |
| Scenery | **** |
| Resort charm | * |
| Off-slope | *** |

**NEWS**

For 2004/05 a Funitel jumbo gondola, the Marmottes III, will go from the top of the existing Marmottes II gondola to the Sarenne glacier, creating a second route to the glacier as part of a plan to make fuller use of it.

For 2003/04 the Lac Blanc chair-lift from the black runs under the Pic Blanc cable-car back up to above the bottom of the cable-car was upgraded to a quad. Chairs were added to the Alpe Auris chair-lift, which links Alpe-d'Huez and the Signal de l'Homme sector.

There is a new chalet development above Les Bergers.

Snowmaking is being increased.



- + Extensive, high, sunny slopes, split interestingly into various sectors
- + Huge snowmaking installation
- + Vast, gentle, sunny nursery slopes right next to the resort
- + Efficient, modern lift system
- + Some good, surprisingly rustic mountain restaurants
- + Short walks to and from the slopes
- + Livelier than most purpose-built resorts
- + Pleasant alternative bases in outlying villages and satellites

- − In late season the many south-facing runs can be icy early and slushy later
- − Some main intermediate runs get badly overcrowded in high season
- − Many of the tough runs are very high, and inaccessible in bad weather
- − Practically no woodland runs to retreat to in bad weather
- − Run gradings can understate difficulty
- − Sprawling resort with a hotchpotch of architectural styles, no central focus and very little charm

**There are few places to rival Alpe-d'Huez for extent and variety of terrain – in good conditions it's one of our favourites. But, in late season at least, despite ever-expanding snowmaking, the 'island in the sun' suffers from the very thing it advertises: strong sun means that ice can spoil mornings on the main slopes, however alluring the prospect of slushy moguls in the afternoons.**

**The village has few fans, but if you don't like the sound of it you always have the alternative of staying in rustic Vaujany (with its mighty cable-car), Villard-Reculas, or in the modern ski-stations of Oz-en-Oisans or Auris. The whole area is increasingly being referred to as the Massif des Grandes Rousses.**

## THE RESORT

Alpe-d'Huez is a large village spread across an open mountainside, high above the Romanche valley, east of Grenoble and has grown in a seemingly unplanned way. Its buildings come in all shapes, sizes and designs (including a futuristic church which hosts weekly organ concerts). Many buildings look scruffy and in need of renovation, although some wood cladding and general smartening-up can now be seen. It is a large, amorphous resort; the nearest thing to a central focus is the main Avenue des Jeux in the middle, where you'll find the swimming pool, ice skating and some of the shops, bars and restaurants. The rest of the resort spreads out in a triangle, with lift stations at two of the apexes.

The bus service around the resort is free with the lift pass, and there's a handy, but slow, bucket-lift (with a piste beneath it) running through the resort to the main lifts at the top. A recent reporter has described the bucket-lift (known locally as the 'lobster pot') as 'dire' because you need to jump on and off it as it moves. It doesn't operate in the evenings. A short distance from the main body of the resort (and linked by chair-lift) are the 'hamlets' – apartment blocks, mainly – of Les Bergers and L'Eclose.

Les Bergers, at the eastern entrance to the resort, is convenient for the slopes (with its own nursery area), but it's a trek from most of the other resort facilities. There are a couple of bar/restaurants and several shops near the slopes. This quarter is expanding uphill with a chalet suburb, convenient for skiing but remote from the village centre. L'Eclose, to the south of the main village, is the least convenient location and has even less to offer. There is accommodation down the hill in the old village of Huez, linked by lift to the resort.

A couple of 2004 reporters remarked how friendly and welcoming the locals were, compared with other French resorts. Outings by road are feasible to other resorts covered on a week's lift pass, including Serre-Chevalier and Les Deux-Alpes (the latter also reachable for the day by helicopter for a surprisingly modest fee).

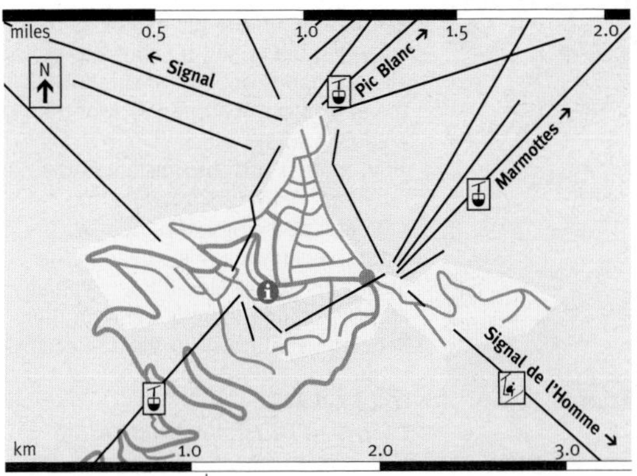


## KEY FACTS

| | |
|---|---|
| **Resort** | 1860m 6,100ft |
| **Slopes** | 1120-3320m 3,670-10,890ft |
| **Lifts** | 87 |
| **Pistes** | 235km 146 miles |
| **Green** | 33% |
| **Blue** | 30% |
| **Red** | 25% |
| **Black** | 12% |
| **Snowmaking** | 55km 34 miles |

## THE MOUNTAINS

Alpe-d'Huez is a big-league resort, ranking alongside giants like Val-d'Isère or La Plagne for the extent and variety of its slopes. Practically all the slopes are above the tree line, and there may be precious little to do when a storm socks in; the runs around Oz are your best bet (if you can get to them).

The piste grading is unreliable. The Hirondelles green run, for example, was commented on by several 2004 reporters as being tricky with a tendency to develop big bumps. Another said, 'The grading is inconsistent – having skied one red run with little difficulty we moved over to the next to find it steeply mogulled halfway down.'

### THE SLOPES
***Several well-linked areas***

The slopes divide into four sectors, with good connections between them, though a 2004 reporter complained of having to pole or walk between lifts and another of poor signposting.

The biggest sector is directly above the village, on the slopes of **Pic Blanc**. There are runs here for everyone, from excellent tough pitches at the top to vast, gentle beginner slopes at the bottom. The huge Grandes Rousses gondola, otherwise known as the DMC (a reference to its clever technology), goes up in two stages from the top of the village. Above it, a cable-car goes up to 3320m/10,890ft on Pic Blanc itself – the top of the Sarenne glacier. A lower area of challenging runs at Clocher de Macle is much more attractive now that it is served by the Marmottes gondola, which is due to go right up to the glacier for 2004/05.

The Sarenne gorge separates the main resort area from **Signal de l'Homme**. A spectacular down-and-up fast chair-lift accesses this area from the Bergers part of the village. From the top you can take excellent north-facing slopes back down towards the gorge, or head south to Auris or west to the old hamlet of Chatelard.

On the other side of town from Signal de l'Homme is the small **Signal** sector, reached by drag-lifts next to the main gondola or by a couple of chairs lower down. Runs go down the other

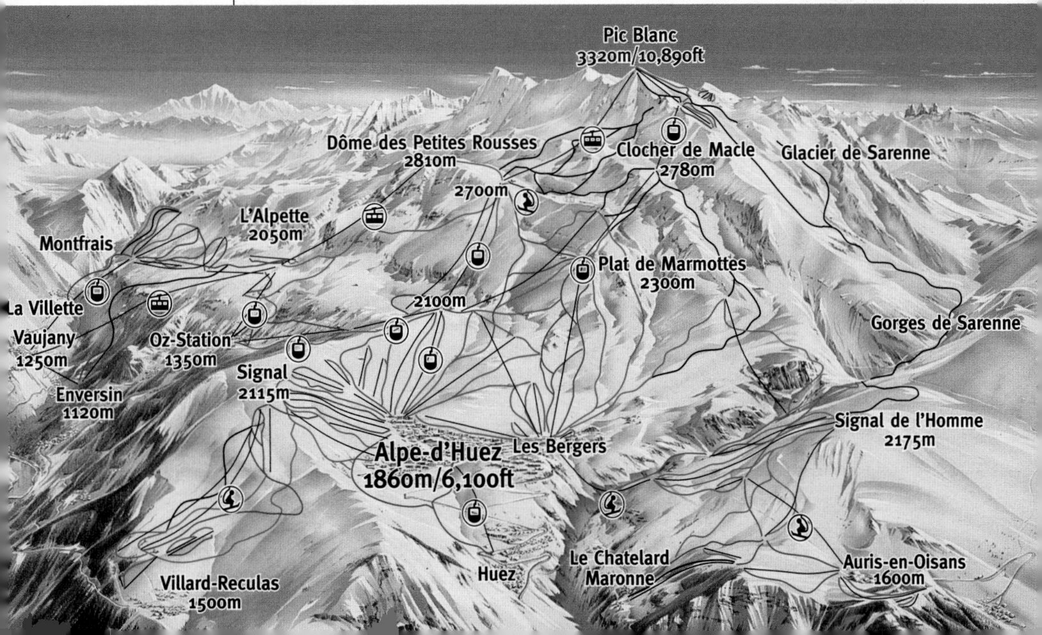

↑ Alpe-d'Huez sits in a very sunny bowl and the slopes get steeper the higher up you go

OT ALPE-D'HUEZ / AGENCE NUTS





## LIFT PASSES

**Visalp**
Covers all lifts in Alpe-d'Huez, Auris, Oz, Vaujany and Villard-Reculas.

**Beginners**
1 day €11

**Main pass**
1 day €34.50
6 days €178.50

**Senior citizens**
Over 60: 6 days €126.50
Over 70: free pass

**Children**
Under 16: 6 days €126.50
Under 5: free pass

**Notes**
Half-day passes available. Two-day plus pass covers sports centre, ice rink, swimming pools, concerts, two museums and shuttle service. Six-day or more pass allows one day's skiing at each of Les Deux-Alpes, Serre-Chevalier, Puy-St-Vincent and the Milky Way in Italy.

**Alternative passes**
Passes for Auris only, Oz-Vaujany only, Villard-Reculas only.

side of the hill to the old village of Villard-Reculas. The Signal blue run back to Alpe-d'Huez is now floodlit three nights a week.

The generally quieter **Vaujany-Oz** sector consists largely of north-west-facing slopes, accessible from Alpe-d'Huez via good red runs from either the mid-station or the top of the DMC gondola. At the heart of this sector is Alpette, the mid-station of the cable-car from Vaujany. From here a disastrously sunny red goes down to Oz, and a much more reliable blue goes north to the Vaujany home slopes around Montfrais. The links back to Alpe-d'Huez are by the top cable-car from Alpette, or a gondola from Oz.

Since the black Fare piste was created from below Alpette to Enversin, just below Vaujany, an on-piste descent of 2200m/7,220ft has been possible – not the biggest vertical in the Alps, but not far short. The area does offer the longest piste in the Alps – the 16km/10 mile Sarenne on the back of the Pic Blanc (see the feature panel later in the chapter).

### TERRAIN-PARKS
#### *A choice*

There's a good boarder-cross course, a 1.5km/1 mile terrain-park and a half-pipe near the main lift base, as well as another terrain-park near Auris.

### SNOW RELIABILITY
#### *Affected by the sun*

Alpe-d'Huez is unique among major purpose-built resorts in the Alps in having mainly south- or south-west-facing slopes. The strong southern sun means that late-season conditions may alternate between slush and ice on most of the area, with some of the lower runs being closed altogether. There are shady slopes above Vaujany and at Signal de l'Homme. The small glacier area on the Pic Blanc has been enlarged, but is still too small to pin all your hopes on. The orientation of the slopes is a real drawback of the area as a whole.

In more wintry circumstances the runs are relatively snow-sure, the natural stuff being backed up by extensive snowmaking, covering the main runs above Alpe-d'Huez, Vaujany and Oz, though there is none on the back of Signal down to Villard-Reculas.

### FOR EXPERTS
#### *Plenty of blacks and off-piste*

This is an excellent resort for experts, with long and challenging black runs (and reds that ought to be black) as well as serious off-piste options.

The slope beneath the Pic Blanc cable-car, usually an impressive mogul-field, is reached by a 300m/1,000ft tunnel from the back side of the mountain. The tunnel exit was altered a few years ago, supposedly creating a less awkward start to the actual slope. The slope itself is of ordinary black steepness, but can be very hard in the mornings because it gets a lot of sun. The run splits up part way down – a couple of variants take you to the Lac Blanc chair back up to the cable-car.

The long Sarenne run on the back of the Pic Blanc is described in a special feature panel later in this chapter. We've never found the black Fare piste to Vaujany open, but a reporter rates it 'great – cold and shady'. Some of the upper red pistes are tough enough to give experts a challenge. These include the Canyon and Balme runs accessed by the Lièvre Blanc chair-lift from the gondola mid-station – runs which are unprepared and south-facing (late in the day, perhaps best tackled on a board), and steep enough to be classified black in many resorts. Above this, the Marmottes II gondola serves another series of steep black runs from Clocher de Macle including the beautiful, long, lonely Combe Charbonniere.

The whole area is full of wonderful off-piste opportunities – see opposite.

### FOR INTERMEDIATES
#### *Fine selection of runs*

Good intermediates have a fine selection of runs all over the area. In good snow conditions the variety of runs is difficult to beat. Every section has some challenging red runs to test the adventurous intermediate. The

## OFF-PISTE FOR ALL STANDARDS IN ALPE-D'HUEZ

The **ESF** is the largest ski school in Alpe-d'Huez, with 370 instructors including English-speakers. It organises group or private lessons for all standards and offers off-piste guiding and instruction.

**t** 00 33 476 803169
www.esf-alpedhuez.com

**'Breathe, you're in Alpe-d'Huez' reads the sign upon arrival in the resort, and one big deep breath is what you'll take as you step off at the top of the Pic Blanc cable-car (pictured here), gateway to the resort's best off-piste, says Ben Langridge, a ski instructor with the ESF there. With Ben's help, we pick out just a few of the many runs to be explored.**

*See our separate feature panel on the Sarenne run – the longest black piste in the Alps. For an adventurous intermediate looking to try off-piste for the first time, the many off-piste variants that can be found on both sides of this valley are ideal. Spectacular scenery abounds and, once you are off the glacier, you'll see no lifts, no pylons, just the magnificent peaks of the Les Oisans area. If you are feeling a bit more adventurous, ask your guide about the Combe du Loup, a beautiful south-facing bowl with views over the Meije. With a black run gradient at the top, this itinerary again offers lots of variants allowing those in the know to find excellent snow whatever the weather. You end up on long, more gentle slopes leading back down to the Sarenne Gorge and linking back into the resort. La Chapelle Saint Giraud, which starts at Signal de l'Homme, is another excellent itinerary for those new to venturing off-piste. Its vertical drop of 630m/2,070ft includes a series of small confidence-boosting bowls, interspersed with gentle rolling terrain; great for finding your feet and balance in the deeper snow. You can descend straight into Auris or pass through the hamlet of Cluy further to the east depending on the snow conditions.*

*For more experienced and adventurous off-piste skiers, the Grand Sablat is a classic which runs through a magnificently wild setting on the eastern face of the Massif des Grandes Rousses. This descent of 2000m/6,560ft vertical includes glacial terrain and some steep couloirs.You can either ski down to the village of Clavans where you can take a pre-booked helicopter or taxi back, or traverse across the slopes above Clavans to the Sarenne huts and back to the Sarenne Gorge. La Combe du Bras, in the Villard sector, is another classic: from the ridge leading to the radar station, there are various routes running down towards the village of Huez (you can also drop off the other side of the ridge for runs to Villard-Reculas).*

*The north-facing Vaujany sector is particularly interesting for experienced off-piste enthusiasts. Having a guide for off-piste skiing is essential (avalanche danger, for example, can be high on some of the runs described above), but nowhere more so than here. Route finding can be very tricky, and although the snow stays fresher in the shade, the avalanche pylons dotted across the entire face provide a constant warning. The huge cliffs and rock bands present even more danger; this is not a place to get lost. From the top of Pic Blanc, a 40-minute hike takes you to Col de la Pyramide at 3250m/10,760ft, the starting point for the classic La Pyramide itinerary. With a vertical drop of over 2000m/6,560ft, the beauty of this run is the variety and once at the bottom of the long and wide Pyramide snow field, you can link into the Vaujany pistes. Head in the direction of the Dôme des Petites Rousses cable-car to take in the various Fare itineraries including the spectacular Canyon de la Fare, a long narrow passage between two huge walls of rock. Or cut off earlier and head towards the Col de Couard for some of the more unknown couloirs and routes, including Couloir 263 for experts only, and the Pylon 10 route.*

*Never venture off-piste without a fully qualified guide or instructor, such as one from the ESF. They will be able to show you the most enjoyable and safest route for your standard of skiing and find you the best snow.*

NUTS.FR / JP NOISILLIER / OT ALPE-D'HUEZ

most challenging are the Canyon and Balme runs, mentioned previously. There are lovely long runs down to Oz and to Vaujany. The Villard-Reculas and Signal de l'Homme sectors also have long challenging reds. The Chamois red from the top of the gondola down to the mid-station is beautiful but quite narrow, and miserable when busy and icy. Fearless intermediates should enjoy most of the super-long black runs from Pic Blanc.

For less ambitious intermediates, there are usually blue alternatives except on the upper part of the mountain. The main Couloir blue from the top of the big gondola is a lovely run, well served by snowmaking, but it does get scarily crowded at times.

There are some great cruising runs above Vaujany; but the red runs between Vaujany and Alpe-d'Huez can be too much for early intermediates. Unless you are prepared to travel via Oz on gondolas, you are effectively confined to one sector or the other.

Early intermediates will also enjoy the gentle slopes leading back to Alpe-d'Huez from the main mountain, and the Signal sector.

**FOR BEGINNERS**
***Good facilities***
The large network of green runs immediately above the village is as good a nursery area as you will find anywhere. Sadly, it gets very crowded and carries a lot of fast through-traffic. A large area embracing half a dozen runs has been declared a low-speed zone, but the restriction is not policed and so achieves very little. And beware of the long Hirondelles run: 'should never be classified green' is the verdict of reporters. But in general the quality of the slopes, the convenience, availability of good lessons, a special lift pass covering 11 lifts, still make Alpe-d'Huez good for beginners.

**FOR CROSS-COUNTRY**
***High-level and convenient***
There are 50km/31 miles of trails, with three loops of varying degrees of difficulty, all at around 2000m/6,560ft and consequently relatively snow-sure.

**QUEUES**
***Generally few problems***
Even in French holiday periods, the modern lift system ensures there are few long hold-ups. Queues can build up for the gondolas out of the village, but the DMC shifts its queue quickly and the bottom section can be avoided by taking alternative lifts to the quieter second-stage, which lots of near-beginners don't use.

The small Pic Blanc cable-car is still queue-prone and is often closed by bad weather; both problems should be relieved by the new Marmottes III gondola, due to open up an alternative route to the glacier for 2004/05.

The inadequate double Lac Blanc chair-lift (to get back up to the Pic Blanc cable-car from black runs from the top) has been replaced by a quad, easing queues there. Although they may not cause queues, there are lots of old drag-lifts scattered around.

A greater problem than lift queues,

**THE LONGEST PISTE IN THE ALPS – AND IT'S BLACK?**

*It's no surprise that most ski runs that are seriously steep are also seriously short. The really long runs in the Alps tend to be classified blue, or red at the most. The Parsenn runs above Klosters, for example – typically 12km to 15km (7 miles to 9 miles) long – are manageable in your first week on skis. Even Chamonix's famous Vallée Blanche off-piste run doesn't include steepness in its attractions.*

*So you could be forgiven for being sceptical about the 'black' Sarenne run from the top of the Pic Blanc to the Sarenne gorge that separates the resort from the Signal de l'Homme sector. Even though the vertical is an impressive 2000m/6,560ft, a run 16km/10 miles in length means an average gradient of only 11% – typical of a blue run. Macho-hype on the part of the lift company, presumably?*

*Not quite. The Sarenne is a run of two halves. The bottom half is virtually flat (boarders beware) but the top half is a genuine black if you take the direct route – a demanding and highly satisfying run (with stunning views) that any keen, competent skier will enjoy. The steep mogul-field near the top can be avoided by taking a newly created easier option; and the whole run can now be tackled by an adventurous intermediate. The run gets a lot of sun, so pick your time with care – there's nothing worse than a sunny run with no sun.*

The resort probably looks better at night than in the day →

NUTS.FR / JP NOISILLIER / OT ALPE-D'HUEZ

over much of the area is that the main pistes can be unbearably crowded. We and many reporters rate the Chamois and Couloir runs from the top of the DMC among the most crowded we've seen. A 2004 reporter said of the blue Couloir, 'I witnessed more collisions in one week than I do in a year working as a traffic police officer on one of Britain's busiest motorways.' To avoid the crowds, head for Vaujany and Oz.

## MOUNTAIN RESTAURANTS

### *Some excellent rustic huts*

Mountain restaurants are generally good – even self-service places are welcoming, and there are many more rustic places with table-service than you'd expect to find in French purpose-built resorts. One of our favourites is the cosy little Chalet du Lac Besson, on one of the cross-country loops north of the DMC gondola mid-station – the route to it now has piste status (the Boulevard des Lacs blue), but is no easier to follow in practice.

The pretty Forêt de Maronne hotel at Chatelard, below Signal de l'Homme, is delightful and has a good choice of traditional French cuisine. The Combe Haute, at the foot of the Chalvet chair in the gorge towards the end of the Sarenne run, is welcoming but gets very busy. The Hermine, at the base of the Fontfroide lift, is recommended for basic but good-value food. The terrace of the Perce-Neige, just below the Oz-Poutran gondola mid-station, attracts crowds. The Plage des Neiges at the top of the nursery slopes is one of the best places available to beginners. The Bergerie at Villard-Reculas has good views and is highly recommended by reporters. Chantebise 2100, at the DMC mid-station, offers slick and cheerful table service. The Cabane du Poutat, halfway down from Plat de Marmottes, is recommended for good food and service. Back in the village, lunch on the terrace at the hotel Christina – by the top of the bucket-lifts – is a pleasant option. The pizzas in the Tetras in Auris get rave reviews. L'Hermine at the bottom of the Fontfroide red below Signal de l'Homme does 'huge bowls of salads and massive tasty burgers, and any dog lover should take a peak at the beautiful huskies kennelled next door'.

The restaurants in the Oz and Vaujany sectors tend to be cheaper. At Montfrais, the Airelles is a rustic hut, built into the rock, with a roaring log fire, atmospheric music and excellent, good-value food (a 'real delight' says a 2004 reporter). The Auberge de l'Alpette also gets enthusiastic reviews emphasising it is 'really good value'.

## SCHOOLS AND GUIDES

### *Contrasting views of the schools*

We have had a couple of reasonable reports on the ESF: 'Good spoken English and good level of instruction.' However, class sizes can be big. One reporter counted 14 in a class. And we've had favourable reports again this year of Masterclass, an independent school run by British instructor Stuart Adamson. Class sizes



**SCHOOLS**

**ESF**
**t** 0476 803169
info@esf-alpedhuez.com

**International**
**t** 0476 804277
mgm.international@wanadoo.fr

**Classes** (ESF prices)
6 days (3hr am and 2½hr pm) €165

**Private lessons**
€34 for 1hr, for 1 or 2 people.

**GUIDES**

**Mountain guide office**
**t** 0476 804255

## boarding

*The resort suits experienced boarders well – the extent and variety of the mountains mean that there's a lot of good free-riding to be had. And, if there's good snow, the off-piste is vast and varied and well worth checking out with a guide. Unfortunately for beginners, the main nursery slopes are almost all accessed by drag-lifts, but these can be avoided once a modicum of control has been achieved. Planète Surf is the main snowboard shop.*

First Choice
discover your choices...
0870 754 3477 firstchoice.co.uk/ski

## CHILDREN

**Les Crapouilloux**
t 0476 113923
Ages 2 to 10; 9.30-5.30

**Les Intrépides**
t 0476 112161
Ages 0 to 3; 8am-6.30

**Les Eterlous** (ESF)
Ages 2½ to 5; 8.45-5.30

**Baby Club (Tonton Mayonnaise)**
(International school)
Ages 2½ to 4; 10am-12 noon

**Jardin d'Enfants** (ESF)
Ages 4 and over; 5½hr per day

**Club des Marmottes**
(International school)
Ages 4 to 12; 9.30-12 noon, 3pm-5pm

**Club Med** nursery
From age 4, with or without lessons





are limited to eight. Advance booking for high season is advised. The Bureau des Guides also has a good reputation.

### FACILITIES FOR CHILDREN
***Positive reports***

Les Crapouilloux day-care centre is 'very well organised' and has been recommended, as has tour operator Crystal's childcare operation.

## STAYING THERE

### HOW TO GO
***Something of everything***

**Chalets** UK tour operators run quite a few chalet-hotels, and some are offering smaller chalets in the new development above Les Bergers.
**Hotels** There are more hotels than is usual in a high French resort, and there's a clear downmarket bias, with more 1-stars than 2- or 3-stars, and only two 4-stars.
((((4) **Royal Ours Blanc** (0476 803550) Central. Luxurious, with good food. Superb fitness centre. Free (but often oversubscribed) minibus to the lifts.
(((3) **Au Chamois d'Or** (0476 803132) Good facilities, modern rooms, one of the best restaurants in town and well placed for main gondola.
(((3) **Cimes** (0476 803431) South-facing rooms, excellent food; close to cross-resort lift and pistes.
(((3) **Grandes Rousses** (0476 803311) A 2004 visitor says 'great atmosphere and Madame, goodish food and a good guitarist'; close to lifts.
((2) **Mariandre** (0476 806603) Comfortable hotel with good food, recommended by readers. Some small rooms. Next to the bucket-lift.
((2) **Gentianes** (0476 803576) Close to the Sarenne gondola in Les Bergers; a range of rooms, the best comfortable.
**Self-catering** There is an enormous choice available. The Pierre et Vacances residence near the Marmottes gondola in Les Bergers offers a high standard of accommodation with good facilities. The Maison de l'Alpe close to the DMC has been recommended for its ideal location and good facilities.

### EATING OUT
***Good value***

Alpe-d'Huez has dozens of restaurants, some of high quality; many offer good value by French resort standards. The Crémaillère, at the bottom end of town, is highly recommended by a frequent visitor. Au P'tit Creux got a similarly positive review for excellent food and ambience, though a reporter thought it was 'getting expensive'. The 'outstanding' Génépi is a friendly old place with good cuisine. The Pomme de Pin is also very popular. The Fromagerie is worth a try; of the pizzerias, L'Origan 'served fabulous pizza and pasta'; Pinocchio 'gets very busy early', says a 2004 reporter, who also liked the 'enormous helpings of good food' at Smithy's Tex-Mex.

### APRES-SKI
***Getting better all the time***

There's a wide range of bars, some of which get fairly lively later on. One complaint is that they are widely dispersed, making pub crawls fairly

## GETTING THERE

**Air** Lyon 150km/93 miles (3hr); Geneva 220km/137 miles (4hr); Grenoble, 99km/62 miles (1½hr).

**Rail** Grenoble (63km/39 miles); daily buses from station.

## ACTIVITIES

**Indoor** Sports centre (tennis, gym, squash, aerobics, swimming, shooting range, climbing wall), cinemas, concerts, theatre, museum

**Outdoor** Ice rink, curling, cleared walking paths, swimming pool, snow-shoeing, micro light flights, sight-seeing flights, ice cave, off-road vehicle tours, hang-gliding, paragliding, ice driving school, all-terrain carts, quad-bikes

**Phone numbers**
From abroad use the prefix +33 and omit the initial '0' of the phone number.

## TOURIST OFFICE

**Alpe-d'Huez**
**t** 0476 114444
info@alpedhuez.com
www.alpedhuez.com

time-consuming. Of the British-run bars, the Roadhouse in Crystal's hotel Vallée Blanche and the Underground in Neilson's hotel Chamois are established favourites. O'Sharkey's (with 'comfortable leather sofas') and the Pacific (sister bar to the one in Val d'Isère) are also popular. Smithy's can get pretty rowdy late on.

The little Avalanche bar is popular with locals and visitors alike, and often has live music. The P'tit Bar de l'Alpe takes some beating for atmosphere, and also has live music. The Sporting is a large but friendly French rendezvous with a live band. The Etalon and Free Ride cafes are also popular. And the Dutch-run Melting Pot does good tapas and is great for a relaxed drink, as is the Zoo.

The **Sporting** (which a 2004 reporter liked for its fine jazz music and view over the ice rink) and Igloo discos liven up whenever the French are in town en masse.

### OFF THE SLOPES

***Good by purpose-built standards***

There is a wide range of facilities, including an indoor pool, an open-air pool (boxer-style cozzies not allowed), Olympic-size ice rink and splendid sports centre – all of this covered by the lift pass. There's also an ice-driving school. Shops are numerous, but limited in range. The helicopter excursion to Les Deux-Alpes is amusing. It's a pity that the better mountain restaurants aren't easily accessible to pedestrians.

## Villard-Reculas

**1500m/4,920ft**

Villard-Reculas is a secluded village, just over the hill (Signal) from Alpe-d'Huez, complete with an old church, set on a small shelf wedged between an expanse of open snowfields above and tree-filled hillsides below. Following the installation of a fast quad chair up to Signal a few years back, the village is becoming more popular as an access point and it is now beginning to find its feet as a 'resort'. Its visitor beds are mainly in self-catering apartments and chalets, booked either through the tourist office or La Source – an English-run outfit which also runs a comfortable catered chalet in a carefully converted stone barn. There is one 2-star hotel, the Beaux Monts (0476 803032). There is a store 'almost like a trading post' and a couple of bars and restaurants.

The local slopes have something for everyone – including a nursery slope at village level – and there is a branch of the Ecole du Ski Français.

But a 2004 reporter warns 'the place is dull at night' and 'beginners will be stuck here because the runs that link to the rest of the wonderful skiing are very undergraded'. Two near-beginners in his party were 'very put off'.

## Oz-en-Oisans

**1350m/4,430ft**

The purpose-built ski station above the attractive old village of Oz-en-Oisans apparently now takes its parent's name and is a 'thriving small resort', says a reporter who has an apartment there. It has a ski school, sports shops, nursery slopes, bars, restaurants, a supermarket and a skating rink. But another reporter complains that there is still no nightlife. There's a large underground car park and attractive new chalets and apartment blocks have been built in a sympathetic style, with much use of wood and stone. There is a hotel, the Hors piste (0476 798662). Two gondolas whisk you out of the resort – one goes to Alpette above Vaujany and the other in two stages to the mid-station of the DMC

**Phone numbers**
From abroad use the prefix +33 and omit the initial '0' of the phone number.

**TOURIST OFFICES**

**Villard-Reculas**
t 0476 804569
info@villard-reculas.com
www.villard-reculas.com

**Oz-en-Oisans**
t 0476 807801
info@oz-en-oisans.com
www.oz-en-oisans.com

**Auris**
t 0476 801352
auris.en.oisans@wanadoo.fr
www.auris-en-oisans.com

**Vaujany**
t 0476 807237
info@vaujany.com
www.vaujany.com





above Alpe-d'Huez. The main run home is liberally endowed with snow-guns, but it needs to be. One clear advantage of staying here is that the slopes above Oz are about the best in the area when heavy snow is falling – and those based elsewhere may not be able to reach them.

## Auris 1600m/5,250ft

Auris is a series of wood-clad, chalet-style apartment blocks with a few shops, bars and restaurants, pleasantly set close to the thickest woodland in the area. It's a fine family resort, with everything close to hand, including a nursery and a ski kindergarten. There's also a ski school. Beneath it is the original old village, complete with attractive, traditional buildings, a church, and all but one of the resort's hotels. Staying here with a car you can drive up to the local lifts or make excursions to neighbouring resorts such as Serre-Chevalier.

Unsurprisingly, evenings are quiet, with a handful of bar-restaurants to choose from. The Beau Site (0476 800639), which looks like an apartment block, is the only hotel in the upper village. A couple of miles down the hill, the traditional Auberge de la Forêt (0476 800601) gives you a feel of 'real' rural France.

Access to the slopes of Alpe-d'Huez is no problem, but there are plenty of local slopes to explore, for which there is a special lift pass. Most runs are intermediate, though Auris is also the best of the local hamlets for beginners.

## Vaujany 1250m/4,100ft

Vaujany is a quiet, small (though growing) village perched on the hillside opposite its own sector of the domain. Hydro-electric riches have financed huge continuing investment. There's a giant 160-person cable-car that whisks you into the heart of the Alpe-d'Huez lift system, a two-stage gondola which takes you to Vaujany's local slopes, a superb sports centre with a 'fantastic' pool and a newish village centre by the lifts (with smart ski shop, cafe, deli and underground car park). Vaujany has a handful of simple hotels – a reporter heartily recommends the Rissiou, run by British operator Ski Peak – and some smart new self-catering developments up the mountainside. Ski Peak also runs comfortable, tastefully decorated catered chalets in Vaujany and La Villette; a minibus service for guests is available. There are some lively bars, and a couple of discos. British, Dutch and Belgian visitors dominate.

A mile or two up the valley (at the mid-station of the gondola) is the even smaller and more rustic hamlet of La Villette (just one tiny bar-restaurant).

There are no village slopes, so even complete beginners have to ride the gondola to Montfrais, which has a mid-station at La Villette. There's a blue run back to La Villette, but it can be tricky enough to reduce early intermediates to tears. You normally have to ride from La Villette down to Vaujany. The local branch of the ESF gets very good reports from readers.

SNOWPIX.COM / CHRIS GILL

# Les Arcs

*Purpose-built convenience, with exciting developments this season*

## COSTS

(1)(2)(3)(4)(5)6

## RATINGS

**The slopes**

| | |
|---|---|
| Snow | **** |
| Extent | *** |
| Expert | **** |
| Intermediate | **** |
| Beginner | **** |
| Convenience | **** |
| Queues | *** |
| Mountain restaurants | ** |

**The rest**

| | |
|---|---|
| Scenery | *** |
| Resort charm | * |
| Off-slope | * |

- \+ A wide range of runs to suit intermediates and experts
- \+ Now has cable-car link to La Plagne
- \+ Excellent woodland runs
- \+ Mainly traffic-free villages with easy access to the slopes from most (but not all) of the apartments
- \+ Option of staying in quiet, more traditional, lower villages
- \+ Very easy rail access from UK
- \+ Splendid views of Mont Blanc massif

- − Main village centres lack charm
- − Few off-slope diversions
- − Few confidence-building easy runs – yet lots of flats to annoy boarders
- − Still lot of slow old chairs and drags
- − Very quiet in the evenings, and limited choice of bars/restaurants
- − Some apartments are quite a walk from the nearest lifts
- − Accommodation in high villages is nearly all apartments

**We've always liked Les Arcs' slopes: they offer impressive variety, including some of the longest descents in the Alps and plenty of steep stuff. The link with La Plagne means the combined Paradiski area can claim an impressive 420km/ 260 miles of runs – in the same league as the Three Valleys and Val-d'Isère/ Tignes. Keen mixed-ability groups should have Les Arcs on their shortlists.**

**The main villages are classic purpose-built resorts – functional but drab. But the new Arc 1950 village offers purpose-built convenience with a lot more style. And there are more traditional (still quiet) options at either extremity of the area.**

## THE RESORT

Les Arcs is made up of four modern resort units, linked by road, high above the railway terminus town of Bourg-St-Maurice. The four villages are all purpose-built and apartment-dominated, and offer doorstep access to the snow with no traffic hazards, but the original three lack Alpine charm, off-slope activities and much evening animation. There's a special feature on the fourth – the new, still-developing Arc 1950 – a couple of pages on.

Reporters repeatedly comment on the friendliness of the locals.

Arc 1600 was the original Arc (it opened in December 1968). For rail travellers it is the obvious choice, with a funicular railway up from Bourg-St-Maurice. 1600 is set in the trees and has a friendly, small-scale atmosphere; and it enjoys good views along the

LES ARCS TOURIST OFFICE

Of the three original Arc villages, 1800 is the best all-round bet, for everything from nursery slopes to nightlife ↓

## NEWS

The Vanoise Express cable-car opened for 2003/04, linking Les Arcs to La Plagne.

At Arc 2000, the Bois de L'Ours chair towards 1800 and the Marmottes drag were replaced by six-packs. An open-topped gondola now connects Arc 1950 to 2000. A new blue piste, Edelweiss, runs from Col des Frettes back to 1950.

A new six-pack is planned for 2004/05 at Peisey-Vallandry (from the village to 2300m/7,550ft). The developments at Arc 1950 will include the Prince des Cimes hotel.





valley and towards Mont Blanc. The central area is particularly good for families: uncrowded, compact, and set on even ground. But it is very quiet in the evening. Above the village, chair-lifts fans out over the lower slopes, leading to links to the other Arcs.

Much the largest of the 'villages' is Arc 1800. It has three sections, though the boundaries are indistinct. Charvet and Villards are small shopping centres, mostly open-air but still managing to seem claustrophobic. Both are dominated by apartment blocks the size of ocean liners (you may do more walking inside your block than outside it). More easy on the eye is Charmettoger, with smaller, wood-clad buildings nestling among trees. There are also apartments up the hillside in Le Chantel. The lifts depart from Villards – chair-lifts to mid-mountain, and a big gondola to Col de la Chal above Arc 2000.

Arc 2000 is just a few hotels, apartment blocks and the Club Med, huddled together in a bleak spot, with little to commend it but immediate access to the highest, toughest skiing. Although some more upmarket apartments have been built over the last couple of years, there is only a handful of restaurants and shops.

Just below Arc 2000 and now linked to it by open-top gondola, the new 'village' of Arc 1950 is part-complete.

There are lifts all around Arc 1950 and 2000, including the Varet gondola up towards the Aiguille Rouge.

At the southern end of the area, linked by pistes but reachable by road only by descending to the valley, is Peisey-Vallandry. The long-awaited cable-car link with La Plagne opened here for 2003/04. At the northern end of the ski area is the rustic hamlet of Le Pré. These outlying options are described at the end of the chapter.

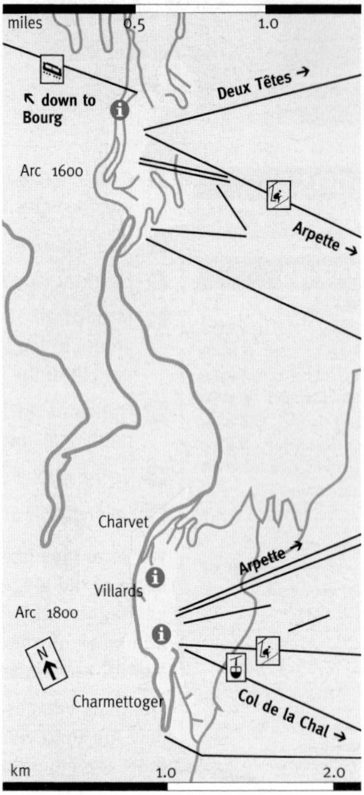

## KEY FACTS

| | |
|---|---|
| **Resort** | 1600-2000m 5,250-6,560ft |
| **Slopes** | 1200-3225m 3,940-10,580ft |
| **Lifts** | 56 |
| **Pistes** | 200km 124 miles |
| **Green** | 1% |
| **Blue** | 51% |
| **Red** | 30% |
| **Black** | 18% |
| **Snowmaking** | 12km 7 miles |

For Paradiski area

| | |
|---|---|
| **Slopes** | 1200-3250m 3,940-10,660ft |
| **Lifts** | 164 |
| **Pistes** | 420km 261 miles |
| **Green** | 5% |
| **Blue** | 54% |
| **Red** | 28% |
| **Black** | 13% |

## PARADISKI FEEDBACK

Three of our reporters made an expedition to La Plagne. Here's what they thought:

'We spent two great days going from Arc 1950 to Champagny and Montalbert – a real sensation of travel!'

'The lift is excellent but it is low – they may need more guns. We just caught the last cable-car back, but had to get a bus from Arc 1800 back to Arc 2000.'

'Leisurely lunch at Roc des Blanchets above Champagny, then an afternoon of superb sunny skiing. The new lift makes a huge difference.'



## THE MOUNTAINS

Les Arcs' terrain is notably varied; it has plenty of runs for experts and intermediates and a good mixture of high, snow-sure slopes and low-level woodland runs ideal for bad weather

Day trips by car to Val-d'Isère-Tignes or the Three Valleys are possible – both covered for a day with a six-day Paradiski or Paradiski Découverte pass. You can also get a reduced-price day pass for La Rosière.

### THE SLOPES
***Well planned and varied***

The slopes are very well laid out, and moving around is quick and easy – though direction-finding can be a problem at times. Arc 1600 and Arc 1800 share a west-facing mountainside laced with runs leading down to one or other village. At the southern end is an area of woodland runs – unusually extensive for a high French area, and a great asset to the area – down to Plan-Peisey and Vallandry .

From various points on the ridge above 1600 and 1800 you can head down into the Arc 2000 bowl – a new option being a blue run to Arc 1950 from the Col des Frettes. On the opposite side of this bowl, lifts take you to the highest runs of the area, from the Aiguille Rouge and the Grand Col. As well as a variety of steep north-west-facing runs back to Arc 2000, the Aiguille Rouge is the start of a lovely long run (over 2000m/6,500ft vertical and 7km/4 miles long) right down to the hamlet of Le Pré near Villaroger. Arc 2000 has runs descending below village level, to the lift-base, restaurant and car park at Pré-St-Esprit, about 200m/660ft lower. You can reach Le Pré from here, via a short drag-lift (often closed, say reporters), and also via the Lanchettes chair at Arc 2000.

### TERRAIN-PARKS
***State of the art***

The terrain-park – Snowp'Arcs, just down from Arpette – was moved and rebuilt recently. It's served by the Clair Blanc chair and you can buy a pass just to use the park, from 1800 or 1600 (23 euros a day in 2003/04). Features change throughout the season, says the resort, and there are two areas. The Games zone has two boarder-cross runs as well as jumps and areas for novices. The more advanced Display zone has a big hip jump and rails, and is by the Altiport restaurant. There is a half-pipe at Arc 2000 (floodlit at night), where you'll also find the Flying Kilometre – a speed skiing run on which you can try your luck travelling at 100kph/63mph or more!

### SNOW RELIABILITY
***Good – plenty of high runs***

A high percentage of the runs are above 2000m/6,500ft and when necessary you can stay high by using lifts that start around that altitude. Most of the slopes face roughly west, which is not ideal. Those from the Col de la Chal and the long runs down to Le Pré are north-facing. There is limited snowmaking on some runs back to 1600, 1800 and Peisey-Vallandry. Reporters are still finding that grooming can be 'economical'.

### FOR EXPERTS
***Challenges on- and off-piste***

Les Arcs has a lot to offer experts – at least when the high lifts are open (the Aiguille Rouge cable-car, in particular, is often shut in bad weather).

There are a number of truly black pistes above Arc 2000, and a couple in other areas. After a narrow shelf near the top (which can be awkward), the Aiguille Rouge-Le Pré run is superb, with remarkably varying terrain throughout its vertical drop of over 2000m/6,500ft. There is also a great deal of off-piste potential. There are steep pitches on the front face of the Aiguille Rouge, and secluded runs on the back side, towards Villaroger – the Combe de l'Anchette, for example. A short climb to the Grand Col from the chair-lift of the same name gives access to several routes, including a quite serious couloir and an easier option. The wooded slopes above 1600 are another attractive possibility – 'great fun skiing between the trees' says a reporter – and there are open slopes all over the place.

### FOR INTERMEDIATES
***Plenty for all abilities***

One strength of the area is that most main routes have easy and more difficult alternatives, making it good for mixed-ability groups. There are plenty of challenges, yet less confident intermediates are able to move around without getting too many nasty surprises. An exception is the solitary Comborcière black from Les Deux Têtes down to Pré-St-Esprit. This long mogul-

## ARC 1950: WHERE NORTH AMERICA MEETS EUROPE

*The first phase of the brand new resort of Arc 1950, a little way down the hill from Arc 2000 and linked to it by gondola, opened for its first winter in December 2003 – two buildings housing 180 apartments. The resort is being designed and built by Canadian company Intrawest, which specialises in developing stylish resort villages incorporating lots of upmarket accommodation. It has developed, for example, Whistler and Tremblant in Canada and the new Village at Squaw Valley in California. This is its first venture into Europe.*

*The buildings are attractively rustic, designed in curving shapes in wood and stone, around a traffic-free, cobbled square. The varied apartments are furnished to a much higher standard than is usual in French resorts, with comfortable easy chairs and sofas. The living rooms are spacious, but they incorporate the tiny kitchens – which do include dishwashers – and the bedrooms conform more to the French norm than the spacious standards you get in North American condos. The outdoor hot-tubs and pools, saunas and steam rooms are added attractions – as are the welcoming reception and the 'animations' planned every evening, such as fireworks, live music and wine tastings.*

*There are a couple of restaurants and bars (we had excellent duck in the restaurant in the Hameau du Glacier), ski and snowboard shops and a ski school – and the gondola to Arc 2000 works until late.*

*Another apartment building is due to open for 2004/05, along with another restaurant and a bakery; and a Radisson SAS luxury hotel will open for 2005/06. All 750 planned apartments are due to be finished by 2008. All the apartments are sold to private purchasers before being built. And most of the owners (around 70% of them British) are leasing them back to a rental management company.*

## LIFT PASSES

**Grand Domaine Les Arcs**
Covers Les Arcs lifts.

**Main pass**
1 day €36.50
6 days €176

**Senior citizens**
Over 60: 6 days €150
Over 72: free pass

**Children**
Under 14: 6 days €132
Under 6: free pass

**Notes**
Half-day pass and one-day Paradiski extension available.

**Paradiski Découverte**
Covers Les Arcs plus one day in La Plagne.

**Main pass**
6 days €190

**Senior citizens**
Over 60: 6 days €162
Over 72: free

**Children**
Under 14: 6 days €143
Under 6: free

**Notes** Extension valid Sat-Tue only, unless bought through certain UK tour operators. Also covers a day in each of the Three Valleys, Val-d'Isère-Tignes, Les Saisies, Pralognan.

**Paradiski**
Covers Les Arcs and La Plagne

**Main pass**
6 days €220

**Senior citizens**
Over 60: 6 days €187
Over 72: free

**Children**
Under 14: 6 days €165
Under 6: free

**Notes** Covers a day in each of the Three Valleys, Val-d'Isère-Tignes, Les Saisies and Pralognan.

field justifies its rating and can be great fun for strong intermediates. Recent reporters also found the Malgovert red, which starts from the same place, to be 'tricky, narrow and mogulled'.

The woodland runs at either end of the domain, above Vallandry and Le Pré, and the bumpy Cachette red down to 1600, are also good for better intermediates. Those who enjoy speed will like the Vallandry area: its well groomed runs have been remarkably uncrowded much of the time (though this may change as more people head down to the cable-car link to La Plagne). Good intermediates can enjoy the Aiguille Rouge-Le Pré run (with red and blue detours available to avoid the toughest bits of the black piste).

The lower half of the mountainside is good for mixed-ability groups, with a choice of routes through the trees. The red runs down from Arpette and Col des Frettes towards 1800 are quite steep but usually well groomed.

Cautious intermediates have plenty of blue cruising terrain. Many of the runs around 2000 are rather bland and prone to overcrowding. Edelweiss is a new blue down to Arc 1950 from Col des Frettes. The blues above 1800 are attractive but also crowded. A favourite blue of ours is Renard, high above Vallandry, usually with excellent snow. And a reporter's favourite is the 'almost deserted' Barmont, 'a good racing blue'.

And of course, there are now the whole of La Plagne's slopes to explore if you get bored locally.

### FOR BEGINNERS

***1800 best for complete novices***

There are nursery slopes conveniently situated just above all three villages. The ones at Arc 1600 are rather steep, while those at 2000 get crowded with intermediate through-traffic at times. The sunny, spacious slopes at 1800 are best. The 'Ski Tranquille' zones at the foot of each village are specially separated areas where novices can practise using the lifts before progressing onto the main runs. There is a lack of attractive, long, easy runs to move on to (there are now no green runs at all). But Mont Blanc, above 1600, is a beautiful, gentle blue, and you can take the gondola up to Col de la Chal and enjoy good snow on easy blues towards 2000.

### FOR CROSS-COUNTRY

***Very boring locally***

Short trails, mostly on roads, is all you can expect unless you travel down to the Nancroix valley's 40km/25 miles of pleasant trails.

## boarding

*Les Arcs calls itself 'the home of the snowboard'. Local boy Regis Rolland played a big part in popularising the sport (not least with his 'Apocalypse Snow' movies), and the resort is constantly developing its boarding facilities – the terrain-park was moved and rebuilt recently and is excellently maintained. There's a park-only pass available (23 euros a day). Boarders are attracted by the great mix of terrain served mainly by boarder-friendly lifts. However, getting around can involve some long traverses on near-flat cat-tracks and some of the blues at Arc 2000 are too flat for comfort. 'I wouldn't stay in Arc 2000 because it's too much of a pain to get to,' says one intermediate reporter. Vallandry has great smooth runs for beginners and carvers. There are a couple of specialist board schools and shops.*

**QUEUES**
***Few problems now***

Reporters have few complaints about queues except in one or two places. In sunny weather, Arc 2000 attracts the crowds and readers comment on non-trivial queues for both the gondola and the chair to Col de la Chal. In bad weather, it's the lifts serving the woodland slopes above Vallandry that cause the problem but the planned new six-pack should help. There are often lengthy waits for the Aiguille Rouge cable-car – 45 minutes complains one high-season reporter; 'Beware, a large proportion of the queue is hidden inside the building,' warns another. A bigger problem than queues is the time taken riding slow old chair-lifts, some of them very long. At peak periods overcrowded pistes can be a problem, too.

The cable-car link to La Plagne seems to cope with demand: 'very impressive', 'smooth, fast and efficient', 'no queues – it doesn't seem to get used much'. However, the lift is low and reporters express concerns about poor snow conditions on the lower slopes and queues for returning chair links.

**MOUNTAIN RESTAURANTS**
***An adequate choice***

Lunch isn't generally a highlight of the day unless you head for the hamlets at the extremes of the area. At the south end, a five-minute taxi-ride from Vallandry will bring you to L'Ancolie, a delightful traditional auberge with superb food (there are only 20 covers, so call 0479 079320 to book). At the north end, the 500-year-old Belliou la Fumée at Pré-St-Esprit is charmingly rustic and given 'top marks' by a reporter. The Ferme, 'simple but excellent value', and Aiguille Rouge down at Le Pré are both friendly, with good food.

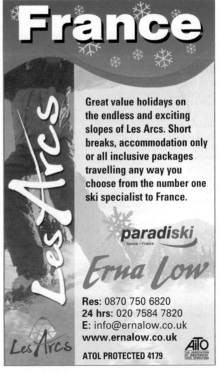

The restaurants scattered here and there on the main slopes are mainly unremarkable. An exception is the Chalets de l'Arc, above Arc 2000 towards Col de la Chal – built in traditional wood and stone and serving good French food. Most reporters are enthusiastic – 'quality all-round,' says one; another rates it as 'a cut above the average' but found the service 'variable'. It's open in the evening, and you can ski back to 1950 or 2000. The little Blanche Murée, just down from the Transarc mid-station, is

## SCHOOLS

**ESF**
esf-arcs-1600@wanadoo.fr

**Arc 1600**
t 0479 074309

**Arc 1800**
t 0479 074031

**Arc 2000**
t 0479 074752

**Arc Aventures (ESI)**
t 0479 074128
arc.aventures@wanadoo.fr

**Virages**
t 0479 077882
viragesmt@aol.com

**New Generation**
t 0479 010318
info@skinewgen.com

**Initial-snow.com** (in Bourg-St-Maurice)
t 0612 457291
infos@initial-snow.com

**Club des Sports**
t 0479 078205
info@sports-lesarcs.com

**Classes** (ESF prices)
6 days (3hr am or pm) €117

**Private lessons**
€33 for 1hr, for 1 or 2 people.

## CHILDREN

**Arc 1600:**
**Garderie La Cachette**
t 0479 077050
8.30 to 6pm; ages 4mnth to 11yr

**Arc 1800:**
**Nurserie Garderie Les Pommes de Pin**
t 0479 042431
ages 1 to 8

**Arc 2000:**
**Les Marmottons**
t 0479 076425
8.30 to 12 noon; 1.30 to 5pm; ages 3 to 6

**Club Med** (at Arc 2000) has full childcare facilities – this is one of their 'family villages'

**Ski school**
The ESF branches in all three stations take children from 3:
6 days (3hr am or pm) €117





consistently recommended – 'friendly service, fantastic food, reasonable prices', but one reporter experienced 'slow service' and 'mediocre food'. The restaurant at Col de la Chal has fabulous views but is otherwise ordinary. Above Vallandry, the Poudreuse has a 'fair choice of meals'. The Solliet above Le Pré has good views across the valley to Le Rosière and Ste-Foy.

### SCHOOL AND GUIDES
***New Brit school for 2003/04***

The ESF here is renowned for being the first in Europe to teach ski évolutif, where you start by learning parallel turns on short skis, gradually moving on to longer skis. We have had reports of several beginners who astonished their experienced friends. One was 'doing perfect parallel turns on steep reds by the end of the week'. But we have reports of a couple being left behind at chair-lifts and limited English being spoken by some instructors. Others have praised the progression made with their instructors. Private boarding lessons with the ESF have been 'very highly recommended'. The International school (Arc Aventures) has impressed reporters over the years: 'Good instruction with English well spoken.' And they are reported to offer 'a good deal in two-hour morning lessons'. We have had glowing reports of the Optimum ski courses, using British instructors, based in a catered chalet in Le Pré.

The big news for 2003/04 was the arrival of the British ski school New Generation (made up of highly qualified young British instructors), which has operated in Courchevel and Méribel for several seasons. But we've had no reports so far.

### FACILITIES FOR CHILDREN
***Good reports***

We have received good reports on the Pommes de Pin facilities in Arc 1800 – 'great care and attention', 'patient approach to teaching'. Comments on children's ski classes are favourable, too – 'nearly all instructors spoke English', 'classes went smoothly'. A children's area was built recently at 1800, complete with moving carpet lifts, a sledging track and a climbing wall. There are also a couple of mauve discovery pistes, at 1800 and 1600, for children to find out about flora and fauna of the Alps.

## STAYING THERE

### HOW TO GO
***New chalets and apartments***

Most resort beds are in apartments. There is a Club Med at Arc 2000.
**Chalets** There are now several catered chalets in the Peisey-Vallandry area (see the end of the chapter), and Le Pré has a couple, but there are hardly any in the high Les Arcs 'villages'.
**Hotels** The choice of hotels in Les Arcs is gradually widening, particularly at the upper end of the market.
((((4 **Mercure Coralia** (1800) (0479 076500) Locally judged to be worth four stars rather than its actual three.
(((3 **Golf** (1800) (0479 414343) An expensive but good 3-star, with sauna, gym, kindergarten, covered parking.
(((3 **Cachette** (1600) (0479 077050) Renovated in the mid-1990s, with something of the style of an American hotel. But it can be 'dominated by kids' says one reporter – not surprising as 1600's childcare facilities are here.
((2 **Aiguille Rouge** (2000) (0479 075707) Daily free ski guiding.
**Self-catering** The original apartments are mostly tight on space, so paying extra for under-occupancy is a sound investment. The MGM Alpages de Chantel apartments above 1800 and the new Arc 1950 apartments (both bookable through Erna Low) are attractive and comfortable by French standards, with pools, saunas and gyms. They are both very convenient for skiing, but the MGM ones not for much else. The Ruitor apartments, set among trees between Villards and Charmettoger, are reported to be 'excellent in all respects'. L'Aiguille Grive has been recommended for spacious apartments and excellent slope access. In Arc 2000 the Chalet des Neiges and Chalet Altitude have 'luxury' apartments, with pool and fitness facilities.

### EATING OUT
***Reasonable choice in Arc 1800***

In Arc 1600 and 2000 there are very few restaurants, but deserving a mention is the Chez Eux (Arc 2000), which received the thumbs-up by a reporter's group this year for the 'excellent' Savoie meals: 'All eight of us were complimentary – a rare event!' 1800 has a choice of about 15 restaurants; an ad-based (so not comprehensive) guide is given away locally. The Petit Zinc restaurant in the

Golf hotel has haute cuisine and high prices; it has a Friday evening seafood buffet. The Gargantus is a good, informal place, although very cramped and one reporter found poor service. Readers have been satisfied by 'enormous portions' at Equipage and 'good food and great service' at the Triangle Noir. Casa Mia is an excellent all-rounder with exceptionally friendly service. The Mountain Café does much more than the Tex-Mex it advertises, and copes well with big family parties. The Chalet de Milou has gourmet cuisine, 'including excellent fish'. Chez les Filles is worth a visit for 'exceptional views' and 'good food'. A popular outing is to drive halfway down the mountain to the welcoming and woody Bois de Lune at Montvenix, which has perhaps the best food in the area (booking advised). And the new village at Arc 1950 has a café, restaurant (Refuge du Montagnard) and bar – all reported to be good.

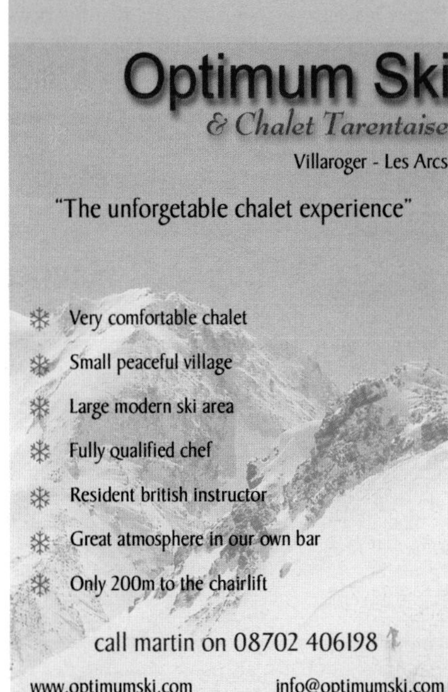


**APRES-SKI**

***Arc 1800 is the place to be***

1800 is the liveliest centre, though even so one reporter calls it 'very, very quiet'. The J.O. bar is open until the early hours and has a friendly atmosphere with live music. The friendly Red Hot Saloon has bar games and 'surprisingly good' live music. 'I danced until I couldn't stand any more,' claimed one recent reporter, who also enjoyed the cocktails, atmosphere and live music at the Jungle Café. The Fairway disco keeps rocking until 4am most mornings and the Apokalypse 'isn't terrible'. Reporters also like the jazz bar in the Hotel Golf.

In 1600 the bar opposite (and belonging to) the hotel Cachette has games machines, pool and live bands, and can be quite lively even in low season, and a reporter has recommended the Beguin, at the top of the village, for 'a rare, truly French experience', whatever that means.

In 2000 the Red Rock is 'good for youngsters but too crowded for grown-ups'; a reporter's verdict is that the Tavern (also at 2000) is 'best all round'. The Whistler Dream, in the Chalet des Neiges, could be worth a try. There is bowling at 1800 and skating at 1800 and 2000.

The cinemas at 2000, 1800 and 1600 have English-language films once or twice a week.

## GETTING THERE

**Air** Geneva 156km/ 97 miles (3½hr); Lyon 200km/125 miles (3½hr); Chambéry 127km/79 miles (2½hr).

**Rail** Bourg-St-Maurice; frequent buses and direct funicular to resort.

## ACTIVITIES

**Indoor** Squash (1800), saunas, solaria, multi-gym (1800), cinemas, games rooms, concert halls, bowling (1800)

**Outdoor** Natural skating rinks (1800/ 2000), tobogganing, organised snow-shoe outings, dog-sledding, 10km/6 miles cleared paths, hang-gliding, horse-riding, sleigh rides, ice grotto, 'snowtubbing' (2000)





**Phone numbers**
From abroad use the prefix +33 and omit the initial '0' of the phone number.

**UK Representative**
Erna Low Consultants
9 Reece Mews
London SW7 3HE
**t** 0870 750 6820
**f** 020 7589 9531
info@ernalow.co.uk
www.ernalow.co.uk

## TOURIST OFFICES

**Les Arcs**
**t** 0479 071257
lesarcs@lesarcs.com
www.lesarcs.com

**Bourg-St-Maurice**
**t** 0479 070492

**Peisey-Vallandry**
**t** 0479 079428
info@peisey-vallandry.com
www.peisey-vallandry.com

### OFF THE SLOPES
***Very poor***

Les Arcs is not the place for an off-the-slopes holiday. There is very little to do; the only pubic pool is at Bourg-St-Maurice, though several of the newer apartment blocks have pools. You can visit the Beaufort dairy and go shopping in Bourg-St-Maurice (cheaper for buying ski equipment), preferably on Saturday for the market, and there are a few walks – nice ones up the Nancroix valley. There's also an ice grotto at the top of the Transarc, which pedestrians can reach.

# Peisey-Vallandry

**1600m/5,250ft**

Plan-Peisey and Vallandry are recently developed lift-base resorts above the old village of Peisey, which has a bucket-lift up to Plan-Peisey. They market themselves as Peisey-Vallandry, and the cluster of villages hereabouts is known collectively as Peisey-Nancroix. Clear as mud, eh?

Both Vallandry and Plan-Peisey are still small and quiet, but more development is planned, including a Club Med (due for 2005) and some MGM apartments. Vallandry attracts a lot of Dutch guests.

The cable-car to La Plagne leaves from Plan-Peisey, which has one hotel, a few shops, bars and restaurants but no real focus other than the lift station. A high-speed six-seater chair takes you into the slopes. Ski Beat has eight chalets here (and one down in Peisey – see below). Family specialist Esprit Ski has five chalets (plus another which houses its comprehensive childcare facilities). The hotel Vanoise (0479 079219) has been recommended by readers for its position, food and 'extremely friendly and helpful staff' – 'very welcoming, very French,' with few British guests. Chez Félix restaurant has 'superb views down the valley'.

Vallandry is a few hundred metres away and linked by shuttle-bus. More development has gone on here recently, with lots of new chalets and a small pedestrian-only square at the foot of the slopes with a small supermarket, a ski shop and several bars and restaurants. Reporters' recommendations include the Calèche for excellent duck, the Chez Feliz (booking advised at weekends), the Refuge and L'Ourson for pizzas and two new restaurants, the Solan and Cordée. There is a crêperie by the Vanoise Express ('good for galettes'). Jimmy's bar is popular but 'noisy'. A fast quad and new six-pack will take you into the slopes. Ski Olympic has a chalet-hotel towards the top of Vallandry with the Forêt, a Beatles-themed bar-restaurant, next to it. Erna Low has self-catered chalets just below the square, with great views.

The old village of Peisey dates back 1,000 years, and has a fine baroque church. The other, mostly old, buildings house locals, a few tourists, a few shops and a couple of bars and restaurants. Ski Hiver has five chalets here and Ski Beat one.

Nancroix is a roadside hamlet notable only for the excellent Ancolie restaurant (a great place for dinner – see 'Mountain restaurants'). Landry is an old village 6km/4 miles down the valley from Peisey.

# Le Pré 1200m/3,940ft

Le Pré is a charming, quiet, rustic little hamlet with three successive chair-lifts (the first two quite slow) up to above Arc 2000. It has a couple of small bar-restaurants and a couple of British-run chalets, including a rustic one that owners Martin and Deirdre Rowe renovated and run themselves under the Optimum brand. We can personally vouch for their good food, free-flowing wine, jolly bar and basic but adequate bedrooms; and the ski courses they run (Martin used to run the school in Andorra) have received rave reviews from reporters. But Le Pré is not at all suitable for beginners.

# Bourg-St-Maurice

**850m/2,790ft**

Bourg-St-Maurice is a real French town, with cheaper hotels and restaurants and easy access to other resorts for day trips. The funicular goes straight to Arc 1600 in seven minutes – but beware, the last one down is currently at 7.30pm. Hostellerie du Pt-St-Bernard (0479 070432) has been reported to be a reasonable 2-star hotel – 'looks tatty but friendly with super food'. Another reporter enjoyed the hospitality and comfort of the cheap and cheerful Savoyard (0479 070403) despite the noise: 'take earplugs to sell to other guests'. A restaurant recommended by a 2004 reporter is the Refuge – 'best food of our stay'.

SNOWPIX.COM / CHRIS GILL

# Avoriaz 1800

*Functional, relatively snow-sure base for the Portes du Soleil circuit*

## COSTS

(1)(2)(3)(4)(5)(6)

## RATINGS

**The slopes**
Snow ***
Extent *****
Expert ***
Intermediate ****
Beginner ****
Convenience ****
Queues ***
Mountain restaurants ****

**The rest**
Scenery ***
Resort charm **
Off-slope *

## NEWS

In 2003/04 the Zore chair-lift, above the gondola up from Morzine, was upgraded to a fast quad.

For 2004/05 the Fornet chair, which serves the Marmotte snow-cross area and the Fornet and Pschott pistes close to the Swiss border, will be replaced by a six-pack.

- + Good position on the main Portes du Soleil circuit, giving access to very extensive, quite varied runs
- + Generally has the best snow in the Portes du Soleil
- + Accommodation right on the slopes
- + Resort-level snow and ski-through, car-free village give Alpine ambience
- + Good children's facilities

- − Much of Portes du Soleil is low for a major French area, with the risk of poor snow or bare slopes low down
- − Can get very crowded at weekends
- − Non-traditional architecture, which some find ugly
- − Little to do off the slopes
- − Few hotels or chalets – mostly no-frills, cramped apartments

**If Avoriaz sounds like the kind of thing you like, you'll probably like it. It differs from most rival purpose-built resorts in being truly car-free, with cars kept completely separate from its snow-covered paths and pistes. And it's a good base for the impressive Portes du Soleil piste circuit, with the bonus of relatively snow-sure local slopes. That's thanks to the altitude, which the resort is making a half-hearted attempt to emphasise by re-branding itself Avoriaz 1800. As for us – we're more at home lower down, in the cosy chalets of Morzine 1000.**

## THE RESORT

Avoriaz 1800 is a purpose-built, traffic-free resort perched above a dramatic, sheer rock face. From the edge of town horse-drawn sleighs or snowcats transport people and luggage from car parks to the accommodation – or you can borrow a sledge for a small deposit and transport your own. The problem of horse mess has been cut since they now wear 'nappies' and staff on snowmobiles scoop up what escapes! Cars are left in paid-for outdoor or underground parking – choose the latter to avoid a chaotic departure if it snows. You can book space.

As our scale plan suggests, it's a compact place, with everything close to hand. But the village is set on quite a slope; elevators inside the buildings (and chair-lifts outside, during the day) mean moving around is no problem except when paths are icy, but if you plan to go out much in the evening it's worth staying near the central focus. Wherever you stay, you can slide down to the main lifts in the mornings.

The village is all angular, dark, wood-clad, high-rise buildings, mostly apartments. But the snow-covered paths and pistes give the place quite a friendly Alpine feel.

The evenings are not especially lively, but reporters have enjoyed 'a good ambience, both day and night', and a 'brilliant parade in half-term week, with a fire-eating display'. Family-friendly events are laid on all season. A floodlit cliff behind the resort adds to its nocturnal charm.

There is accommodation in the lower hamlets of Ardent and Les Prodains.

Avoriaz is on the main lift circuit of the Portes du Soleil – for an overview, look at our separate chapter, later. It has links to Châtel in one direction and Champéry (Switzerland) in the other – both covered in separate chapters. It is above the valley resort of Morzine, to which it is linked by gondola (but not by piste). The slopes of Morzine and Les Gets, on the far side of Morzine, are part of the Portes du Soleil but not on the core circuit; both are now covered in their own chapters. Car trips are possible to Flaine and Chamonix.

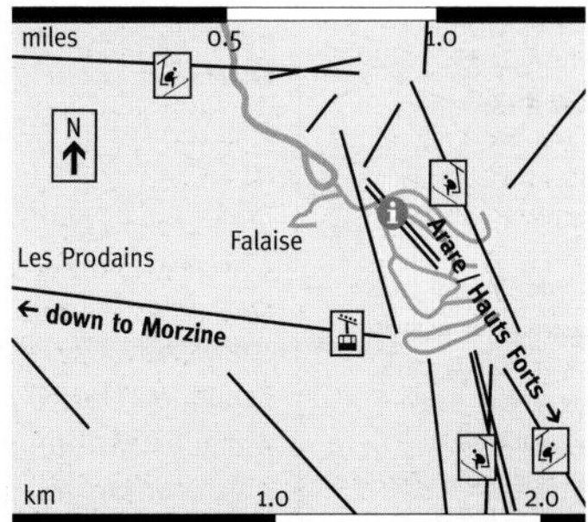

## KEY FACTS

| | |
|---|---|
| **Resort** | 1800m 5,900ft |
| Portes du Soleil | |
| **Slopes** | 975-2275m 3,200-7,460ft |
| **Lifts** | 206 |
| **Pistes** | 650km 400 miles |
| **Green** | 13% |
| **Blue** | 38% |
| **Red** | 39% |
| **Black** | 10% |
| **Snowmaking** | 252 acres |
| Avoriaz only | |
| **Slopes** | 1100-2275m 3,610-7,460ft |
| **Lifts** | 38 |
| **Pistes** | 150km 93 miles |

## LIFT PASSES

**Portes du Soleil**
Covers all lifts in all 12 resorts, and shuttle-buses.

**Main pass**
1 day €35
6 days €171

**Senior citizens**
Over 60: 6 days €137

**Children**
Under 16: 6 days €115
Under 5: free pass

**Alternative passes**
Avoriaz-only pass available. Beginner and snowboarder passes available for limited areas.





## THE MOUNTAINS

The slopes closest to Avoriaz are bleak and treeless, but snow-sure. The main linked Portes du Soleil circuit is easily done by intermediates of all abilities. Going clockwise avoids two snags in Morgins – the excessively sunny lower slopes of Bec de Corbeau, and the uphill walk to the next lift. The booklet-style piste map gives a reasonably clear picture of each resort along the way. Reporters have praised the system of Discovery Routes around the Portes du Soleil – choose an animal that suits your ability and follow the signs displaying it. The circuit breaks down at Châtel, where you need the frequent shuttle-bus.

### THE SLOPES
***Short runs and plenty of them***

The village has lifts and pistes fanning out in all directions. Staying in Avoriaz assures the comfort of riding mostly chairs – some other parts of the Portes du Soleil (especially on the Swiss side) have a lot of drags.

Facing the village are the slopes of **Arare-Hauts Forts** and, when snow conditions allow, there are long, steep runs down to Les Prodains.

The lifts off to the left go to the **Chavanette** sector on the Swiss border – a broad, undulating bowl. Beyond the border is the infamous Swiss Wall – a long, impressive mogul slope with a tricky start, but not the terror it is cracked up to be unless it's icy (it gets a lot of sun). It's no disgrace to ride the chair down – lots of people do. At the bottom of the Wall is the open terrain of Planachaux, above Champéry, with links to the even bigger open area around Les Crosets and Champoussin.

Taking a lift up through the village of Avoriaz (or traversing from some of the highest accommodation) to the ridge behind the village is the way to the prettily wooded **Lindarets-Brocheaux** valley, from where lifts and runs in the excellent Linga sector lead to Châtel.

### TERRAIN-PARKS
***Still leading the way***

In 1993 Avoriaz built the first French terrain-park, and now it boasts three. The Bleue du Lac up in the Arare area is aimed at experts, with advanced jumps such as tabletops, spines and hips, and a variety of rails. The Chapelle, in the resort centre, is better suited to novices. It has boarder-cross features as well as jumps. There's also a snow-skate park here, and a centrally positioned big air jump, where there's a competition at 7pm on Wednesdays. At the foot of the main slopes is the excellent half-pipe, served by its own lift, and recently rebuilt to Olympic standards – 120m/390ft long with 4.5m/15ft walls. There is a special pass for those whose only interest is using the parks and the pipe.

### SNOW RELIABILITY
***High resort, low slopes***

Although Avoriaz itself is high, its slopes don't go much higher – and some parts of the Portes du Soleil circuit are much lower. Considering their altitude, the north-facing slopes below Hauts Forts hold snow well. In general, the snow in Avoriaz is usually much better than over the border on the south-facing Swiss slopes.

Reporters generally say that grooming is good. More snow-guns have been installed, mostly in the Lindarets area, where we have had complaints of lack of snow in the past.

### FOR EXPERTS
***Several challenging runs***

Tough terrain is scattered about. The challenging runs down from Hauts Forts to Prodains (including a World Cup downhill) are excellent. There is a

## boarding

*Avoriaz has always encouraged snowboarding, opening France's first terrain-park in 1993 – there are now three parks including a monster half-pipe (see 'Terrain-parks'). The snowboard pass (29 euros for two days) is excellent value if you're interested only in the parks. There's a specialist snowboard school (Emery) and a snowboard village for children aged 6 to 16. Chalet Snowboard, the first chalet company to target snowboarders rather than skiers, has a couple of chalets at Les Prodains. Only a few (mainly avoidable) drags are left, and the six-pack chairs make for a comfortable ride. The snow-cross free-ride areas (see 'For experts') are a great innovation for riders who enjoy off-piste.*

## SCHOOLS

**ESF**
t 0450 740565
info@esf-avoriaz.com

**International (L'Ecole de Glisse)**
t 0450 740218
info@ecoledeglisse.com

**Emery (snowboard)**
t 0450 741264
ecoledesnowboard emery@wanadoo.fr

**BASS**
t 0450 747691
info@britishskischool.co.uk

**Classes**
(ESF prices)
6 days (2½hr am and pm) €140

**Private lessons**
€30 for 1hr, for 1 or 2 people

tough red, and several long, truly black runs, one of which cuts through trees – useful in poor weather. Two chair-lifts serve the lower runs, which snow-guns help to keep open. The Swiss Wall at Chavanette will naturally be on your agenda, and Châtel is well worth a trip. The black runs off the Swiss side of Mossettes and Pointe de l'Au are worth trying. Four 'snow-cross' runs – ungroomed but avalanche controlled and patrolled – were recently introduced in the Hauts Forts (a 'safe favourite' writes a reporter), Lindarets, Chavanette and Mossettes areas. They are marked on the piste map, closed when dangerous and an excellent idea.

### FOR INTERMEDIATES
***Virtually the whole area***

Although some sections lack variety, the Portes du Soleil is excellent for all grades of intermediates when snow is in good supply. Timid types not worried about pretty surroundings need not leave the Avoriaz sector; Arare and Chavanette are gentle, spacious and above the tree-line bowls. The Lindarets area is also easy, with pretty runs through the trees, but several reporters complain about long, flat sections where poling is required. Champoussin has a lot of easy runs, reached without too much difficulty via Les Crosets and Pointe de l'Au. Better

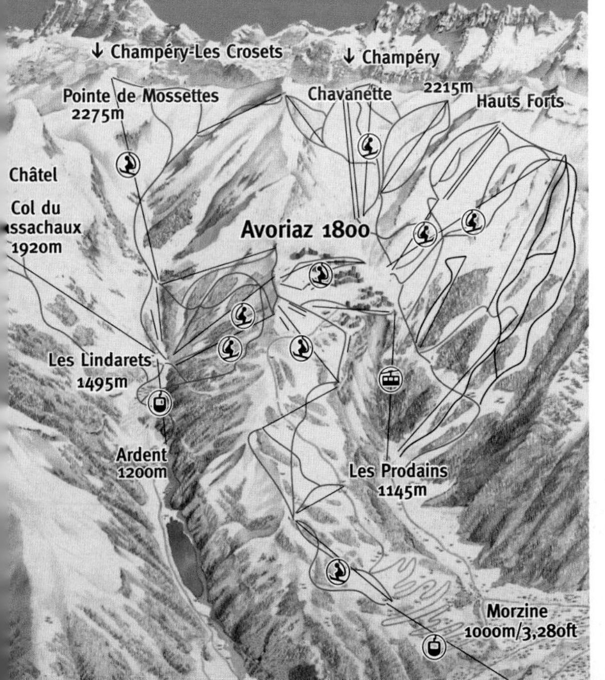




intermediates have virtually the whole area at their disposal. The runs down to Pré-la-Joux and L'Essert on the way to Châtel, and those either side of Morgins, are particularly attractive – as are the long runs down to Grand-Paradis near Champéry when snow conditions allow. Brave intermediates may want to take on the Wall, but Pointe de Mossettes offers an easier route to Switzerland.

### FOR BEGINNERS
***Convenient and good for snow***

The nursery slopes seem small in relation to the size of the resort, but are adequate because so many visitors are intermediates. The slopes are sunny, yet good for snow, and link well to longer, easy runs. The main problem can be the crowded pistes. One reporter in 2003/04 complains crowds and collisions on the Plateau area, made progress 'painfully slow' for novices taking classes there.

### FOR CROSS-COUNTRY
***Varied, with some blacks***

There are 45km/28 miles of trails, a third classified as black, mainly between Avoriaz and Super-Morzine, with other fine trails down to Lindarets and around Montriond. The only drawback is that several trails are not loops, but 'out and back' routes.

### QUEUES
***Main problems now gone***

Most of the bad queues have been eliminated by new high-speed lifts. But there can still be long queues to get out of Les Lindarets towards Châtel on the slow Chaux Fleurie chair-lift to Bassachaux. At weekends crowds on the pistes (especially around the village) can be worse than queues for the lifts, with care having to be taken to avoid collisions.

## GETTING THERE

**Air** Geneva 80km/ 50 miles (2hr); Lyon 200km/124 miles (3½hr).

**Rail** Cluses (42km/ 26 miles) or Thonon (45km/28 miles); bus and cable-car to resort.

## ACTIVITIES

**Indoor** Health centre 'Altiform' (sauna, gym, hot-tub), squash, ice rink, Turkish baths, cinema, bowling
**Outdoor** Ice rink, snake slides, mountain biking on snow, dog-sledding, walking paths, horse-drawn carriage tours, helicopter flights





## CHILDREN

**Les P'tits Loups**
t 0450 740038
9am to 6pm; ages 3mnth to 5yr

**Annie Famose Children's Village and Le Village Snowboard**
t 0450 740446
9am to 5.30 (skiing 9.30 to 12 noon and 1.30 to 4pm); ages 3 to 16; 6 days with meal €204

**Club Med**
This is a 'family village', with comprehensive childcare facilities

**Ski schools**
Take children from 4 to 12 (6 days €120)

**Phone numbers**
From abroad use the prefix +33 and omit the initial '0' of the phone number.

## TOURIST OFFICE

t 0450 740211
info@avoriaz.com
www.avoriaz.com



### MOUNTAIN RESTAURANTS
***Good choice over the hill***

The charming, rustic chalets in the hamlet of Les Lindarets form one of the great concentrations of mountain restaurants in the Alps. A particular Lindarets favourite of ours is the Crémaillière which has wonderful chanterelle mushrooms and great atmosphere. A reporter enjoyed the Terrasse, also at Lindarets. The Pomme de Pin is recommended for its warm welcome and friendly service. The rustic Grenouille du Marais near the top of the gondola up from Morzine has good food, views and atmosphere. The table-service Abricotine does 'excellent galettes'. The Refuge des Brocheaux at Les Brocheaux offers 'efficient service and a good menu'. Pas de Chavanette at the top of the Swiss Wall, and Yéti, at the top of the village, have been recommended.

### SCHOOLS AND GUIDES
***Try BASS***

The ESF has a good reputation; classes can be large, but we have a recent report of 'great instruction'. The British Alpine Ski School (BASS) has British instructors and has been highly recommended, especially for 'quite excellent children's lessons'. This season they will be operating in Ardent, as well as Morzine-Avoriaz. Emery is a specialist snowboard school, but it's small so booking ahead is advised.

### FACILITIES FOR CHILDREN
***'Annie Famose delivers'***

The Village des Enfants, run by ex-downhill champ Annie Famose, is a key part of the family appeal of Avoriaz. Its facilities are excellent – a chalet full of activities and special slopes complete with Disney characters for children aged 3 to 16. There's a snowboard village too.

## STAYING THERE

### HOW TO GO
***Self-catering dominates***

Alternatives to apartments are few.
**Chalets** There are several available – comfortable and attractive but mainly designed for small family groups.
**Hotels** There is one good hotel and a Club Med 'village'.
(((3) **Dromonts** (0450 740811) The original Avoriaz construction in the resort centre, recently taken over and renovated by a celebrity French chef and now in the *Hip Hotels* guidebook. We stayed there in 2003 and liked it.
**Self-catering** Past reporters have said that some apartments needed refurbishing, and others are typically 'basic and cramped'. But the Falaise apart-hotel, Douchka, Sepia and Datcha residences have all been recommended.

### EATING OUT
***Good; booking essential***

There are more than 30 restaurants. The hotel Dromonts has a gastronomic restaurant with an excellent set-price six-course meal and a simpler Table du Marché restaurant. The Bistro and Cabane have been recommended for 'good food and value', as have the Fontaines Blanches and Douchka for Savoyard food, Intrets for 'pizza and pasta', 'table-barbecues and Savoyard fare', and Au Briska, for a cosy night out. You can buy in advance meal vouchers for dinner in a range of five restaurants, when you book Pierre & Vacances apartments. 'Restricted menu but excellent value,' says a reporter.

### APRES-SKI
***Lively, but not much choice***

A few bars have a good atmosphere, particularly in happy hour. The Yeti is busy at 4pm. The Tavaillon attracts Brits and has Sky TV, and the Fantastique is worth a visit. For late-night dancing the Choucas and The Place have bands. Heading to Morzine is a suggested alternative – there is a free bus back to the cable-car, which runs until 10pm.

### OFF THE SLOPES
***Not much at the resort***

Those not interested in the slopes are better off in Morzine – though Avoriaz does have the Altiform Fitness Centre, with saunas and hot-tubs. Pedestrians are not allowed to ride the chair-lifts, which is a shame.

# Chamonix

*Views to die for and slopes that can kill: hire a guide to go off-piste*

**COSTS**

(1)(2)(3)(4)(5)(6)

**RATINGS**

| **The slopes** | |
|---|---|
| Snow | **** |
| Extent | *** |
| Expert | ***** |
| Intermediate | ** |
| Beginner | * |
| Convenience | * |
| Queues | ** |
| Mountain restaurants | ** |
| **The rest** | |
| Scenery | ***** |
| Resort charm | **** |
| Off-slope | ***** |

**NEWS**

For 2003/04 a new six-pack replaced the old Herse chair from Croix de Lognan at the Grands Montets, and a new drag-lift at the top of Flégère was built, giving access to new red and black runs and off-piste bowls.

For 2004/05 a new gondola is due to link Vallorcine to the Tour-Col de Balme ski area, enabling you to ski the long blue run or the off-piste through the trees to Vallorcine without catching the train and bus back to the lifts.

- + A lot of very tough terrain, especially off-piste
- + Amazing cable-car to the Aiguille du Midi, for the famous Vallée Blanche (or just the views – it's on the pass)
- + Stunning views of peaks and glaciers
- + Lots of different resorts and areas covered on Mont Blanc lift pass
- + Town steeped in Alpine traditions, with lots to do off the slopes
- + Easy access by road, rail and air
- + Excellent weekend destination

- − Several separate mountains: mixed ability groups are likely to have to split up, and the bus service is far from perfect – we always take a car
- − Pistes in each individual area are quite limited
- − The few runs to the valley are often closed – and can be dangerous when open
- − Crowds, queues, lots of road traffic
- − Bad weather can shut the best runs

**Chamonix could not be more different from the archetypal high-altitude, purpose-built French resort. Unless you are based next to one mountain and stick to it, you have to drive or take a bus each day. There are all sorts of terrain, but it offers more to interest the expert than anyone else, and to make the most of the area you need a mountain guide rather than a piste map. Chamonix is neither convenient nor conventional.**

**But it is special. The Chamonix valley cuts deeply through Europe's highest mountains and glaciers. The views are stunning and the runs are everything really tough runs should be – not only steep, but high and long. If you like your snow and scenery on the wild side, give Chamonix a try. But be warned: there are those who try it and never go home – including lots of Brits.**



## THE RESORT

Chamonix is a long-established tourist town that over the years has spread for miles along its valley in the shadow of Mont Blanc – the scale map below is one of the biggest in these pages.

On either side of the centre, just within walking distance of it, are lifts to two of the dozen slope areas in the valley – the famous cable-car to the Aiguille du Midi, and a gondola to Le Brévent. Also on the fringe of the centre is the nursery slope of Les Planards. All the other lift bases involve drives or bus-rides – the nearest being the cable-car to La Flégère at the village of Les Praz.

Chamonix is a bustling town with scores of hotels and restaurants, visitors all year round and a lively Saturday market. The car-free centre of town is full of atmosphere, with cobbled streets and squares, beautiful old buildings and a fast-running river. Not everything is rosy: unsightly

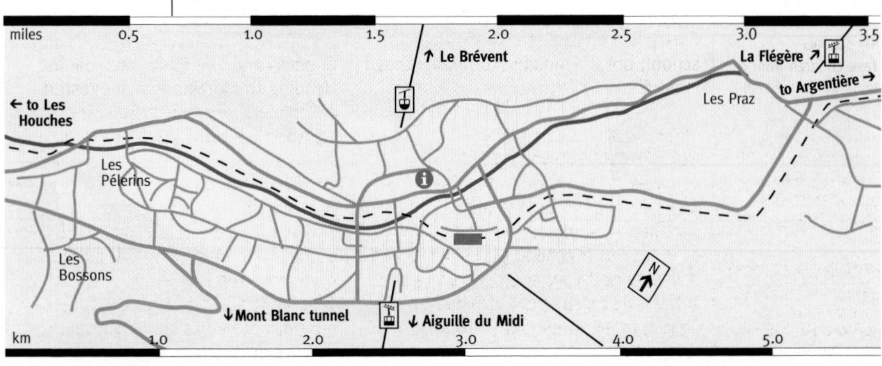

## KEY FACTS

| | |
|---|---|
| Resort | 1035m 3,400ft |
| Slopes | 1035-3840m 3,400-12,600ft |
| Lifts | 47 |
| Pistes | 147km 91 miles |
| Green | 20% |
| Blue | 34% |
| Red | 33% |
| Black | 13% |
| Snowmaking | 96 guns |



modern buildings have been built on to the periphery (especially near the Aiguille du Midi cable-car station), some of the lovely old buildings have been allowed to fall into disrepair, and at busy times traffic clogs the streets around the pedestrianised centre. Most of the day the town squares and pavement cafes are crowded with shoppers and sightseers sipping drinks and staring at the glaciers above. It all makes for a very agreeable ambience, though the resort is in danger of being swamped by Brits (and Yanks): 'In many bars and restaurants I did not hear any French being spoken,' a recent visitor remarks.

Chamonix's shops deal in everything from high-tech equipment to tacky souvenirs. But reporters often comment on the number and excellence of the former, and Chamonix remains essentially a town for mountain people rather than for poseurs.

Strung out for 20km/12 miles along the Chamonix valley are several separate lift systems, some with attached villages, from Les Houches at one end to Le Tour at the other. Regular buses link the lift stations and villages (there's an evening service too) but can get very crowded and aren't always reliable – that to Les Houches is reportedly especially poor. Like many reporters, we rate a car as essential. A car also means you can get easily to other resorts covered by the Mont Blanc pass, such as Megève and Les Contamines, and Courmayeur in Italy.

The obvious place to stay is in downtown Chamonix – it has all the amenities you could want and some of the slopes are close at hand. For those who intend to spend most of their time in one particular area such as Argentière, Le Tour or Les Houches, staying nearby obviously makes sense. Whatever the choice, no location is convenient for everything.

## THE MOUNTAINS

Once you get over the fact that the place is hopelessly disconnected, you come to appreciate the upside – that Chamonix has a good variety of slopes, and that each of the different areas is worth exploring. Practically all the slopes are above the tree line.

### THE SLOPES
***Very fragmented***

The areas within the Chamonix valley – there are 11 in total – are either small, low, beginners' areas or are much higher up, above the wooded slopes that plunge to the valley floor, reached by cable-car or gondola.

↑ You don't have to tackle jumps like this, but you can't help admiring the views

OT CHAMONIX-MONT BLANC

## LIFT PASSES

**Cham'Ski pass**
Covers all areas in the Chamonix Valley and the bus services between them, except Grands-Montets cable-car and Les Houches area.

**Beginners**
Cham'Start 6-day pass covers all valley floor lifts.

**Main pass**
1 day €40
6 days €176

**Senior citizens**
Over 60: 6 days €150

**Children**
Under 15: 6 days €150
Under 11: 6 days €123
Under 4: free pass

**Notes**
6-day passes include two ascents on the Grands Montets cable-car and a day in Courmayeur.

**Alternative passes**
Ski-pass Mont Blanc covers lifts in the 13 resorts of the Mont Blanc area and Courmayeur in Italy.

The modern six-seater gondola for **Le Brévent** departs a short, steep walk from the centre of town, and the cable-car above takes you to the summit. At **La Flégère**, like Le Brévent, the runs are mainly between 1900m and 2450m (6,200ft and 8,040ft), and the stunning views of Mont Blanc are worth the price of the lift pass. The cable-car linking La Flégère and Le Brévent now makes this side of the valley more user-friendly – though reporters have found it's often closed by high winds.

A cable-car or chair-lift take you up to **Les Grands Montets** above Argentière. Much of the best terrain is still accessed by a further cable-car of relatively low capacity. This costs extra – 5 euros a trip in 2003/04 – though two free rides are included in a six-day pass. But it still attracts big queues.

**Le Tour** has an area of mainly easy pistes. It is also the starting point for good off-piste runs, some of which end up over the border in Switzerland.

There is a valley piste map and an informative little Cham'Ski handbook, which includes all the local area piste maps, with brief descriptions of each run and assessments of suitability for different abilities. But for navigation purposes the individual piste maps available at each area are best.

Most of our reporters have been more impressed than they expected with the piste grooming, but not with the signposting of the runs ('virtually non-existent' said one reporter).

### TERRAIN-PARKS
***Competitive***

Head for Argentière and the Grands Montets for the hairiest action – the terrain-park and half-pipe host regular competitions, and there's a boarder-cross course. There's also a natural half-pipe/gully at Le Tour.

### SNOW RELIABILITY
***Good high up; poor low down***

The top runs on the north-facing Grands Montets slopes above Argentière are almost guaranteed to have good snow, and the season normally lasts well into May. The risk of finding the top lift shut because of bad weather is more of a worry (and is the excuse for not including unlimited use of the lift on the main pass). There's snowmaking on the busy Bochard piste and the run to the valley, which can now be kept open late in the season. Le Tour has a snowy location and a good late-season record. The largely south-facing slopes of Brévent and Flégère suffer in warm weather, and the steep runs to the resort are often closed. Don't be tempted to try these unless you know they are in good condition – they can be lethal. Some of the low beginners' areas have snowmaking.

### FOR EXPERTS
***One of the great resorts***

The Grands Montets is justifiably renowned for its extensive steep terrain. To get the best out of the area you really need to have a local guide. Without one you either stick to the relatively small number of pistes or you put your life at risk. There is also lots of excellent off-piste reachable only by ski touring on skins.

The Grands Montets cable-car takes you up to 3235m/10,610ft; if you've got

## boarding

*Chamonix is a place of pilgrimage for advanced boarders, but not the best place to learn. Most areas are equipped mainly with cable-cars, gondolas and chairs. However, there are quite a few difficult drags at Le Tour that cause boarders problems – though you can avoid these if you are ready to contend with cat tracks to take you to other lifts, according to a reporter. If you do the Vallée Blanche, be warned: the usual route is flat in places. If you're ready to tackle tougher off-piste, check out former British champ Neil McNab's excellent extreme backcountry camps (www.mcnab.co.uk) – 'fantastic' says a 2004 reporter.*

the legs and lungs, climb the 121 steep metal steps to the observation platform and take in the stunning views. (But beware: it's 200 more steps down from the cable-car before you hit the snow.)

The ungroomed black pistes from here – Point de Vue and Pylones – are long and exhilarating. The Point de Vue sails right by some dramatic sections of glacier, with marvellous views of the crevasses. The off-piste routes from the top are numerous and often dangerous; the Pas de Chèvre route is serious stuff, eventually joining the Vallée Blanche run. There are many routes down the Argentière glacier.

The Bochard gondola serves a challenging red and a moderate black. Alternatively, head directly down the Combe de la Pendant bowl for 1000m/3,280ft vertical of wild, unpisted mountainside. The continuation down the valley side to Le Lavancher is equally challenging; it suffers frequently from lack of snow.

At Le Brévent there's more to test experts than the piste map suggests – there are a number of variations on the runs down from the summit. 'Superb when open,' said one visitor. Some are steep and prone to ice, and the couloir routes are very steep and very narrow. The runs in the sunny Col de La Charlanon are uncrowded and include one marked red run and lots of excellent off-piste if the snow is good.

At La Flégère there are several good off-piste routes – in the Combe Lachenal, crossed by the linking cable-car, for example – and a pretty tough run back to the village when snow-cover permits. Le Tour boasts little tough terrain on-piste but there are good off-piste routes from the high points to the village and over the back towards Vallorcine or into Switzerland.

Beware of the high avalanche risk off-piste near Col de Balme.

**FOR INTERMEDIATES**
### *It's worth trying it all*

For less confident intermediates, the Col de Balme area above Le Tour is good for cruising and usually free from crowds. There are excellent shady runs on the north side of Tête de Balme, served by a quad.

More adventurous intermediates will also want to try the other three main areas, though they may find the Grands Montets tough going (and crowded). The bulk of the terrain at Le Brévent and La Flégère provides a sensible mix of blue and red runs; at Le Brévent the slopes have been redesigned to achieve this.

If the snow and weather are good, book a guide and do the Vallée Blanche (see feature panel).

A day trip to Courmayeur makes an interesting change of scene, especially when the weather is bad (it can be sunny there when Chamonix's high lifts are closed by blizzards or high winds).

**FOR BEGINNERS**
### *Best to learn elsewhere*

If there is snow low down, the nursery lifts at La Vormaine, Les Chosalets, Les Planards and Le Savoy are fine for first-timers, who will not be bothered by speed-merchants there. But the separation of beginners' slopes from the rest inhibits the transition to real runs, and makes lunchtime meetings of mixed groups difficult. The slopes on the south side of the valley – Les Planards, in particular – can be dark and cold in winter. Le Savoy is sunny, but devoid of restaurants. Better to learn elsewhere, and come to Chamonix when you can appreciate the tough terrain.

**FOR CROSS-COUNTRY**
### *A decent network of trails*

Most of the 42km/26 miles of prepared trails lie along the valley between Chamonix and Argentière. There are green, blue, red and black loops. All these trails are fairly low; they're cold and shady in midwinter, and they fade fast in the spring sun.

**QUEUES**
### *Morning and afternoon problems*

The main lifts from the valley at Chamonix and Argentière produce queues at peak times – and getting down when the home runs are closed can be as bad as getting up the mountain in the morning. At Flégère a

The Vallée Blanche attracts the crowds as much for the spectacular scenery as for the 24km/15 mile run. Once you've negotiated the walk down from the cable-car the run flattens out ↗

OT CHAMONIX-MONT-BLANC

booking system comes into operation at the end of the day.

In poor weather Les Houches gets crowded and the queues for the Bellevue cable-car can then be bad.

There are still long queues for the top cable-car on Les Grands Montets – often all day long. When they reach 30 minutes a booking system operates, so you can go skiing until it's your turn to ride – often an hour or more later. The replacement of the slow Herse chair by a six-pack has relieved the pressure there and on the Bochard gondola – but more reports welcome on this.

**MOUNTAIN RESTAURANTS**
***Surprisingly dull***

The Bergerie de Planpraz on Le Brévent is the most attractive option – built in wood and stone, with self- and table-service. Food and service are 'excellent'; but it gets very busy. The dull little Panoramic at the top enjoys





**THE VALLÉE BLANCHE**

*This is a trip you do for the stunning scenery. The views of the ice, the crevasses and seracs – and the spectacular rock spires beyond – are simply mind-blowing. The run, although exceptionally long, is not steep – mostly effortless gliding down gentle slopes with only the occasional steeper, choppy section to deal with. In the right conditions, it is well within the capability of a confident intermediate. But if snow is sparse, the run can turn tricky – there can be patches of sheet ice, exposed stones and rocks, and narrow snow bridges over gaping crevasses. And if fresh snow is abundant, different challenges may arise. Go in a guided group – dangerous crevasses lurk to swallow those not in the know. The trip is popular – on a busy day 2,500 people do it; book in advance at the Maison de la Montagne or other ski school offices. To miss the worst of the crowds go very early on a weekday, or in the afternoon if you are a good skier and can get down quickly.*

*The amazing Aiguille du Midi cable-car takes you to 3840m/12,600ft. Across the bridge from the arrival station on the Piton Nord is the Piton Central; the view of Mont Blanc from the cafe – a stair-climb higher – should not be missed, and it gives you the opportunity to adjust to the dizzying altitude. A tunnel delivers you to the infamous ridge-walk down to the start of the run. Be prepared for extreme cold up here. There is (usually) a fixed guide-rope for you to hang on to, and many parties rope up to their guides. You may still feel envious of those nonchalantly strolling down in crampons; you may wish you'd stayed in bed.*

*After that, the run seems a doddle. There are variants on the classic route, of varying difficulty and danger. Lack of snow often rules out the full 24km/15 mile run down to Chamonix; a stairway and slow gondola link the glacier to the station at Montenvers, for the half-hour mountain railway ride down to the town.*

## CHILDREN

**Panda Club**
t 0450 550888
panda.bertrand@wanadoo.fr
Ages 3 to 12; 8.30-5pm; includes ski lessons; 6 days €275

**Babysitter list**
Available from the tourist office

**Ski school**
ESF takes children aged 6 to 12 (six 4hr days €135); Evolution 2 takes children from age 3

## SCHOOLS

**ESF**
t 0450 532257
infoski@esf-chamonix.com

**Evolution 2**
t 0450 559022

**Classes**
6 half days: €160

**Private lessons**
€100 for 2hr, for 1 or 2 people





amazing views over to Mont Blanc and the food is fine. Altitude 2000 provides table-service at rip-off prices and a recent reporter has said the attitude of the waiters is 'absolutely terrible'. There's a self-service place at La Flégère with a large terrace and excellent views.

On the Grands Montets the Plan Joran serves good food and does table- and self-service. There's also an indoor picnic area. The restaurant at Lognan has been smartly renovated. The rustic Chalet-Refuge de Lognan, off the Variante Hôtel run to the valley, and overlooking the Argentière glacier, has marvellous food and is very popular.

At the top of the Le Tour gondola, the Chalet de Charamillon is an adequate self-service and there's a picnic area. The Refuge du Col de Balme – a short hike from the lifts – is charming, but has 'appalling' service.

### SCHOOLS AND GUIDES
***The place to try something new***

The schools here are particularly strong in specialist fields – off-piste, glacier and couloir skiing, ski touring, snowboarding and cross-country. English-speaking instructors and mountain guides are plentiful, and specialist Chamonix tour operators can arrange them in advance for guests. At the Maison de la Montagne is the main ESF office and the HQ of the Compagnie des Guides, which has taken visitors to the mountains for 150 years. Both now offer ready-made week-long 'tours' taking clients to a different mountain or resort each day. We have a good report of the ESF Ski Fun Tour where they ski a different Mont Blanc region resort each day, transport included: 'fantastic – we cannot speak highly enough of the guides'. Competition is provided by a number of smaller, independent guiding and teaching outfits.

### FACILITIES FOR CHILDREN
***Better than they were***

The Panda Club is used by quite a few British visitors and reports have been enthusiastic. The Argentière base can be inconvenient for meeting up with children for the afternoons. The Club Med nursery seems to go down well too. UK tour operator Esprit Ski has chalets here, with a nursery in the Sapinière chalet-hotel.

Beware the tendency to keep children on the valley nursery slopes for the convenience of the school when they really should be getting some miles under their skis.

## STAYING THERE

### HOW TO GO
***Any way you like***

There is all sorts of accommodation, and lots of it. The tourist office has a 'useful central booking system'. Call 0450 532333 or email reservation@chamonix.com.

**Chalets** Many are run by small operators that cater for this specialist market. Quality tends to be high and value for money good.

**Hotels** A wide choice, many modestly priced, and the vast majority with fewer than 30 rooms. Bookings for a day or two are no problem – the peak season is summer.

((((4) **Albert 1er** (0450 530509) Smart, 100-year-old chalet-style hotel with 'truly excellent' and 'reasonably priced' food (Michelin stars) but expensive rooms (especially in the farmhouse annexe). Indoor-outdoor pool.

((((4) **Auberge du Bois Prin** (0450 533351) A small modern chalet with a big reputation; great views; bit of a hike into town; closer to Le Brévent.

((((4) **Mont-Blanc** (0450 530564) Central, luxurious.

((((4) **Jeu de Paume** (Lavancher) (0450 540376) Alpine satellite of a chic

## GETTING THERE

**Air** Geneva 86km/ 53 miles (1½hr). Lyon 226km/140 miles (3hr).

**Rail** Station in resort, on the St Gervais-Le Fayet/Vallorcine line.

Direct TGV link from Paris on Friday evenings and weekends.

Parisian hotel: a beautifully furnished modern chalet half-way to Argentière: 'Tasteful, friendly staff ... lovely.'

(4) **Grand Hotel des Alpes** (0450 553780) Newly renovated and re-opened central hotel with pool, sauna, hot-tub and Italian restaurant.

(3) **Alpina** (0450 534777) Much the biggest in town: modernist-functional place just north of centre.

(3) **Gourmets & Italy** (0450 530138) Spot-on central mid-price B&B hotel.

(3) **Labrador** (Les Praz) (0450 559009) Scandinavian-style chalet close to the Flégère lift. Good restaurant.

(3) **Prieuré** (0450 532072) Mega-chalet on northern ring-road – handy for drivers, quite close to centre.

(3) **Vallée Blanche** (0450 530450) Smart, low-priced 3-star B&B hotel, handy for centre and Aiguille du Midi.

(2) **Richemond** (0450 530885) Traditional, comfortable, with good public areas. 'Excellent, very good value, superb food,' says a reporter.

(2) **Arve** (0450 530231) Central, by the river; small rooms. 'Good value and superb service from owners.'

(2) **Pointe Isabelle** (0450 531287) Not pretty, but central; friendly staff, good plain food and well-equipped rooms.

(1) **Faucigny** (0450 530117) Cottage-style; in centre.

**Self-catering** Many properties in UK package brochures are in convenient but cramped blocks in Chamonix Sud. The Balcons du Savoy are a cut above; great view, spacious rooms, use of a pool, a steam room and a solarium. The Splendid & Golf apartments in Les Praz are charming and close to the Flégère cable-car. Erna Low has some luxury places available.

## EATING OUT

### *Plenty of quality places*

The top hotels all have excellent restaurants and there are many other good places to eat. The Sarpé is a lovely 'mountain' restaurant and the Impossible is rustic but smart and features good regional dishes. We always enjoy the Atmosphere, by the river, despite its two-sitting system. The Panier des Quatre Saisons is another favourite – much better than its shopping-gallery setting would suggest.

Reader recommendations include Maison Carrier in the Albert 1er hotel ('Bustling, rustic with great value traditional food'), the Crochon ('Good

## ACTIVITIES

**Indoor** Sports complex (swimming pool, sauna, steam room, tennis, squash ice rink, fitness room, climbing wall), Alpine museum, library, casino, bridge, three cinemas, bowling

**Outdoor** Ice rink, tobogganing, heritage tours, panoramic flights, snow-shoeing, walking paths, ice-climbing, paragliding

**Phone numbers**
From abroad use the prefix +33 and omit the initial '0' of the phone number.

## TOURIST OFFICES

**Chamonix**
t 0450 530024
info@chamonix.com
www.chamonix.com

**Argentière**
t 0450 540214
info@argentiere.com

**Les Houches**
t 0450 555062
info@leshouches.com
www.leshouches.com

Savoyard fare, plus some varied and innovative dishes'), the Cabane next to the Labrador hotel in Les Praz ('Excellent, go before the prices go up'), the Caleche ('Good food, atmosphere and service') and the Bumblebee ('Tiny, excellent, especially for veggies'). The Monchu is good for Savoyard specialities. The Casa Valerio offers 'good Italian at good prices'. The Spiga d'Oro is another recommended Italian, over a 'lovely' deli. There are a number of ethnic restaurants – Mexican, Spanish, Japanese, Chinese, Indian etc – and lots of brasseries and cafes. Cafe Eldorado is 'good and cheap.'

### APRES-SKI
***Lots of bars and music***

Many of the bars around the pedestrianised centre of Chamonix get crowded for a couple of hours at sundown – none more so than the Choucas video bar. During the evening, The Pub ('friendly staff and good British/Irish beer'), Wild Wallabies, the Bar'd Up and the Bar du Moulin are busy. The Chambre Neuf at the Gustavia hotel remains so until late. The Queen Vic is 'nice and dark and dingy with a snug, pool table, good music and Beamish on tap'. For a quiet drink, try the Brit-run Dérapage, with happy hours early and mid-evening. There's a lively variety of nightclubs and discos. The Choucas (again), and Dick's Tea bar are popular. The Cantina sometimes has live music and is open late. Bar Terrasse has live music every night. There are plenty of bars and brasseries for a quieter drink, too. New bars include Privilege, TOF and BPM.

### OFF THE SLOPES
***An excellent choice***

There's more off-slope activity here than in many resorts, though one reader complains that toddlers are not well catered for. Excursion possibilities include Annecy, Geneva, Martigny, Courmayeur and Turin. The Alpine Museum is 'very interesting', the library has a good selection of English language books and there's a good sports centre and swimming pool.

## Argentière 1240m/4,070ft

The old village is in a lovely setting towards the head of the valley – the Glacier d'Argentière pokes down towards it and the Aiguille du Midi and Mont Blanc still dominate the scene down the valley. There's 'more snowmaking on the lower runs', according to one reporter. There's a fair bit of modern development but it still has a rustic appeal. A number of the hotels are simple, inexpensive and handy for the village centre – less so for the slopes – but the Grands-Montets (0450 540666) is a large chalet-style building, right next to the piste and the Panda Club for children. The family-run Montana (0450 541499) provides 'lovely rooms, excellent food'. Restaurants and bars are informal and inexpensive. The Office is always packed with Brits and Scandinavians and has live bands; and 'terrific cooked breakfasts'. The Savoy bar is another traditional favourite – 'lively, friendly, well priced'. The Rusticana is popular with locals and does 'excellent steaks'. The Boomerang is large and packed till 2am and the Stone near the top of the village has a 'great DJ'.

## Les Houches 1010m/3,310ft

Les Houches, 6km/4 miles from Chamonix, is not on the valley pass, but is covered by the regional Mont Blanc pass. It's a pleasant village, sitting in the shade of the looming Mont Blanc massif. There is an old core with a pretty church, but modern developments in chalet style have spread along the road up to Chamonix.

The area above Les Houches is served by a cable-car to Bellevue and a gondola to Prarion. Runs on the back of the mountain towards St-Gervais, and runs of 900m/2,950ft vertical down to Les Houches, make this the biggest single area of pistes in the Chamonix valley – mostly gentle blues and reds, good for building confidence. The largely wooded slopes are popular when bad weather closes other areas.

In good weather the slopes are quiet, and the views superb from the several attractive mountain restaurants, which are noticeably cheaper than others in the valley. Snow-cover on the lower slopes is not reliable, but there is a fair amount of snowmaking.

The village is quiet at night, but there are some pleasant bars and good restaurants including Vieilles Luges and the Terrain. Reporters enjoyed staying in the 3-star Hotel du Bois (0450 545035), with its 'helpful staff and excellent restaurant' and 'a good local band in the bar on Saturday'. Buses run to and from Chamonix all evening.

# Châtel

*A distinctively French base for touring the Portes du Soleil*

## COSTS

①②③④⑤⑥

## RATINGS

**The slopes**

| | |
|---|---|
| Snow | ** |
| Extent | ***** |
| Expert | *** |
| Intermediate | **** |
| Beginner | *** |
| Convenience | ** |
| Queues | *** |
| Mountain restaurants | *** |

**The rest**

| | |
|---|---|
| Scenery | **** |
| Resort charm | *** |
| Off-slope | ** |

## NEWS

For 2003/04, two new drags were installed – one to improve the link between Châtel and Torgon and the other to serve the terrain-park and boarder-cross at Super-Châtel. Five new snow-guns were added.

For 2004/05 the old two-seater chair at Pré-la-Joux will be replaced by a much-needed six-pack.

A new piste, Le Gros Nant, will be constructed to link Vonnes, on the road to Morgins, with the lifts at Linga – previously it took two buses to reach Linga from here.

- + Very extensive, pretty, intermediate terrain – the Portes du Soleil
- + Wide range of cheap and cheerful, good-value accommodation
- + Pleasant, lively, French-dominated old village, still quite rustic in parts
- + Local slopes are among the best in the Portes du Soleil and relatively queue-free
- + Easily reached – one of the shortest drives from the Channel, and close to Geneva, but ...

- – Village congestion can be a problem at weekends and in peak season, as can lift queues in parts of the Portes du Soleil circuit
- – Both the resort and the slopes are low for a French resort, with the resulting risk of poor snow – though snowmaking is now extensive
- – Most main lifts are a bus-ride from village centre
- – Best nursery slope reached by bus or gondola

**Châtel offers an attractive blend of qualities much like that of Morzine – another established valley village in the Portes du Soleil. Morzine is a bit more polished, Châtel (with a claimed 40 working farms) more rustic. But its key advantage is that it is part of the main PdS circuit. There is a gap in the circuit at Châtel, filled by buses; but this is more of an irritant to those passing through than for Châtel residents, for most of whom the excellent local bus services are part of the daily routine. At weekends it's worth trying the slopes of nearby Chapelle d'Abondance, which are pleasantly uncrowded.**

## THE RESORT

Châtel lies near the head of the wooded Dranse valley, at the north-eastern limit of the French-Swiss Portes du Soleil ski circuit.

It is a much expanded but still attractive old village. Modern unpretentious chalet-style hotels and apartments rub shoulders with old farms where cattle still live in winter.

Although there is a definite centre, the village sprawls along the road in from lake Geneva and the diverging roads out – up the hillside towards Morgins and along the valley towards the Linga and Pré-la-Joux lifts.

Lots of visitors take cars and the centre can get clogged with traffic – especially at weekends. Street parking is difficult but there is underground (paid-for) parking and day car parks at Linga and Pré-la-Joux (where the parking can still get very full in peak season despite the provision of new spaces). Other main French Portes du Soleil resorts are easy to reach by piste, but not by road.

The resort bus service is approved by reporters. A central location gives you the advantage of getting on the ski-bus to the outlying lifts before it gets very crowded and simplifies après-ski outings – the night bus finishes at 9.30pm. But there is accommodation near the Linga lift if that's the priority.

A few kilometres down the valley is the rustic village of La Chapelle-d'Abondance (see end of chapter).

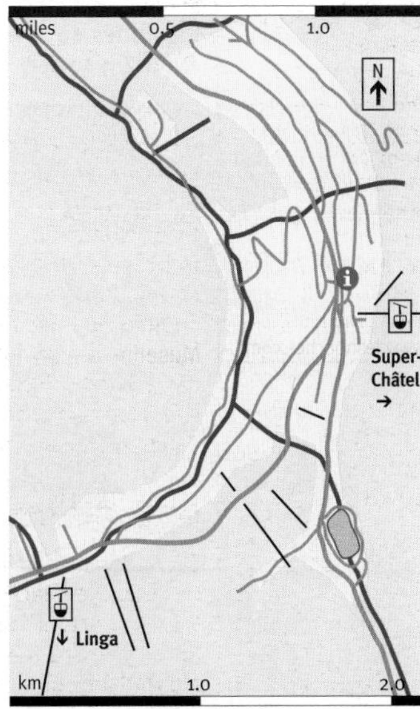

| KEY FACTS | |
|---|---|
| **Resort** | 1200m<br>3,940ft |
| For Portes du Soleil | |
| **Slopes** | 975-2275m<br>3,200-7,460ft |
| **Lifts** | 206 |
| **Pistes** | 650km<br>400 miles |
| **Green** | 13% |
| **Blue** | 38% |
| **Red** | 39% |
| **Black** | 10% |
| **Snowmaking** | 252 acres |
| For Châtel only | |
| **Slopes** | 1100-2205m<br>3,610-7,230ft |
| **Lifts** | 41 |
| **Pistes** | 83km<br>52 miles |





## THE MOUNTAINS

Châtel sits between two sectors of the main Portes du Soleil circuit, each offering a mix of open and wooded slopes, and linked by an 'excellent, practically continuous' free bus service. The circuit is easily done by intermediates of all abilities. Going clockwise avoids two snags in Morgins – the excessively sunny lower slopes of Bec de Corbeau, and the uphill walk to the next lift. The booklet-style piste map gives a reasonably clear picture of each resort along the way. Reporters have praised the system of Discovery Routes around the Portes du Soleil – choose an animal that suits your ability and follow the signs displaying it.

### THE SLOPES
***The circuit breaks down here***

Directly above the village is **Super-Châtel** – an area of easy, open and lightly wooded beginner slopes, accessed by a choice of gondola or two-stage chair. From here you can cross the Swiss border, either to quiet Torgon or clockwise around the Portes du Soleil to Morgins, Champoussin and Champéry, before going back into France above Avoriaz. You can also start from Petit Châtel – successive chairs take you to the link with Torgon. A reader recommended this route, but as the bus doesn't go here you need to be staying locally or have a car.

For intermediates and better, the **Linga** area, accessed by a gondola, has some of the most interesting runs in the Portes du Soleil. The fastest way to Avoriaz is to stay on the bus at Linga and go to Pré-la-Joux. From here a fast quad goes to Plaine Dranse; then it's one more lift and run to Les Lindarets and the lifts to Avoriaz. There is night-skiing on Linga every Thursday.

### TERRAIN-PARKS
***Head for Super Châtel***

There's a terrain-park, with 15 features of varying difficulty, at Super Châtel, plus a 120m/390ft long half-pipe and an 800m/half-mile long boarder-cross course. Music blasts out to help motivate you for the tricks. There's a big air jump on the Stade de Slalom in the Linga sector, and La Chapelle d'Abondance also has a 360m/1,180ft long park with half-pipe.

### SNOW RELIABILITY
***The main drawback***

The main drawback of the Portes du Soleil is that it is low, so snow quality can suffer when it's warm. Châtel is at only 1200m/3,940ft and some runs home can be tricky or shut, especially from Super-Châtel. But a lot of snowmaking has been installed at Super-Châtel and on runs down to resort level. Linga and Pré-la-Joux are mainly north-facing and generally have the best local snow – a regular visitor tells us there is often good snow at Pré-la-Joux until May. But another told us of pistes to Morgins and Lindarets being closed in March.

### FOR EXPERTS
***Some challenges***

The best steep runs – on- and off-piste – are in the Linga and Pré-la-Joux area. Beneath the Linga gondola and chair,

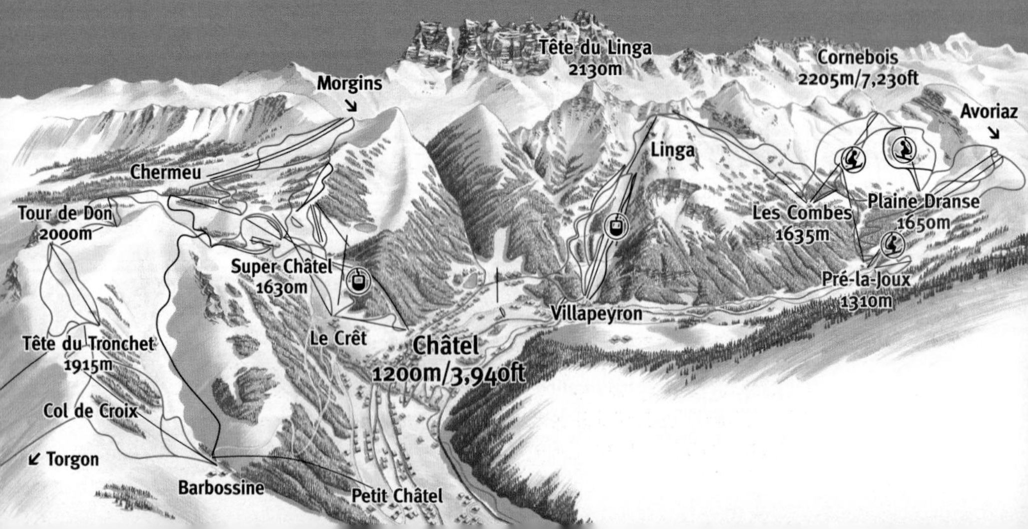

## LIFT PASSES

**Portes du Soleil**
Covers all lifts in all 12 resorts, and shuttle-buses.

**Main pass**
1 day €35
6 days €171

**Senior citizens**
Over 60: 6 days €137

**Children**
Under 16: 6 days €115
Under 5: free pass

**Alternative passes**
As well as Châtel, local pass covers Torgon, Corbeau sector of Morgins and Braitaz sector of La Chapelle d'Abondance.

there's a pleasant mix of open and wooded ground which follows the fall line fairly directly. And there's a mogul field between Cornebois and Plaine Dranse which has been described as 'steeper and narrower than the infamous Swiss Wall in Avoriaz'. An area under the Cornebois chair, known to the locals as Happy Valley, is also popular. There are two blacks from the top of the Morclan chair at Super-Châtel, including a long run down to Barbossine which is quite narrow and tricky at the top. But it can be prone to closure because of avalanche risk. There's also a great off-piste route from Tête du Linga down the valley of La Leiche – hire a guide. Two pistes from the Rochassons ridge are steep and kept well groomed.

### FOR INTERMEDIATES
***Some of the best runs in the area***

When conditions are right the Portes du Soleil is an intermediate's paradise. Good intermediates need not go far from Châtel to find amusement; Linga and Plaine Dranse have some of the best red runs on the circuit. The moderately skilled can do the PdS circuit without problem, and will particularly enjoy runs around Les Lindarets and Morgins. Even timid types can do the circuit, provided they take one or two short-cuts and ride chairs down trickier bits. The chair from Les Lindarets to Pointe de Mossettes leads to a red run into the Swiss area, which is a lot easier than the 'Swiss Wall' from Chavanette and also speeds up a journey round the circuit.

Leaving aside attempts to complete the circuit in both directions, there are rewarding out-and-back expeditions to be made clockwise to the wide open snowfields above Champoussin, beyond Morgins, and anticlockwise to the Hauts-Forts runs above Avoriaz – a preferred option for a reporter this year, who found the circuit to involve more time 'travelling the lift-system and poling along flats and traverses than actually skiing any decent terrain'.

### FOR BEGINNERS
***Three possible options***

There are good beginners' areas at Pré-la-Joux (a bus-ride away) and at Super-Châtel (a gondola-ride). And there are nursery slopes at village level if there is snow there. Recent reporters have praised the Super-Châtel slopes and lifts which 'allow the beginner to progress' and 'safely practise' on gentle gradients away from the main runs. Getting up to them is a bit of an effort, though. The home run to the village at Super-Châtel is not recommended – it is narrow, busy and steep at the end which, coupled with often poor and icy conditions, makes it very tricky for beginners and timid intermediates. The Pré-la-Joux slopes are said to have 'less variety of slopes and quite a steep drag-lift'.

### FOR CROSS-COUNTRY
***Pretty, if low, trails***

There are plenty of pretty trails along the river and through the woods on the lower slopes of Linga, but snow-cover can be a problem. The tourist office produces good maps with suggested routes and trail times.

### QUEUES
***Bottlenecks being eased***

Queues to get to Avoriaz have been eased by the high-speed quad at Pré-la-Joux. But there are still a couple of bottlenecks, which tend to be worse at weekends (although we do have reports of little queuing even during half-term and New Year). The worst is at Les Lindarets, where there is often a lengthy wait for the Chaux Fleurie chair-lift to the Col du Bassachaux on the way back to Châtel – there are reports of this being upgraded in the near future but it is unlikely for 2004/05. But the queue the other way up to Avoriaz has been eased since the introduction of the six-pack. You can face queues to get down from Super-Châtel if the slope back is shut by poor snow. Queues for the gondola out of the village form when school parties

## boarding

*Avoriaz is the hardcore destination in the Portes du Soleil. Châtel is not a bad place to learn or to go to as a budget option, and the terrain-park here might suit non-experts better. But many lifts in the Super-Châtel sector are drags and reporters warn they can be a 'painful experience'. The Linga area also has good, varied slopes and off-piste possibilities, and the Stade de Slalom run there is floodlit every Thursday, is wired for sound and has a big air jump.*

The Linga sector offers widely varying terrain above the trees, as well as some sheltered runs →

OT CHATEL / JEAN-FRANCOIS VUARAND

## SCHOOLS

**ESF**
t 0450 732264
info@est-chatel.com

**International**
t 0450 733192
ski.surf@freesbee.fr

**Stages Henri Gonon**
t 0450 732304
ecole.ski@hotel-arcenciel.fr

**Francis Sports**
t 0450 813251
francis-sports@valdabondance.com

**Snow Ride (Ecole de Glisse)**
t 0608 337651

**Bureau des Moniteurs Virages**
t 0680 028763

**Classes**
(ESF prices)
6 half-days (2½hr am or pm) €105

**Private lessons**
€31 for 1hr, for 1 or 2 people

## CHILDREN

**Le Village des Marmottons**
t 0450 733379
contact@lesmarmottons.com
8.30 to 5.30; ages 3 to 8; ski lessons from age 3

**Mouflets Garderie**
t 0450 813819
ages 3mnth to 6yr

**Ski school**
ESF takes children from 5 to 13 (6 half-days €115); Francis Sport takes children from 3 to 8; International, Henri Gonon and Snow Ride take children from age 8





gather: 'It is common to share your lift with a buzz of hyperactivity,' writes a recent visitor. Reporters have also found lengthy queues at the Tour de Don and Chermeu drag-lifts at certain times of day, causing difficulties for skiers rushing back to Super-Châtel to pick up children from ski school.

### MOUNTAIN RESTAURANTS
***Some quite good local huts***

Atmospheric chalets can be found, notably at Plaine Dranse (the Bois Prin, Chez Crépy, Tân o Marmottes, Vieux Chalet, Chaux des Rosées and Chez Denis have been recommended). In the Linga area the Ferme des Pistes, 'a cosy alpine barn, complete with stable-door', gets the thumbs up for wholesome and hearty mountain meals. The Perdrix Blanche at Pré-la-Joux scarcely counts as a mountain restaurant, but is an attractive (if expensive and crowded) spot for lunch. At Super Châtel the Portes du Soleil at the foot of the Coqs drags is much better than the big place at the top of the gondola. The Escale Blanche is worth a visit.

### SCHOOLS AND GUIDES
***Plenty of choice***

There are now six ski and snowboard schools in Châtel. The International school has been recommended by a reporter, but another was 'very disappointed' with her private lesson and did not learn anything new. The ESF came in for praise, with comments such as 'very helpful and customer-focused instructors', and 'skiing progressed by leaps and bounds', reinforced in 2004 by a regular reporter.

### FACILITIES FOR CHILDREN
***Increasingly sympathetic***

The Marmottons nursery has good facilities, including toboggans, painting, music and videos, and children are reportedly happy there. 'Mini-Montagnards' is a new games room facility based in Vonnes, for children up to 12 years accompanied by an adult. Francis Sports ski school has its own nursery area with a drag lift and chalet at Linga: 'Very organised, convenient and reasonably priced.' The ESF had a rave report again this year, from a regular visitor: 'I continue to be very impressed.' His eight-year old grandson has always received 'sympathetic instruction from English speaking instructors' and made excellent progress.

## STAYING THERE

### HOW TO GO
***A wide choice, including chalets***

Although this is emphatically a French resort, packages from Britain are no problem to track down.

**Chalets** A fair number of UK operators have places here, including some Châtel specialists.

**Hotels** Practically all the hotels are 2-stars, mostly friendly chalets, wooden or at least partly wood-clad. None of the 3-stars is particularly well placed.

(((3 **Macchi** (0450 732412) Modern chalet, most central of the 3-stars.

(((3 **Fleur de Neige** (0450 732010) Welcoming chalet on edge of centre; Grive Gourmande restaurant does about the best food in town.

(((3 **Lion d'Or** (0450 813440) In centre, 'basic rooms, good atmosphere'.

((2 **Belalp** (0450 732439) Very comfortable, with excellent food.

GETTING THERE

**Air** Geneva 75km/47 miles (1½hr).

**Rail** Thonon les Bains (42km/26 miles).

ACTIVITIES

**Indoor** Bowling, cinemas, library

**Outdoor** Ice rink, walks, dog-sledding, bob-sleigh, salto trampolining, farm visits, cheese factory visits, snow-shoe excursions.

**Phone numbers**
From abroad use the prefix +33 and omit the initial '0' of the phone number.

TOURIST OFFICES

**Châtel**
**t** 0450 732244
touristoffice@chatel.com
www.chatel.com

**La Chapelle-d'Abondance**
**t** 0450 735141
ot@lachapelledabondance.com
www.valdabondance.com

① **Kandahar** (0450 733060) One for peace-lovers: a Logis by the river, a walkable distance from the centre.
① **Rhododendrons** (0450 732404) 'Great service, friendly, comfortable, clean.'
**Self-catering** Many of the better places are available through agencies specialising in Châtel or in self-drive holidays. The Gelinotte (out of town but near the Linga lifts and children's village) and the Erines (5 minutes from the centre) look good. The Avenières is right by the Linga gondola. A couple of reporters have mentioned that Châtel's supermarkets are small and over-crowded. There is also a large supermarket out in the direction of Chapelle d'Abondance.

EATING OUT
***Fair selection***

There is an adequate number and range of restaurants. The Vieux Four is beautifully rustic with lots of wooden beams, alcoves and ornaments and does great steaks and 'tempting and tasty Savoyard specialities'. The Fiacre serves similar food and is also popular. The Fleur de Neige hotel has a pricey gastronomic restaurant (La Grive Gourmand). The Pierreir serves Savoyard specialities. The Moroccan chef at the Hotel Soldanelles cooks a 'veritable feast' and the Renard is good for steaks, but is located lower down the valley. The Ripaille, almost opposite the Linga gondola, is popular with the locals and highly rated by reporters, especially for its fish and the 'fantastic local Gamay wines', but booking is essential. The hotel Cornettes in La Chapelle-d'Abondance is worth a trip – see later section.

APRES-SKI
***All down to bars***

Châtel is getting livelier, especially at the weekends. The Tunnel bar is very popular with the British and has a DJ or live music every night (the caramel vodka is recommended). The Avalanche is a very popular English-style pub and has internet facilities. The Godille – close to the Super-Châtel gondola and crowded when everyone descends at close of play – has a more French feel. The 'small and cosy' Isba is the locals' choice, and shows extreme sports videos. The bar in the hotel Soldanelles has been recommended. The bowling alley, the Vieille Grange, also has a good bar.

OFF THE SLOPES
***Better to stay in Morzine***

Those with a car have some entertaining excursions available: Geneva, Thonon and Evian. Otherwise there is little to do but take some pleasant walks along the river, visit the cheese factory and the two cinemas, or join in the daily events organised by the tourist office.

The Portes du Soleil as a whole is less than ideal for those who like to meet their more active friends for lunch: skiers and boarders are likely to be above at some distant resort at lunchtime and very few lifts are accessible to pedestrians.

# La Chapelle-d'Abondance

**1010m/3,310ft**

This unspoiled, rustic farming community, complete with old church and friendly locals, is 5km/3 miles along a beautiful valley from Châtel. 'A car and a bit of French are virtually essential,' says a reporter. It's had its own quiet little north-facing area of easy wooded runs for some years, but has more recently been put on the Portes du Soleil map by a gondola and three chair-lifts that now link it to Torgon in Switzerland and so to Super-Châtel. Taken together with Chapelle's own little area, this spur of the Portes du Soleil is worth exploring – good at weekends, when Châtel gets crowded, and 'excellent for beginners' But a reporter warns of difficult drags on the return from Torgon – 'steep, icy and not child-friendly'.

The mountain restaurants also failed to impress a recent visitor, who queued for 30 minutes at one.

Nightlife is virtually non-existent – just a few quiet bars, a cinema and torchlit descents.

The hotel Cornettes (0450 735024) is an amazing 2-star, run by the Trincaz family since 1894, with 2-star rooms but 4-star facilities, including an indoor pool, sauna, steam room and hot-tubs. It has an atmospheric bar and an excellent restaurant doing extremely good-value menus (but 'disappointing' desserts, comments one reporter). Look out for showcases with puppets and dolls and eccentric touches, such as ancient doors that unexpectedly open automatically. The Alpage and the Chabi are other hotel options. The Airelles apartments have received a favourable report.

OT LA CLUSAZ / MP ROUGE-PULLON

# La Clusaz – Le Gd-Bornand

*Attractive, distinctively French all-rounders; all they lack is altitude*

## COSTS

①②③④⑤⑥

## RATINGS

| | |
|---|---|
| **The slopes** | |
| Snow | ** |
| Extent | *** |
| Expert | *** |
| Intermediate | **** |
| Beginner | **** |
| Convenience | *** |
| Queues | *** |
| Mountain restaurants | **** |
| **The rest** | |
| Scenery | *** |
| Resort charm | **** |
| Off-slope | *** |

## KEY FACTS

| | |
|---|---|
| La Clusaz | |
| **Resort** | 1100m 3,610ft |
| **Slopes** | 1100-2500m 3,610-8,200ft |
| **Lifts** | 55 |
| **Pistes** | 132km 82 miles |
| **Green** | 30% |
| **Blue** | 33% |
| **Red** | 28% |
| **Black** | 9% |
| **Snowmaking** | 74 acres |
| Le Grand-Bornand | |
| **Resort** | 950m 3,120ft |
| **Slopes** | 1000-2100m 3,280-6,890ft |
| **Lifts** | 39 |
| **Pistes** | 90km 56 miles |
| **Green** | 31% |
| **Blue** | 35% |
| **Red** | 27% |
| **Black** | 7% |
| **Snowmaking** | 133 acres |



- + Mountain villages in a scenic setting, retaining traditional character
- + Extensive, interesting slopes – pistes best for beginners and intermediates
- + Very French atmosphere
- + Very short transfer from Geneva, and easy to reach by car from UK
- + Attractive mountain restaurants
- + Good cross-country trails
- + Slopes at La Clusaz and Le Grand-Bornand linked by shuttle-bus

- − Snow conditions unreliable because of low altitude (by French standards)
- − Not many challenging pistes for experts – though there are good off-piste runs
- − Crowded at weekends

**Few other major French resorts are based around what are still, essentially, genuine mountain villages that exude rustic charm and Gallic atmosphere. Combine that with over 200km/125 miles of largely intermediate slopes, above and below the tree line, spread over five linked sectors in the two separate resorts of La Clusaz and Le Grand-Bornand, and there's a good basis for an enjoyable, relaxed week.**

**The area's one big problem is its height, or lack of it. Snowmaking is continually increased, but it's still on a modest scale, and of course makes no difference in mild weather. So pre-booking a holiday here remains a slightly risky business.**

## THE RESORT

**La Clusaz** was once frequented almost entirely by the French. But it has developed into a major international resort – for both summer and winter seasons. And there is a substantial year-round presence of British residents in the area. As one of the most accessible resorts from Geneva and Annecy, it's good for short transfers, but it does get crowded, and there can be weekend traffic jams.

The village is built beside a fast-flowing stream at the junction of a number of narrow wooded valleys, and has had to grow in a rather rambling and sprawling way, with roads running in a confusing mixture of directions. But, unlike so many French resorts, La Clusaz has retained the charm of a genuine mountain village. It's the kind of place that is as attractive in summer as under a blanket of snow in winter.

In the centre is a large old church, and other original old stone and wood buildings; and, for the most part, the new buildings have been built in chalet style and blend in well. Les Etages is a much smaller centre of accommodation south of (and quite a bit higher than) the main town, where two of the mountain sectors meet.

La Clusaz has a friendly feel to it. The villagers welcome visitors every Monday evening in the main square with vin chaud and a variety of local cheeses. There's a weekly market,

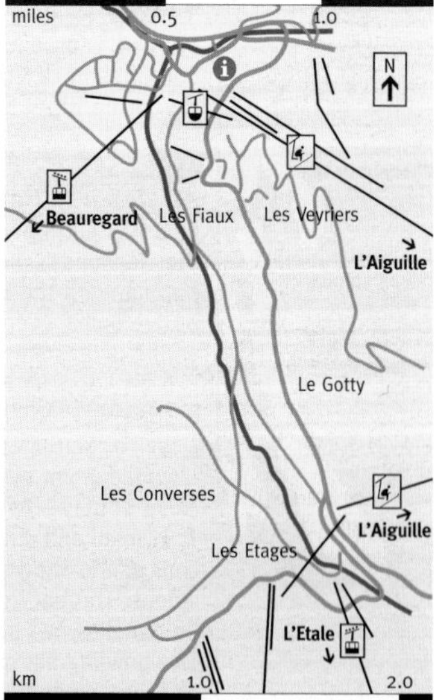

## NEWS

The Beauregard cable-car in La Clusaz was replaced last season, tripling the capacity to 1,500 people an hour. Le Grand-Bornand replaced the Maroly drag-lift with a new six-person chair.

Snowmaking capacity is to be increased in both resorts.

tempting food shops and a wide choice of typically French bars.

For much of the season La Clusaz is a quiet and peaceful place for a holiday. But in peak season and at weekends the place gets packed out with French and Swiss families.

**Le Grand-Bornand**, also covered by the Aravis lift pass, is an even more charming village, with even more sense that it remains a mountain community. This is partly because most of the development as a winter sports resort has gone on up the road at the satellite village of Le Chinaillon, which has been developed in chalet style. Le Grand-Bornand has quite extensive slopes and is well worth exploring for a day or two, or considering as an alternative, quieter base.

Le Grand-Bornand and La Clusaz are linked by free buses doing the 10-minute journey every 30 minutes during the day – these become more erratic in peak-time traffic.

If you are taking a car, you might also consider basing yourself at **St-Jean-de-Sixt** – a small hamlet midway between La Clusaz and Le Grand-Bornand, with a small slope nearby, mainly used for sledging.

## THE MOUNTAINS

Like the village, the slopes at **La Clusaz** are rather spread out – which makes them all the more interesting (and scenic). There are five main areas, each connecting with at least one other. At **Le Grand-Bornand** the slopes can be accessed from either the village or from Le Chinaillon, up the road.

### THE SLOPES
***Pretty and varied***

Several points in **La Clusaz** have lifts giving access to the predominantly west- and north-west facing slopes of **L'Aiguille**. Links between this sector and the slightly higher and shadier slopes of **La Balme** area have improved massively in recent years: a long red and a black piste have replaced the off-piste route from L'Aiguille towards La Balme, and a gondola now returns you to Côte 2000 on L'Aiguille – cutting out the need to take a long, flat run back to La Clusaz. La Balme is a splendid, varied area with good lifts (a high-capacity gondola from the bottom leading to a quad chair); from the top there are wonderful views towards Mont Blanc.

BASILE / JC PIRONON

Le Chinaillon has some genuinely testing slopes ↓

## LIFT PASSES

**Aravis pass**
Covers La Clusaz, Le Grand-Bornand, Saint-Jean-de-Sixt and Manigod, and shuttle service between resorts.

**Main pass**
6 days €149

**Senior citizens**
Over 60: 6 days €123.50

**Children**
Under 15: 6 days €110
Under 5: free pass

**La Clusaz pass**
Covers all lifts in La Clusaz.

**Beginner**
6 days €87

**Main pass**
1 day €26.30
6 days €137.50

**Senior citizens**
Over 60: 6 days €112.50

**Children**
Under 15: 6 days €99
Under 5: free pass

**Le Grand-Bornand pass**
Covers all lifts in Le Grand-Bornand.

**Main pass**
1 day €24.40
6 days €117.30

**Senior citizens**
Over 60: 6 days €110.90

**Children**
Under 15: 6 days €96.90
Under 9: 6 days: €70.00





Going the other way from L'Aiguille leads you to **L'Etale** via another choice of easy runs and the Transval cable-car, which shuttles people between the two areas. From the bottom of L'Etale, you can head back along another path to the village and the cable-car (enlarged for 2003/04) up to the fourth sector of **Beauregard** which, as the name implies, has splendid views and catches a lot of sunshine.

From the top of Beauregard you can link via another easy piste and a two-way chair-lift with the fifth area of **Manigod**. From here you can move on to L'Etale.

The main village at **Le Grand-Bornand** has two gondolas on the outskirts up to a gentle open area of easy runs (including nursery slopes) lying between 1400m and 1500m (4,600ft and 4,920ft). Chairs fan out above this point, one going up to the high point of **Le Lachat,** where there are serious red and black runs. Other lifts and runs go across the mountainside to the slopes above **Le Chinaillon**. Here there is a broad, open mountainside with a row of chairs and drags serving blue and red slopes, and links to the rest of the domain – a wide area of blue and red runs.

### TERRAIN-PARKS

***Twin parks – double the fun***

Both resorts have terrain-parks, although boarders tend to prefer La Clusaz, which is more lively – particularly at weekends. La Clusaz's park is on the Aiguille, while Le Grand-Bornand's area is at Maroly. Both have quarter- and half-pipes, tables, rails and boarder-cross runs.

### SNOW RELIABILITY

***Variable because of low altitude***

Most of the runs are west- or north-west facing and tend to keep their snow fairly well, even though most of the area is below 2000m/6,500ft. The best snow is usually on the north-west-facing slopes at La Balme, where a lift takes you up to 2500m/8,200ft. In late season, the home runs can be dependent on snowmaking – of which there is now virtually blanket coverage. However, the long paths linking La Balme and l'Etale to the village are devoid of snow-guns and can suffer as a result. The main lifts on Beauregard and Crêt du Merle can be used to descend. You can also ride the gondolas down to Le Grand-Bornand and the runs above Le Chinaillon have extensive snowmaking.

## SCHOOLS

La Clusaz

**ESF**
**t** 0450 024083
info@esf-laclusaz.com

**Sno Academie**
**t** 0450 326605
snoacademie@aol.com

**Aravis Challenge**
**t** 0450 028129
aravis-challenge@wanadoo.fr

Le Grand-Bornand

**ESF**
**t** 0450 027910
contact@esf-grand-bo.com

**Starski**
t 0450 270469
esi_starski@yahoo.fr

**Classes**
(ESF prices)
6 days (2hr am and 2hr pm): €135

**Private lessons**
€31 for 1hr for 1 to 3 people

## GUIDES

**Bureau des guides**
**t** 0450 633599

## boarding

*Snowboarding is popular in La Clusaz, and although there are still a lot of drag-lifts, most are avoidable. There are some good nursery slopes, served by chair-lifts, and great cruising runs to progress to. La Balme is a great natural playground for good free-riders. And both La Clusaz and Le Grand Bornand have decent terrain-parks to hang out in.*

### FOR EXPERTS
***Plenty to do, especially off-piste***

The La Clusaz piste map doesn't seem to have a lot to offer experts, but most of the sectors present off-piste variants to the pistes, and there are more serious adventures to undertake – all the more attractive for being ignored by most visitors.

The best terrain is at La Balme, where there are several fairly challenging pistes above mid-mountain. The black Vraille run, which leads to the speed-skiing slope, is seriously steep. On the opposite side of the sector, the entirely off-piste Combe de Bellachat can be reached.

The Noire run down the face of Beauregard can be tricky in poor snow and is often closed. The Tetras on L'Etale and the Mur Edgar bumps run below Crêt du Loup on L'Aiguille have been reclassified as blacks, and rightly so. L'Aiguille has a good off-piste run down the neglected Combe de Borderan and the long Lapiaz black piste runs down the Combe de Fernuy from Côte 2000.

In Le Grand-Bornand there are worthwhile shady black runs on Le Lachat, and on the lower peak of La Floria, above Le Chinaillon.

### FOR INTERMEDIATES
***Good if snow is good***

Most intermediates will love La Clusaz if the snow conditions are good. Early intermediates will delight in the gentle slopes at the top of Beauregard and over on La Croix-Fry at Manigod, where there's a network of gentle tree-lined runs. And they'll be able to travel all over the area on the gentle, green linking pistes, where poling or walking is more likely to be a problem than any fears about steepness.

CHILDREN

La Clusaz:
**Club des Mouflets**
t 0450 326520
Ages 8mnth to 4½yr; 8.30-12 noon, 2pm-6pm; 6 days €109.60

**Club des Champions**
t 0450 326950
Ages 3 to 5; 8.30-12 noon, 2pm-6pm; skiing included

Le Grand-Bornand:
**Les P'tits Maringouins**
t 0450 027905
Ages 3mnth up

**Ski school**
At La Clusaz ESF (Piou-Piou Club) runs lessons for ages up to 5 (€9.50 for 1hr) and for 5 to 11 (6 4hr days €122). At Le Gd-Bornand ESF runs lessons for ages 3 to 8 and for 8 to 12

GETTING THERE

**Air** Geneva 50km/31 miles (1½hr); Lyon 150km/93 miles (2½hr).

ACTIVITIES

**Indoor** Fitness centre, sauna, steam room; hotels with fitness rooms, saunas, etc; library, bridge, cinema
**Outdoor** Ice rink, paragliding, snow-shoe excursions, ice carts, snowmobiling, tobogganing, winter walks, quad-bikes, swimming pool (with indoor jacuzzi), farm visit, town tour, horse and buggy rides

L'Etale and L'Aiguille have more challenging but wide blue runs.

More adventurous intermediates will prefer the steeper red slopes and good snow of La Balme and the long red down Combe du Fernuy from L'Aiguille.

Le Grand-Bornand is full of good cruising blue and red intermediate runs stretching in both directions above Le Chinaillon – well worth a visit for a day or two if you are staying in La Clusaz.

### FOR BEGINNERS
***Splendid beginner slopes***

There is a nursery slope at village level at La Clusaz, and a couple of others just above it, but the best nursery slopes are up the mountain at the top of the Beauregard cable-car and at Crêt du Merle. The Beauregard area has lovely gentle blue runs to progress to, including one long run around the mountain right back to the village. There are also some good beginner slopes at Le Grand-Bornand.

### FOR CROSS-COUNTRY
***Excellent***

The region has much better cross-country facilities than many resorts, with around 70km/43 miles of loops of varying difficulty. In La Clusaz, one good area is near the Lac des Confins, reached by bus. There's also a lovely sunny area at the top of the Beauregard cable-car. At Le Grand-Bornand there are extensive trails in the Vallée du Bouchet and towards Le Chinaillon. In 2003 a new training circuit called the Nordic Park – complete with bumps, gradients and bends – was built. And there are further trails at St-Jean-de-Sixt.

### QUEUES
***Not usually a problem***

Lift queues aren't a problem, except on peak weekends or if the lower slopes are shut because of snow shortage. The chair-lifts up the front face of L'Aiguille are the main weekend black spots; they are avoidable. One reporter complained of racers taking over lifts and pistes.

### MOUNTAIN RESTAURANTS
***High standard***

Mountain restaurants are one of the area's strong points. There are lots of them and most are rustic and charming, serving good, reasonably priced – often Savoyard – food. We have had excellent reports on the Télémark above the chair lift to L'Etale and the Chenons at the bottom of La Balme. There are several other good restaurants higher up in the Aiguille sector, of which the Bercail is said to be the best. The 'very attractive' Chez Arthur at Crêt du Merle has a calm little table-service restaurant tucked away behind the crowded self-service. The restaurant at Beauregard by the cross-country trail is sunny and peaceful, with good views. The Relais de L'Aiguille at Crêt du Loup is also popular. In Le Grand Bornand, the Névé at Le Rosay and the Terres Rouges are recommended. The Vieille Ferme at Merdassier (see Eating out) is also open at lunchtime.

### SCHOOLS AND GUIDES
***Mixed reports***

There are tales of large classes and poor instruction in the ESF, but we've heard from some satisfied customers too – especially those taking private lessons. According to reports, the smaller Sno Academie – with smaller class sizes – is much more reliable.

### FACILITIES FOR CHILDREN
***Good – in theory***

We have had mixed reports about the kindergarten in La Clusaz and none about those in Le Grand-Bornand. But a visitor last year was impressed by the 'variety of activities to encourage the small ones to get used to the snow'. Generally the resorts are places where families can feel at home.

## STAYING THERE

### HOW TO GO
***A fair choice of packages***

La Clusaz is offered mostly by smaller operators, some of which go to Le Grand-Bornand too. The drive from the Channel and the transfer from Geneva airport are as short as they come.

**Chalets** There are some chalets, including some charmingly rustic ones.

**Hotels** Small, friendly 2-star family hotels are the mainstay of the area; luxury is not an option here.

(((3) **Carlina** (0450 024348) A reporter says it's the best; central with pool and grounds.

(((3) **Beauregard** (0450 326800) 'Spacious and comfortable'; on the fringe of the village. A reporter last year enthused about the pool area, the atmosphere and the 'excellent food'.

(((3) **Alp'Hôtel** (0450 024006)

**Phone numbers**
From abroad use the prefix +33 and omit the initial '0' of the phone number.

**TOURIST OFFICES**

**La Clusaz**
t 0450 326500
infos@laclusaz.com
www.laclusaz.com

**Le Grand-Bornand**
t 0450 027800
infos@legrandbornand.com
www.legrandbornand.com

**St-Jean-de-Sixt**
t 0450 022412
infos@saintjeandesixt.com
www.saintjeandesixt.com

**Vallées des Aravis**
t 0450 027874
infos@aravis.com
www.aravis.com

Comfortable modern chalet close to the centre, with good restaurant. Pool.
(((3) **Alpen Roc** (0450 025896) Big but stylish, central and comfortable, although one reporter said his room was 'very cramped'. Pool.
(((3) **Saytels** (0450 022016) Only 3-star in Le Grand-Bornand. Close to church.
(((3) **Cimes** (0450 270038) 3-star in Le Chinaillon.
((2) **Aravis** (0450 026031) Traditional place with 'dated' rooms but 'great' food, in la Clusaz centre, close to lifts.
((2) **Alpage de Tante Pauline** (0450 026328) Dinky chalet at foot of L'Etale slopes (bus stop outside).
**Self-catering** There's quite a good choice, including self-catering chalets as well as apartments. Some are out of town and best for those with a car.

**EATING OUT**
***Good choice***
There's a wide choice of restaurants, some a short drive away, including the Vieux Chalet, which is one of our favourites – good food and service in a splendid, creaky old chalet. The St Joseph at the Alp'Hotel is regarded as the best restaurant in La Clusaz. Ecuelle is the place to go for Savoyard specialities. The Cordée and the Outa are simple places giving great value for money. At the extreme, the Symphonie restaurant in the hotel Beauregard is highly recommended by a reporter.

We're told some of the best food in the area is at the Ferme de Lormay in La Vallée du Bouchet, about 5km/3 miles on from Le Grand-Bornand. But another reporter rates the Vieille Ferme at Merdassier his favourite place in the Alps – an old farm building with 'serious food, classy staff, perfect atmosphere'. The Foly, overlooking the Lac des Confins, is a firm favourite with both tourists and locals alike.

**APRES-SKI**
***La Clusaz getting livelier***
These resorts have always seemed to us typically quiet French family places, with the difference that La Clusaz is definitely the place to stay for a livelier time – especially at the weekend. The Caves du Paccaly, in the centre of La Clusaz, has woody decor and live music. The Pressoir is a focal bar, popular for sports videos. Pub le Salto is run by a British couple and has Sky TV and draught Guinness. The Bali is a more French central recommendation. The Ecluse disco apparently no longer offers views of the floodlit river running beneath its glass dance floor. Club 18 rocks, often with live bands.

**OFF THE SLOPES**
***Some diversions***
The villages are pleasant. It's easy for pedestrians to get around the valley by bus and to several good mountain restaurants for lunch. There are good walks along the valleys, and a day trip to the beautiful lakeside town of Annecy is possible. And La Clusaz has an excellent aquatic centre with indoor and outdoor pools, jacuzzi, sauna and steam rooms.

**STAYING UP THE MOUNTAIN**
***Cheap and panoramic***
There are three places to stay at the top of Beauregard.

OT LES CONTAMINES

# Les Contamines

*A hidden gem: a charming, unspoiled French village with reliable snow*

**COSTS**

(1)(2)(3)(4)(5)(6)

**RATINGS**

| The slopes | |
|---|---|
| Snow | **** |
| Extent | ** |
| Expert | ** |
| Intermediate | *** |
| Beginner | ** |
| Convenience | ** |
| Queues | *** |
| Mountain restaurants | **** |
| **The rest** | |
| Scenery | **** |
| Resort charm | **** |
| Off-slope | ** |

**NEWS**

New for 2004/05 is on-line reservation for lift passes at the resort web site.

The long-rumoured plan to link the slopes with those of Megève seems no nearer to becoming reality.

**KEY FACTS**

| | |
|---|---|
| **Resort** | 1160m 3,810ft |
| For Les Contamines-Montjoie / Hauteluce | |
| **Slopes** | 1160-2485m 3,810-8,150ft |
| **Lifts** | 26 |
| **Pistes** | 120km 75 miles |
| **Green** | 16% |
| **Blue** | 23% |
| **Red** | 40% |
| **Black** | 21% |
| **Snowmaking** | 84 guns |

- + Traditional, unspoiled French village
- + Fair-sized intermediate area
- + Good snow record for its height
- + Lift pass covers several nearby resorts, easily reachable by road

- − Limited scope for experts, and not ideal for beginners
- − Quiet nightlife
- − Lifts a bus-ride from main village
- − Can be some lengthy queues

**Only a few miles from the fur coats of Megève and the ice-axes of Chamonix, Les Contamines is a charming contrast to both, with pretty wooden chalets, impressive old churches, a weekly market in the village square and prices more typical of rural France than of international resorts. Its position at the shoulder of Mont Blanc gives it an enviable snow record. What more could you want?**

## THE RESORT

The core of the village is compact, but the resort as a whole spreads widely, with chalets scattered over a 3km/2 mile stretch of the valley, and the main access lift is 1km/half a mile from the centre. You can stay by the lift at Le Lay or in the charming village centre, a shuttle-bus-ride away. A car is useful, but the Mont Blanc lift pass covers the local buses, as well as the lifts of Chamonix and Megève (among others).

## THE MOUNTAINS

Most of the slopes are above the tree line and there are some magnificent views, though the runs down from Signal are bordered by trees (as is the run from La Ruelle down to Belleville).

**Slopes** From Le Lay a two-stage gondola climbs up to the slopes at Signal. Another gondola leads to the Etape mid-station from a car park a little further up the valley. Above these, a sizeable network of open, largely north-east-facing pistes fans out, with lifts approaching 2500m/ 8,200ft in two places. You can drop over the ridge at Col du Joly to south-west-facing runs down to La Ruelle, with a single red run going on down to Belleville. From Belleville, a 16-person gondola runs back up to La Ruelle. A fast chair takes you the rest of the way back up to Col du Joly.

**Terrain-parks** There is a boarder-cross and a half-pipe on the Tierces slope, accessed by the fast Tierces chair-lift.

**Snow reliability** Many of the shady runs on the Contamines side are above 1700m/5,575ft, and the resort has a justifiable reputation for good snow late into the season, said to be the result of proximity to Mont Blanc. There's snowmaking on the home runs from Signal down to the valley.

**Experts** The steep western section has black runs, which are enjoyable but not terribly challenging except for high mogul fields. The main attraction is the substantial and varied off-piste terrain and visiting the other resorts on the Mont Blanc pass – notably Chamonix.

**Intermediates** Virtually all the runs are ideal for good intermediates, with a mix of blues and reds that one 2004 reporter described as 'very similar – more like purple'. Some of the best run from the gondola's top station to its mid-station and others are served by the Roselette and Bûche Croisée lifts. Given good snow, the south-facing runs down to La Ruelle are a delight. And the black runs are enjoyable for good intermediates. Timid intermediates might find sections of many blue runs too steep for comfort.

**Beginners** In good snow, the village nursery area is adequate for beginners. There are other areas at the mid-station and the top of the gondola. The piste map shows no long greens to progress to but reporters tell of a 'very gentle green run from Col du Joly back to Le Signal' that is not on the map. Beginners will want to take the gondola down to the village at the end of the day as the only run down is red.

**Snowboarding** There is excellent off-piste boarding on offer.

**Cross-country** There are trails of varying difficulty totalling 29km/18 miles. One loop is floodlit twice a week.

**Queues** There can be 15 to 20 minute

Les Contamines is a traditional old village with pretty wooden chalets, a central square and impressive churches →

AGENCE NUTS / OT LES CONTAMINES

peak-period queues for the gondolas, especially if people are bussed in from other resorts with less snow. And the system has bottlenecks – where the gondolas meet for the second stage up to Signal, for example. But we've heard of minimal queues even at weekends.

**Mountain restaurants** There are quite a few lovely rustic mountain restaurants – not all of which are marked on the piste map. The Ferme de la Ruelle is a jolly barn, and the Grange just above it was said by a 2004 reporter to be 'the best but expensive'. Roselette and Bûche Croisée are two cosy chalets and Col du Joly has great views.

**Schools and guides** We have mixed reports on the ESF – one expert this year was 'pleased' with his 'fluent English-speaking' instructor but his brother was lost by the school and 'got a snooty remark' when he rejoined them. Excursions are offered, including trips to the Vallée Blanche. There's an alternative International school, and mountain guides are available.

**Facilities for children** The kindergarten, next to the central nursery slopes, takes children from age one. Children can join ski school from age three.

## STAYING THERE

**How to go** There are some catered chalets and a dozen modest hotels.

**Hotels** The 3-star Chemenaz (0450 470244) at Le Lay is praised by reporters 'Comfortable, and best food in the village.'

**Eating out** There are restaurants and crêperies in town for eating out. Recommendations include the Husky, Auberge du Barattet and the Op Traken – and the Savoisien and the Auberge du Chalézan for Savoie specialities.

**Après-ski** Après-ski is quiet, but there are several bars. The Saxo near the gondola has been recommended, but the Ty Breiz was 'the only lively bar', according to a 2004 reporter. The Labyrinth disco can be lively in peak season. Weekly events are organised, such as music and free vin chaud by the village fountain (on Saturdays) and torchlit descents.

**Off the slopes** There are good walks, a toboggan run, snowmobiling, dog-sledding, snow-shoeing, a climbing wall and a natural ice rink, but St-Gervais, Megève and Chamonix have more to offer.

**Phone numbers**
From abroad use the prefix +33 and omit the initial '0' of the phone number.

## TOURIST OFFICE

**t** 0450 470158
info@lescontamines.com
www.lescontamines.com

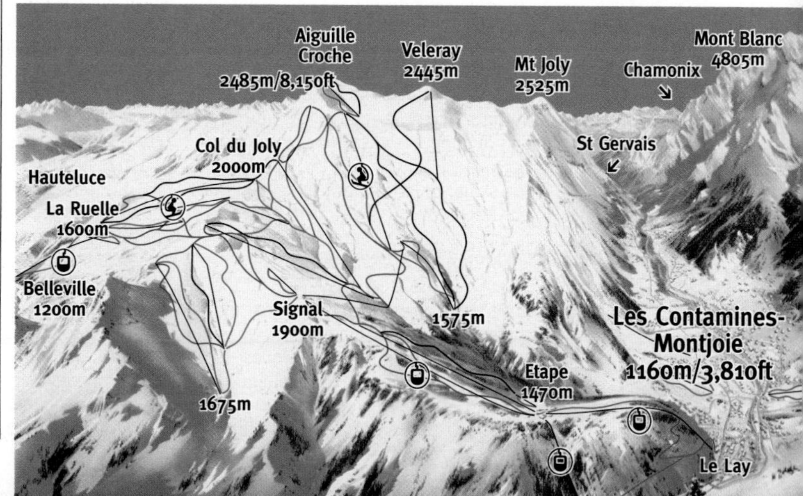

# Courchevel

*Superb skiing and boarding – but the Russians are pushing prices up*

## COSTS

(1)(2)(3)(4)(5)(6)

## RATINGS

**The slopes**

| | |
|---|---|
| Snow | **** |
| Extent | ***** |
| Expert | **** |
| Intermediate | ***** |
| Beginner | **** |
| Convenience | **** |
| Queues | **** |
| Mountain restaurants | **** |

**The rest**

| | |
|---|---|
| Scenery | *** |
| Resort charm | ** |
| Off-slope | *** |

## NEWS

For 2004/05 a new six-pack is planned to replace the Les Tovets drag from 1550 to 1850. The Dou du Midi chair will also be removed. Access to 1650 from 1850 by the Cospillot piste at Pralong will be made easier. The centre of 1850 is being rebuilt, with the new building housing shops and the tourist office. The old Signal hotel in 1650 is being replaced by a new 3-star hotel, Le Seizena, which is owned by the same people who run the luxury Kilimandjaro in 1850. The New Solarium in 1850, which used to be run by Crystal, is being transformed into a 'real' 3-star hotel.

For 2003/04 the Creux and Fruit drag-lifts were replaced by the Gravelles quad to improve the link between 1650 and 1850. The Pralong and Biollay area had more snowmaking installed.



+ Extensive, varied local terrain to suit everyone from beginners to experts – plus the rest of the Three Valleys
+ Lots of slope-side accommodation
+ Impressive lift system, piste maintenance and snowmaking
+ Wooded setting is pretty, and useful in bad weather
+ Choice of four very different villages – only 1850 is notably expensive
+ Some great restaurants, and good après-ski by French standards

- Some pistes get unpleasantly crowded (but they can be avoided)
- Rather soulless villages with intrusive traffic in places
- 1850 has some of the priciest hotels, bars and mountain restaurants in the Alps and its getting pricier
- Losing a little of its French feel as more and more British visitors – and now Russians – discover its attractions
- Little to do away from the slopes, especially during the day

**Courchevel 1850 – the highest of the four components of this big resort – has long been the favourite Alpine hangout of the Paris jet set and they have now been joined by wealthy Russians, who can fly directly in to the mini-airport in the middle of the slopes. Its top hotels and restaurants have always been among the best and the most expensive in the Alps, and the influx of Russians has pushed up prices even further. We've also had reports of the service given to Brits in some restaurants being adversely affected. But don't be put off: a holiday here doesn't have to cost a fortune (especially in the lower villages), the atmosphere is not particularly exclusive, and the slopes are excellent.**

**Courchevel is the most extensive and varied sector of the whole Three Valleys, with everything from long gentle greens to steep couloirs. Many visitors never leave the Courchevel sector; but there is good access to the rest of the Three Valleys, too. Le Praz is an overgrown but still pleasant village, 1550 is quieter and good for families, 1650 has more of a village atmosphere than it seems from the road through, and the posh bits of 1850 are stylishly woody. But overall the resort is no beauty. Well, nothing's perfect. Courchevel's long list of important + points is enough to attract more and more Brits, but it remains much more French than Méribel, over the hill, as well as having better snow.**

## THE RESORT

Courchevel is made up of four varied villages, generally known by numbers supposed to represent their altitudes (but see Altitudes panel in margin later in the chapter). A road winds up the hill, running from Le Praz (1300) past 1550 and through 1650 to 1850. From the skiing point of view, things work a bit differently: runs go down from 1850 to 1550 and 1300, but the slopes of 1650 form a distinct sector.

**1850** is the largest village, and the focal point of the area, with most of the smart nightlife and shops. Two gondolas go over its lower slopes towards the links with Méribel and the rest of the Three Valleys. It's conspicuously upmarket, with some very smooth hotels on the slopes just above the village centre, and among the trees of the Jardin Alpin a suburb is served by its own gondola. There's also a spreading area of smart private chalets. We have always thought the centre of the village a bit of a messy sprawl, and the approach by road shabby; so we were delighted to hear that the centre of town was being rebuilt and smartened up in time for the 2004/05 season.

While some readers 'couldn't afford a second week', others say it's 'not as upmarket as it's made out to be'. You can pay through the nose to eat, drink and stay, but more affordable places are not impossible to find. This year, though, we've had reports of still higher prices and preference being

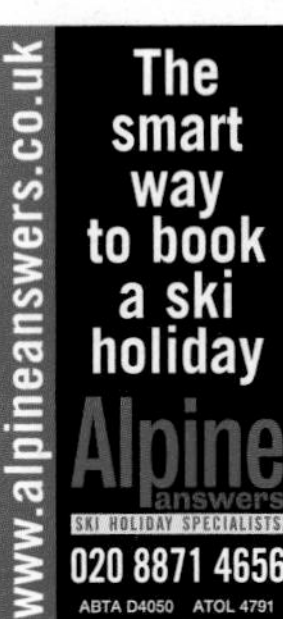


## KEY FACTS

| | |
|---|---|
| **Resort** | 1260-1850m 4,130-6,070ft |
| For the Three Valleys | |
| **Slopes** | 1260-3230m 4,130-10,600ft |
| **Lifts** | 197 |
| **Pistes** | 600km 373 miles |
| **Green** | 21% |
| **Blue** | 33% |
| **Red** | 35% |
| **Black** | 11% |
| **Snowmaking** | 1500 guns |
| For Courchevel/ La Tania only | |
| **Slopes** | 1260-2740m 4,130-8,990ft |
| **Lifts** | 67 |
| Pistes | 150km 93 miles |
| **Green** | 25% |
| **Blue** | 33% |
| **Red** | 32% |
| **Black** | 10% |
| **Snowmaking** | 519 guns |

OT COURCHEVEL / J KELAGOPIAN

The hub of 1850. Three gondolas leave from here; the one in the photo goes to Chenus ↘

given in restaurants to Russian visitors, even to the extent of 'us being moved to a terrible table right by the kitchen. Abysmal service.' Early January is peak time for Russians with one local claiming there were over 18,000 there from 2 to 12 January 2004, making up 95% of resort visitors.

**1650** is 'calm and uncrowded, a world away from 1850', as a reader puts it. The main road up to 1850 cuts through 1650 but there's also an attractive old village centre, lively bars and quietly situated chalets. Its local slopes (whose main access is an escalator-served gondola) are also relatively peaceful. 1650 isn't the most convenient base for exploration of the Three Valleys, but you can still reach Val-Thorens in 90 minutes or less.

**1550** is a quiet dormitory, a gondola or chair ride below 1850. It has the advantage of having essentially the same position as 1850, with cheaper accommodation and restaurants. But it's a long trip to 1850 by road if you want to go there in the evening.

**Le Praz** (or 1300) is an old village set amid woodland and 'excellent for children'. It remains a pleasant spot despite expansion and 'improvements' triggered by the 1992 Olympics – the Olympic ski jump is a conspicuous relic. Ancient gondolas go up over the forest to 1850 and towards Col de la Loze, for Méribel. Near-beginners face rides down as well as up: the pistes back to the village are red and black, and at this altitude snow conditions are often poor.

Free buses run between the villages, and within them a car is of no great value. Champagny is an easy road outing, for access to the extensive slopes of La Plagne.

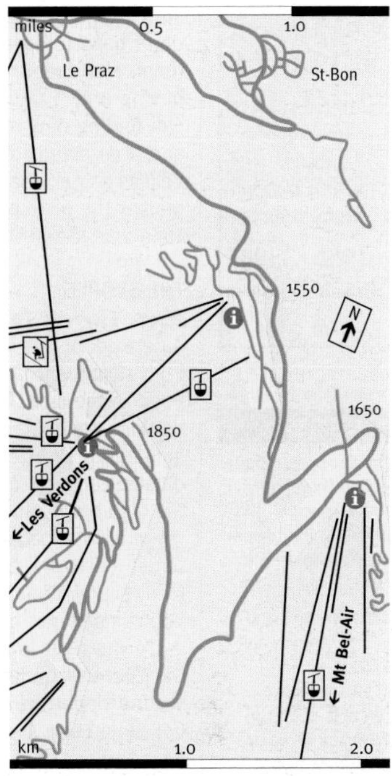


## THE MOUNTAINS

Although there are plenty of trees around the villages, most of the slopes are essentially open, with the notable exception of the runs down to 1550 and to Le Praz, and the valley between 1850 and 1650. These are great areas for experts when the weather closes in. Piste maintenance is good, and daily maps are available, showing which runs have been groomed overnight (normal in America but very rare in Europe). Snowmaking is abundant but the runs to Le Praz are still prone to closure in warm weather. Some slopes

ALTITUDES

The component parts of Courchevel appear to be named by their altitudes. But they are examples of height hype. In fact:

**1300** The lake and village centre are at 1260m
**1550** The village centre is at 1480m
**1650** The lift bases are below 1600m
**1850** The skating rink, below the lift bases, is bang on the 1740m contour.

We revealed these facts in 1999, but our suggestion that new names be adopted – Courchevel ‹1850, for example – has fallen on deaf ears.

above 1850 get very busy, but you don't have to spend much time on them. Many reporters recommend buying only a Courchevel pass ('I was still finding new runs after two weeks') and then extensions for the Three Valleys as necessary. A visitor this year praises the piste marking, which 'above 1650 was the best we've seen'.

**THE SLOPES**
***Huge variety to suit everyone***
A network of lifts and pistes spreads out from **1850**, which is very much the focal point of the area. The main axis is the Verdons gondola, leading to a second gondola to **La Vizelle** and a nearly parallel cable-car up to **La Saulire**. Both the high points give access to a wide range of intermediate and advanced terrain (including a number of couloirs), Méribel and all points to Val-Thorens. You can also get over to 1650 from here.

To the right looking up from 1850 the **Chenus** gondola goes towards a second departure point for Méribel, the Col de la Loze. Easy and intermediate runs go back to 1850, with more difficult runs in the woods above **La Tania** (see separate chapter) and **Le Praz**.

To the left of the Verdons gondola is the Jardin Alpin gondola, which leads to some great beginner terrain, and serves the higher hotels and runs until 8pm. It also gives access to 1650 via the valley of Prameruel.

**1650** offers a good mix of beginner and intermediate slopes away from the crowds and is an ideal area for building confidence. There are still several drag-lifts in this sector, though the trickiest have now been replaced by chairs. Getting to and from Méribel and the rest of the Three Valleys involves slightly more effort than from the rest of Courchevel, because of the intervening valley, but if you run late on the way back you can catch the bus from 1850.

**TERRAIN-PARKS**
***Something for everyone***
The Plantrey terrain-park – just below 1850 and accessed via the Epicea and Ecureuil lifts – is described by the tourist office as for 'experienced boarders' and includes a half-pipe. The Verdons terrain-park, just above 1850, has rolling terrain suitable for all levels of ability to enjoy – as has the smaller Biollay area, which offers 'roller coasters' and 'big moguls to chew up, attack at your own speed, in your own style'. There's a boarder-cross at Pralong.

**SNOW RELIABILITY**
***Very good***
The combination of Courchevel's orientation (its slopes are north- or north-east-facing), its height, an abundance of snowmaking and generally excellent piste maintenance usually guarantees good snow down to at least the 1850 and 1650 villages. A reporter comments: 'On a week when snow was relatively scarce in the Alps, we were pleasantly surprised by the quality and quantity of the snow.' On countless visits we have found that the snow is usually much better than in neighbouring Méribel, where the slopes get the afternoon sun.

**FOR EXPERTS**
***Some black gems***
There is plenty to interest experts, even without the rest of the Three Valleys.

The most obvious expert runs are the couloirs you can see on the right near the top of the Saulire cable-car. The three main ways down were once designated black pistes (some of the steepest in Europe), but now only the Grand Couloir remains a piste – it's the widest and easiest of the three, but you have to pick your way along the narrow, bumpy, precipitous access ridge to reach it.

There is a lot of steep terrain, on- and off-piste, on the shady slopes of La Vizelle, both towards Verdons and towards the link with 1650. Some of the reds on La Vizelle verge on black and the black M piste is surprisingly little used. If you love moguls, don't miss the top of the black Suisses. Chanrossa, which comes towards 1850 from the top of 1650, is quite difficult – the off-piste just next to it is tougher. For a change of scene and a test of stamina, a couple of long (700m/ 2,300ft vertical), genuinely steep blacks cut through the trees to Le Praz.

There is plenty of off-piste terrain to try with a guide and a bit of climbing – high, north-facing slopes right at the top of the 1650 sector, for example (the Vallée des Avals is a great run), and the huge bowl accessed from the Creux Noir chair. Also ask about the mysterious Hidden Valley in 1650. In good snow conditions you can ski all the way down (around 2000m/6,560ft vertical) from La Saulire to Bozel, way below Le Praz, over meadows and through trees on the final section and catch a bus back (we did this in 2004).

**FOR INTERMEDIATES**

***Paradise for all levels***

The Three Valleys is the greatest intermediate playground in the world, but all grades of intermediates will love Courchevel's local slopes too.

Early intermediates will enjoy the gentle Pyramides and Grandes Bosses blues above 1650, and the Biollay and Pralong blues above 1850.

Those of average ability can handle most red runs without difficulty. Our favourite is the long, sweeping Combe de la Saulire from top to bottom of the cable-car – but you have to time it right. Very pleasant first thing, when it's well groomed and free of crowds, it's a different story when it's icy or at the end of the day – cut up snow and very crowded. Creux, behind La Vizelle, is another splendid, long red that gets bumpy and unpleasantly crowded. Marmottes from the top of Vizelle is quieter and more challenging.

The Chenus sector has excellent blues and reds down towards 1850 and 1550, and through the trees towards La Tania – long, rolling cruises 'guaranteed to put a smile on your face'. Over at 1650, the Chapelets and Rochers reds right at the edge of the whole Three Valleys ski area are great fun for fast cruising, and usually quiet.

**FOR BEGINNERS**

***Great graduation runs***

There are excellent nursery slopes above both 1650 and 1850. At the former, lessons are likely to begin on the short drags close to the village, but quick learners will soon be able to go up the gondola. The best nursery

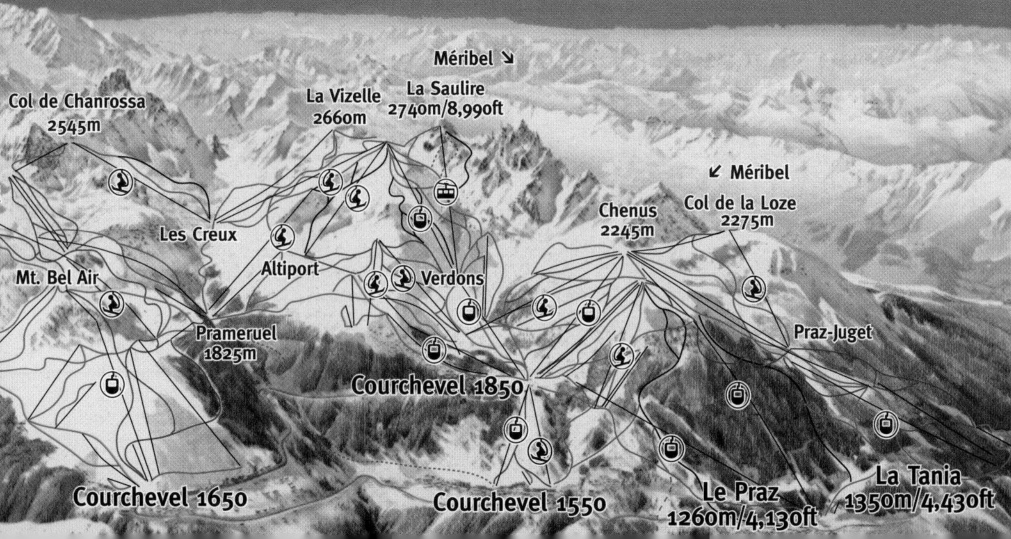

## SCHOOLS

**ESF in 1850**
t 0479 080772
ski@esfcourchevel.com

**ESF in 1650**
t 0479 082608
infos@esf-courchevel1650.com

**ESF in 1550**
t 0479 082107
contact@esf-courchevel.com

**Centre Pralong**
t 0479 011581

**Ski Academy**
t 0479 081199
courchevel@ski-academy.com

**Supreme**
t 0479 082787
(UK: 01479 810800)
info@supremeski.com

**New Generation**
t 0479 010318
info@skinewgen.com

**Magic in Motion**
t 0479 010181
courchevel@magicinmotion.com

**Oxygène**
t 0479 419958
courchevel@oxygene-ski.com

**RTM**
t 06154 85904
info@rtmsnowboarding.com

**Classes**
(ESF 1850 prices)
6 days (2½hr am and pm): €218

**Private lessons**
€58 for 1½hr

## GUIDES

**Mountain guides**
t 0479 010366
guides.courch@wanadoo.com

area at 1850 is at Pralong, above the village, near the airstrip. A reporter points out that getting to it from the village isn't easy, unless you go by road. A green path links this area with chairs to 1650, so adventurous novices can soon move further afield. The Bellecôte green run down into 1850 is an excellent, long, gentle slope – but it is used by skiers returning to the village and does get unpleasantly crowded. It is served by the Jardin Alpin gondola, and a drag that is one of eight free beginner lifts. 1550 and Le Praz have small nursery areas, but most people go up to 1850 for its more reliable snow.

### FOR CROSS-COUNTRY
***Long wooded trails***

Courchevel has a total of 66km/41 miles of trails, the most in the Three Valleys. Le Praz is the most suitable village, with trails through the woods towards 1550, 1850 and Méribel. Given enough snow, there are also loops around the village.

### QUEUES
***There are always alternatives***

Even at New Year and in mid-February, when 1850 in particular positively teems with people, queues are minimal, thanks to the excellence of the lift system. However, as one reporter points out, 'there can be a build-up at 1850 for the gondolas'. At such times 'it's best to avoid skiing back to 1850'. For example, try using the Plantrey chair, below 1850, or the Coqs chair, above it, to get over to the Col de la Loze, Le Praz and La Tania. The Biollay chair is very popular with the ski school (which gets priority) and can also be worth avoiding. Queues for the huge Saulire cable-car are rare. Many lifts have American-style singles lines, which seem to be working better now than when they were first introduced.

### MOUNTAIN RESTAURANTS
***Good but can be very expensive***

Mountain restaurants are plentiful and pleasant, but it is sensible to check the prices; for table-service restaurants reservations may be needed.

There are three expensive places on the fringes of Courchevel 1850 that just about count as mountain restaurants (you can ski away from them after your indulgent lunch). Cap Horn, near the airstrip, has now taken over from Chalet des Pierres as the biggest rip-off, according to a local who says it has a 'scarily' expensive wine list, specifically catering for the rich Russians. A reporter talks of food which was 'cold and dry' and says the place is 'like Cannes in the Alps'. Chalet de Pierres, on the Verdons piste is not far behind, pricewise, with one reporter calling it 'reassuringly expensive' and another forgoing 'a bottle of wine at 9,500 euros (over £6,000)'. But it is a comfortable, smooth place built in traditional style and reporters agree it does good food: 'great unfussy mountain food and very nice staff' is a typical comment. It has a wonderful array of desserts and is easily accessible for pedestrians. The Bergerie on the Bellecôte piste seems to attract a fashionable crowd.

The Verdons is well placed for piste-watching and La Soucoupe is an atmospheric self-service place, with table-service upstairs where food is cooked on a log fire. The Panoramic at the top of Saulire also has self- and table-service restaurants and we had good confit de canard in the latter.

If we're paying the bill, our favourite Courchevel restaurant is the Bel Air, at the top of the gondola above 1650 – good food ('omelettes to die for'), friendly and efficient table-service, and a splendid tiered terrace. The Casserole, at the bottom of the Signal chair, was found to be 'expensive, but efficient'.

## LIFT PASSES

**Three Valleys**
Covers all lifts in Courchevel, La Tania, Méribel, Val-Thorens, Les Menuires and St-Martin-de-Belleville.

**Beginners**
Eight free lifts in the Courchevel valley.

**Main pass**
1 day €40
6 days €198

**Senior citizens**
Over 60: 6 days €158
Over 72: free pass

**Children**
Under 13: 6 days €149
Under 5: free pass

**Notes**
Half-day, family and pedestrian passes available. Six-day pass valid for one day in Espace Killy (Tignes-Val-d'Isère), Paradiski (La Plagne-Les Arcs), Pralognan and Les Saisies.

**Alternative passes**
Courchevel pass covers Courchevel and La Tania only.

## boarding

*For an upmarket resort, Courchevel goes out of its way to attract boarders and last season there were no fewer than four terrain-parks to play in. It's easy to get around the Three Valleys using chairs and gondolas and there is some great free-riding available. RTM is a specialist snowboard school run by Brits that we've had good reports of. The big snowboard hangout in 1850 is 'Prends ta luge et tire toi', a combined shop/bar/internet cafe.*

**SCHOOLS AND GUIDES**

***Size is everything***

Courchevel's branches of the ESF add up to the largest ski school in Europe, with a total of around 500 instructors. We lack recent reports but past reporters have been critical of the standards of teaching and the 'indifference' of the ESF.

Ski Academy is an independent group of French instructors – 'one brilliant, another OK', 'excellent and attentive', said two reporters. Magic in Motion was rated 'good, but not outstanding like the one in La Tania'. Supreme in 1850 (British owned and mainly staffed by British instructors) gets mixed reviews. One 2004 reporter found them 'fantastic and tremendously helpful', while another's eight-year-old daughter had a 'nightmare' experience at the hands of a French instructor, 'leaving her crying' and 'humiliating her' by tying her bib around her legs.

New Generation consists of highly qualified young British instructors committed to giving clients enjoyment as well as technique. We joined a group lesson with them this year and were very impressed by their US-style of teaching: they ask the students to set their goals for the lesson on the gondola ride up and then try to help them achieve them. We nearly all opted for skiing chopped-up, off-piste snow with style and all felt we had improved a lot by the end of the morning. We receive rave reviews about them from reporters, for adults and children alike: 'We had an absolutely brilliant week and our daughter, aged seven, had fun and

## CHILDREN

**Village des Enfants**
(1850) **t** 0479 080847
Ages from 18mnth; 9am-5pm

**Les Pitchounets** (1650)
**t** 0479 083369
Ages from 18mnth; 9am-5pm

**Ski schools**
Most offer lessons from the age of 3 or 4 (ESF 1850 prices €227 for 6 days)



progressed well,' said a 2004 reporter, who was impressed that her daughter's instructor 'talked to parents about progress after every lesson and lent her his goggles for the whole week'. 'Really excellent', 'young and highly motivated', 'learned more in the week than we had over many years previously' are typical comments.

RTM is a specialist boarding school run and staffed by Brits, which a 2004 reporter said was 'great'.

The Bureau des Guides runs all-day off-piste excursions.

### FACILITIES FOR CHILDREN
***Lots of chalet-based options***

In the past reporters have found the ski kindergarten at 1850 over-stretched, with 19 children in a class of five to seven-year-olds. But one reader this year said her three-year-old daughter was happy and 'skiing on reins quite well by the end of the week'. The ESF at 1850 offers VIC (Very Important Children) lessons for English-speaking children between 6 and 12 years with a maximum of six children per group.

Several tour operators run their own nurseries using British nannies – an alternative that many families have found attractive.

## STAYING THERE

### HOW TO GO
***Value chalets and apartments***

Huge numbers of British tour operators go to Courchevel.

**Chalets** There are plenty of chalets and some chalet-hotels available.

In 1850 several operators offer notably comfortable chalets, and a few genuinely luxurious ones. The Beckhams stayed at a Descent International place. FlexiSki and Scott Dunn have several upscale and convenient places. Lotus Supertravel has a number of luxurious 'superchalets' – we loved our stay in the splendid Chalet Founets. Kaluma, a new company last season run by an experienced team, has the splendid Chalet Vizelle. Mark Warner's chalet-hotel Dahu in 1850 is convenient and reported to serve 'excellent food'.

In 1650 Le Ski has 11 good-value chalets; its flagship chalet Rikiki is all en suite and set on the piste and it has two good new chalets for 2004/05. We stayed with them in 2004 and were very impressed with the food, service and ski guiding. Ski Olympic has two chalets and a central chalet-hotel, Les Avals, said to be 'just brilliant', and a chalet-hotel in 1550. Total has a big chalet in 1650 and smaller ones in 1850.

SNOWPIX.COM / CHRIS GILL

The Panoramic restaurant at the top of La Saulire certainly lives up to its name ↘

## GETTING THERE

**Air** Geneva 149km/ 93 miles (3½hr); Lyon 187km/116 miles (3½hr); Chambéry 110km/68 miles (1½hr). Direct flights to Courchevel altiport from London on request only (contact tourist office for details). Also scheduled flights from Geneva to Courchevel.

**Rail** Moûtiers (24km/ 15 miles); transfer by bus or taxi.



Family-specialist Esprit Ski has several chalets down in Le Praz. As does Simply Ski, which also has places in 1850. Thomson's flagship St Louis chalet-hotel is in a great position just across from the Bellecôte piste. Crystal has chalets in all the villages.

**Hotels** There are nearly 50 hotels in Courchevel, mostly at 1850 – including more 4-stars than anywhere else in France except Paris (14 at the last count).

((((⑤ **Les Airelles** (1850) (0479 003838) 'Super flash and over the top. The most expensive hotel in the Alps.' On the Jardin Alpin piste.

((((⑤ **St Joseph** (1850) (0479 081616) Like a plush country house 'with 10 fab rooms and three huge stunning apartments, with awesome views'.

((((⑤ **Mélézin** (1850) (0479 080133) Superbly stylish and luxurious – and in an ideal position beside the bottom of the Bellecôte home slope.

((((⑤ **Carlina** (1850) (0479 080030) Luxury piste-side pad, next to Mélézin.

((((⑤ **Byblos des Neiges** (1850) (0479 009800) Next to first stop on Jardin Alpin gondola; spacious public rooms, good pool, sauna, steam complex.

(((④ **Bellecôte** (1850) (0479 081019) Our favourite among the more swanky places – it offers some Alpine atmosphere as well as sheer luxury.

(((④ **Les Grandes Alpes** (1850) (0479 080335) 4-star on piste by main lifts. Readers enthuse: 'Personal service. Luxurious rooms.' 'Brilliant food.'

((③ **Rond Point** (1850) (0479 080433) Family atmosphere, central position.

((③ **Croisette** (1850) (0479 080900) Next to main lifts above Le Jump bar. 'Simple and clean, staff very helpful.'

((③ **Courcheneige** (1850) (0479 080259) On Bellecôte piste. 'A real find: lovely staff, good food.' Quiet.

((③ **Sivolière** (1850) (0479 080833) Being completely renovated for 2004/05, pleasantly set among pines.

((③ **Golf** (1650) (0479 009292) Rather impersonal 3-star, in a superb position on the piste next to the gondola.

((③ **Ancolies** (1550) (0479 082766) 'A real find,' said a US visitor impressed by the friendly staff and excellent food.

((③ **Peupliers** (1300) (0479 084147) Smartly renovated and expanded, good restaurant, cheap by local standards.

**Self-catering** There's a large selection, though high-season dates can sell out early. As usual in France, check room sizes and book a place advertised for more people than there are of you.

## ACTIVITIES

**Indoor** Artificial skating rink, climbing wall, gymnasium, bowling, exhibitions, concerts, cinemas, language and computer courses, cookery courses, library.
In hotels: health and fitness centres (swimming pools, saunas, steam-room, hot-tub, water therapy, weight-training, massage), bridge (in the Chabichou)

**Outdoor** Hang-gliding, paragliding, flying lessons, snow-shoe excursions, ice-climbing, snowmobile rides, ice karting, horse-drawn sleigh rides, cleared paths, tobogganing, flight excursions, rafting on snow, hot-air ballooning

**Phone numbers**
From abroad use the prefix +33 and omit the initial '0' of the phone number.

## TOURIST OFFICE

**t** 0479 080029
pro@courchevel.com
www.courchevel.com

## EATING OUT
### *Pick your price*

There are a lot of good, very expensive French restaurants in Courchevel.

In 1850, among the best, and priciest, are the Chabichou (a 2004 visitor recommends the mini-dégustation menu of four courses), and the Bateau Ivre – both with two Michelin stars. Recommendations for Savoyard food include the cosy Saulire and the Fromagerie. Other reporters praise the Nuits de Bacchus, Chapelle ('fabulous and filling meal of lamb cooked on an open fire') and 18-50.

A reporter liked the pizzas but not the soup at the Via Ferrata and was concerned to watch the staff smoking in the kitchen. Also mentioned by readers are the Cloche ('good atmosphere'), the Tremplin ('delicious crêpes', but 'snooty and old-style French' in the evening), the Smalto ('great if you are on a budget', but we've had reports of very slow service) and the Cendrée ('a wonderful Italian', 'good value', but 'put Russians before us'). The Potinière does good, cheap pizzas, steaks and pasta. The Locomotive has an American feel, with railway-theme decor and a varied menu, though a reader reckons service is 'a bit surly', and the hotel Tovets is reported to have 'reasonable prices and delicious food'. A local recommends the Grand Café (underneath the hotel St Joseph) for good Asian cuisine.

In 1550, the Oeil du Boeuf is good for grills. The Cortona does good-value pizza. In 1650 the Eterlou, Montagne and the Petit Savoyard ('divine fillet steak and pâté de foie gras dish') do good traditional Savoyard food and cheaper pizza and pasta. In Le Praz, Bistrot du Praz is expensive but excellent. The Ya-ca is small and 'very French'. We had an excellent meal at the Peuplier (very good pepper steak).

## APRES-SKI
### *1850 has most variety*

If you want lots of nightlife, it's got to be 1850. There are some exclusive nightclubs, such as the Caves, with top Paris cabaret acts and sky-high prices. The popular Kalico has DJs and cocktails, and gets packed. The Bergerie has themed evenings – food, music, entertainment – but prices are high.

The Jump at the foot of the main slope is the place to be as the lifts close ('a very cool atmosphere but very expensive') and it does get impossibly packed. One reader comments that there is 'no real large meeting place for après-ski'. The Saulire (aka Chez Jacques) and the cheap and cheerful Potinière are also popular. Piggys is described as 'fur coats, pampered dogs and sky-high prices'; 'Four small beers cost me £45,' says a 2004 reporter. Mangeoire has 'an excellent Piano bar (with high Piggys-style prices) but is extremely lively from about 11pm'.

Cinemas in 1850 and 1650 show English-speaking films.

'Don't choose 1650 if it's nightlife you're after,' said a reporter last year. but this year a reader's 20-something kids had 'plenty to do'. The Bubble is the hub, has satellite TV and internet access. With cheap bar prices, happy hour, some strong local beers and frequent live music, it has a largely British clientele. Rocky's Bar (in chalet-hotel Avals) is popular – and a reporter enjoyed the 'specialities, including flavoured vodkas'. Remonte Pente is a tiny French bar. The Space Bar has pool, games and live music or DJs and the Taverne disco stayed open till 4am delighting a reporter's 20-year-old kids.

In 1550 the Chanrossa bar is British-dominated, with occasional live music, the Taverne also has English owners.

## OFF THE SLOPES
### *1850 isn't bad*

The Forum sports centre in 1850 includes a climbing wall in the shopping centre – good for spectating too. There are a fair number of shops in 1850 plus markets at most levels. There's an ice-driving circuit and an ice-climbing structure. A pedestrian lift pass for the gondolas and buses in Courchevel and Méribel makes it easy for non-slope users to meet up the mountain for lunch. And you can take joyrides from the altiport. A non-skier's guide to Courchevel, Méribel and La Tania is distributed by the tourist office.

OT LES DEUX-ALPES

# Les Deux-Alpes

*It's a long way up to the glacier and a narrow way down*

## COSTS

(1)(2)(3)(4)(5)(6)

## RATINGS

| **The slopes** | |
|---|---|
| Snow | **** |
| Extent | *** |
| Expert | **** |
| Intermediate | ** |
| Beginner | *** |
| Convenience | *** |
| Queues | ** |
| Mountain restaurants | ** |
| **The rest** | |
| Scenery | **** |
| Resort charm | ** |
| Off-slope | ** |

## NEWS

The La Toura chair-lift at mid-mountain has been replaced by a fixed-grip quad with moving carpet to maximise its capacity.

- + High, snow-sure slopes, including an extensive glacier area
- + Varied high-mountain terrain, from motorways to steep off-piste slopes
- + Efficient, modern lift system
- + Excellent, sunny nursery slopes
- + Stunning views of the Ecrins peaks
- + Lively resort with varied nightlife
- + Wide choice of hotels

- − Piste network modest by mega-resort standards – we're sceptical about the claimed 220km/137 miles – and it's badly congested in places
- − The home runs are either steep and icy or dangerously overcrowded – so people queue for a lift down instead
- − Virtually no woodland runs
- − Spread-out, traffic-choked resort
- − Few appealing mountain restaurants

**We have a love–hate relationship with Les Deux-Alpes. We quite like the buzz of the village – arriving here is a bit like driving into Las Vegas from the Nevada desert – and we understand the appeal of its vibrant nightlife. We love the high-Alpine feel of its main mountain, and the good snow to be found on the north-facing runs in the middle of the mountain. But we're very unimpressed by the extent of those slopes, and we hate the piste congestion that results when most of the town's 35,000 visitors are crammed on to them. Crowding apart, keen intermediates spoiled by high-mileage French mega-resorts (and not up to the excellent off-piste) will simply find the usable area of slopes rather small.**

## THE RESORT

Les Deux-Alpes is a narrow village sitting on a high, remote col. Access is from the Grenoble-Briançon road to the north. The village is a long, sprawling collection of hotels, apartments, bars and shops, most lining the busy main street and the parallel street that completes the one-way traffic system. The resort has a lively ambience.

The village has grown haphazardly over the years, and there is a wide range of building styles, from old chalets through 1960s blocks to more sympathetic recent developments. It looks better as you leave than as you arrive, because all the balconies face the southern end of the resort.

Lifts are spread fairly evenly along the village and there is no clear centre, but a couple of focal points are evident. Alpe de Venosc, at the south end of town, has many of the nightspots and hotels, the most character, the fewest cars, the best shops and the Diable gondola up to the tough terrain around Tête Moute. More generally useful is the Jandri Express, now with an improved second stage, from the middle of the resort, where there is a popular outdoor ice rink and some good restaurants and bars. The village straggles north from here, becoming less convenient the further you go.

The free shuttle-bus service saves on some very long walks from one end of town to the other.

The six-day pass covers a day in several nearby resorts including Alpe-d'Huez and Serre-Chevalier. Helicopter trips to Alpe-d'Huez are good value at £40 return – a 'must', says a reporter. More economical is the shuttle-bus service on Wednesdays and Thursdays.

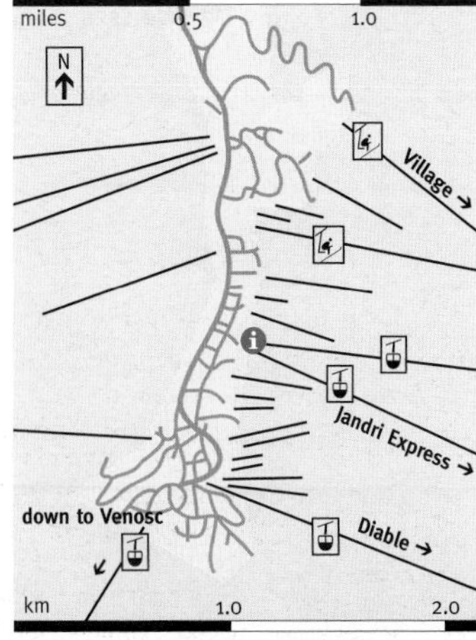

## KEY FACTS

| | |
|---|---|
| **Resort** | 1650m |
| | 5,410ft |
| **Slopes** | 1300-3570m |
| | 4,270-11,710ft |
| **Lifts** | 54 |
| **Pistes** | 220km |
| | 137 miles |
| **Green** | 25% |
| **Blue** | 39% |
| **Red** | 20% |
| **Black** | 16% |
| **Snowmaking** | |
| | 105 guns |

## THE MOUNTAINS

For a big resort, Les Deux-Alpes has a disappointingly small piste area, despite recent improvements. Although extremely long and tall (it rises almost 2000m/6,560ft), the main sector is also very narrow, with just a few runs on the upper part of the mountain, served by a few long, efficient lifts. The piste-grading is rather inconsistent and some runs are graded differently on the map and on the mountain.

### THE SLOPES

***Long, narrow and fragmented***

The western **Pied Moutet** side of Les Deux-Alpes is relatively little-used, although recent improvements in the lift and snowmaking systems have made the area more popular. It is served by lifts from various parts of town but reaches only 2100m/6,890ft. As well as the short runs back to town which get the morning sun, there's an attractive, longer north-facing red run down through the trees to the small village of Bons. The only other tree-lined run in Les Deux-Alpes goes down to another low village, Mont-de-Lans.

On the eastern side of the resort, the broad, steep slope immediately above it offers a series of relatively short, challenging runs, down to the nursery slopes ranged at the bottom. Most of these runs are classified as black, and rightly so: they aren't groomed and are usually mogulled, and often icy when not softened by the afternoon sun. As a result, at the end of the day many visitors are forced to choose between taking the long winding green run, which is extremely crowded, or riding down the gondolas.

The ridge of **Les Crêtes** above the village has lifts and gentle runs along it, and behind it lies the deep, steep Combe de Thuit. Lifts span the combe to the main mid-mountain station at 2600m/8,530ft, at the foot of the slopes on **La Toura**. The middle section of the mountain, above and below this point, is made up primarily of blue cruising runs and is very narrow. At one point, there is essentially just a single run down the mountain – the Grand Nord blue, which is a real bottleneck late in the day. The only alternative is to take the roundabout (partly flat) blue Gours run to the bottom of the combe, where a chair-lift takes you up to Les Crêtes. This pleasant run passes the base of the Fée chair, serving an isolated (and neglected) black run – and a slightly easier parallel run which has now, bizarrely, been classified blue.

The top **Glacier du Mont de Lans**

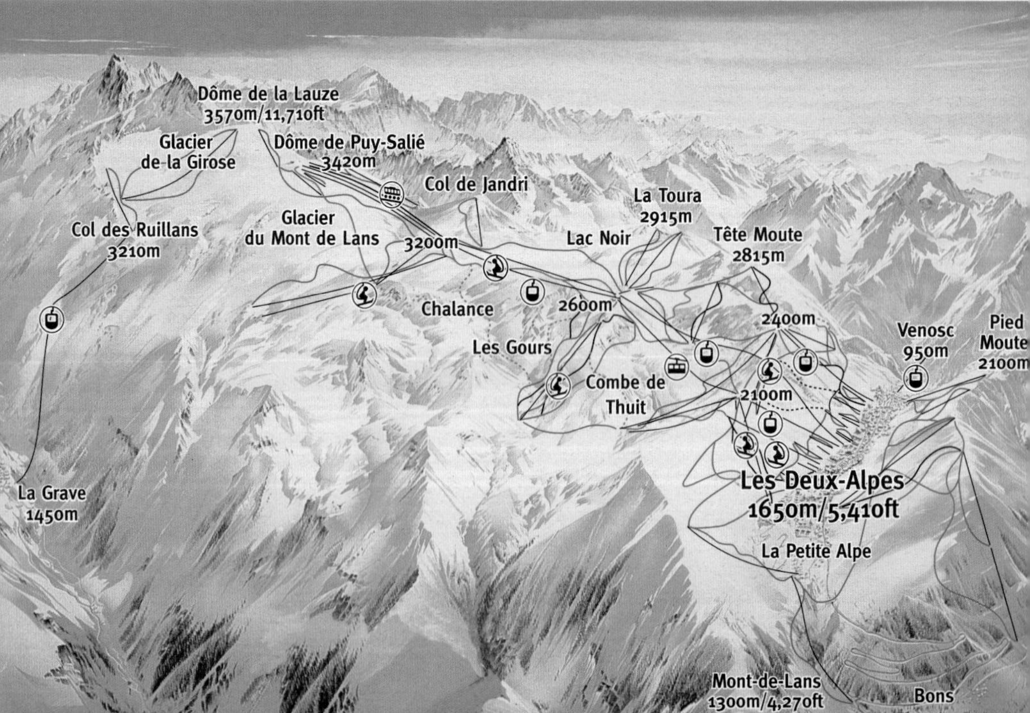

The **European Ski and Snowboard School** does classes and guiding in small groups. Its instructors are of several nationalities, but all speak excellent English.
**t** 00 33 476 797455
europeanskischool@worldonline.fr
www.europeanskischool.co.uk

## OFF-PISTE CHALLENGES FOR EVERYONE FROM NOVICE TO EXPERT

**The off-piste routes in Les Deux-Alpes are numerous and varied in difficulty, the easiest permitting skiers even of an intermediate level to enjoy their first 'free-ride experience'. We've asked Jeremy Edwards of the European Ski and Snowboard School to share some of his favourites.**

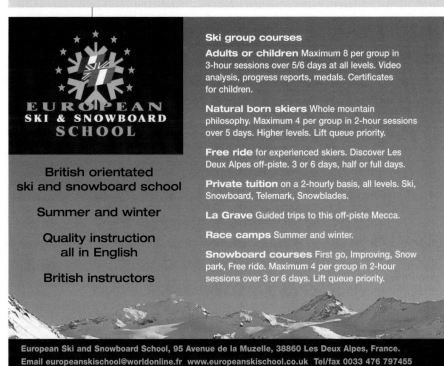

*For something slightly technical, both sides off the Bellecombe red piste – 2800m-2300m (9,190ft-7,550ft) – offer a wide range of varying terrain; it's important to take care here – there are several small cliff faces. For those keen to tackle couloirs – steep, narrow slopes between rocks – this descent offers small ones that are ideal for your first attempts; they can be avoided, though.*

*Traversing across the top of the black Grand Couloir piste leads to the North Rachas area, with off-piste faces that offer cold snow conditions all winter. The first large valley leads to three couloirs – one fairly broad and easy, the other two much narrower and steeper, and certainly not for the timid. Traversing further leads to a much wider descent that avoids the three couloirs.*

*For tree skiing it's best to head for the Vallée Blanche area, reached via the lifts on Pied Moutet. The north-east face, towards the chair-lift at Bons, offers great routes over generally deserted wooded terrain with excellent cold snow conditions.*

*Strong skiers will enjoy the famous Challance run, which starts just below the glacier and descends 1000m/3,280ft vertical to the Gours run; there are several variations, mixing wide open slopes and rocky pitches. These faces are at times subject to quite a high avalanche risk because of wind slab.*

*Traversing above the north face of the Challance leads to the couloir Pylône Électrique – a steep, narrow, 200m/660ft long couloir with the reward below it of an excellent wide powder field of moderate gradient. A rest on the Thuit chair-lift is a must after this adrenalin-charged descent.*

*These routes and many more play a large part in the off-piste free-ride courses offered by the European Ski and Snowboard School.*

## LIFT PASSES

**Super ski pass**
Covers all lifts in Les Deux-Alpes and entry to swimming pool and ice rink.

**Beginners**
Four free lifts

**Main pass**
1 day €33
6 days €158

**Senior citizens**
Over 60: 6 days €118.50
Over 75: free pass

**Children**
Under 14: 6 days €118.50
Under 5: free pass

**Notes**
Half-day passes available. Six-day pass includes access to La grave and one day's skiing in Alpe-d'Huez, Serre-Chevalier, Puy-St-Vincent and the Milky Way.

**Alternative passes**
Ski Sympa covers 21 lifts, Grand Ski covers 32 lifts.

## GETTING THERE

**Air** Lyon 160km/ 99 miles (3½hr); Grenoble 70km/ 43 miles (1½hr); Chambéry 126km/ 78 miles (3hr); Geneva 230km/ 143 miles (4½hr).

**Rail** Grenoble (70km/43 miles); four daily buses from station.





## boarding

*Les Deux-Alpes has been catering for snowboarders for years, and has built up an excellent reputation. There's a specialist Primitive school and lots of boarder-friendly facilities. Most of the lifts on the higher slopes are chairs. The terrain-park is relocated up to the glacier in the summer (access is by T-bar or funicular), which is where the Mondial du Snowboard competition is hosted each year. The ESF offers freestyle classes, using trampolines and a huge air-bag to practise on. But for beginner and timid intermediate boarders the narrow, flat crowded areas in mid-mountain and the routes down to the village are intimidating. There's some great off-piste in the local area for free-riders and the link to La Grave offers some of the best off-piste terrain in the world for advanced riders – hire a guide.*

section, served by drag-lifts and the warmer underground funicular, has some fine, very easy runs which afford great views and are ideal for beginners and the less adventurous. You can go from the top here all the way down to Mont-de-Lans – a descent of 2268m/ 7,440ft vertical which, as far as we know, is the world's biggest on-piste vertical. A walk (or snowcat tow) in the opposite direction takes you over to the slopes of La Grave – a splendid area for advanced skiers with a guide (now covered by the Deux-Alpes pass).

### TERRAIN-PARKS
***Newly improved***

There's a terrain-park with a boarder-cross, a half-pipe, music and a barbecue higher up the mountain in the Toura sector. This is relocated up to the glacier in the summer. There's even a kids' park.

### SNOW RELIABILITY
***Excellent on higher slopes***

The snow on the higher slopes is normally very good, even in a poor winter – one of the main reasons for Les Deux-Alpes' popularity. Above 2200m/7,220ft most of the runs are north-facing, and the top glacier section guarantees good snow. You should worry more about bad weather shutting the lifts, or extremely low temperatures at the top, than about snow shortage. But the runs just above the village face west, so they get a lot of afternoon sun and can be icy at the beginning and end of the day. Snowmaking on some of the lower slopes helps keep them usable.

### FOR EXPERTS
***Off-piste is the main attraction***

With good snow and weather conditions, the area offers wonderful off-piste sport. There are several good off-piste runs within the lift network, including a number of variations from underneath the top stage of the Jandri Express down to the Thuit chair-lift. The best-known ones are marked on the piste map. The Fée chair built a few years ago opened up new off-piste possibilities into the Combe de Thuit. There are also more serious routes that end well outside the lift network, with verticals of over 2000m/6,560ft. One reporter recommends the renowned descent to St-Christophe (hire a guide, who will arrange transport back).

A Free Respect festival is held each year with free advice on off-piste safety and free-ride competitions.

The Super Diable chair-lift, from the top of the Diable gondola, serves the steepest black run around. The brave can also try off-piste variations here.

If the conditions are right, an outing across the glacier to the off-piste slopes of La Grave is a must.

### FOR INTERMEDIATES
***Limited cruising***

Les Deux-Alpes can disappoint keen intermediates. A lot of the runs are either rather tough – some of the blues could be reds – or boringly bland. The steep runs just above the resort put off many. As one of our reporters (who classes himself as an 'advanced' skier) said, 'I myself fell from top to bottom. I was lucky. A girl in a different group broke her back. You cannot afford to be complacent here.'

The runs higher up generally have good snow, and there is some great fast cruising, especially on the mainly north-facing pistes served by the chair-lifts off to the sides. You can often pick gentle or steeper terrain in these bowls as you wish, but avid piste-bashers will explore all there is to offer in a couple of days. Many visitors take the opportunity of excursions to Alpe-d'Huez and Serre-Chevalier.

Less confident intermediates will

↑ There is a lot of good, north-facing off-piste terrain around mid-mountain
AGENCE NUTS / OT LES DEUX-ALPES





## SCHOOLS

**ESF**
t 0476 792121
esf.les2alpes@wanadoo.fr

**International St-Christophe**
t 0476 790421
ecole.ski.internationale@wanadoo.fr

**European**
t 0476 797455
europeanskischool@worldonline.fr

**Primitive**
t 0607 907135

**Ski Privilege**
t 0476 792344

**Easiski**
t 0476 795884

**Burton Connexion**
t 0615 079442

**Classes**
(ESF prices)
6 half days (2¾hr am or pm) €125

**Private lessons**
€31 for 1hr, for 1 to 2 people

## GUIDES

**Guides office**
t 0476 795012
esf.les2alpes@wanadoo.fr

love the quality of the snow and the gentleness of most of the runs on the upper mountain. Their problem might lie in finding the pistes too crowded, especially if snow is poor in other resorts and people are bussed in.

### FOR BEGINNERS
***Good slopes***

The nursery slopes beside the village are spacious and gentle. The run along the ridge above them is excellent, too. The glacier also has a fine array of very easy slopes – but bear in mind that bad weather can close the lifts.

### FOR CROSS-COUNTRY
***Needs very low-altitude snow***

There are three small, widely dispersed areas. La Petite Alpe, near the entrance to the village, has a couple of snow-sure but very short trails. Given good snow, Venosc, reached by a gondola down, has the only worthwhile picturesque ones. Total trail distance is 25km/16 miles. You can ski the Mont de Lans glacier with a qualified guide.

### QUEUES
***Can be a problem***

Les Deux-Alpes has a great deal of hardware to keep queues minimal. But the village is large, and queues at the mid-morning peak can be 'diabolically' long for the Jandri Express and Diable gondolas. The Jandri queue moves quickly and the eight-seat chair from the mid-station to the glacier has reduced the bottleneck for the second stage. Problems can also occur when people are bussed in when snow is in short supply elsewhere. The top lifts are prone to closure if it's windy, putting pressure on the lower lifts. High winds caused one visitor to get stuck on a chair-lift for 10 minutes. 'Others in our chalet reported being stuck on a stationary lift for 45 minutes.' We have repeated reports of queues for the gondolas back to the village when large numbers of people decline to tackle the tricky blacks or the crowded green run back down.

### MOUNTAIN RESTAURANTS
***Still limited***

There are mountain restaurants at all the major lift junctions, but they are generally pretty poor. For years the Pastorale (now closed), at the top of the Diable gondola, was the only recommendable place – then along came the splendid Chalet de la Toura, in the middle of the domain at about 2600m/8,530ft, with a big terrace, a welcoming woody interior and efficient table-service inside and outside. The pizzas are highly rated by one reporter. The Panoramic has been recommended again this year – 'good choice, if a little expensive'.

### SCHOOLS AND GUIDES
***We are all Europeans now***

We get relatively few reports on the many schools operating here. We have a positive recent report on the tuition and organisation of the European school, a dynamic outfit composed of instructors of various nationalities, all (we are assured) speaking good English. Class sizes are small – as few as four pupils if you go for their advanced classes. We have had very good reports in the past of the Primitive snowboard school – for both advanced (off-piste and in the half-pipe) and intermediate riders.

### FACILITIES FOR CHILDREN
***Fine for babies***

Babies from six months to two years old can safely be entrusted to the village nursery. The kindergarten takes kids from two to six years, and there are chalet-based alternatives run by UK tour operators. There are also four free T-bars for children at the village level.

The south end of the resort has great views into the Ecrins national park ➔

OT LES DEUX-ALPES / J CARMONA

## CHILDREN

**Crèche du Clos des Fonds**
**t** 0476 790262
Ages 6mnth to 2yr; 8.30-5.30

**Bonhomme de Neige**
**t** 0476 790677
Ages 2 to 6; 9am-5.30 (also activity centre for ages 6 to 12)

**Jardins des Neiges**
**t** 0476 792121
**t** 0476 790421 (St-Christophe)
Ages 3 to 6; 9.15-12 noon, 2.30-5pm; 6 mornings €105.50

**Ski schools**
Classes for ages 6 to 12 (6 mornings €129.50 with ESF)

## ACTIVITIES

**Indoor** Swimming pool, hot-tub, sauna, sports centres (Club Forme, Tanking Center), cinemas, games rooms, bowling, museum, library, kanata (night in an igloo)

**Outdoor** Ice rink, ice gliders (dodgems), ice driving, donkey rides, sledge outings, helicopter flights, paragliding, quad bikes, snow-shoeing

**Phone numbers**
From abroad use the prefix +33 and omit the initial '0' of the phone number.

## TOURIST OFFICE

**t** 0476 792200
les2alp@les2alpes.com
www.les2alpes.com





## STAYING THERE

### HOW TO GO
***Wide range of packages***

Les Deux-Alpes has something for most tastes, including that rarity in high-altitude French resorts, reasonably priced hotels.

**Chalets** There are a number of catered chalet packages available from UK tour operators, but some use apartments.

**Hotels** There are over 30 hotels, of which the majority are 2-star or below. There's a Club Med 'village' here, too.

(((3) **Bérangère** (0476 792411) Smartest in town (but dreary exterior) with an excellent restaurant and pool; on-piste, at less convenient north end of resort.

((2) **Mariande** (0476 805060) Highly recommended, especially for its 'excellent' five-course dinners. At Venosc end of resort.

((2) **Chalet Mounier** (0476 805690) Smartly modernised. Good reputation for its food, and well placed for the Diable bubble and nightlife.

((2) **Souleil'or** (0476 792469) Looks like a lift station, but pleasant and comfortable, and well placed for the Jandri Express gondola. The rooms and food are reportedly 'fantastic'.

((2) **Brunerie** (0476 792223) 'Basic and cheerful', large 2-star with plenty of parking and quite well positioned.

**Self-catering** Many of the apartments are stuck out at the north end of the resort – well worth avoiding.

### EATING OUT
***Plenty of choice***

The hotel Bérangère has an excellent restaurant and the Chalet Mounier has a high reputation. The Petite Marmite has good food and atmosphere at reasonable prices. Bel'Auberge does classic French and is 'quite superb' – booking is advised. The Patate, the Cloche (formerly the Dahu) and Crêpes à Gogo are also recommended. Visitors on a budget can get a relatively cheap meal at Bleuets bar, the Vetrata or the Spaghetteria and a moderately priced English breakfast at Smokey Joe's Tex-Mex.

### APRES-SKI
***Unsophisticated fun***

Les Deux-Alpes is one of the liveliest of the French resorts, with plenty of bars, several of which stay open until the early hours. The Windsor bar is another noisy British enclave. Corrigans, Smokey Joe's, the Secret Bar and the Baron are recommended. Bar Brésilien has 'great music and tremendous atmosphere'. The Avalanche is the most popular of the discos and the Opera is recommended by locals. There are quieter places, too – the 'cosy, friendly' Bleuets is recommended.

The resort has contrived a couple of ways of dining at altitude – you can snowmobile to the glacier and back, eating on the way, or at full moon you can ski or board back to town after dinner (accompanied by ski patrollers).

### OFF THE SLOPES
***Not recommended***

Les Deux-Alpes is not a particularly good choice for people not hitting the slopes. The pretty valley village of Venosc is worth a visit by gondola, and you can take a scenic helicopter flight to Alpe-d'Huez. There is a good pool and lots of scenic walks. Several mountain restaurants are accessible to pedestrians. Snowcat tours across the glacier provide wonderful views.

OT FLAINE / PHOTOZOOM

# Flaine

*Extensive slopes, with traditional villages but bleak main resort*

## COSTS

①②③④⑤⑥

## RATINGS

**The slopes**

| | |
|---|---|
| Snow | **** |
| Extent | **** |
| Expert | **** |
| Intermediate | ***** |
| Beginner | ***** |
| Convenience | ***** |
| Queues | *** |
| Mountain restaurants | ** |

**The rest**

| | |
|---|---|
| Scenery | **** |
| Resort charm | * |
| Off-slope | * |

## NEWS

A new eight-seat gondola linking the village of Samoëns directly to Samoëns 1600 at mid-mountain was at last built for 2003/04. It leads to a new quad chair replacing the Damoiseaux drag-lift on the nursery slopes at Samoëns 1600.

The Kedeuze gondola out of Les Carroz is to be upgraded to eight-seat cabins, though it's not clear whether this will be finished for 2004/05.

Flaine is spending over a million euros on upgrading its snowmaking system, focusing on the lower ski areas.

There are long-term plans to expand Flaine and perhaps to build a funicular link from Magland, down in the valley, to bring in day visitors.

- ➕ Big, varied area, with off-piste challenges for experts as well as extensive intermediate terrain
- ➕ Reliable snow in the main bowl
- ➕ Compact, convenient, mainly car-free village, right on the slopes
- ➕ Excellent facilities for children
- ➕ Traditional village bases an option
- ➕ Scenic setting, and glorious views
- ➕ Very close to Geneva but ...

- ➖ Weekends can be busy as a result
- ➖ Austere 1960s Bauhaus buildings are not to everyone's taste
- ➖ In bad weather main Flaine bowl offers little to do, and links to outer sectors of the area may be closed
- ➖ No proper hotels in Flaine itself – only club hotels and apartments
- ➖ Nightlife not a highlight
- ➖ Little to do off the slopes

**Flaine is best known as a convenient resort catering particularly well for families, but it has a much broader appeal than that. The Grand Massif may not be quite in the same league as the Three Valleys and the new Paradiski area, but in extent its slopes are almost a match for Val-d'Isère/Tignes.**

**The few hotels in Flaine itself have now all become club hotels run by tour operators such as Club Med and Crystal. But you open up more accommodation options by considering the outlying villages – Samoëns, Morillon and Les Carroz. Not only are they more attractive places to stay in, but also they offer some sheltered slopes for bad weather days.**



## THE RESORT

We have to say we fall in the group that does not find Flaine's Bauhaus architecture attractive. The concrete massifs that form the core of the resort were conceived in the sixties as 'an example of the application of the principle of shadow and light'. They look particularly shocking from the approach road – a mass of blocks nestling at the bottom of the impressive snowy bowl. From the slopes they are less obtrusive, blending into the rocky grey hillside. For us, the outdoor sculptures by Picasso, Vasarely and Dubuffet do little to improve Flaine's austere ambience.

In common with other French Alpine purpose-built resorts, Flaine has improved its looks in recent years. The relatively new development of Hameau-de-Flaine is built in a much more attractive chalet style – but is inconveniently situated 1km/0.5 miles from the slopes and main village.

In Flaine proper, everything is close by: supermarket, sports rental shops, ski schools, main lifts out etc. The resort itself is also easy to get to – only 70km/43 miles from Geneva, and about 90 minutes from the airport.

There are two parts to the main resort. The club hotels, and some apartments, are set in the lower part, Forum. The focus of this area is a snow-covered square with buildings on three sides, the open fourth side blending with the slopes. Flaine Forêt, up the hillside and linked by lift, has its own bars and shops and most of the apartment accommodation.

There are children all over the place; they are catered for with play areas, and the resort is supposed to be traffic-free. In fact, road penetrate the village and you don't have to go far to encounter traffic; but the central Forum itself, leading to the pistes, is pretty safe. A car gives you the option of visiting Chamonix (and Courmayeur via the Mont Blanc tunnel). The bus service to/from Hameau is 'excellent'.

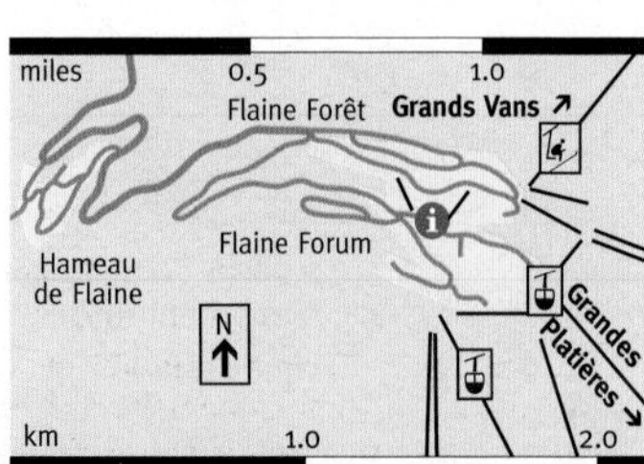

## KEY FACTS

| | |
|---|---|
| **Resort** | 1600m<br>5,250ft |
| Grand Massif ski area (Flaine, Les Carroz, Morillon, Samoëns, Sixt) | |
| **Slopes** | 700-2480m<br>2,300-8,140ft |
| **Lifts** | 78 |
| **Pistes** | 265km<br>165 miles |
| **Green** | 11% |
| **Blue** | 40% |
| **Red** | 38% |
| **Black** | 11% |
| **Snowmaking** | 25% |
| For Flaine only | |
| **Slopes** | 1600-2480m<br>5,250-8,140ft |
| **Lifts** | 28 |
| **Pistes** | 140km<br>87 miles |
| **Green** | 13% |
| **Blue** | 37% |
| **Red** | 42% |
| **Black** | 8% |

# THE MOUNTAINS

With its 265km/165 miles of pistes, the Grand Massif is an impressive area, with plenty of scope for any level of skier or boarder, provided you can get to all of it – the greater part of the domain lies outside the main Flaine bowl and the links can be closed by excessive wind or snow.

## THE SLOPES
### *A big white playground*

The day begins for most people at the **Grandes Platières** jumbo gondola, which speeds you in a single stage up the north face of the Flaine bowl to the high-point of the Grand Massif, and a magnificent view of Mont Blanc.

Most of the runs are reds (though there are some blues curling away to the right as you look down the mountain, and one direct black). There are essentially four or five main ways down the barren, treeless, rolling terrain back to Flaine, or to chairs in the middle of the wilderness going back to the summit.

On the far right, the easy 14km/9 mile, picturesque Cascades blue run (one of the longest in the Alps) leads away from the lift system behind the Tête Pelouse and down to the outskirts of Sixt at 770m/2,530ft (giving a vertical drop of over 1700m/5,580ft). There is no lift back but there is a regular shuttle-bus service to the lifts at Samoëns or Morillon – there may be a lot of people waiting to get on the bus, though. Sixt has its own little west-facing area offering red and black slopes of 700m/2,300ft vertical – and is reachable from the bottom of the Cascades run by drag-lift.

On the other side of the Tête Pelouse, a broad cat-walk leads to the experts-only **Gers** bowl. At the bottom, a flat trail links with the Cascades run or there's a drag back to the ridge.

Back at Platières, an alternative is to head left down the long red Méphisto (many of the runs in this area have diabolic names – Lucifer, Belzébuth etc) to the **Aujon** area. This opens up another sector of the bowl, again mostly red runs but with some blues further down. The lower slopes here are used as slalom courses. This sector is also reachable by gondola or drag-lifts from below the resort.

The eight-seater Grands Vans chair, reached from Forum by means of a slow bucket-lift (aka télébenne), gives access to the extensive slopes of Samoëns, Morillon and Les Carroz. You

There are woodland runs in the Flaine bowl, but they are short and few →

FLAINE TOURIST OFFICE

**LIFT PASSES**

**Grand Massif**
Covers all the lifts in Flaine, Les Carroz, Morillon, Samoëns and Sixt.

**Beginners**
Four free lifts.

**Main pass**
1 day €32
6 days €160

**Senior citizens**
Over 60: 6 days €136
Over 75: free pass

**Children**
Under 16: 6 days €128
Under 12: 6 days €117
Under 5: free pass

**Alternative passes**
Flaine area only – half and day passes available.

come first to the wide Vernant bowl equipped with three fast chair-lifts, one starting from a car park on the road up to Flaine. Beyond here the lie of the land is complicated, and the piste map does not represent it clearly. In good snow there is a choice of blues and reds winding down to **Les Carroz** or **Morillon**, the latter with a halfway point at 1100m/3,610ft. While there is a choice of blue, red and black runs on the top section above **Samoëns 1600**, the runs below here to Vercland are challenging blacks and reds (without snowmaking, so often closed).

We have had past reports of lifts breaking down too often and being too easily closed because of high winds, cutting off links with the lower villages. Piste signing and grooming have, however, been praised. And the piste map has useful lists of the main connecting lifts and pistes between the different resorts.

## TERRAIN-PARKS

### *Cater for kids to experts*

There's a big terrain-park (called the JamPark Pro – standing for Jib and Air Maniacs) in the Aujon area of Flaine. Watch out for the 'downright dangerous' Aujon drag-lift, though, which is reportedly as much of a challenge as the park! There's also an intermediates' park under the Charionde 2 chair on the Samoëns side, with green, red and black options and a variety of rails. And there's a kids' park, JamPark Kids, with a boarder-cross run under the Esserts quad on the Morillon side.

## SNOW RELIABILITY

### *Usually keeps its whiteness*

The main part of Flaine's slopes lie on the wide north- and north-west-facing flank of the Grandes Platières. Its direction, along with a decent height, means that it keeps the snow it receives. There is snowmaking on the greater part of the Aujon sector and on the nursery slopes. The runs towards Samoëns 1600 and Morillon 1100 are

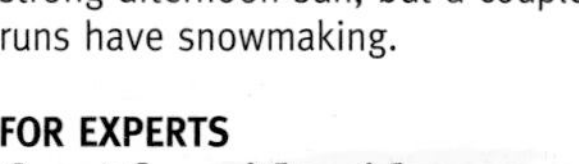

north-facing too, and some lower parts have snowmaking, but below here can be tricky or closed. The Les Carroz runs are west-facing and can suffer from strong afternoon sun, but a couple of runs have snowmaking.

## FOR EXPERTS

### *Great fun with guidance*

Flaine's family-friendly reputation tends to obscure the fact that it has some seriously challenging terrain. But much of it is off-piste and, although some of it looks like it can safely be explored without guidance, this impression is mistaken. The Flaine bowl is riddled with rock crevasses and potholes, and should be treated with the same caution that you would use on a glacier. There have been some tragic cases of off-piste skiers coming across nasty surprises, including a British skier falling to his death only yards from the piste.

All the black pistes on the map deserve their grading. The Diamant Noir, down the line of the main

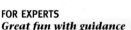

## boarding

*Flaine suits boarders quite well – there's lots of varied terrain and plenty of off-piste with interesting nooks and crannies, including woods outside the main bowl. The key lifts are all now chairs or gondolas – with few unavoidable drag-lifts (beware of the absurdly vicious Aujon drag-lift though, which serves the terrain-park). There are two other terrain-park options, including one for kids. Black Side is the local specialist shop, in the central Forum.*

Grandes Platières isn't very high at 2480m/8,140ft, but it is a fine vantage point ➔

FLAINE TOURIST OFFICE

gondola, is a challenging 850m/2,790ft descent, tricky because of moguls, narrowness and other people rather than great steepness; the first pitch is the steepest, with spectators applauding overhead from the chair-lift.

To the left of the Diamant Noir as you look down are several short but steep off-piste routes through the crags of the Grandes Platières.

The Lindars Nord chair serves a shorter slope that often has the best snow in the area, and some seriously steep gradients if you look for them.

The Gers drag-lift, outside the main bowl beyond Tête Pelouse, serves great expert-only terrain. The piste going down the right of the drag is a proper black, but by departing from it you can find slopes of up to 45°. To the left of the drag is the impressive main Gers bowl – a great horseshoe of about 550m/1,800ft vertical, powder or moguls top to bottom, all off-piste. You can choose your gradient, from steep to very steep. As you look down the bowl, you see more adventurous ways into the bowl from the Grands Vans and Tête de Véret lifts.

There are further serious pistes on the top lifts above Samoëns 1600.

Touring is a possibility behind the Grandes Platières, and there are some scenic off-piste routes from which you can be retrieved by helicopter – such as the Combe des Foges, next to Gers.

## FOR INTERMEDIATES
### *Something for everyone*

Flaine is ideal for confident intermediates, with a great variety of pistes (and usually the bonus of good snow conditions, at least above Flaine itself). As a reporter puts it, 'There may not be many challenging runs, but there are very few dull ones.' The diabolically named reds that dominate the Flaine bowl are not really as hellish as their names imply – they tend to gain their status from short steep sections rather than overall difficulty, and they're great for improving technique. There are gentler cruises from the top of the mountain – Cristal, taking you to the Perdrix chair, or Serpentine, all the way home. The blues at Aujon are excellent for confidence-building, but the drag serving them is just the opposite.

The connections with the slopes outside the main bowl are classified blue but several blue-run reporters have found them tricky because of narrowness, crowds or poor snow. Once the connection has been made, however, all intermediates will enjoy the long tree-lined runs down to Les Carroz, as long as the snow is good. The Morillon slopes are also excellent intermediate terrain – the long green Marvel run to Morillon 1100 is an easy cruise with excellent signs along the way explaining (in English as well as French) about the local wildlife.

## FOR BEGINNERS
### *Fairly good*

There are excellent nursery slopes right by the village, served by free lifts which make a pass unnecessary until you are ready to go higher up the mountain. But a reporter warns that it is also used as a short cut back to the village for other skiers. There are no long green runs to progress to in the Flaine bowl – there is one above Morillon, though, and there are one or two gentle local blues (see 'For intermediates' above).

## SCHOOLS

**ESF**
t 0450 908100
contact@flaine-esf.com

**International**
t 0450 908441
ski.ecole.inter@wanadoo.fr

**Flaine Super Ski**
Advanced skiers only
t 0450 908288
balta2@wanadoo.fr

**Independent instructors**
t 0607 195609
guy.pezet@wanadoo.fr
t 0450 904094
lynnestainbrook@aol.com

**Stages François Simond**
t 0450 908097
simondsports@aol.com

**Classes** (ESF prices)
6 days (3hr per day)
€110

**Private lessons**
€27.50 for 1hr, for 1 or 2 people

## CHILDREN

**Les P'tits Loups**
t 0450 908782
Ages 6mnth to 3yr

**Rabbit Club and Fantaski**
t 0450 908100
Ages 3 to 12; 9am-5pm; 6 days with lunch €215

**La Souris Verte**
t 0450 908441
Ages 3 to 12

**MMV Hotels Flaine and Aujon**
t 0492 126212
Ages 18mnth to 14yr

**Club Med Flaine**
t 0450 908166
For babies aged from 4mnth

**Ski school**
For ages 5 to 12: €83 for 6 days, 2hr per day (ESF prices)

### CROSS-COUNTRY
***Very fragmented***

The Grand Massif claims 64km/40 miles of cross-country tracks but only about 17km/10 miles of that is around Flaine itself. The majority is on the valley floor and dependent on low snow. There are extensive tracks between Morillon and Les Carroz, with some tough uphill sections. Samoëns 1600 has its own tracks and makes the best base for cross-country enthusiasts.

### QUEUES
***A few problems***

Recent investment in new lifts has eliminated some trouble spots, and several reporters had queue-free weeks, even in high season. However you should still expect to wait 10 minutes or more for the Vernant chair to get back to the Flaine bowl late in the afternoon (an alternative is to descend to one of the lift-bases along the road to the resort, and catch a bus). The chair up from Molliets is reported as another bottleneck at the end of the day. A 2004 visitor who managed to get to Gers said skiing was limited by the late opening of the lift and by time spent queuing.

When the resort is full, the main Grandes Platières gondola is prone to queues at the start of the day, but they move quickly. The other main lift into the Flaine bowl, the old Aup de Veran gondola, also gets busy.

Queues elsewhere can build up at weekends (it is very close to Geneva) and when the lifts out of the Flaine bowl are shut due to high winds or when the weather is warm and the lower resorts have poor snow (when this happens, the queues to go down can be worse than those to go up).

### MOUNTAIN RESTAURANTS
***Back to base, or quit the bowl***

In the Flaine bowl, there are few restaurants above the resort's upper outskirts. The Blanchot, at the bottom of the Serpentine run, is popular and rustic, but it can get crowded.

Just scraping into the mountain restaurant category are several chalets close to the resort. At Forum level, across the piste from the gondola, is the welcoming Michet ('definitely worth a visit'), with very good Savoyard food and table service, and the Eloge – 'fast table service, tasty food, reasonable value'. Up the slope a bit, the Cascade is self-service but with a good terrace



and 'very pleasant' proprietors. Epicéa has a rustic atmosphere, a terrace and gets rave reviews. Up at Forêt level, the Bissac has a good atmosphere, traditional decor and excellent food.

Outside the Flaine bowl, we loved the remote Chalet du Lac de Gers (book in advance and ring for a snowcat to tow you up from part way down the Cascades run) – simple food but splendid isolation and views of the frozen lake. We also had an excellent plat du jour at the cosy and rustic Igloo above Morillon. The Chalet les Molliets near the bottom of the Molliets chair is charming and rustic. Reporters have also recommended the Oreade at the top of the gondola from Les Carroz.

### SCHOOLS AND GUIDES
***Getting better***

We've had few reports recently on the ESF but a 9-year old visitor in 2004 was happy to return for a second year. Recent reporters have praised the International school although a 2004 pupil said some found it a little too demanding – 'they refused to take hot chocolate breaks, which led to people dropping out early'. The small specialist Super Ski school apparently has 'small class sizes, good instruction'.

### FACILITIES FOR CHILDREN
***Parents' paradise?***

Flaine prides itself on being a family resort, and the number of English-speaking children around is a bonus. There are some free children's lift passes available in low season weeks.

Club Med has good childcare facilities open to residents only, as does Crystal's hotel Le Totem. The P'tits Loups nursery takes children from six months to three years. Some other accommodation units have kids' clubs of their own.

## GETTING THERE

**Air** Geneva 90km/ 56 miles (1½hr).

**Rail** Cluses (30km/ 19 miles); regular bus service.

## ACTIVITIES

**Indoor** Swimming pool, sauna, solarium, gymnasium, massage, bowling, cinema, billiards, climbing wall, cultural centre with art gallery and library

**Outdoor** Ice rink, snowshoe excursions, dog sledding, paragliding, helicopter rides, snow scooters, quad bikes, ice driving

## STAYING THERE

### HOW TO GO
***Plenty of apartments***

Accommodation is overwhelmingly in self-catering apartments.

**Chalets** There are few catered chalet options, but they include a couple of attractively traditional Scandinavian-style huts in Hameau. Crystal now run the Hotel Totem as a club-hotel and it had a couple of glowing 2004 reports.

**Hotels** All the hotels are now run by tour operators. B&B is available at the Cascade restaurants.

**Self-catering** The best apartments are out at Hameau. In Flaine Forêt, the Forêt and Grand Massif apartment buildings are attractively woody inside and there are hotel facilities.

### EATING OUT
***Enough choice for a week***

The Perdrix Noire in Forêt, a past recommendation, was judged pricey by a 2004 visitor. Its bar is popular. Chez Daniel offers a good range of Savoyard specialities, and is good with kids. The 'lively' Brasserie les Cîmes is recommended for 'excellent food in massive quantities' but it does get very busy later. Try Chez la Jeanne, the Pizzeria in the shopping mall in Forum or La Grange for pizza. A couple of places close to the village and described under 'Mountain restaurants' are open in the evening – the Michet and the Bissac. The Ancolie in Hameau is said to be worth the trip for its 'great food' and 'beautiful wooden chalet interior'. If you have a car, the restaurant at Molliets, just down the mountain, has produced 'rave reviews'.

### APRES-SKI
***Signs of life***

It has long been possible to eat and drink into the early hours here if you move around a bit – but you don't have much choice of venues.

The White Grouse pub has a big screen TV, rock music and punters trying to get pints in before the end of happy hour. The Flying Dutchman is 'very lively 5-7pm, very friendly, tends to wind down around 11'. The bar at the bowling alley has a 'family atmosphere earlier on, turns into a pub after 11' and is 'the only place still serving food until 3am'. The Texa is Flaine's only nightclub but the drinks are 'very expensive' and the 'music not up to much'. The 'very French' Diamant Noir pool hall is open late and sometimes has 'good live music'. The Ski Fun is open late but 'no great shakes,' says a reporter.

### OFF THE SLOPES
***Curse of the purpose-built***

As with most purpose-built resorts, there are few walks, and no town to explore – not recommended for people who don't want to hit the slopes. But there is a great ice-driving circuit where you can take a spin (literally) in your own car or, more sensibly, have a lesson in theirs (as we did). Snowmobile tours and dog-sledding excursions are popular, and there's a cinema, gymnasium and swimming pool. Save your visit to the limited upper gallery shops in Forum for the one evening a week when there is a free hands-on display of large wooden games, enjoyed by visitors of all ages in 2004.

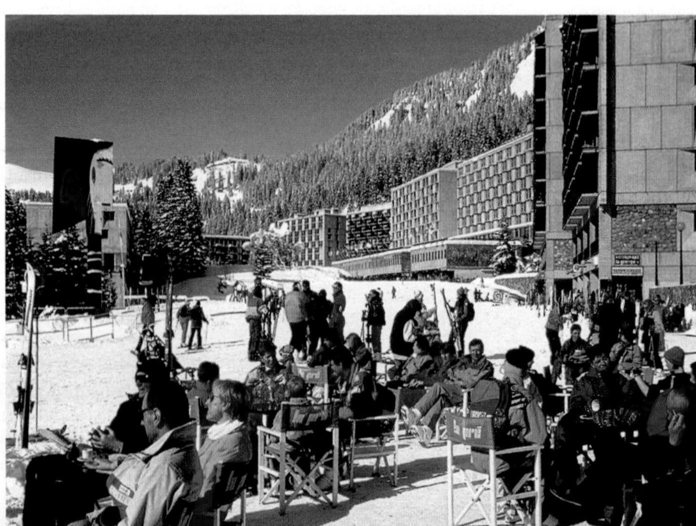

PHOTOZOOM

Flaine Forum – the heart of the resort, leading directly to the snow →

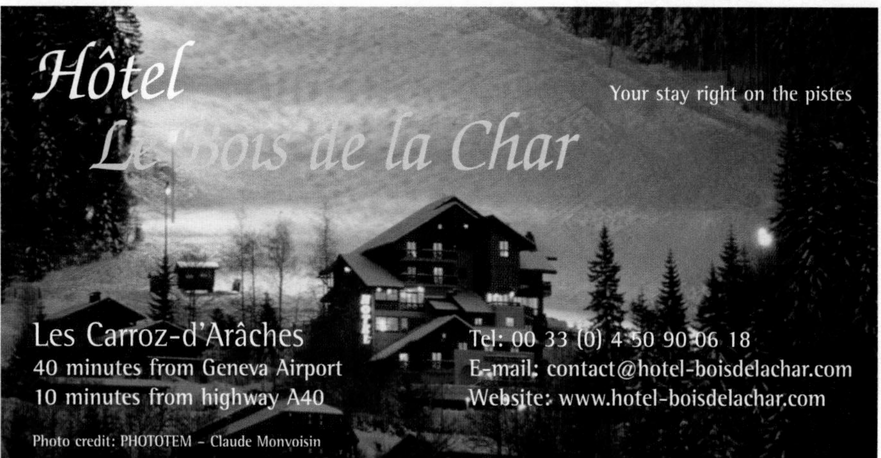




**Phone numbers**
From abroad use the prefix +33 and omit the initial '0' of the phone number.

**TOURIST OFFICES**

**Flaine**
t 0450 908001
welcome@flaine.com
www.flaine.com

**Les Carroz**
t 0450 900004
info@lescarroz.com
www.lescarroz.com

**Samoëns**
t 0450 344028
infos@samoens.com
www.samoens.com

**Morillon**
t 0450 901576
info@ot-morillon.fr
www.ot-morillon.fr

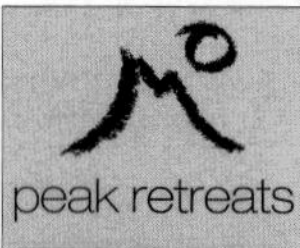


## Les Carroz 1140m/3,740ft

This is a spacious, sunny, traditional, family resort where life revolves around the village square with its pavement cafes, restaurants and interesting little shops. It has a lived-in feel of a real French village, with more animation than Flaine – 'a delight' says a recent visitor, who recommends the 3-star hotel Arbaron (0450 900267) for food, service and views. Even more highly recommended is the 2-star Bois de la Char (0450 900618): 'It is perfectly situated beside the piste. The food was good, the staff friendly and it was excellent value for money.' Apartments include new MGM units with indoor pool, sauna and spa facilities. The Marlow pub 'seems to be the place to go' at close of play.

The gondola and chair-lift go straight into the Grand Massif area, but there's a steep 300m/1,000ft walk up from the centre – the nursery drag is a help or you can catch the free ski-bus.

The ski school's torchlit descent is 'not to be missed' – ending with vin chaud and live jazz in the square.

## Samoëns 720m/2,360ft

This is the only resort in France to be listed as a 'Monument Historique' – once a thriving centre for stone-masons, with their work much in evidence. The traffic-free centre has a pretty square, medieval fountain, rustic old buildings, an ancient church, bars, restaurants and local shops. 'A lovely place to go for a stroll in the evening, with a great family atmosphere,' says a reporter. Despite recent growth on the outskirts, the village retains the feel of 'real' rural France. But it does now have an Irish pub, Covey's, rated by an Irish reporter as 'authentic with a good vibe' – even 'great craic' one night. The Neige et Roc hotel is said to offer 'comfort and good food'.

A reporter recommends the Pizzeria La Louisiane for its wood oven pizzas and 'highly alcoholic' ice creams. Visitors in 2004 enjoyed eating at the Relais Gourmand ('super food') and the Pierrot des Neiges.

The long-awaited 8-person gondola from the village was finally opened last winter. The new base station is still far enough from most accommodation to require transport, but is much nearer than the gondola at Vercland (which is now queue-free, and still the best route up for non-beginners). The new lift arrives at the beginners' area at Samoëns 1600, rated 'one of the best in the Alps' by one reporter, who also strongly recommends the local ESF.

## Morillon 700m/2,300ft

Not quite in the Samoëns league, but still a pretty rustic village, Morillon makes a good base, with an efficient gondola from the upper fringes of the village to the mid-mountain mini-resort of Morillon 1100 (Les Esserts) – also reachable by road. Up here there is a large and 'delightful' ski kindergarten plus good slopes for adult beginners and new apartments right on the piste – it's 'dead as a dodo in the evenings', though, says a reporter. Back in the village, the hotel Morillon is strongly recommended for its 'superb food'.

OT LES GETS

# Les Gets

*Friendly village amid extensive friendly (but low-altitude) slopes*

## COSTS

①②③④⑤⑥

## RATINGS

| **The slopes** | |
|---|---|
| Snow | ** |
| Extent | *** |
| Expert | *** |
| Intermediate | **** |
| Beginner | **** |
| Convenience | *** |
| Queues | *** |
| Mountain restaurants | *** |
| **The rest** | |
| Scenery | *** |
| Resort charm | *** |
| Off-slope | *** |

**Extent rating**
This relates only to the Les Gets/ Morzine slopes, not the whole Portes du Soleil.



## NEWS

Several six-packs have been installed recently – last year, the Perrières lift opened up a new way to La Rosta and Ranfolly, and the Chavannes and Charniaz chairs were replaced, improving links with Morzine.

- + Good-sized, varied local piste area shared with slightly lower Morzine – plus excellent, neglected Mont Chéry
- + Attractive chalet-style village, with through-traffic kept on fringes
- + Relatively short drive from the UK
- + Few queues locally
- + Part of the vast Portes du Soleil ski pass region, but ...

- – To get to Avoriaz and the main Portes du Soleil circuit is a real slog, unless you drive to Ardent
- – Modest altitude means there is always a risk of poor snow, though increased snowmaking has helped
- – Few challenging pistes
- – Weekend crowds

**The area that Les Gets shares with Morzine offers the most extensive slopes in the Portes du Soleil, and in some respects Les Gets is the better base for them. But if the main Portes du Soleil circuit is a priority, stay closer to it.**

## THE RESORT

Les Gets is an attractive, sunny, much-expanded village of traditional chalet-style buildings, on the low pass leading from the A40 autoroute at Cluses to Morzine. The main road bypasses the village centre, which is partly car-free and has plenty of attractive food and other shops and restaurants lining the main street. There's also a popular outdoor ice rink, which adds to the charm.

Although the village has a scattered appearance, most facilities are conveniently close to the main lift station – and the free 'petit train' road-train shuttle is a 'quirky but useful' way of travelling around. It is fairly quiet in the evenings but gets busier and livelier at weekends.

## THE MOUNTAINS

Les Gets is not an ideal base for the Portes du Soleil, but its local slopes are extensive. The local pass saves a fair bit on a Portes du Soleil pass, and makes a lot of sense for many visitors.

**Slopes** The main local slopes – accessed by a gondola and fast chair-lift from the nursery slopes beside the village – are shared with Morzine, and are mainly described in that chapter. On the opposite side of Les Gets is Mont Chéry, accessed by a gondola and parallel chair. The slopes include some of the most challenging in the area, and are usually very quiet. Both sectors offer wooded and open slopes.

**Snow reliability** The nursery slopes benefit from a slightly higher elevation than Morzine, but otherwise our

## KEY FACTS

| | |
|---|---|
| **Resort** | 1170m<br>3,840ft |
| for Portes du Soleil | |
| **Slopes** | 975-2275m<br>3,200-7,460ft |
| **Lifts** | 206 |
| **Pistes** | 650km<br>400 miles |
| **Green** | 13% |
| **Blue** | 38% |
| **Red** | 39% |
| **Black** | 10% |
| **Snowmaking** | 252 acres |
| For Morzine-Les Gets only | |
| **Slopes** | 1000-2020m<br>3,280-6,630ft |
| **Lifts** | 67 |
| **Pistes** | 140km<br>87 miles |

**Piste map**
The whole local area is covered by the map in the Morzine chapter.

**Phone numbers**
From abroad use the prefix +33 and omit the initial '0' of the phone number.

## TOURIST OFFICE

**t** 0450 758080
lesgets@lesgets.com
www.lesgets.com

general reservations about the lack of altitude apply. A lot more snow-guns have improved runs to the resort. The front slopes of Mont Chéry face south-east – bad news at this altitude; but they are 'immaculately groomed', and the other two flanks are shadier.

**Terrain-parks** There's a park on the upper slopes of Mont Chéry called the 'Freestyle District', with five kickers, hip jumps, a gap jump and a couple of quarter-pipes. There are also boarder-cross and slalom courses here.

**Experts** Black runs on the flank and back of Mont Chéry chair are quite steep and often bumped. In good snow there is plenty to do off-piste, including some excellent wooded areas.

**Intermediates** High-mileage piste-bashers might prefer direct access to the main Portes du Soleil circuit, but the local slopes have a lot to offer – including excellent reds on Mont Chéry.

**Beginners** The village nursery slopes are convenient, and there are better, more snow-sure ones up at Chavannes. Although the only longer greens are up the mountain, there are plenty of easy blues lower down.

**Snowboarding** The local Les Gets and Morzine slopes are good for beginners and intermediates.

**Cross-country** There are 18km/11 miles of good, varied loops on Mont Chéry and Les Chavannes.

**Queues** See the Morzine chapter for general observations. Mont Chéry is crowd-free.

**Mountain restaurants** See Morzine.

**Schools and guides** Mixed reports of the ESF – tales of 'instructors shouting at four-year-olds in French' but also of kids enjoying 'a great instructor'. A 2004 reporter had a 'very good' private lesson in 'excellent English'. The 'good but pricey' British Alpine Ski & Snowboard School has a branch here.

**Facilities for children** There are comprehensive resort facilities, and several family-oriented tour operators. The British-run Snowkidz nursery takes babies as well as infant skiers, and is this year reported to be 'superb – absolutely faultless'.

## STAYING THERE

**How to go** Several tour operators have catered chalets, including Ski Activity and Total Ski (which we've heard good reports of).

**Hotels** All the hotels are 3-star and below. The 3-star Crychar (0450 758050), 100m/330ft from central Les Gets at the foot of the slopes, is one of the best. The 2-star Alpen Sports (0450 758055) is a friendly, family-run hotel – 'excellent food and good value for money' says a reporter. We've also had good reports of the the Nagano (0450 797146) and the Marmotte (0450 758033) – both 3-star.

**Self-catering** The tourist office has a list of apartments. A recent reporter was happy with the Lion D'Or.

**Eating out** Most hotels have good restaurants. The Tyrol and the Schuss are good for pizza; the rustic Vieux Chêne for Savoyard specialities. The Flambeau, Tanière and Tourbillon have been recommended. Book ahead, especially at weekends.

**Après-ski** Après-ski is quiet, especially on weekdays. The Pub Irlandaise (with 'an unusual Savoie version of porter'), the Bar Canadie above it, the Boomerang, the Copeaux and the Bush (Scottish owned) are recommended by reporters. The Igloo is a popular disco.

**Off the slopes** There's a well-equipped fitness centre with a pool, and an artificial ice rink. The Mechanical Music Museum is strongly recommended by a reporter (barrel organs and music boxes, for example, with guided tours in English). There is a good selection of shops and outings to Geneva, Lausanne and Montreux are possible.

# La Grave

*A superb mountain for good skiers and free-riders*

## COSTS

(1)(2)(3)(4)(5)(6)

## RATINGS

**The slopes**

| | |
|---|---|
| Snow | *** |
| Extent | * |
| Expert | ***** |
| Intermediate | * |
| Beginner | * |
| Convenience | *** |
| Queues | **** |
| Mountain restaurants | ** |

**The rest**

| | |
|---|---|
| Scenery | **** |
| Resort charm | *** |
| Off-slope | * |

## NEWS

La Grave does not change much, and that is half the charm of the place.



- + Legendary off-piste mountain
- + Usually crowd-free
- + Usually good snow conditions
- + Link to Les Deux-Alpes
- + Easy access by car to other nearby resorts

- − Rather dour village
- − Poor weather spells lift closures – on average, two days per week
- − Suitable for experts only, despite some easy slopes at altitude
- − Nothing to do off the slopes

**La Grave enjoys legendary status among experts. It's a quiet old village with around 500 visitor beds and just one serious lift – a small stop-start gondola serving a high, wild and predominantly off-piste mountainside. The result: an exciting, usually crowd-free area. Strictly, you ought to have a guide, but in good weather many people go it alone.**

## THE RESORT

La Grave is an unspoiled mountaineering village set on a steep hillside facing the impressive glaciers of majestic La Meije. It's rather drab, and the busy road through to Briançon doesn't help. But it has a rustic feel, some welcoming hotels, and prices that are low by resort standards. The village is small and the single lift is just below the centre. Storms close the slopes on average two days a week – so a car is useful for access to nearby resorts.

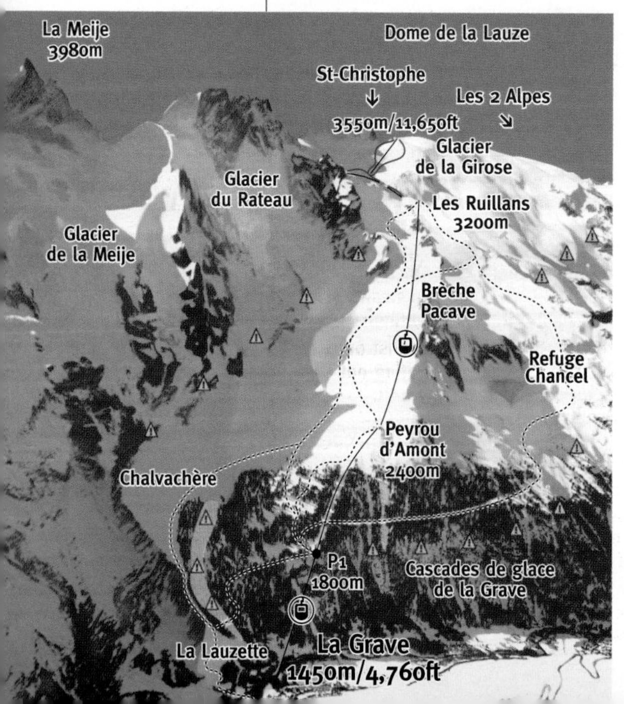


## THE MOUNTAIN

A slow two-stage 'pulse' gondola (with an extra station at a pylon halfway up the lower stage) ascends into the slopes and finishes at 3200m/10,500ft. Above that, a short walk and a drag-lift give access to a second drag serving twin blue runs on a glacier slope of about 350m/1,150ft vertical – from here you can ski to Les Deux-Alpes. But the reason that people come here is to explore the legendary slopes back towards La Grave. These slopes offer no defined, patrolled, avalanche-protected pistes – but there are marked itinéraires of 1400m/4,590ft vertical down to the pylon lift station at 1800m/5,910ft, or all the way down to the valley – 2150m/7,050ft vertical.

**Slopes** The Chancel route is mostly of red-run gradient; the Vallons de la Meije is more challenging but not too steep. People do take these routes without a guide or avalanche protection equipment, but we couldn't possibly recommend it.

There are many more demanding runs away from the itinéraires, including couloirs that range from the straightforward to the seriously hazardous, and long descents from the glacier to the valley road below the village, with return by taxi, bus, or strategically parked car. The dangers are considerable (people die here every year), and good guidance is essential. You can also descend southwards to St-Christophe, returning by bus and the lifts of Les Deux-Alpes.

**Terrain-parks** There aren't any.

**Snow reliability** The chances of powder

## KEY FACTS

| | |
|---|---|
| **Resort** | 1450m 4,760ft |
| **Slopes** | 1450-3550m 4,760-11,650ft |
| **Lifts** | 4 |
| **Pistes** | 5km 3 miles |
| **Green/Blue** | 100% |

The 'difficulty' figure relates to on-piste; practically all the skiing – at least 90% – is off-piste

| | |
|---|---|
| **Snowmaking** | none |

**Phone numbers**
From abroad use the prefix +33 and omit the initial '0' of the phone number.

## TOURIST OFFICE

**t** 0476 799005
ot@lagrave-lameije.com
www.lagrave-lameije.com

snow on the high, north-facing slopes are good, but if conditions are tricky there are no pistes to fall back on apart from the three short blue runs at the top of the gondola.

**Experts** La Grave's uncrowded off-piste slopes have earned it cult status among hard-core skiers.

**Intermediates** The itinéraires get tracked into a piste-like state, and adventurous intermediates could tackle the Chancel.

**Beginners** Novices tricked into coming here can go up the valley to the beginner slopes at Le Chazelet, which has two cannons for snowmaking.

**Snowboarding** There are no special facilities for boarders, but advanced free-riders will be in their element on the open off-piste powder.

**Cross-country** There is a total of 20km/12 miles of loops in the area.

**Queues** Normally, there are short queues only at weekends. If snow conditions back to the valley are poor, queues can build up for the gondola down from the mid and lower stations.

**Mountain restaurants** Surprisingly, there are three decent mountain restaurants; the best is the refuge on the Chancel itinéraire.

**Schools and guides** There are a dozen or so guides in the village, offering a wide range of services through their bureau. See also Hotels below.

**Facilities for children** Babysitting can be arranged through the tourist office.

## STAYING THERE

**How to go** There are several simple hotels.

**Hotels** The Edelweiss (0476 799093) is a friendly 2-star with a cosy bar and restaurant. La Chaumine Skiers Lodge, set 3km/2 miles above La Grave, runs all-inclusive week-long packages, including guiding.

**Self-catering** Bookable through the tourist office.

**Eating out** Most people eat in their hotels, though there are alternatives.

**Après-ski** The standard tea-time après-ski gathering place is the central Glaciers bar, known to habitués as chez Marcel. The Vieux Guide gets crowded later. There's also the Vallons and Bois des Fées.

**Off the slopes** Anyone not using the slopes will find La Grave much too small and quiet.

OT MEGEVE

# Megève

*One of the traditional old winter holiday towns*

## COSTS

①②③④⑤⑥

## RATINGS

**The slopes**

| | |
|---|---|
| Snow | ** |
| Extent | ***** |
| Expert | ** |
| Intermediate | **** |
| Beginner | *** |
| Convenience | ** |
| Queues | **** |
| Mountain restaurants | **** |

**The rest**

| | |
|---|---|
| Scenery | ***** |
| Resort charm | **** |
| Off-slope | **** |

## NEWS

The big news for 2004/05 will be the linking of the slopes of Le Jaillet to La Giettaz – a tiny resort halfway to La Clusaz – via three new runs and two new drag-lifts. The link goes via the backwater of Le Christomet, and there are also plans to upgrade the lifts on the Megève side of this peak – a six-pack to replace the old double chair up to Le Christomet and a quad to replace the Les Près chair back up to Le Jaillet.

New accommodation opened in 2003/04 – the Hameau de Mavarin – is a small cluster of luxury chalets and apartments.



- + Extensive slopes, with miles of easy pistes, ideal for intermediates
- + Scenic setting, with splendid views
- + Charming old village centre, with very swanky shopping
- + Some lovely luxury hotels
- + Both gourmet and simple mountain lunches in attractive surroundings
- + Excellent cross-country trails
- + Different lift pass options cover other worthwhile resorts nearby
- + Great for weekends – co-operative hotels, short drive from Geneva
- + Great when it snows – woodland runs with no one on them
- + Plenty to do off the slopes

- − With most of the slopes below 2000m/6,560ft there's a risk of poor snow, especially on runs to the village – although the grassy terrain does not need a thick covering and snowmaking has improved a lot
- − Three separate mountains, two linked by lift but not by piste, and the third not linked at all
- − Lots of slow, old lifts remain
- − Not many challenging pistes – though there is good off-piste
- − Traffic jams and fumes at weekends and peak season

**Megève is the essence of rustic chic. It has a medieval heart but it was, in a way, the original purpose-built French ski resort – conceived in the 1920s as an alternative to St Moritz. And, although Courchevel took over as France's swank resort ages ago, Megève's smart hotels and chalets still attract 'beautiful people' with fur coats and fat wallets. Happily, you don't need either to enjoy it.**

**The risk of poor snow still makes us wary. But it is true that a few inches of snow is enough to give skiable cover on the grassy slopes – and when a storm socks in this is a great place to be, as we confirmed a couple of years ago.**

**What's more, the list of plus points above is as long as they come.**

## THE RESORT

Megève is in a lovely sunny setting and has a beautifully preserved traditional medieval centre, which is pedestrianised and comes complete with open-air ice rink, horse-drawn sleighs, cobbled streets and a fine church. Lots of smart clothing, jewellery, antique, gift and food shops add to the chic atmosphere.

The main Albertville-Chamonix road bypasses the centre, and there are expensive underground car parks. But the resort's clientele arrives mainly by car and the resulting traffic jams and fumes are a major problem. It's worst at weekends, but can be serious every afternoon in high season.

The clientele are mainly well-heeled French couples and families, who come here as much for an all-round winter holiday and for the people-watching potential as for the slopes themselves. The nightlife is smart rather than lively.

A gondola within walking distance of central Megève gives direct access to one of the three mountains, Rochebrune. This sector can also be reached directly by a cable-car from the southern edge of town. The main

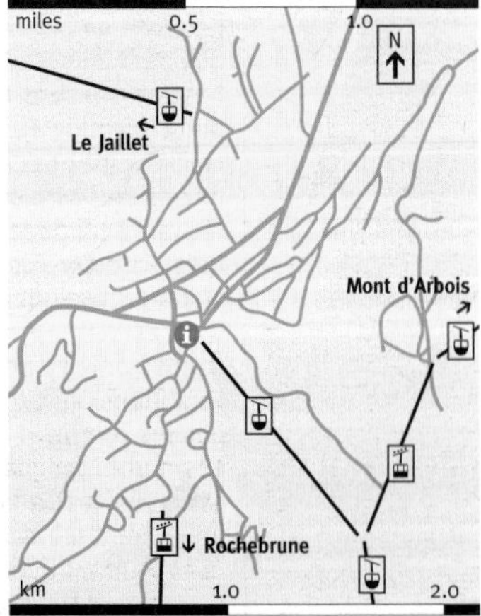

Great views of Mont Blanc from various parts of the area ➔

OT MEGEVE / M BUSCAIL





| KEY FACTS | |
|---|---|
| For Megève only | |
| Resort | 1100m 3,610ft |
| Slopes | 850-2355m 2,790-7,730ft |
| Lifts | 79 |
| Pistes | 300km 186 miles |
| Green | 17% |
| Blue | 30% |
| Red | 40% |
| Black | 13% |
| Snowmaking | 160 acres |



lifts for the bigger Mont d'Arbois sector start from an elevated suburb of the resort – though there is also a cable-car link from Rochebrune. The third sector, Le Jaillet, starts some way out on the north-west fringes of the town, badly served by buses.

Staying close to one of the main lifts makes a lot of sense. Some accommodation is a long walk from the lifts, and the half-hearted free bus services are a source of complaints. Alternative bases on the fringes of the area include St-Gervais (and Le Bettex above it), St-Nicolas, Combloux and now La Giettaz at the far end of the extended Le Jaillet sector. St-Gervais is described at the end of this chapter.

The standard weekly lift pass covers Les Contamines, and the Mont Blanc pass also covers Chamonix and Courmayeur, reached through the Mont Blanc road tunnel. A car is handy for visiting these resorts.

## THE MOUNTAINS

The three different mountains provide predominantly easy intermediate cruising, much of it prettily set in the woods and with some spectacular views. The wooded slopes make it a great resort to head for in poor weather. Some reporters complain that the piste grading is inconsistent.

### THE SLOPES
*Pretty but low*

The biggest, highest and most varied sector is **Mont d'Arbois**, accessible not only from the town but also by a gondola from La Princesse, way out to the north-east of town. It offers some wooded slopes but is mainly open, especially higher up.

Most of the slopes face more-or-less west, but there are north-east-facing slopes to Le Bettex and on down to St-Gervais. A two-stage gondola returns you to the top. You can work your way over to Mont Joux and up to the small Mont Joly area – Megève's highest slopes. And from there you can descend to the backwater village of St-Nicolas-de-Véroce (there's a splendid red run along the ridge with spectacular views of Mont Blanc in front and mile after mile of rolling peaks on both sides); tediously slow chair-lifts bring you back to Mont Joux. Directly behind Mont Joly, further up the same valley as St-Nicolas-de-Véroce, is the substantial resort of Les Contamines.

From the Mont d'Arbois lift base, the Rocharbois cable-car goes across the valley to **Rochebrune**. Alpette is the starting point for Megève's historic downhill course. A network of gentle, wooded, north-east-facing slopes, served by drags and chair-lifts, lead across to the high-point of Côte 2000.

The third area, and much the quietest, is **Le Jaillet**, accessed by gondola from just outside the north-west edge of town. This neglected area is due to be revitalised for 2004/05, thanks to a new link via the sector high-point of Le Christomet to La Giettaz, a tiny resort half-way to La Clusaz. New chair-lifts will take you to and from Le Christomet, and pistes and drag-lifts will link it to Le Torraz (1930m) at the top of Le Giettaz. In the other direction, a series of long, gentle tree-lined runs go down to Combloux.

## LIFT PASSES

**Evasion Mont Blanc**
Covers lifts at Les Contamines as well as Megève.

**Main pass**
1 day €31.50
6 days €151

**Senior citizens**
Over 60: 6 days €136
Over 80: free pass

**Children**
Under 15: 6 days €121
Under 5: free pass

**Notes**
Afternoon pass available.

**Alternative passes**
Day passes for Mégève only; weekly Mont Blanc passes (all resorts in the Mont Blanc area plus Courmayeur in Italy); Jaco pass (Le Jaillet, Christomet and Combloux).

### TERRAIN-PARKS
***Music to motivate***

There is a 320m/1,050ft slope on Mont Joux with a half-pipe, quarter-pipe, pyramid and a section of challenging moguls. A sound system at the bottom helps to motivate the faint-hearted. And there's a small park – Snowtap – on the upper slopes at Combloux.

### SNOW RELIABILITY
***The area's main weakness***

The problem is that the slopes are low, with very few runs above 2000m/ 6,560ft, and partly sunny – the Megève side of Mont d'Arbois gets the afternoon sun. So in a poor snow year, or in a warm spell, snow-cover and quality on the lower slopes can suffer badly – in which case you may need to ride the lifts back down.

Fortunately, the grassy slopes don't need much depth of snow, and the resort has expanded its snowmaking network to 252 snow-guns at the last count. Some runs are now entirely covered, including the long red Olympique run at Rochebrune. There is also a high standard of piste grooming.

### FOR EXPERTS
***Off-piste is the main attraction***

One of Megève's great advantages for expert skiers is that it does not attract many of them, who are instead lured by Chamonix's steeper descents 45 minutes away. As a result you can often make first tracks on challenging slopes many days after a fresh dump.

The Mont Joly and Mont Joux sections offer the steepest slopes. The top chair here serves a genuinely black run, and the slightly lower Epaule chair has some steep runs back down and also accesses some good off-piste, as well as pistes, down to St-Nicolas.

The steep area beneath the second stage of the Princesse gondola can be a play area of powder runs among the trees. Cote 2000 has a small section of steep runs, including good off-piste.

The black run under the Christomet chair is no longer on the map and, given decent snow, could be a good spot to practise off-piste technique.

### FOR INTERMEDIATES
***Superb if the snow is good***

Good intermediates will enjoy the Mont d'Arbois area most. The black runs below the Princesse gondola are perfectly manageable. The runs served by the Grand Vorasset drag and the most direct route between Mont d'Arbois and Le Bettex are also interesting and a reporter liked cruising the 'quiet' area beneath the Etudiants drag. The new link with La Giettaz is expected to mean access to steeper slopes there too.

It's a great area for the less confident. A number of comfortable runs lead down to Le Bettex and La Princesse from Mont d'Arbois, while

## SCHOOLS

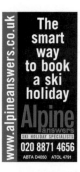

**ESF**
t 0450 210097
info@megeve-ski.com

**International**
t 0450 587888
infos@esimegeve.com

**Freeride**
t 0450 930352
info@ecolefreeride-megeve.com

**White Sensations**
t 0450 911425
info@white-sensations.com

**Classes**
(ESF prices)
5 mornings (2½hr)
€117

**Private lessons**
€35 for 1hr, for 1 or 2 people

## GUIDES

**Compagnie des Guides**
t 0450 215511
guides.megeve@wanadoo.fr



## boarding

*Boarding doesn't really fit with Megève's traditional, rather staid, upmarket image. But free-riders will find lots of untracked off-piste powder for days after new snowfalls. It's a good place to try boarding for the first time, with plenty of fairly wide, quiet, gentle runs and a lot of chair-lifts and gondolas; though there are a fair number of drag-lifts, they are generally avoidable. There are no specialist snowboard schools, but all the ski schools offer boarding lessons. There's a terrain-park on Mont Joux and a smaller one above Combloux.*

nearby Mont Joux accesses long, problem-free runs to St-Nicolas. Alpette and Cote 2000 are also suitable.

Even the timid can get a great deal of mileage in. All main valley-level lifts have easy routes down to them (although the Milloz red run to the Princesse mid-station is a real red). There are some particularly good, long, gentle cruises between Mont Joux and Megève via Mont d'Arbois. But in all sectors you'll find long, easy blue runs.

### FOR BEGINNERS
***Good choice of nursery areas***

There are beginner slopes at valley level, and more snow-sure ones at altitude on each of the main mountains. There are also plenty of very easy longer green runs to progress to – one reporter favoured those at Combloux.

### FOR CROSS-COUNTRY
***An excellent area***

There are 75km/47 miles of varied trails spread throughout the area. Some are at altitude (1300m–1550m/4,270ft–5,090ft), making lunchtime meetings with Alpine skiers simple.

### QUEUES
***Few weekday problems***

Megève is relatively queue-free during the week, except at peak holiday time. But school holidays and sunny Sunday crowds can mean some delays. The Lanchettes drag between Cote 2000 and the rest of the Rochebrune slopes gets busy – as does the cable-car linking the two mountains. Crowded pistes at Mont Joux and Mont d'Arbois can also be a problem. But slow lifts and breakdowns (eg of the gondola from St Gervais) provoke more complaints than queues or crowds.

### MOUNTAIN RESTAURANTS
***Something for all budgets***

Megève has some chic, expensive, gourmet mountain huts but plenty of cheaper options too. Booking ahead is advisable for table-service places.

The Mont d'Arbois area is very well endowed with restaurants. There are two suave places popular with poseurs with small dogs and fur coats – the Club House and the Idéal Sports. Or you can be pampered at the 'expensive but good' Mandarines. If you don't fancy the short ski from the gondola, a snowmobile shuttle can take you there! The Mont d'Arbois self-service is a 'useful meeting point' with a varied menu. Chez Tartine, 'beautifully located' half-way down the Princesse gondola, may be getting too popular for the kitchen to cope. The Ravière, tucked away in the woods near La Croix drag, is a tiny rustic hut which does a set meal and where booking is essential. The Igloo, with wonderful views of Mont Blanc, has both self- and table-service sections. At the base of the Mont Joux lift, Chez Marie du Rosay is recommended.

Prices are lower on the back side of the hill. The hut at the bottom of the Mont Rosset chair offers 'great food' and 'friendly staff'. Alpage at Les Communailles is good, too – although a regular reckons 'the place has lost something' under its new management this year. Above St-Nicolas are several little chalets offering great charm and good food and views at modest prices.

At the foot of the Cote 2000 slopes is the popular Auberge de la Cote 2000, a former farm; Radaz, up the slope a little, enjoys better views but can get busy. Alpette, atop the Rochebrune ridge, offers excellent all-round views outside, a comfortable lounge inside. A reporter enjoyed his Christmas Day lunch at the Super Megève. And Chalet Forestière is a 'cosy' retreat.

At Combloux both restaurants adjacent to the to the top car park 'serve excellent food at acceptable prices', says a reporter. The Auberge du Christomet is highly rated for its 'plats du jour' and 'touches of real originality' about the food. It is also accessible to walkers.

↑ The traffic-free centre is like a stage-set at night

MEGEVE TOURIST OFFICE

## CHILDREN

**Meg'Loisirs**
t 0450 587784
Ages 1 to 6

**Club des Piou-Piou**
t 0450 589765
Ages 3 and 4

**La Princesse**
t 0450 930086
Ages from $2^1/_2$

**Ski schools**
The schools run classes for ages from 3 or 4 (ESF prices: 5 mornings €85 for ages 3 and 4, €104 for ages 5 to 12).

### SCHOOLS AND GUIDES

***Several good options***

The International school has traditionally been more popular with readers than the ESF, but we have several reports of successful private lessons with the ESF. White Sensations is a small school with eight BASI-trained instructors, recommended this year for its 'fun' children's classes – 'my six-year old progressed quickly'. Both main schools offer expeditions to the Vallée Blanche and heli-skiing (in Italy), as well as normal teaching. Individual guides are available. We had a great morning powder skiing in the trees with Alex Périnet (06 8542 8339).

### FACILITIES FOR CHILDREN

***Language problems***

The kindergartens offer a wide range of activities. But lack of English-speaking staff could be a drawback. The slopes are family-friendly and the schools rated by reporters (see above).

## STAYING THERE

### HOW TO GO

***Few packages***

Relatively few British tour operators go to Megève, but there is an impressive range of accommodation.

**Chalets** A few UK tour operators offer catered chalets. For a cheap and very cheerful base, you won't do better than Stanford's Sylvana – a creaky, unpretentious old hotel, reachable on skis, run along chalet lines. Stanford also offers another similar property, the Rond Point, in the centre, as well as a smaller, smarter place. Simon Butler Skiing and SkiBB offer tuition-based holidays combined with chalet accommodation.

**Hotels** Megève offers a range of exceptionally stylish and welcoming hotels. There are simpler places, too.

((((4 **Mont Blanc** (0450 212002) Megève's traditional leading hotel – elegant and fashionable. Right in the centre, and close to the main gondola.

((((4 **Chalet du Mont d'Arbois** (0450 212503) Prettily decorated, former Rothschild family home, now a Relais & Châteaux hotel in a secluded position above town, near the Mont d'Arbois gondola.

((((4 **Fer à Cheval** (0450 213039) Rustic-chic at its best, with a warmly welcoming wood-and-stone interior and excellent food. Close to the centre. 'One of my most memorable hotel stays' writes a reporter.

(((3 **The Prairie** (0450 214855) Central, 'reasonably priced' B&B. Close to the Chamois lift.

## GETTING THERE

**Air** Geneva 70km/43 miles (1hr); Lyon 180km/112 miles (2½hr).

**Rail** Sallanches (12km/7 miles); regular buses from station.

## ACTIVITIES

**Indoor** Palais des Sports (ice rink, tennis, climbing wall, swimming pool, sauna, solarium, gym), beauty treatments, bridge, bowling, language classes, museum, library, cinemas, pottery, casino, concerts

**Outdoor** Cleared paths, snow-shoe excursions, ice rink, curling, sleigh rides, plane and helicopter trips, paragliding, hot-air ballooning, adventure park

**Phone numbers**
From abroad use the prefix +33 and omit the initial '0' of the phone number.

## TOURIST OFFICES

**Megève**
**t** 0450 212728
megeve@megeve.com
www.megeve.com

**St-Gervais**
**t** 0450 477608
welcome@st-gervais.net
www.st-gervais.net

(3) **Coin du Feu** (0450 210494) 'Very well managed' chalet midway between Rochebrune and Chamois lifts.
(3) **Grange d'Arly** (0450 587788) Wrong side of the road, but still quite close to the centre; a beautifully furnished chalet.
(3) **Ferme Hôtel Duvillard** (0450 211462) Smartly restored farmhouse, perfectly positioned for the slopes, at the foot of the Mont d'Arbois gondola.
(2) **Gai Soleil** (0450 210070) Comfortable family-run place – five minutes' walk from the centre of town and the main gondola.
(2) **Mourets** (0450 210476) Entirely inconvenient location but repeatedly recommended by readers: 'basic but spacious with good food and views'; 'very friendly'; 'excellent hosts'.
(2) **Sévigné** (0450 212309) Ten minutes from the centre, but 'really delightful – very quaint, excellent food'.
**Self-catering** There are some very comfortable and well-positioned apartments – not cheap. You can reduce the cost by renting outside town. The tourist office in Combloux is a good starting point.

### EATING OUT
***Very French***

Megève has lots of upmarket restaurants – many recommended in the gastro guides. The Ferme de Mon Père, for example, has three Michelin rosettes. This and the restaurants in all the best hotels are excellent but extremely expensive. The Cintra, also expensive and fashionable, is 'great for fresh seafood'. Michel Gaudin is one of the best in town – 'excellent', with good value set menus.

The Brasserie Centrale is recommended for its 'good value and wide-ranging menu' and the Flocons de Sel for its 'excellent service'. The Prieuré is 'highly recommended – lots of atmosphere, excellent food, good value'. Some reporters wish for more variety. The Phnom-Penh is one of the few less conventional possibilities.

### APRES-SKI
***Strolling and jazz***

Megève is a great place to stroll around after the lifts close. But we found few atmospheric bars for a beer. And those looking for loud disco-bars will also be disappointed. Our favourite place was the Club de Jazz (aka the 5 Rues) – a very popular, if rather expensive, jazz club-cum-cocktail bar, that gets some big-name musicians and opens from tea-time to late. The bar at the Cintra has 'friendly staff' and felt more 'local' according to one visitor. The Cocoon and Rosy Crève Coeur are popular with Brits. The casino has more slot machines than blackjack tables. And there's also a piano bar and disco.

### OFF THE SLOPES
***Lots to do***

There is a 'fantastic' sports centre with pool, an outdoor ice rink, plenty of outdoor activities, three cinemas and a weekly market. Trips to Annecy and Chamonix are possible. And St-Gervais is worth visiting for a spa treatment. Walks are excellent, with 50km/30 miles of marked paths classified for difficulty on a special map. Meeting friends on the slopes for lunch is easy.

### STAYING UP THE MOUNTAIN
***Several possibilities***

As well as mid-mountain Le Bettex, a small collection of hotels, private chalets and modern apartments, there are hotels further up, near the summit of Mont d'Arbois. One is the 3-star Igloo (0450 930584), another the 2-star Chez la Tante (0450 213130).

## St-Gervais 850m/2,790ft

St-Gervais is a handsome 19th-century spa town set in a narrow river gorge, on the far side of Mont d'Arbois, with access to the slopes via a 20-person gondola from just outside the town. It's an urban but pleasant place, with interesting food shops and cosy bars, thermal baths and an Olympic skating rink. Prices are noticeably lower than in Megève. Buses are reported to be regular and convenient. Two hotels convenient for the gondola are the Hostellerie du Nerey (0450 934521), a pleasantly traditional 2-star, and the 'quite charming' 3-star Carlina (0450 934110), the best in town, with a small pool and sauna.

You can go up, on the opposite side of St-Gervais, on a rack-and-pinion railway which in 1904 was intended to go all the way to the top of Mont Blanc but didn't quite make it that far – it actually takes you to the slopes of Les Houches (see Chamonix chapter).

Its position makes St-Gervais a good base for touring the resorts covered by the Mont Blanc regional lift pass, especially if you have a car.

# Les Menuires

*The bargain base for the Trois Vallées – but pick your spot with care*

## COSTS

①②③④⑤⑥

## RATINGS

**The slopes**

| | |
|---|---|
| Snow | **** |
| Extent | ***** |
| Expert | **** |
| Intermediate | ***** |
| Beginner | *** |
| Convenience | ***** |
| Queues | **** |
| Mountain restaurants | *** |

**The rest**

| | |
|---|---|
| Scenery | *** |
| Resort charm | * |
| Off-slope | * |

## NEWS

For 2004/05 a six-pack with covers to Roc des 3 Marches is planned to replace two drag-lifts. It will start from the blue run down from Tougnète and make the run from Méribel and St-Martin to Les Menuires a proper ski rather than a traverse.

For 2003/04 more snowmaking was installed, and a six-pack replaced two drags above Les Menuires.

The resort continues to grow, with attractive new developments such as the MGM Hameau des Airelles, which will replace an existing building that is being demolished.

**Phone numbers**
From abroad use the prefix +33 and omit the initial '0' of the phone number.

## TOURIST OFFICE

**t** 0479 007300
lesmenuires@lesmenuires.com
www.lesmenuires.com



- + The cheapest base for the 3V
- + Great local slopes on La Masse, and quick links with Val-Thorens
- + Extensive snowmaking
- + Lots of slope-side accommodation
- + New, outlying parts of the resort are much more attractive than the core
- + Good specialist food shops, although they are found in ...

- − Gloomy indoor shopping malls
- − Resort core is dominated by big, dreary apartment blocks
- − Main intermediate and beginner slopes get a lot of sun
- − No woodland slopes
- − Some of the lower slopes get dangerously crowded as well as over-exposed to the sun

**Les Menuires is developing in the right way, adding traditional-style satellites where you can ignore the brutal architecture at the core of the resort. And the Belleville valley has a lot of terrain, including the excellent, challenging slopes on La Masse, rarely used by visitors from the other valleys.**

## THE RESORT

The original buildings that surround the main lift base, La Croisette, are among the worst examples of the thoughtless building of the 1960s/70s. The main centre has a particularly dire indoor shopping gallery. But the resort is trying hard to lose its reputation as one of the ugliest in the Alps. In outposts such as Reberty and Hameau des Marmottes, the latest additions are in stone-and-wood chalet style – and there are some luxury developments. These outposts have their own shops and bars – Les Bruyères is now a more-or-less self-contained resort.

## THE MOUNTAINS

Les Menuires is set at about the tree line, with almost entirely open slopes.
**Slopes** The major part of the network spreads across the broad, west-facing mountainside between Les Menuires and St-Martin, with links to the Méribel valley at four points (mostly red runs, but there is one blue) as well as a link up the valley to Val-Thorens. Two fast chairs and a gondola go up from La Croisette. Lifts to La Masse, a more challenging mountain, start below the village – a gondola and a chair-lift.
**Terrain-parks** There's a terrain-park with a half-pipe just above the village.
**Snow reliability** La Masse's height and orientation ensure good snow for a long season. The west-facing slopes have lots of snowmaking but the snow lower down is often icy or slushy.
**Experts** The upper slopes of La Masse are virtually all of stiff red/soft black steepness. Dame Blanche is a particularly fine black, on the front of the hill – we'd love to catch it when groomed, or after fresh snow. There is also a huge amount of off-piste, although a reader this year found it spoiled by the sheer numbers using it. Vallon du Lou is a broad, sweeping route towards Val-Thorens that used to be marked as an itinerary on the piste map. Other off-piste routes go in the opposite direction to various villages. And a reader recommends the descent from Roc de Fer to the village of Béranger.
**Intermediates** With good snow, you may be content with the local slopes, which are virtually all blue and red. In poor snow you can head up to Val-Thorens, and there's blue-run as well as red-run access. Don't miss La Masse – the blacks are not super-steep – but beware the steep Masse drag-lift.
**Beginners** There are wide and gentle slopes and a special lift pass for beginners, but the snow quality on the nursery slopes is a worry. The blue slopes you progress to can get extremely crowded.
**Snowboarding** The number of drags is low and dwindling further year by year; but there are some flattish sections of piste in places. There are huge amounts of terrain to suit free-riders.
**Cross-country** There are 28km/17 miles of prepared trails along the valley floor between St-Martin-de Belleville and Val-Thorens.

If they had built Les Menuires in the pretty chalet style of the newest parts of Reberty right from the start, we'd like the resort a lot more ↗

SNOWPIX.COM / CHRIS GILL

## KEY FACTS

| | |
|---|---|
| **Resort** | 1850m<br>6,070ft |
| for the Three Valleys | |
| **Slopes** | 1260-3230m<br>4,130-10,600ft |
| **Lifts** | 197 |
| **Pistes** | 600km<br>373 miles |
| **Green** | 21% |
| **Blue** | 33% |
| **Red** | 35% |
| **Black** | 11% |
| **Snowmaking** | 1500 guns |
| For Les Menuires / St-Martin only | |
| **Slopes** | 1450-2850m<br>4,760-9,350ft |
| **Lifts** | 41 |
| **Pistes** | 160km<br>99 miles |
| **Green** | 10% |
| **Blue** | 37% |
| **Red** | 39% |
| **Black** | 14% |
| **Snowmaking** | 354 guns |



**Queues** The fast six-packs up from La Croisette seem to have largely solved the problem of queues there, but have perhaps contributed to the worsening problem of acute overcrowding on the slopes down to the resort centre.

**Mountain restaurants** There are few remarkable places in this sector of the 3V. Just above Les Menuires is the very pleasant but quite pricey Etoile. At higher altitude there is 'excellent food and below average prices' at the Alpage, on the 4 Vents piste. Many people head down to the villages for lunch; you retain some sense of being on the mountain at the 'good value' Ferme, beside the piste at Reberty.

**Schools and guides** The ESF has the monopoly here; we lack recent reports.

**Facilities for children** This is very much a family resort, but a visitor reports that no English was spoken at the 'generally grubby' resort nursery and that her children were not allowed to stay together. Family Ski Company has its own nursery in Reberty – and sends a minder with kids going to ski-school, to make up for ESF 'brutality'.

## STAYING THERE

**How to go** Some big UK tour operators offer holidays here, and some chalet operators have a presence in Reberty. There is a Club Med above Reberty, praised by a reporter last year.

**Chalets** Reberty Village has been virtually taken over by UK chalet operators. Family Ski Company has several attractive properties; Cabaniols has a splendid living room.

**Hotels** None of the hotels is above 3-star grading. Ours Blanc (0479 006166) is the best – a chalet-style 3-star on the slopes above Reberty 1850. Maeva Latitudes (0479 007510) is set on the lower fringe of Les Bruyères.

**Self-catering** The newer apartments are more attractive. The Montagnettes and Alpages (with a pool), both in Reberty, are among the best. Résidence les Cotes d'Or is 'very spacious for a French resort'. Choose apartments with care though – a 2004 reporter tells of 'cheap bunk beds, insufficient crockery and linen, a 2ft square bath and nowhere to store or wax a snowboard.'

**Eating out** Though some restaurants lack atmosphere, most serve good food. Alternatives to Savoyard include Italian and Tex-Mex. The Trattoria, with its 'good menu' and 'rustic French' ambience, has been recommended. The set menus at the Snow are 'reasonably priced' with 'particularly good' tartiflette. The La Marmite de Géant has 'excellent food, good prices and pleasant atmosphere'. Chalet-boy night off is no problem in Reberty: La Ferme is one of the best places in the resort.

**Après-ski** There is no shortage of bars in La Croisette, but many are within the dreadful shopping gallery and a 2004 reporter says 'too many had a British feel and advertised big-screen football'. The Taverne bar in Les Bruyères is 'lively and welcoming'. There are discos.

**Off the slopes** This is a resort for keen skiers and boarders.



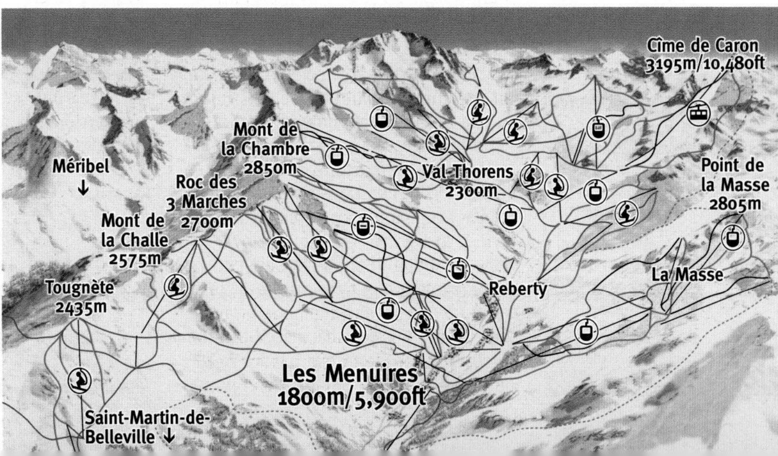

SNOWPIX.COM / CHRIS GILL

# Méribel

*Big chalet-style resort in the centre of the wonderful Three Valleys*



## COSTS

①②③④⑤⑥

## RATINGS

**The slopes**

| | |
|---|---|
| Snow | *** |
| Extent | ***** |
| Expert | **** |
| Intermediate | ***** |
| Beginner | **** |
| Convenience | *** |
| Queues | **** |
| Mountain restaurants | *** |

**The rest**

| | |
|---|---|
| Scenery | *** |
| Resort charm | *** |
| Off-slope | *** |

## NEWS

For 2004/05 a new high-speed chair is planned to replace the slow Plan de l'Homme chair-lift from Méribel to halfway up Tougnète. This will take pressure off the Tougnète gondola in the morning peak.

The red Bouvreuil and two blue pistes, the Sizerin and the flat Ours – in the Mottaret sector linking to and from Mont Vallon – will be remodelled. Snowmaking will be increased, with another 128 machines.



- ➕ In the centre of the biggest linked lift network in the world – ideal for intermediates, great for experts, too
- ➕ Modern, constantly improved lift system means little queueing and rapid access to all slopes
- ➕ Good piste grooming and snowmaking
- ➕ Pleasant chalet-style architecture

- ➖ Not the best snow in the Three Valleys, and pistes can get crowded
- ➖ Main village spreads over a wide area, with lots of accommodation well away from the slopes
- ➖ Expensive
- ➖ Méribel-Mottaret and Méribel Village satellites are rather lifeless
- ➖ Full of Brits

**For keen piste-bashers who like big resorts but dislike tacky purpose-built ones, Méribel is difficult to beat. The Three Valleys can keep anyone amused for a fortnight – and Méribel-Mottaret, in particular, has quick access to every part. And, unlike other purpose-built resorts, Méribel has always insisted on chalet-style architecture. What more could you ask?**

**Well, our ➖ points are mostly non-trivial. And other Three Valleys resorts have the edge in some respects. For better snow opt for Courchevel, and for the best snow Val-Thorens. For less crowded runs, Courchevel 1650. For a smaller village St-Martin or La Tania. For lower prices, Les Menuires. But these other resorts have their drawbacks, of course. Regular visitors love Méribel. And we still have a soft spot for it (one of us learned to ski here).**

## THE RESORT

Méribel occupies the central valley of the Three Valleys system and consists of two main resort villages.

The original resort of Méribel-les-Allues (now simply known as Méribel) is built on a single steepish west-facing hillside with the home piste running down beside it to the main lift stations at the valley bottom. All the buildings are wood-clad, low-rise and chalet style, making this one of the most tastefully designed of French purpose-built resorts. A road winds up from the village centre to the Rond Point des Pistes, and goes on through woods to the outpost of the Altiport (an airstrip with snow-covered runway for little planes with skis).

The resort was founded by a Brit, Peter Lindsay, in 1938, and has retained a strong British presence ever since – 'More like Kensington than France,' commented one visitor last year. It has grown enormously over recent years, and although some accommodation is right on the piste, much of the newer building is more than a walk away – check your location carefully if you don't like having to rely on buses (or tour operator minibuses).

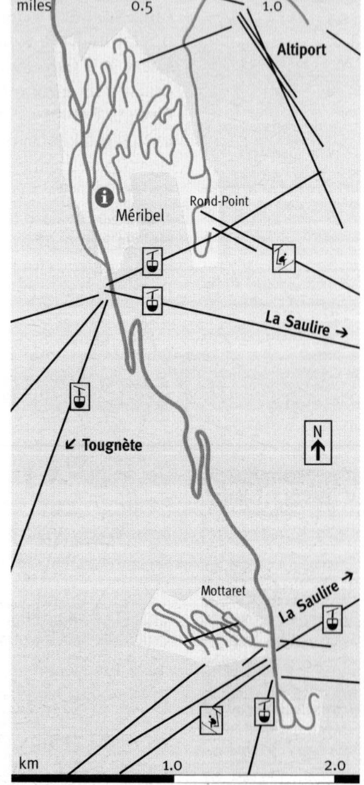

The Tougnète side gets the morning sun; from the top you can drop down to St-Martin or Les Menuires; you can just make out the two half-pipes of the Moon Park at mid-mountain ↗

OT MERIBEL / JEAN-MAURICE GOUEDARD

One clear exception is Belvédère, an upmarket enclave built on the opposite side of the home piste (there's a tunnel for road access). There are collections of shops and restaurants at a couple of points on the road through the resort – Altitude 1600 and Plateau de Morel. The hotels and apartments of Altiport enjoy splendid isolation in the woods, and are convenient for some of the slopes.

The satellite village of Méribel-Mottaret was developed in the early 1970s and is very centrally placed in the Three Valleys ski area, offering swift access in one direction to Courchevel and in another to Mont du Vallon, Val-Thorens and Les Menuires.

The original development was beside the piste on the east-facing slope, but in recent years the resort has spread up the opposite hillside and further up the valley. Both sides are served by lifts for pedestrians – but the gondola up to the original village stops at 7.30pm and it's a long, tiring walk up.

Mottaret looks modern, despite wood-cladding on its apartment blocks. Even so, it's more attractive than many other resorts built for slope-side convenience. It has many fewer shops and bars and much less après-ski than Méribel. Some visitors have found it 'lacking in atmosphere', but we are getting an increasing number of positive reports on it. One 2004 reporter liked it for being 'quieter than Méribel with easier access to the pistes', and another for being 'more cosmopolitan and civilised without the braying Ruperts and Henriettas of Méribel'.

In recent years the hamlet of Méribel-Village, on the road from Méribel to La Tania and Courchevel, has acquired a chair-lift up to Altiport with a blue run back and has developed into a mini-resort. There are some luxury chalets and apartments here but little else apart from a fitness centre, bar, pizzeria and a couple of restaurants; but if nightlife is not a priority it's a pleasant place to stay.

## KEY FACTS

| | |
|---|---|
| **Resort** | 1400-1700m<br>4,590-5,580ft |
| For the Three Valleys | |
| **Slopes** | 1260-3230m<br>4,130-10,600ft |
| **Lifts** | 197 |
| **Pistes** | 600km<br>373 miles |
| **Green** | 21% |
| **Blue** | 33% |
| **Red** | 35% |
| **Black** | 11% |
| **Snowmaking** | 1500 guns |
| For Méribel only | |
| **Slopes** | 1400-2950m<br>4,590-9,680ft |
| **Lifts** | 61 |
| **Pistes** | 150km<br>93 miles |
| **Green** | 15% |
| **Blue** | 45% |
| **Red** | 28% |
| **Black** | 12% |
| **Snowmaking** | 556 guns |





There are some alternative bases lower down the mountain (and the price scale), described at the end of this chapter.

Local buses are free (though some readers complain they are not frequent enough and are overcrowded at peak times), and many UK tour operators run their own minibus services to and from the lifts. A car is mainly of use for outings to other resorts.

Lift passes for six days or more give you a day in Val-d'Isère-Tignes (an hour and a half away by car), Paradiski (La Plagne and Les Arcs, an hour or so away). But these expeditions involve long drives down to the valley and back up to the other resort. Why bother?

## THE MOUNTAINS

Most of the slopes are above the tree line, but there are some sheltered runs for bad-weather days. The lift system is well planned to cut out walks and climbs. Piste grading is not always reliable – there are some testing blues – and in an area where some slopes get the afternoon sun, snow conditions have a huge impact on difficulty. Daily maps are now available, as in Courchevel, showing which runs have been groomed overnight.

The slopes of Courchevel, Les Menuires and Val-Thorens are covered in separate chapters. The last covers the 'fourth valley' – the Maurienne slopes, above Orelle. The links between resorts are not very well signed, and you have to plan your return carefully, taking account of likely queues and the weather. Taxi rides from Courchevel are affordable; the trip from Les Menuires is much longer.

### THE SLOPES
### *Highly efficient lift system*

The Méribel valley runs north-south. On the eastern side, gondolas leave both Méribel and Mottaret for **La Saulire**. From here you can head back down towards either village or down the other side of the ridge towards Courchevel.

From Méribel a gondola rises to **Tougnète**, on the western side of the valley, from where you can get down to Les Menuires or St-Martin-de-Belleville. You can also head for Mottaret from here. From there, a fast chair then a drag take you to another entry point for the Les Menuires runs.

The Mottaret area has seen rapid mechanisation over the last decade. The **Plattières** gondola rises up the valley to the south, ending at yet another entry point to the Les Menuires area. To the east of this is the big stand-up gondola to the top of **Mont du Vallon** (there are wonderful views from the top). A fast quad from near this area goes south up to **Mont de la Chambre**, giving direct access to Val-Thorens.

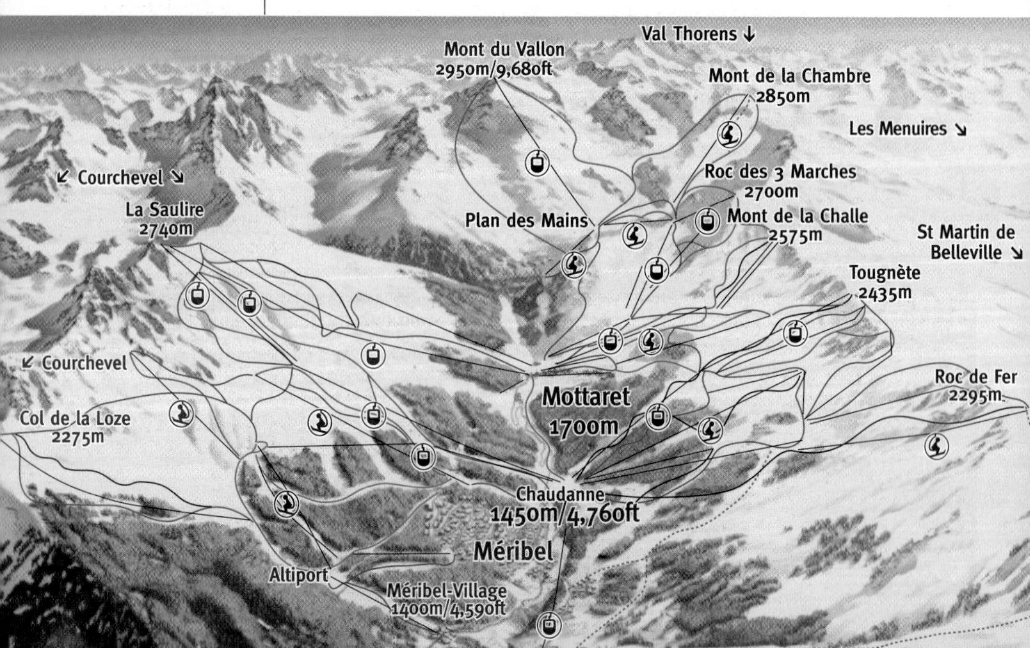

## LIFT PASSES

**Three Valleys**
Covers all lifts in Courchevel, La Tania, Méribel, Val-Thorens, Les Menuires and St-Martin-de-Belleville.

**Main pass**
1 day €40
6 days €198

**Senior citizen**
Over 60: 6 days €158
Over 72: free pass

**Children**
Under 13: 6 days €149
Under 5: free pass

**Notes**
Half-day and pedestrian passes available. Six-day pass and over valid for one day in Espace Killy (Tignes-Val-d'Isère), Paradiski (La Plagne-Les Arcs), Pralognan and Les Saisies.

**Alternative passes**
Méribel pass covers Méribel and Méribel-Mottaret only.

### TERRAIN-PARKS
***There's a choice***

The Plattières terrain-park – accessed from the second stage of the Plattières gondola – has two half-pipes (one for experts, one for novices), two quarter-pipes, three tables, a spine and a 650m/2,130ft boarder-cross. The Moon Park, near the Arpasson drag above the Tougnète gondola mid-station, has two half-pipes and a boarder-cross with various toys to play on.

### SNOW RELIABILITY
***Not the best in the Three Valleys***

Méribel's slopes aren't the highest in the Three Valleys, and they mainly face east or west; the latter get the full force of the afternoon sun. So snow conditions are often better elsewhere. And grooming seems to be rather better in neighbouring Courchevel.

The lower runs now have substantial snowmaking and lack of snow is rarely a problem, but ice or slush at the end of the day can be. The north-west-facing slopes above Altiport generally have decent snow. See For Intermediates for criticisms of the so-called blue runs back into Mottaret.

At the southern end of the valley, towards Les Menuires and Val-Thorens, a lot of runs are north-facing and keep their snow well, as do the runs on Mont du Vallon.

### FOR EXPERTS
***Exciting choices***

The size of the Three Valleys means experts are well catered for. In the Méribel valley, head for Mont du Vallon – voted 'the best skiing in the whole of the Trois Vallées' by one reporter's group last year. The long, steep Combe du Vallon run here is classified red; it's a wonderful, long, fast cruise when groomed, but presents plenty of challenge when mogulled. And there's a beautiful itinéraire (no longer marked on the piste map) in the next valley to the main pistes, leading back to the bottom of the gondola.

The slopes down from the top of the Val-Thorens sector were all off-piste when we old hands first visited Méribel. Since the new lifts were installed up here, there are two pistes back from Val-Thorens, but still plenty of opportunity for getting off-piste in the wide open bowls.

A good mogul run is down the side of the double Roc de Tougne drag-lift which leads up to Mont de la Challe. And there is a steep black run all the way down the Tougnète gondola back to Méribel. Apart from a shallow section near the mid-station, it's unrelenting most of the way.

At the north end of the valley the Face run was built for the women's downhill in the 1992 Olympics. Served by a fast quad, it's a splendid cruise when freshly groomed, and you can terrify yourself just by imagining what it must be like to go straight down.

Nothing on the Saulire side is as steep or as demanding as on the other side of the valley. The Mauduit red run is quite challenging, though – it used to be black.

Throughout the area there are good off-piste opportunities. The ESF runs excellent-value guided groups.

### FOR INTERMEDIATES
***Paradise found***

Méribel and the rest of the Three Valleys is a paradise for intermediates; there are few other resorts where a keen piste-basher can cover so many miles so easily. Virtually every slope in the region has a good intermediate run down it, and to describe them would take a book in itself.

For less adventurous intermediates, the run from the second station of the Plattières gondola above Mottaret back to the first station is ideal, and used a lot by the ski school. It is a gentle, north-facing, cruising run and is generally in good condition. Below that can get tricky and bumpy later in the day; 'carnage when the beginner classes went up,' said a 2004 reporter, who thought 'the problem could be solved by giving the slope a quick groom at lunchtime'. 'People

### boarding

*Méribel is increasingly boarder-oriented. The terrain locally and further afield has lots to offer and you rarely have to take a drag-lift – but there are quite a lot of flat sections on some of the main ways to/from Val-Thorens. The resort hosts a number of big-air and boarder-cross competitions. Specialist shops include Board Brains (in Méribel), and Quiksilver Gotcha Surf (in Mottaret).*

↑ This is a perfect beginner run above Altiport – indeed it was Dave Watts' first-ever run on skis, longer ago than he cares to remember

SNOWPIX.COM / CHRIS GILL

## SCHOOLS

**ESF Méribel**
t 0479 086031
esfmeribel@wanadoo.fr

**ESF Méribel-Mottaret**
t 0479 004949
esfmottaret@wanadoo.fr

**Magic in Motion**
t 0479 085336
meribel@magicinmotion.co.uk

**New Generation**
t 0479 010318
(UK: 01483 205402)
info@skinewgen.com

**Classes**
(ESF prices)
6 half-days (2½hr per day): €148

**Private lessons**
€86 for 2hr for 1 or 2 people

## GUIDES

**Mountain guide office**
t 0479 003038





spreadeagled everywhere, with the bloodwagons overwhelmed,' said another. We think the run into Mottaret on the other side of the valley gets dangerously icy and crowded too. The lift company needs to solve both these problems, which spoil an otherwise ideal intermediate area.

Even early intermediates should find the runs over into the other valleys well within their capabilities, opening up further vast amounts of intermediate runs. Go to Courchevel or Val-Thorens for the better snow.

Virtually all the pistes on both sides of the Méribel valley will suit more advanced intermediates. Most of the reds are on the difficult side.

### FOR BEGINNERS
***Strengths and weaknesses***

Méribel has an excellent slope for beginners, but it's out of the resort at Altiport, which is a bit of a nuisance. There is a small nursery slope at Rond-Point, at the top of the village, mainly used by the children's ski school.

The Altiport area is accessible from the village by the Morel chair-lift, or by free bus. Once you have found your feet, a free drag-lift takes you half-way up one of the best and most attractively situated green pistes we know, the Blanchot – long, gentle, wide and tree-lined, with little through-traffic. Next, a longer drag takes you to the top of the Blanchot, then a chair a bit higher, then another chair higher still, on to an excellent blue usually blessed with good snow.

### FOR CROSS-COUNTRY
***Scenic routes***

There are about 33km/21 miles in total. The main area is in the pine forest near Altiport, a pleasant introduction to those who want to try cross-country for the first time. There's also a loop around Lake Tuéda, in the nature reserve at Mottaret, and for the more experienced an itinéraire from Altiport to Courchevel.

### QUEUES
***3V traffic a persistent problem***

Huge lift investment over the years has paid off in making the area virtually queue-free most of the time, despite the huge numbers of people. Generally, if you do find a queue, there is an alternative quieter route you can take. The real problems result from the tidal flows of people between the three valleys, in the morning (when the tide coincides with the start of ski school) and the late afternoon. One 2004 reporter, who also said the 'lifts kept stopping while I was on them', thought the queues 'horrendous'. Black spots to avoid at these times are: the Tougnète gondola at Méribel towards Les Menuires (though this may be eased by the new fast chair planned for 2004/05); the Plattières gondola at Mottaret towards Les Menuires; the Côte Brune chair to Mont de la Chambre; the Plan des Mains chair (used by everyone returning from Val-Thorens), despite its upgrade to a six-pack.

### MOUNTAIN RESTAURANTS
***Less than wonderful***

There are lots of places on the piste map, but few that are worth singling out – and not enough to meet the demand, so many get very crowded (you might want to take lunch early or late). The Chardonnet, at the mid-station of the Mottaret-Saulire gondola, has table-service and excellent food, but is expensive. The large terrace at the Rhododendrons, at the top of the Altiport drag, remains a popular spot – its varied menu encouraged one reader to eat there several times during his holiday. The Rond Point, just below the mid-point of the Rhodos gondola, offers tasty paninis as well as delicious rösti. The cosy Crêtes, below the top of the Tougnète gondola, continues to provide 'good food and service'. Lower down, at the bottom of the Roc de Tougne drags, the Tougniat has 'very good self-service food'. The pricey Altiport hotel scarcely counts as a mountain restaurant, but has a great outdoor buffet in good weather and the 'best tarts in town'. Two self-service places notable for their views are the Pierres Plates, at the top of Saulire, and the Sittelle ('good choice of cooked and cold buffet lunches')

above the first section of the Plattières gondola. The Blanchot, next to the road to the altiport, is recommended as 'a good place to meet non-skiers'.

**SCHOOLS AND GUIDES**

***No shortage of instructors***

The main schools all have English-speaking instructors.

The ESF is by far the biggest, with over 300 instructors. It has a special international section with instructors speaking good English. Recent reports have been mixed; we've heard tales of instructors adopting the 'follow me' approach, but a 2004 visitor found their instructor 'very thorough'. The ESF offers useful alternatives to standard classes, such as off-piste groups, heli-skiing on the Italian border and tours of the Three Valleys.

Magic in Motion, the second largest school, also offers heli-skiing, couloir and extreme sessions in addition to skiing and boarding lessons. It keeps classes small and generally gets good reports, though a 2003 visitor was not convinced it was any better than ESF.

New Generation, a British school which expanded from Courchevel to Méribel three seasons ago, is now well-established and receives excellent reports. One reader said, 'I cannot recommend them highly enough, they were patient and kept groups small.' See the Courchevel chapter for other reporters' comments.

We've had a couple of damning 2004 reports on Snow Systems, which operates out of Mottaret. An adult and two children were put in classes way below their ability level and the school refused to let them change classes without huge pressure including 'a stand-up row at the meeting point' by a parent who advises, 'Avoid Snow Systems like the plague.'

**FACILITIES FOR CHILDREN**

***Tour operators rule***

We guess readers needing childcare plug into the facilities of chalet operators who run their own nurseries – we rarely get reports on the resort facilities.

## STAYING THERE

**HOW TO GO**

***Huge choice but few bargains***

Package holidays are easy to find, both with big UK tour operators and smaller Méribel specialists. There are three Club Med 'villages', all in their top comfort category, none with the usual children's club facilities.

## CHILDREN

**Les Saturnins**
t 0479 086690
Ages 18mnth to 3yr; 6 days €190

**Les P'tits Loups**
t 0479 086031 (Mér)
t 0479 004949 (Mot)
Ages 3 to 5; 9am-5pm; 6 days €190

**Childminder list**
Available from the tourist office

**Ski school**
The ESF runs classes for ages 5 to 13: 6 half-days (2½hr) €118.

## GETTING THERE

**Air** Geneva 135km/84 miles (3½hr); Lyon 185km/115 miles (3½hr); Chambéry 95km/59 miles (1½hr).

**Rail** Moûtiers (18km/11 miles); regular buses to Méribel.





**Chalets** Méribel has more chalets dedicated to the British market than any other resort, and over 50 operators offering them. What really distinguishes Méribel is the range of recently built luxury chalets. Some are perfectly positioned for the slopes, but many have minibuses on hand to compensate for their inconvenient locations. Méribel specialists include Meriski which has an extensive portfolio, including some of our own favourites, Purple Ski which has two chalets in Mottaret (one with a hot-tub and sauna), one in Méribel-Village (with an outdoor hot-tub) and one in Méribel and a couple of companies in Les Allues (see end of this chapter). At the top of the luxury end of the market, VIP has several sumptuous looking places, mostly with saunas and hot-tubs; sister company Snowline has some not far behind; Kaluma runs the splendid Lodge; and Descent International has a couple of the best chalets. Lotus Supertravel's has a couple of places. Of the few chalet-hotels, Mark Warner's Tarentaise (with a sauna and hot-tub) has a great position, right on the piste at Mottaret. Other companies to check out are listed in our Resort directory / index at the back of the book.

**Hotels** Méribel has some excellent hotels, but they're not cheap.

((((4 **Grand Coeur** (0479 086003) Our favourite almost-affordable hotel in Méribel. Just above the village centre. Welcoming, mature building with plush lounge. Magnificent food. Huge hot-tub, sauna, etc.

((((4 **Altiport** (0479 005232) Modern and luxurious hotel, isolated at the foot of the Altiport lifts. Convenient for Courchevel, not for Val-Thorens.

((((4 **Mont-Vallon** (0479 004400) The best hotel at Mottaret; good food, and excellently situated for the Three Valleys' pistes. Pool, sauna, hot-tub, squash, fitness room, etc.

(((3 **Arolles** (0479 0040400) Right on the slopes at Mottaret. 'Friendly, unpretentious, good food, highly recommended,' says a 2004 visitor. Pool and sauna.

(((3 **Adray Télébar** (0479 086026) Welcoming piste-side chalet with pretty, rustic rooms, good food and popular sun terrace.

((2 **Roc** (0479 086416) A good-value B&B hotel, in the centre, with a bar-restaurant and crêperie below.

**Self-catering** There is a huge number of apartments and chalets to let in both Méribel and Mottaret. Make sure that the place you book is conveniently situated and has enough space. A reader recommends the Merilys apartments in Méribel: 'A fine place with very helpful staff.'

**Phone numbers**
From abroad use the prefix +33 and omit the initial '0' of the phone number.

**EATING OUT**
***Fair choice***

There is a reasonable selection of restaurants, from ambitious French cuisine to relatively cheap pizza and pasta. For the best food in town, in plush surroundings, there are top hotels – Grand Coeur ('so pleased, we ate there several times'), Allodis and Kouisena ('beef fondue excellent') in the Eterlou. Other reader recommendations include: Chez Kiki – 'the best steaks'; the Taverne – 'relaxed atmosphere'; the Tremplin – 'good for families, friendly service, reasonably priced'; the Enfants Terribles – 'wonderful roast beef carvery'; the Refuge – 'lovely crêpes'; and the Cactus Café – 'always busy and friendly, mainly British staff', 'cheap meals, quieter in the evenings'.

Alternatives include the Galette, the Fromagerie, the Cava, the Plantin (on the road out towards La Tania) and Cro-Magnon up the hill in Morel – all popular for raclette and fondue. The Marée Blanche specialises in seafood and the Blanchot, just below Altiport, offers the choice of two dining areas, one dedicated to dishes of the region. Another reader recommends the Crocodile in the Hameau at Mottaret. Scott's does good American-style food.

At Les Allues, the Tsaretta will provide a free taxi service to transport you to enjoy the imaginative creations of the Australian chef. The Chaumière offers 'good value inclusive menus in pleasant, rustic surroundings'. The Chemina is another recommendation as

## ACTIVITIES

**Indoor** Parc Olympique (ice rink, swimming pool, climbing wall, karting on ice), fitness centres in hotels, bowling, library, two cinemas, museum, language and computer courses

**Outdoor** Flying lessons and excursions, snow-mobiles, snow-shoe excursions, cleared paths, paragliding, dog-sledding, hot air ballooning





is the Martagon at Le Raffort between Méribel and Les Allues.

## APRES-SKI

### *Méribel rocks – loudly*

Méribel's après-ski revolves around British-run places. Dick's Tea Bar is well established but is remote from the slopes. At close of play it's the piste-side Rond Point that's packed – happy hour starts around 4pm – and has live music and 'tasty toffee vodka'. The sun terrace of Jack's, near the main lift stations, remains very popular.

The ring of bars around the main square do good business at tea time. The Taverne (run by the same company that owns Dick's Tea Bar) gets packed. Just across the square is the Pub, with videos, pool and sometimes a band. There are a couple of alternatives to the loud pubs complained about in the past. The Poste 'serves the best vin chaud'. The Barometer has a good atmosphere and lots of leather seating.

There is late dancing at Scott's (next to the Pub) and, of course, there's Dick's Tea Bar. One reader was put off by the queues at the Pub, another liked its 'busy atmosphere'.

In Mottaret the bars at the foot of the pistes get packed at tea time – Rastro ('As good as ever,' comments a regular visitor) and Down Town are the most popular, though reporters say that Zig-Zag has lower prices. Later on the Rastro disco gets going. Both villages have a cinema.



## OFF THE SLOPES

### *Flight of fancy*

Méribel is not really a resort for people who want to languish in the village, but it is not unattractive. There's a good public swimming pool and an Olympic ice rink. You can also take joyrides in the little planes that operate from the altiport.

The pedestrian's lift pass covers all the gondolas, cable-cars and buses in the Méribel and Courchevel valleys, and makes it very easy for pedestrians to meet friends for lunch. There are pleasant, marked walks in the Altiport area and a signposted trail through some of the hamlets down to Les Allues (return from there or Le Raffort in the Olympic gondola).

A non-skier's guide to Courchevel, Méribel and La Tania is distributed free by the tourist office.

## STAYING DOWN THE VALLEY

### *Quieter, cheaper choices*

For the 1992 Olympics the competitors were accommodated in **Brides-les-**

Mottaret in the morning sun; it has speedy links to all parts of the Trois Vallées but the runs down to it from both sides of the valley can be tricky →

SNOWPIX.COM / CHRIS GILL

**Bains** (600m/1,970ft), an old spa town way down in the valley, and a gondola was built linking it to Méribel. It is much cheaper than the higher resorts and has some simple hotels, adequate shops and 'plenty of good-value restaurants and friendly bars used by locals', says a reporter. Ski Weekends runs two chalet hotels here. There is a casino, but evenings are distinctly quiet. The long gondola ride to and from Méribel (about 25 minutes) is tedious and can be cold, but in good conditions you can ski off-piste to one or other of the mid-stations at the end of the day. Given a car, Brides makes a good base for visiting other resorts.

Some UK tour operators have places in the old village of **Les Allues**, down the road from the resort and close to a mid-station on the gondola up from Brides-les-Bains. The pick of the chalets is probably Bonne Neige's Les Allodis, a carefully converted barn ('Absolutely brilliant, the best chalet holiday ever, excellent food,' said a 2004 reporter) plus one other chalet – there's a hot-tub and sauna in both. Ski Blanc have six good-looking chalets too, including one with a hot-tub. Next door to one of them is an independent British-run playgroup. There are a couple of bars – and a good-value, well-renovated hotel, the Croix Jean-Claude (0479 086105); rooms are small, though.

**TOURIST OFFICE**

t 0479 086001
info@meribel.net
www.meribel.net

SNOWPIX.COM / CHRIS GILL

# Montgenèvre

*The snowiest part of the Franco-Italian Milky Way circuit*

**COSTS**

①②③④⑤⑥

**RATINGS**

| **The slopes** | |
|---|---|
| Snow | **** |
| Extent | **** |
| Expert | ** |
| Intermediate | **** |
| Beginner | ***** |
| Convenience | **** |
| Queues | **** |
| Mountain restaurants | ** |
| **The rest** | |
| Scenery | *** |
| Resort charm | *** |
| Off-slope | * |

**NEWS**

For 2003/04 the Tremplin drag was replaced by a chair. The new Tremplin red slope was added, too. Snowmaking was extended.



**REPORTS WANTED**

Recently we have had few reports on this resort. If you go there, please do send us a report.

The best reports earn a copy of the next edition, and can lead to free lift passes in future.

See page 10.

- ✚ Good snow record, and local slopes largely north-facing – often the best snow in the Milky Way area
- ✚ Plenty of intermediate cruising and good, convenient nursery slopes
- ✚ Few queues on weekdays, unless people are being bussed in from other resorts with poor snow
- ✚ A lot of accommodation close to the slopes, and some right on them
- ✚ Great potential for car drivers to explore other nearby resorts

- ▬ Poor base for exploring the Italian Milky Way resorts unless you have a car
- ▬ Lots of slow lifts and mainly short runs in local area
- ▬ Busy road lined by tatty bars reduces village charm and family appeal – crossing can be tricky unless you use the travelator
- ▬ Little to challenge experts on-piste

**Montgenèvre is set at one end of the big Milky Way network, reaching over into Italy. It's a time-consuming trek from here to Sestriere and Sauze d'Oulx at the far end (you may have to ride some slow lifts down as well as up). But you can get to these worthwhile resorts much more quickly by car, which also facilitates day trips in the opposite direction to other excellent French resorts such as Serre-Chevalier. You may want to stay on the local slopes shared with Claviere (in Italy, but very close), which will probably have the best snow in the region.**

**The village is quite pleasant once you get away from the main road. Sadly, you can't avoid the road altogether if you want to make use of the bigger area of slopes on the south side of the pass. But most visitors seem to come to terms with it, and don't find that it spoils their enjoyment. When moving between the two slope areas, at least, you can now hop on a travelator.**

## THE RESORT

Montgenèvre is a narrow roadside village set on a high pass only a mile from the Italian border – this is an area where the euro has really simplified things. At first glance the resort appears a rather inhospitable place – a collection of tatty-looking bars and restaurants lining the side of the sometimes windswept and often busy main road over the col. But the cheap and cheerful cafes and bars add an animated atmosphere sometimes missing from French resorts. And tucked away off the main road is a quite pleasant old village, complete with quaint church and friendly natives. The place gets a lot of snow, which adds to the charm factor.

The slopes are convenient, despite the road; most of the accommodation is less than five minutes from a lift. Some of the newer accommodation is uphill, away from the slopes – but there is a free shuttle-bus. The main lifts are gondolas from opposite ends of the village. On the village side of the road are the south-facing slopes of Le Chalvet. The more extensive north-facing slopes of Les Anges and Le Querelay are across the main road, with nursery slopes at the bottom. Both sectors have piste links with Claviere, gateway to the other Italian resorts of the Milky Way – Sansicario, Sestriere and Sauze d'Oulx.

The best way to get to other resorts is to travel by car. Serre-Chevalier and Puy-St-Vincent, with lift pass sharing arrangements, are easily reached, and well worth an outing each. Different lift pass options cater for most needs.

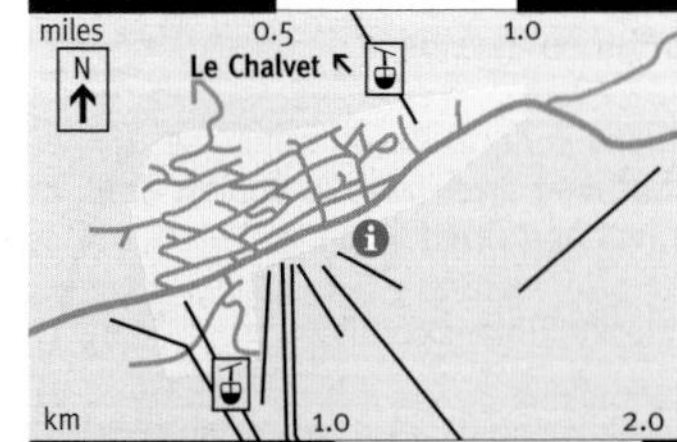

## KEY FACTS

| | |
|---|---|
| **Resort** | 1850m<br>6,070ft |
| For Montgenèvre-Monts de la Lune (Claviere) | |
| **Slopes** | 1850-2630m<br>6,070-8,630ft |
| **Lifts** | 40 |
| **Pistes** | 100km<br>62 miles |
| **Green** | 11% |
| **Blue** | 27% |
| **Red** | 42% |
| **Black** | 20% |
| **Snowmaking** | 10 km<br>6 miles |
| For the whole Milky Way area | |
| **Slopes** | 1390-2825m<br>4,560-9,270ft |
| **Lifts** | 91 |
| **Pistes** | 400km<br>249 miles |
| **Blue** | 25% |
| **Red** | 55% |
| **Black** | 20% |
| **Snowmaking** | 100km<br>62 miles |

## THE MOUNTAINS

Montgenèvre's local slopes are best suited to leisurely intermediates, with lots of easy cruising on blues and greens, both above and in the woods.

Run gradings on the local area and Milky Way piste maps have differed in the past, which can be confusing – however, none of the blacks is much more than a tough red.

### THE SLOPES
***Nicely varied***

The major north-facing Les Anges sector offers easy intermediate slopes above the mid-mountain gondola station, with more of a mix of runs lower down. It has a high-altitude link via Collet Vert (reached by a quad chair) to the slopes above Claviere, in Italy (covered on the Monts de la Lune lift pass). The main complaint about the Claviere area is the number of long, steep and awkward drag-lifts (we have reports of kids 'dropping like flies'). But this whole area around the border is attractively broken up by rocky outcrops and woods and the scenery is quite spectacular.

The runs of the sunny Chalvet sector are mainly on open slopes above its mid-mountain gondola station. When conditions permit, a 'charming' long blue run from this sector goes down to Claviere, for access to Italy. But on the latest resort map we have this run is marked as an itinéraire – there is no explanation, but this would normally mean that it is not patrolled.

### TERRAIN-PARKS
***High and remote***

There's a terrain-park – with quarter-pipe, jump and rope tow – and a boarder cross near the Gondrans chair-lift at the top of the Les Anges sector.

### SNOW RELIABILITY
***Excellent locally***

Montgenèvre has a generally excellent snow record, receiving dumps from westerly storms funnelling up the valley. The high north-facing slopes naturally keep their snow better than the south-facing area but both have snowmaking on the main home pistes.

### FOR EXPERTS
***Limited, except for off-piste***

There are very few challenging pistes in the Montgenèvre-Claviere-Cesana sectors. Many of the runs are overclassified on the map. There is, however, ample opportunity for off-piste excursions, and heli-skiing on the Italian side when conditions are right.

The remote north-east-facing bowl beyond the Col de l'Alpet on the Chalvet side is superb in good snow and has black and red pistes, too. The open section between La Montanina and Sagnalonga on the Italian side is another good powder area. Those with a car should visit Sestriere for the most challenging runs.

### FOR INTERMEDIATES
***Plenty of cruising terrain***

The overclassified blacks are just right for adventurous intermediates, though none holds the interest for very long.



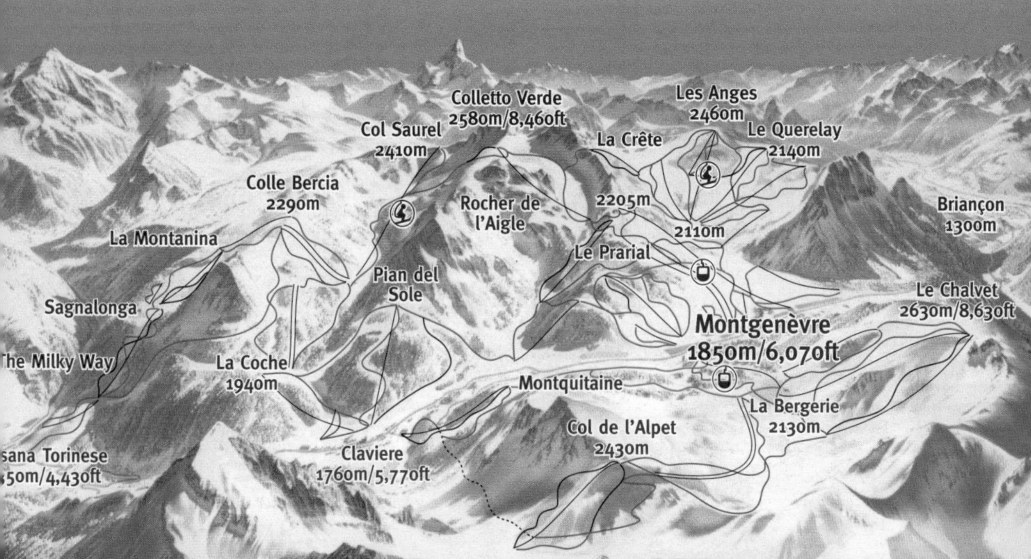

## LIFT PASSES

**Montgenèvre-Monts de la Lune**
Covers Montgenèvre and Claviere lifts.

**Main pass**
1 day €26
6 days €123

**Senior citizens**
Over 60: 6-day pass €98
Over 75: free pass

**Children**
Under 12: 6-day pass €98
Under 6: free pass

**Notes**
6-day and over Galaxie pass allows free day at Alpe-d'Huez, Deux-Alpes, Puy-St-Vincent and Serre-Chevalier.

**Alternative passes**
Montgenèvre only and Voie Lactée area passes available.

## SCHOOLS

**ESF**
**t** 0492 219046
esf.montgenevre@wanadoo.fr

**A-Peak**
**t** 0492 218330
info@a-peak.com

**Classes** (ESF prices)
6 half days (2½hr) €90

**Private lessons**
€31 for 1hr

↑ Good powdery snow on the home slopes is one of the things you hope to find here

OT MONTGENEVRE / A BENE

The pleasantly narrow tree-lined runs to Claviere from Pian del Sole, the steepest of the routes down in the Chalvet sector and the runs off the back of Col de l'Alpet are all fine in small doses.

Average intermediates will enjoy the red runs, though most are short. On the major sector, both the runs from Collet Vert – one into Italy and one back into France – can be great fun.

Getting to Cesana via the lovely sweeping run starting at the top of the Serra Granet double-drag, and heading home from Pian del Sole, is easier than the gradings suggest, and can be tackled by less adventurous intermediates, who also have a wealth of cruising terrain high up at the top of the Les Anges sector. These are served by several upper lifts, but you have the option of continuing right down to town. These long, gentle runs are wonderfully flattering cruises.

Further afield, the run down to Claviere from the top of the Gimont drags, on the Italian side, is a beautifully gentle cruise.

### FOR BEGINNERS
***Good for novices and improvers***

There is a fine selection of convenient nursery slopes with reliable snow at the foot of the north-facing area. Progression to longer runs could not be easier, with a very easy blue starting at Les Anges, leading on to a green and finishing at the roadside 600m/1,970ft below.

### FOR CROSS-COUNTRY
***Having a car widens horizons***

Montgenèvre is the best of the Milky Way resorts for cross-country enthusiasts, but it's useful to have a car. The two local trails, totalling 25km/16 miles, offer quite a bit of variety, but a further 75km/47 miles of track starts in Les Alberts, 8km/5 miles away in the Clarée valley.

### QUEUES
***No problems most of the time***

The slopes are wonderfully uncrowded during weekdays, provided surrounding resorts have snow. Some lifts become crowded at weekends and when nearby Bardonecchia is lacking snow. And queues for the two gondolas out of the village can occur first thing. Links with Italy have improved but some walking can be involved and many of the lifts are still old and slow.

### MOUNTAIN RESTAURANTS
***Head for Italy***

The few mountain restaurants in the Montgenèvre sector are of the large self-service canteen variety – but in the Claviere sector there is a choice of atmospheric little mountain huts, such as the 'cosy' and 'friendly' Montanina Restaurant at the top of the chair lift from Sagnalonga. Alternatively there are plenty of places to eat all along the main road back in the village.

### SCHOOLS AND GUIDES
***Encouraging reports***

Latest reports on the ESF are positive: 'fantastic' teacher 'able to adapt exactly to what we all (four) required' and 'great instructor, good with kids'.

## boarding

*There's plenty to attract boarders to Montgenèvre. There are good local beginner slopes and long runs on varied terrain for intermediates. The only real drawback is that many of the lifts in the area are drags, and you will have to use them to get around – getting over to Sestriere and back involves lots (and some flat sections to skate along as well). There are some excellent off-piste areas for more advanced boarders. Snow Box is the local specialist shop.*

### CHILDREN

**Village kindergarten**
**t** 0492 215250
Ages 6mnth to 5yr; 9am-5pm; €26 per day

**ESF kindergarten**
**t** 0492 219046
Ages 3 to 5

**Ski school**
For ages 5 to 12 (6 half days €87)

### GETTING THERE

**Air** Turin 98km/61 miles (2hr); Grenoble 145km/90 miles (3hr); Lyon 253km/157 miles (4½hr).

**Rail** Briançon (12km/7 miles) or Oulx (15km/9 miles); buses available from both five times a day.

### ACTIVITIES

**Indoor** Library, sauna, cinema

**Outdoor** Natural ice rink, paragliding, snow-shoeing, snowmobiling, tobogganing, walking, horse-riding

**Phone numbers**
From abroad use the prefix +33 and omit the initial '0' of the phone number.

### TOURIST OFFICE

**t** 0492 215252
office.tourisme.montgenevre@wanadoo.fr
www.montgenevre.com

**FACILITIES FOR CHILDREN**
***Pity about the traffic***
The intrusive main road apart, Montgenèvre would seem a fine family resort. Reports on the school's children's classes have been complimentary of both class size and spoken English.

## STAYING THERE

**HOW TO GO**
***Limited choice***
UK tour operators concentrate on cheap and cheerful catered chalets, though some apartments are also available and a few operators also package hotels.
**Hotels** There is a handful of simple places offering good value.
(②) **Valérie** (0492 219002) Central rustic old 3-star.
(②) **Napoléon** (0492 219204) 3-star on the roadside.
① **Alpet** (0492 219006) Basic 2-star near the centre.
① **Chalet des Sports** (0492 219017) Among the cheapest rooms in the Alps.
**Self-catering** Résidences La Ferme d'Augustin are simple, ski-to-the-door apartments on the fringes of the main north-facing slopes, five minutes' walk (across the piste) from town.

**EATING OUT**
***Cheap and cheerful***
There are a dozen places to choose from. The Ca del Sol and the Cesar have been recommended by reporters. The Estable and Transalpin serve good-value traditional fare. Chez Pierrot and the Jamy have an authentic French feel. The 3-star Napoléon is the only hotel with a restaurant open to non-residents – a pizzeria. A trip to Claviere is worthwhile – reporters have testified to the excellence of the restaurants.

**APRES-SKI**
***Mainly bars, but fun***
The range is limited. The Graal is a friendly, unsophisticated place; the Ca del Sol bar is a cosy place with open fire. Pub Chaberton is recommended. The Blue Night disco is popular. The Refuge, the Crepouse and the Jamy are the focal cafe-bars at tea-time.

**OFF THE SLOPES**
***Very limited***
There is a weekly market and you can walk the cross-country routes, but the main diversion is a bus-trip to the beautiful old town of Briançon.

**STAYING UP THE MOUNTAIN**
***Easily arranged, recommended***
The Sport Hotel at Sagnalonga, halfway down the piste to Cesana (on the Italian side of the border) and reached by chair-lift or snowmobile, is recommended by two reporters – 'good-value self-service meals', but 'it's in need of re-decoration'. Even at half-term you get the immaculately groomed local slopes to yourself until skiers based elsewhere arrive, mid-morning. It's quiet in the evenings, but livens up considerably when Italian weekenders arrive to party.

## Claviere 1760m/5,770ft

Claviere is a small, traditional village, barely a mile to the east of Montgenèvre and just over the border in Italy. It's no great beauty, and the main road to Montgenèvre and Briançon that divides it in two has an obvious impact, but visitors seem to like its quiet, relaxed ambience, and are ready to go again.

The slopes of Montgenèvre are as easily reached as those on the Italian side of the border. Stupidly, there is no shared pass sold here; you have to buy day extensions for the French slopes, or go up the road to Montgenèvre, where a shared pass is available.

Claviere's nursery slope is small and steep but usually uncrowded and snow-reliable. We have had mixed reports of its ski school – from 'lovely instructors, brilliant with the kids' to 'only average' and 'big classes'.

OT MORZINE / P JACQUES, FOC

# Morzine

*A lively, year-round resort linked by lift to the Portes du Soleil*

## COSTS

①②③④⑤⑥

## RATINGS

| **The slopes** | |
|---|---|
| Snow | ** |
| Extent | ***** |
| Expert | *** |
| Intermediate | **** |
| Beginner | *** |
| Convenience | ** |
| Queues | *** |
| Mountain restaurants | *** |
| **The rest** | |
| Scenery | *** |
| Resort charm | *** |
| Off-slope | *** |

## NEWS

Morzine and Les Gets have benefited from a lot of new fast lifts recently. In 2003/04 the Perrières six-pack opened up a new access point from the outskirts of Les Gets to the slopes of La Rosta. The Chavannes chair was also replaced by a six-pack, improving the main way out of Les Gets towards Morzine. The slow Charniaz quad on the Morzine side was also upgraded.

Two electric buses were introduced in Morzine in a plan to reduce pollution.

For 2004/05, the Fornet chair on the Swiss border beyond Avoriaz is to be replaced by a six-pack.



- \+ Part of the vast Portes du Soleil
- \+ Larger local piste area than other Portes du Soleil resorts
- \+ Good nightlife by French standards
- \+ Quite attractive old town – a sharp contrast to purpose-built Avoriaz
- \+ One of the easiest drives from the Channel (a car is very useful here)
- \+ Few queues locally

- − Takes a while to get to Avoriaz and the main Portes du Soleil circuit
- − Bus-ride or long walk to lifts from much of the accommodation
- − Low altitude means there is an enduring risk of poor snow, despite increased snowmaking
- − Choice of low-altitude or inconvenient nursery slopes
- − Not a great resort for experts
- − Weekend crowds

**Morzine is a long-established year-round resort, popular for its easy road access, traditional atmosphere and gentle wooded slopes, where children do not get lost and bad weather rarely causes problems. For keen piste-bashers wanting to travel the Portes du Soleil circuit, the main drawback is having to take a bus and cable-car or several lifts to get to Avoriaz and the main circuit.**

**Such problems can be avoided by taking a car or using a tour operator who will drive you around. The little-used Ardent gondola, a short drive from Morzine, is a particularly neat option, giving the alternative of a shorter circuit that misses out Avoriaz, where the worst crowds tend to be found.**

## THE RESORT

Morzine is a traditional mountain town sprawling along both sides of a river gorge. In winter, under a blanket of snow, its chalet-style buildings look charming, and in spring the village quickly takes on a spruce appearance. Morzine is a family resort, and village ambience tends to be fairly subdued – but there is plenty of après-ski action to be found.

The centre is close to the river, around the tourist office. Restaurants and bars line the street up to the Le Pléney lifts, where a busy one-way street runs along the foot of the slopes. Accommodation is widely scattered, and a good multi-route bus service (including two new electric buses, introduced last year) links all parts of the town to outlying lifts, including those for Avoriaz.

As the extensive network of bus routes and a growing number of hotel mini-buses imply, Morzine is a town where getting from A to B can be tricky. The best plan is to stay near the gondola and cable-car to Le Pléney and accept that any trips to the Portes du Soleil circuit are going to involve a bus-ride or a drive.

Our view that the resort suits car drivers is widely shared. But the roads are busy, the one-way system 'takes some getting used to' and although parking problems have been partly relieved by car parks built quite recently near Le Pléney, there is still a lot of competition for space.

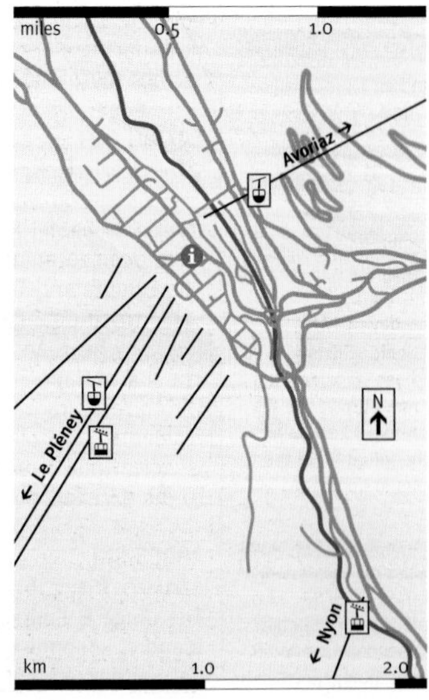

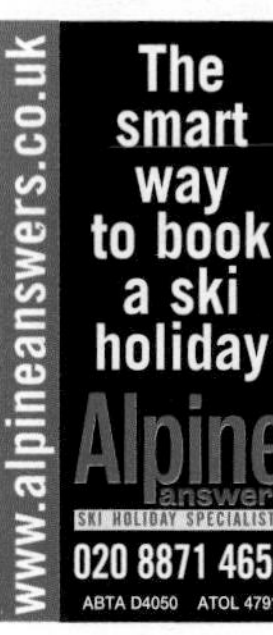

A scenic area, with open and wooded slopes ↗

PIERRE JACQUES / FOC

## KEY FACTS

| | |
|---|---|
| **Resort** | 1000m 3,280ft |
| for Portes du Soleil | |
| **Slopes** | 975-2275m 3,200-7,460ft |
| **Lifts** | 206 |
| **Pistes** | 650km 400 miles |
| **Green** | 13% |
| **Blue** | 38% |
| **Red** | 39% |
| **Black** | 10% |
| **Snowmaking** | 252 acres |
| For Morzine-Les Gets only | |
| **Slopes** | 1000-2020m 3,280-6,630ft |
| **Lifts** | 67 |
| **Pistes** | 107km 66 miles |

## LIFT PASSES

**Portes du Soleil**
Covers all lifts in all 12 resorts, and shuttle-buses.

**Main pass**
1 day €35
6 days €171

**Senior citizens**
Over 60: 6 days €137

**Children**
Under 16: 6 days €115
Under 5: free pass

**Alternative passes**
Morzine-Les Gets pass and Morzine-Avoriaz pass available, also special snowboard pass for Mont Chéry area.

## THE MOUNTAINS

The local slopes suit intermediates well, with excellent areas for beginners and near-beginners too: 'More variety than expected,' said one reporter. Others have praised the system of Discovery Routes around the Portes du Soleil – choose an animal that suits your ability and follow the signs displaying it around the circuit.

### THE SLOPES

***No need to go far afield***

Morzine is not an ideal base for the Portes du Soleil main circuit (described in the Avoriaz, Châtel and Champéry chapters). But it has an extensive local area shared with Les Gets (now covered in a separate chapter).

A cable-car and parallel gondola rise from the edge of central Morzine to **Le Pléney**, where numerous routes return to the valley, including a run down to Les Fys – a quiet junction of chairs which access **Nyon** and, in the opposite direction, the ridge separating Morzine from the Les Gets slopes. The Nyon sector has two peaks – Pointe de Nyon and Chamossière – accessible from Nyon and Le Grand Pré respectively. Nyon can also be accessed by cable-car, situated a bus-ride from Morzine. Beyond Chamossière are two more ridges – Le Ranfolly and La Rosta. In the valley between these two, no less than five chair-lifts have their base stations clustered together – a favourite spot with many readers.

Beyond Les Gets, **Mont Chéry** is notably quiet, and well worth a visit.

Across town from the Le Pléney sector – another handy 'petit train' shuttle service runs between the two – is a gondola leading (via a long chain of lifts and runs) to Avoriaz and the main Portes du Soleil circuit. This is a painless way to get back to Morzine at the end of the day, but a slow way to get to the circuit. Better alternatives are a bus-ride or short drive to either Les Prodains (from where you can get a cable-car to Avoriaz or a chair-lift into the **Hauts Forts** slopes above it) or to Ardent, where a gondola accesses Les Lindarets for lifts towards Châtel, Avoriaz or Champéry. The tree-lined slopes at Les Lindarets are good in poor visibility and the area at the top of the gondola is a good one for mixed ability groups to meet up. Car trips to Flaine and Chamonix are feasible.

### TERRAIN-PARKS

***Mont Chéry, or head for Avoriaz***

There's another boarder-cross, aimed at children, in the Zone Enfant at the top of Les Chavannes. Avoriaz has much more to offer (see Avoriaz chapter).

## boarding

*Avoriaz is the hard-core boarding HQ of the Portes du Soleil. But there's a boarding presence in Morzine, too – Chalet Snowboard, who were the first chalet company to target snowboarders rather than skiers, has Morzine chalets, and former British champ Becci Malthouse teaches with the British Alpine Ski & Snowboard School. With interesting, tree-lined runs and few drags, the local Morzine slopes are good for beginners and intermediates. And there's a terrain-park over in Mont Chéry that might seem less intimidating than the big one in Avoriaz. There's a special snowboarders' pass if you just want to ride that area – 15 euros a day last season – and there's a snow-park map. The specialist shop Misty Fly runs big air comps every Monday – and broadcasts them on the internet.*

**SNOW RELIABILITY**
***Poor***

Morzine has a very low average height, and it can rain here when it is snowing higher up. It had no snow at Christmas and New Year 2002/03, for example. A reporter who visited in January 2004 speaks of 'three days of heavy rain up to 1800m'. There is some snowmaking, most noticeably on runs linking Nyon and Le Pléney, and on the home runs.

**FOR EXPERTS**
***A few possibilities***

The runs down from Pointe de Nyon and Chamossière are quite challenging, as are the black runs down the back of Mont Chéry. Don't overlook the excellent Hauts Forts black runs at Avoriaz. There is plenty of off-piste scope throughout the area; the open slopes of Chamossière offer some of the best local possibilities, and Mont Chéry at Les Gets is also worth exploring. For further off-piste ideas, see the feature box on the facing page.

**FOR INTERMEDIATES**
***Something for everyone***

Good intermediates will enjoy the challenging red and black down from Chamossière. Mont Chéry has some fine steepish runs which are usually very quiet as everyone heads from Les Gets towards Morzine.

Those of average ability have a great choice, though most runs are rather short. Le Pléney has a compact network of pistes that are ideal for groups with mixed abilities: mainly moderate intermediate runs, but with some easier alternatives for the more timid, and a single challenging route for the aggressive.

Less experienced intermediates have lots of options on Le Pléney, including a great away-from-it-all, snow-gun-covered blue cruise from the top to the valley lift station. Heading from Le Ranfolly to Le Grand Pré on the blue is a nice cruise. And the slopes down to Les Gets from Le Pléney are easy when conditions allow (they face south).

The fast chairs on Le Ranfolly and La Rosta now make these sectors more attractive, serving easy blacks and cruising reds.

And, of course, there is the whole of the Portes du Soleil circuit to explore by going up the opposite side of the valley to Avoriaz or via Ardent to Les Lindarets.

**FOR BEGINNERS**
***Good for novices and improvers***

The wide village nursery slopes are convenient, and benefit from snow-guns, though crowds are reported to be a problem. Some of the best progression runs are over at Nyon and

Pointe de Nyon 2020m/6,630ft
Chamossière 2000m
Le Ranfolly 1850m
La Rosta
Pointe de la Turche
Nyon 1420m
Le Grand Pré
Les Chavannes 1485m
La Turche
Les Perrières
Mont Chéry 1850m
Le Pléney 1510m
Les Gets 1170m/3,840ft
Col de l'Encrenaz 1435m
← Avoriaz
Morzine 1000m/3,280ft

The **ESF** Morzine has 155 instructors offering group and private lessons at every level. For off-piste guiding, instructors can be hired for groups of up to six people, by the day and half-day.

**t** 0450 791313
**f** 0450 791770
**e** info@esf-morzine.com
www.esf-morzine.com

## OFF-PISTE RUNS IN THE PORTES DU SOLEIL AREA

**The Portes du Soleil offers a lot of great lift-served off-piste terrain. Here, the ESF Morzine gives us a run-down on some of the highlights on the French side. Like all serious off-piste routes, these runs should not be done without guidance.**

### *Morzine – Nyon/Chamossière area*

*From the Chamossière chair-lift (2000m/6,560ft), heading north brings you to two runs – one on the same north-west slope as the pistes, the other via a col down the north-east slope to the the Nyon cable-car (1020m/3,350ft) in the Vallée de La Manche – a wild area, with a great view of Mont Blanc at first.*

### *Avoriaz area – two suggestions*

*From the the Fornet chair-lift (2220m/7,280ft) on the Swiss border, you head west to descend a beautiful, unspoiled bowl leading down to the village of L'Erigné (1185m/3,890ft). In powder snow you descend the west-facing slopes of the bowl; when there is spring snow, you traverse right to descend the south-facing slopes. Medium-pitch slopes, for skiers and snowboarders.*

*From the top of the Machon chair-lift (2275m/7,460ft) you traverse west, beneath the peaks of Les Hauts Forts, across Les Crozats de la Chaux – a steep, north-facing slope. You then turn north to descend through the forest to the cable-car station at Les Prodains (1150m/3,770ft). Testing terrain, for very good skiers – the traverse is dangerous following a snowfall.*

### *Châtel area*

*From the top of the Linga chair-lift (2040m/6,690ft), you head north-west to cross the ridge on your right at a recognisable col and then head down the La Lèche slope to the drag-lift of the same name (1550m/5,090ft). It's a north-facing slope with powder snow. This run starts in a white wilderness, taking you through trees back to civilisation. Steep slopes – for good skiers only.*

## SCHOOLS

**ESF**
t 0450 791313
info@esf-morzine.com

**International**
t 0450 790516
info@morzineski.fr

**BASS**
t 023 92 528497 (UK)
morzine@britishski school.com

**Classes**
(ESF prices)
6 half days (2½hr am or pm) €113

**Private lessons**
€32 for 1hr for 1 to 3 people

## CHILDREN

**L'Outa nursery**
t 0450 792600
Ages 3mnth to 6yr; ski lessons from 3

**Jack Frost's**
t 07721 912455 (UK)
jackfrostschildcare@email.com
www.jackfrosts.com
Sun-Thu, 9am to 5pm, Fri 9am to 3pm; takes babies upwards

**Club des Piou-Piou**
t 0450 791313
Ages 3 to 12; with ESF instruction and lunch (6 days €308)

**Ski school**
ESF takes children from age 5: 6 half-days €105.





the slopes between Avoriaz and Morzine are also recommended. Adventurous novices also have the option of easy pistes around Le Pléney. Near-beginners can get over to Les Gets via Le Pléney, and return via Le Ranfolly.

### FOR CROSS-COUNTRY
***Good variety***

There is a wide variety of cross-country trails, not all at valley level. The best section is in the pretty Vallée de la Manche beside the Nyon mountain up to the Lac de Mines d'Or, where there is a good restaurant. The Pléney-Chavannes loop is pleasant and relatively snow-reliable.

### QUEUES
***Few problems when snow is good***

Queues are not usually a problem in the local area but we had a report of 'horrendous queues and frequent lift breakdown in the Les Gets area' recently and there are still complaints – doubtless why the resort is building so many fast new lifts. The Nyon cable-car and Belvédère chair-lift (Le Pléney) are weekend bottlenecks. Long waits at the Morzine to Pléney gondola can be avoided by using the adjacent chairs, says a reporter. Queues to and from Avoriaz are much improved in recent times, but are still bad when snow is in short supply.

### MOUNTAIN RESTAURANTS
***Within reach of some good huts***

The nice little place at the foot of the d'Atray chair is perhaps the best local hut. A reporter loved the tiny Lhottys hut, where he ate amazing fresh seafood. We had an enjoyable Savoyard lunch at the rustic Chez Nannon near the top of the Troncs chair between Nyon and Chamossière. The Vaffieu at the top of the Folliets chair has had several recommendations as has the Nabor (Pléney). The self-service on Mont Chéry is 'one of the better examples of the breed'.

### SCHOOLS AND GUIDES
***BASS is worth the premium***

The British Alpine Ski & Snowboard School (BASS), staffed by BASI-qualified instructors, is pricey but gets good reports: 'groups were generally about four in size; very happy with the service,' said a reporter last year. This year a reporter enjoyed the Advanced classes, while the beginners in their party also 'progressed very quickly with their excellent instructor'. Reports on the ESF (which is half the price) are mixed. There are the usual complaints about class sizes. One past reporter told of '22 people in my son's class' in half-term week. This year a reporter says his children 'gave up on the Thursday through boredom'.

### FACILITIES FOR CHILDREN
***Lots of possibilities***

The facilities of the Outa nursery are quite impressive, but we've received reports of poor English and low staff ratios. Jack Frost's is run by a qualified children's nurse from Northern Ireland.

There is a big children's area, the Zone Enfant, in the Les Chavannes area. An ESF childcare centre, Club des Piou-Piou looks after children between the ages of 3 and 12 after skiing. The Dérêches Farm offers days learning about animals, snow-shoeing and tobogganing. The tour operator Esprit Ski has good facilities. Ski Famille and Ski Hillwood are other family specialists, based in Les Gets.

## STAYING THERE

### HOW TO GO
***Good-value hotels and chalets***

The tour operator market concentrates on hotels and chalets.

**Chalets** There's a wide choice, but position varies enormously. Chalet Gueret is an independently run luxury chalet.

**Hotels** The handful of 3-star hotels includes some quite smooth ones; and there are dozens of 2-stars and 1-stars.

((((4) **Dahu** (0450 759292) 3-star linked to centre by footbridge over river; good restaurant; pool. Private shuttle to lifts.

((((4) **Airelles** (0450 747121) Central 3-star close to Pléney lifts and Prodains and Nyon bus routes. Good pool.

((((4) **Champs Fleuris** (0450 791444) Comfy 3-star next to Pléney lifts. Pool.

(((3) **Tremplin** (0450 791231) Also next to the lifts; 'friendly staff, good food' but 'small rooms'.

(((3) **Bergerie** (0450 791369) Rustic chalet, in centre. Friendly staff. Pool.

((2) **Côtes** (0450 790996) Simple 2-star on the edge of town. Pool.

((2) **Equipe** (0450 791143) One of the best 2-stars; next to the Pléney lift.

**Self-catering** The Télémark apartments, close to the Super-Morzine gondola, and the Udrezants, by the Prodains cable-car, have been recommended.

The town spreads up the sunny slope leading down from Avoriaz – just visible at top right →

BERTRAND BODIN/FOC

## GETTING THERE

**Air** Geneva 75km/ 47 miles (1½hr). Lyon 195km/121 miles (3½hr).

**Rail** Cluses or Thonon (30km/19 miles); regular bus connections to resort.

## ACTIVITIES

**Indoor** Ice rink, fitness centre, sauna, hot tub, climbing wall, library, cinemas

**Outdoor** Sleigh rides, snow-shoe classes, fitness trail, helicopter flights, ballooning, snowmobiles, bungee jumping, ice-diving, tobogganing, paragliding, cheese factory visits

**Phone numbers**
From abroad use the prefix +33 and omit the initial '0' of the phone number.

## TOURIST OFFICE

**t** 0450 747272
info@morzine-avoriaz.com
www.morzine.com

## EATING OUT
### *A reasonable choice*

The best restaurant in town is probably the Taverne in hotel Samoyede, which offers traditional and modern cuisine – we enjoyed lobster ravioli, truffle risotto and scallops. The hotel Airelles has a fine restaurant and the hotel Dahu also has good food. The Chamade looks the part (elegant table settings) but reports are mixed. The Grange does 'excellent food, but at a price'. Locals rate the Chalet Philibert highly. The Etale is a good, popular, unpretentious all-rounder with friendly service. Café Chaud – 'a good combination of restaurant and bar' – is popular for fondue and the Pique Feu behind the Mairie does Savoyard food at 'reasonable prices'. The 'friendly' Clin d'Oeil, down by the river, does 'really impressive' food.

## APRES-SKI
### *One of the livelier French resorts*

On Tuesday evenings there's a 'ski retrospective' on the Le Pléney slopes, and on Thursdays there's a torchlight descent, followed by floodlit skiing. There are two cinemas.

Nightlife is good by French resort standards. The Dixie has sport on TV, MTV, a cellar bar and some live music. Between the slopes and the centre, and all in the same building are: the Cavern which is popular with resort staff; the Bowling for arcade games and DJ ... but no longer bowling; the 'relaxed' Boudha Café, with Asian decor, for a quieter drink. At the nearby Crépuscule dancing on the tables in ski boots to deafening music seems compulsory at après time. The tiny Sherpa, on the outskirts of town, is also worth a try as is Pub les Alpes. L'Opéra and the Paradis du Laury's are late-night haunts. L'Opera advertises 'nuits torrides' (striptease and lap dancing).

## OFF THE SLOPES
### *Quite good; excursions possible*

There is an excellent ice rink, which stages ice hockey matches and skating galas. Some hotels have pools, which non-residents can pay to use. Buses run to Thonon for shopping, and car owners can drive to Geneva, Annecy or Montreux. There are lots of very pretty walks, and other activities include horse-drawn sleigh rides, paragliding and a cheese factory visit.

THE DOUBLE BEDROOM, CHALET CHOCOLAT ↑

SELALP

# Paradiski

*The new mega-area formed by linking Les Arcs and La Plagne*

**KEY FACTS**

| For Paradiski area | |
|---|---|
| **Slopes** | 1200-3250m 3,940-10,660ft |
| **Lifts** | 164 |
| **Pistes** | 420km 260 miles |
| **Green** | 5% |
| **Blue** | 54% |
| **Red** | 28% |
| **Black** | 13% |

**December 2003 saw the opening of the world's largest cable-car – a double-decker holding 200 people – which swoops low across a wooded valley to link the French resorts of Les Arcs and La Plagne. The result is that the two resorts can claim a joint ski area, called Paradiski, that is one of the biggest in the world. With 420km/260 miles of pistes and 164 lifts, it beats most of the established mega-areas; only the Three Valleys and the Portes du Soleil are significantly bigger. Add in a lot of off-piste terrain and you could argue the new area is bigger than either.**

The new cable-car, called the Vanoise Express, spans the 2km/1 mile-wide valley between Plan-Peisey (in the Les Arcs area) and a point 300m/980ft above Montchavin (in La Plagne).

The linking of these two major resorts is good news for the great British piste-basher who likes to cover as much ground as possible. In truth, both La Plagne and Les Arcs have enough pistes to keep anyone happy for a week. But readers report that a visit or two to the other resort during the week adds interest and variety. We've included some feedback in our chapters on the two resorts.

For those who like a bit of a challenge, getting from your home base to both far-flung outposts of the Paradiski area – Villaroger in Les Arcs and Champagny-en-Vanoise in La Plagne – would make quite a full day.

The new link is good for expert skiers and boarders based in Les Arcs wanting to tackle the north face of La Plagne's Bellecôte. In the past, you had to get to Montchavin and the La Plagne lift system by taxi. For those doing the run from La Plagne it has benefits, too: you are now able to descend all the way to Nancroix, have lunch at the excellent restaurant Ancolie and catch the free bus or a taxi for the short ride back up to the Vanoise Express.

If you want to make the most of the new link it makes sense to stay near one of the cable-car stations. But once you start to study the piste maps you realise that it's easily accessible from many other bases.

On the Les Arcs side, **Plan-Peisey** and nearby **Vallandry** are in pole position. They are basically small, low-rise, modern developments, but built in a much more sympathetic style than the original Les Arcs resorts. They don't have much more than a handful





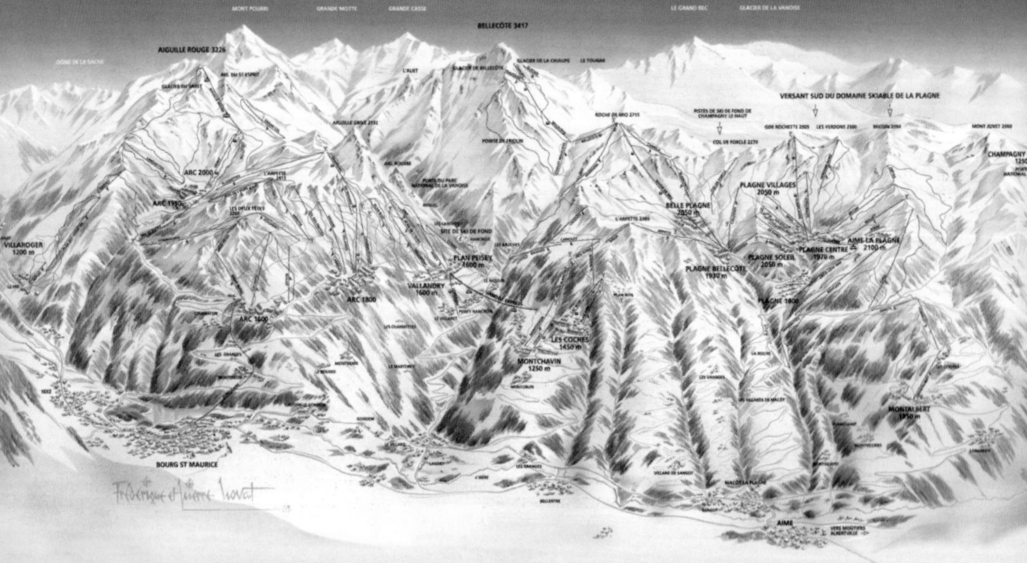

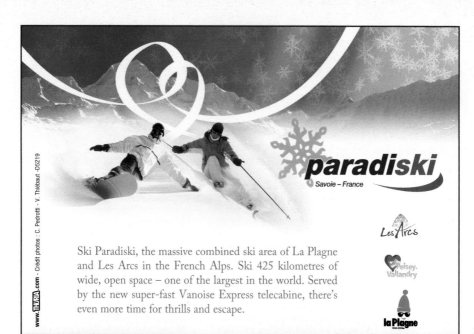

## LIFT PASSES

**Paradiski**
Covers lifts in whole Paradiski area.
6-day pass €220 (over 60 €187; under 14 €165). Also covers a day in the Three Valleys, Val-d'Isère-Tignes, Les Saisies and Pralognan-en-Vanoise.

**Paradiski Découverte**
Covers lifts in Les Arcs area or La Plagne area plus one day Paradiski extension.
6-day pass €190 (over 60 €162; under 14 €143). Extension is valid Sat-Tue only, unless bought through certain UK tour operators. Pass also covers a day in the Three Valleys, Val-d'Isère-Tignes, Les Saisies, Pralognan.

of bars, restaurants and shops at the moment and are quiet places to stay, but a lot of UK tour operators are building chalets here. There is also accommodation in the old village of **Peisey**, 300m/980ft below and linked by bucket-lift to Plan-Peisey. Peisey is still unspoiled by tourism, with two bars and two restaurants.

It's easy to get to the cable-car station at Plan-Peisey from the main resort parts of Les Arcs. One lift and a blue run is all it takes to get there from **Arc 1800,** which is the most attractive of the main resort units. From quieter **Arc 1600,** along the mountainside from 1800, it takes two lifts. **Arc 2000** and the stylish new **Arc 1950** development seem further away, over the ridge that separates them from 1600 and 1800; but all you have to do is ski down a little way and and ride one fast chair to the ridge and enjoy the long blue run down the other side. Beyond and below the bowl of Arc 200, **Le Pré** and **Villaroger** are not going to be ideal starting points.

On the La Plagne side, the obvious place to stay is **Montchavin**, which is well below the Vanoise Express station and easily reached on skis or board. Montchavin is a well-restored traditional old village with modern additions built in traditional style. **Les Coches**, across the mountain from the station, is most easily reached with the help of a lift. Les Coches is entirely modern, but built in a traditional style. Between them Montchavin and Les Coches have eight restaurants, six bars and a nightclub. From either village one lift brings you to the cable-car.

The other parts of La Plagne are some way from the cable-car, over in the main bowl of the area. But one long lift is all it takes to get from monolithic **Plagne-Bellecôte** up to L'Arpette, from which point it's a single long blue descent. The most attractive of the resort villages, **Belle-Plagne**, is only a short run above Plagne-Bellecôte. From the villages further across the bowl – **Plagne-Villages, Plagne-Soleil**, dreary **Plagne-Centre**, futuristic **Aime-la-Plagne** – you have to ride a lift to get to Plagne-Bellecôte. From 'chalet central' below the bowl, **Plagne 1800,** add another lift. From the villages beyond the bowl – rustic, sunny **Champagny-en-Vanoise** and expanding **Montalbert** – it's going to be pretty hard work.

↑ In terms of area, Paradiski is probably the biggest area of linked slopes in the world

SELALP

## RIDING THE VANOISE EXPRESS

The cable-car ride from one resort to the other takes less than four minutes. There are no pylons between the lift-stations. The cabins give spectacular views through the transparent walls. The two cars operate independently, on separate cables, so you don't have to wait for one to fill before the other can set off; and if one is out of action the other can still operate.

The system is designed to be able to operate in bad weather and high winds, so the risk of getting stranded miles from home is low. Each car shifts 1,000 people an hour in each direction – which means the system can shift 2,000 an hour – effectively the same capacity as a small gondola.

Naturally, there is some concern that the system could be overloaded at the end of the day taking people back to the resort they started from. The lift company tells us that they have a cunning plan to prevent such problems: on busy days they will hand out tickets in the morning for a return journey at a particular time in the afternoon. Sounds sensible, but what happens when people miss their allocated slot remains to be seen. None of those who reported to us this year encountered crowds.

The lift company has adopted an innovative pricing system. As you might expect, it offers a six-day pass covering the whole Paradiski region, which is perhaps most likely to appeal to people based in the villages at either end of the lift, who might choose to go in one direction on one day, and the other direction the next. But it also offers a pass (Paradiski Découverte) which includes just one day's use of the Vanoise Express and the lifts in the other resort. When bought in the resort the Découverte extension is valid only Saturday to Tuesday; but when bought through certain tour operators that also arrange your accommodation, you can use the extension on any day of your stay.

You can also buy one-day extensions to a six-day lift pass, and these cost half the normal price at weekends (15 instead of 30 euros).

**UK Representative**
Erna Low Consultants
9 Reece Mews
London SW7 3HE
**t** 0870 750 6820
**f** 020 7589 9531
info@ernalow.co.uk
www.ernalow.co.uk

# La Plagne

*A huge variety of villages spread across a vast playground*

## COSTS

①②③④⑤⑥

## RATINGS

**The slopes**
Snow ****
Extent ****
Expert ***
Intermediate *****
Beginner ****
Convenience *****
Queues ***
Mountain restaurants ***

**The rest**
Scenery ****
Resort charm *
Off-slope *

## NEWS

The Vanoise Express cable-car opened in December 2003 and now links La Plagne with Les Arcs to form Paradiski.

Also for 2003/04 the Roche de Mio gondola received its much-needed renovation.

For 2004/05 access from Montchavin to L'Arpette will be improved by two new six-packs – replacing the Bijolin chair and the two Salla drags.

Snowmaking will also be extended; the top of L'Arpette, above Plagne-Bellecôte and Champagny will all benefit.

- ➕ Extensive intermediate slopes, plus plentiful, excellent off-piste terrain
- ➕ Now linked with Les Arcs
- ➕ Good nursery slopes
- ➕ High and fairly snow-sure – and with some wonderful views
- ➕ Purpose-built resort units are convenient for the slopes
- ➕ Attractive, traditional-style villages lower down share the slopes
- ➕ Wooded runs of lower resorts are useful in poor weather

- ➖ Pistes in the main bowl don't have much to offer experts
- ➖ Pistes get very crowded in places
- ➖ Lower villages can suffer from poor snow – Champagny especially
- ➖ Unattractive architecture in some of the higher resort units
- ➖ Not many green runs for nervous beginners to go on to – though some blues are very easy
- ➖ Nightlife very limited

**With 220km/137 miles of its own slopes and 86% of these being blue or red, the La Plagne area is an intermediate's paradise. And with much-needed lift improvements over the last few years, plus the link with Les Arcs the resort is going up in our estimation. It has a reputation for plug-ugly, soulless, purpose-built villages and some of them justify that view. But there are ten different villages to choose from – and as well as delightful old mountain villages at the foot of the slopes, there are some quite attractive purpose-built centres, too.**

**Experts prepared to hire a guide can have a splendid time off-piste, with some long descents which are often deserted and untracked compared with the classic off-piste runs of more macho resorts like Val-d'Isère.**



## THE RESORT

La Plagne consists of no fewer than 10 separate 'villages'; six are purpose-built at altitude in the main bowl, on or above the tree line and linked by road, lifts and pistes; the other four are scattered around outside the bowl. Each is self-contained, with its own shops, bars, restaurants, schools and lift pass offices.

Even the core resorts vary a lot in character. The first to be built, in the 1960s, was Plagne-Centre – still the focal point for shops and après-ski. Typical of its time, it has ugly blocks and dreary indoor 'malls' that house a reasonable selection of shops, bars and restaurants. Recent developments just above Plagne-Centre are more pleasing to the eye.

Lifts radiate from Centre to all sides of the bowl, the major one being the big twin-cable gondola to Grande Rochette. A cable-car goes to the even more obtrusive 'village' of Aime-la-Plagne – a group of monolithic blocks. Below these two, and a bit of a backwater ('a dormitory', says one reader), is Plagne 1800, where the

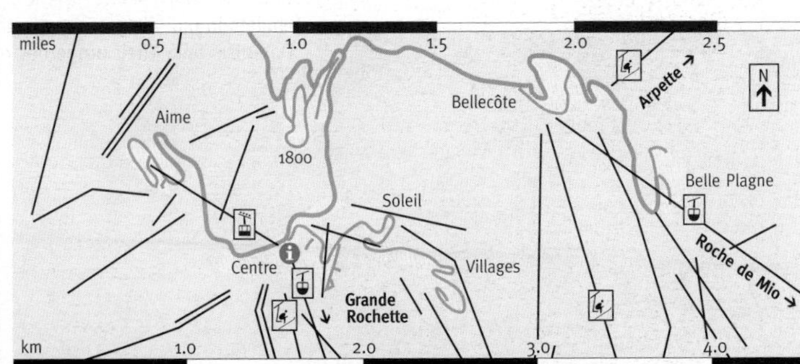

## KEY FACTS

| | |
|---|---|
| **Resort** | 1800-2100m 5,900-6,890ft |
| For La Plagne only | |
| **Slopes** | 1250-3250m 4,100-10,660ft |
| **Lifts** | 108 |
| **Pistes** | 220km 137 miles |
| **Green** | 8% |
| **Blue** | 57% |
| **Red** | 28% |
| **Black** | 7% |
| **Snowmaking** | 70 hectares |
| For Paradiski area | |
| **Slopes** | 1200-3250m 3,940-10,660ft |
| **Lifts** | 164 |
| **Pistes** | 420km 261 miles |
| **Green** | 5% |
| **Blue** | 54% |
| **Red** | 28% |
| **Black** | 13% |





buildings are small-scale and chalet-style – indeed many are offered as catered chalets on the UK market. Access to the main bowl from here is by lifts to Aime-la-Plagne and reporters comment on a drag-lift, the Lovatière, which links with no other lifts.

A little way above Plagne-Centre is the newest development, Plagne-Soleil, with attractive modern chalets. This area is officially attached to Plagne-Villages, which is a rather strung-out but attractive collection of small-scale apartments and chalets in traditional style, handy for the slopes but for nothing else.

The two other core resort units are a bus-ride away, on the other side of a low hill. The large apartment buildings of Plagne-Bellecôte form a wall at the foot of the slopes leading down to it. Some way above it is Belle-Plagne – as its name suggests, easy on the eye, with a neo-Savoyard look, and entirely underground parking. Reporters have complained of exhaustion when moving between the different levels in Belle-Plagne (the bars and other facilities are mainly in the lower part).

Lifts from Plagne-Bellecôte provide links to two of the lower resorts in the valleys outside the bowl – the old village of Montchavin (above which is the cable-car to Les Arcs) and its more recently developed neighbour Les Coches, at the northern extremity of the area. Beyond Grande Rochette, at the southern extremity, is rustic Champagny. Beyond Aime-la-Plagne, at the western extremity, is little Montalbert. For a description of these villages, see the end of this chapter.

A free bus system between the core villages within the bowl runs until after midnight. But you may have to change in Plagne-Centre. Lifts from Belle-Plagne to Plagne-Bellecôte, Aime-la-Plagne to Plagne-Centre, and Plagne-Centre to Plagne-Villages all run until 1am.

Trips by car to Val-d'Isère-Tignes or the Three Valleys are possible – and each is covered for a day with a 6-day Paradiski or Paradiski Découverte pass.

## THE MOUNTAINS

The majority of the slopes in the main bowl are above the tree line, though there are trees scattered around most of the resort centres. The slopes outside the bowl are open at the top but descend into woodland. The gondola up to the exposed glacier slopes on Bellecôte, to the west of the main bowl, is prone to closure by high winds or poor weather, and the top glacier chair-lift is normally shut in winter.

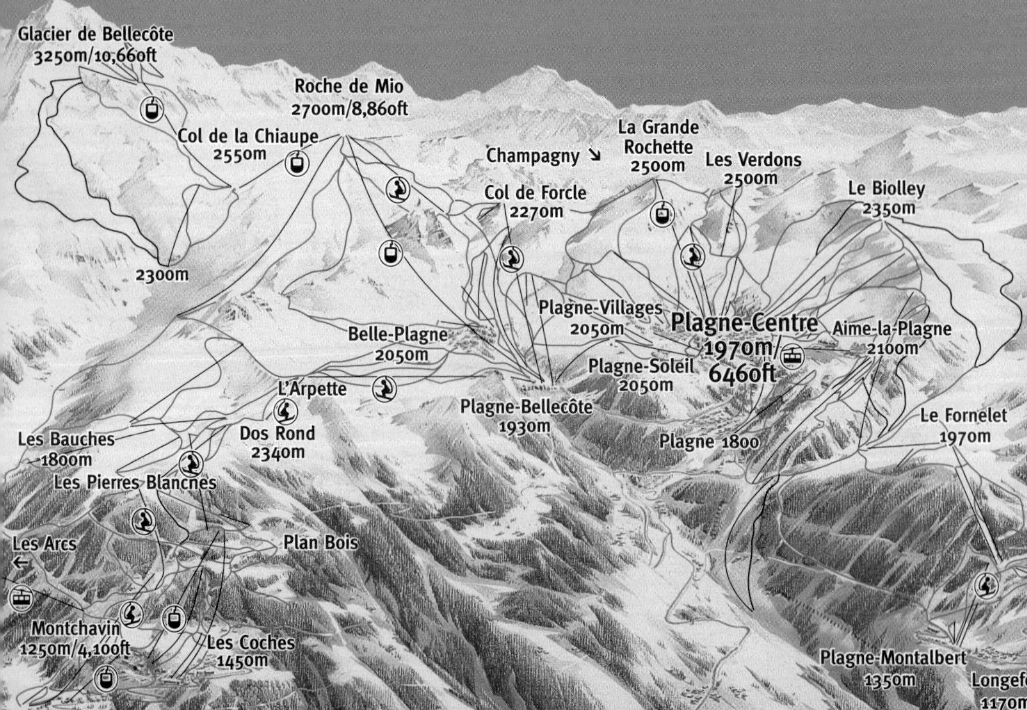

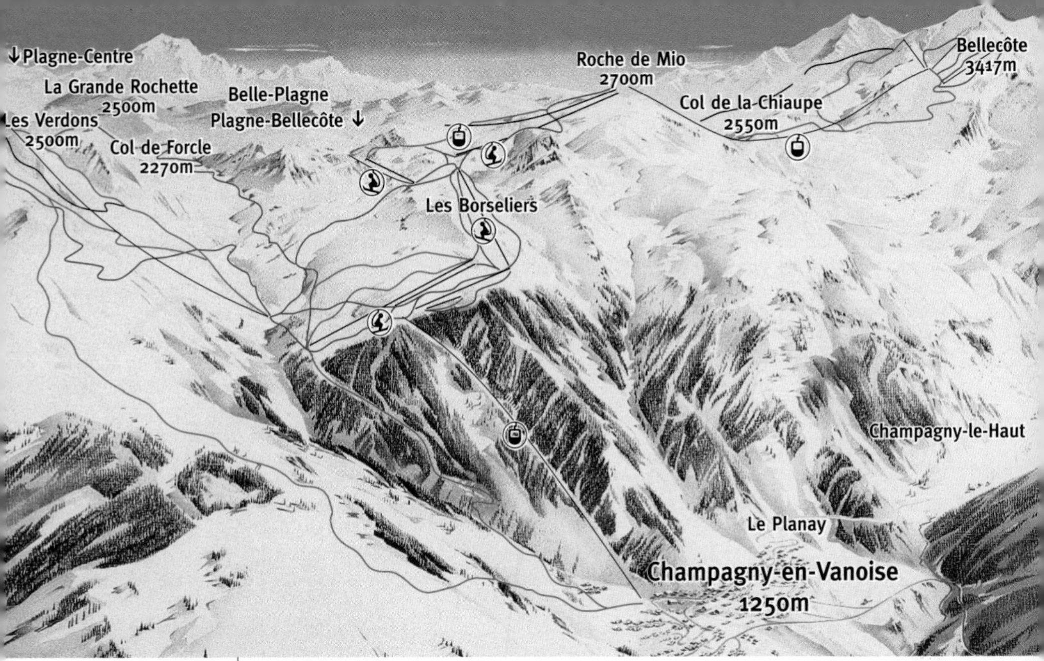

↓Plagne-Centre
La Grande Rochette 2500m
Les Verdons 2500m
Col de Forcle 2270m
Belle-Plagne
Plagne-Bellecôte ↓
Roche de Mio 2700m
Col de la Chiaupe 2550m
Bellecôte 3417m
Les Borseliers
Champagny-le-Haut
Le Planay
Champagny-en-Vanoise 1250m



**PARADISKI FEEDBACK**

Two of our reporters made an expedition to Les Arcs. Here's what they thought:

'It was nice to ski somewhere different – including a fantastic long black from the Aiguille Rouge.'

'We caught a bus from Plagne 1800 to Bellecôte. We were in Plan-Peisey before 10am and had a full day in Les Arcs, taking in the Aiguille Rouge and a good lunch – back in Plagne 1800 for 5pm. The new lift is a great asset; it was well able to cope with the crowds. It was fairly expensive, but for a one-off day it was great fun.'



## THE SLOPES
### *Multi-centred; can be confusing*

La Plagne boasts 220km/137 miles of pistes over a wide area that can be broken down into seven distinct but interlinked sectors. From Plagne-Centre you can take a lift up to **Le Biolley**, from where you can head back to Centre, to Aime-la-Plagne or down gentle runs to **Montalbert**, from where you ride several successive lifts back up. But the main lift out of Plagne-Centre leads up to **La Grande Rochette**. From here there are good sweeping runs back down and an easier one over to Plagne-Bellecôte, or you can drop over the back into the mainly south-facing **Champagny** sector. From the Champagny sector there are great views over to Courchevel.

From Plagne-Bellecôte and Belle-Plagne, you can head up to **Roche de Mio**, and have the choice of the newly refurbished gondola, or the two fast chairs (the first of which also links with the Champagny sector). From Roche de Mio, runs spread out in all directions – towards La Plagne, Champagny or **Montchavin/Les Coches** and the link with Les Arcs. Montchavin/Les Coches can also be reached by taking a chair from Plagne-Bellecôte to L'Arpette. The return from here should be improved when the two Salla drags and the Bijolin chair are replaced by six-packs.

From Roche de Mio you can also take a gondola down then up to the **Bellecôte glacier**. The top chair is often shut in winter – but if open it offers excellent snow and stunning views. You can descend 2000m vertical from the glacier to Montchavin, with a not-difficult off-piste stretch in the middle (we were told wrongly last season that this stretch was being turned into a piste – shown on some piste maps).

Several reporters have complained that run grading is inconsistent; some runs are more difficult than their grading suggests, others are easier.

## TERRAIN-PARKS
### *Spoilt for choice*

There are terrain-parks at Belle-Plagne, Montchavin-Les Coches, and most recently at Champagny. The biggest is at Belle-Plagne, with big air, loads of kickers and rails – plus deckchairs to chill in and shovels to build your own kickers if you want. The other two have a selection of jumps. Plagne-Bellecôte has a 100m/328ft half-pipe and a ski- and boarder-cross run.

## SNOW RELIABILITY
### *Generally good except low down*

Most of La Plagne's runs are snow-sure, being at altitudes between 2000m and 2700m (6,560ft and 8,860ft) on the largely north-facing open slopes above the purpose-built centres. But during the exceptionally poor conditions a couple of seasons ago several reporters commented on poor piste grooming (which still produces complaints), rocks and bare

## LIFT PASSES

**La Plagne**
Covers all lifts in all La Plagne areas.

**Beginners**
Free baby lifts.

**Main pass**
1 day €37
6 days €176

**Senior citizens**
Over 60: 6 days €150
Over 72: free pass

**Children**
Under 14: 6 days €131
Under 5: free pass

**Notes** Also available: individual village-area and half-day passes, and Paradiski extension.

**Paradiski Découverte**
Covers lifts in all La Plagne areas and one-day Paradiski extension.

**Main pass**
6 days €190

**Senior citizens**
Over 60: 6 days €162
Over 72: free

**Children**
Under 14: 6 days €143
Under 6: free

**Notes** Extension valid Sat-Tue only, unless bought through certain UK tour operators; also covers a day in each of the Three Valleys, Val-d'Isère-Tignes, Les Saisies, Pralognan.

**Paradiski**
Covers all lifts in Les Arcs area and La Plagne area

**Main pass**
6 days €220

**Senior citizens**
Over 60: 6 days €187
Over 72: free pass

**Children**
Under 14: 6 days €165
Under 6: free pass

**Notes** Covers a day in each of the Three Valleys, Val-d'Isère-Tignes, Les Saisies, Pralognan.





patches and the need for more snowmaking on the runs into the villages – especially the busy runs into Plagne-Bellecôte. More snowmaking is planned over the next few seasons.

Runs down to the lower resorts can cause more problems – particularly the two sunny runs to Champagny. The north-facing runs to Montchavin/Les Coches and Montalbert, plus a few runs around Plagne-Centre and Plagne-Bellecôte, are the main ones with guns at the moment. But even here cover can be patchy if the weather is warm.

### FOR EXPERTS
***A few good blacks and off-piste***

There are two great black runs from Bellecôte to the chair-lift up to the gondola mid-station at Col de la Chiaupe – both beautiful long runs with a vertical of some 1000m/3,280ft that take you away from the lift system. But these are often closed because of too much or too little snow.

The Les Charmettes black at the end of the long Emile Allais red down from above Aime-la-Plagne is little used, north-facing and very enjoyable in good snow. A couple of drag-lifts take you back up. The Coqs and Morbleu runs also in the Aime-la-Plagne sector are seriously steep.

But experts will get the best out of La Plagne if they hire a guide and explore the vast off-piste potential – which takes longer to get tracked out than in more 'macho' resorts.

### FOR INTERMEDIATES
***Great variety***

Virtually the whole of La Plagne's area is a paradise for intermediates, with blue and red runs wherever you look.

For early intermediates there are plenty of gentle blue motorway pistes in the main La Plagne bowl, and a long, interesting run from Roche de Mio back to Belle Plagne, Les Inversens (involving a tunnel). The blue runs either side of L'Arpette, on the Montchavin side of the main bowl, are glorious cruises. In poor weather the best place to be is in the trees on the gentle runs leading down to Montalbert. The easiest way over to Champagny is from the Roche de Mio area rather than from Grande Rochette.

Better intermediates have lots of delightful long red runs to try. There are challenging red mogul pitches down from the glacier. Roche de Mio to Les Bauches is a drop of 900m/2,950ft – the first half, Le Clapet, is a fabulous varied run with lots of off-piste diversions possible; the second half, Les Crozats, was changed from black to red for 2003/04 – but a reporter comments that it is 'narrow and mogulled' and tricky for timid intermediates. A blue run carries on to Montchavin, but much of this is flattish, and hard work.

The Champagny sector has a couple of tough reds – Kamikaze and Hara-Kiri – leading from Grande Rochette. And the long blue cruise Bozelet has one surprisingly steep section. The long, sweeping Mont de la Guerre red, with 1250m/4,100ft vertical from Les Verdons to Champagny, is also a great run in good snow (a rare event).

### FOR BEGINNERS
***Excellent facilities for the novice***

La Plagne is a good place to learn, with generally good snow and above-average facilities for beginners, especially children. Each of the main centres has nursery slopes on its

## boarding

*La Plagne offers terrain for all levels of rider – there's a good mix of long, easy runs and high, open slopes with some fantastic off-piste options that should be done with a guide. The broad, gentle pistes are ideal for beginners and carvers (crowds permitting). There are also lots of areas to play in between the pistes, as well as three terrain-parks, a boarder-cross and a half-pipe. Whether on- or off-piste, be prepared for some flat areas, including the tunnel in the middle of the Inversens run and the linking blue down to Montchavin from Les Bauches. And while most lifts are gondolas or chairs, there are still some difficult drag-lifts. 'The flat bits are definitely a drawback,' said one reporter, 'but you can get around without using the drags.' More difficult drag-lifts are conveniently marked on the map – it's not a good idea to go all the way down Emile Allais, for example, unless you're very experienced at riding them. Some reporters faced a long walk back to 1800!*

## SCHOOLS

**ESF**
Schools in all centres.
t 0479 900668 (Belle Plagne)

**Oxygène** (Plagne-Centre)
t 0479 090399

**EL Pro** (Belle-Plagne)
t 0479 091162

**Reflex** (Plagne 1800)
t 0613 808056

**Magic in Motion** (Plagne Centre)
t 0617 803311

**Evolution 2** (Montchavin)
t 0479 078185

**Classes** (ESF prices)
6 half-days €94

**Private lessons**
€30 for 1hr

SNOWPIX.COM / CHRIS GILL

There are excellent runs from the top of the system at Bellecôte, both on this side and the shady north face ↓

doorstep. There's a free drag-lift in each resort as well. There are no long green runs to progress to, but no shortage of easy blues. A reporter particularly recommends Les Bouclets at Aime as 'wide and confidence-building'. The Plan Bois area above Les Coches has good gentle slopes. Several reporters have commented that the blue runs back into Plagne 1800 are difficult for novices.

### CROSS-COUNTRY
***Open and wooded trails***

There are 85km/53 miles of prepared cross-country trails scattered around. The most beautiful of these are the 30km/19 miles of winding track set out in the sunny valley around Champagny-le-Haut. The north-facing areas have more wooded trails that link the various centres. It's best to have a car if you want to make the most of it all.

### QUEUES
***Main problems being sorted***

La Plagne used to have some big bottlenecks. Recent lift improvements have eased some of the worst problems, and hopefully the renovation of the Roche de Mio gondola will have reduced the queues for that. But reporters still complain about long waits for the Arpette chair from Plagne-Bellecôte towards Montchavin (partly caused by chairs being allowed to travel up half empty). And there are still several lifts that can generate queues that you can't avoid, once you've descended to them – at Les Bauches for example and in the Champagny sector. The gondola to the glacier is queue-prone when snow is poor lower down. Crowds on the pistes are now as much of a problem as lift queues, particularly above Plagne-Bellecôte in the afternoon, and at Roche de Mio – 'horrific' and 'highly dangerous' were this year's comments.

### MOUNTAIN RESTAURANTS
***An enormous choice***

Mountain restaurants are numerous, varied and crowded only in peak periods, as many people prefer to descend to one of the resorts – particularly Champagny or Montchavin/Les Coches – at the end of the morning. Recommendations by readers include the Bergerie above Plagne-Villages, Crystal des Neiges, Carroley,

## CHILDREN

**Nursery** (Belle-Plagne)
t 0479 090668
Ages 18mnth to 3yr

**Les P'tits Bonnets** (Plagne-Centre)
t 0479 900083
Ages from 10wk

**Marie Christine** (Centre)
t 0479 091181
Ages 2 to 6

**ESF nurseries and snow nurseries** (ages from 2 or 3):
**Aime**: 0479 900475
**Village and Soleil**: 0479 090440
**Belle**: 0479 090668
**Centre**: 0479 090040
**Bellecôte**: 0479 091033
**1800**: 0479 090964

**Ski schools**
Children's classes are available up to 12 or 16 depending on the village: ESF Belle-Plagne 6 full days €129 (€171 during French February school holidays)

Plan Bois and the 'friendly' Plein Soleil on the Montchavin/Les Coches slopes. Two great rustic restaurants in which to hole up in poor weather for a long lunch of Savoyard dishes are the Chez Pat du Sauget, above Montchavin, and Au Bon Vieux Temps, just below Aime-la-Plagne. Reservations may be required at either. Chalet des Colosses above Plagne-Bellecôte and Chalets des Inversens at Roche de Mio ('fabulous views, good food') have been highly recommended. We love Roc des Blanchets at the top of the Champagny gondola – friendly staff, both table- and self-service, beautiful views over to Courchevel from the terrace and good, basic cooking – and a reporter recommends the Borseliers (in the same sector). The little Breton cafe at the bottom of the Quillis lift has been recommended as has the 'very French', newly refurbished Chalet du Friolin at Les Bauches (formerly the Val Santé). The Forperet, an old farm above Montalbert, is also popular and does good tartiflette.

### SCHOOLS AND GUIDES
***Better alternatives to ESF***

Each centre has its own ESF school, offering classes for all abilities. But high-season classes can be much too large (up to 20) and good spoken English cannot be relied upon. One reporter this year was in a 'mainly French class of 14', with an instructor disinclined to speak English. Another received good tuition in her group but her previously keen young daughter 'was left in floods of tears, with her confidence completely destroyed'. But reports about private lessons are generally positive, and the school in Les Coches came in for praise recently. However, the consensus seems to be that the alternatives are preferable. The Oxygène school in Plagne-Centre has impressed reporters: 'Worked very hard with us, and was very patient.' We have had glowing reports on the El Pro school in Belle-Plagne ('good English, asked us what we wanted to do, strong focus on technique and safety'). We have also had good reports on Evolution 2 (based in Montchavin) – 'Wonderful,' said the parent of one junior pupil. Reflex is the newest school (based in 1800), and a reporter noted that group classes are small. Antenne Handicap offers private lessons for skiers with any kind of disability.

### FACILITIES FOR CHILDREN
***Good choice***

Children are well catered for with facilities in each of the villages. The nursery at Belle-Plagne is 'excellent, with good English spoken'. Be wary, however of ESF classes (see 'Schools and Guides'). A Club Med at Aime-la-Plagne is one of their 'family' villages. Several UK chalet operators run childcare services.

## STAYING THERE

### HOW TO GO
***Plenty of packages***

For a resort that is very apartment-dominated, there is a surprising number of attractive chalets available through British tour operators. There are few hotels, but there are some attractive, simple 2-stars in the lower villages. There are two Club Meds. Accommodation in the lower resorts is described at the end of the chapter.

**Chalets** There's a large number available – the majority are fairly simple, small, and located in 1800. But new chalets in the lower villages are proving very popular now that La Plagne is linked with Les Arcs.

**Hotels** There are very few, all of 2-star or 3-star grading.

(2) **Balcons** (0479 557655) 3-star at Belle-Plagne. Pool.

(2) **Eldorador** (0479 091209) Adequate hotel in Belle-Plagne – 'Single rooms tiny, food good but service chaotic.'

(2) **Terra Nova** (0479 557900) Big, 120-room 3-star in Plagne-Centre.

**Self-catering** La Plagne is the ultimate apartment resort, but some are fairly grotty. The best we have seen are the Montagnettes in Belle-Plagne (spacious and attractive with good views) and the MGM Les Hauts Bois apartments in Aime-la-Plagne, which are 'highly recommended' by a reader this year – 'friendly, not a bad size'.

## GETTING THERE

**Air** Geneva 149km/ 93 miles (3½hr); Lyon 196km/122 miles (3½hr); Chambéry 92km/57 miles (2½hr).

**Rail** Aime (18km/ 11 miles) and Bourg-St-Maurice (35km/ 22 miles) (Eurostar service available); frequent buses from stations.

**UK Representative**
Erna Low Consultants
9 Reece Mews
London SW7 3HE
**t** 0870 750 6820
**f** 020 7589 9531
info@ernalow.co.uk
www.ernalow.co.uk

**Phone numbers**
From abroad use the prefix +33 and omit the initial '0' of the phone number.

## EATING OUT

### *A surprising amount of choice*

Throughout the resort there is a good range of casual restaurants including pizzerias and traditional Savoyard places serving raclette and fondue.

Reader recommendations in Plagne-Centre include the Métairie ('the most enjoyable we've encountered in the Alps') and the Refuge ('great meal in charming, rustic atmosphere').

In Plagne-Villages, the Chevrette is good for pizzas and steaks, the Grizzli for Savoyard food. In Plagne 1800, the Loup Garrou, the Petit Chaperon Rouge and the Mama Mia pizzeria have been praised as has the Loup Blanc – 'great food, good service'. At Aime-la-Plagne, Au Bon Vieux Temps (see Mountain restaurants) is open in the evening and the Soupe au Schuss, buried deep in the main block, has 'exceptional' food.

In Plagne-Bellecôte, the Ferme and Chalet des Colosses have been recommended. In Belle-Plagne, so have Pappagone pizzeria, the Chalet Maître Kanter and the Face Nord ('very friendly, lovely rabbit').

## APRES-SKI

### *Bars, bars, bars*

Though fairly quiet during low season, La Plagne has a wide range of après-ski, catering particularly for the younger crowd. In Belle-Plagne, Mat's (an English 'pub') and the Cheyenne are the main bars. The Maître Kanter has been recommended. The King Café (with a massive TV and occasional live music) is the liveliest bar in Plagne-Centre. Plagne-Centre also has night skiing thanks to the floodlights on the Stade de Slalom. Plagne 1800 is fairly quiet at night – though the Mine (complete with old train and mining artifacts) 'does a roaring trade during happy hour', and a reader also recommends upstairs at the Loup Garrou. The Lincoln Pub in Plagne-Soleil is recommended. Plagne-Bellecôte is very limited at night, with only one real bar – Showtime, which is popular for karaoke. But one reporter's group enjoyed the bowling, another the tubing. Aime-la-Plagne is also quiet. Neal's and the Luna (Plagne-Centre), the Jet 73 (Plagne-Bellecôte) and the Saloon (Belle-Plagne) are the main discos. There are cinemas at Aime, Bellecôte and Plagne-Centre.

## OFF THE SLOPES

### *OK for the active*

As well as the sports and fitness facilities, winter walks along marked trails are pleasant. It's also easy to get up the mountain on the gondolas, which both have restaurants at the top. The Olympic bob-sleigh run is a popular evening activity (see feature box). Excursions are limited.

Montchavin makes an excellent rustic base, especially with the link to Les Arcs ↗

OT MONTCHAVIN

## ACTIVITIES

**Indoor** Sauna and solarium in most centres, squash (1800), fitness centres (Belle-Plagne, 1800, Centre, Bellecôte), library (Centre), climbing wall, cinemas, bowling

**Outdoor** Heated swimming pool (Bellecôte), bob-sleigh (La Roche), marked walks, paragliding, snowmobiles, ice-climbing, ice rink, hang-gliding, snow quad-bikes, paintball, snow-shoeing, dog-sledding



## TOURIST OFFICES

**La Plagne:**
t 0479 097979
bienvenue@la-plagne.com
www.la-plagne.com

**Montchavin-Les Coches**
t 0479 078282
montchavin@wanadoo.fr
www.montchavin-lescoches.com

**Montalbert**
t 0479 097733
plagne.montalbert@wanadoo.fr
www.montalbert.com

**Champagny-en-Vanoise**
t 0479 550655
info@champagny.com
www.champagny.com

## STAYING IN THE LOWER RESORTS

### *A good plan*

**Montchavin (1250m/4,100ft)** is based on an old farming hamlet and has an attractive traffic-free centre. The cable-car link with Les Arcs starts from 300m/980ft above the village, and is reached by a fast chair. There are adequate shops, a kindergarten and a ski school. Reaching the La Plagne slopes involves a series of lifts; but the local slopes have quite a bit to offer – pretty, sheltered runs, well endowed with snowmaking, with nursery slopes at village level and up at Plan Bois. Those who venture further can return from Roche de Mio or the Bellecôte glacier (off-piste) in one lovely long swoop. The more usual way home involves some of the trickiest blue runs we have encountered. Après-ski is quiet, but the village doesn't lack atmosphere and has a couple of nice little bars, a nightclub, cinema and night skiing. The Bellecôte hotel (0479 078330) is convenient for the slopes.

**Les Coches (1450m/4,760ft)** is 2km/1 mile away and shares the same slopes. It is a sympathetically designed modern mini-resort that reporters have liked for its 'small, quiet and friendly' feel and its traffic-free centre. It has its own school and kindergarten. The Last One pub is good for après-ski, with a big screen TV and live bands. Poze (for pizza) and Taverne du Monchu are recommended for eating out. There's a shuttle to the cinema in Montchavin.

**Montalbert (1350m/4,430ft)** is a traditional but much expanded village with quicker access into the main area – though it's a long way from here across to the Bellecôte glacier or the Les Arcs link. The local slopes are easy and wooded – a useful insurance against bad visibility. The Aigle Rouge (0479 555105) is a simple hotel.

**Champagny-en-Vanoise (1250m/4,100ft)** is a charming village in a pretty, wooded setting, with its modern expansion done sensitively. It is at the opposite end of the slopes from the link to Les Arcs but well placed for an outing by taxi or car to Courchevel (or the beautiful Vanoise national park, with its 500km/310 miles of marked walking paths). Given good snow, there are lovely runs home (though a reporter doesn't recommend them for near-beginners). There are several hotels, of which the two best are both Logis de France. The Glières (0479 550552) is a rustic old hotel with varied rooms, a friendly welcome and good food. The Ancolie (0479 550500) is smarter, with modern facilities (recommended by a 2004 reporter). The village is quiet in the evenings but the restaurant Pola is highly rated this year for a 'great raclette' in 'lovely surroundings' with good views. A new artificial ice-climbing site in Champagny-le-Haut opened in 2003/04.

## TRY THE OLYMPIC BOB-SLEIGH RUN – YOU CAN NOW DO IT SOLO

*If the thrills of a day on the slopes aren't enough, you can round it off by having a go on the 1992 Winter Olympics bob-sleigh run (open certain nights of the week only). The floodlit 1.5km/1 mile run drops 125m/410ft and has 19 bends. You can go in a proper four-man 'taxi-bob' (90 euros in 2003/04), a special padded driverless bob-raft (33 euros), or, the latest craze, a mono-bob, 95 euros.*

*We tried the mono-bob and hurtled down solo at 100kph/62mph (in excess of the advertised speed!) lying almost horizontally – a great thrill, even if we did close our eyes on a couple of the sharper bends (the pressure in turns can be as high as 3g). Whether it is worth £70 to scare yourself silly is your shout! With the taxi-bob, you are one of three passengers wedged in behind the driver. You reach a maximum advertised speed of 110kph/68mph. Most people find the bob raft's 80kph/50mph quite thrilling enough. Be sure your physical state is up to the ride. It's a good idea to book ahead – and there are minimum age limits. Additional insurance is available (holiday policies may not be valid).*

SNOWPIX.COM / CHRIS GILL

# Portes du Soleil

*Low altitude cross-border cruising*

**The Portes du Soleil vies with the Trois Vallées for the title of World's Largest Ski Area, but its slopes are very different from those of Méribel, Courchevel, Val-Thorens and neighbours. The Portes du Soleil's slopes are spread out over a large area, and most of them are part of an extensive circuit straddling the French-Swiss border; you can travel the circuit in either direction, with a short bus-ride needed at Châtel only. There are smaller areas to explore slightly off the main circuit. The runs are great for keen intermediates who like to travel long distances and through different resorts. There are few of the tightly packed networks of runs that encourage you to stay put in one area – though there are exceptions in one or two places. The area also has some nice rustic mountain restaurants, serving good food in pleasant, sunny settings.**

The lifts throughout the area have been improved in recent years, with several new high-speed chair-lifts eliminating some bad bottlenecks – though there are still plenty of drags and slow chairs. But the slopes are low by French standards, with top heights in the range 2000m to 2300m (6,560ft to 7,550ft), and good snow is far from assured (though snowmaking has been expanded in recent years). When the snow is good you can have a great time racing all over the circuit (as we have been able to do on our last few visits). But the slopes can get very crowded, especially at weekends and in the Avoriaz area.

Purpose-built **Avoriaz** has the most

↑ Great views into Switzerland

PIERRE DEMARCHEZ / FOC





snow-sure slopes and is especially good for families, with a big snow-garden right in the heart of the car-free village. And it is good for snowboarders and freestylers, with three terrain-parks and now snow-cross areas.

The other French resort on the main circuit is **Châtel**. Given good snow, it has some of the best runs in the area – though they are mostly quite short. It is an old and quite characterful village, but it's a busy, traffic-jammed place. It has some good beginner areas – at resort level and up the mountain.

**Morzine** is close to Avoriaz. It is linked by lift but there's no piste all the way back to town. It's a summer as well as a winter resort – a pleasant, bustling little town with good shops and restaurants, busy traffic and long walks to the lifts from much of the accommodation – countered by increasing use of hotel minibuses. The local slopes are extensive, and linked to those of the slightly higher, quieter, traditional village of Les Gets. But they are low, and good snow is certainly not assured. You can use Morzine as a base to ski the main Portes du Soleil circuit, but it's not ideal. **Les Gets** is even further off the main circuit, and if skiing that circuit is a priority you are better off elsewhere – unless you have a car to drive to Ardent's gondola.

On the Swiss side, **Champéry** is a classic, charming, attractive Swiss village – but again just off the main circuit. You have to take a cable-car down from the main slopes as well as up to them – or, if there is enough snow, take a piste that ends out of town and then ride a bus.

**Champoussin** and **Les Crosets** are purpose-built mini-resorts set on the very extensive open slopes between Champéry and Morgins, with fairly direct links over to Avoriaz. **Morgins**, in contrast to Champéry, has excellent village slopes – but they are low and very sunny (one reporter noted that the main blue from Châtel was closed for much of the 2003/04 season), and although its more serious local runs are enjoyable and prettily wooded, they are also limited in extent.

On a spur off the main circuit are the resorts of **La Chapelle d'Abondance** in France (which has one of our favourite hotel-restaurants) and **Torgon** in Switzerland (which has splendid views over Lake Geneva). This area can be reached from above the Super-Châtel area and is usually quiet even when the rest of the circuit is packed.

# Puy-St-Vincent

*Underrated small modern resort with some serious slopes*

## COSTS

(1)(2)(3)(4)(5)(6)

## RATINGS

**The slopes**

| | |
|---|---|
| Snow | *** |
| Extent | ** |
| Expert | *** |
| Intermediate | *** |
| Beginner | *** |
| Convenience | ***** |
| Queues | *** |
| Mountain restaurants | *** |

**The rest**

| | |
|---|---|
| Scenery | *** |
| Resort charm | ** |
| Off-slope | * |

## REPORTS WANTED

Recently we have had few reports on this resort. If you go there, please do send us a report.

The best reports earn a copy of the next edition, and can lead to free lift passes in future.

See page 10.

- ➕ Mostly convenient, purpose-built resort that isn't too hideous
- ➕ Good variety of slopes with challenges for all abilities
- ➕ Low prices by resort standards
- ➕ Friendly locals
- ➕ Some great cross-country routes

- ➖ Slopes very limited in extent
- ➖ Upper village has only apartment-based accommodation
- ➖ Huge queues in French holidays
- ➖ Lots of slow old lifts
- ➖ Limited après-ski/restaurants
- ➖ Not a lot to do off the slopes

**Puy-St-Vincent's ski area may be limited, but we like it a lot – more, to be honest, than we expected before we went. It offers a decent vertical and a lot of variety, including a bit of steep stuff. Provided you pick your spot with care, it makes an attractive choice for a family not hungry for piste miles.**

## THE RESORT

Puy-St-Vincent proper is an old mountain village, not far south-west of Briançon. The modern resort of PSV is a two-part affair – the minor part, Station 1400, is just along the mountainside from PSV proper at 1400m/4,590ft; the major part, Station 1600, is a few hairpins (or a chair-lift ride) further up (yes, at 1600m/5,250ft), and there are buildings in various styles scattered around the hillside. Compact it may be, but 1600 is not perfectly laid out; depending on where you stay, beware walks to the lifts. We and our reporters have found PSV friendly ('even the lift operators') and well run. But it is a small and limited place, where you can expect one day to be pretty much like another.

## THE MOUNTAINS

Within its small area, PSV packs in a lot of variety, with runs from green to black that justify their gradings.

**Slopes** There are gentle slopes between the two villages, but most of the runs are above 1600. A fast quad goes up to the tree line at around 2000m/6,560ft. Entertaining red runs go back down, and a green takes a less direct route. The main higher lift is a long chair to 2700m/8,860ft, serving excellent open slopes of red and genuine black steepness. The shorter Rocher Noir drag serves another steep slope, but also accesses splendid cruising runs that curl around the eastern edge of the area. These runs are also reached by a fast quad chair from just below 1600. Most of the

## KEY FACTS

| | |
|---|---|
| Resort | 1400-1600m<br>4,590-5,250ft |
| Slopes | 1250-2700m<br>4,100-8,860ft |
| Lifts | 16 |
| Pistes | 60km<br>37 miles |
| Green | 16% |
| Blue | 37% |
| Red | 41% |
| Black | 6% |
| Snowmaking | 10km<br>6 miles |





other lifts are drags. The six-day Galaxie pass covers a series of major resorts beyond Briançon. More to the point for most visitors, it also covers a day's skiing above the valley hamlet of Pelvoux, 10 minutes' drive away. This area has blue, red and black runs, often used for race training, and a vertical of over 1000m/3,280ft served by a chair and a drag.

**Terrain-parks** There is a floodlit terrain-park with half-pipe at 1600.

**Snow reliability** The slopes face north-east and are reasonably reliable for snow. Snowmaking has increased and now covers one run down to 1400 and several above 1600.

**Experts** The black runs are short but genuinely black, and are 'totally ungroomed, with serious moguls'. There are off-piste routes to be tackled with guidance. There are itinéraires outside the piste network, including one to the valley.

**Intermediates** Size apart, it's a good area for those who like a challenge – but there aren't many very easy runs.

**Beginners** Beginners should be happy on either of the nursery slopes, and on the long green from 2000m/6,560ft.

**Snowboarding** Boarders are not allowed on the Rocher Noir drag-lift.

**Cross-country** There are 30km/19 miles of cross-country trails, including some splendid routes between 1400m and 1700m (4,590ft and 5,575ft), ranging from green to black difficulty.

**Queues** A 2004 reporter suggests avoiding all French school holidays, as 'the lifts can't cope', leading to 'awful' queues. At other times, no problems.

**Mountain restaurants** There is a modern but pleasantly woody restaurant at mid-mountain, but in good weather the sunny terraces down at 1600 are the natural choice.

**Schools and guides** You have a choice of French and International ski schools, and a British tour operator, Snowbizz, has its own school, which a recent reader found 'excellent'; it provides free guiding in the afternoons, as well as 'good instruction' in 'great English' and in small groups.

**Facilities for children** There are nurseries taking children from 18 months in both villages, and both schools run ski kindergartens.

## STAYING THERE

**How to go** A number of UK operators now offer accommodation here.

**Hotels** There are three cheap hotels in 1400, but none in 1600.

**Self-catering** 1600 consists entirely of apartments, and there are more in 1400. The cheaper apartments may be rather cramped.

**Eating out** The bar-restaurants serve 'a rather monotonous range of dishes'.

**Après-ski** Après-ski amounts to a few bar-restaurants in each village.

**Off the slopes** There are 30km/19 miles of walking and snow-shoe trails. Paragliding, dog-sled rides, floodlit tobogganing and outdoor ice skating (weather permitting) are available. And there is a cinema showing English-speaking films.

**Phone numbers**
From abroad use the prefix +33 and omit the initial '0' of the phone number.

## TOURIST OFFICE

t 0492 233580
courrier@puysaintvincent.net
www.puysaintvincent.com

OT PUY-ST-VINCENT

70% of the lifts are drags ↓

# Risoul

*Villagey modern resort in an attractive setting – and a big shared area*

## COSTS

①②③④⑤⑥

## RATINGS

**The slopes**

| | |
|---|---|
| Snow | *** |
| Extent | *** |
| Expert | ** |
| Intermediate | **** |
| Beginner | **** |
| Convenience | **** |
| Queues | **** |
| Mountain restaurants | *** |

**The rest**

| | |
|---|---|
| Scenery | *** |
| Resort charm | ** |
| Off-slope | * |

## NEWS

A new boarder-cross park was built at 2400m/7,870ft, off Peyrefolle, last winter. It includes a half-pipe, handrail and big air.

- ✚ One of the more attractive and convenient purpose-built resorts
- ✚ Scenic slopes linked with Vars add up to a fair-sized area
- ✚ High resort with reasonable snow reliability
- ✚ Good resort for beginners, early intermediates and families
- ✚ Plenty of good-value places to eat

- ▬ Not many modern lifts – lots of long drag-lifts
- ▬ Not too much to challenge expert skiers and boarders
- ▬ Limited après-ski
- ▬ Little to do off the slopes

**Slowly but surely the international market is waking up to the merits of the southern French Alps. Were they nearer Geneva, Risoul and its linked neighbour Vars would be as well known as Les Arcs and Flaine. The village of Risoul is a lot more attractive than either.**

## THE RESORT

Risoul, purpose-built in the late 1970s, is a quiet, apartment-based resort, popular with families. Set among the trees, with excellent views over the Ecrins national park, it is made up of wood-clad buildings – mostly bulky, but with some concessions to traditional style. It has a busy little main street that, surprisingly, is very far from traffic-free. But the village meets the mountain in classic style with an array of sunny restaurant terraces facing the slopes. Reporters have commented on the friendliness of the natives. The village does not offer many resort amenities. Airport transfers (usually from Turin) are not short.

## THE MOUNTAINS

Together with neighbouring Vars, the area amounts to one of the biggest domains in the southern French Alps – the combined area is marketed as the Forêt Blanche.

**Slopes** The slopes, mainly north-facing, spread over several minor peaks and bowls, and connect with the sunnier slopes of neighbouring Vars via the Pointe de Razis and the lower Col des Saluces. Plans to install a new fast quad from Valbelle up to the Pic de Chabrières above Vars, the area's highest point – providing a third access link between the two – have been put on hold. The upper slopes are open, but those leading back into



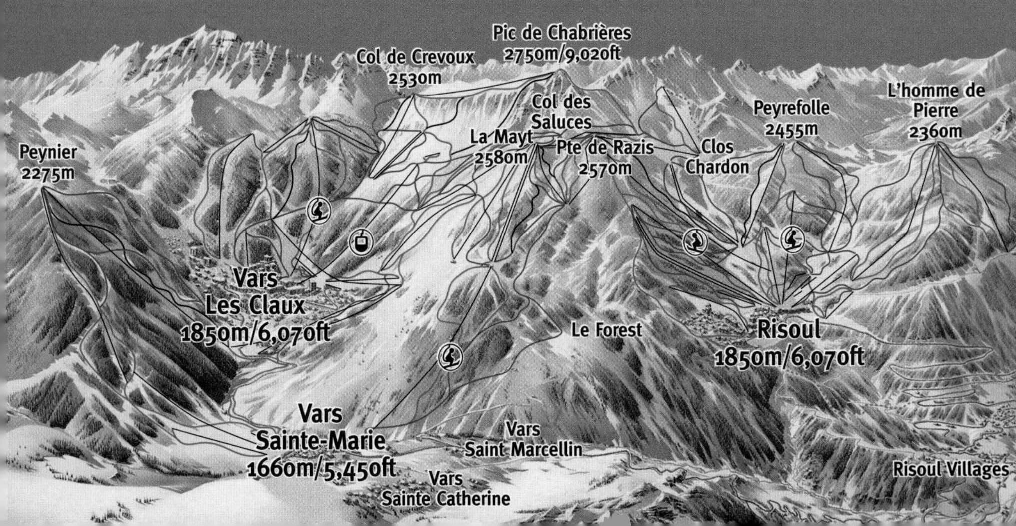

## KEY FACTS

| | |
|---|---|
| **Resort** | 1850m<br>6,070ft |
| For the entire Forêt Blanche ski area | |
| **Slopes** | 1660-2750m<br>5,450-9,020ft |
| **Lifts** | 57 |
| **Pistes** | 180km<br>112 miles |
| **Green** | 16% |
| **Blue** | 38% |
| **Red** | 36% |
| **Black** | 10% |
| **Snowmaking** | 29km<br>18 miles |

## REPORTS WANTED

Recently we have had few reports on this resort. If you go there, please do send us a report.

The best reports earn a copy of the next edition, and can lead to free lift passes in future.

See page 10.





Risoul are attractively wooded, and good for bad-weather days. Recent improvements in the lift system, including the introduction of some fast chairs, mean that the link can now be made in both directions without having to ride any drag-lifts. Nevertheless, reporters still complain that the system as a whole has too many 'long and steep' drag-lifts. Piste grooming is reportedly poor, but the gradings tend to overstate difficulty.

**Terrain-parks** There are two good terrain-parks – with half-pipes, boarder-cross, hand-rail and big air – one near the base, the other up at 2400m/7,870ft.

**Snow reliability** Risoul's slopes are all above 1850m/6,070ft and mostly north-facing, so despite its southerly position snow reliability is reasonably good. Snowmaking is fairly extensive and is being extended. Visitors recommend going over to the east-facing Vars slopes for the morning sun, and returning to Risoul in the afternoon.

**Experts** The pistes in general do not offer much to interest experts. However, Risoul's main top stations access a couple of steepish descents. And there are some good off-piste opportunities if you take a guide.

**Intermediates** The whole area is best suited to intermediates, with some good reds and blues in both sectors. Almost all Risoul's runs return to the village, making it difficult to get lost in even the worst conditions. So intermediate children can be let off the leash without much worry.

**Beginners** Risoul's local area boasts some good, convenient, nursery slopes with a free lift, and a lot of easy longer pistes to move on to.

**Snowboarding** There is a lot of good free-riding to be done throughout the whole area, although beginners might find the large proportion of drag-lifts a problem, and there are weekly competitions.

**Cross-country** There are 45km/28 miles of cross-country trails in the whole domain, of which 20km/12 miles are in Risoul itself. A trail through the Peyrol forest links the two resorts together.

**Queues** Outside French school holidays, Risoul has impressively quiet slopes. There may be a wait to get back from Vars to Risoul at the end of the day.

**Mountain restaurants** The mountain restaurants have increased in quantity and quality – the newish Tetras is a stylish chalet and the Refuge de Valbel is recommended, but most people return to the village terraces.

**Schools and guides** We have had mainly positive reports on the ESF and Internationale schools, but our most recent reporter describes his private ESF instruction as 'most indifferent'.

**Facilities for children** Risoul is very much a family resort. It provides an all-day nursery for children over six months. Both ski schools operate ski kindergartens, slightly above the village, reached by a child-friendly lift. One parent reckons many other drags have a dangerous 'whiplash' effect.

### STAYING THERE

**How to go** Most visitors stay in self-catering apartments, but there are a few hotels and more chalets are becoming available from UK operators.

**Hotels** The Chardon Bleu (0492 460727) is handy for the slopes. You can also stay overnight at the Tetras mountain refuge (0492 460983) at 2000m/6,560ft.

**Self-catering** The Constellation Forêt Blanche apartments are adequate but cramped; the Bételgeuse and Pégase are new.

**Eating out** There's plenty of choice for eating out, from pizza to good French food, and it's mostly good value – the Ecureuil and the Snowboard cafe, at the foot of the slopes, have been highly recommended by reporters. More expensive is the Assiette Gourmande.

**Après-ski** Après-ski is limited to a cinema and a few fairly quiet bars. The best are the Licorne, the Cimbro, the Chérine and the Ecureuil. The Yeti is the liveliest and full of Scandinavians.

**Off the slopes** There is little to do; excursions to Briançon are possible.

# Vars 1850m/6,070ft

### THE RESORT

Vars includes several small, old villages on or near the road running southwards towards the 2110m/6,920ft Col de Vars. But for winter visitors it mainly consists of purpose-built Vars-les-Claux, higher up the road. The resort has convenience and reasonable prices in common with Risoul, but is bigger and has far more in the way of amenities. There are a lot of block-like apartments, but Les Claux is not a complete eyesore, thanks mainly to surrounding woodland. There are two

Plenty of woodland runs above both villages – this is Peynier, at Vars →

SNOWPIX.COM / CHRIS GILL

centres: the original, geographical one – where the main gondola starts and which has most of the accommodation and shopping – and Point Show, a collection of bars, restaurants and shops, 10 minutes' walk away at another main lift station.

**THE MOUNTAINS**

There are slopes on both sides of the village, linked by pistes and by chair-lift at the lower end of Les Claux. Lifts also run up from both sides of Ste-Marie, lower down the mountain.

**Slopes** The wooded, west-facing Peynier area is the smaller sector, and reaches only 2275m/7,465ft – though there are good long descents down to Les Claux and Ste-Marie. The main slopes are in an east-facing bowl beneath the Pic de Chabrières, with direct links to the Risoul slopes at the top and at the Col des Saluces. There's a speed-skiing course at the top (you can have a go on it, via the ski school). Beneath it are easy runs, open at the top but descending into trees, with red runs either side.

**Terrain-parks** There's a terrain-park just above Les Claux.

**Snow reliability** The main slopes get the morning sun, and are centred at around 2000m/6,560ft, so snow reliability is not as good as in Risoul, but snowmaking is widespread.

**Experts** There is little of challenge for experts, though the Crête de Chabrières top section accesses some off-piste, an unpisted route and a tricky couloir at Col de Crevoux. The Olympic red run from the top of La Mayt down to Ste-Marie is a respectable 920m/3,020ft vertical.

**Intermediates** Most of the area is fine for intermediates, with a good mixture of comfortable reds and easy blues, particularly in the main bowl.

**Beginners** There is a nursery area close to central Vars, with lots of 'graduation' runs throughout the area. Quick learners will be able to get over to Risoul by the end of the week.

**Snowboarding** There is good free-riding to be done throughout the area, although beginners might find the number of drag-lifts a problem.

**Cross-country** There are 25km/16 miles of trails in Vars itself. Some start at the edge of town, but those above Ste-Marie are more extensive.

**Queues** Queues are rare outside the French holidays, and even then Vars is not overrun as some family resorts are.

**Mountain restaurants** There are several in both sectors, but a lot of people head back to the villages for lunch.

**Schools and guides** Lack of English-speaking has been a problem.

**Facilities for children** The ski school runs a nursery for children from two years old. There is also a ski kindergarten.

**STAYING THERE**

**How to go** There are a few small hotels, but Les Claux is dominated by apartment accommodation.

**Hotels** The Caribou (0492 465043) is the smartest of the hotels and has a pool. The Ecureuil (0492 465072) is an attractive, modern chalet (no restaurant). There are more hotels in the lower villages, including Ste-Marie.

**Eating out** The range of restaurants is impressive, with good-value pizzerias, crêperies and fondue places. Chez Plumot does proper French cuisine.

**Après-ski** Après-ski is animated at tea-time, less so after dinner – except at weekends when the discos warm up.

**Off the slopes** The amenities are rather disappointing, given the size of Vars: 35km/22 miles of walking paths, a cinema and an ice rink – and that's it.

**Phone numbers**
From abroad use the prefix +33 and omit the initial '0' of the phone number.

**TOURIST OFFICES**

**Risoul**
t 0492 460260
o.t.risoul@wanadoo.fr
www.risoul.com

**Vars**
t 0492 465131
info@otvars.com
www.vars-ski.com

SNOWPIX.COM / CHRIS GILL

# La Rosière

*Pop over to Italy from the sunniest slopes in the Tarentaise*



**COSTS**

①②③④⑤⑥

**RATINGS**

| **The slopes** | |
|---|---|
| Snow | *** |
| Extent | *** |
| Expert | ** |
| Intermediate | *** |
| Beginner | ***** |
| Convenience | *** |
| Queues | *** |
| Mountain restaurants | * |
| **The rest** | |
| Scenery | *** |
| Resort charm | *** |
| Off-slope | * |

**NEWS**

The ski area that La Rosière shares with La Thuile has been named Espace San Bernardo. For 2004/05 two fast six-packs are planned to replace the two slow lifts that were the main ways up the mountain until now – the Roches Noires chair out of the main village and the Les Eucherts drag-lift from the growing bed base there.

- + Attractive purpose-built resort
- + Fair-sized area of slopes linked with La Thuile in Italy
- + Sunny home slopes
- + Heli-skiing over the border in Italy
- + Good nursery slope
- + Gets big dumps of snow when storms are funnelled up the Isère valley from the south-west, but...

- – Winds can be vicious, closing lift links with Italy
- – Snow affected by sun in late season
- – Lots of slow old lifts
- – Few on-piste challenges for experts
- – One run is much like another – though La Thuile is more varied
- – Limited après-ski
- – Few off-slope diversions

**Like Montgenèvre, a long way to the south, La Rosière enjoys a position on the watershed with Italy that brings the twin attractions of big dumps of snow and access to cheap vino rosso. The former is crucial: given the sunny orientation of the slopes – very unusual in a modern French resort – average snowfalls wouldn't do the trick. The Chianti is less significant, because there are few attractive restaurants in which to consume it (see La Thuile chapter).**

## THE RESORT

La Rosière has been built in attractive, traditional chalet style beside the road that zigzags its way up from Bourg-St-Maurice to the Petit-St-Bernard pass to Italy (closed in winter). It's a quiet place with a few shops and friendly locals; but don't expect lively nightlife. The most convenient accommodation is in the main village near the lifts, or just below, in Le Gollet or Vieux Village. There is a growing amount of accommodation by the other main lift, in Les Eucherts.

## THE MOUNTAINS

La Rosière and La Thuile in Italy share a big area of slopes, now called Espace San Bernardo. La Rosière's sunny home slopes are south-facing with great views over the valley to Les Arcs and La Plagne.

**Slopes** The chair and drag out of the village take you into the heart of the slopes, from where a series of drags and chairs, spread across the mountain, takes you up to Col de la Traversette. From there, you can get over the ridge and to the lifts, which link with Italy at Belvedere.

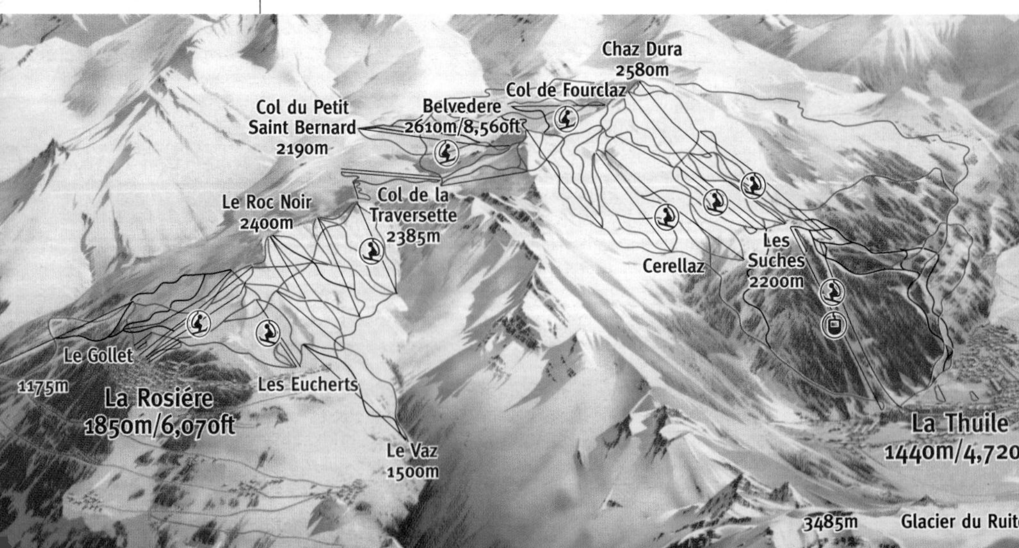

The housing stock includes lots of modern chalets ↗

OT LA ROSIERE / ANNE BADERSPACH

## KEY FACTS

| | |
|---|---|
| Resort | 1850m<br>6,070ft |
| Espace San Bernardo | |
| Slopes | 1175-2610m<br>3,850-8,560ft |
| Lifts | 37 |
| Pistes | 150km<br>93 miles |
| Green | 7% |
| Blue | 40% |
| Red | 38% |
| Black | 15% |
| Snowmaking | 276 guns |
| For La Rosière only | |
| Slopes | 1175-2385m<br>3,850-7,820ft |
| Lifts | 20 |
| Pistes | 47km<br>29 miles |

## REPORTS WANTED

Recently we have had few reports on this resort. If you go there, please do send us a report.

The best reports earn a copy of the next edition, and can lead to free lift passes in future.

See page 10.

**Phone numbers**
From abroad use the prefix +33 and omit the initial '0' of the phone number.

## TOURIST OFFICE

**t** 0479 068051
info@larosiere.net
www.larosiere.net

**Terrain-parks** There is a terrain-park served by the Poletta drag lift, just above the village centre.
**Snow reliability** Surprisingly good, despite its south-facing direction (you may find it has much more snow than the Italian side). Most of the area's snowmaking is in Italy. The link with Italy's slopes is prone to closure because of high winds or heavy snow.
**Experts** Other than excellent heli-skiing from just over the Italian border (including a very long run which ends up near Ste-Foy) and guided off-piste, there is little excitement for experts. The steepest terrain is on the lowest slopes, down the Marcassin run to Le Vaz and down the Ecudets and Eterlou runs to Les Ecudets.
**Intermediates** La Rosière would be nothing special on its own, but there's a fair amount to explore if you take into account La Thuile. Apart from the runs mentioned above, the bottom half of La Rosière's slopes are mainly gentle, open, blue and green runs, ideal for early intermediates to brush up their technique. The top half of the mountain, however, below Le Roc Noir and Col de la Traversette, boasts steeper and more interesting red runs.

The red over the ridge from Col de la Traversette has good snow and views, but is narrow along its top section. Weaker intermediates can avoid it by taking a chair down.
**Beginners** There are good nursery slopes and short lifts near the village and near Les Eucherts.
**Snowboarding** The long drag-lift to Italy means the resort is best-suited to beginners content to stay on the La Rosière side.
**Cross-country** There are 12km/7 miles of trails near the altiport.
**Queues** Queues are not usually a problem – but it is much busier here than over in Italy. The morning queues for the main chair out of the village should be a thing of the past when it becomes a six-pack.
**Mountain restaurants** A reporter recommends the self-service Plan du Repos for its 'friendly staff, huge pasta portions and lovely salads', but found the waiters at the Traversette were 'unable to cope with lunch-time crowds'. There are a couple of bars near the top, which are fine for picnics. The San Bernardo on the border is recommended. Many people descend to the village; reporters recommend the Relais du Petit St Bernard – 'good value, wide menu choice' – and the P'tit Relais – 'lots of choice'.

**Schools and guides** There are three schools. Past reporters have praised Evolution 2 for its 'good teaching, sympathetic instructors and small groups', but reports of the ESF have been less favourable: 'large groups' and 'insufficient supervision of small children'.
**Facilities for children** The Village des Enfants has a snow garden, and British tour operators Esprit and Thomson run nurseries.

## STAYING THERE

**How to go** A number of British tour operators now offer packages here.
**Hotels** There are a few 2-star hotels in the village, and more in the valley.
**Chalets** Of the chalets available we have had reports of Chalethotel Roc Noir ('well placed', 'good food') and of Ferme d'Elisa ('lovely accommodation but a 150m/500ft hike up to the lifts').
**Self-catering** You can book through the resort's central booking service. The relatively new Les Balcons at Les Eucherts offers smart accommodation for larger groups in spacious apartments, some with wood-burning stoves and all with hot-tubs.
**Eating out** The Chalet, Yéti, L'Oustal, Le Plein Soleil and the Ancolie have all been recommended.
**Après-ski** Après-ski is limited to a couple of bars in the village.
**Off the slopes** There are scenic flights and walks, an indoor climbing wall and a cinema. The ski schools offer paragliding and organise various non-skiing expeditions on foot.
**Staying up the mountain** The Hotel San Bernardo, on the border and reachable only on skis, provided a memorable two-night stay for an adventurous reporter last season. 'Simple, comfortable and peaceful', with a 'spectacular collection of grappas'.

SNOWPIX.COM / CHRIS GILL

# Serre-Chevalier

*One of a kind, with a growing band of enthusiastic visitors*

## COSTS

①②③④⑤⑥

## RATINGS

**The slopes**

| | |
|---|---|
| Snow | *** |
| Extent | **** |
| Expert | *** |
| Intermediate | **** |
| Beginner | **** |
| Convenience | *** |
| Queues | *** |
| Mountain restaurants | *** |

**The rest**

| | |
|---|---|
| Scenery | *** |
| Resort charm | *** |
| Off-slope | ** |

## NEWS

For 2003/04 the Bletonet triple chair-lift at the bottom of Chantemerle was replaced by a fast six-pack, doubling capacity.

A new casino is due to open in Briançon in time for the 2004/05 season. So is a new 3-star hotel, the Mont Thabor, just 200m/660ft from the lifts at Villeneuve.



- \+ Big, varied mountain, with something for everyone
- \+ Interesting mixture of wooded runs and open bowls with lots of off-piste
- \+ One of the few big French areas based on old villages with character
- \+ Good-value and atmospheric old hotels, restaurants and chalets
- \+ Lift pass covers days elsewhere
- \+ Generally quiet slopes, but ...

- − Serious crowds in central sectors in French holidays
- − Slow, old lifts on upper mountain – including many drags, some vicious
- − Busy road runs through the resort villages, with traffic jams at times
- − A lot of indiscriminate new buildings
- − Limited nightlife, especially in Le Monêtier and smaller hamlets
- − Few off-slope diversions

**Serre-Chevalier is a big-league resort, but isn't as well known internationally as many of its rivals to the north and west. Maybe that's because it doesn't lend itself to marketing hype – the slopes are not super-high, the lifts are not super-efficient, the hotels are far from super-smooth. But we like it a lot: it's one of the few French resorts where you can find the ambience you might look for on a summer holiday – a sort of Provence in the snow, with lots of small, family-run hotels and restaurants housed in old stone buildings.**

**The slopes are likeable, too. They are split into different segments, so you get a real sensation of travel. What really sets the area apart from the French norm are the woodland runs, making Serre-Chevalier one of the best places to be when snow is falling or wind is blowing – though there are plenty of open runs, too.**

**The lift system, on the other hand, is far from likeable. The resort has invested heavily in lift capacity at resort level but the upper mountain badly needs an injection of six-packs to disperse high-season queues at mid-mountain.**

## THE RESORT

The resort is made up of a string of 13 villages set on a valley floor running roughly north-west to south-east, below the north-east-facing slopes of the mountain range that gives the resort its name. From the north-west – coming over the Col du Lautaret from Grenoble – the three main villages are Le Monêtier (or Serre-Che 1500), Villeneuve (1400) and Chantemerle (1350), spread over a distance of 8km/5 miles. Finally, at the extreme south-eastern end of the mountain, is Briançon (1200) – not a village but a town – the highest in France. Nine smaller villages can be identified, and some give their names to the communes: Villeneuve is in the commune of La Salle les Alpes, for example. Confusing.

Serre-Chevalier is not a smart resort, in any sense. Although each of its parts is based on a simple old village, there is a lot of modern development, which ranges from brash to brutal, and even the older parts are roughly rustic rather than chocolate-box pretty. (A ban on corrugated iron roofs would help.) Because the resort is so spread out, the impact of cars and buses is difficult to escape, even if you're able to manage without them yourself. But when blanketed by snow the older villages and hamlets do have an unpretentious charm, and we find the place as a whole easy to like. Reporters talk of 'wonderfully friendly people' who 'made us very welcome' – unlike in many French resorts.

There are few luxury hotels or notably swanky restaurants; on the other hand, there are more hotels in the modestly priced Logis de France 'club' here than in any other ski resort. This is a family resort, which fills up (even more than most others) with French children in the February high season. You have been warned.

The heart of the resort is **Villeneuve,** which has two gondolas and a fast quad chair going up to widely separated points at mid-mountain. The central area

The top lifts above Le Monêtier serve some great off-piste and mogul runs →

SNOWPIX.COM / CHRIS GILL

of new development near the lifts is brutal and charmless. But not far away is the peaceful and traditional hamlet of Le Bez, which has a third gondola, and across the main road and river is the old stone village of Villeneuve, with its quiet main street lined by cosy bars, hotels and restaurants.

Not far down the valley, **Chantemerle** gives access to opposite ends of the mid-mountain plateau of Serre Ratier via a gondola and a cable-car, both with second stages above. Chantemerle has some tasteless modern buildings in the centre and along the main road. The old sector is a couple of minutes' walk from the lifts, with a lovely church and most of the small hotels, restaurants, bars and nightlife. However, a lot of accommodation is across the main road and 'quite a long walk from the lifts' says a 2004 visitor.

At the top of the valley, **Le Monêtier** has one main access lift – a fast quad chair to mid-mountain, reached from the village by bus or a steepish 10-minute walk, tricky when ice is around (though you can leave your boots at the lift base). Le Monêtier is the smallest, quietest and most unspoiled of the main villages (or 'deadly dull', to put it another way), with a bit of a Provençal feel to its narrow streets and little squares, and new building which is mostly in sympathetic style. Sadly, the through-road to Grenoble, which skirts the other villages, bisects Le Monêtier; pedestrians stroll about bravely, hoping the cars will avoid them.

**Briançon** has a gondola from right in the town to mid-mountain and on almost to the top. The area around the lift station has a wide selection of modern shops, bars, hotels and restaurants, but no character. In contrast, the lovely 17th-century upper quarter is a delight, complete with impressive fortifications, narrow cobbled streets and traditional restaurants, auberges and patisseries. Great views from the top, too.

Regular ski-buses, covered on the free guest card, circulate around each village and link all the villages and lift bases along the valley. But they finish quite early, and taxis aren't cheap.

A six-day area pass (or rather your receipt) covers a day in each of Les Deux-Alpes, Alpe-d'Huez, Puy-St-Vincent and the Milky Way. All of these outings are possible by public transport, but are more attractive to those with a car. If driving from France, you are likely to approach over the high Col du Lautaret, where we needed chains on our 2004 visit and which is very occasionally closed because of avalanche danger.

Turin airport is closer than Lyon, with easier road access.

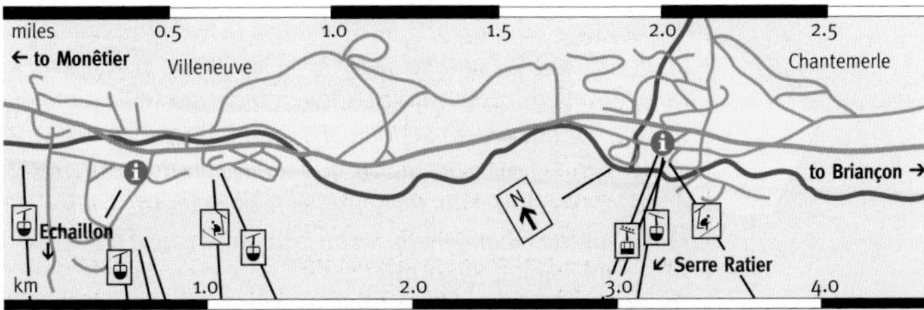

## KEY FACTS

| | |
|---|---|
| **Resort** | 1350-1500m<br>4,430-4,920ft |
| **Slopes** | 1350-2735m<br>4,430-8,970ft |
| **Lifts** | 77 |
| **Pistes** | 250km<br>155 miles |
| **Green** | 17% |
| **Blue** | 29% |
| **Red** | 41% |
| **Black** | 13% |
| **Snowmaking** | 40km<br>25 miles |

## LIFT PASSES

**Grand Serre-Che**
Covers all lifts in Briançon, Chantemerle, Villeneuve and Le Monêtier.

**Beginners pass**
Available

**Main pass**
1 day €32
6 days €158

**Senior citizens**
Over 65: 6 days €112
Over 75: free pass

**Children**
Under 12: 6 days €112
Under 6: free pass

**Notes**
Passes of six days or more give one day in each of Les Deux-Alpes, Alpe-d'Huez, Puy-St-Vincent and Voie Lactée (Milky Way). Reductions for families.

**Alternative passes**
Passes covering individual areas of Serre-Chevalier.





## THE MOUNTAINS

Trees cover almost two-thirds of the mountain, providing some of France's best bad-weather terrain (we had a great day here in 2004, despite the upper lifts all being closed by high winds). The Serre-Chevalier massif is not particularly dramatic, but from the peaks there are fine views of the Ecrins massif, the highest within France (ie not shared with Italy).

The trail map is supposed to have been improved, but it remains infuriatingly unclear and imprecise in places. Readers have found navigation is made even more challenging by 'atrocious' signposting and the tendency of runs to 'change colour halfway down'. We ourselves have found that the signposting at altitude is not up to the job when a storm socks in; take great care.

Piste classification is unreliable – many reds, in particular, could be classified blue, but there are occasional stiff blues, too.

### THE SLOPES
***Interestingly varied and pretty***

Serre-Chevalier's 250km/155 miles of pistes are spread across four main sectors above the four main villages. The sector above **Villeneuve** is the most extensive, reaching back a good way into the mountains and spreading over four or five identifiable bowls. The main mid-station is Fréjus. This sector is reliably linked to the slightly smaller **Chantemerle** sector well below the tree line. The link from Chantemerle to **Briançon** is over a high, exposed col via a six-pack. The link between Villeneuve and **Le Monêtier** is liable to closure by high winds or avalanche danger. Travelling from here towards Villeneuve involves a red run, so timid intermediates have to use the bus.

### TERRAIN-PARKS
***Fully featured***

There are big airs in Briançon and near the Echaillon piste, a boarder-cross in Villeneuve and Chantemerle and a half-pipe in Villeneuve (though it's not always open), all with sound systems.

### SNOW RELIABILITY
***Good – especially upper slopes***

Most slopes face north or north-east and so hold snow well, especially high up (there are lots of lifts starting above 2000m/6,560ft). The weather pattern is different from that of the northern Alps and even that of Les Deux-Alpes or Alpe-d'Huez, only a few miles to the west. Serre-Che can get good snow when there is a shortage elsewhere, and vice versa. There is snowmaking on long runs down to each village. Piste grooming is generally excellent.

### FOR EXPERTS
***Deep, not notably steep***

There is plenty to amuse experts – except those wanting extreme steeps.

The broad black runs down to Villeneuve and Chantemerle are only just black in steepness, but they are fine runs with their gradient sustained over an impressive vertical of around 800m/2,620ft. One or the other may be closed for days on end for racing or training. The rather neglected Tabuc run, sweeping around the mountain away from the lifts to Le Monêtier, has a couple of genuinely steep pitches but is mainly a cruise; it makes a fine end to the day. For moguls, look higher up the mountain to the steeper slopes served by the two top lifts above Le Monêtier and the three above Villeneuve. The runs beside these lifts – on and off-piste – form a great playground in good snow. The more roundabout Isolée black is a reader's favourite – 'scenic and challenging' after a rather scary ridge start.

## boarding

*Serre-Che is a snowboarding hot spot, popular with advanced boarders because of the off-piste, but it is not without problems for others. For beginners, local slopes are limited and drag-lifts must soon be faced; progression from the nursery slope up at Fréjus, for example, is tricky. The diverse pistes, with open and tree-lined runs, also suit intermediates, though there are some annoying flat sections – notably on the way to Le Monêtier – and descents to the valley can involve a choice between winding paths and unpleasantly steep runs. In some areas there are a lot of difficult-to-avoid and violent drag-lifts – one reporter's group stayed mostly in the Chantemerle sector, simply because they could cover a lot of ground using three major chair-lifts.*

There is huge amounts of off-piste terrain throughout the area; on our 2004 visit we had a great morning in the trees above Villeneuve and Chantemerle. There are plenty of more serious off-piste expeditions including: Tête de Grand Pré to Villeneuve (a climb from Cucumelle); off the back of L'Eychauda to Puy-St-André (isolated, beautiful, taxi-ride home); L'Yret to Le Monêtier via Vallon de la Montagnolle; Tabuc (steep at the start, very beautiful). And the experts' Mecca of La Grave is nearby.

**FOR INTERMEDIATES**
***Ski wherever you like***
Serre-Chevalier's slopes ideally suit intermediates, who can buzz around without worrying about nasty surprises on the way. On the trail map red runs far outnumber blues – but most reds are at the easy end of the scale and the grooming is usually good, so even nervous intermediates shouldn't have problems with them.

There's plenty for more adventurous intermediates, though. Many runs are wide enough for a fast pace. Cucumelle on the edge of the Villeneuve sector is a favourite – a beautiful long red, away from the lifts, with a challenging initial section. The red runs off the little-used Aiguillette chair in the Chantemerle sector (which we dubbed the 'Lost Chair' on our last visit because it was so quiet while other areas were packed) are worth seeking out – quiet, enjoyable fast cruises. Aya and Clos Galliard at Le Monêtier and the wonderful long run from the top to the bottom of the gondola at Briançon (with great views of the town) are other favourites.

If the reds are starting to seem a bit tame, there is plenty more to progress to. Unless ice towards the bottom is a problem, the (often well-groomed) blacks on the lower mountain should be first on the agenda, and the bumpier ones higher up can be tackled if snow is good.

**FOR BEGINNERS**
***All three areas OK***
All three main villages have nursery areas (at Chantemerle the area is small, and you generally go up to Serre Ratier or Grand Alpe – both rated as good by a beginner reporter) and there are some easy high runs to progress to. Villeneuve has excellent green runs above Fréjus. Both sectors have green paths down from mid mountain. But they are narrow, and not enjoyable when the runs become rutted and others are speeding along. Le Monêtier's easy runs are at resort level, next to excellent nursery slopes, and beginners have recommended it for 'better snow and fewer people'. But progression to long runs here isn't so easy, and the link to Villeneuve involves the red Cucumelle run.

**FOR CROSS-COUNTRY**
***Excellent if the snow is good***
There are 35km/22 miles of tracks along the valley floor, mainly following the gurgling river between Le Monêtier and Villeneuve and going on up towards the Col du Lautaret.

**QUEUES**
***Investment needed high-up***
A range of big lifts means there are few problems getting out of the valley. But the many old, slow lifts still cause queues at altitude, as well as slowing down the whole process of exploration.

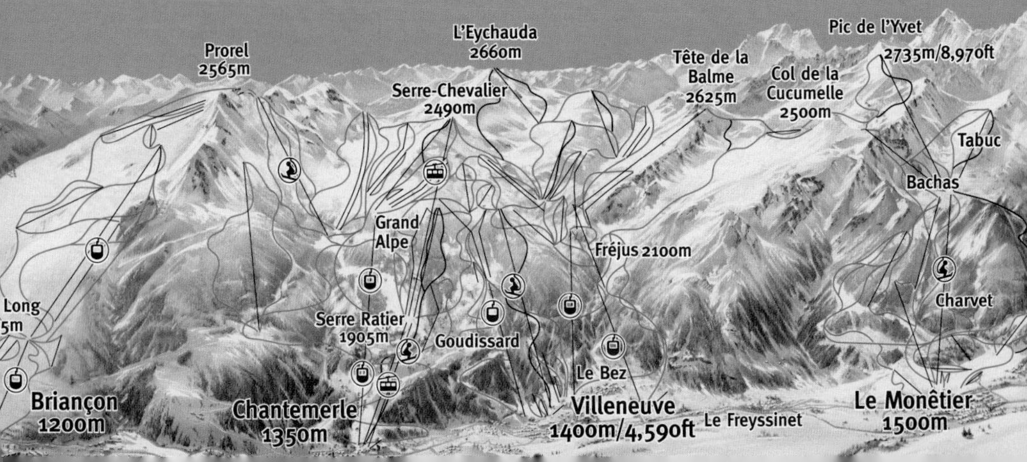

## SCHOOLS

**ESF** In all centres
**t** 0492 92241741
esf-serre-che-1350@wanadoo.fr

**Génération Snow** (1350)
**t** 0492 242151
generation.snow@freesbee.fr

**Evasion** (1350)
**t** 0492 240241

**Buissonnière** (1400)
**t** 0492 247866
ecolebuisse@free.fr

**EurekaSKI**
0674 462484
01326 375710 (in UK)
info@eurekaski.com

**Axesse**
0492 242711
info@axesse.com

**Classes** (ESF prices)
6 half-days €102

**Private lessons**
€31 for 1hr

## GUIDES

**Bureau des Guides** (1200)
**t** 0492 201573
bgb05@club-internet.fr

**Compagnie des Guides de l'Oisans** (1400)
**t** 0492 247590
guides-serrechevalier@wanadoo.fr

**Montagne à la carte** (1400)
**t** 0492 247320
montagnealacarte@free.fr

**Montagne et Ski** (1500)
**t** 0492 244681
tallaron@online.free





The main bottlenecks are the slow and unreliable Balme chair on the way to Le Monêtier, the Fréjus chair above the Pontillas gondola, and the Grande Serre chair to the peak of Serre-Chevalier.

Of course, all these problems are worse in high season. More than most resorts, Serre-Chevalier seems to fill up with French families in the February holidays, producing serious queues, especially in the central sectors – Monêtier and Briançon are quieter.

The lower slopes above Chantemerle, in particular, can get hideously crowded, particularly when snow conditions are poor and progress therefore slow – head for the Aiguillette chair in these circumstances (see 'For Intermediates').

### MOUNTAIN RESTAURANTS
***Choose carefully***

Mountain restaurants are quite well distributed, but if lunch is an important part of your day, you need to plan it carefully.

For a serious lunch, book up at L'Echaillon, just below the the top of the Casse du Boeuf quad from Villeneuve: a rustic interior with open fire, where we had excellent confit de canard and carré d'agneau on our 2004 visit. Just above here, Bivouac de la Casse is reported to be an 'attractive chalet' with both self-service and 'first-class' table-service (inside and out), both doing 'excellent' food. Our previous favourite was Pi Maï in the hamlet of Fréjus, a little way below the Fréjus lift station, which closed down after an explosion but has now re-opened – reports welcome.

In the Chantemerle sector, the 'drab-looking' self-service Soleil has in the past been praised for 'excellent fresh-cooked food' and in 1994 'refused to take payment for two slightly burnt meals', says a reporter.

In the Briançon sector, the Pra Long chalet opened at the gondola mid-station a few seasons ago. Its huge sun deck has great views, food in both table- and self-service sections is 'excellent', and self-service prices are 'very reasonable'. The little chalet just down from the top of Prorel has great views and is reasonably priced.

Above Le Monêtier the choice is between the 'uninspiring' self-service Bachas at mid-mountain and the cosy Peyra Juana much lower down, where we and readers alike have enjoyed excellent service, food and value. Both get packed on bad-weather days.

### SCHOOLS AND GUIDES
***Nearly all good***

We have received a number of reports on the Ecole de Ski Buissonnière over the years – most of them full of praise. But last year a couple of early-intermediate boarders report being put together with a couple of experts, with predictably distressing results.

EurekaSKI is British-run by BASI instructors. Classes with a maximum size of six range from beginner to free-ride masterclass. New for 2004/05 are special one-day Avalanche Awareness courses, including training on how to use transceivers and how to choose the safest routes off-piste, as well as some fun off-piste skiing. There's a satisfaction guarantee for all their classes: if you feel you don't benefit from your first session, your money will be refunded. Our reporters had no need. One who took two private lessons 'learned more than I have previously in a week'. A 2004 reporter found it 'exceptionally' good: 'I booked three lessons and felt I had my money's worth within 30 minutes of my first lesson as the advice had moved my skiing on so far – the positive, good-humoured tuition was appreciated by all.'

## CHILDREN

**Les Schtroumpfs**
(Villeneuve – 1400)
**t** 0492 247095
Ages 6mnth upwards; 9am-5pm

**Les Poussins**
(Chantemerle – 1300)
**t** 0492 240343
Ages 8mnth upwards; 9am-5pm

**Les Eterlous**
(Le Monêtier – 1500)
**t** 0492 244575
Ages 18mnth to 6yr (6mnth to 6yr out of school holidays); 9am-5pm

**Ski school**
Snow gardens for ages 3 to 5; from age 7 children can join ski school classes (ESF 6 half-days €94).

We lack recent reports on the ESF. But a couple of years ago, a near beginner was in a group with eight French and reports: 'By Wednesday I was reduced to tears and we left our class halfway down a blue run.'

On our 2004 visit we skied off-piste for a morning with Bertrand Collet of Axesse ski school and guiding service (which specialises in off-piste and advanced techniques) and had a wonderful time.

### FACILITIES FOR CHILDREN
***Facilities at each village***

We have had no very recent reports, but the Ecole de Ski Buissonnière (see above) has been praised in the past, as has Les Schtroumpfs in Villeneuve.

## STAYING THERE

### HOW TO GO
***A good choice of packages***

There's a wide choice of packages from UK tour operators, offering all kinds of accommodation.

**Chalets** Several operators offer chalets in the different parts of the resort. Equity's chalet Pyrene and Handmade's chalet hotel Rif Blanc have both been approved by readers (and you can book into the latter for a couple of nights locally if there's room). Chez Bear is a wonderful conversion of an 18th-century farmhouse into a luxury chalet for 10 – remotely set above Briançon but the owners will ferry you around in their minibus.

**Hotels** One of the features of this string of little villages is the range of attractive family-run hotels – many of them part of the Logis de France.

**In Monêtier:**

(3) **Auberge de Choucas** (0492 244273) Smart, wood-clad rooms, and 'excellent, seven-course dinners in stone-vaulted restaurant – but mediocre breakfast and erratic service'.

(2) **Europe** (0492 244003) Simple well-run Logis in heart of old village, with pleasant bar and 'good food'.

(2) **Alliey** (0492 244002) 'Excellent rooms with an indoor/outdoor spa.' Our favourite places to eat (see Eating out).

**In Villeneuve:**

(2) **Christiania** (0492 247633) Civilised, family-run hotel on main road, crammed with ornaments.

(2) **Vieille Ferme** (0492 247644) Stylish conversion on the edge of the village.

(2) **Cimotel** (0492 247822) Modern and

SNOWPIX.COM / CHRIS GILL
Old fountains like this add to the charm, even in some of the newer parts (this is Chantemerle – as is the photo overleaf) ↓

↑ The newer parts of Serre-Chevalier (this is by the main lifts at Chantemerle) aren't nearly as attractive as the older parts ... but see previous photo

SNOWPIX.COM / CHRIS GILL





## GETTING THERE

**Air** Turin 108km/ 67 miles (1½hr); Grenoble 92km/ 57 miles (2hr); Lyon 208km/129 miles (3hr).

**Rail** Briançon (6km/ 4 miles); regular buses from station.

**Phone numbers**
From abroad use the prefix +33 and omit the initial '0' of the phone number.

## ACTIVITIES

**Indoor** Swimming pool, sauna, fitness centres, tennis, thermal baths, theatre, cinemas, bowling, libraries, bridge

**Outdoor** Ice rinks, swimming pool, paragliding, cleared paths, snow-shoeing, snowmobiling, ice-driving, quad-bikes, pony rides, hot springs, ski-joring

## TOURIST OFFICE

t 0492 249898
contact@ot-serrechevalier.fr
www.serre-chevalier.com

charmless, with good-sized rooms and 'excellent' food.

① **Chatelas** (0492 247474) Prettily decorated simple chalet by river.

**In Chantemerle:**

②② **Plein Sud** (0492 241701) Modern; pool and sauna.

②② **Boule de Neige** (0492 240016) Comfortable, friendly, in the old centre.

① **Ricelle** (0492 240019) Charming, but across the valley from the slopes in Villard-Laté. Good food.

**Self-catering** There are plenty of modern apartment blocks in Villeneuve, Briançon and Chantemerle. Few have charm.

## EATING OUT
### *Unpretentious and traditional*

In Le Monêtier, there are several good hotel-based options. Our favourite is the panelled restaurant of the Alliey, which offers excellent food at astoundingly moderate prices and an impressive wine list. The Auberge du Choucas considers itself the best in Le Monêtier and is certainly the most expensive. The Europe has reliable French cooking at reasonable prices. The Boîte à Fromages is said to do a 'magnificent' fondue. Barbin is a bit out of town, in a rustic setting.

In Villeneuve the Swedish-run Vieille Ferme is a 'great, stylish eating place'. In the old part of Villeneuve, we have had mixed reports of the food at the Pastorale, a crowded vault with an open-fire grill. The Marotte, a tiny stone building with classic French cuisine, has been highly praised. The Noctambule and the Refuge specialise in fondue and raclette. And there are good crêperies – try the Petit Duc, or the Manouille. Over in Le Bez, the Bidule is said to have 'first-class food and service, at good value'. Two new restaurants which opened last season have been highly recommended: L'Ours Blanc and Passé Simple 1200.

In Chantemerle, the Couch'où is good value for fondue and raclette, and has a pizzeria upstairs. The candlelit Crystal is the smartest, most expensive place in Chantemerle; the rustic Ricelle offers 'amazing value'.

## APRES-SKI
### *Quiet streets and few bars*

Nightlife seems to revolve around bars, scattered through the various villages and several reporters complain of it being too quiet (though that doesn't bother us personally).

In Le Monêtier the Alpen has a happy hour, free nibbles and welcoming staff and the Rif Blanc bar is popular (both are British-run); the Que Tal warms up later on.

In Villeneuve, Loco Loco in the old village is 'the place to go, with funky music and a French atmosphere'; it has a 'comfy sofa area in the loft'. The Frog has 'good local beer'. In Chantemerle the Kitzbühel shows sporting events on TV, 'does good pizzas' and is 'not too full of fellow Brits' (though that may change now that the Underground and Yeti, which used to be run by Thomson, are no more). After everything else has closed, a karaoke bar with 'an erratic door policy' may still let you in.

In Briançon, the Auberge Mont Prorel, right by the gondola base, had live music and was full of Brits and Danes when we paid a tea-time visit.

## OFF THE SLOPES
### *Try the hot baths*

Serre-Chevalier doesn't hold many attractions for non-slope-users, and it's certainly not for avid shoppers, but the old town of Briançon is well worth a visit. There is a leisure complex with pools, sauna, hot-tub and steam room. Briançon also has an ice hockey team – 'a good night out', says a 2004 reporter. Visitors have enjoyed walking in the valley on 'well-prepared trails', and the indoor-outdoor thermal bath in Le Monêtier makes a great place to watch the sun go down – you need to book. The swimming pool in the hotel Sporting in Villeneuve is open to non-residents. Each of the main villages has a cinema. Chantemerle and Villeneuve have outdoor skating rinks.

## STAYING UP THE MOUNTAIN
### *Worth considering*

A possibility is to stay at Pi Maï (0492 248363) in Fréjus, above Villeneuve (see Mountain restaurants).

OT SAINTE-FOY / MARK JUNAK

# Ste-Foy-Tarentaise

*Off-piste haven gradually becoming better-known – get there soon!*

## COSTS

(1)(2)(3)(4)(5)(6)

## RATINGS

**The slopes**

| | |
|---|---|
| Snow | *** |
| Extent | * |
| Expert | **** |
| Intermediate | *** |
| Beginner | ** |
| Convenience | *** |
| Queues | ***** |
| Mountain restaurants | ** |

**The rest**

| | |
|---|---|
| Scenery | *** |
| Resort charm | *** |
| Off-slope | * |

## NEWS

The promised new lifts will not materialise this season. 'We have to wait one more year,' says the tourist office. Rumours continue that Val-d'Isère may buy the lift company. More new chalets and apartments should be ready for 2004/05, including an MGM block by the nursery slope, with pool and spa. Two restaurants and more shops are set to open at the station, and there should be a new boarder-cross course.

For 2003/04 the resort put some snowmaking in place, with a moveable gun on the route down to the resort. The first lift from base was also given more capacity to speed up the rare lift queue.

For 2002/03 the tourist office started a central reservations system, making it easier to book accommodation.

- + No crowds
- + Lots of excellent off-piste and untracked powder
- + Cheap lift pass and good-value lodging
- + Tarentaise mega-resorts nearby for a change of scene

- − Fledgling resort offers few off-slope diversions
- − Very limited piste network for high-mileage piste-bashers
- − To make the most of other resorts it's best to have a car
- − Limited après-ski

**This small area in the Tarentaise has been developed only since 1990, and recently the development has accelerated. The millions who flock to the nearby mega-resorts of Val-d'Isère, Tignes and Les Arcs still rarely give it a thought. But those in the know are well rewarded. It's an uncrowded gem with some wonderful off-piste slopes for experts and intermediates. Lots of ski instructors from the big resorts come here on their days off. And some bring their off-piste groups here for the day to escape the crowds back home.**

## THE RESORT

It is only now developing. Until a couple of seasons ago there was not that much accommodation at the ski station. Now more and more is springing up, with at least three developers working in the area. The good news is it's all tasteful stuff: traditionally constructed chalets and apartment buildings in the Savoyard style of wood and stone. Ste-Foy Station (sometimes called Bonconseil) is set 4km/2.5 miles off the main road between Val-d'Isère and Bourg-St-Maurice: turn off at La Thuile, just after the village of Ste-Foy. A complex at the foot of the lifts houses the tourist and ticket office, a cafe/bar, a pizzeria, a small supermarket and a couple of well-equipped ski/snowboard shops. Zigzags has been there for years and gets wildly differing reports, from 'horrible staff' and 'rudest ski shop in the world' to 'very helpful and well-equipped with everything for off-piste'. The newly established competition is part of the Skiset chain – you can reserve skis online at www.skiset.com.

If you don't have a car it's most convenient to stay at the ski station, as the free buses to and from Ste-Foy village and other local hamlets aren't very frequent. To make the most of the



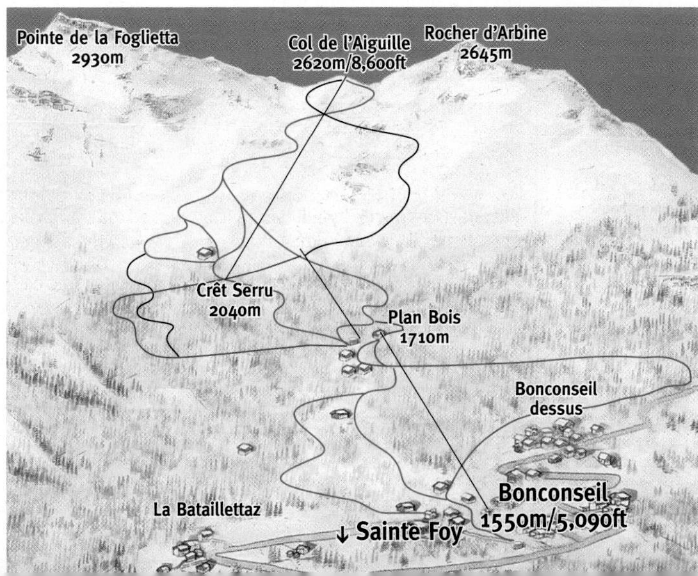

## KEY FACTS

| | |
|---|---|
| **Resort** | 1550m<br>5,090ft |
| **Slopes** | 1550-2620m<br>5,090-8,600ft |
| **Lifts** | 5 |
| **Pistes** | 25km<br>16 miles |
| **Green** | 8% |
| **Blue** | 15% |
| **Red** | 54% |
| **Black** | 23% |
| **Snowmaking** | Minimal |





scattered restaurant scene and nearby resorts, however, it's a good idea to have a car. Parking can be rather challenging and the road tends to be lined with cars.

## THE MOUNTAIN

Off-piste guides from Val regularly impress clients by bringing them to Ste-Foy's deserted slopes, accessed by three quad chairs, rising one above the other to the Col de l'Aiguille. Impressive as the off-piste can be, you may want to spread your wings from the tiny resort during a week's stay, particularly if the snow is unkind. Luckily Val d'Isère, Tignes, Les Arcs (via Villaroger) and La Rosière are all within easy reach (with a car). You are entitled to a day at each of them for 20 euros a time on presentation of a current Ste-Foy six-day pass – which at 96 euros last season was around half the price of neighbouring Val d'Isère. A day pass was a bargain 17.5 euros – compared to 38 in Val. 'Probably the best-value day's skiing I have ever had,' said a reporter last year.

**Slopes** The top lift accesses almost 600m/1,970ft of vertical above the tree line and superb, long off-piste routes on the back of the mountain. The two lower chairs serve a few pleasant green, blue and red runs through trees and back to the base station. Most reporters are amazed by the amount of terrain the few lifts access: 'Most of my ski career I've been in Verbier, Zermatt and Vail. Skiing in Ste-Foy is better.' But don't come here for miles of groomed pistes or modern lifts.

**Terrain-parks** The park wasn't maintained last season and is unlikely to be back, but there is set to be a boarder-cross course in place.

**Snow reliability** The slopes face north or west. Snow reliability is good on the former but can suffer on the latter, especially as there is snowmaking only on the run down to the resort.

**Experts** Experts can pass happy times on and off the sides of Ste-Foy's black and red runs, exploring lots of easily accessible off-piste and trees in the huge bowl (the long black run marked on the piste map is pretty much an off-piste run). If there's been fresh snow, Ste-Foy can't be beaten for snaring first tracks. The top lift may take a while to open, but when it does it is, as one reporter said, 'Awesome. People came from Val-d'Isère, and you could see others ahead of you on the lift. That's a busy day in Ste-Foy.' The lack of crowds means you can still make fresh tracks days after a storm. There's more serious off-piste on offer too, for which you need a guide. There are wonderful runs from the top of the lifts down through deserted old villages, either to the road between Ste-Foy and Val-d'Isère or back to the base, and a splendid route which starts with a hike up to the Pointe de la Foglietta, and takes you through trees and over a stream down to the tiny village of Le Crot. The ESF runs group off-piste trips, and arranges transport back to the station. There's also a Bureau des Guides which can arrange heli-skiing (0614 629024).

**Intermediates** Intermediates can enjoy 1000m/3,280ft vertical of uncrowded reds – ideal for confidence building and sharpening technique. The higher slopes are the more difficult – the red L'Aiguille is a superb test for confident intermediates, who would also be up to the off-piste routes, especially the

OT STE-FOY / MARK JUNAK

A picturesque plod by the river rounds off one of the great off-piste runs →

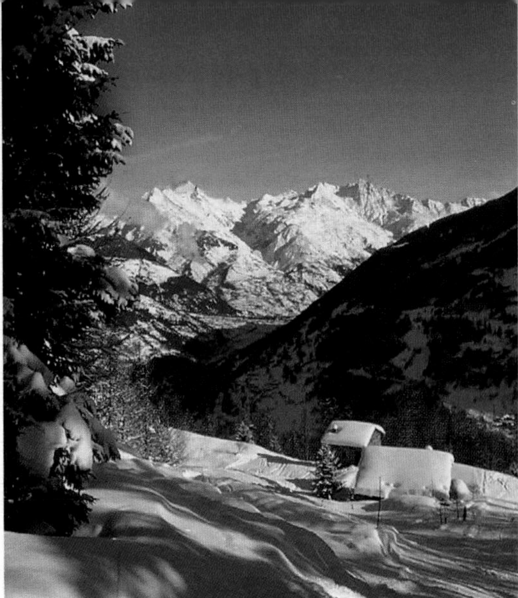

↑ The hordes who arrive in the main valley never give Ste-Foy a thought

OT STE-FOY / MARK JUNAK

Monal route back to base. Anyone who doesn't fancy experimenting with off-piste will tire of the limited runs in a day or two and be champing at the bit to get to Val d'Isère or Les Arcs.

**Beginners** Not the best place, but there is a small nursery drag at the base. After that you can progress to a green run off the first chair and a gentle blue off the second – and the slopes will be pleasantly quiet.

**Snowboarding** Great free-riding terrain, with lots of trees and easily accessed powder between the pistes to play in. 'Loved it,' said a reporter last year.

**Cross-country** No prepared trails, but ask the tourist office about marked itinerary routes such as Planay dessus.

**Queues** Except in peak season and on fresh powder days, you have more chance of winning the lottery than finding a lift queue at Ste-Foy. Even then, it won't be long.

**Mountain restaurants** There are two rustic restaurants at the top of the first chair. A reporter recommends Chez Léon as 'a winner'; you need to book. The Brevettes does good omelettes. The Maison à Colonnes, at the base of the first lift, gets consistently good write-ups. For snacks there's also the Pitchouli bar in the main base building.

**Schools and guides** We've had good reports of ski school, especially for children (from age four). There's a good chance classes will not be large.

**Facilities for children** Under 7s ski free. There is a nursery, Les P'tits Trappeurs, which takes children from age three to eight.

## STAYING THERE

**How to go** Various small tour operators can organise chalets and hotels here – see the list in the resort directory. Ste-Foy is about 20 minutes from the Eurostar terminal at Bourg-St-Maurice.

**Hotels** We have had several glowing reports of Auberge sur la Montagne (0479 069583), just above the turn-off at La Thuile, which has excellent food and atmosphere and is run by an English couple. Recently refurbished, it has a sauna and hot-tub. Yellow Stone Chalet (0479 069606) is a Gîte de France at the ski station run by an American, and has been highly recommended, though some visitors find it rather expensive. Hotel Monal (0479 069007), in Ste-Foy village, is a basic 2-star, with a games room, bar and two restaurants.

**Chalets and self-catering** Gîte de Sainte Foy station and Première Neige both have several chalets and apartments here, with catered and self-catered options. Chalet Number One, in the village of La Masure, is run by British snowboarder Lloyd Rogers, serving good food in comfortable, rustic surroundings. And one of our assistant editors has one of the MGM Fermes de Ste Foy chalets to rent, 100m/330ft from the lift (see www.ste-foy-chalet.co.uk).The tourist office has a brochure and runs a central reservation system (0479 069601).

**Eating out** Book the excellent Chez Mérie, in the village of Le Miroir, well in advance (for lunch, too). In La Thuile, book the Auberge sur la Montagne. In Ste-Foy village, the Grange at the Monal does 'good food'. Chez Léon opens by arrangement in the evenings. At the station the Maison à Colonnes (see Mountain restaurants) is also open in the evenings, and the Bec de l'Ane pizzeria does take-away as well as eat-in.

**Après-ski** Pretty quiet apart from the restaurants. The Pitchouli at the ski station is the place to go for a drink later on, though its liveliness is unpredictable. It has table football and sometimes live music (which one reporter rated 'awful'!). The bar of the Monal can get busy, too, and may have live music.

**Off the slopes** There's not a lot to do off the slopes, but paragliding, dog-sledding and snow-shoeing are available.

**Phone numbers**
From abroad use the prefix +33 and omit the initial '0' of the phone number.

**TOURIST OFFICE**

**t** 0479 069519
stefoy@wanadoo.fr
www.saintefoy.net

# St-Martin-de-Belleville

*Explore the Three Valleys from a traditional old village*

## COSTS

①②③④⑤⑥

## RATINGS

| **The slopes** | |
|---|---|
| Snow | *** |
| Extent | ***** |
| Expert | **** |
| Intermediate | ***** |
| Beginner | *** |
| Convenience | *** |
| Queues | **** |
| Mountain restaurants | **** |
| **The rest** | |
| Scenery | *** |
| Resort charm | **** |
| Off-slope | * |

## KEY FACTS

| | |
|---|---|
| **Resort** | 1400m 4,590ft |
| For the Three Valleys | |
| **Slopes** | 1260-3230m 4,130-10,600ft |
| **Lifts** | 197 |
| **Pistes** | 600km 373 miles |
| **Green** | 21% |
| **Blue** | 33% |
| **Red** | 35% |
| **Black** | 11% |
| **Snowmaking** | 1500 guns |
| For Les Menuires / St-Martin only | |
| **Slopes** | 1450-2850m 4,760-9,350ft |
| **Lifts** | 41 |
| **Pistes** | 160km 99 miles |
| **Green** | 10% |
| **Blue** | 37% |
| **Red** | 39% |
| **Black** | 14% |
| **Snowmaking** | 354 guns |

- \+ Attractively developed traditional village with pretty church
- \+ Easy access to the whole of the extensive Three Valleys network
- \+ Long, easy intermediate runs on rolling local slopes
- \+ Extensive snowmaking keeps local runs open in poor conditions, but ...

- − Snow at resort level suffers from altitude, and sun in the afternoon
- − No green runs for beginners to progress to
- − The climb up from the lower part of the village can be taxing
- − Limited après-ski
- − Few off-slope diversions

**St-Martin is a lived-in, unspoiled village with an old church (prettily lit at night), small square and buildings of wood and stone, a few miles down the valley from Les Menuires. As a quiet, inexpensive, attractive base for exploration of the Three Valleys as a whole, it's unbeatable.**

## THE RESORT

In 1950 St-Martin didn't even have running water or electricity. Later, while new resorts were developed nearby, St-Martin was a bit of a backwater. But in the 1980s chair-lifts were built, linking it to the slopes of Méribel and Les Menuires. The old village has been developed, of course, but the new buildings fit in well, and it remains small – you can walk around it in a few minutes. The main feature of the centre remains the lovely old 16th-century church – prettily floodlit at night. There are some good local shops and few 'touristy' ones. A regular visitor was pleased to report how 'unobtrusive' the newish gondola station is.

## THE MOUNTAINS

The whole of the Three Valleys can be easily explored from here.

**Slopes** A gondola, which opened two seasons ago, followed by a fast quad take you to a ridge from which you can access Méribel on one side and Les Menuires on the other.

**Terrain-parks** There isn't a terrain-park in the St-Martin sector, but you can get to the one above Les Menuires or those above Méribel relatively easily.

**Snow reliability** The local slopes face west and get the full force of the afternoon sun, and the village is relatively low. But there is now snowmaking from top to bottom of the main run to the village, and reporters agree that it is impressively effective at keeping the run open. Many people ride the gondola down if snow is poor.

**Experts** Locally there are large areas of gentle and often deserted off-piste. And access to La Masse for steep north-facing slopes will be improved by the new chair for 2004/05 – see News.

**Intermediates** The local slopes are pleasant blues and reds, mainly of interest to intermediates – including one of our favourite runs in the Three Valleys: the long, rolling, wide Jerusalem red. The Verdet blue from the top of the Méribel lifts is a wonderful easy cruise with great views and is usually very quiet. The whole of the Three Valleys is, of course, an intermediate's paradise.

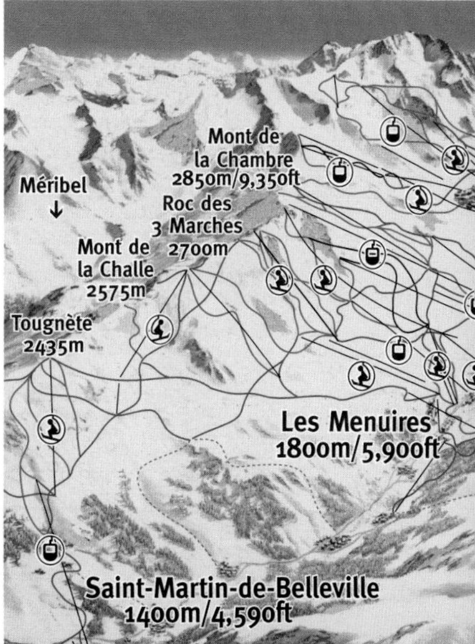

## NEWS

For 2004/05 we are assured that the long-promised improvements to the drag-lift from the church up to the main slope will be ready. And a six-pack with covers to Roc des 3 Marches above St-Martin is planned to replace two drag-lifts. It will start from the blue run down from Tougnète and make the run to Les Menuires a proper ski rather than a traverse.

**Phone numbers**
From abroad use the prefix +33 and omit the initial '0' of the phone number.

## TOURIST OFFICE

**t** 0479 002000
stmartin@st-martin-belleville.com
www.st-martin-belleville.com

**Beginners** St-Martin is far from ideal – there's a nursery slope but no easy green runs to progress to.
**Snowboarding** There is some great local off-piste free-riding available.
**Cross-country** There are 28km/17 miles of trails in the Belleville valley.
**Queues** Queues are not usually much of a problem – 'We didn't queue all week,' comments one visitor, and reporters praise the recent gondola as 'greatly improving access'.
**Mountain restaurants** There are three atmospheric old places on the run down to the village. Chardon Bleu and Corbeleys near the mid-mountain lift junction are good for lunch, and the Loë, lower down, is busy as the lifts close. Brewski's terrace is good for pies and burgers. For a real blow-out, the Bouitte in St-Marcel is one of the best restaurants in the Three Valleys (see Eating out) – you ski to it off-piste, and the owners will ferry you to a lift.
**Schools and guides** The ski school is said to have instructors with good English, but not all past reporters have encountered them.
**Facilities for children** The Piou Piou club and ESF take children from two-and-a-half years old from 9am to 5pm.

## STAYING THERE

**How to go** For a small village there's a good variety of accommodation.
**Hotels** The Alp Hôtel (0479 089282), at the foot of the slope by the main lift and close to the nursery, is deservedly popular. The Saint Martin (0479 008800) is right on the slope, and the Edelweiss (0479 089667) is in the village itself. All are 3-stars. There's simply furnished B&B accommodation slope-side at Brewski's – next to the bar of the same name but now marketed and managed by a German company. Rooms vary widely in size, but all are en suite and most have balconies with views. La Bouitte (0479 089677) in St-Marcel (see Eating out) has five charming rooms for a quiet, civilised break – Kaluma is the only UK tour operator you can book it through.
**Chalets** Les Chalets de St Martin has operated here ever since the first lift was built. But there are now a few other operators too, such as Thomson.
**Self-catering** Les Chalets de St Martin has a variety of self-catered chalets and apartments to rent, and plenty of others are available.
**Eating out** For such a small village there is a good variety of restaurants on hand. Several reader enjoyed the Montagnard's 'fabulous', 'reasonably priced' Savoyard food. The Voûte is good value too and is recommended for its salads and pizzas. Brewski's evening menu has a more French emphasis. The Lachenal is said to do 'good mid-priced food' and the Grenier, in the hotel St Martin, has impressed. The Etoile des Neige is a smart, traditionally French restaurant, but a recent reporter thought that it was a bit over-priced when compared to the Bouitte, just up the road in St-Marcel, which now has a Michelin star. A bit further up the valley, at Les Granges, is the rustic Chez Bidou – popular with locals and 'highly recommended for a Savoyard evening'.
**Après-ski** Après-ski centres around two bars. The Pourquoi Pas? piano bar is delightfully cosy, with a roaring log fire and comfortable easy chairs and sofas. Brewski's is a more animated bar with live bands most nights.
**Off the slopes** If you don't use the slopes, there are better places to base yourself. There are pleasant walks and a sports hall, and classical concerts take place in the church.

ST-SORLIN TOURIST OFFICE

# Les Sybelles

*Extensive linked area but with interestingly varied slopes only in one sector*

## COSTS

(1)(2)(3)(4)(5)(6)

## RATINGS

| **The slopes** | |
|---|---|
| Snow | *** |
| Extent | ***** |
| Expert | ** |
| Intermediate | *** |
| Beginner | **** |
| Convenience | *** |
| Queues | **** |
| Mountain restaurants | ** |
| **The rest** | |
| Scenery | *** |
| Resort charm | |
| – Le Corbier | * |
| – La Toussuire | ** |
| – St-Jean | **** |
| – St-Sorlin | **** |
| Off-slope | * |

+ Extensive area of largely easy intermediate slopes and gentle, uncrowded off-piste
+ Inexpensive by French standards
+ Unusual mixture of stark, purpose-built resorts and old villages

– Hardly any pistes steep enough to interest adventurous intermediates
– Après-ski limited and quiet
– Little luxurious accommodation
– Few off-slope diversions

**Les Sybelles? No, we hadn't heard of it, either, until word began to get around that a group of little-known ski resorts in the Maurienne massif in the French Alps were linking to form an impressively large network for the 2003/04 season. In terms of the extent of pistes, Les Sybelles' 310km/193 miles of pistes puts it straight into the big league, alongside such giants as Val-d'Isère-Tignes, Davos-Klosters and the Sella Ronda. But the similarity ends there. We visited eagerly a few weeks after the new links opened and were disappointed to find the pistes were almost uniformly easy cruising greens and blues, plus reds that should be blues – perfect for near beginners and timid intermediates but terminally dull for those who crave a little excitement. The exception is near St-Sorlin. The lift system, too, was dull – just one high-speed chair among lots of slow chairs and drags (though four more fast chairs are planned for 2004/05).**

**The resorts are sharply contrasting in character. Of the major ones, La Toussuire and Le Corbier are most politely described as functional and modern, selling on price and convenience, particularly for families, while St-Sorlin-d'Arves and St-Jean-d'Arves are largely unspoiled, traditional mountain villages which have recently expanded tastefully and attracted some major UK tour operators.**



The creation of the new linked area involved construction for the 2003/04 season of nine new lifts and five new pistes linking the existing resorts to the hill at the hub of the new area, L'Ouillon. The new links are high – mostly between 2000m and 2600m (6,560ft and 8,530ft) – so they are relatively snow-sure, safe and are easily negotiated by intermediates. The drawback is that getting from one resort to another can be slow going.

### LE CORBIER 1550m/5,090ft

**Le Corbier is centrally placed, with direct links to St-Jean-d'Arves in one direction and La Toussuire in the other, as well as its new link to St-Sorlin-d'Arves via L'Ouillon.**

### THE RESORT

Designed in the 1960s, Le Corbier is a no-compromise functional resort. Most of its accommodation is in eight inner-city-style tower blocks – one as high as 19 storeys – with subterranean shops beneath. To our eye, it looks like a mistake. But it does accommodate its 9,000 visitors efficiently in the

SNOWPIX.COM / CHRIS GILL

Easy intermediate slopes: that's what Les Sybelles is all about. The chair-lift in the distance serves the steepest and most interesting red slopes in the region (from Les Perrons above St-Sorlin) →

↑ Why did the French build monstrosities like Le Corbier in their beautiful mountains? But at least it's family-friendly

SNOWPIX.COM / CHRIS GILL





## NEWS

For 2004/05 four much-needed fast six-seater chair-lifts are planned. Two successive six-packs will go from the lift base at St-Sorlin up to Les Perrons and the link to the rest of Les Sybelles. And in La Toussuire, the existing slow chair from the base to Grande Verdette will be replaced by a six-pack which will meet another new six-pack to take you on to Tête de Ballard and the link to the rest of Les Sybelles.

There will also be some new or replacement drag-lifts on the lower slopes of St-Jean, Le Corbier and La Toussuire. And snowmaking will be increased by over 40%, especially on the slopes linking Le Corbier and St-Jean-d'Arves.

minimum space, and in functional terms it is hard to criticise – it is compact, family-friendly and traffic-free with all ski-in/ski-out accommodation. The apartment blocks line the foot of the slopes and in the other direction the resort's balcony setting gives good views of the valley. It sells itself firmly as a family resort and runs a French Family Championship with teams made up of mother, father and one child. And the resort assures us that all new building will be in traditional style.

## THE MOUNTAIN

Le Corbier's local ski area has 90km/56 miles of gentle pistes. Although the altitudes are modest (top height 2265m/7,430ft, resort 1550m/5,090ft), there are hardly any trees.

**Slopes** Two successive slow chairs rise over 700m/2,300ft vertical to Pte du Corbier from where you use some of the new pistes and lifts along the ridge to Pte de L'Ouillon and the links to St-Sorlin-d'Arves or La Toussuire. Runs spread across a wide, north-east-facing mountainside return to the resort, and there are links at the extremities to La Toussuire and St-Jean-d'Arves. There is a small area of floodlit skiing.

**Terrain-park** There's a park on the lower slopes just above the resort.

**Snow reliability** The mix of reasonable altitude and lack of crowds cutting up the pistes means the snow tends to stay in fairly good condition. The slopes get the morning sun, but there is snowmaking on all the main pistes back to the resort. The sunny link to St-Jean-d'Arves was bare and rocky on our January 2004 visit but should be improved by new snowmaking planned for 2004/05. The low connection from La Toussuire is another problem spot, but there is also a higher link.

**Experts** The area lacks challenges – the one short black piste scarcely deserves a red grading. There are off-piste options in the valley between Le Corbier and La Toussuire.

**Intermediates** Le Corbier's gentle slopes are ideal cruising terrain, though the runs aren't very long and they rather lack variety.

**Beginners** There is an extensive nursery area with a moving carpet right in front of the resort, with gentle progression runs directly above.

**Snowboarding** The wide, open terrain is ideal for riders, as long as they don't want anything too challenging.

**Cross-country** There are narrow loops across the mountainside either side of the resort, one of which leads to La Toussuire and back. It's all a bit bleak.

**Queues** The area is renowned for its uncrowded slopes, and the system is free of bottlenecks.

**Mountain restaurants** A 2004 reporter says Le Charmun, at the foot of the Vadrouille area, 'was the restaurant of the week for us, with delicious crozets with wild mushrooms and lardons' and Chalet 2000 near the top was 'notable for its playful golden labrador as well as its welcome and food'.

**Schools** Our one past reporter judged the ESF 'disdainful, uncaring, very disorganised; bad tuition'.

**Facilities for children** The Baby Club takes children from six months. A reporter praised the ski kindergarten (for age three up): 'Nice, well-equipped ski-park; good instructors'. Its location up on the pistes means a bit of a hike.

## STAYING THERE

**How to go** There are several UK operators selling packages here.

**Chalets** Equity Ski runs its own chalet hotel, described by one reporter as 'clean, comfortable and very good value' and approved by others, too.

**Self-catering** There's nothing larger than cramped two-bedroomed units on offer from central reservations.

**Eating out** Le Grillon, 3km/2 miles away in the Villarembert, makes a pleasant, rustic change from Le Corbier's tower blocks – and serves traditional French food.

**Après ski** Very quiet. The Equity Ski chalet-hotel bar is popular. Roches Blanches restaurant in the centre includes a cosy bar area with an open fire. For dancing, the Président gets busy only on peak holiday periods.

**Off the slopes** There's a nice natural ice rink and a new fitness centre. The outdoor pool opens in winter, and you can go snowmobiling.

| KEY FACTS | |
|---|---|
| Slopes | 1300-2620m<br>4,270-8,600ft |
| Lifts | 76 |
| Pistes | 310km<br>193 miles |
| Green | 17% |
| Blue | 40% |
| Red | 36% |
| Black | 7% |
| Snowmaking | 305 guns |

**LA TOUSSUIRE** 1700m/5,580ft

**La Toussuire, along with Le Corbier, is one of the central resorts of the new network – the two have been linked at low altitude since 1986.**

## THE RESORT

La Toussuire has grown up over many years but is predominantly modern, with a car-free and snow-covered main street lined by dreary-looking buildings dating from the 1960s and 1970s and plagued by piped muzak and a DJ coming via speakers attached to the lamp posts. The resort has now spread widely from here, with recently built wooden chalets as well as older hotels and small apartment blocks scattered across the mountainside.

## THE MOUNTAIN

The local slopes amount to 45km/ 28 miles of piste.

**Slopes** The resort sits in the pit of a wide bowl. Drags and chair-lifts (including two new fast six-packs planned for 2004/05) rise just over 500m/1,640ft vertical to the high point of Tête de Ballard in the centre of the bowl and the link to L'Ouillon and onwards to St-Sorlin. At one end of the bowl is the low-level link to Le Corbier and at the other the start of a long red run to Les Bottières of 900m/2,950ft vertical.

**Terrain-park** There's a boarder-cross course in the centre of the bowl.

**Snow reliability** With every run above 1800m/5,910ft snow-cover is fairly assured, but some of the slopes are rather exposed to the sun – particularly the low-level connection to Le Corbier.

**Experts** There are few challenges here, and not much space left between the pistes. The main interest is the ungroomed black Vallée Perdue run, which descends the valley separating La Toussuire from Le Corbier, away from the lifts. But it gets a lot of sun, and snow conditions can suffer. The new lifts towards L'Ouillon opened up new off-piste routes down this valley.

**Intermediates** This is ideal terrain for cruisers who don't mind mainly short runs. The longer runs that go down to Les Bottières are some of the most appealing in the whole area.

**Beginners** There are nice, gentle nursery slopes immediately above the centre of the village, and good, easy progression slopes.

**Snowboarding** There are quite a few drag-lifts in the area.

**Cross-country** A narrow loop goes to Le Corbier, but it is close to the road and the surroundings are quite bleak.

**Queues** We have not heard of any problems.

**Mountain restaurants** A reporter recommends the Foehn at Le Marolay for its 'friendly service', the good views and an interesting interior of old





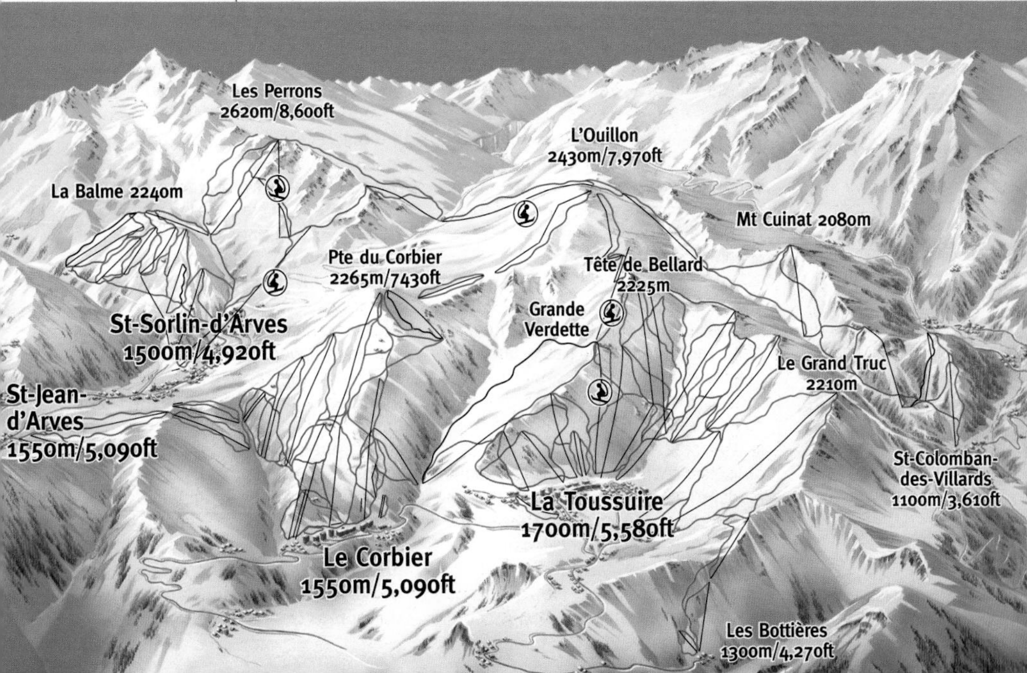

photos, carvings, etc. A 2004 reporter endorses its 'stunning views' and says Les Cigales, near the foot of the bowl, had 'good basic food and was friendly'.
**Schools** A lack of English-speaking tuition can be a problem, though we understand that English classes are often laid on for Dutch visitors. The classes are no larger than 10.
**Facilities for children** The nursery accepts children from three to six. Language may be a problem.

**STAYING THERE**
**How to go** A few UK tour operators serve the resort.
**Hotels** There are several small 3-star and 2-star places. The 3-star Ruade (0479 830179) and Soldanelles (0479 567529) both have pools and saunas.
**Self-catering** The Ecrins chalets are large 3-star apartments. Most others are cheap and not so cheerful.
**Eating out** The options are mostly inexpensive pizzerias and bar-restaurants.
**Après ski** Fairly dire. There are a few bars including the Tonneau. The Alpen Rock nightclub can get busy at peak French holiday time. The ice rink on the roof of a building in the main street pumps out loud music.
**Off the slopes** There's not much to do: snow-shoeing, snowmobiling, dog-sledding, ice skating, hang-gliding and going to the cinema.

**ST-SORLIN D'ARVES** 1500m/4,920ft
**St-Sorlin's only link to the other resorts up to last season was a shuttle-bus to St-Jean, where a chair-lift goes up for access to Le Corbier. The new link to L'Ouillon – and two new high-speed chairs planned for 2004/05 – now make it a much more attractive base, especially as its local slopes are the most interesting for experienced intermediates.**

**THE RESORT**
St-Sorlin-d'Arves is a real, medium-sized village with a year-round life outside skiing. It's a picturesque collection of well-preserved traditional farmhouses, with a baroque church and long-established shops – fromagerie, boulangerie, crafts, etc – alongside more modern resort development. Its setting on a narrow shelf gives fine views of the Aiguilles d'Arves but doesn't allow much room for expansion, so the village has grown in a ribbon-like fashion along its main street. A 2004 reporter warns that the road up from the valley is in poor repair and narrow in places, with precipitous drops and no petrol station. He also warns that, in March at least, the bus link between St-Sorlin and St-Jean stops before the lifts.

**THE MOUNTAIN**
St-Sorlin's local slopes form the biggest single sector of the new network, with 120km/75 miles of piste. Although very much an intermediate mountain, it does offer much more variety, including some steeper options, than the rest of the area.
**Slopes** There are two distinct sections. The lower, gentler left side on La Balme, reached by a choice of slow chairs from the village, is crammed with lots of short, easy runs. The higher, right side on Les Perrons, now reached by two successive fast six-packs due to open for 2004/05, has long, sweeping, generally steeper pistes. The new Vallons run off the back of Les Perrons (which forms the first part of the link to L'Ouillon and from there to La Toussuire, Le Corbier or St-Colomban) and the runs from Petit Perron have added a lot of interest to the local skiing, even for those who have no intention of setting off towards a different resort.
**Snow reliability** Not bad. Les Perrons slopes are the highest in the area and the main runs back to the village are covered by snowmakers.
**Experts** There isn't much on-piste challenge, but Les Perrons had the best off-piste in the whole pre-existing area and the slopes beneath the new Petit Perron chair look interesting.
**Intermediates** The long top-to-bottom reds on both sides of Les Perrons are the best pistes in the whole area. There is only one on the back and a couple on the front, but they have the whole mountain to themselves, giving a great away-from-it-all feel. La Balme has shorter, more leisurely runs.
**Beginners** The nursery slope is right by the village, and there are plenty of slopes to progress to on La Balme.
**Snowboarding** La Balme has a lot of drag-lifts.
**Cross-country** There's a narrow 16km/10 mile loop along a side valley past the foot of La Balme's Alpine area, with good views of the Aiguilles d'Arves.
**Queues** We have received no reports of any problems and the only queue we saw was for the popular but slow chair up to Les Perrons. Pressure on

**Phone numbers**
From abroad use the prefix +33 and omit the initial '0' of the phone number.

The chalet-style development at Le Chal has good nursery slopes and the link to Le Corbier. The old village of St-Jean-d'Arves is on the opposite side of the valley ↗

SNOWPIX.COM / CHRIS GILL

**TOURIST OFFICES**

info@les-sybelles.com
www.les-sybelles.com

**La Toussuire**
t 0479 830606
info@la-toussuire.com
www.la-toussuire.com

**Le Corbier**
t 0479 830404
info@le-corbier.com
www.le-corbier.com

**St-Sorlin-d'Arves**
t 0479 597177
info@saintsorlindarves.com
www.saintsorlindarves.com

**St-Jean-d'Arves**
t 0479 597297
info@saintjeandarves.com
www.saintjeandarves.com

**St-Colomban-des-Villards**
t 0479 562453
info@saint-colomban.com
www.saint-colomban.com

**Les Bottières**
t 0479 832709
bottieres.accueil@worldonline.fr
www.savoie-maurienne.com/lesbottieres

this should be eased by the new fast chairs planned for 2004/05.

**Mountain restaurants** We enjoyed lunch and stunning views of the Aiguilles d'Arves on the sunny terrace of the table-service and rustic Bergerie at the top of the Plan Moulin chair at La Balme.

**Schools** A 2004 visitor reports 'exceptionally friendly and helpful instructors but big classes of up to 20'.

**Facilities for children** The Petits Diables crèche accepts children from three months. The ski kindergarten accepts kids from three-and-a-half years. Language is a likely problem.

## STAYING THERE

**How to go** Some major UK tour operators now offer holidays here – see the index at the back of book.

**Hotels** There are three small 2-star places – all attractive chalets. The Beausoleil (0479 597140) and Balme (0479 597021) look the best bets.

**Self-catering** There are scores of small properties (and the Grignotte bakery sells 'the best bread ever encountered in the Alps', says a 2004 reporter).

**Eating out** The choice is limited to cheap and cheerful pizzerias and raclette/fondue places. The Table de Marie, Beausejour, Gargoulette ('friendly, decent food, but frenetic and disorganised service') and pizza and pasta above the Avalanche bar have been recommended.

**Après-ski** St-Sorlin-d'Arves is even quieter than the other resorts. A 2004 reporter says 'the Avalanche bar was lively with a student-age clientele and the Godille was more frequented by locals but essentially dead. We did not think the guide's warning that there isn't much nightlife or many bars would matter to us oldies, but it did.'

**Off the slopes** There is not much to do. Dog-sledding and snow-shoeing are options, but it's fairly tame territory.

**ST-JEAN-D'ARVES** 1550m/5,090ft
Although small, St-Jean-d'Arves is quite a scattered community. The original old village, with the usual ancient church, is set across the valley from the main slopes, at the foot of a north-facing ridge with two drag-lifts.

Over the valley the mid-mountain hamlet of La Chal, where a tasteful development of new chalet-style buildings is still expanding, is where the lift link to and piste back from Le Corbier is. It is not directly affected by the new lifts; as in the past, it remains linked to Le Corbier by lifts and runs, and by shuttle-bus to St-Sorlin-d'Arves along the valley.

Off-slope diversions are few – dog-sledding, cheese farm visits, snow-shoeing. Après-ski is basic, with a few bars, an Irish pub and night-tobogganing with music. The attractive Chalets Les Marmottes and La Fontaine du Roi apartments are by far the best self-catering option in the whole area.

**ST-COLOMBAN-DES-VILLARDS** 1100m/3,610ft
St-Colomban-des-Villards is a tiny old village in the next valley to La Toussuire, only a few miles up from the Maurienne valley.

In recent years it has developed a chain of drags and chair-lifts on north- and east-facing slopes to the south of the village, with a high point at Mt Cuinat, and for the 2003/04 season it was linked to L'Ouillon, at the hub of Les Sybelles. A battery of snowmakers keeps the home slope down to the village open for most of the season.

**LES BOTTIERES** 1300m/4,270ft
Down the mountain from La Toussuire, this tiny hamlet offers little infrastructure and extremely indirect access to the main network – it takes three lifts to get over to La Toussuire, before setting off for L'Ouillon.

J.M. GOUEDARD

# La Tania

*Small, family-friendly base for exploring the Three Valleys*

**COSTS**

①②③④⑤⑥

**RATINGS**

**The slopes**

| | |
|---|---|
| Snow | *** |
| Extent | ***** |
| Expert | **** |
| Intermediate | ***** |
| Beginner | ** |
| Convenience | **** |
| Queues | **** |
| Mountain restaurants | **** |

**The rest**

| | |
|---|---|
| Scenery | *** |
| Resort charm | *** |
| Off-slope | * |

**NEWS**

Work is allegedly starting on building a much-needed new beginner piste from Courchevel 1850 back into the village, though there's no firm date for its completion. If and when it does open, it will transform the attraction of La Tania for beginners and timid intermediates. Watch this space.

For 2003/04 38 new snow-guns were installed to cover the blue Folyères piste from Praz-Juget down to the centre of the resort.





- ➕ Part of the Three Valleys – the world's biggest linked ski area
- ➕ Quick access to the slopes of Courchevel and Méribel
- ➕ Long, rolling, intermediate runs through woods back to the village
- ➕ Greatly improved snowmaking
- ➕ Attractively developed, small, traffic-free village

- ➖ Small development without much choice of après-ski – and no doctor, pharmacy or cashpoint
- ➖ Main nursery slope is part of the blue run to the village, and gets a lot of through-traffic
- ➖ Runs home are too steep for those progressing from the nursery slopes
- ➖ Some accommodation is a long walk from the centre and the main lifts

**La Tania does not try to compete with its more upmarket neighbours, Courchevel and Méribel. It has carved out its own niche as a good-value, small, quiet, family-friendly base from which to hit the snow-sure slopes of Courchevel and to explore the whole of the Three Valleys. It is prettily set in the trees, and the wood-clad buildings make it one of the more attractive French purpose-built resorts (development started in the early 1990s, by which time lessons had been learned from the resorts that were developed in the 1960s and 70s, with their tiny apartments and uncompromisingly functional architecture). As a budget base for the Three Valleys, it has a lot to be said for it, except for beginners.**

## THE RESORT

La Tania is set just off the minor road linking Le Praz (Courchevel 1300) to Méribel. It has grown into a quiet, attractive, car-free collection of mainly ski-in, ski-out chalets and apartments set among the trees, most with good views. There are few shops other than food and sports shops and not much choice of bars and restaurants. You can walk around the place in a couple of minutes.

A gondola leads up into the slopes, and there are two wonderful sweeping intermediate runs down. The nursery slope is on your doorstep, and visitors say that La Tania is 'very child friendly'. The steepness of the runs back to the village is its key weakness although this should be rectified as we are told that work is starting on a new beginner piste down to the village.

Free buses go to Courchevel which reporters find punctual in the daytime, but one warns that the service is erratic in the evenings. For those with a car Méribel is probably a bigger draw – 1850, Courchevel's main shopping and nightlife focus, is appreciably further.

## THE MOUNTAINS

As well as good, though limited, local slopes, the whole of the Three Valleys can be explored easily from here, with just two lifts needed to get to either the Courchevel or the Méribel slopes.

**Slopes** The gondola out of the village goes to Praz-Juget. From here a drag-lift takes you to Chenus and the slopes above Courchevel 1850 and a fast quad goes to the link with Méribel via Col de la Loze. An alternative way to the slopes above 1850 is to take two successive drag-lifts from the village to Loze. From all these points, varied, interesting intermediate runs take you back into the La Tania sector.

**Terrain-parks** There is no local terrain-park or half-pipe, but you can get to Courchevel's four parks easily.

**Snow reliability** Good snow-cover down to Praz-Juget is usual all season. Snowmaking now covers the whole of the blue run back to the village; some reporters found this satisfactory, but others found the run became icy in the afternoon and preferred to ride the gondola down at times.

**Experts** There are no particular challenges directly above La Tania, but the Jean Blanc and Jockeys blacks from Loze to Le Praz are genuine challenges

**PISTE MAP**

La Tania is covered on the Courchevel map earlier in the France section.

**Phone numbers**
From abroad use the prefix +33 and omit the initial '0' of the phone number.

**TOURIST OFFICE**

**t** 0479 084040
info@latania.com
www.latania.com

and there is good off-piste terrain beneath the Col de la Lose ridge and close by in the Courchevel sector.
**Intermediates** There are two lovely, long, undulating intermediate runs back through the trees to La Tania – though there's little difference in gradient between the blue and the red and timid intermediates may find them too steep for their liking. On the higher slopes you have a choice of three or four pistes. Both Lanches and Dou des Lanches are excellent challenging reds. The quick access to the rest of the Three Valleys' 600km/370 miles of well-groomed pistes makes the area an adventurous intermediate's paradise.

**Beginners** There is a good beginner area and lift right in the village and beginner children, in particular, are well catered for. But there's a lot of through traffic on the main slope and there are no easy, long, local slopes to progress to; the intermediate runs back to the village are quite challenging. Learn elsewhere until the new green run is built.
**Snowboarding** It's easy to get around on gondolas and chairs, avoiding drags.
**Cross-country** There are trails at altitude with links through the woods to Méribel and Courchevel, which has an extensive 66km/41 miles of trails. To our non-specialist eye, this looks a good base.
**Queues** A queue can build up for the village gondola but it is quick-moving, and one of the attractions of La Tania in general is the lack of crowds. Elsewhere in the Three Valleys there are a few remaining bottlenecks.
**Mountain restaurants** The Bouc Blanc, near the top of the gondola out of La Tania, has friendly table-service, good food and a big terrace, though this year a reporter says, 'Maybe I hit it on a bad day, but I was not impressed.' Roc Tania, higher up at Col de la Loze, is tiny, but very pretty inside – good for a scenic coffee stop; one reader found the food good at lunch time, another was disappointed with food and service. Check out the Courchevel and Méribel places, too.
**Schools and guides** Magic in Motion was 'highly thought of' by a reporter last year. We have no recent reports of the other schools that operate out of La Tania – ESF and Snow Ball.
**Facilities for children** We have had excellent reports of tour operator Le Ski's nursery here. The local kindergarten takes non-skiing children from the age of three; the Jardin des Neiges takes skiing children from the age of four. A list of babysitters is available from the tourist office.

## KEY FACTS

| | |
|---|---|
| **Resort** | 1350m<br>4,430ft |
| For the Three Valleys | |
| **Slopes** | 1260-3230m<br>4,130-10,600ft |
| **Lifts** | 197 |
| **Pistes** | 600km<br>373 miles |
| **Green** | 21% |
| **Blue** | 33% |
| **Red** | 35% |
| **Black** | 11% |
| **Snowmaking** | 1500 guns |
| For Courchevel/ La Tania only | |
| **Slopes** | 1260-2740m<br>4,130-8,990ft |
| **Lifts** | 67 |
| Pistes | 150km<br>93 miles |
| **Green** | 25% |
| **Blue** | 33% |
| **Red** | 32% |
| **Black** | 10% |
| **Snowmaking** | 519 guns |

## STAYING THERE

**How to go** Around 30 British tour operators go here.

**Hotels** The Montana (0479 088008) is a slope-side 3-star next to the gondola with a sauna and fitness club. The Mountain Centre (01273 897525 in the UK or www.themountaincentre.com) has 'cheap backpacker-style accommodation and food'.

**Chalets** Several tour operators have splendid newish ski-in, ski-out chalets with fine views, though reporters have complained of 'poor sound-proofing' in some. The choice gets wider every year.

**Self-catering** There are lots of apartments – and most are more spacious and better equipped than usual in France. The Saboia and the Christiania have been recommended. There is a deli and a bakery, as well as a small supermarket.

**Eating out** The Ferme de la Tania gets generally good reviews for its Savoyard fare – 'good service, good food'. The Farçon was considered 'outrageously expensive and not all that good' by several reporters. Pub Le Ski Lodge has 'damn good chilli burgers' and 'will do a deal for groups including all-you-can-eat-and-drink salad, chips and wine'. The Chanterelles is 'highly recommended' for crêpes and pizzas ('first class meals at knockdown prices') and the Taïga does 'very good pizzas and is friendly and quite cheap'. A 2004 reporter recommends the Marmottons for its tartiflette.

**Après-ski** Pub Le Ski Lodge is the focal après-ski place and has live bands. The hotel Montana bar and the Taïga are quieter. But if you want a lively varied nightlife, you need to go elsewhere – La Tania is too small.

**Off the slopes** Unless you have a car, La Tania is not the best place for someone not intending to hit the slopes. However, snowmobile trips, snow-shoeing, paragliding and husky dog-sledding are possibilities, and the hotel Montana has a fitness club with a swimming pool. A non-skier's guide to Courchevel, Méribel and La Tania is distributed free by the tourist office.

SNOWPIX.COM / CHRIS GILL

# Tignes

*Good snow, great varied terrain and a resort that's ... er ... improving*

## COSTS

(1)(2)(3)(4)(5)(6)

## RATINGS

**The slopes**
Snow *****
Extent *****
Expert *****
Intermediate *****
Beginner **
Convenience ****
Queues ****
Mountain restaurants ***

**The rest**
Scenery ***
Resort charm **
Off-slope *

## NEWS

At last: for 2004/05 two lifts on the wide expanse of slopes west of Tignes are being upgraded. The Merle Blanc and Grattalu are to be replaced by fast chairs.

For 2003/4 the terrain-park was moved from Le Lac to Val Claret.

Two new 3-star hotels opened last winter.

A new sports centre and a new cable-car from Les Boisses up to the top of the Chaudannes chair above Le Lac are due to be finished in 2005.

- + Good snow guaranteed for a long season – about the best Alpine bet
- + One of the best areas in the world for lift-served off-piste runs
- + Huge amount of terrain for all abilities, with swift access to the slopes of Val-d'Isère
- + Lots of accommodation close to the slopes (though there is also quite a bit that involves some walking)
- + Efforts to make the resort villages more welcoming are paying off

- − Resort architecture not to everyone's taste (including ours)
- − Bleak, treeless setting – hardly any woodland runs, and many slopes liable to closure during and after storms
- − Still lots of long, slow chair-lifts – though two get upgrades this year
- − Near beginners looking for long green runs have to buy an area pass and go to the Val-d'Isère slopes
- − Limited après-ski

**The appeal of Tignes is simple: good snow, spread over a wide area of varied terrain, shared with Val-d'Isère. Together the two resorts form the enormous Espace Killy – a Mecca for experts, and ideal for adventurous intermediates.**

**We prefer to stay in Val, which is a more human place. But in many ways Tignes makes the better base: appreciably higher, more convenient, surrounded by intermediate terrain, with quick access to the Grande Motte glacier. And the case for Tignes gets stronger as results flow from the resort's campaign to reinvent itself in a more cuddly form. Cars have been largely pushed underground, new buildings are being designed in traditional styles and some old ones are getting a facelift. It all helps to combat the impression that you've landed on the Moon.**

**Tignes built some impressive lifts in the 1990s, but enjoyment of the expansive western side of the Tignes bowl – and some other areas of the Espace Killy, too – is limited by the time you spend riding slow chair-lifts. Upgrades are at last appearing, but many more are still needed.**

**But you keep coming back to the snow. A forecast of 'rain up to 2000m' means 'fresh snow down to village level in Tignes'.**

OT TIGNES / M DALMASSO C TATIN

This shot of Tignes-le-Lac makes the parts of it clear. Left to right: the monstrous slabs of Le Bec Rouge, the tight huddle of Le Rosset, with the new chalets of Les Almes on the slope behind, and the apartment blocks of Le Lavachet →

## KEY FACTS

| Resort | 2100m 6,890ft |
|---|---|
| For entire Espace Killy area | |
| Slopes | 1550-3455m 5,090-11,340ft |
| Lifts | 97 |
| Pistes | 300km 186 miles |
| Green | 15% |
| Blue | 46% |
| Red | 28% |
| Black | 11% |
| Snowmaking | 19km 12 miles |
| For Tignes only | |
| Slopes | 1550-3455m 5,090-11,340ft |
| Lifts | 48 |
| Pistes | 150km 93 miles |





## THE RESORT

Tignes was created before the French discovered the benefits of making purpose-built resorts look acceptable. But things are improving. Traffic is now discouraged (and in places routed underground), and the villages are gradually acquiring a more traditional look and feel.

The original and main village – Tignes-le-Lac – is still the hub of the resort. Some of the smaller buildings in the central part, Le Rosset, are being successfully revamped in chalet style. But the place as a whole is dreary, and the blocks overlooking the lake from the quarter called Le Bec-Rouge will remain monstrous until the day they are demolished. It's at the point where these two sub-resorts meet – now a snowy pedestrian area, with valley traffic passing through a tunnel beneath – that the lifts are concentrated: two slow old chair-lifts up the western slopes and a powerful gondola towards Tovière and Val-d'Isère. Some attractive new buildings are being added both in the centre and on the fringes, in a suburb built on the lower slopes known as Les Almes. A nursery slope separates Le Rosset from the fourth component part, Le Lavachet, below which there are now good fast lifts up both sides of the valley. Like Le Rosset, Le Lavachet is an apartment development, but one that is much easier on the eye.

Val-Claret (2km/1 mile up the valley, beyond the lake) was also mainly developed after Le Rosset, and is a bit more stylish – though we don't side with those readers who claim to actually like the look of it. The main part of the village, Centre, is an uncompromisingly modern-style development on a shelf above the valley floor; a couple of lifts go up the eastern slopes from here. Down on the valley floor there are major lifts up to the Grande Motte glacier, as well as lifts accessing the sides of the bowl and the slopes of Val-d'Isère. Beside the road along the valley to the lifts is a ribbon of more recent development in traditional style, known as Grande Motte. The two levels of Val-Claret are linked by a couple of (unreliable) indoor elevators and stairs, as well as by hazardous paths.

Below the high valley of the main resort villages are two smaller settlements. Tignes-les-Boisses, quietly

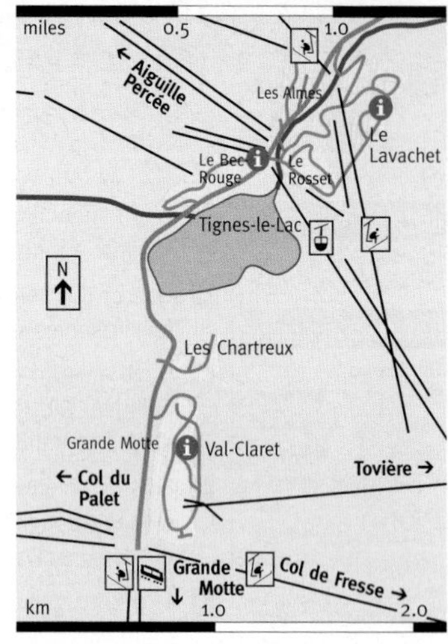


set in the trees beside the road up to the main Tignes villages, consists of a barracks and a couple of simple hotels. Lower Tignes-les-Brévières is a renovated old village at the lowest point of the slopes – a favourite lunch spot, and a friendly place to stay. It has its own nursery slopes.

Location isn't crucial, as a regular and very efficient free bus service connects all the villages until midnight – though in the daytime the route runs along the bottom of Val-Claret, leaving residents of Val-Claret Centre with some uphill hiking.

A six-day pass covers a day in some other resorts, including the newly-linked Les Arcs and La Plagne (Paradiski) area and the Three Valleys, most easily reached with the aid of a car. Preserve your pass and you'll get a loyalty discount off next year's.

## THE MOUNTAINS

The area's great weakness is that it can become unusable in bad weather. There are no woodland runs except immediately above Tignes-les-Boisses and Tignes-les-Brévières, heavy snow produces widespread avalanche risk and wind closes the higher chairs.

Piste classification here is more reliable than in Val-d'Isère.

### THE SLOPES

***High, snow-sure and varied***

Tignes' biggest asset is the **Grande Motte** – and the runs from, as well as on, the glacier. The underground funicular from Val-Claret whizzes you up to over 3000m/9,840ft in seven minutes. There are blue, red and black runs to play on up here, as well as beautiful long runs back to the resort.

The main lifts towards Val-d'Isère are efficient: a high-capacity gondola from Le Lac to **Tovière**, and a fast chair with covers from Val-Claret to **Col de Fresse**. You can head back to Tignes from either: the return from Tovière to Tignes-le-Lac is via a steep black run which is now one of the 'never groomed' set up last year, but there is an easier run to Val-Claret.

Going up the opposite side of the valley takes you to a quieter area of predominantly east-facing slopes split into two main sectors, linked in both directions – **Col du Palet** and **l'Aiguille Percée**. This whole mountainside is spoilt by its strangely antiquated lifts; but two fast chairs are to be built for the 2004/05 season, which is a great step forward. The Col des Ves chair-lift, at the south end of the Col du Palet sector, is not normally opened until high season. You can descend from l'Aiguille Percée to Tignes-les-Brévières, on blue, red or black runs. There's an efficient gondola back.



## TERRAIN-PARKS
### *New location*

Tignes has moved its snow-park to Val-Claret, much to the annoyance of many boarders, we hear, who also feel that it is not as good as previously. There is a quarter-pipe, half-pipe and various bumps, jumps and rails. Restricted passes are available which include the park. For the summer season, Tignes builds a big terrain-park on the Grande Motte glacier.

## SNOW RELIABILITY
### *Difficult to beat*

Tignes has all-year-round runs (barring brief closures in spring or autumn) on its Grande Motte glacier. And the resort height of 2100m/6,890ft generally means good snow-cover right back to base for most of the long winter season – November to May. The west-facing runs down from Col de Fresse and Tovière to Val-Claret suffer from the afternoon sun, although they now have serious snowmaking. Some of the lower east-facing and south-east-facing slopes on the other side of the valley can suffer late in the season, too.

La Grande Motte
3455m/11,340ft
Col de la Leisse
3015m
Col des Ves
2840m
Col du Palet
2695m
Col de Fresse
L'Aiguille Percée
2705m
Tovière
2705m
Val-d'Isère
Val-Claret
Tignes-le-Lac
Le Lavachet
Tignes
2100m/6,890ft
Tignes-les-Boisses
1850m
Tignes-les-Brévières
1550m/5,090ft

**LIFT PASSES**

**L'Espace Killy**
Covers all Tignes and Val-d'Isère.

**Beginners**
Seven free lifts.

**Main pass**
1 day €38
6 days €181

**Senior citizens**
Over 60: 6 days €154
Over 75: free pass

**Children**
Under 13: 6 days €136
Under 5: free pass

**Notes**
Half-day and pedestrian passes available. Discount on presentation of lift pass from previous three seasons. 6-day passes and over are valid for one day in the Three Valleys, one day in Valmorel and one day in La Plagne-Les Arcs, and half-price pass in Ste-Foy.

**Alternative passes**
Tignes-only pass available.

**FOR EXPERTS**

***An excellent choice***

The only serious challenge within the piste network is the long black run from Tovière to Tignes-le-Lac, with steep, usually heavily mogulled sections (the top part, Pâquerettes, is now never groomed). Parts of this run get a lot of afternoon sun. Our favourite black run is the Sache, from Aiguille Percée down a secluded valley to Tignes-les-Brévières, which can become very heavily mogulled at the bottom. The other blacks dotted around the area are not particularly steep – the Ves run was only recently promoted from red status – and how much of a challenge they represent depends on the state of the snow.

But it is the off-piste possibilities that make Tignes such a draw for experts. Go with one of the off-piste groups that the schools organise, and in good snow you'll have a great time. The feature box on the right explains some of the options.

One of the big adventures is to head for Champagny (linked to the La Plagne area) or Peisey-Nancroix (linked to the Les Arcs area) – very beautiful runs, and not too difficult.

The whole western side of the bowl has lots of off-piste possibilities. The terrain served by the Col des Ves chair is often excellent. To the left (looking up) there are wonderfully secluded, scenic and challenging descents. On the right, lower down, is a less heavily used and gentler area, ideal for off-piste initiation. To the north, there are excellent variants on the Sache run to Les Brévières (see below). And just above Les Brévières there is good, under-used tree skiing.

A reader also raves about the off-piste slopes accessed by the Borsat chair over on the Val side.

Schools and guides offer the bizarre French form of heli-skiing: mountaintop drops are forbidden, but from Tovière you can ski down towards the Lac du Chevril to be retrieved by chopper.

**FOR INTERMEDIATES**

***One of the best***

For the keen intermediate piste-basher the Espace Killy is one of the top three or four areas in France, or the world.

Tignes' local slopes are ideal intermediate terrain. The red and blue runs on the Grande Motte glacier nearly always have superb snow. The

There is an **ESF** in each part of Tignes:

Le Lac
**t** 0479 063028

Le Lavachet
**t** 0479 400884

Les Brévières
**t** 0479 065113

www.esf-tignes.com

## A MECCA FOR OFF-PISTE SKIERS

**Tignes is renowned for offering some of the best lift-served off-piste skiing in the world. There is a tremendous choice, with runs to suit all levels, from intermediate skiers to fearless free-riders and off-piste experts. We invited the ESF to give us a guided tour. Although some of these runs are heavily skied, we don't recommend anyone to undertake them without proper guidance.**

*For a first experience of off-piste, perhaps for a family,* ***Lognan*** *is ideal. These slopes – down the mountainside between the pistes to Le Lac and the pistes to Val-Claret – are broad and not very difficult.*

*One of our favourite routes is the* ***Tour de Pramecou****. After few minutes' walking at the bottom of the Grande Motte glacier, we pass around a big rock called Pramecou. There is then a multitude of possibilities, differing in difficulty – so a route can be found for skiers of different abilities.*

***Petite Balme*** *is a run for good skiers only – the access is easy, but brings you to quite challenging north-facing slopes in real high-mountain territory, far from the ski pistes.*

*To ski* ***Oreilles de Mickey*** *(Mickey's Ears) you start from Tovière and walk north along the ridge to the peak of Lavachet, where you get a great view of Tignes.The descent involves three long couloirs, narrow and pretty steep, which bring you back to the village of Le Lavachet.*

*The best place to find fresh snow is the* ***Chardonnet*** *couloirs – they face north, and never get the sun. The snow is always very good here. The route involves a 20-minute walk from the top of the Merle Blanc chair-lift.*

*The* ***Vallons de la Sache*** *is one of the most famous off-piste routes – a descent of 1200m/3,940ft vertical down a breathtaking valley in the heart of the National Park, overlooked by the magnificent Sache glacier. Starting from the Aiguille Percé at 2750m/9,020ft you enter a different world, high up in the mountains, far away from the ski lifts. You arrive several hours later down in Les Brévières at 1550m/5,090ft, below the Tignes dam.*

*This valley offers a multitude of routes to suit intermediate skiers or highly experienced free-riders – gentle slopes, steep slopes, couloirs, rock-faces and tree skiing. The north-facing slopes offer powder skiing while the south-facing slopes are perfect for spring snow skiing. Highly experienced skiers and snowboarders can climb up and pass through the Trou de la Souris (Mouse Hole) to ski the steep slopes of the 3 Murs (3 Walls). And the really fearless can ski through the sheer-sided Gorges de la Sache.*

glacier run from the top of the cable-car has been regraded from blue to red but is wide and mostly easy on usually fabulous snow. The Leisse run down to the chair-lift is now classified black and can get very mogulled but has good snow. The long red run all the way back to town is a delightful long cruise – though often crowded. The roundabout blue alternative (Génépy) is much gentler and quieter.

From Tovière, the blue 'H' run to Val-Claret is an enjoyable cruise and generally well groomed. But again, it can get very crowded.

There is lots to do on the other side of the valley. We particularly like the uncrowded Ves run reached by the low-capacity Col des Ves chair – the highest point of Tignes' non-glacier runs at 2840m/9,320ft. After an initial mogul field (sometimes quite challenging, which we presume is why the run has been reclassified from red to black) it becomes an interesting, undulating and curvy cruise, usually with good snow and a few moguls. The blue runs served by the Grattalu chair have been pleasantly quiet in the past, but this year's upgrade to a fast chair will doubtless change things. The runs down from Aiguille Percée to Tignes-les-Boisses and Tignes-les-Brévières are also scenic and fun. There are red and blue options as well as the beautiful Sache black run – adventurous intermediates shouldn't miss it. The runs down from Aiguille Percée to Le Lac are gentle, wide blues.

### FOR BEGINNERS
***Good nursery slopes, but …***

The nursery slopes of Tignes-le-Lac and Le Lavachet (which meet at the top) are excellent – convenient, snow-sure, gentle, free of through-traffic and served by a slow chair and a drag. The ones at Val-Claret are less appealing:

## SCHOOLS

**ESF**
t 0479 063028
info@esf-tignes.com

**Evolution 2**
t 0479 064378
reservationstignes@evolution2.com

**Snocool**
t 0479 400858
info@snocool.com

**Kebra**
t 0479 064337
kebra.surfing@free.fr

**333**
t 0479 062088
contact@333school.com

**Surf Feeling**
t 0479 065363
surffeeling@aol.com

**Classes** (ESF prices)
6 half days: €129

**Private lessons**
€32 for 1hr

## GUIDES

**Bureau des Guides**
t 0479 064276
bureau@guidesdetignes.com

**Tetra**
t 0479 419707
tetrahp@wanadoo.fr



an unpleasantly steep slope within the village served by a drag, and a less convenient slope served by the fast Bollin chair. All of these lifts are free.

Although there are some fairly easy blues on the west side of Tignes, for long green runs you have to go over to the Val-d'Isère sector. You need an Espace Killy pass to use them, and to get back to Tignes you have a choice between the blue run from Col de Fresse (which has a tricky start) or riding the gondola down from Tovière. And in poor weather, the high Tignes valley is an intimidatingly bleak place – enough to make any wavering beginner retreat to a bar with a book.

### FOR CROSS-COUNTRY
***Interesting variety***

The Espace Killy has 40km/25 miles of cross-country trails. There are tracks on the frozen Lac de Tignes, along the valley between Val-Claret and Tignes-le-Lac, at Les Boisses and Les Brévières and up on the Grande Motte.

### QUEUES
***Very few***

The queues here depend on snow conditions. If snow low down is poor, the Grande Motte funicular generates queues; the fast chairs in parallel with it are often quicker, despite the longer ride time. These lifts jointly shift a lot of people, with the result that the run down to Val-Claret can be unpleasantly crowded. The worst queues now are for the cable-car on the glacier – half-hour waits are common.

Of course, if higher lifts are closed by heavy snow or high winds, the lifts on the lower slopes have big queues.

The famous afternoon queues for the slow Tommeuses chairs bringing Tignes residents back from the Val slopes to Tovière are now a fond memory, thanks to the fast eight-seat replacement. It has also cut queues at the Borsat quad to Col de Fresse, the easiest way back to Val-Claret. Post-lunch queues at Les Brévières are not unknown.

### MOUNTAIN RESTAURANTS
***Adequate***

The restaurants at the top of the Chaudannes chair – the Alpage for self-service and Lo Soli for table-service – represented a huge improvement on the western side of the bowl when they were built a few seasons back. Their adjacent terraces share a superb view of the Grande Motte, and Lo Soli provides 'superb service'.

The opposite side of the bowl has two places offering both table- and self-service. The atmospheric chalet at the top of Tovière is 'fairly basic' but does 'very good portions'. Table-service meals at the modern but pleasantly woody Chalet du Bollin – just a few metres above Val-Claret – are 'first-class', and 'worth the little extra cost'. At the top of the Tichot chair from Val Claret, the Palet 'serves good food at good prices'.

The big Panoramic self-service restaurant at the top of the Grande Motte funicular has great views from its huge terrace, but it is traversed every few minutes by the next funicular-full of people. There's an excellent table-service 'cuisine gourmande' restaurant here too.

There are lots of easily accessible places for lunch in the resorts. One ski-to-the-door favourite of ours in le Lac

### boarding

*This is a big area, with a big boarder reputation, and it's a cheaper place to stay than Val-d'Isère. There are some flat areas to avoid, but the lift system relies more on chairs and gondolas than drags. There are long, wide pistes to blast down, with acres of powder between them to play in. And there's a snow-park (see Terrain-parks). There are three specialist snowboard schools (Kebra, Snocool and Surf Feeling). One reporter was impressed with the Evolution 2 boarding instructors: 'first class, with a really innovative approach'. Hiring a guide and exploring the off-piste is recommended for good free-riders.*

## CHILDREN

**Les Marmottons**
t 0479 065167
info@marmottons-tignes.com
Ages 3 to 8

**Hotel Diva (Val-Claret)**
t 0479 067000
Nursery takes children from age 18mnth

**Ski schools**
Evolution 2 takes children from age 3 and ESF takes children from age 4 (5 half-days €105).

OT TIGNES / M DALMASSO C TATIN

One chair-lift, two destinations. Get in the right queue for this ingenious lift, or you can find yourself being deposited at Col de Fresse on the skyline when you wanted to ride only to the top of the village ↓

is the ground-floor restaurant of the hotel Montana, on the left as you descend from the Aiguille Percée. In Val-Claret the Fish Tank is described as 'very good value', and the Carline self-service restaurant as having 'cheerful staff and hearty portions'. In le Lac, the 'excellent' Arbina is popular (see 'Eating out'). In Les Brévières, a short walk round the corner into the village brings you to places much cheaper than the two by the piste. Sachette, for example, is crowded with artefacts from mountain life and offers 'lots of good cheese dishes' including 'superb tartiflette'. The Etoile des Neiges 'serves great, typical Savoyard food'.

### SCHOOLS AND GUIDES
***Enormous choice***

There are over half-a-dozen schools, including three specialist snowboard schools, plus various independent instructors. Reporters advise that pre-booking is 'essential' at busy times like Easter. The ESF and Evolution 2 are the main schools, with sections in each resort centre. Reports on the ESF this year are mixed. Class sizes are an issue: one reporter complained of her class size of 15, but had to switch to a French group to get a better deal; another rightly judged an off-piste group of '10 people of varying ability' too large. One beginner 'highly recommended' her class, while another had a 'miserable three days', before taking an Evolution 2 private lesson that 'completely transformed her enjoyment of skiing'. Other adult reports on E2 are also positive, for both skiing and boarding ('really took my boarding forward'). We also have a 'strong recommendation' for Snocool.

### FACILITIES FOR CHILDREN
***Mixed reports***

In the past, we have had good reports on the Marmottons kindergartens, and on the 'experienced minders' of the Evolution 2 school in Le Lac. ESF classes can be too large for comfort, but this year it is a report on an Evolution 2 group of only eight that causes concern: a young girl at the back got detached from the group and left on the mountain, to be rescued by passers-by. Another young girl in a different class was 'delivered to her father with white, frost-bitten cheeks'.

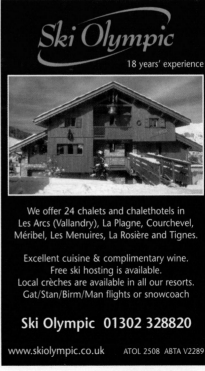

## GETTING THERE

**Air** Geneva 165km/103 miles (3½hr); Lyon 240km/149 miles (3½hr); Chambéry 130km/81 miles (2½hr).

**Rail** Bourg-St-Maurice (30km/19 miles); regular buses or taxi from station.

FRANCE



OT TIGNES / DANIEL ROUSSELOT

Le Lac now has a snowy traffic-free area at its centre, and you can cross from the west to the east slopes on skis ↓

## STAYING THERE

### HOW TO GO

***Unremarkable range of options***

All three main styles of accommodation are available through tour operators, mainly basic, but some options are beginning to appear for those who like more creature comfort.

**Chalets** The choice of catered chalets is increasing. Total Ski has four chalets, and child specialist Esprit Ski now has a chalet hotel here. Ski Olympic's Chalet Rosset has been recommended by reporters: 'Superb, with a lovely lounge with views.' Neilson has a handful of places. Crystal's hotel-style Curling, plumb in the centre of Val-Claret, has neat public areas and spacious bedrooms.

**Hotels** The few hotels are small and concentrated in Le Lac. There are Club Meds at Val-Claret and Les Brévières.

((③ **Campanules** (0479 063436) Smartly rustic chalet in upper Le Lac, with good restaurant. One reporter was impressed enough this year to suggest that it deserved a 4-star rating.

((③ **Village Montana** (0479 400144) Stylishly woody 3-star complex on the east-facing slopes above Le Lac, with new 4-star suites section. Outdoor pool. Reporters praise it for 'delicious and enormous' dinners and 'spacious and comfortable' rooms. 'Lots of children in evidence too,' they say.

((③ **Lévanna** (0479 063294) Smart new 3-star in perfect central position in Le Lac – comfortable, with a 'generous jacuzzi'. Don't cross madame, though.

((③ **Diva** (0479 067000) Biggest in town (120 rooms). On lower level of Val-Claret, a short walk from lifts. 'Very comfy rooms, excellent meals.'

(② **Arbina** (0479 063478) Well-run place close to the lifts in Le Lac, with lunchtime terrace, crowded après-ski bar and one of the best restaurants.

(② **Marais** (0479 064006) Prettily furnished, simple little hotel in Tignes-les-Boisses.

① **Génépy** (0479 065711) Simple but satisfactory Dutch-run chalet in Tignes-les-Brévières.

**Self-catering** MGM's wood-clad L'Ecrin des Neiges apartments in lower Val-Claret are probably the best, with a pool. In upper Val-Claret, close to the Tovière chair, the VVF 'Résidence Le Borsat' apartments are not too cramped, reasonably well equipped and with a communal lounge. The Chalet Club in Val-Claret is a collection of simple studios, but has the benefit

## ACTIVITIES

**Indoor** 'Vitatignes' (sauna, Turkish baths, jacuzzi, etc), Bains du Montana (pool, sauna, etc), Fitness Centre (spa treatments, weight training, fitness), Aquatonic Centre (spa and beauty treatments, fitness etc), cinemas, multisports hall, yoga, bowling, squash, networked games tournaments, computer and video editing lessons

**Outdoor** Natural skating-rink, hang-gliding, paragliding, helicopter rides, snow-mobiles, husky dog-sledding, ice-diving, bungee trampolining, mini quad bikes, snow rafting, ice-climbing, snow-shoeing, aircraft and microlight flights, ski-joring

**Phone numbers**
From abroad use the prefix +33 and omit the initial '0' of the phone number.

## TOURIST OFFICE

**t** 0479 400440
information@tignes.net
www.tignes.net

of free indoor pool, sauna and in-house restaurant and bar. The supermarket at Le Lac is reported to be 'comprehensive but very expensive'.

### EATING OUT
***Good places scattered about***

Each of the main centres has a range of restaurants, although the options in Le Lavachet are rather limited. Reservations are recommended for many restaurants. Finding anywhere with some atmosphere is difficult in Le Lac, though the food in some of the better hotels is good. We and readers have been impressed by two hotels. The Campanules is 'an absolute gastronomic delight' said a reporter this year. The 'superb' Arbina continues to provide 'outstanding food, very good value and first-class service'.

In Val-Claret the Caveau is recommended for a special treat – 'exemplary service' and 'excellent' food. You may also have to wait at Petit Savoyard but the food and service are said to be worth it. The buffet at the Indochine is strongly recommended for the 'excellent choice of Asian dishes' and 'exceptional' quality. Pizza 2000 is recommended for 'reasonable prices, helpful staff, especially with large parties'. The Ski d'Or is a swanky Relais & Châteaux hotel and according to one reporter, 'Its long established reputation is fully justified for its food and service as well as the host's hospitality.' Terrasses du Claret is recommended for big groups.

The Cordée in Les Boisses is said to offer unpretentious surroundings, great traditional French food, modest prices.

### APRES-SKI
***Early to bed***

Tignes is rather quiet at night, though there is no shortage of bars, some doing food as well. Val-Claret has some early-evening atmosphere and happy hours are popular. Reporters differ on the merits of the Crowded House – popular with Brits, but with 'a mixed clientele' – and Brit-dominated Fish Tank ('excellent vin chaud and happy hours'), with the latter getting marginally more votes. Grizzly's is reportedly 'cosy and atmospheric', but you pay for the ambience.

Le Lac is a natural focus for immediate après-ski drinks and this year's favourite is the 'lively' Loop, with pool table. The bar of the hotel Arbina is our kind of spot – adequately cosy, spacious enough to absorb some groups, friendly service. It's a great place to sit outside and people-watch. The Alpaka Lodge is recommended as 'a real gem later on' with 'a staggering array of cocktails'. Embuscade, 'the only proper French bar in town' is reportedly 'very pleasant'. The Red Lion in Les Almes has satellite TV, pool and 'a good range of beers'.

What was the most animated bar in Le Lavachet – Harri's – is now called Censored; we have no recent reports. TC's bar is 'very friendly, with good music'.

Caves du Lac, Café de la Poste and Jack's are popular late haunts.

### OFF THE SLOPES
***Forget it***

Despite the range of alternative activities, Tignes is a resort for those who want to use the slopes, where anyone who doesn't is liable to feel like a fish out of water. Some activities do get booked up quickly as well – a reporter said it was impossible to find a free dog-sledding slot in April. A sports centre is under construction, but meanwhile the big pools at the Village Montana and Suites du Montana are open to the public (though these two may require advance booking).

COURCHEVEL / J. KELAGOPIAN

# Les Trois Vallées

*The biggest lift-linked ski area in the world; and it under-sells itself*

**Despite competing claims, notably from the Portes du Soleil, in practical terms the Trois Vallées cannot be beaten for sheer quantity of lift-served terrain. There is nowhere like it for a keen skier or boarder who wants to cover as much mileage as possible while rarely taking the same run repeatedly. It has a lot to offer everyone, from beginner to expert. And its resorts offer a wide range of alternatives – not only the quite widely known attractions of the big-name mega-resorts but also the increasingly appreciated low-key appeal of the smaller villages.**

**What's more, the area deliberately under-sells itself. It should actually be known as the Quatre Vallées because several years ago it expanded into a fourth valley – the Maurienne. And the figures the individual resorts give us for their local ski areas add up to 630km/391 miles – but the Trois Vallées claims only 600km/373 miles. So we'll forgive the fact that the lifts add up to a mere 199 when 200 are claimed. After spending millions on marketing itself as Three Valleys with 600km of pistes and 200 lifts why should it change? Whatever, it's huge!**

The runs of the Trois Vallées and their resorts are dealt with in six chapters. The four major resorts are Courchevel, Méribel, Les Menuires and Val-Thorens, but we also give chapters to St-Martin-de-Belleville, a small village down the valley from Les Menuires, and La Tania, a relatively recent development between Courchevel and Méribel.

None of the resorts is cheap. **Les**

**Menuires** is the cheapest but it is also the ugliest (though new developments around the original one are now being built in a much more acceptable style). The slopes around the village get too much sun for comfort, but across the valley are some of the best (and quietest) challenging pistes in the Trois Vallées on its north-facing La Masse. Down the valley from Les Menuires is **St-Martin-de-Belleville**, a charming traditional village which has been expanded in a sympathetic style. It has good-value accommodation and improving lift links into the slopes of Les Menuires and Méribel.

Up rather than down the Belleville valley from Les Menuires, at 2300m/7,550ft, **Val-Thorens** is the highest resort in the Alps, and at 3230m/10,600ft the top of its slopes is the high point of the Trois Vallées. The snow in this area is almost always good, and it includes two glaciers where good snow is guaranteed. But the setting is bleak and the lifts are vulnerable to closure in bad weather. The purpose-built resort is very

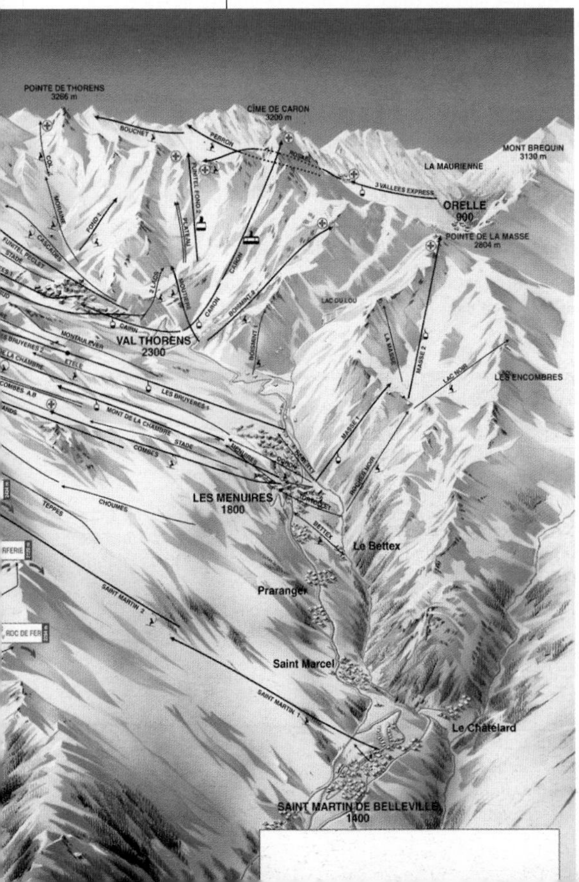

convenient. Visually it is not comparable to Les Menuires, thanks to the smaller-scale design and more thorough use of wood cladding, but it still isn't to everyone's taste.

Méribel is a two-part resort. The higher component, **Méribel-Mottaret**, is the best placed of all the resorts for getting to any part of the Trois Vallées system in the shortest possible time. It's now quite a spread-out place, with some of the accommodation a long way up the hillsides – great for access to the slopes, less so for access to nightlife. **Méribel** itself is 200m/660ft lower and has long been a British favourite, especially for chalet holidays. It is the most attractive of the main Trois Vallées resorts, built in chalet style beside a long winding road up the hillside. Parts of the resort are very convenient for the slopes and the village centre; parts are very far from either. The growing hamlet of **Méribel-Village** has its own chair-lift into the system but is very isolated and quiet.

**Courchevel** has four parts. 1850 is the most fashionable resort in France, and can be the most expensive resort in the Alps (though it doesn't have to cost a fortune to stay there). The less expensive parts – Le Praz (aka 1300), 1550 and 1650 – don't have the same choice of nightlife and restaurants. Many people rate the slopes around Courchevel the best in the Trois Vallées, with runs to suit all standards. The snow tends to be better than in neighbouring Méribel.

**La Tania** was built for the 1992 Olympics, just off the small road linking Le Praz to Méribel. It has now grown into a quiet, attractive, car-free collection of chalets and chalet-style apartments set among the trees, and is popular with families. It has a good nursery slope and lovely long intermediate runs, but there are no very easy runs back to it.

OT VAL-D'ISERE / AGENCE NUTS

# Val-d'Isère

*On- and off-piste playground, with smart new lifts and reliable snow*

## COSTS

①②③④⑤⑥

## RATINGS

**The slopes**

| | |
|---|---|
| Snow | ***** |
| Extent | ***** |
| Expert | ***** |
| Intermediate | ***** |
| Beginner | *** |
| Convenience | *** |
| Queues | **** |
| Mountain restaurants | ** |

**The rest**

| | |
|---|---|
| Scenery | *** |
| Resort charm | *** |
| Off-slope | ** |

## NEWS

For 2003/04 a six-pack replaced the old up-and-over double chair linking Solaise and Col de l'Iseran.

The Plan chair on Solaise was removed, allowing Piste M to be remodelled, making it wider and less steep.

A new four-star luxury hotel, Les Barmes de l'Ours, opened in December 2003 below Bellevarde. And a new mountain hut, the Edelweiss, opened on the way down to Le Fornet.



- ➕ Huge area linked with Tignes, with lots of runs for all abilities
- ➕ Big recent investment in new lifts
- ➕ One of the great resorts for lift-served off-piste runs
- ➕ High altitude of most slopes means snow is more or less guaranteed
- ➕ Wide choice of schools, especially for off-piste lessons and guiding
- ➕ For a high resort, the town is attractive, very lively at night, and offers a good range of restaurants
- ➕ Wide range of package holidays and accommodation
- ➕ Piste grooming and staff attitudes have improved noticeably

- ➖ Many green and blue runs are tricky, and often hazardous for novices – including runs to valley level
- ➖ You're quite likely to need the bus at the start or end of the day
- ➖ Most lifts and slopes are liable to close when the weather is bad
- ➖ Nursery slopes not ideal
- ➖ Still some lifts in need of upgrading
- ➖ Main off-piste slopes get tracked out very quickly
- ➖ Seems at times more British than French – especially in low season
- ➖ Few good mountain restaurants
- ➖ Increasingly pricey, say readers

**Val-d'Isère is one of the world's best resorts for experts – attracted by the extent of lift-served off-piste – and for confident, mileage-hungry intermediates. But you don't have to be particularly adventurous to enjoy the resort, and the village ambience has improved greatly in recent years.**

**The many drawbacks listed above are mainly not serious complaints, whereas most of the plus-points weigh heavily in the balance, both for us and for our many enthusiastic reporters. The clear recent improvement in piste grooming is as welcome as it is surprising. If the lift company would now make a serious attempt to grade its runs sensibly, Val would make more friends than it does at present among nervous intermediates who panic on mogul fields. The piste map encourages novices to expect to ski down to the village, and it shouldn't.**

**Despite the lack of compelling mountain restaurants – normally a key requirement of your editors – this is, in the end, simply one of our favourite resorts in the world.**

## THE RESORT

Val-d'Isère spreads along a remote valley, which is a dead end in winter. The road in from Bourg-St-Maurice brings you dramatically through a rocky defile to the satellite mini-resort of La Daille – a convenient but hideous slope-side apartment complex and the base of lifts into the major Bellevarde sector of the slopes. The outskirts of Val proper are dreary, but as you approach the centre recent improvements become more evident: new wood- and stone-cladding, culminating in the tasteful pedestrian-only Val Village complex. The few remnants of the original old village are tucked away behind this. Many first-

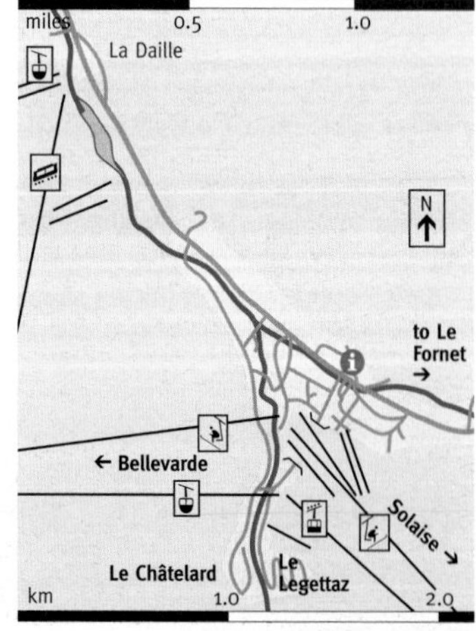

↑ Some of the most attractive parts of the resort are up the side valley south of the village centre – this is Le Joseray

OT VAL-D'ISERE / NUTS

**KEY FACTS**

| | |
|---|---|
| **Resort** | 1850m<br>6,070ft |
| For entire Espace Killy area | |
| **Slopes** | 1550-3455m<br>5,090-11,340ft |
| **Lifts** | 97 |
| **Pistes** | 300km<br>186 miles |
| **Green** | 16% |
| **Blue** | 49% |
| **Red** | 24% |
| **Black** | 11% |
| **Snowmaking** | 26km<br>16 miles |



time visitors find the resort much more pleasant than they expect a high resort to be, and returning visitors generally find things improving.

Turn right at the centre and you drive under the nursery slopes and Val's big lifts up to Bellevarde and Solaise to a lot of new development beyond. Continue up the main valley instead, and you come to Le Fornet – an old village and the third major lift station.

There is a lot of traffic around, but the resort is working to get cars under control and make the centre more pedestrian-friendly.

The location of your accommodation isn't crucial. The main lift stations are linked by efficient free shuttle-buses; even in peak periods you never have to wait more than a few minutes. But in the evening frequency plummets and dedicated après-skiers will want to be within walking distance of the centre. The developments up the side valley beyond the main lift station – Le Châtelard and La Legettaz – are mainly attractive, and some offer ski-in/ski-out convenience. But you pay the price in the evening, when the buses stop running – the farthest-flung places are a long slog from the village. La Daille and Le Fornet have their (quite different) attractions for those less concerned about nightlife.

A car is of no great value around the resort, but simplifies outings to other resorts. A six-day lift pass gives a day in the new Paradiski area (Les Arcs and La Plagne combined) and in the Trois Vallées, and 50% off a pass in Ste-Foy, the locals' favourite outing.

## THE MOUNTAINS

Although there are wooded slopes above the village on all sectors, in practice most of the runs here are on open slopes above the tree line.

Although piste grooming is clearly better than it used to be, this year's reports suggest that the impressive standard achieved in 2002/03 has not been maintained. We continue to get complaints about the poor signing too, particularly at piste junctions – and, especially, of the piste grading. Many blue and even green runs are simply too steep, narrow and even bumpy.

If you plan a return visit, keep your lift pass – those with a week's pass bought in the last three years are entitled to a 'loyal customer' reduction.

The local radio carries weather reports in English as well as French. Precision Ski is a highly-regarded British-run ski shop, which has a Snowtec centre at La Daille where you can test all the latest skis for 25 euros a day (refunded if you buy).

### THE SLOPES
***Vast and varied***

Val-d'Isère's slopes divide into three main sectors. **Bellevarde** is the mountain that is home to Val-d'Isère's famous downhill course – the OK piste, which opens each season's World Cup Alpine circus in December (in 2004, on the weekend of 11/12 December). You can reach Bellevarde quickly by funicular from La Daille, but the powerful new gondola from near the centre of town is now the preferred route for those based near it. From the top you can descend to the valley, play on a variety of drags and chairs at altitude or take a choice of lifts to the Tignes slopes, including the new fast Tommeuses chair-lift.

**Solaise** is the other mountain accessible directly from Val-d'Isère. The Solaise Express fast quad chair-lift takes you a few metres higher than the parallel cable-car. Once up, a short drag takes you over a plateau and down to a variety of chairs that serve this very sunny area of predominantly gentle pistes.

From near the top of this area you can catch the new, fast Leissières six-pack over to the third main area, above and below the **Col de l'Iseran**. The area can also be reached by cable-car from Le Fornet in the valley. The chair-lift ride is spectacular or scary,

**LIFT PASSES**

**L'Espace Killy**
Covers Tignes and Val-d'Isère.

**Beginners**
5 free lifts.

**Main pass**
1 day €38
6 days €181

**Senior citizens**
Over 60: 6 days €154
Over 75: free pass

**Children**
Under 13: 6 days €136
Under 5: free pass

**Notes**
Half-day and pedestrian passes available. Discount on presentation of lift pass from any of previous three seasons. 6-day passes and over are valid for one day in the Three Valleys, Valmorel and Paradiski (La Plagne-Les Arcs), half-price pass in Ste-Foy and reduced price in La Rosière.

**Alternative passes**
There is no separate pass for Val-d'Isère's lifts only.

depending on your head for heights: it climbs over a steep ridge and then drops suddenly down the other side. The runs at Col de l'Iseran are predominantly easy, with spectacular views and access to the region's most beautiful off-piste terrain.

**TERRAIN-PARKS**
***Beginners and experts welcome***

We continue to get rave reports on the very good terrain-park above the La Daille gondola. It is served by the Mont Blanc chair, two drag-lifts and a rope-tow. As well as a half-pipe, quarter-pipes and boarder-cross courses there are assorted bumps, jumps and railslides catering to park-beginners and park-experts alike. 'Enough to keep you entertained for many hours,' said one reporter. 'My sons spent much of the week hanging out there,' another. Four snow-guns are used to ensure good snow-cover.

**SNOW RELIABILITY**
***Difficult to beat***

In years when lower resorts have suffered, Val-d'Isère has rarely been short of snow. Its height means you can almost always get back to the village, especially because of the snowmaking on the main routes home. But even more important is that in each sector there are lots of lifts and runs above mid-mountain, between about 2300m and 2900m (7,550ft and 9,510ft). Many of the slopes face roughly north. And there is access to glaciers at Pissaillas or over in Tignes, although both take a while to get to.

**FOR EXPERTS**
***One of the world's best***

Val-d'Isère is one of the top resorts in the world for experts. The main attraction is the huge range of beautiful off-piste possibilities – see feature panel over the page.

There may be better resorts for really steep pistes – there are certainly lots in North America – but there is plenty on-piste to amuse the expert, despite the small number of blacks on the piste map. Many reds and blues are steep enough to get mogulled.

On Bellevarde the famous Face run is the main attraction – often mogulled from top to bottom, but not worryingly steep. Epaule is the sector's other black run – where the moguls are hit by long exposure to sun and can be slushy or rock-hard too often for our liking (it is prone to closure for these reasons too). There are several challenging ways down from Solaise to the village: all steep, though none fearsomely so.

Wayne Watson of off-piste school Alpine Expérience puts a daily diary of off-piste snow conditions and runs on the web at www.alpineexperience.com.

**FOR INTERMEDIATES**
***Quantity and quality***

Val-d'Isère has even more to offer intermediates than experts. There's enough here to keep you interested for several visits – though there are complaints about crowded high-season pistes, and the less experienced should be aware that many runs are under-classified.

In the Solaise sector is a network of gentle blue runs, ideal for building confidence. And there are a couple of beautiful runs from here through the woods to Le Laisinant – ideal in bad weather, though prone to closure in times of avalanche danger.

Most of the runs in the Col de l'Iseran sector are even easier – ideal for early and hesitant intermediates. Those marked blue at the top of the glacier could really be classified green.

Bellevarde has a huge variety of runs ideally suited to intermediates of all levels. From Bellevarde itself there

## boarding

*Val-d'Isère is good for boarders, though Tignes is a more popular boarder destination. Most of the main lifts are cable-cars, chair-lifts and gondolas, with very few drag-lifts. But there are a few flat areas where you'll need to scoot or walk. Experts will revel in the off-piste. There are several specialist snowboard shops and schools, including Misty Fly. The village nursery area is ideal for trying boarding out and Le Fornet is good to progress to. The terrain-park is great.*

is a choice of green, blue and red runs of varying pitch. And the wide runs from Tovière normally give you the choice of groomed piste or moguls.

A snag for early intermediates is that runs back to the valley can be challenging. The easiest way is to head down to La Daille, where there is a green run – but it should be classified blue (in some resorts it would be red). It gets very crowded and mogulled at the end of the day. None of the runs from Bellevarde and Solaise back to Val itself is really easy. The blue Santons run from Bellevarde takes you through a long, narrow gun barrel, which often has people standing around plucking up courage, making things even trickier. On Solaise there isn't much to choose between the blue and red ways down – they're both narrow in places, though the blue Piste M is supposed to have been improved. At the top, there's no option other than the red run in full view of the lifts. Many early intermediates sensibly choose to ride the lifts down – take the chair for a spectacular view.

### FOR BEGINNERS
***OK if you know where to go***

The nursery slope right by the centre of town is 95% perfect; it's just a pity that the very top is unpleasantly steep. The lifts serving it are free.

Once off the nursery slopes, you have to know where to find easy runs; many of the greens should be blue, or even red. One local instructor admits: 'We have to have green runs on the map, even if we don't have so many green slopes – otherwise beginners wouldn't come to Val-d'Isère.'

A good place for your first real runs off the nursery slopes is the Madeleine green run on Solaise – now served by a fast six-pack. The Col de l'Iseran runs are also gentle and wide, and not overcrowded. There is good progression terrain on Bellevarde, too.

### FOR CROSS-COUNTRY
***Limited***

There are a couple of loops in each of three areas – towards La Daille, on Solaise and out past Le Laisinant. More picturesque is the one going from Le Châtelard (on the road past the main cable-car station) to the Manchet chair. But keen cross-country enthusiasts should go elsewhere.

### QUEUES
***Few problems***

Queues to get out of the resort have been kept in check by new lifts – most recently the big new gondola to Bellevarde. A common complaint, though, is the number of slow chair-lifts at altitude, particularly on the far side of Tignes and at Solaise – the slow Lac chair up to the Tête Solaise can generate queues. Crowded pistes is another complaint in high season.

Getting back from Col de l'Iseran to Solaise at the end of the day should now be no problem, thanks to the new Leissières Express six-pack.

### MOUNTAIN RESTAURANTS
***Getting better – slowly***

The mountain restaurants mainly consist of big self-service places with vast terraces at the top of major lifts. But there are exceptions, and they are gradually growing in number.

### THE BEST LIFT-SERVED OFF-PISTE IN THE WORLD?

*Few resorts can rival the extent of lift-served off-piste skiing in Val-d'Isère.*

*Some runs are ideal for adventurous intermediates looking to try off-piste for the first time. The Tour du Charvet goes through glorious scenery from the top of the Grand Pré chair-lift on the back of Bellevarde. For most of the way it is very gentle, with only a few steeper pitches. It ends up at the bottom of the Manchet chair up to the Solaise area. The Pays Désert is a very easy run from the top of the lift system on the Pissaillas glacier. The views are superb. You end up at the Pays Désert T-bar.*

*For more experienced off-piste skiers, Col Pers is one of our favourite runs. Again, it starts a traverse away from the Pissaillas glacier. You go over a pass into a big, wide, fairly gentle bowl with glorious views and endless ways down. If the snow is good, you can drop down into the Gorges de Malpasset, and ski over the frozen Isère river back to the Le Fornet cable-car.*

*There are endless other off-piste options such as Cugnai and Danaides on Solaise, Banane and the Couloir des Pisteurs on Bellevarde – and of course many more in Tignes.*

*But don't dream of doing any off-piste runs without a fully qualified guide or instructor. Route finding is difficult, avalanche danger can be high and hidden hazards such as cliffs and crevasses lurk.*

The town fills the valley floor ➔

OT VAL-D'ISERE / NUTS

The Fruitière at the top of La Daille gondola, a table-service place kitted out with stuff rescued from a dairy in the valley, is still popular. Reports on the Folie Douce next door range from 'a fine lunch with live music' to 'overpriced'. Later, après-ski starts here. The 'friendly' but busy Trifollet, about halfway down the OK run, 'serves one of the best tartiflettes in the Alps' as well as other 'superb' lunches. If you are in a hurry, Marmottes, in the middle of the Bellevarde bowl, is a 'very efficient' self-service with a big sunny terrace. The 'small and friendly' Bar de L'Ouillette, at the base of the Madeleine chair-lift, does 'good food at reasonable prices' and the Datcha, at the bottom of the Cugnai lift, 'excellent salads, if expensive'. A reporter this year found better value at the Tanière, set between the two chairs going up Face de Bellevarde. It is still popular with the locals, provides 'excellent' food and 'a welcome change from the usual cafeteria crush'. Several reporters this year were excited by the discovery of 'a smashing little place with a nice landlady' and 'very nice cooking' – the 'lovely' and 'pleasantly woody' Edelweiss, above Le Fornet.

There are restaurants on the lower slopes at La Daille that are reachable on snow and by pedestrians. The pizzas at Tufs 'take some beating' and there is a 'good-value buffet on the first floor'. The Toit du Monde just above it offers 'excellent service' and a mix of European and Asian cuisine.

Of course there are lots of places actually in the resort villages. When at Col de l'Iseran, one possible plan for lunch on a wintry day is to descend to the rustic Arolay at Le Fornet.

**SCHOOLS AND GUIDES**

***A very wide choice***

There is a huge choice of schools, guides and private instructors. But they all get busy and at peak periods it's best to book in advance. Practically all the schools run off-piste groups at various levels of competence, as well

## SCHOOLS

**Alpine Expérience**
t 0479 062881 e info@alpineexperience.com

**ESF**
t 0479 060234 e esf.valdisere@wanadoo.fr

**Evolution 2**
t 0479 411672 e valdisere@evolution2.com

**Misty Fly Snowboard**
t 0479 400874

**Mountain Masters**
t 0479 060514

**New Generation**
t 0479 010318
info@skinewgen.com

**Ogier**
t 0479 061893

**Oxygène**
t 0479 419958
valdisere@oxygene-ski.com

**Ski Concept**
t 0688 672563

**Ski Mastery**
t 0479 401768
ski@ski-mastery.com

**Snow Fun**
t 0479 061979
info@snowfun.fr

**Tétra Hors-Piste**
t 0479 419707

**Top Ski**
t 0479 061480
top.ski.val.isere@wanadoo.fr

**Val Gliss**
t 0479 060072

**Classes** (ESF prices)
6 days (3hr am, 2½hr pm) €196

**Private lessons**
€36 for 1hr









as on-piste lessons. Outside the ESF, practically all the instructors and guides speak good English, and many are native English-speakers.

The Oxygène school is well established and seems very popular; make sure you can stick with the same teacher for all your lessons, warns a reporter this year. Over recent years we've heard from lots of satisfied pupils of Snow Fun and Evolution 2. A reporter this year was mightily impressed by Bernard Chesneau of Ski Mastery: 'he transformed the balance of the upper intermediates – and gave confidence to a nervous intermediate'.

The big news in the schools business a couple of years ago was the launch of The Development Centre, based in the Precision Ski shop in the heart of the village. This group of British instructors offers intensive clinics for all levels of skier and has been highly praised.

Mountain Masters is a group of highly-qualified British and French instructors and guides. Misty Fly is a specialist snowboard school.

There are two outfits specialising in guided off-piste groups – an excellent way to get off-piste safely without the cost of hiring a guide as an individual. We have had excellent mornings out with Alpine Expérience (Canadian, French, Italian, British guides) who also do 'excellent off-piste lessons' in the afternoons. Past reports say Top Ski (mostly French guides) is 'highly recommended' and 'efficient' too.

The weekly Henry's Avalanche Talks in Dick's Tea Bar are 'both entertaining and informative'.

Heli-trips can be arranged from over the border in Italy – heli-drops are banned in France.

### FACILITIES FOR CHILDREN

***Good tour op possibilities***

Many people prefer to use the facilities of UK tour operators such as Mark Warner or Ski Beat. But there's a 'children's village' for 3- to 8-year-olds, with supervised indoor and outdoor activities on the village nursery slopes. A past reporter was 'very pleased' with the childcare there: 'The staff speak English, and are very organised, in particular about the children's safety.'

## CHILDREN

**Le Village des Enfants**
**t** 0479 400981
Ages 3 to 8; 9am-5.30 (Sun-Thu); 9am-2pm (Fri).

**Le Petit Poucet**
**t** 0479 061397
Ages from 3; 9am-5.30

**Babysitter list**
Contact tourist office

**Ski schools**
Most offer classes. For example ESF runs classes for ages 5 to 17 (€183 to €233 for 5 days depending on age and ability). Snowfun's Club Nounours takes children aged 3 to 6

## GETTING THERE

**Air** Geneva 180km/112 miles (4hr); Lyon 220km/137 miles (4hr); Chambéry 130km/81 miles (3hr).

**Rail** Bourg-St-Maurice (30km/19 miles); regular buses from station.

## STAYING THERE

### HOW TO GO

***Lots of choice***

More British tour operators go to Val-d'Isère than to any other resort. The choice of chalets and chalet-hotels is vast. There is a Club Med 'village'.

**Chalets** This is Planet Chalet. There is everything from budget chalets – some away from the centre, at Le Châtelard, Le Laisinant and Le Fornet – to the most luxurious you could demand. Some of the most impressive are in the side-valley running south from the village. Companies with properties at the top end of the market include VIP, Scott Dunn (which took over much of the Ski Company portfolio) and Descent International. YSE is a Val d'Isère specialist, with 28 chalets, including some luxury ones and some of the most characterful. Le Ski has seven splendid all-en-suite chalets grouped together just behind the main street. Ski Beat has a smart five-unit chalet at La Daille. Finlays has half-a-dozen properties, the best of them in Le Fornet.

There are several chalet hotels. Mark Warner has four, including the family-friendly Cygnaski, the nightlife hot spot Moris and the Val d'Isère in the centre, which enjoys free use of an outdoor swimming pool.

**Hotels** There are about 40 to choose from, mostly 2- and 3-star, but for such a big international resort surprisingly few are notably attractive.

((((4 **Barmes de L'Ours** (0475 000602) New 4-star 'luxury' hotel. Central, with fitness and beauty centre, indoor pool and children's play area.

((((4 **Christiania** (0479 060825) Big chalet, probably best in town. Chic, with friendly staff. Sauna.

((((4 **Blizzard** (0479 060207) Comfortable. Convenient. Indoor-outdoor pool. Good food.

((((4 **Latitudes** (0479 061888) Modern, stylish. Piano bar, nightclub. Leisure centre: sauna, steam room, whirlpool.

(((3 **Grand Paradis** (0479 061173) Recent refurbishment includes a new, imported Austrian wine cellar! Excellent position. Good food.

(((3 **Savoyarde** (0479 060155) Rustic decor. Newly refurbished leisure centre. Good food. Rooms a bit small.

(((3 **Kandahar** (0479 060239) Smart, newish building above Taverne d'Alsace on main street.

(((3 **Mercure** (0479 061293) Highly recommended by one of our most reliable reporters: 'It doesn't look much from the outside, but the food and the wine list are excellent.'

(((3 **Sorbiers** (0479 062377) Modern but cosy B&B hotel, not far out. 'Clean, comfortable, good-sized rooms.'

(((3 **Samovar** (0479 061351) In La Daille. Traditional, with good food. 'Very friendly and helpful staff.'

**Self-catering** There are thousands of properties to choose from. UK operators offer lots of them, but they tend to get booked up early. The MGM Chalets du Laisinant apartments, out of town on the road to Le Fornet, look good. Local agency Val-d'Isère Agence has a large selection of places and a good brochure. The local supermarkets are well stocked.

### EATING OUT

***Plenty of good, affordable places***

The 70-odd restaurants include Italian, Alsatian, Tex-Mex, even Japanese ones, but most offer good French dishes. A helpful *Guide des Tables* is distributed freely. In high season reservations are essential – especially on Wednesday, when most catered chalet staff get the night off.

There are plenty of pleasant mid-priced places. The 'bustling and busy' Perdrix Blanche is popular, but a 2004 visitor found the 'good, reasonably

**Phone numbers**
From abroad use the prefix +33 and omit the initial '0' of the phone number.

## ACTIVITIES

**Indoor** Swimming pool, sauna, sports hall (badminton, gym etc), weights room, library, fitness and health clubs, pâtisserie classes, bridge, yoga, cinema

**Outdoor** Natural ice rink, quad-bikes, all-terrain karts, snow-shoe outings, farm visits, snowmobiles, paragliding, microlight trips, craft studio visits, dog-sledding, walking





priced' food somewhat overshadowed by the service and attitude of the waiter – 'far from ideal'. Alternatively, head for the Taverne d'Alsace, another old favourite – 'atmospheric and vibrant, good food but pricey'. Tufs and Toit du Monde (formerly the Crêch'ouna) on the snow above La Daille are open in the evenings (see Mountain Restaurants). The 'impressive' Austrian-influenced menu of the Schuss restaurant in the Grand Paradis hotel comes highly recommended this year. Family-run Chez Paolo is praised for its 'excellent pizzas and pastas'.

Our favourite for a special night out – though the flow of supporting reports from readers seems to be drying up – is the Chalet du Crêt, off the road on the northern edge of downtown Val. Set in a 300-year-old stone farmhouse, beautifully renovated by the Franco-British couple who run it, this place serves a fixed-price menu starting with a magnificent hors-d'oeuvres spread. Not cheap, but highly satisfying. A rival for a top-of-the-range meal is the Grande Ourse by the nursery slope.

Those on tight budgets should try Chez Nano (next to Dick's Tea Bar) – reportedly good-value pizza and wine. The Melting Pot also gets good reviews for its unusual menu, which includes Thai dishes and 'a good selection of veggie options' – a rare enough thing in France. The Corniche is recommended for being 'traditional French, very enjoyable'; Casa Scara for 'good food, though the service was slow' and Grand Cocor for 'excellent food and choice'.

### APRES-SKI
***Very lively***

Nightlife is surprisingly energetic, given that most people have spent a hard day on the slopes. There are lots of bars, many with happy hours followed by music and dancing later on.

The Folie Douce, at the top of the La Daille gondola, has become an Austrian-style tea-time rave, with music and dancing; you can ride the gondola down unless it's closed by the

**TOURIST OFFICE**

**t** 0479 060660
info@valdisere.com
www.valdisere.com

toilets and extortionate prices after 11pm and another saying 'so good we were boring and went there all the time'. The nearby Petit Danois is a good alternative and somewhat less frenetic than Dick's. Live music at Café Fats was enjoyed by a 2004 reporter who describes is at 'a haphazard place but nevertheless a good atmosphere'.

On a quieter note, the Pub draws a 'more conversational crowd' and the Lodge is 'quite cosy', or there are hotel bars, piano bars and cocktail lounges.

weather. At La Daille the bar at the Samovar hotel is 'a good spot for a beer after skiing'. In downtown Val, Café Face ('warm and friendly') and the Moris pub (in the Mark Warner chalet) fill up as the slopes close; the 'friendly' Boubou, Bar Jacques and the Perdrix Blanche are popular with locals. Victor's bar is popular before it turns into a restaurant later on – black-and-white decor, stainless steel toilets. The basement Taverne d'Alsace is quiet and relaxing.

Later on, the famous Dick's Tea Bar is the main disco and gets packed, but it receives mixed reports, with one reporter complaining about flooded

### OFF THE SLOPES
***Not much***

Val is primarily a resort for those keen to get on to the slopes – though one non-skiing reporter was 'very satisfied' with the facilities. The sports facilities, renovated swimming pool included, are not particularly impressive. The range of shops is better than in most high French resorts. Lunchtime meetings present problems: the easily accessible mountain restaurants are few, and your friends may prefer lunching miles away in places like Les Brévières. One reporter suggests that it's worth watching out for 'spectacular' firework displays and torchlit descents.

OT VAL-D'ISERE / MARIO COLONEL

A pedestrian development links the nursery slopes to the village centre ↓

# Valmorel

*Pretty, purpose-built resort with fair-sized area of slopes*

## COSTS

①②③④⑤⑥

## RATINGS

**The slopes**
Snow ***
Extent ***
Expert **
Intermediate ****
Beginner *****
Convenience *****
Queues ****
Mountain restaurants **

**The rest**
Scenery ***
Resort charm ****
Off-slope **

## NEWS

For 2004/05, some pistes will be improved and there will be lift pass discounts for weekends and students. The resort is also continuing to expand its snowmaking.

The Gollet drag-lift now starts from nearer the terrain-park.



- + The most sympathetically designed French purpose-built resort
- + Largely slope-side accommodation
- + Beginners and children particularly well catered for

- − Few challenging pistes
- − Fairly low, so snow can suffer
- − Little variety in accommodation or in restaurants and bars
- − Still many slow lifts and some drags

**Built from scratch in the mid-1970s, Valmorel was intended to look and feel like a mountain village: a traffic-free main street with low-rise hamlets grouped around it. The end result is an attractive, friendly sort of place. The slopes are extensive by most standards and with good snow conditions there's enough here to keep everyone except real experts happy. Unashamedly aimed at the middle ground (intermediates, families and mixed-ability groups), Valmorel has considerable appeal because it has been so well put together.**

## THE RESORT

Valmorel is the main resort in 'Le Grand Domaine' – a ski area that links the Tarentaise with the Maurienne, by way of the Col de la Madeleine. Bourg-Morel is the heart of the resort – a traffic-free street where you'll find most of the shops and restaurants. It's pleasant and usually lively, with a distinctly family feel – but a recent reporter says the main street can get very crowded. Scattered here and there on the hillside are the six 'hameaux' with most of the accommodation. Hameau-du-Mottet is convenient – it is at the top of the Télébourg (the cross-village lift) with good access to the main lifts and from the return runs. All the mega-ski areas of the Tarentaise are within driving distance.

## THE MOUNTAINS

Variety is provided by sectors of distinctive character, and the extent is enough to provide interesting day-trips. There are still a few long drag-lifts; you can't get back from Longchamp without taking one.

**Slopes** The pistes are spread over a number of minor valleys and ridges either side of the Col de la Madeleine. The most heavily used route out of the village is the fast Altispace quad chair. From the top, a network of lifts and pistes takes you to the Col de la Madeleine and beyond that to Lauzière or the slopes of St-François and Longchamp. The Mottet sector and the Gollet area have their own runs back towards the village, or you can work your way to the Beaudin and Madeleine sectors.

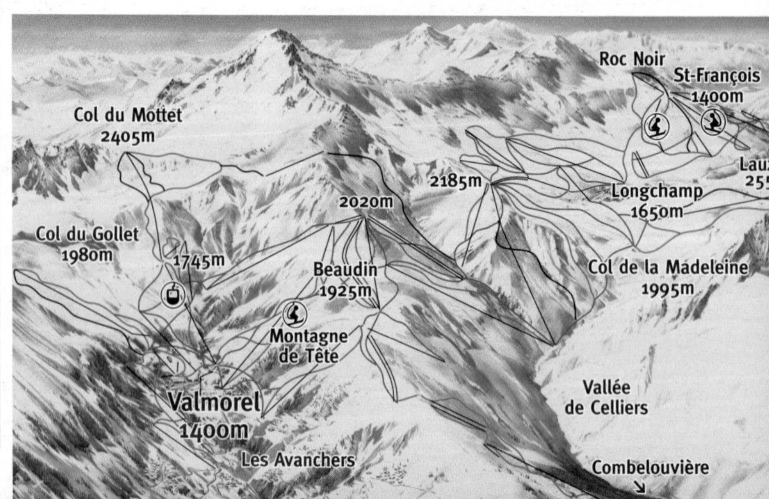

## KEY FACTS

| | |
|---|---|
| **Resort** | 1400m<br>4,590ft |
| For Grand Domaine | |
| **Slopes** | 1250-2550m<br>4,100-8,370ft |
| **Lifts** | 54 |
| **Pistes** | 152km<br>94 miles |
| **Green** | 33% |
| **Blue** | 39% |
| **Red** | 19% |
| **Black** | 9% |
| **Snowmaking** | 220 guns |
| For Domaine de Valmorel only | |
| **Slopes** | 1250-2405m<br>4,100-7,890ft |
| **Lifts** | 38 |
| **Pistes** | 95km<br>59 miles |

**Phone numbers**
From abroad use the prefix +33 and omit the initial '0' of the phone number.

## TOURIST OFFICE

**t** 0479 098555
info@valmorel.com
www.valmorel.com

**Terrain-parks** There's a terrain-park, with a boarder-cross course and half-pipe, at the top of the Crève Coeur chair; a special park-only pass is available. There's a boarder-cross by the Lune Bleue chair-lift at St-François.
**Snow reliability** With many runs below 2000m/6,560ft, good snow is not guaranteed. Mottet is north-facing and usually has the best snow. There's snowmaking on the nursery slopes and the main runs back to base.
**Experts** There are a few challenging pistes, but the off-piste is attractive because the resort does not attract experts, so powder can lie untracked for days after a snowfall. Gollet is usually a good place for moguls. There are steep black runs below the top section of the Mottet chair.
**Intermediates** The whole area except the steepest black runs is ideal, though the red stretch of the main run back to the village can be quite daunting at the end of the day. A 2004 reporter warns that piste grooming is 'erratic', which can make some red runs tricky.
**Beginners** There are dedicated learning areas ('still the best we've seen, 10/10' according to one reporter) right by the village for both adults and children. The long green run to Combelouvière is 'wonderful', says a 2004 reporter.
**Snowboarding** There are decent intermediate runs – but new boarders will find some of the drag-lifts tricky.
**Cross-country** Trails adding up to 23km/14 miles can be reached by bus.
**Queues** There can be 10- to 15-minute waits for the Altispace chair out of town at the morning peak, but those staying in the Mottet or Forêt areas can avoid this by taking the Lanchettes chair. The Frêne drags can't cope when everyone is returning from St-François.
**Mountain restaurants** There are half a dozen or so. Banquise 2000 has a great location at Col de la Madeleine; Prariond has been recommended.
**Schools and guides** We've had some good reports about the school over the years. Teaching for first-timers is a speciality of the resort.
**Facilities for children** Saperlipopette is a comprehensive childcare facility, and children taking ski lessons can have lunch there, too. Advance booking is essential except for very quiet times.

## STAYING THERE

**How to go** Self-catering packages are the norm but there are some catered chalets, mainly aimed at families. One regular prefers staying in Combelouvière below Valmorel – 'sunnier and quieter'.
**Hotels** Planchamp (0479 099700) is the best, with a good French restaurant. A 2004 reporter described the Soleil La Fontaine (0479 098777) as 'excellent; great food, friendly staff, sunny location right on the slopes'.
**Self-catering** The Athamante et Valeriane apartments have been praised.
**Eating out** You can check out most restaurants by wandering along the main street. The Grange and Ski Roc were recommended by a 2003 reporter.
**Après-ski** Immediate après-ski centres on the lively outdoor cafes; after-dark activities centre on the main street.
**Off the slopes** It's very pretty but not a great place to hang around if you're not using the slopes.

# Val-Thorens

*Europe's highest resort, with guaranteed good snow*



## COSTS

①②③④⑤⑥

## RATINGS

**The slopes**

| | |
|---|---|
| Snow | ***** |
| Extent | ***** |
| Expert | **** |
| Intermediate | ***** |
| Beginner | **** |
| Convenience | ***** |
| Queues | *** |
| Mountain restaurants | **** |

**The rest**

| | |
|---|---|
| Scenery | *** |
| Resort charm | ** |
| Off-slope | ** |

## NEWS

For 2003/04 a new gondola – which is able to keep working even in bad weather – replaced the Bouquetin chair towards Méribel, speeding up this journey considerably. It works by three 33-person cabins travelling up together while three more come down. The blue piste to the resort from the top of the new gondola (which is also the way over from Méribel) was improved.

More snowmaking was installed.

The sports centre was renovated to include a new swimming pool, a second hydro pool, a steam room, a sauna, a solarium and a new gym.

In 2002/03 new luxury apartments opened, called L'Oxalys.

Refurbishment work at various hotels and apartment buildings should be taking place for 2004/05.

- + Extensive local slopes to suit all abilities, and good access to the rest of the vast Three Valleys
- + The highest resort in the Alps and one of the most snow-sure, with north-facing slopes guaranteeing good snow for a long season
- + Convenient, gentle nursery slopes
- + Not as much of an eyesore as most high, purpose-built resorts
- + Compact village with direct slope access from most accommodation

- − Can be bleak in bad weather – not a tree in sight
- − Parts of the village are much less attractive to walk through in the evening than to ski past in the day
- − Not much to do off the slopes
- − Some very crowded pistes and dangerous intersections
- − Still some queues – especially for the Cîme de Caron cable-car

**For the enthusiast looking for the best snow in the Alps, it's difficult to beat Val-Thorens. That wonderful snow lies on some pretty wonderful slopes, and the village – always one of the better-designed high-altitude stations – gets more attractive as it continues to develop, and has some smart accommodation now.**

**But we still prefer a cosier base elsewhere in the Three Valleys. That way, if a storm socks in, we can play in the woods around Méribel or Courchevel; if the sun is scorching, we have the option of setting off for Val-Thorens. The formula simply doesn't work the other way round. For a pre-Christmas or an April trip, though, it's the best base.**

## THE RESORT

Val-Thorens is built high above the tree line on a sunny, west-facing mountainside at the head of the Belleville valley, surrounded by peaks, slopes and lifts. The village streets are supposedly traffic-free. Practically all visitors' cars are banished to car parks, except on Saturday. But workers' cars still generate a fair amount of traffic, and weekends can be mayhem with people entering and leaving the resort. Many parts of the resort are designed with their 'fronts' facing the slopes, and their relatively dreary backs facing the streets. There are quite extensive shopping arcades, a fair choice of bars and restaurants, and a good (and recently improved) sports centre.

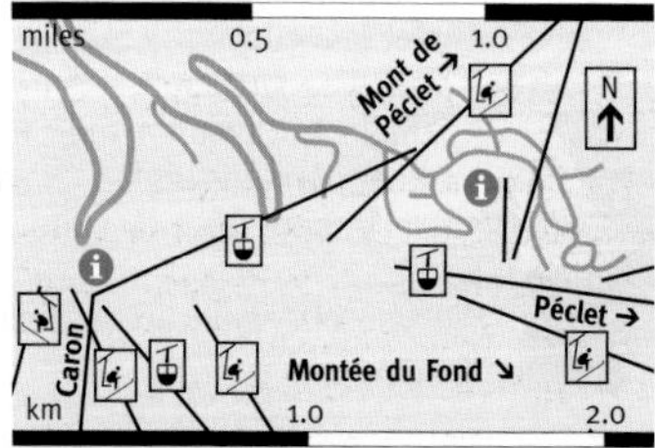


It is a classic purpose-built resort, with lots of convenient slope-side accommodation. It's quite a complex little village; but since it's very compact – our scale plan is one of the smallest in these pages – it doesn't matter much where you stay. At its heart is the snowy Place de Caron, where pedestrians mix with skiers and boarders. Many of the shops and restaurants are clustered here, along with the best hotels, and the sports centre is nearby. The village is basically divided in two by a little slope (with a drag-lift) that leads down from here to the broad main nursery slope running the length of the village. The upper half of the village is centred on the Place de Péclet. A road runs across the hillside from here to the chalet-style Balcons development. The lower half of the village is more diffuse, with the Rue du Soleil winding down from the dreary bus station to the big Temples du Soleil apartments.

Seen from the slopes, the resort is not as hideous as many of its rivals. The buildings are mainly medium-rise and wood-clad; and some are distinctly stylish.

Snow-sure Val-Thorens sits high above the tree line: great on sunny days, not so much fun in a blizzard ↗

SNOWPIX.COM / CHRIS GILL

## KEY FACTS

| | |
|---|---|
| **Resort** | 2300m 7,550ft |
| For the Three Valleys | |
| **Slopes** | 1260-3230m 4,130-10,600ft |
| **Lifts** | 197 |
| **Pistes** | 600km 373 miles |
| **Green** | 21% |
| **Blue** | 33% |
| **Red** | 35% |
| **Black** | 11% |
| **Snowmaking** | 1500 guns |
| For Val-Thorens only | |
| **Slopes** | 1800-3230m 5,900-10,600ft |
| **Lifts** | 30 |
| **Pistes** | 170km 105 miles |
| **Green** | 12% |
| **Blue** | 34% |
| **Red** | 46% |
| **Black** | 8% |
| **Snowmaking** | 200 guns |



## THE MOUNTAINS

Take account of the height, the extent of its local slopes and the easy access to the rest of the Three Valleys, and the attraction of Val-Thorens becomes clear. The main disadvantage is the lack of trees. Heavy snowfalls or high wind can shut practically all the lifts and slopes, and even if they don't close, poor visibility can be a problem.

### THE SLOPES
### *High and snow-sure*

The resort has a wide piste going right down the front of it, leading down to a number of different lifts. The big **Péclet** gondola, with 25-person cabins, rises 700m/2,300ft to the Péclet glacier, with three red runs down. One links across to a wide area of intermediate runs served by lifts to cols either side of the **Pointe de Thorens**. You can take red or blue runs into the 'fourth valley', the Maurienne, from one of these – the **Col de Rosaël,** now served by the Grand Fond jumbo gondola.

In the Maurienne valley two successive chairs go up to 3230m/ 10,600ft on the virgin flanks of **Pointe du Bouchet** – now the highest lift-served point in the Three Valleys and with stunning views. The former black run off the back of here is now off-piste because of crevasse and avalanche danger and the snow gets very windblown and icy – nice!

The cable-car to **Cîme de Caron** is one of the great lifts of the Alps, rising 900m/2,950ft in no time at all. It can be reached by skiing across from mid-mountain, or by coming up on the gondola which starts below the village. From the top there is the choice of red and black pistes down the front, or a black into the Maurienne.

The relatively low **Boismint** sector is overlooked by many visitors, but is actually a very respectable hill, with a total vertical of 860m/2,820ft.

Chair-lifts heading north from the resort serve sunny slopes above the village and also lead to the Méribel valley. Les Menuires can also be reached via these lifts; the alternative Boulevard Cumin along the valley floor is nearly flat, and can be hard work, especially for kids – as the editorial offspring can confirm.

### TERRAIN-PARKS
### *Adequate*

The terrain-park just above the resort, served by a fast chair, has a half-pipe, jumps and a sound system. There is also a boarder-cross course in the Maurienne valley.



## boarding

*The best resort-level snow in Europe appeals to boarders as well as skiers – and pulls in considerable numbers. There are pistes to suit all abilities, and the good snow is great for beginners and carvers. There's plenty of off-piste choice for free-riders, though if you want trees you'll have to travel. The lifts are now mainly chairs and gondolas, although one or two drags remain.*

LIFT PASSES

**Three Valleys**
Covers all lifts in Courchevel, La Tania, Méribel, Val-Thorens, Les Menuires and St-Martin-de-Belleville.

**Beginners**
5 free lifts in Val-Thorens.

**Main pass**
1 day €40
6 days €198

**Senior citizens**
Over 60: 6 days €158
Over 72: free pass

**Children**
Under 13: 6 days €149
Under 5: free pass

**Notes**
Reductions for families. Half-day and pedestrian passes available. 6-day pass valid for one day in Espace Killy (Tignes-Val-d'Isère), Paradiski (La Plagne-Les Arcs), Pralognan and Les Saisies.

**Alternative passes**
Pass for Val-Thorens-Orelle only.





## SNOW RELIABILITY
### *Difficult to beat*

Few resorts can rival Val-Thorens for reliably good snow-cover, thanks to its altitude and generally north-facing slopes. Snowmaking covers a lot of the key pistes, including the crowded south- and west-facing runs on the way back from the Méribel valley, and was extended in 2003/04.

## FOR EXPERTS
### *Lots to do off-piste*

Val-Thorens' local pistes are primarily intermediate terrain. The fast Cascades chair serves a short but steep black run that quickly gets mogulled. The pistes down from the Cîme de Caron cable-car are challenging, but not seriously steep and there's a sunny black run off the back into the fourth valley. The black Chamois and red Falaise (which a reporter called 'horrendous') and Variente runs from Col de Rosaël can get heavily mogulled and challenging. The sunny Marielle run, one of the routes from the Méribel valley, is one of the easiest blacks we've come across.

But there is huge amounts of off-piste to explore with a guide – see the feature panel opposite.

## FOR INTERMEDIATES
### *Unbeatable quality and quantity*

The scope for intermediates throughout the Three Valleys is enormous. It will take a keen intermediate only 90 minutes or so to get to Courchevel at the far end, if not distracted by the endless runs on the way.

The local slopes in Val-Thorens are some of the best intermediate terrain in the region. Most of the pistes are easy reds and blues, made even more enjoyable by the excellent snow.

The snow on the red Col run is always some of the best around. The blue Moraine below it is gentle – 'fine cruising', reports a visitor last year – and popular with the schools. The runs on the top half of the mountain are steeper than those back into the resort. The Grand Fond gondola serves a good variety of red runs. The newly-improved Pluviometre from the Trois Vallées chair is a glorious varied run, away from the lifts. Adventurous intermediates shouldn't miss the Cîme de Caron runs. The black run is not intimidating – it's very wide, usually has good snow and is a wonderful fast cruise when freshly groomed.

## FOR BEGINNERS
### *Good late-season choice*

The slopes at the foot of the resort are very gentle and provide convenient, snow-sure nursery slopes, now with moving walkway lifts. There are no long green runs to progress to, but the blues immediately above the village are easy. The resort's height and bleakness make it cold in midwinter, and intimidating in bad weather.

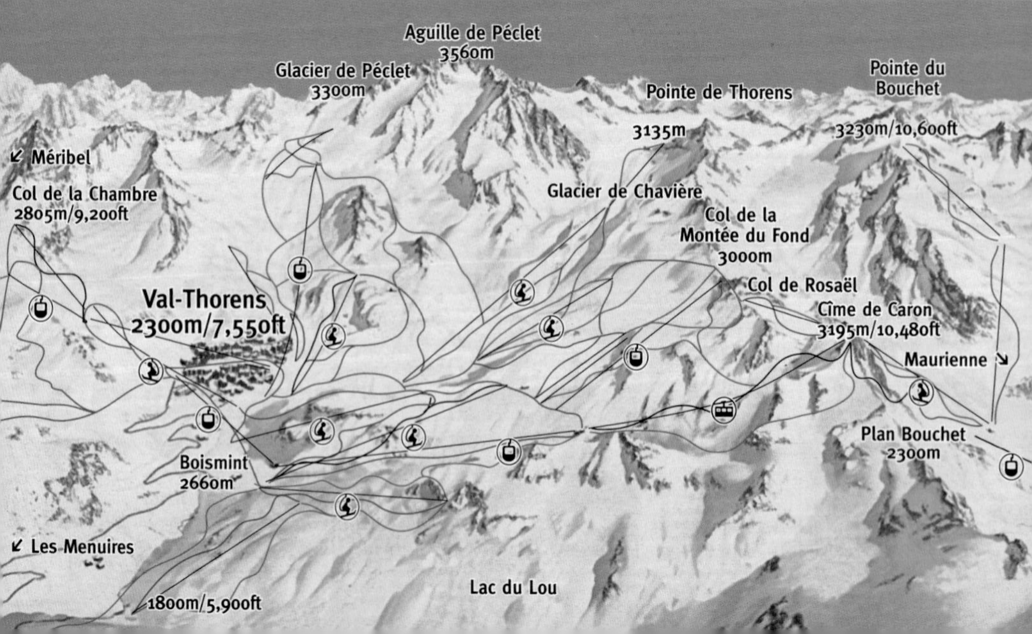

The **ESF** is the largest ski school in Val-Thorens, with 180 English-speaking instructors. It organises group or private off-piste courses, Three Valleys tours, and group and private lessons for every standard of skiers and snowboarder. It runs two mini-clubs and three kindergartens.

**t** 00 33 479 00 02 86
www.esf-valthorens.com

## FABULOUS OFF-PISTE IN VAL-THORENS

**Val-Thorens offers a huge choice of off-piste. And because of the high altitude, the snow stays powdery longer here than in lower parts of the Three Valleys. With the help of Gilbert Smith, Technical Director of the ESF in Val-Thorens, with whom we skied off-piste in 2004, we pick just a few of the runs to be explored.**

*For an adventurous intermediate looking to try off-piste for the first time, or with a little off-piste experience already, the Pierre Lory Pass run is ideal. It is a very large and gentle slope and you access the pass by doing an easy traverse (20 minutes maximum) on the Chavière glacier from the top of the Col chair-lift. When you arrive at Pierre Lory Pass there are breathtaking views of the Aiguilles d'Arves in the Maurienne valley, and you will be just above the Du Bouchet glacier, which you then ski down, rejoining the lift system at Plan Bouchet.*

*For those with more off-piste under their belt already, the Lac du Lou (see below) is a famous off-piste run of 1400m/4,590ft vertical. It is easily accessible from the top of the Cîme de Caron cable-car, from where you have a view of 1,000 summits. The many ways into this long, wide valley allow plenty of variety and opportunities for making first tracks; because many of the slopes face north or north-west it is not unusual to find good powder most of the ski season, even in late April. The views are stunning and you'll notice the quietness and vastness of the whole valley.*

*La Combe sans Nom on the Maurienne side in the 4th Valley, also accessible from the Cîme de Caron cable-car, usually offers superb skiing and snowboard conditions. There's a choice of south-, west- and, on the far side, some east-facing slopes, which makes for excellent spring skiing conditions!*

*For the more adventurous there are many options, including hiking up from the top of the Col chair-lift and skiing a long run over the Gébroulaz glacier down to Méribel.*

*But don't even think about doing any off-piste runs without a fully qualified guide or instructor. Route finding can be difficult, there can be avalanche danger and hidden hazards such as cliffs and crevasses lurk. The ESF offers a wide choice of off-piste programmes and provides avalanche transceivers.*

SNOWPIX.COM / CHRIS GILL

In the distance is the vast expanse of the Lac du Lou run mentioned above in the off-piste feature panel ➔

## SCHOOLS

**ESF**
t 0479 000286
info@esf-valthorens.com

**Ski-Cool**
t 0479 000492
mail@ski-cool.com

**Prosneige**
t 0479 010700
info@prosneige.fr

**International**
t 0479 000196
esi@intl-skischool.com

**Classes** (ESF prices)
6 half-days (3hr am) from €96

**Private lessons**
€31 for 1hr

## GUIDES

t 0689 292336

## CHILDREN

**Le Montana**
t 0479 000286
Ages from 3mnth

**Le Roc**
t 0479 000286
Ages from 18 mnth. Skiing tuition for 3 and over (Bambi club)

**Ski school**
All the schools offer classes for children aged 4 or 5 and over (ESF: 6 mornings from €86)

### FOR CROSS-COUNTRY
***Try elsewhere***

Val-Thorens is a poor base for cross-country, with only 4km/2.5 miles of local trails.

### QUEUES
***Persistent at the Cîme de Caron***

Recent reports suggest that the longest queues are for the largest and most rewarding lifts, notably the Cîme de Caron cable-car, but also the gondolas. The queues move fairly quickly, but reporters warn that visits to the Cîme de Caron really need to be timed to miss the crowds.

The Plein Sud six-pack chair-lift does a good job of getting the crowds out of the village towards Méribel and Courchevel, and now delivers you to just above the new gondola which replaced the Bouquetin chair. But a 2004 reporter says that in the morning there are still massive queues as people head out to the rest of the Three Valleys. Check the Méribel chapter for bottlenecks there.

When snow is in short supply elsewhere, the pressure on the Val-Thorens lifts can increase markedly.

### MOUNTAIN RESTAURANTS
***Lots of choice***

For a high, modern resort, the choice of restaurants is good. The Bar de la Marine, on the Dalles piste, does excellent food (we had good pot au feu), but it's pricey and service can be stretched. The Moutière, near the top of the chair of the same name, is one of the more reasonably priced huts. The Plan Bouchet refuge in the Maurienne valley is very popular and welcoming, but bar service can be slow. You can stay the night there, too. The Chalet Plein Sud, below the chair of the same name, has excellent views but a 'rather limited menu'. The big Chalet de Thorens has been praised for its food and reasonable prices, but is in need of refurbishment, according to one reporter. The Chalets des 2 Lacs is 'still good, friendly and efficient'. In the past we've enjoyed the Chalet de Genépi, on the run down from the Moraine chair – great views and an open fire – but recent reports of the food have been disappointing: 'appalling' and 'bad steak hachée and chips not worth 15 euros'.

### SCHOOLS AND GUIDES
***A mixed bag***

We lack recent reports of the ESF, which has a Trois Vallées group for those who want to cover a lot of ground while receiving lessons – available by the day or the week, and can include off-piste. Reporters recommend the Prosneige classes: 'really excellent – my wife's skiing changed dramatically'; 'good with children'. Ski-Cool class sizes are guaranteed not to exceed 10. They also have off-piste courses. There are several specialist guiding outfits.

### FACILITIES FOR CHILDREN
***Coolly efficient***

Our most recent reporter on the ESF nursery found the facilities convenient and the service efficient. In spite of the fact that the staff were 'not particularly warm or friendly', by the end of the week all the children were 'comfortable' on skis. The Prosneige takes children from the age of five.

## STAYING THERE

### HOW TO GO
***Surprisingly high level of comfort***

Accommodation is of a higher standard than in many purpose-built resorts.
**Chalets** These are catered apartments, and many are quite comfortable.
**Hotels** There are plenty of hotels, and there's a Club Med, too.

Cars and coaches have to be left in parking areas by the access road, leaving the resort largely traffic-free ↗

SNOWPIX.COM / CHRIS GILL

## GETTING THERE

**Air** Geneva 160km/99 miles (3½hr), Lyon 193km/120 miles (3½hr), Chambéry 112km/70 miles (2½hr).

**Rail** Moûtiers (37km/23 miles); regular buses from station.

## ACTIVITIES

**Indoor** Sports centre (spa, sauna, fitness room, hot-tub, tennis, squash, swimming pool, volleyball, table tennis, badminton, football), games rooms, music recitals

**Outdoor** Paragliding, sightseeing flights, snowmobiles, snow-shoe excursions, ice-climbing, walks, tobogganing

**Phone numbers**
From abroad use the prefix +33 and omit the initial '0' of the phone number.

## TOURIST OFFICE

**t** 0479 000808
valtho@valthorens.com
www.valthorens.com

((((5 **Fitz Roy** (0479 000478) The sole 4-star is a swanky but charming Relais & Châteaux place with lovely rooms. Pool. Well placed.
(((4 **Val Thorens** (0479 000433) Welcoming and comfortable; next door to Fitz Roy. 'Good service, good food and an excellent on the slopes location.'
((3 **Sherpa** (0479 000070) Highly recommended for atmosphere and food. Less-than-ideal position at the top of the resort.
((3 **Val Chaviere** (0479 000033) Friendly, convenient, 'good food and plenty of it'.
((3 **Bel Horizon** (0479 000477) Friendly, family-run 3-star, popular with reporters – 'cuisine wonderful'.
**Self-catering** The options include apartments of a higher standard than usual in France. The luxurious Oxalys (with pool, sauna, steam room and open fire in all living rooms), Montagnettes, Chalets du Soleil and Village Montana are all said to be outstanding.

## EATING OUT
### *Surprisingly wide range*

Val-Thorens has something for most tastes and pockets. The Fitz Roy and the Val Thorens hotels do classic French food. But even they have been put in the shade by the new gourmet restaurant in the Oxalys apartment building, which a 2004 reporter says is 'out of this world' and continues: 'In over half a century of French gastronomy I have never had a meal to compare with the inventiveness of this smart but friendly establishment. It is expensive but worth every penny.'

For something more regional, the best bets are the 'excellent' Vieux Chalet and the Chaumière. Other readers' recommendations include the Cabane ('excellent Savoyard fare'), the Ferme de Rosalie ('good but limited menu'), the Montana ('good food and service'), El Gringo's ('great for Tex-Mex food' and 'very popular so get there early'), Auberge des Balcons ('wonderful raclette') and the Joyeuse Fondue. The Galoubet has been recommended for local specialities, including pierrades. The Blanchot is an unusually stylish wine bar with a simple but varied carte and of course an excellent range of wines. Several pizzerias are recommended, including the Grange in the Temples du Soleil.

## APRES-SKI
### *Livelier than you'd imagine*

Val-Thorens is more lively at night than most high-altitude ski-stations. The Red Fox up at Balcons is crowded at close of play, with karaoke. At the opposite extreme the Sherlock in the Temples du Soleil is 'always lively'. The Frog and Roastbeef at the top of the village is a cheerful British ghetto with a live band at tea-time and half-price beer while it plays. It claims to be the highest pub in Europe. The Friends and the Viking pub are all lively bars on the same block. The Underground nightclub in Place de Péclet has an extended happy hour but 'descends into europop' when its disco gets going. The Malaysia cellar bar is recommended for good live bands, and gets very crowded after 11pm. Quieter bars include the 'atmospheric without being over crowded' O'Connells and the cosy Rhum Box (aka Mitch's).

## OFF THE SLOPES
### *Forget it*

There's a good sports centre, which was renovated for last season – see News. You can get to some mountain restaurants by lift, and the 360° panorama from the top of the Cîme de Caron cable-car is not to be missed. But it is not a good bet for a holiday off the slopes.

# The French Pyrenees

*Decent skiing and boarding at half the price of the Alps*

**REPORTS WANTED**

Recently we have had few reports on this resort. If you go there, please do send us a report.

The best reports earn a copy of the next edition, and can lead to free lift passes in future.

See page 10.



**Phone numbers**
From abroad use the prefix +33 and omit the initial '0' of the phone number.

**TOURIST OFFICES**

www.pyrenees-online.fr

**Barèges**
t 0562 921600 /921615
www.tourmalet.fr
www.bareges.com

**La Mongie**
t 0562 919415 / 919084
www.tourmalet.fr
www.bagneresdebigorre-lamongie.com

**Cauterets**
t 0562 925050
www.cauterets.com

**Font-Romeu**
t 0468 306830
www.font-romeu.fr

**St-Lary-Soulan**
t 0562 395081
www.saintlary.com

**It took us a long time to get round to visiting the resorts of the French Pyrenees – mainly because we had the idea that they were second-rate compared with the Alps. Well, it is certainly true that they can't compete in terms of size of ski area with the mega-resorts of the Trois Vallées and Paradiski. But don't dismiss them: they have considerable attractions, including price – hotels cost half as much as in the Alps, and meals and drinks are cheap.**

The Pyrenees are serious mountains, with dramatic picturesque scenery. They are also attractively French. Unlike the big plastic mega resorts, many Pyrenean bases have a rustic, rural Gallic charm.

The biggest ski area – shared by **Barèges** and **La Mongie –** is called **Domaine Tourmalet**. Between them they have 100km/62 miles of runs (70 pistes) and 45 lifts. Most lifts are drags and slow chairs but they have a couple of high-speed chairs.

The runs are best suited to intermediates, with good tree-lined runs above Barèges and open bowl skiing above La Mongie. The best bet for an expert is to try off-piste with a guide – one beautiful run away from all the lifts starts with a scramble through a hole in the rocks. There are two terrain-parks. Rustic mountain huts are scattered around the slopes.

Barèges is a spa village set in a narrow, steep-sided valley, which gets little sun in midwinter; the lift base is at Tournaboup, 4km/2.5 miles up the valley and served by ski-bus. It's the second oldest ski resort in France and the pioneer of skiing in the Pyrenees. Accommodation is mainly in 2-star hotels such as the Igloo, Central and Europe, which reporters recommend for good food and a friendly welcome. One reporter stayed in nearby Luz in the Chimes hotel, describing the food as 'divine'. The rather drab buildings and one main street of Barèges grow on you, though there's little to do in the evenings other than visit the thermal spa and a restaurant. La Mongie, on the other hand, is a modern, purpose-built resort reminiscent of the Alps.

**Cauterets** is another spa town but a complete contrast to Barèges. It is much bigger and set in a wide, sunny valley. It is a popular summer destination, and even in March we were able to sit at a pavement cafe with a drink after dinner. A cable-car goes up to the slopes 850m/2,790ft above the town – you have to ride it down as well as up. There are only 35km/22 miles of slopes (mainly intermediate), and a terrain-park, set in a bowl that can be cold and windy.

But Cauterets' jewel is its cross-country, a long drive or bus-ride from town at Pont d'Espagne and served by a gondola. It is the start of the Pyrenees National Park and the old smugglers' route over the mountains between France and Spain. The 36km/22 miles of snow-sure cross-country tracks run up this beautiful deserted valley, beside a rushing stream and a stunning waterfall.

**Font-Romeu** has 52km/32 miles of pistes and 29 lifts, serving mainly easy and intermediate pistes (15 of its 40 pistes are green) and is popular with families. The slopes get a lot of sun but it has the biggest snowmaking set-up in the Pyrenees. Weekend crowds arrive from nearby Perpignan and over the border from Spain and both lifts and pistes can get crowded. It has 90km/56 miles of cross-country skiing. The village is a bus-ride from the slopes and hotels are mainly 2- and 3-star.

The other major Pyrenean resort is **St-Lary-Soulan**, a traditional village with houses built of stone, with a cable-car at the edge going up to the slopes, of which there are 80km/ 50 miles, mainly suiting intermediates. It has a terrain-park and half-pipe. There's a satellite called **St-Lary-Espiaube**, which is purpose-built and right at the heart of the slopes.

One 2003 reporter also visited other small resorts such as Formiguères, Eyne and Les Angles and suggests staying down in a small valley town and taking an 'ancient, scenic, electric train called Le Petit Train Jaune' and taxis to resorts for a 'different' holiday.

ISOLA 2000 TOURIST OFFICE

# Isola 2000

**An EasyJet flight and a short drive from Nice makes Isola easy and cheap to reach for a short break. It has slope-side accommodation and some snow-sure slopes. But the core of the resort village is dire: block-like and tatty.**

## KEY FACTS

| | |
|---|---|
| **Resort** | 2000m<br>6,560ft |
| **Slopes** | 1840-2610m<br>6,035-8,560ft |
| **Lifts** | 23 |
| **Pistes** | 120km<br>75 miles |
| **Green** | 15% |
| **Blue** | 39% |
| **Red** | 35% |
| **Black** | 11% |
| **Snowmaking** | 15km<br>9 miles |

## TOURIST OFFICE

**t** 04 9323 1515
info@isola2000.com
www.isola2000.com

## THE RESORT

Isola is a small, high, purpose-built resort close to the Côte d'Azur and easy to combine with a couple of days by the sea.

Built by a British property company at the end of the 1960s, the slope-side centre is a complex of block-like apartments, with shops, bars and restaurants in dark and tatty underground tunnels. Various owners have since worked hard to glamourise the image of the resort with new hamlets of more luxurious, wood-clad buildings. The Diva hotel (0493 231771) looks the best place to stay.

## THE RESORT

The ski area spreads around the resort in a horseshoe shape with the main access lift being a gondola to Pélevos at 2320m/7,610ft. But there are still a lot of drag-lifts and slow chairs.

Due to the great base height of Isola – the lowest of the slopes is at 1840m/ 6,035ft – most of the runs are above the tree line. Isola gets different weather from other major French resorts, so it can have masses of snow when the rest of the French Alps have none, and vice versa. Regular visitors say that they never find all the lifts open, but there is always snow – and plenty of sun.

Many of the runs suit confident intermediates best. They and experts will find the toughest runs in the St-Sauveur sector. There is more choice of blue runs in the Pélevos sector and excellent beginner slopes near the resort base. There are some surprisingly attractive restaurants on the slopes, including some just above the base, such as the Bergerie.

VAL-CENIS TOURIST OFFICE

# Val-Cenis

**Val-Cenis is a marketing concept rather than a place. It comprises two quiet villages in the high and remote part of the Maurienne valley – Lanslebourg and Lanslevillard. A good place for half-term holidays, say readers.**

## KEY FACTS

| | |
|---|---|
| **Resort** | 1400m<br>4,590ft |
| **Slopes** | 1400-2800m<br>4,590-9,190ft |
| **Lifts** | 19 |
| **Pistes** | 80km<br>50 miles |
| **Green** | 21% |
| **Blue** | 23% |
| **Red** | 42% |
| **Black** | 14% |
| **Snowmaking** | 84 guns |

## TOURIST OFFICE

**t** 0479 052366
info@valcenis.com
www.valcenis.com

## THE RESORT

Lanslebourg is a long, linear place, spreading along the Route Nationale 6 (a dead end in winter, when the road over the Col du Mont-Cenis becomes a piste). It's pleasant enough, but no great beauty. A bus-ride up the valley, Lanslevillard is more captivating – off the road, randomly arranged and rustic. There are modest hotels and a dozen restaurants in each village, but not much evening action. There's a leisure centre in Lanslevillard. 'Testing but enjoyable' walks are organised.

### THE MOUNTAIN

There are lifts from base stations in and between the two villages – the main one a gondola starting near Lanslevillard. Above mid-mountain is a good range of open runs, served by chairs and drags. Below mid-mountain all the runs are prettily wooded – there is usually an easy blue or green alternative to the various red runs back down as well. Most of the runs are north-facing, and there is snowmaking on the runs back to the base stations. There is ample off-piste but little else to challenge experts. For intermediates there are top-to-bottom cruises of up to 1400m/4,595ft vertical. Beginners have nursery slopes at valley level; higher options include a splendid green following the road from the Col.

There are extensive cross-country trails at Bessans, further up the valley.

Queues are rare, and bearable even at half term – 'mainly at the gondola in the afternoon' – and tend to move quite quickly.

Reports on the ski school are not encouraging – we hear of bored children, and private lessons with moniteurs speaking no English.

BERNARD GRANGE / OT VALLOIRE

# Valloire

**The old mountain village of Valloire is the best known, internationally, of a bunch of resorts sitting high above the Maurienne valley that lie to the south of Val-Thorens and the Trois Vallées.**

## KEY FACTS

| | |
|---|---|
| **Resort** | 1430m<br>4,690ft |
| Valloire/Valmeinier | |
| **Slopes** | 1430-2595m<br>4,690-8,510ft |
| **Lifts** | 32 |
| **Pistes** | 150km<br>93 miles |
| **Green** | 26% |
| **Blue** | 28% |
| **Red** | 38% |
| **Black** | 8% |
| **Snowmaking** | 30% |

## THE RESORT

Valloire still feels like a real mountain village with a year-round population of 1,000, a 17th century baroque church and market square in the centre, crêperies, fromageries and reasonably priced restaurants. Various events such as street markets and ice carving competitions add to its lively ambience, and because the Col du Galibier pass beyond it closes in winter, the place is mercifully free of through-traffic – its one-way system is there only because of its narrow streets. It is 17km/11 miles up a winding road from the valley town of St-Michel-de-Maurienne.

The Aux Oursons hotel (0479 590137) near the centre is comfortable and friendly, and has a small pool, hot-tub and sauna – and teddy bears everywhere (*ourson* means bear). The Galibier (1km/0.5 miles from the centre but close to the piste and a chair-lift) and the central Valmonts apartments are both relatively new, with pool, sauna and steam room.

The Gastilleur restaurant in the Sétaz hotel on the main street is the gourmet choice, while Bistrot Chez Fred serves reasonably priced brasserie food and gets so packed that they erect a canvas awning on the balcony to fit more people in. The Grange crêperie resembles a barn, and the Asile des Fondues serves what you'd expect from the name in a beautiful old building with stone walls. Valloire is not the place to go if you want lively nightlife, though the Touring Bar attracts the teens and 20s with table football, a pool table and loud music.

## THE MOUNTAINS

Two gondolas from different parts of town access Valloire's two linked mountains. The Setaz sector's shady slopes, the lower part tree-lined and the upper section open, generally have the best snow and the toughest slopes. The broad, open, west-facing slopes of Crey du Quart offer a choice of routes to link to the Valmeinier valley (see opposite). A gentle blue heads down from Grand Plateau to Valmeinier 1800, while an even gentler blue or green leads to the Armera chair lift, which goes down and then up to Valmeinier 1500.

Watch out for some tricky drag-lifts, which can lift you in the air at the start – not good for boarders.

Experts will find the area limited. The long Grandes Droze black run down to Valmeinier 1500 can present a challenge when the bumps build up, and the area beyond Valmeinier 1800 served by the Inversins chair-lift and the area from Crey du Quart down into the Valmeinier valley have some decent off-piste if the snow is good.

The vast majority of the slopes are ideal for intermediates of all standards. For easy cruising, head for the Crey du Quart and Valmeinier sectors which have gentle blues and almost-as-gentle reds everywhere. The often deserted, long, gentle Armera blue winds its way delightfully through the trees down from Crey du Quart towards Valmeinier 1500, and the Neuvache blue along the valley from Valmeinier 1800 is flat enough to be a green. The rather out-of-the way red Praz Violette piste from the top of the Combe drag-lift (which, be warned, has some very steep pitches and a huge bend of over 90° in it) can be a wonderful cruise away from the crowds. For more of a challenge, head over to Cretaz and try the highest runs, including the Cascade black, which often has excellent snow.

Valloire suits beginners well, with nursery slopes both at village level and up the mountain at the top of both gondolas, followed by very easy green runs to progress to.

Few of the mountain restaurants are memorable. We had a decent plat du jour and omelette savoyard in the crowded self-service Chateau Ripaille in the Crey du Quart sector.

The six-day lift pass allows a cut-price day in the Trois Vallées (the Val-Thorens sector can be accessed easily by gondola from Orelle in the Maurienne valley, around 30 minutes away by bus).







## TOURIST OFFICE

**t** 0479 590396
infos@valloire.net
www.valloire.net

SNOWPIX.COM / CHRIS GILL

# Valmeinier

**Valmeinier's two villages share slopes which are linked to those of Valloire (see opposite). Purpose-built Valmeinier 1800 attracts most of the visitors, though the lower Valmeinier 1500 was the traditional base.**

## KEY FACTS

| | |
|---|---|
| **Resort** | 1500-1800m<br>4,920-5,900ft |
| Valloire/Valmeinier | |
| **Slopes** | 1430-2595m<br>4,690-8,510ft |
| **Lifts** | 32 |
| **Pistes** | 150km<br>93 miles |
| **Green** | 26% |
| **Blue** | 28% |
| **Red** | 38% |
| **Black** | 8% |
| **Snowmaking** | 30% |

## TOURIST OFFICE

**t** 0479 595369
info@valmeinier.com
www.valmeinier.com

SNOWPIX.COM / CHRIS GILL

For a quiet family holiday, Valmeinier is worth a look ↓

## THE RESORT

The original old village of Valmeinier 1500 has expanded somewhat, with low-rise buildings that blend in well, and is closer to the link with Valloire. But the vast majority of visitors stay up the valley in the purpose-built satellite of Valmeinier 1800, which was started in 1986. Its low-rise chalet-style buildings line the bottom and side of the main slope and fit in well with their surroundings. It is a small, quiet, sunny place that mainly attracts French families on a budget looking for a hassle-free time and undemanding slopes. A reporter who stayed at the hotel Aigle (0479 592431) praised its childcare facilities but found 'over 60 children staying there' too many. The Pierre & Vacances apartments are above average for the chain, right on the piste, with outdoor pool and sauna.

## THE MOUNTAINS

The local slopes get a lot of sun, though the nursery slopes and a fair number of the main pistes have snowmaking. They are served almost entirely by chair-lifts (a welcome contrast with some of the vicious drag-lifts you'll encounter if you head off to the Valloire sector). An easy green route runs from top to bottom of the mountain, and it is difficult to tell the difference in gradient between many of the blues and reds. It suits beginners and undemanding intermediates best. The link to Valloire starts with a chair-lift reached by an almost flat track from Valmeinier 1800 or a down-and-then-up chair from Valmeinier 1500. See opposite for details of the Valloire slopes. There's a shortage of good mountain restaurants. Don't count on English speaking in the ski school.

# Italy

**Italy's popularity as a winter sports destination grew largely because its prices were appreciably lower than those in other Alpine countries. It is no longer quite such a bargain, so it now has to compete in terms of the quality of the holidays offered. And it is trying hard to do so. It has some enduring attractions, such as its food and wine, jolly atmosphere and splendid scenery – especially in the Dolomites. And many resorts now have powerful, modern lifts and huge snowmaking systems.**

Italian resorts vary as widely in their characteristics as they do in location – and they are spread along the full length of the Italian border, from Sauze d'Oulx to the Dolomites. There are high, snow-sure ski stations and charming valley villages, and mountains that range from one-run wonders to some of the most extensive lift networks in the world.

A lot of Italian runs, particularly in the north-west, seem flatteringly easy. This is partly because grooming is immaculate, and partly because piste classification seems to overstate difficulty. Nowhere is this clearer than in the linked area of La Rosière in France and La Thuile – in Italy, despite the French-sounding name. Venturing from the Italian motorways to the French moguls is like moving from the shelter of the harbour to the open sea.



## THE AMAZING DOLOMITI SUPERSKI LIFT PASS

*The Dolomiti Superski lift pass is one of the wonders of the world, covering 45 resorts and 460 lifts. We describe the most important resorts in our chapters on Cortina d'Ampezzo and Selva, but there are countless others worth a visit and we can only touch on a few here.*

*The Superski region, which straddles the provinces of Veneto, Trentino and Alto Adige/Südtirol (predominantly German-speaking, hence the alternative names), is broken down into 12 areas, each embracing a number of resorts.*

*One of the most interesting areas is in the north-east corner of the region, the Val Pusteria/Pustertal, which leads off eastwards towards the Slovenian border from the Brenner motorway. The main town is Brunico/Bruneck; we have fond memories of one of our first weeks on skis, spent near here on Plan de Corones/ Kronplatz – an extraordinary dome-shaped mountain with easy, open slopes around its bare summit, and more testing stuff lower down. Brunico now has lift access to the mountain by gondola from an outlying suburb, and what looks like an exciting black run through the woods to the base.*

*Just to the east is the area known as the Alta Val Pusteria/Hochpustertal. There are three small towns dotted along the valley. Westernmost is Villabassa/Niederdorf, chiefly of interest to cross-country skiers. At the watershed of the gently sloping valley, where it starts to descend towards Slovenia, is Dobbiaco/Toblach, with some short slopes on its fringes and very scenic cross-country trails. And further east is San Candido/Innichen, with a long chair-lift serving intermediate slopes.*

*Up an elevated side valley from here (again with scenic cross-country trails) is the main resort of this area, the village of Sesto/Sexten. This has nursery slopes all around it, and two major lifts. From close to the village a cable-car gives access to a variety of open intermediate slopes on Gallo Cedrone/Hahnspiel, with a long red of 1100m/3,610ft vertical to the base of a gondola up from the Val Pusteria.*

SNOWPIX.COM / CHRIS GILL

← The scenery in many Italian resorts is impressive – this is on the back of the hill at Courmayeur; strangely, there is no restaurant at the bottom of this lift

Most Italian lifts are, thankfully, more modern and powerful than this ↗

SAUZE D'OULX TOURIST OFFICE

Many Italians based in the northern cities ski mainly at weekends, and it's very noticeable that many resorts become busy only at weekends. It's a great advantage for those of us who are there for the whole week. This pattern is especially noticeable at the chic resorts, such as Cortina, Courmayeur and Madonna, and resorts which have not yet found international fame such as the Monterosa region; it's much less pronounced in parts of the Dolomites favoured by German visitors who, like Brits, tend to go for a week.

In general, Italians don't take their skiing or boarding too seriously. A late start, long lunch and early finish is the norm – leaving the slopes delightfully quiet for the rest of us. Almost everywhere mountain restaurants are welcoming places, encouraging leisurely lunching. Pasta – even in the most modest establishment –

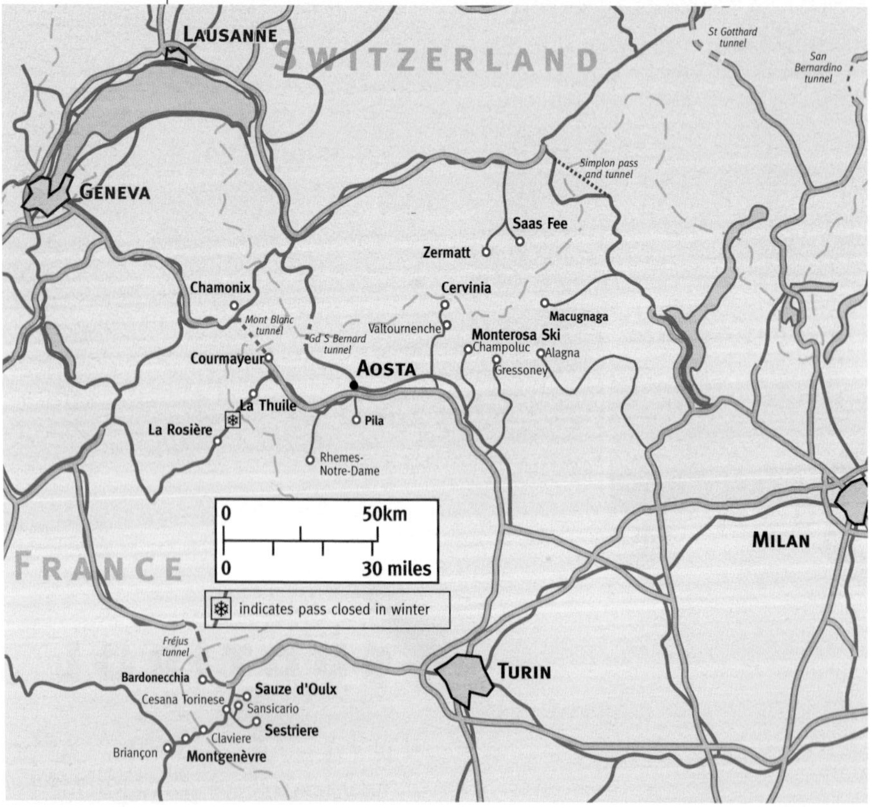

LAUSANNE
SWITZERLAND
St Gotthard tunnel
San Bernardino tunnel
Simplon pass and tunnel
GENEVA
Saas Fee
Zermatt
Chamonix
Cervinia
Macugnaga
Mont Blanc tunnel
Gd S Bernard tunnel
Valtournenche
Monterosa Ski
Champoluc
Alagna
Gressoney
Courmayeur
AOSTA
La Thuile
Pila
La Rosière
Rhemes-Notre-Dame
0 50km
0 30 miles
MILAN
FRANCE
indicates pass closed in winter
Fréjus tunnel
Bardonecchia
TURIN
Cesana Torinese
Sauze d'Oulx
Sansicario
Sestriere
Claviere
Briançon
Montgenèvre

is delicious. And eating and drinking on the mountain is still cheaper than in other Alpine resorts. But one drawback that nearly all reporters remark upon is the inexplicably primitive hole-in-the-ground toilets that are the norm in mountain restaurants (and sometimes in resorts too). If they can have proper sit-down loos a few metres over the border in Switzerland or France, why not in Italy too?

One thing that Italian resorts do have to contend with is erratic snowfall. While the snow in the northern Alps tends to come from the west, Italy's tends to come from storms arriving from the south. So it can have great conditions when other countries are suffering; or vice versa. Italian resorts have extensive snowmaking, and our observation is that they tend to use it more effectively than other Alpine countries. We have skied in Courmayeur and in the Dolomites when little natural snow had fallen, and in each case there was excellent cruising on man-made snow.

## DRIVING IN THE ITALIAN ALPS

There are four main geographical groupings of Italian resorts, widely separated. Getting to some of these resorts is a very long haul, and moving from one area to another can involve very long drives (though the extensive motorway network is a great help).

The handful of resorts to the west of Turin – Bardonecchia, Sauze d'Oulx, Sestriere and neighbours in the Milky Way region – are easily reached from France via the Fréjus tunnel from Modane, or via the good road over the pass that the resort of Montgenèvre sits on.



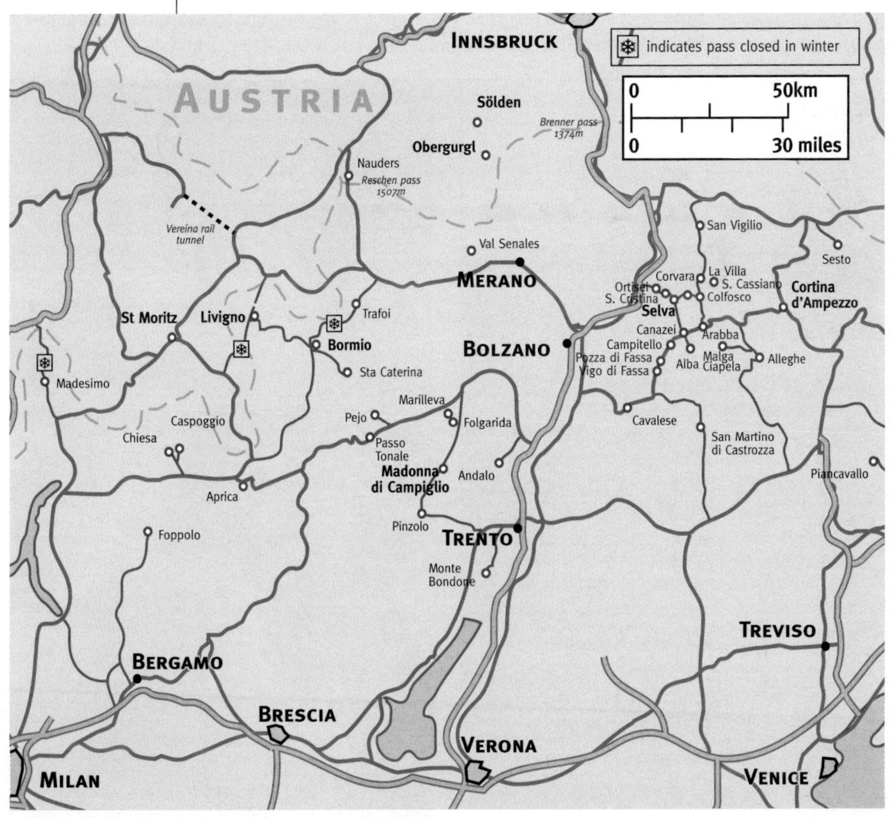

Further north, and somewhat nearer to Turin than Milan, are the resorts of the Aosta valley – Courmayeur, Cervinia, La Thuile and the Monterosa area are the best known. These (especially Courmayeur) are the easiest of all Italian resorts to reach from Britain (via the Mont Blanc tunnel from Chamonix in France). The Aosta valley can also be reached from Switzerland via the Grand St Bernard tunnel. The approach is high and may require chains. The road down the Aosta valley is a major thoroughfare, but the roads up to some of the other resorts are quite long, winding and (in the case of Cervinia) high.

To the east is a string of scattered resorts, most close to the Swiss border, many in isolated and remote valleys involving long drives up from the nearest Italian cities, or high-altitude drives from Switzerland. The links between Switzerland and Italy are more clearly shown on our larger-scale Switzerland map at the beginning of that section than on the map of the Italian Alps included here. The major routes are the St Gotthard tunnel between Göschenen (near Andermatt) and Airolo – the main route between Basel and Milan – and the San Bernardino tunnel reached via Chur.

Finally, further east still are the resorts of the Dolomites. Getting there from Austria is easy, over the Brenner motorway pass from Innsbruck. But getting there from Britain is a very long drive indeed – allow at least a day and a half. We wouldn't lightly drive there and back for a week's skiing, though we routinely do as part of a longer tour including some Austrian resorts. It's also worth bearing in mind that once you arrive in the Dolomites, getting around the intricate network of valleys linked by narrow, winding roads can be a slow business – it's often quicker to get from village to village on skis. Impatient Italian driving can make it a bit stressful, too.







APT VAL DI FASSA / STEFANO ZARDINI

The scenery in many Italian resorts is impressive; in the Dolomites it's simply fabulous ↘

# Bormio

*A tall, narrow mountain above a very unusual, historic resort town*

**COSTS**

(1)(2)(3)(4)(5)(6)

**RATINGS**

**The slopes**

| | |
|---|---|
| Snow | *** |
| Extent | ** |
| Expert | * |
| Intermediate | *** |
| Beginner | ** |
| Convenience | *** |
| Queues | *** |
| Mountain restaurants | **** |

**The rest**

| | |
|---|---|
| Scenery | *** |
| Resort charm | **** |
| Off-slope | **** |

**NEWS**

For 2004/05 two new chair-lifts will access Cima Bianca from mid-mountain. Last year the queue-prone cable-car from the base to Bormio 2000 was replaced by a gondola.

Bormio has been chosen to host the Alpine World Ski Championships in 2005, 20 years after it first staged them. They take place 28 Jan to 13 Feb.

- + Good mix of high, open pistes and woodland runs adding up to some good long descents
- + Worthwhile neighbouring resorts
- + Attractive medieval town centre – quite unlike any other winter resort
- + Good mountain restaurants

- − Slopes all of medium steepness
- − Rather confined main mountain, with second area some way distant
- − Still many slow old lifts
- − Long airport transfers
- − Crowds on Sundays
- − Central hotels inconvenient

**If you like ancient Italian towns and don't insist on a traditional Alpine resort atmosphere, you'll find the centre of Bormio very appealing – though you're unlikely to be staying right in the centre. Given the limited slopes of Bormio's own mountain, plan on taking the free bus out to the Valdidentro area and perhaps make longer outings, to Santa Caterina at least.**

## THE RESORT

Bormio, a spa since Roman times, has a splendid 17th-century town centre, with narrow cobbled streets and grand stone facades – very colourful during the evening promenade. It is in a remote spot, close to the Swiss border – though road improvements have cut the airport transfer to three hours.

The town centre is a 15-minute walk from the gondola station across the river to the south. There are reliable free shuttle-buses, but many people walk. Closer to the lifts is a suburban sprawl of hotels for skiers. Several major hotels are on Via Milano, leading out of town, which is neither convenient nor atmospheric.

na Bianca
om/9,880ft
2550m
2200m
Valdidentro
Val di Sotto
Isolaccia
Oga
1475m
Bormio 2000
Le Motte
1430m
Ciuk
1620m
Bormio
1225m/4,020ft

## THE MOUNTAINS

There's a nice mix of high, snow-sure pistes and lower wooded slopes. The main slopes are tall (vertical drop 1800m/5,900ft) and narrow. Most pistes face north-west.

Both the piste map and the piste marking need substantial improvement. Reporters have complained about the abundance of slow old lifts, and the resort policy of opening certain lift links only at weekends and busy times (which amounts to the same thing).

The Valdidentro area, a short bus-ride out of Bormio, shouldn't be overlooked. The open and woodland runs are very pleasant and usually empty (and have great views). Day trips to Santa Caterina (20 minutes by bus) and Livigno (90 minutes) are covered by the Alta Valtellina lift pass. A six-day pass entitles you to a discount rate on a one-day pass in St Moritz (3 hours away).

**Slopes** The main access lift is now an eight-seat gondola to the mid-mountain mini-resort of Bormio 2000, with a cable-car going on up to the top at over 3000m/9,840ft. An alternative gondola goes to Ciuk, and new chair-lifts to the top from this area are planned for this season.

**Terrain-parks** There aren't any.

**Snow reliability** Runs above Bormio 2000 are usually snow-sure, and there is snowmaking on the lower slopes, though this doesn't necessarily help in late March. The Valdidentro area is more reliable, and the high, shaded,

↑ It's a lovely old town, quite unlike any other ski resort

APT VALTELLINA





## KEY FACTS

| | |
|---|---|
| **Resort** | 1225m 4,020ft |
| For Bormio and Valdidentro | |
| **Slopes** | 1225-3010m 4,020-9,880ft |
| **Lifts** | 27 |
| **Pistes** | 44km 27 miles |
| **Blue** | 28% |
| **Red** | 65% |
| **Black** | 7% |
| **Snowmaking** | 30km 19 miles |
| For Bormio only | |
| **Slopes** | 1225-3010m 4,020-9,880ft |
| **Lifts** | 15 |
| **Pistes** | 25km 16 miles |

## REPORTS WANTED

Recently we have had few reports on this resort. If you go there, please do send us a report.

**Phone numbers**
From abroad use the prefix +39 (and do **not** omit the initial '0' of the phone number).

## TOURIST OFFICE

t 0342 903300
aptbormio@provincia.so.it
www.valtellinaonline.com

north-facing slopes of Santa Caterina usually have good snow.

**Experts** There are a couple of short black runs in the main area, but the greatest interest lies in off-piste routes from Cima Bianca to both east and west of the piste area.

**Intermediates** The men's downhill course starts with a steep plunge, but otherwise is just a tough red, ideal for strong intermediates. Stella Alpina, down to 2000, is also fairly steep. Many runs are less tough – ideal for most intermediates. The longest is a superb top-to-bottom cruise. The outlying mountains are also suitable for early intermediates.

**Beginners** The nursery slopes at Bormio 2000 offer good snow, but there are no very easy longer pistes to move on to. Novices are better off at nearby Santa Caterina.

**Snowboarding** The slopes are too steep for novices, and there's little to attract experienced boarders either.

**Cross-country** There are some trails either side of Bormio, towards Piatta and beneath Le Motte and Valdidentro, but cross-country skiers are better off at snow-sure Santa Caterina.

**Queues** The new gondola which replaced the cable-car from the main car park to Bormio 2000 in 2003/04 should have dealt with the problems low-down, and the new chairs planned to go up to Cima Bianca should relieve the pressure on the top cable-car. There should now be few problems outside carnival week.

**Mountain restaurants** The mountain restaurants are generally good. Even the efficient self-service at Cafe Bormio 2000 has a good choice of dishes. At the Rocca, above Ciuk, there is a welcoming chalet and a smart, modern place with table- or self-service. Cedrone, at Bormio 2000, has a good terrace and a play area for children. Several reporters recommend the very welcoming Baita de Mario, at Ciuk, as a great place for a long lunch.

**Schools and guides** The only recent report we have is of the Nazionale school, which offered 'satisfactory lessons in English'.

**Facilities for children** The ski school takes children from the age of three, from 10am to 4pm. The Bormio 2000 branch of the school has a roped-off snow garden at mid-mountain with a moving carpet lift.

## STAYING THERE

**How to go** There are plenty of apartments, but hotels dominate the package market.

**Hotels** Most of Bormio's 40-plus hotels are 2- and 3-star places. The 4-star Palace (0342 903131) is the most luxurious in town. The Posta (0342 904753) is in the centre of the old town – rooms range from adequate to very good. The Baita dei Pinti (0342 904346) is the best placed of the top hotels – on the river, between the lifts and centre. The Ambassador (0342 904625) is close to the gondola to Ciuk.

**Self-catering** The modern Cristallo apartments have been recommended.

**Eating out** There's a wide selection of restaurants. The atmospheric Taulà at Valfurva does excellent modern food with great service. The Kuerc and the Vecchia Combo are also popular. The Rododendri (at Valfurva) is recommended and there are excellent pizzerias, including the Jap.

**Après-ski** The après-ski starts on the mountain at the Rocca, and there are popular bars around the bottom lift stations. The Clem Pub, Gordy's, Cafe Mozart and the Aurora are popular. Shangri-La is a friendly bar. The King's Club is said to be the best disco.

**Off the slopes** Diversions include thermal baths – apparently now including reopened Roman baths – riding and walks in the Stelvio National Park. There is also an excellent sports centre, ice rink and 'superb' swimming pool. St Moritz and duty-free Livigno are popular excursions.

**Staying up the mountain** The modern Girasole 2000 (0342 904652), at Bormio 2000, is simple but well run by an Anglo-Italian couple; lots of events for evening entertainment.

SNOWPIX.COM / CHRIS GILL

# Cervinia

*Mile after mile of high-altitude, easy, snow-sure cruising*

## COSTS

①②③④⑤⑥

## RATINGS

**The slopes**

| | |
|---|---|
| Snow | ***** |
| Extent | *** |
| Expert | * |
| Intermediate | **** |
| Beginner | ***** |
| Convenience | *** |
| Queues | *** |
| Mountain restaurants | *** |

**The rest**

| | |
|---|---|
| Scenery | **** |
| Resort charm | ** |
| Off-slope | * |

## NEWS

For 2003/04 a tunnel was built under the road so you can ski down to the gondola station in Valtournenche (if there's enough snow for the run to be open).

For 2004/05 a new kindergarten will open.

+ Extensive mountain with miles of long, consistently gentle runs – ideal for early intermediates and anyone wary of steep slopes or bumps
+ High, sunny and snow-sure slopes amid impressive scenery
+ Link with Zermatt in Switzerland provides even more spectacular views and good lunches

- Very little to interest good or aggressive intermediates and above
- Almost entirely treeless, with little to do in bad weather
- Lifts prone to closure by wind, particularly early in the season
- Link with Zermatt has its drawbacks
- Steep uphill walk to main lifts, followed by lots of steps in station
- Few off-slope amenities

**If there is a better resort for those who like gentle, late-season cruising on mile after mile of easy, snow-sure, well-groomed, sunny slopes we have yet to find it. And all this at the foot of the southern side of the Matterhorn (Monte Cervino), with the easiest of Zermatt's slopes just over the Swiss border and linked by lift and piste. But Breuil Cervinia (as the resort styles itself) will not suit everyone. It can be cold and bleak in early season and the top lifts and link with Switzerland can close. The more adventurous will get bored by the easy slopes and find that Zermatt's most interesting challenges are out of range for a relaxing day trip. And the resort itself is a bit of an eyesore. Oh ... and the hole-in-the ground mountain loos tend to go down very badly with our readers.**

## THE RESORT

Cervinia is at the head of a long valley leading off the Aosta valley on the Italian side of the Matterhorn. The old climbing village developed into a winter resort in a rather haphazard way, and it has no consistent style of architecture. It's an uncomfortable hotchpotch, neither pleasing to the eye nor as offensive as the worst of the French purpose-built resorts. The centre is pleasant, compact and traffic-free. But ugly surrounding apartment blocks and hotels make the whole place feel less friendly and welcoming.

A lot of people stay near the village centre, at the foot of the nursery slopes. You can take a series of slow drags and chairs from here into the slopes, or peel off after the first and ski down to the main gondola and cable-car to Plan Maison. Otherwise these main lifts are an awkward uphill walk away, above the village. There are no resort ski buses but some hotels run their own shuttle-bus. Once at the main lift base you can't avoid the steps (120, counted one reporter) up to where you load the gondola. There is more accommodation further out at the Cieloalto complex and on the road up to it – but some of these buildings are among the worst eyesores.

At weekends, the resort can fill up with day trippers and weekenders from Milan and Turin. There are surprisingly few off-slope amenities, such as marked walks and spa facilities.

The slopes link to Valtournenche further down the valley (covered by the lift pass) and Zermatt in Switzerland (covered by a daily supplement, or a more expensive weekly pass). More about this later in the chapter.

Day trips by car are possible to Courmayeur, La Thuile and the Monterosa Ski resorts of Champoluc and Gressoney (all covered by the Aosta valley lift pass).

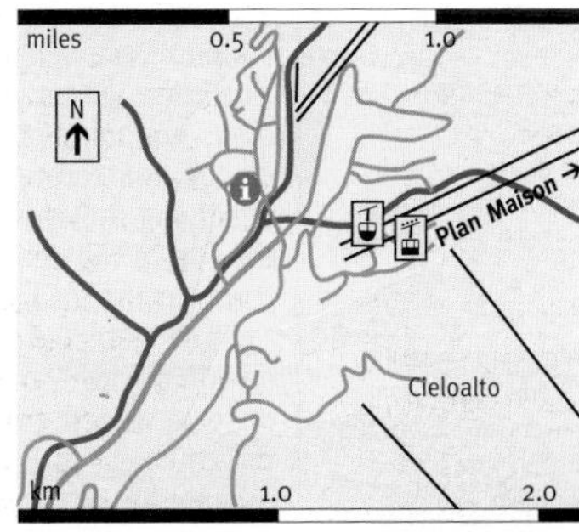

## KEY FACTS

| | |
|---|---|
| **Resort** | 2050m 6,730ft |
| For Cervinia/ Valtournenche | |
| **Slopes** | 1525-3480m 5,000-11,420ft |
| **Lifts** | 28 |
| **Pistes** | 200km 124 miles |
| **Blue** | 30% |
| **Red** | 59% |
| **Black** | 11% |
| **Snowmaking** | 21km 13 miles |
| For Cervinia/ Valtournenche/ Zermatt combined | |
| **Slopes** | 1525-3820m 5,000-12,530ft |
| **Lifts** | 62 |
| **Pistes** | 394km 245 miles |
| **Blue** | 27% |
| **Red** | 54% |
| **Black** | 19% |
| **Snowmaking** | 69km 43 miles |





## LIFT PASSES

**Breuil-Cervinia**
Covers all lifts on the Italian side of the border including Valtournenche.

**Beginners**
Pass for three beginner lifts.

**Main pass**
1 day €30
6 days €163

**Senior citizens**
Over 65: 6 days €123

**Children**
Under 12: 6 days €123
Under 8: 6 days €41

**Notes**
Half-day pass and individual section passes available. Also daily extension for Zermatt lifts.

**Alternative passes**
International pass covers all lifts on the Italian side plus Zermatt.

## THE MOUNTAINS

Cervinia's main slopes, which are high, open, sunny and mostly west-facing, are split into two sections by a gorge which runs from top to bottom of the mountain, and are linked by piste only at the top. The area has Italy's highest pistes and some of its longest (a claimed 13km/8 miles from Plateau Rosa to Valtournenche, with only a short drag-lift partway – but see 'Snow reliability'). Nearly all the runs are accessible to average intermediates. The weather is more of a problem than steepness. If it's bad, the top lifts often close because of high winds. And even the lower slopes may be unusable because of poor visibility. There are few woodland pistes.

### THE SLOPES
***Very easy***

Cervinia has the biggest, highest, most snow-sure area of easy, well groomed pistes we've come across, but we're very sceptical of the claimed total of 200km/124 miles. The high proportion of red runs on the piste map is misleading: most of them would be classified blue elsewhere. The slopes just above the village are floodlit some evenings.

The main lifts take you to the mid-mountain base of **Plan Maison**. From there a further gondola then a giant cable-car go up to **Plateau Rosa** and a link with Zermatt. (Confusingly Plateau Rosa is called Testa Grigia on the Zermatt piste map. We welcome the newish handy piste map that has both Cervinia and Zermatt's slopes on it.) Three successive fast quads (all with covers) from Plan Maison go up to a slightly lower point on the border, and another link with Zermatt. Between the fast quads and Plateau Rosa, and going all the way back to the village, is a deep gorge that separates Cervinia's slopes into two main sections, which you can get between on skis only from Plateau Rosa at the top.

On the left as you look at the piste maps are some of Cervinia's easiest slopes (marked red at the top but not deserving that grading), leading from the top of the chairs to Plan Maison or down to the village. If instead you turn right at Plateau Rosa you take the splendid wide Ventina run (which does deserve its red grading). You can use the cable-car to do the top part repeatedly, or go all the way down to Cervinia (8km/5 miles and over 1400m/4,600ft vertical). Or you can branch off left down towards **Valtournenche**. The slopes here are served by a number of slow old lifts above the initial modern gondola from Valtournenche to Salette. You can't get back to Plan Maison from this sector except by riding down the gondola.

There is also the very small, little-used **Cieloalto** area, served by a slow old chair to the south of the cable-car at the bottom of the Ventina run. This has some of Cervinia's steeper pistes and the only trees in the area. But since another chair and several runs were taken out of service it is now a tiny area. And the only way back to the main area is a 150m/490ft downhill walk to the main lift base.

Several reporters have criticised the 'inadequate' piste map.

### TERRAIN-PARKS
***Winter and summer***

The terrain-park at Plan Maison has jumps, rails, boxes, a boarder-cross course and a half-pipe, and the resort claims it is designed for everyone from beginners to experts. But a boarding reporter this year thought it was 'intimidating for non-experts'. Another who is a skier had a go but saw a sign saying 'no skiers'. There's an even bigger park over the Swiss border on Zermatt's Klein Matterhorn glacier slopes, open all year round.

### SNOW RELIABILITY
***Superb***

The mountain is one of the highest in Europe and, despite getting a lot of afternoon sun, can usually be relied on to have good snow conditions. Lift closures due to wind are a bigger worry. Several reporters have complained about this and about the biting winds.

The village nursery slopes, the bottom half of the Ventina run and the runs under the top chair-lifts down to Plan Maison have snowmaking. But the run below the top of the gondola to lower-lying Valtournenche doesn't – and so is prone to bare patches and closure. In our 2003 and 2004 March visits it was closed both years, despite excellent snow elsewhere.

### FOR EXPERTS
***Forget it***

This is not a resort for experts. There is little readily accessible off-piste and high winds can blow the snow off what

## SCHOOLS

**Cervino**
t 0166 949034
info@scuolacervino.com

**Breuil**
t 0166 940960
info@scuolascibreuil.com

**Cervinia**
t 0166 948451
info@scuolascicervinia.com

**Classes**
(Cervino prices)
6 days (2hr 45min per day) €155

**Private lessons**
€32 for 1hr for 1 person

## boarding

*Cervinia has great slopes for learning to snowboard – gentle, wide and usually with good snow. And the main lifts around the area are chairs, gondolas and cable-cars, but there are a lot of drag-lifts and some long flat bits as well. There's not much to interest better boarders – just as there's not much to interest better skiers.*

there is (though good heli-drops with guides can be arranged). There are a few black runs scattered here and there, but most of them would be classified red elsewhere. Many reporters head over to Zermatt for more challenging slopes but don't necessarily find them – see 'The Zermatt Connection'.

### FOR INTERMEDIATES
***Miles of long, flattering runs***

Virtually the whole area can be covered comfortably by average intermediates. But as a 2004 reporter so aptly put it, 'Strong, aggressive intermediates will get bored quickly.' If you like wide, easy, motorway pistes, you'll love Cervinia: it has more long, flattering runs than any other resort. The easiest slopes are on the left as you look at the mountain. From top to bottom there are gentle blue runs and almost equally gentle reds in the beautiful scenery at the foot of the south face of the Matterhorn. But a reporter warns that the start of the run from Plan Maison has been regraded from red to blue but is 'very tricky in parts and I saw children in trouble'.

The area on the right as you look at the mountain is best for adventurous intermediates. The Ventina run is a particularly good fast cruise. The long run down to Valtournenche is mostly easy, though the snow conditions on the lower part can be challenging.

### FOR BEGINNERS
***Pretty much ideal***

Complete beginners will start on the good village nursery slope, and should graduate quickly to the fine flat area around Plan Maison and its gentle blue runs. Fast learners will be going all the way from the top to the bottom of the mountain by the end of the week.

### FOR CROSS-COUNTRY
***Hardly any***

There are a couple of short trails, but this is not a cross-country resort.

### QUEUES
***Not as bad as they were***

Our 2004 reporters did not find queues

## THE ZERMATT CONNECTION

If the weather is good, you'll be tempted to go over to Zermatt. And quite right – the restaurants are simply the best, and it's only from the Swiss side that you get the classic view of the Matterhorn. But there are snags.

For a start, the two lift companies don't convey clearly where you can cross over. Testa Grigia on one side of the joint map becomes Plateau Rosa on the other; Theodulpass becomes nameless. Disgraceful.

Then there are the top runs. You come first of all to even gentler glacier motorways than on the Cervinia side. There are more challenging pistes once you get below Trockener Steg and you can have enjoyable days cruising here and from Schwarzsee. But to get to Zermatt's classic terrain on Gornergrat, Stockhorn and Rothorn you have to make the long descent to the village, and then bus, walk, or take a taxi the length of the village to other lifts.

You could do this, but you couldn't do it enjoyably – mainly because you have to set off back early to make sure of the lift links back to the border. There can be long queues for the Trockener Steg-Klein Matterhorn cable-car. And the alternative involves a very exposed T-bar, which there may be queues for as well.

You can get a very enjoyable taste of Zermatt from Cervinia, but you're unlikely to get your fill.





a problem. Although the main lifts are now fast and efficient, there are still some antiquated lifts around: the series of slow lifts back up from Valtournenche is a particular source of complaint. The two main access lifts from Cervinia to Plan Maison can get crowded at the peak morning rush, especially on Sundays, and the alternative series of drags and chairs need upgrading. There can also be queues for many lower lifts when upper lifts are shut due to wind.

### MOUNTAIN RESTAURANTS
***OK if you know where to go***

The mountain restaurants are not as appealing as you might expect in an Italian resort (and the toilet facilities are generally primitive hole-in-the-ground affairs), so some reporters head over to Zermatt for lunch.

However, the Châlet Etoile, beneath the Rocce Nere chair-lift at Plan Maison, is highly recommended by reporters: 'The best mountain restaurant I've been to,' says one, and 'Top quality cuisine in an authentic Italian style,' said another last year. So is the more basic table-service section of Rifugio Teodulo near the link with Zermatt reached by chair-lifts – excellent pasta. Booking is recommended at both.

Other reporter recommendations include the British-run Igloo, near the top of the Bardoney chair just off the Ventina piste, which serves huge burgers and has 'a UK-style toilet'. Baita Cretaz, near the bottom of the Cretaz pistes, is good value. The Bontadini at the top of the Fornet chair was praised again last year ('good value and superb view').

The restaurants are cheaper and less crowded on the Valtournenche side. The Motta, at the top of the drag-lift of the same name, does excellent food, including goulaschsuppe that is 'out of this world' and Lo Baracon dou Tene near the top of the Becca d'Arran chair-lift does a 'magnificent polenta con funghi'.

### SCHOOLS AND GUIDES
***Generally positive reports***

Cervinia has three main schools, Cervino, Breuil and Nuova Cielo Alto. Reports are fairly positive and a 2004 reporter found the Breuil school 'great value at around 30 euros for a private lesson, with friendly instructors who speak good English'. But a reporter last year complained of asking for an English instructor but getting an Italian. She also recommended pre-booking as demand was high – even in mid-March.

### FACILITIES FOR CHILDREN
***Could be better***

The Cervino ski school runs a ski kindergarten. And there's a babysitting and kindergarten area at Plan Maison. A new kindergarten, Biancaneve, opens this season. The slopes, with their long gentle runs, should suit families.

## STAYING THERE

### HOW TO GO
***Plenty of hotel packages***

Most of the big operators come here, offering a wide selection of hotels, though other types of accommodation are rather thin on the ground.

**Hotels** There are almost 50 hotels, mostly 2- or 3-stars, but there are a few 4-stars. Unless they run their own mini-bus to the slopes, choose your location with care – being near a lift base is important.

((((4 **Hermitage** (0166 948998) Small, luxurious Relais et Château just out of the village on the road up to Cieloalto. Great views, pool, free bus to lifts. 'First class, good ambiance and service,' says a 2004 reporter.

(((3 **Excelsior Planet** (0166 949426) Regularly recommended by reporters: 'Fantastic in all respects with food second to none,' said one this year. Pool, spa facilities and minibus to lift. In centre near Cretaz lifts.

(((3 **Sporthotel Sertorelli** (0166 949797) Excellent food, sauna and hot-tub. Ten minutes from lifts.

(((3 **Europa** (0166 948660) Friendly and family run; near Cretaz lifts. Pool.

((2 **Astoria** (0166 949062) Right by main lift station. Family run and simple. 'Comfortable but that's all,' says a reporter.

((2 **Marmore** (0166 949057) Friendly, family run, with 'quite good food'; on main street – an easy walk to the lifts.

**Self-catering** There are many apartments in the resort, but few are available through British tour ops.

### EATING OUT
***Plenty to choose from***

Cervinia's 50 or so restaurants allow plenty of choice. The Chamois and Matterhorn are excellent, but quite expensive. The Grotta belies its name

↑ Monte Cervino (aka the Matterhorn) as seen from the Ventina run – the rope is there to stop you venturing into the gorge that splits the ski area in two

SNOWPIX.COM / CHRIS GILL

## CHILDREN

**Kinderheim**
**t** 0166 940201
Ages 2 to 8; 8.30-5.30 daily

**Biancaneve**
**t** 0166 940201
Ages 2 to 8

**Ski school**
Classes for children over 5

## GETTING THERE

**Air** Turin 118km/73 miles (2½hr); Geneva 220km/137 miles (2½hr).

**Rail** Châtillon (27km/17 miles); regular buses from station.

## ACTIVITIES

**Indoor** Hotels with swimming pools and saunas, fitness centre, squash, bowling, climbing wall

**Outdoor** Natural ice rink, paragliding, hang-gliding, hiking, mountaineering, snowmobiles, snow-shoeing, ice climbing, ice cave visits

**Phone numbers**
From abroad use the prefix +39 (and do **not** omit the initial '0' of the phone number).

## TOURIST OFFICE

**t** 0166 949136
breuil-cervinia@montecervino.it
www.montecervino.it
www.cervinia.it

with good food ('best kids' pizza,' says a reader). Casse Croute also serves good pizzas. The Copa Pan has a lively atmosphere and is again recommended by several reporters. The Bricole and the Nicchia have also been praised, and the Maison de Saussure does 'very good local specialities – quite cosy'. The Givola does 'an excellent pizza and is lively' and you'll find 'good pizza and pasta' at Capanna Alpina. An evening out at the Baita Cretaz mountain hut makes a change.

## APRES-SKI
### *Disappoints many Brits*

Plenty of Brits come here looking for action but find there isn't much to do except tour the mostly fairly ordinary bars. 'The best thing to do is take a good book,' said a 2004 reporter. But the Copa Pan (see 'Eating out') is lively, good value and serves generous measures. The Dragon Bar is popular with Brits and Scandinavians and has satellite TV and videos ('It's great if you're homesick,' says a reporter). Lino's (by the ice rink) ('excellent food and music'), the Yeti, Labatt and Café des Guides (with mementos of the owner's Himalayan mountaineering trips) are all recommended by reporters. The discos liven up at weekends. There are events organised by tour-op reps, such as snowmobiling on the old bob-sled run, quiz nights, bowling and fondue nights.

## OFF THE SLOPES
### *Little attraction*

There is little to do for those who don't plan to hit the slopes. The pleasant town of Aosta is a four-hour round trip. Village amenities include hotel pools, a fitness centre and a natural ice rink. The walks are disappointing. The mountain restaurants that are reachable by gondola or cable-car are not special.

## STAYING UP THE MOUNTAIN
### *To beat the queues*

Up at Plan Maison, the major lift junction 500m/1,640ft vertical above the resort, Lo Stambecco (0166 949053) is a 50-room 3-star hotel ideally placed for early nights and early starts. Less radically, the Cime Bianche (0166 949046) is a rustic 3-star chalet on the upper fringes of the resort (in the area known as La Vieille).

## STAYING DOWN THE VALLEY
### *Great home run*

Valtournenche, 9km/5.5 miles down the road, is cheaper than Cervinia, has a genuine Italian atmosphere and a fair selection of simple hotels, of which the 3-star Bijou (0166 92109) is the best.

A newish gondola speeds you out of town. But the slow lifts above it mean it takes quite a time to reach the top. The exceptionally long run back down is a nice way to end the day – when it is all open (the bottom section is often closed due to lack of snow). The main street through the village is very busy with cars going to and from Cervinia.

CORTINA TURISMO / DG BANDION

# Cortina d'Ampezzo

*The scenery will take your breath away even if the slopes don't*

**COSTS**

(1)(2)(3)(4)(5)(6)

**RATINGS**

**The slopes**

| | |
|---|---|
| Snow | *** |
| Extent | *** |
| Expert | ** |
| Intermediate | *** |
| Beginner | ***** |
| Convenience | * |
| Queues | **** |
| Mountain restaurants | **** |

**The rest**

| | |
|---|---|
| Scenery | ***** |
| Resort charm | **** |
| Off-slope | ***** |

**NEWS**

For 2004/05 the old Pian di Ra Bigontina chair-lift at Faloria, above Rio Gere, will be replaced by a fast quad.

Also for 2004/05, 10 km/6 miles of new cross-country tracks will be opened at Passo Tre Croci, bringing the total in the area to 85km/53 miles.

You can now arrive in style – helicopter transfers will be available to whisk you from Venice (Marco Polo) to the resort in 35 minutes.



- ➕ Magnificent Dolomite scenery – perhaps the most dramatic anywhere
- ➕ Marvellous nursery slopes and good long cruising runs
- ➕ Access to the vast area covered by the Dolomiti Superski pass
- ➕ Attractive, although rather towny, resort, with lots of upmarket shops
- ➕ Good off-slope facilities
- ➕ Remarkably uncrowded slopes

- ➖ Several separate areas spread around all sides of the resort and linked by buses
- ➖ Erratic snow record
- ➖ Expensive by Italian standards
- ➖ Gets very crowded in town and in restaurants during Italian holidays
- ➖ Very little to entertain experts
- ➖ Mobile phones and fur coats may drive you nuts

**Cortina is one on its own. Sure, it has a quantity of well-maintained, enjoyable intermediate slopes, and in one or two sectors it has efficient lifts. But you shouldn't even think about a holiday here if matters like these are top of your agenda – if skiing or riding from dawn to dusk is your priority.**

**If, on the other hand, you like lazy days centred around long lunches on sunny terraces, gazing at scenery that is just draw-droppingly wonderful, this is the place. Dramatic pink-tinged cliffs and peaks rising vertically from the top of the slopes ring the town, giving picture-postcard views wherever you look. Every time we go back, the memory has faded and our jaws drop again.**

**Cortina has a regular upmarket clientele from Rome and Milan, many of whom have second homes here and enjoy the strolling, shopping, people-watching and lunching as much as the slopes. A good proportion of visitors don't go near the slopes except to drive up to a 'mountain restaurant' for lunch.**

**As an occasional change from serious ski resorts, we love it.**

## THE RESORT

In winter, more people come to Cortina for the clear mountain air, the stunning views, the shopping, the cafes and to pose and be seen than for the winter sports – 70 per cent of all Italian visitors don't bother taking to the slopes. Cortina attracts the rich and famous from the big Italian cities. Fur coats and glitzy jewellery are the norm.

The resort itself is a widely spread town rather than a village, with exclusive chalets scattered around the outskirts. The centre is the traffic-free, Corso Italia, full of chic designer clothes, jewellery and antique shops, art galleries and furriers – finding a ski shop can seem tricky. The cobbles and picturesque church bell tower add to the atmosphere. By 5pm, hardly anyone is still in ski gear; the streets are packed with people parading up and down in their evening finery and gesticulating into their mobile phones.

Unlike the rest of the Dolomites,

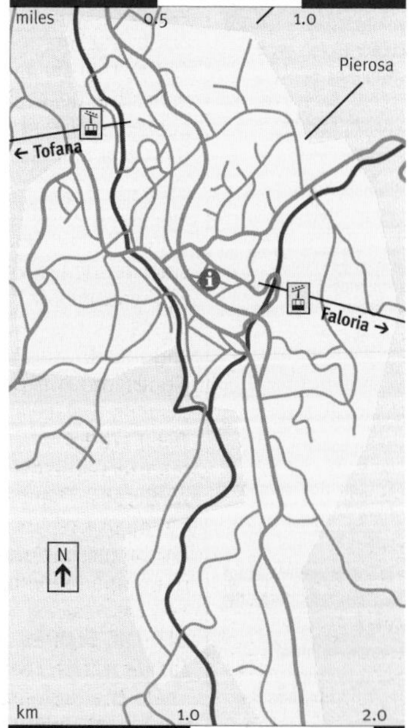

The kind of thing you may see from your bedroom window ↗

CORTINA TURISMO





Cortina is pure Italy. It has none of the Germanic traditions of the Sud Tirol.

Surrounding the centre is a horrendous one-way system, often traffic-clogged and a nasty contrast to the stunning scenery everywhere else you look. The lifts to the two main areas of slopes are a fair way from the centre, and at opposite sides of town. Other lifts are bus-rides away. There's a wide range of hotels in the centre and scattered on the outskirts. Staying centrally is best. The local bus service is good, and free to ski-pass holders. A car can be useful, especially for getting to the outlying areas and to make the most of other areas on the Dolomiti Superski pass. San Cassiano is not far to the west, with links from there to Corvara and the other Sella Ronda resorts (see Selva chapter).

## THE MOUNTAINS

Cortina first leapt to fame as host of the 1956 Winter Olympics. At the time, it was very modern; now its facilities feel dated. There is a good mixture of slopes above and below the tree line.

### THE SLOPES

***Inconveniently fragmented***

All Cortina's smallish separate areas are a fair trek from the town centre. The largest is **Socrepes**, accessed by chair- and drag-lifts a bus-ride away. You can reach it by piste from **Tofana**, Cortina's highest area, accessed by cable-car from near the Olympic ice rink.

On the opposite side of the valley is the tiny **Mietres** area. Another two-stage cable-car from the east side of town leads to the **Faloria** area, from where you can head down to chairs that lead up into the limited but dramatic runs beneath **Cristallo**.

Other areas are reachable by road. The cable-car from Passo Falzarego up to Lagazuoi accesses a beautiful red run to Armentarola, which takes you away from all signs of civilisation through the stunning scenery of the Hidden Valley. On the way to Passo Falzarego is the tiny but spectacular Cinque Torri area. Its excellent, north-facing slopes are accessed by a high-speed quad, followed by a one-person chair and a rope tow. It's worth taking them for the long red run down the back to Passo Giau. Another excellent red run down from Lagazuoi takes you back to the cable-car, or to the tiny Col Gallina area, from where you can take a pleasant green to Cinque Torri.

Reporters consistently praise the excellent grooming and quiet slopes but complain about other things: the piste map not showing some runs, the way runs are named on the mountain but numbered on the map, poor piste marking, World Cup races disrupting January skiing, having to take some cable-cars down as well as up if snow is poor or you want to avoid poling. They occasionally comment on the number of very fast skiers tearing down the slopes – perhaps because the grooming is so good.

One way to tour the area is to use special ski itineraries, maps for which are available at the tourist and ski pass offices. 'Skitour Olympia' takes

## KEY FACTS

| | |
|---|---|
| **Resort** | 1225m<br>4,020ft |
| **Slopes** | 1225-2930m<br>4,020-9,610ft |
| **Lifts** | 49 |
| **Pistes** | 140km<br>87 miles |
| **Blue** | 33% |
| **Red** | 62% |
| **Black** | 5% |
| **Snowmaking** | 133km<br>83 miles |

## boarding

*Despite its upmarket chic, Cortina is a good resort for learning to board. The Socrepes nursery slopes are wide, gentle and served by a fast chair-lift. And progress on to other easy slopes is simple because you can get around in all areas using just chairs and cable-cars – though there are drags, they can be avoided. A specialist snowboard shop, Boarderline, organises instruction as well as equipment hire. There's little off-piste to interest experienced boarders, but the best is to be found off the back of Cinque Torri, and the tiny Col Gallina area. There are some nice trees and natural undulations under the one-person chair at Cinque Torri.*

### LIFT PASSES

**Dolomiti Superski**
Covers 450 lifts and 1220km/758 miles of piste in the Dolomites, including all Cortina areas.

**Main pass**
1 day €37
6 days €182

**Senior citizens**
Over 60: 6 days €155

**Children**
Under 16: 6 days €127

**Alternative pass**
Cortina d'Ampezzo covers all lifts in Cortina, San Vito di Cadore, Auronzo and Misurina, and ski-buses.





you on the 1956 Olympic downhill, GS and slalom courses and the Bobsled run. 'Skitour Romantic Views' covers the Lagazuoi-Cinque Torri area.

### TERRAIN-PARKS
***Not bad for first-timers***

There is a terrain-park at Faloria which has some decent kickers and rails, and a half-pipe. We're told it's open to all, although there was a sign up saying 'snowboarders only' when we visited.

### SNOW RELIABILITY
***Lots of artificial help***

The snowfall record is erratic – it can be good here when it's poor on the north side of the Alps (and vice versa). But over 90 per cent of the pistes are now covered by snowmaking, so cover should be good if it is cold enough to make snow. When we visited a few years ago, the link from Tofana to Socrepes was closed because of lack of snow on a key south-facing slope – which made the areas even more fragmented. Two years ago, however, though natural snow was scarce temperatures were low, and the pistes had ample artificial cover.

### FOR EXPERTS
***Limited***

The run down from the second stage of the Tofana cable-car at Ra Valles is deservedly graded black; it goes through a gap in the rocks, and a steep, narrow, south-facing section gives wonderful views of Cortina. It can be tricky in poor snow conditions.

Cortina's other steep run goes from the top of the Cristallo area at Forcella Staunies. A chair-lift takes you to a south-facing couloir which is often shut due to avalanche danger or poor snow.

Other than these two runs there are few challenges. There are some great long red runs though, and if it snows you'll also have very little competition for first tracks. Heli-skiing is available.

### FOR INTERMEDIATES
***Fragmented and not extensive***

To enjoy Cortina you must like cruising in beautiful scenery, and not mind doing runs repeatedly.

The runs at the top of Tofana are short but normally have the best snow. The highest are at over 2800m/9,190ft and mainly face north. But be warned: the only way back down is by the

## SCHOOLS

**Cortina**
t 0436 2911
info@scuolascicortina.it

**Azzurra Cortina**
t 0436 2694
azzurracortina@libero.it

**Cristallo**
t 0436 870073
scicristallo@dolomiti.it

**Classes**
(Cortina prices)
6 days (2½hr per day) €195

**Private lessons**
€40 for 1hr; each additional person €12

## CHILDREN

**Kinderheim at the Pocol ski area**
For ages 3mnth to 3yr; 9.30 to 4.30

**Ski school**
The schools offer all-day classes for children



tricky black run described above or by cable-car. The reds from the linked Pomedes area offer good cruising.

Faloria has a string of fairly short north-facing runs – we loved the Vitelli red run, round the back away from the lifts. And the Cristallo area has a long blue run served by a fast quad.

It is well worth making the trip to Cinque Torri for wonderful, deserted fast cruising on usually excellent north-facing snow. The very easy Hidden Valley red run from Lagazuoi at the top of the Passo Falzarego cable-car to Armentarola is a must – one of the most beautiful runs we've come across, which consistently delights reporters. It offers isolation amid sheer pink-tinged Dolomite peaks and frozen waterfalls. Make time to stop at the atmospheric Scotoni rifugio ('an absolute must' writes a reporter) near the end, then it's a long pole, skate or walk to the welcome sight of a horse-drawn sled (with ropes attached) which tows the weary to Armentarola. Shared taxis take you back to Passo Falzarego (if you've time, try the slopes of Alta Badia, accessed from Armentarola).

## FOR BEGINNERS
***Wonderful nursery slopes***

The Socrepes area has some of the biggest nursery slopes and best progression runs we have seen. Some of the blue forest paths can be icy and intimidating. But you'll find ideal gentle terrain on the main pistes.

## FOR CROSS-COUNTRY
***One of the best***

Cortina has around 85km/57 miles of trails suitable for all standards, mainly in the Fiames area, where there is a cross-country centre and school. Trails include a 30km itinerary following an old railway from Fiames to Cortina, and there is a special beginner area equipped with snowmaking. Passo Tre Croci offers more challenging trails, and 10km/6 miles of new ones will open there in 2004/05.

## QUEUES
***No problem***

Most Cortina holidaymakers rise late, lunch lengthily and leave the slopes early – if they get on to them at all. That means few lift queues and generally uncrowded pistes – a different world from the crowded Sella Ronda circuit. 'Lack of queues was one of the highlights of our holiday,' said one reporter. Another visitor was delighted to find the slopes got emptier in the afternoons, as the Italians left the slopes, but that lifts stayed open as late as 5pm.

## MOUNTAIN RESTAURANTS
***Good, but get in early***

Lunch is a major event for many Cortina visitors. At weekends you often need to book or turn up very early to be sure of a table. Many restaurants can be reached by road or lift, and fur coats arrive as early as 10am to sunbathe, admire the views and idle the time away on their mobile phones.

Although prices are high in the swishest establishments, we've found plenty of reasonably priced places, serving generally excellent food. In the Socrepes area, the Rifugio Col Taron is highly recommended and the Pié de Tofana, Rifugio Pomedes and El Faral are also good. At Tofana, the Col Drusciè has re-opened and there will be a new restaurant for 2004/05, El Sorêi, by the Olympic chair above Lacedèl.

At Cristallo the Rio Gere at the base of the quad chair and Rifugio Son Forca, with fabulous views at the top of it (and owned by Alberto Tomba's former trainer), are both worth a visit.

The restaurants at Cinque Torri, the Scoiattoli ('magnificent home-made pastas') and the Rifugio Averau, offer fantastic views as well as good food, and are non-smoking. The Rifugio Fedare, over the back of Cinque Torri, is also recommended and non-smoking. Rifugio Lagazuoi, a short hike up from the top of the Passo Falzarego cable-car, also has great views.

## SCHOOLS AND GUIDES
***Mixed reports***

Of the three ski schools, we've had mixed reports of the Cortina school over the years – though we lack recent reports. The Gruppo Guide Alpine offers off-piste and touring.

## FACILITIES FOR CHILDREN
***Better than average***

By Italian standards childcare facilities are outstanding, with a choice of all-day care arrangements for children of practically any age. However, given the small number of British visitors, you can't count on good spoken English. And the fragmented area can make travelling around with children difficult.

Whichever sector you are on, there are great views of the others; this is Tofana, seen from Faloria →

CORTINA TURISMO

## GETTING THERE

**Air** Venice 160km/100 miles (2hr). Treviso 132km/82 miles (1¾hr). Saturday and Sunday transfers available for hotel guests; advance booking required.

**Rail** Calalzo (35km/22 miles) or Dobbiaco (32km/20 miles); frequent buses from station.

## ACTIVITIES

**Indoor** Swimming pool, saunas, health spa, fitness centre, ice stadium, museums, art gallery, cinema, indoor tennis court, library

**Outdoor** Rides on Olympic bob run, snowrafting down Olympic ski jump, crazy sledging, snow-shoe tours, sleigh rides, horse-riding school, 6km/4 miles of walking paths, tobogganing

**Phone numbers**
From abroad use the prefix +39 (and do **not** omit the initial '0' of the phone number).

## TOURIST OFFICE

**t** 0436 866252
cortina@dolomiti.org
www.cortina.dolomiti.org





## STAYING THERE

### HOW TO GO
***Now with more packages***

Hotels dominate the market but there are some catered chalets.

**Hotels** There's a big choice, from 5-star luxury to 1-star and 2-star pensions.

(5) **Miramonti** (0436 4201) Spectacularly grand hotel, 2km/1 mile south of town. Pool.

(5) **Cristallo** (0436 881111) Newish, with a spa-health clinic. A hike from the lifts and town centre, but there's a shuttle bus.

(4) **Poste** (0436 4271) Reliable 4-star, at the heart of the town.

(4) **Ancora** (0436 3261) Elegant public rooms. On the traffic-free Corso Italia.

(4) **Parc Victoria** (0436 3246) Rustic 4-star with small rooms but good food, at the Faloria end of the town centre.

(4) **Corona** (0436 3251) Family run 4-star, very friendly with good food and lots of original art. Near Tofana lift.

(4) **Park Faloria** (0436 2959) Near ski jump, splendid pool, good food.

(3) **Olimpia** (0436 3256) Comfortable B&B hotel in centre, near Faloria lift.

(3) **Menardi** (0436 2400) Welcoming roadside inn, a long walk from centre and lifts.

(3) **Villa Resy** (0436 3303) Small and welcoming, just outside centre, with British owner.

(2) **Montana** (0436 862126) 'Excellent B&B. Amazing value and central location,' says a reporter.

**Self-catering** There are some chalets and apartments – usually out of town – available for independent travellers.

### EATING OUT
***Huge choice***

There's an enormous selection, both in town and a little way out, doing mainly Italian food. The very smart and expensive El Toulà is in a beautiful old barn, just on the edge of town. Many of the best restaurants are further out – such as the Michelin-starred Tivoli, Meloncino, Leone e Anna, Rio Gere and Baita Fraina. Reasonably priced central restaurants include the Cinque Torri and the Passetto for pizza and pasta. The Tavernetta is a new restaurant in the centre. You can also arrange a night-time jaunt for a meal at a rifugio, travelling by snowmobile and sledge.

### APRES-SKI
***Lively in high season***

Cortina is a lively social whirl in high season, with lots of well-heeled Italians staying up very late.

The Lovat is one of several high-calorie tea-time spots. There are many good wine bars: Enoteca has 700 wines and good cheese and meats; Osteria has good wines and local ham; and Villa Sandi and Brio di Vino have been recommended. The liveliest bar is the Clipper, with a bob-sleigh by the door. The Dok-Dall' Ava is a new wine bar. Discos liven up after 11pm.

### OFF THE SLOPES
***A classic resort***

Cortina attracts lots of people who don't use the slopes. The setting is stunning, the town attractive, the shopping extensive and many mountain restaurants are accessible by road (a car is handy). And there's plenty more to do, such as swimming, ice skating and dog-sledding.

There is an observatory at Col Drusciè which has star-gazing tours (call 0436 3146 to book). You can have a run (with driver!) down the Olympic bob-sleigh run. There's horse jumping and polo on the snow occasionally. Excursions to Venice are easily organised.

SNOWPIX.COM / CHRIS GILL

# Courmayeur

*Seductive village, stunning scenery, limited slopes*

## COSTS

(1)(2)(3)(4)(5)(6)

## RATINGS

**The slopes**

| | |
|---|---|
| Snow | **** |
| Extent | ** |
| Expert | *** |
| Intermediate | **** |
| Beginners | ** |
| Convenience | * |
| Queues | *** |
| Mountain restaurants | **** |

**The rest**

| | |
|---|---|
| Scenery | **** |
| Resort charm | **** |
| Off-slope | *** |

## NEWS

For the 2003/04 season, a new 500m/1,640ft boarder-cross run was created by the Plan de la Gabba chair – the first special facility for boarders or freestylers. A new school called Snowboard & Ski School Courmayeur was also set up and the snowmaking capacity was increased.

The Swiss International City Ski Championships in association with Momentum Ski are run here annually. This season's dates are 17 to 20 March 2005. For more details see chapter on corporate ski trips.

- + Charming old village, with car-free centre and stylish shops and bars
- + Stunning views of Mont Blanc massif
- + Pleasant range of intermediate runs
- + Day trips to Chamonix (including doing the Vallée Blanche run) possible
- + Good base for heli-skiing
- + Comprehensive snowmaking
- + Good mountain restaurants

- – Lack of nursery slopes and easy runs for beginners to progress to
- – No tough pistes
- – Relatively small area, with mainly short runs; high-mileage piste-bashers will get bored in a week
- – Slopes very crowded on Sundays
- – Tiresome walk and cable-car journey between village and slopes

**Courmayeur is very popular, especially at weekends, with the smart Italian set from Milan and Turin. It's easy to see why: it's very easy to get to and certainly the most captivating of the Val d'Aosta resorts.**

**The scenery, the charm of the village, the stylish bars and restaurants and the nightlife are big draws. The main slopes are fine but nothing special given their limited range of difficulty, inconvenient location across the valley from the village and their limited size; a keen piste-basher will cover Courmayeur in a day. But a day trip to Chamonix is easy, via the Mont Blanc tunnel.**

**The resort is good for short breaks and could make a jolly week for those who want to party as much as hit the slopes. It also appeals to those with quite different ambitions, who want to explore the spectacular Mont Blanc massif with the aid of a guide and other local peaks with the aid of a helicopter.**



## THE RESORT

Courmayeur is a traditional old Italian mountaineering village that, despite the nearby Mont Blanc tunnel road and modern hotels, has retained much of its old-world feel.

The village has a charming traffic-free centre of attractive shops, cobbled streets and well-preserved buildings. An Alpine museum and a statue of a long-dead mountain rescue hero add to the historical feel.

The centre has a great atmosphere, focused around the Via Roma. As the lifts close, people pile into the many bars, some of which are very civilised. Others wander in and out of the many small shops, which include a salami specialist and a good bookshop. At weekends people-watching is part of the evening scene, when the fur coats of the Milanese and Torinese take over.

The village is quite large and its huge cable-car is right on the southern edge of town, a fair distance from much of the accommodation. There is no shuttle-bus alternative to walking, but you can leave skis, boards and boots in lockers at the top – highly recommended by reporters. There is another short walk from the top to the other lifts before you can get going.

Having accommodation close to the

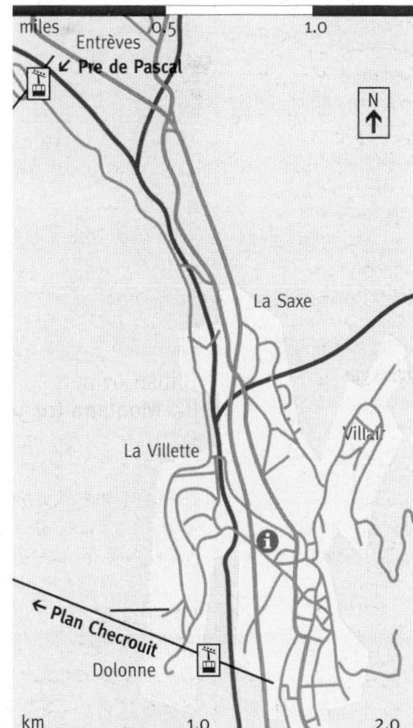

## KEY FACTS

| | |
|---|---|
| Resort | 1225m<br>4,020ft |
| Slopes | 1210-2755m<br>3,970-9,040ft |
| Lifts | 16 |
| Pistes | 100km<br>62 miles |
| Blue | 26% |
| Red | 57% |
| Black | 17% |
| Snowmaking | 18km<br>11 miles |

## LIFT PASSES

**Courmayeur Mont Blanc**
Covers all lifts in Val Veny and Checrouit, and the lifts on Mont Blanc up to Punta Helbronner.

**Beginners**
Two free nursery lifts.

**Main pass**
1 day €34
6 days €175

**Senior citizens**
Over 65: 6 days €131

**Children**
Under 12: 6 days €131
Under 8: €87.50

**Notes**
Single ascent on some lifts and half-day pass available. Passes for four days plus allow for at least one day in the Aosta valley, Flaine and Chamonix.





village cable-car is handy. Parking at the cable-car is very limited, but drivers can go to Entrèves, a few kilometres away, where there is a large car park at the Val Veny cable-car. Buses, infrequent but timetabled, link Courmayeur with La Palud, just beyond Entrèves, for the Punta Helbronner-Vallée Blanche cable-car.

## THE MOUNTAINS

The pistes suit intermediates, but are surprisingly limited for such a well-known, large resort. They are varied in character, if not gradient. Piste marking could be improved.

### THE SLOPES
***Small but interestingly varied***

The slopes are separate from the village: you have to ride a cable-car to them and either take it down or take a bus from Dolonne at the end of the day. The cable-car arrives at the bottom of the slopes at Plan Checrouit (where you can store your equipment).

There are two distinct sections, both almost entirely intermediate. The north-east-facing **Checrouit** area accessed by the Checrouit gondola catches morning sun, and has open, above-the-tree-line pistes. The 25-person, infrequently running Youla cable-car goes to the top of Courmayeur's pistes. There is a further tiny cable-car to Cresta d'Arp. This serves only long off-piste runs but it is no longer compulsory to have a guide with you to go up it.

Most people follow the sun over to the north-west-facing slopes towards **Val Veny** in the afternoon. These are interesting, varied and tree lined, with great views of Mont Blanc and its glaciers. Connections between the Checrouit and Val Veny areas are good, with many alternative routes. The Val Veny slopes are also accessible by cable-car from Entrèves, a few miles outside Courmayeur.

A little way beyond Entrèves is La Palud, where a cable-car goes up in three stages to Punta Helbronner, at the shoulder of **Mont Blanc**. There are no pistes from the top, but you can do the famous Vallée Blanche run to Chamonix from here without the horrific ridge walk on the Chamonix side – you catch a bus or a taxi back from Chamonix through the Mont Blanc tunnel. Or you can tackle the tougher off-piste runs on the Italian side of

## boarding

*Courmayeur's pistes suit intermediates, and most areas are easily accessible by novices as the main lifts are cable-cars, chairs and gondolas – but it's all a bit steep for absolute beginners. The biggest draws for the more experienced are the off-piste routes to be done with a guide. And from the 2003/04 season there's a boarder-cross run – the first special facility for boarders.*

Mont Blanc. None of these glacier runs should be done without a guide.

La Thuile and Pila are an easy drive to the south, and Cervinia is reachable.

**TERRAIN-PARKS**
***At last, there's a boarder-cross***
Like a lot of Italian resorts, Courmayeur has no terrain-park or half-pipe. However, the resort created a 500m/1,640ft boarder-cross run for 2003/04 near the top of the Plan de la Grabba high-speed chair.

**SNOW RELIABILITY**
***Good for most of the season***
Courmayeur's slopes are not high – mostly between 1700m and 2250m (5,600ft and 7,400ft). Those above Val Veny face north or north-west, so keep their snow well, but the Plan Checrouit side is rather too sunny for comfort in late season. There is snowmaking on most main runs, so good coverage in early- and mid-season is virtually assured – we were there in the January 2002 snow drought and enjoyed decent skiing entirely on man-made snow.

**FOR EXPERTS**
***Off-piste is the only challenge***
Courmayeur has few challenging pistes. The only black – the Competizione, on the Val Veny side – is not hard, and few moguls form elsewhere. But if you're lucky enough to find fresh powder – as we have been several times – you can have fantastic fun among the trees.

Classic off-piste runs go from Cresta d'Arp, at the top of the lift network, in three directions – a clockwise loop via Arp Vieille to Val Veny, with close-up views of the Miage glacier; east down a deserted valley to Dolonne or Pré St Didier; or south through the Youla gorge to La Thuile.

On Mont Blanc, the Vallée Blanche is not a challenge (though there are more difficult variations), but the Toula glacier route on the Italian side from Punta Helbronner to Pavillon most certainly is, often to the point of being dangerous. There are also heli-drops available, including a wonderful 20km/12 mile run from the Ruitor glacier down into France – you catch the lifts back up from La Rosière and ski or board down to La Thuile (a taxi-ride from Courmayeur). And you can do a day trip to Chamonix through the Mont Blanc tunnel.

**FOR INTERMEDIATES**
***Ideal gradient but limited extent***
The whole area is suitable for most intermediates, but it is small. The avid piste-basher will find it very limited for a week's holiday.

The open Checrouit section is pretty much go-anywhere territory, where you can choose your own route and make it as easy or difficult as you like. The blue runs here are about Courmayeur's gentlest. In Val Veny, the reds running the length of the Bertolini chair are more challenging and very enjoyable. They link in with the pretty, wooded slopes heading down to Zerotta.

The Zerotta chair dominates Val Veny, with lots of alternatives from the top – good for mixed abilities since runs of varying difficulty meet up at several places on the way down.

The Vallée Blanche, although off-piste, is easy enough for adventurous, fit intermediates to try. So is the local heli-skiing (from £90 a drop including a guide); you are picked up on the piste so there's no wasted time.

**FOR BEGINNERS**
***Consistently too steep***
Courmayeur is not well suited to beginners. There are several nursery slopes, none ideal. The area at Plan Checrouit gets crowded, and there are few easy runs for the near-beginner to progress to. The small area served by the short Tzaly drag, just above the Entrèves cable-car top station, is the most suitable beginner terrain, and it tends to have good snow.

**FOR CROSS-COUNTRY**
***Beautiful trails***
There are 35km/22 miles of trails scattered around Courmayeur. The best are the four covering 20km/12 miles at

## SCHOOLS

**Monte Bianco**
t 0165 842477
montebianco@maestridisci.com

**Courmayeur**
t 0165 848254
info@scuolascicourmayeur.it

**Classes**
(Monte Bianco prices)
5 days (3hr per day)
€142

**Private lessons**
€32 to €41 for 1hr for 1 person; each additional person €6

## CHILDREN

**Kinderheim at Plan Checrouit**
t 0165 842477
From age 6mnth; 9.30 to 4pm

**Kinderheim at the Sports Centre**
From age 6mnth

**'Fun park' at Dolonne**
9am-4.30

**Ski schools**
Takes children from age 4 and can be looked after for the whole day (lesson am, play pm) (6 days incl. lunch €180)

## GETTING THERE

**Air** Geneva 105km/65 miles (2hr); Turin 150km/93 miles (2hr).

**Rail** Pré-St-Didier (5km/3 miles); regular buses from station.

Val Ferret, served by bus. Dolonne has a couple of short trails.

### QUEUES
***Sunday crowds pour in***

The Checrouit and Val Veny cable-cars suffer queues only on Sundays, and even these can be beaten with an early start. There can be queues to go down as well as up. Patience is needed when waiting for the infrequent Youla cable-car – 'Not sure it's worth waiting more than 15 minutes for the one steep red,' said a reporter. Overcrowded slopes on Sundays, particularly down to Zerotta, can also be a problem.

### MOUNTAIN RESTAURANTS
***Lots – some of them good***

The area is lavishly endowed with 27 establishments ranging from rustic little huts to larger self-service places. Most huts do table-service of delicious pizza, pasta and other dishes and it is best to reserve tables in advance. But there are also snack bars selling more basic fare and relying on views and sun to fill their terraces.

Several restaurants are excellent. Maison Vieille, at the top of the chair of the same name and run by the charming mountain man Giacomo, is our favourite – a welcoming rustic place with superb home-made pastas. Chiecco, next to the drag-lift with the same name at Plan Checrouit, has good food and friendly service. The pick of the Plan Checrouit places is the Christiania – book a table downstairs.

On the other side of the mountain in Val Veny is another clutch of places worth experiencing. The jolly Grolla has good food and a sunny terrace with excellent views; La Fodze (just below Grolla) is a nice snack bar with some hot food; the Zerotta, at the foot of the eponymous chair has a sunny terrace and good food; the nearby Petit Mont Blanc has also been recommended.

One of the better snack bars is Courba Dzeleuna, with incredible views and delicious home-made myrtle grappa (beware of the alcohol-soaked berries left in the bottom of your glass if you want to hit the slopes again), just below the top of Dzeleuna chair.

### SCHOOLS AND GUIDES
***Good reports***

'We had the best instructor for ages – possibly ever,' said a reporter about the Monte Bianco ski school. There is a thriving guides' association ready to help you explore the area's off-piste; it has produced a helpful booklet showing the main possibilities.

### FACILITIES FOR CHILDREN
***Good care by Italian standards***

Childcare facilities are well ahead of the Italian norm, but Courmayeur is far from an ideal resort for a young family.

## STAYING THERE

### HOW TO GO
***Plenty of hotels***

Courmayeur's long-standing popularity ensures a wide range of packages (including some excellent weekend deals), mainly in hotels. Tour op Interski has cheap hotels out of town, and buses people in. One or two UK operators have catered chalets.

**Hotels** There are nearly 50 hotels, spanning the star ratings.

((((4 **Grand Hotel Courmaison** (0165 831400) Luxury new hotel 2km/1 mile from town, with 'excellent food'. Pool.

((((4 **Gallia Gran Baita** (0165 844040) Luxury place with antique furnishings, panoramic views and 'superb food'. Pool. Shuttle-bus to cable-car.

((((4 **Pavillon** (0165 846120) Comfortable 4-star near cable-car, with a pool. Friendly staff.

(((3 **Auberge de la Maison** (0165 869811) Small atmospheric 3-star in Entrèves under same ownership as Maison de Filippo (see Eating Out).

(((3 **Bouton d'Or** (0165 846729) Small, friendly B&B near main square.

(((3 **Berthod** (0165 842835) Friendly, family-run hotel near centre.

(((3 **Grange** (0165 869733) Rustic, stone-and-wood farmhouse in Entrèves.

(((3 **Triolet** (0165 846822) 'Excellent location near lift. Comfy, well- furnished.'

((2 **Edelweiss** (0165 841590) Friendly, cosy, good-value; close to the centre.

((2 **Lo Scoiattolo** (0165 846721) Good rooms, good food, shame it's at the opposite end of town to the cable-car.

**Self-catering** There is quite a lot available to independent bookers.

### EATING OUT
***Jolly Italian evenings***

There is a great choice, both in downtown Courmayeur and within taxi range; there's a handy promotional booklet describing many of them (in English as well as Italian). The touristy but very jolly Maison de Filippo in Entrèves is famous for its fixed-price, 36-dish feast. Also in Entrèves, the

↑ The slopes above Plan Checrouit get the morning sun (this photo was taken in the afternoon) and are linked by cable-car to Courmayeur in the valley below

SNOWPIX.COM / CHRIS GILL



**ACTIVITIES**

**Indoor** Swimming pool and sauna at Pré-St-Didier (5km/ 3 miles), Alpine museum, cinema, library, sports centre with climbing wall, ice rink, curling, fitness centre, indoor golf, squash, tennis

**Outdoor** Walking paths in Val Ferret, paragliding, snow-biking, dog-sledding

**Phone numbers**
From abroad use the prefix +39 (and do **not** omit the initial '0' of the phone number).

**TOURIST OFFICE**

**t** 0165 842060
aiat.montebianco@psw.it
www.courmayeur.net

Brenva has now added a separate Steakhouse serving huge steaks. We've been impressed by the traditional Italian cuisine of both Pierre Alexis and Cadran Solaire. The Terrazza ('excellent pasta and very friendly, jolly service') is a rising star. The Tunnel pizzeria, Mont-Frety ('good value', 'its antipasti is a must'), La Padella ('great pizza, raclette and fondue') and Le Vieux Pommier ('the place to go for fondue and raclette') have been recommended by reporters. Restaurants tend to be busy, so book well in advance.

## APRES-SKI
### *Stylish bar-hopping*

Courmayeur has a lively evening scene, centred on stylish bars with comfy sofas or armchairs to collapse in. Our favourites are the Roma (reporters have been very taken with the free canapés), the back room of the Caffè della Posta and the Bar delle Guide. The Cadran Solaire is where the big money from Milan and Turin hangs out. Le Prive is excellent for cocktails. The American Bar has good music and a fine selection of wines. Bar de Linge has a popular terrace. Poppys has been recommended for dancing. Maquis is the better of the two night clubs in Entrèves.

## OFF THE SLOPES
### *Lots on for non-slope users*

If you're not interested in hitting the snow you'll find the village pleasant – parading up and down is a favourite pastime for the many non-slope users the resort attracts (especially at weekends). You can go by cable-car up to Punta Helbronner, by bus to Aosta, or up the main cable-car to Plan Checrouit to meet friends for lunch. The huge sports centre is good (indoor tennis, climbing wall, ice skating, squash, golf practice, gym, sauna, steam, but no pool).

## STAYING UP THE MOUNTAIN
### *Why would you want to?*

Visiting Courmayeur and not staying in the charming village seems perverse – if you're that keen to get on the slopes in the morning, this is probably the wrong resort. But at Plan Checrouit, the 1-star Christiania (0165 843572 – see 'Mountain restaurants') has simple rooms and the 3-star Baita (0165 843570) is smarter; you need to book way in advance.

# Livigno

*Lowish prices and highish altitude – a tempting combination*

## COSTS

①②③④⑤⑥

## RATINGS

| The slopes | |
|---|---|
| Snow | **** |
| Extent | ** |
| Experts | ** |
| Intermediates | *** |
| Beginners | **** |
| Convenience | ** |
| Queues | **** |
| Mountain restaurants | *** |
| **The rest** | |
| Scenery | *** |
| Resort charm | *** |
| Off-slope | ** |

## NEWS

For 2003/04 a six-pack replaced a drag-lift in the Federia sector.



## REPORTS WANTED

**Recently we have had few reports on this resort. If you go there, please do send us a report.**

**The best reports earn a copy of the next edition, and can lead to free lift passes in future.**

**See page 10.**

## KEY FACTS

| | |
|---|---|
| **Resort** | 1815m<br>5,950ft |
| **Slopes** | 1815-2800m<br>5,950-9,190ft |
| **Lifts** | 33 |
| **Pistes** | 115km<br>71 miles |
| **Blue** | 25% |
| **Red** | 58% |
| **Black** | 17% |
| **Snowmaking** | 70km<br>43 miles |

- + High altitude plus snowmaking ensures a long season and a good chance of snow to resort level
- + Large choice of beginners' slopes
- + Impressive modern lift system
- + Cheap by the standards of high resorts, with the bonus of duty-free shopping – a great place to treat yourself to new equipment
- + Cosmopolitan, friendly and quite smart village with some Alpine atmosphere
- + Long, snow-sure cross-country trails

- − No challenging pistes
- − Long airport transfer – around 5hr
- − Slopes split into two quite widely separated areas
- − Village is very long and straggling
- − Few off-slope amenities
- − Bleak setting – wind can easily close upper lifts
- − Not many really comfortable hotels bookable through UK tour operators
- − Nightlife can disappoint

**Livigno offers the unusual combination of a fair-sized mountain, high altitude and fairly low prices. Despite its vaunted duty-free status, hotels, bars and restaurants are not much cheaper than in other Italian resorts, but shopping is – there are countless camera and clothes shops. As a relatively snow-sure alternative to the Pyrenees or to the smallest, cheapest resorts in Austria, Livigno seems attractive. But don't overlook the long list of drawbacks.**

## THE RESORT

Livigno is an amalgam of three villages in a wide, remote valley near the Swiss border – basically a string of hotels, bars, specialist shops and supermarkets lining a single long street. The buildings are small in scale and mainly traditional in style, giving the village a pleasant atmosphere. The original hamlet of San Antonio is the nearest thing Livigno has to a centre, and the best all-round location. Here, the main street and those at right angles linking it to the busy bypass road are nominally traffic-free. The road that skirts the 'traffic-free' area is constantly busy, and becomes intrusive in the hamlets of Santa Maria, 1km/0.5 miles to the north, and San Rocco, a bit further away to the south (and uphill).

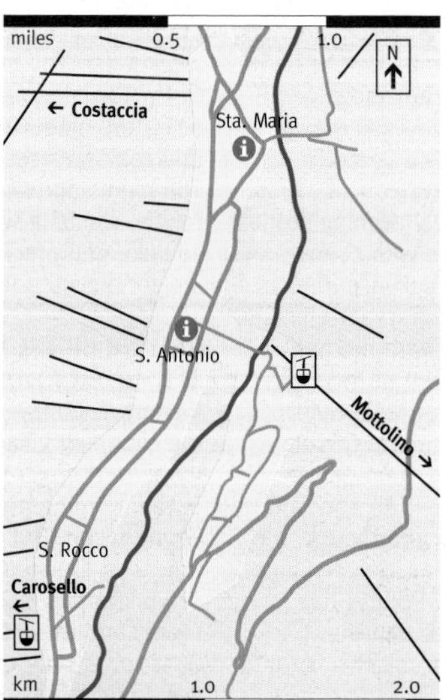


Lifts along the length of the village access the western slopes of the valley. The main lift to the eastern slopes is directly across the flat valley floor from the centre.

The bus services, on three colour-coded routes, are free and fairly frequent, but can get overcrowded at peak times and stop early in the evening. Taxis (including minibus taxis for groups) are an affordable alternative.

The lift pass covers Bormio and Santa Caterina, an easy drive or free bus-ride if the high pass is open, and a six-day pass entitles you to a discount rate on a one-day pass in St Moritz, reached via a road tunnel – a 'fantastic' day out, says a reader.

The airport transfer from Bergamo is long – five hours with a snack stop.

## LIFT PASSES

**Alta Valtellina**
Covers all lifts in Livigno, Bormio, Valdidentro and Valfurva

**Main pass**
1 day €31
6 days €154

**Senior citizens**
Over 60: 6 days €107

**Children**
Under 13: 6 days €107
Under 8: free pass

**Notes**
6-day pass entitles you to a discount on a 1-day pass for St Moritz.

**Alternative passes**
Half-day passes for Livigno only are available. Natura skipass classic covers lift pass, tuition, ski hire and a full day's pass for St Moritz.

## boarding

*Livigno attracts a fair number of boarders. There are some good, long, high runs for free-riders and carvers, as well as ample off-piste opportunities for intermediate riders. Most of the resort can be accessed by cable-cars and chairs; however, the excellent beginner slopes are mainly served by drags.*

## THE MOUNTAINS

The mainly open slopes, on either side of the valley, are more extensive than in many other budget destinations.

### THE SLOPES
***Improved links***

There are three sectors, all of them suitable for moderate and leisurely intermediates, and two of them are reasonably well linked.

A two-seater chair from the nursery slopes at the north end of the village take you up to **Costaccia**, where a long fast quad chair-lift goes along the ridge towards the **Carosello** sector. The blue linking run back from Carosello to the top of Costaccia is flat in places and may involve energetic poling if the snow conditions and the wind are against you. Carosello is more usually accessed by the optimistically named Carosello 3000 gondola at San Rocco, which goes up, in two stages, to 2750m/9,020ft. Most runs return towards the village, but there are a couple on the back of the mountain, on the west-facing slopes of Val Federia – where the double drags have recently been replaced by a six-pack.

The ridge of **Mottolino** is reached by an efficient gondola from Teola, a tiresome walk or a short bus-ride across the valley from San Antonio. From the top, you can descend to fast quads on either side of the ridge or, if you must, take a slow antique chair up the ridge to Monte della Neve. There is now the alternative of a fast quad starting a little way along the valley, and linking with a six-pack to Monte della Neve.

Signposting is patchy and the piste map isn't always entirely accurate.

### TERRAIN-PARKS
***There, but empty***

There's a half-pipe, a beginner's half-pipe and a good, if underused, terrain-park/boarder-cross in the Mottolino area.

### SNOW RELIABILITY
***Very good, despite no glacier***

Livigno's slopes are high (you can spend most of your time around 2500m/8,200ft), and with snow-guns on the lower slopes of Mottolino and Costaccia, the season is long.





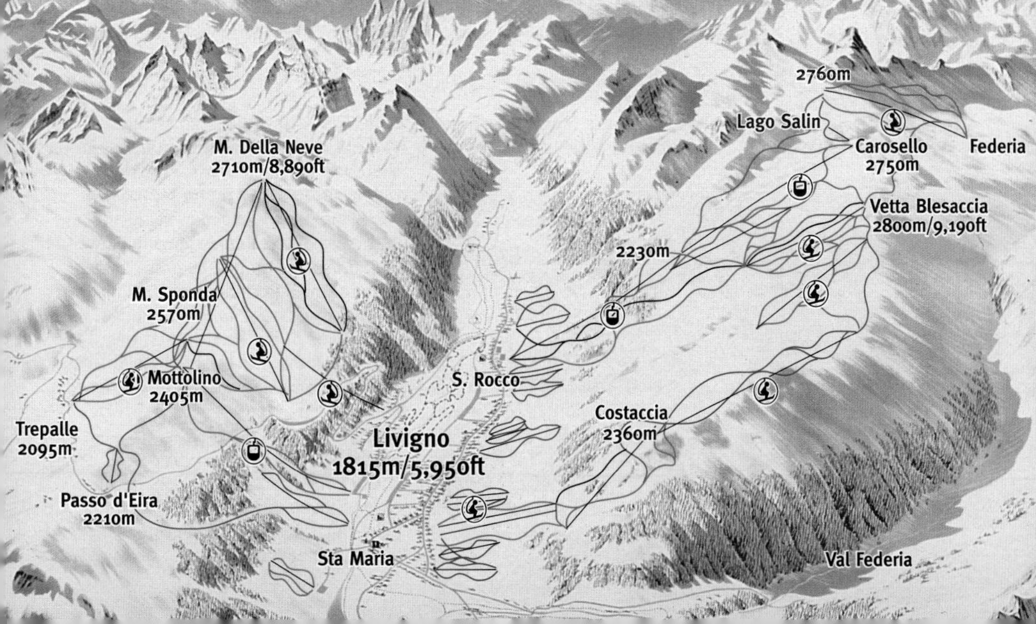

## SCHOOLS

**Livigno Inverno/Estate**
t 0342 996276
info@scuolascilivigno.com

**Azzurra Livigno**
t 0342 997683
info@azzurra.info

**Livigno Italy**
t 0342 996739
mail@livignovacanze.it

**Livigno Soc Coop**
t 0342 970300
info@sisl.it

**Top Club Mottolino**
t 0342 970822
scuolasci@livignotopclub.it

**Classes**
(Livigno Inverno/Estate prices)
6 days (2hr per day) €80

**Private lessons**
€29 for 1hr; each additional person €6





### FOR EXPERTS
***Not recommended***

The piste map shows a few black runs but these are not particularly steep. Even the all-black terrain served by the six-pack on Monte della Neve is really no more than stiff red in gradient. There is off-piste to be done, but guidance would be needed.

### FOR INTERMEDIATES
***Flattering slopes***

Good intermediates will be able to tackle all the blacks without worry. The woodland black run down from Carosello past Tea da Borch is narrow in places and can get mogulled and icy at the end of the day. The red runs at Federia are challenging, and bumpy. Moderate intermediates have virtually the whole area at their disposal. The long run beneath the Mottolino gondola is one of the best – and there is also a long, under-used blue going less directly to the valley. Leisurely types have several long cruises available. The run beneath the Valandrea-Vetta fast chair, at the top of the Costaccia sector, is a splendid slope for confidence-building.

### FOR BEGINNERS
***Excellent but scattered slopes***

A vast array of nursery slopes along the sunny lower flanks of Costaccia, and other slopes around the valley, make Livigno excellent for novices – although some of the slopes at the northern end are steep enough to cause difficulties. There are lots of longer runs to progress to.

### CROSS-COUNTRY
***Good snow, bleak setting***

Long snow-sure trails (40km/25 miles in total) follow the valley floor, making Livigno a good choice, provided you don't mind the bleak scenery. There is a specialist cross-country school, and the resort organises major cross-country races.

APT LIVIGNO / L MARTINELLI

San Antonio is the heart of the long village ↓

### QUEUES
***Few problems these days***

Despite reports of queues for the Costaccia chair at midday and short delays for the Carosello gondola in peak season, lift queues are not generally a problem. A total of eight fast chairs is impressive for an area of this size. A bigger problem is that strong winds often close the upper lifts, causing overcrowding lower down.

### MOUNTAIN RESTAURANTS
***More than adequate***

On Mottolino, the refuge at the top of the gondola is impressive, with smart self- and table-service sections, a solarium and a nursery, but 'immense' lunch-time queues. The rustic restaurants at Passo d'Eira and Trepalle are a good option for a quiet stop. And there are some more charming places lower down. The welcoming Tea del Vidal is at the base of the same sector. Costaccia's Tea del Plan is pleasantly rustic and sunny, with good food and a great atmosphere. The self-service place at the top of Carosello is acceptable and Tea da Borch, in the trees lower down, serves great food in a Tirolean-style atmosphere, though the run down can be tricky. Lunch in the valley at the hotel Sporting (near the Carosello gondola) is popular. The terrace at the hotel Möta, at the base of the Costaccia lifts, is also recommended.

### SCHOOLS AND GUIDES
***Watch out for short classes***

There are several schools. English is widely spoken, and recent reports are complimentary. A common complaint is that most of the classes are short (two-hours). Another is that beginners spend too long on the nursery slopes before progressing up the mountain. It also seems to be the case that the schools on the Costaccia-Carosello side avoid the Mottolino sector altogether.

### FACILITIES FOR CHILDREN
***Not bad for Italy***

The schools run children's classes. The Livigno Inverno/Estate school's Alì-Babà nursery offers all-day care and the staff speak English.

## CHILDREN

**Alì Babà**
t 0342 978050
Ages 3 and over

**Miniclub Top Club Mottolino**
t 0342 970025

**Spazio Gioco Peribimbi**
t 0342 970711
Ages 18mnth to 3yr

## GETTING THERE

**Air** Bergamo 200km/124 miles (5hr).

**Rail** Tirano (48km/ 30 miles), Zernez (Switzerland, 28km/ 17 miles); regular buses from station, weekends only.

## ACTIVITIES

**Indoor** Saunas and fitness rooms (in hotels), swimming pool (hotel Spöl), badminton, basketball, billiards, climbing wall, bowls, bowling, cinema

**Outdoor** Cleared paths, ice rink, snow-shoeing, horse-riding, ice climbing, ice driving, dog sledding, paragliding

**Phone numbers**
From abroad use the prefix +39 (and do **not** omit the initial '0' of the phone number).

## TOURIST OFFICE

**t** 0342 996379
info@aptlivigno.it
www.aptlivigno.it

## STAYING THERE

### HOW TO GO

***Lots of hotels, some apartments***

Livigno has an enormous range of hotels and a number of apartments. There are some attractively priced catered chalets from UK operators.

**Hotels** Most of the hotels are small 2- and 3-star places, with a couple of 4-stars out of the centre.

(3) **Intermonti** (0342 972100) Modern 4-star with all mod cons (including a pool); some way from the centre, on the Mottolino side of the valley.

(2) **Bivio** (0342 996137) The only hotel in central Livigno with a pool.

(2) **Steinbock** (0342 970520) Nice little place, far from major lifts but a short walk from some nursery slopes.

(2) **Loredana** (0342 996330) Modern chalet on the Mottolino side. 'Pleasant food, good rooms.'

(2) **Larice** (0342 996184) Stylish little 3-star B&B well placed for Costaccia lifts and slopes.

(2) **Montanina** (0342 996060) Good central 3-star.

(2) **Alpi** (0342 996408) In San Rocco, not far from Carosello gondola. 'Absolutely the best; exquisite food.'

(2) **Camana Veglia** (0342 996904) Charming old wooden chalet. Popular restaurant, well placed in Santa Maria.

(2) **Silvestri** (0342 996255) 2-star in the San Rocco area. 'Great staff, comfortable rooms, filling meals.'

**Self-catering** All the big tour operators that come here have apartment options. Most are cheap and cheerful.

### EATING OUT

***Improving, still value for money***

Livigno has lots of traditional, unpretentious restaurants, many hotel-based. Hotel Concordia has some of the best cooking in town. Mario's has one of the largest menus, serving seafood, fondue and steaks in addition to the ubiquitous pizza and pasta. Bait dal Ghet and the Bivio restaurant are popular with the locals, and the Rusticana does wholesome, cheap food. Pesce d'Oro is good for seafood and Italian cuisine. The Bellavista, Ambassador, Mirage, Grolla and the Garden are also recommended.

### APRES-SKI

***Lively, but disappoints some***

It's not that there isn't action in Livigno, but simply that the scene is quieter than some people expect in a duty-free resort. Pas de la Casa it is not – to the relief of most reporters. Also, the best places are scattered about, so the village lacks evening buzz. At tea time many people return to their hotels for a quiet drink. But Tea del Vidal, at the bottom of Mottolino, gets lively, as does the Stalet bar at the base of the Carosello gondola. The Caffè della Posta umbrella bar, near the centre, is also popular. We hear Europe's highest brewery is in production at the Echo. Nightlife gets going only after 10pm. Galli's pub, in San Antonio, is 'a full-on party pub', popular with Brits. The Kuhstall under the Bivio hotel is an excellent cellar bar with live music, as is the Helvetia, over the road. The San Rocco end is quietest, but Daphne's ('good fun') and Marco's are popular. The stylish Art Cafe is also recommended. Kokodi and the Cielo are the main discos.

### OFF THE SLOPES

***Look lively, or go shopping***

Livigno offers a small range of outdoor alternatives to skiing and boarding – horse-riding among them. Walks are uninspiring and there is no sports centre or public swimming pool. However, the duty-free shopping more than makes up for this. Trips to Bormio and St Moritz are popular.

# Madonna di Campiglio

*Extensive, easy slopes amid stunning scenery*

## COSTS

(1)(2)(3)(4)(5)(6)

## RATINGS

**The slopes**

| | |
|---|---|
| Snow | *** |
| Extent | *** |
| Expert | ** |
| Intermediate | **** |
| Beginner | **** |
| Convenience | *** |
| Queues | **** |
| Mountain restaurants | *** |

**The rest**

| | |
|---|---|
| Scenery | **** |
| Resort charm | *** |
| Off-slope | *** |

## NEWS

In 2003/04 a fast quad with covers replaced two old chair-lifts serving the slopes between Monte Vigo and Pradalago and was extended to meet the Monte Vigo connection.

For 2004/05 a new six-pack is planned for the top Groste slopes, replacing the two parallel chairs Groste I & II.



## REPORTS WANTED

**Recently we have had few reports on this resort. If you go there, please do send us a report.**

**The best reports earn a copy of the next edition, and can lead to free lift passes in future.**

**See page 10.**

- + Pleasant town in a pretty valley with splendid views at altitude
- + Fairly extensive network of slopes, best for beginners and intermediates
- − Spread-out village and infrequent shuttle-bus service
- − Quiet après-ski

**Like Cortina, Madonna is a pleasant Dolomite town with an affluent, almost exclusively Italian, clientele – though the scenery isn't in quite the same league. Folgarida and Marilleva, to which Madonna's slopes are linked, are quite different – and are covered in our new chapter on Trentino.**

## THE RESORT

Madonna is a long-established, traditional-style but now largely modern town, set in a prettily wooded valley beneath the impressive Brenta Dolomites, with slopes in three linked sectors. The centre is fairly compact: the cable-car to Cinque Laghi (to the west) and the gondola to Pradalago (to the north) bracket most of the central hotels, and are about a five-minute walk apart. Five minutes outside the centre is a gondola to Monte Spinale, leading to the Grostè sector, to the east; there is another gondola to Grostè starting a short bus-ride outside the town, to the north. Beyond this lift station are the main nursery slopes at Campo Carlo Magno. The town spreads a long way south from the centre, past a frozen lake.

Madonna attracts an affluent, young, Italian clientele; it has lots of smart shops. Many visitors stay around the village all day, and promenading is an early evening ritual.

The free ski-bus runs to a timetable, but is not frequent. Some hotels run minibuses.

↑ The scenery may not be quite in the Cortina league – but by normal standards it is splendid

APT MADONNA DI CAMPIGLIO

## KEY FACTS

| | |
|---|---|
| **Resort** | 1520m 4,990ft |
| Madonna, Folgarida, and Marilleva combined area | |
| **Slopes** | 1520-2505m 4,990-8,220ft |
| **Lifts** | 45 |
| **Pistes** | 120km 75 miles |
| **Blue** | 35% |
| **Red** | 50% |
| **Black** | 15% |
| **Snowmaking** | 90% |

**Phone numbers**
From abroad use the prefix +39 (and do **not** omit the initial '0' of the phone number).

## TOURIST OFFICE

**t** 0465 442000
info@campiglio.net
www.campiglio.net

## THE MOUNTAINS

The Pradalago sector is linked by lift and piste to Monte Vigo, and so to the slopes of Folgarida and Marilleva.
**Slopes** The terrain is mainly intermediate, both above and below the tree line. Recent reporters were very impressed with the grooming. Some recommend skiing the Marilleva and Folgarida slopes in the afternoon to avoid crowds of ski school classes.
**Terrain-parks** The Ursus park, at Grostè, includes boarder-cross, half- and quarter-pipes and big air jumps, .
**Snow reliability** Although many of the runs are sunny, they are at a fair altitude, and there has been hefty investment in snowmaking. As a result, snow reliability is reasonable. Grooming is excellent.
**Experts** Experts should plan on heading off-piste. The trees under the Genziana chair are 'a good spot for untracked snow'. But the 3-Tre race course and the Spinale Direttissima are steep. Pista Nera, above Folgarida, can be a challenging mogul field. And a recent reporter enjoyed the Orti/ Marilleva black at Marilleva.
**Intermediates** Cinque Laghi, Madonna's racing mountain, is ideal: early or timid intermediates will love the area and have no difficulty exploring most of the network, though the connection to Folgarida is a bit trickier. Grostè and Pradalago have long, easy runs, though the former can get crowded.
**Beginners** The nursery slopes at Campo Carlo Magno are excellent, but do involve a bus-ride. Progression to longer runs is easy.
**Snowboarding** The resort is popular with boarders and some major events have been held here.
**Cross-country** There are 30km/19 miles of pretty trails through the woods.
**Queues** Two 2004 reporters did not find queuing a worry, but there are one or two bottlenecks. The Cinque Laghi cable-car is called 'Express' and like all cable-cars is quick, but its capacity is tiny; it produces half-hour queues which can be avoided by using the two nearby chairs.
**Mountain restaurants** The Malga Montagnoli in the lower part of Grostè is a 'charming old refuge with a decent self-service'. Other recommendations include the Cinque Laghi ('stunning views') and the Boch.
**Schools and guides** One group 'got on well' with the Nazionale school this year – an improvement on the past.
**Facilities for children** Very limited.

## STAYING THERE

**How to go** There is a wide choice of hotels and some self-catering.
**Hotels** The 4-star Spinale (0465 441116) is convenient. The Savoia Palace (0465 441004) is also 4-star but without a pool; 'comfortable and friendly', but the location can be noisy. The central Arnica (0465 440377) does only breakfast but does it very well and gets a rave review this year – 'super', with 'very friendly owners' and a new wellness centre. The central 3-star Milano (0465 441210) is also recommended. At Campo Carlo Magno the Zeledria (0465 441010) is 'a good 4-star with friendly staff' but was undergoing refurbishment in 2003/04.
**Eating out** There are around 20 restaurants. 'All the ones we tried were good,' says a reporter, and Belvedere, the Antica Focolare, the Roi and Stube Diana have all been recommended. A 2004 reporter enjoyed the 'artistic dishes' at the pricey Alfiero, and Locanda degli Artisti is 'worth the expense for a special night out'. Some of the mountain huts are also open.
**Après-ski** Après-ski is quiet. At tea-time, the Maturi is said to have the 'best cakes and chocolates in town'. Franz-Joseph Stube (now non-smoking), Bar Suisse and Cantina del Suisse are recommended, as is the Bowling bar – and the Alpes is perhaps the smartest club. There's also a well-known disco – the Zangola – which reportedly gets going very late.
**Off the slopes** Window-shopping, skating on the lake and walking are popular. There's also paragliding. A reporter recommends taking the bus out to Campo Carlo Magno for lunch.

# Monterosa Ski

*Europe's best kept secret – an undiscovered gem*

## COSTS

(1)(2)(3)(4)(5)(6)

## RATINGS

**The slopes**

| | |
|---|---|
| Snow | *** |
| Extent | **** |
| Expert | *** |
| Intermediate | **** |
| Beginner | ** |
| Convenience | **** |
| Queues | **** |
| Mountain restaurants | ** |

**The rest**

| | |
|---|---|
| Scenery | **** |
| Resort charm | *** |
| Off-slope | * |

## NEWS

From 2004/05 Alagna should at last be linked to and from Gressoney by piste Up till now the link both ways has only been off-piste. A new 100-person cable-car from the heart of Alagna's slopes at Pianalunga to Passo dei Salati at the top of the gondola from Gressoney should have been in place for last season but we are now assured it will be there for 2004/05. A blue piste is planned from the top to the mid-station and a red from there to Pianalunga. There will still be an off-piste route down.

There are plans to build another cable-car in a couple of years' time from Passo dei Salati to Cresta Rosa at 3500m/11,480ft, above Punta Indren. This will open up some stunning off-piste and remove the need to use the tiny, ancient cable-car to Punta Indren.



- + Fairly extensive network of pistes
- + Fabulous intermediate and advanced off-piste, including heli-skiing
- + Slopes usually very quiet weekdays
- + Beautiful scenery
- + Good snow reliability and grooming
- + Quiet, pretty, unspoiled villages

- – Few steep pistes – mainly easy cruising
- – High winds can close link between Champoluc and Gressoney valleys
- – Few off-slope diversions
- – Limited après-ski

**Monterosa Ski is Italy's little-known and less extensive answer to France's Trois Vallées and has a good lift system which is being developed further as the result of two lift companies merging. Yet it is hardly heard of on the international market. It is popular with Italians at weekends, when they drive up for the day from Milan and Turin. But during the week it is empty. The pistes are mostly intermediate and set amid impressive scenery. And the off-piste is fabulous (and usually deserted). It is the only major ski area we have come across in Europe where there is no real well-developed resort to stay in. The villages that access the slopes have avoided commercialisation and still retain a friendly, small-scale, local ambience. Our advice is to get there soon before all this changes.**

## THE RESORT

The main resorts are Champoluc in the western valley, Gressoney in the central valley, and Alagna to the east.

Champoluc is set towards the end of a long, winding road up from the Aosta valley motorway. It is strung out along the road for quite a distance but retains a certain quiet charm and very Italian feel. The first part you come to is the attractive old village centre with the church and a fast-running river.

Small shops and hotels line the road between here and the gondola, several minutes' walk away. You can store boots and skis/board there overnight. More accommodation is on the road to Frachey, where there is a chair-lift into the slopes.

Gressoney La Trinité is a quiet, neat little village, with cobbled streets, wooden buildings and an old church. It is about 800m/0.5 miles from the chair-lift into the slopes, where there are a few convenient hotels. It is a bus-ride from the outpost of Stafal at the head of the valley, which is the link between the Gressoney and Champoluc slopes and has a few rather soulless blocks. Gressoney St Jean, a bigger village, is 5km/3 miles down the valley and has its own separate slopes.

The main resort in the east valley is Alagna, a strange place with some large, deserted and dilapidated buildings as well as smaller charming wooden buildings and church.

Trips to Cervinia, La Thuile and Courmayeur (covered by the Aosta Valley pass) are possible by car.

## THE MOUNTAINS

The slopes of Monterosa Ski are relatively extensive, and very scenic. The pistes are almost all intermediate (and well groomed), and the lifts are mainly chairs and gondolas, with few drag-lifts. The terrain is undulating and runs are long, but many lifts serve only one or two pistes.

The piste map is poor: 'Woefully inadequate,' said one reporter, and 'In need of radical surgery to improve it,' said another. But the signposting on the pistes is clear. Several reporters, who visited at different times, said the top lifts and the connection between Champoluc and Gressoney closed due to high winds, severely restricting the available terrain.

**Slopes** A gondola from Champoluc followed by two slow chairs takes you up to the steep, narrow, bumpy link with the rest of the slopes (which a lot of timid intermediates find very

← Almost 40% of the pistes are covered by snowmaking and grooming is good

JON SIMS



difficult). Taking the bus to the Frachey chair is a quicker way into the main cruising runs and the link via Colle Bettaforca with Stafal in the Gressoney valley, and avoids the tricky top run.

At Stafal a cable-car followed by a high-speed chair take you back to the Champoluc slopes and two successive gondolas opposite take you to Passo dei Salati. From there runs lead back down to Stafal and to Gressoney La Trinité and Orsia, both served by chair-lifts. Or you can head towards Alagna on the new piste planned for 2004/05.

From Alagna a modern gondola goes to Pianalunga at mid-mountain. For 2004/05 a new two-stage cable-car from here is planned to take you to Passo dei Salati. Before this, the only way further up was by a two-person chair-lift up to a tiny, ancient cable-car, which accesses the high slopes around Punta Indren; the only ways back to Gressoney from there are off-piste. On the Alagna side of the cable-car there is lots of off-piste and an ungroomed black run that leads to an antique bucket lift that you jump into while it is moving (it goes back to the bottom of the cable-car).

Gressoney St Jean and Antagnod, near Champoluc, have their own small areas of slopes. The St Jean slopes have only one lift but two 2004 reporters enjoyed half-days there: one said, 'Choice of blue, red and splendid black.' Antagnod is used by local instructors on bad-weather days and has some good off piste terrain in between the intermediate runs.

**Terrain-parks** There were big air jumps near the top of the Champoluc gondola on our last visit.

**Snow reliability** Generally good, thanks to extensive snowmaking, altitude and good grooming.

**Experts** The attraction is the off-piste, with great runs from the high-points of the lift system in all three valleys and



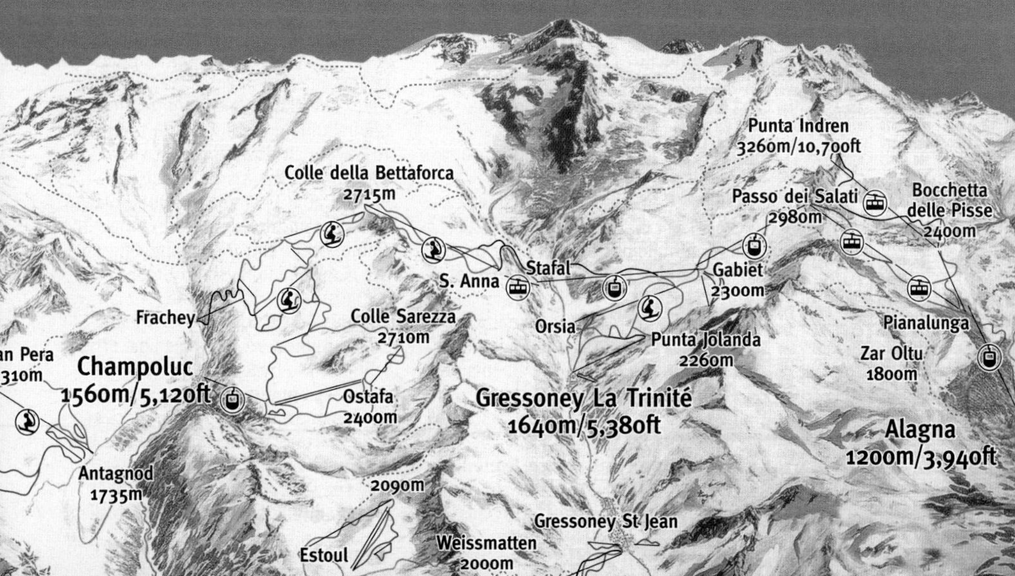

↑ Typical mid-week crowds on the pistes of the Monterosa ski area

JON SIMS

**KEY FACTS**

| | |
|---|---|
| **Resort** | 1640m<br>5,380ft |
| **Slopes** | 1200-3260m<br>3,940-10,700ft |
| **Lifts** | 36 |
| **Pistes** | 180km<br>112 miles |
| **Blue** | 29% |
| **Red** | 63% |
| **Black** | 8% |
| **Snowmaking** | 70km<br>43 miles |



some excellent heli-drops. A mountain guide is essential for getting the best out of the area. We had two fabulous days on our last visit – one exploring the runs from Punta Indren and the other a heli-drop on Monte Rosa, skiing down to Zermatt and returning off-piste from the top of the Cervinia area. The bowls above Gressoney are little used and snow can lie untracked for days. Alagna is a cult area for expert off-piste. There are a few black pistes but none of them really deserve their grading.

**Intermediates** For those who like to travel on easy, undemanding pistes, the area is great, with long cruising runs from the ridges down into the valleys. There isn't much on-piste challenge for more demanding intermediates, but those willing to take a guide and explore some of the gentler off-piste will have a great time. If you stick to the pistes, a weekend or mid-week break rather than a full week might be worth trying: 'It's great for a short break,' said a reporter.

**Beginners** The high nursery slopes at the top of the gondola at Champoluc, served by two moving pavements, are better than the lower ones at Gressoney. But neither area has ideal gentle runs to progress to.

**Snowboarding** There is great off-piste free-riding.

**Cross-country** There are long trails around St Jean, and shorter ones up the valley; Brusson, in the Champoluc valley, has the best trails in the area.

**Queues** Usually it's only at weekends, when the hordes from Turin and Milan arrive, that there are any queues. The worst bottleneck is the tiny top cable-car on the Alagna side, where waits of over an hour are possible and where queues can form even in mid-week. The double chair to Belvedere on the way back from Frachey/ Bettaforca to Champoluc can have long queues at the end of the day. Pistes can get crowded at weekends, too, but the off-piste is still delightfully quiet.

**Mountain restaurants** The mountain restaurants are basic. The Edelweiss, Vieux Crest and Belvedere (one of the few mountain restaurants in the region to have a sit-down loo), above Champoluc, the Mandria above Frachey, the Chamois at Punta Jolanda, Bedemie on the way to Gressoney from Gabiet, Del Ponte above Gabiet, and the Guglielmina, Lys and Gabiet refuges are recommended.

**Schools and guides** We have had mixed reports on the Italian ski schools ('One of the best instructors I have had,' says one reporter; 'suitable abilities not put together' and 'classes large, mixed nationalities, not much teaching' say others) but universally good reports about the Monterosa mountain guides ('Absolutely excellent day,' said a 2004 reporter) and the ski school run by tour operator Ski2 ('Superb, especially Ali, as good as North America.')

**Facilities for children** There is a special kids' ski school and snow-park at Antagnod near Champoluc and a mini-club at Gressoney St Jean.

## STAYING THERE

**How to go** More tour operators are discovering the area. We've had good reports of Monterosa specialists Ski 2 ('great from pick-up to drop-off').

**Hotels** At Champoluc the Castor (0125 307117) in the old centre is 'an absolute gem' with 'good food and magnificent puddings' and is managed by a British guy who married into the family that has owned it for generations. At the hotel California (0125 307977 – the owners speak no English) every room is dedicated to a pop star or group (eg the Byrds, Bob Dylan, Joan Baez, the Doors) and their music plays whenever you turn on the light. It's quite a way out of the centre. Two 2004 reporters stayed at the newly built Le Rocher (0125 308711), which they both thought friendly and welcoming with good food, but set a bit remotely.

The Breithorn (0125 08734), two minutes from the gondola, is an excellent luxury 4-star, converted from a 100-year-old building with wonderful beamed bedrooms and good spa facilities. 'It's a gem,' says one well-travelled reporter. 'The service was better than any 5-star hotel I have stayed in.' The owner also has the luxury renovated Mascognaz chalet in a deserted village reached only by snowmobile – you can stay or have dinner up there for a supplement.

At Gressoney La Trinité several reporters recommend the Jolanda Sport (0125 366140), with gym and sauna, and right by the lift. Another says of the nearby Residence (0125 366148), 'Friendliest hotel I've ever stayed at in the Alps.' Dufour (0125 366139) has also been mentioned. In Alagna, try the Monterosa (0163 923209) or Cristallo (0163 91285).

**Eating out** Both Gressoney and Champoluc have a few stand-alone restaurants; most are in hotels. The Walserchild in Gressoney got a good review from a 2004 reporter.

**Après-ski** Après-ski is quiet. In Champoluc, the bar of the hotel Castor is cosy and popular with seasonnaires and resort workers; the Golosono is a small atmospheric, authentic Italian wine bar; the Galion opposite the gondola is busy as the lifts close; the West Road in the California has karaoke some nights. At weekends, the disco beneath hotel California gets going. Gressoney is even quieter; 'Schnee Blume bar is the best, but it has nothing to beat,' says a reporter, 'and the tour-op organised wine tasting at Hirschstube was excellent.'

**Off the slopes** There is little to amuse those who don't head for the slopes.

**Phone numbers**
From abroad use the prefix +39 (and do **not** omit the initial '0' of the phone number).

**TOURIST OFFICE**

**t** 0125 303111
kikesly@monterosa-ski.com
www.monterosa-ski.com

SAUZE D'OULX TOURIST OFFICE

# Sauze d'Oulx

*'Suzy does it' still, but with more dignity than in the past*

**COSTS**

①②③④⑤⑥

**RATINGS**

**The slopes**

| | |
|---|---|
| Snow | ** |
| Extent | **** |
| Expert | ** |
| Intermediate | **** |
| Beginner | ** |
| Convenience | ** |
| Queues | *** |
| Mountain restaurants | *** |

**The rest**

| | |
|---|---|
| Scenery | *** |
| Resort charm | ** |
| Off-slope | * |

**NEWS**

Turin has been chosen to host the 2006 Olympic Winter Games; freestyle events will be at Sauze d'Oulx, the women's downhill, super-G and combined events at Sansicario.

This has triggered a rash of improvements in the Sansicario sector. Last season a new piste was made for the women's races; the Soleil Boeuf chair was replaced by the fast Ski Lodge quad; and the drags on the nursery slopes were replaced by a slow quad. For 2004/05 two new lifts are planned. One is the gondola up from Cesana, promised for last year. The other is at the top of the area, on M Fraiteve.



- ✚ Extensive and uncrowded slopes, great intermediate cruising
- ✚ Linked into Milky Way network
- ✚ Mix of open and tree-lined runs is good for all weather conditions
- ✚ Entertaining nightlife
- ✚ Some scope for off-piste adventures
- ✚ One of the cheapest major resorts there is – and more attractive than its reputation suggests

- ━ Still lots of ancient lifts, making progress around the slopes slow
- ━ Erratic snow record – and still far from comprehensive snowmaking
- ━ Crowds at weekends
- ━ Getting to the French end of the Milky Way takes forever
- ━ Very few challenging pistes – and hardly a mogul to be seen
- ━ Mornings-only classes, and the best nursery slopes are at mid-mountain
- ━ Steep walks around the village, and an inadequate shuttle-bus service

**If you're looking for a cheap holiday in a resort with extensive slopes, put Sauze on your shortlist. In the 1980s it became known as prime lager-lout territory; but it always was a resort of two halves – young Brits on a budget alongside mature second-home owners from Turin – and these days the two halves seem to be much more in balance, especially at weekends. It still has lively bars and shops festooned in English signs, but sober Brits like you and us need not stay away. When we visit, we like it more than we expect to – as do many reporters.**

**We are slightly haunted, though, by the memory of the bare slopes of our first visit, in the mid-1980s, and the thin cover four seasons ago: Sauze is a resort that needs comprehensive snowmaking, and doesn't yet have it.**

## THE RESORT

Sauze d'Oulx sits on a sloping mountain shelf facing north-west across the Valle di Susa, with impressive views of the towering mountains forming the border with France. Most of the resort is modern and undistinguished, made up of block-like hotels relieved by the occasional chalet, spreading down the steep hillside from the foot of the slopes. Despite the shift in clientele described above, the centre is still lively at night; the late-closing bars are usually quite full, and the handful of discos do brisk business – at the weekend, at least.

Sauze also has an attractive old core, with narrow, twisting streets and houses roofed with huge stone slabs. There is a central car-free zone, but traffic roams freely through most of the village, which can be congested morning and evening. The roads have few pavements and can become icy and treacherous at night.

Out of the bustle of the centre, where most of the bars and nightclubs are located, there are quiet, wooded residential areas full of secluded apartment blocks, and a number of good restaurants are also tucked out of the way of the front line. Chair-lifts go from the top of the village and from two points on its fringes. There's also a chair from nearby Jouvenceaux.

Most of the hotels are reasonably central, but the Clotes lift is at the top of the village, up a short but steep hill, and the Sportinia chair is an irritatingly long walk beyond that. Buses (not covered by the lift pass) are infrequent and can't cope with high-season crowds. The service around lunch-time is particularly poor.

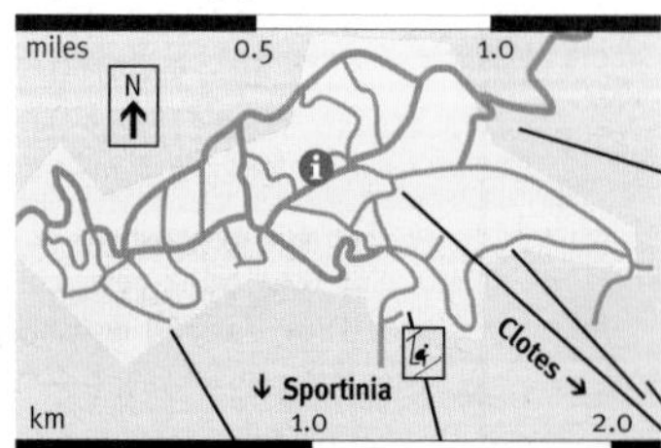

## KEY FACTS

| | |
|---|---|
| **Resort** | 1510m<br>4,950ft |
| For Milky Way | |
| **Slopes** | 1390-2825m<br>4,560-9,270ft |
| **Lifts** | 88 |
| **Pistes** | 400km<br>249 miles |
| **Blue** | 25% |
| **Red** | 55% |
| **Black** | 20% |
| **Snowmaking** | 120km<br>75 miles |
| For Sauze d'Oulx-Sestriere-Sansicario only | |
| **Slopes** | 1390-2825m<br>4,560-9,270ft |
| **Lifts** | 51 |
| **Pistes** | 300km<br>186 miles |
| **Snowmaking** | 90km<br>56 miles |

There is excellent intermediate terrain above Sansicario – broad, long cruises ↗

SNOWPIX.COM / CHRIS GILL

## LIFT PASSES

**La Via Lattea**
Covers all lifts in Sauze d'Oulx, Sestriere, Sansicario, Cesana and Claviere.

**Main pass**
1 day €31
6 days €155

**Senior citizens**
Over 75: free pass

**Children**
Under 12: 6-day pass €77.50
Under 10: free pass

**Notes**
Half-day pass available; also one-day extension for Montgenèvre.

## THE MOUNTAINS

Sauze's mountains provide excellent intermediate terrain. The piste grading fluctuates from year to year, if you believe the resort's map – and we're never sure we've caught up with the latest changes from blue to red and red to blue. But most reporters agree that many runs graded red or even black should really be graded blue; challenges are few and far between. (The same might be said of the whole extensive Milky Way area, of which Sauze is one extreme.)

### THE SLOPES
***Big and varied enough for most***

Sauze's local slopes are spread across a broad wooded bowl above the resort, ranging from west- to north-facing. The main lifts are chairs, from the top of the village up to **Clotes** and from the western fringes to **Sportinia** – a sunny mid-mountain clearing in the woods, with a ring of restaurants and hotels (see 'Staying up the mountain') and a small nursery area.

The high point of the system is **Monte Fraiteve**. From here you can travel west on splendid broad, long runs to **Sansicario** – and on to chair-lifts near **Cesana Torinese** that link with **Claviere** and then **Montgenèvre**, in France, the far end of the Milky Way (both are reached more quickly by car).

You normally get to **Sestriere** from the lower point of Col Basset, on the shoulder of M Fraiteve – but snow cover is unreliable and in our experience you normally have to use the gondola to descend the bottom half of the mountain. In bad weather, on the other hand, the gondola may be closed by strong winds. The alternative of descending the slope from M Fraiteve itself has been reinstated, at least in theory; but snow again is not reliable, and our attempts to check out this slope last winter were frustrated by closure of the piste.

As in so many Italian resorts, piste marking, direction signing and piste map design are not taken seriously.

The slopes of Montgenèvre and Sestriere are covered in other chapters. Montgenèvre is best reached by car.

### TERRAIN-PARKS
***Not in Sauze***

There's no park or pipe here. The nearest is in the Sises sector of Sestriere.

### SNOW RELIABILITY
***Can be poor, affecting the links***

The area is notorious for erratic snowfalls, occasionally suffering acute droughts. Another problem is that many of the slopes get a lot of afternoon sun. At these modest altitudes, late-season conditions are far from reliable. Reporters have found icy, bare slopes at vital link points earlier in the season, too – particularly from M Fraiteve. There's snowmaking on a couple of slopes, notably the key home run from P Rocca via Clotes to the village.

### FOR EXPERTS
***Head off-piste***

Very few of the pistes are challenging. The best slopes are at virtually opposite ends of Sauze's local area – a short, high, north-facing run from the shoulder of M Fraiteve, and the sunny slopes below M Moncrons.

The main interest is in going off-piste. There are plenty of minor opportunities within the piste network, but the highlights are long, top-to-bottom descents of up to 1300m/ 4,270ft vertical from M Fraiteve, ending (snow permitting) at villages dotted along the valleys. The best known of these runs (which used to be marked on the piste map but is no longer – presumably to encourage the use of guides) is the Rio Nero, down to the road near Oulx. When snow low down is poor, some of these runs can be cut short at Jouvenceaux or Sansicario.

## boarding

*Sauze has good snowboarding slopes – it's got local tree-lined slopes (with space in the trees, too), high, undulating, open terrain, and links to other resorts in the Milky Way. But although it has a fair number of chair-lifts, there are also lots of drags – a serious drawback for novice riders.*

### FOR INTERMEDIATES
***Splendid cruising terrain***

The whole area is ideal for confident intermediates who want to clock up the kilometres. For the less confident, the piste map doesn't help because it picks out only the very easiest runs in blue – there are many others that are manageable. The Belvedere and Moncrons sectors at the east of the area are served only by drags but offer some wonderful, uncrowded high cruising, some of it above the tree line.

The long runs down to Jouvenceaux are splendid, confidence-boosting intermediate terrain.

The slopes above Sansicario are also excellent – and are now served by two fast quad chair-lifts, installed for the benefit of Olympic racers – but the link via the steep shoulder of M Fraiteve is problematic for those lacking confidence. You have to tackle a seriously steep drag-lift on the way out, and a short but genuine black run – the steepest pitch in the whole area – on the way back. This is a serious shortcoming in the circuit, which ought to have been rectified years ago by installation of a chair-lift.

At the higher levels, where the slopes are above the tree line, the terrain often allows a choice of route. Lower down are pretty runs through the woods, where the main complication can be route-finding. The mountainside is broken up by gullies, and pistes that appear to be quite close together but may in fact have no easy connections between them.

### FOR BEGINNERS
***There are better choices***

Sauze is not ideal for beginners: its village-level slopes are a bit on the steep side and the main nursery area is up the mountain, at Sportinia. Equally importantly, the mornings-only classes don't suit everyone. Once off the nursery slopes, the main problem is a psychological one – that most of the mountain is graded red. It would help if more of the easy reds were graded blue.

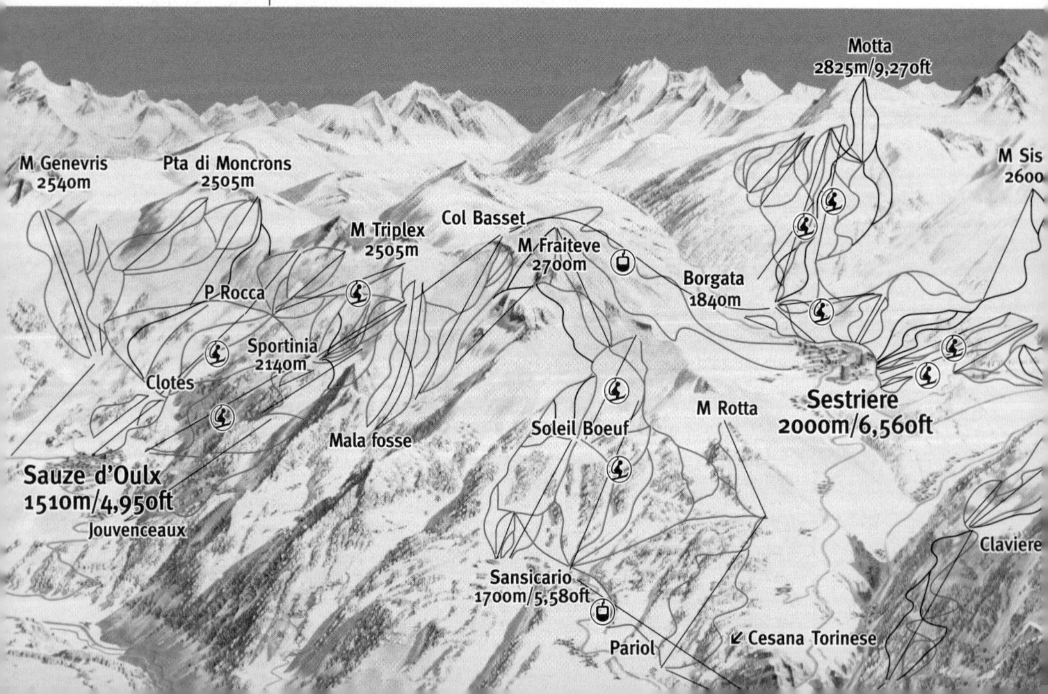

Motta 2825m/9,270ft
M Genevris 2540m
Pta di Moncrons 2505m
M Sis 2600
M Triplex 2505m
Col Basset
M Fraiteve 2700m
Borgata 1840m
P Rocca
Sportinia 2140m
Clotes
M Rotta
Sestriere 2000m/6,560ft
Soleil Boeuf
Mala fosse
Sauze d'Oulx 1510m/4,950ft
Jouvenceaux
Claviere
Sansicario 1700m/5,580ft
Pariol
Cesana Torinese

Most of the terrain is easy-intermediate stuff – one of the main exceptions being the slope from which this shot was taken. This is an obstacle to timid intermediates based in Sauze, who would relish the long runs down to Sansicario that lie beyond it ➔

SNOWPIX.COM / CHRIS GILL

## SCHOOLS

**Sauze Sportinia**
**t** 0122 850218
info@scuolasci sauzesportinia.com

**Sauze d'Oulx**
**t** 0122 858084

**Sauze Project**
**t** 0122 858942
info@sauzeproject.it

**Classes**
(Sauze Sportinia prices)
6 3hr days: €135

**Private lessons**
€30 for 1hr

## GUIDES

**Marco Degani**
**t** 0335 398984

## CHILDREN

**La Cinciarella**
**t** 0328 644 5146
lacinciarella@tin.it
Ages over 13mnth; Mon-Sat; 9am-5pm

**Ski school**
Sauze Sportinia offers classes (6 half-days €165)

### FOR CROSS-COUNTRY
***Severely limited, even with snow***
There is very little cross-country skiing, and it isn't reliable for snow.

### QUEUES
***Slow lifts the biggest problem***
There can be irritating waits at Sportinia especially when school classes set off, or just after lunch; otherwise the system has fewer, though still some noticeable, bottlenecks. Despite the introduction of fast quads over recent years, most of the lifts are ancient and terribly slow. The chair-lift from the village to Clotes is an extreme case: a museum-piece which requires you to carry your skis in your lap and hit the ground running at the top. This lift is simply inadequate. Breakdowns of elderly lifts may also be a nuisance. And a February visitor reports that several lifts were opened only at weekends, when the Italian crowds arrive.

### MOUNTAIN RESTAURANTS
***Some pleasant possibilities***
Restaurants are numerous and generally pleasant, though few are particularly special. If you like a civilised table-service lunch head for the hotel Capricorno, at Clotes. It is not cheap, and midweek in low season it can be amazingly quiet. The Ciao Pais, further up the hill, is 'a superb rustic restaurant, ideal when the weather closes in'. Pian della Rocca and Clot Bourget have also pleased visitors. There are several places at Sportinia; reporters are not generally impressed by what they deliver, but Capanna Kind does 'an awesome all-day breakfast'. The Marmotta on M Triplex is one reader's tip for 'drinks and service with a smile'. The Soleil Boeuf above Sansicario is 'good value, with a nice sun terrace'.

### SCHOOLS AND GUIDES
***Lessons variable, large classes***
A reporter this year found his daughter enthusiastic about her lesson (in a group of eight, in low season), though past reports have been mixed.

### FACILITIES FOR CHILDREN
***Tour operator alternatives***
The village kindergarten, La Cinciarella, can be booked for evenings so long as there are at least three children using the facility. You might also want to look at the nursery facilities offered by some of the major UK tour operators in the chalets and chalet-hotels that they run here – Crystal and Neilson, for example.

## STAYING THERE

### HOW TO GO
***Packaged hotels dominate***
All the major mainstream operators offer hotel packages here, but there are also a few chalets.

**Hotels** Simple 2-star and 3-star hotels form the core of the holiday accommodation, with a couple of 4-stars and some more basic places.

(((3) **Torre** (0122 858301) Cylindrical 4-star landmark 200m/650ft below the centre. Excellent rooms, 'good food', 'plenty of choice'; mini-buses to lifts.

((2) **Hermitage** (0122 850385) Neat chalet-style hotel beside the home piste from Clotes.

## GETTING THERE

**Air** Turin 84km/ 52 miles (1½hr).

**Rail** Oulx (5km/ 3 miles); frequent buses.

## ACTIVITIES

**Indoor** Bowling, cinema, games room, sauna, solarium, massage

**Outdoor** Ice rink, snowmobiling, snow-shoeing

**Phone numbers**
From abroad use the prefix +39 (and do **not** omit the initial '0' of the phone number).

## TOURIST OFFICES

**Sauze d'Oulx**
**t** 0122 858009
sauze@montagnedoc.it
www.montagnedoc.it
www.vialattea.it

**Cesana Torinese (Sansicario)**
**t** 0122 89202
cesana@montagnedoc.it

(2) **Gran Baita** (0122 850183) Comfortable place in quiet, central backstreet, with excellent food and good rooms, some with sunset views.
(2) **Biancaneve** (0122 850160) Pleasant, with smallish rooms. Near the centre.
(2) **Amis** (0122 858488) Down in Jouvenceaux, but near bus stop; simple hotel run by Anglo-Italian couple.
(2) **Stella Alpina** (0122 858731) Between Clotes and Sportinia lifts. Friendly Anglo-Italian family doing 'excellent food'.
**Self-catering** Apartments and chalets available, some through UK operators.

### EATING OUT
***Caters for all tastes and pockets***

Typical Italian banquets of five or six courses can be had in the upmarket Godfather and Cantun restaurants. The Falco does a particularly good three-course 'skiers' menu'. In the old town, the Borgo and the Griglia are popular pizzerias. The Lampione is the place to go for 'pub grub' – good-value Chinese, Mexican and Indian food. Sugo's spaghetteria provides delicious, filling and economic fare. The Pecore Nere also gets good reviews. Reservations are generally recommended.

### APRES-SKI
***Suzy does it with more dignity***

Once favoured almost solely by large groups of youngsters, some of whom were very rowdy, Sauze's bars now impress reporters young and old.

The Assietta terrace is popular for catching the last rays of the sun at the end of the day. The New Scotch bar in the hotel Stella Alpina is also popular, as is the Lampione, in the old town.

After dinner, more places warm up. One of the best is the smart, atmospheric cocktail bar Moncrons, which holds regular quiz nights. Reporters also like the Village Café (first beer free with freely available vouchers); you can eat here too ('excellent pizzas'). The Cotton Club provides good service, directors' chairs, video screen and draught cider. Miravallino is a 'very Italian' cafe bar. Paddy McGinty's offers 'a good variety of meals including Mexican and steaks'. The 'very cosy' Derby is nice for a quiet drink and a 'civilised chillout'. The Grotta offers free sandwiches with your drinks. Of the discos, the Bandito is a walk away, and popular with Italians. Schuss runs theme nights and drink promotions – entrance is normally free.

Tour operators' resort reps organise the usual range of activities.

### OFF THE SLOPES
***Go elsewhere***

Sauze is not a particularly rewarding place in which to while away the days if you don't want to hit the slopes. Shopping is limited, there are no gondolas or cable-cars for pedestrians and there are few off-slope activities. Turin or Briançon are worth a visit.

### STAYING UP THE MOUNTAIN
***'You pays your money ... '***

In most resorts, staying up the mountain is an amusing thing to do and is often economical – but usually you pay the price of accepting simple accommodation. Here, the reverse applies. The 4-star Capricorno (0122 850273), up at Clotes, is one of the most comfortable hotels in Sauze, certainly the most attractive and by a wide margin the most expensive. It's a charming little chalet beside the piste, with a smart restaurant and terrace and only eight bedrooms.

Not quite in the same league are the places up at Sportinia. Reporters who stayed here enjoyed the isolation and easy access to the slopes – but access to the village depends on expensive skidoo taxis.

## Sansicario 1700m/5,580ft

If any resort is ideally placed for exploration of the whole Milky Way, it is Sansicario. It is a modern, purpose-built, self-contained but rather soulless little resort, mainly consisting of apartments around the small shopping precinct. The 45-room Rio Envers (0122 811333) is a comfortable, expensive hotel. Visitors recommend the Enoteca in the evening for fondue and grappa.

# Selva/Sella Ronda

*Endless intermediate slopes amid spectacular Dolomite scenery*

## COSTS

①②③④⑤⑥

## RATINGS

| The slopes | |
|---|---|
| Snow | **** |
| Extent | ***** |
| Expert | *** |
| Intermediate | ***** |
| Beginner | **** |
| Convenience | *** |
| Queues | *** |
| Mountain restaurants | **** |
| **The rest** | |
| Scenery | ***** |
| Resort charm | *** |
| Off-slope | *** |

## KEY FACTS

| | |
|---|---|
| **Resort** | 1565m 5,130ft |

For the linked lift network of Val Gardena, Alta Badia, Arabba, and the Canazei and Campitello slopes of Val di Fassa

| | |
|---|---|
| **Slopes** | 1235-2520m 4,050-8,270ft |
| **Lifts** | 186 |
| **Pistes** | 395km 245 miles |
| **Blue** | 38% |
| **Red** | 53% |
| **Black** | 9% |
| **Snowmaking** | 276km 172 miles |

For Val Gardena-Alpe di Siusi only

| | |
|---|---|
| **Slopes** | 1005-2520m 3,300-8,270ft |
| **Lifts** | 81 |
| **Pistes** | 175km 109 miles |
| **Blue** | 30% |
| **Red** | 60% |
| **Black** | 10% |
| **Snowmaking** | 90km 56 miles |

- + Vast network of connected slopes – suits intermediates particularly well
- + Stunning, unique Dolomite scenery
- + Superb snowmaking and grooming
- + Jolly mountain huts with good food
- + Lift system now pretty efficient
- + Mix of open and wooded slopes
- + Good nursery slopes
- + Excellent value

- − Very few tough runs
- − Crowds on Sella Ronda circuit
- − Most runs are rather short
- − Selva is not the ideal base in the area for novices
- − Bus services are far from ideal
- − Erratic snow record; slopes vulnerable to warm weather

**This is an area unlike any other. The Sella Ronda is an amazing circular network of lifts and pistes taking you around the spectacular Gruppo Sella – a mighty limestone massif with villages scattered around it, the biggest of them being Selva (aka Wolkenstein) in Val Gardena (aka Gröden). As well as this impressive main circuit, there are major lift systems leading off it at four main points. In overall scale, the network rivals the famed Trois Vallées in France.**

**The Dolomite scenery is fabulous. But the geology that provides the visual drama also dictates the nature of the slopes. Sheer limestone cliffs rise out of gentle pasture-land; you spend your time on the latter, gazing at the former. There is scarcely a black run to be seen, and runs of more than 500m/1,640ft vertical are rare, whereas runs of under 300m/980ft vertical are not.**

**Don't overlook the several alternatives to Selva as a base. Experts and confident intermediates should consider Arabba, where classic Dolomite terrain gives way to longer, steeper slopes. For less confident intermediates the obvious choice is Corvara, where the gentlest part of the Sella Ronda meets the Alta Badia.**

## THE RESORT

Selva is a long roadside village at the head of the Val Gardena, almost merging with the next village of Santa Cristina. It suffers from traffic but has traditional-style architecture and an attractive church. The valley is famed for wood carvings, which are on display (and sale) wherever you look.

The village enjoys a lovely setting under the impressive pink-tinged walls of Sassolungo and the Gruppo Sella – a fortress-like massif about 6km/4 miles across that lies at the hub of the Sella Ronda circuit (see the feature box later in the chapter). Despite the World Cup fame of Val Gardena and animated atmosphere, Selva is neither upmarket nor brash. It's a good-value, civilised family resort – and the biggest and liveliest of the places to stay right on the Sella Ronda circuit.

For many years the area was part of Austria, and reporters admire the Tirolean charm of the resort. German is

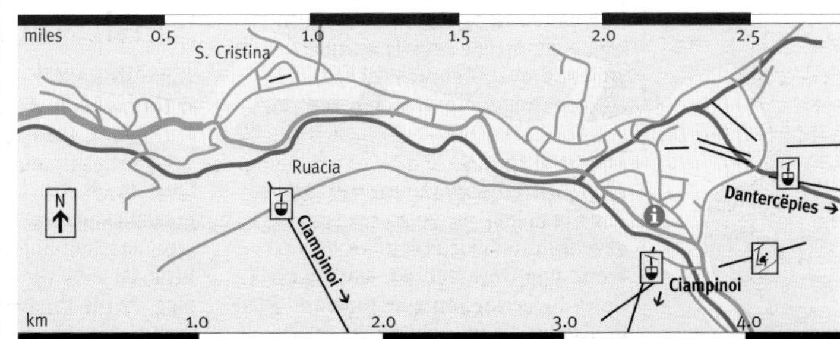

## NEWS

There is continuing investment in new fast lifts. These are recent and imminent highlights.

For 2004/05 a link between Ciampinoi and Col Raiser/ Seceda is planned – a new underground funicular across the valley at S Cristina.

Last year Alpe di Siusi gained a lift up from the village of Siusi – a 16-person gondola. One of the last remaining drags here, the Floralpina, is be replaced by a fast quad this year.

In Alta Badia, the Piz chair out of San Cassiano is to be replaced by an eight-seat gondola. Last year the old Biok lift became a fast quad. Above Corvara the Vallon chair was upgraded to a fast two-seater.

Last year the Burz chair out of Arabba was upgraded to a fast quad. A couple more drags here are to be replaced by chairs for 2004/05. Over on Marmolada, the cable-car to the glacier is to be upgraded – hopefully for 2004/05.





the main language, not Italian, and most visitors are German, too. Most places have two names: Selva is also known as Wolkenstein and the Gardena valley as Gröden. We do our bit to help with Italian unity by using the Italian place names. The local dialect, Ladin, also survives.

Ortisei is the administrative centre of Val Gardena but it is not so convenient for the Sella Ronda slopes. For a brief description of this and the other villages on or near the circuit, see the end of this chapter.

From Selva, gondolas rise in two directions. The Dantercëpies gondola, starting an irritating distance from the main village at the top of the nursery slopes, goes east towards Colfosco and Corvara, forming the start of the clockwise Sella Ronda route. The Ciampinoi gondola goes south from near the centre of the village to start the anti-clockwise route. The most convenient position is near one of these gondolas. There are regular buses until early evening – 2 euros for a weekly card – but they generate lots of complaints from reporters about infrequency, inadequate capacity, poorly sited stops, lack of services to Corvara and Plan de Gralba. There are taxis – but these are expensive.

The Dolomiti Superski pass covers not only the Sella Ronda resorts but dozens of others. It's an easy road trip to Cortina – worth it for the fabulous scenery alone. But many other drives in this area are very tortuous and slow – it's often quicker on skis.

## THE MOUNTAIN

The slopes cover a vast area, all amid stunning scenery and practically all ideally suited to intermediates. There are different piste maps for different areas, and nearly every reporter complains that they are inadequate and confusing. Piste marking and signing also come in for criticism, though the Sella Ronda route itself is well signposted. Several reporters note with approval that most of the lifts stay open until 5pm in high season.

### THE SLOPES
*High mileage piste excursions*

The **Ciampinoi** gondola accesses several pistes, including the famous World Cup Downhill run, leading back down to Selva, **Santa Cristina** and **Plan de Gralba** – and leads to the anti-clockwise Sella Ronda circuit via **Passo Sella** and **Canazei**.

The Dantercëpies gondola serves the Ladies' Downhill course and accesses the clockwise Sella Ronda circuit. From the top you head down to **Colfosco**, then lifts link with **Corvara**.

At the far corner of the circuit, opposite Selva, is **Arabba**.

At Passo Pordoi, between Canazei and Arabba, is the one breach in the defences of the Gruppo Sella: a cable-car goes up to Sass Pordoi at 2950m/9,680ft, giving access to off-piste routes – and spectacular views.

There are several linked areas that are not directly on the Sella Ronda circuit that are worth exploring. The biggest is the **Alta Badia** area to the west of Corvara – a lovely area of gentle slopes from which you can go down to **La Villa** or to **San Cassiano** and Armentarola on the road to Cortina. You can go by taxi from here to Passo Falzarego to ride the Lagazuoi cable-car and do the famously lovely Hidden Valley run, described in the Cortina chapter.

Not far from Selva is the **Col Raiser/ Seceda** area, accessed by a gondola on the outskirts of Santa Cristina. Traditionally reached by bus, this area will now be accessible by descending from Ciampinoi to ride an underground funicular across the valley. Runs descend to S Cristina or to **Ortisei**. And from Ortisei a cable-car goes up the other side of the valley to **Alpe di Siusi** – a gentle elevated area of quiet, easy runs, cross-country tracks and walks. This area can also be accessed via the big new gondola from the village of **Siusi,** to the west.

The **Marmolada** glacier beyond Arabba is open most of the winter and is included on the main lift pass. It's a trip to do more for its spectacular views than for skiing, though the red run from top to bottom is a notable 1490m/4,900ft vertical. The inadequate antique cable-car is currently being replaced – hopefully for 2004/05.

### TERRAIN-PARKS
*A few widely spread options*

Near Selva, there are boarder-cross runs at Passo Sella by the Grohmann-Cavazes chair and at Piz Sella by the Comici chair, and there's a natural half-pipe near the Sotsaslong lift at Piz Sella. At Alpe di Siusi, there's a half-pipe by the Laurin chair and a kids' terrain-park by the Euro chair. Alta

## LIFT PASSES

**Dolomiti Superski**
Covers 450 lifts and 1220km/758 miles of piste in the Dolomites, including all Sella Ronda resorts.

**Main pass**
1 day €37
6 days €182

**Senior citizens**
Over 60: 6 days €155

**Children**
Under 16: 6 days €127
Under 8: free pass

**Alternative pass**
Val Gardena pass covers all lifts in Selva Gardena, S Cristina, Ortisei and Alpe di Siusi.

Badia has a terrain-park near the Brancia restaurant and the Dolomites Fun Park at Piz la Villa. There's a half-pipe, boarder-cross and new kids' park at Belvedere above Canazei. Timed slalom runs are located in several areas – free to try.

## SNOW RELIABILITY
### *Excellent when it's cold*

The slopes are not high – there are few above 2200m/7,220ft and most are between 1500m and 2000m (5,000ft and 6,500ft). And natural snowfalls are erratic. But the area has one of the largest snowmaking systems in Europe, and we have enjoyed excellent pistes here in times of severe natural snow shortage. Most areas have snow-guns on the main runs to the resorts. World-class piste grooming adds to the effect. Typical reporter comments on the snowmaking are 'a revelation – quite superb', 'wonderful' and 'stunning'.

Problems arise only in poor snow years if it is too warm to make snow.

## FOR EXPERTS
### *A few good runs*

In general, experts may find the region too tame, especially if they're looking for lots of steep challenges or moguls.

Arabba has the best steep slopes (and snow). North-facing blacks and reds from Porta Vescovo back to Arabba are served by an efficient high-capacity gondola and are great fun. The black run down to La Villa is worth a visit, too – 'long, consistently steep, but crowded', writes a reporter. Another enjoyed the short black at Colfosco. The Val Gardena World Cup piste, the 'Saslonch', is one of several steepish runs between Ciampinoi and both Selva and Santa Cristina. Unlike many World Cup pistes it is kept in racing condition for Italian team practices, but it is open to the public much of the time. It's especially good in January, when it's not too crowded. The unpisted trail down to Santa Cristina, accessed from the Florian chair on Alpe di Siusi, is not difficult, but is pleasantly lonely.

**REPORTS WANTED**

Recently we have had few reports on this resort. If you go there, please do send us a report.

The best reports earn a copy of the next edition, and can lead to free lift passes in future.

See page 10.

Off-piste is limited because of the sheer-drop nature of the mountain tops in the Dolomites, but for the daring – and with a guide – there is excitement to be found. The itinerary from Sass Pordoi back to the cable-car station is not too difficult; the much longer route to Colfosco ends in a spectacular narrow descent through the Val de Mesdi.

### FOR INTERMEDIATES

***A huge network of ideal runs***

The Sella Ronda region is famed for easy slopes. For early or timid intermediates, the runs from Dantercëpies to Colfosco and Corvara, and over the valley from there in the Alta Badia, are superb for cruising and confidence-boosting. They're easy to reach from Selva, but returning from Dantercëpies may be a little daunting. Riding the gondola down is an option.

Nearer to Selva, the runs in the Plan de Gralba area are gentle – but the red run to get there from Ciampinoi is a real obstacle – steep and crowded. The Alpe di Siusi above Ortisei is ideal for confidence-building – very gentle, quiet, amid superb scenery. A 2004 reporter loved the 'long red' down to Saltria from Punta d'Oro and those at Spitzbuhl were 'enjoyable and never busy'. The runs at Mont de Seura, between this area and Ciampinoi, are also recommended for avoiding the crowds. On the rather neglected Seceda sector there is a splendid easy blue back to S Cristina (the lower half is marked red on some maps but is of blue gradient).

**THE SELLA RONDA**

*The Sella Ronda is one of the world's classic intermediate circuits. The journey around the Sella massif is easily managed in a day by even an early intermediate. The slopes you descend are almost all easy, and take you through Selva, Colfosco, Corvara, Arabba and Canazei. You can do the circuit in either direction by following very clear coloured signs. The clockwise route is slightly quicker and offers more interesting slopes; but at Porta Vescovo above Arabba timid intermediates should be sure to find the red run and not struggle down the black. There are two free maps available; map-literate people will want the proper topographical one with contour lines, from the tourist office (not lift stations).*

*The runs total around 23km/14 miles and the lifts around 14km/9 miles. The lifts take a total of about two hours (plus any queuing). We've done it in just three and a half hours plus some diversions and hut stops; five or six hours is a realistic time during busy periods, when there are crowds both on the pistes and on the lifts. If possible, choose low season or a Saturday, and set out early.*

*Not everyone likes it. 'It's a bit of a slog,' said one reporter. Others have found the circuit 'boring', and 'a bit of a rat race', but agree that 'it is a good way to get to other areas'. Boarders beware: there are quite a few flat bits.*

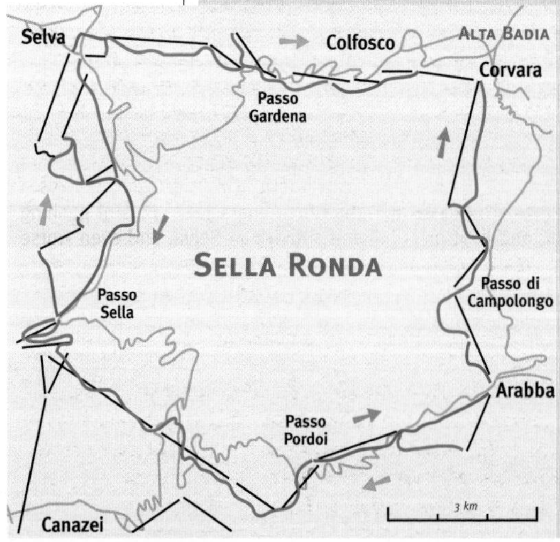


*If you set out early, you can make more of the day by taking some diversions from the circuit. Among the most entertaining segments are the long runs down from Ciampinoi to Santa Cristina and Selva, from Dantercëpies to Selva, from the top of the Boe gondola back down to Corvara and from the top of the Arabba gondola. Take in all those in a day doing the circuit and you'll have had a good day.*

*Intermediates could take time out to explore the off-the-circuit Alta Badia area from Corvara. Groups of different abilities can do the circuit and arrange to meet along the way at some of the many welcoming rifugios.*

The stunning scenery is a major attraction of this whole area →

APT VAL DI FASSA

## SCHOOLS

**Selva Gardena**
**t** 0471 795156
info@ski-factory.it

**2000**
**t** 0471 773125
snowboardvalgardena@val-gardena.com

**Peter Runggaldier**
**t** 0471 773282
info@peterrunggaldier.com

**Classes**
(Selva prices)
6 days (5 half days and one full day)
€151

**Private lessons**
€41 for 1hr

Average intermediates have a very large network of suitable pistes, though there are few long runs. One notable one is the beautiful red swoop Cucasattel on Seceda to Ortisei. The Plan de Gralba area, the runs from the Florian chair on Alpe di Siusi and the main pistes to San Cassiano and La Villa in the Alta Badia area are other recommended cruises. Don't neglect the Edelweiss valley, off the Sella Ronda circuit at Colfosco – 'nice, gentle slopes' and 'uncrowded and peaceful' said two recent reporters.

Several reporters also enjoyed the area above Canazei, below the Belvedere: 'Efficient lifts and good snow. The red to Lupo Bianco is a beautiful run through the trees.'

The runs back to Selva direct from Ciampinoi are a bit more challenging, as are the descents from Dantercëpies to Selva. Those at Arabba can be tricky and a reporter warns of the red run from Passo Padon – narrow, steep and unnerving in places – which is the only way back from Marmolada.

The spectacular Hidden Valley on the way to Cortina is also worth a visit. See the Cortina chapter for details.

### FOR BEGINNERS
***Great slopes, but ...***

The village nursery slopes are excellent – spacious, convenient, and kept in good condition. In the area as a whole, near-beginners have lots of splendid gentle long runs to progress to but Selva isn't the ideal base for access to them – Corvara or Colfosco are much better placed.

### FOR CROSS-COUNTRY
***Beautiful trails***

There are 98km/61 miles of trails, all enjoying wonderful scenery. The 12km/7 mile trail up the Vallunga-Langental valley is particularly attractive, with neck-craning views all around. Almost half the trails have the advantage of being at altitude, running between Monte Pana and Seiseralm, and across Alpe di Siusi.

### QUEUES
***Still a few problems***

New lifts have vastly improved the area, and there are now fewer bottlenecks. Most recently, the fast quad out of Arabba has greatly improved matters there, and the new gondola out of San Cassiano should solve the serious queue problem there. The chairs from Corvara towards Selva remain 'unacceptable bottlenecks'; other problems reported this year are the Dantercëpies gondola and the Sass Becè six-pack to Passo Pordoi. You may find the length of queues on the Sella Ronda circuit less of a problem than their character – 'Lots of pushing and shoving at Selva, and even worse at Corvara,' says one reporter – and the crowds on the pistes. The trip from

### boarding

*Snowboarding is not particularly big in the area, but things are becoming more boarder-friendly. The main lifts out of Selva are all gondolas or chairs and more drag-lifts are being replaced by chairs and gondolas. If you want to do the Sella Ronda, there are some frustratingly flat sections where you have to scoot or walk – reporters recommend the anti-clockwise route as best.*

## CHILDREN

**Kindergarten**
(run by ski school)
For ages 2 up; skiing available for ages 3 upwards

**Ski school**
6 days (4 half days and two full days) €172 at Selva school

## GETTING THERE

**Air** Verona 190km/118 miles (3hr); Bolzano 40km/25 miles (45min); Treviso 130km/81 miles (2½hr).

**Rail** Chiusa (27km/17 miles), Bressanone (35km/22 miles), Bolzano (40km/25 miles); frequent buses from station.





Arabba to Marmolada is getting less painful: the antiquated cable-car to the glacier, which regularly provokes complaints, is finally being replaced, hopefully for 2004/05.

### MOUNTAIN RESTAURANTS
***One of the area's highlights***

There are lots of huts all over the area, and virtually all of them are lively, with helpful staff, good food, plenty of character and modest prices.

In Val Gardena the Panorama is a small, cosy, rustic suntrap at the foot of the Dantercëpies drag. On the way down to Plan de Gralba from Ciampinoi, the Vallongia Rolandhütte is tucked away on a corner of the piste. In the Plan de Gralba area the top station of the cable-car does excellent pizza; the Comici is atmospheric, with a big terrace. Piz Seteur has 'superb lasagne' and is also recommended late in the day (see Après-ski).

The trio of little huts in the Colfosco area – Forcelles (now non-smoking), Edelweiss and Pradat – are all very pleasant but can get very busy.

At Alta Badia the Piz Sorega above San Cassiano gets very crowded. La Brancia does 'wonderful polenta and delicious blackberry grappa'. The Saraghes is 'friendly and popular' and 'serves generous portions'. Cherz above Passo di Campolongo has great views of Marmolada. The Pralongia is 'welcoming and cosy' with 'a wonderful array of pastries and strudels'.

Around Arabba, Bec de Roces and Col de Burz are both suntraps (with 'amazing Bombardinos' at the latter). The rifugio at the top of the Porta Vescovo lifts has been recommended for 'excellent food' and 'stunning panoramic views'. But a favourite of a 2004 visitor was the 'lively' Rifugio Plan Boè. And Capanna Bill, near the Marmolada lifts, is a good beer stop on the way back to Arabba.

In the Seceda sector there are countless options. The cosy Sangon 'has bags of atmosphere', though another reporter pronounces Baita Gamsblut her favourite: 'Super rustic hut with a good menu and a warm, friendly atmosphere.' The Seceda does 'wonderful food, served by waitresses in miniskirts or leather shorts', which brightened our reporter's day.

On Alpe di Siusi the rustic Sanon refuge gets a good review, particularly since 'the barman came out to serenade us with his accordion'. The table-service restaurant at the bottom of the Monte Piz lift is also highly rated – 'good value', 'huge portions'. And the Williams hut at the top of the Florian chair has 'superb views'.

Above Canazei there are at least six huts scattered around the Belvedere bowl. Baita Belvedere is 'a good place for lunch, with excellent service' and a 'superb view'. Rifugio Salei offers table or self-service and is recommended. Lower down, Lupo Bianco is a notable rendezvous point and suntrap. As well as restaurants, there are lots of little snow bars for a quick grappa.

### SCHOOLS AND GUIDES
***Mixed views***

The Selva school is capable of good instruction, provided you get into a suitable group. One reporter found that the level of tuition was good 'but groups tended to alter on a daily basis, dependent on numbers'. The emphasis seemed to be on economic grouping rather than learners' needs. Another visitor calls the ski school at Pecol, above Canazei, 'excellent'.

### FACILITIES FOR CHILDREN
***Good by Italian standards***

There are comprehensive childcare arrangements, but German and Italian are the main languages here and English is not routinely spoken. That said, in the past we have had reports of very enjoyable lessons and of children longing to return.

## STAYING THERE

### HOW TO GO
***A reasonable choice***

These resorts now feature in quite a few tour op brochures. Arabba is increasingly popular with reporters.

**Chalets** There is a fair choice of catered chalets, including some good ones with en suite bathrooms.

**Hotels** There are a dozen 4-stars, over 30 3-stars and numerous lesser hotels. Few of the best are well positioned.

(((3) **Gran Baita** (0471 795210) Large, luxurious sporthotel, with lots of mod cons including indoor pool. A few minutes' walk from centre and lifts.

(((3) **Aaritz** (0471 795011) Best-placed 4-star, opposite the Ciampinoi gondola, and with an open fire.

((2) **Astor** (0471 795207) Family-run chalet in centre. Good value.

((2) **Continental** (0471 795411) 3-star situated right on the nursery slopes.

## ACTIVITIES

In Val Gardena:

**Indoor** Swimming pool, sauna, bowling, squash, ice rink, ice hockey, museum, concerts, cinema, billiards, tennis, climbing wall, fitness centre

**Outdoor** Sleigh rides, snow-shoeing, toboggan runs, paragliding, extensive cleared paths, climbing

**Phone numbers**
From abroad use the prefix +39 (and do **not** omit the initial '0' of the phone number).

## TOURIST OFFICES

**VAL GARDENA**
**t** 0471 792277
www.valgardena.it

**Selva**
**t** 0471 795122
selva@valgardena.it

**Ortisei**
**t** 0471 796328
ortisei@valgardena.it

**ALTA BADIA**
www.altabadia.org

**Corvara**
**t** 0471 836176
corvara@altabadia.org

**Colfosco**
**t** 0471 836145
colfosco@altabadia.org

**San Cassiano**
**t** 0471 849422
s.cassiano@altabadia.org

**La Villa**
**t** 0471 847037
lavilla@altabadia.org



(2) **Linder** (0471 795242) 'Friendly, family-run with good food.'
(2) **Olympia** (0471 795145) Well positioned 3-star.
(2) **Pralong** (0471 795370) An uphill walk from the centre, but 'one of the best hotels we've visited', says a reporter – endorsed again in 2004.
(2) **Solaia** (0471 795104) 3-star chalet, superbly positioned for lifts and slopes.
**Self-catering** There are plenty of apartments to choose from. We have had excellent reports of the Villa Gardena (0471 794602) and Isabell (0471 794562) apartments.

### EATING OUT
***Plenty of good-value choices***

Selva offers both Austrian and Italian food at prices to suit all pockets. The higher-quality restaurants are mainly hotel-based. The Bellavista is good for pasta and Costabella for Tirolean specialities and 'large measures of spirits'. Rino's has 'excellent pizza'.

### APRES-SKI
***Above average for a family resort***

Nightlife is lively and informal, though the village is so scattered there is little on-street atmosphere. La Stua is an après-ski bar on the Sella Ronda route, with live music on some nights. For an early drink we are told that the Piz Seteur bar, above Plan de Gralba, is worth a little detour from the route – 'fun, loud and a bit raunchy' (you may find scantily clad girls dancing on the bar). For a civilised early drink try the good-value ski-school bar at the base of the Dantercëpies piste. Or the Costabella – cosy, serving good gluhwein. Café Mozart on the main street is 'a great place for cakes'.

For thigh-slapping in Selva later on, the Laurinkeller has good atmosphere though it's 'quite expensive', while the popular Luislkeller is 'very German', 'lively' with loud music and barmaids in Tirolean garb.

The Bula has 'a DJ and great music'. The hotel Stella disco next door has a 'good crowd and is well used by Brits'.

### OFF THE SLOPES
***Good variety***

There's a sports centre, snow-shoeing, lovely walks, tobogganing and sleigh rides on Alpe di Siusi. There is a bus to Ortisei, which is well worth a visit for its large hot-spring swimming pool (recently renovated and improved), shops, restaurants and lovely old buildings.

Pedestrians can reach numerous good restaurants by gondola or cable-car. Car drivers have Bolzano and Innsbruck within reach and tour operators do trips to Cortina.

## Ortisei 1235m/4,050ft

Ortisei is an attractive, prosperous market town with a life of its own, and its local slopes aren't on the main Sella Ronda circuit. It's full of lovely buildings, pretty churches and pleasant shops. The lift to the Seceda slopes is easily reached from the centre by a 300m/980ft-long series of underground moving walkways and escalators; the Alpe di Siusi lifts are a similar distance out, but more of an effort, involving a steep, icy uphill walk. The nursery area, school and kindergarten are at the foot of these slopes, but there's a fair range of family accommodation on the piste side of the road. The fine public indoor pool and ice rink are also here.

There are hotels and self-catering to suit all tastes and pockets and many good restaurants, mainly specialising in local dishes. A reporter recommends the Hotel Alpenheim (0471 796515): 'luxurious rooms', 'excellent food' but not central. Après-ski is quite jolly, and many bars keep going till late.

## Corvara 1570m/5,150ft

Corvara is the most animated village east of Selva, with plenty of hotels, restaurants, bars and sports facilities.

It's well positioned, with village lifts heading off to reasonably equidistant Selva, Arabba and San Cassiano, and has gentle slopes for beginners. The main shops and some hotels cluster around a small piazza, but the rest of the place sprawls along the valley floor. The Posta Zirm in Corvara does a ski-boot tea dance but support may depend on tour ops organising group transport back to other villages. The hotel Posta Zirm has a large new spa facility. There's a covered ice rink, indoor tennis courts and an outdoor artificial climbing wall. The hotel Table is recommended by reporters for its piano bar and good cakes.

## Colfosco 1645m/5,400ft

Colfosco is a smaller, quieter version of Corvara, 2km/1 mile away. It has a fairly compact centre with a sprawl of large hotels along the road towards Selva. It's connected to Corvara by a horizontal-running chair-lift. In the opposite direction, a gondola heads off to Passo Gardena, from where you can then press on to Selva.

## Arabba 1600m/5,250ft

Arabba is a small, traditional-style village. But it is growing fast, as the market wakes up to its excellent position – well placed for exploring the Sella Ronda circuit while avoiding the worst of the crowds starting from Selva and Corvara, and set at the foot of high, north-facing slopes, which have the best natural snow and steepest pistes in the Dolomites. It is not a good choice for beginners or timid intermediates – there is a small nursery slope, but access to longer easy runs is tricky.

Of the dozen or so hotels, reporters recommend the 3-star Portavescovo (0436 79139): 'Excellent: wonderful food, nicely furnished rooms and a well-equipped fitness centre' (with the only pool in the village). The 3-star B&B hotel Royal (0436 79293) offers 'incredible value for money' – large rooms, sauna, hot-tub and Turkish bath. Chalets and self-catering accommodation are available.

The après-ski is limited – but it is cheap. The atmospheric Rifugio Plan Boè up the mountain is good for a last drink on the pistes before heading back to the village – 'loud 70s, 80s and Europop music', The 'friendly' Bar Peter and cosy hotel bars are the focal points in the village. The lively Stube bar attracts tour op reps and young teenagers, say recent reporters. The Hotel Portavescovo's happy hour is very good value and the Albergio Pordoi has 'the biggest selection of drinks in town'. Restaurant choice is limited, too. The central hotels all have busy restaurants. 7 Sass does 'wonderful enormous pizzas and little else'. Al Table is recommended for its 'great food', 'wide range' and 'good value'. You can go up to Rifugio Plan Boè by snowmobile for a 'special' 3-course dinner and dancing – 'the best meal we had'.

## San Cassiano 1530m/5,020ft

San Cassiano is a pretty little village, set in an attractive, tree-filled valley. It's a quiet, slightly upmarket resort, full of well-heeled Italian families and comfortable hotels. The local slopes, the sizeable and attractive Alta Badia, form a spur off the main Sella Ronda circuit. Adventurers who want to do the circuit repeatedly will find getting to it a tiresome business. At least the new gondola, planned to replace the main chair out of the village, will get you off to a quick start. Trips to the Hidden Valley are also easily arranged.

The best hotel is the 4-star Rosa Alpina (0471 849500). Mountainsun has a jumbo chalet here – 'brilliantly located' on the piste, according to one guest. Après-ski starts up the mountain with loud music at Las Vegas. Nightlife is very limited: the Rosa Alpina has dancing and there's a bowling alley. Walking in the pretty scenery is the main off-slope activity; swimming is the other.

## La Villa 1435m/4,710ft

La Villa is similar to neighbouring San Cassiano in most respects – small, quiet, pretty, unspoiled – but it is slightly closer to Corvara, making it rather better placed for the main Sella Ronda circuit. The home pistes are challenging – genuine red and black. Village amenities include a pool and skating on a frozen lake.

## Canazei 1465m/4,810ft

Canazei is a sizeable village at the south-west corner of the Sella Ronda circuit. It is covered in the new chapter on Trentino.

## Campitello 1445m/4,740ft

Campitello is a pleasant, unremarkable village, smaller and quieter than next-door Canazei and still unspoiled. It is covered in the chapter on Trentino.

**Phone numbers**
From abroad use the prefix +39 (and do **not** omit the initial '0' of the phone number).

**TOURIST OFFICES**

**VAL DI FASSA**
www.fassa.com

**Canazei**
**t** 0462 601113
infocanazei@fassa.com

**Campitello**
**t** 0462 750500
infocampitello@fassa.com

**ARABBA**
**t** 0436 780019
info@arabba.it
www.arabba.it

# Sestriere

*Altitude is the main attraction – maybe the only attraction*

**COSTS**

(1)(2)(3)(4)(5)(6)

**RATINGS**

| **The slopes** | |
|---|---|
| Snow | *** |
| Extent | **** |
| Expert | *** |
| Intermediate | **** |
| Beginner | *** |
| Convenience | **** |
| Queues | *** |
| Mountain restaurants | ** |
| **The rest** | |
| Scenery | *** |
| Resort charm | * |
| Off-slope | * |

**NEWS**

For 2004/05 the Clos dell'Acqua drag is to be replaced. Last year the Garnel drag was replaced by a quad chair and the Trebials chair from Borgata was replaced by a fast quad.

Turin is to host the 2006 Olympic Winter Games; Sestriere will host the men's Alpine events.

**KEY FACTS**

| | |
|---|---|
| **Resort** | 2000m 6,560ft |
| For Milky Way | |
| **Slopes** | 1390-2825m 4,560-9,270ft |
| **Lifts** | 88 |
| **Pistes** | 400km 249 miles |
| **Blue** | 25% |
| **Red** | 55% |
| **Black** | 20% |
| **Snowmaking** | 120km 75 miles |
| For Sestriere-Sauze d'Oulx-Sansicario | |
| **Slopes** | 1390-2825m 4,560-9,270ft |
| **Lifts** | 51 |
| **Pistes** | 300km 186 miles |
| **Snowmaking** | 90km 56 miles |

- \+ Snow reliability is usually good, with extensive snowmaking back-up
- \+ Local slopes suitable for most levels, with some tougher runs than most neighbouring resorts
- \+ Part of the extensive Franco-Italian Milky Way area, but ...

- − Situated at one extreme of the Milky Way area – so inconvenient for exploration of the whole network
- − The purpose-built village is an eyesore, and much of it is rather scruffy, though likely to improve for the 2006 Winter Olympics
- − Weekend and peak-period queues
- − Little après-ski during the week

**Sestriere was built for snow – high, with north-west-facing slopes – and it has very extensive snowmaking, too. So even if you are let down by the notoriously erratic snowfalls in this corner of Italy, you should be fairly safe here – certainly safer than in Sauze d'Oulx, over the hill. Whether this is a sensible basis for choosing to stay here is another question. When we go to Italy, we generally aim to go somewhere a bit more captivating.**

## THE RESORT

Sestriere was the Alps' first purpose-built resort, developed by Giovanni Agnelli in the 1930s. It sits on a broad, sunny and windy col, and neither the site nor the village, with its large apartment blocks, looks very hospitable – though the buildings have benefited from recent investment. New building work, including a large residential building close to the Cit Roc chair, is already in evidence in preparation for the 2006 Olympics. There are some interesting buildings, but much of the village still seems rather scruffy. This is not the most convenient of purpose-built resorts, but location is not crucial. The satellite of Borgata, 200m/660ft lower, is less convenient for nightlife and shops.

## THE MOUNTAINS

Sestriere is at one extreme of the big Franco-Italian Milky Way area. The local slopes have two main sectors: Sises, directly in front of the village, and more varied Motta, above Borgata – to the north-east and 225m/740ft higher.

**Slopes** There are mainly drag- and chair-lifts on the local north-west-facing slopes. Access to Sansicario and the rest of the Milky Way is via gondola from Borgata to Col Basset, at the top of the Sauze d'Oulx area, and a drag-lift back up to Monte Fraiteve. In theory the return to Sestriere is via the red run down from Monte Fraiteve to the northern side of the village or via a long red from the top of the gondola at Col Basset, but we've yet to see these runs open and usually you have to ride the gondola down. Signposting and the piste map are poor. There's night skiing twice a week.

**Terrain-parks** The terrain-park next to the Cit Roc chair on Sises was rebuilt and enlarged a couple of seasons ago.

**Snow reliability** With most of the local slopes facing north-west and ranging from 1840m to 2825m (6,040ft to 9,270ft), and an extensive snowmaking network covering most of the Sises sector and half of Motta, snow-cover is usually reliable for most of the season. The notoriously erratic snowfalls in the Milky Way often leave the rest of the area seriously short of snow while the extensive snowmaking in Sestriere provides fairly reliable cover. The sunny runs down from Sauze do not benefit from any artificial back-up.

**Experts** There is a fair amount to amuse experts – steep pistes served by the drags at the top of both sectors (though don't go hoping for moguls, which are erased religiously), and off-piste slopes in several directions from here and Monte Fraiteve.

**Intermediates** Both sectors also offer plenty for confident intermediates, who can explore practically all of the Milky Way areas, conditions permitting.

**Beginners** The terrain is good for beginners, with several nursery areas

There are resorts that look worse than Sestriere; but they are few, and most are more conveniently arranged ➔

SNOWPIX.COM / CHRIS GILL





## PISTE MAP

Sestriere is covered on the Sauze d'Oulx map a few pages back.

## REPORTS WANTED

Recently we have had few reports on this resort. If you go there, please do send us a report.

The best reports earn a copy of the next edition, and can lead to free lift passes in future.

See page 10.

**Phone numbers**
From abroad use the prefix +39 (and do **not** omit the initial '0' of the phone number).

## TOURIST OFFICE

**t** 0122 755444
sestriere@montagnedoc.it
www.sestriere.it
www.montagnedoc.it
www.vialattea.it

and the gentlest of easy runs down to Borgata. However, one reporter points out that there is a lack of easy intermediate runs to progress to.
**Snowboarding** Sestriere has a reasonable number of chairs, but there are also lots of drag-lifts.
**Cross-country** There are two loops covering a total of 10km/6 miles.
**Queues** The lifts are mainly modern, though there are still some inadequate old ones. But queues for the main lifts occur at the weekends and holidays. The lifts from Borgata to Sestriere should now be less of a bottleneck at the end of the day. Queues occur when poor weather closes the gondola link to Sauze. Reporters here, as in Sauze, complain that some lifts may be kept closed during the week, either to conserve money or snow.
**Mountain restaurants** The Raggio di Sole in the Anfiteatro sector is a 'cosy log cabin'. Another reporter recommends the Tana della Volpe at the top of the Banchetta chair, but on the whole the local mountain restaurants are only fair. There are better ones further afield.
**Schools and guides** Lack of spoken English can be a problem.
**Facilities for children** There are no special facilities for children.

## STAYING THERE

**How to go** Most accommodation is in apartments.
**Hotels** There are a dozen hotels, mostly 3-star or 4-star. The Savoy Edelweiss (0122 77040) and the Du Col (0122 76990) are central, and just out of the village is the luxurious Principi di Piemonte (0122 7941). The distinctive towers in the centre are the Club Med quarters.
**Eating out** There are plenty of options. Try Lu Periol for home-made ravioli and atmosphere. Tre Rubinetti has been highly recommended for 'outstanding Italian cooking' and an enormous wine list. Last Tango and the Baita are also well regarded.
**Après-ski** Après-ski is quiet during the week but becomes lively at weekends: the Prestige and Palace are two of the many little bars that liven up. The Pinky is one of the best of the bars that double as eateries, with lots of low sofas in the classic Italian casual-chic style, an antipasto buffet and 'great choices of pizzas'.
**Off the slopes** There are some smart shops and there's a fitness centre, an ice rink and a sports centre. A swimming pool was built in 2003.

CONSORZIO OPERATORI TURISTICA LA THUILE

# La Thuile

*Little-known resort with extensive, easy slopes and link with France*

## COSTS

①②③④⑤⑥

## RATINGS

**The slopes**

| | |
|---|---|
| Snow | **** |
| Extent | *** |
| Expert | ** |
| Intermediate | **** |
| Beginner | **** |
| Convenience | *** |
| Queues | **** |
| Mountain restaurants | * |

**The rest**

| | |
|---|---|
| Scenery | *** |
| Resort charm | *** |
| Off-slope | ** |

## NEWS

For 2004/05, two fast six-packs are planned to replace the two slow lifts that were the main ways back up the mountain from La Rosière (see the La Rosière chapter).

The area including La Rosière's slopes has been renamed Espace San Bernardo.

For 2003/04 a new black piste (n33), by the Arnouvaz chair, was supposed to have replaced the existing red piste, but the slope was still red on all the piste maps we saw – very Italian! And a new mountain restaurant called Le Melèze opened.

**Phone numbers**
From abroad use the prefix +39 (and do **not** omit the initial '0' of the phone number).

## REPORTS WANTED

Recently we have had few reports on this resort. If you go there, please do send us a report.

- + Fair-sized area with good lift system linked to La Rosière in France
- + Free of crowds and queues
- + Excellent beginner and easy intermediate slopes
- + Some slope-side accommodation

- – Most of the seriously tough pistes are low down, and most of the low, woodland runs are tough
- – Mountain restaurants are generally disappointing
- – Not the place for lively après-ski

**La Thuile deserves to be better known internationally. The slopes best suit beginners and intermediates not seeking challenges, but are not devoid of interest for experts, particularly if the snow conditions are good.**

**When you venture over the border to La Rosière, you'll notice that the grooming is better on the Italian side and that the Italian piste classification often overstates difficulty. Moving from gentle red runs to bumpy blues may be a shock.**

## THE RESORT

La Thuile is a resort of parts. At the foot of the lifts is the modern Planibel complex, with places to stay, a leisure centre, bars, shops and restaurants – like a French purpose-built resort, but with a distinctly Italian atmosphere. But many people find this rather soulless and prefer to stay in the old town across the river (served by a regular free bus service). Much of the old town has been restored and new buildings (and an underground car park) tastefully added. There are reasonable restaurants and bars.

The slopes link with La Rosière, over the border in France. Courmayeur is easily reached by car, and Cervinia is about an hour away.

## THE MOUNTAINS

La Thuile has quite extensive slopes, with the great attraction that they are normally very uncrowded. Many runs are marked red, but deserve no more than a blue rating. The lift system is excellent in general: a fast chair or gondola takes you up the mountain, and there are high-speed chairs to the top. There may be some queues at the gondola first thing, but not usually at the alternative chair. One reporter describes La Thuile as 'like Heaven' compared to La Rosière for lifts and slope maintenance.

**Slopes** The lifts out of the village take you to Les Suches, with shady black runs going back down directly to the village through the trees, and reds taking a more roundabout route. From here chairs and drags take you to Chaz Dura for access to a variety of gentle bowls facing east. You can go off westwards from here to the Petit St Bernard road. From both sides there are lifts back to the ridge, the high-point of Belvedere being the launch pad for excursions via the Col de la Traversette to La Rosière in France. The French slopes are largely south-facing and tend to be steeper.

**Terrain-parks** There are no specific facilities.

**Snow reliability** Most of La Thuile's slopes are north- or east-facing and above 2000m/6,560ft, so the snow generally keeps well. There's also a decent amount of snowmaking.

**Experts** The only steep pistes are those down through the trees from Les Suches: the steepest – the Diretta and Tre – are serious stuff. The area above the Petit St Bernard road has some genuinely black terrain and plenty of off-piste – the fast quad means you can do quick circuits in this area.

Heli-lifts are available. One of the best, to the Ruitor glacier, has a 20km/12 mile run into France ending near Ste-Foy, a short taxi ride from La Rosière and the lifts back to La Thuile.

**Intermediates** La Thuile has some good intermediate runs, and its link with La Rosière adds adventure; but the start of the route back from La Rosière is a fairly tricky red, and most of La Rosière is quite challenging. The bowls above Les Suches have many gentle blue and red runs, ideal for cruising and practising. There are also long reds

↑ One of La Thuile's many gentle runs, which make it good for early intermediates and beginners

CONSORZIO OPERATORI TURISTICA LA THUILE

## KEY FACTS

| | |
|---|---|
| **Resort** | 1440m 4,720ft |
| For Espace San Bernardo (La Rosière and La Thuile) | |
| **Slopes** | 1175-2610m 3,850-8,560ft |
| **Lifts** | 37 |
| **Pistes** | 150km 93 miles |
| **Green** | 7% |
| **Blue** | 40% |
| **Red** | 38% |
| **Black** | 15% |
| **Snowmaking** | 276 guns |

## TOURIST OFFICE

t 0165 884179
info@lathuile.it
www.lathuile.it

through the trees back to the resort. The red runs on the other side of the top ridge, down towards the Petit St Bernard road, offer a greater challenge.

**Beginners** There are nursery slopes at village level and up at Les Suches. There's a good gentle green run above there, and easy blues. Promenade is 'a very easy blue and good for beginners', but is served by drag-lifts. You ride the gondola back down.

**Snowboarding** These are great slopes for learning. You need ride only chair-lifts and the gondola, and most of the slopes are easy. For the more experienced there are great tree runs, and the link with France offers off-piste possibilities. There is good free-riding, and some good carving runs.

**Cross-country** La Thuile has four loops of varying difficulty on the valley floor, adding up to 20km/12 miles of track.

**Queues** The resort has a very effective lift system for the number of visitors, and all our reporters comment that they never had to queue.

**Mountain restaurants** There are few notable places – disappointing, for Italy. In the Riondet (on Chaz Dura) a reporter found 'genuinely good food and hospitality'. The place at the foot of the Chalets chair lift does 'tasty, reasonably priced food' and has a 'good atmosphere'. A new restaurant called Le Melèze opened near the top of the gondola last season – reports welcome please.

**Schools and guides** Reporters say the ski school has reasonably sized classes and fair instruction in good English.

**Facilities for children** There's an 'excellent' nursery, a Miniclub, and children over the age of five can join adult ski classes.

## STAYING THERE

**How to go** The number of tour operators going there is increasing.

**Hotels** The choice is between the characterless 4-star Planibel, a few 3-stars and some simpler places. Hotel du Glacier, a short walk to the slopes above the lifts, is described as a 'quiet, friendly, family-run, with good buffet breakfasts' by a 2004 reporter.

**Self-catering** The Planibel apartments are spacious, right by the lifts and great value. Some 'have been refurbished and are quite smart', but others are 'tired and urgently need refurbishing'.

**Eating out** Reader recommendations include the Bricole 'expensive but well worth it', the Fordze (French/Italian local dishes) and the Rascard (pizza).

**Après-ski** Nightlife is 'not vibrant' and 'even quieter' than one recent reporter expected. The Cage aux Folles is popular from 4pm till late. The Lord Whymper pub has been recommended. The Bricole is the busiest and liveliest bar. The Fantasia disco at the Planibel warms up well after midnight.

**Off the slopes** The Planibel complex has a good pool, but there are few attractive walks or shops. Pedestrians can ride up the gondola for lunch.

# Trentino

*A winter playground that deserves to be better known in Britain*

**Trentino is a fabulously scenic area that is rather neglected by the British. It has a great many small ski areas that you won't have heard of, as well as a few large ones that are better known. The following guide is not comprehensive; but it certainly includes all the places that are likely to be of international interest, and more. Several areas spread across the borders of Trentino into Alto Adige, Lombardia or Veneto.**

## EAST OF TRENTO

Skiers doing the famous Sella Ronda circuit – usually from a base in Val Gardena, such as Selva – stray into Trentino on the slopes above Canazei and Campitello in the Val di Fassa, in the extreme north-east of Trentino.

### CANAZEI 1465m/4,810ft

**Canazei is a sizeable, bustling, pretty, roadside village of narrow streets, rustic old buildings, traditional-style hotels and nice little shops, set in the Sella Ronda's most heavily wooded section of mountains. There's plenty going on generally – and it has been recommended by many reporters.**

There are no really luxurious hotels, but the grand 3-star Dolomiti (0462 601106) in the middle of town is one of the original resort hotels. The chalet-style Diana (0462 601477) is charming, and five minutes from the village centre.

There are numerous restaurants. The Stala, Melester and Te Cevana are all worth a try. And après-ski is really animated. La Stua di Ladins serves good local wines. The Husky and Roxy bars are worth a visit.

Off-slope entertainment consists of beautiful walks and shopping. There's also a pool, sauna, Turkish baths and skating in neighbouring Alba.

A 12-person gondola is the only mountain access point, but it shifts the queues (which can be long) quickly.

A single piste back to the village is linked to runs returning from both Selva and Arabba (see Selva chapter), but it is often closed. The local Belvedere slopes are easy, with mountain restaurants scattered here and there. The village nursery slope is

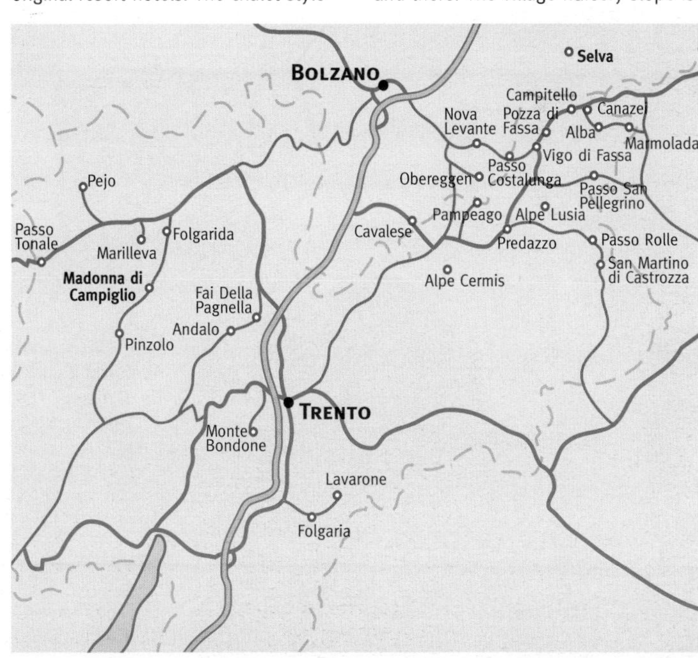

In Trentino.
A holiday on and
off the slopes.

good but inconvenient, and so unlikely to be used after day one.

Lack of spoken English in the school and kindergarten can be a problem.

**CAMPITELLO 1445m/4,740ft**

**Campitello is a pleasant, unremarkable village, smaller and quieter than next-door Canazei, and still unspoiled. It's quiet during the day, having no slopes to the village (though you can take the piste to Canazei and catch a bus).**

A reporter recommends the 4-star hotel Soroghes (0462 750060): 'Superb food and accommodation, helpful staff, excellent facilities.' Another enjoyed a stay at the hotel Sella Ronda (0462 750525). Campitello is quite lively – we've had trouble getting near the bar of the throbbing Da Giulio in the early evening, and a reporter suggests that it's even busier later on. There's an ice rink. But there appear to be no children's facilities. A cable-car takes you up into the Sella Ronda circuit.

Nearby, **Alba** has its own little area of slopes. A bit further away is the well-known glacier of **Marmolada**, on the border with Veneto, reachable on skis from Arabba on the Sella Ronda circuit (see Selva chapter). A little way down the Val di Fassa, **Pozza di Fassa** and **Vigo di Fassa** have lifts on either side of the valley. Not far from the valley town of Moena is the lift system of **Alpe Lusia**, but off to the east are more extensive slopes at **Passo San Pellegrino**, linked with **Falcade** – again, over the border in Veneto. Off to the east is another fair-sized lift network at **Passo Costalunga**, linked with **Nova Levante** (Welschnofen) in Alto Adige.

Continuing downstream, you are now in the Val di Fiemme. Near **Predazzo** there is a lift up to the slopes shared with **Pampeago** and with **Obereggen**, across the border in Alto Adige. Finally, the major town of **Cavalese** has lifts up to the slopes of **Alpe Cermis**.

To the south of the Val di Fassa/Val di Fiemme axis, a steep road over the high **Passo Rolle** – where there is a small network of drags and chairs serving easy slopes on either side of the road – leads down to the resort of **San Martino di Castrozza** (1470m/4,820ft). San Martino has a fabulous setting beneath a wall of Dolomite cliffs and peaks – the Pale di San Martino – soaring to over 3000m/9,840ft. The village is not notably cute – there are quite a few large, block-like buildings – but it is pleasant enough. The slopes, modest in extent and entirely intermediate in difficulty, are split into three sectors, only two of them linked (at altitude). Restaurant terraces in two of these sectors give magnificent views of the Pale.

## AROUND TRENTO

Trento's local hill – only a few minutes' drive from the town – is **Monte Bondone**. And for a local hill it is excellent: half a dozen roadside chair-lifts serve partly wooded slopes here on Palon (2090m/6,860ft), with a longest run of 4km/2.5 miles dropping 800m/2,620ft and served by a fast quad chair. About 90% of the small area is covered by snowmaking. There's a new terrain-park. And great views north-west to the Brenta Dolomites around Madonna.

To the south-east of Trento, and closer to the town of Rovereto, are the small resorts of **Folgaria** (1165m/3,820ft – not to be confused with Folgarida near Madonna) and **Lavarone**. Lavarone has a handful of lifts, but Folgaria has more like 20, serving 60km/37 miles of runs with 100% snowmaking cover.

To the north-west are the slopes on Paganella (2125m/6,970ft) shared by **Fai della Paganella** (1000m/3,280ft) and **Andalo** (1050m/3,440ft). Andalo is a sizeable, pleasant-enough resort that appears in one or two UK package brochures. Runs radiate from the peak, and end up in one of the two resorts. The direct red run to Fai, 1100m/3,610ft vertical and almost directly north-facing, is a reader's favourite, with great Dolomite views.

## WEST OF TRENTO

Trentino's largest and best-known ski area is here in the Brenta Dolomites, shared by the big resort of **Madonna di Campiglio** (which has its own separate chapter) and the much smaller resorts of **Marilleva** and **Folgarida**.

Marilleva is a modern resort, the main part (largely consisting of a few functional low-rise buildings) built on a mid-mountain shelf at 1400m/4,590ft and reached by road or gondola from the lower part of the resort at 900m/2,950ft, on the valley floor. From 1400, lifts diverge to Doss della Pesa (2230m/7,320ft) and Monte Vigo, where the slopes link with those of Folgarida and Madonna. Folgarida is also a purpose-built two-part resort, but both parts are at about the same altitude beside the road up to Madonna – clustered around gondola stations at 1300m/4,270ft and at 1400m/4,590ft – and the resort is more traditional in style.

A 20-minute drive south of Madonna – and possibly to be linked one day by lifts and pistes – is **Pinzolo** (780m/2,560ft), not a conventional ski resort but the main town of the Val Rendena, with half-a-dozen lifts on Doss del Sabion (2100m/6,890ft). There are great views of the Brenta massif from the top, and some quite challenging terrain.

Further up the Val di Sole is **Pejo** (1400m/4,590ft), a spa village with a narrow but tall slope area close to the border with Lombardia. Actually straddling the border is high, snow-sure Passo Tonale, described below.

## PASSO TONALE 1885m/6,180ft

**Passo Tonale offers that all too rare combination of a fair-sized, uncrowded, snow-sure ski area and slope-side hotels at a bargain price. The resort lacks many traditional ski-village amenities, but who cares? Reporters are unanimous that it's a great place for beginners.**

Passo Tonale sits on a wide, treeless pass. The village is a compact, functional affair, purpose built for skiing, with its hotels, shops, bars and restaurants spread along both sides of the busy through-road. There are 26 hotels, almost all of which are in the 2- to 3-star category. Practically everyone stays on half-board terms, so there are few restaurants other than in hotels. Although there are plenty of bars and restaurants, we and reporters agree that they seem very quiet. Snowmobiles are for hire and there's a good swimming pool and skating rink down in Ponte di Legno.

Tonale's slopes are spread over two unconnected sections, far enough apart at their bases to be linked by efficient buses. The broad, south-facing area is much the larger, starts right in the village and is entirely novice and intermediate terrain served by a well-laid-out mix of chairs and drags, mostly between 2000m and 2400m (6,560ft and 7,870ft). The north-facing area is steeper, narrower and taller. First, there is a a cable car of



700m/2,300ft vertical; above that a double chair-lift; and at the top, four drag-lifts on the Presena glacier going just over the 3000m mark (just short of 10,000ft). Both areas are completely open terrain, but down in the village of Ponte di Legno is a tree-lined area that's good for poor visibility days.

Given a glacier, no low altitude slopes and a lot of snowmaking, Tonale is difficult to beat for snow.

It's an excellent resort for novices. The sunny lifts on gentle slopes right by the village are ideal for beginners, and there are good longer progression runs higher up. Reports on the ski schools are good, too.

For intermediates, Tonale is rather limited. The south-facing slopes offer gentle terrain ideal for cruising; the 4.5 km/3 mile Alpino piste down a deserted valley to the village is a highlight. The glacier runs are short and easy, while the rest of the north-facing side is more challenging but not extremely so. The obvious solution would be to use the regional pass and visit the Marilleva/Madonna area a little way down the valley.

Experts will need to look off-piste. The black piste down the cable-car is not seriously steep except at the top, but the more direct ski route next to it is more of a challenge. In the right conditions there are epic off-piste runs to be done from the glacier, including the impressive 16km/10 mile Pisgana run towards Ponte di Legno (a vertical of 1650m/5,410ft). Guidance needed.

The lift system is impressive – well able to cope with the demand, and with half-a-dozen fast chairs in key positions it provides fast uplift. The cable-car is due to be replaced for this season. Unlike many Italian resorts, Tonale does not seem to get invaded at weekends.

The half-dozen mountain restaurants generally meet with readers' approval.

BARDONECCHIA TOURIST OFFICE

## KEY FACTS

| | |
|---|---|
| **Resort** | 1310m<br>4,300ft |
| **Slopes** | 1290m-2750m<br>4,230-9,020ft |
| **Lifts** | 23 |
| **Pistes** | 140km<br>87 miles |
| **Blue** | 41% |
| **Red** | 49% |
| **Black** | 10% |
| **Snowmaking** | 20km<br>12 miles |

## TOURIST OFFICE

**t** 0122 99032
bardonecchia@montagnedoc.it
www.comune.bardonecchia.to.it

# Bardonecchia

**A fairly extensive area worth considering as a base for touring other nearby French and Italian resorts. The local slopes, and the town itself, tend to be fairly quiet during the week, but lots of weekenders pour in from Turin.**

## THE RESORT

Bardonecchia is a sizeable old railway town, lacking alpine charm and with a somewhat run-down feel (maybe that will change, as it is due to stage some events for the 2006 Winter Olympics). Après-ski is quiet ('nil', said our most recent reporter, who recommends the Crot di Ciulin wine bar and 'superb' La Ciaburna di Viarengo Mario restaurant in Melezet). The resort is right by the Fréjus road tunnel to France. The Three Valleys can be reached from Orelle on the French side, and Valloire, the Milky Way resorts (Sauze etc) and Serre-Chevalier are reachable by car.

## THE MOUNTAINS

Two separate areas of slopes either side of town are each a free bus-ride away, and reporters complain of the antiquated lift system. The larger area is a wide section of low (little above 2000m/6,560ft), tree-lined, north-facing runs above three valley lift stations – Campo Smith, Les Arnauds and Melezet. The other – Jafferau – is a tall, thin mountain of long, partly open, west-facing runs. The area's snow record isn't particularly good, but there are plenty of relatively snow-sure runs above the middle stations and some snowmaking top to bottom. There is little challenge for experts, but virtually the whole area is suitable for intermediates. Campo Smith and Melezet have nursery areas for beginners. For boarders there is a terrain-park and half-pipe but there are a lot of awkward drag-lifts to cope with. Although the lifts are antiquated there are few queues during the week. Mountain restaurants are generally pleasant and uncrowded.

MACUGNAGA TOURIST OFFICE

## KEY FACTS

| | |
|---|---|
| **Resort** | 1325m<br>4,350ft |
| **Slopes** | 1325-2800m<br>4,350-9,190ft |
| **Lifts** | 12 |
| **Pistes** | 37km<br>23 miles |
| **Blue** | 30% |
| **Red** | 65% |
| **Black** | 5% |
| **Snowmaking** | some |

## TOURIST OFFICE

**t** 0324 65119
sviva@libero.it
www.macugnaga-online.it

# Macugnaga

**Macugnaga consists of a pair of quiet villages dramatically set at the head of a remote valley, only a few miles from the lifts of Zermatt and Saas-Fee. It's a place for a cheap holiday away from it all, with some skiing thrown in.**

## THE RESORT

The villages of Staffa and slightly higher Pecetto have a lot of traditional charm and enjoy a splendid setting close to the the towering east wall of Monte Rosa. Reporters remark on the friendly people and the good food. There is a 'lovely' wine shop, too.

There are a dozen small hotels: most manage 3-star status. The place rarely features in tour op brochures. Neilson offers three simple hotels.

## THE MOUNTAINS

The slopes are in two separate sectors above the two villages.

Pecetto's lifts run up to Belvedere (1930m/6,330ft), at the foot of the Belvedere glacier beneath Monte Rosa. A gently rising chair-lift from the village takes you to Burky, in the middle of the small, woody area of gentle red and blue runs.

Staffa has a couple of nursery drags beside the village and a two-stage cable-car going from a station on the village fringe over sunny slopes almost to the Swiss border. Drag-lifts up here serve short blue and slightly longer red and black runs, and there are good, varied red runs down the 1100m/3,610ft vertical of the top cable-car – the longest curling well away from the lifts to notch up 7.5km/5 miles. In the right conditions off-piste possibilities from the top of the cable-car are considerable, including a run north ending below Saas-Fee. Whether it's worth the three-hour bus-ride back ...

Reporters have approved of the piste grooming, the lack of queues, the 'very patient' ski instructors and the 'lovely, inexpensive' lunches in the several mountain restaurants.

SNOWPIX.COM / CHRIS GILL

## KEY FACTS

| | |
|---|---|
| Resort | 1545m 5,070ft |
| Slopes | 1545-2880m 1545-9,450ft |
| Lifts | 16 |
| Pistes | 55km 34 miles |
| Blue | 30% |
| Red | 55% |
| Black | 15% |
| Snowmaking | some |

## TOURIST OFFICE

t 0343 57039
consorzioturistico@valchianvenna.com
www.madesimo.com

# Madesimo

**Madesimo's mountain is great for Italian weekenders, who arrive in numbers. If you're planning a week, it's far from ideal. But we have a sneaking affection for the place – and we'd really like to do the run to Fraciscio.**

## THE RESORT

Madesimo sits in a remote, pretty side valley, a three-hour drive north from Bergamo that ends in a very dramatic hairpin-bend ascent. The village has some old farm buildings, but is mainly a piecemeal modern development. The delightful central church, narrow streets and little shops appear to be overlooked by an airport control tower (the hotel Torre). A fair choice of hotels is available; we liked the Andossi, now a 4-star. Eating out is a highlight. Après-ski is fairly quiet.

## THE MOUNTAINS

A two-stage cable-car is the primary lift to the slopes, with chair alternatives to the first section. There are runs to the village, or you can cut across the wide mountainside to the open slopes above Motta, now equipped with fast quads to deal with the weekend influx on the funicular from the valley town of Campodolcino. The runs – facing almost east and west – get too much sun for snow to be very reliable. One run that keeps its snow well is the famous Canalone, a long, sweeping run beneath the top cable-car – an easy black, classed as an off-piste route. In theory there is also a route of 1600m/5,250ft vertical to Fraciscio, next to Campodolcino. The best intermediate runs are on the back of the mountain, but the reds from the cable-car mid-station are very pleasant, passing through pretty woodland. The nursery slopes are fine, but beginners have few really easy pistes to graduate to.

There are weekend queues for the cable-car, but otherwise few lift delays. The mountain restaurants are not particularly appealing.

PILA TOURIST OFFICE

## KEY FACTS

| | |
|---|---|
| Resort | 1800m 5,910ft |
| Slopes | 1550-2710m 5,090-8,890ft |
| Lifts | 12 |
| Pistes | 70km 43 miles |
| Blue | 12% |
| Red | 72% |
| Black | 16% |
| Snowmaking | 15km 9 miles |

## TOURIST OFFICE

t 0165 521055
info@pilaturismo.it
www.pilaturismo.it

# Pila

**Pila is little known outside Italy and offers a worthwhile surprise to those who visit. A fair-sized area of well-groomed, snow-sure slopes rises around a purpose-built resort, linked by gondola to an old Roman town below.**

## THE RESORT

Pila is a car-free, purpose-built, ski-in ski-out resort, with a mix of chalet-style buildings and large apartment blocks typical of a French resort. Après-ski is quiet. Below the resort at 570m/1,870ft, and connected by an 18-minute gondola ride or an 18km/11 mile drive on a winding road, is Aosta, founded by the Romans in 25 BC. The centre is traffic-free, with cobbled streets lined with shops and cafes (catering largely for locals), a church and a huge square. The resort attracts large numbers of British school groups.

## THE MOUNTAINS

The terrain is an interesting mix of mainly red-graded slopes above and below the tree line, with stunning views from the top: from Mont Blanc in the west to the Matterhorn and Monte Rosa in the east. Chair-lifts (some fast) and a cable-car fan out from the village and there are runs for all standards. A keen piste-basher could cover all the runs in a day or two, but there is more variety here than in nearby Courmayeur. Most of the slopes are north- or north-east facing and above 2000m/6,560ft, so snow reliability is good (as is the grooming). Except at weekends, when Italians in the know pour on to the slopes, there are few queues. We have had good reports of both the local ski school and the one run by (mainly schools) tour operator Interski.

There are several good rustic mountain restaurants. At Lo Bautson (which means cow shed) the penne all'Arrabiata was excellent. La Châtelaine does excellent plats du jour, and you might get a free grappa afterwards from the friendly owner.

# Switzerland

**Switzerland is home to some of our favourite resorts. For sheer charm and spectacular scenery, the essentially traffic-free villages of Wengen, Mürren, Saas-Fee and Zermatt take some beating. Many resorts have impressive slopes, too – including some of the biggest, highest and toughest runs in the Alps as well as a lot of good intermediate terrain. For fast, queue-free lift networks, Swiss resorts rarely match French standards – but the real bottlenecks are steadily disappearing. And there are compensations – the world's best mountain restaurants, for example.**

**People always seem to associate Switzerland with high prices. In the recent past, we haven't found most Swiss resorts appreciably more expensive than most French ones – though some Swiss resorts, such as Zermatt, Verbier and St Moritz, do tend to be pricey. What is clear is that what you get for your money in Switzerland is generally first class.**

GRINDELWALD TOURISMUS / SWISS-IMAGE.CH

← Knockout scenery is a Swiss speciality. This is Grindelwald – but no, it's not the Eiger, which casts a long shadow over the village and the slopes. The Wetterhorn is easier to get in the frame, because it's not quite so close

While France is the home of the purpose-built resort, Switzerland is the home of the mountain village that has transformed itself from traditional farming community into year-round holiday resort. Many of Switzerland's most famous mountain resorts are as popular in the summer as in the winter, or more so. This creates places with a more lived-in feel to them and a much more stable local community. Many villages are still dominated by a handful of families lucky or shrewd enough to get involved in the early development of the area.

This has its downside as well as advantages. The ruling families are able to stifle competition and prevent newcomers from taking a slice of their action. Alternative ski schools, competing with the traditional school and pushing up standards, are much less common than in other Alpine countries, for example.

Switzerland means high living as well as high prices, and the swanky grand hotels of St Moritz, Gstaad, Zermatt and Davos are

beyond the dreams of most ordinary holidaymakers. Even in more modest places, the quality of the service is generally high. The trains run like clockwork to the advertised timetable (and often they run to the top of the mountain, doubling as ski-lifts). The food is almost universally of good quality and much less stodgy than in neighbouring Austria. In Switzerland you get what you pay for: even the cheapest wine, for example, is not cheap, but it is reliable.

## GETTING AROUND THE SWISS ALPS

Access to practically all Swiss resorts is fairly straightforward when approaching from the north – just pick your motorway. Many of the high passes that are perfectly sensible ways to get around the country in summer are closed in winter, which can be inconvenient if you are moving around from one area to another.

There are very useful car-carrying trains in various places. One key link is between the Valais (Crans-Montana, Zermatt etc) and Andermatt via the Furka tunnel, and another is from Andermatt to the Grisons (Flims, Davos etc) via the Oberalp pass – closed to road traffic in winter but open to trains except after very heavy snowfalls. Another rail tunnel that's very handy is the Lötschberg, linking Kandersteg in the Bernese Oberland with Brig in the Valais.

St Moritz is more awkward to get to than other resorts. The main road route is over the Julier pass. This is normally kept open, but at 2285m/7,500ft it is naturally prone to heavy snowfalls that can shut it for a time. Fallbacks are car-carrying rail tunnels under the Albula pass and the Vereina tunnel from near Klosters.

These car-carrying rail services are painless unless you travel at peak times, when there may be long queues – particularly for the Furka tunnel from Andermatt, which Zürich residents use to get to the Valais resorts. There is a car-carrying rail tunnel linking Switzerland with Italy – the Simplon. But most routes to Italy are kept open by means of road tunnels. See the Italy introduction.

To use Swiss motorways (and it's difficult to avoid doing so if you're driving serious distances) you have to buy a permit to stick on your windscreen (costing SF40 in 2004). They are sold at the border, and are, for all practical purposes, compulsory.

ANDERMATT TOURIST OFFICE

# Andermatt

*An old-fashioned resort with some great off-piste (and snow)*

## COSTS

①②③④⑤⑥

## RATINGS

**The slopes**

| | |
|---|---|
| Snow | **** |
| Extent | * |
| Expert | **** |
| Intermediate | ** |
| Beginner | * |
| Convenience | *** |
| Queues | ** |
| Mountain restaurants | * |

**The rest**

| | |
|---|---|
| Scenery | *** |
| Resort charm | **** |
| Off-slope | ** |

## NEWS

A new shuttle-bus between Gemsstock and Winterhorn came into operation last season.

Snowmaking was extended last winter and more is to be added for 2004/05.

- ➕ Attractive, traditional village
- ➕ Excellent snow record
- ➕ Some excellent steep pistes, and great off-piste terrain

- ➖ Three separate areas of slopes are all fairly limited if you stay on-piste
- ➖ Unsuitable for beginners
- ➖ Limited off-slope diversions
- ➖ Little English spoken
- ➖ Cable-car queues at weekends

**Little old Andermatt was rather left behind in the mega-resort boom of the 1960s and 70s. But its attractions have not faded for those who like their mountains tall, steep and covered in deep powder. At first sight, quick access from Zürich makes it a tempting destination for a weekend break – but you'll be joined by the residents of Zürich, who arrive by the coachload and trainload.**

## THE RESORT

Andermatt is quite busy in summer and gets weekend winter business, but at other times seems deserted apart from groups of soldiers from the local barracks. The town is quietly attractive, with wooden houses lining the dog-leg main street that runs between railway and cable-car stations, and some imposing churches. The railway is the only link in winter with the Grisons to the east and the Valais to the west – trains carry cars. There are good road and rail links from Zürich. The town is fairly small, and there are now buses around the town going to Gemsstock and Winterhorn.

## THE MOUNTAINS

Andermatt's skiing is split over three unlinked mountains. The slopes are almost entirely above the trees, and the individual areas are all limited in extent. You buy a pass covering the three mountains and trains between them. The Gotthard-Oberalp lift pass also covers the nearby resorts of Sedrun and Disentis – reached by train over the Oberalp pass.

**Slopes** A two-stage cable-car from the edge of the village serves magnificent, varied slopes on the open, steep and usually empty slopes of Gemsstock. Across town is the gentler Nätschen/Gütsch area. And a bus- or train-ride

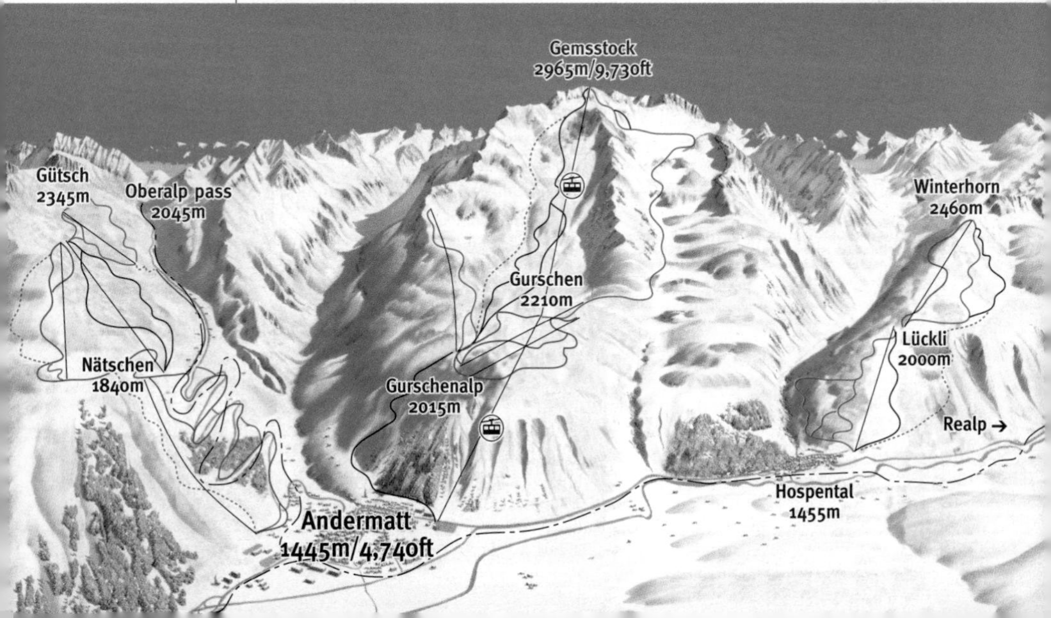

Gemsstock 2965m/9,730ft
Gütsch 2345m
Oberalp pass 2045m
Winterhorn 2460m
Gurschen 2210m
Lückli 2000m
Nätschen 1840m
Gurschenalp 2015m
Realp →
Hospental 1455m
Andermatt 1445m/4,740ft

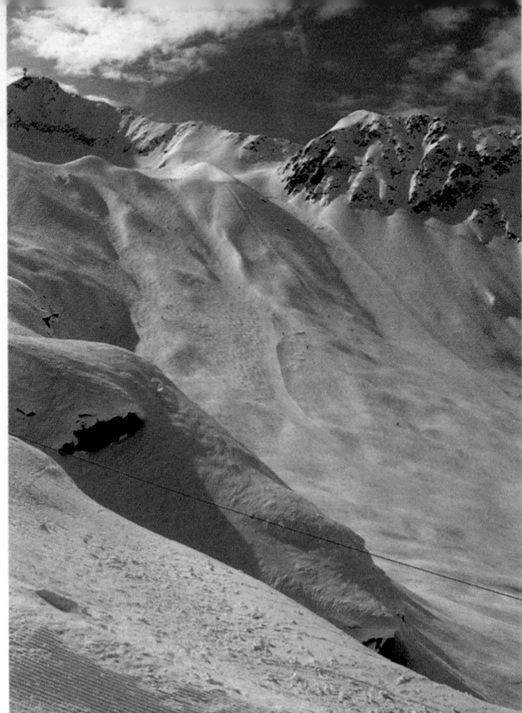

↑ 900m/2,950ft vertical of powdery black run
SNOWPIX.COM / CHRIS GILL

## KEY FACTS

| | |
|---|---|
| **Resort** | 1445m<br>4,740ft |
| **Slopes** | 1445-2965m<br>4,740-9,730ft |
| **Lifts** | 13 |
| **Pistes** | 74km<br>46 miles |
| **Blue** | 12% |
| **Red** | 48% |
| **Black** | 40% |
| **Snowmaking** | 7km<br>4 miles |

## REPORTS WANTED

Recently we have had few reports on this resort. If you go there, please do send us a report.

**Phone numbers**
From elsewhere in Switzerland add the prefix 041.
From abroad use the prefix +41 41.

## TOURIST OFFICE

**t** 887 1454
info@andermatt.ch
www.andermatt.ch

along the valley is Winterhorn (above Hospental). There is also an isolated nursery slope further along at Realp. Piste marking is slack, which on such a steep hill is bad news in a white-out.
**Terrain-parks** There are facilities (park and pipe) on Gemsstock.
**Snow reliability** The area has a justified reputation for reliable snow. Piste grooming is generally good.
**Experts** It is most definitely a resort for experts. The north-facing bowl beneath the top Gemsstock cable-car is a glorious, long, steep slope (about 900m/2,950ft vertical), usually with excellent snow, down which there are countless off-piste routes and one marked run, which branches into two. Outside the bowl, the Sonnenpiste is a fine open red run curling around the back of the mountain to the Gurschen mid-station, also flanked by off-piste opportunities. From Gurschen to the village there is a black run, not too steep but heavily mogulled. Routes off the back of Gemsstock lead to the village, or to Hospental. Nätschen and Winterhorn both have black pistes and off-piste opportunities.
**Intermediates** Intermediates needn't be put off Gemsstock: the Sonnenpiste can be tackled (especially as there are immaculately groomed sections of the piste 'created especially for carvers'), and there is a pleasant red run and some short blues at mid-mountain. Winterhorn's modest lift system offers pistes to suit all abilities down the 1000m/3,280ft vertical, while Nätschen's south and west-facing mountain is perfect for confidence-building – and for first experiments off-piste.
**Beginners** The lower half of Nätschen has a good, long, easy run. But this is not a good resort for beginners.
**Snowboarding** The cable-car accesses some great free-ride terrain.
**Cross-country** There is a 20km/12 mile loop along the valley towards Realp.
**Queues** The Gemsstock cable-car can generate morning queues in the village and at mid-mountain when conditions are attractive, especially at weekends. Things take a while to get going after heavy snow.
**Mountain restaurants** Present, but unremarkable. Plans for a new one at Gurschen have been postponed.
**Schools and guides** Alpine Adventures Mountain Reality, a guiding outfit run by local big wheel Alex Clapasson, is very pricey, and a reporter this year did not regret hiring a guide from the Swiss ski school instead.
**Facilities for children** There there are slopes they can handle at Nätschen and the Swiss school does classes.

## STAYING THERE

**How to go** Andermatt's accommodation is in cosy 2- and 3-star hotels.
**Hotels** Gasthaus Sternen (887 1130) is an attractive central chalet with a cosy restaurant and bar. The 3-star Sonne (887 1226), between the centre and the lift, is welcoming and comfortable. The neighbouring 2-star Bergidyll (887 1455) is a British favourite. Alpenhotel Schlüssel (888 7088) is 'good value', with spacious rooms.
**Eating out** A recent reporter recommends the Sternen for 'hearty, good value' meals and the Kronen hotel's 'quite formal' Tre Passi restaurant for 'good game'.
**Après-ski** Après-ski revolves around cosy bars. The Spycher is liveliest. Later on, try the Piccadilly and the bars at the hotel Monopol ('great cocktails, stays open late'). At weekends the Gotthard disco is said to be 'lively'.
**Off the slopes** There's a toboggan run at Nätschen. The churches and the museum of local history are worth a visit. The fitness centre at the hotel Drei König is open to the public. There are maintained footpaths.

# Arosa

*Classic all-round winter resort – walkers are as welcome as skiers*

## COSTS

①②③④⑤⑥

## RATINGS

**The slopes**

| | |
|---|---|
| Snow | *** |
| Extent | ** |
| Expert | * |
| Intermediate | *** |
| Beginner | **** |
| Convenience | *** |
| Queues | **** |
| Mountain restaurants | **** |

**The rest**

| | |
|---|---|
| Scenery | *** |
| Resort charm | ** |
| Off-slope | **** |

## NEWS

November 2003 saw the opening of the Alpine Club Mickey Mouse. Thirteen 'family friendly' hotels, the Swiss ski school and Disney are collaborating to provide 'a constant stream of surprises and entertainment' – skiing features, too.

Plans for lifts to link Arosa to Lenzerheide-Valbella hold out the prospect of a hugely increased area from 2006. The top of Arosa's Hörnli lifts is only about 2km/1 mile from the top of the Valbella lifts. The combined area will offer around 250km/155 miles of pistes, propelling Arosa into the big league.

- + Classic winter sports resort ambience, with lots going on other than skiing and boarding
- + Some of the best cross-country loops in the Alps
- + Few queues
- + Relatively good snow reliability
- + Prettily wooded setting, but ...

- − Some very block-like buildings in main village
- − Spread-out village lacks a heart, and means some accommodation is inconveniently situated
- − Slopes too limited for mileage-hungry intermediates
- − Few challenging pistes for experts – though there is good off-piste

**The classic image of a winter sports resort is perhaps an isolated, snow-covered Swiss village, surrounded by big, beautiful mountains, with skating on a frozen lake, horse-drawn sleighs jingling along snowy streets and people in fur coats strolling on mountain paths. Arosa is exactly that. It's just a pity that many of its comfortable hotels date from a time when pitched roofs were out of fashion.**

## THE RESORT

High and remote, Arosa is in a sheltered basin at the head of a beautiful wooded valley, in contrast to the open slopes above it. It's a long, winding drive or splendid rail journey from Chur (both take under an hour). The main resort development is around Obersee – a pretty spot, spoilt by the surrounding block-like buildings. Lifts go up from here into the Weisshorn sector of the slopes. The rest of Arosa is scattered, much of it spreading up the hill separating Obersee from the older, prettier Inner-Arosa, where lifts from opposite extremities go up into both sectors of the slopes. Arosa is quiet; its relaxed ambience attracts an unpretentiously well-heeled clientele of families and older people. Very few of them are British.

Some accommodation is a long walk from the lifts, but there is an excellent free shuttle-bus.



## THE MOUNTAINS

Arosa's slopes are situated in a wide, open bowl, facing north-east to south-east, with all the runs returning eventually to the village at the bottom. All the slopes are above the tree line, except the home runs to Obersee.

**Slopes** The slopes are spread widely over two main sectors. Although the

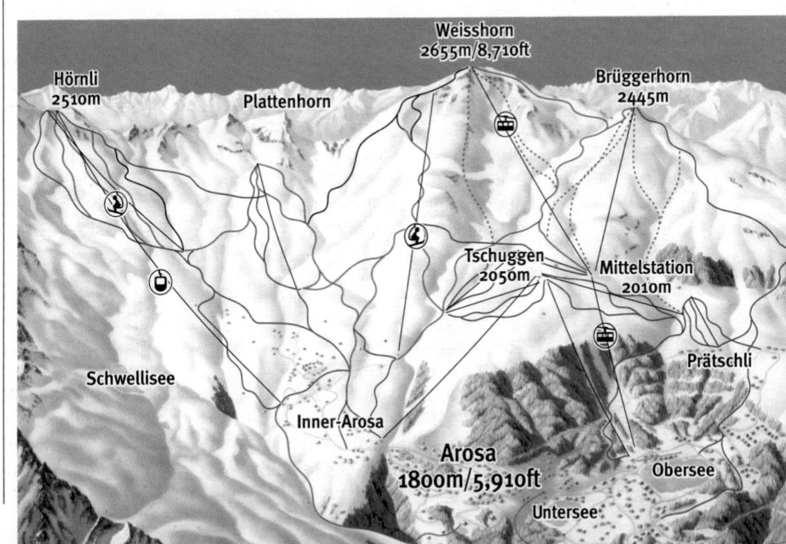

↑ There are easier ways to get to lunch on the mountain than skiing
AROSA TOURIST OFFICE

## KEY FACTS

| | |
|---|---|
| Resort | 1800m<br>5,910ft |
| Slopes | 1800-2655m<br>5,910-8,710ft |
| Lifts | 13 |
| Pistes | 60km<br>37 miles |
| Blue | 27% |
| Red | 60% |
| Black | 13% |
| Snowmaking | 15km<br>9 miles |





## REPORTS WANTED

Recently we have had few reports on this resort. If you go there, please do send us a report.

The best reports earn a copy of the next edition, and can lead to free lift passes in future.

See page 10.

**Phone numbers**
From elsewhere in Switzerland add the prefix 081.
From abroad use the prefix +41 81.

## TOURIST OFFICE

t 378 7020
arosa@arosa.ch
www.arosa.ch

very poor piste map doesn't show it, the major lift junction in the Weisshorn sector is Tschuggen, 500m/1,640ft away from the Mittelstation of the Weisshorn cable-car, and reachable from both Obersee and Inner-Arosa. From Mittelstation, you can take a chair to the lower peak of Brüggerhorn. A slow gondola from below Inner-Arosa is the main access to the Hörnli sector. Well used walking paths wind across the mountainsides, and great care is needed where they cross the pistes.
**Terrain-parks** There is a park and a half-pipe.
**Snow reliability** Arosa has relatively good snow reliability. The sunnier slopes are quite high, and the shadier Hörnli slopes hold their snow well. Grooming is good, and snowmaking on the home runs is often put into use.
**Experts** Arosa isn't the resort for a keen expert. The two black runs barely deserve their grading, but you can ski off-piste to and from Lenzerheide – with a guide. And there are several ungroomed 'free-ride' routes.
**Intermediates** This is a good area for intermediates who aren't looking for high mileage or huge challenges. The 'free-ride' routes offer an easy way into off-piste. The blue runs through woods to Obersee are particular pleasures – particularly the 'staggeringly beautiful' one from the Brüggerhorn via Prätschli.
**Beginners** The Tschuggen nursery slopes are excellent and usually have good snow, but they get a lot of through traffic. Inner-Arosa has a quieter area for children.
**Snowboarding** There is a specialist school.
**Cross-country** Arosa's modest 25km/16 miles of loops include some of the best and most varied in the Alps.
**Queues** Arosa does not suffer from serious queues. There can be waits for the Weisshorn cable-car, though recent reporters have had no problems.
**Mountain restaurants** The mountain restaurants can get crowded in peak season, but practically all get good reviews. The rustic little Carmennahütte is our favourite; the similarly attractive Tschuggenhütte is expanding into a new log cabin for 2004/05. Alpenblick does 'very good food' and Hörnli is a 'welcoming hut in a dramatic position' at the top of the gondola.
**Schools and guides** Swiss and ABC are the main schools. Class sizes can be large. There's a lot of demand for private lessons.
**Facilities for children** Arosa's appeal as a family resort has led to Disney endorsement, with 13 hotels and the Swiss Ski school forming the Alpine Club Mickey Mouse.

## STAYING THERE

**How to go** Arosa is a hotel resort, with a high proportion of 3- and 4-stars.
**Hotels** The sensitively modernised 4-star Waldhotel National (378 5555) with 'really special food' and direct access to the slopes is 'quite delightful'. The 4-star Sporthotel Valsana (377 0275) is recommended.
**Eating out** Most restaurants are hotel-based, some with a very high reputation. The Kachelofa-Stübli at the Waldhotel National is excellent. Another recommendation is the Orchidee Palaste – a 'very good' Chinese at the Hotel Merkur.
**Après-ski** Après-ski is quite lively. The Carmenna hotel by the ice rink has a popular piano bar. The Sitting Bull is busy and cheerful. Recommended bars include the Grischuna for grown-ups and Mexicalito for kids (both with restaurants attached). The Casino is 'good fun' and its bars are 'lively'.
**Off the slopes** There are plenty of outdoor alternatives. You can get a pedestrian's lift pass, and many mountain restaurants are reachable via 60km/37 miles of cleared, marked walks (map available). Sleigh rides in the mountains are popular, and there's a busy outdoor ice rink.

# Champéry

*Picture-postcard village, with access to the Portes du Soleil*

**COSTS**

① ② ③ ④ ⑤ ⑥

**RATINGS**

| **The slopes** | |
|---|---|
| Snow | ** |
| Extent | ***** |
| Expert | *** |
| Intermediate | **** |
| Beginner | ** |
| Convenience | * |
| Queues | **** |
| Mountain restaurants | *** |
| **The rest** | |
| Scenery | **** |
| Resort charm | **** |
| Off-slope | *** |

**KEY FACTS**

| | |
|---|---|
| **Resort** | 1050m<br>3,440ft |
| For Portes du Soleil | |
| **Slopes** | 975-2275m<br>3,200-7,460ft |
| **Lifts** | 206 |
| **Pistes** | 650km<br>400 miles |
| **Green** | 13% |
| **Blue** | 38% |
| **Red** | 39% |
| **Black** | 10% |
| **Snowmaking** | 252 acres |
| For Swiss side only | |
| **Slopes** | 1,050-2275m<br>3,440-7,460ft |
| **Lifts** | 35 |
| **Pistes** | 100km<br>62 miles |

+ Charmingly rustic mountain village
+ Cable-car takes you into the very extensive Portes du Soleil slopes
+ Quiet, relaxed – yet plenty to do off the slopes

- Local slopes suffer from the sun
- No runs back to the village – and sometimes none back to the valley
- Not good for beginners
- Not many tough slopes nearby

**With good transport links and sports facilities, Champéry is great for anyone looking for a quiet time in a lovely place, especially if they have a car – but not if they're beginners. Not bad access to the Portes du Soleil: Avoriaz is fairly easy to get to – and there may be fresh powder there when Champéry is suffering.**

## THE RESORT

Set beneath the dramatic Dents du Midi, Champéry is a village of old wooden chalets. Friendly and relaxed, it would be ideal for families if it wasn't separated from its slopes by a steep, fragmented mountainside.

Down a steepish hill, away from the main street, are the cable-car, sports centre and railway station.

## THE MOUNTAINS

Once you get up to them, the local slopes are open, friendly and relaxing.

**Slopes** Champéry's sunny slopes are part of the extensive Portes du Soleil circuit. The village cable-car or a chair-lift from Grand Paradis, a short free bus-ride from Champéry, go to the bowl of Planachaux. If snow is good there are a couple of pistes back to Grand Paradis, but no pistes back to Champéry. The Portes du Soleil circuit goes clockwise via Avoriaz or anticlockwise via Les Crosets. For more on the Portes du Soleil, see Avoriaz and Châtel chapters.

**Terrain-parks** There is a good terrain park at Les Crosets (which a reporter rates as the best in the area), half of which is natural. The 17 features include a quarter-pipe, gaps and kickers. There's also a half-pipe that's floodlit on Wednesday and Saturday evenings. At Morgins there's a snow-skate park in the village. Avoriaz, over in France now has three parks.

**Snow reliability** The snow on the north-facing French side of the link with Avoriaz is usually better than on the sunnier Swiss side to the south. The local Champéry area would benefit from more snowmaking.

**Experts** Few local challenges and badly placed for most of the tough Portes du Soleil runs. The Swiss Wall, on the Champéry side of Chavanette, is intimidatingly long and steep, but not that terrifying. There's scope for off-piste at Chavanette and on the broad slopes of Les Crosets and Champoussin.

**Intermediates** Confident intermediates have the whole Portes du Soleil at their disposal. Locally, the runs home to Grand Paradis are good when the



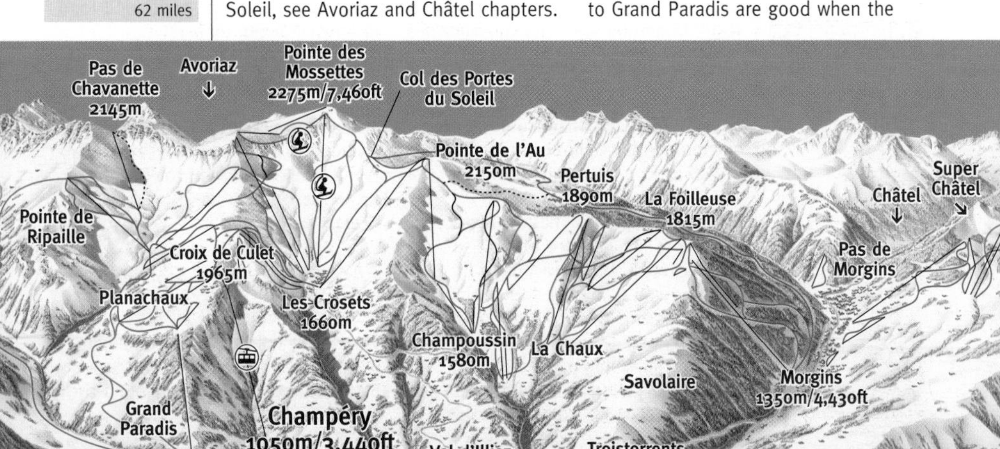

↑ The famous Swiss Wall is not as fearsome as it looks
CHAMPERY TOURIST OFFICE

## NEWS

Various lifts planned for the Morgins/ Champoussin area are being delayed by objections.

For 2004/05 a National Ice Sports Centre will open in Champéry.

## REPORTS WANTED

Recently we have had few reports on this resort. If you go there, please do send us a report.

**Phone numbers**
From elsewhere in Switzerland add the prefix 024.
From abroad use the prefix +41 24.

## TOURIST OFFICES

**Champéry**
t 479 2020
info@champery.ch
www.champery.ch

**Les Crosets**
t 479 1400
lot.illiez@chablais.info
www.valdilliez.ch

**Champoussin**
t 477 2727
champoussintourisme@bluewin.ch
www.valdilliez.ch

**Morgins**
t 477 2361
touristoffice@morgins.ch
www.morgins.ch

snow conditions allow, and the return bus to Champéry 'works well'. Les Crosets is a junction of several fine runs. Also worth trying are the slightly tougher pistes down from Mossettes and Pointe de l'Au, Champoussin's leisurely cruising, and runs to Morgins – delightful tree-lined meanders. A highlight is the beautiful, long blue direct from Col des Portes du Soleil to Morgins via the 'cute' little restaurant at Tovassière.

**Beginners** The Planachaux runs, where lessons are held, are steepish and limited in extent.

**Snowboarding** Not ideal for beginners, and access to the Portes du Soleil circuit involves drag-lifts, many of which are quite steep. Good terrain parks for experts though, and some good between-the-pistes powder areas.

**Cross-country** It's advertised as 10km/ 6 miles with 4km/2 miles floodlit every night, but it's very unreliable snow.

**Queues** Few local problems but Les Crosets is still a bottleneck at peak times. If snow is good, avoid end-of-the-day queues for the cable-car down by taking one of the valley runs.

**Mountain restaurants** Chez Coquoz at Planachaux is recommended as is Chez Gaby above Champoussin – 'marvellous rösti'. Under the same management is a new restaurant, Ferme à Gaby, at the top of the Champeys drag. The tiny Lapisa on the way to Grand Paradis is delightfully rustic (they make cheese and smoke their own meats on-site) and Chez Hermann's above Lechereuse also deserves a mention.

**Schools and guides** The few reports that we've had are free of criticism. ESS has received praise from a reporter who enjoyed a 'very helpful' private lesson. The Freeride Company provides healthy competition.

**Facilities for children** The tourist office has a list of childminders. The Swiss ski school takes three- to six-year-olds.

## STAYING THERE

**How to go** Limited packages available. Easy access for independent travellers.

**Chalets** Tour op Piste Artiste has some.

**Hotels** Prices are low compared with smarter Swiss resorts. The Beau Séjour (479 5858 ) is friendly, family-run, with 'large rooms'. The National (479 1130) has 'friendly staff, lovely breakfast'. The Auberge du Grand Paradis (479 1167) is 'charmingly rustic but noisy'.

**Self-catering** Some apartments are available to independent travellers.

**Eating out** A fair choice. Two of the best for local specialities are just outside the village: Cantines des Rives and Auberge du Grand Paradis. Locally, try the the Farinet for pizza, or the Nord. Mitchell's bar has a good restaurant and the Café du Centre serves Asian food – 'good menu in modern surroundings'. The Vieux Chalet (hotel Beau-Séjour) is recommended ('excellent fondue'), as is the bistro in the hotel National. Twice a week, the slopes are floodlit and the restaurant at the top of the cable-car opens.

**Après-ski** Mitchell's has big sofas and a fireplace. Below the 'rather seedy' Pub, the Crevasse disco is one of the liveliest places. The Café du Centre has its own micro brewery. Try the Bar des Guides in the hotel Suisse, or the Farinet's spacious cellar nightclub.

**Off the slopes** Walks are pleasant and the railway allows excursions to Montreux, Lausanne and Sion. There's a sports centre, an interesting church, a bell foundry and even a perfumery.

## Les Crosets 1660m/5,450ft

A good base for a quiet time and slopes on the doorstep. The Télécabine hotel (479 0300) is homely, with good food in a rustic dining room.

## Champoussin 1580m/5,180ft

A good family choice – no through traffic, near the slopes, no noisy late-night revellers and the comfortable Royal Alpage Club hotel (pool, gym, disco, two restaurants – 476 8300).

## Morgins 1350m/4,430ft

A fairly scattered, but attractive, quiet resort. The hotel Reine des Alpes (477 1143) is well thought of, and there are catered chalets. A reporter found the ski school 'very satisfactory'.

SNOWPIX.COM / CHRIS GILL

# Crans-Montana

*Sun-soaked slopes, stunning long-distance views and big town base*

**COSTS**

(1)(2)(3)(4)(5)(6)

**RATINGS**

| **The slopes** | |
|---|---|
| Snow | ** |
| Extent | *** |
| Expert | ** |
| Intermediate | **** |
| Beginner | *** |
| Convenience | ** |
| Queues | *** |
| Mountain restaurants | *** |
| **The rest** | |
| Scenery | **** |
| Resort charm | ** |
| Off-slope | **** |

**NEWS**

For 2004/05 the Toula chair-lift is being upgraded to a high-speed six-seater. A new black run, the Toula, is being created off the Toula chair.

For 2003/04 the Verdets beginners area was improved with a moving carpet. Three new picnic areas were added. The casino was refurbished.

- + Large, varied piste area
- + Splendid setting and views
- + Fair number of woodland slopes – good in bad weather
- + Modern, well-designed lift system, with few queues
- + Excellent, gentle nursery slopes
- + Excellent cross-country trails
- + Very sunny slopes, but ...

- – Snow badly affected by sun – ice in morning and slush in afternoon
- – Large town (rather than village) composed partly of big chalet-style blocks but mainly of dreary cubic blocks – and therefore entirely without Alpine atmosphere
- – Bus- or car-rides to lifts from much of the accommodation
- – Few challenges except off-piste

**When conditions are right – clear skies above fresh, deep snow – Crans-Montana takes some beating: the mountains you bounce down are charmingly scenic, the mountains you gaze at are mind-blowing, and you can forgive Crans-Montana its inconvenient, linear layout and the plain, towny style of its twin resort centres. Sadly, conditions are more often wrong. Except in the depths of winter, the strong midday sun bakes the pistes.**

## THE RESORT

Set on a broad shelf facing south across the Rhône valley, Crans-Montana is really two towns, their centres a mile apart and their fringes merging. Strung along a busy road, the resort's many hotels, villas, apartments and smart shops are mainly dull blocks with little traditional Alpine character, though the resort's many trees help to screen the buildings, and make some areas positively attractive.

The resort is reached by good roads, and by a fast funicular railway from Sierre. It depends heavily on summer conference business, so hotels tend to be formal, and visitors dignified. Crans is the more upmarket; Montana has somewhat cheaper restaurants and bars. The main gondola stations are above the main road – there is a free shuttle-bus during the day but it can get very crowded.

There are other gondola base stations and places to stay at Les Barzettes and at Aminona. Anzère is nearby, though the slopes aren't linked. You can get to Zermatt, Saas-Fee and Verbier by road or rail.

CRANS-MONTANA TOURISME

Gondolas from both Crans and Montana arrive at Cry d'Er ↓

## THE MOUNTAINS

Crans-Montana has slopes with few challenges and no nasty surprises, and there is a pleasant mix of open and wooded slopes.

**The slopes** The slopes are spread over three well-linked areas and the views over the valley to the peaks on the other side are breathtaking. Cry d'Er is the largest – an open bowl descending into patchy forest, directly above Montana. The next sector is focused on Les Violettes, from which the jumbo gondola goes up to the Plaine Morte glacier. The third, Petit Bonvin, sector is served by a gondola up from Aminona. Some of the runs down to the valley are narrow woodland paths, and signing is ridiculously slack.

**Terrain-parks** Aminona has a terrain-park, and there's a half-pipe in the more central Cry d'Er area.

**Snow reliability** The runs on the Plaine Morte glacier are limited and practically

## KEY FACTS

| | |
|---|---|
| **Resort** | 1500m<br>4,920ft |
| **Slopes** | 1500-3000m<br>4,920-9,840ft |
| **Lifts** | 30 |
| **Pistes** | 140km<br>87 miles |
| **Blue** | 38% |
| **Red** | 50% |
| **Black** | 12% |
| **Snowmaking** | 17km<br>11 miles |

## REPORTS WANTED

Recently we have had few reports on this resort. If you go there, please do send us a report.

The best reports earn a copy of the next edition, and can lead to free lift passes in future.

See page 10.

**Phone numbers**
From elsewhere in Switzerland add the prefix 027.
From abroad use the prefix +41 27.

## TOURIST OFFICE

**t** 485 0404
information@crans-montana.ch
www.crans-montana.ch

all the other slopes get a lot of direct sun. There is snowmaking on the main runs, but we have never found good snow on the runs down to the valley.

**For experts** There are few steep pistes and the only decent moguls are on the short slopes at La Toula. There's plenty of off-piste, particularly beneath Chetseron and La Tza.

**For intermediates** Pistes are mostly wide, and many of the red runs don't justify the grading. They tend to be uniform in difficulty from top to bottom, with few surprises. Avid piste-bashers enjoy the length of many runs, plus the fast lifts and good links that allow a lot of mileage. The 11km/7 mile run from Plaine Morte to Les Barzettes starts with top-of-the-world views and powder, and finishes among pretty woods. The Piste Nationale downhill course is a good test of technique.

**For beginners** There are three excellent nursery areas, with slopes of varying difficulty. Near-beginners can try the little run up at Plaine Morte.

**Snowboarding** Despite the resort's staid image, boarding is very popular. There are a number of specialist shops and the Stoked snowboard school. The main lifts are chairs and gondolas, and the drag-lifts are usually avoidable.

**For cross-country** There are 40km/25 miles of cross-country trails altogether, including snow-sure ones on the glacier.

**Queues** Investment in gondolas has helped, though bottlenecks can occur at the Nationale drag-lifts.

**Mountain restaurants** There are 20 mountain restaurants; the Merbé is one of the most attractive. Bella-Lui's terrace offers good views, as does the Chetseron eatery and Petit Bonvin, at the top of the Aminona sector. The Cabane des Violettes has had rave reviews (be there early for a seat).

**Schools and guides** The Swiss schools have attracted mainly favourable comments over the years.

**Facilities for children** These seem adequate, but we lack recent reports.

## STAYING THERE

**How to go** There is a wide choice of hotels and apartments.

**Hotels** This conference resort has over 50 mainly large, comfortable, expensive hotels. Pas de l'Ours (485 9333) is our favourite – chic, attractive, wood and stone. Aïda Castel (485 4111) is also beautifully furnished in chic rustic style. Beau-Site (481 3312) is a friendly, family-run hotel.

**Self-catering** There are many apartments available.

**Eating out** There is a good variety of places, from French to Lebanese. The best is the Bistrot in the Pas de l'Ours hotel. The Chalet, the Plaza and the Padrino are also recommended.

**Après-ski** Amadeus 2006 and Chez Nanette are tents on Cry d'Er serving close-of-play vin chaud. The George & Dragon in Crans is one of the liveliest bars. Reporters recommend Bar 1900 and the Grange.

**Off the slopes** There are swimming pools (in hotels), an ice rink and a cinema. Sierre and Sion are close.

SWISS-IMAGE / DAVOS TOURISMUS

# Davos

*A big, grey town surrounded by a glorious Alpine playground*

## COSTS

①②③④⑤⑥

## RATINGS

**The slopes**

| | |
|---|---|
| Snow | **** |
| Extent | ***** |
| Expert | **** |
| Intermediate | ***** |
| Beginner | ** |
| Convenience | ** |
| Queues | ** |
| Mountain restaurants | *** |

**The rest**

| | |
|---|---|
| Scenery | **** |
| Resort charm | ** |
| Off-slope | ***** |

## NEWS

For 2003/04 a new 8km/5 mile toboggan run opened on Madrisa, with a bus for the return from Saas to Klosters. On the Jakobshorn snowmaking was installed on the Gämpen piste down to Bolgen.

The Klosters bypass road is due for completion in 2005.

- + Very extensive slopes
- + Some superb, long, and mostly easy pistes away from the lifts
- + Lots of accessible off-piste terrain, with several marked itineraries
- + Good cross-country trails
- + Plenty to do off the slopes – from sports to shopping
- + Some cute mountain restaurants
- + Klosters is an attractively villagey alternative base
- + New funicular out of Davos two years back was a huge improvement

- − Dreary block-style buildings of Davos spoil the views
- − Davos is a huge, city-like place, plagued by traffic, lacking Alpine atmosphere and après-ski animation
- − The slopes are spread over five separate areas
- − Preponderance of T-bars is a problem for some visitors
- − Only pistes back to Davos from main Parsenn area are blacks finishing on the outskirts

**Davos was one of the original mega-resorts, with slopes on a scale that few resorts can better, even today. But it's a difficult resort to like. It's easy to put up with slopes spread over separate mountains, some queue-prone lifts and lots of T-bars if that's the price of staying in a captivating Alpine village. But Davos is far from that.**

**Whether you forgive the flaws probably depends on how highly you value three plus-points: the distinctive, super-long runs of the Parsenn area; being able to visit different sectors daily; and the considerable off-piste potential. We value all three, and we always look forward to visiting, especially now that the upgraded funicular to the main slopes on the Parsenn has removed what was the Alps' worst lift queue.**

**You don't have to stay in Davos to enjoy its slopes: Klosters offers a much more attractive alternative. Despite royal connections, it is not particularly exclusive. But it is less well placed than Davos for exploring all the mountains, and its cable-car still produces queues.**

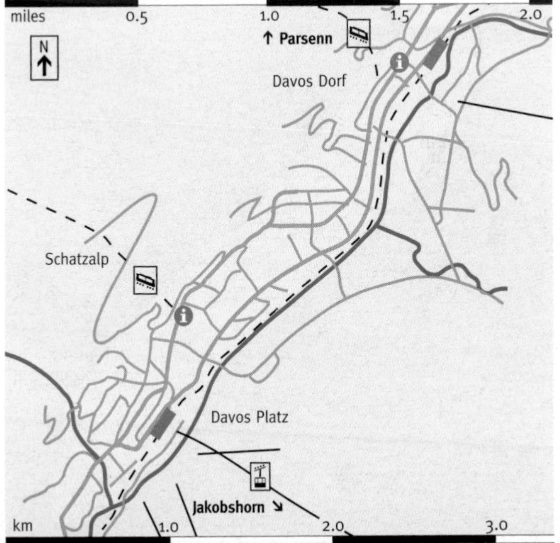


## THE RESORT

Davos is set in a high, broad, flat-bottomed valley, with its lifts and slopes either side. Arguably it was the very first place in the Alps to develop its slopes. The railway up the Parsenn was one of the first built for skiers (in 1931), and the first drag-lift was built on the Bolgen nursery slopes in 1934. But Davos was already a health resort; many of its luxury hotels were built as sanatoriums.

Sadly, that's just what they look like. There are still several specialist clinics and it is for these, along with its conferences and sporting facilities, that Davos has become well known. The place has the grey, neat, rectilinear feel of a Swiss city rather than that of a mountain village.

## KEY FACTS

| | |
|---|---|
| Resort | 1550m<br>5,090ft |
| Slopes | 810-2845m<br>2,660-9,330ft |
| Lifts | 50 |
| Pistes | 310km<br>193 miles |
| Blue | 19% |
| Red | 43% |
| Black | 38% |
| Snowmaking | 19km<br>12 miles |

It has two main centres, Dorf and Platz, about 2km/1 mile apart. Although transport is good, with buses around the town as well as the railway linking Dorf and Platz to Klosters and other villages, location is important. Easiest access to the slopes is from Dorf to the main Parsenn area, via the funicular railway; Platz is better placed for the Jakobshorn area, the big sports facilities, the smarter shopping and evening action.

Davos shares its slopes with the famously royal resort of Klosters, down the valley – an attractive village with good links into the Parsenn area and its own separate sector, the sunny Madrisa. Klosters is described in more detail at the end of this chapter.

Trips are possible by car or rail to St Moritz (the Vereina rail tunnel offers access to the Engadine area without having to negotiate the snowy Flüelapass) and Arosa, and by car to Flims-Laax and Lenzerheide.

## THE MOUNTAINS

The slopes here have something for everyone, though experts and nervous intermediates need to choose their territory with care.

### THE SLOPES
*Vast and varied*

You could hit a different mountain around Davos nearly every day for a week, but the out-of-town areas tend to be much quieter than the ones directly accessible from the resort. Lots of reporters remark on the immaculate grooming of the slopes.

The new Parsennbahn funicular from Davos Dorf ends at mid-mountain, where a choice of fast six-pack or old funicular take you on up to the major lift junction of Weissfluhjoch, at one end of the **Parsenn**. The only run back to the valley is a black to the outskirts of Dorf. At the other end of the wide, open Parsenn bowl is Gotschnagrat, reached by cable-car from the centre of Klosters. There are excellent, exceptionally long intermediate runs down to Klosters, and to other villages (see feature panel). From Davos Platz, a funicular goes up to Schatzalp, where there is a hotel, but the lifts above here are now closed.

Across the valley, **Jakobshorn** is reached by cable-car or chair-lift from Davos Platz; this is popular with snowboarders but good for skiers too. **Rinerhorn** and **Pischa** are reached by bus or (in the case of Rinerhorn) train.

Beyond the main part of Klosters, a gondola goes up from Klosters Dorf to the sunny, scenic **Madrisa** area.

There are too many T-bars for the comfort of some reporters – Rinerhorn, Pischa and Madrisa have little else.

### TERRAIN-PARKS
*Lots of choice*

The Jakobshorn has traditionally been the main boarder hang-out and has two half-pipes, one near the bottom in the Bolgen area and another at the top at Jatz – which is 100m/330ft long. There is also a terrain-park, a boarder-cross course and the funky Jatz Bar nearby. The Rinerhorn and Pischa each have a park and the Parsenn a half-pipe.

## LIFT PASSES

**Davos/Klosters**
Covers all Davos and Klosters, the railway in the whole region and buses between the resorts.

**Main pass**
1 day SF61
6 days SF279

**Senior citizens**
Over 65 (63 for women): 6 days SF251

**Children**
Under 18: 6 days SF187
Under 13: 6-days SF93
Under 6 (with adult): free pass

**Notes** Afternoon passes available.

**Alternative passes**
A confusing array of passes is available for individual and combined areas (Parsenn/Gotschna, Jakobshorn, Pischa/Rinerhorn/Madrisa).
Midday and afternoon ski passes were introduced last season.

## THE PARSENN'S SUPER-RUNS

*The runs from Weissfluhjoch that head north, on the back of the mountain, make this area special for many visitors. The pistes that go down to Schifer and then to Küblis, Saas and Serneus, and the one that curls around the mountain to Klosters, are classified red but are not normally difficult – though the latter parts can be challenging if they are not groomed. What marks them out is their sheer length (10-12km/6-7 miles) and the sensation of travel they offer – plus the welcoming huts in the woods towards the end. You can descend the 1100m/3,610ft vertical to Schifer as often as you like and take the gondola back. Once past there, the return journey is by train (included in the lift pass).*

### SNOW RELIABILITY
***Good, but not the best***

Davos is high by Swiss standards. Its mountains go respectably high, too – though not to glacial heights. Not many of the slopes face directly south, but not many face directly north either. Snow reliability is generally good higher up but can be poor lower down – you may have to take the lifts down after using the Parsenn slopes. Snowguns cover a couple of the upper runs on the Parsenn and several on the Jakobshorn, and the home runs from the Parsenn to Davos Dorf and Klosters. And piste grooming is excellent, helping to preserve snow.

### FOR EXPERTS
***Plenty to do, on- and off-piste***

A glance at the piste map may give the misleading impression that this is an intermediate's resort – there aren't many black runs. But there are some excellent runs among them – the Meierhofer Tälli run to Wolfgang is a favourite. There are also half a dozen off-piste itineraries (marked but not prepared or patrolled). These are a key feature, adding up to a lot of expert terrain that can be tackled without expensive guidance. Some are on the open upper slopes, some in the woods lower down, some from the peaks right to the valley. Two of the steepest routes go from Gotschnagrat down beside the infamous Gotschnawang slope – Drostobel and Chalbersäss.

There is also excellent 'proper' off-piste terrain, for which guidance is needed, and some short tours. Arosa can be reached with a bit of help from a train or taxi and from there you can travel on snow to Lenzerheide, but you'll need a train back. From Madrisa you can make tours to Gargellen in Austria. A reader also recommends the descent to St Antönien, north of Küblis, not least for 'spectacular views', returning by bus and train.

### FOR INTERMEDIATES
***A splendid variety of runs***

For intermediates of any temperament, this is a great area. There are good cruising runs on all five mountains, so you would never get bored in a week. This variety of different slopes taken



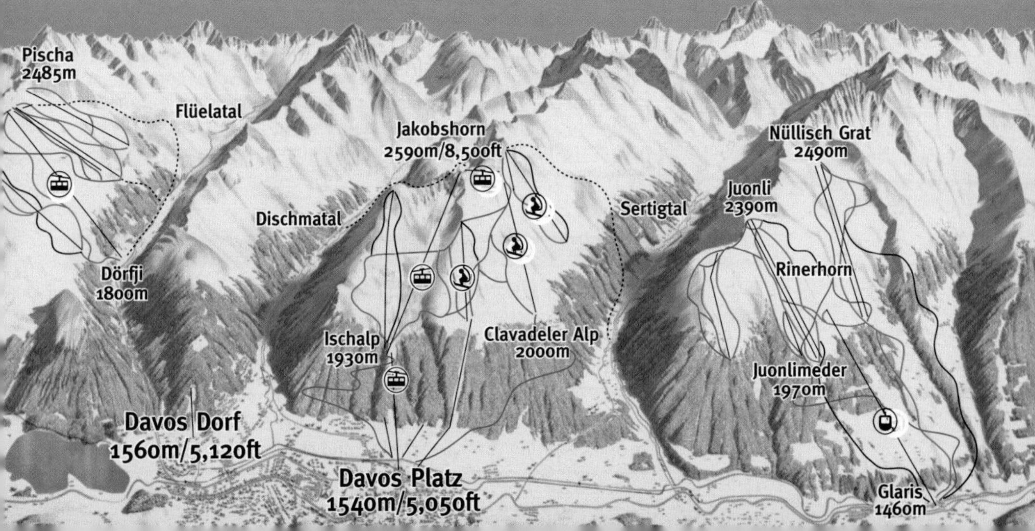

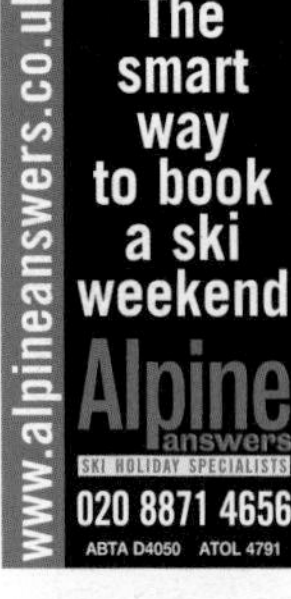




## SCHOOLS

**Swiss Davos**
t 416 2454

**New Trend**
t 413 2040
info@newtrenddavos.ch

**Teachers**
t 413 5113

**Telemark**
t 420 1477

**Wiesen**
t 404 1200

**Top Secret (snowboard)**
t 413 4043
info@topsecretdavos.ch

**Classes**
(Swiss prices)
5 4hr days SF240

**Private lessons**
Half day SF190

## CHILDREN

**Pischa nursery**
t 079 660 3168
Ages from 3

**Bobo Club**
t 416 5969
Ages 4 to 7; 10am-noon, 2pm-4pm; SF60 per day

**Madrisa Kids' Land**
t 410 2330
Ages 2 to 6

**Kinderhotel Muchetta**
(at Wiesen)
t 404 1424
Ages from 6mnth

**Babysitter list**
At tourist office

**Ski school**
Takes ages 5 to 14 (5 days SF218)





together with the wonderful long runs to the valleys makes it a compelling area with a unique character.

The epic runs to Klosters and other places (described in the feature panel) pose few difficulties for a confident intermediate or even an ambitious near-beginner (one of your editors did the run to Klosters on his third day on skis, and we have heard from reporters who did the run to Küblis on their second holiday). And there are one or two other notable away-from-the-lifts runs to the valley. In particular, you can travel from the top of Madrisa back to Klosters Dorf via the beautiful Schlappin valley (it's an easy black – classified red until the mid-1990s).

Pischa is a relatively gentle area whereas the Jakobshorn has some genuine challenges. Rinerhorn comes somewhere between the two.

### FOR BEGINNERS
***Platz is the more convenient***

The Bolgen nursery slope is adequately spacious and gentle, and a bearable walk from the centre of Platz. But Dorf-based beginners face more of a trek out to Bünda – unless staying out at the hotel of the same name.

There is no shortage of easy runs to progress to, spread around all the sectors. The Parsenn sector probably has the edge, with long, early intermediate runs in the main Parsenn bowl, as well as in the valleys down from Weissfluhjoch.

### FOR CROSS-COUNTRY
***Long, scenic valley trails***

Davos has a total of 75km/47 miles of trails running in both directions along the main valley and reaching well up into Sertigtal, Dischmatal and Flüelatal. There is a cross-country ski centre and special ski school on the outskirts.

### QUEUES
***Worst one now gone***

Some of the longest queues in the Alps were ended two seasons ago, with the replacement of the first stage of the Parsennbahn, tripling the lift's capacity. The existing lifts from the mid-station — a six-pack and the existing railway — seem to be coping with the increased loading, too. Queues can build up elsewhere for some cable-cars (including the one out of Klosters) at peak periods – a wait of 30 to 60 minutes at peak times in Klosters is not unknown.

### MOUNTAIN RESTAURANTS
***Stay low down***

The main high-altitude restaurants are dreary self-service affairs. The main exception is the highest of all – Bruhin's at Weissflügipfel is a great place for a hang-the-cost blow-out on a snowy day, with table-service of excellent rustic as well as gourmet dishes, and some knockout desserts.

There are other compelling places lower down in the Parsenn sector. A reader recommends 'big portions of chicken and noodles' at the Höhenweg bar outside the mid-station of the Parsennbahn. The old favourites, the rustic 'schwendis' in the woods on the way down to the Klosters valley from the Parsenn, still attract crowds. 2004 reporters recommend the 'super sun terrace' or the 'very cosy interior' of the Chesetta. Lower down, the 'excellent' Berghaus Schwendi offers 'freshly cooked' oriental dishes. These are fun places to end up as darkness falls – some sell wax torches to illuminate your final descent.

## boarding

*Intermediate and advanced boarders will get the most out of Davos's vast terrain and off-piste potential. The established boarder mountain is the Jakobshorn, with its pipe and park facilities and funky Jatz bar. But there are some lengthy flattish bits, including on the long runs down the Schifer gondola on the main Parsenn area. Top Secret is a specialist snowboard shop and school. There are several cheap hotels specially for boarders, including the 180-bed Bolgenhof near the Jakobshorn, the Snowboardhotel Bolgenschanze and the Snowboarder's Palace.*

Davos is more like a small city than a mountain village ↗

DAVOS TOURISMUS / SWISS-IMAGE

On Jakobshorn the Jatzhütte near the boarders' terrain-park is wild – with changing scenery such as mock palm trees, parrots and pirates. The Chalet Güggel on Jakobshorn is 'small and cosy with a nice atmosphere but slow service'. Both restaurants on the Madrisa slopes have been pronounced 'disappointing' in terms of food choice and quality. On Pischa, the Mäderbeiz at Flüelameder is a friendly and spacious woody hut, cheering on a cold day. On the Rinerhorn, the Hubelhütte is the best bet.

**SCHOOLS AND GUIDES**

***Decent choice***

A reporter says that 'nearly all instructors spoke English and were skilled and friendly — both my kids had a terrific time'. There is an alternative ski school called New Trend (maximum of six in a class) and Top Secret is the competing snowboard school.

**FACILITIES FOR CHILDREN**

***Not ideal***

Davos is a rather spread-out place in which to handle a family – and indeed the school's nursery is in a rather isolated spot, at Dorf's Bünda nursery slope. A reporter tells us the nursery is 'well organised, but even good instructors forget at times that your child doesn't speak German'.

## STAYING THERE

**HOW TO GO**

***Hotels dominate the packages***

Although most beds are in apartments, hotels dominate the UK market.

**Hotels** A dozen 4-star places and about 30 3-stars form the core of the Davos hotel trade, though there are a couple of 5-stars and quite a few cheaper places, including B&Bs. You can book any hotel by calling 415 2121.

((((5) **Flüela** (410 1717) The more atmospheric of the 5-star hotels, in central Dorf. Pool.

(((4) **Waldhuus** (416 8131) Convenient for langlaufers. Quiet, modern, tasteful. Pool.

(((4) **Davoserhof** (414 9020) Best in town. Small, old, beautifully furnished, with excellent food; well placed in Platz.

(((4) **Sunstar Park** (413 1414) At far end of Davos Platz. Pool, sauna, games room. Recommended for 'excellent' food.

## GETTING THERE

**Air** Zürich 144km/ 89 miles (2hr by car, 3hr by rail or bus).

**Rail** Stations in Davos Dorf and Platz. 20 minutes from Davos to Klosters.

## ACTIVITIES

**Indoor** Ice rink, fitness centre, tennis, squash, swimming pool, sauna, solarium, wellness centres, cinema, casino, galleries, museums, libraries, massage, badminton, pool, golf-driving range

**Outdoor** Over 80km/ 50 miles of cleared paths (mostly at valley level), snow-shoe trekking, tobogganing, ice rink, curling, horse-riding, sleigh rides, hang-gliding, paragliding

**Phone numbers**
From elsewhere in Switzerland add the prefix 081.
From abroad use the prefix +41 81.

## TOURIST OFFICES

**Davos**
t 415 2121
info@davos.ch
www.davos.ch

**Klosters**
t 410 2020
info@klosters.ch
www.klosters.ch





③ **Parsenn** (416 3232) Right opposite the Parsenn railway in Dorf. An attractive chalet marred by the big McDonald's on the ground floor.
③ **Berghotel Schatzalp** (415 5151) On the tree line 300m/1,000ft above Platz; reached by funicular (free to guests).
② **Alte Post** (414 9020) Traditional and cosy; in central Platz. Popular with boarders.
② **Hubli's Landhaus** (417 1010) 5km/3 miles out at Laret, towards Klosters. Quiet country inn with sophisticated, expensive food.
① **Snowboarder's Palace** (414 9020) Close to Schatzalp funicular, offers good-value dormitory accommodation.

### EATING OUT
***Wide choice, mostly in hotels***

In a town this size, you need to know where to go – if you just walk around hoping to spot a suitable place to eat, you may starve. For a start, get the tourist office's Gastroführer booklet. The more ambitious restaurants are mostly in hotels. There is a choice of two good Chinese restaurants – the lavish Zauberberg in the Europe and the Zum Goldener Drachen in the Bahnhof Terminus. Good-value places include the jolly Al Ponte (pizza and steak both approved of), La Carretta (good for home-made pasta), the small and cosy Gentiana (with an upstairs stübli), and the Hotel Dischma's Röstizerria. For local specialities try Heidi's und Haui's Bündnerstübli. An evening excursion for dinner out of town is popular. A reporter this year enjoyed a fondue evening at Höhenweg, half-way up the Parsenn – 'excellent food, very friendly and good service' – but warns that your ski pass isn't valid in the evening. Schatzalp (reached by a funicular), the Schneider and Landhaus in Frauenkirch have also been recommended.

### APRES-SKI
***Lots on offer, but quiet clientele***

There are plenty of bars, discos and nightclubs, and a large casino in the hotel Europe. But we're not sure how some of them make a living – Davos guests tend to want the quiet life. At tea-time, mega-calories are consumed at the Weber – 'remains excellent' says a 2004 visitor – and Scala has a popular outside terrace. The liveliest place in town is the rustic little Chämi bar (popular with locals); it has 'the best atmosphere later in the evening', according to a reporter. The smart Ex Bar attracts a mixed age group. Nightclubs tend to be sophisticated, expensive and lacking atmosphere during the week. The most popular are the Cabanna and the Cava Grischa (both in the hotel Europe), the Rot Liecht, Paulaner's and Bar Senn.

Bolgenschanze and Bolgen are popular boarder hang-outs.

### OFF THE SLOPES
***Great apart from the buildings***

Provided you're not fussy about building style, Davos can be unreservedly recommended for those not planning to hit the slopes. The towny resort has shops and other diversions, and transport along the valley and up on to the slopes is good – though the best of the mountain restaurants are well out of range for pedestrians. The sports facilities are excellent; the natural ice rink is said to be Europe's biggest, and is supplemented by artificial rinks, both indoor and outdoor. Spectator events include speed skating as well as hockey. And there are lots of walks up on the slopes as well as around the lake and along the valleys.

# Klosters 1190m/3,900ft

In a word association game, Klosters might trigger 'Prince of Wales'. The enlarged cable-car to Gotschna – and the Parsenn – is named after him.

Don't be put off. We don't know why HRH likes to ski in Klosters particularly, but it is certainly not because the place is the exclusive territory of royalty. Most of the really smart socialising goes on behind closed doors, in private chalets.

### THE RESORT

Klosters is a comfortable, quiet village with a much more appealing Alpine flavour than Davos. Klosters Platz is the main focus – a collection of upmarket, traditional-style hotels around the railway station, at the foot of the steep, wooded slopes of Gotschna. Traffic on the road through, leading to Davos, is a problem; a bypass is being built and is due for completion in 2005.

The village spreads along the valley road for quite a way before fading into the countryside; there's then a second concentration of building in the even quieter village of Klosters Dorf.

## THE MOUNTAIN

**Slopes** A cable-car takes you to the Gotschnagrat end of the Parsenn area and a gondola from Klosters Dorf takes you up to the scenic Madrisa area.

**Terrain-parks** The Madrisa area has a park, and there are more options on the other mountains.

**Snow reliability** It's usually reliable higher up but can be poor lower down – you may have to take the lifts down after using the Parsenn slopes.

**Experts** The off-piste possibilities are the main appeal for experts.

**Intermediates** There are excellent cruising runs in all five ski areas shared with Davos.

**Beginners** There are some nursery lifts at valley level, but the wide sunny slopes of Madrisa are more appealing.

**Snowboarding** Local slopes are good, but more boarders stay in Davos.

**Cross-country** There are 35km/22 miles of trails and a Nordic ski school offers lessons. Further trails are easily accessible at Davos.

**Queues** Queues for the Gotschna cable-car have been reduced by a doubling of its capacity, but can still be a problem at weekends and peak holiday times.





**Mountain restaurants** There are a number of atmospheric huts in the woods above the village.

**Schools and guides** There is a choice of three ski and snowboard schools. One reader recommends the Saas, with 'excellent English-speaking instructors'.

**Facilities for children** The ski schools offer classes for children from the age of four and the Madrisa Kids' Club takes children aged two to six.

## STAYING THERE

**How to go** There is a wide choice of packages offered by UK tour operators.

**Hotels** There are some particularly attractive hotels – all bookable on the central reservations phone number, 410 2020. The central Chesa Grischuna (422 2222) is still a firm favourite, combining traditional atmosphere with modern comfort – and a lively après-ski bar. The Albeina (423 2100) is cheaper than the other 4-stars, runs a mini-bus to the lifts, has a good spa and is 'friendly, with good food' says a a fourth-time visitor. We get good reports of the 3-star Cresta (422 2525). The very cosy old Wynegg (422 1340) is popular with British visitors.

**Eating out** Good restaurants abound, but a reporter comments that there is a shortage of the cheap and cheerful variety. Top of the range is the Walserhof. Al Berto's serves the best pizza in town and the rösti at the Alpina is recommended. The Chesa Selfranga is 20 minutes' walk from the centre of town, but is noted for fondue.

**Après-ski** In the village, the Chesa Grischuna is a focus from tea-time onwards, with its live music, bowling and restaurant. A reporter enjoyed the music 'at a volume which allowed you to converse'. The hotel Vereina is recommended for its piano bar.

Gaudy's at the foot of the slopes is a popular stop after skiing, as is the lively bar at the four-star Alpina and the warmly panelled Wynegg.

The Casa Antica is a small disco that livens up on Saturday night. The Kir Royal, under the hotel Silvretta Park, is bigger and more brash.

**Off the slopes** Klosters is an attractive base for walking and cross-country skiing. There is a sport and leisure centre, and some hotels have pools. There are spas in the hotel Bad Serneus just down the valley and further afield at Scuol Tarasp. You can take the train to the interesting old town of Chur.

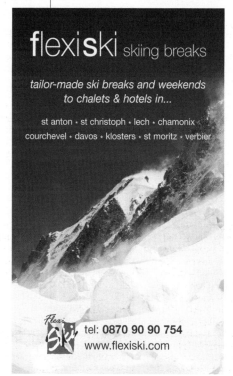

SWISS-IMAGE / MOUNTAIN MARKETING AG

# Flims

*Splendid slopes that deserve to be better known outside Switzerland*

## COSTS

(1)(2)(3)(4)(5)(6)

## RATINGS

| **The slopes** | |
|---|---|
| Snow | *** |
| Extent | **** |
| Expert | *** |
| Intermediate | ***** |
| Beginner | **** |
| Convenience | *** |
| Queues | *** |
| Mountain restaurants | *** |
| **The rest** | |
| Scenery | *** |
| Resort charm | *** |
| Off-slope | *** |

## KEY FACTS

| | |
|---|---|
| **Resort** | 1100m 3,610ft |
| **Altitude** | 1100-3020m 3,610-9,910ft |
| **Lifts** | 29 |
| **Pistes** | 220km 137 miles |
| **Blue** | 35% |
| **Red** | 40% |
| **Black** | 25% |
| **Snowmaking** | 13km 8 miles |

## NEWS

For 2005/06 – not the coming season, note – a six-seat chair is to replace the two Mutta Rodunda drags.





- ➕ Extensive, varied slopes ideal for intermediates, shared with Laax
- ➕ Impressive lift system
- ➕ Virtually queue-free on weekdays
- ➕ Just 90 minutes from Zürich airport

- ➖ Sunny orientation can cause icy or slushy pistes and shut lower runs
- ➖ Village very spread out, which can mean long walks or bus-rides
- ➖ Weekend crowds in high season

**Flims is virtually unknown outside the Swiss and German market and deserves much more international recognition. It has an impressive 220km/137 miles of mainly intermediate pistes and some good off-piste. The resort is popular with weekenders but can be very quiet during the week.**

## THE RESORT

Flims is set on a sunny mountain terrace and has two parts: Dorf sprawls along a busy road, while Waldhaus is set in the trees. The slopes spread across to a lift station at Murschetg, an outpost of Laax. There's also a high-speed quad at Falera, 5km/3 miles from Waldhaus. The better hotels in Waldhaus run efficient courtesy buses to and from the slopes.

## THE MOUNTAINS

Flims has extensive, varied slopes and some high, exposed peaks, including a small glacier. In poor visibility there are plenty of tree-lined runs. Trips are possible by car to Lenzerheide, Davos-Klosters and Arosa.

After fooling around with a unique system for piste grading the resort has reverted to the standard system, but with useful additions. It marks some flattish link runs in orange (green on our map for clarity), and marks recognised off-piste areas in yellow with US-style black-diamond grades of difficulty. You are told to 'take notice of avalanche bulletins' at various places. The piste map shows the time it takes to ride each lift – useful for meeting others on time. Sadly, piste marking on the ground is nowhere near as thoughtful or thorough.

**Slopes** There are powerful gondolas going into the heart of the slopes from both Flims Dorf and Murschetg (where there's a cable-car too). Above mid-mountain, there is a complex web of lifts and runs.

**Terrain-parks** The resort claims to have Europe's best terrain-park at Crap Sogn Gion. As well as the two half-pipes, the walls of which can be built to 6.7m/22ft, there are drops and jumps, quarter-pipes, rails for all levels and a boarder-cross. A Pipe & Park day pass is available. There's a boarder-cross and a half-pipe on the Vorab Glacier.

**Snow reliability** Upper runs are snow-sure, but those back to Flims can suffer from sun. There is snowmaking on the main runs from Crap Sogn Gion, from Segnes-Hütte to Flims and on part of the run to Alp Ruschein.

**Experts** The few black pistes are not seriously steep except in patches, but the identified and graded off-piste areas mean there is a lot of excellent off-piste to tackle without a guide.

**Intermediates** This is a superb area for all intermediates. There are easy snow-sure blue runs on the Vorab glacier and good blue cruising lower down. For the more adventurous and confident, there are plenty of reds and some blacks worth trying – especially the superb, long Sattel run from the top of the Vorab glacier, and the men's World Cup Downhill piste from Crap Sogn Gion to Larnags, which is often beautifully groomed. Flims is also a good area to learn off-piste.

**Beginners** There's a nursery area in Dorf, and alternatives at Startgels and Nagens if snow is poor. The Foppa area has good confidence-building runs to move on to. Getting the bus to the easy runs above Falera is possible.

**Snowboarding** This is a snowboard hot spot. Crap Sogn Gion is a popular meeting point, with loud music from the Rock Bar and the No-Name Café, which overlook half-pipes. Traverses on the piste map are usefully marked as 'not ideal for snowboarders'.

**Cross-country** There are 60km/37 miles of trails scattered around.

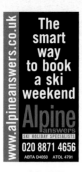

Not Flims but Falera – an attractively rustic alternative base ↗

SWISS-IMAGE / MOUNTAIN MARKETING CORP

**Phone numbers**
From elsewhere in Switzerland add the prefix 081.
From abroad use the prefix +41 81.

## TOURIST OFFICES

**Flims**
t 920 9200

**Laax**
t 921 8181

**Falera**
t 921 3030

For all three resorts:
tourismus@alpenarena.ch
www.alpenarena.ch

**Queues** There is little queuing during the week, but at weekends coach loads of day visitors arrive at Murschetg. Lifts closing because of wind has been a common complaint.
**Mountain restaurants** These are numerous, with a useful short summary of each on the piste map. We prefer the rustic huts lower down (especially the Tegia hut at Larnags).
**Schools and guides** The school has a good reputation. It offers several innovative programmes such as special free-riding and park-and-pipe courses.
**Facilities for children** Children aged three and over can be looked after at one of the Dreamland centres. And there is a Snow Kids Village in the ski school. Nannies are available.

## STAYING THERE

**How to go** Only a handful of UK tour operators feature Flims.
**Hotels** The top hotels are in Waldhaus. Reporters recommend the Adula (928 2828) and Cresta (911 3535). The Park Hotel (928 4848) opened a new fitness and spa facility for 2004. The high tech Riders Palace (927 9700) at Murschetg is a trendy place to stay – with dorm as well as normal rooms.
**Self-catering** The tourist office has a long list of available apartments.
**Eating out** Most Flims restaurants are in hotels. Reporters recommend the Alpina (Waldhaus) and the Pomodoro.
**Après-ski** Flims is, in general, very quiet but the new Legna bar, at the base of the gondola, is reportedly 'very good'. If you want lots of action, head for Murschetg and the Crap Bar, the Riders Palace bar and its Ministry of Sound-run club. The Iglu and Stenna bars are packed when the slopes close. Casa Veglia has live bands.
**Off the slopes** There's an enormous sports centre and 60km/37 miles of marked walks. Historic Chur is a bus-ride away.

## Laax 1020m/3,350ft

Laax is a quiet, characterful old farming community, with most of its modern development a bus-ride away at Murschetg at the base of the lifts. Restaurants and bars are hotel-based and nightlife is limited.

## Falera 1220m/4,000ft

This tiny village is quiet and traffic-free and has good views over three valleys. Most accommodation is in apartments. Two successive fast quad chairs take you to the heart of the slopes.

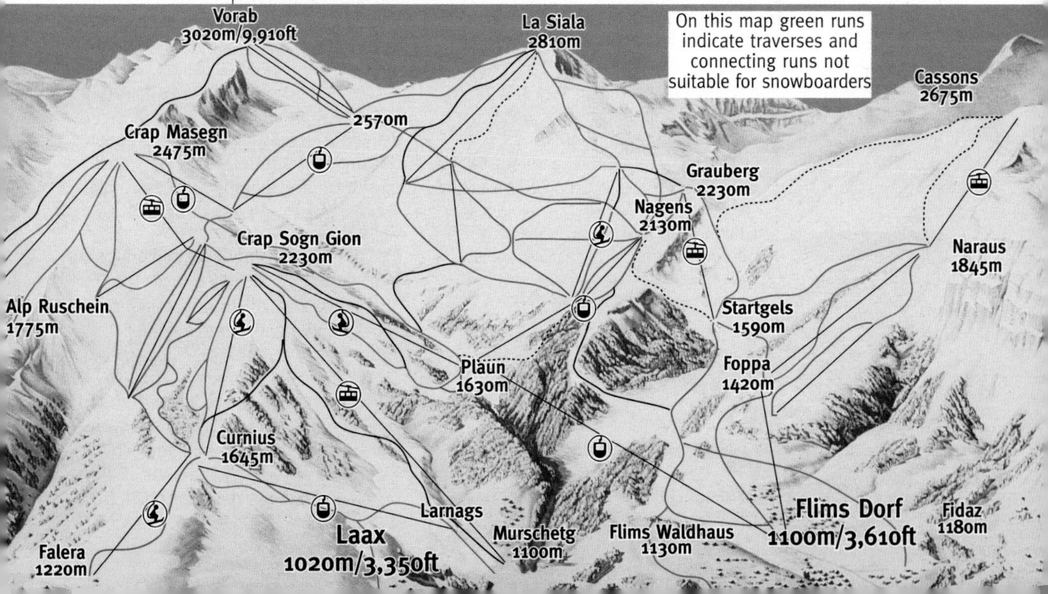

On this map green runs indicate traverses and connecting runs not suitable for snowboarders

Vorab 3020m/9,910ft
La Siala 2810m
Cassons 2675m
2570m
Crap Masegn 2475m
Grauberg 2230m
Nagens 2130m
Crap Sogn Gion 2230m
Naraus 1845m
Alp Ruschein 1775m
Startgels 1590m
Foppa 1420m
Plaun 1630m
Curnius 1645m
Larnags
Laax 1020m/3,350ft
Murschetg 1100m
Flims Waldhaus 1130m
Flims Dorf 1100m/3,610ft
Fidaz 1180m
Falera 1220m

GRINDELWALD TOURIST OFFICE

# Grindelwald

*Traditional town in spectacular scenery at the foot of the Eiger*



## COSTS

①②③④⑤⑥

## RATINGS

| **The slopes** | |
|---|---|
| Snow | ** |
| Extent | *** |
| Expert | ** |
| Intermediate | **** |
| Beginner | *** |
| Convenience | ** |
| Queues | ** |
| Mountain restaurants | *** |
| **The rest** | |
| Scenery | ***** |
| Resort charm | **** |
| Off-slope | **** |

## NEWS

The railway from Grindelwald to the Kleine Scheidegg is to get new rolling stock and a 'more sophisticated' timetable for 2004/05.

For 2003/04 the Läger double chair-lift on Männlichen was replaced by a fast quad with covers, doubling capacity.

On First a new black run, the Black Dream, was made. It goes from Oberjoch down towards the side of the Schilt quad chair. It is marked but not groomed. And snowmaking was installed on the Grindel run.

- + Dramatically set in magnificent scenery, directly beneath the towering north face of the Eiger
- + Lots of long, gentle runs, ideal for intermediates, with links to Wengen
- + Pleasant old village with long mountaineering history, though the tourist trade now sets the tone
- + Fair amount to do off the slopes, including splendid walks and recently expanded toboggan runs

- – Village gets very little midwinter sun
- – Few challenging pistes for experts
- – Inconvenient for visiting Mürren
- – Snow-cover unreliable
- – Major area accessed by a painfully slow gondola, very queue-prone especially at weekends, and by slow and trains (which *may* improve somewhat – see News)

**For stunning views from your hotel window and from the pistes, there are few places to rival Grindelwald, and two of them are just over the hill. The village is nowhere near as special as Wengen or Mürren, but staying here does give you direct access to Grindelwald's own First area. But you can spend ages queueing for, waiting for or sitting in the gondola or trains up into the Kleine Scheidegg area shared with Wengen. (The gondola ride takes over half an hour. We'll reserve judgement on the forthcoming train improvements until we try them.) Grindelwald regulars accept all this as part of the scene.**

## THE RESORT

Grindelwald is set either side of a road along a narrow valley. Buildings are mainly traditional chalet-style. Towering mountains rise steeply from the valley floor, and the resort and main slopes get very little sun in January.

Grindelwald can feel very jolly at times, such as during the ice-carving festival in January, when huge ice-sculptures are on display along the main street. The village is livelier at night than the other Jungfrau resorts of Wengen and Mürren. There's live music in several bars and hotels, but it isn't a place for bopping until dawn.

The main lifts into the slopes shared with Wengen are at Grund, right at the bottom of the sloping village. Near the opposite end of the village, a gondola goes to the separate First area. Trains run between the centre and Grund, and buses link the lift stations – but these get congested at times and reporters say they are too infrequent.

The most convenient place to stay for the slopes is at Grund. But this is out of the centre and rather charmless. There's a wide range of hotels in the heart of the village, handy enough for everything else, including the First area, at the foot of which are nursery slopes, ski school and kindergarten.

Trips to other resorts are not very easy, but you can drive to Adelboden. Getting to the tougher, higher slopes of Mürren is a lengthy business unless you go to Lauterbrunnen by car.

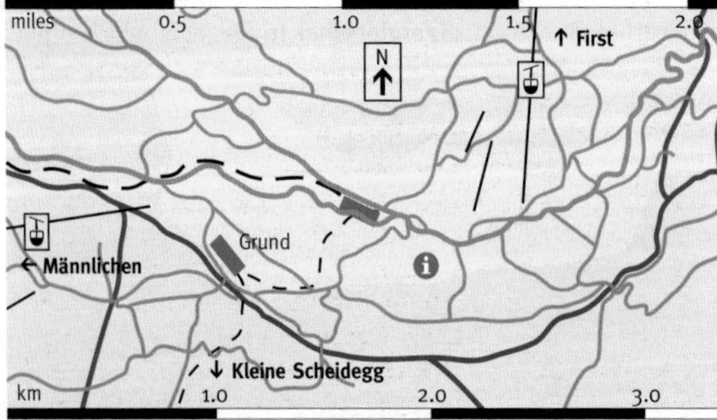


## THE MOUNTAINS

The major area of slopes is shared with Wengen and offers a mix of wooded slopes and open slopes higher up. The smaller First area is mainly open, though there are wooded runs to the village. The Aletsch glacier which can be seen from the Jungfraujoch station (see feature panel later in this chapter) has been declared a UNESCO World Nature Heritage Site.

The view from First: on the right, the gentle slopes of Kleine Scheidegg and Männlichen; on the left, the precipitous north face of the Eiger ➔

SNOWPIX.COM / CHRIS GILL

**KEY FACTS**

| | |
|---|---|
| **Resort** | 1035m 3,400ft |
| For Jungfrau region | |
| **Slopes** | 945-2970m 3,100-9,740ft |
| **Lifts** | 42 |
| **Pistes** | 213km 133 miles |
| **Blue** | 25% |
| **Red** | 61% |
| **Black** | 14% |
| **Snowmaking** | 60km 37 miles |
| For First-Männlichen-Kleine-Scheidegg only | |
| **Slopes** | 945-2485m 3,100-8,150ft |
| **Lifts** | 30 |
| **Pistes** | 150km 93 miles |

**LIFT PASSES**

**Jungfrau Top Ski Region**
Covers Grindelwald, Wengen and Mürren lifts, trains between them and Grindelwald ski-bus.

**Main pass**
1 day SF55
6 days SF282

**Senior citizens**
Over 62: 6 days SF254

**Children**
Under 20: 6 days SF226
Under 16: 6 days SF141
Under 6: free pass

**Notes**
Day pass price is for Grindelwald and Wengen area only.

**Alternative passes**
Passes available for Grindelwald and Wengen only and for Mürren only. Non-skiers pass available.

## THE SLOPES
### *Broad and mainly gentle*

From Grund, near the western end of town, you can get to **Männlichen** by an appallingly slow two-stage gondola or to **Kleine Scheidegg** by an even slower cog railway (due for improvement for 2004/05 – reports please from 2005 visitors). The slopes of the separate south-facing First area are reached by a long, slow three-stage gondola starting a bus-ride east of the centre. From all over the slopes there are superb views, not only of the Eiger but also of the Wetterhorn and other peaks. Piste marking is poor, and one reporter complains that from First it is difficult to determine which run you are on – and therefore easy to end up at the wrong point in the valley.

## TERRAIN-PARKS
### *First things first*

There is a terrain-park at Oberjoch and a huge super-pipe at Schrekfeld, both on First.

## SNOW RELIABILITY
### *Poor*

Grindelwald's low altitude (the slopes go down to below 1000m/3,280ft and few are above 2000m/6,560ft) and the lack of much snowmaking (though it is increasing) mean this is not a resort to book far in advance. And it's not the place for a late-season holiday. First is sunny, and so even less snow-sure than the main area. We have also had reports of poor piste grooming.

## FOR EXPERTS
### *They are trying*

The area is quite limited for experts. The black run on First beneath the gondola back to town is quite tough, especially when the snow has suffered from too much sun. A new black was created near the top of First last season. There are now two ungroomed itineraries from the Lauberhorn chair, widening the options slightly.

Heli-trips with mountain guides are organised if there are enough takers.

## FOR INTERMEDIATES
### *Ideal intermediate terrain*

In good snow, First makes a splendid intermediate playground, though the general lack of trees makes the area less friendly than the larger Kleine Scheidegg-Männlichen area. The runs to the valley are great fun. Nearly all the runs from Kleine Scheidegg are long blues or gentle reds. On the Männlichen there's a choice of gentle runs down to the mid-station of the gondola up from Grund. In good snow, you can get right down to the bottom on easy red runs – 'barely deserving the grade', says a reporter (and one of these runs used to be marked black).

For tougher pistes, head for the top of the Lauberhorn lift and the runs to Kleine Scheidegg, or to Wixi (following the start of the downhill course). You could also try the north-facing run from Eigergletscher to Salzegg, which often has the best snow late in the season.

## FOR BEGINNERS
### *Depends where you go*

The Bodmi nursery slope at the bottom of First is scenic but can suffer from the sun and its low altitude – a 2004 reporter said Grindelwald instructors used it despite it being icy, full of craters and spoiled by fast skiers and tobogganers racing through. Kleine

## SCHOOLS

**Grindelwald Sports**
t 854 1280
info@
grindelwaldsports.ch

**Swiss Snowboard**
t 853 3353

**Snowsports Kleine Scheidegg**
t 855 1545

**Classes**
(Sports prices)
5 full days SF255

**Private lessons**
SF80 for 1hr

## CHILDREN

**Kinderhort Sunshine**
t 853 0440
Ages from 1mnth; 9.30-4pm

**Kidsclub Bodmi**
t 854 1280
Ages from 3; 9.15-3.30; SF50 per day

**Ski school**
Takes children from age 3 (5 days SF255)

## GETTING THERE

**Air** Zürich 195km/121 miles (3hr); Bern 70km/43 miles (1½hr).

**Rail** Station in resort.





## boarding

*Intermediates will enjoy the area most – the beginners' slopes can be bare, while experts will hanker for Mürren's steep, off-piste slopes. First is the main boarders' mountain, not only because of the terrain-park and big pipe but also the open free-ride terrain accessed via the top lifts. There are still quite a few drag-lifts.*

Scheidegg has a better, higher beginner area and splendid long runs to progress to, served by the railway.

### FOR CROSS-COUNTRY
***Good but shady***

There are over 25km/16 miles of prepared tracks. Almost all of this is onothe valley floor, so it's very shady in midwinter and may have poor snow later in the season.

### QUEUES
***Can be dreadful at peak times***

The queues for the gondola and train at Grund can be very bad in high season, especially at weekends. A reporter last year speaks of half-hour waits for the gondola; the mid-station at Holenstein is closed until the queues down in Grindelwald have cleared. In the past this produced long queues for chairs in the Männlichen sector – but the upgrading of the Läger chair last season has 'revolutionised the area', says a 2004 reporter. You may find long waits for the gondola down from First when the lower runs are closed. Queues for the Oberjoch chair on First have been eased by the Schilt quad (new for 2002/03).

### MOUNTAIN RESTAURANTS
***Wide choice***

See the Wengen chapter for options around Kleine Scheidegg and down towards Wengen. Brandegg, on the railway, is recommended for 'wonderful' apple fritters and its sunny terrace. Berghaus Bort does very good rösti, but the 'best rösti anywhere' is at the Jägerstubli, off the Rennstrecke piste.

### SCHOOLS AND GUIDES
***Mixed views***

One report declares the main school, Grindelwald Sports, 'very good'; spoken English is normally excellent. But a 2004 reporter criticised them for taking her children to the First beginner area (see For Beginners) when the Kleine Scheidegg 'is better and more convenient for families who want to ski together'.

### FACILITIES FOR CHILDREN
***Good reputation***

See above, but a past reporter who put four children through the Grindelwald mill praised caring and effective instructors. The First mountain restaurant runs a day nursery, which is a neat idea.

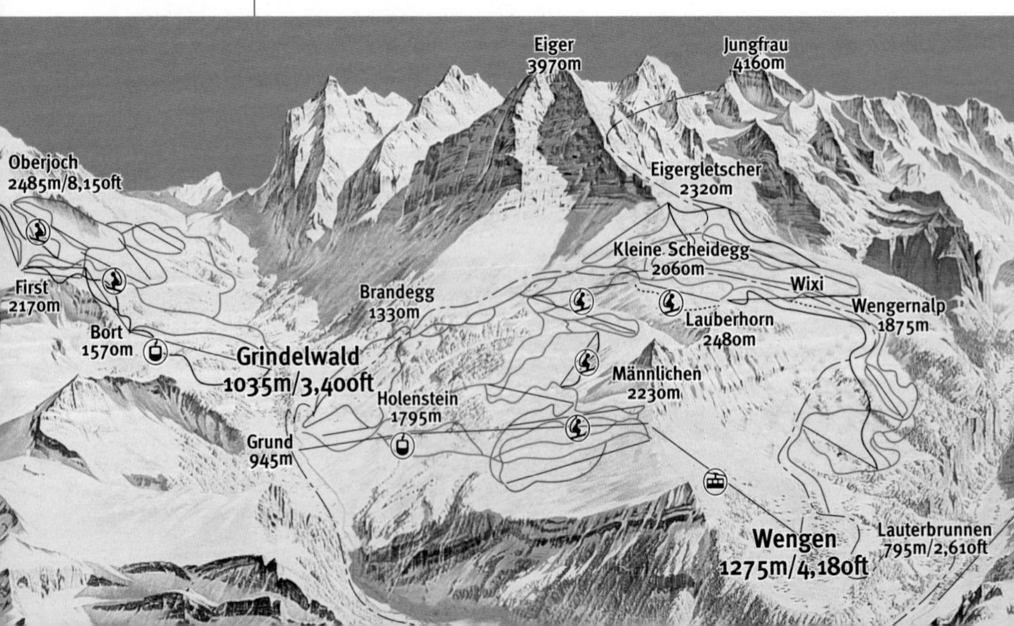

## ACTIVITIES

**Indoor** Sports centre (swimming pool, sauna, steam, fitness room, games room), indoor ice rink, curling, concerts, cinema

**Outdoor** 80km/ 50 miles of cleared paths, train rides to Jungfraujoch, ice rink, tobogganing, snow-shoe excursions, climbing, snow tubing, paragliding, glacier tours, ice climbing, husky rides

**Phone numbers**
From elsewhere in Switzerland add the prefix 033.
From abroad use the prefix +41 33.

## TOURIST OFFICE

**t** 854 1212
touristcenter@grindelwald.ch
www.grindelwald.ch

## REPORTS WANTED

Recently we have had few reports on this resort. If you go there, please do send us a report.

The best reports earn a copy of the next edition, and can lead to free lift passes in future.

See page 10.

## STAYING THERE

### HOW TO GO
***Limited range of packages***

The hotels UK tour operators offer are mainly at the upper end of the market.
**Hotels** One 5-star, a dozen 4-stars, and plenty of more modest places are available.
(((((5) **Grand Regina** (854 8600) Big and imposing 5-star; right next to the station. Nightly music in the bar. Pool.
((((4) **Belvedere** (854 5757) Family-run, close to the station, 'wonderful' pool.
((((4) **Schweizerhof** (853 2202) Beautifully decorated 4-star chalet at west end of the centre, close to the station. Pool.
((((4) **Bodmi** (853 1220) Little chalet right on the village nursery slopes.
(((3) **Hirschen** (854 8484) Family-run 3-star by nursery slopes. Good food.
(((3) **Fiescherblick** (854 5353) Hospitable chalet on the eastern fringe, five minutes from the First gondola.
(((3) **Derby** (854 5461) Popular, modern 3-star next to station, with 'first-class' service, good food and great views.
((2) **Tschuggen** (853 1781) Modest chalet in a central position below the nursery slopes.
(1) **Hotel Wetterhorn** (853 1218) Cosy, simple chalet way beyond the village, with great views of the glacier.
**Self-catering** A reporter recommends the apartments of the hotel Hirschen (854 8484) for comfort and space. Another rates those in the hotel Eiger (854 3131) 'excellent, great value'.

### EATING OUT
***Hotel based***

There's a wide choice of good hotel restaurants, but cheaper pizzeria-style places are in short supply. The Latino does home-made Italian cooking. Among the more attractively traditional places are: the Swiss Chalet in the Eiger; Schmitte in the Schweizerhof; Challi-Stübli in the Kreuz; and the Alte Post. The Fiescherblick's Swiss Bistro is repeatedly recommended – 'brilliant but expensive'. The Kirchbühl and Oberland are good for vegetarians, the Bahnhof in the Derby for fondue and raclette. Hotel Spinne has many options: Italian, Mexican, Chinese and the candlelit Rôtisserie for a special romantic meal.

### APRES-SKI
***Relaxed***

There are at least three discos and a handful of bars that aim to keep going late. There's also a cinema, plus ice hockey and curling matches to watch. There's an excellent sports centre with pool. Tobogganing and tubing are organised on First, and some evenings a 'Sledge Express' train takes people up to Brandegg/Alpiglen for fondues and tobogganing.

### OFF THE SLOPES
***Plenty to do, easy to get around***

There are many cleared paths with magnificent views, especially around First – and there's a special (though expensive) pedestrian bus/lift pass. A trip to Jungfraujoch is spectacular (see below), and excursions by train are easy to Interlaken and possible to Bern. Tobogganing has undergone a bit of a renaissance, with runs up to 15km/9 miles on First (Europe's longest) and 57km/35 miles of runs in total. Helicopter flights from Männlichen are recommended.

### STAYING UP THE MOUNTAIN
***Several possibilities***

See the Wengen chapter for details of rooms at Kleine Scheidegg. The Berghaus Bort (853 3651), at the gondola station in the middle of the First area, is an attractive alternative.

### THE JOURNEY TO THE TOP OF EUROPE

*From Kleine Scheidegg you can take a train through the Eiger to the highest railway station in Europe – Jungfraujoch at 3454m/11,332ft. The journey is a bit tedious – you're in a tunnel except when you stop to look out of a gallery carved into the sheer north face of the Eiger, where there are magnificent views over to Männlichen and the villages. At the top is a big restaurant complex. There's an 'ice palace' carved out of the glacier, with ice sculptures and slippery walkways, an outdoor 'plateau' to wander around and a viewing tower from which you have fabulous views of the Aletsch glacier (a UNESCO World Heritage Site).*

*The cost is SF49.50 with a Jungfrau lift pass for three days or more. At the top the air is thin, and some people have breathing or balance problems.*

SNOWPIX.COM / CHRIS GILL

# Mürren

*Stupendous views, an epic run, and a chocolate-box village*

**COSTS**

1 2 3 4 5 6

**RATINGS**

| **The slopes** | |
|---|---|
| Snow | *** |
| Extent | * |
| Expert | *** |
| Intermediate | *** |
| Beginner | ** |
| Convenience | *** |
| Queues | *** |
| Mountain restaurants | ** |
| **The rest** | |
| Scenery | ***** |
| Charm | ***** |
| Off-slope | *** |

**NEWS**

There isn't much that changes in Mürren. That's one of the things that makes it so special.



**REPORTS WANTED**

Recently we have had few reports on this resort. If you go there, please do send us a report.

The best reports earn a copy of the next edition, and can lead to free lift passes in future.

See page 10.

+ Tiny, charming, traditional 'traffic-free' village, with snowy paths and chocolate-box chalets
+ Stupendous scenery, best enjoyed on the challenging run from the panoramic Schilthorn
+ Good sports centre
+ Good snow high up, even when the rest of the region is suffering

− Extent of local pistes very limited, no matter what your level of expertise
− Lower slopes can be in poor condition
− Quiet, limited nightlife

**Mürren is one of our favourite resorts. There may be other mountain villages that are equally pretty, but none of them enjoys views like those from Mürren across the deep valley to the rock faces and glaciers of the Eiger, Mönch and Jungfrau: simply breathtaking. Then there's the Schilthorn run – 1300m/4,270ft vertical with an unrivalled combination of varied terrain and glorious views.**

**Our visits are normally one-day affairs; holidaymakers, we concede, are likely to want to explore the extensive intermediate slopes of Wengen and Grindelwald, across the valley. And you have to accept that getting there takes time.**

**It was in Mürren that the British more or less invented modern skiing. Sir Arnold Lunn organised the first ever slalom race here in 1922. Some 12 years earlier his father, Sir Henry, had persuaded the locals to open the railway in winter so that he could bring the first winter package tour here. Sir Arnold's son Peter, who first skied here in November 1916, still skis here with his children and grandchildren. He still takes part in the annual Inferno race and you may bump into him around the village bars.**

## THE RESORT

Mürren is set on a shelf high above the Lauterbrunnen valley floor, across from Wengen, and can be reached only by cable-car from Stechelberg (via Gimmelwald) or funicular and then railway from Lauterbrunnen. Once you get there you can't fail to be struck by Mürren's tranquillity and beauty. The tiny village is made up of paths and narrow lanes weaving between tiny wooden chalets and a handful of bigger hotel buildings. The roofs and paths are normally snow-covered.

Two further stages of the cable-car take you up to the high slopes of Birg and the Schilthorn. Nearby lifts go to the main lower slopes, and a recently modernised funicular halfway along the village accesses the other slopes.

Mürren's traffic-free status is being somewhat eroded and there are now a few delivery trucks. But the place still isn't plagued by electric carts and taxis in the way that most other traditional 'traffic-free' resorts now are.

It's not the place to go for lively nightlife, shopping or showing off your latest gear to admiring hordes. It is the place to go if you want tranquillity and stunning views. The village is so small that location is not a concern. Nothing is more than a few minutes' walk.

## THE MOUNTAIN

Mürren's slopes aren't extensive (53km/33 miles in total). But it has something for everyone, including one of our favourite runs, and a vertical of some 1300m/4,270ft. And those happy to take the time to cross the valley to Wengen-Grindelwald will find plenty of options. These resorts are covered by the Jungfrau lift pass.

### THE SLOPES

***Small but interesting***

There are three connected areas around the village, reaching no higher than 2145m/7,040ft. The biggest is **Schiltgrat**, served by a fast quad chair behind the cable-car station. You can

## KEY FACTS

| Resort | 1650m<br>5,410ft |
|---|---|
| For Jungfrau region | |
| Altitude | 945-2970m<br>3,100-9,740ft |
| Lifts | 42 |
| Pistes | 213km<br>133 miles |
| Blue | 25% |
| Red | 61% |
| Black | 14% |
| Snowmaking | 60km<br>37 miles |
| For Mürren-Schilthorn only | |
| Slopes | 1650-2970m<br>5,410-9,740ft |
| Lifts | 12 |
| Pistes | 53km<br>33 miles |

also get there from the top of the modernised funicular that goes from the middle of the village to the nursery slope at **Allmendhubel** – from where a run and a fast chair take you to the slightly higher **Maulerhubel**. Runs go down from here to the Winteregg stop on the railway. These lower slopes take you up to around 2000m/6,560ft.

Much more interesting are the higher slopes reached by cable-car. The first stage takes you to Birg and the **Engetal** area, where an old T-bar serves short, steep, shady slopes. Two chair-lifts below the Engetal serve some snow-sure intermediate slopes. But plans for a third chair, back up to Birg, have been shelved. To get back to the Birg cable-car station and avoid the tricky black run down to the village, you face an annoying walk up from these chairs to the old T-bar.

The final stage of the cable-car takes you up to the summit of the **Schilthorn** and the Piz Gloria revolving restaurant, made famous by the James Bond film *On Her Majesty's Secret Service.* In good snow you can go all the way from here to Lauterbrunnen – almost 16km/10 miles. The Inferno race (see separate box) takes place over this course, conditions permitting. Below Winteregg it's all boring paths.

### TERRAIN-PARKS
***Affirmative***

There are a half-pipe and a terrain-park on the lower slopes of Schiltgrat.

### SNOW RELIABILITY
***Good on the upper slopes***

The Jungfrau region does not have a good snow record – but Mürren always has the best snow in the area. When Wengen-Grindelwald (and Mürren's lower slopes) have problems, the Schilthorn and Engetal often have packed powder snow because of their height and orientation – north-east to east. The run from below Engetal to Allmendhubel and parts of the lower slopes have snowmaking – and a 2004 reporter complains of it being left on at midday forming 'lumps of wet icing sugar' while another tells of bare patches on the lower slopes being left that way.

### FOR EXPERTS
***One wonderful piste***

The run from the top of the Schilthorn starts with a steep but not terrifying slope, in the past generally mogulled but now often groomed. It flattens into a schuss to Engetal, below Birg. Then there's a wonderful, wide run with stunning views over the valley to the

## LIFT PASSES

**Jungfrau Top Ski Region**
Covers Wengen, Mürren and Grindelwald, trains between them and Grindelwald ski-bus.

**Main pass**
1 day SF55
6 days SF282

**Senior citizens**
Over 62: 6 days SF254

**Children**
Under 20: 6 days SF226
Under 16: 6 days SF141
Under 6: free pass

**Notes**
Day pass price is for Mürren-Schilthorn area only.

**Alternative passes**
Passes available for Grindelwald and Wengen only and for Mürren. Non-skiers pass available.





## SCHOOLS

**Swiss**
t 8551247

**Classes**
6 2hr days SF135

**Private lessons**
SF110 for 2hr for 2 persons



## boarding

*Like many Swiss resorts, Mürren has a traditional image, but it is trying to move with the times and offer a more snowboard-friendly attitude – and the major lifts are cable-cars and chair-lifts. The terrain above Mürren is suitable mainly for good free-riders – it's steep, with a lot of off-piste. Intermediates will find the area tough and limited; nearby Wengen is ideal, and much better for beginners.*

Eiger, Mönch and Jungfrau. Since the chair-lifts were built here you can play on these upper runs for as long as you like. Below the lifts you hit the Kanonenrohr (gun barrel). This is a very narrow shelf with solid rock on one side and a steep drop on the other – protected by nets. After an open slope and scrappy zig-zag path, you arrive at the 'hog's back' and can descend towards the village on either side of Allmendhubel.

From Schiltgrat a short, serious mogul run – the Kandahar – descends towards the village, but experts are more likely to be interested in the off-piste runs into the Blumental – both from here (the north-facing Blumenlucke run) and from Birg (the sunnier Tschingelchrachen) – or the adventurous runs from the Schilthorn.

### FOR INTERMEDIATES
***Limited, but Wengen nearby***

Keen piste-bashers will want to make a few trips to the long cruising runs of Wengen-Grindelwald. The best easy cruising run in Mürren is the north-facing blue down to Winteregg. The reds on the other low slopes can get mogulled, and snow conditions can be poor. The area below the Engetal normally has good snow, and you can choose your gradient.

### FOR BEGINNERS
***Not ideal, but adequate***

The nursery slopes at Allmendhubel, at the top of the funicular, are on the steep side. And there are not many easy runs to graduate to – though the blue down the Winteregg chair is easy, and a couple of blues are served by the long Gimmeln drag and the less tiring Schiltgrat chair.

### FOR CROSS-COUNTRY
***Forget it***

There is one small loop above the village in the Blumental, and more extensive loops down at Lauterbrunnen or Stechelberg. But snow is unreliable at valley height.

### QUEUES
***Generally not a problem***

Mürren doesn't get as crowded as Wengen and Grindelwald, except on sunny Sundays. There can be queues for the cable-cars – usually when snow shortages bring in people from lower resorts. The top stage has only one cabin.

### MOUNTAIN RESTAURANTS
***Nothing outstanding***

Piz Gloria revolves once an hour, displaying a fabulous 360° panorama of peaks and lakes. We don't like the ambience here, but a 2004 reporter tells of 'a very nice goulash soup' and says, 'It is incredible value for money just for the view (and cheaper than Méribel).' By the Engetal chair-lifts, the Schilthornhütte is small and rustic and 'does excellent special coffees'.

Lower down, the Suppenalp in the Blumental is rustic and quietly set but gets no sun in January and a reporter this year had very poor service. As you

### THE INFERNO RACE

*Every January 1,800 amateurs compete in Mürren's spectacular Inferno race. Conditions permitting, and they usually don't, the race goes from the top of the Schilthorn right down to Lauterbrunnen – a vertical drop of 2175m/7,140ft and a distance of almost 16km/10 miles, incorporating a short climb at Maulerhubel. The racers start individually at 12 second intervals; the fastest finish the course in around 15 minutes, but anything under half an hour is very respectable.*

*The race was started by Sir Arnold Lunn in 1928 when he and his friends climbed up to spend the night in a mountain hut and then raced down in the morning. For many years the race was organised by the British-run Kandahar Club, and there is still a strong British presence among the competitors.*

An idyllic hideaway, and one of our favourite places for a short stay ➔

SNOWPIX.COM / CHRIS GILL

## CHILDREN

**Snowgarden**
Ages 1mnth to 5yr; SF54 per day.

**Ski school**
Takes ages 5 and over (6 2hr days SF135).

## GETTING THERE

**Air** Zürich 195km/ 121 miles (3½hr); Bern 70km/43 miles (1½hr).

**Rail** Lauterbrunnen; transfer by mountain railway and tram.

## ACTIVITIES

**Indoor** Alpine Sports Centre: swimming pool, sauna, solarium, steam bath, massage, fitness room, gymnasium, squash, library, museum

**Outdoor** Ice rink, curling, ice-climbing, tobogganing, 12km/7 miles cleared paths, snow-shoeing

**Phone numbers**
From elsewhere in Switzerland add the prefix 033.
From abroad use the prefix +41 33.

## TOURIST OFFICE

**t** 856 8686
info@muerren.ch
www.wengen-muerren.ch

might expect, Sonnenberg is sunnier and a reporter enjoyed 'tasty and filling rösti'. Gimmeln is a self-service place with a large terrace, famous for its apple cake. Winteregg does something similar, as well as 'superb rösti' and 'the best burger east of the Rockies'. Both have little playgrounds to amuse kids.

### SCHOOLS AND GUIDES
***Long tradition***

We lack recent reports but the school has a long tradition of teaching British guests.

### FACILITIES FOR CHILDREN
***Adequate***

There is a baby slope with a rope tow. And there is a children's club at the sports centre. The ski school takes children from five years.

## STAYING THERE

### HOW TO GO
***Mainly hotels, packaged or not***

A handful of operators offer packages to Mürren.

**Hotels** There are fewer than a dozen hotels, ranging widely in style.

((((4 **Anfi Palace** (856 9999) Victorian pile near station.

((((4 **Eiger** (856 5454) Plain-looking 'chalet' blocks next to railway station, widely recommended; good blend of efficiency and charm; good food; pool.

(((3 **Alpenruh** (856 8800) Attractively renovated chalet next to the cable-car.

(((3 **Edelweiss** (856 5600) Block-like but friendly; good food and facilities.

(((3 **Jungfrau** (855 4545) Perfectly placed for families, in front of the baby slope and close to the funicular.

((2 **Alpenblick** (855 1327) Simple, small, modern chalet near station.

**Self-catering** There are plenty of chalets and apartments in the village for independent travellers to rent.

### EATING OUT
***Mainly in hotels***

The main alternative to hotels is the rustic Stägerstübli – a bar as well as restaurant. The locals eat in the little diner at the back. The food at the Eiger hotel is good, and the Bellevue and Alpenruh get good reports.

### APRES-SKI
***Not devoid of life***

The Eiger Bar (in the Eiger guest house, not the hotel) is the Brits' meeting place. The tiny Stägerstübli is cosy, and the place to meet locals. Other activities are hotel-based. The Anfi Palace's Balloon bar is an attempt at a trendy cocktail bar; it also has a weekend disco, the Inferno. The Bliemli Chäller disco in the Blumental caters for kids, the nightly Tachi disco in the Eiger for a more mixed crowd.

### OFF THE SLOPES
***Tranquillity but not much else***

There isn't a lot to amuse people who don't want to hit the slopes. But there is a very good sports centre, with an outdoor ice rink. Excursions by car or train to Interlaken and to Bern are easy. It's no problem for friends to return to the village for lunch. The only problem with meeting at the top of the cable-car instead is the expense.

### STAYING DOWN THE VALLEY
***A cheaper option***

Lauterbrunnen is a good budget base. It has a resort atmosphere and access to and from both Wengen and Mürren until late. We've happily stayed at the Schützen (855 3026) and Oberland (855 1241) on several occasions. And the Silberhorn (856 2210) is recommended as 'good and outstanding value'.

SNOWPIX.COM / CHRIS GILL

# Saas-Fee

*Beautiful, car-free village with slopes on top of the world*

## COSTS

(1)(2)(3)(4)(5)(6)

## RATINGS

| **The slopes** | |
|---|---|
| Snow | ***** |
| Extent | ** |
| Expert | *** |
| Intermediate | **** |
| Beginner | ***** |
| Convenience | *** |
| Queues | *** |
| Mountain restaurants | *** |
| **The rest** | |
| Scenery | **** |
| Charm | ***** |
| Off-slope | **** |

## NEWS

Family lift pass offers were introduced last season, with second and all further children skiing free when two adults purchase passes for 6 days or more.

The Ferienart Resort Hotel, formerly the Walliserhof, has achieved 5-star status.



## KEY FACTS

| | |
|---|---|
| **Resort** | 1800m 5,910ft |
| **Slopes** | 1800-3500m 5,910-11,480ft |
| **Lifts** | 22 |
| **Pistes** | 100km 62 miles |
| **Blue** | 25% |
| **Red** | 50% |
| **Black** | 25% |
| **Snowmaking** | 8km 5 miles |

- + Spectacular setting amid high peaks and glaciers
- + Traditional, 'traffic-free' village
- + Most of the runs are at exceptionally high altitude, and snow-sure
- + Good off-slope facilities – even a mountain specially for walking and tobogganing

- − Disappointingly small area of slopes, with mainly easy runs
- − Glacier limits off-piste exploration
- − Much of the area is in shadow in midwinter – cold and dark
- − Bad weather can shut the slopes
- − Long village can mean quite a bit of walking to and from the slopes
- − Some visitors suffer altitude problems at top of mountain

**Saas-Fee is one of our favourite places. It oozes Swiss charm, and the setting is stunning – spectacular glaciers and 4000m/13,120ft peaks surround the place. And good snow is guaranteed, even late in the season: the altitude you spend most of your time at – between 2500m and 3500m (8,200ft and 11,480ft) – is unrivalled in the Alps.**

**But we tend to drop in for a couple of days at a time, so the limited extent of the slopes never becomes a problem; for a week's holiday, it would. Top to bottom there is an impressive 1800m/5,900ft vertical – but there aren't many alternative ways down. Keen, mileage-hungry intermediates should look elsewhere, as should experts (except those prepared to go touring). For the rest, it's a question of priorities and expectations. Over to you.**

## THE RESORT

Like nearby Zermatt, Saas-Fee is a high-altitude mountain village centred on narrow streets lined by attractive old chalets and free of cars (there are car parks at the resort entrance) but not free of electric milk floats posing as taxis. On most other counts, Saas-Fee and its more exalted neighbour are a long way apart in style.

There are some very smart hotels (plus many more modest ones) and plenty of good eating and drinking places. But there's little of the glamour and greed that, for some, spoil Zermatt – and even the electric taxis here are driven at a more considerate pace. Saas-Fee still feels like a village, with its cow sheds more obviously still containing cows. The village may be chilly in January, but when the spring sun is beating down, Saas-Fee is a quite beautiful place in which to just stroll around and relax, admiring the impressive view.

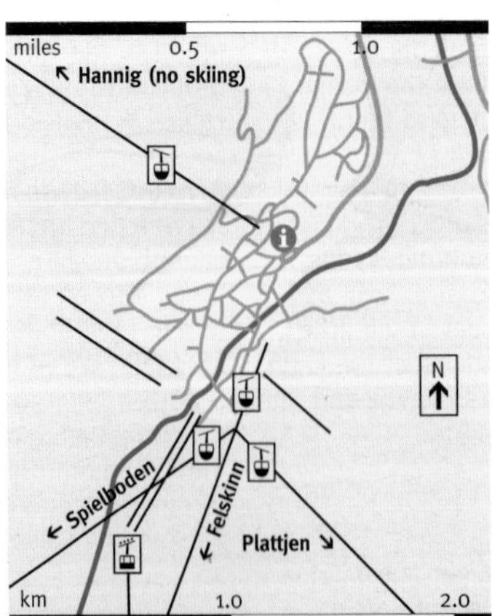


Depending on where you're staying and which way you want to go up the mountain, you may do more marching than strolling. It's a long walk from one end of the spread-out village to the other, though your hotel may run a courtesy bus to and from the lifts. Three major lifts start from the southern end of the village, at the foot of the slopes, and lots of the hotels and apartments are 1km/0.5 miles or more away. The modern Alpin Express starts below the centre, though, quite near the entrance to the resort.

The village centre has the school and guides' office, the church and a

## LIFT PASSES

**Saas-Fee area**
Covers all lifts in Saas-Fee only.

**Beginners**
Cheap pass for nursery lifts.

**Main pass**
1 day SF60
6 days SF294

**Children**
Under 16: 6 days SF176
Under 6: free pass

**Notes**
Single and return tickets on most main lifts. Afternoon pass available. Free passes for second and all further children when two adults purchase for 6 days or more.

**Alternative passes**
Separate passes for each of the other Saastal ski areas (Saas-Grund, Saas-Almagell, Saas-Balen). Pass for all four villages also available; includes ski-bus between them.

few more shops than elsewhere, but it doesn't add up to much. On a sunny day, though, the restaurant terraces fronting the nursery slopes at the far end of the village are a magnet, with breathtaking views up to the ring of 4000m/13,120ft peaks – you can see why the village is called 'The Pearl of the Alps'.

Staying near a main lift makes most sense. If you do end up at the wrong (north) end of the village – and most budget accommodation is there – ease the pain by storing kit near the lifts.

The slopes of Saas-Almagell and Saas-Grund are not far away, and you can buy a lift pass that covers all these resorts and buses between them. There is a footpath down to Saas-Almagell, which one reporter enjoyed skiing down. Day trips by car/train to Zermatt are also possible.

## THE MOUNTAIN

The area is a strange mixture of powerful modern lifts (a two-stage 30-person gondola followed by an underground funicular which take you up 1700m/5,580ft vertical) and a lot of old-fashioned T-bars (there's only one chair-lift). Blame the glaciers, which can move downhill by 100m/330ft a year; drag-lift pylons can be moved to cope, but chair-lifts are not practicable. Readers complain about the 'walks and climbs' involved in getting from one lift to another. Take it easy when climbing out of the top lift station: the altitude of 3500m/ 11,480ft means some people feel faint because of the thin air.

The upper slopes are largely gentle, while the lower mountain, below the glacier, is steeper and rockier, needing good snow-cover. There is very little shelter here in bad weather: during and after heavy snowfalls you may find yourself limited to the nursery area.

Saas-Fee is one of the leading resorts for mountaineering and ski touring from valley to valley. Several nearby peaks can be climbed, and the extended Haute Route from Chamonix via Zermatt ends here.

### THE SLOPES
***A glacier runs through it***

There are two routes up to the main **Felskinn** area. The efficient 30-person Alpin Express jumbo gondola, starting across the river from the main village, takes you to Felskinn via a mid-station at Morenia (where you have to change cabins). The alternative is a short drag

↑ For close-up views of glaciers, there is nowhere like it

SNOWPIX.COM / CHRIS GILL

across the nursery slope at the south end of the village, and then the Felskinn cable-car. From Felskinn, the Metro Alpin underground funicular hurtles up to Mittelallalin. From below here, the top two drag-lifts access the high point of 3500m/11,480ft.

Also from the south end of the village, a gondola leaves for Spielboden. This is met by a cable-car which takes you up to **Längfluh**.

Between Felskinn and Längfluh is an off-limits glacier area. A very long drag-lift from Längfluh takes you to a point where you can get down to the Felskinn area. These two sectors are served mainly by drag-lifts, and you can get down to the village from both.

Another gondola from the south end of the village goes up to Saas-Fee's smallest area, **Plattjen**.

**TERRAIN-PARKS**
***Well developed***

Saas-Fee was early into the fun-park business, and has well-established facilities in the Felskinn sector including a big half-pipe, a fun-park and a boarder-cross. The nearby Morenia bar is the place for a break.

**SNOW RELIABILITY**
***Good at the highest altitudes***

Most of Saas-Fee's slopes face north and many are above 2500m/8,200ft, making this one of the most reliable resorts for snow in the Alps. The glacier is open most of the year. Visitors tell us that the substantial recent investment in snow-guns still doesn't completely ensure good coverage on the rocky lower slopes. Piste grooming is 'excellent'.

**FOR EXPERTS**
***Not a lot to keep your interest***

There is not much steep stuff, except on the bottom half of the mountain where the snow tends not to be as good. There is a short black run from Felskinn that certainly deserves its grading. The slopes around the top of Längfluh often provide good powder, and there are usually moguls above Spielboden. The blacks and trees on Plattjen are worth exploring. The glacier puts limits on the local off-piste even with a guide – crevasse danger is extreme. But there are extensive touring possibilities, especially late in the season.

**FOR INTERMEDIATES**
***Great for gentle cruising***

Saas-Fee is ideal for early intermediates and those not looking for much of a challenge. For long cruises, head for Mittelallalin. The top of the mountain, down as far as Längfluh in one direction, and as far as Morenia in the other, is ideal, with usually excellent snow. Gradients range from gentle blues to slightly steeper reds which can build up smallish bumps. For more of a challenge, head across to the chair-lift at Längfluh.

The 1800m/5,900ft vertical descents from the top to the village are great tests of stamina – or, if you choose, an enjoyable long cruise with plenty of view stops. The lower runs have steepish, tricky sections and can have poor snow, especially if it isn't cold enough to make artificial snow – timid intermediates might prefer to take a lift

## boarding

*Saas-Fee encourages boarding in a big way. In summer, in particular, its glacier slopes are dominated by boarders. While the gentle glacier slopes are ideal for learning, only main access lifts are boarder-friendly (gondolas, cable-cars and a funicular); nearly all the rest are drags. There are a couple of specialist schools. Expert free-riders may be frustrated by the limits imposed on off-piste riding by the glacier. The slopes above Längfluh offer great carving space. The Popcorn board shop and bar is popular.*

down from mid-mountain.

Plattjen has a variety of runs, all of them fine for ambitious intermediates and often underused.

### FOR BEGINNERS
***Usually a nice place to start***

There's a good, large, out-of-the-way nursery area at the edge of the village, as snow-sure as any you will find. Those ready to progress can head for the gentle blues on Felskinn just above Morenia – it's best to return by the Alpin Express. There are also gentle blues at the top of the mountain, from where you can head down to Längfluh. Again, use the lifts to return to base.

A useful beginners' pass covers all the short lifts at the village edge, for those not ready to go higher.

### FOR CROSS-COUNTRY
***Good local trail and lots nearby***

There is one short (8km/5 mile) pleasant trail at the edge of the village. It snakes up through the woods, providing about 150m/490ft of climb and nice views. There are more options in the Saas valley.

### QUEUES
***Persistent problems***

Reporters this year still complain of an 'uncomfortable scrum' to get on the Alpin Express first thing in the morning, and note that the whole journey to the top may take over an hour – but then it is quite a long way. Further queues were experienced for the drag lifts at the top of the mountain, which are persistent offenders.

### MOUNTAIN RESTAURANTS
***Fair choice, but it's no Zermatt***

The restaurants at the main lift stations are functional; at least Mittelallalin revolves – see separate box. The best places are slightly off the beaten track: the Berghaus Plattjen (just down from Plattjen) and the cosy Gletschergrotte, halfway down from Spielboden (watch for the arrow from the piste). A reporter says it does 'good food but is popular, so you have to wait'. If you're up for a trek – about 15 minutes each way – the Britanniahütte is special: a real climbing refuge, with atmosphere and views. The restaurant at the top of Plattjen has 'friendly service and the best rösti in the resort'. At Spielboden there's 'lovely food, traditional and very tasty', a terrace and views of tricky slopes. At Längfluh the large terrace has spectacular views of huge crevasses but a 2004 reporter found it 'basic and expensive', and Popcorn Plaza nearby is 'cosy with a fire on bad days' but has 'limited food'. At mid-mountain the Morenia has 'cheap and very good' pizza.

### EUROPE'S HIGHEST LUNCH?

*There is something beautifully Swiss about the idea of a revolving restaurant – and all three pivoting pubs in the Alps are in Switzerland. 'Customers not getting a share of the views? Can't have that. Only one thing for it: spin the whole restaurant about once an hour.' Actually, they spin only the bit of floor with the tables on it; the stairs stay put (along with the windows – watch your gloves). Only the table-service section revolves; there is stationary self-service downstairs.*

*This is the world's highest revolving restaurant – a good 500m/ 1,640ft higher than the famous original on Mürren's Schilthorn. We don't rate the views from Mittelallalin all that highly, but it's an amusing novelty that most visitors enjoy, and lunch is OK too – a reporter this year rates the place highly for food, service and value. To reserve a table next to the windows phone 957 1771.*

*And the third spinning speisesaal? At Leysin.*

### SCHOOLS

**Swiss**
t 957 2348

**Eskimos Snowboard**
t 957 4404

**Classes**
5 3hr days SF172

**Private lessons**
SF59 for 1hr for 1 or 2 people

### CHILDREN

**BärenKlub (Bears club)**
t 957 2484
hotel.berghof@saas-fee.ch
8.45-4pm; SF60 per day

**Kindertagesstätte Murmeli (Marmots Club)**
t 957 4057
Ages 1mnth to 6yr; 9am-5pm; SF50 per day

**Glückskäfer**
t 9587574
In Hotel Schweizerhof

**Ski school**
From age 4 (from SF75 per day). Full junior ski school from age 5 (5-day ski courses including lunch SF390)

## GETTING THERE

**Air** Sion 70km/ 43 miles (1hr); Geneva 234km/ 145 miles (3½hr); Zürich 246km/153 miles (4hr); Milan 250km/155 miles (3hr).

**Rail** Brig (38km/ 24 miles); regular buses from station.





## ACTIVITIES

**Indoor** Bielen leisure centre (swimming, hot-tub, steam bath, whirlpool, solarium, sauna, aerobics, massage, tennis, badminton, gym, bodyforming, aquafitness), cinema, museums

**Outdoor** 30km/ 19 miles of cleared paths, ice rink (skating, curling, snowbowling), tobogganing, snow tubing, climbing, ice-climbing, snow-shoeing, dog-sledding

**Phone numbers**
From elsewhere in Switzerland add the prefix 027.
From abroad use the prefix +41 27.

## TOURIST OFFICE

t 958 1858
to@saas-fee.ch
www.saas-fee.ch

### SCHOOLS AND GUIDES
***No choice; mixed reactions***

For skiing, it's the Swiss school or nothing. Reports this year range from an instructor who was 'shockingly rude, aggressive and demanding', providing only commands in limited English, to another whose lessons were enjoyable, encouraging a 'real leap of confidence'.

### FACILITIES FOR CHILDREN
***Good reports***

The school takes children from four years old, and most of the reports we have had have been positive. A 2004 visitor says her children 'raved about' their instructor, who spoke good English and 'made an adventure out of learning'. But classes of as many as 15 have been spotted. One solution for younger ones is to stay at a hotel with an in-house kindergarten.

## STAYING THERE

### HOW TO GO
***Check the location***

Quite a few UK tour operators sell holidays to Saas-Fee. But there are surprisingly few chalet holidays.

**Hotels** There are over 50.

((((5) **Fletschhorn** (957 2131) Elegant chalet in woods, with original art and individual rooms, a trek from the village and lifts, but fabulous food.

((((5) **Ferienart** (958 1900) Formerly the Walliserhof. Lovely relaxed place, despite 5-star status. Central, with excellent facilities including swish spa.

(((4) **Schweizerhof** (958 7575) Stylish, in quiet position above the centre. 'Fantastic food, friendly staff, excellent kindergarten, wonderful service.' Pool and new health facilities.

((3) **Beau-Site** (958 1560) 'First-rate' if quiet 4-star in central, but not convenient, position. Good food. Pool and relaxation suite.

((3) **Alphubel** (958 6363) At the wrong end of town, praised by reporters for its own 'brilliant nursery'.

((3) **Waldesruh** (958 6464) Strongly recommended by a reporter: 'Best situation for the Alpin Express.'

((3) **Astoria** (957 1133) 'Very handy for the Alpin Express, excellent, friendly' says reporter. Whirlpool and sauna.

((3) **Hohnegg** (957 2268) Small rustic alternative to the Fletschhorn, in a similarly remote spot.

((3) **Jägerhof** (957 1310) Adjacent to nursery slopes. 'A truly excellent place', says a 2004 visitor.

((2) **Belmont** (958 1640) The most appealing of the hotels looking directly on to the nursery slopes.

**Self-catering** Most apartments featured by UK operators are at the north end of the village, but they are generally spacious and well equipped.

### EATING OUT
***Good variety – but book a table***

Gastronomes will want to head for the highly acclaimed Fletschhorn – expensive but excellent. Our favourite is the less formal Bodmen along a path into the woods. It has great food (from rösti to fillet steak) and rustic ambience. We had a delicious Thai meal in one of the Walliserhof's several restaurants. Boccalino is cheap and does pizzas – book or get there early. Alp-Hitta specialises in rustic food and surroundings. The hotel Dom's restaurant specialises in endless varieties of rösti. The Ferme is 'excellent'. Arvu Stuba, Zur Mühle, Gorge and Feeloch have all been recommended. Booking is generally necessary.

### APRES-SKI
***Excellent and varied***

Late afternoon, Nesti's Ski-Bar, Zur Mühle and the little snow-bars near the lifts are all pretty lively, especially if the sun's shining. The Black Bull, with outdoor seating only, is reportedly the 'in place' at the moment. Later on, Nesti's and the Alpenpub keep going till 1am. Popcorn is as popular as ever. The new night club, Poison (formerly Go-Inn), advertises 'legendary parties' fuelled by shots and shakers. The Metro Bar is like being in a 19th-century mine shaft; Why-Not, a 'Guinness-themed' pub, is popular. The Metropol has the Crazy Night disco and a couple of other bars.

### OFF THE SLOPES
***A mountain for pedestrians***

The whole of the Hannig mountain is dedicated to walking, tobogganing and paragliding. It offers 'great views' of the glacial slopes. In the village, the splendid Bielen leisure centre boasts a 25m/80ft pool, indoor tennis courts and a lounging area with sunlamps. There's also the interesting Saas museum and the Bakery Museum, where children can make bread. Don't miss the largest ice pavilion in the world, carved out of the glacier at Mittelallalin.

# St Moritz

*Luxury living – on and off the flatteringly easy slopes*

## COSTS

①②③④⑤⑥

## RATINGS

| **The slopes** | |
|---|---|
| Snow | **** |
| Extent | ***** |
| Expert | **** |
| Intermediate | **** |
| Beginner | ** |
| Convenience | ** |
| Queues | ** |
| Mountain restaurants | **** |
| **The rest** | |
| Scenery | **** |
| Resort charm | * |
| Off-slope | ***** |

- ➕ Wonderful panoramic scenery
- ➕ Off-slope activities second to none
- ➕ Extensive, mainly intermediate slopes
- ➕ Fairly snow-sure
- ➕ Good après-ski, for all tastes
- ➕ Good mountain restaurants, some with magnificent views
- ➕ Painless rail access via Zürich

- ➖ Some hideous block buildings
- ➖ A sizeable town, with little traditional Alpine character
- ➖ Several unlinked mountains, with a bus, train or car needed to most
- ➖ Runs on two main mountains all fairly easy and much the same
- ➖ Expensive

**St Moritz is Switzerland's most famous 'exclusive' winter resort: glitzy, expensive, fashionable and, above all, the place to be seen – a place for an all-round winter holiday, with an unrivalled array of wacky diversions such as polo, golf and cricket on snow, and gourmet and music festivals. It has long been popular with upper-crust Brits, who stay in the top hotels. The slopes on the two main mountains are almost uniformly easy intermediate – experts must venture off-piste for their fun. But for cross-country, it is superb.**

**The town of St Moritz doesn't have the chocolate-box image of a Swiss mountain resort, all wooden huts and cows with bells round their necks. Many buildings resemble council flats (extremely neat and clean ones – it is Switzerland, after all).**

**But you may find, as some readers have, that St Moritz's spectacular setting blinds you to the town's aesthetic faults. This is one of those areas where our progress on the mountain is regularly interrupted by the need to stand and gaze. And the cross-country skiing, walking and other activities on the frozen lake give it a real 'winter wonderland' feel.**



## THE RESORT

St Moritz has two distinct parts. Dorf is the fashionable main part, on a steep hillside above the lake. It has two main streets – lined with boutiques selling Rolex watches, Cartier jewellery and Hermes scarves – a few side lanes and a small main square. A funicular takes you from Dorf to the slopes of Corviglia, also reached by gondola from down the road at Celerina, and by cable-car from Dorf's other half, the spa resort of St Moritz Bad, spread around one end of the lake.

Everything in Bad is less prestigious. Many of the modern buildings are uncompromisingly rectangular and spoil otherwise superb views. In winter the lake is used for eccentric activities including horse and greyhound racing, show jumping, polo, 'ice golf' and even cricket. It also makes a superb setting for walking and cross-country skiing.

Other downhill slopes, at Corvatsch, are reached via lifts at Surlej and Sils

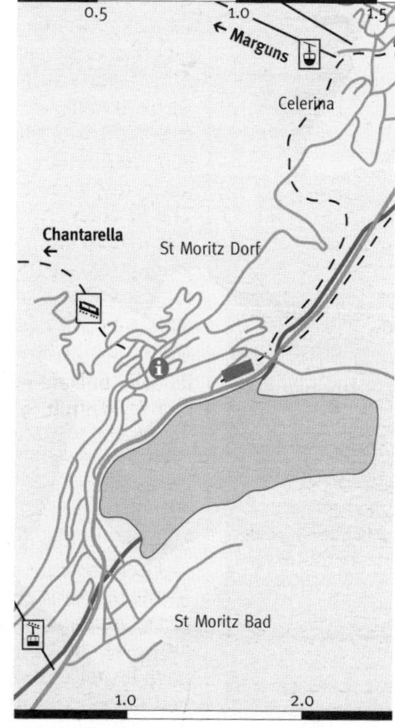

| KEY FACTS | |
|---|---|
| Resort | 1770m<br>5,810ft |
| Slopes | 1730-3305m<br>5,680-10,840ft |
| Lifts | 56 |
| Pistes | 350km<br>217 miles |
| Blue | 16% |
| Red | 71% |
| Black | 13% |
| Snowmaking | 70km<br>43 miles |
| For Corviglia only | |
| Slopes | 1730-3055m<br>5,680-10,020ft |
| Lifts | 23 |
| Pistes | 158km<br>98 miles |

Maria. Cross-country skiing is the main activity around the outlying villages of Samedan and Pontresina.

The town's clientele is typified by the results of a Cresta Run race we saw on one of our visits. In the top 29 were three Lords, one Count, one Archduke and a Baronet. But the race was won by a local Swiss guy.

For high society and a better choice of bars and restaurants, stay in Dorf. Bad has the advantage that you can get back to it from Corvatsch and Corviglia. Celerina is the obvious alternative, and an attractive one, but there are other options – a reader this year heartily recommends 'chocolate-box-pretty' Sils Maria, with immediate access to the Corvatsch slopes.

## THE MOUNTAINS

Like the resort, most of the slopes are made for posing. There are lots of long, wide, well-groomed runs, with varied terrain – practically all on open slopes above the trees. The piste map is poor, with 'several pistes not marked' according to one reporter. The several distinct areas add up to a substantial 350km/217 miles of pistes. The main slopes, shown on our maps, are nearby Corviglia-Marguns and Corvatsch-Furtschellas, a bus-ride away (you can get back to Bad on snow). But some of the more distant slopes are well worth an outing. It helps to have a car, although the free bus service is reported to be fairly efficient. Trips to other resorts such as Klosters and Davos (around 90 minutes by train or car) and Livigno (around an hour by car) are possible.

### THE SLOPES
*Big but broken up*

From St Moritz Dorf a two-stage railway goes up to **Corviglia**, a fair-sized area with slopes facing east and south. The peak of Piz Nair, reached from here by a cable-car, splits the area – sunny runs towards the main valley, and less sunny ones to the north. From Corviglia you can head down (snow permitting) to Dorf and Bad, and via the lower lift junction of Marguns to Celerina.

From Surlej, a few miles from St Moritz, a two-stage cable-car takes you to the north-facing slopes of **Corvatsch**. From the mid-station at Murtèl you have a choice of reds to Margun-Vegl and Alp Margun. From the latter you can work your way to **Furtschellas**, also reached by cable-car from Sils Maria.

Diavolezza (2980m/9,780ft) and Lagalb (2960m/9,710ft), the main additional areas, are on opposite sides of the road to the Bernina pass to Italy, less than half an hour away by bus. **Diavolezza** has excellent north-facing pistes of 900m/2,950ft vertical, down under its big 125-person cable-car, and a very popular and spectacular off-piste route off the back, across a glacier and down a valley beneath Piz Bernina to Morteratsch. **Lagalb** is a smaller area with quite challenging slopes, and an 80-person cable-car serving the west-facing front slope of 850m/2,790ft vertical.

### TERRAIN-PARKS
*Not a clear picture*

The resort's information is inconsistent, and it doesn't have a great record of delivering what it promises in this area, but we believe on Corviglia there is a half-pipe above the Signal area and a terrain park towards Marguns. The boarders' guide also marks, not at all clearly, 'natural freestyle' and 'secret spots' on some mountains.

### SNOW RELIABILITY
*Improved by good snowmaking*

This corner of the Alps has a rather dry climate, but the altitude means that any precipitation is likely to be snowy. The top runs at Corvatsch are glacial. There is snowmaking in every sector and piste grooming is excellent.

### FOR EXPERTS
*Dispersed challenges*

If you're looking for challenges, you're liable to find St Moritz disappointing on-piste. Red runs (many of which should really be classified blue) far outnumber black, and mogul-fields are scarce. The few serious black runs are scattered about in different sectors and few are seriously steep; those at Lagalb and Diavolezza are the most challenging. The Minor run down the Lagalb cable-car has 850m/2,790ft vertical of non-stop moguls. But there is good off-piste terrain, and it doesn't get tracked out as it does in more macho resorts. There is an excellent north-facing slope immediately above Marguns, for example. Experts often head for the tough off-piste runs on Piz Nair or the Corvatsch summit. More serious expeditions can be undertaken – such as down the Roseg valley from

Corvatsch. To get the most out of the area, you will need to hire a guide.

**FOR INTERMEDIATES**
***Good but flattering***
St Moritz is great for intermediates. Most pistes on Corviglia and Corvatsch are very well groomed, easyish reds that could well have been classified blue – ideal cruising terrain. A reporter this year takes the view that Corvatsch is the more varied and interesting area, and we don't dispute that; it is certainly higher and wider, and well worth the excursion from St Moritz. If you're lucky with the snow, you can end the day there with the splendid Hahnensee run, from the northern limit of the Corvatsch lift system at Giand'Alva down to St Moritz Bad – a black-classified run that is of red difficulty for most of its 6km/4 mile length and 900m/2,950ft vertical drop. It's a five-minute walk from the end of the run to the cable-car up to Corviglia.

Diavolezza is mostly intermediate stuff, too. There is an easy open slope at the top, served by a fast quad, and a splendid long intermediate run back down under the lift. The popular off-piste run to Morteratsch requires a bit of energy and nerve. After a gentle climb, you cross the glacier on a narrow ledge, with crevasses waiting to gobble you up on the right. When we last did it, there were ice picks and shovels at intervals along the path, put there by the enterprising proprietors of the beautifully laid out, welcoming ice bar which greets you at the end of the 30-minute slog. After that, it's downhill through the glacier, with splendid views. Lagalb has more challenging pistes.



**FOR BEGINNERS**
***Not much to offer***
St Moritz is not ideal for beginners. It sits in a deep, steep-sided valley, with very little space for nursery slopes at the lower levels. Beginners start up at Salastrains or Corviglia, or slightly out of town, at Suvretta. Celerina has good, broad nursery slopes at village level. Progression from the nursery slopes to intermediate runs is rather awkward – these always include a difficult section.

**FOR CROSS-COUNTRY**
***Excellent***
The Engadine is one of the premier regions in the Alps for cross-country, with 180km/112 miles of trails,



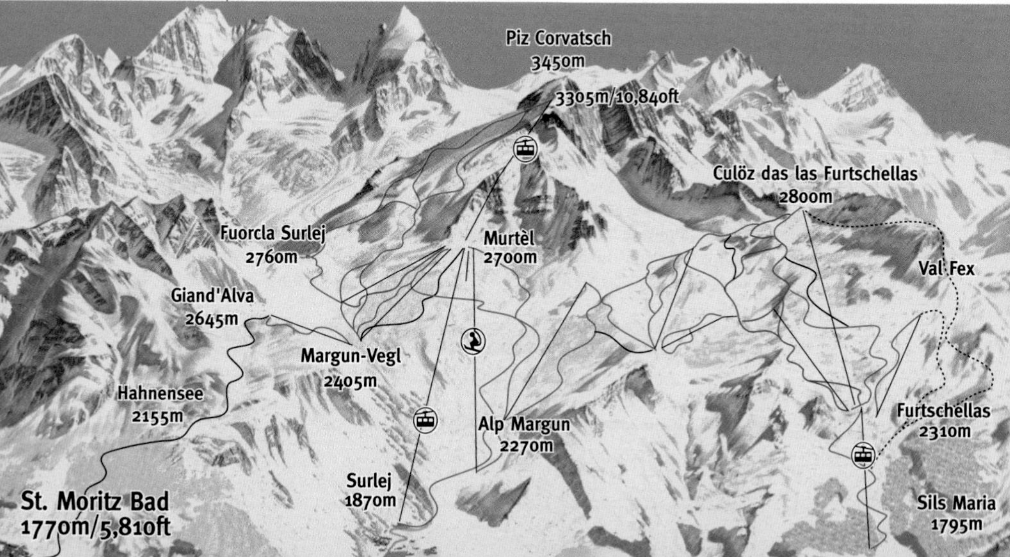

↑ There's not much skiing to be done up at Muottas Muragl, but the hotel-restaurant enjoys a fab view

ST MORITZ TOURIST OFFICE





## LIFT PASSES

**Upper Engadine**
Covers all lifts in Corviglia (St Moritz, Celerina, Samedan), Corvatsch (Silvaplana, Sils, Surlej), Diavolezza-Lagalb (Pontresina), and Zuoz.

**Main pass**
1 day SF68
6 days SF322

**Children**
Under 20: 6 days SF290
Under 16: 6 days SF161
Under 6: free pass

**Alternative passes**
Half-day and day passes available for individual areas within Upper Engadine.

## SCHOOLS

**Swiss**
t 830 0101
info@skischool.ch

**Suvretta**
t 836 3600
info@sssc.ch

**Classes**
(Swiss prices)
6 2hr days SF230

**Private lessons**
SF180 for 2hr

including floodlit loops, amid splendid scenery and with fairly reliable snow. A reporter recommends the lessons at the Langlauf Centre near the Hotel Kempinski. The Engadine Ski Marathon is held here every March – over 12,000 racers take part. Pontresina makes a great base for cross-country.

## QUEUES

***Not much of a problem***

St Moritz has invested heavily in new lifts in recent years. Once you get up the mountain, Corviglia has fast chairs everywhere. But the area as a whole has a lot of cable-cars – both for getting up the mountain from the resort and for access to peaks from mid-mountain. Queues can result, though reporters have had good experiences lately – the enlarged cable-car from Surlej to Murtèl is a big improvement at Corvatsch, although a 2003 reporter recommends avoiding Surlej and going to Sils Maria instead. The upgraded cable-car to Piz Nair seems to have cut the queues there. The top Corvatsch cable-car can generate queues. Happy reporters comment that many St Moritz visitors are late risers and don't ski after lunch, leaving the slopes quiet at the start and end of the day. 'Peak period is 11 to 12.30, when congestion can be a problem above Marguns on Corviglia and on the run down from Murtèl on Corvatsch,' says a reporter.

## MOUNTAIN RESTAURANTS

***Some special places***

Mountain restaurants are plentiful, and include some of the most glamorous in Europe. Prices can be high, and reservations are advisable. But there are plenty of cheaper places too.

On Corviglia, the gourmet highlight is the Marmite; but it is outrageously expensive. And it is housed in the Corviglia lift station, known locally as the highest post office in Switzerland because of its bright yellow paint. Much better for charm is the Paradiso, with glorious panoramic views from the terrace; or the inviting terrace of the Chamanna, or the Lej de la Pêsch, down in the valley behind Piz Nair. A reader recommends Mathis for 'first-class food and wine'.

On the Corvatsch side, we've heard good reports about the self-service place at the top of the area and of the sunny bar, with live music, at the bottom of Rabguisa. Fuorcla Surlej is delightfully secluded, as is Hahnensee, on the lift-free run of the same name down to Bad – a splendid place to pause in the sun on the way home at the end of the day. On stormy days, most captivating is the rustic Alpetta, near Alp Margun – 'nice food, lovely atmosphere and a great bar' (table-service inside).

The hotel-restaurant up at Muottas Muragl, between Celerina and Pontresina, is well worth a visit. It has truly spectacular views overlooking the valley – a fabulous sunset, if you are lucky – as well as good food.

Morteratsch restaurant (at the end of the off-piste run from Diavolezza) is splendid – sunny, by the cross-country area and tiny railway station, and with excellent, good-value food.

## SCHOOLS AND GUIDES

***Internal competition***

As well as the St Moritz and Suvretta schools, there is The Wave snowboarding school and The St Moritz Experience, for heli-trips. Some hotels have their own instructors for private lessons.

## boarding

*Despite the high prices and its glitzy image, the terrain in St Moritz is boarder-friendly and there's a special boarders' booklet with lots of good information and profiles of local riders. The Corvatsch area has links that rely on drags – otherwise, most lifts are chairs, gondolas, cable-cars and trains. There are several specialist snowboard shops, including Playground in Paradise.*

**CHILDREN**

**Schweizerhof hotel**
Ages from 3; 9am-5.30; SF34 per day

**Ski school**
Ages from 4; pick-up service and all-day care available

**GETTING THERE**

**Air** Zürich 200km/124 miles (3hr); Upper Engadine airport 5km/3 miles.

**Rail** Mainline station in resort.

### FACILITIES FOR CHILDREN

***Choose a hotel with a nursery***

Children wanting lessons have a choice of schools, but others must be deposited at a hotel nursery. Club Med has its usual good facilities.

## STAYING THERE

### HOW TO GO

***Several packaged options***

Packages are available, but many people make their own arrangements. There is a Club Med – its all-inclusive deal cuts the impact of high prices. The tourist office can provide a list of apartments.

**Hotels** Over half the hotels are 4-stars and 5-stars – the highest concentration of high-quality hotels in Switzerland. We don't like any of the famous 5-stars or their jacket-and-tie policies. If made to choose we'd prefer the glossy, secluded Carlton or even more secluded Suvretta House to the staid Kulm or Gothic Badrutt's Palace.

((((4 **Crystal** (836 2626) Big 4-star in Dorf, as close to the Corviglia lift as any. Recently renovated and now part of the 'Small Luxury Hotels' group.

((((4 **Schweizerhof** (837 0707) 'Relaxed' 4-star in central Dorf, five minutes from the Corviglia lift, with 'excellent food and very helpful staff'.

((((4 **Albana** (836 6161) 4-star in Dorf, with walls adorned with big game trophies bagged by proprietor's family.

(((3 **Monopol** (837 0404) Good value (for St Moritz) 4-star in centre of Dorf. Excellent breakfasts. hot-tub, sauna.

(((3 **Steinbock** (833 6035) 'Friendly, understated, comfortable,' says a reporter. In Dorf.

(((3 **Nolda** (833 0575) One of the few chalet-style buildings, close to the cable-car in St Moritz Bad.

((2 **Bellaval** (833 3245) A two-star between the station and the lake.

flexiski skiing breaks
tailor-made ski breaks and weekends to chalets & hotels in...
st anton • st christoph • lech • chamonix
courchevel • davos • klosters • st moritz • verbier
Flexi Ski
tel: 0870 90 90 754
www.flexiski.com

### EATING OUT

***Mostly chic and expensive***

It's easy to spend £50 a head eating out in St Moritz – without wine – but you can eat more cheaply. We liked the excellent Italian food at the down-to-earth Cascade in Dorf and the, pricier, three restaurants in the Chesa Veglia (though one reporter tells of it being 'a rip-off, and the staff were disinterested when we only ordered two pizzas and turned down the wine which started at £35 a bottle'). Another reporter had a 'week of gourmet eating'. The two top restaurants, Jöhri's Talvo at Champfèr and Bumann's Chesa Pirani in La Punt, both approach the top restaurants in London or Paris for quality and price – we spent SF200 a head in each. We also liked the rustic Landhotel Meierei, in a bay of the lake opposite Bad. If you want something less pricey and like fondue, reporters recommend the restaurant in the hotel Schweizerhof.

Try an evening up at Muottas Muragl for the spectacular views, splendid sunset and unpretentious dinner. The food at the Chesa Rosatsch hotel at Celerina attracts non-resident diners and is recommended this year.

### APRES-SKI

***Caters for all ages***

There's a big variety of après-skiing age groups here. The fur coat count is high – people come to St Moritz to be seen.

At tea time, head for Hanselmann's 'fabulous tea and strudels' but 'the place is a bit dull'. Or try Café Hauser.

The pub-style Bobby's Bar (with internet access), and the Prince (with a 'disco/lounge') attract a young crowd, as does the loud music of the Stübli, one of three bars in the Schweizerhof: the others are the Muli, with a country

↑ St Moritz looks no better from above than from ground level

ST MORITZ TOURIST OFFICE

**Phone numbers**
From elsewhere in Switzerland add the prefix 081.
From abroad use the prefix +41 81.

## ACTIVITIES

**Indoor** Swimming pool, sauna, solarium, golf driving range, tennis, squash, museums, cinema (with English films), beauty farm, health centre, casino, library,

**Outdoor** Ice skating, sleigh rides, ski jumping, curling, cricket on snow, tobogganing, hang-gliding, paragliding, golf on frozen lake, bobsleigh rides, Cresta run, 180km/112 miles cleared paths, greyhound racing, horse-riding, polo tournaments

## TOURIST OFFICES

**St Moritz**
t 837 3333
information@stmoritz.ch
www.stmoritz.ch

**Celerina**
t 830 0011
info@celerina.ch
www.celerina.ch

**Pontresina**
t 838 8300
info@pontresina.com
www.pontresina.com

and western theme and live music, and the chic Piano Bar. The Cresta, at the Steffani, is popular with the British, while the Cava below it is louder, livelier and younger. Readers rate the piano bar at the Albana Hotel 'cosy and welcoming'. It is also amusing to put on a jacket and tie and explore bars in Badrutt's Palace and the Kulm.

The two most popular discos are Vivai (expensive) at the Steffani, and King's at Badrutt's Palace (even more expensive; jackets and ties required). And if they don't part you with enough of your cash, try the casino.

### OFF THE SLOPES
***Excellent variety of pastimes***

Even if you lack the bravado for the Cresta Run, there is lots to do. In midwinter the snow-covered lake provides a playground for bizarre events (see earlier in chapter) but in March the lake starts to thaw. There's an annual 'gourmet festival', with chefs from all over the world.

Some hotels run special activities, such as a curling week. Other options are hang-gliding, indoor tennis and trips to Italy (Milan is four hours by car). There's a public pool in Bad.

St Moritz gets a lot of sun – 322 sunny days a year, they claim – so lounging on sunny terraces is popular. One reporter was bowled over by a train trip on the Bernina Express, with 'amazing bends, gradients and scenery. The high-spot of our visit.'

### STAYING UP THE MOUNTAIN
***Excellent possibilities***

Next door to each other at Salastrains are two chalet-style hotels, the 3-star Salastrains (833 3867), with 60 comfy beds, and the slightly simpler and much smaller Chesa Chantarella (833 3355). Great views, and no queues.

## Celerina 1730m/5,680ft

At the bottom end of the Cresta Run, Celerina is unpretentious and villagey, if quiet, with good access to Corviglia. It is sizeable, with a lot of second homes, many owned by Italians (the upper part is known as Piccolo Milano). There are some appealing small hotels (reporters recommend Chesa Rosatsch 837 0101) and a couple of bigger 4-stars.

## Pontresina 1805m/5,920ft

Pontresina is small and sedate, and an excellent base for the extensive cross-country skiing on its doorstep. It's a sheltered, sunny village with one main street, spoiled by the predominant sanatorium-style architecture. Pontresina's own hill, Languard, has a single long piste.

It can be somewhat cheaper to stay here than St Moritz and there is a Club Med (offering its usual all-inclusive deal). Dining is mostly hotel-based and nightlife is quiet. A 2003 reporter found medium-priced eating out here compared favourably with back home and recommends the Bernina Hotel restaurant and the Thai restaurant at the Collina Hotel.

### THE CRESTA RUN

*No trip to St Moritz is really complete without a visit to the Cresta Run. It's the last bastion of Britishness (until recently, payment had to be made in sterling) and male chauvinism (women have been banned since 1929 – unless you can secure an invitation from a club member for the last day of their season).*

*Any adult male can pay around £200 for five rides on the famous run (helmet and lunch at the Kulm hotel included). Watch out for Shuttlecock corner – that's where most people come off and the ambulances ply for trade. You lie on a toboggan (aptly called a 'skeleton') and hurtle head-first down a sheet ice gully from St Moritz to Celerina. David Gower and Sandy Gall are among the Cresta's many addicts.*

VERBIER TOURIST OFFICE

# Verbier

*Paradise for nightlife-loving powder hounds with cash*

## COSTS

(1)(2)(3)(4)(5)(6)

## RATINGS

**The slopes**

| | |
|---|---|
| Snow | *** |
| Extent | ***** |
| Expert | ***** |
| Intermediate | *** |
| Beginner | ** |
| Convenience | ** |
| Queues | *** |
| Mountain restaurants | *** |

**The rest**

| | |
|---|---|
| Scenery | **** |
| Resort charm | *** |
| Off-slope | *** |

## NEWS

For 2003/04 a new snow bridge was built at Col Brunet to avoid congestion and collisions. Skiers arriving from Attelas can now ski over the bridge to La Chaux, while those coming from La Chaux ski under the bridge.

The last stretch of the run down to Médran has been extended.

New marked trails for snow-shoeing are planned for 2004/05.

A new hotel, the Central, is being built in the Place Centrale.

Two pistes solely for slower skiers are planned – one on Savoleyres and one at La Chaux. Whether these will be adequately policed remains to be seen.

- + Extensive, challenging slopes with a lot of off-piste potential and some good bump runs
- + Upper slopes offer a real high-mountain feel plus great views
- + Pleasant, animated village in a sunny, panoramic setting
- + Lively, varied nightlife
- + Wide range of chalet holidays
- + Good advanced-level lessons
- + Much improved lift system
- + Much improved piste grooming
- + Hardly any drag-lifts in the Verbier sector but ...

- − Still many slow chair-lifts and drag-lifts and some serious queues, particularly on 4 Valleys links
- − Overcrowded pistes and lots of people going too fast in certain areas
- − The 4 Valleys network is much less wonderful than it looks on paper
- − Sunny lower slopes will always be a problem, even with snowmaking
- − Signposting and piste map still hopelessly inadequate
- − Busy traffic (and fumes) in centre
- − Some long walks/rides to lifts
- − Lots of off-piste is tracked out quickly
- − Pretty expensive

**There is no doubt that Verbier is trying hard to retain its international visitors, improving over the last few years its grooming, snowmaking, ski schools and lifts. But major grouses remain. Some are down to the organisation of the slopes: the kind of piste signing shown later in the chapter is infuriating, and the new clearer piste map introduced last year still fails to identify pistes by name or number. But other problems are down to the lie of the land.**

**For experts prepared to hire a guide to explore off-piste, Verbier is one of the big names. With its claimed 410km/255 miles of pistes, Verbier also seems at first sight to rank alongside the French mega-resorts that draw keen piste skiers, such as Courchevel and La Plagne. But it doesn't; the 4 Valleys network is an inconveniently sprawling affair, while Verbier's local pistes are surprisingly confined and crowded. Of course, piste skiers who have not been spoilt by the mega-resorts can have a satisfying holiday here – but you can do that in scores of minor resorts from Alpbach to Zell am See. Whether they can match Verbier's sheer style and famously vibrant nightlife is another question.**



## THE RESORT

Verbier is an amorphous sprawl of chalet-style buildings, without too much concrete in evidence, in an impressive setting on a wide, sunny balcony facing spectacular peaks. It's a fashionable, informal, very lively place that teems with cosmopolitan visitors. Most are younger than visitors to other big Swiss resorts.

Most of the shops and hotels (but not chalets) are set around the Place Centrale and along the sloping streets stretching down the hill in one direction and up it in the other to the main lift station at Médran 500m/1,640ft away. Much of the nightlife is here, too, though bars are rather scattered. These central areas get unpleasantly packed with cars at busy times, especially weekends.

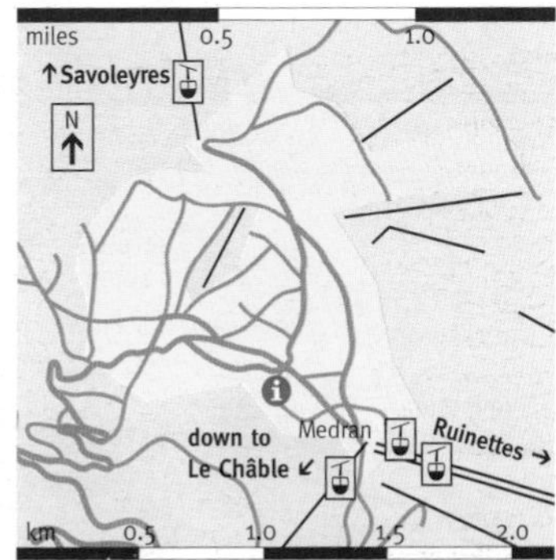

## KEY FACTS

| | |
|---|---|
| **Resort** | 1500m<br>4,920ft |

For 4 Valleys area

| | |
|---|---|
| **Slopes** | 1500-3330m<br>4,920-10,930ft |
| **Lifts** | 94 |
| **Pistes** | 410km<br>255 miles |
| **Blue** | 33% |
| **Red** | 41% |
| **Black** | 26% |
| **Snowmaking** | 50km<br>31 miles |

For Verbier, Bruson and Tzoumas/ Savoleyres sectors only (covered by Verbier pass)

| | |
|---|---|
| **Slopes** | 1500-3025m<br>4,920-9,920ft |
| **Lifts** | 38 |
| **Pistes** | 150km<br>93 miles |
| **Blue** | 33% |
| **Red** | 33% |
| **Black** | 34% |
| **Snowmaking** | 20km<br>12 miles |

More chalets and apartments are built each year – which means building sites spoil the views in places – with newer properties inconveniently situated along the road to the lift base for the secondary Savoleyres area, about 1.5km/1 mile from Medran.

The Médran lift station is a walkable distance from the Place Centrale, so staying there has attractions. There is accommodation close to the Médran lift station, which is sufficiently distant from nightlife to avoid late-night noise. If nightlife is not a priority, staying somewhere near the upper (north-east) fringes of the village may mean that you can almost ski to your door – and there is a piste linking the upper nursery slopes to the one in the middle of the village.

But in practice most people just get used to using the free buses, which run efficiently on several routes until 7pm. Some areas have quite an infrequent service. We are told that from 7pm to 8.30 there is a special taxi service that will drop you at any of the usual bus stops within the resort for five francs per person.

Verbier is at one end of a long, strung-out series of interconnected slopes, optimistically branded the 4 Valleys and linking Verbier to Nendaz, Veysonnaz, Thyon and other resorts.

These other resorts have their own pros and cons. All are appreciably cheaper places to stay than Verbier, and some are more sensible bases for those who plan to stick to pistes rather than venture off-piste – the Veysonnaz-Thyon sector, in particular, is much more intermediate-friendly than Verbier. As bases for exploration of the whole 4 Valleys, only Siviez is much of an advance on Verbier. They are much less lively in the evening.

You can also stay down in the valley village of Le Châble, which has a gondola up to Verbier and on into the slopes. Across the valley, Bruson is more attractive as a place to visit for a day than to stay in.

These alternatives are all described at the end of the chapter.

Chamonix and Champéry (Portes du Soleil) are within reach by car. But a car can be a bit of a nuisance in Verbier itself. Parking is tightly controlled; your chalet or hotel may not have enough space for all guests' cars, which means a hike from the free parking at the sports centre or paying for garage space.

## THE MOUNTAINS

Essentially this is high-mountain terrain. There are wooded slopes directly above the village, but the runs here are either bumpy itinéraires or winding paths. There is more sheltered skiing in other sectors – particularly above Veysonnaz.

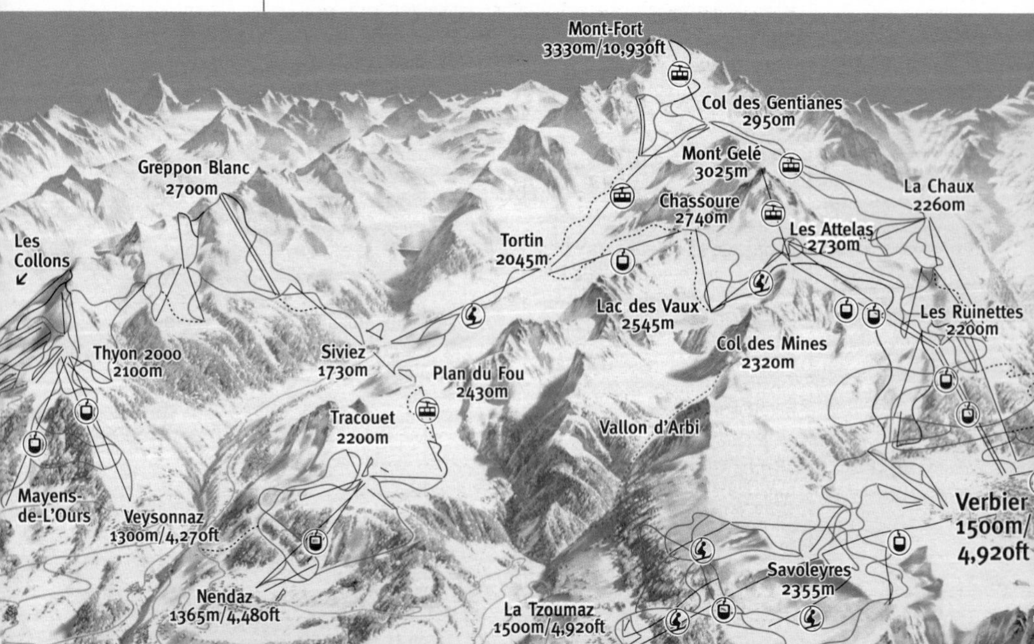

↑ There are great views down to town from many of the slopes

VERBIER TOURIST OFFICE / FRANCOIS PERRAUDIN

### THE SLOPES
***Very spread out***

**Savoleyres** is the smaller area, reached by a gondola from the north-west end of the village. This area is underrated and generally underused. It has open, sunny slopes on the front side, and long, pleasantly wooded, shadier runs on the back. You can take a catwalk across from Savoleyres to the foot of Verbier's main slopes. These are served by lifts from Médran, at the opposite end of the village.

Two gondolas rise to **Les Ruinettes** and then on to **Les Attelas**. From Les Attelas a small cable-car goes up to Mont Gelé, for steep off-piste runs only. Heading down instead, you can go back westwards to Les Ruinettes, south to La Chaux or north to Lac des Vaux. From here chairs go back to Les Attelas and on to Chassoure, the top of a wide, steep and shady off-piste mogul field leading down to **Tortin,** with a gondola back.

La Chaux is served by two slow chair-lifts and is the departure point of a jumbo cable-car up to Col des Gentianes and the glacier area. A second, much smaller cable-car then goes up to **Mont-Fort,** the high point of the 4 Valleys. From the glacier is another off-piste route down to Tortin, a north-facing run of almost 1300m/ 4,270ft vertical. A cable-car returns to Col des Gentianes.

Below Tortin is the gateway to the rest of the 4 Valleys, **Siviez**, where one chair goes off into the long, thin **Nendaz** sector and another heads for the **Thyon-Veysonnaz** sector, via a couple of lifts and a lot of catwalks.

Allow plenty of time to get to and from these remote corners – the taxi-rides home are expensive.

The slopes of **Bruson** are described briefly at the end of this chapter.

### TERRAIN-PARKS
***A couple of options***

There are two terrain-parks – one at La Chaux and another one at Savoleyres.

### SNOW RELIABILITY
***Improved snowmaking***

The slopes of the Mont-Fort glacier always have good snow. The runs to Tortin are normally snow-sure too. But nearly all of this is steep, and much of it is formally off-piste. Most of Verbier's main local slopes face south or west and are below 2500m/8,200ft – so they can be in poor condition at times. There is snowmaking on the main run down all the way from Attelas to Médran. But the north-facing slopes of Savoleyres and Lac des Vaux are normally much better.

### FOR EXPERTS
***The main attraction***

Verbier has some superb tough slopes, many of them off-piste and needing a guide – see the separate feature panel on this. There are few conventional black pistes; most of the runs that might have this designation are now defined as itinéraires – see our feature panel on finding your way around. The blacks that do exist are mostly indistinguishable from nearby reds. The front face of Mont-Fort is an exception: a long mogul field, with a choice of



### boarding

*As with its skiing, Verbier is one of Europe's best off-piste and extreme boarding resorts for those able and willing to pay for a guide or to join a group. The main area is served by gondolas, cable-cars and chairs, with no drag-lifts at all. Less experienced boarders should try Savoleyres, though there are a few drag-lifts. To see some real experts in action, hang around the resort in March, when the world's best congregate here for both the Verbier Ride and the Xtreme contest. There is a special pass allowing use of and access to lifts for the La Chaux terrain-park (CHF40 in 2003/04) and a couple of specialist snowboard shops.*

## LIFT PASSES

**4 Valleys/Mont-Fort**
Covers all lifts and ski-buses in Verbier, Mont-Fort, Bruson, La Tzoumaz, Nendaz, Veysonnaz and Thyon.

**Main pass**
1-day SF59
6 days SF306

**Senior citizens**
Over 65: 6-days SF214

**Children**
Under 20: 6-days SF260
Under 16: 6-days SF214
Under 6: free pass

**Notes**
Afternoon pass available. Reductions for families.

**Alternative passes**
Verbier pass, La Tzoumaz/Savoleyres pass and Bruson only pass available.





gradient from seriously steep to intimidatingly steep. The World Cup run at Veysonnaz is a steepish, often icy red, ideal for really speeding down. The two itinéraires to Tortin are both excellent in their different ways. The one from Chassoure is just one wide, steep slope, normally a huge mogul field. The north-facing itinéraire from Gentianes is longer, less steep, but feels much more of an adventure. There is an entertaining itinéraire from Greppon Blanc, at the top of the Veysonnaz-Thyon sector, into the next valley. There are five buses a day from the end of the run to the lifts of Les Collons, below Thyon.

### FOR INTERMEDIATES
***Hit Savoleyres – or Veysonnaz***

Many mileage-hungry intermediates find Verbier disappointing. The intermediate slopes in the main area are concentrated between Les Attelas and the village, above and below Les Ruinettes, plus the little bowl at Lac des Vaux and the sunny slopes served by the chairs at La Chaux. This is all excellent and varied intermediate territory, but there isn't much of it – to put it in perspective, this whole area is no bigger than the tiny slopes of Alpbach – and it is used by the bulk of the visitors staying in one of Switzerland's largest resorts. So it is often very crowded, especially the otherwise wonderful sweeping red from Les Attelas to Les Ruinettes served by the big gondola. Even early intermediates should taste the perfect snow on the glacier. The red run from Col des Gentianes to La Chaux is not too difficult, but its high-mountain feel can be unnerving and it's no disgrace to ride the cable-car down instead.

Intermediates should exploit the under-used Savoleyres area. This has good intermediate pistes, usually better snow and far fewer people (especially on Sundays). It is also a good hill for mixed abilities, with variations of many runs. The Thyon-Veysonnaz and Nendaz sectors are worth exploring (those not willing to take on the itinéraires will have to ride down to Tortin; and down from Plan du Fou if they want to get to Nendaz).

The Verbier slopes present difficulties for early intermediates, as editorial daughter Laura can confirm.

### FINDING YOUR WAY AROUND THE SLOPES OF VERBIER

*It isn't easy. The main area is complicated, and difficult to represent on a single map. Téléverbier's traditional hopeless map has been replaced by one that makes a better job of showing the mountain; but it still fails to show Savoleyres and La Chaux sensibly, and it still fails to identify the pistes. So although the signs on the mountain religiously use numbers to identify pistes, there is no way to connect the signs to the map – insane. The problem is compounded by a strange faith in the kind of 'motorway' signs shown here. We and most of our readers find these impossible to relate to the real choices of route. One 2004 reporter describes the map as 'virtually fictitious' and 'absolutely hazardous' for her group.*

*Life is further complicated by confusion over which runs it is prudent to tackle. For years now, runs that once were black pistes have been defined as 'itinéraires à ski' (eg both runs down to Tortin) or 'itinéraires de haute-montagne' (eg the Col des Mines run home from Lac des Vaux). We've long campaigned for these runs – especially the former category – to be restored to piste status.*

**Adrenaline** ski and snowboard school organises off-piste and heli-skiing groups and provides safety equipment. It also offers ski-touring, freestyle lessons in the park and pipe, ice-climbing, snow-shoeing and group and private lessons for every standard of skier and snowboarder.

**t** 00 41 27 771 74 59
www.adrenaline-verbier.ch

## OFF-PISTE FOR ALL

**Verbier has some of the best, most extensive and varied off-piste in the world, and major free-ride competitions are held there every year. Here, with the help of Luca Voisin from Adrenaline, we pick out just a few of the runs on offer.**

*For adventurous intermediates who want to try off-piste for the first time, Adrenaline ski school runs off-piste courses, including avalanche transceiver training and the use of wide skis specially designed to make off-piste easier. Then you can try relatively easy runs such as Col des Mines and Vallon d'Arby (both start from Lac des Vaux and are marked on the piste map as high mountain tours) – the former is a long, open slope back to Verbier and the latter a very beautiful run in a steep-sided valley down to La Tzoumaz. Stairway to Heaven starts with a steep climb up near Col de Gentianes, taking you into the next valley to the well-known itinéraire to Tortin with usually excellent snow and no crowds. Or try the Rock Garden, which starts with a 20-minute walk from Lac des Vaux, or Col de la Mouche, which starts from Chassoure with a traverse over the normal Tortin itinéraire to a wide, quieter alternative.*

*Experts have endless off-piste to choose from. From the top of the Mont Fort cable-car you can drop off the back and negotiate a very, very steep initial pitch followed by crevasses before dropping into a beautiful deserted valley and ending up at Siviez. If you'd like to follow in the tracks of the best free-riders in the world, you can try the legendary Bec des Rosses, where the Xtreme free-ride contest takes place each year. Or head for the very steep couloirs between Mont Gelé and Les Attelas.*

*Heli-skiing is permitted in Switzerland and allows you to reach virgin slopes on which you can make first tracks – magic if there's fresh powder. Some of the most famous runs are Petit-Combin, Trient and Rosablanche, and prices start at around SF350 including a guide.*

*Off-piste skiing is great fun, but don't even think about going off-piste without a fully qualified guide or instructor and the right safety equipment: route finding is difficult, avalanche danger can be high and hidden hazards such as cliffs and crevasses lurk. Adrenaline ski school can provide all you need.*





There is excellent easy blue-run skiing at La Chaux (but reporters tell of the linking piste being used 'as a motorway by good skiers going at top speed, causing wipe-outs and ski rage' – let's hope this is sorted out by the promised 'slow skiing' piste and adequate policing); but there is no easy way back to Les Ruinettes. From Savoleyres there is an easy way to Médran but there may be no easy way down to that link from the top of Savoleyres. In both cases, we had to take quite challenging red runs. Laura managed, but in a properly run resort the difficulties would have been foreseen and sorted out.

### FOR BEGINNERS
***Progression is the problem***

There are sunny nursery slopes close to the middle of the village and at Les Esserts, at the top of it. These are fine provided they have snow (they have a lot of snowmaking, which helps). The problem is what you do after the nursery slopes. There are easy blues on the back side of Savoleyres, and at La Chaux, but they are not easy to get back from (see above).

### FOR CROSS-COUNTRY
***Surprisingly little on offer***

Verbier is limited for cross-country. There's a 4km/2.5 mile circuit in Verbier, 4km/2.5 miles at Les Ruinettes-La Chaux and 30km/19 miles down at Le Châble/Val de Bagnes.

### QUEUES
***Not the problem they were***

Verbier's queue problems have been greatly eased by recent investment. The jumbo gondola to Les Attelas – its capacity increased recently – has cut queues at Les Ruinettes, but it has increased the overcrowding on the pistes back down. The mega-queues at Tortin for Chassoure are a thing of the past, thanks to the upgraded gondola. The fast chair at Lac des Vaux has greatly eased the bottleneck there. But the cable-car from Tortin to Col des Gentianes can produce queues, and the Mont-Fort cable-car above it can still generate very long ones.

Some queues at the main village lift station at Médran can arise if Sunday visitors fill one of the gondolas down in the valley at Le Châble. The recent upgrade of this gondola has helped.

www.alpineanswers.co.uk
The smart way to book a ski holiday
Alpine answers
SKI HOLIDAY SPECIALISTS
020 8871 4656
ABTA D4050 ATOL 4791

## CHILDREN

**Schtroumpfs**
t 771 6585
Ages 3mnth to 4yr; 8.30 to 5.30; SF50 per day

**Kids Club**
t 775 3363
From age 3; 8.30-5pm; 6 days SF435 including lunch

**Ski school**
Takes children aged 4 to 12 (5 2½hr days SF155)

There are continuing reports of queues for outdated double chairs and for inadequate drag-lifts in the outlying 4 Valleys resorts – notably the Greppon Blanc drags on the way to Veysonnaz – and at La Chaux when crowds descend from the glacier. Overall, though, recent reporters find the lift system much improved.

## MOUNTAIN RESTAURANTS

***Disappointing in main area***

There are not enough huts, which means queues and overcrowding in high season. Savoleyres is the best area. The Poste hotel by the Tzoumaz chair takes some beating for value and lack of crowds. Also worth trying are Chez Simon ('simple and cheap'), Au Mayen (beneath the Combe 1 chair – 'good service, sunny terrace') and the rustic Marmotte ('wicked, excellent rösti'). Le Sonalon, on the fringe of the village, is 'excellent, with great views', but reached off-piste.

In the main area, the rustic Chez Dany at Clambin, on the off-piste run on the southern fringe of the area, is about the best, and gets packed – booking needed. Carrefour, with a large terrace, is popular and well-situated at the top of the village. The restaurants at Les Ruinettes – table-service upstairs – have big terraces with splendid views. The Olympique at Les Attelas is a good table-service restaurant. Everyone loves the Cabane Mont Fort – a proper mountain refuge off the run to La Chaux from Col des Gentianes; cosy on a bad day, and great views on a good one, but very busy – get there early or book a table.

## SCHOOLS AND GUIDES

***Good reports***

Verbier is an excellent place for advanced skiers, in particular, to get lessons. Several reporters have praised off-piste lessons with the Swiss ski school. Of the others, Adrenaline gets rave reviews, particularly for its private lessons; a reader this year said it was 'the one bright spot about the resort – highly recommended'. Another reader had a private lesson with European Snowsport and found the English instructor 'was brilliant at spotting faults and an excellent communicator'. British instructor Warren Smith runs his Ski Academy here (www.warrensmith-skiacademy.com).

The Les Esserts nursery slopes at the top of the village are good for children →

VERBIER TOURIST OFFICE / RICO FRANKFORT

## SCHOOLS

**Swiss (Maison du Sport)**
t 775 3363
info@maisondusport.ch

**Fantastique**
t 771 4141
lafantastique@verbier.ch

**Adrenaline**
t 771 7459
info@adrenaline-verbier.ch

**Altitude**
t 771 6006
info@altitude-verbier.com

**European Snowsport**
t 771 6222

**Classes**
(Swiss prices)
5 2½hr days SF200

**Private lessons**
SF140 for 2hr for 1 or 2 people

## GUIDES

**Bureau des guides**
t 775 3363
info@maisondusport.ch

**Olivier Roduit**
t 771 5317
o.roduit@mountain-guide.ch

## GETTING THERE

**Air** Geneva 170km/106 miles (2hr).

**Rail** Le Châble (7km/4 miles); regular buses to resort or gondola.

### FACILITIES FOR CHILDREN
***Wide range of options***

The Swiss school's facilities in the resort are good, and the resort attracts quite a lot of families. The playground up at La Chaux has also received favourable reports. Space on the bus back is limited, and priority is given to school groups. The possibility of leaving very young babies at the Schtroumpfs nursery is valuable.

There are considerable reductions on the lift pass price for families on production of your passports.

## STAYING THERE

### HOW TO GO
***Plenty of options***

Given the size of the place there are surprisingly few apartments and pensions available, though those on a budget have inexpensive B&B options in Le Châble. Hotels are expensive in relation to their grading. Given a sleeping bag you can bed down at the sports centre for about £10 a night – and that includes the use of the pool.

**Chalets** Verbier is the chalet-party capital of the Alps. Companies large and small have properties here, including Verbier specialists such as Ski Verbier who have ten chalets including one with an indoor pool and another with steam, sauna and outdoor hot-tub. Flexiski has the deeply comfortable chalet Bouvreuil. Right at the top of the market, Descent has two superb chalets.

**Hotels** There is one 5-star hotel, five 4-star, 14 3-star and a few simpler places.

((((5 **Chalet d'Adrien** (771 6200) The best-in-town: a beautifully furnished low-rise 25-room chalet, with top-notch cooking to match. Right next to the Savoleyres lift.

(((4 **Rosalp** (771 6323) The great attraction is the food in Roland Pierroz's Michelin-starred restaurant, which is as good as you'll find in any Swiss resort. Good position midway between centre and Médran.

(((4 **Montpelier** (771 6131) Very comfortable 4-star, but out of town (a courtesy bus is provided). Pool.

(((4 **Vanessa** (775 2800) Central 4-star with spacious apartments as well as rooms; 'Great food,' says a reporter.

((3 **Rotonde** (771 6525) Much cheaper, well positioned 3-star between centre and Médran; some budget rooms.

((3 **Verbier Lodge** (771 6666) Novel log-built B&B with stylish modern fittings, offering packages with tuition or heli-skiing. On southern fringe, beyond Médran – reachable on skis.

((3 **Poste** (771 6681) Well placed 3-star midway between centre and Médran; pool. Some rooms rather small.

((3 **Verbier** (775 2121) Central 3-star, popular with tour operators and their clientele; renowned for good food; atmospheric and traditional, with helpful owners and staff.

(2 **Farinet** (771 6626) Central 3-star hotel, British-owned, with a focal après-ski bar on its elevated terrace.

**Self-catering** Few UK tour operators offer apartments, but they can be booked locally.

## EATING OUT

***Plenty of choice***

There is a very wide range of restaurants; a pocket guide is given away locally which would be much more useful if all its advertisers gave some clues about price.

Hotel Rosalp is clearly the best (and most expensive) in town, and among the best in Switzerland, with an awesome wine cellar to match its excellent Michelin-starred food – splash out on the seven-course Menu Gastronomique if you can afford it. The Pinte bistro in the hotel basement is a less expensive option – worth trying. The 5-star Chalet d'Adrien also has two tempting options, with a starred chef at work in the gastronomique Astrance. The Grange is another place serious about its food.

King's is one of our favourites – innovative food in a stylish, clublike setting. We've also had excellent meals in the stylish Millénium, above the Toro Negro steak-house – itself recommended for 'a big spread of good food'.

For Swiss specialities, try the Relais des Neiges, the Robinson, the Caveau, Au Vieux Verbier by the Médran lifts or Esserts by the nursery slopes. Le Mignon does an 'excellent fondue,' says a reporter this year. The ever-popular Fer à Cheval does reasonably priced pizza and other simple dishes. Arguably the best-value Italian food in town is at Al Capone out near the Savoleyres gondola. Harold's Snack internet cafe is Verbier's burger joint.

You can be ferried by snowmobile up to Chez Dany or the Marmotte for a meal, followed by a torchlit descent.

## APRES-SKI

***Throbbing but expensive***

It starts with a 4pm visit to the Offshore Café at Médran, for people-watching, milk shakes and cakes. The nearby Big Ben pub is 'great and lively on a sunny afternoon'. Au Mignon at the bottom of the golf course has become popular since it was given a large sun deck.

Then if you're young, loud and British it's on to the Pub Mont-Fort – there's a widescreen TV for live sporting events. The Nelson is popular with locals. The Farinet is particularly good in spring, its live band playing to the audience on a huge, sunny terrace – there's a conservatory-type cover

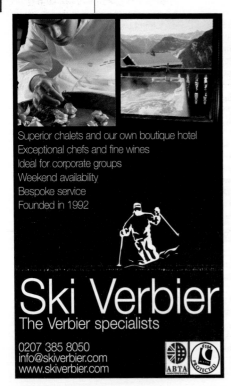

**Phone numbers**
From elsewhere in Switzerland add the prefix 027.
From abroad use the prefix +41 27.

**ACTIVITIES**

**Indoor** Sports centre (swimming pools, ice rink, curling, squash, sauna, solarium, steam bath, hot-tub), cinema, ice hockey, indoor golf

**Outdoor** 25km/16 miles of cleared walking paths, paragliding, hang-gliding, ice-climbing, snow-shoeing, horse-riding, tobogganing, mountaineering

**TOURIST OFFICES**

**Verbier**
t 775 3888
info@verbier.ch
www.verbier.ch

**Nendaz**
t 289 5589
info@nendaz.ch
www.nendaz.ch

**Siviez**
www.siviez-nendaz.ch

**Veysonnaz**
t 207 1053
tourism@veysonnaz.ch
www.veysonnaz.ch

**Thyon 2000 / Les Collons**
t 281 2727
info@thyon-region.ch
www.thyon-region.ch

**Le Châble** and **Bruson**
t 776 1682
bagnestourisme@verbier.ch

over it when it's cold. Fer à Cheval is a fun place full of regulars.

After dinner the Pub Mont-Fort is again popular (the shots bar in the cellar is worth a visit). Crok No Name has good live bands or a DJ and is entertaining for its cosmopolitan crowd. Murphy's Irish bar in the Garbo hotel is popular, with a good resident DJ. The much-loved King's is a quiet candlelit cellar bar with 60s' decor – 'hip crowd, good music'. New Club is a sophisticated piano bar, with comfortable seating and a more discerning clientele. Jacky's is a classy piano bar frequented by big spenders on their way to the seriously expensive Farm Club – on Friday and Saturday packed with rich Swiss paying SF220 for bottles of spirits. You'll find us having a quiet nightcap in the basement Bar'Jo, across the road.

The Casbah, in the basement of the Farinet hotel, has a North African theme. Taratata is a friendly club that seems to be growing in popularity. Scotch is the cheapest disco in town and popular with teenagers and snowboarders. Big Ben is 'lively, crowded and friendly'.

### OFF THE SLOPES
***No great attraction***

Verbier has an excellent sports centre, some nice walks and a big alpine museum, but otherwise not much to offer if you don't want to hit the slopes. Montreux is an enjoyable train excursion from Le Châble, and Martigny is worth a visit for the Roman remains and art gallery. The spa complex at Lavey-les-Bains has been highly recommended by a reporter. Various mountain restaurants are accessible to pedestrians. Both toboggan runs – on the shady side of Savoleyres and from Les Ruinettes – are an impressive 10km/6 miles long. The nursery slope at Les Esserts is floodlit for tubing etc on Saturday and Sunday evenings.

## Nendaz 1365m/4,480ft

Nendaz is a big resort with over 17,000 beds, but is little-known in Britain. Although it appears to be centrally set in the 4 Valleys, getting to and from the other sectors – particularly the Verbier slopes – is a slow business unless you drive/take a bus to Siviez. In other respects it has attractions, relatively low prices among them. Airport transfers are quick.

### THE RESORT

Nendaz itself is a large place on a shelf above and with great views of the Rhône valley. Most of the resort is modern but built in traditional chalet-style and the original old village of Haute-Nendaz is still there, with its narrow streets, old houses and barns, and baroque chapel dating from 1499.

### THE MOUNTAIN

Nendaz has its own area of slopes and a rather tenuous link with rest of the 4 Valleys via Siviez.

**Slopes** There's a 12-person gondola straight to the top of the local north-facing slopes at Tracouet. Here there are good, snow-sure nursery slopes plus blue and red intermediate runs back to town through the trees.

Intermediate and better skiers and boarders can head off down the back of Tracouet to a cable-car which takes you to Plan du Fou at 2430m/7,970ft. From there you can go down to Siviez and the links to Verbier one way and Thyon and Veysonnaz in the other.

**Terrain-parks** There is a terrain-park.

**Snow reliability** Nendaz sits on a north-facing shelf so its local slopes don't get the sun that affects Verbier.

**Experts** Access to the tough stuff is a bit slower from here than from Verbier.

**Intermediates** The local slopes are quite varied, but not very extensive.

**Beginners** There are good nursery slopes at Tracouet.

**Snowboarding** There is a half-pipe.

**Cross-country** There are 17km/11 miles of cross-country tracks.

**Queues** There may be queues at Siviez at the end of the day.

**Mountain restaurants** The most compelling are in the Verbier area.

**Schools and guides** Families seemed pleased with the school.

**Facilities for children** The school has a nursery area at Tracouet.

### STAYING THERE

**How to go** Interhome has properties.

**Hotels** There are a few traditional hotels. Reporters recommend the Sourire (288 2616): 'Simple, but good food.'

**Self-catering** There is no shortage of apartments bookable locally.

**Eating out** Readers recommend the hotel Sourire and the Mont Rouge.

**Après-ski** There are plenty of bars and four discos; a 17-year-old reporter recommends the Cactus Saloon and the Bodega as the liveliest spots.

**Off the slopes** Nendaz has 70km/43 miles of winter walks, an open-air rink, a fitness centre and squash courts.

## Siviez 1730m/5,680ft

Siviez is a small huddle of buildings in an isolated spot, where the slopes of Verbier, Nendaz and Veysonnaz/Thyon meet. Among them is the 2-star hotel de Siviez (288 1623). Not surprisingly, this is an ideal base from which to explore the whole 4 Valleys lift network. But, being set a little way down the valley from Tortin, at the foot of the steep itinerary runs from Chassoure and Mont-Fort, it is also an excellent base for exploration of the tough skiing of Verbier – you can end the day with a descent of 1600m/5,250ft vertical from Mont-Fort; no noise in the evenings; perfect.

## Veysonnaz 1300m/4,270ft

Veysonnaz is a small, quiet resort, sunny in the afternoon, at the foot of an excellent long red slope from the ridge above Thyon. It is an attractive old village complete with church. It has adequate bars, cafes and restaurants, a disco and a 'good' sports centre with swimming pool. Accommodation is mainly in apartments. Of the two hotels, the 'very comfortable' Chalet Royal (208 5644) is preferable to the 'tired-looking' Magrappé, which is the focus of noisy après-ski. Taking a car means you can drive to Siviez for quick access to the Verbier or Nendaz slopes – a slow business by lift and piste.

## Thyon 2000 2100m/6,890ft

Thyon 2000 (why not Thyon 2100, we wonder?) is a functional, purpose-built collection of plain, medium-rise apartment blocks just above the tree line at the centre of the Thyon-Veysonnaz sector of the 4 Valleys. It has the basics – bakery, supermarket, newsagent, a couple of bar-restaurants. There's a kindergarten as well as a ski school, and an indoor pool.

## Les Collons 1800m/5,910ft

At the foot of a broad, east-facing slope down from Thyon 2000, Les Collons could hardly be more different – a couple of strings of chalets along roads following the hillside, mostly apartments but also a couple of modest hotels including the 3-star Cambuse (281 1883). There's a much wider range of bars, restaurants and other diversions than up in Thyon.

## Le Châble 820m/2,690ft

Le Châble is a busy roadside village in the valley, at the bottom of the hairpin road up to Verbier. It is linked to Verbier by a queue-free gondola that goes on (without changing cabins) to Les Ruinettes and Les Attelas, which means access to the slopes can be just as quick as from Verbier. Le Châble is on the rail network, and is also convenient for drivers who want to visit other resorts in the Valais or further afield. And it is handy for Bruson, just a short bus-ride up the mountainside facing Verbier. There are several modest hotels, of which the 2-star Giétroz (776 1184) is the pick.

## Bruson 1000m/3,280ft

Bruson is a small village on a shelf just above Le Châble, and reached by a short free bus-ride. Its lifts are covered by the Verbier pass. From the village a slow chair goes up over gentle east-facing slopes dotted with chalets to Bruson les Forêts (1600m/5,250ft).

The open slopes above Bruson les Forêts are served by a quad chair up to the ridge, on the far side of which is a short drag-lift serving a tight little bowl. This may not sound much, but in addition to the intermediate pistes served by these lifts there are large amounts of underused off-piste terrain, notably through woods on the front side accessed by the drag on the back side. Off-piste descents down the back towards Orsières are possible, with the return by train. For years there have been great plans to develop Bruson – building a lift from Le Châble to mid-mountain, extending the lift network across the north-east-facing slopes of Six Blanc and on to the shoulder of Mt Rogneux at 2800m/9,190ft, and building a lift up from Orsières. For now, it remains a great place to escape Verbier crowds.

SNOWPIX.COM / CHRIS GILL

# Villars

*Traditional old resort with a much-needed but far-flung glacier*

**COSTS**

(1)(2)(3)(4)(5)(6)

**RATINGS**

| **The slopes** | |
|---|---|
| Snow | ** |
| Extent | *** |
| Expert | ** |
| Intermediate | *** |
| Beginner | **** |
| Convenience | *** |
| Queues | *** |
| Mountain restaurants | *** |
| **The rest** | |
| Scenery | *** |
| Resort charm | **** |
| Off-slope | **** |

**Phone numbers**
From elsewhere in Switzerland add the prefix 024.
From abroad use the prefix +41 24.

- ➕ Pleasant, relaxing year-round resort
- ➕ Fairly extensive intermediate slopes linked to Les Diablerets
- ➕ Good nursery slopes
- ➕ Quite close to Geneva airport
- ➕ Good range of off-slope diversions

- ➖ Unreliable snow-cover
- ➖ Overcrowded mountain restaurants
- ➖ Getting up the mountain means a slow, often crowded train journey or a bus-ride from the town centre to the gondola

**With its mountain railway and gentle low-altitude slopes, Villars is the kind of place that has been overshadowed by modern mega-resorts. But for a relaxing and varied family holiday the attractions are clear – and the link with Les Diablerets and its high glacier, now known as Glacier 3000, adds to the appeal.**

## THE RESORT

Villars sits on a sunny shelf, looking across the Rhône valley to the Portes du Soleil. A busy high street lined with a variety of shops gives it the air of a pleasant small town; all around are chalet-style buildings, with just a few block-like hotels. You can travel to the centre of Villars on a picturesque cog train which goes on up to the slopes. It leaves from Bex in the valley, which is served by direct trains from Geneva airport (as is Aigle, a bus-ride from Villars). A gondola at one end of town is the main lift; stay nearby if you can, since shuttle-buses get crowded at peak times. You can also stay in Gryon.

The Glacier-Alpes Vaudoises pass covers Villars, the linked slopes of Les Diablerets and Glacier 3000, plus Leysin and Les Mosses, both of which are easy jaunts by rail or road. Other resorts (eg Champéry and Verbier) are within driving distance. Les Diablerets, Leysin and Les Mosses have extended entries in our resort directory, at the back of the book.

Gstaad Reusch
Glacier 3000
Floriettaz 2120m/6,960ft
Cabane 2525m
Scex Rouge 2970m/9,740ft
Iseneau 1760m
Col du Pillon 1545m
Le Meilleret 1950m
Les Diablerets 1200m/3,940ft
Croix des Chaux 2020m/6,630ft
Petit Chamossaire 2035m/6,680ft
Laouissalet
Chaux de Conches
Les Chaux 1750m
Grand Chamossaire 2120m
Alpe des Chaux
Chaux Ronde 1985m
Les Fracherets 1515m
Roc d'Orsay 2000m
Bretaye 1805m
Sodoleuvre
Col de Soud 1525m
La Rasse 1350m
Villars 1300m/4,270ft
Barboleuse 1200m/3,940ft
Gryon 1115m/3,660ft

The classic chocolate-box view of Villars. If only there was always this much snow around! ↗

VILLARS TOURIST OFFICE



## NEWS

For 2003/04, a new terrain-park was made on the top of Chaux Ronde with three difficulty levels – and jumps, hips and rails. A snow bar opened at the bottom.

A new high-speed chair is planned (for 2005/06 at the earliest) to replace the Villars-Roc d'Orsay gondola, increasing capacity by 30%.

## KEY FACTS

| | |
|---|---|
| **Resort** | 1300m<br>4,270ft |
| For Villars, Gryon and Les Diablerets, but excluding Glacier 3000 | |
| **Slopes** | 1115-2120m<br>3,660-6,960ft |
| **Lifts** | 36 |
| **Pistes** | 100km<br>62 miles |
| **Blue** | 40% |
| **Red** | 50% |
| **Black** | 10% |
| **Snowmaking** | 10km<br>6 miles |

## TOURIST OFFICE

t 495 3232
information@villars.ch
www.villars.ch

## THE MOUNTAINS

There's a good mix of open and wooded slopes throughout the area.

**Slopes** The train goes up to the col of Bretaye, which has intermediate slopes on either side, with a maximum vertical of 300m/980ft back to the col and much longer runs back to the village. To the east, open slopes (often spoilt by sun) go to La Rasse and the link to the Les Chaux sector. The gondola from town takes you to Roc d'Orsay, from where you can head for Bretaye or back to Villars. From Bretaye you can head for the slow two-way chair-lift which is the connection to Les Diablerets. The piste map and marking are both poor. 'If you don't know the resort, skiing in bad visibility would be stressful,' says a reader this year.

**Terrain-parks** There's a terrain-park at Les Chaux and a new one on Chaux Ronde (see News).

**Snow reliability** Low altitude and sunny slopes mean snow reliability isn't good. There is some snowmaking but the SF12m investment planned is badly needed. If local snow is poor, head for Glacier 3000 – a long trek.

**Experts** The main interest for experts is off-piste. Heli-skiing is available.

**Intermediates** The local slopes and Les Diablerets offer a good variety and add up to a fair amount of terrain. The lengthy trip to Glacier 3000 for the splendid red run down the Combe d'Audon is worth it for the adventurous.

**Beginners** Beginners will enjoy the village nursery slopes and riding the train to Bretaye. There are gentle runs here, too, but it's also very crowded.

**Snowboarding** Villars is home to a big end-of-season snowboarders' party (visit www.snowbombing.com).

**Cross-country** The trails up the valley past La Rasse are long and pretty, and there are more in the depression beyond Bretaye (44km/27 miles in all).

**Queues** Queues appear for the lifts at Bretaye mainly at weekends and peak periods and the buses and train can get overcrowded. A reader this year found queues at the Laouissalet drag between Villars and Les Diablerets.

**Mountain restaurants** They are often oversubscribed especially at Bretaye and the Meilleret sector of Les Diablerets. The Golf is expensive but good, as is the Col-de-Soud ('best rösti ever'); Lac des Chavonnes (open at peak periods) is worth the walk.

**Schools and guides** The Villars ski school – aka Ecole Moderne (using the ski évolutif method) – and the Swiss ski school get good reports. A past reporter gave the Swiss School '10 out of 10'. Riderschool is a specialist snowboard outfit.

**Facilities for children** Both ski schools run children's classes. There is also a non-ski nursery for children up to six and a Club Med with good facilities.

## STAYING THERE

**How to go** Several tour operators offer packages here. We have received glowing reports on the Club Med here.

**Hotels** The Golf (496 3838) is popular ('great, family tries hard'). The Eurotel Victoria (495 3131) lacks style but is near the gondola. The Bristol (496 3636) is not, but offers 'comfort, good food and service'. All are 4-star.

**Eating out** Many restaurants are hotel-based. Apart from these, the Sporting is recommended for pizza and the Vieux-Villars for local specialities.

**Après-ski** Charlie's, the Central, the Sporting and the Mini-Pub are popular bars. The bowling can be a laugh; El Gringo and Fox are the discos.

**Off the slopes** Paragliding and hang-gliding are available, plus tennis, skating, curling, swimming, 'excellent' walks, and trips on the train – to Lausanne for instance.

SNOWPIX.COM / CHRIS GILL

# Wengen

*Charming village, stunning views and extensive intermediate terrain*

**COSTS**

①②③④⑤⑥

**RATINGS**

| **The slopes** | |
|---|---|
| Snow | ** |
| Extent | *** |
| Expert | ** |
| Intermediate | **** |
| Beginner | *** |
| Convenience | *** |
| Queues | *** |
| Mountain restaurants | **** |
| **The rest** | |
| Scenery | ***** |
| Charm | ***** |
| Off-slope | **** |

**NEWS**

For 2004/05 the old double chair from Innerwengen to Allmend is to be replaced by a high-speed quad.

For 2003/04 the slow Läger double chair on Männlichen was replaced by a fast quad.



- ＋ Some of the most spectacular scenery in the Alps
- ＋ Traditional, nearly traffic-free Alpine village, reached only by cog railway
- ＋ Lots of long, gentle runs, ideal for intermediates, leading down to Grindelwald
- ＋ Rebuilt cable-car an attractive alternative to slow trains up to the slopes above Grindelwald
- ＋ Nursery slopes in heart of village
- ＋ Calm, unhurried atmosphere

- − Limited terrain for experts and adventurous intermediates
- − Despite some snowmaking, snow conditions are unreliable – especially on the sunny home run and village nursery slope
- − Trains to slopes from here and from Grindelwald are slow
- − Getting to Grindelwald's First area can take hours
- − Subdued in the evening, with little variety of nightlife

**Given the charm of the village, the friendliness of the locals and the drama of the scenery, it's easy to see why many people – including large numbers of middle-aged British people who have been going for decades – love Wengen. But non-devotees should think carefully about the lack of challenge, the unreliable snow and the number of slow lifts before signing up.**

**The Männlichen cable-car station, destroyed in the devastating avalanches of 1999, was rebuilt in the heart of the village, where it is not only less vulnerable to avalanche but also much more convenient. Of course, it is now more popular, and gets queues at peak times but it does offer a useful alternative to living with the train timetable.**

## THE RESORT

Wengen is set on a shelf high above the Lauterbrunnen valley, opposite Mürren, and reached only by a cog railway, which carries on up the mountain as the main lift. Wengen was a farming community long before skiing arrived; it is still tiny, but it is dominated by sizeable hotels, mostly of Victorian origin. So it is not exactly pretty, but it is charming and relaxed, and almost traffic-free. The only traffic is electric hotel taxi-trucks, which gather at the station to pick up guests, and a few ordinary engine-driven taxis. (Why, we wonder?)

The short main street is the hub of the village. Lined with chalet-style shops and hotels, it also has the ice rink and village nursery slopes right next to it. The nursery slopes double as the venue for floodlit ski-jumping and parallel slalom races.

The views across the valley are stunning. They get even better higher up, when the famous trio of peaks comes fully into view – the Mönch (Monk) protecting the Jungfrau (Maiden) from the Eiger (Ogre).

The main way up the mountain is the regular, usually punctual, trains from the southern end of the street to Kleine Scheidegg, where the slopes of Wengen meet those of Grindelwald. The cable-car is a much quicker way to the Grindelwald slopes, and now starts conveniently close to the main street.

Wengen is small, so location isn't as crucial as in many other resorts. The main street is ideally placed for the station. There are hotels on the home piste, convenient for the slopes. Those who don't fancy a steepish morning climb should avoid places down the hill below the station.

You can get to Mürren by taking the train down to Lauterbrunnen, followed by a funicular and connecting train up the other side, or a bus-ride to Stechelberg followed by a cable-car up (this route is usually quicker and also avoids a walk through Mürren to the main lifts). The Jungfrau lift pass covers all of this. Outings further afield aren't really worth the effort.

## LIFT PASSES

**Jungfrau Top Ski Region**
Covers Wengen, Mürren and Grindelwald, trains between them and Grindelwald ski-bus.

**Main pass**
1 day SF55
6 days SF282

**Senior citizens**
Over 62: 6 days SF254

**Children**
Under 20: 6 days SF226
Under 16: 6 days SF141
Under 6: free pass.

**Notes**
Day pass price is for First-Kleine Scheidegg-Männlichen area only.

**Alternative passes**
Passes available for Grindelwald and Wengen only and for Mürren only. Non-skiers pass available.

## THE MOUNTAINS

Although it is famous for the fearsome Lauberhorn Downhill course – the longest and one of the toughest on the World Cup circuit – Wengen's slopes are best suited to early intermediates. Most of the Downhill course is now open to the public. But the steepest section (the Hundschopf jump) can be avoided by an alternative red route, for those who don't fancy it.

The majority of Wengen's runs are gentle blues and reds, ideal for cruising.

### THE SLOPES
***Picturesque playground***

Most of the slopes are on the Grindelwald side of the mountain. From the railway station at Kleine Scheidegg you can head straight down to Grindelwald or work your way across the mountain with the help of a couple of lifts to the top of the Männlichen. This area is served by drag- and chair-lifts, and can be reached directly from Wengen by the improved cable-car.

There are a few runs back down towards Wengen from the top of the Lauberhorn, but below Kleine Scheidegg there's really only one.

### TERRAIN-PARKS
***Couple of options***

There's a Jumpers' Corner under the top of the Wixi chair and Jump Street by the Bumps T-bar, below Wengernalp.

### SNOW RELIABILITY
***How well do they use the guns?***

Most slopes are below 2000m/6,560ft, and at Grindelwald they go down to less than 1000m/3,280ft. Very few slopes face north and the long blue run back to the village suffers from sun and lack of altitude. In the past reporters have been critical of the resort's use of snowmaking: a 2003 report said, 'At least three machines were parked up and decorating the landscape at Kleine Scheidegg and never moved all week while the field below Wengernalp was 500 yards of sheet ice.' But a 2004 reporter said that they 'appeared to be using snow-machines smartly'. We have also had reports of poor piste grooming. More reports please!

While we've found wonderful snow a couple of times in late March, we've also struggled to find decent snow to ski on in January.

### FOR EXPERTS
***Few challenges***

Wengen is quite limited for experts. The only genuine black runs in the area are parts of the Lauberhorn World Cup Downhill (which, for most of its length, is merely of intermediate red run gradient) and a couple of pistes from Eigergletscher towards Wixi including Oh God (which used to be off-piste). There are now two 'itinerary' runs from the Lauberhorn chair-lift.

There are some decent off-piste



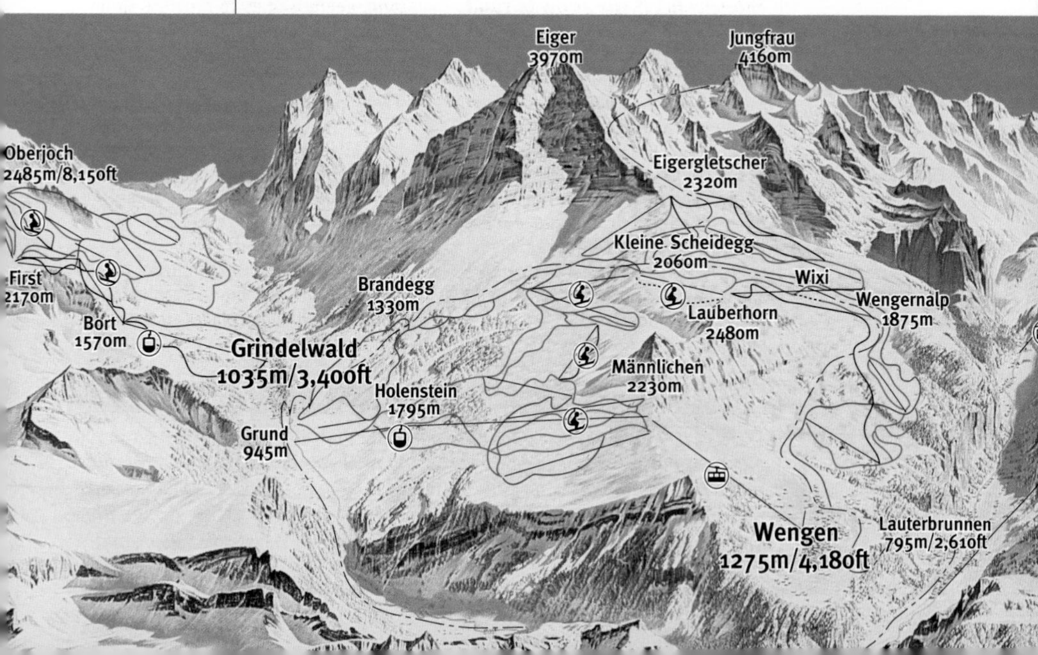

↑ The gentle terrain in the valley is where the train winds its way up and you ski back to the village through trees and meadows

WENGEN TOURIST OFFICE



**KEY FACTS**

| | |
|---|---|
| **Resort** | 1275m 4,180ft |
| For Jungfrau region | |
| **Slopes** | 945-2970m 3,100-9,740ft |
| **Lifts** | 42 |
| **Pistes** | 203km 126 miles |
| **Blue** | 25% |
| **Red** | 61% |
| **Black** | 14% |
| **Snowmaking** | 60km 37 miles |
| For First-Männlichen-Kleine-Scheidegg only | |
| **Slopes** | 945-2485m 3,100-8,150ft |
| **Lifts** | 30 |
| **Pistes** | 150km 93 miles |

runs such as White Hare from under the north face of the Eiger and more adventurous runs from the Jungfraujoch late in the season.

For more serious challenges it's well worth going to nearby Mürren, around an hour away. Heli-trips with mountain guides are organised if there are enough takers.

**FOR INTERMEDIATES**

***Wonderful if the snow is good***

Wengen and Grindelwald share superb intermediate slopes. Nearly all are long blue or gentle red runs – see Grindelwald chapter. The run back to Wengen is a relaxing end to the day, as long as it's not too crowded.

For tougher pistes, head for the top of the Lauberhorn lift and then the runs to Kleine Scheidegg, or to Wixi (following the start of the Downhill course). You could also try the north-facing run from Eigergletscher to Salzegg, which often has the best snow late in the season.

**FOR BEGINNERS**

***Not ideal***

There's a nursery slope in the centre of the village – it's convenient and gentle, but the snow is unreliable. There's a beginners' area at Wengernalp and another on the Grindelwald side of Kleine Scheidegg, but to get back to Wengen you either have to take the train or tackle the run down, which can be tricky. There are plenty of good, long, gentle slopes to progress to on the Grindelwald side.

**FOR CROSS-COUNTRY**

***There is none***

There's no cross-country in Wengen itself. There are 17.5km/11 miles of tracks down in the Lauterbrunnen valley, where the snow is unreliable.

**QUEUES**

***Improving, but a long way to go***

The Männlichen cable-car has helped cut the queues for the trains but both can still be crowded at peak periods. It

**boarding**

*Wengen is not a bad place for gentle boarding – the nursery area is not ideal, but beginners have plenty of slopes to progress to, with lots of long blue and red runs served by the train and chair-lifts. Getting from Kleine Scheidegg to Männlichen means an unavoidable drag-lift though. And the slope back to Wenegen is narrow and almost flat in places, so you may have to scoot. For the steepest slopes and best free-riding, experts will want to head for Mürren.*

## GETTING THERE

**Air** Zürich 195km/121 miles (3½hr); Bern 70km/43 miles (1½hr).

**Rail** Station in resort.

## SCHOOLS

**Swiss**
**t** 855 2022
ski.school@wengen.com

**Privat**
**t** 8555005
privat@wengen.com

**Kleine Scheidegg**
t 8551545

**Classes**
(Swiss prices)
6 3hr days SF232

**Private lessons**
SF72 for 1hr

## CHILDREN

**Little Playhouse**
**t** 855 3681
Ages 2 to 7; 8.30-5pm; Sun-Fri

**Sunshine nursery**
**t** 853 0440
Ages 1mnth upwards

**Ski school**
The Swiss school takes ages 4 up (6 3hr days SF232)

is best to avoid travelling up at the same time as the ski school. Weekend invasions can increase the crowds on the Grindelwald side, especially. Queues up the mountain have been alleviated a lot in the last few years by the installation of fast chairs. A reader who visited at Easter found no queues. But plenty of slow old lifts remain.

### MOUNTAIN RESTAURANTS
***Plenty of variety***

A popular but pricey place for lunch is the Jungfrau hotel at Wengernalp, where the rösti is excellent and the views of the Jungfrau are superb. The highest restaurant is at Eigergletscher. If you get there early on a sunny day, you can grab a table on the narrow outside balcony and enjoy magnificent views of the glacier. The station buffet at Kleine Scheidegg gets repeated rave reviews, so it's not surprising that it also gets packed – the take-away rösti and sausage are a popular option. The Grindelwaldblick is a worthwhile trudge uphill from Kleine Scheidegg, with great food and views of the Eiger.

The Allmend, near the top of the Innerwengen chair and the train stop, is reportedly 'delightful', with 'friendly service' and wonderful views of the valley from the terrace. We've had conflicting reviews for Mary's Cafe situated at the end of the World Cup runs. One 2004 reporter says it is 'cosy and serves excellent food', another found it had 'lost its character now it is owned by the Regina hotel'. For restaurants on the slopes down towards Grindelwald, see that chapter.

### SCHOOLS AND GUIDES
***Healthy competition***

A reporter says, 'The Swiss school is definitely trying harder than a few years ago.' The lessons and the standard of English are usually good. The independent Privat school has been recommended for private lessons. Guides are available for heli-trips and powder excursions.

### FACILITIES FOR CHILDREN
***Apparently satisfactory***

Our reports on children's facilities are from observers rather than participants, but are all favourable. It is an attractive and reassuring village for families, with the baby slope in the very heart of the village.

The train gives easy access to higher slopes.

## STAYING THERE

### HOW TO GO
***Wide range of hotels***

Most accommodation is in hotels. There is only a handful of catered chalets (and no especially luxurious ones). Self-catering apartments are few, too.

**Hotels** There are about two dozen hotels, mostly 4-star and 3-star, with a handful of simpler places.

((((4 **Beausite Park** (856 5161) Reputedly the best in town. Good pool, steam and massage. But poorly situated at top of nursery slopes – a schlep up from the main street.

((((4 **Wengener Hof** (856 6969) No prizes for style or convenience, but recommended for peace, helpful staff and spacious, spotless rooms with good views.

((((4 **Sunstar** (856 5200) Modern hotel on main street right opposite cable-car. Comfortable rooms which are gradually being refurbished; lounge has a log fire. Live music most evenings. Pool with views. 'Excellent meals, friendly.'

((((4 **Regina** (856 5858) Quite central. Smart, traditional atmosphere. 'Best food in Wengen.' Carousel nightclub.

((((4 **Silberhorn** (856 5131) Comfortable, modern 4-star in central position opposite station, with a choice of restaurants, frequently praised by reporters.

((((4 **Caprice** (856 0606) Small, smartly furnished chalet-style hotel across the tracks from the Regina. Sauna and steam room. 'Comfortable and friendly'; 'fabulous views, children's menu'. Kindergarten.

(((3 **Belvédère** (856 6868) Some way out, but we have good reports of buffet-style meals ('good for families'), spacious rooms and grand art nouveau public rooms.

(((3 **Alpenrose** (855 3216) Long-standing British favourite; eight minutes' climb to the station. Small, simple rooms, but good views; 'first-class' food; friendly staff.

(((3 **Eiger** (856 0505) Very conveniently sited, right next to the station. Focal après-ski bar. Comfy modern rooms.

((2 **Falken** (856 5121) Further up the hill. Another British favourite, known affectionately as 'Fawlty Towers'.

**Self-catering** The hotel Bernerhof's decent Résidence apartments are well positioned just off the main street, and hotel facilities are available to guests.

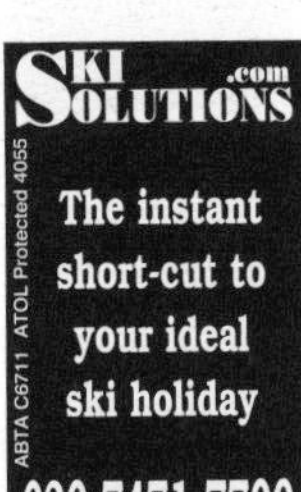




**ACTIVITIES**

**Indoor** Swimming pool (in Beausite Park and Sunstar hotels), sauna, solarium, whirlpool, massage (in hotels), cinema (with English films), billiards

**Outdoor** Ice rink, curling, 50km/ 31 miles of cleared paths, tobogganing, snow-shoeing, paragliding, glacier flights, sledging excursions, hang-gliding, ice-climbing, helicopter flights

**REPORTS WANTED**

Recently we have had few reports on this resort. If you go there, please do send us a report.

The best reports earn a copy of the next edition, and can lead to free lift passes in future.

See page 10.

**Phone numbers**
From elsewhere in Switzerland add the prefix 033.
From abroad use the prefix +41 33.

**TOURIST OFFICE**

**t** 855 1414
info@wengen.ch
www.wengen-muerren.ch




## EATING OUT
### *Lots of choice*

Most restaurants are in hotels. They offer good food and service. The Eiger has a traditional restaurant and a stube with Swiss and French cuisine. The Bernerhof has good-value traditional dishes. The little hotel Hirschen has good steaks. There's no shortage of fondues in the village. Several bars do casual food, including good-value pizza at Sina. Cafe Gruebi has been recommended again this year for 'the most wonderful cakes'. The Jungfrau at Wengernalp has an excellent restaurant – but you have to get back on skis or on a toboggan.

## APRES-SKI
### *It depends on what you want*

People's reactions to the après-ski scene in Wengen vary widely, according to their expectations and appetites. If you're used to raving in Kitzbühel or Les Deux-Alpes, you'll rate Wengen dead, especially for young people. If you've heard it's dead, you may be pleasantly surprised to find that there is a handful of bars that do good business both early and late in the evening. But it is only a handful of small places. The Schnee-Bar, at the Bumps section of the home run, is a popular final run stop-off. And the stube at the Eiger hotel and the tiny, 'always welcoming' Eiger Bar are popular at the end of the day. The traditional Tanne and the funky Chili's, almost opposite on the main street, are generally lively. Sina's, a little way out by Club Med, usually has live music. The Caprice bar is also recommended. There are discos and live music in some hotels. The cinema often shows English-language films.

## OFF THE SLOPES
### *Good for a relaxing time*

Wengen is a superb resort for those who want a completely relaxing holiday, with its unbeatable scenery and pedestrian-friendly trains and cable-car (there's a special, though expensive, pass for pedestrians). There are some lovely walks, ice skating and a curling club. Several hotels have health spas. Excursions to Interlaken and Bern are possible by train, as is the trip up to the Jungfraujoch (see the Grindelwald chapter). Helicopter flights from Männlichen are recommended.

## STAYING UP THE MOUNTAIN
### *Great views*

You can stay at two points up the mountain reached by the railway: the expensive Jungfrau hotel (855 1622) at Wengernalp – with fabulous views – and at Kleine Scheidegg, where there are rooms in the big Scheidegg-Hotels (855 1212) and dormitory space above the Grindelwaldblick restaurant (855 1374) and the station buffet. The big restaurant at Männlichen has rooms.

## STAYING DOWN THE VALLEY
### *The budget option*

Staying in a 3-star hotel like the Schützen (855 2032) or Oberland (855 1241) down in Lauterbrunnen will cost about half as much as similar accommodation in Wengen. The trains from Wengen run until 11.30pm and are included in your lift pass. Staying in Lauterbrunnen also improves your chances of getting a seat on the morning train to Kleine Scheidegg rather than joining the scramble at Wengen – though of course it also means a much longer journey time. Lauterbrunnen is also much better placed for visits to Mürren.

You can save even more by staying in Interlaken. Choose a hotel near Interlaken Ost station, from which you can catch a train to Lauterbrunnen (22 minutes) or Grindelwald (36 minutes). Driving can take longer at weekends, when the roads get very busy.

## THE BRITISH IN WENGEN

*There's a very strong British presence at Wengen. Many Brits have been returning for years to the same rooms in the same hotels in the same week, and treat the resort as a sort of second home. There is an English church with weekly services, and a British-run club, the DHO (Downhill Only) – so named when the first Brits persuaded the locals to keep the summer railway running up the mountain in winter so that they would no longer have to climb up in order to ski down again. That greatly amused the locals, who until then had regarded skiing in winter as a necessity rather than a pastime to be done for fun. The DHO is still going strong and organises regular events throughout the season.*

SNOWPIX.COM / CHRIS GILL

# Zermatt

*Magical in many respects – both on and off the slopes*

**COSTS**

(1)(2)(3)(4)(5)(6)

**RATINGS**

**The slopes**

| | |
|---|---|
| Snow | **** |
| Extent | **** |
| Expert | ***** |
| Intermediate | **** |
| Beginner | * |
| Convenience | * |
| Queues | *** |
| Mountain restaurants | ***** |

**The rest**

| | |
|---|---|
| Scenery | ***** |
| Charm | ***** |
| Off-slope | **** |

**NEWS**

For 2003/04 two new fast six-seater chair-lifts were built. One goes from Trockener Steg to Furggsattel, replacing the queue-prone T-bar here, the other from Riffelberg to Gifthittli, below Gornergrat, replacing another T-bar.

For 2004/05 more snowmaking is planned in five key areas.

A large investment programme will begin in 2005/06. First, the ancient Sunnegga-Blauherd gondola will be replaced with a lift that mixes eight-person gondola cabins and six-seat high-speed chairs. Further out, there are plans for a much needed link between Furi and Riffelberg and a link between Sunnegga and Gornergrat via Findeln and Breitboden – we'd be sad about this latter link because it would spoil the wonderful deserted runs from Gornergrat and Hohtälli to Gant.

+ Wonderful, high and extensive slopes and three varied areas
+ Spectacular high-mountain scenery, dominated by the Matterhorn
+ Charming, if rather sprawling, old mountain village, largely traffic-free
+ Reliable snow at altitude
+ World's best mountain restaurants
+ Extensive helicopter operation
+ Nightlife to suit most tastes
+ Smart shops
+ Linked to Cervinia in Italy

− Main lifts may be a long walk, or a crowded bus- or taxi-ride from home
− Beginners should go elsewhere
− Europe's most expensive lift pass
− Some restaurants and hotels very expensive – so choose carefully
− One-way link only between Rothorn/ Gornergrat and the Klein Matterhorn
− Slow train up to Gornergrat annoys some people, but can be avoided
− Some lift queues at peak periods
− Annoying electric taxis detract from the car-free village ambience

**You must try Zermatt before you die. Few places can match its combination of excellent advanced and intermediate slopes, reliable snow, magnificent scenery, Alpine charm and mountain restaurants with superb food and stunning views.**

**Zermatt has its drawbacks – see the long list above. But for us, and for virtually all our reporters (after taking a few days to get used to its inconvenience, in some cases), these pale into insignificance compared to its attractions, which come close to matching perfectly our notion of the ideal winter resort. It's one of our favourites – and one of the editors regularly takes his annual holiday here.**



## THE RESORT

Zermatt started life as a traditional mountain village, developed as a mountaineering centre in the 19th century, then became a winter resort. Summer is as important as winter here.

Zermatt is big business and most restaurants and hotels are owned by a handful of families. Many of the workers are brought in from outside the area – but that is probably one of the reasons many reporters have remarked on the increased friendliness and improved service in recent years.

The village sprawls along either side of a river, mountains rising steeply on each side. It is a mixture of chocolate-box chalets and modern buildings, most in traditional style. You arrive by rail or taxi from Täsch, where cars have to be left for a fee. They can be left for free at more distant Visp, from where you can also get a train. The main street runs past the station, lined with luxury hotels, shops and restaurants. Many of the narrow side-streets and paths are hilly and treacherous if icy.

Zermatt doesn't have the relaxed, quaint feel of other car-free resorts, such as Wengen and Saas-Fee. That's partly because the electric vehicles are more intrusive and aggressive, and partly because the clientele is more overtly part of the jet set.

For a resort with such good and extensive slopes, there's a remarkably high age profile. Most visitors seem to be over 40, and there's little of the youthful atmosphere you get in rival resorts with comparable slopes, such as Val-d'Isère, St Anton and Chamonix.

The main street has the station near one end, with the cog railway to

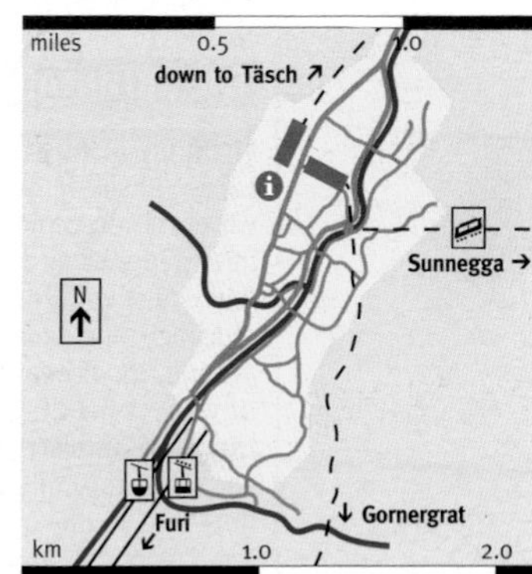

Gornergrat leaving from the other side of the square. The underground funicular to Sunnegga is a few minutes' walk away and the gondola to the Klein Matterhorn area (and the link to Cervinia) is a 15-minute trek, a crowded bus-ride or a taxi-ride (you can keep taxi costs down by sharing).

Choosing where to stay is very important in Zermatt. The solar-powered shuttle-buses get crowded. Walking from one end of the village to the furthest lifts can take 15 to 20 minutes and can be unpleasant because of treacherous icy paths. If you rent equipment from Flexrent they will transport it free overnight between their shops near the Sunnegga and Klein Matterhorn lifts if you tell them which area you want to use next day.

The best spot to stay is near the Gornergrat and Sunnegga railways, near the end of the main street. Some accommodation is up the steep hill across the river in Winkelmatten – you can ski back to it from all areas and it has its own reliable bus service.

Getting up to the village from Täsch is no problem. The trains run on time and have automatically descending ramps that allow you to wheel luggage trolleys on and off. You are met at the other end by electric and horse-drawn taxis and hotel shuttles.

## THE MOUNTAINS

There are slopes to suit all abilities except absolute beginners, for whom we don't recommend the resort. For intermediates and experts Zermatt has few rivals, with marvellously groomed cruising trails, some of the best moguls around, long, beautiful scenic runs out of view of the lift system, exciting heli-trips and off-piste possibilities, as well as the opportunity to get down into Italy for the day and lunch on pasta and chianti. On our recent visits we have been impressed with the service improvements: the lift staff are polite and helpful, there are useful announcements in several languages (including English) on the train and some cable-cars and there are free tissues at most lift stations (just as in America). The large 'self-ripping' piste-map was complained of by a reporter (there's another very compact version which shows Cervinia's slopes, too).

The whole area around Stockhorn is now a 'free-ride' area served by 'ski runs' rather than pistes; after scouring the map we discovered this seems to mean 'protected' (from avalanches we presume) 'and marked, but not prepared and not checked at the end of the day'. There are several other 'ski runs' elsewhere in Zermatt's ski area.

### THE SLOPES
***Beautiful and varied***

Zermatt consists of three separate areas, two of which are now well linked. The **Sunnegga-Blauherd-Rothorn** area is reached by the underground funicular starting about five minutes' walk from the station. This shifts large numbers rapidly but can lead to queues for the subsequent gondola – you can take a run down to a high-speed quad alternative.

From the top of this area you can make your way – via south-facing slopes served by snowmaking – to Gant in the valley between Sunnegga and the second main area, **Gornergrat–Hohtälli–Stockhorn**. A 125-person cable-car opened a few seasons ago linking Gant to Hohtälli in just seven minutes – a vast improvement on two gruelling steep T-bars that were the only links before. A gondola makes the link back from Gant to Sunnegga. Gornergrat can be reached direct from Zermatt by cog railway trains which leave every 24 minutes and take 30 or 40 minutes to get to the top – arrive at

## boarding

*Boarders in soft boots have one big advantage over skiers in Zermatt – they have much more comfortable walks to and from the lift stations! Even so, there aren't many snowboarders around. The slopes are best for experienced free-riders, because tough piste and off-piste action is what Zermatt is really about; plus there's the world-class terrain-park. There is, however, an excellent little beginner area at Blauherd, complete with moving carpet lift, which we've seen many beginner snowboarders having lessons on. The main lifts are boarder-friendly: train, funicular, gondolas and cable-cars and there aren't too many flat bits. But there are still a few T-bars. Stoked is a specialist snowboard school.*

### KEY FACTS

| | |
|---|---|
| **Resort** | 1620m<br>5,310ft |
| For Zermatt only | |
| **Slopes** | 1620-3820m<br>5,310-12,530ft |
| **Lifts** | 34 |
| **Pistes** | 194km<br>121 miles |
| **Blue** | 27% |
| **Red** | 47% |
| **Black** | 26% |
| **Snowmaking** | 48km<br>30 miles |
| For Zermatt-Cervinia-Valtournenche combined | |
| **Slopes** | 1525-3820m<br>5,000-12,530ft |
| **Lifts** | 62 |
| Pistes | 394km<br>245 miles |
| **Blue** | 27% |
| **Red** | 54% |
| **Black** | 19% |
| **Snowmaking** | 69km<br>43 miles |

the station early to get a seat on the right-hand side and enjoy the fabulous views. It can be an uncomfortable journey if you have to stand.

From Gornergrat there's a piste, followed by a short walk, to Furi to link up with the third and highest area, **Klein Matterhorn–Trockener Steg–Schwarzsee**. But you can't yet do the journey in the opposite direction: once on the Klein Matterhorn, moving to a different mountain means heading down and getting from one end of the village to the other to catch a lift up. (A gondola from Furi to Riffelberg is planned for '2008 at the latest'). The Klein Matterhorn gives access to Cervinia – you need to buy an 'international pass' or pay a daily supplement to your Zermatt lift pass.

There are pistes back to the village from all three areas – though some of them can be closed or tricky due to poor snow conditions. They can be hazardous at the end of the day due to crowds and speeding skiers.

### TERRAIN-PARKS
***Two fun winter options***

There's a world-class terrain-park (Gravity Park) between the new six-pack and T-bar above Trockener Steg in the Klein Matterhorn area. It includes kickers, rails, wall ride, box, rainbow, boarder-cross course and 'a wondrous pipe' says a reporter. There's an excellent park just a bit higher up the glacier in the summer.

### SNOW RELIABILITY
***Good high up, poor lower down***

Zermatt has rocky terrain and a relatively dry climate. But it also has some of the highest slopes in Europe, and quite a lot of snowmaking.

All three areas go up to over 3000m/9,840ft, and the Klein Matterhorn area has summer glacier skiing. There are loads of runs above 2500m/ 8,200ft, many of which are north-facing, so guaranteeing decent snow except in freak years.

Snowmaking machines serve some of the pistes on all three areas, from

about 3000m to under 2000m (about 10,000ft down to under 6,500ft). The runs back to the village can still be patchy, as can the lower part of the south-facing run from Rothorn to Gant (which got more snow-guns in 2003/04). Piste grooming is excellent.

**FOR EXPERTS**
***Good – with superb heli-trips***

If you've never been, Zermatt has to be on your shortlist. If you have been, we're pretty sure you'll want to return.

If you love long mogul pitches, the slopes at Triftji, below Stockhorn, which no longer has official pistes, just 'ski runs' (see previous page) are the stuff of dreams. 'A great playground,' says a reader this year. From the top of the Stockhorn cable-car there's a run down to the T-bar that serves a wide 2km/1 mile long face. The whole mountainside here can be one vast mogul field – steep, but not extremely so. Being north-facing and lying between 3400m and 2700m (11,150ft and 8,860ft), the snow keeps in good condition long after a new snowfall. But be warned: this whole area does not open until February (the lifts are closed). There are other great 'ski runs' down from Hohtälli to Gant.

And two wonderful 'ski runs' from Rothorn have spectacular views of both the village and the Matterhorn. But they need good snow-cover to be really enjoyable.

On the Klein Matterhorn, the best area for experts is Schwarzsee, from where there are several steep north-facing gullies through the woods. Access to these runs is much improved by the new gondola.

There are marvellous off-piste possibilities from the top lifts in each sector, but they aren't immediately obvious to those without local knowledge. They are also dangerous because of rocky and glacial terrain. You can join daily ski touring groups but there aren't standard off-piste groups as there are in resorts such as Val-d'Isère and Méribel; you have to hire a guide privately for a full day. The Ski Club of Great Britain usually hires a guide for off-piste skiing once a





**THE WORLD'S BEST MOUNTAIN RESTAURANTS**

*Even reporters who don't normally stop long for lunch usually succumb to temptation here. The choice of restaurants is enormous, the food usually excellent (but it helps not to be vegetarian), the small hut-based places very atmospheric (some with spectacular views), the table-service friendly (if over-worked). It is impossible to list here all those worth a visit – so don't limit yourself to those we mention. It is best to book; check prices are within your budget when you do!*

*Down at Findeln below Sunnegga are several attractive, busy, expensive, rustic restaurants, including Findlerhof (aka Franz & Heidy's) where we had excellent lamb in 2003, Chez Vrony ('fab lunch with wine for about SF40' says a 2004 reporter), Paradies and Enzian ('less busy than others'). The simple hut at Tuftern has great views from the terrace, sells good Heida wine from the highest vineyard in Europe and does a basic menu of home-made soup, cheese and cold sausage (but a reporter complains of 'watery hot chocolate in a plastic cup').*

*The restaurants at Fluhalp (which often has live music) and Grünsee have beautiful, isolated situations, and the large terraces at Sunnegga and Rothorn have great views. All these are part of the Matterhorn Group and do decent food.*

*At Furi, the Restaurant Furi (excellent rösti and scrumptious tarts) and Simi's on the road below both have large sun terraces and good food. The hotel at Schwarzsee is right at the foot of the Matterhorn, with staggering views and endless variations of rösti. Round the back from here Stafelalp is simple, but it is charmingly situated. Up above Trockener Steg, Gandegghütte has stunning views of the glacier. On the way back to the village below Furi, Zum See is a charming old hut serving the best mountain food in Zermatt (which means it is world-class: we had delicious beef, lamb and raspberry tart here). Blatten is good, too.*

*The Kulmhotel, at 3100m/10,170ft at Gornergrat, has both self-service and table-service restaurants, with amazing views of lift-free mountains and glaciers. 'But beware of dive-bombing birds when eating outside!' says a reporter. Wherever you go, don't miss the local alcoholic coffee – in its many varieties.*

**LIFT PASSES**

**Zermatt**
Covers all lifts on the Swiss side of the border.

**Main pass**
1 day SF64
6 days SF320

**Senior citizens**
Over 65 : 6 days SF272

**Children**
Under 20: 6 days SF272
Under 16: 6 days SF160
Under 9: free pass

**Notes**
Half-day passes and single-ascent tickets on some lifts also available.

**Alternative passes**
Combined passes available for Zermatt and Cervinia and for Klein Matterhorn, Schwarzsee and Cervinia.

week – a 2004 reporter had 'an awesome day of powder' with them.

Zermatt is the Alps' biggest heli-trip centre; the helipad resembles a bus station at times, with choppers taking off every few minutes. There are only three main drop-off points, so this can mean encountering one or two other groups on the mountain, even though there are multiple ways down. From all three points there are routes that don't require great expertise. The epic is from Monte Rosa, at over 4000m/13,120ft, an easy run down through wonderful glacier scenery to Furi. If there isn't much snow, getting off the end of the glacier can be scary though; last year we needed the help of both our guide and a rope that's fixed to the rocks to navigate a short, almost vertical section.

**FOR INTERMEDIATES**
***Mile after mile of beautiful runs***

Zermatt is ideal for adventurous intermediates. Many of the blue and red runs tend to be at the difficult end of their grading. There are very beautiful reds down lift-free valleys from both Gornergrat (Kelle) and Hohtälli (White Hare) to Gant – we love these first thing in the morning, before anyone else is on them. A variant to Riffelalp (Balmbrunnen) ends up on a narrow wooded path with a sheer cliff and magnificent views to the right.

On Sunnegga, the 5km/3 mile Kumme run, from Rothorn to the bottom of the Patrullarve chair, also gets away from the lift system and has an interesting mix of straight-running and mogul pitches. On Klein Matterhorn, the reds served by the Hörnli drag and the fast quad chair from Furgg are all long and gloriously set at the foot of the Matterhorn. The Matterhornpiste red reached from the new Furggsattel chair has the most stunning views of the mountain it is named after (and is of blue gradient for much of its length).

For less adventurous intermediates, the blues on Sunnegga and above Riffelberg on Gornergrat and the runs between Klein Matterhorn and Trockener Steg are best. Of these, the Riffelberg area often has the best combination of good snow and easy cruising, and is popular with the school. Sunnegga gets a lot of sun, but the snowmaking means that the problem is more often a foot or more of heavy snow near the bottom than bare patches.

On the Klein Matterhorn most of the runs, though marked red on the piste map, are very flat and represent the easiest slopes Zermatt has to offer, as well as the best snow. The problem here is the possibility of bad weather because of the height – high winds, extreme cold and poor visibility can make life very unpleasant. To get to Cervinia, you set off from Testa Grigia (confusingly, called Plateau Rosa on the Cervinia piste map) with a choice of two routes – even an early intermediate should find the easier 10km/6 mile route (on the left as you look at the Cervinia piste map) down to the village manageable. The red Ventina run is a delightful cruise for better intermediates.

Beware of the run from Furgg to Furi

SNOWPIX.COM / CHRIS GILL

Zermatt is a great place for a relaxing holiday even if you don't venture onto skis or board →

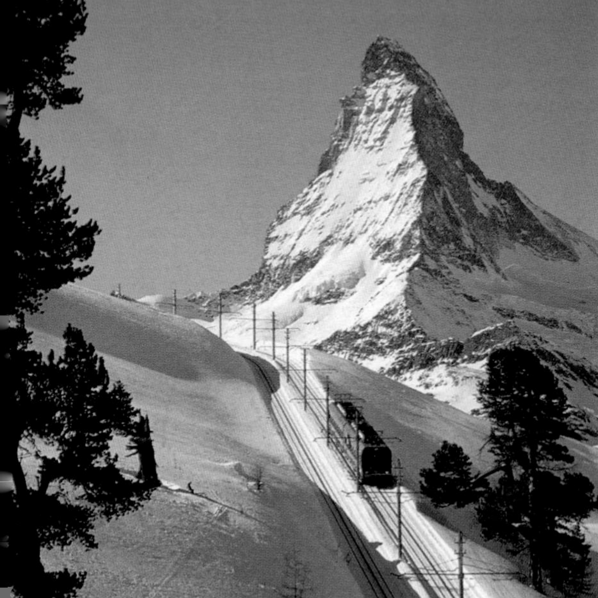

↑ The train might be a slow way up the mountain but sit back, relax and enjoy the stupendous views on the way (sit on the right for the best views)

ZERMATT TOURIST OFFICE / TONI MOHR





at the end of the day, when it can be chopped up, mogulled in places and very crowded (the only reason it is graded black that we can see, because it isn't very steep). A much more relaxed way is the beautifully scenic Weiss Perle run (the Stafelalp variant is even more scenic but has a short uphill section). Or you can catch the gondola down from Schwarzsee.

**FOR BEGINNERS**
***Learn elsewhere***
Zermatt is to be avoided by beginners. The best snow-sure nursery slope area is at Blauherd. But there are no long easy runs to progress to except above Trockener Steg, which can be bitterly cold and windy.

**FOR EVERYONE**
***Spectacular cable-car and ice cave***
The Klein Matterhorn cable-car is an experience not to miss if the weather is good. The views from the left side down to the glacier and its crevasses, as the car swings steeply into its hole blasted out of the mountain at the top, are stupendous. When you arrive, you walk through a long tunnel, to emerge on top of the world for the highest piste in Europe – walk slowly, the air is thin here and some people have altitude problems. The ice grotto cut into the glacier here is well worth a visit, with 'incredible ice carvings'. The top drag-lifts are open in the summer only.

**FOR CROSS-COUNTRY**
***Fairly limited***
There's a 4km/2.5 mile loop at Furi, 3km/2 miles of trails near the bottom of the gondola to Furi and another 12 to 15km/7 to 9 miles down at Täsch (don't count on there being snow). There are also 'ski walking trails', best tackled as part of an organised group.

**QUEUES**
***Main problems being solved***
Zermatt has improved its lift system hugely in recent years, eliminating major bottlenecks. But a few problems remain. The high-speed quad from Furgg can get busy now that the new gondola is dumping people nearby. And the Klein Matterhorn cable-car has queues much of the time. You may find there's only standing room on the Gornergrat train, which can be tiring and uncomfortable: 'Better to wait for the next one,' says a reporter. One thing we love about Zermatt is getting the 8am train with the lifties and restaurant staff. It arrives at the top just as they are dropping the rope to open the pistes and you can enjoy deserted slopes for an hour or two, before the crowds join you.

The T-bars to Testa Grigia have an annoying gap between them. And the run down from Furgg is overcrowded at the end of the day (see 'For intermediates' for a better way down) – as are the buses back to town from the end of the piste home.

**SCHOOLS AND GUIDES**
***Welcome competition at last***
The main Swiss school has a poor reputation: 'In three days the instructor taught us the same exercises over and over again, mainly on the same slopes, and made fun of our enthusiasm over talent,' says a reporter this year.

There's a separate Stoked snowboard school, which we have good reports of. This has now combined with The SkiSchool, which started in 2000/01 and is made up of talented young instructors, some of whom are British and all of whom speak good English. A reporter who took a private instructor highly recommends them and another was impressed by group lessons (with a British instructor). This year a reader says they had 'a complete beginner confident on reds after three lessons'. Their programme includes freestyle classes (tricks in the terrain-park).

## SCHOOLS

**Swiss**
t 966 2466
info@
skischulezermatt.ch

**Stoked**
t 967 7020
info@stoked.ch
info@stoked.ch

**Classes** (Swiss prices)
5 days (10am to 3.30 with lunch break)
SF295

**Private lessons**
SF160 for 2hr for 1-2 people

## CHILDREN

**Kinderparadies**
t 967 7252
Ages from 3mnth; 9am-5pm

**Hotel Nicoletta**
t 966 0777
Ages 2 to 8, 9am-5pm

**Kinderclub Pumuckel (Hotel Ginabelle)**
t 966 5000
Ages from 30mnth; 9am-5pm

**Kinderhort (Stoked)**
t 967 7020
Ages from 3; 9am-3.30

**Snowflakes (Stoked)**
t 967 7020
Ages from 4; 9am-3.30

**Private babysitters**
Tourist office has list

**Ski school**
The Swiss school takes ages 4 and over (4 to 6 in Snow Kids Village Riffelberg);5 days SF385

### FACILITIES FOR CHILDREN

***Good hotel nurseries***

The Nicoletta and Ginabelle hotels have nurseries. The Kinderparadies, 200m/660ft from the station, takes children from three months. Stoked/ The SkiSchool runs Snowflakes, for children aged at least four years old, at Trockener Steg and a kindergarten for kids from three years at Schwarzsee.

## STAYING THERE

### HOW TO GO

***A wide choice, packaged or not***

**Chalets** Several operators have places here, many of the most comfortable contained in large apartment blocks. Reporters have praised Total Ski's operation here. And Simply Ski has some good-looking small places.

**Hotels** There are over 100 hotels, mostly comfortable and traditional-style 3-stars and 4-stars, but taking in the whole range.

((((5 **Mont Cervin** (966 8888) Biggest in town. Elegantly traditional. Good pool.

((((5 **Zermatterhof** (966 6600) Traditional 'grand hotel' style with piano bar and pool.

((((5 **Riffelalp Resort** (966 0555) Up the mountain, recent smart extension, pool and spa, own evening trains.

(((4 **Alex** (966 7070) Close to station. Reporters love it. 'Wonderful,' says one. Pool. Dancing.

(((4 **Ambassador** (966 2611) Peaceful position near Gornergrat station. Large pool; sauna. 'Excellent food and attentive staff,' says one of our reporters.

(((4 **Monte Rosa** (966 0333) Well-modernised original Zermatt hotel, near southern end of village – full of climbing pictures and mementos.

(((4 **Ginabelle** (966 5000) Smart pair of chalets not far from Sunnegga lift; has own ski nursery as well as day care.

(((4 **Nicoletta** (966 0777) Modern chalet quite close to centre, with nursery.

(((4 **Sonne** (966 2066) Traditionally decorated, in quiet setting away from main street; 'Roman Bath' complex.

(((4 **Beau-Site Parkhotel** (966 6868) Highly recommended by a 2004 reporter. 'Faultless service with nouvelle meals of four to five courses.'

((3 **Julen** (966 7600) Charming, modern-rustic chalet over the river, with Matterhorn views from some rooms.

((3 **Butterfly** (966 4166) 'Small, friendly, as well furnished as the Alex, but much better food,' says a reporter.

(2 **Atlanta** (966 3535) No frills, but 'friendly service'; close to centre, with Matterhorn views from some rooms.

(2 **Alpina** (967 1050) Modest but very friendly, and close to centre.

(2 **Bahnhof** (967 2406) Right by Gornergrat station. Recently refurbished. Cheapest place to stay in town (SF95 a night for twin room with shower, SF30 a night for a dormitory bed; with use of communal kitchen).

**Self-catering** There is a lot of apartment accommodation, but not much finds its way to the UK package market. We have enjoyed staying in the hotel Ambassador apartments, with free use of all its facilities such as a pool and a sauna. The Vanessa complex was recommended by a reporter. The tourist office web site has apartments.

### EATING OUT

***Huge choice at all price levels***

There are over 100 restaurants to choose from, ranging from top-quality haute cuisine, through traditional Swiss food, Chinese, Japanese and Thai to egg and chips and even a McDonald's.

Mood's (see Après-ski) does excellent fish. The Mazot is highly rated and highly priced. At the other end of the scale, Café du Pont has good-value pasta and rösti; Grampi's ('sensibly priced'), Broken and Postli do good pizzas. The Schwyzer Stübli

## GETTING THERE

**Air** Geneva 222km/138 miles (4hr by rail); Zürich 245km/152 miles (5hr by rail); Sion 80km/50 miles (1½hr).

**Rail** Station in resort.

## ACTIVITIES

**Indoor** Sauna, tennis, squash, hotel swimming pools (some open to public), salt water pool, fitness centre, indoor golf, climbing wall, casino, billiards, bowling, gallery, library, concerts, Alpine museum, cinema

**Outdoor** Ice rinks, curling, sleigh rides, 30km/19 miles cleared paths, snow-shoeing, helicopter flights, paragliding, climbing, ice-climbing

**Phone numbers**
From elsewhere in Switzerland add the prefix 027.
From abroad use the prefix +41 27.

## TOURIST OFFICE

t 966 8100
zermatt@wallis.ch
www.zermatt.ch





has local specialities and live Swiss music and dancing.

Rua Thai in the basement of the hotel Abana Real has been recommended for excellent food and beautiful decor. Fuji in the same building is a good Japanese.

Chez Heini serves excellent lamb and the owner sings after dinner. Giuseppe's doesn't look much, but has the best Italian food in town – book before your trip, it gets so busy. Avena is recommended by a local for curry.

Da Mario, Casa Rustica, Baku (see Après-ski), the Old Spaghetti Factory (in the hotel Post complex), the Stockhorn Grill ('excellent local lamb'), Tony's Grotta ('expensive but excellent Italian') and the Whymperstube have all been recommended by readers.

### APRES-SKI
***Lively and varied***

There's a good mix of sophisticated and informal fun, though it helps if you have deep pockets. On the way back from the Klein Matterhorn there are lots of restaurants below Furi for a last drink and sunbathe. Hennu Stadl blasts out loud music in a very un-Zermatt-like fashion but attracts huge crowds ('a beer and toffee vodka chaser sets you up to tackle the slush below,' says a 2004 reporter) – we preferred the delicious red wine and fruit tarts at Zum See. Visitors rave about the Baku, on the way back to Winkelmatten. It's got a wigwam outside, so you can't miss it. On the way back from Sunnegga, Othmar's Hütte has great views and organises dinners (followed by tobogganing down) and the Olympia Stübli often has live music. Near the church at Winkelmatten, the Sonnenblick is 'a great place to watch the sun set'.

In town the Papperazi is one of the few popular early places (it's crowded after dinner, too). Elsie's bar is wood-panelled, atmospheric and gets packed with an older crowd both early and late. The North Wall is frequented by seasonal workers. Promenading the main street checking out expensive shoes and watches is popular.

Later on, the hotel Post complex has something for everyone, from a quiet, comfortable bar (Papa Caesar's) to a lively disco (Broken) and live music (Pink) and a selection of restaurants.

Grampi's has dancing. Z'Alt Hischi (in an old house, serves huge measures of spirits) and the Little Bar (crowded if there are ten people in) are good for a quiet drink. The Hexenbar is cosy too. The hotel Alex draws a mature clientele for eating, drinking and dancing. The Hotel Pollux has 'lively music in its bar' says a reporter.

The Vernissage is our favourite bar in town for a quiet evening drink. It is an unusual and stylish modern place, with the projection room for the cinema built into the upstairs bar and displays of art elsewhere. Mood's was designed by the same guy and is run by the team that used to run the Post complex. There's a good cocktail bar downstairs, wood-panelled restaurant above and a comfortable bar done out in nautical fashion at the top.

### OFF THE SLOPES
***Considerable attractions***

Zermatt is an attractive place to spend time. As well as pricey watch and clothes shops, there are interesting food and wine shops and book and art stores. It is easy (but expensive) for pedestrians to get around on the lifts and meet others for lunch and there are some nice walks. The Ice Grotto at Klein Matterhorn (recommended by several readers this year) and the Alpine museum in town are worth seeing. You can take a helicopter trip around the Matterhorn. There is a cinema, and a reader tells us the free village guided tour is 'well worth doing'.

### STAYING UP THE MOUNTAIN
***Comfortable seclusion***

There are several hotels at altitude, of which the pick is the Riffelalp Resort at the first stop on the Gornergrat railway (see Hotels above) – but you might find its limited evening train service a bit restricting. At the top of the railway, at 3100m/10,170ft, is the Kulmhotel Gornergrat (966 6400) – an austere building with basic rooms.

### STAYING DOWN THE VALLEY
***Attractive for drivers***

In Täsch, where visitors must leave their cars, there are five 3-star hotels, costing less than half the price of the equivalent in Zermatt. The Täscherhof (966 6262) ('very comfortable, good food and spa facilities', says a 2004 reporter) is next to the station; the City (967 3606) is close by. It's quiet at night, a 13-minute ride from Zermatt, with trains every 20 minutes for most of the day; the last train down is 11.10. Taxis can go to the edge of Zermatt.

# WHERE *to* SKI AND Snowboard 2006

## Get next year's edition **free!**

### by reporting on your holiday

**There are too many resorts for us to visit them all every year, and too many hotels, bars and mountain restaurants for us to see. So we are very keen to encourage more readers to send in reports on their holiday experiences. As usual, we'll be giving 100 copies of the next edition to the writers of the best reports.**

There are five main kinds of feedback we need:

- what you particularly **liked and disliked** about the resort
- what aspects of the resort came as a **surprise** to you
- your other suggestions for **changes to our evaluation** of the resort – changes we should make to the ratings, verdicts, descriptions etc
- your experience of **queues** and other weaknesses in the lift system, and the **ski school** and associated childcare arrangements
- your feedback on **individual facilities** in the resort – the hotels, bars, restaurants (including mountain restaurants), nightspots, equipment shops, sports facilities etc.

You can send your reports to us in three ways. In order of preference, they are:

- by e-mail to: reports@snow-zone.co.uk (don't forget to give us your postal address)
- word-processed and printed on paper
- handwritten on a form that we can provide.

Consistently helpful reporters are invited to become 'resort observers', which means that when possible we'll arrange free lift-passes in your holiday resorts, in exchange for detailed reports on those resorts.

**Our postal address is:**

Where to Ski and Snowboard, FREEPOST SN815,
The Old Forge, Norton St Philip, Bath BA2 7ZZ

ADELBODEN TOURIST OFFICE

# Adelboden

**For intermediates who find relaxing, pretty surroundings more important than convenience for the slopes, chocolate-box-pretty Adelboden has a lot of appeal. The slopes are extensive, and the lifts are impressive.**

### KEY FACTS

| | |
|---|---|
| Resort | 1355m<br>4,450ft |
| Slopes | 1070-2355m<br>3,510-7,730ft |
| Lifts | 56 |
| Pistes | 170km<br>106 miles |
| Blue | 41% |
| Red | 52% |
| Black | 7% |
| Snowmaking | 40km<br>25 miles |

### TOURIST OFFICE

t 033 673 8080
info@adelboden.ch
www.adelboden.ch

## THE RESORT

Adelboden is a classic Swiss mountain village: old chalets line the quiet main street (cars are discouraged), with a backdrop of 3000m/9,840ft peaks. The village is compact, with efficient buses to the outlying areas. There are some 30 pensions and hotels (mainly 3- and 4-star). The après-ski is low-key, based on bars and tea rooms. Eating out possibilities are varied, and include a couple of mountain restaurants. There is a fair bit to do off the slopes, including skating and curling.

## THE MOUNTAINS

Adelboden's slopes are split into five sectors – two of them a bus-ride away. The others are linked, by piste if not by lift, and stretch across the mountain to Lenk in the next valley.

Most pistes are below 2000m/ 6,560ft and snowmaking is limited – so snow reliability is not ideal. At Geils there are some genuine black pistes, and good off-piste possibilities down to both Adelboden and Lenk that are under-used. All five sectors deserve exploration by intermediates. At Geils there is a lot of ground to be covered – including trips across to Lenk's own gentle Betelberg area. There are good nursery slopes in the village and at nearby sectors. At Geils there are long, glorious, easy runs to progress to.

There are extensive cross-country trails along the valley and up at snow-sure Engstligenalp.

The main gondola isn't entirely free of queues. And the old Hahnenmoos gondola is a bottleneck, overdue for replacement. There are pleasant mountain restaurants with terraces in the Geils sector.

ENGELBERG TOURIST OFFICE

# Engelberg

**Engelberg is an easy 2.5 hour train ride from Zürich airport (even less by car), which makes it great for short breaks. It has one of the biggest verticals in the Alps, awesome off-piste and some good intermediate slopes.**

### KEY FACTS

| | |
|---|---|
| Resort | 1050m<br>3,440ft |
| Slopes | 1050-3020m<br>3,440-9,910ft |
| Lifts | 24 |
| Pistes | 82km<br>51 miles |
| Blue | 30% |
| Red | 68% |
| Black | 2% |
| Snowmaking | some |

### TOURIST OFFICE

t 041 639 7777
welcome@engelberg.ch
www.engelberg.ch

## THE RESORT

Engelberg was popular with Brits in the early 20th century but its grand Victorian hotels have a faded look and have been joined by chalet-style buildings and concrete blocks. It is more of a town than a village. The 12th-century monastery and its cheese-making shop are worth a visit. It's a bus-ride or long walk to the lifts from most hotels. The Europe (041 639 7575) is central, the Terrace (041 639 6666) is served by a funicular and run on club-hotel lines. The Yucatan is the main après-ski bar.

## THE MOUNTAINS

The main slopes rise almost 2000m/ 6,560ft above the town by three successive lifts: a gondola and two cable-cars, the top one rising above glacial crevasses and rotating 360° on the way. Weekend queues can be long.

Pistes are limited and fragmented by the glaciers and rugged terrain, and they suit strong intermediates best: most runs are steep reds and there are few easy cruises. Beware of the seriously steep and usually mogulled black between Titlis and Stand. There's a good isolated beginner area near the mid-station of the gondola.

There is superb off-piste for experts who hire a guide. The classic Laub run is 1000m/3,280ft vertical down an immensely wide face with a consistent pitch and magnificent views of town. But we enjoyed even more the 2000m/ 6,560ft vertical Galtiberg run, which starts over glaciers and ends among mountain streams and trees: we saw only three other people on it. There's plenty more off-piste, too. The Ritz (at the bottom of the Laub) and Jochpass mountain restaurants are rustic.

SNOWPIX.COM / CHRIS GILL

# Gstaad

**Despite its exclusive reputation, Gstaad is an attractive, traditional village where anyone could have a relaxing holiday. But the slopes are very fragmented, and not snow-sure – most are below 2100m/6,890ft.**

## KEY FACTS

| | |
|---|---|
| **Resort** | 1050m<br>3,440ft |
| **Slopes** | 950-3000m<br>3,120-9,840ft |
| **Lifts** | 66 |
| **Pistes** | 250km<br>155 miles |
| **Blue** | 48% |
| **Red** | 36% |
| **Black** | 16% |
| **Snowmaking** | 12km<br>7 miles |

## TOURIST OFFICE

**t** 033 748 8181
gst@gstaad.ch
www.gstaad.ch

## THE RESORT

Gstaad is a year-round resort in a spacious, sunny setting amid friendly, wooded mountains, its traffic-free main street lined by chalet-style hotels, smart shops and cafes. Most of the accommodation is in private chalets and apartments, the rest in 3-star hotels and above – including the landmark 5-star Palace. Restaurants are mainly hotel-based, and expensive. In season après-ski is lively. Off-slope activities are good – the tennis centre and pool complex are impressive.

## THE MOUNTAINS

There are four main areas of slopes, covered by a single, confusing map. Most slopes are below the tree line.

Three sectors are accessed via lifts scattered around the fringes of Gstaad and served by a shuttle-bus. The largest sector is accessed from lifts reached by train at Saanenmöser and Schönried, which also has a separate sunny area of slopes across the valley.

Low altitude means that snow-cover can be unreliable except on the Glacier des Diablerets – also covered by the area pass, but 15km/9 miles away.

Few runs challenge experts. Black runs rarely exceed red or even blue difficulty. There is off-piste potential – some steep. Given good snow, this is a superb area for intermediates, with long, easy descents in the major area to the villages scattered around its edges. The nursery slopes at the bottom of Wispile are adequate, and there are plenty of runs to progress to. Time lost on buses or trains is more of a problem than queues. Mountain restaurants are plentiful, and most are attractive.

LENZERHEIDE TOURIST OFFICE / PHOTOPRESS

# Lenzerheide

**Lenzerheide is the senior partner with Valbella in an extensive area of intermediate slopes in a pretty setting around a lake, all at a decent altitude – worth considering, although the villages are not chocolate-box pretty.**

## KEY FACTS

| | |
|---|---|
| **Resort** | 1470m<br>4,820ft |
| **Slopes** | 1230-2865m<br>4,040-9400ft |
| **Lifts** | 28 |
| **Pistes** | 155km<br>96 miles |
| **Blue** | 35% |
| **Red** | 45% |
| **Black** | 20% |

## TOURIST OFFICE

**t** 081 385 1120
info@lenzerheide.ch
www.lenzerheide.ch

## THE RESORTS

Lenzerheide is a sprawling village – a pleasant enough place away from the minor but quite busy through-road that is at its centre. The road runs past a prettily wooded lake to Valbella, a more amorphous collection of holiday accommodation on the sunny slopes north of the lake. There are plenty of comfortable hotels, and a wonderful luxury rustic retreat in the Guarda Val. An influx of weekend visitors enlivens the après-ski scene.

## THE MOUNTAINS

The slopes are on the two sides of the valley, facing due east and west. Links across the valley are by bus, but within each sector there are links across the mountainside – so a circuit is possible. All around the circuit there are separate lifts serving the wooded lower slopes and the open upper slopes – with lots of restaurants dotted around at the mid-mountain stations where they meet. The east-facing, morning-sun slopes are mainly fairly gentle, with top heights around the 2300m/7,550ft mark. The west-facing slopes have more character, both in skiing and visual terms, with a couple of runs on the back of the dramatic peak of the Rothorn (2865m/9,400ft), reached by cable-car. There are off-piste runs to Arosa from this sector, and increasingly concrete plans for a lift link.

The lift system as a whole is not the most modern; although there are a couple of six-packs there are also quite a few old chairs and drags. But queues are rare except at weekends. Snow reliability is reasonable, at least on the upper east-facing slopes. There are plenty of reliable mountain restaurants.

# USA

**In general, people who try American skiing and snowboarding for the first time are captivated by the experience and by the contrasts with European resorts. Nearly everyone is struck by the high standards of service and courtesy, the relatively deserted pistes, the immaculate piste grooming and the quality of accommodation. Depending on the resort, you may also be struck by the cute Wild West ambience and the superb quality of the snow.**

**But don't fall into the trap of lumping all US resorts together – they differ enormously. That's one reason why we have organised our American chapters in regional sections – California, Colorado, Rest of the West (now incorporating Utah) and New England. US skiing does have some distinct disadvantages, too. Read on.**

Most American resorts receive serious amounts of snow – average snowfall is typically in the region of 6m to 12m (20ft to 40ft) in a season. And most have serious snowmaking facilities too. What's more, they use them well – they lay down a base of snow early in the season, rather than patching up shortages later.

There are wide differences in quantity and quality of snowfall, both between individual resorts and between regions – we discuss some of these in our regional introductions.

Piste grooming is taken very seriously – most American resorts set standards that the best Alpine resorts are only now attempting to match. Every morning you can expect to step out on to perfect 'corduroy' pistes. But this doesn't mean that there aren't moguls – far from it. It's just that you get moguls where the resort says you can expect moguls, not everywhere. Some resorts even go so far as to groom half the width of some runs, leaving the other half mogulled.



The slopes of most American resorts are blissfully free of crowds – a key advantage that becomes more important every year as the pistes of Europe become ever more congested. If you want to let those new skiercross skis travel at the speeds they were designed for, take them to the States. And, because the slopes are mostly below the tree line, they offer good visibility in bad weather.

Most American resorts offer free guided tours of the area. Lift queues are short, partly because they are highly disciplined: spare seats on chair-lifts are religiously filled, with the aid of cheerful, conscientious attendants. Piste maps and tissues are freely available at the bottom of most lifts. Mountain 'hosts' are on hand to advise you about the best possible routes to take. School standards are uniformly high, with the added advantage that English is the native language. And facilities for children are impressive, too.

Many Europeans have the idea that American resorts don't have off-piste terrain, but this seriously misrepresents the position. It's true that resorts practically always have a boundary, and that venturing beyond it into the 'backcountry' may be discouraged or forbidden (though in some resorts you just have to go through gates). But within the boundary there is often very challenging terrain that is very much like off-piste terrain in an Alpine resort, but with the important advantage that it is patrolled and avalanche-

SNOWPIX.COM / CHRIS GILL

← Classic Rockies stuff – perfect packed powder on crowd-free trails cut through forest on rounded hills. This is Vail – the most crowd-prone of Colorado resorts – on a weekday in March

controlled – so you don't need to hire a guide. We rate this as one of the great attractions of American resorts.

There are drawbacks to the US, of course. One is that many resorts have slopes that are very modest in extent compared with major Alpine areas. But many US resorts (in Colorado and California, in particular) are very close to each other – so if you are prepared to travel a bit, you won't get bored. Roads are good, and car hire is cheap (though you should budget for buying snow-chains – we've yet to find a US rental company that will provide them). A more serious problem is that the day is ridiculously short. The lifts often shut at 3pm or 3.30. That may explain another drawback for those who like a good lunch – the dearth of decent mountain restaurants. The norm is monster self-service refuelling stations – designed to minimise time off the slopes. Small restaurants with table-service and decent food are rare.



It's also true that in many resorts the terrain is slightly monotonous. You don't get the spectacular mountain scenery and the distinctive high-mountain runs of the Alps. Most trails have clearly been cut through the forest; whereas in the Alps the artificial nature of the runs is rarely obvious when they are blanketed by snow, in the Rockies it is inescapable.

The grading of pistes (or trails, to use the local term) is different from that in Europe. Red runs don't exist. The colours used are combined with shapes. Green circles correspond fairly closely to greens in Europe (that is, in France, where they are mainly found). American blue squares largely correspond to blues in Europe, but also include tougher intermediate runs that would be red in the Alps; these are sometimes labelled as double-blue squares, although in some resorts a hybrid blue-black grading is used instead. Black diamond runs correspond to steeper European reds and easier European blacks. But then there

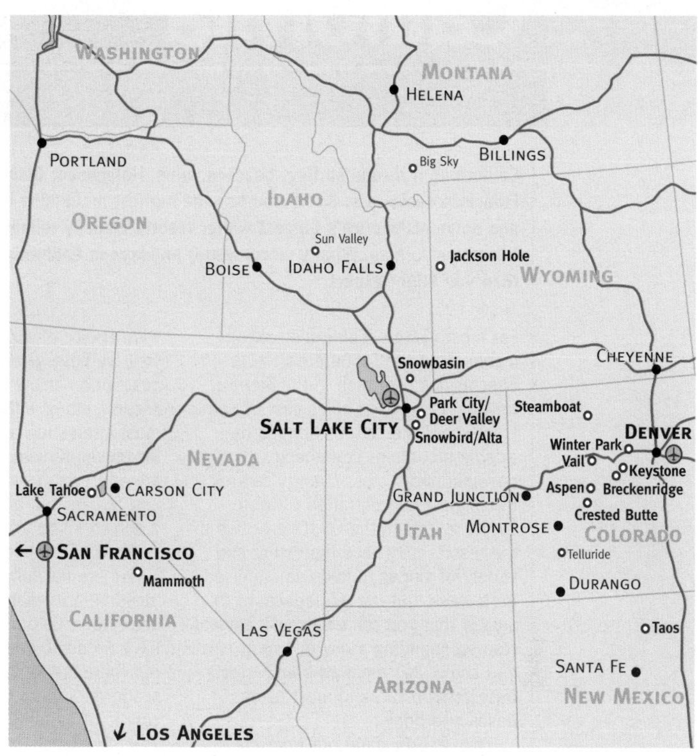






are multiple diamonds. Double-diamond runs are seriously steep – often steeper than the steepest pistes in the Alps – and include high, open bowls. A few resorts have wildly steep triple-diamonds.

US resort towns vary widely in style and convenience. There are old restored mining towns such as Telluride, Crested Butte and Aspen, genuine cowboy towns such as Jackson Hole, purpose-built monstrosities such as Snowbird, and even skyscraping gambling dens such as Heavenly. There is an increasing number of cute, car-free base villages such as Keystone's River Run, Copper Mountain's revamped base and the fledgling village at Squaw Valley. Two important things that they all have in common are good-value, spacious accommodation and good, reasonably priced restaurants. One drawback for young people is that the legal age for buying or consuming alcohol is 21; and the law is rigorously enforced – anyone under 40 is well advised to carry evidence of age.

In the end, your reaction to skiing and snowboarding in America may depend mainly on your reaction to America. If repeated cheerful exhortations to have a nice day wind you up – or if you like to be left in silence on chair-lifts – perhaps you'd better stick to the Alps.

What about the cost? It's never going to be cheap, but the basic cost of getting there is lower than you might think: you can get room-plus-hire-car February packages to California for under £600; with the £1 at over $1.75 eating out is not expensive; and it's not difficult to find rooms with kitchenettes where you can economise by doing some of your own catering. But lift passes, tuition and childcare are very expensive by European standards (they can be double the cost). You can often save, especially on lift passes, by buying in advance through tour operators – look out for these deals.

SNOWPIX.COM / CHRIS GILL

# California

**California? It means surfing, beaches, wine, Hollywood, Disneyland and San Francisco cable-cars. But it also has the highest mountains in continental USA and some of America's biggest winter resorts, usually reliable for snow from November to May. What's more, winter holidays in California are less expensive than you might expect.**

For most visitors, Californian skiing means the Lake Tahoe area. Spectacularly set high in the Sierra Nevada 322km/200 miles east of San Francisco, Lake Tahoe is ringed by skiable mountains containing 14 downhill and 7 cross-country centres – the highest concentration of winter sports resorts in the US. One or two of the resorts may have the extent and variety of slopes to keep you amused for a week, but the real appeal of this area is that you can easily visit several resorts, spending a day or two at each. You could visit them all from a single base using a car, and most using buses and boats.

Two resorts stand out from the herd, at least in terms of size. **Heavenly** (covered in detail in its own chapter) is the biggest in the area, and has at the foot of its slopes much the biggest development – the bizarre gambling-based town of South Lake Tahoe. It makes an obvious base for visiting a range of resorts, both south and north of the lake. **Squaw Valley**, the biggest north-shore resort, comes a close second to Heavenly in terms of area, but is only now developing a wide choice of accommodation. This year we have given it a half-page description at the end of the California section, along with the three next-most-interesting resorts – **Alpine Meadows, Kirkwood** and **Northstar**. All are appreciably smaller than Heavenly and Squaw, but all offer a worthwhile 2,000 to 2,500 acres of terrain.

Most of the minor resorts around Tahoe are not fully formed 'destination' resorts of the kind that you find in Colorado or the Alps. A few have no nearby accommodation at all; but there are lots of B&Bs and motels scattered around the lake, and a couple of quite pleasant small towns. The obvious alternative to staying in South Lake Tahoe is the small tourist town of Tahoe City, on the lake's north shore. It has a range of touristy shops and some good restaurants and bars. Our regular Tahoe reporter suggests Incline Village at the north-east corner of the lake (handy for Diamond Peak and Mount Rose) for its 'country charm and ambience, and friendly people'.

**Sierra-at-Tahoe** is only a half-hour drive from South Lake Tahoe – though the road passes over the 2250m/

SNOWPIX.COM / CHRIS GILL

One of the attractions of the Tahoe area is the mixture of open and lightly wooded slopes – and another is the interestingly varied terrain. This is Squaw Valley →

7,380ft Echo Summit, which may require chains. It's a densely wooded area with a vertical of 675m/2,210ft and nine lifts including two fast quads, and nothing at the base but a day lodge and a car park. Sierra claims an average of 480 inches of snow a year – almost a match for better-known Kirkwood. The Backside area is gentle, but slopes are generally quite challenging. **Sugarbowl** (460m/1,510ft vertical, lifts include four fast quads) is said by an experienced local reporter to be a place 'for serious skiers'. Visitors recommend **Diamond Peak** (560m/1,840ft vertical, six chairs, one fast) for its 'breathtaking views and fab restaurant' and the relatively high and steep **Mount Rose** (440m/1,440ft vertical, seven lifts including a six-pack) for its 'great snow always and carving runs' – and both are recommended for their quiet slopes. Mount Rose has a major expansion planned for this coming season. At least one reporter reckons **Homewood** (500m/1,640ft vertical, eight lifts) has the best views of all, as well as the quietest slopes.

The other Californian resort we cover in detail, **Mammoth**, has the real drawback that it is rather isolated – it's a long drive from Tahoe, or from Los Angeles airport. But it is an impressive mountain that is worth considering – it's much higher than the Tahoe resorts, for one thing – and it's well placed if you fancy a couple of days at Disneyland as part of the trip.

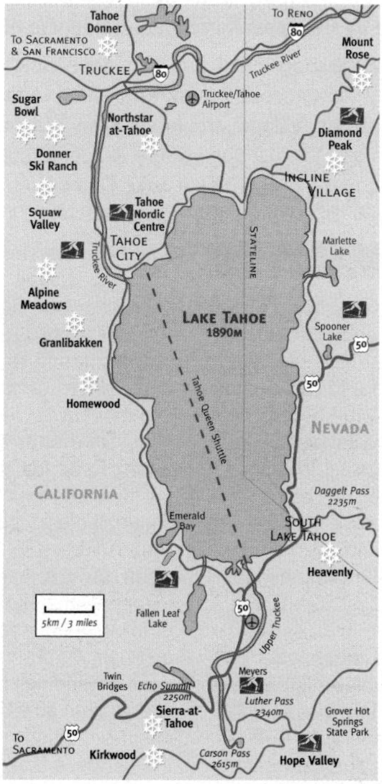

Holidays in California are relatively cheap because winter is low season for much of the accommodation and also for scheduled flights from Britain into Los Angeles and San Francisco. There is huge capacity available for the massive summer tourist trade to the Lake Tahoe area, in particular, and hotel owners and airlines are happy to offer cut-price deals to keep a contribution coming in towards their overheads.

California's mountains get a lot of snow. In several recent seasons, Californian resorts have recorded the deepest snow-cover in North America. Connoisseurs of Rockies powder are inclined to brand the snow that falls in California as wet 'Sierra Cement'. Our fat file of reports from visitors has some complaints about that – especially late in the season – but most people have found the snow just fine. So have we: in March 2002 we enjoyed two of the best days of our season skiing powder in the trees of Heavenly and Mammoth.

Most of the resorts mainly attract weekend visitors from the cities of California's coastal area. Peak weekends apart, the slopes are uncrowded, and queues are rare.

In the past our main reservation has been the character of the resorts themselves; they don't have the traditional mountain-town ambience that we look for in the States. That's partly because this is California, where walking is regarded as an eccentric way to get around. In compensation, Heavenly, at least, offers uniquely big-time entertainment in its casinos.

But things are changing, with several new pedestrian 'villages' being developed. At Heavenly a gondola now goes from a new car-free 'village' in the centre of South Lake Tahoe right into the heart of the slopes. The new village at Squaw Valley continues to develop, making this an increasingly attractive base. Kirkwood and Northstar have developed small, attractive slope-side villages. And a new pedestrian village opened last season in Mammoth, too, linked to the slopes by gondola.

HEAVENLY SKI RESORT / SCOTT MARKEWITZ

# Heavenly

*Knockout views over Lake Tahoe, and a unique nightlife scene*

## COSTS

①②③④⑤⑥

## RATINGS

| The slopes | |
|---|---|
| Snow | **** |
| Extent | *** |
| Expert | *** |
| Intermediate | **** |
| Beginner | **** |
| Convenience | * |
| Queues | **** |
| Mountain restaurants | * |
| **The rest** | |
| Scenery | **** |
| Resort charm | * |
| Off-slope | ** |

## NEWS

Vail Resorts, which owns Heavenly, is continuing to invest in the area. Last season they replaced the Canyon three-person chair on the California side with a high-speed quad and created a 15-acre beginner area at the top of the Heavenly gondola served by a new chair, moving carpet and drag-lift. A 120m/400ft-long super-pipe was constructed.

The new 'village' at the bottom of the gondola – with accommodation, shops and a few bars and restaurants – opened in December 2002 and is still developing.

For 2004/05 the slow Powderbowl and Waterfall chairs on the California side will be replaced by a fast six-pack, there will be increased capacity on the Heavenly gondola and the beginner area will be expanded and will include snowmaking.



- ➕ Spectacular setting, with amazing views of Lake Tahoe and Nevada
- ➕ Fair-sized mountain which offers a sensation of travelling around – common in the Alps, not in the US
- ➕ Large areas of widely spaced trees, largely on intermediate slopes – fabulous in fresh powder
- ➕ Some serious challenges for experts
- ➕ Numerous other worthwhile resorts within an hour's drive
- ➕ A unique nightlife scene
- ➕ Good snow record plus impressive snowmaking facilities
- ➕ Gondola from downtown South Lake Tahoe and pedestrian 'village' are real improvements

- ➖ South Lake Tahoe, where you stay, is a bizarre and messy combination of high-rise casino-hotels, low-rise motels and shops and restaurants that spreads for miles along a busy highway. The new resort 'village' has not transformed the whole place
- ➖ No trail back to South Lake Tahoe, so it's a gondola ride or bus-ride home if you're based there
- ➖ Gondola can be stopped by high winds
- ➖ Very little traditional après-ski activity – though the new 'village' is helping to put that right
- ➖ If natural snow is in short supply, most of the challenging terrain is likely to be closed

**A resort called Heavenly invites an obvious question: just how close to heaven does it take you? Physically, close enough: with a top height of 3070m/10,070ft and vertical of 1075m/3,530ft, it's the highest and biggest of the resorts clustered around scenic Lake Tahoe (see start and end of this California section for more on these). Metaphorically, it's not quite so close. In particular, anyone who (like us) is drawn to Heavenly partly by its exceptionally scenic setting is likely to be dismayed by the appearance and atmosphere of South Lake Tahoe.**

**The official line is that the place has been transformed into something like a European ski resort by the gondola from downtown up to the mountain, and by the opening of a pedestrian 'village' around its base. We don't buy that. Unless you stay there, the 'village' is just somewhere to spend time and money at the end of the day – the general feel of South Lake Tahoe isn't much affected. Accommodation, though, is plentiful and reporters think it good value.**

## THE RESORT

Heavenly is on California's border with Nevada, at the south end of Lake Tahoe. Other resorts around the lake are described elsewhere in this section.

Heavenly's base-town – South Lake Tahoe – is primarily a summer resort. In this respect it is unusual, but not unique. What really sets it apart is that its economy is driven by gambling. The Stateline area at its centre is dominated by a handful of monstrous hotel-casinos located just inches on the Nevada side of the line. These brash but comfortable hotels offer good-value accommodation (subsidised by the gambling), swanky restaurants and big-name entertainers, as well as roulette wheels, craps and card games – and endless slot machines into which gambling-starved Americans feed bucketloads of quarters.

The casinos are a conspicuous part of the amazing lake views from the lower slopes (though not from above mid-mountain). They look like a classic American downtown area, which you'd expect to be full of shops and bars. But they are actually just a cluster of high-rise blocks bisected by the seriously busy US Highway 50. The rest of the town spreads for miles along this pedestrian-hostile road – dozens of low-rise hotels and motels (some quite smart, but many rather shabby), stores, wedding chapels and so on. The general effect is less dire than it might be, thanks to the camouflage of the tall trees that blanket the area.

↑ 'A Heavenly view of Lake Tahoe,' says the ski resort; the gentle off-piste in the trees looks pretty heavenly, too

HEAVENLY SKI RESORT

## KEY FACTS

| | |
|---|---|
| **Resort** | 1995m 6,540ft |
| **Slopes** | 1995-3070m 6,540-10,070ft |
| **Lifts** | 29 |
| **Pistes** | 4,800 acres |
| **Green** | 20% |
| **Blue** | 45% |
| **Black** | 35% |
| **Snowmaking** | 70 % |

## LIFT PASSES

**Heavenly**
Covers all lifts on Heavenly mountain.

**Main pass**
1 day $62
6 days $372

**Senior citizens**
Over 65: 6 days $222

**Children**
Under 19: 6 days $306
Under 13: 6 days $174
Under 5: free pass

**Notes**
Discounts if purchased in advance. Half-day passes available.

The still-developing new 'village' built on the California side of the stateline is an improvement, providing an après-ski focus and pedestrianised area that the resort has lacked and this is now the obvious place to stay – right next to the base of the gondola into the heart of the slopes.

Some of the casino-hotels are within five minutes' walk of the 'village' and gondola, making these an attractive choice even for those not keen on the gambling and entertainment, but others are enough of a hike away to justify using the shuttle buses. And much of the cheaper accommodation is literally miles away. If that's where you're staying, you may prefer to access the mountain from the original lift base, the refurbished California Lodge, up a heavily wooded slope 2km/1 mile out of South Lake Tahoe.

Like the town, the slopes spread across the border into Nevada – and there are two other lift bases, which can easily be reached by road, around the mountain in Nevada. There are 'adequate' free shuttle-bus services to the three out-of-town bases. A car is still handy to explore the other resorts around Lake Tahoe and to get to many of the best bars and restaurants.

An amusing way to visit Squaw Valley is to go by boat on the skier/boarder shuttle. The service runs from Tuesday to Friday from 7am.

## THE MOUNTAIN

Most of Heavenly's slopes suit intermediates best, but there are also good beginner slopes. Experts can find genuine challenges on the Nevada side – as well as lots of fun in acre upon acre of widely spaced trees. As always in America, this off-piste terrain is avalanche controlled. But it's 'patrolled' only by hollering; since collision with a tree may render you unconscious, don't ski the trees alone.

### THE SLOPES
### *Interestingly complex*

Heavenly's mountain is quite complicated, and getting from A to B requires more careful navigation than is usual on American mountains. Quite a few of the links between different sectors involve flat tracks.

There is a fairly clear division between the California side of the mountain (the slopes directly above South Lake Tahoe) and the Nevada side (above Stagecoach Lodge and Boulder Lodge). The gondola is efficient and will have additional capacity for this season but it can be closed by high winds (two 2004 reporters complained of this). Strangely there's 'an annoying uphill walk' from the top of it to the fast Tamarack six-seater chair, which gives access to either side. Near the Nevada border you can see beautiful views over Lake Tahoe in one direction and the arid Nevada 'desert' in the other.

On the California side there are four main sectors, all to be served by fast chairs from 2004/05: blue runs from the Tamarack chair; black and blue runs from the Sky and Canyon quads; everything from black to green runs from the Powderhorn six-pack; and the lower slopes served by the Tramway and Gunbarrel chair – unrelenting steep black runs down the front face, often heavily mogulled, with the alternative of the narrow, blue Roundabout trail snaking its way down the mountain. Right at the California Lodge base is a great beginner area.

On the Nevada side there are three main bowls. The central one, above East Peak Lodge, is an excellent intermediate area, served by two fast quad chairs, with a downhill extension of the bowl served by the Galaxy chair. On one side of this central bowl is the steeper, open terrain of Milky Way Bowl, leading to the seriously steep Mott and Killebrew canyons, served by the Mott Canyon chair. On the other side is the North Bowl, with lifts up from Nevada's two base lodges. There are no really easy runs on the Nevada side, apart from limited nursery slopes at the base.

**TERRAIN-PARKS**

***Big improvements***

Recent expansion has resulted in three good terrain-parks on the Groove, High Roller and Cascade runs. The resort boasted the country's first tri-level box and has a new 120m/390ft super-pipe.

**SNOW RELIABILITY**

***No worries***

Heavenly was one of the first resorts to invest heavily in snowmaking, which proved its value when a severe snow drought hit in the late 1980s and early 1990s. The system now covers around 70% of the trails and ensures that most sections are open most of the time. In recent years Californian resorts have consistently recorded some of the deepest snow-cover of any North American resorts – and Heavenly is now able to claim a five-year average of an impressive 360 inches. Our (and reporters') most recent visits have been blessed by excellent conditions.

**FOR EXPERTS**

***Some specific challenges***

The black runs under the California base lifts – including The Face and Gunbarrel (often used for mogul competitions) – are seriously steep and challenging. Ellie's, at the top of the mountain, may offer continuous moguls too. There's even steeper stuff on the Nevada side. Milky Way Bowl provides a gentle single-diamond introduction to the emphatically double-diamond terrain beyond it. The extremely steep Mott and Killebrew canyons have roped gateways and the less expert are steered to lower gates. The Mott Canyon chair is slow, but you may welcome the rest it affords.

All over the mountain there is excellent off-piste among widely spaced trees – tremendous fun when conditions are right. Some wooded slopes are identified on the trail map, but you are not confined to those. The trail map gives a good indication of the density of trees, and the grading of nearby trails gives a good idea of steepness.

**FOR INTERMEDIATES**

***Lots to do***

Heavenly is excellent for intermediates, who are made to feel welcome and

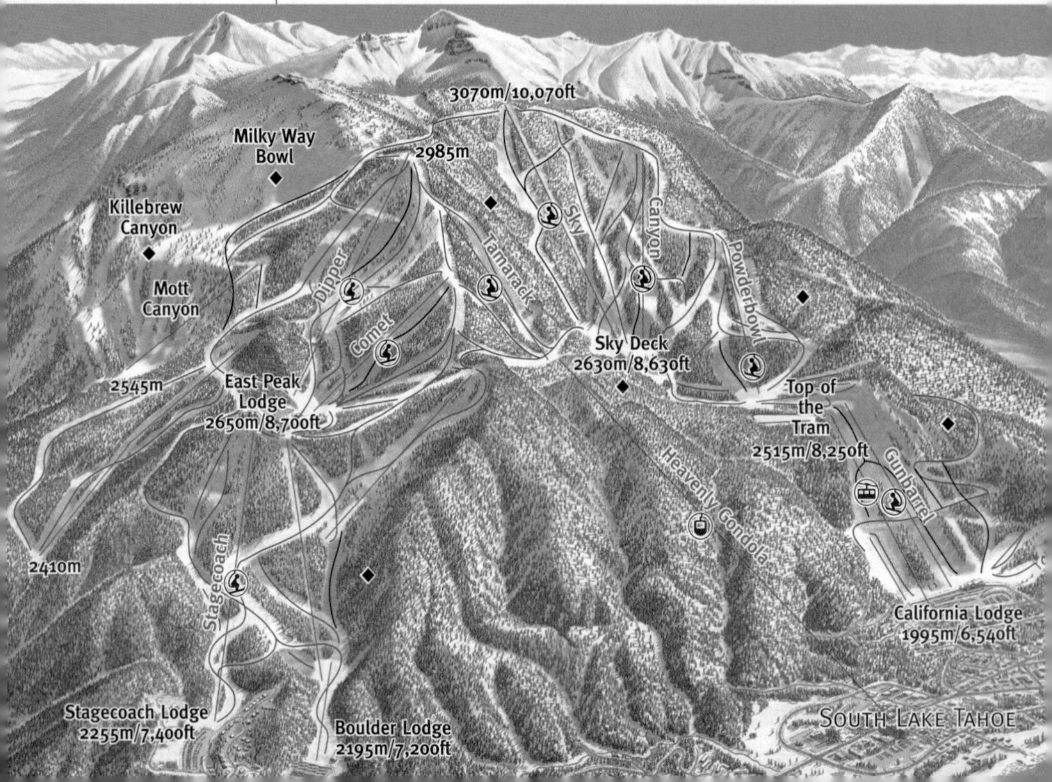

**SCHOOLS**

**Heavenly**
775 586 4400

**Classes**
One (2¾hr) lesson
$58

**Private lessons**
$175 for 2hr

**CHILDREN**

**Day Care Center**
t 775 586 7000
Ages 6wk to 6yr; 8.30-4pm; $96 including lunch; book ahead

**Ski school**
For ages 4 to 13 (snowboarding 7 to 13); full 5hr day (including lesson, equipment, pass and lunch) $129

secure by excellent piste grooming and signposting. The California side offers a progression from the relaxed cruising of the long Ridge Run, starting right at the top of the mountain, to more challenging blues dropping off the ridge towards the Sky Deck restaurant. Confident intermediates will want to spend more time on the Nevada side, where there is more variety of terrain, some longer runs down to the lift bases and more carving space.

**FOR BEGINNERS**
***An excellent place to learn***

We have had no first-hand experience or reports of the new beginner area at the top of the gondola (see News). But it sounds good and there's a link to the California side, where gentle green runs are served by the Pioneer drag-lift and the Powderbowl chair at the top of the cable-car. There are good nursery slopes at the California base lodge too.

**FOR CROSS-COUNTRY**
***A separate world***

You can try it at Adventure Peak at the top of the gondola. But the serious stuff is at the Spooner Lake Cross Country Area located close to Tahoe: an extensive meadow area of over 100km/60 miles and 21 prepared trails. Organised moonlit tours are a popular.

**QUEUES**
***Some at weekends***

Lift lines are generally not a problem, except during some weekends and public holidays when the entire Tahoe area gets busy. Thanks to the recent gondola, the key lifts moving people out from the base lodges are now under less pressure on busy days.

**MOUNTAIN RESTAURANTS**
***Even refuelling is problematic***

We have long considered the on-mountain catering grossly inadequate, especially in bad weather; our 2004 reporters wholeheartedly endorse this view. The only recommendable restaurant is the table-service Lake View Lodge at the top of the tram from California Lodge (reservations necessary). The other options consist of outdoor decks serving BBQs and pizzas (hugely unenjoyable in a blizzard as we can testify) and grossly overcrowded cafeterias.

**SCHOOLS AND GUIDES**
***Innovative programmes***

A 2004 reporter joined the school for two days and was delighted to find only two in her class. Programmes on offer include Guided Adventures such as four hours on runs not marked on the trail map and skiing corduroy before the lifts officially open.

**FACILITIES FOR CHILDREN**
***Comprehensive***

We lack recent feedback but a past reporter praised the day care and ski school facilities: 'Excellent – very convenient and very professionally run. I would thoroughly recommend it.'

**boarding**

*Lake Tahoe is quickly becoming known as the snowboarding hub of North America and, as you would expect, boarders are very well catered for at Heavenly. The off-piste in trees and double-black-diamond bowls make a great playground for good free-riders. Beginners and intermediates will enjoy great cruising runs and the easy-to-ride chair-lifts. There are a couple of specialist shops in South Lake Tahoe. Learn some 'hot new moves' in Pipe and Park classes offered by the school.*

↑ The only way to get away from lake views like this is to head over to the Nevada side and look down to the 'desert' far below

HEAVENLY SKI RESORT / SCOTT MARKEWITZ



## GETTING THERE

**Air** San Francisco 274km/170 miles (3½hr); Reno 89km/55 miles (1¼hr); South Lake Tahoe, 15min.

## ACTIVITIES

**Indoor** Casinos, art galleries, museums

**Outdoor** Lake cruises, snowmobiling, snow-shoeing, sleigh rides, dog-sledding, hot springs, fishing, hot-air ballooning, factory outlet visits

**Phone numbers**

Different area codes are used on the two sides of the stateline. For this chapter, therefore, the area code is included with each number.

From distant parts of the US, add the prefix 1. From abroad, add the prefix +1.

## TOURIST OFFICE

**t** 775 586 7000
heavenlyinternational@vailresorts.com
www.skiheavenly.com

## STAYING THERE

### HOW TO GO

***Hotel or motel?***

Accommodation in the South Lake Tahoe area is abundant and ranges from the glossy casinos to small motels. Rooms are easy to find mid-week, but weekends can be busy.

**Chalets** UK tour operators run some good catered chalets, including some lakeside ones.

**Hotels** Of the main casino hotels, Harrah's (775 558 6611) and Harveys (775 558 2411) are the closest to the gondola. Rooms booked on the spot are expensive; packages are cheaper.

((((4 **Embassy Suites** (530 544 5400) Luxury suites in a modern, traditional-style building close to the gondola.

((((4 **Marriott's Timber Lodge** (530 542 6600) Part of the new 'village'.

(((3 **Forest Suites** (530 541 6655) Right by the gondola, pools, hot-tubs, 'enormous rooms, very luxurious'.

(((3 **Holiday Inn Express** (530 544 5900) 'Eight minutes walk to gondola, modern, comfortable, plenty of facilities.'

((2 **Holiday Lodge** (530 544 4101) Opposite the gondola. 'Clean, comfortable, breakfast included, indoor and outdoor pools, hot-tub.'

((2 **Station House Inn** (530 542 1101) 'Very good, near the gondola.'

((2 **Tahoe Chalet Inn** (530 544 3311) Clean, friendly, near casinos. Back rooms (away from highway) preferable.

((2 **Timber Cove Lodge** (530 541 6722) Bland but well run, with lake views from some rooms.

**Self-catering** Plenty of choice. Some are available from tour operators. We've had a rave report about The Ridge Tahoe condos near Stagecoach Lodge: 'Luxury accommodation. The bathroom was big enough for waltzing.' There's an indoor-outdoor pool and hot-tub – and a private gondola to whisk you to the slopes.

### EATING OUT

***Good value***

The casino hotels' all-you-can-eat buffets offer fantastic value. They have some more ambitious 'gourmet' restaurants too – some high enough to give superb views (try Harrah's 18th floor). At the new 'village' Fire and Ice (with an outdoor seating area with fires and heaters) was 'heartily recommended' by a 2004 visitor. The sprawling resort area offers a great choice, from cosy little pizza houses to large, traditional American diners, Mexican tequila-and-tacos joints, and English and Irish pubs. Visitors' suggestions include Applebees ('very good food'), Hunan Garden ('best Chinese buffet ever') and Fresh Ketch at Tahoe Keys Marina for 'wonderful fresh fish and harbour views'.

### APRES-SKI

***Extraordinary***

The casinos on the Nevada side of the stateline aren't simply opportunities to throw money away: top-name pop and jazz stars, comedians, circus acts and Broadway revues are also to be found in them – designed to give gamblers another reason to stay. You can dance and dine your way across the lake aboard an authentic paddle steamer. As one reporter comments, 'It's impossible to be bored.'

### OFF THE SLOPES

***Luck be a lady***

If gambling is your weakness, you're in luck. Or then again, perhaps not. If you want to get away from the bright lights, try a boat trip on Lake Tahoe, snowmobiling a short drive from South Lake Tahoe, or a hot-air balloon ride.

Pedestrians can use the cable-car or the gondola to share the lake views and at Adventure Peak at the top of the gondola you can try tubing, snow-biking, tobogganing and snow-shoeing.

# Mammoth Mountain

*A big, sprawling mountain above a car-oriented, sprawling resort*

## COSTS

(1)(2)(3)(4)(5)(6)

## RATINGS

**The slopes**

| | |
|---|---|
| Snow | **** |
| Extent | *** |
| Expert | **** |
| Intermediate | **** |
| Beginner | **** |
| Convenience | ** |
| Queues | **** |
| Mountain restaurants | * |

**The rest**

| | |
|---|---|
| Scenery | *** |
| Resort charm | ** |
| Off-slope | * |

## NEWS

The first phase of the Village at Mammoth was officially opened in 2003/04, with a big gondola up to the Canyon Lodge lift base area. Various shops, restaurants, bars and lodgings have opened.

Free night shuttle-buses were introduced, running until 1am. The Village is the hub of the seven routes.

Terrain-park changes included the addition of 'The Wall' – a 5m/16ft tall steel wall for advanced jibbers.

For 2004/05 a fast quad will replace the old triple Chair 17, serving the easy runs and family fun-park above Canyon Lodge.

A new condo-hotel, the Grand Sierra Lodge, will open at the Village this season.

- + One of North America's bigger ski hills, with something for everyone
- + Good mix of open Alpine-style bowls and classic American wooded slopes
- + Combination of location and altitude means a good snowfall record
- + Uncrowded slopes except on peak-season weekends
- + Mightily impressive terrain parks
- + Good views, including more Alpine drama than usual in the US

- − Mammoth Lakes, though not unpleasant, is a rather straggling place with no focus, where life generally revolves around your car
- − Most accommodation is miles from the slopes – though development is taking place at the lift bases
- − Weekend crowds in high season
- − Trail map and signing still poor
- − Wind can close high lifts, and upper runs can be icy and windblown

**Mammoth may not be giant in Alpine terms – from end to end, it measures less than one-third of the size of Val-d'Isère-Tignes, in area more like one-sixth – but it is among the bigger resorts in the US, and big enough to amuse many people for a week. It can be a superb mountain for anyone who is happy in deep snow, but is equally suited to families and mixed-ability groups looking for groomed runs. The main thing it lacks is a real village at the base.**

**Enter Intrawest, owner of Whistler and now of various key plots of land (and the majority of development rights) here. Intrawest is investing heavily, planning to create 10,000 more guest beds over the next decade. It opened the first stage of slope-side development, Juniper Springs, a few years ago, and the first (quite limited) phase of the new pedestrian 'village' on the edge of the town of Mammoth Lakes was opened for the start of the 2003/04 season.**

**For most visitors, though, we don't expect the 'village' to have a huge impact. Mammoth Lakes will essentially remain what it has always been: a resort that expects you to arrive by car, and get around by car.**

MAMMOTH MOUNTAIN SKI AREA

There is no piste down to the new Village, but a gondola goes up through the trees to the slopes →

| KEY FACTS | |
|---|---|
| **Resort** | 2425m<br>7,950ft |
| Mammoth only | |
| **Slopes** | 2425-3370m<br>7,950-11,050ft |
| **Lifts** | 27 |
| **Pistes** | 3,500 acres |
| **Green** | 25% |
| **Blue** | 40% |
| **Black** | 35% |
| **Snowmaking** | 477 acres |
| June Mountain only | |
| **Slopes** | 2290-3100m<br>7,510-10,170ft |
| **Lifts** | 8 |
| **Pistes** | 500 acres |
| **Green** | 35% |
| **Blue** | 45% |
| **Black** | 20% |
| **Snowmaking** | none |





## THE RESORT

The mountain is set above Mammoth Lakes, a small year-round resort town that spreads over a wide area of woodland. The place is entirely geared to driving, with no discernible centre – hotels, restaurants and little shopping centres are scattered along the four-lane highway called Main Street and Old Mammoth Road, which crosses it. The buildings are generally timber-clad in traditional style – even McDonald's has been tastefully designed – and are set among trees, so although it may be short on resort ambience, the place has a pleasant enough appearance – particularly when under snow.

The town meets the mountain at two lift bases, both a mile or two from most of the hotels and condos. The major base is Canyon Lodge, with a big day lodge and four chair-lifts; there are hotels, condos and individual homes in the area below the lodge. Not far from here, Intrawest is building its new pedestrian 'village', which is now linked to Canyon Lodge by a gondola. The minor base, with a single six-pack lift, is Eagle Lodge (previously Little Eagle – also known as Juniper Springs, which strictly is the name of the condos built at the base).

A road runs along the north fringe of the mountain past an anonymous chair-lift base to two major base areas: The Mill Cafe, with two fast chairs, and Main Lodge, a mini-resort with three fast access lifts and a big day lodge. You can stay here, in the Mammoth Mountain Inn; but who wants to be based four miles from practically all of the resort's 50 restaurants? Not us.

Shuttle-buses run on several colour-coded routes serving the lift bases (though they are reported to be erratic in the mornings). Night buses were introduced last year, running via the Village until 1am. A car is useful.

The Mammoth lift pass also covers June, a small mountain half an hour's drive north, chiefly attractive for its astonishingly people-free slopes. See feature box, later in this chapter.

The drive up from Los Angeles takes six hours (more in poor conditions); but it is not without interest. You pass through the Santa Monica mountains close to Beverly Hills, then the San Gabriel mountains and Mojave Desert (with the world's biggest jet-plane parking lot) before reaching the Sierra Nevada range.

There are plans to extend Mammoth Lakes' small airport to take jet flights, but progress seems slow.

## THE MOUNTAIN

The 27 lifts access an impressive area, suitable for all abilities. The highest runs are almost all steep bowls and chutes for experts. In general, the lower down you go, the easier the terrain gets – as well as more sheltered.

Finding your way around is not easy at first. Many of the chair-lifts now have names (the traditional practice was to give them numbers), but the trail map still shows trails by means of isolated symbols, not continuous lines, so it's difficult to see where a run starts and finishes. The signposting of runs on the mountain leaves a lot to be desired, too. On the lower part of the mountain this doesn't matter a lot:

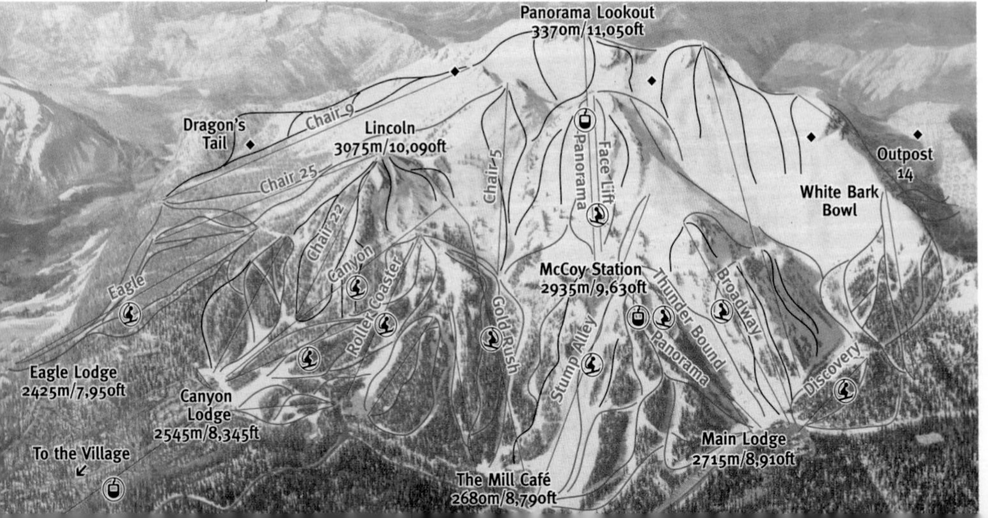

## LIFT PASSES

**Mammoth Mountain**
Covers all lifts at Mammoth and June Mountains.

**Beginners**
Pass covering Chair 7 and Discovery only.

**Main pass**
1 day $62
6 days $279

**Senior citizens**
Over 65: 6 days $141
Over 80: free pass

**Children**
Under 19: 6 days $210
Under 13: 6 days $141
Under 7: free pass

**Notes**
Afternoon pass available.

**Alternative passes**
Pass covering June Mountain only.

head downhill, and you'll come to a lift. But higher up there are real dangers, especially in poor visibility. The map uses a six-point trail difficulty scale, with intermediate green/blue and blue/black categories – rather pointless precision when the poor signposting means that you often end up on entirely the wrong trail anyway.

### THE SLOPES
***Interesting variety***

From **Main Lodge** the two-stage Panorama gondola goes via McCoy Station right to the top. The views are great, with Nevada to the north-east and the jagged Minarets to the west. From the top, there are essentially three ways down. The first, on which there are countless variations, is down the front of the mountain, which ranges from steep to very steep – or vertical if the wind has created a cornice, as it often does. The second is off the back, down to **Outpost 14**, whence chairs 14 or 13 bring you back to lower points on the ridge. The third is to follow the ridge, which eventually brings you down to the Main Lodge area. This route brings you past an easy area served by a double chair, and a very easy area served by the Discovery fast quad.

McCoy Station can also be reached using the Stump Alley fast chair from **The Mill Cafe**, on the road up from town. The fast Gold Rush quad from here takes you into the more heavily wooded eastern half of the area. This has long, gentle runs served by lifts up from **Canyon Lodge** and **Eagle Lodge** and seriously steep stuff as well as some intermediate terrain on the subsidiary peak known as Lincoln (un-named on the resort trail map) served by lifts 25 and 22.

### TERRAIN-PARKS
***Among the best***

Mammoth initially set out to attract boarders to its sister mountain June, where there are three good terrain-parks and a half-pipe. But Mammoth itself now has three impressive 'Unbound' terrain-parks and half-pipes for different abilities – more than 60 acres in all. Novices get a taster at the Family park, and there's an ever-expanding selection of urban-style rails, jumps and 'impressively large kickers' at Unbound South and Main. The astonishing Super-Duper pipe, 183m/600ft long and boasting 7m/22ft walls, was introduced two years ago, and 2003/04 saw the debut of 'The Wall' – a 5m/16ft tall steel structure for advanced jibbers.

### SNOW RELIABILITY
***A long season***

Mammoth has an impressive snow record – an annual average of 385 inches, which puts it in the second rank, ahead of major Colorado resorts and about on a par with Jackson Hole (but a long way behind Alta and Snowbird). Mammoth is appreciably higher than other Californian resorts, and it has an ever-expanding array of snow-guns, so it enjoys a long season – staying open as late as 4 July in many years. The mountain faces roughly north; the relatively low and slightly sunny slopes down to Eagle Lodge are affected by warm weather before those down to the other bases. Strong winds can be a problem on the upper mountain; some lifts are kept going in surprisingly breezy conditions. One reporter was blown over and another complains of 'extreme skiing conditions'. The snow quality can be affected by these strong winds, too.

### JUNE MOUNTAIN: THE WORLD'S QUIETEST SLOPES?

*June Mountain, a scenic half-hour drive from Mammoth, is a small resort in the same ownership and covered by the Mammoth lift pass. It makes a pleasant day out, especially if Mammoth is busy. When Mammoth isn't busy, June is quite incredibly quiet; when we visited on a March weekday morning we rode chair after chair, skied run after run, without seeing another person.*

*A double chair goes up from the car park at 2290m/7,510ft over black slopes that are often short of snow to the main lodge, June Meadows Chalet. From here, a quad chair serves a gentle blue-run hill, and a double chair goes right over very gentle green runs to the foot of a quad serving short but genuinely black slopes on June Mountain itself (3100m/10,175ft). There are a couple of double-diamond runs, but they don't really deserve the grading. June is very sensibly going for the freestyle market, with three terrain-parks, two jib-parks and a super-pipe.*

#### FOR EXPERTS
***Some very challenging terrain***

The steep bowls that run the width of the mountain top provide wonderful opportunities for experts. There are one or two single-diamond slopes, but runs such as Hangman's Hollow and Wipe-Out Chutes are emphatically double-diamond affairs requiring a lot of bottle. Route-finding can be tricky – marking is virtually non-existent.

There is lots of challenging terrain lower down, too; Chair 5, Chair 22 and Broadway are often open in bad weather when the top is firmly shut, and their more sheltered slopes may in any case have the best snow. (The top of Chair 22 is higher than the very top of Heavenly, remember.) There are plenty of good slopes over the back towards Outpost 14, too.

Many of the steeper trails are short by Alpine standards (typically under 400m/1,300ft vertical), but despite this we've enjoyed some great powder days here (with guidance).

#### FOR INTERMEDIATES
***Lots of great cruising***

Although there are exceptions, most of the lower mountain, below the tree-line, is intermediate cruising territory. What's more, Mammoth's piste maintenance is generally good, and many slopes that might become mogulled are kept easily skiable. 'Very flattering', says one visitor.

As you might hope, the six-point trail difficulty scale – which we haven't tried to replicate on our own small trail map – is a good guide to what you'll find on the mountain.

Some of the mountain's longest runs, blue-blacks served by chairs 9 and 25, are ideal for good intermediates. There are also some excellent, fairly steep, woodland trails down to The Mill Cafe.

Most of the long runs above Eagle Lodge, and some of the shorter ones above Canyon Lodge, are easy cruises. There is a variety of terrain, including lots of gentle stuff, at the western extremity of the slopes, both on the front side and on the back side, down to Outpost 14.

June mountain is great for a leisurely day out – see feature box.

#### FOR BEGINNERS
***Excellent***

Chair 7 and the new fast Chair 17 replacement at Canyon Lodge and Discovery Chair at Main Lodge serve quiet, gentle green runs – so as soon as you're off the nursery slopes you can get an encouraging taste of real skiing. Excellent instruction, top-notch grooming and snow quality usually make progress speedy.

#### FOR CROSS-COUNTRY
***Very popular***

Two specialist centres, Tamarack and Sierra Meadows (ungroomed), provide lessons and tours. There are 70km/43 miles of trails in all, including some through the pretty Lakes Basin area, and lots of scenic ungroomed tracks.

#### QUEUES
***Normally quiet slopes***

During the week the lifts and slopes are usually very quiet, with no queues; 'empty', 'deserted', say reporters. But even the efficient lift system can struggle when 15,000 visitors arrive from LA on fine peak-season weekends. That's the time to try the wonderfully uncrowded June Mountain, half an hour away.

#### MOUNTAIN RESTAURANTS
***Not a lot of choice***

The only real mountain restaurants are at mid-mountain McCoy Station. This offers 'a good choice' of roasts, Italian, Asian and other dishes – but does get 'very busy'. The Parallax table-service restaurant next door does satisfying food with a calm atmosphere and a splendid view. The other on-mountain possibility in good weather is the primitive outdoor BBQ at Outpost 14.

Most people eat at the lift bases. Talons at Eagle Lodge has its fans. The Mill Cafe is 'pleasant' but the 'choice of food was limited', according to a

#### boarding

*Mammoth's slopes are ideal for all abilities, with some excellent free-riding in the high bowls and perfect beginner and intermediate runs below. There's only one tiny drag-lift, and none of the flat linking runs that make some American resorts hard work to get around. Competent boarders will revel in the resort's extensive terrain parks (see above).*

**REPORTS WANTED**

Recently we have had few reports on this resort. If you go there, please do send us a report.

The best reports earn a copy of the next edition, and can lead to free lift passes in future.

See page 10.

## SCHOOLS

**Mammoth Mountain**
info@mammoth-mtn.com

**Classes**
1 3hr morning $60

**Private lessons**
$130 for 1hr for 1 to 5 people

## CHILDREN

**Small World**
**t** 934 0646
Ages newborn to 12; 8am-4.30; $70 per day

**Ski school**
Takes ages 4 to 6 at **Woollywood** ($45 for 2hr; $109 all day (10am-3pm) and ages 7 to 12 at **Canyon Kids** ($109 for a day (10am-3pm).

## GETTING THERE

**Air** Los Angeles 494km/307 miles (5hr); Reno 270km/168 miles (3hr).

## ACTIVITIES

**Indoor** Mammoth museum, art galleries, cinema, concerts

**Outdoor** Ice rink, snowmobiling, snow-shoeing, dog-sledding, tubing, hot air balloon rides

**Phone numbers**
From distant parts of the US, add the prefix 1 760.
From abroad, add the prefix +1 760.

## TOURIST OFFICE

**t** 934 0745
info@mammoth-mtn.com
www.mammothmountain.com

2004 visitor. The Mountain Side Grill at the newly revamped Mammoth Mountain Inn is also recommended. And Canyon Lodge offers Mexican, Italian, Asian and more.

### SCHOOLS AND GUIDES
***Excellent reports***

Past and recent reporters alike are favourably impressed by the school, which apparently contains growing numbers of Scottish instructors. There is the general American problem that you usually get a different instructor every day. There are some special 'camps' for experts, and for women.

### FACILITIES FOR CHILDREN
***Family favourite***

Mammoth is keen to attract families. The Woollywood school, based in the Panorama gondola station, works closely with the nearby Small World childcare centre. We've had glowing reports; one reporter noted the 'family feel of the resort'. Another rated the facilities as 'second to none'.

## STAYING THERE

### HOW TO GO
***Good value packages***

A good choice of hotels (none very luxurious or expensive) and condos. The condos tend to be out of town, near the lifts or on the road to them.
((((4) **Mammoth Mountain Inn** (934 2581) Way out of town at Main Lodge. Handy for the gondola, but dreary.
(((3) **Quality Inn** (934 5114) Good main street hotel with a big hot-tub.
(((3) **Alpenhof Lodge** (934 6330) Comfortable and friendly, in central location. Shuttle-bus stop and plenty of restaurants nearby.
(((3) **Austria Hof** (934 2764) Ski-out location near Canyon Lodge, recommended by a reporter despite modest-sized rooms.
(((3) **Sierra Nevada Rodeway Inn** (934 2515) Central, good value, 'great spa'.
(((3) **Holiday Inn** (924 1234) Central location, large, comfortable rooms and 'great restaurant'. Pool.
**Self-catering** The Juniper Springs Lodge is near lifts and town. Close to the Canyon Lodge base-station, the 1849 Condominiums are spacious and well equipped. The Mammoth Ski and Racquet Club, a 10-minute walk from the same lifts, is very comfortable. There is an 'excellent' supermarket in the Minaret Mall, with good discounts.

### EATING OUT
***Outstanding choice***

Reporters continue to be impressed by the wide choice available – over 50 restaurants, scattered over a wide area, catering for most tastes and pockets. Start with a copy of the local menu guide, and book what you fancy. One reporting couple had a great time dining in a different restaurant every day for a fortnight. Meshing their findings with other reports, we offer the following guidance: Slocums Grill – very good meal in wood-panelled room; Angel's – popular, good-value diner; Matterhorn – excellent Swiss-style food, good service; Ocean Harvest – great atmosphere and wonderful fish; Nevados – best in town, excellent modern cooking; Charthouse – excellent seafood, varied meat dishes; Alpenrose – intimate chalet-style place, good food; Matsu – small, simple, with delicious Thai food; Old Mammoth Grill – traditional family diner, 'good bar'. Also recommended are Shogun for Japanese and Gomez's for Mexican. We've had excellent dinners at Skadi and Whiskey Creek, too. Several new eateries have opened in the Village.

### APRES-SKI
***Lively at weekends***

The liveliest immediate après-ski spot is the Yodler, at the Main Lodge base – a chalet transported from Switzerland (so they say). Later on, things revolve around a handful of bars, which come to life at weekends. The Clocktower cellar is reported to be 'best in town – lively, friendly, good music, great choice of beers'. Whiskey Creek is the liveliest (and stays open latest); it has live bands at weekends, and Wild Wednesday discos. Slocums is popular with locals and 'ideal for an after-dinner drink'. Grumpy's is a sports bar (big-screen TVs). Dublin's Irish Bar (with nightclub), Hennessey's and the Hawaiian-style Lananuki's are new at the Village.

### OFF THE SLOPES
***Mainly sightseeing***

There are various things to be done outdoors, including skating. Or you can go sightseeing by car (preferably 4WD). The town of Bishop, 40 minutes' drive south, makes an amusing day out. Factory shopping is recommended for bargains. Mono Lake is reported to be 'well worth a visit'.

SNOWPIX.COM / CHRIS GILL

# Alpine Meadows

**Squaw Valley's next-door neighbour has similar, lightly wooded terrain, with runs of all classifications and an impressive snow record, but a modest total vertical of 550m/1,800ft. There's nothing but a day lodge at the base.**

## KEY FACTS

| | |
|---|---|
| **Resort** | 2085m<br>6,840ft |
| **Slopes** | 2085-2635m<br>6,840-8,640ft |
| **Lifts** | 12 |
| **Pistes** | 2,000 acres |
| **Green** | 25% |
| **Blue** | 40% |
| **Black** | 35% |
| **Snowmaking** | 220 acres |

## TOURIST OFFICE

**t** 530 583 4232
info@skialpine.com
www.skialpine.com

## THE RESORT?

There is no resort in the European sense of the word. The base day-lodge has 'uninspiring' self-service and table-service restaurants. Lots of lodgings close-by in lakeside Tahoe City.

## THE MOUNTAIN

The base is surrounded by excellent beginner slopes with a variety of slow lifts. The major mountain access lifts are a fast quad going half-way up the broad bowl under Ward Peak, and a six-pack to the top of it; this accesses a wide range of black runs (single and double diamond) at the top of the bowl, some of them involving long traverses, but there are also blue runs down to the generally blue terrain lower down the bowl. There is also a double chair on the upper slopes.

Separated from Ward Peak by a low saddle is Scott Peak; a double chair goes up over the steep black slopes on the front, and on the back pleasant blue runs are served by a triple. A second triple serves part of the open slopes on the back of Ward Peak, with steeper areas accessed by the Alpine Bowl chair on the front of the hill. The resort boundary is open – expeditions require guidance, of course.

There's a terrain-park, a half-pipe and a super-pipe just above the base. With a top-notch average snowfall of 495 inches, Alpine Meadows is known for its long season and excellent spring snow – but when it closes depends on ticket sales.

There is a little Mid-Mountain Chalet on the hill – self-service, but pleasantly woody and welcoming.

A regular visitor warns of 'ten-minute lift lines on weekends'.

KIRKWOOD MOUNTAIN RESORT

# Kirkwood

**Kirkwood is renowned for its powder, and has a lot to offer experts and confident intermediates. The drive from South Lake Tahoe involves two passes. The small base village includes a growing range of condos.**

## KEY FACTS

| | |
|---|---|
| **Resort** | 2375m<br>7,800ft |
| **Slopes** | 2375-2985m<br>7,800-9,800ft |
| **Lifts** | 12 |
| **Pistes** | 2,300 acres |
| **Green** | 15% |
| **Blue** | 50% |
| **Black** | 35% |
| **Snowmaking** | 55 acres |

## TOURIST OFFICE

**t** 209 258 6000
info@kirkwood.com
www.kirkwood.com

## THE RESORT

Kirkwood is reached from South Lake Tahoe over two high passes; heavy snowfall often closes the road. There is a cheap shuttle bus arriving at 9.30.

A small 'village' with ski-in, ski-out apartment accommodation is taking shape at the base. There are several bars and restaurants. There is a recreation centre with outdoor pool, spa and sun deck. There is an ice rink on the edge of the village plaza, also snow-skating and tubing. Après-ski is very limited.

## THE MOUNTAIN

The resort sits at the centre of a semicircle of slopes, lightly wooded at the top, more densely at the bottom. The lift system consists almost entirely of slow chair-lifts. One goes up to the top of the main bowl above the base, as does the resort's one fast quad. These two long lifts also give access to bowls to left and right of the main one. All three bowls have black slopes at the top, and easier runs lower down, served by their own shorter chairs. Beyond the left-hand bowl is a lightly wooded mountainside of blue/black gradient served by two more chairs, with a range of fairly adventurous ways back to the front of the mountain.

Kirkwood is an excellent resort for experts and adventurous intermediates, and fine for beginners, but rather limited for less confident intermediates who are not happy to tackle black runs. Deep snow is part of the attraction: Kirkwood claims an annual average snowfall of over 500 inches, which puts it right in the first rank, alongside Utah's Alta and Snowbird.

SNOWPIX.COM / CHRIS GILL

# Northstar-at-Tahoe

**Northstar is a classic US-style mountain with runs cut through dense forest. It's locally regarded as a friendly, well-run resort – a good bet for families. The lift system is slicker than at other minor resorts in the Tahoe area.**

## KEY FACTS

| | |
|---|---|
| Resort | 1930m 6,330ft |
| Slopes | 1930-2625m 6,330-8,610ft |
| Lifts | 17 |
| Pistes | 2,420 acres |
| Green | 25% |
| Blue | 50% |
| Black | 25% |
| Snowmaking | 50 % |

## TOURIST OFFICE

**t** 530 562 1010
verticalplus@skinorthstar.com
www.skinorthstar.com

## THE RESORT

Northstar's tiny 'village' is a pleasant, car-free affair in two parts – one angular and wooden, the other more traditional. Both have apartments and hotel-style rooms (though no recognisable hotel) over shops, a couple of restaurants and a couple of bars. The gondola station is at one end of the village, a short walk from the highly organised drop-off zone and the premium ($15 a day) parking lot – free parking is a bit further away, served by buses.

## THE MOUNTAIN

The whole area is very sheltered and good for bad-weather days. It enjoys long views in various directions.

A short gondola goes up to a mid-mountain lodge at Big Springs, only 160m/525ft above the village. From this point two fast chairs and one slow one radiate to serve a broad bowl with some short steep pitches at the top, with easier blue runs lower down and around the ridges – these giving excellent runs to the village of almost 700m/2,300ft vertical. On the back-side of the mountain is a second, steeper bowl with a central fast quad chair rising 575m/1,880ft; on either side of it are three or four runs that are at the easy end of the black spectrum (especially when groomed).

A fast quad serves the most recently opened area – another four black runs with a modest vertical of 390m/1,280ft on Lookout Mountain. The two runs close to the chair are seriously steep; the less steep outer runs (groomed when we visited) are still genuine blacks. You can eat on the hill – there are several options at Big Springs.

SQUAW VALLEY SKI CORP / NATHAN KENDALL

# Squaw Valley

**The major resort at the north end of Lake Tahoe, with 4,000 acres of open and lightly wooded bowls on six linked peaks. The small base village has undergone major development by Intrawest, with considerable success.**

## KEY FACTS

| | |
|---|---|
| Resort | 1890m 6,200ft |
| Slopes | 1890-2760m 6,200-9,050ft |
| Lifts | 33 |
| Pistes | 4,000 acres |
| Green | 25% |
| Blue | 45% |
| Black | 30% |
| Snowmaking | 360 acres |

## TOURIST OFFICE

**t** 530 583 6985
squaw@squaw.com
www.squaw.com

## THE RESORT

Until recently, Squaw has had very little accommodation at the base. The main options were Squaw Valley Lodge and the self-contained, luxurious conference-oriented Resort at Squaw Creek, linked into one end of the lift network by its own chair-lift. But a new resort village has been built by Intrawest, of Whistler fame, and with phase 2 complete reporters tell us it now has a real village atmosphere.

## THE MOUNTAINS

There are two powerful lifts from the base – a twin-cable jumbo Funitel gondola (as in Verbier and Val-Thorens) and a big cable-car. Both rise 610m/2,000ft to the twin mid-mountain stations of Gold Coast and High Camp – an incredible mid-mountain complex (open in the evening), with bars and restaurants, outdoor pool, ice skating, tennis, bungee jumping and tubing. Above these two points is a superb area of long, gentle, snow-sure beginner slopes. Intermediates have a choice of some lovely cruises in the Emigrant and Snow King sectors, and a top-to-bottom three-mile run. The possibilities for experts are huge, with lots of steep slopes, chutes and big mogul fields. There are several distinct sectors, each offering different challenges. Some sectors – notably the steep slopes down the Silverado chair – we wouldn't go into without a guide.

The peaks and high bowls of the area are treeless, but much of the terrain is lightly wooded – a very attractive compromise between the usual US wooded terrain and the open Alpine style of terrain. The average snowfall is an impressive 450 inches.

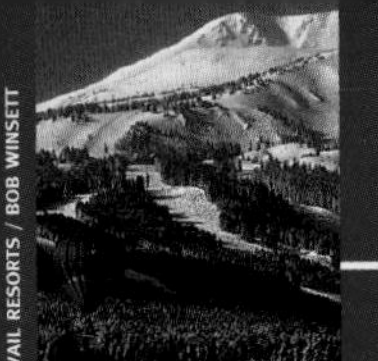
VAIL RESORTS / BOB WINSETT

# Colorado



**Colorado was the first US state to market its resorts internationally and is still the most popular American destination for UK visitors. And justifiably so: it has the most alluring combination of attractive resorts, slopes to suit all abilities and excellent, reliable snow – dry enough to justify its 'champagne powder' label. It also has direct flights (by British Airways) from London to Denver.**

Colorado has amazingly dry snow. Even when the snow melts and refreezes, the moisture seems to be magically whisked away, leaving it in soft powdery condition. Even in times of snow shortage, the artificial snow is of a quality you'll rarely find in Europe.

Colorado resorts vary enormously, both in the extent and variety of slopes and in the character of the villages. If you want cute restored buildings from the mining boom days of the late 1800s, try the dinky old towns of Telluride or Crested Butte – the latter now covered in one of our new short entries at the end of the Colorado section – or the much bigger Aspen. Others major on conveniece – such as Aspen's modern satellite, Snowmass, which for the first time is covered in its own chapter. Like most north American rivals, Colorado resorts generally have excellent, steep, ungroomed terrain that has enormous appeal to the adventurous.

Some resorts, such as Steamboat, Crested Butte and Telluride, are rather isolated, but there is a cluster of resorts west of Denver which can be combined in a holiday tour by car. As well as the resorts we cover in detail, you could think about quick visits to some others – notably high, steep Arapahoe Basin, up the valley from Keystone; and snow-sure Loveland, which you can see from the main I70 highway. If visiting Crested Butte, you could take in Monarch, which has snowcat as well as lift-served slopes

Further south, Durango (which used to be called Purgatory) now gets a half-page entry. If approaching from the north, be warned: the road over Red Mountain pass is quite the scariest we have driven – do it only in daylight and good weather. We hear good things about Silverton, with steep, ungroomed runs that you tackle in guided groups, and Wolf Creek, which claims the most snow in Colorado – an average of 465 inches a year.

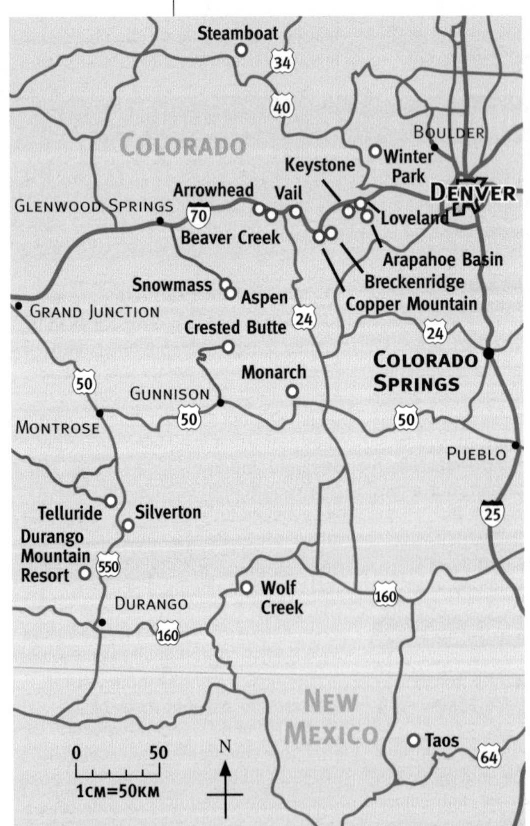

# Aspen

*Don't be put off by the ritzy image – this is America's best resort*

## COSTS

①②③④⑤⑥

## RATINGS

**The slopes**
Snow *****
Extent ****
Expert *****
Intermediate *****
Beginner *****
Convenience **
Queues ****
Mountain restaurants ***

**The rest**
Scenery ***
Resort charm ****
Off-slope ****

Our extent rating relates to the whole Aspen-Snowmass area. Aspen alone would rate **

## NEWS

For 2004/05 a fast quad will replace the old Buttermilk West chair. A mid-station will allow easier access to the beginner terrain on the mountain. On Aspen Mountain it's time to say goodbye to the oldest chair in the resort – the F.I.S., which was installed in 1958, is due to be replaced by a new two-seater.

Your choice of swanky hotels near the lift base widens further in spring 2005 with the opening of the Hyatt Grand Aspen.

On Aspen Mountain, 2003/04 saw improvements to the Ajax Express lift. And the Sundeck restaurant gained a table-service area.

- + Notably uncrowded slopes, even by American standards
- + Attractive, characterful old mining town, with lots of smart shops
- + Lively, varied nightlife
- + Great range of restaurants
- + Excellent Snowmass just up the road

- − Slopes split over three separate mountains (four if you count Snowmass, as you should), though there's efficient, free transport
- − Some accommodation in Aspen town is a bus-ride from the lifts
- − Expensive

**Aspen is our favourite American resort. It has been for years, and we confirmed it again last winter. We admit that this affection depends heavily on the presence of Snowmass a little way down the valley, which for the first time we are covering in a separate chapter – so to get to the most extensive slopes you have to ride a bus. That doesn't put us off, and doesn't seem to worry readers who report on the place – so it shouldn't deter you, either.**

**You can forget the film-star image. Yes, many rich and famous guests jet in to the local airport, and for connoisseurs of cosmetic surgery the bars of Aspen's top hotels can be fascinating places. But most celebs keep a low profile; and, like all other 'glamorous' ski resorts, Aspen is actually filled by ordinary holidaymakers.**

## THE RESORT

In 1892 Aspen was a booming silver-mining town, source of one-sixth of the USA's silver, with 12,000 inhabitants, six newspapers, an opera house and a red-light district. But Aspen's fortunes took a nose-dive when the silver price plummeted in 1893, and by the 1930s the population had shrunk to 700 or so, and handsome Victorian buildings – such as the Hotel Jerome – had fallen into disrepair.

Development of the skiing started on a small scale in the late 1930s. The first lift was opened shortly after the Second World War, and Aspen hasn't looked back since. Now, the historic centre – with a typical American grid of streets – has been beautifully renovated to form the core of the most fashionable ski town in the Rockies. There's a huge variety of bars, restaurants, shops and art galleries – some amazingly upmarket. Spreading out from this centre, you'll find a mixture of developments, ranging from the homes of the super-rich to the mobile homes for the workers. Though the town is busy with traffic, it moves slowly and pedestrians effectively have priority in much of the central area.

Aspen is very unusual in being a cute town with a major lift close to the centre: the Silver Queen gondola straight to the top of Aspen Mountain is only yards from some of the top hotels, and the streets running away from the lift base are lined by the restaurants and shops that make Aspen what it is. Stay close to this lift if you can. Downtown Aspen is quite compact by American resort standards, but it spreads far enough to make the free ski-bus a necessity for many visitors staying less centrally.

Aspen Highlands, a couple of miles out of town, now has limited accommodation. Twelve miles away is Snowmass, which now gets its own chapter. Buses for these mountains and Buttermilk leave from near the gondola station.

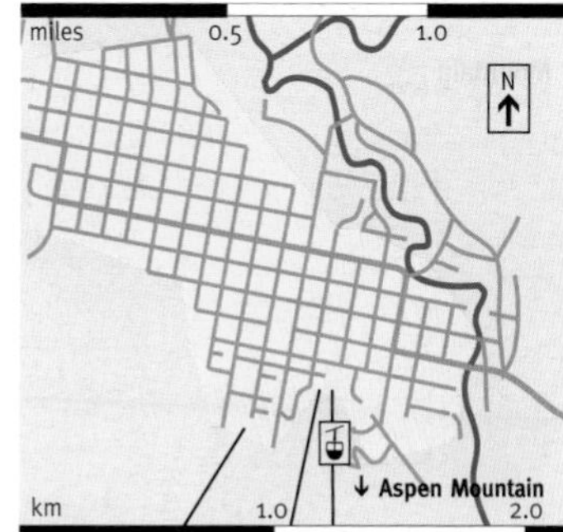

## LIFT PASSES

**Four Mountain Pass**
Covers Aspen Mountain, Aspen Highlands, Buttermilk and Snowmass, and shuttle-bus between the areas.

**Beginners**
Included in price of beginners' lessons.

**Main pass**
1 day $72
6 days $432

**Senior citizens**
Over 65: 6 days $384
Over 70: Unlimited period $189

**Children**
Under 18: 6 days $384
Under 13: 6 days $258
Under 7: free pass

**Notes**
Substantial savings on lift passes for 4 days or more if you purchase them more than 7 days in advance or through certain tour operators.

## THE MOUNTAINS

Aspen has lots for every ability; you just have to pick the right mountain. All of them have regular, free, guided tours, given by excellent amateur ambassadors. The ratio of acres to visitor beds is high, and the slopes are usually blissfully uncrowded. Lift passes are discounted heavily for purchase in advance or through tour operators – check out your options well in advance of travelling.

### THE SLOPES
***Widely dispersed***

Each of the three local mountains is worth a visit – though novices should note that Aspen Mountain has no green runs. Most of the slopes are in the trees. Much the most extensive mountain is at Snowmass – see separate chapter.

Once you are up the gondola, a series of chairs serves the ridges of **Aspen Mountain**. In general, there are long cruising blue runs along the valley floors and short, steep blacks down from the ridges.

**Buttermilk** is the least challenging mountain, served by a fast quad from the fairly primitive main base lodge. The runs fan out from the top in three directions – back to the base, or down to the slow Tiehack chair, or down to the new fast quad at West Buttermilk.

**Aspen Highlands** consists essentially of a single ridge served by three fast quad chairs, with easy and intermediate slopes along the ridge itself and steep black runs on the flanks – very steep ones at the top. And beyond the lift network is Highland Bowl, where gates give access to a splendid open bowl of entirely double-black gradient. There are free snowcat rides from the top of the lifts to the first access gate of Highland Bowl, but if these are not operating, it's a 20-minute hike. All the other gates require further hiking. The views from the upper part of Highlands are the best that Aspen has to offer – the famous Maroon Bells that appear on countless postcards. There is a base lodge with underground parking and a Ritz-Carlton aparthotel.

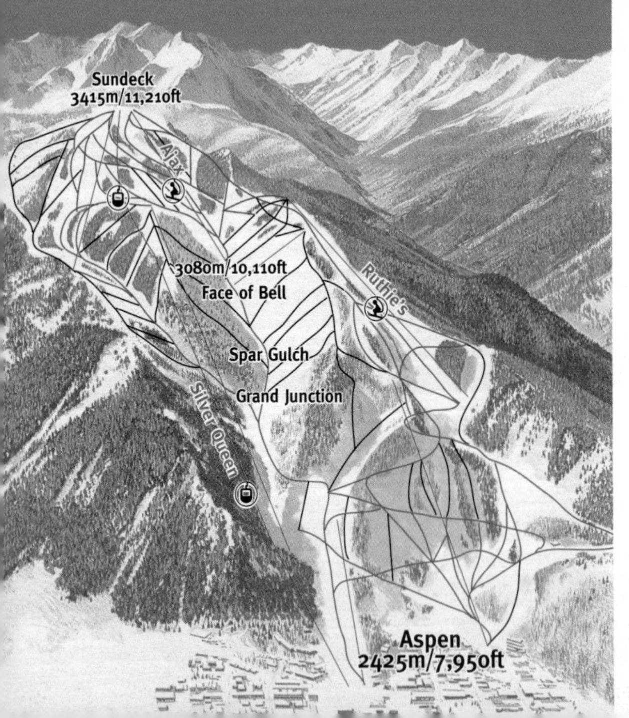


### TERRAIN-PARKS
***Some of the world's best***

Buttermilk has a 3km/2 mile-long terrain-park (claimed to be the world's longest) with a beginner and intermediate area, more than 30 rails and 25 jumps, a boarder-cross course, a 100m/330ft long super-pipe and 'motivating' sound system. The park is currently home to the ESPN Winter X games and now incorporates a permanent X Games-style course.

### SNOW RELIABILITY
***Rarely a problem***

Aspen's mountains get an annual average of 300 inches of snow – not in the front rank, but not far behind. In addition, all areas have substantial snowmaking. Immaculate grooming adds to the quality of the pistes.

### FOR EXPERTS
***Buttermilk is the only soft stuff***

There's plenty to choose from – all the mountains except Buttermilk offer lots of challenges.

Aspen Mountain has a formidable array of double-black-diamond runs. From the top of the gondola, Walsh's, Hyrup's and Kristi are on a lightly wooded slope and link up with Gentleman's Ridge and Jackpot to form the longest black run on the mountain. A series of steep glades drops down from Gentleman's Ridge. The central Bell ridge has less extreme single-diamonds on both its flanks. On the opposite side of Spar Gulch is another

| KEY FACTS | |
|---|---|
| Resort | 2425m 7,950ft |
| Aspen Mountain | |
| Slopes | 2425-3415m 7,950-11,210ft |
| Lifts | 8 |
| Pistes | 673 acres |
| Green | 0% |
| Blue | 48% |
| Black | 52% |
| Snow-guns | 210 acres |
| Aspen Highlands | |
| Slopes | 2450-3560m 8,040-11,680ft |
| Lifts | 4 |
| Pistes | 790 acres |
| Green | 18% |
| Blue | 30% |
| Black | 52% |
| Snow-guns | 110 acres |
| Buttermilk | |
| Slopes | 2400-3020m 7,880-9,900ft |
| Lifts | 7 |
| Pistes | 429 acres |
| Green | 35% |
| Blue | 39% |
| Black | 26% |
| Snow-guns | 108 acres |
| Total with Snowmass | |
| Slopes | 2400-3815m 7,880-12,510ft |
| Lifts | 40 |
| Pistes | 4,900 acres |
| Green | 10% |
| Blue | 48% |
| Black | 42% |
| Snow-guns | 608 acres |

row of double-blacks collectively called the Dumps, because waste was dumped here in the silver-mining days.

At Highlands there are challenging runs from top to bottom of the mountain. Consider joining a guided group as an introduction to the best of them. Highland Bowl, beyond the top lift, is superb in the right conditions: a big open bowl with pitches from a serious 38° to a terrifying 48° – facts you can check in the very informative Highlands Extreme Skiing Guide leaflet. Within the lift system, the Steeplechase area consists of a number of parallel natural avalanche chutes, and their elevation means the snow stays light and dry. The Olympic Bowl area on the opposite flank of the mountain has great views of the Maroon Bells and some serious moguls. Thunderbowl chair from the base serves a nice varied area that's often underused.

### FOR INTERMEDIATES
***Grooming to die for***

Most intermediate runs on Highlands are concentrated above the mid-mountain Merry-Go-Round restaurant, many served by the Cloud Nine fast quad chair. But there are good slopes higher up and lower down – don't miss the vast, neglected expanses of Golden Horn, on the eastern limit of the area.

Aspen Mountain has its fair share of intermediate slopes, but they tend to be tougher than on the other mountains. Copper Bowl and Spar Gulch, running between the ridges, are great cruises early in the morning but can get crowded later. Upper Aspen Mountain, at the top of the gondola, has a dense network of well-groomed blues. The unusual Ruthie's chair – a fast double, apparently installed to rekindle the romance that quads have destroyed – serves more cruising runs and the popular Snow Bowl, a wide, open area with moguls on the left but groomed on the right and centre.



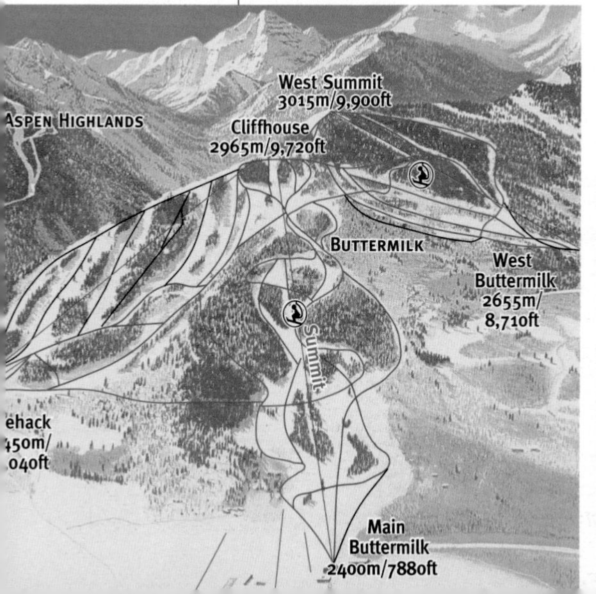


SNOWPIX.COM / CHRIS GILL

Iguana's at the Highlands base is a popular après-ski spot ↓

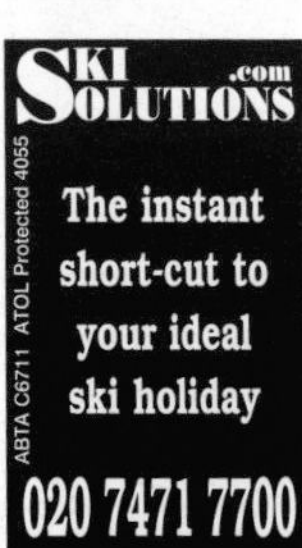


## SCHOOLS

**Aspen**
t 990 6346
breakthrough@aspensnowmass.com

**Classes**
Full day (5hr) $123, incl.tax

**Private lessons**
$329 for a half day (3hr) for up to 5 people.

The Main Buttermilk runs offer good, easy slopes to practise on. And good intermediates should be able to handle the relatively easy black runs – when groomed, these are a real blast on carving skis. It's also a great place for early experiments off-piste.

### FOR BEGINNERS
***Can be a great place to learn***

Buttermilk is a great mountain for beginners. West Buttermilk has beautifully groomed, gentle runs which will be served by a new quad for 2004/05. The easiest slopes of all, though, are at the base of the Main Buttermilk sector – on Panda Hill.

Despite its macho image, Highlands boasts the highest concentration of green runs in Aspen.

### FOR CROSS-COUNTRY
***Backcountry bonanza***

There are 60km/37 miles of groomed trails between Aspen and Snowmass in the Roaring Fork valley – the most extensive maintained cross-country system in the US. And the Ashcroft Ski Touring Centre maintains around 35km/21 miles of trails around Ashcroft, a mining ghost-town. The Pine Creek Cookhouse – excellent food and accessible by ski, snowshoe or horse-drawn sleigh only – has reopened following a devastating fire. Aspen is at one end of the famous Tenth Mountain Division Trail, heading 370km/230 miles north-east almost to Vail, with 12 huts for overnight stops.

### QUEUES
***Few problems***

There are rarely major queues on any of the mountains. At Aspen Mountain, the gondola can have delays at peak times, but you have alternative lifts to the top. Aspen Highlands is almost always queue-free, even at peak times. The two lifts out of Main Buttermilk sometimes get congested.

### MOUNTAIN RESTAURANTS
***Good by American standards***

On Aspen Mountain the recently expanded Sundeck has 'one of the best self-service restaurants you'll find', with great views. And last season a table-service area – Benedict's – was opened, offering 'wonderful food'.

At Highlands the Cloud Nine Alpine bistro is the nearest thing you will find in the States to a cosy Alpine hut, with great views and excellent food – thanks to an Austrian chef.

On Buttermilk the mountaintop Cliffhouse is known for its 'Mongolian Barbecue' stir-fry bar and great views.

### SCHOOLS AND GUIDES
***Simply the best?***

There's a wide variety of specialised instruction – mountain exploration groups, off-piste tours, adrenaline sessions, women's groups, and so on. Reporters rave about the small group lessons ('they say average of three people, but we did five days and my wife had one-to-one the whole time'; 'the best class ever'; 'wonderful instruction'). The Wizard Ski Deck is an indoor ski and snowboard simulator used in combination with some classes or available for a private lesson.

### FACILITIES FOR CHILDREN
***Choice of nurseries***

We have no recent reports, but past reports on the childcare arrangements have always been first class. Young children are bused to and from Buttermilk's very impressive Fort Frog. The Kids' Trail Map is a great idea. But Snowmass has clear advantages for families with young children.

### GET THE BEST OF THE SNOW, ON- AND OFF-PISTE

*Aspen offers special experiences for small numbers of skiers or riders.*

**Fresh Tracks** *The first eight skiers to sign up each day get to ride the gondola up Aspen Mountain at 8am the next morning, and to get first tracks on perfect corduroy or fresh powder. Free!*

**Off-piste Tours** *On Fridays backcountry guides lead expert skiers and riders around the famous expert terrain of Highlands – the same deal is available in Snowmass on Wednesdays. 10am–3pm, $109 (2003/04).*

**Powder Tours** *Spend the day finding untracked snow in 1,500 acres of backcountry beyond Aspen Mountain, with a 10-passenger heated snowcat as your personal lift. You're likely to squeeze in about 10 runs in all. You break for lunch at an old mountain cabin. Full day, $295 (2003/04).*

Highland Bowl has wonderful steep, ungroomed runs that are avalanche controlled. The dot in the middle of this pic is a skier, resting →

SNOWPIX.COM / CHRIS GILL

## STAYING THERE

### HOW TO GO

***Accommodation for all pockets***

There's a mixture of hotels, inns, B&Bs, lodges and condos.

**Chalets** Several UK tour operators have chalets here – some very luxurious.

**Hotels** There are places for all budgets. Sadly, our favourite, the intimate Sardy House, is no longer operating as a hotel. A new hotel by the gondola, the Hyatt Grand Aspen, is scheduled to open in spring 2005.

((((5 **St Regis Aspen** (920 3300) Opulent city-type hotel, near gondola. A fancy new spa facility is due to open for 2004/05.

((((5 **Little Nell** (920 4600) Stylish, modern hotel right by the gondola with popular bar. Fireplaces in every room, outdoor pool, hot-tub, sauna.

((((5 **Jerome** (920 1000) Step back a century: Victorian authenticity combined with modern-day luxury. Several blocks from the gondola.

(((4 **Lenado** (925 6246) Smart modern B&B place with open-fire lounge, individually designed rooms.

((3 **Innsbruck Inn** (925 2980) Tirolean-style hotel, 10 minutes from lifts. Liked by many reporters, but 'the new management has dropped the muesli'.

((3 **Hotel Aspen** (925 3441) Best 'moderate' place in town, 10 minutes from lifts; comfortable, pool, hot-tubs.

((3 **The Mountain Chalet** (925 7797) Convenient and cosy lodge at the base of the slopes; breakfast included. Pool, sauna and fitness room.

**Self-catering** The standards here are high, even in US terms. Many of the smarter developments have their own free shuttle-buses. The Gant is luxurious and close to the gondola. Chateau Roaring Fork and Eau Claire, four blocks from the gondola, are spacious and well furnished. The Tamarack Townhouses, Terrace House and Top of the Village have all been highly recommended by reporters. A reader says the two small supermarkets are 'exceptionally well stocked'.

### EATING OUT

***Dining dilemma***

As you'd expect, there are excellent upmarket places, but also plenty of cheaper options – and an easy way to economise in many smarter places is to choose from the bar menu.

Piñons serves innovative American food. Syzygy is a suave upstairs place with live jazz from 10pm. Conundrum



## CHILDREN

**Buttermilk: Powder Pandas**
**t** 920 0935
Ages 3 to 6 (5 to 7 for snowboarding); shuttle-bus from Aspen.

**Snowmass: Big Burn Bears**
**t** 923 0570
From age 3½

**Snow Cubs**
**t** 923 0563
Ages 8wk to 3½yr

**Nighthawks**
**t** 923 0570
Ages 3 to 10; 4pm to 11pm.

**Grizzlies**
**t** 923 0580
Ages 5 and 6 (snowboarding for 5 to 7).

**All-day non-skiing nurseries**
Several

**Ski school**
Takes ages 7 to 12, US$389 for 5 days (5¾hr per day, lunch included).

## boarding

*There is great snowboarding for every ability. The ban on snowboarding on Aspen Mountain was lifted back in April 2001. All the mountains offer excellent boarding, with few flat sections and almost all lifts being chairs or gondolas. There are two world-class terrain-parks, and regularly hosting the Winter X Games has boosted Aspen's image as boarder-friendly.*

## GETTING THERE

**Air** Aspen 5km/3 miles; Eagle 113km/70 miles (1½hr); Denver 355km/220 miles (4hr).

**Rail** Glenwood Springs (63km/40 miles).

## ACTIVITIES

**Indoor** The Aspen Club and Spa (racquetball, swimming, weights, aerobics, sauna, steam, hot-tubs, ice skating); new Aspen Recreation Centre (swimming complex and ice rink), cinemas, theatre, naturalists' evenings, paintballing

**Outdoor** Ice skating, snowcat tours, snow-shoe tours, sleigh rides, dog sledding, tubing, snowmobiles, tours of mines

**Phone numbers**
From distant parts of the US, add the prefix 1 970.
From abroad, add the prefix +1 970.

## TOURIST OFFICE

t 925 1220
intlres@skiaspen.com
www.aspensnowmass.com





(modern American food, expensive) and Pacifica Seafood Brasserie are top-notch. The basement Steak Pit is a long-established and reliable favourite. The Elevation is new, featuring 'original Andy Warhol artworks on the wall' and 'superb modern food'. L'Hostaria, The Mother Lode, Campo de Fiori and new Umbria are good Italians. Cache Cache does good-value Provençal. Ute City Bar & Grill is good for local game.

Cheaper recommendations include: Bentley's (main courses $8 upwards), Boogie's (a 50s-style diner, great for families), Main Street Bakery & Café, Mezzaluna, Red Onion, Hickory House ('very good ribs'), the Skier's Chalet steak house and Woody Creek Tavern – apparently a favourite of famous Aspen resident Hunter S Thompson.

### APRES-SKI
***Lots of options***

As the lifts shut, a few bars at the bases get busy. At Highlands the terrace of Iguana's is busy. In Aspen the Ajax Tavern is popular. The Greenhouse bar at the Little Nell is a great place for gazing at face-lifts.

Many of the restaurants are also bars – Jimmy's (spectacular stock of tequila), Mezzaluna, Red Onion, and Ute City, for example. The J-bar of the Jerome hotel still has a traditional feel. Shooters Saloon is a splendid country-and-western dive with pool and line-dancing. For pool in more suave circumstances, there's Aspen Billiards adjoining the fashionable Cigar Bar, with its comfortable sofas (and smoking permitted!). The Popcorn Wagon is the place for munchies after the bars close. We're told the new place to be seen sipping a botox Martini is the swanky 39 Degrees (located in the Sky Hotel). You can get a week's membership of the famous members-only Caribou club.

### OFF THE SLOPES
***Silver service***

Aspen has lots to offer, especially if you've got a high credit card limit. There are literally dozens of art galleries, some of them world-class, as well as the predictable clothes and jewellery shops. Just wandering around town is pleasant. It's a shame that all the best mountain restaurants are awkward for pedestrians to get to. Many hotels have excellent spa facilities. The new Aspen Recreation Centre at the base of Highlands has a huge swimming complex and indoor ice-rink.

SNOWPIX.COM / CHRIS GILL

Downtown Aspen is a pleasure to explore, particularly if your flexible friend is in good shape →

JACK AFFLECK

# Beaver Creek

*The Rolls Royce of resorts: very expensive but smooth and spacious*

**COSTS**

**RATINGS**

**The slopes**

| | |
|---|---|
| Snow | ***** |
| Extent | ** |
| Expert | **** |
| Intermediate | **** |
| Beginner | ***** |
| Convenience | **** |
| Queues | ***** |
| Mountain restaurants | ** |

**The rest**

| | |
|---|---|
| Scenery | *** |
| Resort charm | ** |
| Off-slope | *** |

**NEWS**

For 2004/05 a new base area, Beaver Creek Landing, will be created close to the valley town of Avon. Two fast quads will link to the main slopes at the top of Strawberry Park via Bachelor Gulch.

In 2003/04 the Westfall chair was replaced by the fast Birds of Prey quad.

- ➕ Blissfully quiet slopes, in sharp contrast to nearby Vail
- ➕ Mountain has it all, from superb novice runs to daunting mogul-fields
- ➕ Fast chair-lifts all over the place
- ➕ Compact, traffic-free village centre

- ➖ Rather urban feel to the village core – far from the Wild West atmosphere Europeans might look for
- ➖ Very expensive
- ➖ Disappointing mountain restaurants – the best ones are members-only

**In contrast to its better-known neighbour, Vail, Beaver Creek is a haven of peace – both on and off the slopes. It gets rather overshadowed by big sister, but we wouldn't dream of making a trip to Vail without spending a day or two in Beaver. But we're not really tempted to do it the other way round – not least because of the prices in this most exclusive of Colorado resorts.**

## THE RESORT

Beaver Creek, 10 miles to the west of Vail, was developed in the 1980s. It is unashamedly exclusive, with a choice of top-quality hotels and condos right by the slopes. It centres on a smart but rather severe pedestrian area with escalators to the slopes, exclusive shops, exquisite bronze statues and an open-air ice rink. The lift system spreads across the mountains through Bachelor Gulch, with its Ritz-Carlton, to Arrowhead, which has luxury condos at the base of the mountain. Most of the nightlife, bars and restaurants are in Beaver Creek and the choice is much more limited than in Vail, a 25-minute bus-ride away. Staying in the valley town of Avon will become much more attractive this season with the opening nearby of a new lift base, Beaver Creek Landing, with fast new chairs linking to the heart of the Beaver Creek slopes. This will also form the natural access point for day visitors.

SNOWPIX.COM / CHRIS GILL

Beaver Creek village always strikes us as feeling more like a small city than a ski resort ↓

## THE MOUNTAINS

Beaver Creek, Bachelor Gulch, Arrowhead and now Beaver Creek Landing offer a small-scale version of the linked lift networks of the Alps. Free mountain tours are held four days a week. British guests may get the opportunity to ski the area with Martin Bell, Britain's best-ever downhiller, who now lives in Vail and is UK ski ambassador for Vail Resorts.



**Slopes** The slopes immediately above Beaver Creek divide into two sectors, each accessed by a fast quad chair. The major sector is centred on Spruce Saddle, with lifts above it reaching 3485m/11,440ft. The other is Strawberry Park, which forms the link with Bachelor Gulch and the other lift bases. Between these two sectors is Grouse Mountain.

Resorts within a two-hour drive include Breckenridge and Keystone (owned by Vail Resorts and covered by multi-day lift passes), Aspen, Steamboat and Copper Mountain.

**Terrain-parks** There are three: Park 101 is a small beginner's park, Moonshine includes a 120m/400ft long super-pipe and the Zoom Room is for progressing intermediates and beginners. Park-ology is a new park and pipe programme designed to offer tuition mainly to kids.

**Snow reliability** An impressive annual snow record (average 310 inches) plus extensive snowmaking means you can relax. Grouse Mountain can suffer from thin cover (some call it Gravel Mountain). Grooming is excellent.

**Experts** There is quite a bit of intimidatingly steep double-diamond

## KEY FACTS

| | |
|---|---|
| Resort | 2470m 8,100ft |
| Slopes | 2255-3485m 7,400-11,440ft |
| Lifts | 15 |
| Pistes | 1,625 acres |
| Green | 34% |
| Blue | 39% |
| Black | 27% |
| Snowmaking | 624 acres |

## REPORTS WANTED

Recently we have had few reports on this resort. If you go there, please do send us a report.

## LIFT PASSES

See Vail chapter.

**Central reservations phone number**
1 800 427 8308
(toll free from within the US).

**Phone numbers**
From distant parts of the US, add the prefix 1 970.
From abroad, add the prefix +1 970.

## TOURIST OFFICE

**t** 845 9090
bcinfo@vailresorts.com
www.beavercreek.com





terrain. In the Birds of Prey and Grouse Mountain areas most runs are long, steep and mogulled from top to bottom. The Larkspur Bowl area has three short steep mogul runs.

**Intermediates** There are marvellous long, quiet, cruising blues almost everywhere you look, including top to bottom runs with a vertical of 1000m/3,280ft from the top of the Cinch chair. The Larkspur and Strawberry Park chairs serve further cruising runs – and lead to yet more ideal terrain served by the Bachelor Gulch and Arrowhead fast chairs.

**Beginners** There are excellent nursery slopes at resort level and at altitude (there's a family zone at the top of the Cinch chair). And there are plenty of easy longer runs to progress to, including runs from top to bottom of the mountains.

**Snowboarding** Good riders will love the excellent gladed runs and perfect carving slopes. The resort is great for beginners, too, with special teaching methods and equipment that claim to help you learn quicker.

**Cross-country** There's a splendid, mountain-top network of tracks at McCoy Park (over 32km/20 miles), reached via the Strawberry Park lift.

**Queues** The slopes are delightfully deserted and virtually queue-free, even at peak times – it is amazing that more skiers don't come here from Vail.

**Mountain restaurants** There's not much choice. The 'pleasant' and 'good-value' Spruce Saddle at mid-mountain is the main place – a food court in a spectacular log and glass building. Red Tail Camp does decent barbecues. The Broken Arrow at Arrowhead base is recommended.

**Schools and guides** The school has an excellent reputation.

**Facilities for children** Small World Play School looks after non-skiing kids from two months to six years from 8.30 to 4.30. We've had good reports on the children's school and there are splendid adventure trails and play areas.

## STAYING THERE

**How to go** There's a reasonable choice of packages.

**Hotels** There are lots of upmarket places, including the Ritz-Carlton, Inn at Beaver Creek and Hyatt Regency.

**Self-catering** There's a wide choice of condos available.

**Eating out** SaddleRidge is luxurious and packed with photos and Wild West artefacts. A good evening out is to take a sleigh ride to one of the beautiful log cabins that are open for dinner – Beano's, Allie's or Zach's. Toscanini's, the Golden Eagle, Dusty Boot, and Blue Moose have all been recommended.

**Après-ski** Beaver Creek Tavern and the Coyote Cafe are decent bars. The Whiskey Elk is said to have a good selection of bourbon, port and wine.

**Off the slopes** There are smart boutiques and galleries, an impressive ice rink, hot-air balloon rides and some great shows and concerts.

**Staying up the mountain** Trappers Cabin is a luxurious private enclave up the mountain, which a group can rent (for a small fortune) by the night.

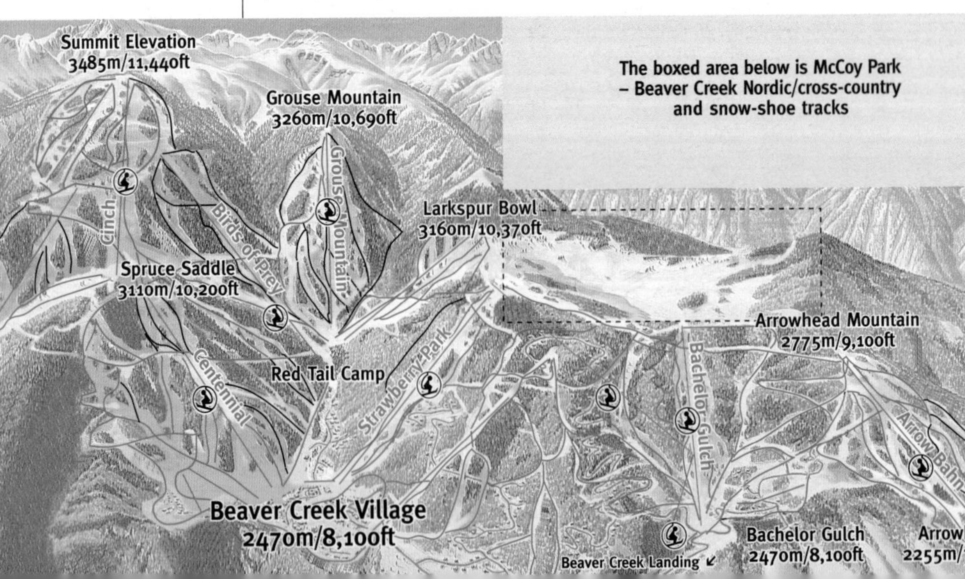

VAIL RESORTS INC / BOB WINSETT

# Breckenridge

*Four linked mountains, reached from a village with Wild West roots*

## COSTS

①②③④⑤⑥

## RATINGS

**The slopes**

| | |
|---|---|
| Snow | ***** |
| Extent | ** |
| Expert | **** |
| Intermediate | **** |
| Beginner | **** |
| Convenience | *** |
| Queues | **** |
| Mountain restaurants | ** |

**The rest**

| | |
|---|---|
| Scenery | *** |
| Resort charm | *** |
| Off-slope | *** |

## NEWS

Long-term plans have been approved to build new villages at the bases of Peaks 7 and 8. They will be linked to parking lots in the valley by a new gondola.

## KEY FACTS

| | |
|---|---|
| **Resort** | 2925m<br>9,600ft |
| **Slopes** | 2925-3700m<br>9,600-12,140ft |
| **Lifts** | 27 |
| **Pistes** | 2,208 acres |
| **Green** | 15% |
| **Blue** | 33% |
| **Black** | 52% |
| **Snowmaking** | 516 acres |

- ➕ Local mountains have something for all abilities
- ➕ Shared lift pass with nearby Keystone and Arapahoe Basin and not-so-nearby Vail and Beaver Creek
- ➕ Efficient lifts mean few queues
- ➕ Lively bars, restaurants and nightlife by US standards
- ➕ Some slope-side accommodation
- ➕ Restored Victorian mining town, with mainly sympathetic new buildings
- ➕ One of the nearest major resorts to Denver, so relatively short transfer

- ➖ Limited intermediate terrain, and few long runs
- ➖ Best advanced slopes can be windy
- ➖ At 2925m/9,600ft the village is one of the highest you will encounter. At this extreme altitude there is a real risk of sickness for visitors coming straight from lower altitudes
- ➖ The 19th-century style gets a bit overblown in places, and there are some out-of-place modern buildings
- ➖ Main Street is just that – always busy with traffic

**Breckenridge is very popular with first-time visitors to Colorado, and it's not a bad introduction to the place. We're not registered fans, though – no doubt partly because our first visit was spoiled by altitude sickness, and partly because some of our subsequent attempts to explore the steep stuff at the top have been thwarted by high winds – a regular feature, apparently.**

**For intermediates not interested in tackling the steep stuff, the slopes lack character as well as extent. If you base yourself here for a week or more, you should do so with the expectation that you'll want to explore other resorts (covered by the lift pass) by car or bus.**



## THE RESORT

Breckenridge was founded in 1859 and became a booming gold-mining town. The old clapboard buildings have been well renovated and form the bottom part of Main Street. New shopping malls and buildings have been added in similar style – though they are obvious modern additions.

The town centre is lively in the evening, with over 100 restaurants and bars. Christmas lights and decorations remain throughout the season, giving the town an air of non-stop winter festivity. This is enhanced by a number of real winter festivals such as Ullr Fest – a carnival honouring the Norse God of Winter – and Ice Sculpture championships, which leave sculptures for weeks afterwards.

Hotels and condominiums are spread over a wide, wooded area and are linked by regular, free shuttle-buses (less frequent in the evening). If you stay in a condo and don't have a car, shopping at the local supermarket can be hard work – it is not in the centre of town. Although there is a lot of slope-side accommodation – more than any other Colorado resort, it is claimed – there is also a fair amount that's inconveniently distant from Main Street and the lift base-stations.

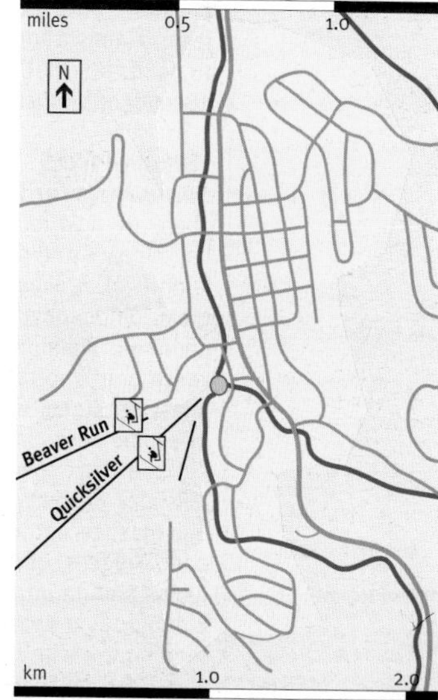

The Lake Chutes are serious stuff. The jump's the easy part: the slope you land on can be as steep as a terrifying 50° →

VAIL RESORTS, INC / CHADD DAMICO





## THE MOUNTAINS

The slopes are mainly cut through the forest, with some open runs at the top. Breckenridge is in the same ownership as Vail, Beaver Creek, Keystone and Arapahoe Basin. A multi-day lift ticket covers all five resorts. Copper Mountain is not covered by the same ticket. All six of these resorts are linked by regular buses (free except for the trips to Vail or Beaver Creek).

### THE SLOPES
***Small but fragmented***

There are four sectors, linked by lift and piste, named Peaks 7, 8, 9 and 10 – going from right to left as you look at the mountain. The grooming is excellent and the signposting very clear. There are free mountain tours at 9.30 daily.

Two high-speed chair-lifts go from the top end of town up to **Peak 9**, one accessing mainly green runs on the lower half of the hill, the other mainly blues higher up. From there you can get to **Peak 10**, which has a large number of blue and black runs served by one high-speed quad.

The **Peak 8** area – tough stuff at the top, easier lower down – can be reached by a fast quad from Peak 9. The base lifts of Peak 8 at the Bergenhof can also be reached by the town shuttle-bus or the Snowflake lift from the edge of town. Beyond here the lower slopes of **Peak 7** are served by a single six-pack. A T-bar on Peak 8 gets you to the resort's open ski-anywhere bowls, on 8 and 7. The resort claims a top height of 3963m/12,998ft, but that involves a hike of 260m/850ft vertical.

### TERRAIN-PARKS
***Something for everyone***

There are now four terrain-parks and half-pipes – one of the best in the US is on Peak 8, Freeway, with a series of great jumps, obstacles and an enormous championship half-pipe, which one reporter described as 'massive, steep, well kept and awesome'. Less intimidating is the park on Peak 9, with jumps and railslides designed for intermediates. The most recent addition is the small park, Trygves, on Peak 8, with gentle jumps and an introductory pipe. Eldorado is a boarders-only mini-terrain-park with half-pipe on Peak 9 (see Boarding).

### SNOW RELIABILITY
***Excellent***

With its high altitude, Breckenridge boasts an excellent natural snow record – annual average 300 inches. That is supplemented by substantial snowmaking (used mainly early in the season to form a good base). There are a lot of east- and north-east-facing slopes, which hold snow well.

### FOR EXPERTS
***Quite a few short but tough runs***

A remarkable 55% of Breckenridge's runs are classified black – either 'most difficult' (single-black-diamond) or 'expert' (double-black-diamond) terrain. That's a higher proportion than the famous 'macho' resorts, such as Jackson Hole, Taos and Snowbird. But it's a high proportion of a fairly small area – and you have to hike to get to much of it.

From the top of the T-bar on Peak 8 traversing or hiking up takes you to great steep, shady runs on Peak 7, or to the steepest slopes in Imperial Bowl and Lake Chutes. Without hiking you can reach good open terrain on Peak 8 in Horseshoe and Contest bowls, where the snow is normally good.

We particularly liked the lightly wooded back bowls of Peak 8, accessed from the T-bar or Chair 6 – picturesque and not too steep. Steep black mogul fields lead further to the

## LIFT PASSES

**The Colorado Ticket**
Covers all Vail, Beaver Creek, Breckenridge and Keystone resorts, plus Arapahoe Basin.

**Main pass**
1 day $73
6 days $318

**Senior citizens**
Over 65: 6 days $286
Over 70: season pass $299

**Children**
Under 13: 6 days $180
Under 5: free pass

**Notes**
Half-day pass available. The Colorado ticket is available only to visitors who pre-book through a UK tour operator. It is not available at the ticket window in the resort. Prices quoted are regular season rates.

junction with Peak 9.

Peak 9's North Slope under Chair E has very steep blacks (so steep that we have never seen them retaining good snow). The double diamond Peak 9 chutes are reached by hiking up from the peak.

On Peak 10, at the edge of the area, is a network of interlinking steep mogul runs. To skier's left of the chair is a lovely, lightly wooded off-piste area called The Burn.

### FOR INTERMEDIATES
***Nice cruising, limited extent***

Breckenridge has some good blue cruising runs for all intermediates. The development of Peak 7 increased the intermediate terrain by 30%. But dedicated piste-bashers are still likely to find the runs short and limited in extent. Peak 9 has the easiest slopes. It is nearly all gentle, wide, blue runs at the top and almost flat, wide, green runs at the bottom. And the ski patrol enforces slow-speed skiing in narrow and crowded areas. Peak 10 has a couple of more challenging runs classified blue-black, such as Crystal and Centennial, which make for good fast cruising. Peaks 7 and 8 both have a choice of blues on trails cut close together in the trees. Adventurous intermediates will also like to try some of the high bowl runs).

### FOR BEGINNERS
***Excellent***

The bottom of Peak 9 has a big, virtually flat area and some good gentle nursery slopes. There's then a good choice of green runs to move on to. Beginners can try Peak 8 too, with another selection of green runs and a choice of trails back to town. Reporters praise the good-value beginner package which includes lessons, equipment rental and lift pass.

## boarding

*Breckenridge is pretty much ideal for all standards of boarder and hosts several major US snowboarding events. Beginners have ideal nursery slopes, easy greens to progress to and – if taking lessons – the opportunity to learn on a boarders-only slope, the Eldorado run, on Peak 9. There is also a boarders-only mini terrain-park and a warming hut. Intermediates have great cruising runs, all served by chairs. The powder bowls at the top of Peaks 7 and 8 make for great riding – unfortunately accessed only by an awkward T-bar, which does not. Boarders of all levels will enjoy the choice of excellent terrain-parks and half-pipes (see Terrain-parks). Nearby Arapahoe Basin is another area for hardcore boarding in steep bowls and chutes. Breckenridge pays homage to the early pioneers of the sport with a history of snowboarding display in the Vista Haus restaurant on Peak 8.*

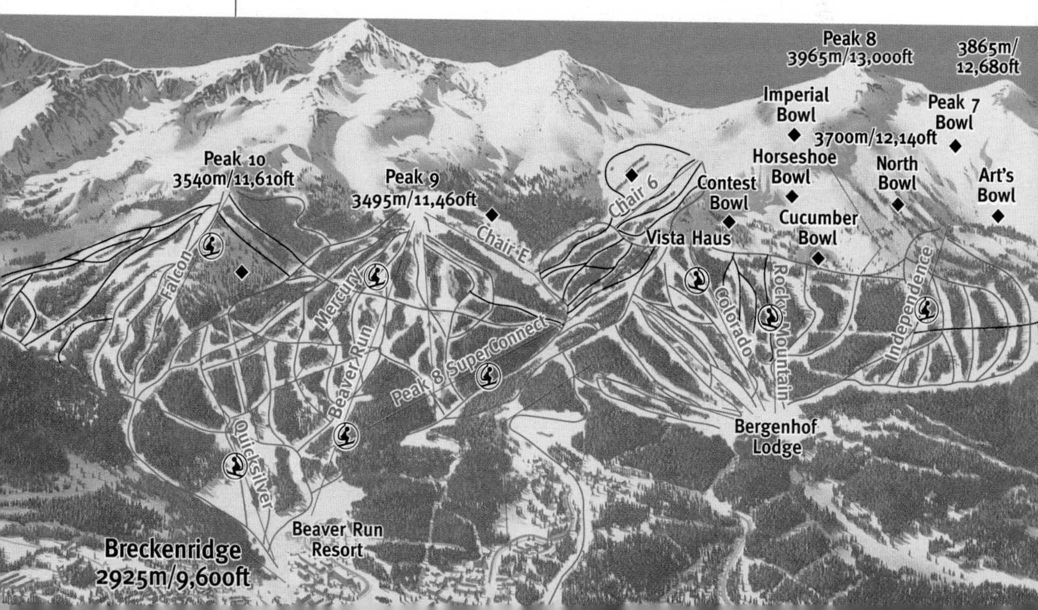

↑ Some of the lodgings are distant from the lift bases

VAIL RESORTS, INC / BOB WINSETT





## SCHOOLS

**Breckenridge**
t 453 3272
lrn2ski@vailresorts.com

**Classes**
Half day (2¼hr) $65

**Private lessons**
$140 for 1hr for up to 6 people.

## CHILDREN

**Children's Center, Peak 8**
t 453 3258

**Children's Center, Peak 9**
t 496 7449

Complex array of options for all-day care from 8.30 to 4.30 for children from age 2mnth – prior reservation essential

**Ski school**
For ages 3 to 12, 9.45 to 3.45 daily.

### FOR CROSS-COUNTRY
***Specialist centre in woods***

There are 50km/31 miles of groomed trails in total. Breckenridge's Nordic Center is prettily set in the woods between the town and Peak 8 (served by the shuttle-bus). It has 32km/20 miles of trails and 16km/10 miles of snow-shoeing trails. Other trails are located at the golf course.

### QUEUES
***Not normally a problem***

Breckenridge's eight high-speed chair-lifts make light work of peak-time crowds. Neither we nor our reporters have come across serious queues, except at exceptional times, such as President's Day weekend and on powder days – when the T-bar at Peak 8 can get crowded.

### MOUNTAIN RESTAURANTS
***Varied but nothing special***

Breckenridge is making an effort to improve on the standard US cafeterias: both Tenmile Station, where Peak 9 meets 10, and the Vista Haus at the top of Peak 8 are food-court operations. Border Burritos ('huge portions') is now located at Vista Haus.

### SCHOOLS AND GUIDES
***Excellent reports***

Our reporters are unanimous in their praise for the school: classes of five to eight (sometimes smaller), doing what the class, not the instructor, wants. Special clinics include bumps, telemark and powder.

### FACILITIES FOR CHILDREN
***Excellent facilities***

Every report on the children's school and nursery is full of plaudits. Typical comments: 'excellent, combining serious coaching with lots of fun', 'our boys loved it', 'so much more positive than ski schools in Europe'.

## STAYING THERE

### HOW TO GO
***Lots of choice***

A lot of tour operators feature Breckenridge.

**Chalets** Several tour operators have very comfortable chalets. A reporter described Whispering Pines (sold through Ski All America) as, 'an absolutely top notch place to stay'. Ski Independence's two traditional chalets look good – and we have been impressed by their efficiency.

**Hotels** There's a good choice of style and price range.

((((4) **Great Divide** (453 4500) Owned by Vail Resorts. Prime location, vast rooms. Pool, tubs.

((((4) **Lodge at Breckenridge** (453 9300) Stylish luxury spa resort set out of town among 32 acres, with great views. Private shuttle-bus. Pool, tubs.

((((4) **Little Mountain Lodge** (453 1969) Luxury B&B near ice rink.

(((3) **Beaver Run** (453 6000) Huge, resort complex with 520 spacious rooms. Great location, by one of the main lifts up Peak 9. Pool, hot-tubs.

(((3) **Williams House** (453 2975) Beautifully restored, charmingly furnished four-room B&B on Main St.

(((3) **Village** (547 5725) Central 3-star. 'Good value with spacious rooms,' says a recent visitor.

**Self-catering** There is a huge choice of condominiums, many set conveniently off the aptly named Four O'Clock run. There are lots of houses to rent, too.

### EATING OUT
***Over 100 restaurants***

There's a very wide range of eating places, from typical American food to 'fine dining'. The Breckenridge Dining Guide lists a full menu of most places.

The Brewery is famous for its enormous portions of 'appetisers' such as buffalo wings – as well as its

## GETTING THERE

**Air** Denver 167km/ 104 miles (2½hr).

## ACTIVITIES

**Indoor** Spas, theatre, museum, ice skating, recreation centre (pool, tubs, gym, tennis, climbing wall) on the outskirts of town – accessible by bus

**Outdoor** Horse-drawn sleigh rides, dog-sledding, fishing, snowmobiles, snow-shoeing, ice skating, hot-air balloon rides

**Phone numbers**
From distant parts of the US, add the prefix 1 970.
From abroad, add the prefix +1 970.

## TOURIST OFFICE

**t** 453 5000
breckguest@vailresorts.com
www.breckenridge.com

splendid brewed-on-the-spot beers – and is still 'the liveliest spot in town'.

Poirrier's at the Wellington and the sophisticated food at both Café Alpine and Pierre's Riverwalk Café have been recommended. Sushi Breck and Mi Casa (Mexican) have had good reviews as has the Kenosha steakhouse – 'specials at great prices'. The Hearthstone is said to do 'lovely food in good surroundings', the Blue River Bistro to offer 'a wide selection of food at affordable prices', and Bubba Gump Shrimp Company to have 'good food and exceptional service'. Michael's Italian is recommended for 'extensive menu, large portions and reasonable prices'. Rasta Pasta offers pasta dishes with a Jamaican twist. Two recent arrivals are Mountain Flying Fish (sushi) and Mrs E & Me (steaks).

### APRES-SKI
***The best in the area***

The Breckenridge Brewery, Tiffany's, Liquid Lounge, Fatty's and Sherpa & Yetti's are popular. The Gold Pan saloon dates from gold rush days, and is reputedly the oldest bar west of the Mississippi. Cecilia's serves good cocktails; Gracy O'Malleys is an Irish bar and Downstairs at Erics is a disco sports-bar. Mount Java is a relaxed cafe-bookshop with Internet access.

### OFF THE SLOPES
***Pleasant enough***

Breckenridge is a pleasant place to wander around with plenty of souvenir and gift shops. Silverthorne (about 30 minutes away) has excellent bargain factory outlet stores – 'well worth a visit' writes a reporter. It is easy to get around and visit other resorts.

### STAYING DOWN THE VALLEY
***Good for exploring the area***

Staying in Frisco makes sense for those touring around or on a tight budget. It's a small town with decent bars and restaurants. There are cheap motels, a couple of small hotels and some B&Bs; Hotel Frisco (668 5009) has been recommended.

VAIL RESORTS, INC

A cute town buried in powder – what could be better? ➔

# Copper Mountain

*Great terrain for all ability levels, above a born-again resort*

**COSTS**

(1)(2)(3)(4)(5)(6)

**RATINGS**

| **The slopes** | |
|---|---|
| Snow | ***** |
| Extent | ** |
| Expert | **** |
| Intermediate | **** |
| Beginner | **** |
| Convenience | **** |
| Queues | **** |
| Mountain restaurants | * |
| **The rest** | |
| Scenery | *** |
| Resort charm | ** |
| Off-slope | * |

**NEWS**

For 2003/04 the Cirque Lodge condo complex at Union Creek was opened, with two outdoor pools.

A new restaurant, Alexander's on the Creek, opened in the Village.

**KEY FACTS**

| | |
|---|---|
| **Resort** | 2955m 9,700ft |
| **Slopes** | 2955-3750m 9,700-12,300ft |
| **Lifts** | 23 |
| **Pistes** | 2,433 acres |
| **Green** | 21% |
| **Blue** | 25% |
| **Black** | 54% |
| **Snowmaking** | 380 acres |



- ➕ Convenient purpose-built resort, transformed by new owners Intrawest (of Whistler fame)
- ➕ Fair-sized mountain, with good runs for all abilities
- ➕ Several other good resorts nearby
- ➕ Few queues on weekdays, but ...

- ➖ Can be long lift queues at weekends
- ➖ Village still very limited
- ➖ Black-diamond bowls at the top offer only limited vertical
- ➖ Risk of altitude sickness for visitors coming straight from sea level
- ➖ One mediocre mountain restaurant

**Copper's slopes are some of Colorado's best, and now there's a much-improved village at the base. But expect weekend queues, and watch out for that altitude sickness; Copper's village is even higher than Breckenridge.**

## THE RESORT

Rather like the French resorts of the 1960s, Copper Mountain was originally high on convenience, low on charm. But its new owner, Intrawest, has done a typically thorough job with the new Village at Copper, a small group of wood-and-stone-clad condo buildings with shops, restaurants and car-free walkways and squares, forming the heart of the resort. There is also the separate East Village – with some accommodation and base lodge. A regular free shuttle-bus runs between these bases and the family skiing and beginners' area at Union Creek.

Keystone, Breckenridge and Arapahoe Basin are all nearby, and Vail is within an hour's drive.

## THE MOUNTAIN

The area is medium-sized by American standards, and has great runs for all ability levels, with an attractive mix of wooded, gladed and open slopes. Guided tours are available daily.

**Slopes** The area divides into slopes below Copper Peak and below Union Peak, with fast quads towards each from the main base area. Between the two is Union Bowl, and on the back of the hill are the high Spaulding and

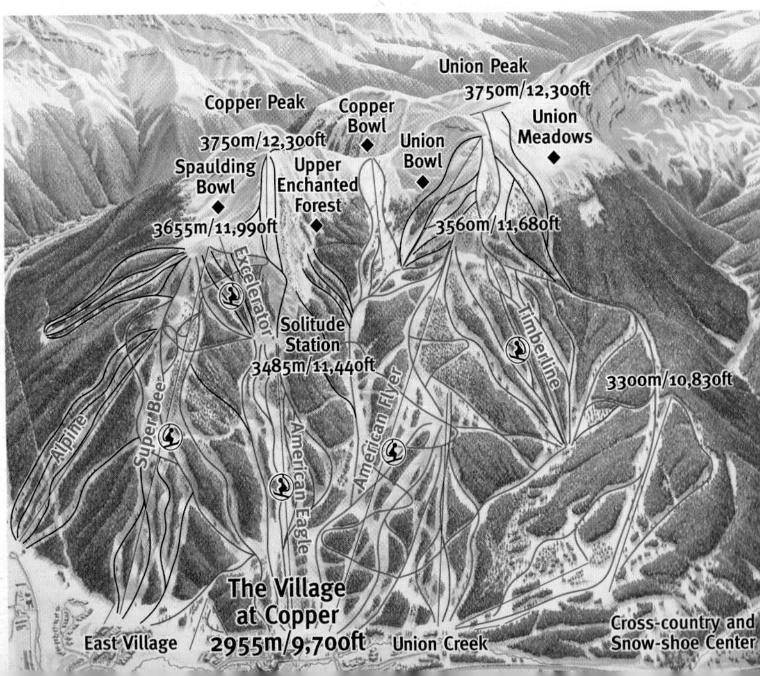

Copper Bowls – open slopes, in contrast to the wooded lower runs.

**Terrain-parks** There are three. The main park is beside the American Flyer chair and has areas for beginners, intermediates and experts, plus a super-pipe and 62m/100ft rail. There's also a special kid's park, and a park for experts, with big jumps.

**Snow reliability** Height and extensive snowmaking give Copper an early opening date and excellent reliability. Snowfall averages 280in a year.

**Experts** There is a lot of good expert terrain. Spaulding and Copper bowls offer gradients ranging from moderate to seriously steep, but with limited vertical. The wooded bump runs lower down are much longer.

**Intermediates** There are runs to suit everyone, from top-to-bottom greens on the right of the map through similarly long blues to easy black runs in various sectors.

**Beginners** The nursery slopes are excellent, and there are plenty of very easy green runs to graduate to.

**Snowboarding** There are great slopes for all abilities, plus three terrain-parks.

**Cross-country** There are 25km/15 miles of trails through the White River forest.

**Queues** On weekdays you may find no queues, but weekend visitors pour in from Denver and cause 20-minute queues. You can buy a (pricey) Beeline Advantage pass to jump the queues.

**Mountain restaurants** Grim. The only place worth considering is a food court at Solitude Station.

**Schools and guides** The school offers a wide variety of courses and has a fine reputation, especially for children.

**Facilities for children** The Belly Button childcare facility takes children from two months old and ski school takes children from age three. On the mountain, there are dedicated fun trails and a special kid's map.

## STAYING THERE

**How to go** A number of tour operators offer packages to Copper.

**Hotels and condos** There are no hotels but some condos are splendidly luxurious, with outdoor hot-tubs, etc.

**Eating out** The new Alexander's on the Creek does excellent sophisticated food. Blue Moose pizza, Endo's and JJ's Rocky Mountain Tavern are popular. Sleigh rides take people out to Western-style dinners in tents.

**Après-ski** Après-ski is lively as the lifts close. Later on, Endo's Adrenaline cafe and JJ's Rocky Mountain Tavern (with live music) are popular. Pravda is a Russian-style club and Larkin's Cross a traditional Irish pub. McGillycuddy's is a new Irish bar, with live music.

**Off the slopes** There's a fine sports club, with a huge pool and indoor tennis, and ice skating on the lake.

**Central reservations**
Call 968 2882.
Toll-free number (from within the US) 1 888 263 5302.

**Phone numbers**
From distant parts of the US, add the prefix 1 970.
From abroad, add the prefix +1 970.

### TOURIST OFFICE

t 968 2882
copper-marketing@coppercolorado.com
www.coppercolorado.com

SNOWPIX.COM / CHRIS GILL

Union Bowl – with gradients from green to double-black – and sunny Copper Bowl on the left ➔

KEYSTONE / BEN BLANKENBURG

# Keystone

*For those who want a peaceful, quiet, pampered time*

## COSTS

①②③④⑤⑥

## RATINGS

| **The slopes** | |
|---|---|
| Snow | ***** |
| Extent | ** |
| Expert | *** |
| Intermediate | **** |
| Beginner | **** |
| Convenience | ** |
| Queues | **** |
| Mountain restaurants | *** |
| **The rest** | |
| Scenery | *** |
| Resort charm | ** |
| Off-slope | ** |

## NEWS

During the 2003/04 Keystone gained permission to expand its terrain by 860 acres by operating snow cats to access Erickson Bowl and Little Bowl, beyond The Outback.

For 2003/04 the terrain-park moved to a new spot (where it has its own chair-lift) and trebled in size.



- + Good mountain for everyone but the double-diamond diehard
- + Huge night-skiing operation
- + Other nearby resorts on lift pass
- + Luxurious condominiums

- − Very scattered resort, with a lot of bussing or driving for most visitors, and no village atmosphere except in small River Run development
- − Risk of altitude sickness for visitors coming straight from sea level

**Keystone's slopes are impressive from many points of view, but there isn't a proper village at the foot of them. Luxurious condos are scattered over a wide area, and the nearest thing to a 'village' is the limited River Run development. We prefer to stay elsewhere and visit Keystone's slopes for a day.**

## THE RESORT

Keystone is a sprawling resort of condominiums spread around a partly wooded valley floor. It has no clear centre and is divided into seven 'neighborhoods'. Some are little more than groups of condos, while others have shops, restaurants and bars (though no supermarkets or liquor stores – they are on the main highway).

River Run, at the base of the main gondola, is the nearest thing to a conventional ski resort village, with condo buildings, a short main street, a square and a few restaurants, bars and shops. A second lift base area half a mile to the west, Mountain House, is much less of a village. Another mile west is Keystone Village, which is not a village at all but a hotel and condo complex, weirdly lacking animation, beside a lake – a huge natural ice rink.

Buses link all the component parts. At weekends, overflow parking lots come into operation and the bus services become overstretched.

SNOWPIX.COM / CHRIS GILL

The resort spreads widely across the valley floor ↓

## THE MOUNTAINS

By US standards Keystone offers extensive intermediate slopes and some challenging steeper stuff, further expanded this year with the opening of Erickson and Little Bowls. The resort is owned by Vail Resorts, and the lift pass covers Vail, Beaver Creek, Breckenridge and Arapahoe Basin (a few minutes away by road). Copper Mountain is also nearby.

**Slopes** Three wooded mountains form Keystone's local slopes. Lifts depart from Mountain House and River Run to the one above the resort, now named Dercum Mountain. The front face of the mountain has Keystone's biggest network of lifts and runs by far, mainly of easy and intermediate gradient. From the top you can drop over the back down to Keystone Gulch, where there are lifts back on to the next hill, North Peak. Or you can ride the Outpost gondola directly to the shoulder of North Peak. Beyond North Peak is the third peak, The Outback. Keystone has the biggest floodlit skiing operation in the US, covering Dercum Mountain top to bottom up to 8pm on certain nights of the week.

**Terrain-parks** The terrain-park was moved to a new location for 2003/04 – and trebled in size, with features for all levels including a half-pipe and super-pipe. The park has its own chair-lift, and is floodlit several nights a week.

**Snow reliability** Shortage of snow is rarely a problem, and Keystone has one of the world's biggest snowmaking systems.

**Experts** Keystone has a lot of steeper, ungroomed terrain. The Windows is a 60-acre area of experts-only glade runs

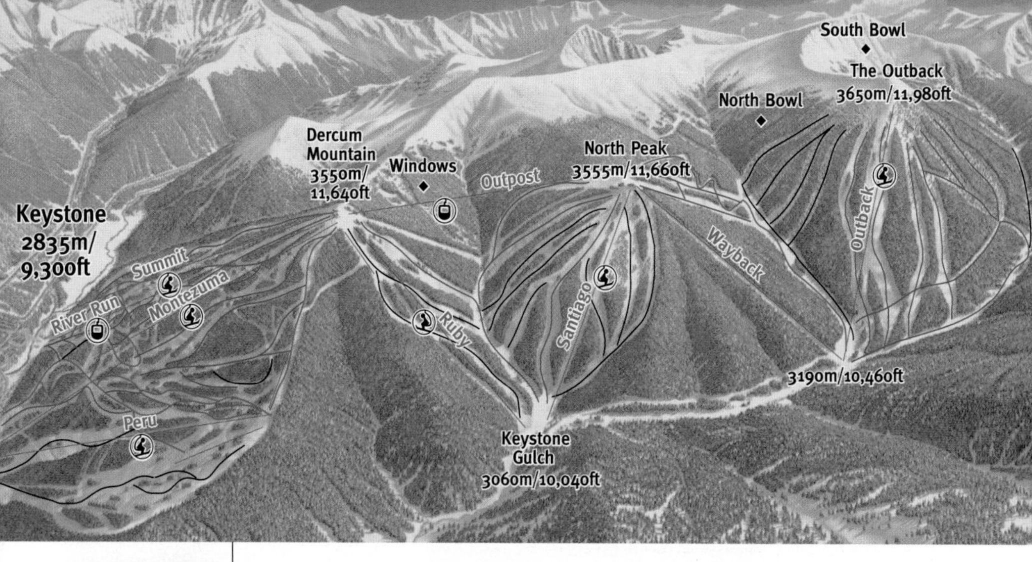


## KEY FACTS

| | |
|---|---|
| **Resort** | 2835m<br>9,300ft |
| **Slopes** | 2835-3650m<br>9,300-11,980ft |
| **Lifts** | 20 |
| **Pistes** | 1,860 acres |
| **Green** | 12% |
| **Blue** | 29% |
| **Black** | 59% |
| **Snowmaking** | 956 acres |

Skiable area excludes terrain accessed by snowcats not covered by lift pass

## REPORTS WANTED

Recently we have had few reports on this resort. If you go there, please do send us a report.

**Central reservations phone number**
1 800 427 8308
(toll free from within the US).

**Phone numbers**
From distant parts of the US, add the prefix 1 970.
From abroad, add the prefix +1 970.

## TOURIST OFFICE

**t** 496 2316
keystoneinfo@vailresorts.com
www.keystoneresort.com

on Dercum Mountain's back side. From The Outback there are black runs with all sorts of challenges, route-finding being one of them. You can access open and glade runs in the North and South Bowls. The newly opened Erickson Bowl and Little Bowl add more terrain, but you pay extra for the snowcat access and guidance.

**Intermediates** Keystone is ideal. The front face of Dercum Mountain itself is a network of beautifully groomed blue and green runs through the trees. The Outback and North Peak also have easy cruising blues. Some of the blacks are groomed, and are tremendous fun early in the day.

**Beginners** There are good nursery slopes at the top and bottom of Dercum Mountain, although a reporter found the area at the top rather 'disorganised' and a 'little daunting' for novices arriving from the gondola. There are excellent long green runs to progress to.

**Snowboarding** Keystone is ideal for beginners and intermediates, with mainly chair-lifts and gondolas, good beginner areas and cruising runs. Expert riders will love The Outback.

**Cross-country** There are 16km/10 miles of groomed trails and 50km/31 miles of unprepared trails.

**Queues** Except at the morning peak, there are few queues and the trails are usually beautifully quiet, except for Mozart, the only blue run down from Dercum Mountain to North Peak.

**Mountain restaurants** The table-service Alpenglow Stube (North Peak) is a delightfully cosseting place, and one of our favourites in the US: the fixed-price lunch is a bargain at about $20. The alternatives, at the top of Dercum and at the lift base between the two hills, are not appealing.

**Schools and guides** As well as the normal lessons, there are bumps, race and various other advanced classes. A 2004 reporter enjoyed 'excellent' instruction in very small groups.

**Facilities for children** These are excellent, with programmes tailored to specific age groups. Children have their own teaching areas. Kids' nights out are also organised.

## STAYING THERE

**How to go** Regular shuttles operate from Denver airport. Most accommodation is in condominiums.

**Hotels** There isn't a great choice but they're all of a high standard.

**Self-catering** All the condominiums are large and luxurious – and we've stayed in some fabulous ones.

**Eating out** Disappointing: the restaurants are scattered around, and there isn't the range of mid-market restaurants that makes eating out such a pleasure in many American resorts. You can eat up the mountain at the Summit House or Alpenglow Stube.

**Après-ski** The Summit House has live music and caters for night skiing customers too. But this is not the resort for late-night revellers.

**Off the slopes** There are plenty of activities, including skating on the frozen lake, tubing and indoor tennis. Silverthorne has a leisure centre and swimming pool as well as the factory outlet shopping.

ASPEN/SNOWMASS PICTURE LIBRARY

# Snowmass

*Aspen's modern satellite – with impressively varied and extensive slopes*

## COSTS

①②③④⑤⑥

## RATINGS

**The slopes**

| | |
|---|---|
| Snow | ***** |
| Extent | **** |
| Expert | ***** |
| Intermediate | ***** |
| Beginner | ***** |
| Convenience | **** |
| Queues | **** |
| Mountain restaurants | *** |

**The rest**

| | |
|---|---|
| Scenery | **** |
| Resort charm | ** |
| Off-slope | *** |

Our extent rating relates to the whole Aspen-Snowmass area. Snowmass alone rates ***

## NEWS

There are plans for a new base village to be built in collaboration with the famous Intrawest corporation.

## KEY FACTS

| | |
|---|---|
| **Resort** | 2565m 8,420ft |
| Snowmass | |
| **Slopes** | 2470-3815m 8,100-12,510ft |
| **Lifts** | 21 |
| **Pistes** | 3,010 acres |
| **Green** | 7% |
| **Blue** | 55% |
| **Black** | 38% |
| **Snowmaking** | 180 acres |
| Aspen + Snowmass | |
| **Slopes** | 2400-3815m 7,870-12,510ft |
| **Lifts** | 40 |
| **Pistes** | 4,900 acres |
| **Green** | 10% |
| **Blue** | 48% |
| **Black** | 42% |
| **Snowmaking** | 608 acres |



- ＋ Big, varied mountain with a vertical of 1340m/4,400ft – biggest in the US
- ＋ Aspen's three mountains also accessible by frequent free bus
- ＋ Uncrowded slopes
- ＋ Lots of slope-side lodgings

- − Snowmass 'village' offers very limited shopping and nightlife
- − Diversions of Aspen town are a bus-ride away

**The slopes of Snowmass are a key part of the attraction of nearby Aspen as a destination. Whether Snowmass makes sense as a base depends on what's more important to you: great bars and restaurants, or great nursery slopes and green runs on your doorstep. For many families, the choice is clear.**

## THE RESORT

Snowmass is a modern, purpose-built resort with most of the accommodation in low-rise buildings set alongside the gentle home slope. At the heart of these buildings is Snowmass Village Mall, with a small cluster of shops and restaurants. There are also lots of private homes set along roads that wind up into the lower slopes.

The Mall contains the essentials of resort life, but not much more. There are plans to build a new base village which would make the place a more rounded resort, with a broader appeal.

Aspen is some 12 miles away, its Highlands and Buttermilk mountains slightly less. Efficient free bus services link the resorts and mountains. The service to Aspen town runs to 1am.

## THE MOUNTAIN

Snowmass has over 60% of the total acreage covered by the Aspen ski pass – it is almost five miles across, and has the biggest vertical in the US. Many of the Snowmass runs are wide, sweeping cruisers. But it also has some of the toughest terrain in the Aspen portfolio. Most of the slopes are in the forest, but the higher ones are open or only lightly wooded.

**Slopes** Chair-lifts fan out from the purpose-built village at the base towards four linked sectors – Elk Camp, High Alpine, Big Burn and Sam's Knob. There is also access from Two Creeks, which is much nearer to Aspen town and has free slope-side parking.

**Terrain-parks** The Snowmass Pipeline terrain-park is now 2.5km/1.5 miles long and incorporates a 90m/300ft long half-pipe. A new rail yard was added for 2003/04. There are also separate parks for beginners and kids

**Snow reliability** With 300 inches a year plus snowmaking, it's good.

**Experts** Our favourite area is around the Hanging Valley Wall and Glades – beautiful scenery and wonderful tree-covered slopes, and steep enough everywhere to satisfy the keenest. The other seriously steep area is the Cirque. The Cirque drag-lift takes you well above the tree line to Aspen's highest point. From here, the Headwall is not terrifyingly steep, but there are also narrow, often rocky, chutes – Gowdy's is one of the steepest in the whole area. All these runs funnel into a pretty, lightly wooded valley. Consider joining a guided group as an introduction to the best of Snowmass.

**Intermediates** Snowmass is the best mountain in the Aspen area for intermediates. The Big Burn is a cruising paradise – a huge, lightly wooded area with a satisfying variety of terrain, including the Powerline Glades for the adventurous. The easiest intermediate slopes are from the Elk Camp lift all the way down to Two Creeks. Long Shot is a glorious, ungroomed, 5km/3 mile run, lost in the forest, and well worth the short hike up to get to the start. In the centre of the area, the two chair-lifts below High Alpine serve yet more intermediate slopes – a little trickier and more varied. The Sam's Knob sector offers slightly more challenge, including some regularly groomed single-black runs. And Green Cabin, from the High Alpine lift, is a magical top-to-bottom cruise.

## REPORTS WANTED

Recently we have had few reports on this resort. If you go there, please do send us a report.

The best reports earn a copy of the next edition, and can lead to free lift passes in future.

See page 10.

**Phone numbers**
From distant parts of the US, add the prefix 1 970.
From abroad, add the prefix +1 970.

## TOURIST OFFICE

**t** 925 1220
intlres@skiaspen.com
www.aspensnowmass.com

**Beginners** In the heart of the resort is a broad, gentle beginners' run. An even easier slope is the wide Assay Hill, at the bottom of Elk Camp. From Sam's Knob there are long, gentle cruises leading back to the resort.
**Snowboarding** A great mountain, whatever your inclination.
**Cross-country** Excellent trails between here and Aspen – see Aspen chapter.
**Queues** Snowmass has so many alternative lifts and runs that you can normally avoid problems. Some long, slow chairs can be cold in mid-winter. The home slope gets very crowded.
**Mountain restaurants** There are refuelling stops at several key points, but also some places worth seeking out. Gwyn's High Alpine is an elegant table-service restaurant serving above-average food. The best views are from Sam's Knob, with self-service and table-service restaurants. Cafe Suzanne on Elk Camp has a French flavour and does 'exceptionally good crêpes'.
**Schools and guides** A 2004 reporter had three rewarding days, but warns that the advertised off-piste groups turned out to be just standard school classes, which will go off-piste only if the whole group is up to it.
**Facilities for children** We lack recent reports, but the facilities for kids here look good to us. Above the village is a special Family Zone with special fun trails, race course and terrain park.

## STAYING THERE

**How to go** Most accommodation is self-catering.
**Hotels** The focal hotel is the Silvertree (923 3520) – an ocean liner parked next to the home slope and the Mall. Excellent top-floor Brothers' Grille restaurant; pools. Stonebridge Inn (923 2420) is a good-value alternative; nice restaurant, pool, hot-tub.
**Self-catering** Lots of condos close to the slopes.
**Eating out** The choice is adequate. As well as the excellent Brothers' Grille and a nearby steakhouse there are Italian, Tex-Mex, Provençal and 'pan-Asian' restaurants. The Blue Door (below) does Cajun food.
**Après-ski** The Cirque next to the home slope has live bands most days. The restaurants (above) have bars – the Margarita keeps 30 tequilas. The Blue Door is a new nightclub, sometimes offering live music.
**Off the slopes** Diversions include tubing on Assay Hill 1pm to 8pm, snow-shoe trails, nature tours, piste basher rides, paintball, dog-sled rides.

Elk Camp
3450m/11,320ft
High Alpine
3590m
The Cirque
3815m/12,510ft
Big Burn
3610m/11,830ft
Hanging Valley
Sam's Knob
3240m/10,630ft
Elk Camp
Alpine Springs
Big Burn
Sam's Knob
Cafe Suzanne
Ullrhof
3005m
Coney Glade
Two Creeks
Fanny Hill
Snowmass
2565m/8,420ft
Two Creeks
2470m/8,100ft

STEAMBOAT / LARRY PIERCE

# Steamboat

*Where they invented the term Champagne Powder™*

## COSTS

①②③④⑤⑥

## RATINGS

**The slopes**

| | |
|---|---|
| Snow | **** |
| Extent | *** |
| Expert | *** |
| Intermediate | **** |
| Beginner | ***** |
| Convenience | *** |
| Queues | **** |
| Mountain restaurants | *** |

**The rest**

| | |
|---|---|
| Scenery | *** |
| Resort charm | ** |
| Off-slope | ** |

## NEWS

For 2004/05 a new triple chair will replace the old Burgess Creek double. It will be the first new lift in the resort for six years.

$1.8 million is being invested to give the Gondola Square area a major revamp.



STEAMBOAT / LARRY PIERCE

The terrain looks gentle, but it includes some challenging slopes ↓

- + Excellent easy runs
- + Famed for its gladed powder terrain
- + Good snow record
- + Table-service mountain restaurants
- + Plenty of slope-side lodging
- + Town has some Western character

- − Town is a drive from the slopes
- − Modern base 'village' is sprawling, with some eyesore buildings
- − Not enough runs to amuse keen intermediates for a week
- − Not a huge amount of double-black terrain – some of it is a hike away

**Sadly, there is very little of the Wild West about Steamboat's base village – and the 'cattle town' of Steamboat Springs doesn't merit more than the occasional excursion. The mountain may not match some of its competitors for extent, but it's one of the best for powder fun among the trees.**

## THE RESORT

The resort village is a 10-minute bus-ride from the old town of Steamboat Springs. Near the gondola there are a few shop- and restaurant-lined multi-level squares, some of which will receive a much-needed face-lift over the next few years. Some lodgings are up the sides of the piste, but the resort also sprawls across the valley. The old town can be a bit of a disappointment. It may be a working cattle town, but the Wild West isn't much in evidence. The wide main street is lined with bars, hotels and shops in a mixture of styles, from old wooden buildings to concrete plazas.

## THE MOUNTAINS

Steamboat's slopes are prettily set among trees, with extensive views over rolling hills and the wide Yampa valley. The place is relatively isolated, but you could combine it with resorts west of Denver, from Winter Park to Vail.

**Slopes** The slopes can be divided into five sectors. The gondola from the village rises to the low peak of Thunderhead. Beyond it are lifts on the twin heights Storm Peak and Sunshine Peak. On the back of the hill is the Morningside Park area, with a lift up to the top height of Mt Werner also accessing some of the highest runs on the front side. Below these is an area served by the Pony Express chair.

**Terrain-parks** The Bashor lift serves the SoBe terrain-park, with rails, jumps and mini-pipe, and the Mavericks super-pipe, claimed to be the longest in North America. Beehive is a special park for the kids. Park and Pipe clinics can help you on your way.

**Snow reliability** Steamboat is low for Colorado but it has an excellent snow record with a 10-year annual average of 335 inches. The term Champagne Powder™ was invented here. There is snowmaking from top to bottom, too.

**Experts** The main attraction is the challenging terrain in the glades. A great area is on Sunshine Peak below the Sundown chair. Morningside Park and Pioneer Ridge also have excellent gladed runs. Three steep chutes are easily accessed via the lift back from Morningside, and a short hike gets you to the tree skiing of Christmas Tree Bowl. For bumps, try the series of runs off Four Points.

**Intermediates** Much of the mountain is ideal, with long cruising blue runs. Morningside Park is a great area for easy black as well as blue slopes. The

## KEY FACTS

| | |
|---|---|
| Resort | 2100m<br>6,900ft |
| Slopes | 2100-3220m<br>6,900-10,570ft |
| Lifts | 20 |
| Pistes | 2,939 acres |
| Green | 13% |
| Blue | 56% |
| Black | 31% |
| Snow-guns | 438 acres |

## REPORTS WANTED

Recently we have had few reports on this resort. If you go there, please do send us a report.

**Central reservations phone number**
1 800 922 2722 (toll free in the US).

**Phone numbers**
Calling long-distance, add the prefix 1 970. From abroad, add the prefix +1 970.

## TOURIST OFFICE

**t** 879 0740
info@steamboat.com
www.steamboat.com

Sunshine area is very gentle. Keen intermediates will find the area is limited in extent.

**Beginners** There's a big nursery area at the base of the mountain, with a variety of gentle greens to progress to.

**Snowboarding** There's a special learning area, gentle slopes to progress to and you can get around using chair-lifts and the gondola. For experienced riders, riding the glades in fresh powder is unbeatable.

**Cross-country** A free shuttle service takes you to 30km/20 miles of groomed tracks at the Touring Center.

**Queues** Queues form for the gondola first thing, but they move quickly; the slow Sunshine lift can be crowded. Noticeboards indicate waiting times.

**Mountain restaurants** There are food courts and table-service restaurants at both Thunderhead and Rendezvous Saddle – much better than the American fast-food norm.

**Schools and guides** Reports are very positive. 'Very good indeed ... even by the standards of the USA,' enthused a couple who had separate lessons.

**Facilities for children** Arrangements are exceptional, including evening entertainment. Kids under 12 ski free with a parent or grandparent buying a pass for at least five days.

## STAYING THERE

**How to go** A fair number of UK tour operators feature Steamboat.

**Chalets** There are some catered chalets run by UK tour operators.

**Hotels** There are smart hotels at the resort, more characterful ones in town. The Rabbit Ears Motel (879 1150) has been recommended.

**Self-catering** There are countless condos, many with good pool/tub facilities, all on a free bus route. Ski Inn Condos at the base of the gondola have been recommended.

**Eating out** There are over 70 bars and restaurants. Pick up a dining guide booklet to check out the menus. You can dine in three restaurants up the mountain. In downtown Steamboat Springs try the Apogee for French-style food, Old West Steakhouse, or the Cottonwood Grill for its 'fabulously tasty Pacific Rim cuisine'. For a budget meal, head for Double Z.

**Après-ski** The old town is quiet in the evening – the base lodge area is livelier. At close of play the Slopeside Grill is popular or you could try the Bear River Bar with its comedy club.

**Off the slopes** Getting to Thunderhead restaurant complex is easy for pedestrians. Visiting town is, too.

The yellow line shows the Pioneer Ridge Expansion area. In the long term 500 acres are due to be developed and another lift installed.

TELLURIDE SKI & GOLF CO. / DOUG BERRY

# Telluride

*One of the best Colorado has to offer, in every respect except size*

**COSTS**

(1)(2)(3)(4)(5)(6)

**RATINGS**

| **The slopes** | |
|---|---|
| Snow | **** |
| Extent | ** |
| Expert | **** |
| Intermediate | *** |
| Beginner | ***** |
| Convenience | **** |
| Queues | ***** |
| Mountain restaurants | * |
| **The rest** | |
| Scenery | **** |
| Resort charm | **** |
| Off-slope | ** |

**NEWS**

For 2003/04 the Air Garden terrain-park trebled in size and new features were added. Unconfirmed plans for 2004/05 are to add a new super-pipe and offer guided backcountry tours.



- + Charming restored Victorian mining town with a Wild West atmosphere
- + Slopes for all, including experts
- + Dramatic, craggy mountain scenery – unusual for Colorado

- – Isolated location
- – Despite expansion, still a small area
- – Mountain Village a little quiet
- – Limited mountain restaurants

**We love the old town of Telluride and always enjoy its scenic, varied slopes; but their limited extent makes the place difficult to recommend for a holiday except in combination with another resort – which means travelling some distance.**

## THE RESORT

Telluride is an isolated resort in south-west Colorado. The town first boomed when gold was found – and Butch Cassidy robbed his first bank here. The town's old red-brick and timber buildings have been well restored, and it has more Wild West charm than any other resort. Shops and restaurants have gone decidedly up-market since its 'hippy' days of a few years ago and a lot of celebrities have plush holiday-homes in the area now. But Telluride is still friendly and small-scale. On the slopes, the Mountain Village is a development of lavish modern condos and hotels. A gondola links the town and village and runs until midnight.

## THE MOUNTAINS

There is something for everyone here.

**Slopes** Two chair-lifts and a gondola serve steep wooded slopes above the town, and access the bowl beyond which leads down to Mountain Village. This bowl is almost all wooded, with steep open slopes at the very top.

**Terrain-parks** The huge, 10-acre Sprite Air Garden terrain-park above the Mountain Village has a big half-pipe and all the features you could dream of. There are also two separate Freestyle Terrain areas to pull tricks in and Ute Park is suitable for beginners.

**Snow reliability** With an average of 309 inches of snow a year and some snowmaking, reliability is good, but there have been some slow starts to recent seasons.

**Experts** The double-black bump runs are well-known tests, and there are steep gladed runs from all along the ridge between Giuseppe's and Gold Hill – no longer a hike, thanks to the Gold Hill lift. Gold Hill has some truly challenging terrain, from wide open steeps to narrow chutes and gnarly wooded trails. Helitrax claims to be Colorado's only heli-skiing operation.

**Intermediates** There are ideal blue cruising runs with awesome views from the top down to Mountain Village (including the aptly-named See Forever). Some of the blacks above the town get groomed – worth catching if you can. Prospect Bowl, opened in 2001, added a lot of good intermediate terrain, with dozens of rolling pitches that meander and weave their way through thickets of trees – a very relaxing and pretty area. Even so, keen piste-bashers could get bored after a couple of days.

**Beginners** There are ideal runs in the Meadows below Mountain Village, and

## KEY FACTS

| | |
|---|---|
| Resort | 2665m<br>8,750ft |
| Slopes | 2665-3735m<br>8,750-12,260ft |
| Lifts | 16 |
| Pistes | 1,700 acres |
| Green | 24% |
| Blue | 38% |
| Black | 38% |
| Snowmaking | 204 acres |

**Central reservations**
Call 728 7507.
Toll-free number (from within the US) 1 888 827 8050.

**Phone numbers**
From distant parts of the US, add the prefix 1 970.
From abroad, add the prefix +1 970.

## TOURIST OFFICE

**t** 728 3041
skitelluride@telski.com
www.telski.com

## REPORTS WANTED

Recently we have had few reports on this resort. If you go there, please do send us a report.

The best reports earn a copy of the next edition, and can lead to free lift passes in future.

See page 10.

splendid long greens and blues served by the Sunshine fast chair.
**Snowboarding** The lift system means it is easy to get about, and the huge terrain-park offers plenty of scope.
**Cross-country** The beauty of the area makes it splendid for cross-country – both in the valley and at altitude – there are 10km/6miles of trails at the wonderfully elevated Topaten Centre.
**Queues** These are rarely a problem.
**Mountain restaurants** Gorrono Ranch is the main on-mountain restaurant, with a big terrace, live music and a BBQ. There are a couple of snack shacks higher up, with great views. Allred's, a civilised table-service place at St Sophia gondola station, is meant to be members only – but there's no harm in asking if they can squeeze you in.
**Schools and guides** The resort is proud of its Telluride Teaching System. Bump clinics are a speciality.
**Facilities for children** The Adventure Club provides indoor and outdoor play before and after children's lessons. The Mountain Village Activity Center has a nursery for toddlers.

## STAYING THERE

Telluride is tricky to get to from the UK, involving two or three flights or a long 335-mile drive from Denver.
**How to go** Packages fly into nearby Montrose or the tiny Telluride airport (prone to closure by the weather).
**Hotels** Hotel Columbia is luxurious, as is the plush yet friendly Camel's Garden Hotel and Spa. The New Sheridan is actually old – a Main Street USA classic, and comfortable too. The Wyndham Peaks Resort in the Mountain Village is enormous but has a spectacular lounge area and impressive spa facilities.
**Self-catering** There are plenty of condos. The Inn At Lost Creek in Mountain Village is the most lavish of the self-catering options.
**Eating out** The Cosmopolitan in the Hotel Columbia is renowned as the best in town. Other sophisticated options include the Marmotte and Harmon's (in the old station). Allred's at the top of the gondola is open for gourmet dining in the evenings.
**Après-ski** There's a lively bar-based après-ski scene. The West End Tavern has replaced Leimgruber's. The New Sheridan has a lovely old bar. The Last Dollar has been recommended by locals. The Fly Me to the Moon Saloon has live music and stays open late. There's a swanky candlelit lounge called the Noir Bar attached to the Blue Point Restaurant. There are often concerts at the historic Sheridan Opera House. The Nugget Theatre shows latest cinema releases. Thrill Hill at the Mountain Village has floodlit tubing, sledding and snowbiking.
**Off the slopes** There's quite a lot to do around town if you are not skiing or boarding, such as dog sledding, horse riding, snow-shoeing, ice skating, and glider rides. The Golden Door Spa in the Wyndham Peaks Resort was voted one of the top 10 spas in the world by *Condé Nast Traveller* readers.

← The lower black runs give great views of the town below. This run, Cat's Paw, gets much steeper lower down

SNOWPIX.COM / CHRIS GILL

# Vail

*Luxury living, high prices and the US's biggest single ski area*

**COSTS**

(1)(2)(3)(4)(5)(6)

**RATINGS**

| **The slopes** | |
|---|---|
| Snow | ***** |
| Extent | **** |
| Expert | **** |
| Intermediate | ***** |
| Beginner | *** |
| Convenience | *** |
| Queues | ** |
| Mountain restaurants | ** |
| **The rest** | |
| Scenery | *** |
| Resort charm | *** |
| Off-slope | *** |

**NEWS**

For 2004/05 a yurt will be built at Two Elk, providing additional seating for the children's ski school and for picnic lunches. Snowmaking will be improved on eastern areas of Golden Peak.

At Lionshead, future plans include a luxury hotel complex and a pedestrian-friendly plaza with shops, restaurants and outdoor ice rink.

In 2003/04 a moving carpet was added to the beginners' area at Eagle's Nest. And there were two new terrain-parks.



- + Biggest area in the US – great for confident intermediates, especially
- + The Back Bowls are big areas of treeless terrain – unusual in the US
- + Fabulous area of ungroomed, wooded slopes at Blue Sky Basin
- + Largely traffic-free resort centres, very pleasant in parts – but ...

- − Resort as a whole is a vast sprawl, and Lionshead is a dreary mess
- − Slopes can be crowded by American standards, with some lift queues even in low season
- − Blue Sky Basin and the Back Bowls may not be open in early season; warm weather can close the Bowls
- − Inadequate mountain restaurants
- − Expensive

**Blue Sky Basin, an area of shady, wooded, largely ungroomed slopes, has transformed Vail's attraction for good skiers and riders. Not only does it bring a much-needed bit of spice to the resort, but it gets you away from the crowds that are Vail's most serious drawback.**

**Vail's slopes are undeniably compelling, especially when you take account of nearby sister-resort Beaver Creek (see separate chapter). What continues to push Vail down our American shortlist are its style and its atmosphere – a curious mixture of pseudo-Tirol and sprawling, anonymous suburbs. The resort works well, largely thanks to the efficient buses. But if you hope to be captivated, Vail can't compete with the distinctive Rockies resorts based on old mining or cowboy towns. If we're going that far West, we like it to be a bit Wild.**

## THE RESORT

Standing in the centre of Vail Village, surrounded by chalets and bierkellers, you could be forgiven for thinking you were in the Tirol – which is what Vail's founder, Pete Seibert, intended back in the 1950s. But Vail Village is now just part of an enormous resort, mostly built in anonymous modern style, stretching for miles beside the I-70 freeway running west from Denver.

The vast village benefits from a free and efficient bus service, which makes choice of location less than crucial. But there's no denying that the most convenient – and expensive – places to stay are in mock-Tirolean Vail Village, near the Vista Bahn fast chair, or in functional Lionshead, near the gondola – a much less attractive area that really needs the revamp that is now being planned for it. There is a lot of accommodation further out – the cheapest tends to be across I-70.

Beaver Creek, ten miles away, is covered by the lift pass and is easily reached by bus (see separate chapter). A short drive gets you to Breckenridge and Keystone (both owned by Vail Resorts and covered by the lift pass), and Copper Mountain.

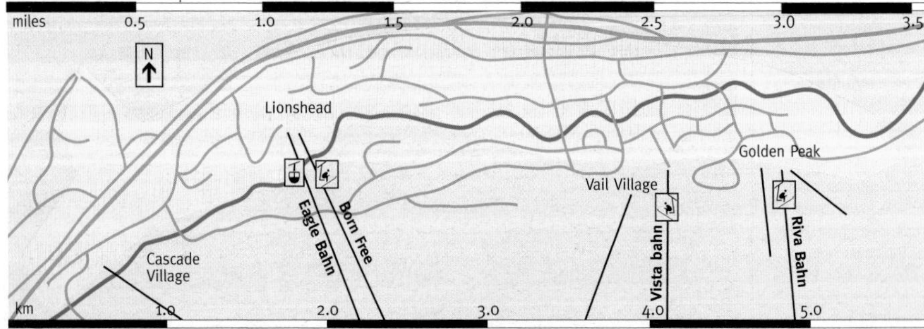

↑ Game Creek bowl tends to be less busy than the front face of the mountain, and has excellent terrain for intermediates. The chalet just off the trail is a restaurant, open to the public only for dinner

SNOWPIX.COM / CHRIS GILL

## KEY FACTS

| | |
|---|---|
| **Resort** | 2500m<br>8,200ft |
| **Slopes** | 2475-3525m<br>8,120-11,570ft |
| **Lifts** | 34 |
| **Pistes** | 5,289 acres |
| **Green** | 18% |
| **Blue** | 29% |
| **Black** | 53% |
| **Snowmaking** | 390 acres |

## THE MOUNTAINS

Vail has the biggest area of slopes in the US, with immaculately groomed trails and ungroomed terrain in open bowls and among the trees. There are runs to suit every taste, and you get a real sense of travelling around the mountain – something missing in many smaller American resorts. The main criticism is that some of the runs (especially blacks) are overclassified. Trail marking has been praised – 'good directions', 'large map boards'.

### THE SLOPES
***Something for everyone***

The slopes above **Vail** can be accessed via three main lifts. From right next to Vail Village, the Vista Bahn fast chair goes up to the major mid-mountain focal point, Mid-Vail; from Lionshead, the Eagle Bahn gondola goes up to the Eagle's Nest complex; and from the Golden Peak base area just to the east of Vail Village, the Riva Bahn fast chair goes up towards the Two Elk area.

The front face of the mountain is largely north-facing, with well-groomed trails cut through the trees. At altitude the mountainside divides into three bowls – Mid-Vail in the centre, with Game Creek to the south-west and Northeast Bowl to the, er, north-east. Lifts reach the ridge at three points, all giving access to the **Back Bowls** (mostly ungroomed and treeless) and through them to the **Blue Sky Basin** area (mostly ungroomed and wooded).

The slopes have yellow-jacketed patrollers who stop people speeding recklessly. There's a 'new technology center' where you can test the latest equipment. British guests may get the chance of skiing with Martin Bell, Britain's best-ever downhiller and now UK ski ambassador for Vail Resorts (he lives in Vail).

### TERRAIN-PARKS
***Head for Golden Peak***

There is an excellent terrain-park and a super-pipe (130m/425ft long with 5.5m/18ft walls) at Golden Peak, accessed by the Riva Bahn Express. The park has over 30 rails and lots of jumps and was recently expanded. There's also a deck where you can chill out. Two smaller parks were added for 2003/04 – Mule Skinner (also at River Bahn) has four jumps, boxes and two rails whilst Bwana Park, under the Eagle Bahn gondola, has a few more. The schools will also use the parks for their new 'speciality' classes.

### SNOW RELIABILITY
***Excellent, except in the Bowls***

As well as an exceptional natural snow record, Vail has extensive snowmaking facilities, normally needed only in early

## BLUE SKY BASIN

*This is the one of biggest expansion developments in any Colorado ski area for years – 645 acres of terrain, served by three fast quads. The prospect of it caused outrage among environmental groups, and there were some arson attacks.*

*When we skied the Basin we loved it. There are some easy blue runs that are frequently groomed, but most of the area is left ungroomed and the runs among the trees – some widely spaced, some very tight – are delightful for strong skiers and boarders. Few of the runs are very steep, but because you are basically finding your own way much of the time, there is a great feeling of adventure. The snow is usually much better than in the Back Bowls because of the shelter given by the trees and the generally north-facing aspect. A recent reporter recommends the free daily tours which start at 10am at the Blue Sky Basin sign at the top of the Mountaintop and Northwoods Express lifts.*

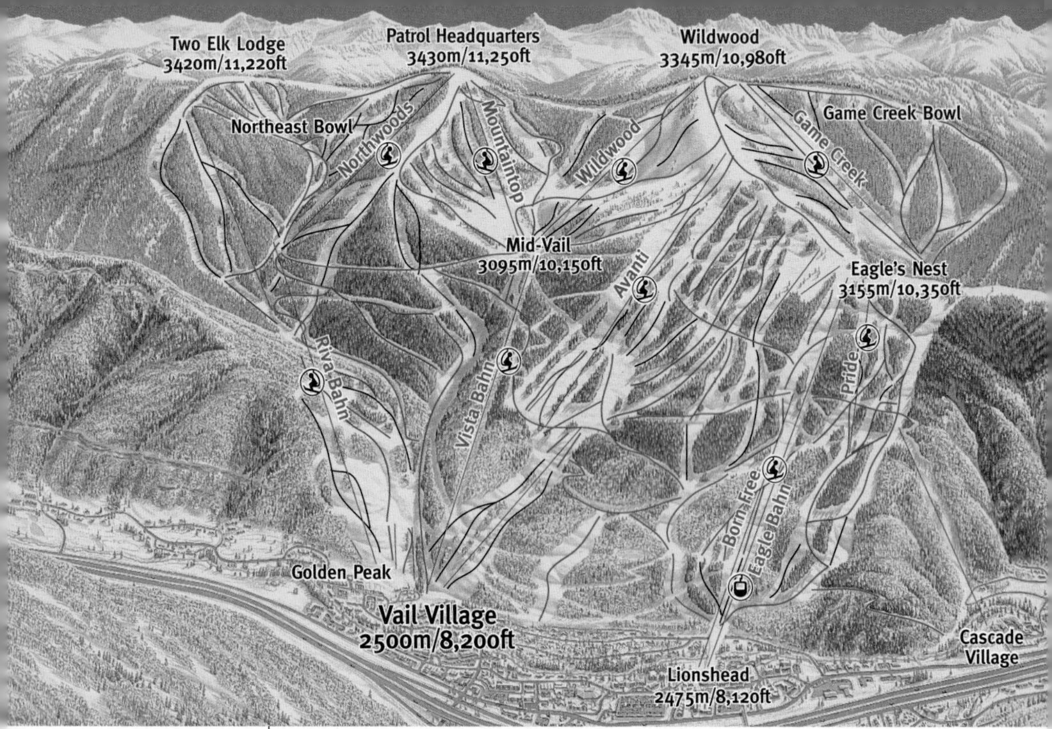

Two Elk Lodge
3420m/11,220ft
Patrol Headquarters
3430m/11,250ft
Wildwood
3345m/10,980ft
Game Creek Bowl
Northeast Bowl
Northwoods
Mountaintop
Wildwood
Game Creek
Mid-Vail
3095m/10,150ft
Avanti
Eagle's Nest
3155m/10,350ft
Riva Bahn
Vista Bahn
Pride
Born Free
Eagle Bahn
Golden Peak
Vail Village
2500m/8,200ft
Cascade Village
Lionshead
2475m/8,120ft





Game Creek Bowl
Patrol Headquarters
3430m/11,250ft
Two Elk Lodge
3420m/11,220ft
China Bowl
Sun Down Bowl
Sun Up Bowl
Siberia Bowl
Outer Mongolia Bowl
Inner Mongolia Bowl
Orient Express
Tea Cup Bowl
Tea Cup
3000m/9,840ft
Pete's
2865m/9,400ft
2915m/9,560ft
Skyline
Blue Sky Basin

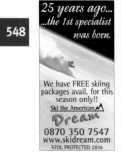

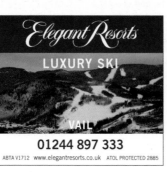

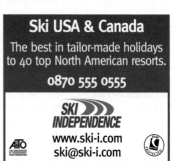

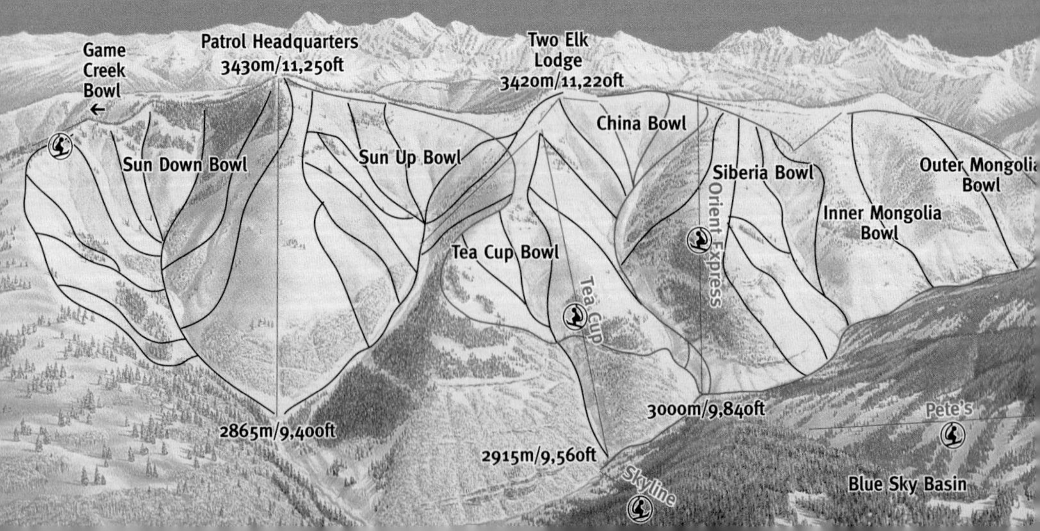

## boarding

*Vail has been wooing boarders with excellent facilities for years. With beautifully groomed, gentle slopes and lots of high-speed chairs, this is a great area for beginners, and there's plenty for experts too, including some wonderful gladed runs. There are specialist board shops and good instruction. Vail's Burton Learn to Ride Program uses special equipment designed to help you learn. It claims to minimise falls and accelerate the learning curve. There's a Burton test centre at the New Technology Centre at the top of the Mountaintop Express chair. And there are now three terrain-parks to jib in.*

season. Both the Back Bowls and Blue Sky Basin usually open later in the season than the front mountain. Blue Sky is largely north-facing (and wooded) and keeps its snow well, but the Bowls are sunny, and in warm weather snow can deteriorate to the point where they are closed.

### FOR EXPERTS
***Transformed by Blue Sky Basin***

Vail's Back Bowls are vast areas, served by three chair-lifts and a couple of short drag-lifts. You can go virtually anywhere you like in the half-dozen identifiable bowls, trying the gradient and terrain of your choice. There are interesting, lightly wooded areas, as well as the open slopes that dominate the area. 87 per cent of the runs in the Back Bowls are classified black but are not particularly steep, and they have disappointed some of our more confident reporters.

Blue Sky Basin has some great adventure runs in the trees – see feature panel.

On the front face there are some genuinely steep double-black-diamond runs which usually have great snow; they are often mogulled but sometimes groomed to make wonderful fast cruising. The Highline lift on the extreme east of the area serves three – a 2004 reporter had 'great fun' here on 'deserted' trails. Prima Cornice, served by the Northwoods Express, is one of the steepest runs on the front side.

If the snow is good, try the back-country Minturn Mile – you leave the ski area through a gate in the Game Creek area for an off-piste run starting with a powder bowl and finishing on a path by a river – ending up at the atmospheric Saloon (see Après-ski).

### FOR INTERMEDIATES
***Ideal territory***

The majority of Vail's front face is great intermediate territory, with easy cruising runs. Above Lionshead, especially, there are excellent long, relatively quiet blues – Born Free and Simba both go from top to bottom. Game Creek Bowl, nearby, is excellent, too. Avanti, underneath the chair of the same name, is a nice cruiser.

As well as tackling some of the

## LIFT PASSES

**The Colorado Ticket**
Covers all Vail, Beaver Creek, Breckenridge and Keystone resorts, plus Arapahoe Basin.

**Main pass**
1 day $73
6 days $318

**Senior citizens**
Over 65: 6 days $286
Over 70: season pass $299

**Children**
Under 13: 6 days $180
Under 5: free pass

**Notes**
Half-day pass available. The Colorado ticket is available only to international visitors who pre-book through a UK tour operator. It is not available at the ticket window in the resort. Prices quoted are regular season rates.

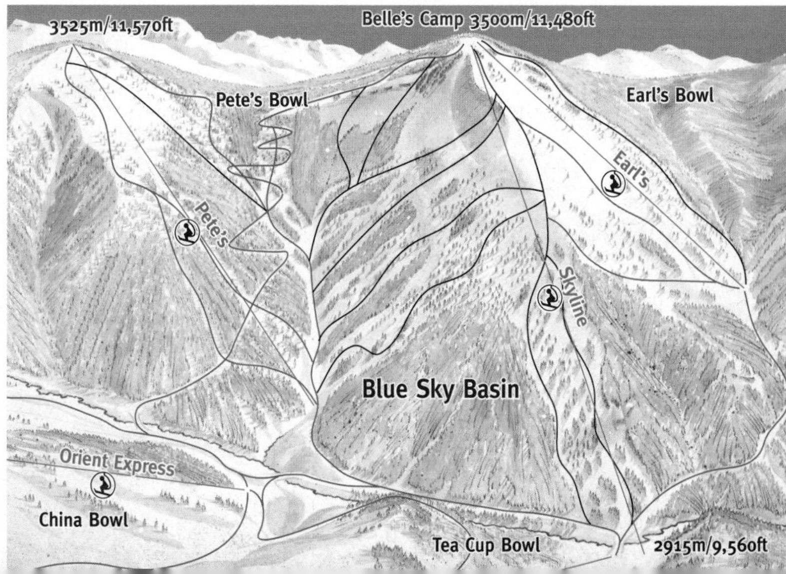

↑ Blue Sky Basin is a great area for experts and adventurous intermediates, with better snow than the sunny Back Bowls in the distance

SNOWPIX.COM / CHRIS GILL

## SCHOOLS

**Vail**
t 476 3239

**Classes**
Full day (9.45-3.30) $100

**Private lessons**
$135 for 1hr for 1 to 6 people

## CHILDREN

**Small World Play School**
t 479 3285
Ages 2mnth to 6yr; 8am to 4.30; reservations essential

**Ski school**
Ages 3 to 14 at Golden Peak and Lionshead (full day including lift pass and lunch US$145): Mini-Mice (for age 3) to Mogul Mice (from age 4), Super Stars (for 3 to 6) and lessons (for 7 to 14)

easier front-face blacks, intermediates will find plenty of interest in the Back Bowls (given good visibility). Some of the runs are groomed and several are classified blue, including Silk Road, which loops around the eastern edge, with wonderful views. Some of the unpisted slopes make the ideal introduction to powder. Confident intermediates will also enjoy Blue Sky Basin's clearly marked blue runs.

### FOR BEGINNERS
***Good but can be crowded***

There are excellent nursery slopes at resort level and at altitude and easy longer runs to progress to. But they can be rather crowded.

### FOR CROSS-COUNTRY
***Some of the best***

Vail's cross-country areas are at the foot of Golden Peak and at the Nordic Center on the golf course. Cross-country and telemark lessons are available at Golden Peak.

### QUEUES
***Can be bad***

Vail has some of the longest lift queues we've hit in the US, especially at weekends because of the influx from Denver. At Mid-Vail, waits of 15 minutes are common, and we have reports of 45-minute waits both here and for the slow chairs in the Back Bowls. The Northwoods Express lift can also be very busy because the alternative Highline lift is so slow.

### MOUNTAIN RESTAURANTS
***Surprisingly poor (though pricey)***

As other major American resorts are gradually improving their mountain restaurants, Vail's are slipping further behind: demand is increasing to the point where the major self-service restaurants can be unpleasantly crowded from 11am to 2pm. They are also expensive (especially Two Elk, where a reporter said 'a hot dog, fries and coke cost £10'). There's table-service (with limited menu) at Eagle's Nest – book ahead. Buffalo's 'served the purpose' for one reporter – basic, good value choices.

### SCHOOLS AND GUIDES
***Among the best in the world***

The Vail-Beaver Creek school generates many glowing reports. Class sizes are usually small – as few as four is not uncommon. One reporter's class was 'really excellent – good technical advice without too much standing around' – though another's private instructor was 'very low key', with little advice volunteered. There are specialist half-day workshops in, for example, bumps and powder. You can sign up on the mountain.

### FACILITIES FOR CHILDREN
***Excellent***

The comprehensive arrangements for young children look excellent, and we've had good reports on the children's school. There are splendid children's areas with adventure trails and themed play areas, most of which received a revamp for 2003/04 – animal characters will guide you around. There's even a special kids cafe area at Mid Vail. The Night Owl programme gives parents an evening off and includes supervised activities and dinner at Adventure Ridge at the top of the gondola.

## GETTING THERE

**Air** Eagle 56km/35 miles (1hr); Denver 177km/110 miles (2½hr).

## ACTIVITIES

**Indoor** Athletic clubs and spas, massage, ski museum, cinema, artificial skating rink

**Outdoor** Skating, ice hockey, sleigh rides, mountaineering, fishing, snowmobiles, snow-shoe excursions, snowcat tours, dog-sledding, paragliding, tubing hill, ski biking, thrill-sledding, laser tag

**Central reservations phone number**
Call 1 800 404 3535 (toll-free from within the US).

**Phone numbers**
From distant parts of the US, add the prefix 1 970.
From abroad, add the prefix +1 970.

## TOURIST OFFICE

**t** 476 5601
vailinfo@vailresorts.com
www.vail.com

## STAYING THERE

### HOW TO GO
***Package or independent***

There's a big choice of packages to Vail. It's easy to organise your own visit, with regular airport shuttles.

**Chalets** Several UK tour operators offer catered chalets. Many are out of the centre at East Vail or West Vail or across the busy I70 freeway.

**Hotels** Vail has a fair choice of hotels, though most tend to be expensive. Check online for the best deals.

(((((5) **Vail Cascade** One of the best in town. A resort within a resort – lots of facilities and a chair-lift right outside.

(((((5) **Sonnenalp Bavaria Haus** Very smart and central. Large spa and splendid piano bar-lounge.

(((((5) **Lodge at Vail** Owned by Vail Resorts, right by the Vista Bahn in Vail Village. Some standard rooms small. Huge buffet breakfast. Outdoor pool. 'A real treat' writes a reporter.

(((((5) **Marriot Mountain Resort** Also owned by Vail Resorts, near the Eagle Bahn gondola. Impressive spa facilities

((((4) **Evergreen Lodge** Cheaper (for Vail!) option. Between village and Lionshead. Outdoor pool. Sports bar.

**Self-catering** The Racquet Club at East Vail has lots of amenities. Mountain Haus has high-quality condos in the centre of town.

### EATING OUT
***Endless choice***

Whatever kind of food you want, Vail has it – but most of it is distinctly pricey. Booking in advance is essential.

Fine-dining options include the Wildflower, in the Lodge, the Tour (modern French) – recommended highly by a 2004 reporter – and Ludwig's, in the Sonnenalp Bavaria Haus. Other recommendations for good food and service in an Alpine ambience are the Alpenrose and Pepi's in the hotel Gramshammer.

For better value, we've always found Blu's 'contemporary American' food satisfactory; a reader recommends the Ore House and Billy's Island Grill ('superb steaks at moderate prices'). Bart & Yeti's or Bogart's Bar and Bistro are good for local ales and no-frills, filling American food.

Recommendations from readers include May Palace (Chinese) in West Vail, Sapphire (seafood), Montauk (seafood), the Bistro at the Racquet Club, Los Amigos, Russell's, La



Bottega, and Vendetta's. For a bit of a treat try Game Creek Lodge, reached by snowcat from the top of the gondola.

### APRES-SKI
***Fairly lively***

Lions Den (formerly Powderhounds) at Lionshead is popular at the end of the day, with live music. Nearby Garfinkel's has a DJ, sundeck and happy hour. The Red Lion in the village centre is popular, with big-screen TVs and huge portions of food. The George tries to be an English-style pub. The Ore House serves 'mean margaritas and hot wings'. The Tap Room in the Vista Bahn building is a relaxed woody bar – 'good range of wines by the glass'.

King's Club is the place to go for high-calorie cakes, and becomes a piano bar later; and Los Amigos and Bogart's Bar and Bistro are other lively places at four o'clock.

You can have a good night out at Adventure Ridge at the top of the gondola. As well as bars and restaurants, there's lots to do on the snow – though a reporter reckons the tubing hill is no match for Keystone's.

Later on, Fubar is a popular disco. 8150 is also good, with a suspended floor that moves with the dancing; the Bully Ranch at the Sonnenalp has great 'mudslide' drinks; The Bridge is a snowboard hangout; Vendetta's does good pizza and beer. The Sanctuary club is above the Tap Room bar.

Out of town in Minturn, the Saloon is worth a trip – genuine old-West style with photos of famous skier patrons.

### OFF THE SLOPES
***A lot to do***

Getting around on the free bus is easy, and there are lots of activities to try. Balloon rides are popular. The factory outlets at Silverthorne are a must for shopaholics who can't resist a bargain.

# Winter Park

*Good value, great terrain, huge snowfalls, unpretentious town*

## COSTS

①②③④⑤⑥

## RATINGS

| The slopes | |
|---|---|
| Snow | ***** |
| Extent | *** |
| Expert | **** |
| Intermediate | **** |
| Beginner | ***** |
| Convenience | *** |
| Queues | **** |
| Mountain restaurants | *** |
| **The rest** | |
| Scenery | *** |
| Resort charm | ** |
| Off-slope | * |

## NEWS

For 2004/05 Intrawest plans to invest $4 million to improve the learning zone in Sorensen Park, at the base of the mountain, expanding it to cover 5 acres and installing new lifts.

For 2003/04 terrain-park features at Rail Yard were expanded to include a super-pipe. And a new bridge was built to enable easier access to the lower section.



- ➕ The best snowfall record of all Colorado's major resorts
- ➕ Superb beginner terrain and lots of groomed cruises
- ➕ Lots for experts, including countless mogul slopes and great tree skiing – at least when conditions are right
- ➕ Quiet on weekdays, and impressive lift system copes with weekends
- ➕ Leading resort for teaching people with disabilities to ski and ride
- ➕ Largely free of inflated prices and ski-resort glitz, but ...

- ➖ Also lacking the range of shops and restaurants you might expect
- ➖ Town is a bus-ride from the slopes, and strung-out along the main road
- ➖ 'Village' at the lift base is still very limited, and dead in the evening
- ➖ Access to high advanced/expert terrain depends on conditions
- ➖ Trails tend to be either easy cruises or stiff mogul fields
- ➖ One or two slow lifts in key spots
- ➖ The nearest big resort to Denver, so can get crowded at weekends

**When we first visited Winter Park – developed for the recreation of the citizens of nearby Denver, and still owned by the city – we were surprised by what we found: a mountain of world class. Now there seems to be the prospect of a world-class resort at the base, too: dynamic Intrawest (developers of famously wonderful Whistler) has signed a long-term agreement to operate and develop the whole resort. The future looks bright.**

**For the present, if value for money and snow are more important to you than glamour or variety of shops and restaurants, the place should be high up on your Colorado shortlist. Some of our reporters rate it their favourite Colorado resort, partly because it makes such a refreshing change from the norm. Both the mountain and the town have a distinct character, which even Intrawest will be hard pushed to iron out.**

## THE RESORT

Winter Park started life around the turn of the century as a railway town, when Rio Grande railway workers climbed the slopes to ski down. One of the resort's mountains, Mary Jane, is named after a legendary 'lady of pleasure' who is said to have received the land as payment for her favours.

The railway still plays an important part in Winter Park's existence, with a station right at the foot of the slopes where trains deposit Denverites every Saturday and Sunday morning; there's apparently quite an après-ski party on the homebound leg.

Most accommodation is a shuttle-bus-ride away in spacious condos scattered around either side of US highway 40, the road through the town of Winter Park, or a few miles down the road around the town of Fraser. Drive into Winter Park at night, and it seems to resemble an established ski resort town, with brightly lit shops, motels, bars and restaurants along the road – but in the daytime it's clear that the place doesn't amount to much.

In the last few years, stylish accommodation has been developed at or near the foot of the slopes, including a car-free mini-resort known as The Village at Winter Park Resort.

Confusingly, an area between the mountain and the town is known as Old Town.

Shuttle-buses (reportedly rather primitive, with unhelpful drivers) run between the town and the lift base, and the hotels and condos also provide shuttles. A car simplifies getting around what is a very spread-out resort area as well as day trips to Denver or other resorts such as Copper Mountain, Breckenridge and Keystone.

The approach road is more like the Alps than Colorado, going over the Continental Divide at Berthoud Pass (3450m/11,320ft). Sadly, the mini-resort that operated here in the past – most recently using snowcats – has closed.

| KEY FACTS | |
|---|---|
| Resort | 2745m<br>9,000ft |
| Slopes | 2745-3675m<br>9,000-12,060ft |
| Lifts | 21 |
| Pistes | 2,762 acres |
| Green | 9% |
| Blue | 34% |
| Black | 57% |
| Snowmaking | 119 hectares<br>294 acres |

## THE MOUNTAINS

Winter Park has a mountain that's big by US standards, and an excellent mix of terrain that suits all abilities – when it's all open.

### THE SLOPES

***Interestingly divided***

There are five distinct, but well-linked, sectors. From the main base, a fast quad takes you to the peak of the original **Winter Park** mountain. From there, you can descend in all directions. Runs lead back towards the main base and over to the **Vasquez Ridge** area on the far right, served by the Pioneer fast quad.

You can also descend to the base of **Mary Jane** mountain, where four chairs up the front face serve tough runs; other chairs serve easier terrain on the flanks. From the top you can head up to **Parsenn Bowl**, via the slow Timberline chair, for intermediate terrain above and in the trees. This chair is exposed at the top, and can be closed for long periods in bad weather. From here, conditions permitting, you can hike for up to half an hour to access the advanced and extreme slopes of **Vasquez Cirque**. A long ski-out takes you to the bottom of Vasquez Ridge and the Pioneer lift.

### TERRAIN-PARKS

***Bigger and better...***

Winter Park has recently expanded and improved its terrain-parks. The Rail Yard park, with over 12 rails, 15 jumps, and new 130m/420ft long super-pipe, runs down much of the front of Winter Park mountain for over 1110m/ 3,650ft. Halfway down it crosses a new bridge so that those on the Cranmer Cutoff

## boarding

*There is some great advanced and extreme boarding terrain and a high probability of fresh powder to ride. The Rail Yard park (see Terrain-parks) makes Winter Park even more attractive to advanced riders. The resort is also an ideal beginner and intermediate boarder area, with excellent terrain for learning. A good school provides classes for all levels, including 'Ride Festival' for perfecting park and freeride skills, and special lessons for children aged 7-15.*



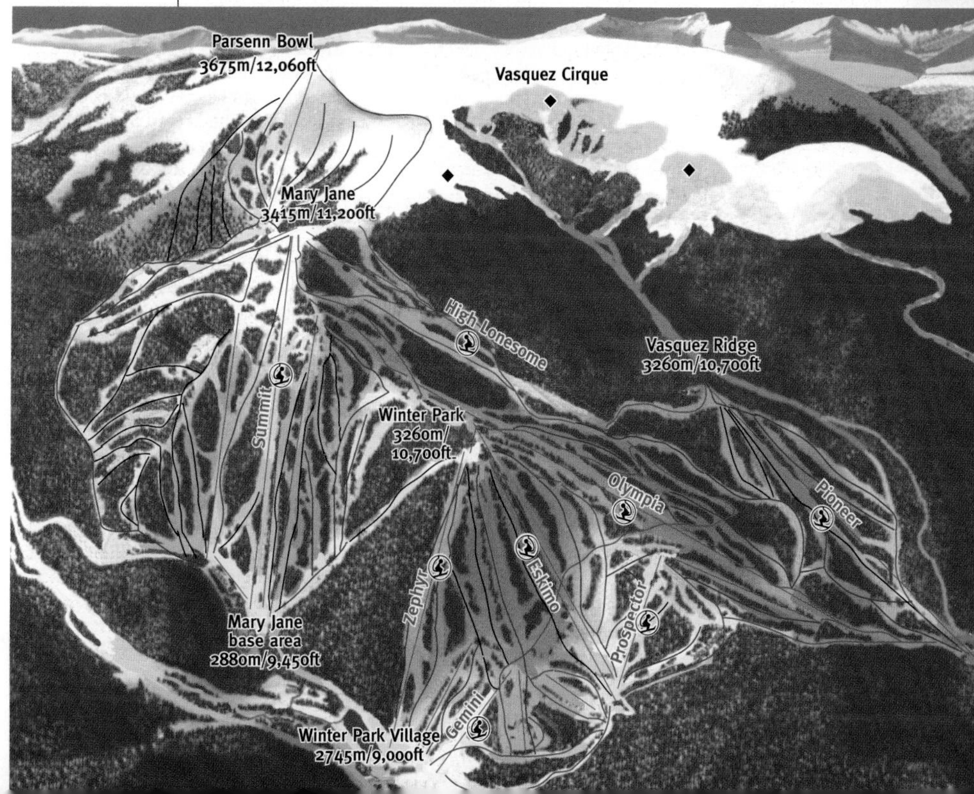

↑ The Continental Divide dominates the skyline from the majority of runs

WINTER PARK RESORT





## LIFT PASSES

**Winter Park Resort**
Covers all lifts in Winter Park.

**Main pass**
1 day $65
6 days $354

**Senior citizens**
Over 62: 6 days $324
Over 70: free pass (Mon-Thu)

**Children**
Under 14: 6 days $180
Under 6: free pass

**Notes**
Half-day passes available. Special rates for disabled skiers.

green run can cross the park safely. For the lower half, you can choose to continue on traditional park features such as table-tops and spines or go on the slope-style park designed for skier- and boarder-cross events. There's also a beginner's park at Jack Kendrick's – newly improved for 2003/04 – and a mini-park in the Discovery area.

### SNOW RELIABILITY
***Among Colorado's best***

'Copious amounts of beautiful, dry powder,' enthuses a reporter. 'So much snow, we were delayed a day getting to the resort,' says another. Winter Park's position, close to the watershed of the Continental Divide, gives it an average yearly snowfall of over 350 inches – the highest of any major Colorado resort. Snowmaking covers a lot of Winter Park Mountain's runs.

### FOR EXPERTS
***Some hair-raising challenges***

Mary Jane has some of the steepest mogul fields, chutes and hair-raising challenges in the US. On the front side are a row of long black mogul fields that are quite steep enough for most of us. There are some challenges on Winter Park Mountain, too.

Some of the best terrain is open only when there is good snow and/or good weather – so it's particularly unreliable early in the season. The fearsome chutes of Mary Jane's back side – all very steep, narrow and bordered by rocks – are accessed by a control gate. Parsenn Bowl, served by the high, exposed Timberline chair, has superb blue/black gladed runs and tougher tree skiing on the back side. Vasquez Cirque, the least reliably open area, has excellent ungroomed expert terrain with extensive views. You don't get much vertical before you hit the forest, though.

### FOR INTERMEDIATES
***Choose your challenge***

From pretty much wherever you are on Winter Park mountain and Vasquez Ridge you can choose a run to suit your ability. Most are well groomed every night, giving you perfect early morning cruising on the famous Colorado 'corduroy' pistes.

For bumps, try Mary Jane's front side. Parsenn Bowl has grand views and some gentle cruising pistes as well as more challenging ungroomed terrain. It's also an ideal place to try ungroomed powder for the first time.

### FOR BEGINNERS
***About the best we've seen***

Discovery Park is a 25-acre dedicated area for beginners, reached by a high-speed quad and served by two more chairs. As well as a nursery area and longer green runs, it has an adventure trail through trees and a special terrain park. Once out of the Park, there are easy runs back to base. And the learning zone at Sorensen is to be expanded and improved for 2004/05.

### FOR CROSS-COUNTRY
***Lots of it***

There are several different areas, all with generally excellent snow, totalling over 200km/125 miles of groomed trails, as well as backcountry tours.

### QUEUES
***Rarely a problem***

During the week the mountain is generally quiet. 'We had whole runs to ourselves for a couple of miles,' says one delighted reporter. However, there may be a crowd waiting for the opening of the Zephyr Express from the main base and there can be queues on the slow chair up Parsenn

Downtown Winter Park is a bit more sophisticated than this (the outskirts of Fraser), but not a whole lot more →

BYRON HETZLER / WINTER PARK RESORT

## SCHOOLS

**Winter Park**
t 1 800 729 7907
skischool@skiwinterpark.com

**National Sports Center for the Disabled**
t 726 1518
Special programme for disabled skiers and snowboarders

**Classes**
Half day (2½hr) $46

**Private lessons**
$249 for 2hr for 1 or 2 people

## CHILDREN

**Children's Center**
t 1 800 729 7907
Ages 2mnth to 5yr; $99 per day

**Ski school**
Takes ages 3 to 17 ($109 per day including lift ticket)

Bowl. At weekends the Denver crowds arrive – even then the network of more than 20 lifts (including eight fast quads) makes light work of the people.

### MOUNTAIN RESTAURANTS
***Some good facilities***

The highlight is the Lodge at Sunspot, at the top of Winter Park mountain. This wood and glass building has a welcoming bar with a roaring log fire, a table-service restaurant and very good self-service food – but it gets very busy. Lunch Rock Cafe at the top of Mary Jane does quick snacks and has a deli counter, and there is a self-service at Snoasis, by the beginner area. Mama Mia's Pizzeria is on the lower level of Snoasis – you can order food in advance from a special kiosk on top of Winter Park Mountain so that the food is waiting for you on arrival. Otherwise, it's down to the bases. The Club Car at the base of Mary Jane offers table-service and 'a good atmosphere and more varied menu' than the American norm. The Boxcar Deli at the newly revamped West Portal Station does sandwiches, pastries and coffees. Moffat Market food court (also at West Portal) now offers a wider selection in a railway-themed setting.

### SCHOOLS AND GUIDES
***A good reputation***

'The ski school was a delight and class sizes averaged three!' says a recent reporter. As well as standard classes there are ideas such as Family Private, for different abilities together; themed lessons such as Mogul Mania and Bump Jamboree, as well as men- or women-only clinics.

### FACILITIES FOR CHILDREN
***Some of the best***

The Children's Center at Winter Park base area houses day-care facilities and is the meeting point for children's classes, which have their own areas, including moving carpets. 'They couldn't do enough for children,' says our most recent reporter.

### NATIONAL SPORTS CENTER FOR THE DISABLED

*If you are able-bodied, the most striking and humbling thing you'll notice as you ride your first chair-lift is the number of people with disabilities hurtling down the mountain faster than many of us could ever hope to. There are blind skiers, skiers with one leg, people with paralysis – whatever their problem, they've cracked it.*

*That's because Winter Park is home to the US National Sports Center for the Disabled (NSCD) – the world's leading centre for teaching skiing and snowboarding to people with disabilities. As well as full-time instructors, there are 1,000 trained volunteers who help in the programme. More than 40 disabilities are specially catered for. If you are disabled and want to learn to ski or snowboard, there's no better place to go. It's important to book ahead so that a suitable instructor is available. The NSCD can help with travel and accommodation arrangements:*

*NSCD, PO Box 36, Winter Park, CO 80482, USA. Tel: 726 1540.*

## GETTING THERE

**Air** Denver 137km/ 85 miles (1½hr).

**Rail** Denver, Sat and Sun only. Journey time 2hr.

## ACTIVITIES

**Indoor** Fitness clubs, hot-tubs, comedy club, aerobics

**Outdoor** Dog-sledding, ice rink, snow-shoeing, sleigh rides, tubing, snowmobiling, snowcat tours, hot air ballooning, hot springs

**Central reservations**
Call 726 5587.
Toll-free number (from within the US)
1 800 729 5813.

**Phone numbers**
From distant parts of the US, add the prefix 1 970.
From abroad, add the prefix +1 970.

## TOURIST OFFICE

**t** 726 5514
wpinfo@skiwinterpark.com
www.skiwinterpark.com

WINTER PARK RESORT

The Lodge at Sunspot, up the mountain, is open some evenings for dinner ↓

## STAYING THERE

### HOW TO GO
***Fair choice***

Several UK operators offer Winter Park.

**Chalets** Several operators offer them.

**Hotels** There are a couple of outstanding hotel/condo complexes.

(((4 **Iron Horse Resort** Slope-side, comfortable, condo-style. Recommended by a 2004 reporter.

(((4 **Vintage** Near resort entrance; good facilities but some poor past reports of it.

((3 **Winter Park Mountain Lodge** Inconveniently positioned across the valley from the lifts; incorporates a micro-brewery; gets mixed reports.

**Self-catering** There are a lot of comfortable condos, including the slope-side Zephyr Mountain Lodge. 'Large comfortable rooms and couldn't be more convenient,' says a reporter.

### EATING OUT
***A fair choice***

The range of options is gradually improving, but still isn't a match for that in more established 'destination' resorts. Get hold of the giveaway Grand County menu guide – but don't expect to find the contents wildly appetising unless you're starving for a 16oz steak. Reporters are keen on the long-established Deno's – seafood, steaks etc (also popular après-ski bar). Smokin' Moe's offers sports TV and grills plus 'a great salad bar'. Nearby in the Cooper Creek Square area is New Hong Kong (for 'tasty' Chinese) and the Divide Grill (for pasta, seafood and grills). Readers also recommend the Shed ('excellent steak and seafood, reasonably priced'), for Tex-Mex Carlos and Maria's, for pizza/pasta the 'dark but rustic' Hernandos, with open fires. Gasthaus Eichler does 'very good' German-influenced food, at slightly higher prices. Try the Crooked Creek Saloon at Fraser for atmosphere and typical American food. The Lodge at Sunspot, up the mountain, is open some nights, with a 'fantastic' five-course fine-dining option on Saturday. They put gondola cabins on the chair-lift to get you up there in comfort.

### APRES-SKI
***If you know where to go ...***

At close of play, there's action at the Kickapoo Tavern and 'quite jolly' Derailer Bar at the main lift base, as well as the Club Car at the base of Mary Jane. Later on, the Shed and Randi's Irish Saloon can be lively. The Crooked Creek is popular with locals and the Winter Park Pub attracts the younger crowd. Buckets is a funky new sports-bar.

### OFF THE SLOPES
***Mainly the great outdoors***

Most diversions involve getting about on snow in different ways. If you like shopping, you'll rapidly exhaust the local possibilities and want to visit Silverthorne's factory outlet stores (90 minutes away on Interstate 70, near Keystone and other resorts).

SNOWPIX.COM / CHRIS GILL

# Crested Butte

**Crested Butte has one of the cutest old Wild West towns in Colorado and its mountain enjoys cult status among experts who enjoy steep, gnarly terrain. But keen, mileage-hungry intermediates will find there isn't enough suitable terrain.**

### KEY FACTS

| | |
|---|---|
| **Resort** | 2860m<br>9,380ft |
| **Slopes** | 2775-3620m<br>9,100-11,880ft |
| **Lifts** | 14 |
| **Pistes** | 1,058 acres |
| **Green** | 15% |
| **Blue** | 44% |
| **Black** | 41% |
| **Snowmaking** | 300 acres |

### TOURIST OFFICE

t 970 349 2286
info@cbmr.com
www.crestedbutteresort.com

## THE RESORT

This small town in a remote corner of Colorado takes its name from the local mountain – an isolated peak (a butte, pronounced 'beaut') with a distinctive shape. It was a mining town in the late 1800s and is now one of the cutest resorts in the Rockies – a few narrow streets with beautifully restored wooden buildings and sidewalks and a good selection of bars and restaurants. The mountain is a couple of miles away, with the modern, characterless resort 'village' of Mount Crested Butte at its foot. You can stay in town or village.

## THE MOUNTAINS

It's a small area, but it packs in an astonishing mixture of perfect beginner slopes, easy cruising runs and expert terrain. Two fast quad chairs leave the base. Snowfall is modest by Colorado standards – an average of 240 inches compared with over 300 for many other resorts. But for those who like steep, ungroomed terrain, if the snow is good, Crested Butte is idyllic – the 448 acres of the Extreme Limits at the top of the mountain offer seriously steep, prettily wooded terrain; but it is not unusual for it to be closed until late January to allow the snowpack to build up. Though there are also some 'ordinary' black runs, these are few.

Good intermediates will find the area limited, with few challenging groomed trails. For early intermediates, there are lots of wide, fairly gentle, well-groomed and normally uncrowded cruising runs. There are excellent nursery slopes near the village and lots of good long runs to progress to. The ski school has an excellent reputation and there are a couple of mountain restaurants.

SNOWPIX.COM / CHRIS GILL

# Durango

**Durango Mountain Resort (not to be confused with Durango, a nearby city) is not a resort you would cross the Atlantic to visit – but if you're passing, you could do worse than give it a day or two.**

### KEY FACTS

| | |
|---|---|
| **Resort** | 2680m<br>8,795ft |
| **Slopes** | 2680-3300m<br>8,795-10,820ft |
| **Lifts** | 11 |
| **Pistes** | 1,200 acres |
| **Blue** | 25% |
| **Red** | 50% |
| **Black** | 25% |
| **Snowmaking** | 250 acres |

### TOURIST OFFICE

t 970 247 9000
info@durangomountainresort.com
www.durangomountainresort.com

## THE RESORT

The heart of the resort is Purgatory Village, a modern, purpose-built affair with hotel and condo accommodation – as convenient and soulless as the many similar developments in France. Evening options in the 'village' are extremely limited. Fortunately, Hamilton's Chop House down on the roadside at The Inn at DMR is a surprisingly competent restaurant. There is tubing and snowmobiling. The city of Durango has a historic district and is worth a look. Other diversions a drive away include hot springs, Sky Ute Casino and a steam railroad.

## THE MOUNTAIN

Practically all the runs are cut through dense forest. It's a small area even by US standards, and won't amuse most non-beginners for more than a day or two. Directly above the resort is a steepish slope served by a six-pack, with a slow double chair off to the right serving gentle green runs. Both link to the shady mountainside that forms the main part of the area, served by a row of three chairs with a vertical of not much over 350m/1,150ft. The first, a fast quad, serves a handful of pleasant blue runs. The others serve steeper terrain that provides some genuine blacks – including a nice little gladed area – and some very short double-diamond pitches. Snowcat skiing is said to operate from the top.

The snowfall record isn't Colorado's best, but an average of 260 inches is not bad. There are two terrain-parks with all the usual features, including a half-pipe. Amazingly, the mountain restaurants include a highly regarded table-service place, Café de los Piños.

JACKSON HOLE / GORAN ASSNER

# Rest of the West

**This section covers a varied group of resorts in different parts of the great Rocky Mountain chain that stretches the length of the United States from Montana and Idaho down through Wyoming, Utah and Colorado to New Mexico. Each has its own unique character – and 12 of them are covered later in this section.**

Sun Valley, Idaho, was America's first purpose-built resort, developed in the 1930s by the president of the Union Pacific Railway. It quickly became popular with the Hollywood jet set and has managed to retain its stylish image and ambience; it has one of our favourite luxury hotels.

If you don't mind a bit of a cross-state drive, you might combine a visit to Sun Valley with a visit to the famously snowy resorts of Utah (see below) or to Jackson Hole in Wyoming – another resort with an impressive snow record. Jackson is the nearest there is to a resort with a genuine Wild West cowboy atmosphere.

A little way north of Jackson, just inside Montana, is Big Sky, not to be confused with Big Mountain at the far northern end of the state. Big Sky has one of the biggest verticals in the US. Bridger Bowl, a 90-minute drive away, boasts broad, steep, lightly wooded slopes which offer wonderful powder descents after a fresh snowfall.

Going south from Jackson you reach the Utah resorts, which hit the headlines when they hosted the 2002 Winter Olympics, centred around Salt Lake City. Car number plates here used to bear the slogan 'The Greatest Snow on Earth'; sadly, state policy has now changed to target broader markets. But the claim stands. The Colorado resorts dispute it and have figures to prove that their famous powder is drier. What they can't dispute is that some Utah resorts do get huge dumps – up to twice the amount, over the season, that falls on some big-name Colorado resorts. In any case, by Alpine standards the snow here is wonderful. If you like the steep and deep, you should at some point make the pilgrimage to Utah – in particular to Snowbird and Alta, which receive the biggest dumps (an average of 500 inches a year). Park City, Utah's main 'destination' resort, and upmarket Deer Valley next door hosted the lion's share of the Olympic events. These resorts, and The Canyons nearby, are only a few miles from Alta/Snowbird, but they get 'only' 300 to 350 inches (still more than most Colorado resorts). But it was unknown Snowbasin (400 inches) that got the prestige downhill Olympic events. In recent years, the snow record of Alta and Snowbird has almost been matched by those of near-neighbours Brighton and Solitude, where the snow gets tracked out less quickly, because the resorts attract far fewer experts. Separate chapters follow on these eight Utah resorts, and the Utah Passport ski pass, available through UK tour operators, covers them all. If you enjoy seeing different resorts, you can construct a compelling holiday by staying in Park City (by far the liveliest resort) or Salt Lake City (with a big-city rather than a ski-resort ambience) and driving to a different resort each day.

There are other Utah resorts that are well worth visiting, too. One that gets a bit of international attention – not least because it's owned by Robert Redford – is Sundance. Another is Powder Mountain: it is the biggest ski area in Utah, yet it remains under-developed, with a welcoming, down-to-earth atmosphere. Both these have extended entries in our Resort index / directory at the back of the book.

A long way south of all these resorts, Taos in New Mexico is the most southerly major resort in America, and because of its isolation it is largely unknown on the international market.





**TOURIST OFFICE**

**Ski Utah**
www.skiutah.com

ALTA / SUNSPOT

# Alta

*Cult powder resort, now sharing one of America's biggest areas*

## COSTS

(1)(2)(3)(4)(5)(6)

## RATINGS

| **The slopes** | |
|---|---|
| Snow | ***** |
| Extent | *** |
| Expert | ***** |
| Intermediate | *** |
| Beginner | *** |
| Convenience | **** |
| Queues | *** |
| Mountain restaurants | ** |
| **The rest** | |
| Scenery | *** |
| Resort charm | ** |
| Off-slope | * |

## KEY FACTS

| | |
|---|---|
| **Resort** | 2600m 8,530ft |
| For Alta and Snowbird combined area see Snowbird | |
| For Alta only | |
| **Slopes** | 2600-3215m 8,530-10,550ft |
| **Lifts** | 13 |
| **Pistes** | 2,200 acres |
| **Green** | 25% |
| **Blue** | 40% |
| **Black** | 35% |
| **Snowmaking** | 50 acres |

## REPORTS WANTED

Recently we have had few reports on this resort. If you go there, please do send us a report.

- + Phenomenal snow and steep terrain mean cult status among experts
- + New link to Snowbird, making one of the largest ski areas in the US
- + Very cheap local lift pass
- + Ski-almost-to-the-door convenience
- + Easy to get to other Utah resorts

- – 'Resort' is a scattering of lodges – not much après-ski atmosphere and few off-slope diversions
- – No snowboarding allowed
- – Still a lot of old slow chair-lifts
- – Limited groomed runs for intermediates, though the link with Snowbird doubled the terrain

**Alta has long been famous for remarkable amounts of powder snow arriving with great regularity and for one of the cheapest lift passes around ($42 a day). It used to be famous for its stubborn refusal to develop or modernise. But things have changed on that front: the Sunnyside fast triple chair, installed a few years ago specially for beginners, was followed in 2001 by the resort's first fast quad, to connect Alta to Snowbird. Now another fast quad is being installed. And last season they built their first terrain-park. How long, we wonder, before Alta really joins the modern world, and admits snowboarders to its hallowed slopes?**

## THE RESORT

Alta, which celebrated its 65th year of operation last season, sits at the craggy head of Little Cottonwood Canyon, 2km/1 mile beyond Snowbird and less than an hour's drive from downtown Salt Lake City. Both the resort and the approach road are prone to avalanches and closure: visitors can be confined indoors for safety. The peaceful location was once the scene of a bustling and bawdy mining town. The 'new' Alta is a strung-out handful of lodges and parking areas, and nothing more; life revolves around the two separate lift base areas – Albion and Wildcat – linked by a bi-directional rope tow along the flat valley floor. There are about a dozen places to stay.

## THE MOUNTAINS

Alta's slopes are still served by mainly slow double and triple chairs, though things are improving. Check out the Snowbird chapter for the linked slopes.

**Slopes** The dominant feature of Alta's terrain is the steep end of a ridge that separates the area's two basins. To the left, above Albion Base, the slopes stretch away over easy green terrain towards the blue and black runs from Point Supreme and from the top of the Sugarloaf quad; to the right, above Wildcat Base, is a more concentrated bowl with blue runs down the middle and blacks either side. These two sectors are linked at altitude, and by the flat rope tow along the valley floor.

**Terrain-parks** A park was built for the first time last season.

**Snow reliability** The quantity and quality of the snow and the northerly orientation put Alta in the top rank.

**Experts** Even without the Snowbird link Alta had cult status among local experts, who flocked to the high ridges after a fresh snowfall. There are dozens of steep slopes and chutes – and with the link, the area is among the world's best for powder hounds.

**Intermediates** Adventurous intermediates who are happy to try ungroomed slopes and learn to love

SNOWPIX.COM / CHRIS GILL

← The access road; you can see why it's prone to closure by avalanche danger

## NEWS

For 2004/05 the resort's third fast chair (a quad) is set to replace the Collins and Germania chairs. The start of the Wildcat chair will also be moved, and you won't have to walk up a hill before you get on a lift. There will be a mid-station in the new lift at Watson's Shelter.

For 2002/03 guided snowcat skiing and boarding (yes, boarding) for advanced/expert levels only were introduced in Grizzly Gulch, next to the main area. Five runs cost $225 including breakfast.

**Phone numbers**
From distant parts of the US, add the prefix 1 801.
From abroad, add the prefix +1 801.

## TOURIST OFFICE

t 359 1078
info@alta.com
www.alta.com

powder should like Alta, too. There are good blue bowls in both Alta and Snowbird and not-so-tough blacks to progress too. But if it is miles of perfectly groomed piste you are after, there are plenty of better resorts.
**Beginners** Timid intermediates and beginners will be happy on the Albion side. But it's hard to recommend such a narrowly focused resort to beginners.
**Snowboarding** Boarding is banned (but see News for snowcat boarding).
**Cross-country** There's a 5km/3 mile groomed track and the Alta Nordic Centre offers lessons and equipment.
**Queues** Bottlenecks are not unknown at Alta, especially in spring and on sunny weekends, but the slopes remain uncrowded.
**Mountain restaurants** There's a basic mountain restaurant in each sector of the slopes, offering mainly fast food. Alf's on the Albion side 'serves very good sandwiches'. Watson's Shelter on the Wildcat side serves 'fantastic burgers'. Upstairs, the small table-service Collins Grill has a limited menu but gets booked up anyway. Several lodges at the base open for lunch.
**Schools and guides** The ski school naturally specialises in powder lessons – though there are regular classes, too.
**Facilities for children** Day care for children over three months is available at the Children's Center at Albion Base.

## STAYING THERE

**How to go** None of the hotels is luxurious in US terms. Most get booked up well in advance by repeat visitors. Unusually for America, most lodges (as they're called) operate half-board deals, with dinner included.
**Hotels** The Alta Lodge (742 3500) is one of Alta's oldest, and feels rather like an over-crowded chalet-hotel in the Alps, but has 'great atmosphere and food'. It has recently started offering four-day Powder Tracks packages, including instruction. Rustler Lodge (742 2200) is more luxurious, with a big outdoor pool, but impersonal. The comfortable, modern Goldminer's Daughter (742 2300) and the basic Peruvian Lodge (742 3000) are cheaper. The Snowpine Lodge (742 2000) is 'convenient, comfortable and friendly' but rather 'old-fashioned'.
**Eating out** It is possible, but eating in is the routine.
**Après-ski** This rarely goes beyond a few drinks and possibly a video in the lodge. The Goldminer's Daughter has the main après-ski bar. The cocktail bar in the Rustler Lodge is recommended for a pre-dinner drink.
**Off the slopes** There are few options other than a sightseeing trip to Salt Lake City, or the spa at Snowbird.

BIG SKY RESORT

# Big Sky

*Vast, empty slopes for all abilities and a purpose-built village*

## COSTS

①②③④⑤⑥

## RATINGS

**The slopes**

| | |
|---|---|
| Snow | **** |
| Extent | *** |
| Expert | **** |
| Intermediate | **** |
| Beginner | **** |
| Convenience | **** |
| Queues | ***** |
| Mountain restaurants | * |

**The rest**

| | |
|---|---|
| Scenery | *** |
| Resort charm | ** |
| Off-slope | ** |

## NEWS

For 2004/05, a fourth high-speed quad chair is planned, on Andesite mountain, replacing the triple Southern Comfort and giving faster access to intermediate and beginner cruisers.
The resort is also taking legal steps to sever ties with neighbouring Moonlight Basin (see end of chapter), meaning that the Iron Horse quad and small area of surrounding runs would no longer be used by Big Sky.
There should also be more improvements to the terrain-parks.

In 2003/04, three new gladed runs were cut on Andesite mountain, all single blacks, taking the number of new glades up to eight in four years.

BIG SKY RESORT

Big Sky's trails are blissfully deserted (but were the lifts open when this was taken, we wonder?) →

- ➕ Extensive ski area with runs for all abilities, including great expert runs
- ➕ Excellent snow reliability
- ➕ Big vertical by US standards
- ➕ Few queues, empty slopes

- ➖ Resort village is fairly limited and it can be quiet in the evenings
- ➖ Some slow, old chair-lifts
- ➖ Only one fast-food mountain eatery

**Big Sky is renowned for its powder, steeps and big vertical, and has blissfully empty gentler slopes and tree skiing, too. The mountain village is not much more than three hotels (including a luxury 5-star), with a few shops, bars, restaurants, and an increasing number of condos and cabins extending out around them.**

**There is a curious new development next-door to Big Sky. Moonlight Basin, once a small development with a lift linking it to Big Sky, has become an independent resort, on the north face of Lone Mountain. Last season the areas overlapped, but next season it looks as though they will be completely separate.**

## THE RESORT

Big Sky, which celebrated its 30th anniversary in 2004, is famous for huge snowfalls, big vertical (for North America), and fabulous, deserted slopes. It's a big draw for locals and US visitors, and deserves to be better known internationally.

The resort is set amid the wide open spaces of Montana, one hour's drive from the airport town of Bozeman. At the foot of the slopes is Mountain Village – with three hotels, some slope-side condos and ski shops. There are more bars, shops and restaurants in the Mountain Mall. Some outlying condos and chalets are served by a lift to the slopes, others by free buses, but it's most convenient to stay near the main access lifts.

## THE MOUNTAINS

The slopes cover a big area spread over two linked mountains, with long runs for all abilities. There should be four fast quad chairs operating for next season, but many of the chairs are still old triples and doubles. There are daily free mountain tours.

**Slopes** Lone Mountain provides the resort's poster shot, with steep, open upper slopes that can cause even the hardiest expert to take a sharp intake of breath. The Lone Peak chair leads to the Lone Peak Tram – a tiny 15-person cable-car to the top and fabulous 360° views (go up for the view even if you don't fancy the chutes – there are blue routes from the bottom). Lone Mountain's lower slopes are wooded and varied, as are those of Andesite Mountain, which has less vertical, but is home to three of the fast lifts.

**Terrain-parks** There are two terrain-parks, a half-pipe on Andesite served by the Ramcharger fast quad, and a natural half-pipe on Lone Mountain.

**Snow reliability** Snowfall averages 400+ inches, which puts Big Sky ahead of most Colorado resorts and alongside Jackson Hole. Grooming is good, too.

**Experts** Most of the terrain accessed from the Tram is double-black diamond and some of the steepest stuff, such as the Big Couloir can only be done if you've checked in with patrol and have avalanche safety equipment. The easiest way down is the single black Liberty Bowl, which is wider than most of the runs but long and often bumped up. If the tram is taking its time to open, take a few runs down the wide open Bowl, off the Lone Peak Triple.

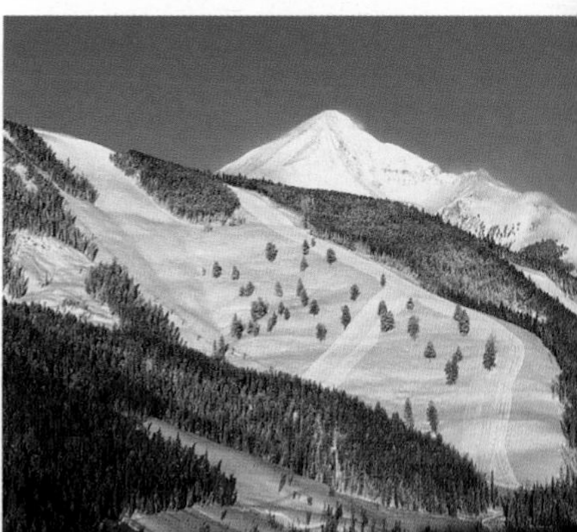

| KEY FACTS | |
|---|---|
| Resort | 2285m 7,500ft |
| Slopes | 2070-3400m 6,800-11,150ft |
| Lifts | 17 |
| Pistes | 3,600 acres |
| Green | 17% |
| Blue | 25% |
| Black | 58% |
| Snowmaking | 350 acres |

**REPORTS WANTED**

Recently we have had few reports on this resort. If you go there, please do send us a report.

The best reports earn a copy of the next edition, and can lead to free lift passes in future.

See page 10.

**Central reservations**
Call 1 800 548 4486 (toll-free within US).

**Phone numbers**
From distant parts of the US, add the prefix 1 406. From abroad, add the prefix +1 406.

**TOURIST OFFICE**

t 995 5000
info@bigskyresort.com
www.bigskyresort.com





More challenges await from the Shedhorn and Challenger chairs; you can also hike to the long, narrow A-Z Chutes from the latter. On Andesite, the new gladed runs are testing too.

**Intermediates** There is lots of cruising terrain on Andesite – the runs from the Ramcharger chair are splendid – and on Lone Mountain, especially from the Swift Current Express.

**Beginners** There's a good nursery area at the base and long greens to progress to, such as Mr K on Lone Mountain, and the runs served by the Southern Comfort lift on Andesite.

**Snowboarding** There's great free-riding and good terrain features.

**Cross-country** There are 65km/40 miles of trails at Lone Mountain Ranch. There are also trails at West Yellowstone.

**Queues** The tiny tram attracts serious queues on busy days. Queues are rare otherwise – and the runs are deserted.

**Mountain restaurants** The Dug Out, on Andesite does fast food and BBQs. Or you can head back to base to eat.

**School and guides** The ski school receives excellent reviews. Guides are available to help you take on the challenges.

**Facilities for children** Handprints nursery in the slope-side Snowcrest lodge takes children from age six months ('perfection,' says a reporter). Children 10 years and under ski for free (up to two kids free per paying adult), and there's also an evening kids' club.

## STAYING THERE

**Hotels** The slope-side Summit (spa baths in the rooms, sculptures in the foyer) is 'hugely impressive'. Huntley Lodge and Buck's T-4 Lodge, 11km/7 miles away, have been recommended

**Self-catering** The good-value Stillwater condos have been recommended, along with Arrowhead, Beaverhead, Snowcrest Lodge, Big Horn and, way out of town, Powder Ridge Cabins.

**Eating out** Huntley Lodge has a smart restaurant; The Peaks (in the Summit) and Dante's Inferno are popular. Shuttle-buses and courtesy cars run to far-flung places such as Buck's T-4 and Timbers restaurant at Moonlight Basin.

**Après-ski** Chet's bar has live music and pool. The Carabiner in the Summit and the Black Bear are also popular.

**Off the slopes** There's snowmobiling, snow-shoeing, sleigh rides, visiting Yellowstone national park.

# Moonlight Basin

If you think Big Sky's slopes are quiet, try Moonlight – when we visited last season, at times we were outnumbered by hosts and patrollers. Last season, Moonlight was linked to Big Sky but it is unlikely to be for 2004/05 (see News). It has some serious chutes and good cruising. Moonlight Lodge was recommended by a reporter for luxury accommodation and good food.

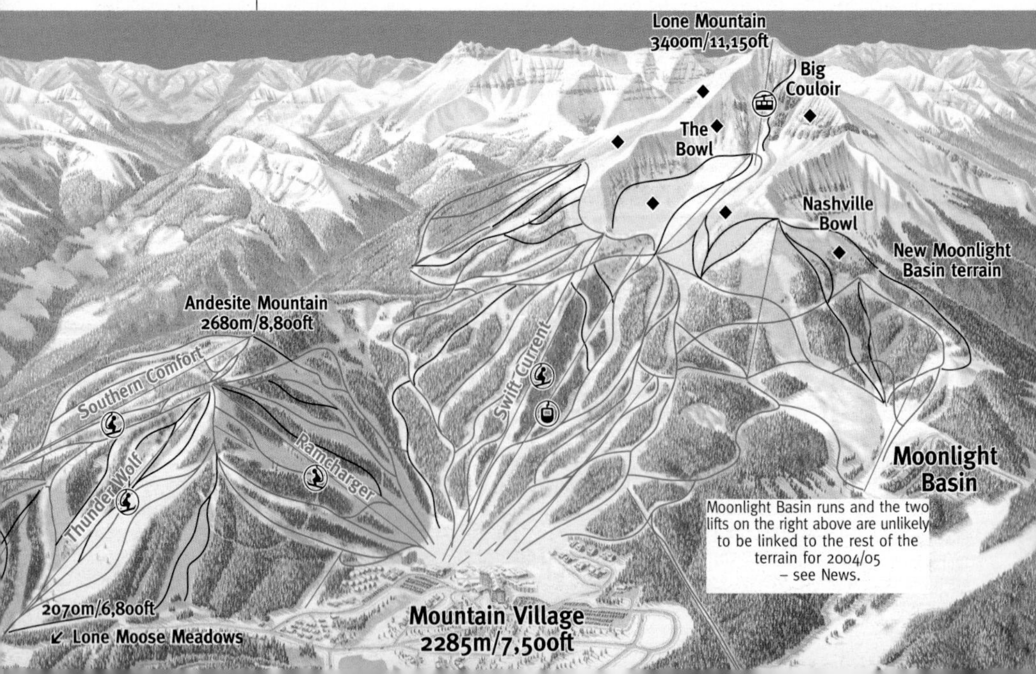


Moonlight Basin runs and the two lifts on the right above are unlikely to be linked to the rest of the terrain for 2004/05 – see News.

THE CANYONS / HUGHES MARTIN

# The Canyons

*Potentially the biggest mountain in the US, and already impressive*

## COSTS

①②③④⑤⑥

## RATINGS

| **The slopes** | |
|---|---|
| Snow | **** |
| Extent | *** |
| Experts | *** |
| Intermediate | *** |
| Beginner | *** |
| Convenience | **** |
| Queues | **** |
| Mountain restaurants | *** |
| **The rest** | |
| Scenery | *** |
| Resort charm | ** |
| Off-slope | ** |

## NEWS

For 2003/04, the terrain-park was moved to a higher 16-acre location by the Snow Canyon lift, meaning it's more likely to have good snow-cover. The on-mountain Lookout Cabin table-service restaurant now has a bar too, open for après-ski from 2.30 until 4pm.

- ➕ Extensive area of slopes for all abilities – and could grow further
- ➕ Modern lift system with few queues
- ➕ Convenient new purpose-built resort village taking shape at the base
- ➕ Park City is nearby – an entertaining alternative base with its own slopes
- ➕ Easy access to other Utah resorts
- ➕ Excellent snow in general, but ...

- ➖ Snow on the many south-facing slopes often not up to the usual Utah standards
- ➖ Because the area is a series of canyons (valleys) many runs are short and the area is a bit disjointed
- ➖ Resort village offers limited après-ski and dining possibilities, and few off-slope diversions

**The American Skiing Company's ambitious plans to make The Canyons' slopes the most extensive in the US are gradually being implemented: the area has already more than doubled in size over the seven seasons the American Skiing Company has owned it and is sixth biggest in the US – amazing, considering its low international profile. The lift system is virtually new; the snow, if not out of the top Utah drawer, is great by normal standards; a new slope-side resort village is up and running. But we'd rather stay in Park City and visit for the day.**

## THE RESORT

The Canyons' car-free village has really taken shape over the past few years, and there is now a basic selection of shops, bars and restaurants as well as accommodation at the base of the main access gondola. Although the accommodation at the resort village is convenient, staying in Park City may suit many people better – regular shuttle-buses run to the resort, and there is also a car park below the resort from which you get a cabriolet lift to the village.

## THE MOUNTAINS

The Canyons gets its name from the valleys between the eight mountains that make up the ski area.

**Slopes** Red Pine Lodge, at the heart of the slopes, is reached by an eight-person gondola from the village. From here you can move in either direction across a series of ridges and valleys. Runs come off both sides of each ridge and generally face north or south. Most runs finish on the valley floors with some long, relatively flat run-outs. Five of the major lifts are fast quads. Free daily mountain tours start at 10.30am.

## KEY FACTS

| | |
|---|---|
| Resort | 2075m<br>6,800ft |
| Slopes | 2075-3045m<br>6,800-9,990ft |
| Lifts | 16 |
| Pistes | 3,500 acres |
| Green | 14% |
| Blue | 44% |
| Black | 42% |
| Snowmaking | 160 acres |

## REPORTS WANTED

Recently we have had few reports on this resort. If you go there, please do send us a report.

The best reports earn a copy of the next edition, and can lead to free lift passes in future.

See page 10.

**Central reservations**
Call 1 866 604 4171 (toll-free from within the US).

**Phone numbers**
From distant parts of the US, add the prefix 1 435.
From abroad, add the prefix +1 435.

## TOURIST OFFICE

**t** 649 5400
info@thecanyons.com
www.thecanyons.com

**Terrain-parks** There are six natural half-pipes across the mountain. The terrain park, which includes a super-pipe as well as jumps and rails, was moved for 2003/04 (see News).

**Snow reliability** Snow is not the best in Utah. The Canyons gets as much on average as Park City (350 inches) and more than Deer Valley. But the south-facing slopes suffer in late-season sun.

**Experts** There is steep terrain all over the mountain. We particularly liked the north-facing runs off Ninety Nine 90, with steep double-black-diamond runs plunging down through the trees to a pretty but almost flat run-out trail. There is also lots of double-diamond terrain on Murdock Peak. The runs off the Peak 5 chair are more sheltered.

**Intermediates** There are groomed blue runs for intermediates on all the main sectors except Ninety Nine 90. Some are quite short, but you can switch from valley to valley for added interest. Reporters recommend the runs off the Super Condor fast chair, and the Dreamscape area can be blissfully quiet.

**Beginners** There are areas just for beginners by Red Pine Lodge. But the run you progress to gets very busy with through-traffic.

**Snowboarding** It's a great area, with lots of natural hits. Canis Lupis is a mile-long, tight gully with high banked walls and numerous obstacles – like riding a bob-sleigh course.

**Cross-country** There are prepared trails on the Park City golf course and the Homestead Resort course.

**Queues** The gondola can be busy at peak times.

**Mountain restaurants** Red Pine Lodge is a large, attractive log-and-glass building with a busy self-service cafeteria and a table-service restaurant. Reporters found the Dreamscape Grill 'much quieter and more relaxing, with good soup'. The Lookout Cabin has wonderful views, and we've had excellent table-service food there.

**Schools and guides** The ski school uses the American Skiing Company's Perfect Turn formula, which focuses on an individual's strengths and builds on them (rather than correcting faults). The 'Perfect Kids' clinics are available for children from 2 to 12 years.

**Facilities for children** There's day care for children from 6 weeks to 4 years, located in the Grand Summit Hotel.

## STAYING THERE

**How to go** Accommodation at the resort village is still fairly limited.

**Hotels** The luxurious Grand Summit is right at the base of the gondola, and has a pool on the roof.

**Self-catering** The Sundial Lodge condos are in the resort village, with a rooftop hot-tub and plunge pool.

**Eating out** The Cabin restaurant, in the Grand Summit, serves eclectic US cuisine; Smokie's in the village is more casual. The Westgate Grill does steak and seafood. There is a Viking yurt for 'gourmet' dining after a sleigh ride.

**Après-ski** The Cabin Lounge in the Grand Summit has live entertainment, and Smokie's is good for après-ski.

**Off the slopes** There's a factory outlet mall nearby and a fair bit going on in Salt Lake City and Park City (see that chapter for more details).

THE CANYONS

It's not all as wild and bumpy as Ninety Nine 90; there is lots of intermediate cruising, too →

DEER VALLEY RESORT

# Deer Valley

*The ultimate upmarket ski resort*

**COSTS**

(1)(2)(3)(4)(5)(6)

**RATINGS**

**The slopes**

| | |
|---|---|
| Snow | **** |
| Extent | ** |
| Expert | *** |
| Intermediate | **** |
| Beginner | **** |
| Convenience | **** |
| Queues | **** |
| Mountain restaurants | **** |

**The rest**

| | |
|---|---|
| Scenery | *** |
| Resort charm | *** |
| Off-slope | ** |

**NEWS**

For 2004/05 two new chair-lifts are planned – one a fourth high-speed quad to the top of Flagstaff, the other a short triple linking Flagstaff to Bald Mountain. Two new intermediate runs are to be cut from the top of Flagstaff. And there should be new glade skiing for Empire Canyon and on Flagstaff, and more snowmaking.

- + Highly convenient, upmarket resort with superb skier services
- + Immaculate piste grooming, good snow record and lots of snow-guns
- + Good tree skiing
- + No queues
- + Easy access to Park City, The Canyons and other Utah resorts

- − No snowboarding allowed
- − Relatively expensive
- − Deer Valley itself is quiet at night – though Park City is right next door

**Deer Valley prides itself on pampering its guests, with valets to unload your skis, gourmet dining, immaculately groomed slopes, limited numbers on the mountain, no snowboarding. But there's more to it than that – it has some excellent slopes, with interesting terrain for all abilities, including plenty of ungroomed stuff. It hosted the freestyle and slalom competitions in the 2002 Olympics, and the 2003 Freestyle World Championships.**

**The slopes of Deer Valley and Park City are separated by nothing more than a fence which, given Deer Valley's ethos, seems likely to be permanent. Any skier visiting the area should try both; for most people, Park City is the obvious base – but there are some seductive hotels here at mid-mountain Silver Lake.**

## THE RESORT

Just a mile from the end of Park City's Main Street, Deer Valley is unashamedly upmarket – famed for the care and attention lavished on both slopes and guests. It's very obviously aimed at people who are used to being pampered and can pay for it.

The lodgings – luxurious private chalets and swanky hotels – are scattered around the fringes of the slopes, with more concentrated clusters on the valley floor near the main lift base and at Silver Lake Lodge (mid-mountain but accessible by road). There is no village as such. For any real animation you need to head for Park City, and many visitors prefer to stay there. There are free buses.

DEER VALLEY RESORT

Deer Valley's slopes are a great mixture of perfectly groomed trails, high bowls and chutes and excellent tree skiing ↓

## THE MOUNTAINS

The slopes are varied and interesting. Deer Valley's reputation for immaculate grooming is justified, but there is also a lot of exciting tree skiing (great when snow is falling) – and some steep mogul runs, too.

**Slopes** Two fast quads take you up to Bald Eagle Mountain, just beyond which is the mid-mountain focus of Silver Lake Lodge. You can ski from here to the isolated Little Baldy Peak, served by a gondola and a quad chair-lift, with mainly easy runs to serve property developments there, and also some short black runs. But the main skiing is on three linked peaks beyond Silver Lake Lodge, all served by fast quads – Bald Mountain, Flagstaff Mountain and Empire Canyon. The top of Empire is just a few metres from the runs of the Park City ski area.

**Terrain-parks** There aren't any as such, but there is a skier-cross course on Empire Canyon and a slalom course on Bald Mountain. You can take a run down them for a small charge.

**Snow reliability** As you'd expect in Utah, snow reliability is excellent, and there's plenty of snowmaking too.

**Experts** Despite its image of pampered luxury there is excellent expert terrain on all three main mountains, including

## KEY FACTS

| | |
|---|---|
| Resort | 2195m 7,200ft |
| Slopes | 2000-2915m 6,570-9,570ft |
| Lifts | 21 |
| Pistes | 1,750 acres |
| Green | 15% |
| Blue | 50% |
| Black | 35% |
| Snowmaking | 500 acres |

## REPORTS WANTED

Recently we have had few reports on this resort. If you go there, please do send us a report.

**Central reservations**
Call 645 6528.
**Phone numbers**
From distant parts of the US, add 1 435.
From abroad, add the prefix +1 435.

## TOURIST OFFICE

**t** 649 1000
marketing@deervalley.com
www.deervalley.com

fabulous glade skiing, bumps, chutes and open bowl slopes. And the snow doesn't get skied out quickly.

**Intermediates** There are lots of immaculately groomed blue runs all over the mountains.

**Beginners** There are nursery slopes at Silver Lake Lodge as well as the base, and gentle green runs (some, like Bandana, with great views from the top) to progress to on all mountains.

**Snowboarding** Boarding is banned.

**Cross-country** There are prepared trails on the Park City golf course and the Homestead Resort course, just out of town. There is also lots of scope for backcountry trips.

**Queues** Waiting in lift lines is not something that Deer Valley wants its guests to experience, so it limits the number of lift tickets sold.

**Mountain restaurants** There are attractive wood-and-glass self-service places at both Silver Lake and the base lodge, with free valet ski storage (you can store them free overnight too). The food is fine (but expensive). The grill restaurant at the recently opened Empire Canyon Lodge has been recommended. For a bit of a treat, try the restaurants at Stein Eriksen Lodge (including an all-you-can-eat buffet which was 'very highly recommended' by a 2004 reporter) or the Goldener Hirsch.

**Schools and guides** The ski school is doubtless excellent. Classes have a maximum of four pupils. Telemark lessons were introduced last season.

**Facilities for children** Deer Valley's Children's Center gives parents complimentary pagers. New last season was the free 'early drop' system. Leave your kids at 8.30am so you can get on the hill sooner. They'll be looked after and escorted to their lesson.

## STAYING THERE

**How to go** A car is useful for visiting the other nearby Utah resorts, though Deer Valley, Park City and The Canyons are all linked by regular shuttle-buses.

**Hotels** Stein Eriksen Lodge and the Goldener Hirsch at Silver Lake are two of the plushest hotels in any ski resort.

**Self-catering** There are many luxury apartments and houses to rent.

**Après-ski** The Lounge of the Snow Park Lodge at the base area is the main après-ski venue, with live music. There are lively bars and restaurants around Main Street in Park City.

**Eating out** Of the gourmet restaurants, the Mariposa is the best. The Seafood Buffet is also recommended. 'Fireside Dining' evenings at the Empire Canyon Lodge are held two days a week.

**Off the slopes** Park City has lots of shops, galleries etc. Salt Lake City has concerts, sights and shopping. Balloon rides and snowmobiling are popular.

# Jackson Hole

*Wild West town, exciting slopes and rapidly changing resort village*

**COSTS**

(1)(2)(3)(4)(5)(6)

**RATINGS**

**The slopes**

| | |
|---|---|
| Snow | **** |
| Extent | *** |
| Expert | ***** |
| Intermediate | ** |
| Beginner | *** |
| Convenience | *** |
| Queues | *** |
| Mountain restaurants | * |

**The rest**

| | |
|---|---|
| Scenery | *** |
| Resort charm | *** |
| Off-slope | *** |

**NEWS**

Jackson Hole has long had comfortable and good-value accommodation. But now it has truly luxurious options too, right by the slopes. The Teton Mountain Lodge, which opened in 2002/03, was upstaged in 2003/04 by the decadently luxurious Four Seasons Resort, whose 5-star accommodation boasts a fine dining restaurant, private health club and heated outdoor pool.

A yurt has opened in a backcountry location at Rock Springs and offers lunches and overnight stays.

Flight time to Jackson from the UK has improved with American Airlines (via Dallas) and Northwest (via Minneapolis) offering one-stop routes.

- + Big, steep mountain, with some real expert-only terrain and one of the US's biggest verticals: 1260m/4,140ft
- + Jackson town has an entertaining Wild West ambience
- + Unspoiled, remote location with impressive scenery and wildlife
- + Excellent snow record
- + Even more snow (and empty slopes) 90 minutes away at Grand Targhee
- + Luxurious new slope-side hotels plus lots of budget options
- + Plenty to do off the slopes
- + Airport is only minutes from town

- − Intermediates lacking the confidence to tackle ungroomed black runs will find the area very limited
- − Inadequate mountain restaurants
- − The cable-car serving the top runs still generates long queues
- − Low altitude, and slopes face roughly south-east, so snow can deteriorate quickly (and good snow is needed on steep slopes like these)
- − Town is 15 minutes from the slopes, though the slope-side village has lodgings and is growing quickly
- − Getting there from the UK involves two or (more often) three flights

**For those who like the idea of steep slopes smothered in deep powder or plastered with big bumps, Jackson Hole is Mecca. Like many American mountains, Jackson has double-diamond steeps that you can't find in Europe except by going off-piste with a guide. What marks it out from the rest is the sheer quantity of terrain that is classified black, and the scale of the mountain.**

**Utah devotees will tell you that the snow here isn't as light as at Alta/Snowbird; but it's light enough, and falls in quantities somewhere between those found in Colorado and those in Alta – the average annual total is around 400 inches, but in recent seasons it has often been around or above the 500-inch mark.**

**With its wooden sidewalks, country-music saloons and pool halls, tiny Jackson is a determinedly Western town – great fun, if you like that kind of thing. We do. A couple of luxurious slope-side hotels have opened in the last two seasons.**



## THE RESORT

The town of Jackson sits at the south-eastern edge of Jackson Hole – a high, flat valley surrounded by mountain ranges, in north-west Wyoming. Jackson gets many more visitors in summer than in winter (thanks to the nearby national parks). This is real 'cowboy' territory, and to entertain summer tourists the town strives to maintain its Wild West flavour, with traditional-style wooden buildings and sidewalks, and a couple of 'cowboy' saloons. It has lots of clothing and souvenir shops as well as upmarket galleries appealing to second-home owners. In winter it's half-empty and accommodation prices come down.

The slopes, a 15-minute drive or $2 bus-ride north-east, rise abruptly from the flat valley floor. At the base is Teton Village, with purpose-built lodgings, shops and restaurants in a pleasantly woody setting, some neo-Alpine but, increasingly, in local style. Teton Village has expanded rapidly over the last three years to become a much more attractive base with two new luxury hotels and an increased choice of restaurants and bars.

## THE MOUNTAINS

Jackson Hole has long been recognised as one of the world's most compelling resorts for advanced and expert skiers. With recent improvements to the lifts and the new buildings at Teton Village, the resort may seem to have a broader appeal. Don't be fooled: the beginner slopes are fine, but intermediates wanting to build up confidence should look elsewhere. Trail gradings are accurate: our own small map doesn't distinguish black from double-black-

## boarding

*Jackson Hole is a cult resort for expert snowboarders: the steeps, cliffs and chutes make for a lot of high-adrenalin thrills for competent free-riders. It's not a bad resort for novices, with the beginner slopes served by a high-speed quad. Intermediates not wishing to venture off the groomed runs will find the resort limited. There are some good snowboard shops, including the Hole-in-the-Wall at Teton Village.*

diamond runs, but the distinction matters once you are there – 'expert only' tends to mean just that. Some of the double-black runs are simply steep; but there are also cliffs, bumps, jumps and couloirs, including the infamous Corbet's.

### THE SLOPES
***One big mountain, one small one***

One big mountain makes Jackson Hole famous – **Rendezvous.** The summit, accessed by a mid-sized cable-car (the Tram), provides a 1260m/4,130ft vertical – exceptional for the US. Conditions and thighs permitting, you can go from top to almost bottom on black slopes. From the top of the Tram you can also access the backcountry of Cody Bowl. It can be incredibly cold and windy at the top of the Tram even when it's warm and calm below.

To the right looking up is **Apres Vous** mountain, with half the vertical and mostly much gentler runs, accessed by the short Teewinot and the longer Apres Vous fast quads.

Between these two peaks is a broad mountainside split by gullies, accessed by the Bridger gondola. This gives speedy access to the Thunder and Sublette quad chairs serving some of the steepest terrain on Rendezvous.

To get your bearings, take the Rendezvous Trail from the top of the Tram. This turns into South Pass traverse and goes all the way past the main lifts to the far end of the area on Apres Vous. There are complimentary tours of the mountain daily.

**Snow King** is a separate area right by Jackson town. Locals use it lunch-time and evenings (it's partly floodlit).

### TERRAIN-PARKS
***They exist***

There's a terrain-park and a half-pipe, and Dick's Ditch is a natural pipe, but you really come to Jackson for the steeps and deeps of the free-riding.

### SNOW RELIABILITY
***Steep lower slopes can suffer***

The claimed average of 402 inches of 'mostly dry powder' snow is much more than most Colorado resorts claim – and for a core three-month season conditions are likely to be reasonable. But the base elevation is relatively low for the Rockies, and the slopes are quite sunny – they basically face south-east. If you're unlucky, you may find the steep lower slopes like the Hobacks in poor shape, or even shut (we have). Locals claim that you can expect powder roughly half the time.

### KEY FACTS

| | |
|---|---|
| **Resort** | 1925m 6,310ft |
| Jackson Hole | |
| **Slopes** | 1925-3185m 6,310-10,450ft |
| **Lifts** | 12 |
| **Pistes** | 2,500 acres |
| **Green** | 10% |
| **Blue** | 40% |
| **Black** | 50% |
| **Snowmaking** | 180 acres |
| Grand Targhee | |
| **Slopes** | 2310-3050m 7,600-10,000ft |
| **Lifts** | 5 |
| **Pistes** | 2,000 acres (plus 1,000 acres served by snowcat) |
| **Green** | 10% |
| **Blue** | 70% |
| **Black** | 20% |
| **Snowmaking** | none |

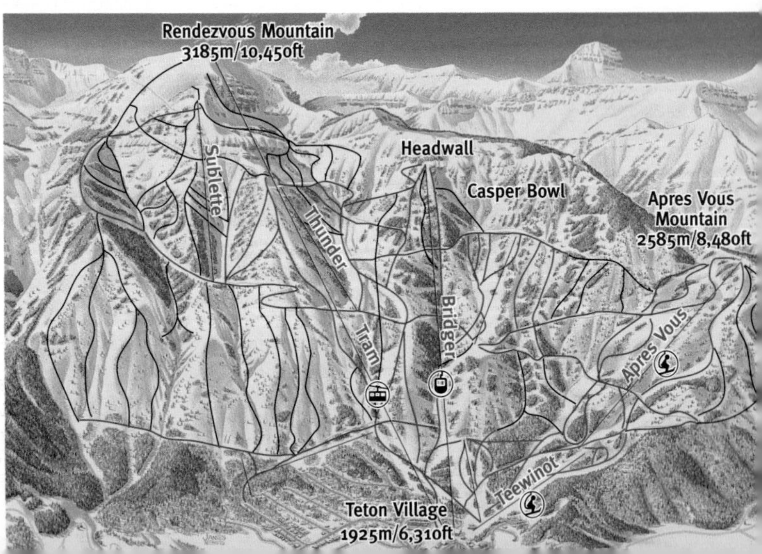

When conditions are like this in the backcountry, who could resist hiring a guide to find fresh tracks like these guys have? →

WADE MCKOY / FPI

## LIFT PASSES

**Jackson Hole**
Covers all lifts in Jackson Hole

**Main pass**
1 day $64
6 days $348

**Senior citizens**
Over 65: 6 days $174

**Children**
Under 22: 6 days $268
Under 15: 6 days $174

**Notes**
Half-day pass available. Prices may be cheaper when booked in advance through UK tour operators.

**Alternative passes**
Grand Targhee; Snow King Mountain

## FOR EXPERTS
***Best for the brave***

For the good skier or boarder who wants challenges without the expense of hiring a guide to go off-piste, Jackson is one of the world's best resorts – maybe even the best. Rendezvous mountain offers virtually nothing but black and very black slopes. The routes down the main Rendezvous Bowl are not particularly fearsome; but some of the alternatives are. Go down the East Ridge at least once to stare over the edge of the notorious Corbet's Couloir. The Tram passes right above it, giving a great view of people leaping off the lip. It's the jump-in that's special; the word is that the slope you land on is a mere 50° to the horizontal. One reporter last season survived a run down Corbet's but said that part of the lip at the top had worn away so you could slide down rather than take a leap of faith. His guide referred to the easier route down as 'the Four Seasons approach', referring to the new luxury hotel.

Below Rendezvous Bowl, the wooded flanks of Cheyenne Bowl offer serious challenges, at the extreme end of the single-black-diamond spectrum. If instead you take the ridge run that skirts this bowl to the right, you get to the Hobacks – a huge area of open and lightly wooded slopes, gentler than those higher up, but still black.

Corbet's aside, most of the seriously steep slopes are more easily reached from the slightly lower quad chairs. From Sublette, you have direct access to the short but seriously steep Alta chutes, and to the less severe Laramie Bowl beside them. Or you can track over to Tensleep Bowl – pausing to inspect Corbet's from below – and on to the less extreme (and less chute-like) Expert Chutes, and the single black Cirque and Headwall areas. Casper Bowl – accessed through gates only – is recommended for untracked powder. Thunder chair serves further steep, narrow, north-facing chutes.

Again, the lower part of the mountain here offers lightly wooded single-black slopes.

The gondola serves terrain not without interest for experts. In particular, Moran Woods is a splendid, under-utilised area. And even Apres Vous itself has an area of serious single blacks in Saratoga bowl.

The gates into the backcountry access over 3,000 acres of amazing terrain; you should hire a guide to take you there. You can now stay out overnight at the new backcountry yurt. There are some helicopter operations.

## FOR INTERMEDIATES
***Exciting for some***

There are great cruising runs on the front face of Apres Vous, and top-to-bottom quite gentle blues from the gondola. But they don't add up to a great deal of mileage, and you shouldn't consider Jackson unless you want to tackle the blacks. It's then important to get guidance on steepness and snow conditions. The steepest single blacks are steep, intimidating when mogulled and fearsome when hard. The daily grooming map is worth consulting.

## FOR BEGINNERS
***Fine, up to a point***

There are a few broad, gentle runs: fine for getting started. The progression to the blue Werner run off the Apres Vous chair is gradual enough – but few other runs will help build confidence.

## FOR CROSS-COUNTRY
***Lots of possibilities***

There are three centres, and one at Grand Targhee, offering varied trails. The Spring Creek Nordic Center has

## SCHOOLS

**Jackson Hole**
t 739 2663
mountainsports@
jacksonhole.com

**Classes**
Full day (5½hr) $70

**Private lessons**
Half day (3hr) $265

## CHILDREN

**Kids' Ranch**
t 739 2691
kidsranch@
jacksonhole.com
Wranglers: 8.30-4.30; ages 6mnth to 2yr; $95 per day.
Rough Riders: 9am-3.30; ages 3 to 6; includes skiing; $95 per day

**Ski school**
Explorers: ages 7 to 14; 9am-3.30; $95 per day
Team Extreme: ages 12 to 17; 8.50-3.30; $115 per day.

some good beginner terrain and moonlight tours. The Nordic Center at Teton has 17km/11 miles of trails and organises trips into the National Parks.

### QUEUES
***Always queues for the Tram***

The Bridger gondola relieved some of the pressure on the Tram, which is now over 30 years old. But the Tram is still the quickest way up, still the only way to the very top and still not able to keep up with demand; there may be queues all day (10 to 30 minutes, at different times of day). The tram used to take 60 people a time but since the backcountry gates have been opened it now only takes 55 because more and more people are wearing backpacks and carrying shovels. You can access all of the mountain except Rendezvous Bowl via the Sublette chair.

### MOUNTAIN RESTAURANTS
***Head back to base***

There's only one real restaurant on the mountain – at the base of the Casper chair-lift; it does a good range of self-service food, but gets very crowded. There are simple snack bars at four other points on the mountain.

### SCHOOLS AND GUIDES
***Learn to tackle the steeps***

As well as the usual lessons, there are also special types – steep and deep, women-only, for example – on certain dates. You can book Early Tram lessons and be first on the slopes. Backcountry guides can be hired.

### FACILITIES FOR CHILDREN
***Just fine***

The area may not seem to be one ideally suited to children, but in fact there are enough easy runs and the 'Kids' Ranch' care facilities are good. There are various classes catering for ages 3 to 17.

## STAYING THERE

### HOW TO GO
***In town or by the mountain***

Teton Village is convenient and has varied accommodation. But stay in Jackson if you want the cowboy atmosphere.

**Hotels** Because winter is low season, prices are low.

((((5 **Four Seasons Resort** (332 3442) Stylish luxury in Teton Village with a health club and one of the most impressive outdoor pools, set amid landscaped boulders with waterfalls, we have seen.

((((5 **Amangani Resort** (734 7333) Hedonistic luxury in isolated position way above the valley.

(((4 **Teton Mountain Lodge** (734 7111) Very comfortable ski in, ski out hotel in Teton Village. Good indoor and outdoor pool and fitness centre.

(((4 **Alpenhof** (733 3242) Tirolean-style, with varied rooms. Recently extended and refurbished. Good food. Pool, sauna, hot-tub.

(((4 **Wort** (733 2190) Comfortable, right in the centre of town, above the lively Silver Dollar Bar. Hot-tub.

(((4 **Rusty Parrot Lodge** (733 2000) A stylish place in town, with a rustic feel and handcrafted furniture. Hot-tub.

(((4 **Snake River Lodge & Spa** (732 6000) At Teton Village. Smartly welcoming as well as comfortable and convenient, with fine spa facilities.

(((4 **Spring Creek Ranch** (733 8833) Exclusive retreat between town and slopes; cross-country on hand. Hot-tub.

(((4 **Huff House Inn** (733 4164) Charming old inn – the best of Jackson's many luxury B&B places.

(((4 **Painted Porch** (733 1981) Gorgeous B&B full of antiques.

((3 **Jackson Hole Lodge** (733 2992) Western-style place on fringe of Jackson town. Comfortable mini-suite rooms, and free breakfast/après-ski munchies. Pool, sauna, hot-tubs.

((3 **Parkway Inn** (733 3143) Friendly, family-run, central in Jackson town; big rooms, antique furniture, pool, hot-tubs. Recommended by a reporter.

(2 **Hostel x** (733 3415) Basic, good value, at Teton Village. Recommended by a reporter.

(2 **Trapper Inn** (733 2648) Friendly, good value, a block or two from Town Square. Hot-tubs.

**Self-catering** There is lots of choice around Jackson and at Teton Village.

## GETTING THERE

**Air** Jackson 19km/ 12 miles (½hr).

## ACTIVITIES

**Indoor** Cinemas, fitness centres, swimming, tennis, theatre, library, wildlife art and other museums

**Outdoor** Snowmobiles, ice skating, snow-shoeing, sleigh rides, dog-sledding, paragliding, ballooning, wildlife tours

**Phone numbers**
From distant parts of the US, add the prefix 1 307.
From abroad, add the prefix +1 307.

## TOURIST OFFICES

**Jackson Hole**
**t** 733 2292
info@jacksonhole.com
www.jacksonhole.com

**Grand Targhee**
**t** 353 2300
info@grandtarghee.com
www.grandtarghee.com

### EATING OUT
***A reasonable range of options***

Teton Village has pizza, Mexican, Japanese, a steakhouse and a number of good hotel restaurants (a 2004 reporter enjoyed 'scallops to die for' at the Alpenhof Bistro). The Mangy Moose is good value and good fun. In Jackson town there is more choice. The cool art-deco Cadillac Grille does good food. The Blue Lion is small and casually stylish. The 'saloons' do hearty meals and good steaks. A reporter praises Antony's Italian and 'for a treat' the Rusty Parrot Lodge. The cute log cabin Sweetwater serves 'Greek-inspired' food. The Snake River brew-pub is good value – not to be confused with the expensive Snake River Grill. The Old Yellowstone Garage has 'superb Italian food in an elegant setting', Rendezvous Bistro 'excellent cuisine'. Nikai Sushi, which turns into a city-style nightclub on Friday nights, is popular with the younger set wanting an urban fix. The Grill at Amangani has 'a supremely stylish setting, stunning food and is not nearly as expensive as expected from a 5-star establishment.'

### APRES-SKI
***Amusing saloons***

For immediate après-ski at Teton Village, the Mangy Moose is a big, happy, noisy place, often with live music. For a quieter time head for Dietrich's bar at the Alpenhof.

In Jackson there are two famous 'saloons'. The Million Dollar Cowboy Bar features saddles as bar stools and a stuffed grizzly bear, and is usually the liveliest place in town, with live music and dancing some nights. The Silver Dollar around the corner is more subdued; there may be ragtime playing as you count the 2032 silver dollars inlaid into the counter. The Rancher is a huge pool-hall. The Shady Lady saloon sometimes has live music. The Virginian saloon is much quieter and a locals' hangout ('If you like guns, ammo and beer, you will be in good company,' says one). For a night out of town, join the locals at the Stagecoach Inn at Wilson, especially Sundays for Church: 'A real western and blue grass swing night with music from a band that has not missed a night since 1969.'

### OFF THE SLOPES
***'Great' outdoor diversions***

Yellowstone National Park is 100km/60 miles to the north. You can tour the park by snowcat or snowmobile, but you'll be roaring along in the company of several hundred other smelly snowmobiles – 'more like a Grand Prix than a wilderness', says one reporter.

The National Elk Refuge, next to Jackson and across the road from the National Museum of Wildlife Art, has the largest elk herd in the US and 'you can get really close to the elk on a sled ride organised by the centre,' says a reporter. In town there are some 40 galleries and museums and a number of outlets for Indian and Western arts and crafts.

### A DAY OUT IN GRAND TARGHEE 2440m/8,000ft

*We'd recommend any adventurous visitor to make the hour-and-a-half trip over the Teton pass to Grand Targhee, especially if there's been a recent big dump. The average snowfall here is over 500 inches – 25% greater than Jackson, and on a par with Utah's best – and the slopes are usually blissfully empty and much easier than at Jackson. Locals call it Grand Foggee, because there is often low cloud even when it's not snowing. A 2004 reporter said 'I had one of my best ski days ever, with run after run of fresh powder and barely a soul in sight.'*

*On the main Fred's Mountain, the 1,500 acres can all be accessed from a central fast quad. The wide area of open and lightly wooded blue and black runs has a respectable 610m/2,000ft vertical. A long slow double serves a splendid area of tough blues and easy blacks. Lower down, a slow quad serves an excellent area of short green runs. One-third of neighbouring Peaked Mountain is accessed by a fast quad and has a vertical of only 390m/1,280ft and four short blue and blue-black trails, as well as some wooded terrain. Two-thirds is reserved for guided snowcat skiing – over 1,000 acres, mainly great gladed runs in pristine powder.*

*Daily buses to Targhee pick up from various hotels around town and Teton Village and you can buy a combined bus/lift ticket for $65. Snowcat skiing or boarding costs $299 a day (including lunch), $225 a half day. You can also stay at Grand Targhee – there's a small, quiet, modern village right at the base.*

SNOWPIX.COM / CHRIS GILL

# Park City

*An entertaining base for excursions into Utah's famous powder*

## COSTS

①②③④⑤⑥

## RATINGS

| **The slopes** | |
|---|---|
| Snow | **** |
| Extent | *** |
| Expert | **** |
| Intermediate | **** |
| Beginner | **** |
| Convenience | *** |
| Queues | **** |
| Mountain restaurants | ** |
| **The rest** | |
| Scenery | *** |
| Resort charm | *** |
| Off-slope | *** |

## NEWS

For 2003/04 a fourth terrain-park was created and 'fast lanes' introduced on four lifts. You can use them for free with a pass of four days or more. The resort also bought more grooming machines, and the Summit House mountain restaurant got a new heated patio.



## KEY FACTS

| | |
|---|---|
| **Resort** | 2105m 6,900ft |
| **Slopes** | 2105-3050m 6,900-10,000ft |
| **Lifts** | 15 |
| **Pistes** | 3,300 acres |
| **Green** | 18% |
| **Blue** | 44% |
| **Black** | 38% |
| **Snowmaking** | 475 acres |

- ✚ Increasingly touristy Wild West-style Main Street, convenient for slopes
- ✚ Lots of bars and restaurants make nonsense of Utah's Mormon image
- ✚ Well maintained slopes, good snow record, and lots of snowmaking
- ✚ Good lift system, with four six-packs
- ✚ Good base for visiting other major Utah resorts – Deer Valley and The Canyons are effectively suburbs and other resorts less than an hour away

- ▬ Rest of town is an enormous (still expanding) sprawl and doesn't have the same charm as Main Street
- ▬ The blue and black runs tend to be rather short – most lifts give a vertical of around 400m/1,300ft
- ▬ Although the snowfall record is impressive by normal standards, it comes nowhere near that of Alta and Snowbird, a few miles away
- ▬ Lack of spectacular scenery

**Park City has clear attractions, particularly if you ignore its sprawling suburbs and stay near the centre to make the most of the lively bars and restaurants in its beautifully restored and developed Main Street. But the place really comes into its own as a base for touring other resorts as well.**

**Deer Valley is separated from Park City's slopes by a fence between the tops of two lifts, and by separate ownership with quite different objectives. All that is required to link them is to remove the fence – a small step that is unlikely to be taken, given Deer Valley's exclusive nature. To European eyes, all very strange.**

**The Canyons is only a little further away, on the outskirts of town, and reached by free buses. And then there are the famously powdery resorts of Snowbird and Alta, less than an hour away by car or bus. Even the Olympic downhill slopes of Snowbasin are within easy reach if you have a car.**

## THE RESORT

Park City is about 45 minutes by road from Salt Lake City. It was born with the discovery of silver in 1872. By the turn of the century it boasted a population of 10,000, a red-light district, a Chinese quarter and 27 saloons. Careful restoration has left the town with a splendid historic centrepiece in Main Street.

The old wooden sidewalks and clapboard buildings are now filled with a colourful selection of art galleries, shops, boutiques, bars and restaurants – though it is getting rather touristy, with some tacky shops selling T-shirts and souvenirs. New buildings have been tastefully designed to blend in smoothly. But away from the centre the resort lacks charm, sprawls over a wide area and is still expanding.

The Town Lift is a triple chair up to the slopes from Lower Main Street, but the main lift base is Resort Center, on the fringes, with modern buildings and its own bars, restaurants and lodgings.

Deer Valley and The Canyons are

## LIFT PASSES

**Park City**
Covers all lifts in Park City Mountain Resort, with free ski-bus.

**Main pass**
1 day $67
6 days $354

**Senior citizens**
Over 65: 1 day $36
Over 70: free

**Children**
Under 13: 6 days $192
Under 7: free

**Notes**
Half-day pass available. Lower multi-day pass prices if purchased in advance with lodging.

**Alternative passes**
Utah passport covering Park City, The Canyons, Deer Valley, Snowbird, Solitude, Sundance, Brighton and Alta is available through UK tour operators.

PARK CITY CVB

↙ Main Street is based on the original 19th century silver mining town and the old buildings have been well restored

almost suburbs of Park City, but all three retain quite separate identities. They are linked by free shuttle-buses, which also go around town and run until late. A trolley-bus runs along Main Street. A car is useful for visiting other ski areas on the good roads.

If you're not hiring a car, pick a location that's handy for Main Street and the Town chair or the free bus.

## THE MOUNTAIN

Mostly the area consists of blue and black trails cut through the trees on the flanks of rounded mountain ridges, with easier runs running along the ridges and the gullies between. The more interesting terrain is in the lightly wooded bowls and ridges at the top of the resort's slopes.

### THE SLOPES
***Bowls above the woods***

A fast six-seat chair-lift whisks you up from Resort Center, and another beyond that up to Summit House, the main mountain restaurant.

Most of the easy and intermediate runs lie between the Summit House and the base area, and spread along the sides of a series of interconnecting ridges. Virtually all the steep terrain is above Summit House in a series of ungroomed bowls, and accessed by the McConkey's six-pack and the old Jupiter double chair.

There are free twice daily Mountain History Tours of the slopes, looking at the area's silver mining heritage (including old mine workings). A long floodlit run and a floodlit terrain-park and half-pipe are open until 7.30pm.

### TERRAIN-PARKS
***Is four enough?***

There are four terrain-parks created with the help of a team of big name skiers and snowboarders – the Park City All Stars – who regularly ride them, and two half-pipes (including the 105m/350ft long Eagle Superpipe that was used in the 2002 Olympics).

### SNOW RELIABILITY
***Not quite the Greatest on Earth***

Utah is famous for the quality and quantity of its snow. Park City's record doesn't match those of Snowbird and Alta, but an annual average of 350 inches is still impressive, and ahead of most Colorado figures. And snowmaking covers about 15% of the terrain.

### FOR EXPERTS
***Lots of variety***

There is a lot of excellent advanced and expert terrain at the top of the lift system. It is now all marked as double-diamond on the trail map but there are

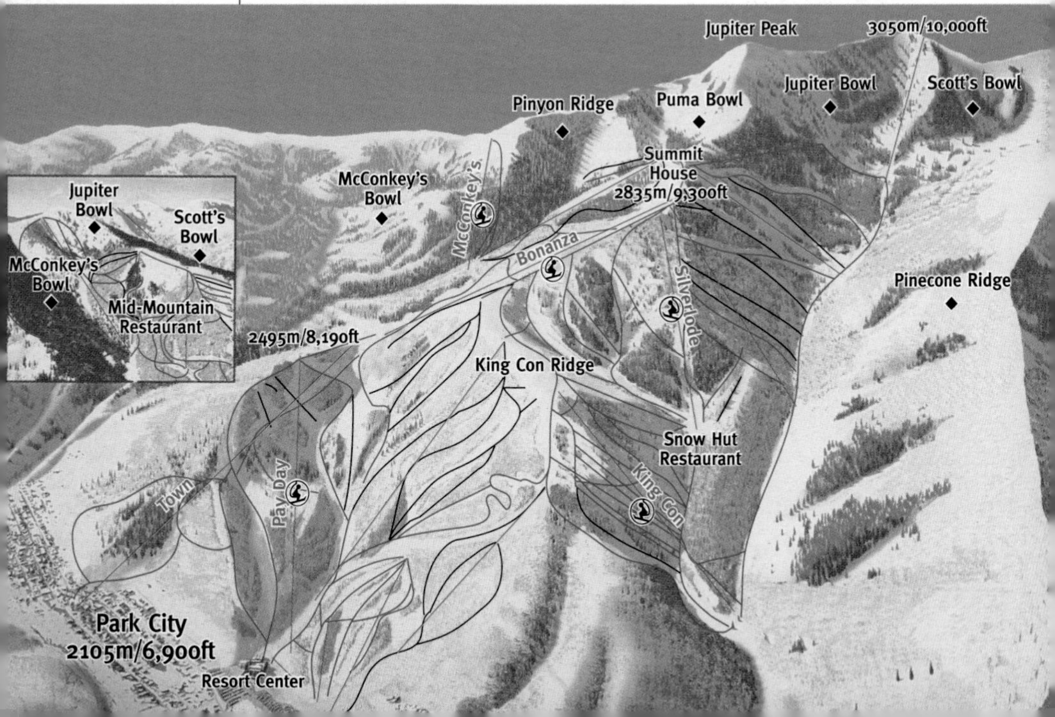

**REPORTS WANTED**

Recently we have had few reports on this resort. If you go there, please do send us a report.

The best reports earn a copy of the next edition, and can lead to free lift passes in future.

See page 10.

## boarding

*It's difficult to believe that boarding was banned here until the late 1990s. 'Great boarding area,' says a 2004 reporter; and no wonder – the resort has wonderful free-ride terrain and high powder bowls. Beginners have their own excellent area, good easy cruising and a lift system which is entirely chair-lifts. And now there are no fewer than four terrain-parks and the Olympic half-pipe.*

many runs that deserve only a single-diamond rating – so don't be put off. We particularly like the prettily wooded McConkey's Bowl, served by a six-pack and offering a range of open pitches and gladed terrain. The old Jupiter lift accesses the highest bowls, which include some serious terrain – with narrow couloirs, cliffs and cornices – as well as easier wide-open slopes. The Jupiter bowl runs are under the chair, but there is a lot more terrain accessible by traversing and hiking – turn left for West Face, Pioneer Ridge and Puma Bowl, right for Scott's Bowl and the vast expanse of Pinecone Ridge, stretching literally for miles down the side of Thaynes Canyon.

Lower down, the side of Summit House ridge, serviced by the Thaynes and Motherlode chairs, has some little-used black runs, plus a few satisfying trails in the trees. There's a zone of steep runs towards town from further round the ridge. And don't miss Blueslip Bowl near Summit House – so called because in the past, when it was out of bounds, ski company employees caught skiing it were fired, and were given their notice on a blue slip.

Good skiers (no snowboarders, due to some long flat run-outs and hikes) should not miss the Utah Interconnect – see feature panel. For bigger budgets, Park City Powder Guides offers heli-skiing on 20,000 acres of private backcountry land.

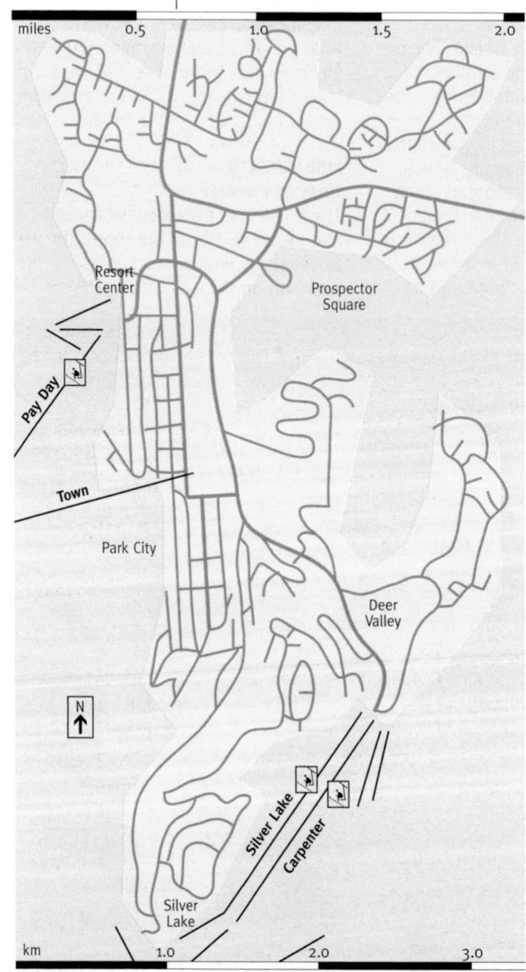


### FOR INTERMEDIATES
***OK for a day***

There are blue runs served by all the main lifts, apart from Jupiter (the blue Jupiter Access is worth a go though, even if you don't ride the chair, for the sight of people coming down the chutes). The areas around the King Con high-speed quad and Silverlode high-speed six-pack have a dense network of great (but fairly short) cruising runs. There are also more difficult trails close by, for those looking for a challenge.

But there are few long, fast cruising runs – most trails are around 1 to 2km/0.5 to 1 mile, and many have long, flat run-outs. The Pioneer and McConkey's chair-lifts are off the main drag and serve some very pleasant, often quiet runs. The runs under the Town lift have great views of the town.

Intermediates will certainly want to visit The Canyons and Deer Valley for a day or two (see separate chapters).

### FOR BEGINNERS
***A good chance for fast progress***

Novices get started on short lifts and a dedicated beginners' area near the

Just a fraction of Park City's sprawling suburbs, with Resort Center sitting at the foot of the slopes →

PARK CITY CVB

**SCHOOLS**

**Park City**
t 1-800-227-2754
pcinfo@pcski.com

**Classes**
3 3hr days $215

**Private lessons**
$120 for 1hr

**CHILDREN**

**Little Groomers**
(run by ski school)
t 1 800 227 2754
9am-3pm or 9.45-3.45; ages 3½ to 5; 5 days $650, includes ski tuition, lunch and indoor activities

**The Clubhouse**
t 940 1607
Licensed day care centre

**Guardian Angel**
t 783 2662
Babysitting service

**Ski school**
The school offers classes for ages 6 to 13, 9.30-3.30, $122 per day including lunch

base lodge. The beginners' classes graduate up the hill quite quickly, and there's a good, very gentle and wide 'easiest way down' – the three-and a half-mile Home Run – clearly marked all the way from Summit House. It's easy enough for most beginners to manage after only a few lessons. The Town chair can be ridden down.

### FOR CROSS-COUNTRY
***Some trails; lots of backcountry***

There are prepared trails on both the Park City golf course, next to the downhill area, and the Homestead Resort course, just out of town. There is lots of scope for backcountry trips.

### QUEUES
***Peak period problems only***

Lift queues aren't normally a problem with so many six-packs. But it can get pretty crowded (on some trails as well as the lifts) at weekends, particularly on the Payday lift from Resort Center. With a pass for four days or more, the Fast Track system means you can jump the queues on four main lifts.

### MOUNTAIN RESTAURANTS
***Standard self-service stuff***

The Mid-Mountain Lodge is a 19th-century mine building which was heaved up the mountain to its present location near the bottom of Pioneer chair. The food is standard self-service fare but most reporters prefer it to the alternatives. The Summit House is cafe-style – serving chilli, pizza, soup etc. The Snow Hut is a smaller log building and usually has an outdoor grill. Caffé Amante is a coffee house halfway down the Bonanza chair-lift. There's quite a choice of restaurants back at the base area, including the 'impersonal' food court at the Legacy Lodge. The Brewhouse serves pizzas and a range of local and imported beer.

### SCHOOLS AND GUIDES
***Thorough, full of enthusiasm***

The school offers performance workshops (Moguls and Beyond, Dealing with the Diamonds) and Power Clinics (for strong intermediates) as well as beginner and private lessons. A 2004 reporter who booked two snowboard group lessons was the only one on both occasions: 'Great value.'

### FACILITIES FOR CHILDREN
***Well organised; ideal terrain***

There are a number of licensed carers who operate either at their own premises or at visitors' lodgings. The ski school takes children from the age of three. Book in advance.

**THE UTAH INTERCONNECT**

*Good skiers should not miss this excellent guided backcountry tour that runs four days a week from Park City to Snowbird. (Three days a week it runs from Snowbird, but only as far as Solitude.) When we did it we got fresh tracks in knee-deep powder practically all day. After a warm-up run to weed out weak skiers, you head up to the top of the Jupiter chair, go through a 'closed' gate in the area boundary and ski down a deserted, prettily wooded valley to Solitude. After taking the lifts to the top of Solitude we did a short traverse, then down more virgin powder towards Brighton. After more powder runs and lunch back in Solitude, it was up the lifts and a 30-minute hike up the Highway to Heaven to north-facing, tree-lined slopes and a great little gully down into Alta. How much of Alta and Snowbird you get to ski depends on how much time is left.*

*The price ($150) includes two guides – one leading, another at the rear – lunch, lift tickets for all five resorts you pass through and transport home.*

## GETTING THERE

**Air** Salt Lake City 58km/36 miles (½hr).

## ACTIVITIES

**Indoor** Park City Racquet Club (tennis, racquetball, swimming pool, hot-tub, gym); Silver Mountain Spa sports club (pools, hot-tubs, sauna, steam room, tennis, racquetball, gym); other fitness clubs, spa treatments, art galleries, museum, theatre

**Outdoor** Ice skating, snowmobiles, dog sledding, sleigh rides, ballooning, ski jumping, bob-sleigh and ice rocket (luge) track, snow-shoeing, snow tubing, winter fly fishing, horse riding

**Phone numbers**
From distant parts of the US, add the prefix 1 435.
From abroad, add the prefix +1 435.

## TOURIST OFFICE

**t** 649 8111
info@pcski.com
www.parkcitymountain.com
www.parkcityinfo.com

## STAYING THERE

### HOW TO GO
***Packaged independence***

Park City is the busiest and most atmospheric of the Utah resorts, and a good base for visiting the others. We prefer to stay near Main Street but outlying areas such as Kimball Junction are convenient (but soulless) if you have a rental car and want to visit a different resort each day.

**Hotels** There's a wide variety, from typical chains to individual little B&Bs. We had a scathing 2004 report on the Yarrow, so have dropped it.

(4) **Silver King** (649 5500) Deluxe hotel/condo complex at base of the slopes, with indoor-outdoor pool.

(4) **Radisson Inn Park City** (649 5000) Excellent rooms and indoor-outdoor pool, but out of town.

(4) **Washington School Inn** (649 3800) 'Absolutely excellent' historic inn with 'fantastic service' say reporters. In a great location near Main Street.

(3) **Best Western Landmark Inn** (649 7300) At Kimball Junction. Pool.

(3) **Old Miners' Lodge** (645 8068) 100-year-old building next to Town lift, restored and furnished with antiques.

(2) **Chateau Apres Lodge** (649 9372) Close to the slopes: comfortable, faded, cheap.

(2) **1904 Imperial Inn** (649 1904) Quaint B&B at the top of Main Street.

**Self-catering** There's a big range available. The Townlift studios near Main Street and Park Avenue condos are both modern and comfortable and the latter have outdoor pool and hot-tubs. Silver Cliff Village is adjacent to the slopes and has spacious units and access to the facilities of the Silver King Hotel. Blue Church Lodge is a well-converted 19th-century Mormon church with luxury condos and rooms.

### EATING OUT
***Book in advance***

There are over 100 restaurants but they can get busy, so book in advance if you can. Zoom is the old Union Pacific train depot, now a trendy restaurant owned by Robert Redford. Riverhorse is in a beautiful, high-ceilinged first-floor room with live music. Chimayo has great south-west cuisine. Chez Betty is small and has perhaps the best food in town – expensive though. Other reporter favourites include the Prime Steakhouse ('best steak ever'), the Grub Steak Restaurant, Cisero's and Grappa (Italian), Wasatch Brew Pub (good value and interesting range of beers) and Baja Cantina (Mexican). The new Butchers Chop House has been recommended for 'amazing beef'.

### APRES-SKI
***Better than you might think***

Although there are still some arcane liquor laws in Utah, provided you're over 21 and can prove it, the laws are never a serious barrier to getting a drink. At the bars and clubs that are more dedicated to drinking (ie don't feature food but do serve spirits or beer stronger than 3.2% alcohol) membership of some kind is required. This may involve one of your party handing over $4 or more – one member can introduce numerous 'guests' – or else there'll be some old guy at the bar already organised to 'sponsor' you (sign you in) for the price of a beer (not exactly legal). A membership lasts three weeks, but a reporter points out that the system can be very expensive if you visit different resorts most days and just want a quick beer before hitting the road. Places with tavern licences serve 3.2% beer and don't operate as clubs – but you do still need to be 21.

As the slopes close, Legends and the Brewhouse are the places to head for at the Resort Center. In Main Street, the Wasatch Brew Pub makes its own ale. The Claimjumper, JB Mulligans and the scruffy Alamo are lively and there's usually live music and dancing at weekends. Harry O's and Cisero's nightclub are good too. The Monkey Bar, new for 2003/04, has DJs and pole dancing.

### OFF THE SLOPES
***Should be interesting***

There's a factory outlet mall at Kimball Junction. Balloon flights and excursions to Nevada for gambling are popular. Snowmobiling is big. In January there's Robert Redford's Sundance Film Festival, in February Winterfest is a 10-day celebration of the 2002 Olympics including concerts and snow sculpture.

There are lots of shops and galleries. The museum and old jail house are worth a visit. Salt Lake City has some good concerts, shopping and Mormon heritage sites. The Capitol Building, open until 8pm, gives good views of the city.

You might like to learn to ski-jump or try the Olympic bob track at the Winter Sports Park down the road.

# Snowbird

*One of the best spots for powder hounds, linked to Alta*

## COSTS

(1)(2)(3)(4)(5)(6)

## RATINGS

**The slopes**

| | |
|---|---|
| Snow | ***** |
| Extent | *** |
| Expert | ***** |
| Intermediate | *** |
| Beginner | ** |
| Convenience | ***** |
| Queues | ** |
| Mountain restaurants | * |

**The rest**

| | |
|---|---|
| Scenery | *** |
| Resort charm | * |
| Off-slope | * |

## NEWS

For 2004/05 there is to be a new super-pipe next to the intermediate Big Emma terrain-park. This continues the terrain-park expansions of the previous two seasons. There will also be yet more snowmaking.

## KEY FACTS

| | |
|---|---|
| **Resort** | 2470m 8,100ft |

For Snowbird and Alta combined area

| | |
|---|---|
| **Slopes** | 2365-3350m 7,760-11,000ft |
| **Lifts** | 26 |
| **Pistes** | 4,700 acres |
| **Green** | 22% |
| **Blue** | 39% |
| **Black** | 39% |
| **Snowmaking** | 125 acres |

Snowbird only

| | |
|---|---|
| **Slopes** | 2365-3350m 7,760-11,000ft |
| **Lifts** | 13 |
| **Pistes** | 2,500 acres |
| **Green** | 27% |
| **Blue** | 38% |
| **Black** | 35% |
| **Snowmaking** | 75 acres |

+ Quantity and quality of powder snow unrivalled
+ Link to Alta makes one of the largest ski areas in the US
+ Fabulous ungroomed slopes, with steep and not-so-steep options
+ Luxurious accommodation
+ Slopes-at-the-door convenience
+ Easy to get to other Utah resorts

− Limited groomed runs for intermediates
− Tiny, claustrophobic resort 'village'
− Stark modern architecture
− Frequent queues for main cable-car
− Avalanche risk can close the road and slopes and keep you indoors
− Very quiet at night

**There can be few places where nature has combined the steep with the deep better than at Snowbird and neighbouring Alta, and even fewer places where there are also lifts to give you access. The two resorts have been linked since the 2001/02 season and the combined area is one of the top powder-pig paradises in the world and one of the US's biggest lift-linked ski areas. So it is a shame that Snowbird's concrete, purpose-built 'base village' is so lacking in charm and ski resort ambience. Snowboarders are banned from Alta's slopes, so cannot take advantage of the link.**

## THE RESORT

Snowbird lies 40km/25 miles from Salt Lake City in Little Cottonwood Canyon – just before Alta. The setting is rugged and rather Alpine – and both the resort and (particularly) the approach road are prone to avalanches and closure: visitors are sometimes confined indoors for safety. The resort buildings are mainly block-like – but they provide high-quality ski-in, ski-out lodging.

The resort area and the slopes are spread along the road on the south side of the narrow canyon. The focal Snowbird Center (lift base/shops/restaurants) is towards the eastern, up-canyon end. All the lodgings and restaurants are within walking distance. The main cable-car (Tram) station is central and the other main Gad lifts can be reached on snow. There are regular shuttle-buses, including a service up to Alta.

↑ The rooftop pool at the Cliff Lodge has fabulous mountain views

CHRIS GOODYEAR / SNOWBIRD





**REPORTS WANTED**

Recently we have had few reports on this resort. If you go there, please do send us a report.

The best reports earn a copy of the next edition, and can lead to free lift passes in future.

See page 10.

**TOURIST OFFICE**

t 742 2222
info@snowbird.com
www.snowbird.com

## THE MOUNTAINS

Snowbird's recent link with Alta forms one of the largest ski areas in the US.
**Slopes** The north-facing slopes rear up from the edge of the resort. Six access lifts are ranged along the valley floor, the main ones being the 125-person cable-car (the Aerial Tram) to Hidden Peak, and the fast Gadzoom quad chair. To the west, in Gad Valley, there are runs ranging from very tough to nice and easy. Mineral Basin, on the back of Hidden Peak, offers 500 acres of terrain for all abilities. A fast quad there forms the link with Alta.
**Terrain-parks** There are two terrain-parks, a huge one for experts and one for intermediates. A new super-pipe is being built for 2004/05.
**Snow reliability** Snowbird and Alta average 500 inches of snowfall a year – twice as much as some Colorado resorts and around 50% more than the nearby Park City area. Snowmaking ensures excellent cover in busy areas.
**Experts** Snowbird was created for experts; the trail map is liberally sprinkled with double-black-diamonds, and some of the gullies off the Cirque ridge – Silver Fox and Great Scott, for example – are exceptionally steep and frequently neck-deep in powder. Lower down lurk the bump runs, including Mach Schnell – a great run straight down the fall line through trees. There is wonderful ski-anywhere terrain in the bowl beneath the high Little Cloud chair, and the Gad 2 lift opens up attractive tree runs. Fantastic go-anywhere terrain under the High Baldy traverse is controlled by gates – catch the area as the ski patrol opens them after a snowfall and you're in for a real treat. Mineral Basin has more expert terrain. Backcountry tours and heli-lifts are available.
**Intermediates** The winding Chip's Run on the Cirque ridge provides the only comfortable route down from the top. For adventurous intermediates wanting to try powder skiing, the bowl below the Little Cloud lift is a must. There are some challenging runs through the trees off the Gad 2 lift and some nice long cruises in Mineral Basin. But if you want miles of perfectly groomed piste, there are plenty of better resorts.
**Beginners** Beginners have the Chickadee lift right down in the resort and the Mountain Learning area by the Big Emma green run.
**Snowboarding** Competent free-riders will have a wild time in Snowbird's powder. Alta does not allow boarders.
**Cross-country** There are no prepared cross-country trails.
**Queues** For much of the season queues of up to 40 minutes for the Tram are common. The Gadzoom fast quad and the slow and exposed Little Cloud chair above it are the only alternative for getting to the top.
**Mountain restaurants** It's the Mid-Gad Lodge self-service cafeteria or back to base. A reader recommends the sit-down Forklift at Snowbird Centre.'
**Schools and guides** The ski school offers a range of lessons and speciality clinics – such as women-only clinics, terrain-park skills, over-50s lessons and experts-only programmes
**Facilities for children** The 'kids ski free' programme allows two children (12 and under) to ski for free ($15 a day extra for use of the Tram) with each adult buying an all-day lift ticket. Camp Snowbird offers day care.

## STAYING THERE

**How to go** A few UK tour operators feature Snowbird.
**Hotels** There are several lodges, and smaller condo blocks. Cliff Lodge is a huge luxury hotel with a splendid rooftop pool. The Lodge at Snowbird was completely renovated for 2003/04.
**Eating out** Cliff Lodge and Snowbird Center are the focal points, and there's a wide range. Readers recommend the Steak Pit in Snowbird Center and the fine dining Aerie in the Cliff Lodge.
**Après-ski** Après-ski tends to be a bit muted. The Tram Club and the Keyhole Cantina are lively as the slopes close.
**Off the slopes** Apart from spas in the various lodges, a skating rink and a family tubing hill, there's little else here. Salt Lake City is easily reached.

SNOWPIX.COM / CHRIS GILL

# Brighton/Solitude

**These linked neighbours in the valley next to famous Alta and Snowbird get much the same amount of lovely powder snow. Solitude has come on a lot in recent years, and in some ways is now an attractive destination.**

### KEY FACTS

| | |
|---|---|
| **Resort** | 2435/2665m<br>7,990/8,755ft |
| **Slopes** | 2435-3200m<br>7,990-10,500ft |
| **Lifts** | 15 |
| **Pistes** | 2,250 acres |
| **Blue** | 20% |
| **Red** | 45% |
| **Black** | 35% |
| **Snowmaking** | |
| Brighton | 200 acres |
| Solitude | 18 runs |

### TOURIST OFFICE

**Brighton**
**t** 801 532 4731
info@skibrighton.com
www.skibrighton.com

**Solitude**
**t** 801 534 1400
info@skisolitude.com
www.skisolitude.com

## THE RESORTS

Solitude is the obvious place to stay – a smart neo-Alpine mini-village with an ice rink in the centre and a choice of condos (some quite luxurious) or the 46-room Inn at Solitude. There are several restaurants, including one doing French gourmet cuisine and a family-friendly Italian. Brighton offers little other than slope-side Brighton Lodge – rooms with breakfast. In either, you're in for a quiet time.

## THE MOUNTAINS

The key recent development is that the two resorts now offer a joint lift pass. The total acreage is half that of Alta/Snowbird, but is fair by general US standards. This valley attracts fewer people – experts, in particular – so the powder doesn't get tracked out in hours, as it does over the hill.

Brighton, at the head of the canyon, has the slicker lift system, with three fast chairs, including one serving the resort's maximum vertical of 530m/1,740ft on Clayton Peak. This and the slightly lower Mt Millicent are almost all expert terrain, but other lifts serve a wide spectrum of runs.

Most (not all) of the slopes immediately above Solitude are easy or intermediate, including a wide area served by the one fast quad. But the top lift accesses lots of steeps in Honeycomb Canyon, on the back of the hill, now with a short quad to bring you back to the front face.

The resorts' boundaries are open, and there are excellent backcountry adventures to be had. The Solitude ski patrol runs guided groups of 10, with all necessary safety kit provided – at $150, including lift pass, good value.

SNOWPIX.COM / CHRIS GILL

# Snowbasin

**The 2002 Olympics put Snowbasin on the map. It's a great hill, and it gets great snow (usually). All it needs is a great village – and we don't doubt it will get one. For now, it makes a great day out from Park City, for example.**

### KEY FACTS

| | |
|---|---|
| **Resort** | 1950m<br>6,390ft |
| **Slopes** | 1785-2850m<br>5,860-9,350ft |
| **Lifts** | 11 |
| **Pistes** | 2,650 acres |
| **Green** | 20% |
| **Blue** | 50% |
| **Black** | 30% |
| **Snowmaking** | 580 acres |

### TOURIST OFFICE

**t** 620 1000
info@snowbasin.com
www.snowbasin.com

## THE RESORT

There is no resort, in the European sense of a village with accommodation. A plush base lodge was built for the 2002 Olympics. Big investment is expected over the next few years, but for now you have to stay elsewhere – in the town of Ogden on the Salt Lake plain, or nearer the mountain in the backwater of Huntsville. The drive from Park City takes less than an hour.

## THE MOUNTAIN

Snowbasin's slopes cover a lot of pleasantly varied terrain and its 11 lifts include a fast quad chair and two gondolas, all running bottom to top. A new terrain-park, Porcupine Face, made its debut in 2003/04, with features covering about 10 acres.

This is a great mountain for experts. All the lifts serve worthwhile terrain. The downhill course, designed by Bernhard Russi, drops 885m/2,900ft and is already claimed to be a modern classic. Between the race course and the area boundary is a splendid area of off-piste wooded glades and gullies, served by the fast John Paul chair. This is where most experts will want to spend their time. It's good for intermediates, too. The Strawberry gondola accesses mainly long open blue runs but also leads to a lightly wooded steeper slope at the extremity of the area. Middle Bowl is great terrain for the adventurous, with a complex network of blues and blacks. There is a nursery slope, and a few green runs to progress to.

At 400 inches the average snowfall is in the usual Utah class.

There are two smart, recently built self-service mountain restaurants.

SUN VALLEY RESORT

# Sun Valley

**Built in the 1930s, Sun Valley was the US's first luxury, purpose-built winter resort and soon became popular with the stars. For a peaceful, relaxing time, it's hard to beat. For skiing and boarding alone, there are better resorts.**

## KEY FACTS

| | |
|---|---|
| **Resort** | 1750m<br>5,750ft |
| **for Bald Mountain** | |
| **Slopes** | 1750-2790m<br>5,750-9,150ft |
| **Lifts** | 15 |
| **Pistes** | 2,054 acres |
| **Green** | 36% |
| **Blue** | 42% |
| **Black** | 22% |
| **Snowmaking** | 70+% |

## TOURIST OFFICE

**t** 208 786 8259
ski@sunvalley.com
www.sunvalley.com

## THE RESORT

Sun Valley is based around the old mining village of Ketchum, and its current owner has pumped millions of dollars into the mountain to restore it to state-of-the-art luxury. The town retains its old-world charm and has atmospheric bars, restaurants and shops; you can sometimes find Clint Eastwood in the Pioneer Saloon. The stylish Sun Valley Lodge is one of our favourite ski hotels, and its corridors are lined with photos of film-star guests. Shuttle-buses link the slopes to most accommodation.

## THE MOUNTAINS

The slopes of Bald Mountain (known locally as Baldy) are accessed from one of two luxurious base lodge complexes at River Run and Warm Springs. Of the lifts, seven are high-speed quads. The separate Dollar Mountain has good beginner slopes. The resort has an erratic natural snow record, but snowmaking covers over 70% of the runs. There are a few tough slopes for experts, but nothing beyond single-black-diamond pitch. Most of the terrain is ideal for intermediates, with lots of runs at a consistent pitch. There are good blue bowl runs with great views from the top ridge as well as well-groomed cruisers through the trees. Dollar is the place for beginners, with gentle, green runs to progress to. Snowboarding is now allowed, but Sun Valley doesn't have a snowboard culture – it built its first half-pipe last season. The mountain restaurants and base lodges have to be seen to be believed. They are way ahead of most US on-slope facilities. There are good cross-country facilities.

TAOS SKI VALLEY

# Taos

**Set high above an arid New Mexico valley, Taos Ski Valley is the most southerly of North America's major ski areas. It offers some good expert terrain but snowboarders are banned from sampling its slopes.**

## KEY FACTS

| | |
|---|---|
| **Resort** | 2805m<br>9,210ft |
| **Slopes** | 2805-3600m<br>9,210-11,820ft |
| **Lifts** | 12 |
| **Pistes** | 1,295 acres |
| **Green** | 24% |
| **Blue** | 25% |
| **Black** | 51% |
| **Snowmaking** | 100% of green/blue slopes |

## TOURIST OFFICE

**t** 505 776 2291
tsv@skitaos.org
www.skitaos.org

## THE RESORT

Taos Ski Valley, at the foot of the slopes, is tiny. It has around 1,000 beds in a handful of hotels and condos, with little room for expansion and no room for the swimming pools, ice rinks, galleries and boutiques you find in larger places. The Inn at Snakedance, Hotel St Bernard and the Edelweiss all offer good slope-side accommodation. 18 miles down the valley, the traditional adobe town of Taos with its art and craft galleries and shops makes an alternative base.

## THE MOUNTAINS

When you hit Taos Ski Valley the first thing you will see is Al's run, a steep mogul field rising sheerly out of the resort. To allay people's fears a prominent sign reads 'Don't panic! You're looking at 1/30 of Taos Ski Valley. We have many easy runs too.' But it's good skiers who will get the most out of the resort. There are numerous long steep runs through the trees, and many of the best runs require a hike from the top lifts.

There's enough to keep intermediates happy for a few days, especially if they're willing to tackle some of the steeper runs, too. Beginners have their own dedicated area and easy green runs to progress to. And the ski school has an extremely high reputation. Snowfall averages over 300 inches, on a par with some Colorado resorts but not in the premier league; and all the green and blue runs are covered by snowmaking.

There are a couple of basic mountain restaurants but many people head back to base for lunch.

AMERICAN SKIING COMPANY / NATHAN BLOW

# New England

**You go to Utah for the deepest snow, to Colorado for the lightest powder and swankiest resorts, to California for the mountains and low prices. You go to New England for ... well, for what? Extreme cold? Rock-hard artificial snow? Mountains too limited to be of interest beyond New Jersey? Yes and no: all of these preconceptions have some basis, but they are an incomplete and unfair picture.**

Yes, it can be cold: one of our reporters recorded −27°C, with wind chill producing a perceived −73°C. Early in the season, people wear face masks to prevent frostbite. It can also be warm – another reporter had a whole week of rain that washed away the early-season snow. The thing about New England weather is that it varies. Not as much as in Scotland, maybe, but the locals' favourite saying is: 'If you don't like the weather in New England, wait two minutes.'

New England doesn't usually get much super-light powder or deep snow to play in. But the resorts have big snowmaking installations, designed to ensure a long season and to help the slopes to 'recover' after a thaw or spell of rain. They were the pioneers of snowmaking technology; and 'farming' snow, as they put it, is an art form and a way of life – provided the weather is cold enough. Many of the resorts get impressive amounts of natural snow too – in some seasons.

The mountains are not huge in terms of trail mileage (the largest, Killington, is smaller than all except one of the resorts we feature in western US). But several have verticals of over 800m/2,620ft (on a par with Colorado resorts such as Keystone) and most have over 600m/1,970ft (matching Breckenridge), and are worth considering for a short stay, or even for a week if you like familiar runs. For more novelty, a two- or three-centre trip is the obvious solution. Most resorts suit snowboarders well, often having more than one terrain-park.

You won't lack challenge – most of the double-black-diamond runs are seriously steep. And you won't lack space: most Americans visit over weekends, which means deserted slopes on weekdays – except at peak holiday periods. It also means the resorts are keen to attract long-stay visitors, so UK package prices are low.

But the big weekend and day-trip trade also means that few New England resorts have developed atmospheric resort villages – just a few condos and a hotel, maybe, with places to stay further out geared to car drivers.

New England is easy to get to from Britain – a flight to Boston, then perhaps a three- or four-hour drive to your resort. And there are some pretty towns to visit, with their clapboard houses and big churches. You might also like to consider spending a day or two in Boston – one of America's most charming cities. And you could have a shopping spree at the factory outlet stores that abound in New England.

We cover three of the most popular resorts on the UK market in the chapters that follow. But there are many other small areas, too. And if you are going for a week or more, we recommend renting a car and visiting a few resorts. In this introduction, we outline the main possibilities.

From Killington (by far the biggest resort), you can go south to a range of smaller resorts. **Okemo** competes with Smugglers' Notch for the family market. Okemo mountain has southern Vermont's biggest vertical (655m/2,150ft) and longest trail (over 7km/4.3 miles). The slopes are largely intermediate or easy – though there are a dozen black runs and a couple of short double-black-diamonds. Two seasons ago the area was expanded considerably by construction of a new fast quad on the next-door mountain, Jackson Gore. A new base development is being built, and, once completed, there will be 16 new trails, two gladed areas, four chairs and a gondola – adding 30% to Okemo's terrain. There's an extensive terrain-park leading into a half-pipe and almost 100% snowmaking cover. We have reports of serious queues for the main fast quad at peak times.

**Mount Snow** is a one-peak resort,

with a long row of lifts on the front face serving easy and intermediate runs of just over 500m/1,640ft vertical, and a separate area of black runs on the north face – including one short but serious double-black. (The sister resort of **Haystack**, a short drive away, has more steep slopes.) Mount Snow has some of the best terrain-parks in the east. There are 2,000 beds at the base, some in hotels.

**Stratton** offers something like the classic Alpine arrangement of a village at the foot of the lifts: a smart, modern development with a car-free shopping street. The slopes – mostly easy and intermediate, with some blacks and some short double-black pitches – is spread widely around the flanks of a single peak, served by modern lifts, including a 12-person gondola (which reportedly produces queues) and four fast six-seat chairs. Stratton calls itself the 'snowboarding capital of the east', with no fewer than six terrain-parks. The Pro Power Park was new for 2003/04 and has a super-pipe.

You may find more interest in **Sugarbush**, to the north of Killington, midway between Killington and Stowe, Sugarbush is a fast-developing resort, with one of the larger ski areas. The main sector is an extensive bowl below Lincoln Peak, with lifts up to six points on the rim; a long up-and-over chair-lift links the Mt Ellen area – smaller, but with more altitude and more vertical (810m/2,650ft). The easy runs are confined to the lower slopes; higher up, the direct runs are seriously steep. There are terrain-parks in both areas. Most of the accommodation is in the historic village of Waitsfield, but a village is developing at the base.

**Mad River Glen** next door is a cult resort with locals, owned for several years now by a co-operative, with some tough ungroomed terrain, a few well-groomed intermediate trails and old-fashioned lifts – it still has a single-person chair-lift. And snowboarding is still banned.

Further north, near the Canadian border, is **Jay Peak**. It gets crowded at weekends but is quiet in the week. It has Vermont's only cable-car, which takes you to the summit and to views of four US states plus Canada. It gets a lot of snow (350 inches on average) and has some good runs for advanced skiers and adventurous intermediates – notably 100+ acres of glades. Longer-term plans exist for an expansion into the West Bowl – 250 acres of intermediate terrain, some of which they hope to have open for 2006/07. There is slope-side accommodation.

**Sugarloaf** in Maine already has a much better developed village at the base than most small New England resorts. But the mountain is small and a keen piste-basher could ski it out in a day or two. There is something for everybody, with genuine steeps up around and above the tree line and gentle terrain lower down in the woods. Two new glades were built for 2003/04 – one black and one double black. The resort is also building a third terrain-park and a super-pipe.





SUNDAY RIVER / NORM HERSOM

Sunday River's trails spread right along the slopes of eight linked peaks, with lots of car parking for day visitors ↓

## TOURIST OFFICES

**Okemo**
www.okemo.com

**Mount Snow/Haystack**
www.mountsnow.com

**Stratton**
www.stratton.com

**Sugarbush**
www.sugarbush.com

**Mad River Glen**
www.madriverglen.com

**Jay Peak**
www.jaypeakresort.com

**Sugarloaf**
www.sugarloaf.com

**Sunday River**
www.sundayriver.com

**Bretton Woods**
www.brettonwoods.com

**Cannon**
www.cannonmt.com

**Loon Mountain Resort**
www.loonmtn.com

**Waterville Valley**
www.waterville.com

Still in Maine, **Sunday River** has a vertical of 710m/2,330ft with terrain for every standard – from double-black-diamond glades to excellent beginner areas – and four terrain-parks. It was one of the pioneers of snowmaking and over 90% of trails are served by it. Its eight linked peaks have several base areas and quite a bit of slope-side accommodation. The small town of Bethel is a 10-minute drive. The resort attracts quite a lot of British school groups, especially late-season.

New Hampshire has several small resorts scattered along the Interstate 93 highway. **Bretton Woods** is one of the smaller areas, 460m/1,510ft vertical on a single mountain face, but it is highly rated, particularly by families, who relish the top-to-bottom easy trails. There is a good mix of terrain, and snowmaking is comprehensive. There are a few places to stay near the base, with the grand old Mount Washington hotel five minutes away. A new quad and 12 new pistes are being built for 2004/05. The base lodge is being expanded, and there are plans for new shops and restaurants to help to create a village feel.

**Cannon** is a ski area and nothing more – lifts from its two base areas converge on the summit 650m/2,130ft above. This is the state's biggest vertical and the slopes are mainly intermediate. There are quite a few black runs, but no double-blacks. It's a few minutes' drive to hotels and motels in Franconia in one direction and to Lincoln in the other. Seven new beginner and intermediate trails were cut and a new quad was installed to service them for 2003/04. There are also two new glades for experts.

**Loon Mountain Resort** is a small, smart, modern resort just outside the sprawling town of Lincoln. The mountain (640m/2,100ft vertical) is mostly intermediate, though some fall-line runs merit their black grading. A new fast quad is planned for 2004/05.

**Waterville Valley** is a compact area with runs dropping either side of a broad, gentle ridge rising 615m/2,020ft above the lift base. There are a couple of short but genuine double-black-diamond mogul fields, but most of the slopes are intermediate. The village is a Disneyesque affair a couple of miles away down on the flat valley bottom.

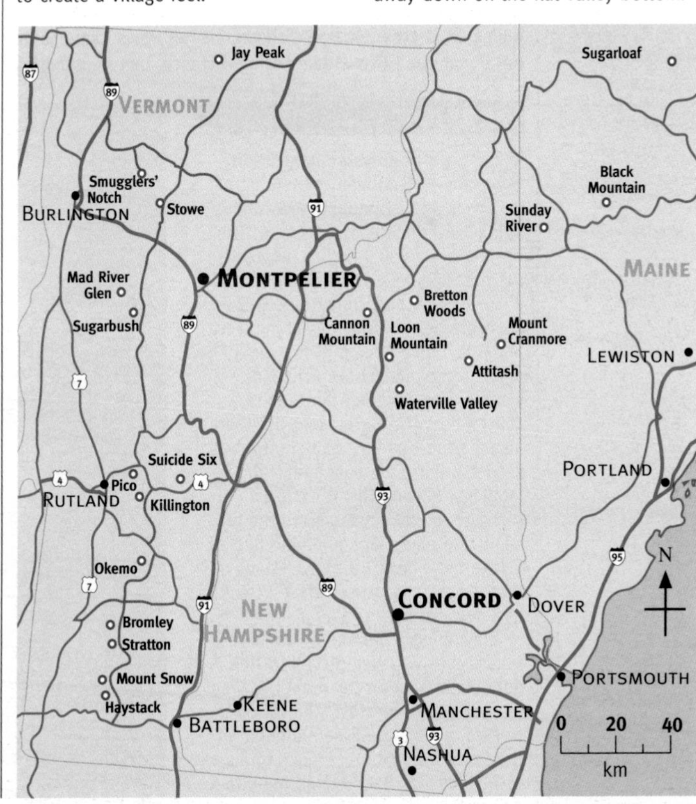

AMERICAN SKIING COMPANY / NATHAN BILOW

# Killington

*Good slopes, great après-ski, no village*

## COSTS

①②③④⑤6

## RATINGS

**The slopes**

| | |
|---|---|
| Snow | *** |
| Extent | ** |
| Expert | *** |
| Intermediate | *** |
| Beginner | **** |
| Convenience | * |
| Queues | **** |
| Mountain restaurants | * |

**The rest**

| | |
|---|---|
| Scenery | *** |
| Resort charm | * |
| Off-slope | * |

## NEWS

For 2003/04 the children's learning area at Ram's Head doubled in size – a new moving carpet and nursery area were opened.

An area of easy gladed terrain was also opened.

Plans for 2004/05 include terrain-park improvements.

- The biggest mountain in the east, matching some Colorado resorts
- Lively après-ski, with lots of bar-restaurants offering happy hours and late-night action
- Excellent nursery slopes
- Comprehensive and very effective snowmaking
- Good childcare, although it's not a notably child-oriented resort

- No resort village: hotels, condos and restaurants are widely spread, mostly along the five-mile access road – a car is almost a necessity
- New England weather – highly changeable and can be very cold
- The trail network is complex, and there are lots of trail-crossings
- Terminally tedious for anyone who is not a skier or boarder

**It's difficult to ignore Killington. It claims to have the largest mountain, the largest number of quad chairs, the largest grooming fleet and longest season in the east, and the world's biggest snowmaking installation. (It tries to be the first resort in America to open, in October, but often shuts again shortly afterwards.) It also claims to have America's longest lift and longest trail (a winding 16km/10 miles) and New England's steepest mogul slope (Outer Limits – average gradient 46%).**

**But it also has weekend and public holiday crowds, and New England's changeable weather. And it has nothing resembling a resort village. It has grown up to suit car drivers arriving for a day or a weekend. Most accommodation is well away from the slopes on the long approach road.**

**Killington is great for New Yorkers, just as Nevis Range is great for Glaswegians. But if you don't live within driving distance, there are more attractive places.**



## THE RESORT

Killington is an extraordinary resort, especially to European eyes. Most of its hotels and restaurants are spread along a five-mile approach road. The nearest thing you'll find to a focus is the occasional set of traffic lights with a cluster of shops, though there is a concentration of buildings along a two-and-a-half mile stretch of the road. The resort caters mainly for weekend visitors who drive in from the east-coast cities. The car is king; but there's also a good free day-time shuttle-bus service around the base areas and lodgings. Beyond this it costs $2.

There are lodgings around the lift base, and plans for something like a village there should be revived, now that the resort's owners have brought in a new partner.

Staying near the end of the access road leaves you well placed for the gondola station on the main highway leading past the resort, and for outings to Pico, a separate little mountain in the same ownership, perhaps one day to be linked to Ram's Head mountain.

KILLINGTON RESORT

Killington Peak is big for New England, rising a respectable 500m/1,640ft from the base →

## KEY FACTS

| | |
|---|---|
| **Resort** | 670m |
| | 2,200ft |
| **Slopes** | 355-1285m |
| | 1,165-4,220ft |
| **Lifts** | 31 |
| **Pistes** | 1,182 acres |
| **Green** | 30% |
| **Blue** | 39% |
| **Black** | 31% |
| **Snowmaking** | |
| | 70% of trails |

## THE MOUNTAINS

Runs spread over a series of wooded peaks, all quite close together but giving the resort a basis for claiming to cover six mountains – or seven if you count Pico. An impressive number of runs and lifts are crammed into a modest area. The result is a complex network of runs, and signposting isn't always clear – Skye Peak is particularly confusing. To some extent the terrain on each sector suits a different ability level. But there are also areas where a mixed ability group would be quite happy, and there are easy runs from top to bottom of each peak.

Some runs of all levels are left to form bumps; there is half-and-half grooming on selected trails; and terrain features – ridges etc – are created. There are also Fusion Zones – thinned-out forest areas, not groomed or patrolled, where you pick your own line. They come in blue and single- and double-black-diamond grades. We found them great fun.

### THE SLOPES
*Complicated*

The Killington Base area has chairs radiating to three of the six peaks – **Snowdon, Killington** (the high-point of the area) and **Skye** – the last also accessible by gondola starting beside US highway 4. Novices and families head for the other main base area, which has two parts: Snowshed, at the foot of the main beginner slope, served by several parallel chairs; and Rams Head, just across the road up to



Killington Base, where there's a Family Center at the foot of the entirely gentle **Rams Head** mountain – the nursery slopes were extended for 2003/04.

The two remaining peaks are behind Skye Peak; they can be reached by trails from Killington and Skye, but each also has a lift base accessible by road. **Bear Mountain** is the experts' hill, served by two quad chairs from its mid-mountain base area. The sixth 'peak', **Sunrise**, is a slight blip on the mountainside, with a short triple chair up from the Sunrise Village condos.

### TERRAIN-PARKS
*Lots of possibilities*

There's a good choice, including early and late season parks (plus one at Pico). The Beach at Snowshed is the main park, with rails, jumps and quarter-pipe. Timberline on Ram's Head is better suited to intermediates and was extended for 2003/04. And there's a kids-only mini-park. There are various other terrain features scattered around the area.



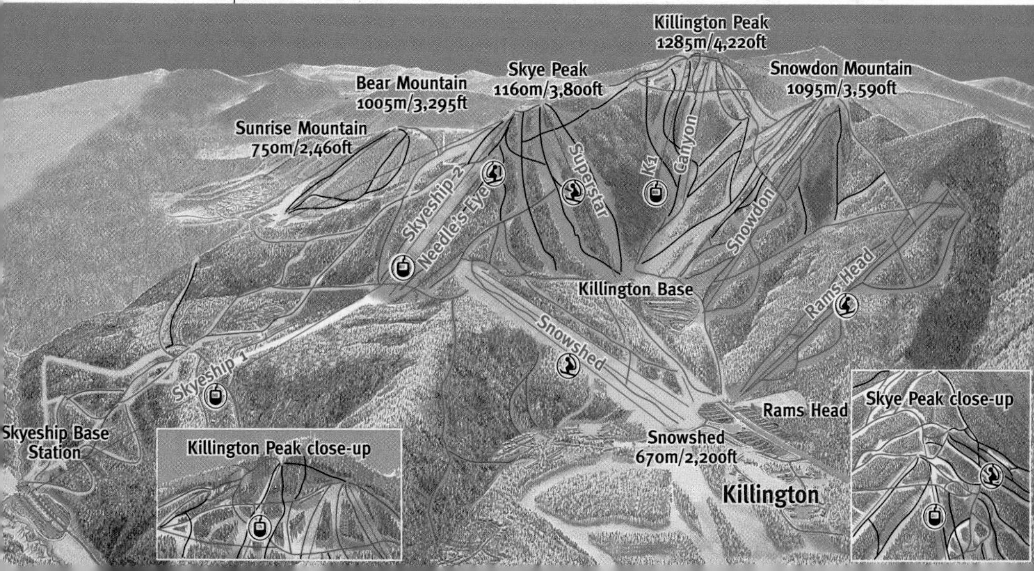

## LIFT PASSES

**Killington Mountain Pass**
Covers all lifts in the Killington and Pico ski areas. Prices include sales tax.

**Main pass**
1 day $67
6 days $312

**Senior citizens**
Over 65: 6 days $204

**Children**
Under 19: 6 days $264
Under 13: 6 days $204
Under 6: free

**Notes**
Discount if you book online 14 days in advance. Special prices for combinations of lift pass, equipment and lessons.

## SCHOOLS

**Perfect Turn**
t 1-800-923-9444

**Learn to ski clinics**
(including lift pass, equipment and use of Discovery Centre)
1 day $80
3 days $185

**Classes**
One 2hr group lesson $39

**Private lessons**
$89 for 1hr





## boarding

*A cool resort like Killington has to take boarding seriously, and it does. There are terrain features scattered around the area,with lots of interest for all levels, and parts of the mountain have been reshaped to cut out some of the unpleasant flats on green runs. There are excellent beginner slopes, and plenty of friendly high-speed (ie slow-loading) chair-lifts – and the Perfect Turn Discovery Center caters just for beginners. Several big-name board events are held here.*

### SNOW RELIABILITY
***Good if it's cold***

Killington has a good snowfall record and a huge snowmaking system (although a 2004 reporter was surprised to find this little used during his peak season visit, despite low temperatures). But even that is no good if temperatures are too high to operate it. Bad weather can ruin a holiday even in mid-season. A reporter who had new powder each night on a March visit went back at the same time the following year to find people skiing in shorts and T-shirts on the few runs that were open. A February visitor told of 'everything from frostbite warnings to pouring rain'. Grooming was also reported to be poor in 2004 – 'only a couple of trails groomed per peak'.

### FOR EXPERTS
***Some challenges***

The main areas that experts head for are Killington Peak, where there is a handful of genuine double-diamond fall-line runs under the two chair-lifts, and Bear Mountain. Most of the slopes here are single blacks but Outer Limits, under the main quad chair, is a double-diamond, claimed to be 'the steepest mogul slope in the east'. We suspect there are steeper runs at Stowe and Smugglers' Notch. There are two or three worthwhile blacks on Snowdon and Skye, too. Also the Fusion Zones on Skye and Snowdon are well worth seeking out.

### FOR INTERMEDIATES
***Navigation problems?***

There are lots of easy cruising blue and green runs all over the slopes, except on Bear Mountain, where the single blacks present a little more of a challenge for intermediates. Snowdon is a splendid area for those who like to vary their diet although a reporter favoured the trails on Skye. There's a blue-classified Fusion Zone on Rams Head. Finding your way around the complicated network of trails may be tricky, though. One reporter liked Pico but complained that the blue run down was more difficult than some blacks.

### FOR BEGINNERS
***Splendid***

The facilities for complete beginners are excellent. The Snowshed slope is one vast nursery slope served by three chair-lifts and a very slow drag-lift. Rams Head also has excellent gentle slopes, recently extended. The ski school runs a special, purpose-built Discovery Center just for first-time skiers and boarders – they introduce you to the equipment, show you videos and provide refreshments.

### FOR CROSS-COUNTRY
***Two main options***

Extensive cross-country loops are available at two specialist 'resorts' – Mountain Meadows, down on US highway 4, and Mountain Top Ski Touring, just a short drive away at Chittenden.

### QUEUES
***Weekend crowds***

Killington gets a lot of weekend and holiday business, but at other times the slopes and lifts are likely to be quiet. A recent holiday visitor found long lines for the Rams Head chair, the K1 gondola and the Bear Mountain chair. Overcrowded slopes are more of a problem than lift queues – the approaches to Bear Mountain lift base were singled out by a reporter.

### MOUNTAIN RESTAURANTS
***Bearable base lodges***

There are only two real mountain restaurants. We have mixed reports on the one at the top of Killington Peak, in what was the top station of the old gondola. Max's Place, on Sunrise, has table-service burgers, pasta, salad etc, and is highly recommended by a reporter for 'escaping the squalor of the other on-mountain eating places'. Each of the lift base stations has an eatery; when there are crowds, they get crowded.

Moguls are available, but also avoidable →

KILLINGTON RESORT

## CHILDREN

t 888-765-7758

**Friendly Penguin Nursery & Day Care**
Ages 6wk to 6yr

**First Tracks**
Ages 2 to 3; 8.30-4.30; $95 a day; includes skiing

**Ministars/Lowriders**
Ages 4 to 6; 8.30-3pm; $90 a day; includes skiing

**Ski school**
'Superstars' for ages 7 to 12 and 'Snowzone Teen' for ages 13 to 18 ($69 for a full day)

## GETTING THERE

**Air** Boston 251km/ 156 miles (2½hr).

## ACTIVITIES

**Indoor** Killington Grand Resort Hotel has massage, fitness centre, outdoor pool, hot-tub, sauna; cinemas, bowling, at Rutland; climbing wall at Snowshed base

**Outdoor** Ice rink, snow-shoeing, tubing, climbing

**Central reservations phone number**
Call 1 800 621 6867 (toll-free from within the US).

**Phone numbers**
From distant parts of the US, add the prefix 1 802.
From abroad, add the prefix +1 802.

## TOURIST OFFICE

t 422 3333
info@killington.com
www.killington.com

### SCHOOLS AND GUIDES

***In search of the Perfect Turn***

The philosophy of the Perfect Turn school is to build on your strengths rather than correct your mistakes, and it seems to work for most people. Beginners start and finish their day in a dedicated beginners' building with easy chairs, coffee, videos and help with choosing and fitting your equipment.

### FACILITIES FOR CHILDREN

***Fine in practice***

There is a Family Center at the Rams Head base, which takes kids from six weeks and will introduce them to skiing from age two years. Classes are reported to be small. The daughter of one of your editors learned to ski here, at the age of four, and approved of it.

## STAYING THERE

### HOW TO GO

***Wide choices***

There is a wide choice of places to stay. As well as hotels and condos, there are a few chalets.

**Hotels** There are a few places near the lifts, but most are a drive or bus-ride away, down Killington Road or on US4.

((((4 **Cortina Inn** (773 3333) 20 minutes away on US4, near Pico; pool, 'excellent food, poor soundproofing'.

((((4 **Grand Resort** (422 6888) Swanky resort-owned place at Snowshed, with outdoor pool and health club.

((((4 **Inn of the Six Mountains** (422 4302) Couple of miles down Killington Road; 'spacious rooms, good pool'.

(((3 **Red Rob Inn** (422 3303) Short drive from slopes – 'good restaurant, a cut above the usual motel style'.

(((3 **North Star Lodge** (422 4040) Well down Killington Road; 'good budget accommodation'.

### EATING OUT

***You name it***

There are all sorts of restaurants spread along the Killington Road, from simple pizza or pasta through to 'fine dining' places. They get very crowded at weekends; many don't take reservations. Many of the places in the Après-ski section serve food.

The local menu guide is essential reading. Claude's Choices, the 'excellent' Grist Mill, Hemingway's, Charity's, the Cortina Inn and Red Rob Inn have been recommended. Sugar and Spice is reported to serve good breakfasts, as does Peppers, which also has 'good burgers' and desserts.

### APRES-SKI

***The beast of the east***

Killington has a well-deserved reputation for a vibrant après-ski scene; many of its short-stay visitors are clearly intent on making the most of their few days (or nights) here.

Although there are bars at the base lodges, keen après-skiers head down Killington Road to one of the lively places scattered along its 8km/5 mile length. From 3pm it's cheap drinks and free munchies, then in the early evening it's serious dining time, and later on the real action starts (and admission charges kick in). Most of the places mentioned here would also rate a mention in Eating out.

The train-themed Casey's Caboose is said to have the best 'wings' in town. Charity's is another lively bar, with an interior apparently lifted from a late-19th-century Parisian brothel. The Wobbly Barn ('expensive' but 'very good' food) is a famous live-music place that rivals Jackson's Mangy Moose for the position of America's leading après-ski venue. The Pickle Barrel caters for a younger crowd, with theme nights and loud music. The Outback complex has something for everyone, from pizzas and free massages to disco and live bands.

### OFF THE SLOPES

***Rent a car***

If there is a less amusing resort in which to spend time off the slopes, we have yet to find it. Make sure you have a car, as well as a book.

# Smugglers' Notch

*Fine fun for families – but those not saddled with kids should stay away*

## COSTS

(1)(2)(3)(4)(5)6

## RATINGS

| The slopes | |
|---|---|
| Snow | *** |
| Extent | * |
| Expert | *** |
| Intermediate | *** |
| Beginner | **** |
| Convenience | ***** |
| Queues | **** |
| Mountain restaurants | * |
| **The rest** | |
| Scenery | *** |
| Resort charm | ** |
| Off-slope | * |

## NEWS

2004/05 will see snowmaking added to the Snowsnake Trail on Morse Mountain and further gladed areas opened up on Sterling Mountain.

Last season the resort opened an additional 40 acres of glades to celebrate 40 years of skiing on Madonna Mountain. The six new areas are graded intermediate.

Another terrain-park was added to Sterling Mountain with features best suited to advanced users.



- + Excellent children's facilities
- + Lots of slope-side accommodation
- + Varied slopes with runs for all abilities
- + No queues
- + Great for beginners, with excellent ski school

- − Family orientation may be too much for some child-free visitors
- − New England weather – highly changeable, and can be very cold
- − Limited local slopes
- − No proper mountain restaurants
- − Slow chair-lifts
- − No hotels – condos only
- − Little après-ski atmosphere

**Smuggs hits the family target squarely, with a constant round of early-evening activities, sympathetic instructors, comprehensive childcare, a generally child-friendly layout and some long, quiet, easy runs. There are challenging slopes, too, but mileage-hungry intermediates should go elsewhere.**

## THE RESORT

Smugglers' Notch is about the nearest thing you'll find in the US to a French-style purpose-built family resort – except that it doesn't look so bad. The village isn't genuinely traffic-free but it comes close, and once installed in your condo you can happily do without a car (much of the accommodation is near to or on the slopes).

The resort is energetically managed and produces a constant flow of developments designed to tighten its grip on the family market, on which it is entirely focused. Most years it seems to get voted 'North American family resort of the year' by at least one American skiing publication. Those not afflicted with children would find the family orientation of the resort a bit overpowering – and even those with kids may find the village has little to offer in the evenings.

## THE MOUNTAIN

Smuggs has varied and satisfying slopes, spread over three hills – Morse, above the village (with the Morse Highlands area off to the left), Madonna (which opened 40 acres of new glades in 2003/04) and Sterling off to the right, reached by green links. From Sterling you can ski to Stowe (see separate chapter), but the on/off lift pass-sharing arrangement with Stowe is currently off, and the run is classified as a backcountry route.

**Slopes** There are some real challenges as well as easy cruising, and a worthwhile vertical of 800m/2,610ft. But one visitor found skiing together as a family and meeting for lunch was very difficult: different levels of ability meant being on different mountains. It's blissfully quiet except at weekends and holidays.

**Terrain-parks** There are now three impressive terrain-parks to suit all abilities and an Olympic-size super-pipe. And the beginners' terrain-garden will suit children and adults alike.

**Snow reliability** Snow reliability is good, subject to the inherent variability of New England weather. Snowmaking has been improved.

**Experts** There are challenges for experts. We were impressed by the two or three double-diamond runs on Madonna – and The Black Hole is the only triple-diamond run in the east, they say. You can go off into the trees – but these areas are not patrolled.

**Intermediates** There are intermediate runs of every grade; there just aren't many of them.

**Beginners** It's a great area for beginners. One of the chair-lifts out of the village runs at half speed, and the runs it accesses are of an ideal gradient. Morse Highlands adds another tailor-made novice area. And the higher lifts take you to long easy runs that even 'never-evers' can tackle during their first week.

**Snowboarding** Smuggs encourages snowboarding. Night school at St.

## KEY FACTS

| | |
|---|---|
| Resort | 315m<br>1,030ft |
| Altitude | 315-1110m<br>1,030-3,640ft |
| Lifts | 8 |
| Pistes | 1,000 acres |
| Green | 19% |
| Blue | 57% |
| Black | 24% |
| Snowmaking | 167 acres |

**Central reservations phone number**
Call 644 8851.
From the UK ring 0800 169 8219.

**Phone numbers**
From distant parts of the US, add the prefix 1 802.
From abroad, add the prefix +1 802.

## TOURIST OFFICE

**t** 644 8851
smuggs@smuggs.com
www.smuggs.com

## REPORTS WANTED

Recently we have had few reports on this resort. If you go there, please do send us a report.

The best reports earn a copy of the next edition, and can lead to free lift passes in future.

See page 10.

Henry's is popular with beginners. There's a snowboard camp specially tailored for four- to five-year-olds.
**Cross-country** The 27km/17 miles of trails may be a bit limited for experts.
**Queues** We encountered no queues, and away from weekends we'd be surprised if anyone else did.
**Mountain restaurants** There are no real mountain restaurants, but there are warming huts with snacks at the top of Sterling and Madonna Mountains and another at the top of the Prohibition terrain-park.
**Schools and guides** The ski school (or 'Snow Sport University') has often been voted the best in North America. Readers rate it 'outstanding', and 'Our best yet – we all improved a lot'. Among its bright ideas are private lessons for a parent and child, with the idea that the parent learns how to help the child develop while having fun. There's also a new Adult camp for Intermediates and above – four days' tuition in small groups.
**Facilities for children** The mountain is child-friendly, offering excitement with safety – with a special jolly kids' trail map. There's a terrain-park for kids, and little forest glades where even tinies can be taken 'off-piste'. The Treasures Child Care Centre is a comprehensive nursery. It now has an on-slope location, which offers parents ski-in/ski-out access. The school arrangements are very good, too, with childcare before and after sessions.

## STAYING THERE

**How to go** There are no hotels in the resort itself – though there are some within driving distance.
**Self-catering** There are lots of comfortable condos on or near the slopes, none very far from the snow. Ours had a TV in every room – bathroom included.
**Eating out** Options are very limited: there are a couple of restaurants in the resort, including the cosy Hearth and Candle (with separate family-friendly and adults-only dining rooms), and others a short drive down the road to the outside world – we and the kids enjoyed Banditos. Babysitters can be arranged.
**Après-ski** The adult après-ski possibilities are about the most limited we have come across. We hear good reports of the teen centres and there's an indoor fun zone with activities for the whole family. Camp fires and hot chocolate are popular with the youngsters as the lifts close.
**Off the slopes** The off-slope options are not numerous, but include tubing, a floodlit outdoor skating rink and an indoor pool. Organised day trips to Vermont or Montreal are possible. Dog-sledding and snowmobiling (kids free with a parent) are easily arranged and a visit to Ben & Jerry's might amuse – the ice-cream factory is nearby (though you can taste the goods at an outlet in the resort).

# Stowe

*Charming Vermont town some way from its small but serious mountain*

## COSTS

(1)(2)(3)(4)(5)(6)

## RATINGS

| **The slopes** | |
|---|---|
| Snow | *** |
| Extent | * |
| Expert | *** |
| Intermediate | **** |
| Beginner | **** |
| Convenience | * |
| Queues | **** |
| Mountain restaurants | ** |
| **The rest** | |
| Scenery | *** |
| Resort charm | **** |
| Off-slope | * |

## KEY FACTS

| | |
|---|---|
| **Resort** | 475m 1,560ft |
| **Slopes** | 390-1110m 1,280-3,640ft |
| **Lifts** | 12 |
| **Pistes** | 480 acres |
| **Green** | 16% |
| **Blue** | 59% |
| **Black** | 25% |
| **Snowmaking** | 350 acres |



+ Cute tourist town in classic New England style
+ Some good slopes for all abilities, including serious challenges
+ Few queues
+ Excellent cross-country trails
+ Great children's facilities

− Slopes a bus-ride from town
− Slopes limited in extent, and split into two unlinked sectors
− New England weather – highly changeable, and can be very cold
− Weekend queues
− No après-ski atmosphere

**Stowe is one of New England's cutest little towns, its main street lined with dinky clapboard shops and restaurants; you could find no sharper contrast to the other New England resorts we feature. Its mountain, six miles away, is another New England classic: something for everyone, but not much of it.**

## THE RESORT

Stowe is a picture-postcard New England town – and a popular spot for tourists year-round, with bijou shops and more 3- and 4-diamond hotels and restaurants than any other place in New England except Boston. The slopes of Mount Mansfield, Vermont's snow-capped (though mainly wooded) highest peak, are a 15-minute drive away and much of the accommodation is along the road out to it. There's a good day-time shuttle-bus service but a car is recommended for flexibility (and excursions).

## THE MOUNTAIN

There are three sectors, two linked, the third a short shuttle-bus ride away. There are free daily mountain tours.

**Slopes** The main sector, served by a trio of chair-lifts from Mansfield Base Lodge, is dominated by the famous Front Four – a row of double-black-diamond runs. But there is plenty of easier stuff, too. An eight-seat gondola serves the next sector. The third area, Spruce Peak, has the main nursery area at the bottom – though now in a more secluded position. A fast quad now heads up to mid-mountain. The

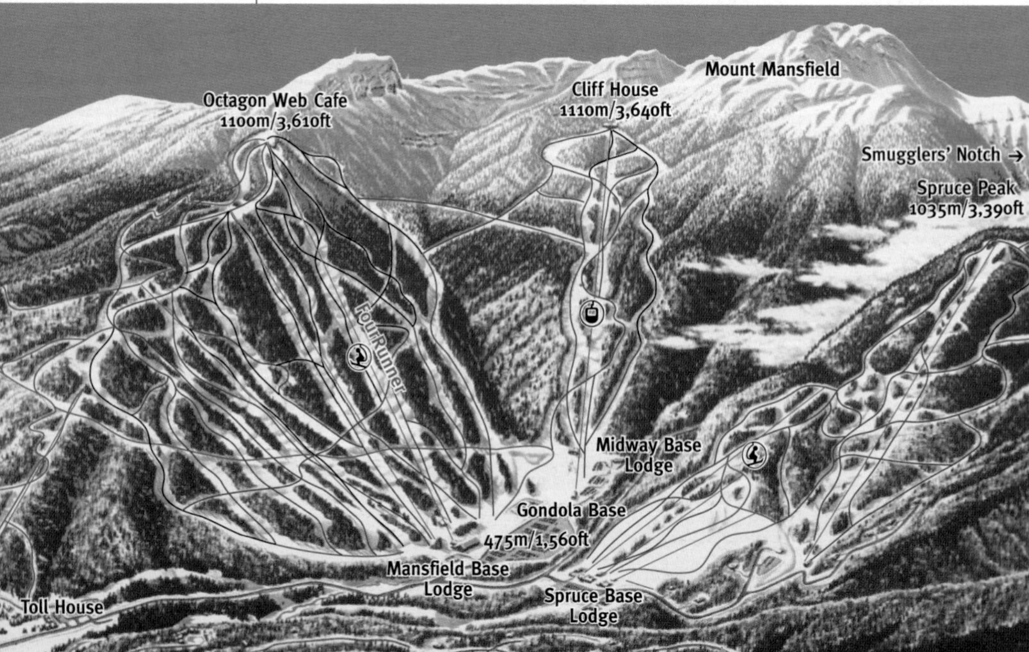

## NEWS

Work has begun on a major scheme to develop Spruce Peak over 10 to 15 years – plans include a hotel, restaurants, and a link to the other slopes.

For 2004/05 a new fast quad will replace the Little Spruce Double, cutting queues. A triple chair will be installed to serve a new self-contained learning area.

**Central reservations phone number**
Call 1 877 317 8693 (toll-free from within the US).
From within the UK call 0800 731 9279.

**Phone numbers**
From distant parts of the US, add the prefix 1 802.
From abroad, add the prefix +1 802.

## TOURIST OFFICE

**t** 253 3500
info@stowe.com
www.stowe.com

old link with Smugglers' Notch, from the top of this sector over the hill, is now a backcountry route.

**Terrain-parks** Stowe has three terrain-parks and a half-pipe: one is for beginners, the others are best suited to advanced users.

**Snow reliability** This is helped by snowmaking on practically all the blue (and some black) runs of the main sectors, and on lower Spruce Peak.

**Experts** The 'scarily narrow' and seriously steep Front Four and their variants on the top half of the main sector present a real challenge (if they are open) – and there are others nearby. There are various gladed areas.

**Intermediates** The usual New England reservation applies: the terrain is limited in extent; there's also a severe shortage of ordinary black runs (as opposed to double diamonds).

**Beginners** The nursery slopes and long green runs are great. 'Spruce Peak is one of the best beginner/early skier areas we've seen,' says a reporter. In the main sector there are splendid long green runs down to Toll House base.

**Snowboarding** Stowe attracts many snowboarders. Beginners learn on special customised boards at the Burton Method Center on Spruce Peak. There's a snowboarder-specific resort web site: www.ridestowe.com

**Cross-country** There are excellent centres scattered around (including one at the musically famous Trapp Family Lodge) – 150km/93 miles of groomed and 100km/62 miles of backcountry trails form the largest network in the eastern US.

**Queues** The area is largely queue-free mid-week but we've had reports of 25-minute queues at weekends.

**Mountain restaurants** Cliff House, at the top of the gondola, is a lofty room with table-service and good food and views. Next-best is Midway Café near the base of the gondola, with a BBQ deck and table-service inside.

**Schools and guides** A reporter was disappointed, but this was partly because he had a different instructor every day, which is common in the US. You can try out the latest equipment, with instruction, at the Stowe Toys Demo Centre.

**Facilities for children** Facilities are excellent and the nursery takes children from age six months to six years.

## STAYING THERE

**How to go** There are hotels in and around Stowe itself and along the road to the slopes, some with Austrian or Scandinavian names and styles.

**Hotels** 1066 Ye Olde England Inne is recommended (despite the appalling name), as are Stowehof Inn, Green Mountain Inn and the 'pleasant' and welcoming Stowe Inn. The Golden Eagle has 'excellent breakfasts', pool and hot-tub. The smart Inn at the Mountain, at Toll House, is the only slope-side accommodation, with chair-lift access to the main sector of slopes.

**Self-catering** There is a reasonable range of condos available for rent.

**Eating out** There are restaurants of every kind. The Whip in the Green Mountain Inn, the Shed ('good ribs') and an Italian restaurant Trattoria La Festa have all been recommended.

**Après-ski** Après-ski is muted – Stowe reportedly goes to bed early. The Matterhorn, Shed and Rusty Nail on the access road are popular. There's a good cinema with new releases.

**Off the slopes** Stowe is a pleasant town in which to spend time off the slopes – at least if you like shopping. The Vermont Ski Museum is 'worth a visit', says a reporter; and a trip to the Burlington shopping mall and a tour (with samples) of Ben & Jerry's ice cream factory just down the road have also been recommended.

# Canada

**Canada is now more popular with British skiers and snowboarders than the USA. In many ways it combines the best that the US has to offer – good service, a warm welcome, relatively quiet slopes, good lift systems with lots of high-speed chairs, heavy dumps of snow, great grooming and a high standard of accommodation – with more spectacular scenery and lower prices. It also has the advantage that you can get direct flights to its main airports, without having to change planes and go through customs part way through your journey. And this season the charter flights and direct Air Canada and British Airways flights will be joined by the new budget scheduled airline Zoom which flies from Gatwick and Glasgow. We've enjoyed many of our best days on skis in western Canada – including some, a couple of seasons back, when locals were complaining about snow conditions being the worst in living memory. Basically, people in western Canada don't really know what bad snow conditions are. And when the snow is good it is phenomenal.**

SNOWPIX.COM / CHRIS GILL

← A rare thing on Canadian slopes – a decent mountain restaurant. This is Temple Lodge, at Lake Louise, which has a good table-service section

In an average year Whistler, for example, gets 360 inches of snow and it snows (or rains, at resort level) for half the days in the season. That makes for superb conditions on the slopes. Inland at Banff-Lake Louise you might not get quite the same frequency of snow, but it stays in great condition because the air is drier and temperatures are lower. You get a better chance of blue skies there – but also a higher chance of a day or two of very low temperatures ( –20°C or less).

So you go to Canada for the skiing or boarding, not the sunbathing. If you prefer long lunches on sun-drenched mountain restaurant terraces, stick to March in the Alps. If you want a good chance of hitting powder, put western Canada high on your list of possible destinations. The east is different: expect snow and extremes of weather more like in New England. The main attraction of Québec for us is the French culture, which makes for a unique ambience; it also has the advantage of a shorter flight time.

If you really want untracked powder and are feeling flush, there is nothing to beat Canada's amazing heli-skiing and snowcat skiing operations. It is the leading country for both these activities and you can expect run after run in virgin snow. The main difference is that the former is faster paced and more expensive than the latter. You can do it by the day, but the hedonistic option is to book a few days or a week in a luxury lodge run by the heli-skiing or snowcat operation, eating gourmet dinners and stepping out of the door each morning straight into the chopper or snowcat.

But if you resist heli-skiing or snowcat heaven, you'll find a holiday in Canada can be very cheap. Package prices start at well under £600 for a week to western Canada. And once you get there you'll find the cost of meals and drinks very low compared with the Alps. Lift passes fall midway between Alpine and American price levels.

Both east and west have the disadvantage for young people that laws about buying and consuming alcohol are more strictly enforced than in the UK. The legal age is 18 in Alberta and Québec but 19 in British Columbia; carrying your passport as evidence of age is a good idea even if you are well over the required age. People unable to prove their age may be refused entries to bars and clubs but will usually be allowed in restaurants (though not to drink alcohol).

Another disadvantage that many reporters comment on is that, as in the USA, lifts close much earlier than in Europe – as early as 3pm in some cases.

SNOWPIX.COM / CHRIS GILL

# Western Canada

**For international visitors to Canada, the main draw is the west. It has fabulous scenery, good snow and a wonderful sense of the great outdoors. The big names of Whistler, Banff and Lake Louise capture most of the British market but there are lots of worthwhile smaller resorts that more adventurous travellers are now starting to explore. We recommend renting a car and combining two or more of these, with a couple of days on virgin powder served by helicopters or snowcats as well, perhaps. We've done this on several occasions but visiting seven or eight resorts on each trip; it's tiring but rewarding. Take it a bit easier than we do (we're working, of course) and you'll have the holiday of a lifetime.**

The three big resorts mentioned above and nine of the smaller ones you're most likely to want to visit for a while get their own write-ups in this section of the book. There are big differences between them, so be sure to read each one. For example, Whistler is the busiest and most developed, Kicking Horse the quietest and least developed (so far). Fernie has great steep powder terrain for experts, Big White great gentle powder terrain to learn how to ski it. Sun Peaks is a fairly new, compact, purpose-built resort with a vaguely Tirolean feel and the second-biggest (to Whistler) ski area in British Columbia. Panorama is a longer-established, purpose-built resort undergoing a renaissance and boasting the second-biggest (to Whistler) vertical in Canada. Banff and Lake Louise are very different bases from which to ski three separate areas, which you need transport to reach.

Jasper, Kimberley, Red Mountain and Silver Star are of more limited interest for a variety of very different reasons and get shorter write-ups.

There are other resorts in the west, of course. One of the ones we were most surprised by on our 2004 tour of the west was Apex – and that has an extended entry in the Resort index / directory at the back of the book.

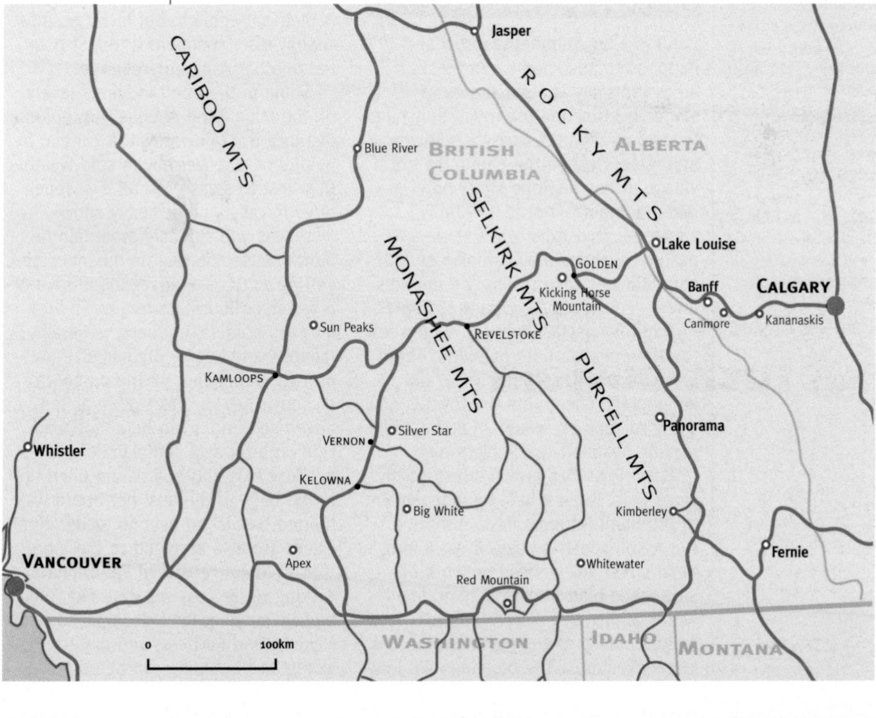

SNOWPIX.COM / CHRIS GILL

# Banff

*A winter wonderland with wildlife*

## COSTS

(1)(2)(3)(4)(5)(6)

## RATINGS

| **The slopes** | |
|---|---|
| Snow | **** |
| Extent | **** |
| Expert | **** |
| Intermediate | **** |
| Beginner | *** |
| Convenience | * |
| Queues | **** |
| Mountain restaurants | *** |
| **The rest** | |
| Scenery | **** |
| Resort charm | *** |
| Off-slope | ***** |

## NEWS

In Sunshine Village a new high-speed quad has replaced the previous slow chair up to Mount Standish and there is a new green run from the top. Sunshine also expanded its terrain by 158 acres with four new expert runs on Goat's Eye Mountain. There are plans to open another very steep area called the Wild West on Goat's Eye, conditions permitting, from 2004/05 – as with Delirium Dive, you'll need a companion, avalanche transceiver and shovel to be allowed in.



- \+ Spectacular high-mountain scenery – quite unlike the Colorado Rockies
- \+ Lots of wildlife around the valley
- \+ Lots of touristy shops
- \+ Good-value lodging because winter is the area's low season
- \+ Late season holidays
- \+ Extensive slopes with excellent snow record at Sunshine, but ...

- − Sunshine is a 20-minute drive away
- − You'll probably want to take in Lake Louise, too – a 45-minute drive
- − Can be very cold; most lifts have no covers and waiting for shuttle-buses can be unpleasant
- − Banff lacks ski resort atmosphere – though it's not an unattractive town
- − Resort can seem over-full of Brits

**Huge numbers of British skiers and boarders go to Banff. Price has been a key factor in getting us to make the trip, but that's only half the story: most visitors are delighted with what they find, and are keen to go back.**

**It's not difficult to see why. The landscape is one of glaciers, jagged peaks and magnificent views, and the valleys are full of wildlife that you'll never see in Europe. The slopes have something for everyone, from steep couloirs to gentle cruising. The snow is some of the coldest, driest and most reliable you'll find anywhere in the world, and there's a lot of it (at Sunshine Village, at least). And there are the standard Canadian assets of people who are friendly and welcoming, and low prices for meals and other on-the-spot expenses.**

**For us, these factors count for more than the drawbacks. But then we, luckily, have never encountered the extremely low temperatures (–35°C is not unknown) that have left some early-season reporters feeling less convinced.**

## THE RESORT

Banff is a big summer resort that happens to have some nearby ski areas. Norquay is a small area of slopes overlooking the town. Sunshine Village, 20 minutes away, is a bigger mountain; despite the name, it's not a village (it has just one small hotel at mid-mountain) – nor is it notably sunny. Most visitors buy a three-area pass that means they can also spend some time at Lake Louise, 45 minutes away – covered by a separate chapter.

Banff is spectacularly set, with a few towering peaks on its outskirts. There is lots of wildlife, especially elk and long-horned sheep (but the town is now trying to keep elk away). In spring there may be bears along the highways.

Banff town has grown substantially since 1990, when it became independent of the Banff National Park authority. But it still consists basically of a long main street and a small network of side roads built in grid fashion, lined with clothing and souvenir shops (aimed mainly at summer visitors) and a few ski shops. The buildings are low-rise and some are wood-clad. The town is pleasant enough, but lacks genuine charm; it's a commercial tourist town, not another Aspen or Telluride.

Some of the Banff lodgings (even on the main Banff Avenue) are quite a distance from downtown. A car can be helpful here, especially in cold weather (it's best to splash out on a 4-wheel drive in case you hit heavy snow).

Unless you stay mid-mountain on Sunshine (see Staying up the mountain), getting to the slopes means a drive or a bus-ride. Buses are free to Tri-area lift pass holders, frequent, generally reliable, and 'highly organised' – though, depending on the number of pickups, they can take twice as long as advertised and it can be a cold wait. One reporter also complained that because skis and boards are piled up in the belly of the bus, her board was 'ruined; scratched beyond recognition'. Buses are also arranged to the more distant major resorts of Panorama and Kicking Horse (see separate chapters) and the smaller (and closer) resorts of Nakiska and Fortress, and day-trip heli-skiing and boarding can be organised.

## KEY FACTS

| | |
|---|---|
| **Resort** | 1380m<br>4,530ft |
| For Norquay, Sunshine and Lake Louise, covered by the Tri-area pass | |
| **Slopes** | 1630-2730m<br>5,350-8,950ft |
| **Lifts** | 29 |
| **Pistes** | 7,748 acres |
| **Green** | 23% |
| **Blue** | 39% |
| **Black** | 38% |
| **Snowmaking** | 1,840 acres |
| For Norquay only | |
| **Slopes** | 1630-2135m<br>5,350-7,000ft |
| **Lifts** | 5 |
| **Pistes** | 190 acres |
| **Green** | 20% |
| **Blue** | 36% |
| **Black** | 44% |
| **Snowmaking** | 85% |
| For Sunshine only | |
| **Slopes** | 1660-2730m<br>5,440-8,950ft |
| **Lifts** | 12 |
| **Pistes** | 3,358 acres |
| **Green** | 22% |
| **Blue** | 31% |
| **Black** | 47% |
| **Snowmaking** | none |

## THE MOUNTAINS

The Sunshine Village slopes are set right on the Continental Divide and as a result get a lot of snow. Most of the slopes above the village are above the tree line and can be very cold and bleak during a snowfall or cold snap. Although there is a wooded sector served by the second section of the gondola and a couple of chairs, in bad weather you're better off elsewhere. It is great, however, for late-season skiing, which goes on until May.

Norquay is much smaller. But it's worth a visit, especially in bad weather – it has wooded slopes to suit all abilities and the trails can be delightfully quiet. One reporter who visited late last season said that for most of the day they were almost the only people on the mountain.

### THE SLOPES
***Lots of variety***

The main slopes of **Sunshine Village** are not visible from the base station: you ride a two-stage gondola, first to the base of Goat's Eye Mountain, and then on to Sunshine Village itself.

Goat's Eye is served by a fast quad rising 580m/1,900ft. Although there are some blue runs, this is basically a black mountain, with some genuine double-blacks at the extremities.

Lifts fan out in all directions from Sunshine Village, with short runs back from Mount Standish and longer ones from Lookout Mountain. Lookout is

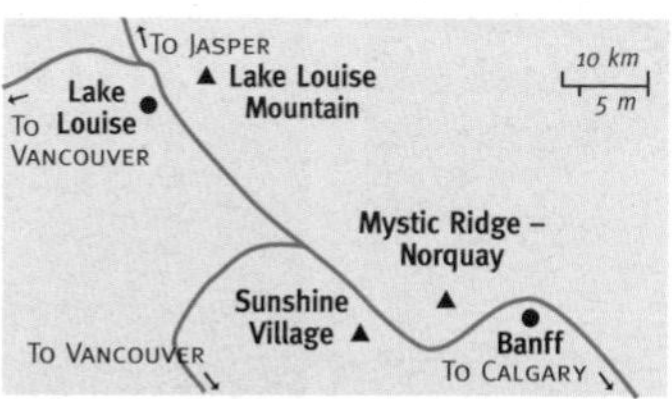


where the Continental Divide is, with the melting snow flowing in one direction to the Pacific and in the other to the Atlantic. From the top here experts can pass through a gate (you need an avalanche transceiver to get through) and hike up to the extreme terrain of Delirium Dive.

Many people ride the gondola down at the end of the day. But the 2.5km/1.5 mile green run to the bottom is a pretty cruise. If you go down while the lifts are running you can take the Jackrabbit chair to cut out a flat section, but the run gets crowded and is much more enjoyable if you delay your descent a bit. The Canyon trail provides a scenic alternative for more advanced skiers and riders. Though marked black diamond, it's not steep – just a bit narrow in places.

The slopes at **Norquay** are served by a row of five parallel lifts and has floodlit trails on Friday nights.

### TERRAIN-PARKS
***Park – and ride...***

Both Sunshine and Norquay have good half-pipes and terrain-parks offering a vast array of rails, table-tops and

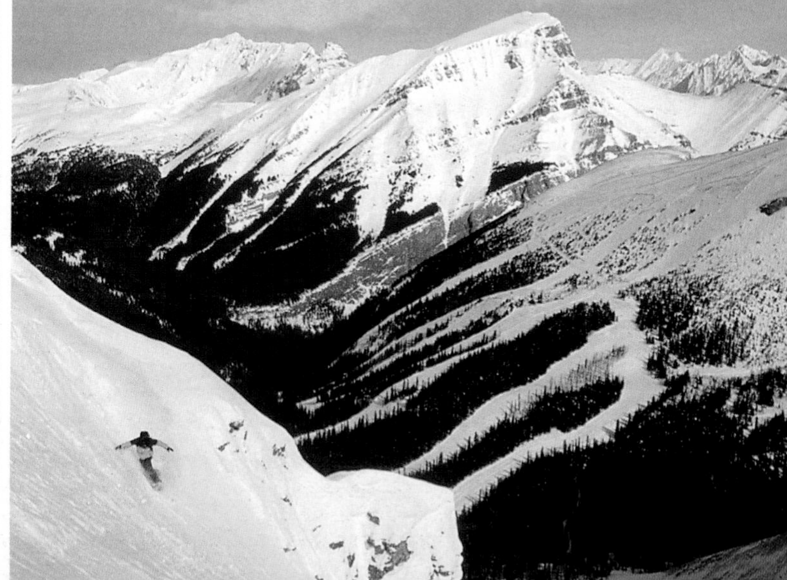

SKI BANFF/LAKE LOUISE / BILL MARSH

Sunshine has some great expert terrain. This guy is heading down Delirium Dive and that's Goat's Eye on the right →

## LIFT PASSES

**Tri-area lift pass**
Covers all lifts and transport between Banff, Lake Louise, Norquay and Sunshine Village.

**Main pass**
3 days C$199
6 days C$398

**Senior citizens**
Over 65: 6 days C$356

**Children**
Under 13: 6 days C$128
Under 6: free pass

**Notes**
Prices above include taxes. Three-day minimum.

**Alternative passes**
One-day and half-day passes available for individual areas.



boxes. Norquay's park is floodlit on a Friday night and the area offers a lift ticket for those who want to use only the park and pipe.

### SNOW RELIABILITY
***Excellent***

Sunshine Village claims '100% natural snow', a neat reversal of the usual snowmaking hype. In a poor snow season, some black runs can remain rocky but the blues are usually fine. 'Three times the snow' is another Sunshine slogan – a cryptic reference to the fact that the average snowfall here is 360 to 400 inches (depending on which figures you believe) – as good as anything in Colorado – compared with a modest 140 inches at Lake Louise and 120 inches on Norquay. But we're told the Sunshine figures relate to Lookout, and that Goat's Eye gets less. There is snowmaking on 90% of pistes at Norquay. So all in all, lack of snow is unlikely to be a problem in a normal season and late-season snow on Sunshine is usually good.

### FOR EXPERTS
***Pure pleasure***

Both areas have satisfying terrain for good skiers and boarders.

Sunshine has plenty of open runs of genuine black steepness above the tree line on Lookout, but Goat's Eye is much more compelling. It has a great, and still expanding, area of expert double-black-diamond trails and chutes, both above and below the tree line. But the slopes are rocky and need good cover, and the top can be windswept.

There are short, steep runs on Mount Standish, too. One particular novelty is a pitch known as the Waterfall run – because you do actually ski down over a snow-covered frozen fall. But a lot of snow is needed to cover the waterfall and prevent it reverting to ice. Also try the Shoulder on Lookout Mountain; it is sheltered and tends to accumulate powder; stay high to make the traverse out easier.

Real experts will want to get to grips with Delirium Dive on Lookout Mountain's north face. You are allowed to hike up to it only if you have a companion, an avalanche transceiver and a shovel – and a guide is recommended. ('Book in advance' and 'rent your transceiver and shovel in Banff – you can't at Sunshine' advise disappointed reporters.) But a local expert says: 'The patrol neurotically carpet-bombs the entire cirque and closes it upon sighting the first tiny fog-bank, making Delirium the safest off-piste on the planet. The mandatory transceiver routine is pure theatre.' The

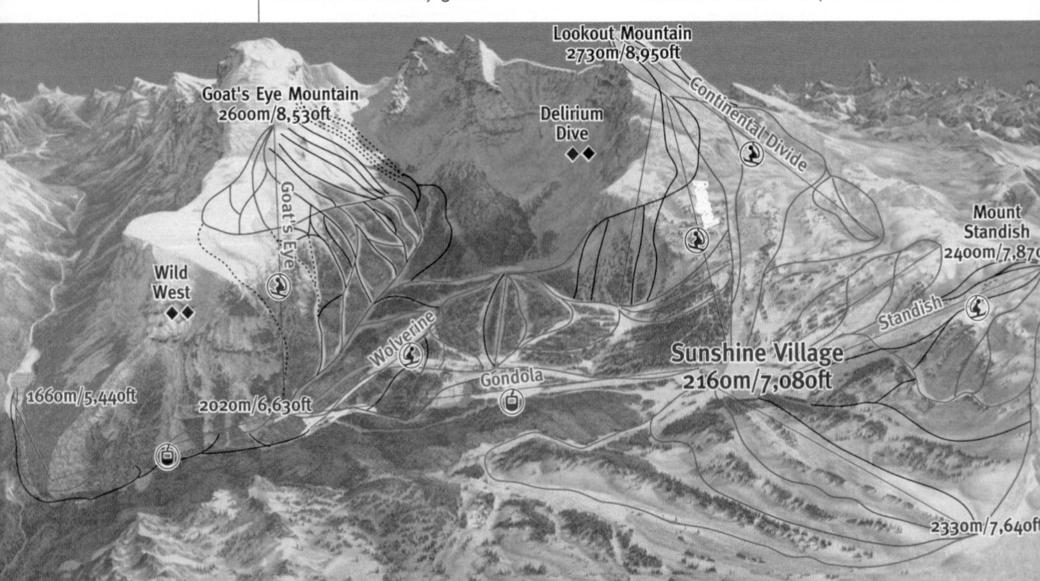

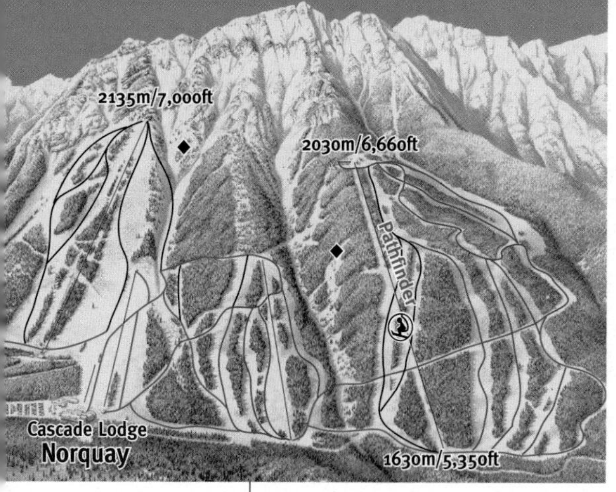


walk to where you drop in is 'pretty scarey' according to another reporter.

Norquay's two main lifts give only 400m/1,300ft vertical, but both serve black slopes and the North American chair accesses a couple of double-diamond runs that justify their grading.

Heli-skiing is available from bases outside the National Park in British Columbia – roughly two hours' drive.

### FOR INTERMEDIATES
***Ideal runs***

Half the runs on Sunshine are classified as intermediate. Wherever you look there are blues and greens – some of the greens as enjoyable (and pretty much as steep) as the blues.

We particularly like the World Cup Downhill run, from the top of Lookout to the mid-mountain base. The slow Wawa chair gives access to the Wawa Bowl and Tincan Alley. This is a good area for intermediates and offers tree-lined protection from bad weather. There's a delightful wooded area under the second stage of the gondola served by Jackrabbit and Wolverine chairs. The blue runs down Goat's Eye are good cruises too.

The Pathfinder fast quad at Norquay serves a handful of quite challenging tree-lined blues and a couple of sometimes-groomed blacks – great for a snowy day or a 'first day warm-up'.

### FOR BEGINNERS
***Pretty good terrain***

Sunshine has a good area by the mid-mountain base, served by a moving carpet. The long Meadow Park green is a great, long, easy run to progress to.

Norquay has a good small nursery area with a moving carpet and gentle greens served by the Cascade chair.

Banff is not the ideal destination for a mixed party of beginners (who may want to stay in one area) and more experienced friends (who are likely to want to visit other places).

### FOR CROSS-COUNTRY
***High in quality and quantity***

It's a good area for cross-country. There are trails near Banff, around the Bow River, and on the Banff Springs golf course. But the best area is around Lake Louise. Altogether, there are around 80km/50 miles of groomed trails within Banff National Park. Beware of the wildlife though: a few seasons ago a cross-country skier was killed by a mountain lion.

### QUEUES
***No problem most of the time***

Half the visitors come for the day from cities such as Calgary – so it's fairly quiet during the week. We have never encountered any serious queues but a 2003 reporter, who was there at UK half-term and a Canadian bank holiday, tells of a 45-minute queue for the Sunshine gondola one day and 15- to 30-minute queues on the mountain.

### MOUNTAIN RESTAURANTS
***Quite good***

Sunshine Village has a choice of eating places at its mid-mountain base. The Day Lodge offers three different styles of food on three floors (table service in the top-floor Lookout Lounge, with great views). Mixed reports of the food but the buffalo stew is recommended. Mad Trapper's Saloon is a jolly western-style place in Old Sunshine Lodge, serving good beer and different food on its two levels (shame about

### boarding

*Boarders will feel at home in Banff and there is some excellent free-riding terrain. 'There are so many natural ledges, jumps and tree gaps to play with that the terrain-park seems almost unnecessary!' said a reporter last year. But Sunshine also has some flat areas to beware of where scooting or walking is required (such as the green run to the base) and the blue traverse on Goat's Eye is tedious. There are two specialist snowboard shops: Rude Boys and Unlimited Snowboards.*

the disposable plates though). The Sunshine Inn hotel has the best food – table-service snacks in the Chimney Corner Lounge or a full lunch in the Eagle's Nest Dining Room. At the bottom of Goat's Eye Mountain there's a temporary tent-like structure; we've had mixed reports of the food here.

At the base of Norquay, the big, stylish, timber-framed Cascade Lodge is excellent – it has great views and a table-service restaurant upstairs as well as a self-service cafeteria.

## SCHOOLS

**ClubSki and ClubSnowboard**
**t** 762 4561
info@banffskischool.com

**Classes**
3 days guided tuition of the three areas (4½hr per day) C$229 incl. tax.

**Private lessons**
Half day (3hr) C$341, incl. tax.

### SCHOOLS AND GUIDES
***Some great ideas***

Both mountains have their own school. But recognising that visitors wanting lessons won't want to be confined to just one mountain, the resorts have organised an excellent Club Ski and Club Snowboard Program – three-day courses starting on Mondays and Thursdays that take you to Sunshine, Norquay and Lake Louise on different days, offering a mixture of guiding and instruction and including free video analysis, a fun race and a group photo. Reporters rave about it: 'absolutely brilliant', 'a great way to meet other people', 'improved more in three days than in a week anywhere else'. All abilities are catered for, including beginners. One reporter recommends booking a midweek group lesson: 'Normally only one or two people; I did an excellent Black Diamond class.' We also have a fat file full of praise for the free mountain tours by friendly local volunteer snow hosts.

## CHILDREN

**Tiny Tigers (Sunshine)**
**t** 762 6563
Ages 19mnth to 6yr; 8.30-4.30

**Kid's Place (Norquay)**
**t** 760 7709
Ages 19mnth to 6yr; 9.00 to 4.00

**Ski school**
Takes ages 6 to 12 (3 days C$229, incl. tax and lunch)

### FACILITIES FOR CHILDREN
***Excellent***

One reporter who used Sunshine, Norquay and Lake Louise said: 'I'd recommend all three.'

## STAYING THERE

### HOW TO GO
***Superb-value packages***

A huge amount of accommodation is on offer – especially hotels and self-catering, but also a few catered chalets.

**Hotels** Summer is the peak season here. Prices halve for the winter – so you can stay in luxury at bargain rates.

((((4) **Fairmont Banff Springs** (762 2211) A late 19th-century, castle-style property, well outside town. It's virtually a town within itself – it can sleep 2,000 people, has over 40 shops, numerous restaurants and bars, a nightclub and a superb health club and spa (which costs extra).

((((4) **Rimrock** (762 3356) Spectacularly set, out of town, with great views and a smart health club. Luxurious.

(((3) **Inns of Banff** (762 4581) About 20 minutes' walk from town, but good for buses; praised by reporters for large rooms, comfort, room service and fitness facilities; 'very large' hot-tub.

(((3) **Banff Park Lodge** (762 4433) Best-quality central hotel, with hot-tub, steam room and indoor pool.

((2) **Banff Caribou Lodge** (762 5887) On the main street, slightly out of town. A variety of wood-clad, individually designed rooms, sauna and hot-tub and a good restaurant and bar. Repeatedly recommended by reporters.

((2) **Timberline Inn** (762 2281) At foot of Norquay and reachable on skis. Comfortable, good views, hot-tub. Recently renovated and expanded.

((2) **Pension Tannenhof** (762 4636) Central, with comfortable rooms and plusher attic suites. Highly recommended by a 2003 reporter. Very friendly. Breakfast included.

((2) **Banff King Edward** (762 2202) Right in the town centre, set above shops; large rooms and surprisingly quiet for its position.

(1) **Banff International Hostel** (762 5521) A bit out of town but cheap ('£60 for the week,' said a reporter).

**Self-catering** Don't expect the choice or luxury you find in many North American resorts. But there are some decent options. The Banff Rocky Mountain Resort is set in the woods on the edge of town, with indoor pool, squash and hot-tubs. Reporters have also recommended the Douglas Fir resort for families – though it's 'a bit out of town' – and Woodland Village.

### EATING OUT
***Lots of choice***

Banff boasts over 100 restaurants, from McDonald's to fine dining in the Banff Springs hotel. Many get crowded and don't take bookings. Reader recommendations include Earl's (burgers and ethnic dishes, very popular and lively), Magpie & Stump (Mexican, with Wild West decor and 'jars' of ale), Giorgio's (Italian), Caramba in the Banff Ptarmigan Inn (Mediterranean, 'well worth the money'), the Keg ('quality steaks'), Seoul Country (Korean), Wild Bill's ('the biggest and best burgers in town', dancing and live entertainment),

## GETTING THERE

**Air** Calgary 122km/ 76 miles (1½hr).

## ACTIVITIES

**Indoor** Film theatre, museums, galleries, swimming pools (one with water slides), gym, squash, racquetball, weight training, bowling, hot-tub, sauna, climbing wall

**Outdoor** Swimming in hot springs, ice rink, sleigh rides, dog-sled rides, snowmobiles, curling, ice hockey, ice fishing, helicopter tours, snow-shoeing

**Phone numbers**
From distant parts of Canada, add the prefix 1 403.
From abroad, add the prefix +1 403.

## TOURIST OFFICE

**Banff**
**t** 762 4561
info@sblls.com
www.skibig3.com

Melissa's ('good steaks', 'excellent choice of beers'), Caboose at the train station ('best steak,' 'superb crab'), Bumpers ('big slabs of rib'), Grizzly House ('fondues and fun', 'great selection of meats') and the Old Spaghetti Factory ('great for families'). Tommy's Neighbourhood Pub 'is a must for great food and good beer'. Sunday brunch at the Banff Springs hotel is highly recommended by one reporter. Designer-cool Saltlik does good game, steak and fish.

### APRES-SKI
***Livens up later on***

One of the drawbacks of the area is that tea time après-ski is limited because the resort is a drive from the slopes. But Mad Trapper's Saloon at the top of the Sunshine gondola is popular during the close of play happy hour (with endless free peanuts). They also do evenings with tobogganing, a buffet, live music and dancing, followed by a gondola ride down. In town later, Wild Bill's has live country and western music and line dancing. The Rose & Crown has live music and gets crowded. The Barbary Coast nightclub is popular. And Outabounds attracts a young lively crowd, while Aurora is for more serious clubbing. The St James Gate Irish pub has 'great atmosphere, good-value food and a wide range of beers'. Melissa's and Saltlik are popular.

### OFF THE SLOPES
***Lots to do***

For those who do not intend to hit the slopes, Banff has lots to offer: plenty of wildlife to see, lovely walks (including ice canyon walks), and you can go snow-shoeing, dog-sledding, skating and snowmobiling. There are 'excellent' sightseeing tours, several interesting museums to visit and natural hot springs to try although one reporter said they were a let-down ('you are limited to 20 minutes in a pool, and it is just that, a pool'). Another reporter enjoyed an evening in Calgary watching the Flames play ice hockey ('sit back and enjoy the fights').

### STAYING UP THE MOUNTAIN
***Worth considering***

We loved spending a night on the slopes of Sunshine Village at the Sunshine Inn (762 6550). Luggage is transported for you in the gondola while you hit the slopes. Rooms vary in size. Big outdoor hot-pool. Sauna. Good restaurant.

SKI BANFF/LAKE LOUISE / MALCOLM CARMICHAEL

From Norquay's top slopes you have great views over the town of Banff to the dramatic Mount Rundle →

BIG WHITE SKI RESORT / KLAUS GRETZMACHER

# Big White

*Big by local standards, white by any standard*

**COSTS**

①②③④⑤⑥

**RATINGS**

| **The slopes** | |
|---|---|
| Snow | ***** |
| Extent | *** |
| Expert | *** |
| Intermediate | **** |
| Beginner | **** |
| Convenience | **** |
| Queues | ***** |
| Mountain restaurants | * |
| **The rest** | |
| Scenery | *** |
| Resort charm | ** |
| Off-slope | ** |

**KEY FACTS**

| | |
|---|---|
| **Resort** | 1755m<br>5,760ft |
| **Slopes** | 1510-2320m<br>4,950-7,610ft |
| **Lifts** | 15 |
| **Pistes** | 2,800 acres |
| **Green** | 18% |
| **Blue** | 56% |
| **Black** | 26% |
| **Snowmaking** In new terrain-park only | |



+ Combination of a good snow record and gentle gladed terrain makes it great for learning to ski powder
+ Extensive, varied slopes, quiet except at weekends and holidays
+ Convenient, purpose-built village

– Visibility can be poor, especially on the upper mountain, because of snow, cloud or freezing fog
– Few off-slope diversions – and isolated without a car
– Limited après-ski

**'It's the snow' says the Big White slogan. And as slogans go, it's spot on. If you want a good chance of skiing powder on reasonably easy slopes, put Big White high on the shortlist. The locals call it 'Big White Out' because the mountain often has a cloud sitting on it while the plains around are bathed in sunshine. So if you want a sun tan (or lively après-ski, or extensive steep bowls and chutes) look elsewhere. If you're an intermediate looking to learn powder and try gladed skiing for the first time, there can be few better places. Consider combining it with another BC resort such as Sun Peaks or Silver Star for variety.**

## THE RESORT

Big White is a modern, rapidly growing, purpose-built resort 45 minutes from Kelowna airport. The village is rather piecemeal but attractive in wood and stone and built slightly above the main chair-lift bases so that much of the accommodation is ski-in/ski-out. A lot of the resort's business comes from day visitors, who can park near the lift bases. Silver Star resort is under the same ownership and there are day trips by bus (Thursdays) or helicopter.

## THE MOUNTAINS

Much of the terrain is heavily wooded. But the trees thin out towards the summits, leading to almost open slopes in the bowls at the top. There's at least one green option from the top of each lift but the one from Gem Lake is narrow and can be tricky and busy.
**Slopes** Fast chairs run from points below village level to above mid-mountain, serving the main area of wooded beginner and intermediate runs above and beside the village.

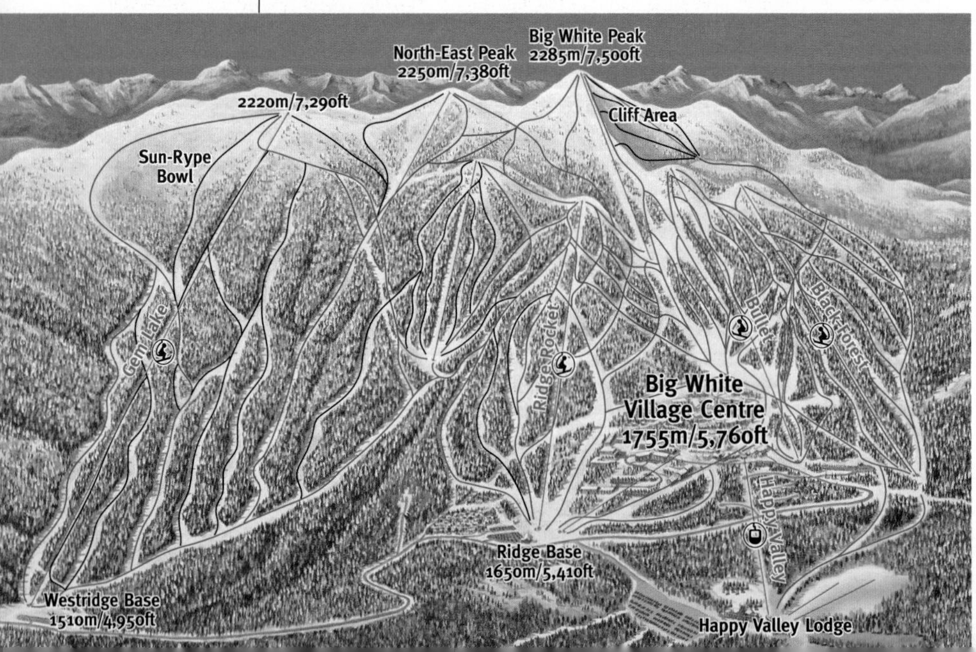

The village centre ↗

BIG WHITE / KLAUS GRETZMACHER

## NEWS

For 2004/05 a two-person chair-lift will serve the steep Cliff area, avoiding going to the bottom after each run. The area will also include more steep runs on East Peak (right of the Cliff area).

Six new intermediate runs will be cut in the Gem Lake area.

A new terrain-park is being built above the village, served by a new two-person chair and by Big White's first snowmaking. It will include a half-pipe, and expert and intermediate parks and rails – and a super-pipe and a boarder-cross course of Olympic standard. It will also have race courses for skiers and boarders and will be floodlit at night. A new mountain restaurant overlooking the park will be built.

**Central reservations**
Call 765 8888; toll-free (within Canada) 1 800 663 1772.

**Phone numbers**
From distant parts of Canada, add the prefix 1 250. From abroad, add +1 250.

## TOURIST OFFICE

t 765 3101
bigwhite@bigwhite.com
www.bigwhite.com

Slower lifts – a T-bar and four chairs – serve the higher slopes. Quite some way across the mountainside is the Gem Lake fast chair, serving a range of long top-to-bottom runs; with its 710m/2,330ft vertical, this lift is in a different league from the others. 'Snow Hosts' (highly praised by reporters) run twice daily guided ski tours.

**Terrain-parks** See News for the new world-class facility being built.

**Snow reliability** Big White has a reputation for great powder; average snowfall is about 300 inches, which is similar to many Colorado resorts. The top of the mountain can suffer from freezing fog, which means the top trees usually stay white all winter; they are known as snow-ghosts and make visibility tricky in a white out (but are great fun to ski between on clear days).

**Experts** The Cliff area at the top right of the ski area is of serious double-black pitch; the runs are short but you will be able to ski them repeatedly (along with the new East Ridge runs) using the new chair (see News). The Sun-Rype bowl at the opposite edge of the ski area is more forgiving. There are some long blacks off the Gem Lake chair and several shorter ones off the Powder and Falcon chairs. There are glades to explore and bump runs too.

**Intermediates** The resort is excellent for cruisers and families, with long blues and greens all over the hill. Good intermediates will enjoy the easier black runs too. In general the runs get steeper from right to left as you look at the mountain. The Black Forest area has some marvellous easy skiing among the trees, while some of the blues off the Gem Lake chair are quite steep, narrow and challenging.

**Beginners** There's a good dedicated nursery area in the village and lots of long easy runs to progress to.

**Snowboarding** There's some excellent free-riding terrain. There will also be the new terrain-park to try. Novices can use long, chair-lift-served green runs.

**Cross-country** Trails total 25km/16 miles.

**Queues** With four fast quads and few visitors still, queues are pretty rare. The new Cliff chair should ease the pressure on the Alpine T-bar.

**Mountain restaurants** The new mountain restaurant will be Big White's first.

**School and guides** A 2003 reporter was wildly enthusiastic about the ski school for both adults and children.

**Facilities for children** The excellent Kids' Centre takes children from 18 months. Evening activities are organised.

## STAYING THERE

**How to go** There's an increasing range of packages to Big White.

**Hotels** The White Crystal Inn was recommended over the Inn at Big White by a 2004 reporter.

**Self-catering** Standards are high but grocery shopping is limited. We stayed at the Stonebridge condos in 2004 and loved them – big, central, well-furnished, private hot-tub on the balcony.

**Eating out** We had good meals in the Copper Kettle in the White Crystal Inn (great fillet steak) and the Kettle Valley Steakhouse at Happy Valley (varied cuisine, some dishes with an oriental flavour, and 'flights' of four different glasses of local wines to try). Reporters also recommend Snowshoe Sam's ('wonderful flamed black cherries and alcoholic gun barrel coffee'), Powder Keg (Greek), Swiss Bear in the Chateau Big White (Swiss!), Frank's Chinese Laundry (take-away or eat-in).

**Après-ski** The atmospheric Snowshoe Sam's has a DJ, live entertainment and dancing. Raakel's in the Hopfbrauhaus has live music and dancing.

**Off the slopes** Happy Valley has tubing hills, ice skating, snowmobiling, snow-shoeing and dog-sledding. Helicopter tours and two health spas are popular.

SNOWPIX.COM / CHRIS GILL

# Fernie

*Lots of snow and lots of steeps – best with a guide*

**COSTS**

①②③④⑤⑥

**RATINGS**

| **The slopes** | |
|---|---|
| Snow | ***** |
| Extent | *** |
| Expert | ***** |
| Intermediate | ** |
| Beginner | **** |
| Convenience | **** |
| Queues | **** |
| Mountain restaurants | * |
| **The rest** | |
| Scenery | *** |
| Resort charm | ** |
| Off-slope | ** |

**NEWS**

For 2004/05 more glading to thin out the trees will be done in three areas. And better access is planned from Currie Bowl to the fast Great Bear chair, cutting out the need to ski all the way back to the slow Elk chair to change areas. An extra grooming machine may result in more and better grooming. Improvements to make the Day Lodge food area brighter are also promised.

For 2003/04 more snowmaking was installed. Downtown, a Japanese sushi restaurant, Yama Goya, opened.



- ✚ Good snow record, with less chance of rain than at Whistler (and less chance of Arctic temperatures than at resorts up in the Rockies)
- ✚ Great terrain for those who like it steep and deep, with lots for confident intermediates too
- ✚ Snowcat operations nearby
- ✚ Some good on-slope accommodation available, but ...

- ▬ Mountain resort is very limited
- ▬ Lift system still a weakness, especially for experts
- ▬ After a dump it can take time to make the bowls safe
- ▬ Little groomed cruising for timid or average intermediates
- ▬ Poor trail map and signposts
- ▬ No decent mountain restaurants

**Fernie has long had cult status among Alberta and BC skiers for its steep gladed slopes and superb natural snow. In the last six years there has been a lot of investment in the development of the village at the foot of the slopes – though it remains small, without many facilities. Some visitors would rather see more investment in the mountain, to cut down the amount of hiking and traversing to the best steep terrain, and to hasten reopening after a serious snowfall. We see their point, but most reports we get are dominated by excitement at Fernie's combination of snow and terrain – 'just like Jackson Hole' and 'the hiking and traversing isn't that bad; Fernie's not for expert wimps', to quote two reporters. You'll enjoy Fernie most if you are a good skier or rider wanting adventure.**

## THE RESORT

Fernie Alpine Resort is set at the lift base a little way up the mountainside from the flat Elk Valley floor and a couple of miles from the little town of Fernie. It has grown considerably from very little in the past few years, but there's still not much there other than convenient accommodation, a few bars and restaurants and a few small shops. It is quiet at night.

The town of Fernie is named after William Fernie – a prospector who discovered coal here and triggered a boom in the early 1900s. Much of the town was destroyed by fire in 1908 but some downtown stone and brick buildings survived and are still there. It is primarily a town for locals not tourists. There are some lively bars, decent places to eat and good outdoor shops. It is down to earth rather than charming and reporters' reactions to it vary: 'Like staying in an industrial estate,' said one; 'I liked the way it felt like real Canada and enjoyed staying in a town with some history,' said another. All reporters this year stress how they loved the friendliness of the locals.

There are buses between the town and the mountain, which run at half-hourly intervals at peak times and cost C$3 one way (you can buy books of tickets for about C$10 for four).

Outings to Kimberley are possible; a coach does the trip every Thursday – the drive takes about 90 minutes. (there's also a helicopter option).

## THE MOUNTAINS

Fernie's 2,500 acres pack in a lot of variety, from superb green terrain at the bottom to ungroomed chutes (that will be satisfyingly steep to anyone but the extreme specialist) and huge numbers of steep runs in the trees. A lot of the runs have the rare quality of consistently steep pure fall lines.

### THE SLOPES
#### *Bowl after bowl*

What you see when you arrive at the lift base is a trio of impressive mogul slopes towering above you. The slow Deer chair approaches the foot of these slopes, but goes no further. You get to them by traversing and hiking from the main Lizard Bowl, on the right, or you can take a high traverse from Currie Bowl, skirting the boundary. Lizard Bowl is a broad snowfield reached by a series of lifts:

↑ There's still not much at Fernie Alpine Resort; this is the new building that sells lift tickets and houses the rental shop

SNOWPIX.COM / CHRIS GILL

| KEY FACTS | |
|---|---|
| Resort | 1065m<br>3,490ft |
| Slopes | 1065-1925m<br>3,490-6,320ft |
| Lifts | 10 |
| Pistes | 2,500 acres |
| Green | 30% |
| Blue | 40% |
| Black | 30% |
| Snowmaking | 125 acres |

the slow Elk quad (which reporters continue to complain about stopping frequently, as they do the Deer chair); the fast Great Bear quad; and finally the short Face Lift, a dreadful rope tow. It often doesn't run, because of either too little or too much snow, and when it does is well known for shredding gloves. This is also the main way into Cedar Bowl and to Snake Ridge beyond it. The only lift here is the Haul Back T-bar, which brings you out. You can still traverse into the lower parts of both Lizard and Cedar Bowls when the Face Lift isn't working – or if you just can't deal with it. There is a mini-bowl between them, served by the Boomerang chair.

The Timber Bowl fast quad chair gives access to Siberia Bowl and the lower part of Timber. But for access to the higher slopes and to Currie Bowl you must take the White Pass quad. A long traverse from the top gets you to the steeper slopes on the flanks of Currie (our favourite area), which are otherwise reached by hiking from the main Lizard Bowl. From there you have to go right to the bottom, and it takes quite a while to get back for another go.

There are free tours of the area in groups of different abilities for two hours twice a day, but the hosts can only take you on blue and green runs. For the steeper, deeper stuff you need to hire a guide or join the Steep and Deep tours. Using these services to get your bearings is a good idea. Going with someone who knows the area makes it hugely more enjoyable. We found both signs and trail map dangerously inadequate – see feature panel later in this chapter.



## TERRAIN-PARKS
### *Two to choose from*

There's a good half-pipe at the bottom of the mountain, served by the Deer chair, and a terrain-park on the Falling Star trail near the top of the Timber Chair in Siberia Bowl, with berms jumps, rollers, table top, large hip and box and curved rails and boarder-cross features. There are also two kids' rails.

## SNOW RELIABILITY
### *A key part of the appeal*

Fernie has an excellent snow record – with an average of 350 inches per year, better than practically all of Colorado. But the altitude is modest – rain is not unknown, and in warmer weather the lower slopes can suffer. Snowmaking has increased in recent years, and now covers most of the base area. Reporters found piste maintenance poor in the snow drought season and others said that, while some runs were well groomed after a snowfall, some blue runs were just

## boarding

*Fernie is a fine place for good boarders (and there are a lot of local experts here). Lots of natural gullies, hits and endless off-piste opportunities – including some adrenalin-pumping tree-runs and knee-deep powder bowls – will keep free-riders of all abilities grinning from ear to ear. And, as one reader commented, 'The only flat sections are at the base and coming out of Falling Star.' The main board shops, Board Stiff and Edge of the World, are in downtown Fernie, the latter with an Internet connection and an indoor skate park to use while your board gets tuned. But beginners and faint-hearted intermediates should stay away.*

### LIFT PASSES

**Fernie**

**Main pass**
1 day C$62
6 days C$360

**Senior citizens**
Over 65: 6 days C$282

**Children**
Under 18: 6 days C$250
Under 13: 6 days C$122
Under 6: free pass

**Notes**
Prices include taxes. Half-day pass available from noon. Mighty Moose lift pass available for beginners.

never groomed at all. A reader this year found 'a lot less grooming than expected'.

### FOR EXPERTS
***Wonderful – deep and steep***

The combination of heavy snowfalls and abundant steep terrain with the shelter of trees makes this a superb mountain for good skiers. There are about a dozen identifiable faces offering genuine black or double-black slopes, each of them with several alternative ways down. Currie and Timber Bowls both have some serious double-diamonds but mainly have single-diamonds. However, as one of our regular reporters says, 'The majority of the single blacks are tough. Some of them are so steep that I can't work out how you could get anything harder without falling off the mountain ... just like Jackson Hole but without the cliffs.' Another reporter this year also likened it to Jackson Hole. Even where the trail map shows trees to be sparse, expect them to be close enough together, and where there aren't any, expect alder bushes unless there's lots of snow. And see our warning in the feature panel below about the trail map and signposting.

There are backcountry routes you can take with guidance (some include an overnight camp) and snowcat operations in other nearby mountains – see feature panel opposite.

### FOR INTERMEDIATES
***Far from ideal***

Although there are intermediate runs both low down and high up, they don't add up to a lot of mileage. Most high runs are not groomed, and one reporter said, 'The blues in all bowls except Timber would be black in most resorts.' Adventurous, strong intermediates willing to give the ungroomed terrain a try will enjoy the area. But if you want miles of groomed cruising, go elsewhere.

### FOR BEGINNERS
***Excellent***

There's a good nursery area served by two lifts (a moving carpet and a drag) and the lower mountain served by the Deer and Elk chairs has lots of wide, smooth trails to gain confidence on. But the green runs from the top of the

### THE TRAIL MAP

*We have complained about many trail maps over the years. But we have rarely come across one as useless as Fernie's. Couple that with completely inadequate signposting on the mountain and you get a dangerous combination, especially if you are heading off on a tree run. When we tried to find the long black Diamond Back run from the top of the White Pass quad, we failed and ended up in tight trees on a slope of triple-diamond steepness – scary. Comments from 2004 reporters include: 'you can often find yourself on unexpected terrain, which is fine if you are a competent skier and can handle most things, otherwise it could lead to some unpleasant situations', 'this is an issue the resort needs to address, especially for timid intermediates, who are going to have a hard time there anyway', and 'I don't think the map is that bad unless you are heading along the ridges for the long blacks'. As one past reporter said, 'It's great to go out with someone who knows where they're going' and 'to make the most of the area you've almost got to stop worrying about following what's on the map'.*

*Fine, as long as you know where you are going and how steep the terrain will be. Others would prefer a more helpful map and on-mountain directions.*

## RIDE THE SNOWCATS – HELI-SKIING AT AN AFFORDABLE PRICE

*Good skiers who relish off-piste should consider treating themselves to some cat skiing; there are several operations in this area. The best-known is Island Lake Lodge (423 3700), which does three- or four-day all-inclusive packages. The Lodge is a cosy chalet 10km/6 miles from Fernie, amid 7,000 acres of spectacular bowls and ridges. It has 36 beds, and four snowcats to act as lifts. In a day you might do eight powder runs averaging 500m/1,640ft vertical, taking in all kinds of terrain from gentle open slopes to some very Alpine adventures. We've heard they can be booked solid up to three years in advance. You can do single days without accommodation, but only on a standby basis; we managed this once and loved it, but our second attempt failed. A reader tells us that Fernie Wilderness Adventures (423 6704) offers 'an excellent alternative' to Island Lake Lodge. Others have been less convinced. 'It's billed as intermediate level,' said one, 'but it's not – there's a lot of tree skiing, some steep and tight, and we were always skiing in a big crowd.'*

mountain are usually just cat-tracks, which nonetheless have tough parts to them, plus more experienced skiers and boarders travelling fast.

### FOR CROSS-COUNTRY
***Some possibilities***

There are 14km/9 miles of trails marked out in the forest adjacent to the resort, and the Fernie golf and country club allows enthusiasts on to their white fairways.

### QUEUES
***Not usually a problem***

Unless there are weekend crowds from Calgary, or heavy snow keeps part of the mountain closed, queues are rare. The slopes are delightfully quiet too.

### MOUNTAIN RESTAURANTS
***What mountain restaurants?***

Bear's Den at the top of the Elk chair is an open-air fast-food kiosk. A welcome stop for coffee and hot chocolate say some readers, but it's not a mountain restaurant, so it's back to base for lunch – the ancient Day Lodge is grim, busy but cheap and serves good soups and sandwiches to order, and Lizard Creek is good for Sunday brunch ('It's a must,' says a reporter this year). Look at the places recommended in 'Eating out', too.

### SCHOOLS AND GUIDES
***Highly praised***

Reporters have praised the Winter Sports school and its small classes. One tried telemarking and described the lessons as 'outstanding' and 'best ever', with only two people in the class. Others loved the beer, snacks and video session that is part of the deal if you book a ski week. A reader this year had snowboard lessons and 'was amazed to be the only student on the first day and that there were three

### SCHOOLS

**Fernie**
**t** 423 4655

**Classes**
Half day C$45 (incl. taxes)

**Private lessons**
C$125 (incl. taxes) for 1hr for up to 5 people

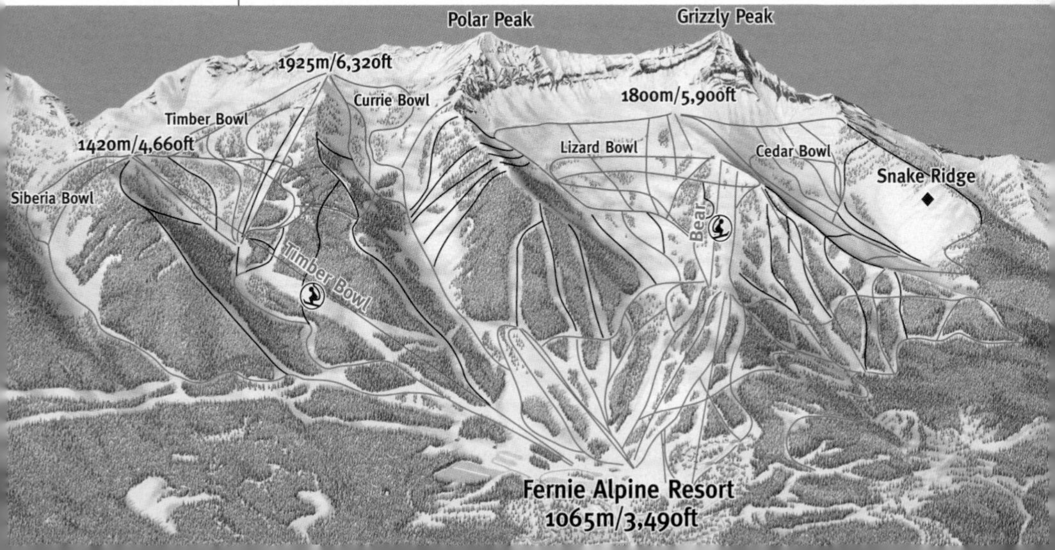

## CHILDREN

**Day care centre**
t 423 2430
Newborn to age 6; 8.30 to 4.30; ski lessons available for ages 3 and 4

**Ski school**
For ages 5 to 12 (C$68, incl. taxes, per day)

## GETTING THERE

**Air** Calgary 322km/200 miles (3½hr).

## ACTIVITIES

**Indoor** Museum, galleries, aquatic centre, saunas, bowling, fitness centre, ice skating, cinema, curling

**Outdoor** Sleigh rides, snowmobiling, dog-sledding, snow-shoe excursions, ice fishing

**Central reservations phone number**
For all resort accommodation call 1 800 258 7669 (toll-free from within Canada).

**Phone numbers**
From distant parts of Canada, add the prefix 1 250.
From abroad, add the prefix +1 250.

## TOURIST OFFICE

t 423 4655
info@skifernie.com
www.skifernie.com





of us with two instructors on the second'. We've also had good reports of the Steep and Deep camps and private lessons. 'First Tracks' gets you up the mountain at 7.45am for two hours, but when we tried it the instructor didn't know which lifts were open and there was a lot of wasted time.

### FACILITIES FOR CHILDREN
***Good day care centre***

There's a day care centre in the Cornerstone Lodge, which a reporter found 'very well run'. There are also 'Kids' Activity Nights' for children age six to twelve.

## STAYING THERE

### HOW TO GO
***More packages***

Fernie is increasingly easy to find in tour operator brochures. Unless stated, accommodation listed is at the resort.

**Chalets** Some UK tour operators run chalets. Beavertail Lodge (www.beavertaillodge.com) is run along chalet lines and received rave reviews from a 2004 reporter: 'The best chalet I have ever stayed in and the food is equal to any Michelin starred restaurant I have ever eaten in'. Canadian Powder Tours has a chalet and includes in the price guiding by locals who know the mountain well. 'Food was excellent. I am a novice off-piste skier but had a brilliant time,' says a reporter this year.

**Hotels and condos** As the resort develops, the choice is widening and shifting upmarket.

((((4 **Lizard Creek Lodge** Luxury ski-in, ski-out condo hotel. Spa, outdoor pool and hot-tub. We stayed there and highly recommend it.

(((3 **Cornerstone Lodge** Condo hotel in the village core.

(((3 **Best Western Fernie Mountain Lodge** Next to golf course near town. Recommended by reporters. Pool, hot-tub, fitness room.

(((3 **Griz Inn Sport Hotel** Condo-hotel with good facilities. Pool.

((2 **Wolf's Den Mountain Lodge** 'Simple but comfortable,' say reporters. Indoor hot-tub, games room and small gym. At base of slope.

((2 **Timberline Lodges** Very comfortable condos a shuttle-ride from the lifts.

((2 **Cedar Lodge** Motel on road to town. 'Comfortable and clean, but not very welcoming,' said reporters.

((2 **Alpine Lodge** B&B recommended by a reporter, with a Japanese-inspired restaurant.

### EATING OUT
***Not a highlight***

At the base, the Lizard Creek Lodge is expensive but serves gourmet food (in small portions). A reporter this year says the food in Beavertail Lodge (which takes outsiders if it's not full) is worth a Michelin star. Kelsey's (part of a chain) is casual and offers Asian dishes as well as standard burgers, steaks and pasta, but we've had very mixed reports on it. The Wood in the Hill opened last season and should be good (it's under the same ownership as Wood in town – see below). Gabriella's does cheap and cheerful Italian, and lots of readers have enjoyed it. The Mean Bean coffee shop in the Cornerstone Lodge has been recommended.

In Fernie, there are quite a few options. A reporter enjoyed the grills and pasta in the Old Elevator, a converted grain store. Jamochas is a coffee house that does meals. Other reader recommendations include the Curry Bowl (various Asian styles), the Royal hotel, Rip'n Richard's Eatery (south-western food and a lively atmosphere). The current favourite is the Wood bistro and tapas bar – 'Good but expensive. You need to book.' The new Japanese restaurant, Yama Goya does 'good sushi' says a reader.

### APRES-SKI
***Have a beer***

The Grizzly bar in the Day Lodge is quite lively when the lifts close – with live bands sometimes. During the week, the bars are pretty quiet later on. In town, the bars of the Royal hotel are popular with locals. Other recommendations are the Park Place Lodge Pub, the bar in the Grand Central hotel and the Eldorado Lounge for later on (it's under the Wood). The resort offers barbecue at the Bear's Den two days a week, with a torchlit descent.

### OFF THE SLOPES
***Get out and about***

There is a heritage walking tour of historic Fernie and the old railroad station is now the Art Station. You could take in an ice-hockey game. But the main diversion is the great outdoors.

# Kicking Horse

*Powdery adventure high above a fledgling resort village*

## COSTS

①②③④⑤⑥

## RATINGS

**The slopes**

| | |
|---|---|
| Snow | **** |
| Extent | *** |
| Expert | **** |
| Intermediate | *** |
| Beginner | *** |
| Convenience | * |
| Queues | ***** |
| Mountain restaurants | ** |

**The rest**

| | |
|---|---|
| Scenery | *** |
| Resort charm | * |
| Off-slope | * |

## TOURIST OFFICE

**t** 439 5400
guestservices@kickinghorseresort.com
www.kickinghorseresort.com

- ＋ A good bet for powder high up
- ＋ Great terrain for experts and some for adventurous intermediates
- ＋ Big vertical served by a fast lift
- ＋ Splendid mountaintop restaurant
- ＋ Now a few places to stay

- − Resort village in very early stages
- − Golden, the resort substitute, is neither attractive nor convenient
- − Single-stage gondola suits summer visitors, not skiers and riders
- − Few groomed intermediate runs

**In 2000/01, a tiny local hill with lifts only on the lower slopes was transformed by a new gondola rising 1150m/3,770ft to the top of high, powdery bowls and chutes. A smart base lodge and mountaintop restaurant were also built. In 2002 came a new quad chair-lift (slow, sadly) serving more high slopes. This year a couple of lodges will open and form the first stage of a mountain village at the lift base, which will eventually make this a real destination resort. It suits experts best and makes a good day trip from Banff or Lake Louise for adventurous intermediates. But it's a shame there's no gondola mid-station so you could ski the top half repeatedly without depending on less reliably good snow below.**

## THE RESORT

Eight miles from the small logging town of Golden, Kicking Horse is in the very early stages of development. When we visited in 2003 there were just a few houses and condos in the trees, a smart new base lodge and a portacabin housing the rental shop near the base of the gondola. The first phase of a real resort village at the gondola base is due to open for 2004/05 (see News); this is also due to house ski shops (rental and sales) and a 'cafe cum sushi' place. Daily round-trip buses run from Banff and Lake Louise to Kicking Horse: they will cost C$82 (plus sales tax) in 2005 including a lift pass.

Golden is a spread-out place beside the transcontinental highway. It has no real centre – it's the kind of place where you travel from motel to shops to restaurant by car. There's a shuttle-bus from some hotels to the slopes.

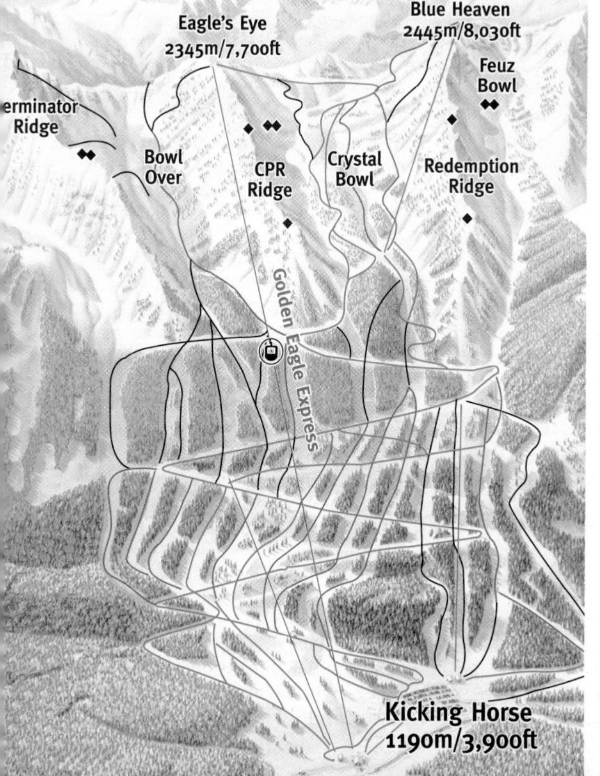


## THE MOUNTAINS

The lower two-thirds of the hill are wooded, with trails cut in the usual style. The upper third is a mix of open and lightly wooded slopes.

**Slopes** The only way up to the top part of the mountain is by the eight-seater gondola to Eagle's Eye. Despite the serious vertical of 1150m/3,770ft, this lift goes up in a single stage – to give summer sightseeing visitors a quick ascent. In winter, the lack of a mid-station is a real drawback: unless you ride the slow Stairway to Heaven chair to the slightly higher peak of Blue Heaven all the time, you have to make the full descent (and the snow conditions on the lower slopes may be

↑ This is what you come to Kicking Horse for: great powder in Bowl Over in the foreground and from the lightly tree-covered CPR Ridge

SNOWPIX.COM / CHRIS GILL

## NEWS

For 2004/05 two ski-in, ski-out lodges, forming the first part of the village centre planned for the foot of the gondola, will be open. Glacier Lodge will have 55 condo units and Vagabond Lodge, which opened this summer, has 10 suites. The next phase, the 51-unit Mountaineer Lodge, will be under construction during the winter. The village is expected to be complete by 2010.

2003/04 saw the 12-roomed Highland Lodge open.

## KEY FACTS

| | |
|---|---|
| **Resort** | 1190m<br>3,900ft |
| **Slopes** | 1190-2445m<br>3,900-8,030ft |
| **Lifts** | 5 |
| **Pistes** | 2,750 acres |
| **Green** | 20% |
| **Blue** | 20% |
| **Black** | 60% |
| **Snowmaking** | None |

**Central reservations phone number**
For resort accommodation call 1 250 439 5400 (toll-free from within Canada).

**Phone numbers**
From distant parts of Canada, add the prefix 1 250.
From abroad, add the prefix +1 250.

poor). As well as the marked runs, there are literally hundreds of ways down through the bowls, chutes and trees. The plan is that hardly any of the terrain will be groomed – making the area a paradise for powder pigs. Two chair-lifts from near the base serve the lower runs that formed the original Whitetooth ski area.

**Terrain-park** There isn't one.

**Snow reliability** It gets an average of 275 inches of snow a year; not enough to put it in the very top flight, but not far off. The top part of the mountain usually has light, dry powder. The lower part, however, may have cruddier snow and thin cover. It is a real shame that there is no gondola mid-station so you could stick to the top half.

**Experts** It's advanced skiers and riders who will get the most out of the area. From CPR ridge, drop off to skier's right through trees or to skier's left through chutes – there are endless options. If it's open you can also hike to Terminator Ridge (often closed due to avalanche danger). The Stairway to Heaven quad chair to Blue Heaven opens up easier ski-anywhere terrain down into Crystal Bowl. From the top you can also drop down into the steeper but wonderfully wide Feuz Bowl. The lower half of the mountain has fine black runs on cleared trails through the trees, some with serious moguls. Do six or seven laps on the gondola in a day and you'll sleep well that night.

**Intermediates** Adventurous intermediates will have a fine time learning to play in the powder from Blue Heaven down to Crystal Bowl. Most of it is open but you can head off into trees if you want to. But don't expect many groomed runs. Piste-bashers and timid intermediates should go elsewhere. The only easy, groomed way down the mountain is a 10km/6 mile winding road called It's a Ten.

**Beginners** We can't imagine why a UK-based beginner would come here.

**Snowboarding** Free-riders will love this powder paradise.

**Cross-country** There are 12km/7 miles of trails at Dawn Mountain and a 5km/3 mile loop on the golf course.

**Queues** None of our 2004 reporters experienced any large queues.

**Mountain restaurants** The Eagle's Eye table-service restaurant at the top of the gondola serves excellent food in stylish log-cabin surroundings and has splendid views. The base lodge is also newly built with logs and beams and has a small self-service restaurant. A yurt (tent) in Crystal Bowl serves snacks.

**Schools and guides** Two 2003 reporters booked group lessons and each was the only pupil. 'Excellent,' they both said. Another joined a free mountain tour and again was the only one. In 2004 a boarder met an instructor who gave him some free tips, and a skier took an avalanche safety course which 'was worth every penny; a truly memorable day'.

**Facilities for children** The school teaches children from the age of three.

## STAYING THERE

**How to go** Try the new lodges or condos at the slopes (a reporter said the Whispering Pines town homes were 'the most luxurious ski accommodation we've had') or stay in Golden.

**Hotels** In Golden, the Prestige Inn (344 7990) is a functional hotel with a small pool just off the main highway. Sisters and Beans (344 2443) has some well kept rooms – see below. Moberly Mountain Lodge (344 5544) is a luxury B&B that we've had good reports of.

**Eating out** In Golden, we enjoyed the cosy Sisters and Beans (pasta, steaks, Asian). The Kicking Horse Grill and the out-of-town Cedar House Cafe are highly rated. Eagle's Eye at the top of the gondola opens some nights.

**Après-ski** The Mad Trapper is the main drinking spot in Golden – a lively pub.

**Off the slopes** There is snowmobiling, snow-shoeing, ice-climbing and dog-sledding. But for someone who isn't going to hit the slopes, Golden is a dire place to stay.

SKI BANFF / LAKE LOUISE / ALEC PYTLOWANY

# Lake Louise

*Knockout views from Canada's second-biggest mountain*

## COSTS

(1)(2)(3)(4)(5)(6)

## RATINGS

| The slopes | |
|---|---|
| Snow | *** |
| Extent | **** |
| Expert | **** |
| Intermediate | **** |
| Beginner | *** |
| Convenience | * |
| Queues | **** |
| Mountain restaurants | ** |
| **The rest** | |
| Scenery | ***** |
| Resort charm | *** |
| Off-slope | **** |

- ➕ Spectacular high-mountain scenery – the best of any North American resort
- ➕ Slopes are the largest in the Canadian Rockies
- ➕ Snowy slopes of Sunshine Village within reach (see Banff chapter)
- ➕ Lots of wildlife around the valley
- ➕ Good value for money

- ➖ Local slopes are a short drive away from the 'village', Banff areas further
- ➖ Snowfall modest by local standards – though snowmaking is extensive
- ➖ Can be very cold – and the chair-lifts have no covers
- ➖ 'Village' is just a few hotels and shops dotted around a road junction
- ➖ Slopes can seem full of Brits

**If you care more for scenery than for après-ski action, Lake Louise is worth considering for a holiday. We've seen a few spectacular mountain views, and the view from the Fairmont Chateau Lake Louise hotel, of the lake and the Victoria Glacier behind it, is as spectacular as they come; it is simply stunning.**

**Even if you prefer the more animated base of Banff, you'll want to make expeditions to Lake Louise during your holiday. It can't compete with Sunshine Village for quantity of snow, but it's a big and interesting mountain. And from the slopes you get a distant version of that view.**

## THE RESORT

Although it's a small place, Lake Louise is a resort of parts. First, there's the lake itself, in a spectacular setting beneath the Victoria Glacier. Tom Wilson, who discovered it in 1882, declared, 'As God is my judge, I never in all my exploration have seen such a matchless scene.' Neither have we. And it can be appreciated from many of the rooms of the vast Fairmont Chateau Lake Louise hotel on the shore. Then there's Lake Louise 'village' – a collection of a few hotels, condos, petrol station, liquor store and shops, a couple of miles away on a road junction. Finally, a mile or two across the valley is the lift base station. A car helps, especially in cold weather. Buses to the Lake Louise ski area run every half hour, but a lot less frequently to the Banff areas of Sunshine and Norquay. Bus trips to the more distant resorts of Panorama and Kicking Horse and the small resorts of Nakiska and Fortress are possible. Day trip heli-skiing can also be arranged.



SKI BANFF/ LAKE LOUISE/ CRAIG FARISH

A high-speed quad from the bottom takes you up over easy beginner slopes (and the terrain-park and super-pipe) ↓

## NEWS

For 2003/04 75 new snow-guns were installed. Grooming was also expanded. A three-year plan to improve food and facilities at the four mountain lodges got under way, too. For 2002/03 the Top of the World chair at the top of the Front Side was upgraded from a fast quad to a six-pack.

## KEY FACTS

| Resort | 1645m 5,400ft |
|---|---|
| For Sunshine, Norquay and Lake Louise, covered by the Tri-area pass | |
| Slopes | 1630-2730m 5,350-8,950ft |
| Lifts | 29 |
| Pistes | 7,748 acres |
| Green | 23% |
| Blue | 39% |
| Black | 38% |
| Snowmaking | 1,840 acres |
| For Lake Louise only | |
| Slopes | 1645-2635m 5,400-8,650ft |
| Lifts | 12 |
| Pistes | 4,200 acres |
| Green | 25% |
| Blue | 45% |
| Black | 30% |
| Snowmaking | 40% |



## THE MOUNTAINS

The Lake Louise ski area is big, with a mixture of high open slopes, low trails cut through forest and gladed slopes between the two. Reporters are usually full of praise for the free guided tours given by volunteer 'Ski Friends'. There has been some criticism of inconsistent piste grading 'with some blues being more like blacks' and lots about cold lifts with no covers.

### THE SLOPES
*A wide variety*

One of two fast quads takes you up the **Front Side** (also called the South Face) to mid-mountain; from here, a six-pack goes to the top. From there, as elsewhere, there's a choice of green, blue or black runs to other lifts. The tree line comes about halfway up the top lift, but there are alternative lifts that stop a bit lower, so you can stay in the trees in bad weather. From mid-mountain, the long Summit drag-lift takes you to the high-point of the area, at the shoulder of Mount Whitehorn – there's a stunning view of peaks and glaciers including Canada's Matterhorn lookalike, Mount Assiniboine.

From either the top chair or the drag you can go over the ridge and into Lake Louise's almost treeless **Back Bowls** – open, predominantly north-facing and mainly steep.

From the bottom of the bowls you can take the Paradise lift back to the top again or continue on to the separate **Larch** area, served by a fast quad chair. With a lift-served vertical of 375m/1,230ft it's not huge, but it has pretty wooded runs of all grades. From the bottom you can return to the top of the main mountain via the Ptarmigan chair or take a long green path back to the main base area.

### TERRAIN-PARKS
*Huge and varied*

The resort redeveloped its terrain-park completely for 2002/03, and increased its size again last season. Now called

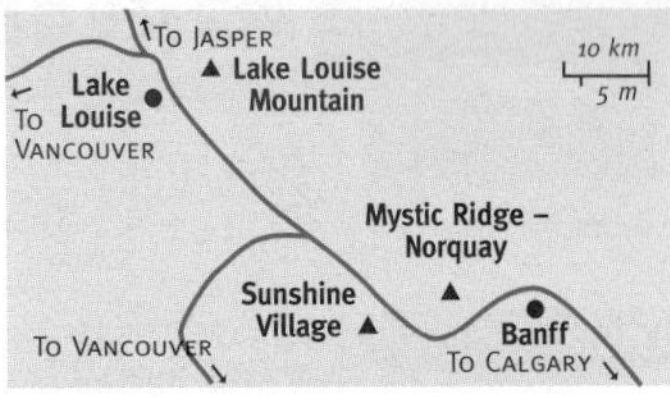


Showtime, it has nine varied rails, nine jumps and there's a quarter-pipe at the bottom. There's also an Olympic-sized super-pipe, a boarder-cross course and a beginner park with a small half-pipe, rollers and banked turns.

### SNOW RELIABILITY
*Usually OK*

Lake Louise gets around 140 inches a year on the Front Side, which by the standards of western Canada is not a lot. But it is usually enough, and there is snowmaking on 40% of the pistes. The north-facing Back Bowls and Larch hold the snow pretty well.

### FOR EXPERTS
*Widespread pleasure*

There are plenty of steep slopes. On the Front Side, as well as a score of marked black-diamond trails in and above the trees, there is the alluring West Bowl, reached from the Summit drag – a wide open expanse of snow outside the area boundary. Because this is National Park territory, you can in theory go anywhere. But outside the boundaries there are no patrols and, of course, no avalanche control. A guide is essential. 'You get a real feel of being in the middle of nowhere. The return through thick woods with small plunges and over-hanging branches is great fun,' says a recent reporter.

Inside the boundaries, going over to the Back Bowls opens up countless black mogul/powder runs. If it is open, try the Whitehorn 2 area directly behind the peak. This gave our Ozzie editor what she called 'some of the most exciting in-bounds skiing in North America' – a row of extreme chutes, almost 1km/0.5 miles long.

## boarding

*Lake Louise is a great mountain for free-riders, with all the challenging terrain in the bowls and glades. The Summit drag-lift is a tricky one to ride (very long and with a difficult start and steep pitches), but it's worth it to access the Back Bowls and the views. The long green run that goes from the Larch area back to the base is to be avoided – it's really flat. In Banff, two specialist snowboard shops are Rude Boys and Unlimited Snowboards.*

## LIFT PASSES

**Tri-area lift pass**
Covers all lifts and transport between Banff, Lake Louise and Sunshine Village.

**Main pass**
3 days C$199
6 days C$398

**Senior citizens**
Over 65: 6 days C$356

**Children**
Under 13: 6 days C$128
Under 6: free pass

**Notes**
Prices above include taxes. Three days minimum.

**Alternative passes**
One-day and half-day passes available for individual areas.

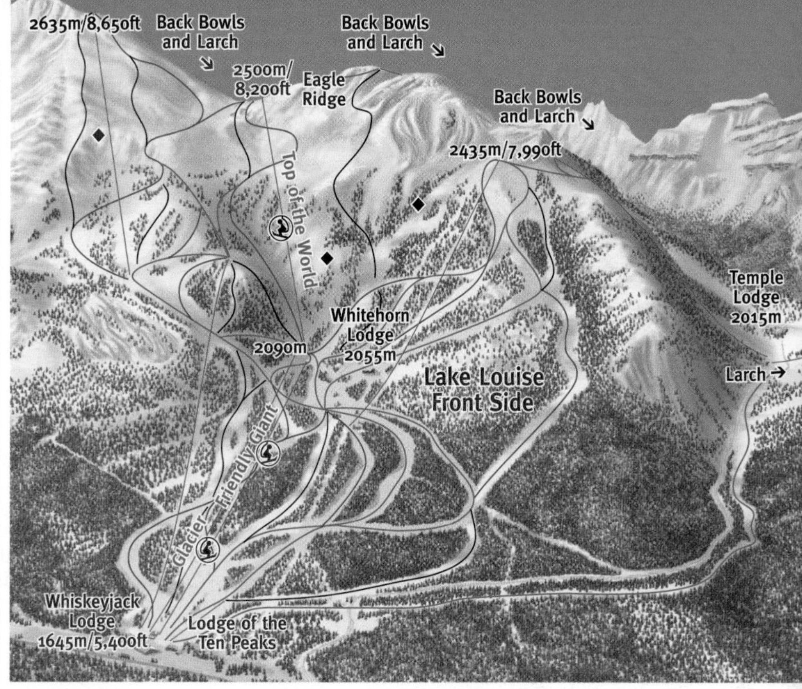


The Top of the World six-pack takes you to the very popular Paradise Bowl, served by its own triple chair – there are endless variants here. From the Summit drag you can access wide open Back Bowl slopes that take you right away from all signs of lifts. The seriously steep slope served by the Ptarmigan quad chair provided many of the logs for the newest base lodge, and offers great gladed terrain as a result. It's a good place to beat the crowds and find good snow, suggests one reporter. The Larch area has some steep double-diamond stuff in the trees, and open snowfields at the top for those with the energy to hike up. Heli-skiing is available from bases outside the National Park.

### FOR INTERMEDIATES
***Some good cruising***

Almost half the runs are classified as intermediate. But from the top of the Front Side the blue runs down are little more than paths in places, and there are only two blue and two green routes marked in the Back Bowls. Once you get part way down the Front Side the blues are much more interesting. And when groomed, the Men's and Ladies' Downhill black runs are great fast cruises on the lower half of the mountain. Juniper is a wonderful cruising run in the same area. Meadowlark is a beautiful tree-lined run to the base area – to find it from the Eagle chair, first follow Eagle Meadows. The Larch area has some short but ideal intermediate runs – and reporters have enjoyed the natural



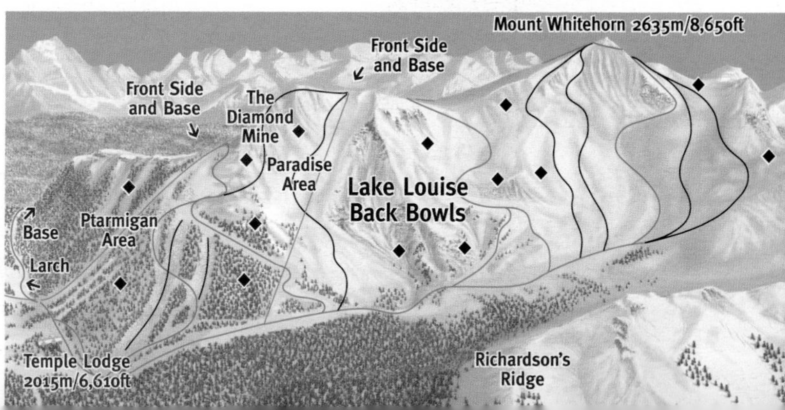

## SCHOOLS

**ClubSki and ClubSnowboard**
t 762 4561
info@banffskischool.com

**Classes**
3 days guided tuition of the three areas (4½hr per day) C$229 incl. tax.

**Private lessons**
Half day (3hr) C$341, incl. tax.





lumps and bumps of the aptly named blue, Rock Garden. The adventurous should also try the blue-classified Boomerang, which starts with a short side-step up from the top of the Summit drag, and some of the ungroomed Back Bowls terrain.

### FOR BEGINNERS
***Excellent terrain***

Louise has a good nursery area near the base, which has attracted praise, served by a short T-bar, which has not. You progress to the gentle, wide Wiwaxy, Pinecone Way and the slightly more difficult Deer Run or Eagle Meadows (all designated 'slow skiing zones'). There are even green slow-skiing zones round the back bowls and in the Larch area – worth trying for the views, though some do contain slightly steep pitches. A past reporter lost confidence on these, and found that people still skied fast in the slow areas and that they were quite crowded.

### FOR CROSS-COUNTRY
***High in quality and quantity***

It's a very good area for cross-country, with around 80km/50 miles of groomed trails within Banff National Park. There are excellent trails in the local area (and on Lake Louise itself). And Emerald Lake Lodge 40km/25 miles away has some lovely trails and has been highly recommended as a place to stay for a peaceful time.

### QUEUES
***Not unknown***

Half of the area's visitors come for the day from nearby cities such as Calgary – so it can have queues at weekends, especially for the slow chairs on the back of the mountain.

### MOUNTAIN RESTAURANTS
***Good base facilities***

There's not much choice up the mountain. Temple Lodge, near the bottom of Larch, is built in rustic style with a big terrace. Sawyer's Nook is its calm table-service restaurant. 'We were impressed with both food and prices,' said a reporter. The self-service cafeteria can get very crowded. Whitehorn Lodge, at mid-mountain on the Front Side, is a cafeteria with fine views from its balcony. At the base, the Lodge of the Ten Peaks is a hugely impressive, spacious, airy, modern, log-built affair with various eating, drinking and lounging options. The neighbouring Whiskeyjack building has the good Northface table-service

SKI BANFF/ LAKE LOUISE/ ALEC PYTLOWANY

A classic view over the frozen Lake Louise, with the Chateau at its edge and the Victoria Glacier rising up beyond it ↓

### CHILDREN

**Telus Play Station & Daycare**
t 522 3555
Ages 18 days to 6yr; 8am to 4.30.

**Ski school**
Takes ages 6 to 12 (3 days C$229, incl. tax and lunch).

### GETTING THERE

**Air** Calgary 177km/110 miles (1½hr).

### ACTIVITIES

**Indoor** Mainly hotel-based pools, saunas and hot-tubs, bowling, cinema, museums

**Outdoor** Ice rinks, walking, ice fishing, swimming in hot springs, sleigh rides, dog-sled rides, snowmobiles, helicopter rides, snow-shoeing

**Phone numbers**
From distant parts of Canada, add the prefix 1 403.
From abroad, add the prefix +1 403.

### TOURIST OFFICE

t 762 4561
info@sblls.com
www.skibig3.com

restaurant and buffet, including a breakfast menu that 'sets you up for the whole day'. The Kokanee Kabin has BBQ food – but a reporter complained of long queues and poor food.

**SCHOOLS AND GUIDES**
***Generally good reports***
'The best teaching we've encountered' is how a reporter described his 'bumps' lesson at Lake Louise. A 2003 reporter enjoyed the lessons, but said she could not get afternoon-only classes. And her five-year-old daughter did not like being put in classes with eight- to ten-year-olds. See the Banff chapter for details on the excellent three-day, three-mountain Club Ski and Club Snowboard Program.

**FACILITIES FOR CHILDREN**
***Varying reports***
A reporter who used Lake Louise, Sunshine and Norquay facilities said: 'I'd recommend all three and advise booking in advance at Lake Louise.'

## STAYING THERE

**HOW TO GO**
***Good value accommodation***
**Hotels** Summer is the peak season here. Prices halve for the winter – so you can stay in luxury at bargain rates.
((((4) **Fairmont Chateau Lake Louise** (522 3511) Isolated position with stunning views over frozen Lake Louise, 500 rooms, lots of shops, groups of Japanese tourists, pool, hot-tub, steam room. 'Could not be faulted.'
((((4) **Post Hotel** (522 3989) Small, comfortable Relais & Châteaux place in the village with good restaurant (huge wine list) and pool, hot-tub, sauna.
((2) **Lake Louise Inn** (522 3791) Cheaper option in the village, with pool, hot-tub and sauna. 'Comfortable rooms', 'good food', but 'staff with an attitude problem'.
((2) **Deer Lodge** (522 3747) Charming old hotel next to the Chateau, good restaurant, rooftop hot-tub.
**Self-catering** Some is available but local shopping is limited. The Baker Creek Chalets (522 3761) were highly recommended by 2003 reporters on their honeymoon ('really romantic').

**EATING OUT**
***Limited choice***
The Post hotel has a good reputation. The Fairview Dining Room at the Chateau is also top notch. The Outpost (in the Post hotel) does inexpensive pub food. The Station restaurant is in an atmospheric old station building. The small bakery/coffee shop in the village has had praise from reporters and is good for breakfast.

**APRES-SKI**
***Lively at tea time, quiet later***
There are several options at the bottom of the slopes. The Sitzmark Lounge in Whiskeyjack Lodge is popular – with an open fire and often a live band. The upstairs part of The Lodge of the Ten Peaks has lovely surroundings, an open fire, a couple of bars and a relaxed atmosphere. The Kokanee Kabin has live music on Spring afternoons. Twice a week there's live music and dancing and a buffet dinner at the mid-mountain Whitehorn Lodge. You ski or ride there as the lifts close and the evening ends with a torchlit descent. It is hugely popular with British visitors, and we loved it. Reporters recommend the Sleigh Ride to Dinner, with BBQ and dancing.

Later on, things are fairly quiet. But the Glacier Saloon, in Chateau Lake Louise, with traditional Wild West decor, often has live music until late. Explorer's Lounge, in the Lake Louise Inn, has entertainment. The Post hotel's Outpost Pub is worth a look.

**OFF THE SLOPES**
***Beautiful scenery***
Lake Louise makes a lovely, peaceful place to stay for someone who does not intend to hit the slopes. The lake itself makes a stunning setting for walks, snow-shoeing, cross-country skiing and ice skating. There are plenty of other things to do and lots of wildlife to see. You can go on ice canyon walks, sleigh rides, dog-sledding, tobogganing, sightseeing tours and visit natural hot springs.

For a more lively day or for shopping you can visit Banff.

Lake Louise is near one end of the Columbia Icefields Parkway, a three-hour drive to Jasper through National Parks, amidst stunningly beautiful scenery of high peaks and glaciers – one of the world's most beautiful drives.

**STAYING UP THE MOUNTAIN**
***Try ski touring***
Skoki Lodge (522 3555) is 11km/7 miles on skis from Temle Lodge. Built in the 1930s, it sleeps 22 in the lodge and cabins and allegedly has 'gourmet food'. Reports welcome.

# Panorama

*Great views, some challenging runs, a rapidly developing resort*

## COSTS

①②③④⑤⑥

## RATINGS

| **The slopes** | |
|---|---|
| Snow | *** |
| Extent | ** |
| Expert | **** |
| Intermediate | *** |
| Beginner | **** |
| Convenience | **** |
| Queues | **** |
| Mountain restaurants | * |
| **The rest** | |
| Scenery | *** |
| Resort charm | ** |
| Off-slope | * |

## KEY FACTS

| | |
|---|---|
| **Resort** | 1160m 3,800ft |
| **Slopes** | 1160-2380m 3,800-7,800ft |
| **Lifts** | 9 |
| **Pistes** | 2,847 acres |
| **Green** | 15% |
| **Blue** | 55% |
| **Black** | 30% |
| **Snowmaking** | 40% |



- ➕ Increasing amount of slope-side accommodation, plus a lower village linked by lift till 10pm
- ➕ Fair-sized area with big vertical drop and challenging runs for all abilities
- ➕ Runs are usually deserted
- ➕ Two new quads for 2003/04 make getting to the top much quicker
- ➕ Heli-skiing by the day on hand

- ➖ May be too challenging for timid intermediates – not many cruisers
- ➖ Snowfall record not impressive by high local standards
- ➖ Not many lifts serve the upper runs
- ➖ No real mountain restaurants
- ➖ Village still quiet with no real focus

**Panorama has benefited from a huge investment in the past few years. New slope-side accommodation has been built, along with outdoor hot-pools and a skating rink. And last season saw two new quads replacing two T-bars and a slow, queue-prone chair – the source of many complaints by reporters. The mountain's vertical of 1220m/4,000ft is one of the biggest in North America, and it has some excellent terrain for experts and adventurous intermediates. It's good for beginners too. But timid intermediates may find some of the runs intimidating and prefer to stick to the rather limited lower mountain. And the resort is quiet – a better place for families than singles looking for nightlife.**

## THE RESORT

Panorama is a small, quiet, purpose-built resort above the lakeside town of Invermere in eastern BC, about two hours' scenic drive south-west of Banff. Accommodation is concentrated mainly in two car-free areas. There are attractive lodges with a hot-pool complex and a skating rink at the foot of the main slopes and, with ski-in, ski-out convenience, this is the best place to stay. But a lot of accommodation is in a 'lower village' which lacks character or life. This is now linked to the 'upper village' and the slopes by a bucket lift which runs until 10pm. There are also houses spread widely around the hillside and the village as a whole lacks a central focus or hub.

Outings by car are possible to Kimberley, less than two hours south, or to Lake Louise or Kicking Horse, slightly further away to the north. The resort runs day trips to Lake Louise and Kicking Horse.

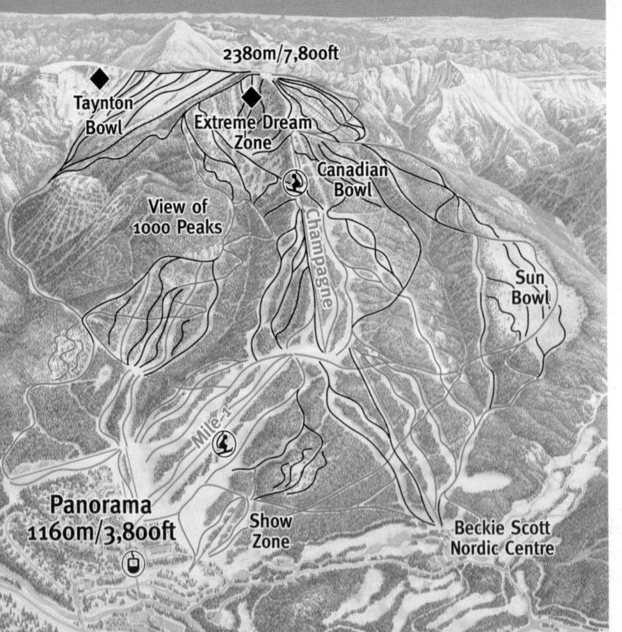


## THE MOUNTAIN

The slopes basically follow three ridges, joined at top and bottom. Almost all of the terrain is wooded. Daily mountain tours are available. And some runs are open for floodlit skiing and riding Thursday to Sunday.

**Slopes** From the upper village, a fast quad goes over gentle slopes to mid-mountain. Above this a fast quad (new for 2003/04) serves both expert and intermediate slopes. Then the also new

Don't panic: you can take much easier lines down Taynton Bowl than this ➔

PANORAMA MOUNTAIN VILLAGE

## NEWS

For 2003/04 two new quad chairs were built which makes getting to the top of the mountain quicker and easier. The Champagne Express high-speed quad replaced the slow, queue-prone, two-person Horizon chair and the Champagne T-bar above it. And the Summit T-bar to the top was replaced by a fixed-grip quad.

New snowmaking was installed on several of the long cruising pistes.

The two terrain-parks received a few new features and for 2004/05 the intermediate terrain-park will have more wide learning rails, while the expert park will receive new expert rails.

There is new slope-side hotel and condo accommodation in the upper village: 1000 Peaks Lodge and the adjacent 1000 Peaks Summit, complete with skating rink and BBQ area.

fixed-grip quad takes you to the summit. From the summit there is only one blue run (appropriately named Getmedown). The other runs are all single- or double-black diamonds. There are long runs down the two outer ridges as well as the central one. Those on the right bring you to a triple-chair near the base of the mountain, which also serves its own bunch of runs. Either way, the whole vertical is usable. At the top, between the left and central ridges, is the double-black-diamond Extreme Dream Zone. Off the back is the 'Outback' area in Taynton Bowl – 700 acres of lightly wooded expert terrain which opened in the 2000/01 season (it was previously used for heli-skiing). This funnels down to a long, flattish blue run back to the village.

**Terrain-parks** There are two: the Blue intermediate jib park for beginner freestylers and kids and the main Showzone terrain-park. Both were improved last season with the addition of a rainbow funbox, battleship rail and flatdown funbox. There is a half-pipe too. They are floodlit Thursday to Sunday evenings.

**Snow reliability** Annual snowfall is low by local standards – less than half the Fernie figure. But snowmaking covers 40% of trails and grooming is good.

**Experts** There are genuine black runs scattered all over the mountain, and some expert-only areas. At the very top of the mountain and accessed through a gate is the Extreme Dream Zone – seriously steep trails with cliffs as well as tight trees, said to contain the best snow on the mountain. Off the back of the summit is the Taynton Bowl area, with challenging but (even though it is marked double-black diamond on the map) less extreme terrain – hiking over to the far runs can be worth it for fresh tracks. There are often good bumps on the blacks at mid-mountain. On the extreme right of the mountain is an area of gentler glades, where you can pick the density of trees and steepness of slope to try. Then there's the local heli-skiing – see Intermediates.

**Intermediates** For adventurous intermediates the terrain is excellent – there are easy blacks all over the mountain, some of them regularly groomed. The black View of 1000 Peaks, which turns into Stumbock's or the blue Messerli's Mile, has fabulous views but can be a bit tricky in parts. Both this and Getmedown from the top

which runs into Schober's Dream are beautiful and long for North America (up to 3.5km/2 miles). Sun Bowl is a good introduction to a powder bowl and Millennium (black running into blue) is a great roller-coaster.

But the less confident may find all this uncomfortably challenging. The blues in the centre of the area such as World Cup Way, Skyline and Rollercoaster are gentler but they don't add up to a lot. RK Heli-Skiing operates from a base right next to the village and specialises in one-day sessions for first-time heli-skiers – well worth a go. 'We got in eight runs on the glacier in shin-deep powder. The whole experience was first class with excellent guides and a fine lunch on a ridge with phenomenal alpine views in all directions,' says a 2003 reporter. But this year we had a report of some-one being put in a group that was too strong for her, spoiling the day.

**Beginners** There are a couple of nursery lifts and a moving carpet serving a quiet and gentle nursery area. Then there are good, longer runs to progress to served by the Mile 1 quad.

**Snowboarding** There is good steep terrain and tree runs for expert free-riders. And it's great news that the two top T-bars have been replaced by

chairs. The two terrain-parks offer something for all standards. Beginners have several good long green runs to practise on but the main nursery slopes are served by drag-lifts.
**Cross-country** There are 30 km/19 miles of trails starting from the Nordic Centre, which you can reach on downhill skis and where you can rent cross-country gear.
**Queues** The two new quads last season seem to have eliminated the only queues on the mountain as we have 2004 reports of very few queues, even in a school holiday week. And the trails are usually delightfully deserted.
**Mountain restaurants** There are no real mountain restaurants, just two huts offering basic refreshments. But the Ski Tip day lodge at the base is an excellent modern affair.
**Schools and guides** We have mainly had glowing reports of the ski school. 'Universally agreed as superb by all who tried it' and 'massive leap in skiing – felt great' are typical comments. But one reporter who joined an all-day free-skiing group thought it 'didn't live up to the publicity and we were disappointed'. Multi-day courses include BBQ lunches at the mid-mountain rustic Elkhorn Cabin.
**Facilities for children** Wee Wascals is the childcare centre, taking children from 18 months. Snowbirds is for three to five year olds, and the Adventure Club caters for kids from 5 to 14. Kid's Nights for 6 to 13 year olds and a Teen Nightclub for 13 to 18 year olds are arranged some evenings to let parents have a night out. Evening babysitters are also available.

## STAYING THERE

**How to go** The better places are the newer ones in the upper village.
**Hotels** Panorama Springs is right on the slopes with a big outdoor hot-pool and sauna facility. Next door Tamarack and Ski Tip have been recommended. And the new 1000 Peaks Lodge and 1000 Peaks Summit units, built around a public skating rink, look good. The Pine Inn in the lower village is a budget option, which reporters have criticised (one moved out after one night); Toby Creek seems a better bet.
**Self-catering** There are plenty of condo blocks and town homes. The store is inadequate, so stock up in Invermere.
**Eating out** Eating out options are mainly unexciting and in the lodges. The Heli Plex restaurant has great views of the mountain, a shooter bar sculpted from ice and is frequently recommended by reporters. The ski school organises BBQs at Elkhorn Cabin followed by a torchlight descent. There's a horsedrawn wagon ride followed by chilli around a campfire. There's a shuttle-bus to the restaurants down in Invermere, which leaves at 7.15pm and comes back around 10pm.
**Après-ski** Après-ski revolves around the T-bar and Grill in the Pine Inn and the Jackpine pub in the Horsethief Lodge. The Ski Tip Lodge terrace is popular on sunny afternoons. The Heli Plex is 'good for a relaxing drink'. The Glacier is the nightclub.
**Off the slopes** The hot-pool facility, with thermal baths, a swimming pool, slides and sauna is excellent, but it gets rather taken over by kids. There are snowmobile tours, ice fishing excursions, snow-shoeing and skating.

**Central reservations**
1 800 663 2929 (toll-free within Canada).

**Phone numbers**
From distant parts of Canada, add the prefix 1 250. From abroad, add +1 250.

### TOURIST OFFICE

**t** 342 6941
paninfo@intrawest.com
www.skipanorama.com

PANORAMA MOUNTAIN VILLAGE

The hot pools are great, so long as they aren't overrun by kids →

# Sun Peaks

*Attractive new village at the foot of rapidly expanded slopes*

## COSTS

(1)(2)(3)(4)(5)(6)

## RATINGS

**The slopes**

| | |
|---|---|
| Snow | **** |
| Extent | *** |
| Expert | *** |
| Intermediate | **** |
| Beginner | **** |
| Convenience | **** |
| Queues | ***** |
| Mountain restaurants | * |

**The rest**

| | |
|---|---|
| Scenery | *** |
| Resort charm | *** |
| Off-slope | ** |

## NEWS

For 2003/04 there were two new black runs on Mt Morrisey, a new blue on Sundance, more cross-country trails and a new floodlit tubing park.

For 2004/05 a new moving carpet will be installed at the tubing hill and there will be extra snowmaking and three new grooming machines.

## KEY FACTS

| | |
|---|---|
| **Resort** | 1255m<br>4,120ft |
| **Slopes** | 1200–2080m<br>3,930–6,820ft |
| **Lifts** | 10 |
| **Pistes** | 3,491 acres |
| **Green** | 20% |
| **Blue** | 61% |
| **Black** | 19% |
| **Snowmaking** | 40 acres |

+ Some great terrain for all standards
+ Excellent glades for intermediates as well as experts
+ Slopes very quiet during the week
+ Attractive new slope-side village with some smart shops

− Village may be too small and quiet for some tastes
− Snow on some of the lower steep terrain can suffer from the sun
− Although the second largest ski area in BC, it's not big by Alpine standards

**Sun Peaks has sprung from the drawing board in the last ten years and we have been increasingly impressed on each of three successive visits. It now has an almost complete small village and a fair amount of varied terrain. Former Olympic slalom champion Nancy Greene and husband Al Raine, who were instrumental in developing Whistler years ago, have made Sun Peaks their new project. Al runs a hotel here and Nancy is Director of Skiing and skis with guests daily.**

## THE RESORT

Until 1993 Sun Peaks was known as Tod Mountain, a local hill for the residents of nearby Kamloops. Since then the company that bought it has overseen the development of a small, attractive resort village with low-rise pastel-coloured buildings with a vaguely Tirolean feeling to them. The traffic-free main street is lined with accommodation, restaurants and shops including a smart art gallery, great chocolate shop and good coffee bar.

## THE MOUNTAINS

With almost 3,700 acres of skiable terrain, Sun Peaks is the second biggest ski area in BC (Whistler is the biggest). There are free guided tours twice a day and every day at 11am you can ski for free with former Olympic champion and Canada's Female Athlete of the 20th Century Nancy Greene (don't miss it – she is great fun!).

**Slopes** There are three distinct sectors, each served by a high-speed quad. One goes from the centre of the village to mid-mountain on Sun Peaks' original ski hill, Mt Tod. This has mainly black runs but there are easier blues and greens. A tiny snowcat offers day-long backcountry skiing here. Also reached from the village centre, the Sundance area has mainly blue and green cruising runs. Both Sundance and Tod have some great gladed areas (12 of them marked on the trail map). Mt Morrisey is reached by a long green run from the top of Sundance. It has a delightful network of easy blue runs with trees left uncut in the trails, making them effectively groomed glade runs.

**Terrain-park** There's a park, boarder-cross and half-pipe on Sundance.
**Snow reliability** Sun Peaks gets an average snowfall of 220 inches a year; not in the top league but better than some. The snow can suffer on the lower part of Mt Tod's south-facing slopes, especially later in the season.
**Experts** Mt Tod has most of the steep terrain, though some of the blacks on Mt Morrisey are long mogul runs too.
**Intermediates** This is great terrain for early intermediates, with the easy groomed glades of Mt Morrisey, lovely swooping blues on Sundance and the long 5 Mile run from Mt Tod. More adventurous intermediates can tackle the easier glades (such as Greene's) and blacks (such as Peek-A-Boo).
**Beginners** There are nursery slopes right in the village centre, with long easy greens to progress too.
**Snowboarding** Boarders can explore the whole mountain. But beware the flat green run back from Mt Morrisey.
**Cross-country** There are 28km/17 miles of groomed trails.
**Queues** Weekdays are usually very quiet; it's only at peak weekends that you might find short queues.
**Mountain restaurants** The Sunburst Lodge is the only option; its cinnamon buns are highly recommended.
**Schools and guides** Reporters have been impressed with a multi-day ski school course which included après-ski activities and the 'ladies mornings'
**Facilities for children** The playschool takes kids from age 18 months and the ski school from 3 years.

## STAYING THERE

**How to go** There's a lot of self-catering accommodation as well as hotels.
**Hotels** Nancy Greene's Cahilty Lodge is a friendly and comfortable ski-in, ski-out base and you get the chance to ski with her and Al Raine (former Canadian ski team coach) at 9am most days. The Delta Sun Peaks Resort (outdoor pool and hot-tub) is in the village centre.
**Eating out** For a small resort, there's a good choice of restaurants. Macker's Bistro is popular and we had great Thai-style sea bass there. Powder Hounds does good steaks and The Val and Servus more sophisticated food.
**Après-ski** Bottoms, Masa's and Macker's are the main après-ski bars. At weekends MackDaddy's nightclub in The Delta can get lively. There are fondue evenings with torchlit descents, winter bonfires and tobogganing.
**Off the slopes** There's skating, tubing, snowmobiling and dog-sledding.

**Phone numbers**
From distant parts of Canada, add the prefix 1 250.
From abroad, add the prefix +1 250.

### TOURIST OFFICE

**t** 578 7222
info@sunpeaksresort.com
www.sunpeaksresort.com





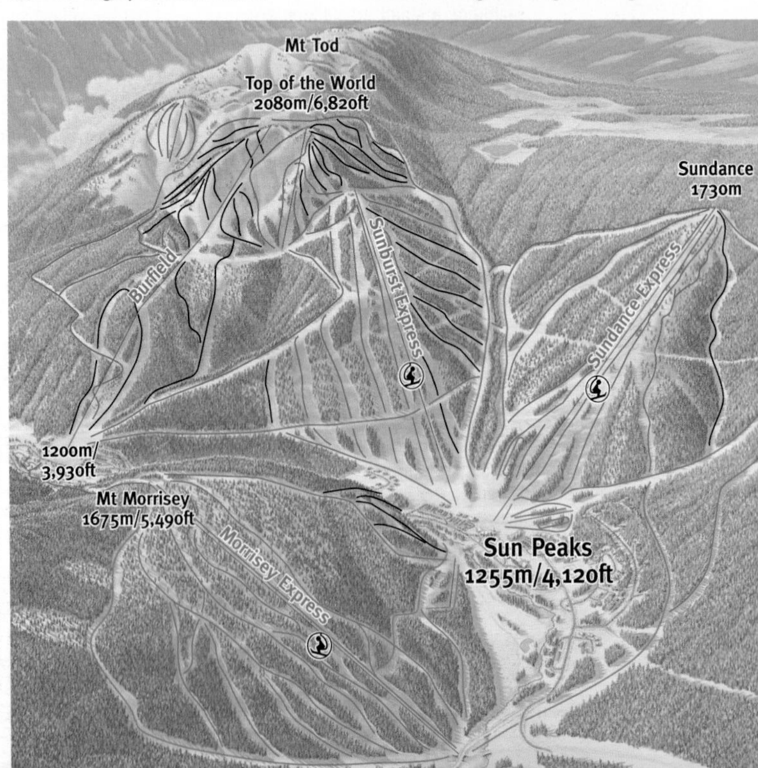

# Whistler

*North America's biggest mountain with terrain to suit every standard*

## COSTS

(1)(2)(3)(4)(5)(6)

## HOW IT RATES

| **The slopes** | |
|---|---|
| Snow | **** |
| Extent | **** |
| Expert | ***** |
| Intermediate | ***** |
| Beginner | *** |
| Convenience | **** |
| Queues | *** |
| Mountain restaurants | ** |
| **The rest** | |
| Scenery | *** |
| Resort charm | *** |
| Off-slope | ** |

## KEY FACTS

| | |
|---|---|
| **Resort** | 675m 2,210ft |
| **Altitude** | 650-2285m 2,140-7,490ft |
| **Lifts** | 33 |
| **Pistes** | 8,171 acres |
| **Green** | 18% |
| **Blue** | 55% |
| **Black** | 27% |
| **Snowmaking** | 565 acres |

- \+ North America's biggest, both in area and vertical (1610m/5,280ft)
- \+ Good slopes for most abilities, with an unrivalled combination of high open bowls and woodland trails
- \+ Good snow record
- \+ Almost Alpine scenery, unlike the rounded Rockies of Colorado
- \+ Attractive modern villages at the foot of the slopes with car-free centres, one with lively après-ski
- \+ Good range of restaurants and bars (though not enough of them)
- \+ Easy access from the UK – non-stop flights to Vancouver, short transfer
- \+ Excellent heli-operation nearby

- − Proximity to the ocean means a lot of cloudy weather and, with the low altitude, when it's snowing on the mountain it's often raining at resort level
- − Two separate mountains are linked only at resort level
- − Some runs get very crowded
- − Lift queues are often a problem
- − Mountain restaurants are mostly functional (and overcrowded)
- − Whistler is in danger of becoming a victim of its own success – attracting more people than the mountain or the village facilities (restaurants in particular) can cope with

**Whistler is unlike any other resort in North America. It's bigger, both in terms of vertical drop and skiable area. The town is big too. Combine that with hordes of people pouring in from Vancouver on powder days and weekends and you can get lengthy lift queues and crowded trails – unusual for North America. The facilities in town can get overstretched too, with tables in restaurants difficult to come by. If you want to get away from the crowds, you should go elsewhere.**

**But a lot of people will put up with the crowds for Whistler's other attractions. There are some fine up-market hotels and a good variety of restaurants. And the mountain is simply the best that North America has to offer. Great open bowls, steeps and deeps, tree-lined intermediate cruising and good beginner slopes. The ski schools are excellent. The lifts are generally fast and efficient. And the snow on the upper half of the mountain is as reliable and powdery as you'll find. But be prepared for rain at resort level and poor snow on the lower slopes.**

**Whistler will host many events during the 2010 Winter Olympics, and it seems set to expand facilities even more before then. This season sees an increase in terrain of more than some smaller North American resorts such as Crested Butte have in total. And we look forward to seeing the revamped Whistler Creekside.**

## THE RESORT

Whistler Village sits at the foot of its two mountains, Whistler and Blackcomb, a scenic 115km/71 mile drive from Vancouver on Canada's west coast. Whistler started as a locals' ski area in 1966 with a few ramshackle buildings in what is now the revamped Whistler Creek (aka Creekside). Whistler Village, a 10-minute bus-ride away, developed in the late 1970s. And another village spread up the lower slopes of Blackcomb Mountain in the 1980s; this village, a 10-minute walk from Whistler, is now known simply as Upper Village.

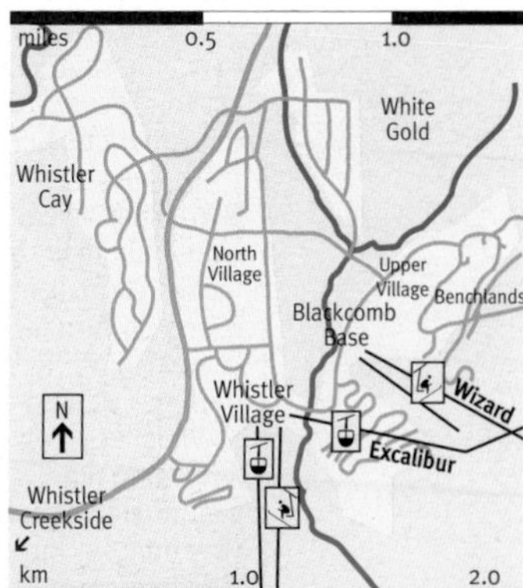

## NEWS

For 2004/05 another 1,100 acres of terrain is due to open on Whistler Mountain. Four new runs (one intermediate and three advanced/ expert trails) with a vertical descent of over 1500m/4,920ft from the Peak down to Whistler Creekside will open. As will 700 acres of formerly out-of-bounds terrain in Flute Bowl, a short hike up from the top of either the Peak or Harmony chair.

Creekside will be re-launched after a four-year face-lift and expansion as a smaller, quieter, family-friendly, traffic-free alternative to the main Whistler village. A new 5-star Four Seasons hotel is due to open near the base of Blackcomb.

A new super-pipe is being built on Blackcomb mountain for the 2005 Snowboard World Championships and Blackcomb's terrain-park is being upgraded.





The centres of all the villages are traffic-free. The architecture is varied and, for a purpose-built resort, quite tasteful. There are lots of chalet-style apartments on the hillsides. The centres have individually designed wood and concrete buildings, blended together around pedestrian streets and squares. There are no monstrous high-rise blocks – but there are a lot of large five- or six-storey buildings.

Whistler Village has most of the bars, restaurants and shops, and two gondolas (one to each mountain). Whistler North, further from the lifts, is newer and has virtually merged with the original village, making a huge car-free area of streets lined with shops, condos and restaurants. Upper Village is much smaller and quieter. Its huge Fairmont Chateau Whistler hotel dominates the views of the village from the mountain.

Whistler Creek (aka Creekside) has been revamped and expanded and it will play an important role in the Olympics, with many of the alpine events finishing here.

There is a free bus between Whistler and Upper Village but, if you're staying near the base of Blackcomb, it's just as quick to walk. Staying further out means paying for buses or taxis – which are not expensive. Some hotels have free shuttle-buses, which you can get to pick you up as well as take you to restaurants and nightlife.

The most convenient place to stay is Whistler Village as you can access either mountain by gondola. Creekside, though convenient for Whistler Mountain, is less so for Blackcomb. Some lodging is an inconvenient walk or bus-ride from the villages and slopes.

Whistler is now getting very busy and some reporters have found the central area around Village Square very noisy in the early hours. Creekside is quieter.

## THE MOUNTAINS

The area has acquired a formidable and well-deserved reputation among experts. But both Whistler and Blackcomb also have loads of well-groomed intermediate terrain. Together they have over 200 marked trails, and form the biggest area of slopes, with the longest runs, in North America.

Many reporters enthuse about the mountain host service and the 'go slow' patrol – some find the latter 'over zealous', but crowded slopes, especially on the runs home ('a human slalom'), mean they're often needed. A 2004 visitor praised the 'very good signposting with large piste map and lift operation indicator boards'.

But reporters also comment on the early closing times for lifts (3pm until end-January, 3.30 in February and 4pm thereafter). Upper lifts may close earlier.

### THE SLOPES
*The best in North America*

**Whistler Mountain** is accessed from Whistler Village by a two-stage, 10-person gondola that rises over 1100m/3,610ft to Roundhouse Lodge, the main mid-mountain base. There is an alternative of two consecutive fast quads, which take you slightly lower; they are a good choice when queues for the gondola are long.

Runs back down through the trees fan out from the gondola – cruises to the Emerald and Big Red fast chairs, longer runs to the gondola mid-station.

From Roundhouse you can see the jewel in Whistler's crown – magnificent above-the-tree-line bowls, served by the fast Peak and Harmony quads. The bowls are mostly go-anywhere terrain for experts but there are groomed trails, so anyone can appreciate the views.

A six-person gondola from Creekside also accesses Whistler Mountain.

Access to **Blackcomb** from Whistler Village is by an eight-seater gondola, followed by a fast quad. From the base of Blackcomb you take two consecutive fast quads up to the main Rendezvous restaurant. From the arrival points you can go left for great cruising terrain and the Glacier Express quad up to the Horstman Glacier area, or right for steeper slopes, the terrain-park or the 7th Heaven chair. The 1610m/5,280ft vertical from the top of 7th Heaven to the base is the largest in North America (and big even by Alpine standards). Or you can go into the

glacier area. A T-bar from the Horstman Glacier brings you (with a very short hike) to the Blackcomb Glacier in the next valley – a beautiful run which takes you away from all lifts.

Fresh Tracks is a deal that allows you to ride up Whistler Mountain (at extra cost) from 7.15am, have a buffet breakfast and get to the slopes as they open – very popular with many reporters. A good tip is to hit the slopes first and breakfast after – that way you find the slopes at their quietest.

Free guided tours of each mountain are offered twice a day.

**TERRAIN-PARKS**
***For high-fliers and mere mortals***

The resort has an array of different-ability parks. Novices can start in the Big Easy Terrain Garden on Blackcomb, with its unthreatening rails, rollers and hits. Next up in terms of difficulty is the Chipmunk park on Whistler, which doubled in size last season, and has lots of rails, plus there's a half-pipe at the top of the Emerald chair. The main park on Blackcomb, next to the Catskinner chair, has slightly bigger hits and rails, fun-boxes, hips, spines and banks. True experts can head into the Highest Level park – to be allowed in you need to wear a helmet and buy a special pass. A new super-pipe on Blackcomb is being built for the 2005 Snowboard World Championships.

**SNOW RELIABILITY**
***Excellent at altitude***

Snow conditions at the top are usually excellent – the place gets around 360 inches of snow a year, on average.

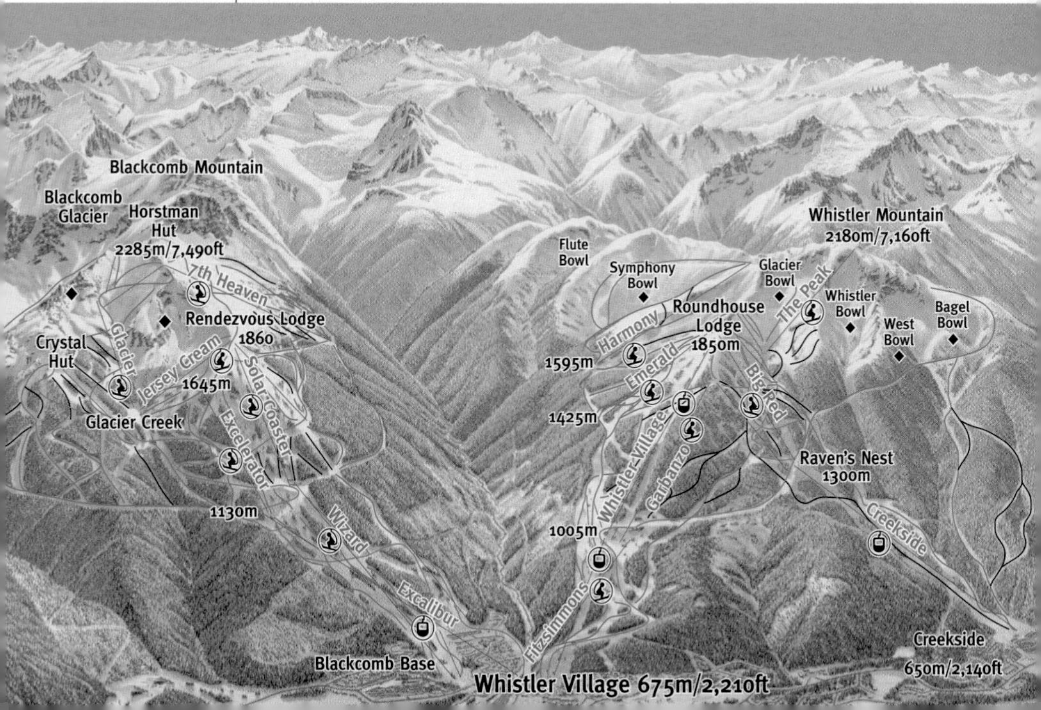

**LIFT PASSES**

**Whistler/Blackcomb**
Covers all lifts on both Whistler and Blackcomb mountains.

**Main pass**
1 day C$76
6 days C$430

**Senior citizens**
Over 65: 6 days C$366

**Children**
Under 19: 6 days C$366
Under 13: 6 days C$225
Under 7: free pass

**Notes**
Prices include 7% sales tax.

But because the resort is low and close to the Pacific, the bottom slopes can be wet, icy or unskiable. People may 'download' from the mid-stations due to poor snow, especially in late season.

### FOR EXPERTS
***Few can rival it***

Whistler Mountain's bowls are enough to keep experts happy for weeks. Each has endless variations, with chutes and gullies of varied steepness and width. The biggest challenges are around Glacier, Whistler and West Bowls, with runs such as The Cirque and Doom & Gloom – though you can literally go anywhere in this high, wide area.

Blackcomb's slopes are not as extensive as Whistler's, but some are more challenging. From the top of the 7th Heaven lift, traverse to Xhiggy's Meadow, for sunny bowl runs.

If you're feeling brave, go in the opposite direction and drop into the extremely steep chutes down towards Glacier Creek, including the infamous 41° Couloir Extreme, which can have moguls the size of elephants at the top. Or try the also serious, but less frequented, steep bowls reached by hiking up Spanky's Ladder, after taking the Glacier Express lift.

Both mountains have challenging trails through trees. This season you'll be able to explore the new 400 acre Peak to Creek area from below Whistler's West Bowl to Creekside. If all this isn't enough, there's also out-of-bounds backcountry guiding (see Schools and guides), and local heli-skiing available by the day.

### FOR INTERMEDIATES
***Ideal and extensive terrain***

Both mountains are an intermediate's paradise. In good weather, good intermediates will enjoy the less extreme variations in the bowls on both mountains.

One of our favourite intermediate runs is down the Blackcomb Glacier, from the top of the mountain to the bottom of the Excelerator chair over 1000m/3,280ft below. This 5km/3 mile run, away from all lifts, starts with a two-minute walk up from the top of the Showcase T-bar. You drop over the ridge into a wide, wide bowl – not too suddenly or you'll get a short, sharp shock in the very steep double-diamond Blowhole. The further you traverse, the shallower the slope.

You are guaranteed good snow on the Horstman Glacier too, and typically

### boarding

*Both mountains are excellent for every level of boarder. All the main lifts are chairs and gondolas and terrain ranges from gentle green runs to wide open bowls and heart-stopping cliff drops and chutes. And snowboarders have one advantage over skiers in Whistler – when the snow gets slushy lower down, it's easier and more fun to ride it on a board! There are T-bars on the glacier, but they're not vicious and any discomfort is worth it for the powder. The resort is popular with snowboarders and known for its summer boarding camps. The school runs a lot of specialist classes, including freestyle lessons and women's camps, and Canada's Olympic gold medallist, Ross Rebagliati, is on the team of coaches – he's available on request. The resort regularly hosts big snowboard events, and the 2005 Snowboard World Championships are taking place in January. Specialist snowboard shops include Showcase and Katmandu Boards.*

Whistler's high ski-anywhere bowls are being expanded this season by opening up 700 acres in the formerly out-of-bounds Flute Bowl ↗

INTRAWEST / PAUL MORRISON

gentle runs. The blue runs served by the 7th Heaven chair are 'heavenly on a sunny day', as a reporter put it. Lower down there are lots of perfect cruising runs through the trees – ideal when the weather is bad.

On Whistler Mountain, there are easy blue pistes in Symphony, Harmony and Glacier bowls. Even early intermediates should try them, since there's always an easy way down. The Saddle run from the top of the Harmony Express lift is a favourite with many of our reporters. The blue Highway 86 path, which skirts West Bowl from the top of the Peak chair, has beautiful views over a steep valley and across to the rather phallic Black Tusk mountain. The green Burnt Stew Trail also has great views.

Lower down the mountain there is a vast choice of groomed blue runs with a series of efficient fast chairs to bring you back up to the top of the gondola. It's a cruiser's paradise – especially the aptly named Ego Bowl. A great long run is the fabulous Dave Murray Downhill all the way from mid-mountain to the finish at Whistler Creek. Although it will be the Olympic men's downhill course and is marked black on the map, it's a wonderful fast and varied cruise when it has been groomed. There is also the new groomed blue in the Peak to Creek area to try this season.

**FOR BEGINNERS**
***OK if the sun shines***

Whistler has excellent nursery slopes by the mid-station of the gondola, as does Blackcomb, down at the base area. Both have facilities higher up too.

The map has a guide to easy runs, and slow zones are marked. On Whistler, after progressing from the nursery slopes, there are some gentle first runs from the top of the gondola. Their downside is other people speeding past. You can return by various chairs or continue to the base area on greens. Check the latter are in good condition first, and maybe avoid them at the end of the day, when they can get very crowded.

On Blackcomb, Green Line runs from the top of the mountain to the bottom. The top part is particularly gentle, with some steeper pitches lower down. As a recent reporter said, 'A tentative beginner in our group found it hard to move around with confidence because of the varying steepness of green runs.'

Another reservation is – you guessed – the weather. Beginners don't get a lot out of heavy snowfalls, and might be put off by rain and unpredictable conditions.

**FOR CROSS-COUNTRY**
***Picturesque but low***

There are over 28km/17 miles of cross-country tracks around Lost Lake, starting by the river, on the path between Whistler and Blackcomb. But it is low altitude here, so conditions can be unreliable. There's a specialist school, Cross-Country Connection (905 0071) offering lessons, tours and rental. Keen cross-country merchants can catch the train to better areas.

**QUEUES**
***An ever-increasing problem***

Whistler is becoming a victim of its own success. Even with 15 fast lifts – more than any other resort in North

America – the mountains are queue-prone, especially at weekends when people pour in from Vancouver. There are noticeboards displaying waiting times at different lifts, and although readers find them useful, most people would prefer shorter queues.

Some reporters have signed up with the ski school just to get lift priority. Others have visited Vancouver at the weekend to avoid the crowds.

The routes out of Whistler Village in the morning can be busy. Creekside is less of a problem. Some of the chairs higher up both mountains produce long queues – especially Harmony (where even the singles line seems to take ages). And we had a report of a 45-minute wait for The Peak chair on an early-January 2003 Sunday. Visiting the resort outside peak season may not help – we found some lifts, including the gondola to Blackcomb, were kept closed in an early-December visit and readers have also reported closed lifts in late season. Crowds on the slopes, especially the runs home, can be annoying too.

### MOUNTAIN RESTAURANTS
***Overcrowded***

The main restaurants sell decent, good-value food but are charmless self-service stops with long queues. They're huge, but not huge enough. 'Seat-seekers' are employed to find spaces, but success is not guaranteed.

Past reporters have stressed the need to lunch early. But even that no longer works – 'They're packed by 11.30,' say recent reporters. Late lunches don't work either, because the lifts close early; so the answer may be a big breakfast, ski through the day and eat later.

Blackcomb has the Rendezvous, mainly a big (850-seat) self-service place but also home to Christine's, a table-service restaurant – the best on either mountain. Glacier Creek Lodge, at the bottom of the Glacier Express, is a better self-service place. But even this (1,496 seats) gets incredibly crowded. Whistler has the massive (1,740-seat) Roundhouse Lodge; Steeps Grill is its table-service refuge.

Reporters generally prefer the smaller places – but they're still packed unless you time it right, and may be closed early and late season. On Blackcomb, Crystal Hut at the top of the Crystal Ridge chair ('nice cosy interior') and Horstman Hut at the top of the mountain are tiny with great views.

On Whistler, Raven's Nest, at the top of the Creekside gondola, is a small and friendly deli/cafe. And the Chic Pea near the top of the Garbanzo chair-lift is 'funky and rustic' for pizza and barbecue. There's also the Harmony Hut, specialising in stews and cider, at the top of the Harmony lift. You can of course descend to the base – the table-service Dusty's at Whistler Creek has good sandwiches and soup and doesn't get too crowded. There's also a Snack-Shack on each mountain, if all you fancy is a quick drink and hot-dog.

### SCHOOLS AND GUIDES
***A great formula***

Ski Esprit and Ride Esprit programmes run for three or four days and combine instruction with showing you around the mountains – with the same instructor daily. Many of our reporters have joined these groups (usually small), and all reports are glowing: 'Big improvement in confidence and skill' is typical. 'Tuition very good, 9 out of 10,' says a reader this year. There are specialist clinics and snowboard classes, too.

Extremely Canadian specialises in guiding and coaching adventurous advanced intermediates upwards in Whistler's steep and deep terrain. A lot

**SCHOOLS**

**Whistler and Blackcomb**
t 932 3434

**Extremely Canadian**
t 938 9656

**Classes**
(Whistler and Blackcomb prices, incl. taxes)
3 days (beginner): C$308

**Private lessons**
Half day (3hr): C$427

**GUIDES**

**Whistler Guides**
t 938 3228

## CHILDREN

**Whistler Kids**
**t** 1 800 766 0449
Ages 3mnth to 3yr; from 8am; non-skiing; C$112 per day (incl. taxes)

**Ski school**
Offers Adventure Camps for ages 3 to 12 and **Ride Tribe** programme for ages 13 to 17 (C$593 (incl. taxes) for 5 days for 3 to 4 year olds)

## GETTING THERE

**Air** Vancouver 115km/71 miles (2hr).

WHISTLER RESORT ASSOCIATION / PAUL MORRISON

It would be great if there was always fresh snow like this at village level; sadly, it rains down here too often for our liking ↓

of its coaches compete in free-ride and skier-cross competitions. We have been with them a few times and they really are great! As a reporter said, 'You end up skiing places that other people don't even know about – we were very impressed.' They run two- and four-day clinics and also have their own catered chalet you can stay at.

Backcountry day trips or overnight touring are available with Whistler Guides.

### FACILITIES FOR CHILDREN

***Impressive***

Blackcomb's base area has a special slow-moving Magic Chair to get children part-way up the mountain. Whistler's gondola mid-station has a splendid kids-only area. A reporter found the staff 'friendly and instilled confidence'.

Kids Adventure Zones feature castles and forts, enchanted forests and animals to keep them entertained. A recent reporter was enthusiastic about 'climb and dine', where children can spend a few fun hours at the climbing centre, including a meal, while parents go out to eat.

## STAYING THERE

### HOW TO GO

***High quality packages***

A lot of British tour operators go to Whistler and some run catered chalets.

**Hotels** There is a very wide range.

(((((5) **Fairmont Chateau Whistler** (938 8000) Well run and luxurious at the foot of Blackcomb. Excellent spa with pools and tubs. The Gold floor is expensive and especially cosseting.

(((((5) **Westin Resort & Spa** (905 5000) Luxury all-suite hotel at the foot of Whistler mountain next to the lifts.

((((4) **Pan Pacific** (905 2999) Luxury, all-suite, at Whistler Village base. Pool/sauna/tub.

((((4) **Lost Lake Lodge** (932 2882) 'Excellent' place: studios and suites, out by the golf course. Pool/tub.

((((4) **Crystal Lodge** (932 2221) Has been renovated. 'Comfortable, friendly, convenient', in Whistler Village. Pool/sauna/tub.

(((3) **Glacier Lodge** (932 2882) In Upper Village. 'Big rooms, quiet area, recommended.' Pool/tub.

**Self-catering** There are plenty of spacious, comfortable condominiums in both chalet and hotel-style blocks.

## ACTIVITIES

**Indoor** Sports arena (ice rink, pool, hot-tubs), museum, art galleries, tennis, spa and health clubs, library, cinemas, climbing wall

**Outdoor** Flightseeing, snow-shoe excursions, snowmobiling, fishing, dog-sledding, sleigh rides

**Phone numbers**
From distant parts of Canada, add the prefix 1 604.
From abroad, add the prefix +1 604.

## TOURIST OFFICE

**t** 932 3434
wbres@intrawest.com
www.mywhistler.com
www.whistler-blackcomb.com

## EATING OUT

### *High quality and plenty of choice*

Reporters are enthusiastic about the range, quality and value of places to eat, but do book well ahead: there simply aren't enough restaurant seats to meet demand. Some cheaper places won't take bookings for small groups, meaning long waits. One 2003 reporter 'gave up trying to find a table at Easter weekend and ate in the hotel bar'. Bars serve decent food, too. But if you've got kids, as one reporter found, 'Some places don't allow under-19s in, or even to sit outside, and we had to wait up to two hours elsewhere.'

At the top of the market, Umberto's in Whistler Village has classy Italian cuisine. The Rimrock Café at Whistler Creek serves 'the best seafood we have ever eaten', says a reporter.

Good mid-market Whistler Village places include Araxi (Italian/Pacific), the Keg ('great value' steak and seafood), Teppan Village (Japanese), Mongolie (Asian) and Kypriaki Norte ('excellent duck'). We've had mixed reports on Crab Shack (seafood). Reporters have also suggested La Bocca (Italian: 'excellent home-made pasta, good value') and the Bearfoot Bistro (European: 'the best gourmet restaurant, with a stellar wine list').

In Village North: the good-value Brewhouse has a lively atmosphere (steaks, burgers), Caramba has 'good Mediterranean food at reasonable prices', and the Tandoori Grill has 'Indian just like at home'. Hy's Steakhouse has the best steaks ('melt in your mouth'). Sushi-Ya and Quattro (Italian) are good. In Upper Village, Thai One On is 'excellent', and Monk's Grill has 'very good steaks'.

There are plenty of budget places, including the bars mentioned under Après-ski. Uli's Flipside at Creekside and The Old Spaghetti Factory in Whistler Village ('very good value') have been recommended for pasta.

## APRES-SKI

### *Something for most tastes*

Whistler is very lively. Most of the après bars seem to compete to see who can serve the biggest dustbin lid of nachos. Popular at Whistler are the Longhorn, with a huge terrace, and the Garibaldi Lift Company. The Dubh Linn Gate Irish pub has 'great live music and Guinness'. Tapley's seems 'the nearest thing to a locals' bar'. Merlin's is the focus at Blackcomb base, though readers also recommend the Monk's Grill, and Dusty's is the place at Creekside – good beer, loud music.

Later on, Buffalo Bill's is lively and loud and the Amsterdam is worth a look. Tommy Africa's, Maxx Fish, the Savage Beagle, Garfinkel's and Moe Joe's are the main clubs. Try the Mallard bar in Chateau Whistler and the Crystal Lodge piano bar for a quieter time.

Bars and clubs are for over-19s only, and readers have found it's advisable to carry age ID. Smoking is generally not allowed in bars, although most have a smoking area outside, sometimes heated. Garfinkel's and the Mallard have inside smoking areas.

## OFF THE SLOPES

### *Not ideal*

Whistler is a long way to go if you don't intend to hit the slopes. Meadow Park Sports Centre has a full range of fitness facilities. There are also several luxurious spas. Reporters have recommended walks around the lake, the Great Wall Underground climbing centre and a shop where you can paint your own pottery. There's an eight-screen cinema in Whistler Village. And Ziptrek Ecotours (935 0001) offers three-hour ecological journeys through the forest between Whistler and Blackcomb mountains, using cables and suspension bridges. Excursions to Squamish (famous for its eagles) are easy, as are day trips to Vancouver.

# Jasper

**Set in the middle of Jasper National Park, Jasper appeals more to those keen on scenery and wildlife (and perhaps cross-country skiing) than piste mileage. It could be combined with a stay in Whistler, Banff or Lake Louise.**

JASPER PARK LODGE

## KEY FACTS

| | |
|---|---|
| **Resort** | 1065m 3,500ft |
| **Slopes** | 1705-2600m 5,590-8.530ft |
| **Lifts** | 8 |
| **Pistes** | 1,500 acres |
| **Green** | 30% |
| **Blue** | 30% |
| **Black** | 40% |
| **Snowmaking** | 10 acres |

## TOURIST OFFICE

**t** 780 852 3816
info@skimarmot.com
www.skimarmot.com

## THE RESORT

Jasper is a low-key, low-rise little town. One of the most beautiful drives in the world is the three-hour trip to or from Lake Louise on the Columbia Icefields Parkway through the Banff and Jasper National Parks – past glaciers, frozen waterfalls and lakes.

Most accommodation is out of town or on the outskirts and the local slopes are a 30-minute drive. The Fairmont Jasper Park Lodge (852 3301) is a set of luxurious log cabins set 4km/2 miles out of town around a lake.

## THE MOUNTAINS

The slopes are very limited in size and are at Marmot Basin, in the heart of the unspoiled National Park. A high-speed quad takes you to mid-mountain, with four slow chairs above that. The highest Knob chair ends way below the 2600m/8,530ft peak that the area includes in its claim of almost 900m/2,950ft vertical. Snowfall is modest by North American standards and cover has been sparse on both our visits. There is lots of steep expert terrain but it can be unskiable if snow conditions are not good. Keen piste-bashers will cover all the groomed runs in half a day and find the area very small. Less adventurous intermediates will be happy to cruise the greens and blues for a day or two. There are excellent nursery slopes and gentle greens to progress to. At mid-mountain the Paradise Chalet has a big self-service cafe and the Eagle Chalet is a cosy table-service place. At the base the rebuilt Caribou Chalet is attractive.

The area has 300km/186 miles of cross-country trails set amid delightful scenery.

# Kimberley

**A fledgling new mountain village sits at the foot of limited slopes a few miles from a bizarre (to European eyes) 'Bavarian' town. By all means include it for a day or two on a trip to several resorts but we wouldn't spend a week here.**

RCR INC

## KEY FACTS

| | |
|---|---|
| **Resort** | 1230m 4,035ft |
| **Slopes** | 1230-1980m 4,040-6,500ft |
| **Lifts** | 10 |
| **Pistes** | 1,800 acres |
| **Green** | 20% |
| **Blue** | 45% |
| **Black** | 35% |

## TOURIST OFFICE

**t** 250 427 4881
info@skikimberley.com
www.skikimberley.com

## THE RESORT

The original base area is not quite at the bottom of the hill, with a range of lodgings, including the 'lovely' NorthStar condos. Below this, a new village is being built, served by a fast quad that is the resort's staple lift. The Trickle Creek Residence Inn (250 427 5175) is comfortable and convenient and the Polaris condos 'superb'. But both bases are very limited and quiet, and bars and restaurants are few. Trickle Creek Golf Resort is transformed into Trickle Creek Winter Adventure Park each winter – facilities include a skating rink, cross-country skiing, snow-shoeing and campfires. The town of Kimberley, about five minutes' drive away, is known for its indescribably naff 'Bavarian theme'. But it is reported to have some good restaurants, including the Old Bauernhaus.

## THE MOUNTAINS

Kimberley's terrain offers a mix of blue and black runs (plus the occasional green) and a vertical of 750m/2,460ft. In addition to the lifts up the front there are two other slow chairs (one is a double discarded from Lake Louise). The runs – all in forest of varying density – are spread over two rather featureless hills. There are only a few short double-diamonds, but grading tends to understate difficulty, and many of the single diamonds are quite challenging. When we last visited, using the chair from the new village meant descending a steep, traffic-polished and congested final slope to get back to the lower level. The resort has a reputation for good powder, although it doesn't get huge amounts by the standards of this region. Further expansion is planned.

RED MOUNTAIN RESORTS INC

## KEY FACTS

| | |
|---|---|
| Resort | 1185m<br>3,890ft |
| Slopes | 1185-2075m<br>3,890-6,800ft |
| Lifts | 5 |
| Pistes | 1,585 acres |
| Green | 10% |
| Blue | 45% |
| Black | 45% |
| Snowmaking | none |

## TOURIST OFFICE

t 250 362 7384
info@ski-red.com
www.ski-red.com

# Red Mountain

**The tiny town of Rossland has produced more members of the Canadian ski team than anywhere else. You'll understand why when you see its local mountain, where the kids learn to ski on double-black diamonds in the trees.**

## THE RESORT

Currently there's a smattering of accommodation at the base of the ski hill, but a new owner has plans for a proper village there. On our 2004 visit we stayed at the Rams Head Inn (250 362 9577) – a homely B&B with hot-tub a couple of minutes' walk from the lifts (the owner will guide guests around the mountain). Gypsey at Red, an excellent new restaurant, is nearby. The sleepy small town of Rossland a couple of miles away has a few hotels and restaurants and the cool Gold Rush bookshop/coffee bar.

## THE MOUNTAINS

Red Mountain attracts a few experts from afar but you'll mainly find locals on the hill. Its 300 inch average snowfall is up there with many Colorado resorts but not in the super league. There are a few green and blue runs to warm up on (don't believe the 45% statistic they put out), but it's the black and double-black stuff that is the real attraction. The tough stuff is marked on the map but not really on the mountain; and it's mostly in trees, with cliffs and gnarly narrow bits, so you need a guide. There are plenty of friendly local snow hosts who are only too pleased to show you around; many of them are retired and phenomenally good skiers, and they ignore the trail map completely. The main mountain is Granite, a conical peak with more-or-less separate faces of blue, black and double-black steepness – all served by a few slow chairs. Next-door Red Mountain itself is half the size and has a double chair. Paradise Lodge is an on-mountain snackery but most people head back to base for lunch.

SILVER STAR RESORT / DON WEIXL PHOTOGRAPHY

## KEY FACTS

| | |
|---|---|
| Resort | 1610m<br>5,280ft |
| Slopes | 1155-1915m<br>3,780-6,280ft |
| Lifts | 11 |
| Pistes | 2,725 acres |
| Green | 20% |
| Blue | 50% |
| Black | 30% |

## TOURIST OFFICE

t 250 542 0224
www.skisilverstar.com

# Silver Star

**This quiet, family-friendly resort has a tiny traffic-free centre resembling a 19th-century mining town. There are slopes to suit everyone and it's easy to combine a stay here with one at Big White, which has the same owners.**

## THE RESORT

Silver Star is a small, recently developed resort built in the style of an 1890s mining town right on the slopes. The centre is a compact car-free area of brightly painted Victorian-style buildings with wooden sidewalks and pseudo gas lights. It's rather Disneyesque but works surprisingly well. Big chalets are dotted in the trees. Putnam Station does good steaks in a room decorated with railway memorabilia and with a model train running around the walls. Après-ski is quiet.

## THE MOUNTAINS

The wooded mountain has two main linked faces. The south face around the village has mainly easy intermediate slopes served by a six-pack, which starts below the main village.

There are a few short black runs on the south side, but the main challenges are on the back, on the north face. Easy trails run along three ridges, with black and double-black trails dropping from them to meet the Powder Gulch fast quad, including some seriously steep double-black-diamond runs and lots of moguls. But you can stick to blue and (one) green alternatives, too. Because of the north-facing aspect of most of the runs here the snow normally keeps in good condition.

We were impressed with the extent of the slopes served by just two main fast chairs. But there are also lots of flat areas, including the link with the back side, which make life difficult for snowboarders.

Cross-country is very popular here; they claim their 55km/34 miles of groomed trails are 'The Best Nordic Skiing in North America'.

STONEHAM / JEAN VAUDREUIL

# Eastern Canada

**NEWS**

For 2003/04 a third terrain-park and three new steep black runs through the trees in the Black Forest were opened in Mont-Sainte-Anne.

Stoneham celebrated its 40th birthday by naming all its runs, which had been previously numbered, and by extending its terrain-park.

For 2004/05 the new owner of Le Massif is planning to replace a double chair with a high-speed quad, create six new runs, widen some existing gladed runs and increase the snowmaking capacity. Last season a new terrain-park was built.

**For us the main attraction of skiing or riding in eastern Canada is the French culture and language that are predominant in the province of Québec. It really feels like a different country from the rest of Canada – as indeed many of its residents want it to become. It is also only a six-hour flight from the UK, compared with 10 for Canada's west. Tremblant is the main destination resort and is one of the cutest purpose-built resorts we've seen (though it is now in danger of being spoiled by expansion). The other main base is Québec city, which dates from the 17th century and is full of atmosphere and Canadian history. Slopes of the main resorts are small both in extent and in vertical drop, and the weather can be perishingly cold in early and mid-winter. But at least this means that the extensive snowmaking systems that all the resorts have can be effective for a long season. Be prepared for variable snow conditions and don't go expecting light, dry powder – if that's what you want, head west.**

There are lots of ski and snowboard areas in Ontario – Canada's most populated province – but most of them are tiny and cater just for locals. For people heading on holiday for a week or more, eastern Canada really means the province of Québec. Québec and its capital, Québec city, are heavily dominated by the French culture and language. Notices, menus, trail maps and so on are usually printed in both French and English. Many ski area workers are bilingual or just French-speaking. And French cuisine abounds.

The weather is very variable, rather like New England's – but it can get even colder. Hence the snow, though pretty much guaranteed by snowmaking, can vary enormously in quality. When we were there one April we were slush skiing in Tremblant one day and rattling along on a rock-hard surface in Mont-Sainte-Anne the next. One reporter who visited Mont-Sainte-Anne, Stoneham and Le Massif in late January experienced mild temperatures and several perfect blue-sky days.

The main destination resort is Tremblant (see separate chapter), about 90 minutes' drive from Montreal. Other areas near here popular with locals include **Mont Blanc** (with only 300m/980ft of vertical, hardly a competitor to the Franco-Italian version) and the **Saint-Sauveur** valley (five areas, each with around 200m/660ft of vertical and with interchangeable lift passes).

The other main place to stay for easy access to several ski resorts is **Québec city**. Old Québec, at the city's heart, is North America's only walled city and is a World Heritage site. Within the city walls are narrow, winding streets and 17th and 18th century houses. It is situated right on the banks of the St Lawrence river. In January/February there is a famous two-week carnival, with an ice castle, snow sculptures, dog-sled and canoe races, night parades and grand balls. But most of the winter is low season for Québec city, with good-value rooms available in big hotels. Because of this, the area is popular with British school

TREMBLANT RESORT

In Eastern Canada it's usual for the trees to go right to the top. This is Tremblant ➔

groups, especially in late season. Non-skiers, or those who like the option to do other activities, won't be bored whatever time of year they go.

There are several ski and snowboard areas close to Québec city, and a Carte Blanche pass which covers the three main areas: a total of 106 runs, 26 lifts and Canada's largest night skiing area. A car is handy, but there are buses to some areas.

The biggest and most varied area (though easily skied in a day by a good skier) is **Mont-Sainte-Anne**, 30 minutes away and with some accommodation of its own. A gondola takes you to the top, and slopes lead down the front (south) and back (north) sides. The views from the front over the ice-flows of the St Lawrence are spectacular. There are intermediate cruising runs on both sides and some steep blacks (including World Cup runs) through the trees on the front among its 63km/39 miles of trails. Last season three new steep expert runs through the trees opened in the Black Forest area. There are some easy top-to-bottom runs and good nursery slopes at the base. In spring you can stop by the Sugar Shack and try fresh maple toffee. The resort has three terrain-parks, including a new one last year, and a 600m/1,970ft boarder-cross course. Fifteen trails are floodlit until 10pm seven nights a week (five in January). Over 80% of the runs are covered by snowmaking, which was increased last season. It also has the largest cross-country centre in Canada, with 223km/139 miles of trails.

**Stoneham** is the closest resort to Québec city, around 20 minutes away and celebrated its 40th birthday last season. It also has its own small village with accommodation and an impressive base lodge with bar, restaurant and big wooden deck. Après-ski in the lodge can be lively, and there is often live music. It is a small area, with only around 30km/19 miles of runs spread between three faces and a vertical of 420m/1,380ft. But it is very sheltered in a sunny setting protected from wind. It suits families well, with mainly intermediate and beginner terrain. It has a special learn to ski area equipped with a moving carpet. Snowboarders, freestylers and freeskiers are attracted to the area by the resort's impressive terrain-park with 15 rails and 10 table-tops, its 1000m/3,280ft boarder-cross course, and a super-pipe. Stoneham also has the biggest night-skiing operation in Canada, with two of the three faces lit top to bottom. Some 85% of the area has snowmaking.

**Le Massif** is around an hour away from Québec city and is a cult area with locals. It is in a UNESCO World Biosphere Reserve, and is just metres from the St Lawrence. The views of the ice-flows are stunning, and you feel you are heading straight down into them when you are on the pretty, tree-lined trails. The area of slopes, though small, has the largest vertical drop in the east. There are a couple of steep double black diamond runs and some good, well-groomed black and blue cruising runs, including a run designed to meet International Ski Federation World Cup standards. They have Québec's longest high-speed quad chair and for 2004/05 another fast chair and six more runs are planned – see News.

**TOURIST OFFICES**

**Mont Blanc**
www.ski-mont-blanc.com

**Saint-Sauveur**
www.montsaintauveur.com

**Québec city**
www.quebecregion.com

**Mont-Ste-Anne**
www.mont-sainte-anne.com

**Stoneham**
www.ski-stoneham.com

**Le Massif**
www.lemassif.com

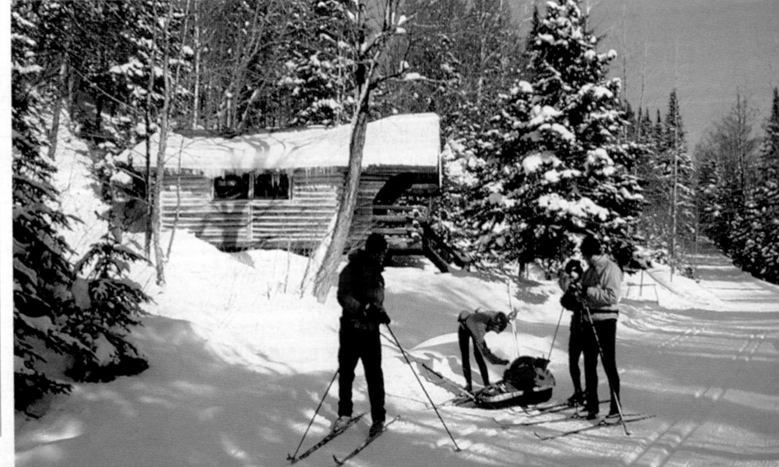

MONT-STE-ANNE / SEBASTIEN LAROSE

Mont-Sainte-Anne has the largest cross-country centre in Canada →

# Tremblant

*Charming, traffic-free village at the foot of a small area of slopes*

**COSTS**

①②③④⑤⑥

**RATINGS**

| The slopes | |
|---|---|
| Snow | **** |
| Extent | * |
| Expert | ** |
| Intermediate | *** |
| Beginner | **** |
| Convenience | **** |
| Queues | *** |
| Mntn restaurants | ** |
| **The rest** | |
| Scenery | *** |
| Resort charm | **** |
| Off-slope | *** |

**KEY FACTS**

| | |
|---|---|
| **Slopes** | 230-875m |
| **Lifts** | 13 |
| **Pistes** | 77km |
| **Green** | 17% |
| **Blue** | 33% |
| **Black** | 50% |
| **Snowmaking** | 76% |

- ➕ Charming purpose-built core village
- ➕ Slope-side accommodation
- ➕ Good snow reliability with extensive artificial back-up
- ➕ Some good runs for all abilities
- ➕ Good variety of restaurants and bars

- ➖ Limited area for keen piste-bashers
- ➖ Can be perishingly cold in midwinter
- ➖ Weekend queues and overcrowding
- ➖ New building on edge not in keeping with cute original style – and huge expansion plans

**Tremblant is eastern Canada's main destination resort and attracts quite a lot of Brits. But for keen piste-bashers the limited slopes don't really do justice to the cute and lively little core village, which has been built in traditional style.**

## THE RESORT

Tremblant has been transformed in recent years from a day or weekend ski area for locals to being eastern Canada's leading ski resort. Intrawest (which also owns Whistler and several other North American resorts) developed a charming purpose-built village in the traditional style of old Québec. Buildings in bright, vibrant colours line narrow, cobbled traffic-free streets and squares, and it has a very French feel to it.

## THE MOUNTAINS

In its small area, Tremblant has a good variety of pleasantly wooded terrain.

**Slopes** A heated gondola takes you to the top, from where there are good views over the village and a 14km/9 mile lake on the so-called South Side, and over National Park wilderness on the North Side. The North Side is really north-east facing and gets the morning sun – a high-speed quad brings you back and there are two other chairs to play on. The slow Edge lift accesses another summit, serving mainly expert terrain. On the South Side (really south-west facing and so good for the pm sun) you can go right back to town on blue or green runs, or use two high-speed quads to explore the top and bottom halves. The Versant Soleil area is more directly south-facing and has one top-to-bottom blue run with all the rest being black runs and tree runs.

**Terrain-parks** The excellent 18-acre Gravité terrain-park plus a super-pipe is located on the top half of the North Side. There's a mini Gravité park here too. The resort built a third park for 2003/04, on the South Side.

**Snow reliability** Canada's east coast doesn't get as much snow as the west, but over 75% of the trails are covered by snowmaking. Grooming is excellent.

**Experts** Half the runs are classified as suitable for advanced skiers and riders. But we found many of the blacks did not deserve their grading. There are steep top-to-bottom bump runs on the North Side and great gladed tree runs off the Edge lift. The Versant Soleil area has more black runs and some tough runs in the trees. However, the gladed runs really need decent, and preferably fresh, snow to be fun.

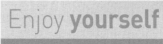

**Central reservations phone number**
Call 425 8681.

**Phone numbers**
From distant parts of Canada, add the prefix 1 819.
From abroad, add the prefix +1 819.

## TOURIST OFFICE

**t** 681 2000
info_tremblant@intrawest.com
www.tremblant.ca

**Intermediates** Both North and South Sides have good cruising and we found the North Side less crowded. There are blue-classified runs in the trees as well as on groomed trails.
**Beginners** The 2-acre beginner area is excellent and there are long, easy top-to-bottom green runs to progress to.
**Snowboarding** The slopes are good for beginners, but better boarders can't count on fresh natural snow to play in. A specialist shop, Adrénaline, runs a Burton learn-to-ride programme.
**Cross-country** There are around 100km/62 miles of trails, some at the top of the mountain, with great views.
**Queues** At weekends there can be queues but they tend to move quickly. We found crowds on the main run back to the village more of a problem.
**Mountain restaurants** The main Grand Manitou restaurant has good views and decent food but can get crowded. Many people go back to town for lunch.
**Schools and guides** Reporters praise the school – 'excellent – a four-year-old was skiing greens after a week'.
**Facilities for children** Children from age 1 to 12 can be cared for until 9.30pm.

## STAYING THERE

**How to go** There's no shortage of packages from the UK.
**Hotels and condos** The luxurious Fairmont Tremblant and the condos in the Place St Bernard, the Tour des Voyagers and the Chouette have been recommended. But the nearest supermarket is a car or bus-ride away.
**Eating out** Try the Forge, Ya'ooo Pizza Bar, Shack, Casey's, Mexicali Rosa's and The Loup Garou at the Fairmont.
**Après-ski** Octobar Rock is popular with Brits, the Forge is good as the slopes close, the Shack brews its own beer. There is often live music and a good atmosphere in the main square. There are floodlit slopes some nights.
**Off the slopes** The Aquaclub La Source pool complex resembles a lake set in a forest, but reporters complain it's pricey. For adults only, the 'excellent' Scandinavian Baths offers sauna, steam, outdoor hot-tubs and waterfalls. You can also go ice-climbing, horse-riding, ice skating, snow-shoeing, snowmobiling, dog-sledding and swimming – and visit Montreal ('highly recommended').

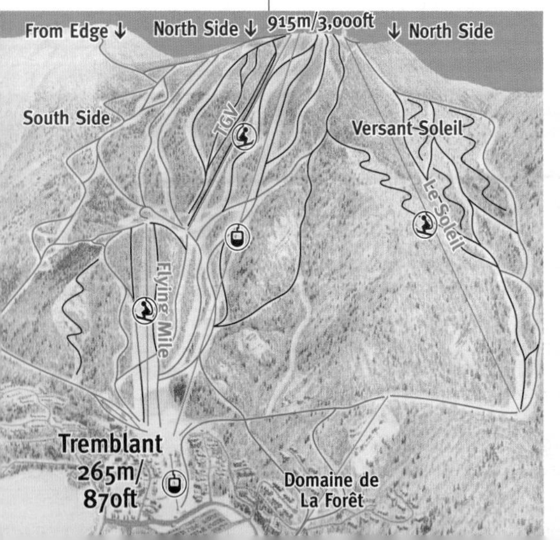


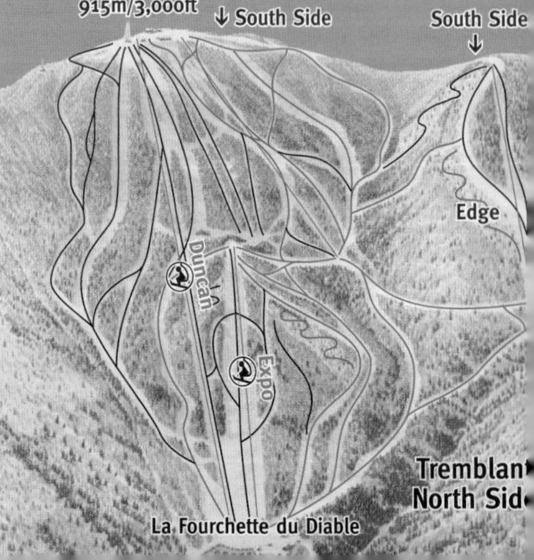

# Spain

## NEWS

At Sierra Nevada a new triple chair from Borreguiles and a new quad on the slow ski area on Loma de Dîlar were installed for 2003/04. There was also a new moving carpet and more snowmaking.

**These days it's dangerous to generalise about Spanish resorts – which is why we don't provide the lists of + and – points that we do for other second-division countries. There are now some well equipped Pyrenean resorts with fine, snow-sure slopes that compare favourably with mid-sized places in the Alps. Two resorts are certainly not downmarket – Sierra Nevada and Baqueira-Beret (see next chapter) are both frequented by the King of Spain. Winter sports are becoming more popular with the prosperous Spanish themselves, and as a result many of the smaller resorts are continually improving.**

The general ambience of Spanish resorts is attractive – not unlike that of Italy, with eating, posing and partying taken seriously and late starts to the ski day the norm.

**Sierra Nevada** (2100m/6,890ft) is in the extreme south of Spain, between Granada (well worth a visit and much quieter than in the summer) and the Costa del Sol, with views from the very top to the Atlas mountains in Morocco.

The hub of the resort is Pradollano, a stylish modern development with shops and a few restaurants and bars set around traffic-free open spaces – likened by one reporter to Whistler. There is a huge but expensive underground car-park here, and parking elsewhere can be difficult.

Most of the accommodation is in older, less smart buildings set along a road winding up the steep hillside. A two-stage chair-lift also goes up the hillside, with red runs back down to the main lift stations at Pradollano. Choose your location with care; the hotel Telecabina is, not surprisingly, ideally placed for the gondolas and is also 'warm, friendly, with good food'.

From Pradollano an old 4-person gondola and a newer 14-person one go up to Borreguiles, at the heart of the slopes. Here there are excellent nursery slopes, and lifts going up to the broad upper slopes beneath the peak of Veleta. There are three identifiable sectors, well linked, with a good range of easy and intermediate runs, some reasonably long. The snow is well groomed, but it is not a big area, and there is not a lot for experts.

Queues can develop at Pradollano when buses arrive from lower towns, and higher up there are quite a lot of slow old lifts that cause queues at ski school time and after lunch. The chair up the village slope gets the biggest queues of all. Most chairs have singles lines, though. The run back to town at the end of the day can get crowded.

Sierra Nevada's weather can be a problem. The resort's natural snow arrives via completely different weather patterns from those supplying the Alps and the Pyrenees; in 1990, when the Alps were disastrously snowless, Sierra Nevada had the best conditions in Europe. But the much-fêted World Championships in the mid-1990s had to be postponed by a year. The slopes face generally north-west, but some get the full force of the afternoon sun. And when the wind blows, as it does, the slopes close; there are no trees.

A reporter this year liked the 'nice restaurants in the village, but not the cafeteria on the mountain'.

There is a group of worthwhile resorts in the western Pyrenees, between Pau and Huesca.

**Formigal** is working hard to improve its standing, but the 57km/35 miles of pistes are windswept. When the wind blows, retreat to nearby Panticosa – a charming old village with 34km/21 miles of sheltered pistes. **Candanchu** and nearby **Astún**, with almost 100km/62 miles of pistes between them, are popular on the Spanish market. They offer a wide range of lodging set in some of the Pyrenees' most stunning scenery. Candanchu has some tough runs.

The other resorts of international interest are just east of Andorra. The 50km/31 miles of runs at **La Molina** and its purpose-built satellite Supermolina (1700m/5,580ft) are now linked to those of Masella, over the mountain, via a gondola and six-pack. The whole area, called Alp 2500, now extends over 100km/62 miles of mainly intermediate skiing.



## REPORTS WANTED

We would welcome more reports on Spanish resorts. If you go there, please do send us a report.

The best reports earn a copy of the next edition, and can lead to free lift passes in future.

See page 10.

## TOURIST OFFICES

**Sierra Nevada**
www.sierranevadaski.com

**Formigal**
www.formigal.com

**Candanchu**
www.candanchu.com

**Astún**
www.astun.com

**La Molina**
www.lamolina.com

BAQUEIRA TOURIST OFFICE

# Baqueira-Beret

*Spain's leading winter resort – fit for their king*

**COSTS**

①②③④⑤⑥

**RATINGS**

| The slopes | |
|---|---|
| Snow | *** |
| Extent | ** |
| Expert | *** |
| Intermediate | **** |
| Beginner | ** |
| Convenience | *** |
| Queues | *** |
| Mountain restaurants | ** |
| **The rest** | |
| Scenery | *** |
| Resort charm | ** |
| Off-slope | * |

**KEY FACTS**

| | |
|---|---|
| **Resort** | 1500m 4,920ft |
| **Slopes** | 1500-2510m 4,920-8,230ft |
| **Lifts** | 30 |
| **Pistes** | 93km 58 miles |
| **Green** | 7% |
| **Blue** | 47% |
| **Red** | 37% |
| **Black** | 9% |
| **Snowmaking** | 35km 22 miles |



- + Compact modern resort
- + Efficient lifts with few queues
- + Reasonable snow reliability
- + Some good off-piste potential
- + Lots of good intermediate slopes
- + Friendly, helpful locals

- − Drab high-rise blocks dominate the main village, though new developments are more attractive
- − Resort is not cleverly laid out, and suffers from traffic around the lift base station
- − Few off-slope diversions

**Baqueira is in a different league from other resorts in the Spanish Pyrenees – a smart, family-oriented resort with a wide area of north-facing slopes that gives a real feeling of travel. It attracts an almost entirely Spanish clientele (which regularly includes the royal family), so don't count on English being spoken.**

## THE RESORT

Baqueira was purpose-built in the 1960s and has its fair share of drab, high-rise blocks; these are clustered below the road that runs through to the high pass of Port de la Bonaigua, while the main lift base is just above it. But up the steep hill from the main base are some newer, smaller-scale stone-clad developments. At the very top is an alternative chair-lift into the slopes. The most convenient base is close to the main chair-lift, but the village is small enough for location not to be too much of an issue. There is a lot of accommodation spread down the valley, and a big car park with road-train shuttle up to the lift base.

BAQUEIRA TOURIST OFFICE

There are open slopes further away from the base ↓

## THE MOUNTAINS

There is an extensive area of long, mainly intermediate, runs, practically all of them on open, treeless slopes and facing roughly west.

**Slopes** The slopes are split into three distinct but well-connected areas – Baqueira, Beret and Bonaigua. From the base station at Baqueira, a fast quad which you ride without skis (which fit in to slots in the back of the chair in front) takes you up to the nursery slopes at 1800m/5,910ft. Fast chairs go on up to Cap de Baqueira. From here there is a wide variety of long runs, served by chairs and drags – including, a long black down to Orri. From several points you can descend into the Bonaigua sector, leading over to the summit of the Bonaigua pass. You can now ride a new chair from the pass to get to new slopes (a red, a blue and an itinerary) descending to the east of the pass and served by a new fast quad. This is the main part of the expansion area (see News).

From the opposite extremity of the Baqueira sector at Orri a triple chair takes you off to the Beret sector, where a series of more-or-less parallel chairs serve mainly blue and red runs. A fast quad and a drag-lift serve a fourth sector across the valley from the Beret slopes, with three blue and a red piste and an itinerary. Beret, Orri and Bonaigua are accessible by road.

**Terrain-parks** There's a terrain park with half-pipe in the Beret area.

**Snow reliability** Most of the slopes are above 1800m/5,910ft and there is extensive snowmaking, but afternoon sun is a problem in spring. Grooming

## NEWS

2003/04 saw the first phase of an expansion of the Bonaigua area, with three new chair-lifts (including two fast quads), three new runs and two itineraries.

For 2004/05 a new high-speed quad is planned, which will access Beret from Baqueira and will be good for beginners.

A new British ski school plans to open with three BASI qualified instructors.

## REPORTS WANTED

**Recently we have had few reports on this resort. If you go there, please do send us a report.**

**Phone numbers**
From abroad use the prefix +34.

## TOURIST OFFICE

**t** 973 639010
baqueira@baqueira.es
www.baqueira.es

is good – too good for one reporter.
**Experts** Experts will find few on-piste challenges, but there's plenty of off-piste, some needing guidance. The Escornacrabes itinerary, from the top of Cap de Baqueira, is steep and narrow. Cheap heli-lifts are available.
**Intermediates** It's excellent, with lots of varied blues and some classic long red runs such as Muntanyo down to Port de la Bonaigua and Mirador above town. Less daring intermediates will enjoy the Beret and Bonaigua areas best.
**Beginners** There are some good nursery runs above Baqueira but some of the blues you move on to can be a bit tough. Beret (reachable by road) has an excellent nursery slope and gentle blues and is due to be served by a new chair from Baqueira for 2004/05.
**Snowboarding** The main nursery slopes are served by drags and some blue runs are a bit tricky for novices.
**Cross-country** There are 7km/4 miles of trails between Orri and Beret.
**Queues** Weekdays are quiet but at weekends some waits can be 10 minutes.
**Mountain restaurants** Most have decent, good-value food and pleasant terraces. You can get table service at Cap del Port, at the Bonaigua pass, at Baqueira 2200 and at Beret.
**Schools and guides** The school gets good reports – some spoken English. This season a new British school is due to open – see News.
**Facilities for children** The kindergarten takes children from three months but lack of spoken English is a problem. Ski school classes start from age four.

## STAYING THERE

**How to go** There is a reasonable choice of hotels and apartments locally. Ski Miquel has a catered chalet.
**Hotels** In the main village three have been recommended – the 4-star Montarto (973 639001) with 'pool and wonderful food' and two 3-stars: the 'very satisfactory' Tuc Blanc (973 644350) with pool and Val de Ruda (973 645258). The 5-star Royal Tanau looks good (973 644446). The Parador (973 640801) down the valley in Arties and the 2-star Husa Vielha (973 640275) further down in Vielha have been recommended.
**Eating out** The more interesting restaurants are down the valley in Salardu, Arties and Vielha. Reporters have enjoyed the local tapas bars.
**Après-ski** There are lots of pubs and discos in the valley. Tiffany's and Pacha are in the main village. They get going very late (ie 1am or 2am).
**Off the slopes** Pool and spa facilities are available in some hotels. Vielha, 15km/9 miles away, has a sports centre.




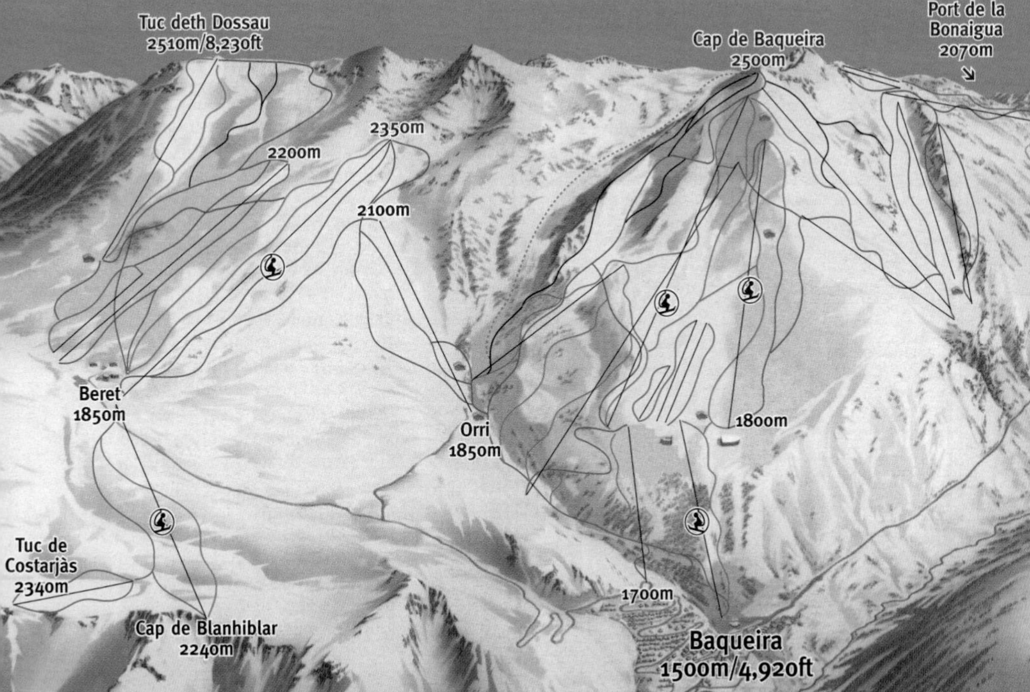

# Bulgaria

**COSTS**

①②③④⑤⑥

**NEWS**

Practically all Bansko's lifts have been installed in the last few years and include a gondola and three high-speed quad chair-lifts.

In Pamporovo, a new triple and a quad chair and three new runs are planned for 2004/05. Work has also begun on a new 4-star hotel in the centre of the resort.

In Borovets, for 2003/04 new snowmaking systems were installed and new grooming machines bought. For 2004/05 two new fast quads are planned to replace a single chair and a drag. A new green run is planned, which should add another 12km/7 miles of pistes. More snowmaking is also planned.



- ➕ Very cheap
- ➕ A different winter holiday, with the chance to experience a fascinating, although depressed, culture
- ➕ Very friendly, welcoming people
- ➕ Good ski schools

- ➖ Poor snow record and not enough snowmaking (Bansko is best)
- ➖ Generally poor piste and lift maintenance
- ➖ Small ski areas
- ➖ Borovets hotels and food poor

**Bulgaria has traditionally attracted beginners and early intermediates on a tight budget: the basic flight-and-hotel-package, equipment rental, school and lift pass are all very cheap. So is alcohol when you get there. Drawbacks include limited slopes (and up till now old lifts) and mountain and hotel food that can have you reaching for the Mars bars. There are compensations, mostly listed above. But now Bansko has sprung from nowhere three years ago to being Bulgaria's leading resort after spending more than £20 million on smart new lifts, snowmaking and even a hands-free lift pass system. It outstrips traditional favourites Borovets and Pamporovo for size and variety of ski area and modern lifts. Now those two are starting the fightback, both announcing new lifts for 2004/05. Even so, keen piste-bashers, gourmets, posers and those wanting creature comforts should look elsewhere or be prepared for a shock.**

## Bansko 935m/3,070ft

### THE RESORT

Bansko, set on a flat valley floor circled by spectacular peaks, looks like a giant goods yard on the outskirts – more of an industrial town than a tourist destination. But at its heart lurks a beautiful old centre, with architecture straight out of Disney's *Beauty And The Beast*. There are few outward signs of commercial tourism except for hotels, which nestle unobtrusively between homes, shops, restaurants and churches. However, while the area around the town square is quiet and charming, a new hub with apartments and hotels is developing near a newly opened gondola.

The cuisine in Bansko is firmly Bulgarian – no burgers and chips here. Instead the mehanas (traditional inns) sell traditional food very cheaply: things like Shopska salad (a salad with goats' cheese), chicken, stews and soup, with Macedonian musicians providing the live entertainment rather than the ubiquitous electric organs of rival resorts.

BALKAN HOLIDAYS

Mountain restaurants and bars at Bansko are a cut above the Bulgarian norm ↓

### THE MOUNTAIN

Before last season, the pistes in the Pirin National Park were accessible only by army jeeps and minibuses up a tortuous 12km/7 mile road. Now a new eight-seater gondola ferries skiers to Bunderishka at 1,635m/5,360ft and 56km/35 miles of pistes.

**Slopes** From Bunderishka two successive fast quad chairs take you up mainly north-facing slopes to the high point of 2560m/8,400ft. From there you can ski down reds or blues to Shiligarnika, or a red followed by a black (called Alberto Tomba after the man who opened the revamped ski area at the start of last season) to Bunderishka. 'Ski roads' (easy tracks cut through the woods) link the main lift bases and a new chair-lift planned for the 2004/05 season will link Bunderishka and Shiligarnika, making

↑ New hotels such as the Strazhite have been built in an attractive style near the gondola base
BALKAN HOLIDAYS

getting around easier if the top lifts are shut because of high winds. There are a few slopes near the mid-station of the gondola and another area with one red run that was closed during last season for improvements. There are still some old drag-lifts, which can break down. There are good views of the UNESCO-protected national park.
**Terrain-parks** There's a half-pipe.
**Snow reliability** They claim that 80% of the pistes are covered by snowmaking. Together with good grooming (by Bulgarian standards) and north-facing slopes, this means more reliable snow than the Bulgarian norm. But the ski run to the bottom of the gondola has no snowmaking and can get icy, according to a local.
**Experts** There is little in the way of challenging pistes.
**Intermediates** Medium-to-difficult reds come straight down the face from the top of the mountain and varied blues go round to skiers' right.
**Beginners** The nursery slopes near the top of the gondola are good, with little through-traffic. There are blue runs served by drag-lifts at the top of the mountain and the long ski road back from top to bottom of the gondola is gentle and easy if the snow is good.
**Queues** Bansko is the least busy and has the best lifts of the Bulgarian resorts, so queues are not bad.
**Mountain restaurants** A fair sprinkling, including some modern ones with outdoor bars, mostly serving a peppery form of gluwein, chips and grills. The best are in the Shiligarnika area.
**Schools and guides** 'Not many English-speaking classes, and quite chaotically organised at first,' says a reporter. 'Instructors tend to err on the side of caution and take the easiest routes. Classes go on most of the day and instructors often dine with students.'
**Facilities for children** Classes include parents and children.

**STAYING THERE**
There are a growing number of new hotels, mostly around the gondola. 'The best hotel is the Pirin, near the town square,' says a reporter. 'This has recently undergone a facelift and the pool, steam room, sauna and hot-tub are good, as is the bar area. Sadly the food in the restaurant is average. Eating out is recommended.' The Strazhite, near the gondola, has similar leisure facilities, plus bowling alleys and a games room. Another popular hotel is the Bansko, though it lacks the charm of the Pirin. Most hotels offer a shuttle-bus service to the gondola.
**Eating out** There are scores of authentic mehanas with roaring fires, attentive waiters and real Bulgarian food. The best restaurant is the Chardaka Lialeu near the main square.
**Après-ski** Generally sedate with drinks back at the hotel bars. The main nightclub is Amnesia.
**Off the slopes** Excursions to the Rila monastery and trips across the border into Greece are possible.

## Pamporovo 1650m/5,410ft

**THE RESORT**
Despite the bus-ride to the lifts, visitors praise Pamporovo. The purpose-built village has 'everything to hand'.

**THE MOUNTAIN**
Pamporovo is Bulgaria's best bet for beginners and early intermediates, with mostly easy runs. Others are likely to find 17.5km/11 miles of mainly short runs too limited, despite the three new runs planned for this season.
**Slopes** The slopes are pretty and sheltered, with pistes starting at a high point of 1925m/6,320ft and cutting through pine forest.
**Terrain-parks** There are none.
**Snow reliability** Late-season snow-cover is unreliable.

**TOURIST OFFICES**

www.bulgaria.com
www.bulgariaski.com
**Bansko**
www.banskoski.com

**REPORTS WANTED**

We would welcome more reports on Bulgarian resorts. If you go there, please do send us a report.
The best reports earn a copy of the next edition, and can lead to free lift passes in future.
See page 10.

**Experts** Experts will find little to challenge them in this limited ski area.
**Intermediates** The slopes are too limited for most intermediates.
**Beginners** Book a 'learn to ski' package through your tour operator, saving up to 80% on local prices.
**Snowboarding** The Snow Shack is best for snowboard rental and lessons.
**Mountain restaurants** The best bets are the Lodge and the Spider restaurant.
**Schools and guides** The ski schools are repeatedly praised by reporters – instructors are patient, enthusiastic and speak good English, and class sizes are usually quite small.
**Facilities for children** The English-speaking nursery is well regarded.

### STAYING THERE

**Hotels** The main hotels are in the centre of the handy, purpose-built village. Hotel Pamporovo offers the best accommodation in the resort. It's close to the village centre, and facilities include an indoor swimming pool, a hot-tub and a gym. More basic are the Perelik (also with a pool) and Murgavets – both in the centre.
**Eating out** The food can be poor. You are best off sticking to local Bulgarian stew dishes, which can be delicious. Breakfast buffets offer a fair choice.
**Après-ski** The nightlife is fairly lively, although limited to a handful of bars and discos – BJ's, White Hart, Dak's and the Havana club are popular.
**Off the slopes** The organised evening events are recommended by reporters.

## Borovets 1307m/4,290ft

### THE RESORT

Borovets is a collection of large, modern hotels, with bars, restaurants and shops housed within them. There is a ramshackle selection of quirkier bars, shops and eating places. The beautiful wooded setting provides a degree of Alpine-style charm, and hides some of the worst architecture.

### THE MOUNTAIN

The 40km/25 miles of piste (due to go up to 52km/32 miles with the new run for 2004/05) are spread over three sectors – two loosely linked.
**Slopes** The two largest sectors have fairly steep and awkward slopes. The gondola rises over 1000m/3,280ft to service both the small, high, easy slopes of Markoudjika (up to 2500m/8,200ft), and the mainly long, steepish Yastrebets pistes. A little drag-lift and path connect the two and the new green run will go all the way back to town. The third sector – Baraki – is accessed by several lifts. Runs are short, with just 550m/1,800ft of vertical drop.
**Terrain-parks** We're told 'there is a special snowboard track for all abilities'.
**Snow reliability** Reliable cover is by no means guaranteed.
**Experts** There's little of real challenge.
**Intermediates** The runs are best suited to good intermediates. Less confident skiers may find the mainly tough red runs a bit intimidating.
**Beginners** The slopes are not ideal for novices; nursery slopes are inadequate and after the Markoudjika blue runs progressing means going on to reds.
**Queues** These can be bad – especially for the gondola (down as well as up). Grooming is erratic and signing poor.
**Mountain restaurants** Mostly basic little snack bars with limited seating, serving large portions of very simple fare.
**Schools and guides** Repeatedly praised by virtually all reporters.
**Facilities for children** Reports of the ski kindergarten have been complimentary. The non-ski nursery is in the Rila hotel.

### STAYING THERE

**Hotels** Most reporters stayed at the Rila or the Samokov – both huge and impersonal. Typical verdicts on the Rila's food: 'horrid' and 'absolutely terrible'. Late-night noise from the street can be a problem.
**Eating out** Reporters recommend Katy's Bar for steaks.
**Après-ski** The nightlife caters well to an 18-30 type crowd. Tour operator reps organise pub crawls, folklore evenings and dinner in a local village. The Black Tiger pub (with karaoke), the Buzz Bar and the Titanic are lively.
**Off the slopes** Excursions to the Rila monastery by coach and to Sofia by coach or helicopter are interesting.

## Vitosha 1800m/5,900ft

This is no more than a few widely scattered hotels with very limited, bland runs and a top height of 2290m/7,510ft. The hotels are fairly dour, and most are a bus-ride from the lifts. The resort is just over 20km/12 miles from Sofia, allowing short transfers and easy excursions, but the slopes get overrun at weekends. The slopes are north-facing and have a decent snow record.

**Phone numbers**
From abroad use the prefix +359.

**TOURIST OFFICES**

www.bulgaria.com
www.bulgariaski.com
**Pamporovo**
www.bulgariaski.com
**Borovets**
www.borovets-bg.com
**Vitosha**
www.bulgariaski.com

# Romania

**COSTS**

①②③④⑤⑥

- ➕ Extremely cheap
- ➕ Interesting excursions and friendly local people
- ➕ Good standard of affordable lessons

- ➖ Primitive facilities
- ➖ Uninspiring food
- ➖ Limited slopes with few real challenges

**Like Bulgaria, Romania sells mainly on price. On-the-spot prices, in particular, are very, very low. Provided you have correspondingly low expectations – and provided you go to Poiana Brasov and not Sinaia – you'll probably come back content. If you have any interest in good living, and particularly good lunching, stay away. It's a place for beginners and near-beginners. Reporters have commented on the friendliness of the people, and most recommend exploring beyond the confines of the resorts. Bucharest is 'not to be missed'.**

**It's some years since we visited the country. The abiding impression we brought back then was one of resources stretched to their limits. To judge by the few reports we have since received, post-revolutionary Romania has, sadly, not made much progress.**

**REPORTS WANTED**

We would welcome more reports on Romanian resorts. If you go there, please do send us a report.

The best reports earn a copy of the next edition, and can lead to free lift passes in future.

See page 10.

Romania's two main resorts are in the Carpathian mountains, about 120km/75 miles north-west of the capital and arrival airport, Bucharest. They are very different places, but have one or two things in common apart from low prices: patient instruction, with excellent spoken English, and small classes; and very basic mountain restaurants, with primitive toilets.

The main resort is **Poiana Brasov** (1030m/3,380ft), near the city of Brasov. It is purpose-built, but not designed for convenience: the hotels are scattered about a pretty, wooded plateau, served by regular buses and cheap taxis. The place has the air of a spacious holiday camp.

The main slopes (approximately 12km/7 miles of pistes in total) consist of decent intermediate tree-lined runs of about 750m/2,460ft vertical, roughly following the line of the main cable-car and gondola, plus an open nursery area at the top. There are also some nursery lifts at village level. A black run takes a less direct route down the mountain, which means that on average it is less steep than the red run under the lifts; it has one steepish pitch towards the end. There's a terrain-park and half-pipe. Night-skiing is also now available. The resort gets weekend crowds from Brasov and Bucharest, and queues result.

**Phone numbers**
From abroad use the prefix +40 and omit the initial '0' of the phone number.



The Bradul (0268 262252) and recently refurbished Sport (0268 262252) hotels are handy for the lower nursery slopes and for one of the cable-cars. The Tirol (0268 262460) and the Alpin (0268 262343) get good reports. The Ciucas (0268 262181) is a 'good, basic' place with satellite TV. Après-ski revolves around the hotel bars and discos and can be quite lively at times. The nightclub puts on cheap cabarets. Off-slope facilities are limited; there is a good-sized pool, and bowling. A trip to the Carpathian Stag in Brasov for an evening of tasting in the wine cellars, dinner and a folklore show has been recommended. An excursion to nearby Bran Castle (Count Dracula's home) is also popular.

You may be offered holidays in **Sinaia** – a small town on the busy road from Bucharest to Brasov. When we visited it some years ago the town seemed to us a rather depressing place, and reporters since have been shocked and saddened by the evident poverty. But there are now chalets and a 4-star Holiday Inn.

## COSTS

- Good value for money
- Beautiful scenery
- Good beginners' slopes and lessons

- Limited, easy slopes on the whole
- Mainly antiquated lifts
- Uninspiring food, but improving

**Slovenia offers good value for money 'on the sunny side of the Alps'. The main resorts are popular with economy-minded British and Dutch visitors and with visitors from neighbouring Italy and Austria, giving quite a cosmopolitan feel.**

## REPORTS WANTED

We would welcome more reports on Slovenian resorts. If you go there, please do send us a report.

The best reports earn a copy of the next edition, and can lead to free lift passes in future.

See page 10.



Slovenia is a small country bordering Italy to the west and Austria to the north. It was the first state to break away from former Yugoslavia and managed to escape the turmoil that engulfed the Balkans. The economy is improving steadily, and there is a positive feel to the resorts – along with a warm and hospitable welcome.

The main resorts are within two and a half hours' bus-ride of the capital, Ljubljana. The ski areas are generally small, with fairly antiquated lifts but few queues. The mountain restaurants are mainly unappealing, while the ski schools are of a high standard and cheap, with reputedly good English. Hotel star ratings tend to be a trifle generous, but standards of service and hygiene are high. Snow reliability is not particularly good, but some resorts have snowmaking.

**Kranjska Gora** (810m/2,660ft), not far from the Austrian and the Italian borders, is the best-known resort. The pretty village is dominated by the majestic Julian Alps. The Lek, Kompas and Larix hotels – with pools – are the best placed for slope-side convenience. A 2004 reporter enjoyed varied food and 'amazing breakfasts' at the Larix.

There are 30km/20 miles of mainly intermediate slopes, rising up to 1570m/5,150ft. The only challenging slopes are a couple of short runs in the Podkoren area and the World Cup slalom run. For those wanting a change of slopes, trips to Arnoldstein in Austria are available. Snow reliability is not good, despite snowmaking and a northerly exposure. The lift system is rather antiquated (17 of the 22 lifts are T-bars), but at least queues are rare, except at New Year and on local holidays. Mountain restaurants are poor and most people choose to lunch in the village. There are 40km/25 miles of cross-country trails. Although it is family orientated, there is a good selection of bars and discos for Austrian-style après-ski.

**Vogel** (1535m/5,040ft), in the beautiful **Bohinj** basin, has the best slopes and conditions in the area. The 18km/11 miles of slopes are reached by a cable-car up from the valley. There's a collection of small hotels and restaurants at the base. Pistes of varying difficulty run from the high point at 1800m/5,910ft back into a central bowl with a small beginner area. When conditions permit, there is a long run to the bottom cable-car station. For a change of scene, **Kobla**, with 23km/14 miles of wooded runs, is a short bus-ride away.

**Bled**, with its beautiful lake and fairly lively nightlife, is an attractive base. Its local slopes are very limited, but free buses run to Vogel (about 20km/12 miles) and Kobla (a bit nearer).

**Kanin** (980m/3,210ft), offers 15km/9 miles of pistes between 1600m and 2300m (5,250ft and 7,550ft).

Slovenia's second city, **Maribor** (265m/870ft), in the north-east, is 6km/4 miles from its local slopes – the biggest ski area in the country, with 64km/40 miles of runs, 28km/17 miles of cross-country and 21 lifts. There are several atmospheric old inns serving good, Hungarian-influenced food.

## TOURIST OFFICES

www.slovenia-tourism.si

**Kranjska Gora**
www.kranjska-gora.si

**Vogel (Bohinj)**
www.bohinj.si/vogel

**Kobla (Bohinj)**
www.bohinj.si/kobla

**Bled**
www.bled.si

**Kanin (Bovec)**
www.bovec.si

**Maribor**
www.maribor.si

## COSTS

## NEWS

For 2004/05 in Levi the Himmeriikki lift is being moved to the southern side of the mountain and will be called the Sun lift. Three new pistes – a red and two blues – are being created for it and will suit families.

More snowmaking and night skiing is planned, bringing the total pistes for each to 15.

In Ruka, for 2003/04, a super-pipe was built to FIS regulations.

A new conference centre and apartment hotel, the Rukariutta, complete with grocery store, were built.

In Ylläs, in 2003/04, the slopes were enlarged with the addition of two new lifts. And more snowmaking was added.

## REPORTS WANTED

We would welcome more reports on Finnish resorts. If you go there, please do send us a report.

The best reports earn a copy of the next edition, and can lead to free lift passes in future.

See page 10.

- + Peace, quiet and Lapp charm
- + Ideal terrain for cross-country and gentle downhilling
- + Reliable late snow
- + Jolly outings

- − Cold
- − Small ski areas
- − Quite expensive
- − Uninspiring food

**For skiers with no appetite for the hustle and hassle of Alpine resorts in high season – perhaps especially for families – escape to the white silence of Lapland may be an attractive alternative. Finland has the lion's share of Lapland and has successfully marketed it, not only for day-trip visits to Santa in his home environment but also for ski holidays. With limited downhill slopes but limitless cross-country the resorts compete with the established resorts in Norway, the most important difference being that Finnish resorts lie far to the north. Of half a dozen 'main' resorts only Ruka is south of the Arctic Circle (by 80km/50 miles).**

The weather, snow and timing of the season are accordingly different, and ski holidays in Finland have an extra ingredient of folklorish charm, plus a good chance of seeing the Northern Lights (three times in the January week when one reporter visited). The main resorts are **Levi** and **Ylläs**, respectively 17km/10 miles north and 50km/31 miles west of Kittilä, which has direct charter flights from Britain.

Ylläs mountain has two gateways, of which the major one is Äkäslompolo – a traditional lakeside Lapp settlement, two miles from the lifts. It has a more relaxing atmosphere and longer runs than Levi, whose great appeal is convenience: it is a purpose-built village of hotels and cabins at the foot of the slopes, with more nightlife and commercial development.

The Arctic landscape of flat and gently rolling forest punctuated by many lakes and the occasional treeless hill is a paradise for cross-country skiing. Weather permitting, it also offers good beginner and intermediate downhilling, albeit on a small scale. In fine weather it is a land of great beauty, but don't expect drama.

The resorts usually open a few runs in late November. For two months in midwinter, the sun does not rise; at least, not at ground level – even at Christmas (a quiet time) the sun may be visible from the slopes for a period of pale daylight between 10am and 2pm. Most of the ski areas have floodlit runs. The mountains do not open fully until mid-February, when a normal skiing day is possible and Finnish schools have holidays that usually coincide with ours – a busy time. Finland comes into its own at the end of the season, with friendlier temperatures and long daylight hours. Understandably, Easter is extremely popular, and the slopes are crowded.

Conditions are usually hard-packed powder or fresh snow from the start of the season to the end (early May).

The temperature can be extremely variable, yo-yoing between zero and minus 30°C several times in a week. The fine days are the coldest, but usually the best for skiing: it may be 10 to 15 degrees warmer on the slopes than at valley level. 'Mild' days of cloud and wind are much worse on the hill. Face masks are widely sold.

None of the ski areas has significant vertical by alpine standards. Ylläs is the largest in Finland with 463m/1,520ft vertical and, having lifts and pistes on two broad flanks of the mountain, gives plenty of scope for skiers just off the nursery slopes. Second- and third-week skiers will rapidly conquer the benign black runs. Levi hosted a women's World Cup event in 2004 and the 'Levi Black', which was created for it, is challenging.

The staple Finnish lift is the T-bar. Ruka has some chairs, and Levi has Finland's only gondola, which must be a godsend in bitter weather. Pistes are wide, uncomplicated and well maintained, with good nursery slopes. The Finns are great boarders and consider their terrain-parks far superior to those in the Alps. Levi has a terrain park with super-pipe and half-pipe and Ruka built a super-pipe last season.

The runs are so short that there is no great need for mountain restaurants – on a Finnish piste you are never far from the base lodge, with its shops and self-service restaurant. The ski areas also have shelters or 'kotas' – log-built teepees with an open fire and a smoke hole in the roof – where you can eat a snack or grill some food. Ylläs has a welcoming, snow-encrusted, round restaurant – the highest in the country, at 718m/2,360ft – on the flat top of the mountain, with an open fire, reindeer skins on the benches, and alcohol.

Ski school is good, with English widely spoken. All ski areas have indoor playrooms for small children, but they may be closed at weekends.

Cross-country skiing makes sense of a resort such as Äkäslompolo, transforming it from awkward sprawl to doorstep ski resort of limitless scope. People ski alongside the main road, from their cabins to the hotel or supermarket (pulling children on sledges); up to the base of the lifts where trails fan out around the mountain; across the frozen lake and away through the endless forest. Levi has 230km/143 miles of trails, many floodlit, which are 'well signposted' says a reporter this year.

Excursions are common – husky-sledding, snowmobile safaris, a reindeer sleigh ride and tea with the Lapp drivers in their tent. 'The whole experience is wonderful,' says a typically enthusiastic participant. A reporter thought the trip to the Ice Hotel in Sweden 'truly memorable,' and worth the four-hour trip each way.

Hotels are self-contained resorts, large and practical rather than stylish, typically with a shop, a cafe, a bar with dance floor, and a pool/sauna with outdoor cooling-off area. Hotel supper is served no later than seven, typically, sometimes followed by a children's disco or dancing to a live band.

Finns usually prefer to stay in cabins, and tour operators offer the compromise of staying in a cabin but taking half-board at a nearby hotel. Cabins vary, but are mostly spacious and well equipped, with a sauna and heated drying cupboard as standard. The Hillankukka log cabins at Äkäslompolo are exceptionally good, but the 10-minute walk to and from meals at the Äkäs hotel (016 553000) is not to be underestimated. A reporter praises the hotel itself – 'beautiful hotel, excellent hydrotherapy pool'. Levi's biggest hotel, Levitunturi (016 646301), is rated 'great' by a reporter this year, with 'excellent' facilities including a big pool, tennis, children's activity centre and a golf simulator.

Restaurants in Levi recommended by reporters are the Steak House, Myllyn Aija ('good value'), Arran and (for a treat) the White Reindeer. Recommended bars are the Panimo (a microbrewery), Crazy Reindeer (karaoke), Arran ('more sophisticated').

The southernmost of Finland's resorts, **Ruka** lies 80km/50 miles south of the Arctic Circle, 27km/17 miles from Kuusamo airport and only 25km/15 miles from the Russian border, in a region known for abundant and enduring snow. Finns think nothing of driving the 800km/500 miles from Helsinki, despite the proximity of Kuusamo airport. The ski area, a mixture of open and forest terrain, has 18 lifts (including four chairs), and 28 runs (22 floodlit, 24 with snowmaking, a mogul run and several black runs, none of them steep), and the vertical range is 200m/660ft. The Freestyle World Championships will be held here in March 2005 and a super-pipe was built in 2003/04. The cross-country scope is vast: they advertise 500km/310 miles of trails, of which 40km/25 miles are floodlit.

The atmosphere at the resort and on the slopes is upbeat – with live music in the Wunderbar and sun terraces outside the Piste, very popular in spring. Hotels include the Rukahovi (08 85910), only 50m/160ft from the slopes, and the Royal Ruka (08 868 6000), the resort's flagship property; both of these are popular conference venues. The best accommodation is in cabins. Good restaurants include Riipinen Riistaravintola, which has bear, boar and capercaillie on the menu, Vanha Karhu, and Kalakeidas, an intimate little fish restaurant.

**Pyhä**, 150km/93 miles north-east of Rovaniemi, has seven lifts (including two chairs) and 10 runs on a mountain, much of which is a National Park. The vertical is only 280m/920ft and there is no steep terrain, but it has good off-piste. The best powder runs are on both sides of a long T-bar on the north slope. The Hotel Pyhätunturi (016 856111) is at mid-mountain.

**Phone numbers**
From abroad use the prefix +358 and omit the initial '0' of the phone number.

**TOURIST OFFICES**

**Levi**
www.levi.fi

**Ylläs**
www.yllas.fi

**Ruka**
www.ruka.fi

**Pyhä**
www.pyha.fi

# Norway

COSTS

①②③④⑤⑥

- ➕ Probably the best terrain and facilities in Europe for serious cross-country skiing
- ➕ The home of telemark – plenty of opportunities to learn and practise
- ➕ Complete freedom from the glitziness and ill-mannered lift queues of the Alps
- ➕ Quiet atmosphere that suits families and older people
- ➕ Impressive snowboard parks
- ➕ Usually reliable snow conditions throughout a long season

- ➖ Very limited downhill areas – small, and mostly with few challenges
- ➖ Mountain restaurants that are little more than pit stops
- ➖ Prohibitively high prices (because of high taxes) for alcoholic drinks
- ➖ Unremarkable scenery
- ➖ Après-ski that is either deadly dull or irritatingly rowdy
- ➖ Short daylight hours in midwinter
- ➖ Highly changeable weather
- ➖ Limited off-slope activities

**Norway and its resorts are very different from the Alps, or indeed the Rockies. Some people find the place very much to their taste. For downhillers who dislike the usual ski-resort trappings, and prefer a simpler approach to winter holidays, it could be just the place. For families with young children, in particular, the drawbacks are less pronounced than for others; you'll have no trouble finding junk food for the kids to eat – the mountain restaurants serve little else.**

**Speaking for ourselves, any one of the first three ➖ points we've listed above would probably be enough to put us off. Combine these in a single destination – then add in the other non-trivial negative points – and you can count us out.**



From the 1960s to the 1980s, Norway's popularity with British skiers declined steadily, until the country was attracting only 1,500 or so – about one-tenth of the peak number. So in 1988 the tourist agencies launched an initiative to reverse the trend. Aided by the Alpine snow shortages at the turn of the decade and the award of the 1994 Olympic Winter Games to Lillehammer, the campaign has been a success – bookings from the UK have grown appreciably, with a sizeable number doing cross-country skiing.

There is a traditional friendship between Norway and Britain, and we think of Norwegians as welcoming people, well disposed towards British visitors. We have to say that our visits have repeatedly left us underwhelmed by the warmth of welcome. But at least English is widely spoken – universally spoken, in our experience.

For the Norwegians and Swedes, skiing is a weekend rather than a special holiday activity, and not an occasion for extravagance. So at lunchtime they tend to haul sandwiches out of their backpacks, and in the evening they cook in their apartments. Don't expect a tempting choice of restaurants – 'extremely basic' was the verdict from a reporter recently visiting Lillehammer.

The Norwegians have a problem with alcohol. Walk into an après-ski bar at 5pm on a Saturday and you may find young men already inebriated – and by that we mean not merry but incoherent. And this is despite – or, some say, because of – prohibitively high taxes on booze. Restaurant prices for wine are ludicrous, and shop prices may be irrelevant – Hemsedal has no state-controlled liquor store. Our one attempt at self-catering (well, OK, our one takeaway meal) was an unusually sober affair as a result. Crystal, cutely, offers free wine with dinner in some of its hotels. Other prices are generally not high by Alpine standards.

Cross-country skiing comes as naturally to Norwegians as walking; and even if you're not that keen, the fact that cross-country is normal, and not a wimp's alternative to 'real' skiing, gives Norway a special appeal. Here, cross-country is both a way of

REPORTS WANTED

We would welcome more reports on Norwegian resorts. If you go there, please do send us a report.

The best reports earn a copy of the next edition, and can lead to free lift passes in future.

See page 10.

getting about the valleys and a way of exploring the hills. Although you can plod around short valley circuits as you might in an Alpine resort, what distinguishes Norway for the keen cross-country skier is the network of long trails across the gentle uplands, with refuges along the way where backpackers can pause for refreshment or stay overnight. This network of mountain huts offers basic but cheap accommodation which can turn touring into a week-long adventure away from the crowds. Several tour operators now offer ski-touring packages, or they can be arranged on the spot.

More and more Norwegians are taking to telemarking (a bit like cross-country, with a free-heel binding, but with broader skis) for both downhill and backcountry skiing trips.

Snowboarding is very popular – local youths fill the impressive terrain-parks at weekends.

For downhill skiing, the country isn't nearly so attractive. Despite the fact that it is able to hold downhill races, and despite the successes of its Alpine racers during the 1990s, Norway's Alpine areas are of limited appeal. The most rewarding resort is Hemsedal, which we cover in the next chapter.

The site of the 1994 Olympics, the little lakeside town of **Lillehammer** (200m/660ft), is not actually a downhill resort at all. There is plenty of cross-country terrain around, but the nearest downhill runs are 15km/9 miles north at Hafjell (230m/750ft). This is a worthwhile little area, 'good for beginners', with a vertical of 830m/2,720ft, 12 lifts, and pistes totalling 33km/20 miles. The Olympic slalom events were held here; but the downhill and super-G races went to Kvitfjell, about 35km/22 miles further north, developed specially for the purpose. It's steeper but a bit smaller – 19km/12 miles of pistes.

Norway's other internationally known resort is **Geilo** (800m/2,620ft). This is a small, quiet, unspoiled community on the railway line that links Bergen, on the coast, to Oslo. It provides all the basics of a resort – a handful of cafes and shops clustered around the railway station, a dozen or so hotels more widely spread around the wide valley, children's facilities and a sports centre.

Geilo is a superb cross-country resort. As the Bergen-Oslo railway runs through the town it is possible to go for long tours and return by train.

Geilo is very limited for downhillers, but it does lay claim to having Scandinavia's only super-pipe. The 32km/20miles of piste are spread over two small hills – one, Vestlia, a bus-ride away from Geilo, with a good, informal hotel and restaurant at its foot. For 2004/05 this area will be extended by a six-pack link to a new family beginners' area, Kikutheisene. None of the runs is really difficult.

Clearly the best hotel, and one of the attractions of staying in Geilo, is the Dr Holms Hotel (call central reservations on 320 95940) – smartly white-painted outside, beautifully furnished and spacious inside. This is the centre for après-ski, but prices are steep. All the other hotels we have seen can be recommended. The resort is quiet at the end of the day, but the main hotels provide live entertainment.

A long way north of the other resorts is **Oppdal** (550m/1,800ft), with more downhill runs than any of its rivals (55km/34 miles). The total vertical is 790m/2,590ft, but this is misleading – most runs are short.

There are slightly more extensive slopes at **Trysil** (460m/1,510ft), off to the east, on the border with Sweden, and the runs are longer (up to 4km/2 miles and 685m/2,250ft vertical). The runs here are all around the conical Trysilfjellet, some way from Trysil itself – though there is some accommodation at the hill.

In complete contrast to all of these resorts is **Voss** (50m/160ft), a sizeable lakeside town quite close to the sea which 'pleasantly surprised' our 2004 reporter. A cable-car links the town to the slopes on Hangur and Slettafjell, with a total of 40km/25 miles of pistes – 'excellent' for intermediates, 'good' for beginners and 'no queues'. There are plenty of excursion possibilities, in particular the spectacular Flåm railway.



**Phone numbers**
From abroad use the prefix +47.

**TOURIST OFFICES**

**Lillehammer**
www.lillehammerturist.no

**Geilo**
www.geilo.no

**Oppdal**
www.oppdal.com

**Trysil**
www.trysil.com

**Voss**
www.skiinfo.no/voss/

SNOWPIX.C

*The place for Alpine skiing in Norway – though we prefer the Alps*

## COSTS

(1)(2)(3)(4)(5)(6)

## RATINGS

**The slopes**

| | |
|---|---|
| Snow | **** |
| Extent | * |
| Expert | ** |
| Intermediate | **** |
| Beginner | *** |
| Convenience | ** |
| Queues | **** |
| Mountain restaurants | * |

**The rest**

| | |
|---|---|
| Scenery | ** |
| Resort charm | ** |
| Off-slope | * |

## NEWS

In 2003/04 a new button lift was installed between the Welcome centre and the children's area.

For 2004/05 a new eight-seat chair is planned to replace the Holvinheisen lift from the base to the mid-mountain. And the children's area is due to expand – two new lifts and three slopes.

- ＋ Impressive snow reliability because of northerly location
- ＋ Increasing amounts of convenient slope-side accommodation
- ＋ Extensive cross-country trails compared to the Alps
- ＋ Some quite challenging slopes, and mountains with a slightly Alpine feel

- − Not much of a village
- − Limited slopes
- − Exposed upper mountain prone to closure because of bad weather
- − Weekend queues
- − One abysmal mountain restaurant
- − No liquor store for miles
- − Après-ski limited during the week and rowdy at weekends

**Hemsedal's craggy terrain is reminiscent of a small-but-serious Alpine resort. Most people not resident in Scandinavia would be better advised to go for the real thing, but if you like the sound of Norway, Hemsedal is the place for downhill skiing. Go after the February school holidays, if possible.**

## THE RESORT

Hemsedal is both an unspoiled valley and a village, also referred to as Trøym and Sentrum ('Centre'), which amounts to very little – a couple of apartment/hotel buildings, a few shops, a bank and a petrol station (but, note, no liquor store). Though there has been talk of a lift from Trøym to the slopes, for now the lift base is a mile or two away, across the valley.

There are self-catering apartments and houses beside the slopes – with a newish development called Skarsnuten linked to the main network by its own lift and red piste – and in a pleasantly woody separate cluster a walkable distance down the hill from the lifts.

A ski-bus links these points, and others in the valley, and was improved for 2003/04; but really, the place is geared to weekend visitors arriving by car or by coach.

## THE MOUNTAINS

Hemsedal's slopes pack a lot of variety into a small space. They are shaded in midwinter, and can be very cold.

**Slopes** With no fewer than four fast chairs to play on, you can pack a lot of runs into the day. And there's night-skiing until 11pm, Tuesdays to Fridays. The lift pass also covers smaller Solheisen, a few miles up the valley. A small supplement is required to ski at Geilo, an hour away.

**Terrain-parks** There's an impressive and 'very well maintained' terrain-park and two half-pipes and new mini-park for beginners and children.

**Snow reliability** The combination of latitude, altitude and orientation makes for impressive snow reliability – and there's extensive snowmaking. The season runs until early May.

**Experts** There is quite a bit to amuse experts – several black pistes of



HEMSEDAL TOURIST OFFICE

This is as dramatic as Norwegian ski resort scenery gets →

## KEY FACTS

| | |
|---|---|
| Resort | 650m<br>2,050ft |
| Slopes | 670-1450m<br>2,200-4,760ft |
| Lifts | 19 |
| Pistes | 42km<br>26 miles |
| Green | 33% |
| Blue | 21% |
| Red | 26% |
| Black | 20% |
| Snowmaking | 14km<br>9 miles |

## REPORTS WANTED

Recently we have had few reports on this resort. If you go there, please do send us a report.

The best reports earn a copy of the next edition, and can lead to free lift passes in future.

See page 10.





**Phone numbers**
From abroad use the prefix +47.

## TOURIST OFFICE

**t** 320 55030
info@hemsedal.com
www.hemsedal.com

450m/1,480ft vertical served by a fast eight-seat chair (or the adjacent 'very steep and very bumpy' t-bar) from the base (one left as a mogul slope) – and wide areas of gentler off-piste terrain served by drags above the tree line.

**Intermediates** Mileage-hungry piste-bashers will find Hemsedal's runs very limited. There are quite a few red and blue runs to play on, but the difference in difficulty is slight.

**Beginners** There's a gentle nursery area for absolute beginners. And there are splendid long green runs – but they get a lot of traffic, some of it irresponsibly fast. Some long blues and reds also suit near-beginners.

**Snowboarding** There is plenty of free-riding terrain, and some pistes are suitable for carving. The park is popular.

**Cross-country** By Alpine standards there is lots to do – 130km/80 miles of prepared trails in the valley and forest and (later in the season) 80km/50 miles at altitude. There is a special trail map. Most of the trails are a few miles down the valley at the Gravset centre, served by one bus a day.

**Queues** Hemsedal is Norway's premier downhill resort, and it is only a three-hour drive from Oslo, the capital. Good weekend weather fills the car parks, leading to queues for the main access lifts after mid-morning, and possibly for others. But during the week it is quiet. The upper lifts are very exposed, and are easily closed by bad weather, producing crowds lower down.

**Mountain restaurants** There is one functional self-service mountain restaurant doing dreary fast food, plus two or three kiosks with benches.

**Schools and guides** Our most recent reporter was greatly impressed: 'Lots of one-to-one, very encouraging.'

**Facilities for children** The facilities at the lift base are good, with day care for children over three months, free to parents in ski school. The kids' nursery slope is admirably gentle and is being expanded for 2004/05 – and now has a lift from the Welcome Centre.

## STAYING THERE

**How to go** Most of the accommodation is in apartments, varying widely in convenience. Catered chalets are available through certain UK operators.

**Hotels** The best hotel is the Skogstad (320 60333) in central Hemsedal – comfortable, but noisy at weekends. Other hotels along the valley are used by UK tour operators. The hotel Skarsnuten, on the mountain, is stylishly modern (with no smoking).

**Self-catering** The Alpin apartments, a walk from the lift base, are satisfactory if you don't fill all the beds. The adjacent Tinden ones are quite smart.

**Eating out** There are half-a-dozen restaurants down in the village.

**Après-ski** It's minimal in the week, rowdy at weekends and holidays.

**Off the slopes** Diversions include sleighs and snowmobiling. The hotel Skogstad pool is open to the public.

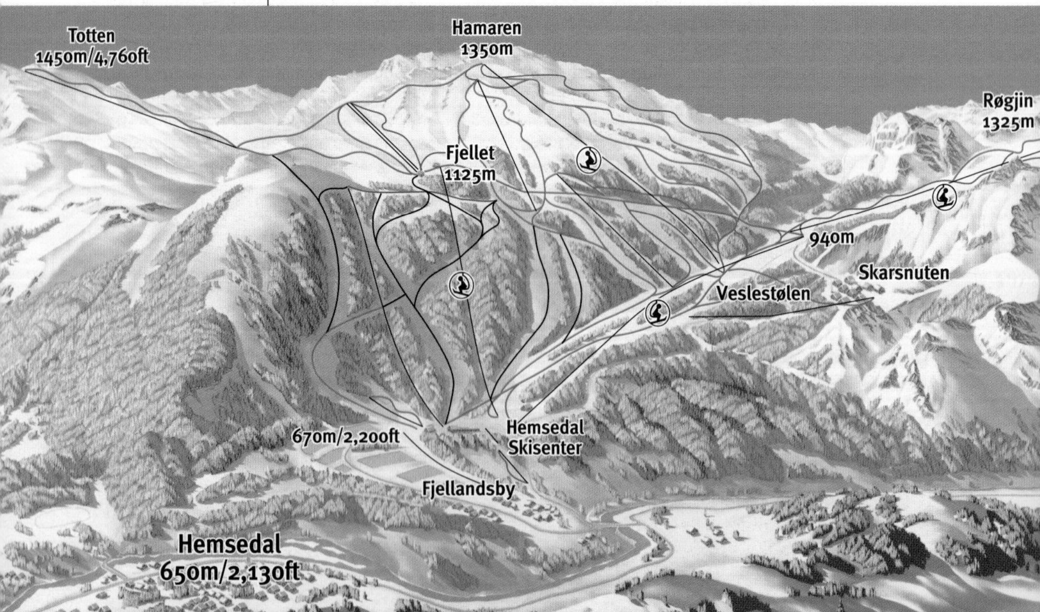

## COSTS

①②③④⑤⑥

- Snow-sure from December to May
- Unspoiled, beautiful landscape
- Uncrowded pistes and lifts
- Vibrant (but regimented) après-ski
- Good range of non-skiing activities

- Limited challenging downhill terrain
- Small areas by Alpine standards
- Lacks the dramatic peaks and vista of the Alps
- Short days during the early season

**Sweden's landscape of forests and lakes and miles of unspoiled wilderness is entirely different from the Alps' grandeur and traffic-choked roads. Standards of accommodation, food and service are good and the people welcoming, lively and friendly. There are plenty of off-slope activities, but most of the downhill areas are limited in size and challenge. Sweden is likely to appeal most to those who want an all-round winter holiday in a different environment and culture. Don't be put off by the myths that Sweden is expensive, dark and cold – see below.**

## REPORTS WANTED

We would welcome more reports on Swedish resorts. If you go there, please do send us a report.

The best reports earn a copy of the next edition, and can lead to free lift passes in future.

See page 10.

Holidaying in Sweden is a completely different experience, culturally as well as physically, from a holiday in the Alps. The language is generally incomprehensible to us and, although virtually everyone speaks good English, the menus and signs are often written only in Swedish. The food is delightful, especially if you like fish and venison. And resorts are very family-friendly.

One of the myths about Sweden is that it is expensive. Sweden is significantly cheaper than neighbouring Norway, especially for alcohol, and prices are pretty much on a par with the main Alpine countries.

Another myth is that it is dark. It is true that the days are very short in December and early January. But from early February the lifts generally work from 9am to 4.30pm and by March it is light until 8.30pm. And most resorts have floodlit pistes for night skiing.

On the down side, downhill slopes are generally limited in both challenge and extent and the lift systems tend to be dominated by T-bars. But there is lots of cross-country and backcountry skiing. Snowboarding is also popular, with parks and pipes in most resorts.

Après-ski is taken very seriously – with live bands from mid- to late-afternoon. But it stops suddenly, dinner is served and then the nightlife starts. There is plenty to do off the slopes: snowmobile safaris, ice fishing, dog-sled rides, ice-climbing, and saunas galore. You can also visit a local Sami village.

The main resort is Åre (see separate chapter). **Sälen** is Scandinavia's largest winter sports area – and is made up of four separate sets of slopes totalling 144km/89 miles of piste. Most slopes are very gentle, suiting beginners and early or timid intermediates best. Lindvalen and Högfjället are vaguely linked by a lift and a long cross-country slog. But you need the unreliable bus service to the others.

**Vemdalen** has two main areas of slopes 18km/11 miles apart by road. **Björnrike** is great for families, beginners and early intermediates, with eight lifts and 15km/9 miles of mainly gentle pistes. There is a hotel right on the slopes, built in modern style. **Vemdalsskalet** has more advanced intermediate terrain, 10 lifts and 13km/8 miles of pistes. The Högfjällshotell at the base is large, dates from 1936 and prides itself on its lively après-ski.

**Riksgränsen**, 250km/155 miles north of the Arctic Circle, is an area of jagged mountain peaks and narrow fjords. The season starts in mid-February and ends in June – when you can be on the slopes under the midnight sun. There are only six lifts and 21km/13 miles of piste. But there is some good off-piste and midnight heli-skiing.

**Björkliden**, also above the Arctic Circle, is famous for its subterranean skiing inside Scandinavia's largest cave system. You need to go with a guide.

**Ramundberget** is a good, small, quiet family resort with ski-in/ski-out accommodation. It gets large amounts of snow and its 22km/14 miles of pistes are mainly easy or intermediate. There is a special children's area with its own lift. The cross-country is vast, with 300km/186 miles of prepared trails.

## TOURIST OFFICES

www.visit-sweden.com

**Sälen**
www.skistar.com

**Vemdalen (Björnrike, Vemdalsskalet)**
www.skistar.com

**Riksgränsen**
www.riksgransen.nu

**Björkliden**
www.bjorkliden.com

**Ramundberget**
www.ramundberget.se

ÅRE RESORT / OLSSON

# Åre

*Sweden's best slopes, strung out along a frozen lake*

## COSTS

①②③④⑤⑥

## RATINGS

| **The slopes** | |
|---|---|
| Snow | *** |
| Extent | ** |
| Expert | ** |
| Intermediate | **** |
| Beginner | **** |
| Convenience | *** |
| Queues | **** |
| Mountain restaurants | *** |
| **The rest** | |
| Scenery | *** |
| Resort charm | *** |
| Off-slope | *** |

## KEY FACTS

| | |
|---|---|
| **Resort** | 380m<br>1,250ft |
| **Slopes** | 380-1275m<br>1,250-4,180ft |
| **Lifts** | 40 |
| **Pistes** | 97km<br>60 miles |
| **Green** | 12% |
| **Blue** | 39% |
| **Red** | 39% |
| **Black** | 5% |
| **Unpatrolled** | 5% |

## NEWS

Work has started in the Olympia area on building a new run for the ladies' downhill and super-G events of the Alpine World Ski Championships to be held in Åre in 2007.

In 2002/03 a six-pack was installed next to the main cable-car from town, replacing the slow double chair. This feeds a quad chair, also new for 2002/03, which replaced a T-bar and two double chairs.



- + Cute little town centre
- + Good snow reliability
- + Good intermediate and beginner runs
- + Extensive cross-country trails
- + Excellent children's facilities
- + Lively après-ski scene
- + Lots of off-slope diversions

- − Lots of T-bars
- − Exposed upper mountain prone to closure because of bad weather
- − High winds detrimental to snow conditions
- − Few expert challenges
- − High season and weekend queues

**Åre has the biggest area of linked slopes in Sweden and some of its most challenging terrain. But it suits beginners, intermediates and families best. It has a dinky little town centre and a long area of slopes set along a frozen lake.**

## THE RESORT

Åre is a small town made up of old, pretty, coloured wooden buildings and some larger, modern additions. When we were there the main square had a roaring open fire to warm up by. As well as accommodation in town, there is lots spread out along the valley, with a concentration in the Duved area. All the slopes and accommodation are set on the shore of a huge, long lake, frozen in the winter months.

## THE MOUNTAINS

The terrain is mainly green and blue tree-lined slopes, with a couple of windswept bowls above the trees.

**Slopes** There are two main areas. The largest is accessed by a funicular from the centre of town or by a six-pack or cable-car a short climb above it. This takes you to the hub of a network of runs and (mainly) T-bars that stretches for 10km/6 miles from end to end. The cable-car is often shut because it goes to the top of the above-the-tree-line slopes (known as the 'high zone'), which often suffers from howling gales. A gondola also accesses the high zone from a different point. You can get back on-piste right into the town square. A separate area of slopes is above Duved and served by a high-speed chair. There are four floodlit slopes, each open on a different night.

**Terrain-parks** There's a 1.4km/1 mile long boarder/skier-cross course, a half-pipe and a big terrain-park, plus two smaller parks for beginner freestylers.

**Snow reliability** Snow reliability is good from November to May. But high winds can blow fresh snow away. They also mean that artificial snow is often deliberately made wet so that it doesn't blow away – it then compacts to a hard, icy surface (and certainly had when we tried the Olympia night skiing area – the top was sheet ice).

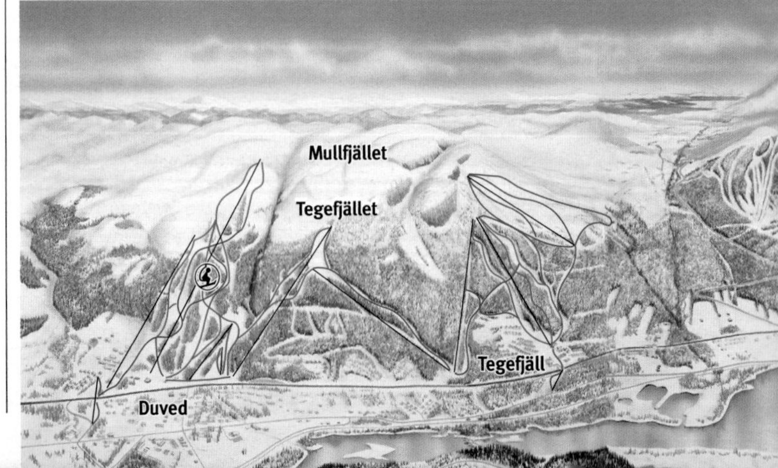

**REPORTS WANTED**

Recently we have had few reports on this resort. If you go there, please do send us a report.

The best reports earn a copy of the next edition, and can lead to free lift passes in future.

See page 10.

**Central reservations phone number**
For all resort accommodation call 17700.

**Phone numbers**
From elsewhere in Sweden add the prefix 0647.
From abroad use the prefix +46 647.

**TOURIST OFFICE**

t 17720
info@areresort.se
www.skistar.com

**Experts** Experts will find Åre's slopes limited, especially if the 'high zone' is closed. If it is open, there is a lot of off-piste available, including an 8km/5 mile run over the back, accessed by a snowcat service in high season. On the main lower area the steepest (and iciest when we were there) pistes are in the Olympia area. There are also steep black and red runs back to town.
**Intermediates** The slopes are ideal for most intermediates, with pretty blue runs through the trees. Because they tend to be more sheltered, the blue runs also often have the best snow. You can get a real sense of travelling from hill to hill on the main area.
**Beginners** There are good facilities, both on the main area and at Duved.
**Snowboarding** There's good varied terrain for boarders, plus three terrain parks (see above). But there are a lot of drag-lifts (31 out of a total of 40).
**Cross-country** There's an amazing 300km/185 miles of cross-country trails, both on prepared tracks and unprepared trails marked with red crosses. Some trails are floodlit.
**Queues** In high season there can be queues for some lifts, especially in the central area immediately above Åre.
**Mountain restaurants** There are some good ones. Our favourite was the rustic Buustamons, tucked away in the woods near Rödkulleomradret.
**Schools and guides** The ski school has a good reputation – and a 2004 reporter who had a private snowboard lesson said the instructor was 'patient and explained things clearly'.
**Facilities for children** There are special children's areas and under eight-year-olds get free lift passes if wearing helmets. There's a kindergarten that takes children from the age of two.

## STAYING THERE

**How to go** Neilson is the only big UK tour operator to offer packages to Åre.
**Hotels** The main central hotels are the delightful old Åregarden – 'good breakfast, nice rooms and helpful staff' – and the simpler Diplomat Ski Lodge. The slope-side Tott Hotel & Spa has good spa facilities. The Renen in Duved is popular with families.
**Self-catering** There are plenty of cabins and apartments; reporters have recommended the ones at Åre Fjällby.
**Eating out** The Bistro is good and there are plenty of alternatives, but a 2004 reporter found traditional Swedish restaurants expensive.
**Après-ski** Après-ski is amazingly lively. The Diplomat is packed from 3pm and has live bands. Later on, the Country Club and Bygget also have live bands and there are plenty of bars for a quiet drink. One reporter recommended the concerts held in igloos by the Tannforsen frozen waterfall.
**Off the slopes** Lots to do, including dog- or reindeer-sled rides, skating, ice fishing, tobogganing, ice-driving, ice-climbing, snowmobiling, paragliding.



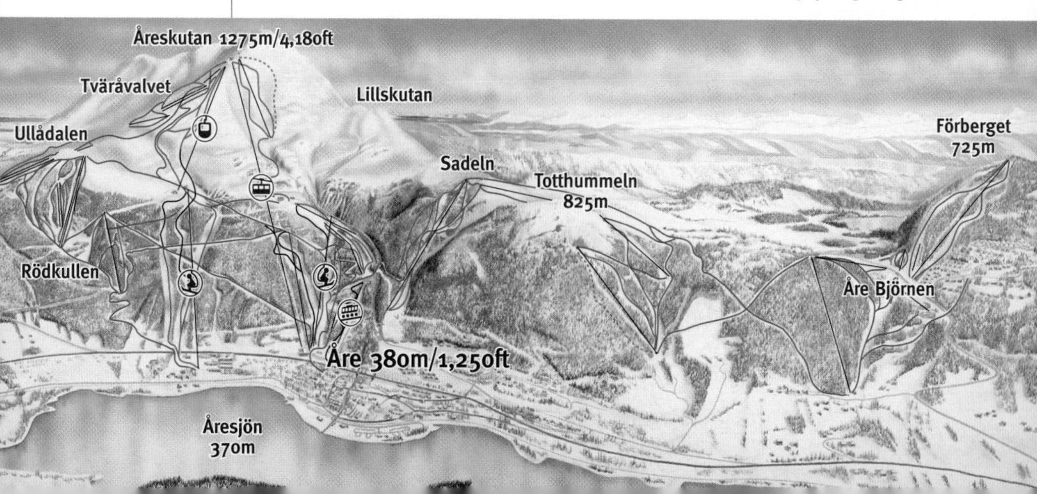

## NEWS

The future looked uncertain for Glencoe in 2003/04 with the place up for sale and opening only at weekends, but we hear a buyer has now been found.

At the Lecht, the new day lodge is due to open for 2004/05.

At Cairngorm there are plans to move two button lifts to the Ptarmigan Bowl to improve access for novices.

A limited number of Scotland-wide season tickets are now available.



## FURTHER INFORMATION

The VisitScotland brochure, *Scottish Snow*, has all the information you need to fix up a trip.

**t** 0131 332 2433
info@visitscotland.com
www.visitscotland.com
www.ski-scotland.com

- ➕ Easy to get to from northern Britain
- ➕ It is possible to experience perfect snow and stirring skiing
- ➕ Decent, cheap accommodation and good-value packages are on offer
- ➕ Mid-week it's rarely crowded
- ➕ Extensive ski-touring possibilities
- ➕ Lots to do off the slopes

- ➖ Weather is extremely changeable and sometimes vicious
- ➖ Snowfall is erratic, to say the least, and pistes can be closed through lack of snow
- ➖ Slopes are limited; runs mainly short
- ➖ Queueing can be a problem
- ➖ Little ski village ambience and few memorable mountain restaurants

**Conditions in Scotland are unpredictable, to say the least. If you are willing to take a chance, or if you live nearby and can go at short notice when things look good, fine. But don't look on it as a replacement for your usual week in the Alps. If you try it, you'll either love it or hate it; but at least you'll know.**

For novices who are really keen to learn, Scotland could make sense, especially if you live nearby. You can book instruction via one of the excellent outdoor centres, many of which also provide accommodation and a wide range of other activities. The ski schools at the resorts themselves are also very good.

Most of the slopes in most of the areas fall around the intermediate level. But all apart from The Lecht offer one or two tough or very tough slopes.

Snowboarding is popular and most of the resorts have some special terrain features, but maintaining these facilities in good nick is problematic. The natural terrain is good for free-riding when the conditions are right.

**Cairngorm** is the best-known resort, with 16 lifts and 37km/23 miles of runs. Aviemore is the main centre (with a shuttle-bus to the slopes), but you can stay in other villages in the Spey valley. The slopes are accessed by a funicular from the main car park up to Ptarmigan at 1100m/3,610ft.

**Nevis Range** is the highest Scottish resort and opened in 1989. It has 12 lifts and 35km/22 miles of runs on the north-facing slopes of Aonach Mor – Britain's eighth highest peak. You get up to the slopes by means of a long six-seat gondola. There are many B&Bs and hotels in and around Fort William, 10 minutes away by shuttle-bus.

**Glenshee** boasts 23 lifts and 40km/25 miles of runs, spread out over three minor parallel valleys. Glenshee remains primarily a venue for day-trippers, though there are hotels, hostels and B&Bs in the area.

**Glencoe's** more limited slopes (seven lifts, 20km/12 miles of runs) lie just east of moody Glen Coe itself. You have to ride a double chair-lift and a button lift to get to the main slopes, including the nursery area. The isolated Kings House Hotel is 2km/1 mile away.

**The Lecht** is largely a beginners' area, with 14 lifts and 20km/12 miles of runs on the gentle slopes beside a high road pass with a series of parallel lifts and runs just above the car parks. With a maximum vertical of only 200m/660ft, runs are short. The Lecht also has a dry slope. And there's a new day lodge at the base. The village of Tomintoul is 10km/6 miles away.

# Australia

- + Offers skiing and boarding during the European summer
- + In one holiday you can also take in a visit to tropical northern Australia
- + Some of the resorts are year-round destinations offering upmarket slope-side accommodation

- − It's a long way from anywhere except New Zealand and south-east Asia
- − Mountains are rather low, and lift/ trail networks are small by Alpine standards
- − Day lift passes are very expensive

**Even more than New Zealand, Australia offers resorts that are basically of local interest, but which might amuse people with other reasons to travel there – catching up with those long-lost relatives, say. Skiing among snow-laden gum trees is also a unique experience for northern hemisphere skiers, plus there is often the chance to see kangaroos, emus, echidnas and wombats.**

**The major resorts are concentrated in the populous south-east corner of the country, between Sydney and Melbourne, with the largest in New South Wales (NSW) – in the National Park centred on Australia's highest mountain, Mt Kosciusko (2230m/7,320ft), about six hours' drive from Sydney. Skiing has been going on here since the early 1900s – as in the next-door state of Victoria, where there are several resorts within three or four hours' drive of Melbourne.**

The Australian ski season generally runs from early June to mid-October. The big snows rarely arrive before late July, and August and September are the most reliable months.

**Thredbo**, established in 1955, is a relatively upmarket Alpine village in NSW. It hosted the only World Cup race event held in Australia, thanks to a vertical of 670m/2,200ft.

Thredbo is rather like a small and quite smart French purpose-built resort – user-friendly, and mostly made up of modern apartments, many new luxury ski-in/ski-out chalets and lodges run by clubs. But there are many more bars than you would find in the French equivalent, and the party atmosphere thrives. The Austrian flavour brought by Thredbo's founders is now giving way to modern, casual-elegant restaurants and bars. It's a steep little place, with stiff climbs to get around from one part to another. Road access is easy, but it costs A$16 a day just to enter the park.

The slopes, prettily wooded with gum trees, rise up across the valley from the village, served by a regular shuttle-bus through the resort. The runs are many and varied. The dozen lifts include three fast quad chairs, and the trails include Australia's highest (2037m/ 6,680ft) and longest (6km/4 miles). While the blacks are not difficult – except for one called Funnelweb, after Australia's most poisonous spider – they offer variety, and on the higher lifts there are off-piste variants. Thredbo's slopes are now dotted with terrain features.

Heavy investment has produced an abundance of luxury architect-designed apartments, an attractive pedestrian mall with good shopping and some high-class restaurants – Segreto and Sante are top favourites – both on and off the mountain. There is also an impressive sports training complex open to the public, with an Olympic-size pool. The 700m/2,300ft public bob-sleigh track is popular.

On the other side of the mountain range is the large **Perisher Blue** resort complex, with a pass covering 51 lifts – more than anywhere else in Australia – but a vertical of less than 400m/1,310ft. The main area is Perisher/Smiggins, where lifts and runs – practically all easy or intermediate – range over three lightly wooded sectors. The resort is reachable by road, or by the Skitube, a rack railway that tunnels up from Bullocks Flat and goes on to the second area, **Blue Cow/Guthega**, where the slopes offer more challenges.

Perisher Blue is doing its best to catch up with Thredbo by upgrading hotels and building more facilities. The resort is very spread out and has no village heart, but work on a $100 million pedestrian village is scheduled to start next season. Despite the lack of a central focus, Perisher has no trouble attracting the crowds. Perisher also has more ski-in/ski-out accommodation than Thredbo, although it does appeal more to the masses, with its shopping-mall-style village centre filled with every manner of shop, bar and fast food restaurant. Its main advantage over Thredbo is its snow, thanks to its position further within the mountain ranges and its altitude: Perisher's lift bases are about as high as Thredbo's mid-station. New this season are a super pipe with 4.5m/15ft high walls, a Snow Deck Park and a Mini Terrain Park for kids.

Many on a budget choose to stay in the apartments or hotels in the lakeside town of Jindabyne, a half-hour drive from both Thredbo and Perisher, with a lively youth-oriented nightlife scene. There are also some rather upmarket chalets along the Alpine Way, which leads to Thredbo.

From Perisher, a snowcat can take you on an 8km/5 mile ride to the isolated chalets of Australia's highest resort, **Charlotte Pass** (1760m/5,770ft), with five lifts but only 200m/660ft vertical. People visit the Pass more for its charm than for the skiing, although it is a favourite with families. The major hotel is the historic and turreted Kosciusko Chalet, a good spot for romantic weekends. Mt Kosciusko, Australia's highest point, is easily reached on cross-country skis.

In Victoria, resorts are not as high as in NSW but many have good snow since they are set well within the ranges. You're better off flying and coaching to these resorts – most Victorian ski fields are approached by tricky winding mountain roads.

**Mount Hotham** has a justified reputation for good snow. An airport just 20 minutes' drive from the ski field makes it the most accessible resort in Australia, with 10 flights a week from Sydney alone. The 13 lifts serve a complete range of runs with plenty of variety. The longest run is 2.5km/1.5 miles and there is more consistently steep terrain here than at any other area in Australia. A free snowcat service tows skiers out to nearby backcountry slopes. The village is built along the top of a ridge, with the slopes below it. The place is also distinguished by its Hotham Heights Chalets, a nest of upscale multi-storey buildings atop the slopes. The focus of the village is Mount Hotham Central, comprising apartments, shops and eateries including a few excellent restaurants. You can also stay 15 minutes' drive away at Dinner Plain, a rather stunning settlement of architect-designed chalets set prettily among gum trees. There are a few restaurants and bars here, many cross-country trails and horse riding.

There is also a six-minute helicopter link from Mount Hotham to another resort nearby (and covered by the same lift pass), **Falls Creek**, that costs all of A$94 return. Falls Creek is the most alpine of Australia's resorts, completely snow-bound in winter. Guests not arriving by chopper are taken there by snowcat from the car park. There are 18 lifts, though the area is smaller than Mount Hotham's and the runs are mostly intermediate. New last season was Australia's first super-pipe, 120m/390ft long with 6m/20ft high walls. Terrain features are dotted around, and there are snow bikes, a tubing park and night skiing.

For some, the big attraction at Falls Creek is being able to access Australia's steepest skiing on the adjacent **Mt McKay** – 365m/1,200ft vertical of true black diamond terrain. Guided snowcat trips from take place twice a day. It's well worth the trip.

The other Victorian resort of note is the isolated peak of **Mt Buller**. This place is to Melbourne, only a two-hour drive away, what the Hamptons are to Manhattan – a magnet for old money. Big-time entrepreneurs have poured millions into Mt Buller, creating a proper resort village with a luxury hotel, a new pampering spa, Australia's highest cinema complex and even a university campus. Draped around the mountain are 25 lifts – the largest network in Victoria, including 13 chair-lifts. Mt Buller annually hosts the World Aerials. New for the 2004 season was a 100m/330ft long half-pipe with 3m/10ft walls. Be aware there's a hefty resort entry fee.

**Mt Buffalo** is worth visiting mainly to stay in the historic Mt Buffalo Chalet, with its dramatic views over the craggy Victorian alps. The Chalet is done up in true 1930s style and offers gourmet dining. The slopes, a short drive away, are in an Alpine basin surrounded by boulders, with five lifts almost purely for beginners.

**TOURIST OFFICES**

**Thredbo**
www.thredbo.com.au

**Perisher Blue**
(for Perisher, Smiggins, Blue Cow, Guthega)
www.perisherblue.com.au

**Charlotte Pass**
www.charlottepass.com.au

**Mount Hotham**
www.hotham.com.au

**Falls Creek**
(for Falls Creek and Mt McKay)
www.fallscreek.com.au

**Mt Buller**
www.mtbuller.com.au

**Mt Buffalo**
www.mtbuffalochalet.com.au

# New Zealand

- ➕ For Europeans, more interesting than summer skiing on glaciers
- ➕ For Australians, conveniently close, with flights from Sydney
- ➕ Huge areas of off-piste terrain accessible by helicopter on the South Island
- ➕ Some spectacular scenery, as seen in *The Lord of the Rings* movies

- ➖ It's a long way from anywhere except Australia
- ➖ Limited on-mountain restaurants – though these are being upgraded
- ➖ Half-hour-plus drives from accommodation up to the ski areas
- ➖ Highly changeable weather
- ➖ No trees, so skiing in bad weather is virtually impossible

**The number of keen skiers and boarders from New Zealand found kicking around the Alps gives a clue that there must be some decent slopes back home – and indeed there are. The resorts are rather different from those of the Alps or the Rockies – generally, you don't stay near the slopes – and the networks of lifts and runs are rather limited by those exalted standards. If Whakapapa and Turoa on the North Island ever build their link, taken together they will be a match for smaller European resorts. Even so, Alpine glaciers will probably remain a more practical destination for Europeans – unless of course you've got some other reason to visit New Zealand, as many of us have.**

**But the heli-skiing around the Mt Cook region on the South Island is definitely worth writing home about. For Europeans already spending a lot to travel to New Zealand, the extra cost of a day or two's heli-drops around the Methven area is well worth while.**



Skiing at almost every New Zealand ski resort involves at least a half-hour drive from a nearby town – usually below the snowline – to the ski field itself. Coach transfers from the hotels and towns to the ski fields are generally well organised. The ski fields will have a base lodge, usually with a restaurant and a cafeteria, equipment rental and one or two shops, as well as the main lifts. The only on-snow accommodation is in luxury apartments at Cardrona on the South Island, and some private lodges at the base of Whakapapa on the North Island.

There are resorts on both North Island and South Island. The main concentration on South Island is around the scenic lakeside town (and year-round resort) of Queenstown, covered in detail in the next chapter.

In what follows, we describe the most prominent resorts (apart from Queenstown and its two local mountains), but there are a number of other possibilities. The main commercial ones are described briefly in our directory at the back of the book, but there are also other ski fields run by clubs. Don't expect groomed trails, restaurants or other luxuries: club fields are pretty primitive, involving stiff walks to get to the base and crude rope tows or at best T-bars when you get there. Craigieburn on the South Island, near Mt Hutt, wins the vote for the most impressive terrain out of the selection.

Any of the major resorts is worth a day or two of your time if you're in the area and the conditions are right. But if your credit card is also in good condition, don't miss the heli-skiing; even if you're no expert off-piste, with powder skis it's a doddle, and tremendously satisfying.

We recommend Methven or Wilderness Heliski (03 302 8108). Both are operated by the same company but fly to different regions around the main spine of mountains in the Mt Cook area; they offer the longest and most spectacular runs for serious skiers and snowboarders. The cost for about five runs is around NZ$745. There are several other companies operating on South Island. Harris Mountain Heliskiing (03 442 6722), operating out of Queenstown and Wanaka, caters mainly for the large Japanese market,

**Phone numbers**
From abroad use the prefix +64 and omit the initial '0' of the phone number.

## KEY FACTS

| Whakapapa | |
|---|---|
| **Altitude** | 1630-2300m<br>5,350-7,550ft |
| **Lifts** | 14 |
| **Pistes** | 550 hectares<br>1,360 acres |
| **Blue** | 25% |
| **Red** | 50% |
| **Black** | 25% |
| **Snowmaking** | some |

| Mount Hutt | |
|---|---|
| **Altitude** | 1405-2075m<br>4,610-6,810ft |
| **Lifts** | 9 |
| **Pistes** | 365 hectares<br>900 acres |
| **Green** | 25% |
| **Blue** | 50% |
| **Black** | 25% |
| **Snowmaking** | 42 hectares<br>104 acres |

| Treble Cone | |
|---|---|
| **Altitude** | 1200-1860m<br>3,940-6,100ft |
| **Lifts** | 5 |
| **Pistes** | 550 hectares<br>1,360 acres |
| **Green** | 15% |
| **Blue** | 45% |
| **Black** | 40% |
| **Snowmaking** | 50 hectares<br>125 acres |

| Cardrona | |
|---|---|
| **Altitude** | 1670-2060m<br>5,480-6,760ft |
| **Lifts** | 8 |
| **Pistes** | 320 hectares<br>791 acres |
| **Green** | 25% |
| **Blue** | 55% |
| **Black** | 20% |
| **Snowmaking** | none |



and the three-run days are generally very easy skiing, with long waits between lifts. The other major Queenstown operation, Southern Lakes Heli-Ski (03 442 6222) is more amenable to exciting skiing as is Alpine Guides (03 435 1834). Try to leave the arrangements loose, to cope with the highly changeable weather.

An alternative adventure is to fly by plane to ski 10km/6 miles down the length of the Tasman Glacier. For a gentle schuss the cost is high – about NZ$800-900 for the day. The main draw is the immense grandeur of the place, along with the ski-plane flights over stunning blue ice-flows and the close proximity of Mt Cook. The Tasman is also one of the few glaciers in the world where it is possible to walk through the eery ice-blue glacial caves – quite a surreal experience.

As in the northern hemisphere, the season doesn't really get under way until midwinter – mid or late June; it runs until some time in October. Mount Hutt aims to open first, in mid-May, and disputes the longest-season title with Whakapapa, which generally stays open until mid-November.

Snowboarding is very popular in New Zealand, and most of the major resorts have special terrain-parks.

**Whakapapa** (pronounced Fukapapa) is on the slopes of the active volcano Mt Ruapehu, which has occasionally erupted in recent years, leaving the slopes black with volcanic ash. Until the late 1990s the volcano had not caused havoc since the 1950s, when an eruption carried away a bridge.

Mt Ruapehu is in the middle of the North Island and within four hours' drive of both Auckland and Wellington. Whakapapa, New Zealand's largest ski field, is located on the north-facing slopes, with a vertical of 670m/2,200ft served by 14 lifts including one fast quad. Terrain is typified by large, wide open cruisers plus challenging off-piste. Next to the base lodge is an extensive beginners' area, Happy Valley, with half a dozen rope tows, a chair-lift that was new last season and snowmaking that allows this particular section to open early in the season. The resort's lifts and runs range across craggy terrain made especially interesting because of the twists, turns and drops of the solidified lava on which it sits. There is a mix of deep gullies, superb natural half-pipes for snowboarders and narrow chutes. There is a handful of mountain restaurants and a new cafe at the nearby Turoa ski field. Views from both resorts are of the surrounding volcanic peaks and wide open fields of tundra – quite surreal.

Accommodation is mostly 6km/4 miles away at Whakapapa village, with the best middle-of-the-road property being a motel named the Skotel. There is on-snow accommodation in ski lodges at the base. A complete anomaly in this area of rustic lodges is the Chateau, a hotel in the grand style of the 1920s, with overly high ceilings, sweeping drapes over picture windows, a marble foyer and formal dining room with grand piano.

Worth knowing about is the hike to



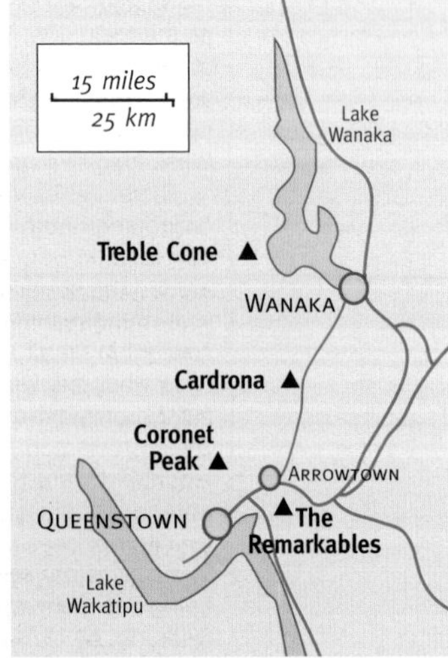

**Phone numbers**
From abroad use the prefix +64 and omit the initial '0' of the phone number.

## TOURIST OFFICES

**Whakapapa**
t 07 892 3738
info@mtruapehu.com
www.mtruapehu.com

**Mount Hutt**
t 03 308 5074
service@nzski.com
www.nzski.com

**Treble Cone**
t 03 443 7443
tcinfo@treblecone.co.nz
www.treblecone.co.nz

**Cardrona**
t 03 443 7411
info@cardrona.com
www.cardrona.com

Mt Ruapehu's fizzing Crater Lake. Ask a ski patrol for directions or, better, talk them into taking you on a guided trip. This involves about a half-hour (500m/1,640ft) hike up from the top of the highest T-bar, and then a long traverse across a large flat tundra-like area. A few lefts and rights and you are staring into the mouth of a volcano. Awesome views and neighbouring volcanos give this area an other-worldly feel.

On the south-western slope of Mt Ruapehu is **Turoa** – now under the same ownership as Whakapapa. You can ski both on the same ticket, which cost NZ$62 last season, the cheapest deal in NZ skiing. And there is now a trail that links both – but the snow must be perfect and you must be guided by a ski patroller. Turoa is smaller, but with an impressive 722m/2,370ft vertical – the biggest in Australasia. The longest run is 4km/2.5 miles. There's plenty of off-piste scope away from the gentle intermediate runs, plus the chance to ski on the Mangaehuehu Glacier. Accommodation is 20 minutes away in Ohakune.

The South Island has 15 ski areas, including five club fields. **Mt Hutt**, an hour west of Christchurch in the northern part of the island, has a 670m/2,200ft vertical and some of the country's most impressive, consistently steep, wide-open terrain – all within view of the Pacific Ocean. On a clear day you can even see the sandy beaches in the distance beyond the patchwork Canterbury plains – in fact it often snows on the beaches here. The lift system is half the size of Whakapapa's and a few more fast chair-lifts would not go amiss. The main area is an open bowl with gentle terrain in the centre served by chairs and drags and steeper terrain around the outside, some of which requires a short hike to the top. An impressive big base lodge was built for the 2000 season, including a spacious, welcoming cafe and brasserie with a glorious outdoor terrace, plus a well-stocked rental shop. Mt Hutt Helicopters (03 302 8401) offers six-run days in the mountains beyond for NZ$600. The helicopter departs from the heli-pad right in the car park – just wander up to the heli hut and book in. There is no accommodation on-mountain – most people stay in the little town of **Methven**, where there are several truly comfortable up-market B&Bs as well as motels and apartments. The very British South Island capital of Christchurch, an hour and a half away, is also an option.

About six hours' drive south of Christchurch is the quiet lakeside town of Wanaka, which is also 90 minutes from Queenstown, and there are two resorts accessible from here.

**Treble Cone**, 20km/12 miles from Wanaka, has more advanced slopes than any other NZ ski area, plus the advantage of a better lift system, including the first six-pack in the southern hemisphere. There are two well-maintained intermediate trails, one 3.5km/2 miles, the other 2km/1.2 miles. Both on the main flank and off to the side in Saddle Basin there are long natural half-pipes which are great fun when snow is good, as well as smooth, wide runs for cruising. Treble Cone is reached by a long and winding dirt track that adds to the excitement. The ski field offers stunning views across Lake Wanaka, with snowcapped Alpine-style peaks in the distance. There's a cosmopolitan cafe at the lift base, quite a discovery in such a far flung place. An enormous sundeck sharing that view was added last season. The resort is also adding another chair-lift in 2004 in its advanced Saddle Basin area, and a fancy cafe to match. The food here and at Cardrona is generally far better than at the other resorts.

**Cardrona**, 34km/21 miles from Wanaka, is famous for its dry snow. The terrain is noted for its well-groomed, flattering cruisers. But there are some serious if short chutes, and the middle basin, Arcadia, hosts the New Zealand Extreme Skiing Championships. The total vertical is a modest 390m/1,280ft. Millions have been poured into the resort by its family owners over the past few years, resulting in a large base area focused around an odd clock tower. New for the 2004 season were another fast quad chair, a bigger 1.2km/0.75 mile long terrain-park – the largest in the Southern Hemisphere, with four half-pipes – plus a learners' terrain-park and more facilities at the Children's Alpine Centre. There's a bar and brasserie-style restaurant, a new ski-in/ski-out noodle bar with sundeck overlooking the nursery slopes, large rental facility and a licensed childcare centre, plus 10 modern apartments at the base (but bring all your own supplies). Learners are looked after well, with three moving carpets.

# Queenstown

*Lively base for sampling a range of South Island resorts*

**RATINGS**

| **The slopes** | |
|---|---|
| Snow | ** |
| Extent | * |
| Experts | *** |
| Intermediates | *** |
| Beginners | *** |
| Convenience | * |
| Queues | *** |
| Mountain restaurants | * |
| **The rest** | |
| Scenery | **** |
| Resort charm | ** |
| Off-slope | ***** |

- For Europeans, more interesting than summer skiing on glaciers
- For Australians, conveniently close, with short flights from Sydney
- Huge areas of off-piste terrain accessible by helicopters
- Lots to do off the slopes, especially for adrenalin junkies
- Lively town, with lots going on and good restaurants
- Grand views locally, and the spectacular 'fjord' country nearby

- Slopes (in two separate areas locally) are a drive from town
- Limited lift-served slopes in each area
- It's a long way from anywhere except Australia
- Highly changeable weather
- No trees, so skiing in bad weather is virtually impossible

**If you want a single destination in New Zealand – as opposed to visiting a few different mountains on your travels – Queenstown is probably it, especially if you can cope with the cost of a few heli-drops. Although the resorts of North Island are impressive, the Southern Alps are, in the end, more compelling – and their resorts are free of volcanic interruptions. Mount Hutt may be a slightly more impressive area than either of Queenstown's local fields – Coronet Peak and The Remarkables – but it's a rather isolated place. From Queenstown you have a choice of the two local fields plus the option of an outing to Treble Cone and Cardrona, perhaps with a few nights in Wanaka.**



## THE RESORT

Queenstown is a winter-and-summer resort on the shore of Lake Wakatipu. (There is a map of the area in the introductory chapter on New Zealand.) Although the setting is splendid, with views to the peaks of the aptly named Remarkables range beyond the lake, the town itself is no beauty – it has grown up to meet tourists' needs, and has a very commercial feel. Shopping is good, of course.

In recent years much effort has been put into smartening up the town, with such additions as the classy new Steamer Wharf complex by the lake and lots of lakeside luxury apartments and hotels. It has a lively, relaxed feel, and makes a satisfactory base, with more than 160 licensed bars and cafes, some good restaurants, and lots of touristy clothes shops. It's the base for adventure activities, offering bungee jumping, jet boating, river surfing and horse-trekking.

There are four lift-served mountains – all small by Alpine standards – that you can get to from Queenstown. The two described here – Coronet Peak and The Remarkables – are close by (about a 30-minute drive). The others – Treble Cone and Cardrona – are a more serious drive away (at least 90 minutes), near Wanaka – another lakeside town with accommodation, but much quieter.

## THE MOUNTAINS

At each base area you'll find a mini-resort – a ski school, a ski rental shop, a functional self-service restaurant, but no accommodation except at Cardrona.

All the areas have something for all abilities of skier or boarder, with off-piste opportunities as well as prepared and patrolled trails. They use the American green/blue/ black convention for run classification, not the European blue/red/black.

### THE SLOPES
***Not the height of convenience***

**The Remarkables,** true to their name, are a dramatic range of craggy peaks visible across the lake from some parts of Queenstown. The slopes are tucked in a bowl right behind the largest visible peak, a 45-minute drive from

| KEY FACTS | |
|---|---|
| **Resort** | 310m 1,020ft |
| The Remarkables | |
| **Slopes** | 1580-1935m 5,180-6,350ft |
| **Lifts** | 5 |
| **Pistes** | 220 hectares 545 acres |
| **Green** | 30% |
| **Blue** | 40% |
| **Black** | 30% |
| **Snowmaking** | 25 acres |
| Coronet Peak | |
| **Slopes** | 1230-1650m 4,040-5,410ft |
| **Lifts** | 6 |
| **Pistes** | 280 hectares 690 acres |
| **Green** | 20% |
| **Blue** | 45% |
| **Black** | 35% |
| **Snowmaking** | 200 acres |

## boarding

*Boarding is popular in New Zealand, and although the two mountains close to Queenstown don't seem to have quite such a hold on the boarding market as Cardrona (see New Zealand introduction), they have everything you need, including equipment and tuition. You needn't go anywhere near a drag-lift, and there are no flats to worry about except on the lowest green at The Remarkables.*

town. This resort is fine for families and beginners, (though there is limited extreme skiing for experts), with the emphasis on taking it easy and enjoying entertainment on the restaurant's sundecks during the week. Children under 10 ski for free at The Remarkables.

Two chairs go up from the base. The slow Alta lift has been replaced with a fast quad which serves easy runs and accesses the higher Sugar Bowl chair. This chair accesses mainly long, easy runs, an enormous new terrain park, 150m/490ft long super pipe and a children's terrain-park, plus a couple of black chutes. The Shadow Basin chair leads to steeper terrain, including three hike-accessed, expert-only chutes that drop down to Lake Alta, and the Homeward Run – a broad, fairly gentle, unprepared slope down to the resort access road, where a shuttle-truck takes you back to the base.

**Coronet Peak**, about 25 minutes' drive from Queenstown, is a far more satisfying resort, especially for intermediates and above. Again, there are three main chair-lifts, one a fast quad that accesses practically all the runs. A novice trail was added a few seasons ago to appeal to beginner skiers and boarders. The main mountainside is a pleasantly varied intermediate slope, full of highly enjoyable rolling terrain that snowboarders adore, though it steepens near the bottom. A fourth lift, a T-bar, serves another mainly intermediate area to one side. There are also drags for beginners. Night skiing runs from July to September on Fridays and Saturdays only. For the 2004 season the resort added 30 new guns on the 1.8km/1.1 mile main trail.

**TERRAIN-PARKS**
***Coronet rules***
Coronet Peak has two half-pipes and a terrain-park. The Remarkables has only a kids' adventure terrain-park plus the Ozone Tubing Park.

**SNOW RELIABILITY**
***Good overall, but unpredictable***
The New Zealand weather is highly variable, so it's difficult to be confident about snow conditions – though the mountains certainly get oodles of snow. The South Island resorts are at the same sort of latitude as the Alps, but are much more influenced by the ocean; fortunately, their ocean is a lot

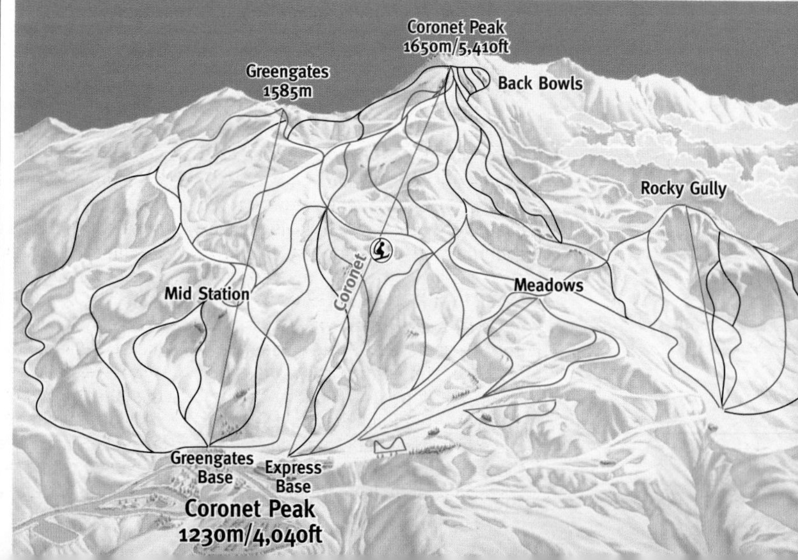

colder than ours. Coronet tends to receive sleet and/or rain even when it's snowing in The Remarkables. But Coronet Peak has snowmaking on practically all its intermediate terrain, from top to bottom of the mountain.

### FOR EXPERTS
***Challenges exist***

Both areas have quite a choice of genuinely black slopes. Coronet's Back Bowls is an experts-only area, and there are other black slopes scattered around the mountain. The main enjoyment comes from venturing off-piste all over the place. The Remarkables' Shadow Basin chair serves some excellent slopes. And The Remarkables' hike-up expert chutes are truly world-class.

### FOR INTERMEDIATES
***Fine, within limits***

There's some very enjoyable intermediate skiing in both areas – appreciably more at Coronet, where there are also easy blacks to go on to. But remember: these are very small areas by Alpine standards.

### FOR BEGINNERS
***Excellent***

There are gentle slopes at both areas, served by rope tows, and longer green runs served by chairs. And many other diversions if you decide it's a drag.

### FOR CROSS-COUNTRY
***Unremarkable***

There is a short loop around a lake in the middle of The Remarkables area, but the only serious cross-country area is the elevated plateau of Waiorau Snow Farm, near Cardrona.

### QUEUES
***It depends***

Coronet and The Remarkables can suffer a little from high-season crowds – there are certainly enough beds locally to lead to queues at peak times. But they aren't normally a major worry.

### MOUNTAIN RESTAURANTS
***Er, what mountain restaurants?***

Both areas have a simple cafeteria at the base, and Coronet has a brasserie facing the slopes, but nothing up the mountain. The Remarkables cafeteria has a big sunny deck, often visited by the large local mountain parrots, called keas, and entertainment most days.

### SCHOOLS AND GUIDES
***All the usual classes***

The schools are well organised, with a wide range of options, including 'guaranteed' beginner classes.

### FACILITIES FOR CHILDREN
***Look good***

Childcare looked okay to us. At both resorts there is a nursery for children aged from two to five years old. Coronet Peak has a Skiwiland Club for children aged four to six with morning and afternoon sessions. The Remarkables has Skiwipak for four and five year olds, also with morning and afternoon sessions. There's also a wide range of kid's activities on offer each day. The Queenstown nursery can take younger children all day.

## STAYING THERE

### HOW TO GO
***Sheer luxury?***

There are lots of big, luxury hotels – all either new or refurbished – built to meet the big summer demand for beds in this popular lakeside resort.
**Hotels** Some hotels are quite some way from central Queenstown – inconvenient for après-ski unless there's a shuttle-bus. In town they range from the very simple to the glossily pretentious Millennium (03 441 8888). Aim to get a room with a view across Lake Wakatipu and the mountains – the view is worth the extra dollars. Two of the best boutique-style places to stay are the Heritage Hotel (03 442 4988) or the Mercure Grand Hotel St Moritz (03 442 4990).

### EATING OUT
***Lots of choice***

We're told there are now over 160 bars and restaurants – a quite astonishing figure. Restaurants include Chinese, Italian, Malaysian, Japanese – you name it, Queenstown has it. The Boardwalk in the Steamer Wharf complex overlooking the lake is the place to go for seafood, and the upmarket Copper Club nearby is also excellent. A dining experience with a difference is the Bath House, located in a 1911 Victorian bath house right on the lakeshore. Solero Vino has delicious Mediterranean food and a rustic bar, and McNeill's is an excellent brew-pub with a range of tasty beers, housed in a stone cottage. The Bunker

Lots of NZ areas offer great view like this (you can just make out parts of Queenstown in this shot from the Remarkables →

NZ SKI MARKETING NETWORK

does excellent local cuisine such as Bluff oysters and lamb. Gantley's, a little way out of town, is a classic restaurant in an historic home. At the other end of the scale, pizza-lovers crowd into The Cow, a cosy barn-like place where you sit on logs around a fire waiting for tables or takeaways. Lone Star offers big servings of satisfying American-style food.

**APRES-SKI**

***Lively little town***

Queenstown has a good range of bars and clubs that stay open late, with disco or live music. A small upmarket casino opened in 1999 in the plush Steamer Wharf, which also holds a classy cigar bar and good duty-free shopping.

**OFF THE SLOPES**

***Scare yourself silly***

There are lots of scary things to do – see the feature box. Just to the west is the spectacularly scenic 'fjord country', and you can go on independent or guided walks. By all reports, the sightseeing flights by plane or helicopter are to be preferred to the slow bus-ride – but the weather can ruin your plans. A marvellous thing to do is to take the Skyline gondola 400m/1,310ft above Queenstown for the great view; try a spin down the public go-cart track, too. Cruise the lake on an historic steamship or go wine tasting. Arrowtown is interesting for a quick visit – a cute, touristy old mining town where you can kit yourself out to go panning for gold. The Winter Festival, held in mid-July, is an annual 'action-packed week of mayhem'.



**GET THAT ADRENALIN RUSH**

*The streets of Queenstown are lined by agencies offering various artificial thrills. We've sampled just a few.*

*AJ Hackett's bungee jump at Kawarau Bridge is where this crazy activity got off the ground – you plunge towards the icy river, but are pulled up short by your bungee cord and lowered into an inflatable boat. You can now also jump off a platform near the sightseeing gondola above town, giving you the illusion of leaping out over the lake and Queenstown.*

*The Shotover Jet Boat experience is less demanding. You get chauffeured at high speed along the rocky river in a boat that can get along in very shallow water, execute high-speed 360° turns and pass very close to cliffs and trees.*

*The whitewater rafting is genuinely thrilling – and not as uncomfortable as you'd expect, thanks to the full wet-suit, helmet, boots and gloves, and to the exertion involved. The rivers have some exciting rapids. One route even passes through a tunnel excavated in the gold-mining days, after which comes a small but steep waterfall where your souvenir shots are snapped.*

**Phone numbers**

From abroad use the prefix +64 and omit the initial '0' of the phone number.

**TOURIST OFFICES**

**The Remarkables**
**t** 03 442 4615
service@theremarkables.co.nz
www.nzski.com

**Coronet Peak**
**t** 03 442 4620
service@coronetpeak.co.nz
www.nzski.com

# Reference section

**A classified listing of the names, numbers and addresses you are likely to need.**

## TOUR OPERATORS

**360 Sun and Ski**
*Family holidays in Les Carroz*
**Tel** 0870 068 3180
info@360sunandski.com
www.360sunandski.co.uk

**Absolute Ski**
*Chalet in Méribel*
**Tel** 01788 822100
holiday@absoluteski.com
www.absoluteski.com

**Airtours**
*Mainstream operator*
**Tel** 0800 916 0623
www.airtours.co.uk

**Albus Travel**
*St Anton specialist*
**Tel** 01449 711952
info@albustravel.com
www.albustravel.com

**Alpine Action**
*Chalets in Les Trois Vallées*
**Tel** 01273 597940
sales@alpineaction.co.uk
www.alpineaction.co.uk

**Alpine Answers Select**
*Tailor-made holidays*
**Tel** 020 8871 4656
select@alpineanswers.co.uk
www.alpineanswers.co.uk

**The Alpine Club**
*Chalet in St-Martin-de-Belleville*
**Tel** 0797 746 5285
info@thealpineclub.co.uk
www.thealpineclub.co.uk

**Alpine Escapes**
*Catered chalets in Morzine*
**Tel** 00 33 450 747392 / 020 8859 6327
alpineescapes@yahoo.com
www.alpine-escapes.com

**Alpine Events**
*Corporate ski specialist*
**Tel** 01962 829777
alpine@offsiteevents.com
www.alpineevents.co.uk

**Alpine Tours**
*Group and schools holidays, mainly in Austria and Italy*
**Tel** 01227 738388
sales@alpinetours.co.uk



**Alpine Weekends**
*Weekends in the Alps*
**Tel** 020 8944 9762
info@alpineweekends.com
www.alpineweekends.com

**AmeriCan Ski**
*Hotels and apartments in France and North America*
**Tel** 01892 511894
ian@awwt.co.uk
www.awwt.co.uk

**American Ski Classics**
*Holidays in major North American resorts*
**Tel** 020 8392 6660
sales@holidayworld.ltd.uk
www.americanskiclassics.com

**Aravis Alpine Retreat**
*Chalet in St Jean-de-Sixt (La Clusaz)*
**Tel** 020 8878 8760
info@aravis-retreat.com
www.aravis-retreat.com

**Avant-ski**
*Mainly holidays in France*
**Tel** 0191 285 8141
sales@avant-ski.com
www.avant-ski.com

**Balkan Holidays**
*Holidays in Bulgaria, Slovenia, Romania and Serbia*
**Tel** 0845 130 1114
res@balkanholidays.co.uk
www.balkanholidays.co.uk

**Barrelli Ski**
*Chalets in Champagny and Les Houches*
**Tel** 0870 220 1500
whiplash@barrelliski.co.uk
www.barrelliski.co.uk

**Belvedere Chalets**
*Luxury chalets in Méribel*
**Tel** 01264 738257
info@belvedereproperties.net
www.belvedereproperties.net

**Bigfoot Travel**
*Variety of holidays in Chamonix*
**Tel** 0870 300 5874
reservation@bigfoot-travel.co.uk
www.bigfoot-winters.com



**Bladon Lines**
*Chalet arm of Inghams*
**Tel** 020 8780 8800
bladonlines@inghams.co.uk
www.inghams.co.uk

**Board and Lodge**
*Catered snowboarding holidays in Chamonix*
**Tel** 020 7916 2275
info@boardnlodge.com
www.boardnlodge.com

**Bonne Neige Ski Holidays**
*Catered chalets in Méribel*
**Tel** 01270 256966
ukoffice@bonne-neige-ski.com
www.bonne-neige-ski.com

**Borderline**
*Specialist in Barèges*
**Tel** 00 33 562 926895
info@borderlinehols.com
www.borderlinehols.com

**Canadian Powder Tours Chalet Holidays**
*Chalet holidays in Western Canada*
**Tel** +1 250 423 3019
cdnpowder@elkvalley.net
www.canadianpowdertours.com

**Canterbury Travel**
*Holidays in Finland*
**Tel** 01923 457017
reservations@laplandmagic.com
www.laplandmagic.com

**Chalet Chez Bear**
*Chalet in Serre-Chevalier*
**Tel** 00 33 492 211170
www.chezbear.com

**Chalet Chocolat**
*Chalet in Morzine*
**Tel** 01872 580814
www.chalet-chocolat.co.uk

**The Chalet Company**
*Catered chalets in Morzine and Ardent (Avoriaz)*
**Tel** 0871 717 4208 / 00 33 450 79 68 40
moran@thechaletco.com
www.thechaletco.com

**The Chalet Group**
*Chalet holidays in the French Alps*
**Tel** 00 33 479 013500
kate@chaletgroup.com
www.chaletgroup.com

**Chalet Gueret**
*Luxury chalet in Morzine*
**Tel** 01884 256542
info@chaletgueret.com
www.chaletgueret.com

**Chalet Kiana**
*Chalet in Les Contamines*
**Tel** 00 33 450 915518 / 01689 838558
chaletkiana@aol.com
www.chaletkiana.com

**Chalet Limited**
*Chalet in Ste-Foy and apartment in Val-d'Isère*
**Tel** 01291 673898
richard.hawkins@chalet.co.uk
www.chalet.co.uk

**Chalet Number One**
*Chalet in Ste-Foy*
**Tel** 01572 717259 / 0033 479069533
info@chn1.co.uk
www.chn1.co.uk

**Les Chalets de St Martin**
*Chalets in St-Martin*
**Tel** 01202 569015
les.chalets@virgin.net
www.leschalets.co.uk

**Chalet Snowboard**
*Snowboard holidays in Morzine*
**Tel** 0870 800 4020
info@csbmountainholidays.com
www.csbmountainholidays.com

**Chalets 'Unlimited'**
*Chalets worldwide*
**Tel** 0191 285 8141
sales@avant-ski.com
www.avant-ski.com

**Chalet World**
*Chalets in big-name resorts*
**Tel** 01743 231199
chaletworld@yahoo.co.uk
www.chaletworldski.co.uk

**Challenge Activ**
*Chalets and apartments in Morzine*
**Tel** 0871 717 4113
info@challenge-activ.com
www.challenge-activ.com

**Chamonix Lodge**
*Chalet in Chamonix*
**Tel** 00 33 674 601167
chamonixlodge@hotmail.com
www.chamonixlodge.com

**Chez Jay Ski Chalets**
*Chalet in Villaroger (Les Arcs) and Montchavin (La Plagne)*
ski@chezjayski.com
www.chezjayski.com

**Classic Ski Limited**
*Holidays for 'mature' skiers/beginners*
**Tel** 01590 623400
info@classicski.co.uk
www.classicski.co.uk

**Club Europe Schools Skiing**
*Schools trips to Europe*
**Tel** 0800 496 4996
ski@club-europe.co.uk
www.club-europe.co.uk

**Club Med**
*All-inclusive holidays in 'ski villages'*
**Tel** 08453 676767
admin.uk@clubmed.com
www.clubmed.co.uk

**Club Pavilion**
*Affordable ski holidays*
**Tel** 0870 241 0427
info@conceptholidays.co.uk
www.conceptholidays.co.uk

**Collineige**
*Chamonix valley specialist*
**Tel** 01276 24262
sales@collineige.com
www.collineige.com

**Connick Ski**
*Chalet in Châtel*
**Tel** 00 33 450 732212
nick@connickski.com
www.connickski.com

**Contiki Holidays**
*Coach-travel holidays for 18-35s*
**Tel** 020 8290 6422
travel@contiki.co.uk
www.contiki.com

**Cooltip Mountain Holidays**
*Chalets in Méribel*
**Tel** 01964 563563
ski@cooltip.com
www.cooltip.com

**The Corporate Ski Company**
*Corporate specialists*
**Tel** 020 7627 5500
ski@vantagepoint.co.uk
www.thecorporateskicompany.co.uk

**Crystal**
*Major mainstream operator*
**Tel** 0870 160 6040
skires@crystalholidays.co.uk
www.crystalski.co.uk

**Descent International**
*Luxury chalets in France and Switzerland*
**Tel** 020 7384 3854
sales@descent.co.uk
www.descent.co.uk





**Directski.com**
*Holidays in Austria, France, Italy and Andorra*
**Tel** 0800 587 0945
sales@directski.com
www.directski.com

**Elegant Resorts**
*Luxury ski holidays*
**Tel** 01244 897333
enquiries@elegantresorts.co.uk
www.elegantresorts.co.uk

**Equity School Ski**
*School group holidays*
**Tel** 01273 886886
schoolski@equity.co.uk
www.equityschooltravel.co.uk

**Equity Ski**
*All-in holidays*
**Tel** 01273 298298
travel@equity.co.uk
www.equityski.co.uk

**Erna Low**
*Hotel and self-catering holidays in the Alps and North America*
**Tel** 0870 750 6820
info@ernalow.co.uk
www.ernalow.co.uk

**Esprit Ski**
*Families specialist in Europe and North America*
**Tel** 01252 618300
www.esprit-holidays.co.uk

**The Family Ski Company**
*Family holidays in France*
**Tel** 01684 540333
enquiries@familyski.co.uk
www.familyski.co.uk

**Finlays**
*Mainly chalets in France*
**Tel** 01573 226611
info@finlayski.com
www.finlayski.com

**First Choice Ski**
*Major mainstream operator*
**Tel** 0870 754 3477
sales@fcski.co.uk
www.firstchoice.co.uk/ski

**FlexiSki**
*Flexible breaks in chalets and hotels in Europe*
**Tel** 0870 909 0754
reservations@flexiski.com
www.flexiski.com

**Fraser Ralston**
*Self-catering accommodation in Chamonix*
**Tel** 028 9042 4662
fraser_ralston@hotmail.com
www.chamonix.uk.com

**Freedom Holidays**
*Tailormade holidays to Châtel*
**Tel** 01798 861888
freedomhols@hotmail.com
www.freedomholidays.co.uk

**French Freedom Holidays**
*Self-catered apartments/ chalets in the French Alps*
**Tel** 01724 290660
info@french-freedom.co.uk
www.french-freedom.co.uk

**Frontier Ski**
*Holidays in Canada and Alaska*
**Tel** 020 8776 8709
info@frontier-travel.co.uk
www.frontier-ski.co.uk

**Frosty's Ski and Snowboard Holidays**
*Chalet in St-Jean-de-Sixt*
**Tel** 00 33 450 023728
info@frostys.co.uk
www.frostys.co.uk

**Frozenplanet.co.uk**
*Chalets and apartments, mostly in the Alps*
**Tel** 07947 331606
www.frozenplanet.co.uk

**Haig Ski**
*Hotels with guiding in Châtel and Morzine*
**Tel** 00 33 450 811947
sales@haigski.com
www.haigski.com

**Handmade Holidays**
*Tailor-made specialists*
**Tel** 01285 642555
travel@handmade-holidays.co.uk
www.handmade-holidays.co.uk

**Hannibals**
*Holidays in Serre-Chevalier*
**Tel** 01233 813105
sales@hannibals.co.uk
www.hannibals.co.uk

**Headwater Holidays**
*Cross-country skiing holidays*
**Tel** 01606 720199
info@headwater.com
www.headwater.com

**High Mountain Holidays**
*Holidays in Chamonix valley*
**Tel** 01993 775540
info@highmountain.co.uk
www.highmountain.co.uk

**Huski**
*Chalet holidays in Chamonix*
**Tel** 020 7938 4844
ski@huski.com
www.huski.com

**Improve Your Skiing**
*Holidays with tuition*
**Tel** 0870 1225549 / 01840 860956
philsmith@improveyourskiing.com
www.improveyourskiing.com

**Independent Ski Links**
*Tailor-made holidays mainly in France*
**Tel** 01964 533905
info@ski-links.com
www.ski-links.com

**Inghams**
*Major mainstream operator*
**Tel** 020 8780 4433
reservations@inghams.co.uk
www.inghams.co.uk

**Inntravel**
*Cross-country skiing holidays*
**Tel** 01653 617920
winter@inntravel.co.uk
www.inntravel.co.uk

**Inspired to Ski**
*Holidays with tuition in France*
**Tel** 0870 128 8989
sally@inspiredtoski.co.uk
www.inspiredtoski.co.uk

**Interhome**
*Apartments and chalets in Europe*
**Tel** 020 8891 1294
info@interhome.co.uk
www.interhome.co.uk

**Interski**
*Group holidays with tuition in Italy*
**Tel** 01623 456333
email@interski.co.uk
www.interski.co.uk

**James Orr Heliski**
*Heli-skiing packages in Canada*
**Tel** 01799 516964
james.orr@btinternet.com
www.heliski.co.uk

**Jeffersons Private Jet Holidays**
**Tel** 0870 850 8181
info@jeffersons.com
www.jeffersons.com

**Kaluma Ski**
*Holidays in the Alps*
**Tel** 0870 442 8044
enquiries@kalumatravel.co.uk
www.kalumatravel.co.uk

**Kuoni**
*Holidays in Switzerland*
**Tel** 01306 747000
switzerland.sales@kuoni.co.uk
www.kuoni.co.uk

**Lagrange Holidays**
*Ski holidays in Europe*
**Tel** 020 7371 6111
info@lagrange-holidays.co.uk
www.lagrange-holidays.co.uk

**The Last Resort**
*Chalet and apartments in St Jean-de-Sixt*
**Tel** 0800 652 3977
thelastresort@cario.fr
www.lastresort.info

**Le Ski**
*Chalets in Courchevel, Val-d'Isère and La Tania*
**Tel** 0870 754 4444
email@leski.com
www.leski.com

**Lotus Supertravel**
*Upmarket European and North American holidays*
**Tel** 020 7962 9933
ski@lotusgroup.co.uk
www.supertravel.co.uk

**Made to Measure Holidays**
*Wide variety of tailor-made holidays*
**Tel** 01243 533333
sales@mtmhols.co.uk
www.mtmhols.co.uk

**Mark Warner**
*Chalet-hotel holidays in big-name resorts*
**Tel** 0870 770 4226
sales@markwarner.co.uk
www.markwarner.co.uk

**MasterSki**
*Christian holidays*
**Tel** 020 8942 9442
holidays@mastersun.co.uk
www.mastersun.co.uk

**McNab Mountain Sports**
*Snowboarding holidays based around Argentière*
**Tel** 01546 830243
info@mcnab.co.uk
www.mcnab.co.uk

**Meriski**
*Chalet specialist in Méribel*
**Tel** 01285 648518
sales@meriski.co.uk
www.meriski.co.uk

**MGS Ski**
*Apartments in Val-Cenis*
**Tel** 01799 525984
skimajor@aol.com
www.mgsski.com

**Momentum Ski**
*Tailor-made specialists*
**Tel** 020 7371 9111
sales@momentumski.com
www.momentumski.com

**Moswin Tours**
*Small German programme*
**Tel** 0116 271 9922
germany@moswin.com
www.moswin.com

**Mountain Highs**
*Chalet specialist in Morzine*
**Tel** 0121 550 9321
mhighs@dircon.co.uk
www.mountainhighs.co.uk

**Mountain Sun**
*Chalets in Paradiski and Alta Badia*
**Tel** 07941 196517
mail@mountainsunltd.com
www.mountainsunltd.com

**Mountain Tracks**
*Ski safaris mainly based on Chamonix and Monterosa Ski*
**Tel** 020 8877 5773
info@mountaintracks.co.uk
www.mountaintracks.co.uk

**Neilson**
*Major mainstream operator*
**Tel** 0870 333 3347
sales@neilson.com
www.neilson.com

**Neilson School Groups**
*School trips to North America and Europe*
**Tel** 0870 333 3620
infoschools@neilson.com
www.skiersworld.com

**Optimum Ski**
*Chalet and tuition in Les Arcs*
**Tel** 08702 406198
info@optimumski.com
www.optimumski.com

**The Oxford Ski Company**
*Chalets in France and Switzerland*
**Tel** 0870 754 2275
rupert@oxfordski.com
www.oxfordski.com

**Panorama Holidays**
*Budget-oriented holidays in Europe*
**Tel** 08707 505060
panoramaski@phg.co.uk
www.panoramaski.co.uk

**Peak Leisure**
*Chalet in Ste-Foy*
**Tel** 01256 397010
info@peak-leisure.co.uk
www.peak-leisure.co.uk

**Peak Retreats**
*Holidays to the lesser-known Alpine resorts*
**Tel** 0870 770 0408
bonjour@peakretreats.co.uk
www.peakretreats.co.uk

**Peak Ski**
*Chalets in Verbier*
**Tel** 01442 832629
peakski@which.net
www.peak-ski.co.uk

**PGL Ski Europe**
*Specialist in school group holidays*
**Tel** 0870 1626622
ski@pgl.co.uk
www.pgl.co.uk

**PGL Teenski**
*Holidays for teenagers*
**Tel** 08700 507507
holidays@pgl.co.uk
www.pgl.co.uk

**Piste Artiste Ltd**
*Self-catered chalets in Champéry*
reserve@pisteartiste.com
www.pisteartiste.com

**Powder Byrne**
*Luxury hotel holidays*
**Tel** 020 8246 5300
enquiries@powderbyrne.co.uk
www.powderbyrne.com

**Powder Skiing in North America Limited**
*Heli-skiing holidays in Canada*
**Tel** 020 7736 8191
info@psna.co.uk

**Premiere Neige**
*Chalets/apartments in Ste-Foy*
**Tel** 0709 2000 300
ski@premiere-neige.com
www.premiere-neige.com

**Purple Ski**
*Chalet holidays in Méribel*
**Tel** 01494 488633
michael@purpleski.com
www.purpleski.com

**Pyrenees Ski Experience**
*Chalets in the Pyrenees*
**Tel** 00 33 468 041879
info@pyrenees-ski-experience.co.uk
www.pyrenees-ski-experience.co.uk

**Ramblers Holidays**
*Cross-country holidays*
**Tel** 01707 331133
info@ramblersholidays.co.uk
www.ramblersholidays.co.uk

**Re-lax Holidays**
*Hotel holidays in Switzerland*
**Tel** 020 8360 1185
sarah@re-laxholidays.co.uk
www.re-laxholidays.co.uk

**Rocketski**
*All-in holidays online*
**Tel** 01273 262626
info@rocketski.com
www.rocketski.com

**Scott Dunn Latin America**
*Tailor-made holidays to South America*
**Tel** 020 8682 5030
latin@scottdunn.com
www.scottdunn.com

**Scott Dunn Ski**
*Upmarket holidays*
**Tel** 020 8682 5050
ski@scottdunn.com
www.scottdunn.com

**Silver Ski**
*Chalet holidays in France*
**Tel** 01622 735544
karen@silverski.co.uk
www.silverski.co.uk

**Simon Butler Skiing**
*Holidays with instruction in Megève*
**Tel** 0870 873 0001
info@simonbutlerskiing.co.uk
www.simonbutlerskiing.co.uk

**Simply Ski**
*Specialist chalet operator in big-name resorts*
**Tel** 020 8541 2209
ski@simply-travel.com
www.simplyski.co.uk

**Ski 2**
*Monterosa specialists*
**Tel** 01962 713330
info@ski-2.com
www.ski-2.com

**Ski Activity**
*Holidays in big-name resorts*
**Tel** 01738 840888
sales@skiactivity.com
www.skiactivity.com

**Ski Addiction**
*Chalets and hotels in Châtel, St Anton and Gressoney*
**Tel** 01580 819354
sales@skiaddiction.co.uk
www.skiaddiction.co.uk

**Ski All America**
*US, Canadian and South American holidays*
**Tel** 08701 676 676
sales@skiallamerica.com
www.skiallamerica.com



**Skialot**
*Chalet in Châtel*
**Tel** 020 8363 8326
stuey@skialot.com
www.skialot.com

**Ski The American Dream**
*Major operator to North America*
**Tel** 0870 350 7547
holidays@skidream.com
www.skidream.com

**Ski Amis**
*Catered chalet and self-catered holidays in the French Alps*
**Tel** 020 7692 0850
info@skiamis.com
www.skiamis.com

**Ski Arrangements**
*Chalets/apartments in Europe and North America*
**Tel** 08700 110565
info@skiarrangements.com
www.skiarrangements.com

**Ski Balkantours**
*Holidays in Eastern Europe*
**Tel** 028 9024 6795
mail@balkan.co.uk
www.balkan.co.uk

**Ski Barrett-Boyce**
*Chalet in Megève with tuition*
**Tel** 01737 831184
info@skibb.com
www.skibb.com

**Ski Basics**
*Chalets in Méribel*
**Tel** 01225 444143
sales@skibasics.co.uk
www.skibasics.co.uk

**Ski Beat**
*Chalets in the French Alps*
**Tel** 01243 780405
ski@skibeat.co.uk
www.skibeat.co.uk

**Ski Blanc**
*Chalet holidays in Méribel*
**Tel** 020 8502 9082
sales@skiblanc.co.uk
www.skiblanc.co.uk

**Ski Bon**
*Chalets in Méribel*
**Tel** 01604 247723
sales@skibon.com
www.skibon.com

**SkiBound**
*Schools division of First Choice*
**Tel** 0870 900 3200
sales@skibound.co.uk
www.skibound.co.uk

**Ski Chamois**
*Holidays in Morzine*
**Tel** 01302 369006
sales@skichamois.co.uk
www.skichamois.co.uk

**Ski Cuisine**
*Chalets in Méribel*
**Tel** 01702 589543
info@skicuisine.co.uk
www.skicuisine.co.uk

**Ski Deep**
*Chalets in La Tania and Le Praz*
**Tel** 01483 722706 / 00 33 479 081905
info@skideep.com
www.skideep.com

**Ski Etoile**
*Chalets and hotels in Montgenèvre*
**Tel** 01588 640442
info@skietoile.co.uk
www.skietoile.co.uk

**Ski Expectations**
*Hotels and chalets in Europe*
**Tel** 01799 531888
ski.expectations@virgin.net
www.skiexpectations.com

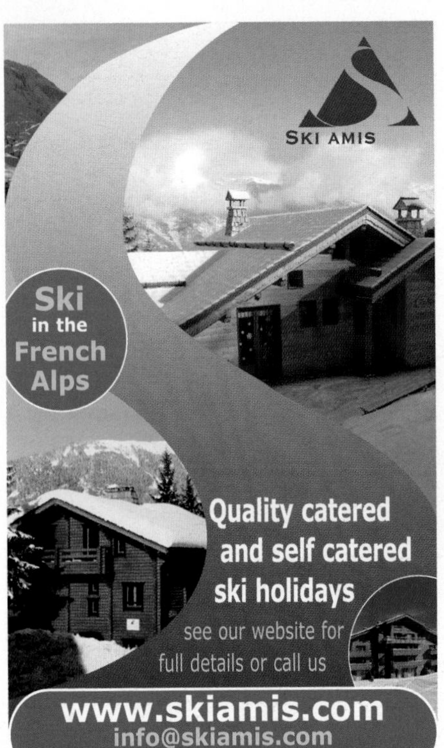


**Ski Express**
*Weekend breaks by coach to France*
**Tel** 01268 783878
info@ski-express.net
www.ski-express.net

**Ski Famille**
*Family holidays in Les Gets*
**Tel** 0845 644 3764
info@skifamille.co.uk
www.skifamille.co.uk

**Ski France**
*Chalets and catered apartments in France*
**Tel** 0870 787 3402
ski@skifrance.co.uk
www.skifrance.co.uk

**Ski FreshTracks**
*Holidays run by Ski Club of GB*
**Tel** 0845 458 0784
skiers@skiclub.co.uk
www.skifreshtracks.co.uk
www.skiclub.co.uk

**SkiGower**
*School trips mainly to Switzerland*
**Tel** 01527 851411
peter@gowstrav.demon.co.uk
www.skigower.co.uk

**Ski Hame**
*Catered chalets in the Three Valleys*
**Tel** 01875 320157
powderpigs@skihame.co.uk
www.skihame.co.uk

**Ski Hillwood**
*Austrian, French and Canadian family holidays*
**Tel** 01923 290700
sales@hillwood-holidays.co.uk
www.hillwood-holidays.co.uk

**Ski Hiver**
*Chalets in Peisey (Paradiski)*
**Tel** 023 9242 8586
skihiver@aol.com
www.skihiver.co.uk

**Ski Independence**
*USA and Canada and self-drive to France and Switzerland*
**Tel** 0870 555 0555
ski@ski-i.com
www.ski-i.com

**Ski La Cote**
*Chalet in La Chapelle d'Abondance*
**Tel** 01482 668357
adrian@ski-la-cote.karoo.co.uk
www.ski-la-cote.karoo.net

**Ski Leisure Direction**
*Mainly self-catering in France*
**Tel** 0870 442 9842
sales@leisuredirection.co.uk
www.leisuredirection.co.uk

**Ski Life**
*Self-drive holidays to France*
**Tel** 0870 429 2180
skilife@frenchlife.co.uk
www.frenchlifeski.co.uk

**Ski Line**
*Chalet holidays in Europe and North America*
**Tel** 020 8313 3999
angus@skiline.co.uk
www.skiline.co.uk

**Ski Link**
*Holidays in Courchevel*
**Tel** 01706 828245 / 00 33 479 083549
skilinkuk@aol.com
www.ski-link.co.uk

**Ski McNeill**
*Tailor-made to USA and European weekends*
**Tel** 0870 600 1359
contact@skimcneill.com
www.skimcneill.com

**Ski Miquel**
*Small but eclectic programme*
**Tel** 01457 821200
ski@miquelhols.co.uk
www.miquelhols.co.uk

**Ski Morgins Holidays**
*Chalet holidays in Morgins*
**Tel** 01568 770681
info@skimorgins.com
www.skimorgins.com

**Ski Morzine**
*Accommodation in Morzine*
**Tel** 01372 470104
info@skimorzine.com
www.skimorzine.com

**Ski 'n' Action**
*Chalet in Le Praz (Courchevel )*
**Tel** 01707 251696
info@ski-n-action.com
www.ski-n-action.com

**Ski Olympic**
*Chalet holidays in France*
**Tel** 01302 328820
info@skiolympic.co.uk
www.skiolympic.com

**Ski Peak**
*Specialist in Vaujany*
**Tel** 01428 608070
info@skipeak.com
www.skipeak.com

**SkiPlan Travel Service**
*Schools programme of Tops Travel*
**Tel** 01273 774778
sales@topstravel.co.uk

**Ski Power**
*Chalets in La Tania*
**Tel** 01737 823232
info@skipower.co.uk
www.skipower.co.uk

**Ski Rosie**
*Catered chalet in Morgins and self-catered apartments in Châtel*
**Tel** 00 33 450813100
rosie@skirosie.com
www.skirosie.com

**Ski Safari**
*Canadian/US specialist, but also Chile*
**Tel** 01273 223680
info@skisafari.com
www.skisafari.com

**Skisafe Travel**
*Mainly holidays in Scotland*
**Tel** 0141 812 0925
info@osatravel.co.uk
www.osatravel.co.uk

**Ski Scott James**
*Chalets in Argentière*
**Tel** 01845 501139
jamie@skiscottjames.co.uk
www.skiscottjames.co.uk

**Ski Solutions**
*Tailor-made holidays*
**Tel** 020 7471 7777
alc@skisolutions.com
www.skisolutions.com

**Ski St Anton**
*St Anton specialist*
**Tel** 01276 61072
office@skistanton.net
www.skistanton.net

**Ski Supreme**
*Coach and self-drive holidays to France*
**Tel** 01355 260547
info@skisupreme.co.uk
www.skisupreme.co.uk

**Skitopia**
*Holidays to the southern French Alps*
**Tel** 01872 272767
www.skitopia.com

**Ski Tracer**
*Val-Thorens specialist*
**Tel** 0870 420 5782
sales@skitracer.com
www.skitracer.com

**Ski-Val**
*Holidays in France and Austria*
**Tel** 0870 746 3030
reservations@skival.co.uk
www.skival.co.uk

**Ski Verbier**
*Specialists in Verbier*
**Tel** 020 7385 8050
info@skiverbier.com
www.skiverbier.com

**Ski Weekend**
*Weekend and ten-day holidays*
**Tel** 0870 060 0615
sales@skiweekend.com
www.skiweekend.com

**Ski Weekends & Board Breaks**
*3- and 6-day holidays to Les Trois Vallées*
**Tel** 01375 396688 / 0870 4423400
sales@harris-travel.com
www.skiweekends.com

**Ski Wild**
*Specialise in Austria and Norway*
**Tel** 0870 746 9668
info@skiwild.co.uk
www.skiwild.co.uk

**Ski with Julia**
*Hotels and catered chalets in Verbier*
**Tel** 01386 584478
julia@skijulia.co.uk
www.skijulia.co.uk

**Skiworld**
*European and North American programme*
**Tel** 0870 241 6723
sales@skiworld.ltd.uk
www.skiworld.ltd.uk

**Ski Yogi**
*Holidays in Italy*
**Tel** 01799 531886
ski.expectations@virgin.net
www.skiexpectations.com

**Sloping Off**
*Schools and group holidays by coach*
**Tel** 01725 552833
hilary@sloping-off.co.uk
www.sloping-off.co.uk

**Slovenija and Austrian Pursuits**
*Accommodation in Slovenija and Austria*
**Tel** 0870 220 0201
enquiries@slovenijapursuits.co.uk
www.slovenijapursuits.co.uk

**Snowbizz**
*Holidays in Puy-St-Vincent*
**Tel** 01778 341455
wendy@snowbizz.co.uk
www.snowbizz.co.uk

**Snowcoach**
*Holidays to Austria and France*
**Tel** 01727 866177
info@snowcoach.co.uk
www.snowcoach.co.uk

**Snowfocus**
*Chalet in Châtel*
**Tel** 01392 479555
action@snowfocus.com
www.snowfocus.com

**Snowlife**
*Catered chalet in La Clusaz*
**Tel** 01534 863630
info@snowlife.co.uk
www.snowlife.co.uk

**Snowline**
*Chalet holidays in France*
**Tel** 08701 123118
ski@snowline.co.uk
www.snowline.co.uk

**Snow Monkey Chalets**
*Quirky chalets in the Paradiski area*
**Tel** 020 7387 0095
enquiries@snowmonkeys chalets.co.uk
www.snowmonkeychalets.co.uk

**Snowscape**
*Flexible trips to Austria*
**Tel** 01905 357760
skiandboard@snowscape.co.uk
www.snowscape.co.uk

**Snowstar Holidays**
*Catered chalets in Tignes*
**Tel** 0870 068 6611
info@snowstarholidays.com
www.snowstarholidays.com

**Solo's**
*Singles' holidays for 25 to 69s*
**Tel** 08700 720700
travel@solosholidays.co.uk
www.solosholidays.co.uk

**La Source**
*Chalet and accommodation in Villard-Reculas*
**Tel** 01707 655988
lasourcefrance@aol.com
www.lasource.org.uk

**Stanford Skiing**
*Megève specialist*
**Tel** 01223 477644
info@stanfordskiing.co.uk
www.stanfordskiing.co.uk

**St Anton Ski Company**
*Hotels and chalets in St Anton*
**Tel** 00 43 676 495 3438
jonathanverney@compuserve.com
www.atlas.co.uk/ski

**Susie Ward Alpine Holidays**
*Flexible-length holidays to Châtel*
**Tel** 01872 553055
susie@susieward.com
www.susieward.com

**Swiss Travel Service**
*Hotels in Switzerland*
**Tel** 0870 191 7175
swiss@bridge-travel.co.uk
www.swisstravel.co.uk

**Switzerland Travel Centre**
*Specialists in Swiss resorts*
**Tel** 020 7734 0383
sales@stc.ch
www.switzerlandtravelcentre.co.uk

**Thomson Ski & Snowboarding**
*Major mainstream operator*
**Tel** 0870 606 1470
info@thomson-ski.com
www.thomson-ski.co.uk

**Tops Ski Chalets and Club Hotels**
*Chalets and hotels in French resorts*
**Tel** 01273 774666
sales@topstravel.co.uk
www.topstravel.co.uk

**Total**
*Chalet holidays in Europe and Canada*
**Tel** 08701 633633
www.skitotal.com

**Trail Alpine**
*Chalet in Morzine*
**Tel** 0870 750 6560
info@trailalpine.co.uk
www.trailalpine.co.uk

**Trailfinders**
*North American programme*
**Tel** 0845 050 5900
www.trailfinders.com

**United Vacations Ski Freedom USA & Canada**
*US and Canada programme*
**Tel** 0870 606 2222
uvuk@unitedvacations.com
www.unitedvacations.co.uk

**Val d'Isère A La Carte**
*Specialists in Val d'Isère hotels and self-catering holidays*
**Tel** 01481 236800
skialacarte@aol.com
www.skivaldisere.co.uk

**Vanilla Ski**
*Chalet in Seez (near La Rosière and Les Arcs)*
**Tel** 01932 860696
sam@vanillaski.com
www.vanillaski.com

**Vertical Reality at Verbier Ltd**
*Chalets in Verbier*
**Tel** 01268 452337
info@verticalrealityverbier.com
www.verticalrealityverbier.com

**VIP**
*Chalets in Val d'Isère and Méribel*
**Tel** 08701 123119
ski@vip-chalets.com
www.vip-chalets.com

**Virgin Snow**
*Holidays to America*
**Tel** 0870 990 4212
brochure.requests@virginholidays.co.uk
www.virgin.com/holidays

**Waymark Holidays**
*Cross-country skiing holidays*
**Tel** 01753 516477
enquiries@waymarkholidays.com
www.waymarkholidays.com

**Weekends in Val d'Isère**
*Weekends – and not just in Val d'Isère*
**Tel** 020 8944 9762
info@alpineweekends.com
www.alpineweekends.com

**White Heat Skiing**
*Davos specialist*
**Tel** 020 989 3281
info@whiteheatski.biz
www.whiteheatski.biz

**White Roc**
*Weekends and tailormade hotel holidays*
**Tel** 020 7792 1188
snow@whiteroc.co.uk
www.whiteroc.co.uk

**Wood Advent Farm**
*Chalet in Les Gets*
**Tel** 01984 640920
www.skilesgets.com

**YSE**
*Variety of holidays in Val-d'Isère*
**Tel** 020 8871 5117
sales@yseski.co.uk
www.yseski.co.uk

## AIRLINES

**Air Canada**
**Tel** 0871 220 1111
www.aircanada.ca

**Air France**
**Tel** 0845 359 1000
www.airfrance.com/uk

**Air New Zealand**
**Tel** 0800 028 4149
www.airnewzealand.co.uk

**Alitalia**
**Tel** 0870 544 8259
www.alitalia.co.uk

**American Airlines**
*08547 789789 outside London*
**Tel** 020 7365 0777
www.aa.com

**Austrian Airlines**
**Tel** 0870 124 2625
www.austrianairlines.co.uk

**bmibaby**
**Tel** 0870 264 2229
www.bmibaby.com

**British Airways**
*Flight enquiries:*
*0870 55 111 55*
**Tel** 0870 850 9850
www.britishairways.com

**Continental Airlines**
**Tel** 01293 776464
www.continental.com

**Delta Airlines**
**Tel** 0800 414767
www.delta.com

**EasyJet**
*Flights to Geneva, Zurich, Nice*
**Tel** 0870 6 000 000
www.easyjet.com

**FlyBE**
**Tel** 0871 700 0535
www.flybe.com

**KLM**
**Tel** 08705 074074
www.klmuk.co.uk

**Lufthansa**
**Tel** 0870 837 7747
www.lufthansa.com

**Qantas**
**Tel** 0845 774 7767
www.qantas.com.au

**Ryanair**
**Tel** 0871 246 0000
www.ryanair.com

**Swiss International Air Lines**
**Tel** 0845 601 0956
contactus@swiss.com
www.swiss.com

**United Airlines**
**Tel** 0845 844 4777
www.unitedairlines.co.uk

**Virgin Atlantic Airways**
*Flight information:*
*0871 222 3767*
**Tel** 0870 380 2007
www.virgin-atlantic.com

**Zoom Airlines**
*Flights to Canada*
**Tel** 0870 240 0055
www.flyzoom.com

## AIRPORTS

**Aberdeen**
**Tel** 0870 040 0006
www.baa.co.uk

**Belfast**
**Tel** 028 9448 4848
info.desk@bial.co.uk
www.bial.co.uk

**Birmingham**
**Tel** 08707 335511
info@bhx.co.uk
www.bhx.co.uk

**Bournemouth**
**Tel** 01202 364000
feedback@bournemouth
airport.co.uk
www.flybournemouth.com

**Bristol**
**Tel** 0870 121 2747
feedback@bristolairport.com
www.bristolairport.co.uk

**Cardiff**
**Tel** 01446 711111
infodesk@cwl.aero
www.cial.co.uk

**Dublin**
**Tel** +353 1 814 1111
customer.relations-
dublin@aer-rianta.ie
www.dublin-airport.com

**East Midlands**
**Tel** 01332 852852
www.eastmidlandsairport.com

**Edinburgh**
**Tel** 0870 040 0007
www.baa.co.uk

**Exeter**
**Tel** 01392 367433
marketing@exeter-
airport.co.uk
www.exeter-airport.co.uk

**Glasgow**
**Tel** 0870 040 008
www.baa.co.uk

**Leeds-Bradford**
**Tel** 0113 250 9696
www.lbia.co.uk

**London Gatwick**
**Tel** 0870 000 2468
www.baa.com

**London Heathrow**
**Tel** 0870 000 0123
www.baa.co.uk

**London Luton**
**Tel** 01582 405100
info@london-luton.co.uk
www.london-luton.com

**London Stansted**
**Tel** 0870 000 0303
www.baa.co.uk

**Manchester**
**Tel** 0161 489 3000
www.manchesterairport.co.uk

**Newcastle**
**Tel** 0870 122 1488
kmw@newcastleairport.com
www.newcastleairport.com

**Southampton**
**Tel** 0870 040 0009
www.baa.co.uk

**Teesside**
**Tel** 01325 332811
www.teessideairport.com

## AIRPORT TRANSFERS

**Airport Transfer Service**
*Geneva transfers*
**Tel** +33 450 536397

**AlpineCab**
**Tel** 00 33 450 731938
info@alpinecab.com
www.alpinecab.com

**Fraser Ralston Airport Transfers**
**Tel** 028 9042 4662
fraser_ralston@hotmail.com
www.chamonix.uk.com

## BREAKDOWN INSURANCE

**AA Five Star Europe**
**Tel** 0800 085 2840
customer.services@theAA.com
www.theAA.com

**Autohome**
**Tel** 0800 371 280
www.autohome.co.uk

**Direct Line Rescue**
**Tel** 020 8686 3313
www.directline.com/rescue

**Europ Assistance**
**Tel** 0870 737 5720
customerservices@europ-
assistance.co.uk
www.europ-assistance.co.uk

**Green Flag**
**Tel** 0800 400 638
european-sales@
greenflag.com
www.greenflag.com

**Leisurecare Insurance Services**
**Tel** 01793 750150

**Mondial Assistance UK**
**Tel** 0800 777148
enquiries@mondial-
assistance.co.uk
www.mondial-assistance.co.uk

**RAC Travel Services**
**Tel** 0800 550055
traveladmin@rac.co.uk
www.rac.co.uk

## CAR HIRE

**Alamo Rent A Car**
**Tel** 0870 599 4000
international@goalamo.com
www.alamo.com

**Avis Rent A Car**
**Tel** 08700 100 287
www.avis.co.uk

**Budget Car and Van Rental**
**Tel** 08701 565656
reservations@budget-uk.com
www.budget-uk.com

**Europcar UK**
**Tel** 0870 607 5000
www.europcar.co.uk

**Hertz UK Ltd**
**Tel** 08708 448844
www.hertz.co.uk

**Holiday Autos International Ltd**
**Tel** 0870 400 4447
www.holidayautos.com

**Suncars**
**Tel** 0870 500 5566
customerservices@suncars.com
www.suncars.com

## CAR WINTER EQUIPMENT

**Brindley Chains Ltd**
*Pewag snowchains*
**Tel** 01925 825555
enquiries@brindley-chains.co.uk
www.brindley-chains.co.uk

**GT Towing Ltd**
*Ski boxes and snowchains*
**Tel** 01707 652118
sales@gttowing.co.uk
www.gttowing.co.uk

**Lakeland Roof Box Centre**
*Roof boxes, snowchains*
**Tel** 08700 766326
www.roofbox.co.uk

**Latchmere Motor Spares**
*Snowchains, roof bars, ski clamps, boxes*
**Tel** 020 7228 3907

**Motor Traveller**
*Thule racks and boxes; Milz snowchains*
**Tel** 01753 833442
info@carbox.freeserve.co.uk
www.carbox.co.uk

**The Roof Box Company**
**Tel** 08700 766326
www.roofbox.co.uk

**RUD Chains Ltd**
*Snowchains*
**Tel** 01227 276611
sales@rud.co.uk
www.rud.co.uk

**skidrive.co.uk**
*Thule roof systems, Karrite boxes, Skandibox, Konig snowchains*
**Tel** 01223 323488
skidrive@dapcambridge.co.uk
www.skidrive.co.uk

**Snowchains Ltd**
*Thule ski boxes, roof bars and ski racks; Weissenfels snowchains*
**Tel** 01732 884408
info@snowchains.co.uk
www.snowchains.co.uk

**Spikes Spider**
**Tel** 01706 819365
pparkinson@ndirect.co.uk
www.spikesspider.com

**Thule Ltd**
**Tel** 01275 340404
www.thule.co.uk

## CROSS-CHANNEL TRAVEL

**Brittany Ferries**
*Portsmouth–Caen*
**Tel** 08703 665 333
reservations@brittany-ferries.com
www.brittanyferries.co.uk

**Eurotunnel**
*Folkestone–Calais/Coquelles via the Channel Tunnel*
**Tel** 08705 35 35 35
www.eurotunnel.com

**Hoverspeed**
*Dover–Calais; Dover–Ostend; Newhaven–Dieppe*
**Tel** 0870 240 8070
www.hoverspeed.com

**Norfolkline**
*Dover–Dunkerque*
**Tel** 01304 218400
doverpax@norfolkline.com
www.norfolkline.com

**P&O Ferries**
*Hull–Zeebrugge, Hull–Rotterdam*
**Tel** 08705 202020
www.ponsf.com

**P&O Ferries**
*Portsmouth–Cherbourg; Portsmouth–Le Havre; Portsmouth-Caen*
**Tel** 08705 202020
reservations.admin@poportsmouth.com
www.poportsmouth.com

**P&O Ferries**
*Dover–Calais*
**Tel** 08705 202020
customer.services@posl.com
www.poferries.com

**SeaFrance**
*Dover–Calais*
**Tel** 08705 711 711
enquiries@seafrance.com
www.seafrance.com

**SpeedFerries**
*Dover-Boulogne*
**Tel** 01304 203000
mail@speedferries.com
www.speedferries.com

**Stena Line**
*Harwich--Hook of Holland*
**Tel** 08704 006798
www.stenaline.co.uk

## DRY SKI SLOPES

### SOUTH-WEST ENGLAND

**Christchurch Ski Centre**
Matchams Lane, Hurn, Christchurch, Dorset
**Tel** 01202 499155
info@christchurch-skicentre.com
www.newforest-online.co.uk/christchurch_ski

**Exeter and District Ski Club**
Clifton Hill Sports Ground, Belmont Road, Exeter
**Tel** 01392 211422
exeterskiclub@ntlworld.com
homepage.ntlworld.com/exeterskiclub/

**High Action Avon Ski Centre**
Lyncombe Lodge, Churchill, North Somerset
**Tel** 01934 852335
info@highaction.co.uk
www.highaction.co.uk

**John Nike Leisuresport – Plymouth**
Plymouth Ski Centre, Alpine Park, Marsh Mills, Plymouth
**Tel** 01752 600220
ski-plymouth@nikegroup.co.uk
www.jnll.co.uk

**Torquay Alpine Ski Club**
Barton Hall, Kingskerswell Road, Torquay, Devon
**Tel** 01803 313350
info@skitorquay,co.uk
www.skitorquay.co.uk

**Warmwell Ski Centre**
Warmwell, Dorchester, Dorset
**Tel** 01305 853245

**Yeovil Ski Centre**
Addlewell Lane, Nine Springs, Yeovil, Somerset
**Tel** 01935 421702

### SOUTH-EAST ENGLAND

**Alpine Snowsports Aldershot**
Gallwey Road, Aldershot, Hants
**Tel** 01252 325889
info@alpinesnowsports.co.uk
www.alpinesnowsports.co.uk

**Bowles Outdoor Centre**
Eridge Green, Tunbridge Wells
**Tel** 01892 665665
admin@bowles.ac
www.bowles.ac

**Bromley Ski Centre**
Sandy Lane, St Paul's Cray, Orpington, Kent
**Tel** 01689 876812
management@bromleyski.co.uk
www.c-v-s.co.uk/bromleyski/

**Calshot Activities Centre**
Calshot Spit, Fawley, Southampton
**Tel** 023 8089 2077
calshot.ac@hants.gov.uk
www.hants.gov.uk/calshot

**Christ's College Ski Club**
Larch Avenue, Guildford, Surrey
**Tel** 01483 504988
www.ccski.co.uk

**Folkestone Sports Centre Ski Slope**
Radnor Park Avenue, Folkestone, Kent
**Tel** 01303 850333
www.folkestonesports.ndo.co.uk/swimski.html

**John Nike Leisuresport – Bracknell**
Bracknell Ski Centre, Amen Corner, Bracknell, Berkshire
**Tel** 01344 789000
ski-bracknell@nikegroup.co.uk
www.jnll.co.uk

**John Nike Leisuresport – Chatham**
Chatham Ski and Snowboard Centre, Alpine Park, Capstone Road, Gillingham, Kent
**Tel** 01634 827979
ski-chatham@nikegroup.co.uk
www.jnll.co.uk

**Sandown Ski Centre**
More Lane, Esher, Surrey
**Tel** 01372 467132
sandown@sandownsports.co.uk
www.sandownsports.co.uk

**Southampton Alpine Centre**
The Sports Centre, Bassett, Southampton
**Tel** 023 8079 0970
info@southampton-alpine-centre.co.uk
www.southampton-alpine-centre.co.uk

**Wycombe Summit**
Abbey Barn Lane, High Wycombe, Bucks
**Tel** 01494 474711
info@wycombesummit.co.uk
www.wycombesummit.co.uk

### MIDDLE ENGLAND

**The Ackers**
Golden Hillock Road, Small Heath, Birmingham
**Tel** 0121 772 5111
www.ackers-adventure.co.uk

**Gloucester Ski and Snowboard Centre**
Jarvis International Hotel and Country Club, Robinswood Hill, Matson Lane, Gloucester
**Tel** 08702 400375
www.gloucesterski.com

**John Nike Leisuresport – Swadlincote**
Swadlincote Ski Centre, Hill Street, Swadlincote, Derbyshire
**Tel** 01283 217200
ski-swadlincote@nikegroup.co.uk
www.jnll.co.uk

**Kidsgrove Ski Centre**
Bathpool Park, Kidsgrove, Stoke-on-Trent
**Tel** 01782 784908
matt.wall@skier71.fsnet.co.uk
www.ski-kidsgrove.co.uk

**Snozone**
Xscape, 602 Marlborough Gate, Central Milton Keynes
**Tel** 0871 222 5670
info@snozonemk.co.uk

**Stoke Ski Centre**
Festival Park, Stoke-on-Trent
**Tel** 01782 204159
wilsonpb@postmaster.co.uk
www.stokeskicentre.co.uk

**Tallington Ski and Snowboard Centre**
Tallington Lakes Leisure Park, Barholm Road, Tallington, Stamford, Lincs
**Tel** 01778 344990
sales@waspdirect.com
www.waspdirect.com

**Tamworth Snowdome**
Leisure Island, River Drive, Tamworth, Staffordshire
**Tel** 08705 000011
info@snowdome.co.uk
www.snowdome.co.uk

**Telford Ski Centre**
Court Street, Madeley, Telford, Shropshire
**Tel** 01952 586862
madeleyskicentre@telford.gov.uk
www.telfordleisure.co.uk

## EASTERN ENGLAND

**Brentwood Park Ski and Snowboard Centre**
Warley Gap, Brentwood, Essex
**Tel** 01277 211994
info@brentwoodskicentre.co.uk
www.brentwoodskicentre.co.uk

**Gosling Ski Centre**
Stanborough Road, Welwyn Garden City, Hertfordshire
**Tel** 01707 331056
info@goslingsports.co.uk
www.goslingsports.co.uk

**Hemel Ski Centre**
St Albans Hill, Hemel Hempstead, Herts
**Tel** 01442 241321
communicate@hemel-ski.co.uk
www.hemel-ski.co.uk

**Norfolk Ski Club**
Whitlingham Lane, Trowse, Norwich, Norfolk
**Tel** 01603 662781
info@norfolkskiclub.co.uk
www.norfolkskiclub.co.uk

**Suffolk Ski Centre**
Bourne Hill, Wherstead, Ipswich
**Tel** 01473 602347
enquiries@suffolkskicentre.co.uk
www.suffolkskicentre.co.uk

## NORTHERN ENGLAND

**Alston Training and Adventure Centre**
High Plains Lodge, Alston, Cumbria
**Tel** 01434 381886
alstontraining@btconnect.com
www.alstontraining.co.uk

**Halifax Ski and Snowboard Centre**
Sportsman Leisure, Bradford Old Road, Swalesmoor Ploughcroft, Halifax
**Tel** 01422 340760
skislope@ridehalifax.co.uk
www.ridehalifax.co.uk

**Kendal Ski Club**
Canal Head North, Kendal, Cumbria
**Tel** 01539 732948
sec@kendalski.co.uk
www.kendalski.co.uk

**Pendle Ski Club**
Clitheroe Road, Sabden, Clitheroe, Lancs
**Tel** 01200 425222
info@pendleskiclub.org.uk
www.pendleskiclub.org.uk

**Runcorn Ski and Snowboard Centre**
Town Park, Palace Fields, Runcorn, Cheshire
**Tel** 01928 701965
info@runcornskicentre.co.uk
www.runcornskicentre.co.uk

**Sheffield Ski Village**
Vale Road, Parkwood Springs, Sheffield
**Tel** 0114 276 9459
www.sheffieldskivillage.co.uk

**Ski Rossendale**
Haslingden Old Road, Rawtenstall, Rossendale, Lancashire
**Tel** 01706 226457
info@ski-rossendale.co.uk
www.ski-rossendale.co.uk

**Whickham Thorns Outdoor Centre**
Market Lane, Dunston
**Tel** 0191 433 5767
whickhamthorns@leisure.gatesheadmbc.gov.uk
www.gateshead.gov.uk/leisserv/whickhamthorns.htm

## WALES

**Cardiff Ski & Snowboard Centre**
Fairwater Park, Fairwater Rd, Cardiff
**Tel** 029 2056 1793
info@skicardiff.com
www.skicardiff.com

**Dan-yr-Ogof Ski Slopes**
Glyn Tawe, Abercraf, West Glamorgan
**Tel** 01639 730284
www.showcaves.co.uk/english/fr_ski.html

**John Nike Leisuresport – Llandudno**
Wyddfyd Road, Great Orme, Llandudno
**Tel** 01492 874707
ski-llandudno@nikegroup.co.uk
www.jnll.co.uk

**Plas y Brenin**
Capel Curig, Gwynedd
**Tel** 01690 720214
www.pyb.co.uk

**Pontypool Ski Centre**
Pontypool Leisure Park, Pontypool, Gwent
**Tel** 01495 756955

**Rhiwgoch Ski Centre**
Bronaber, Trawsfynydd, Gwynedd
**Tel** 01766 540219
staff@logcabinswales.co.uk
www.logcabins-skiwales.co.uk

**Ski Pembrey**
Pembrey Country Park, Burry Port, Llanelli, Dyfed
**Tel** 01554 834443

## SCOTLAND

**Alford Ski Centre**
Greystone Road, Alford, Aberdeenshire
**Tel** 01975 563024
keith.morris@aberdeenshire.gov.uk

**Ancrum Outdoor Education Resource Centre**
10 Ancrum Road, Dundee, Tayside
**Tel** 01382 435911
ancrum.centre@dundeecity.gov.uk

**Bearsden Ski & Board**
Stockiemuir Road, Bearsden, Glasgow
**Tel** 0141 943 1500
info@skibearsden.co.uk
www.skibearsden.co.uk

**Firpark Ski Centre**
Tillicoultry, Clackmannanshire
**Tel** 01259 751772
www.clacksleisure.co.uk/facilities/fsc.php

**Glasgow Ski & Snowboard Centre**
Bellahouston Park, 16 Dumbreck Road, Glasgow
**Tel** 0141 427 4991
info@ski-glasgow.org
www.ski-glasgow.org

**Glenmore Lodge**
Scottish National Sports Centre, Aviemore, Inverness
**Tel** 01479 861256
enquiries@glenmorelodge.org.uk
www.glenmorelodge.org.uk

**Loch Rannoch Outdoor Activity Centre**
Kinloch Rannoch, Perthshire
**Tel** 01882 632201
enquiries@lochrannoch-hotel.co.uk
www.lochrannoch-hotel.co.uk

**Midlothian Ski Centre**
Hillend, near Edinburgh
**Tel** 0131 445 4433
ski@midlothian.gov.uk
www.midlothian.gov.uk/services_home.asp

**Polmonthill Ski Centre**
Polmont, Falkirk
**Tel** 01324 503835
ski@polmonthill.freeserve.co.uk

## NORTHERN IRELAND

**Craigavon Golf and Ski Centre**
Turmoyra Lane, Silverwood, Lurgan, Co Armagh
**Tel** 028 3832 6606
golf.ski@craigavon.gov.uk
www.craigavon.gov.uk

## INSURANCE COMPANIES

**ABC Holiday Extras**
**Tel** 0870 844 4020
insurance@abcmail.co.uk
www.abctravelinsurance.co.uk

**Atlas Insurance**
**Tel** 020 7609 5000
sales@travel-insurance.co.uk
www.atlasdirect.net

**AUL**
**Tel** 01206 577770
enquiries@aul.co.uk
www.aul.co.uk

**Best Ski Insurance**
**Tel** 0870 458 2985
sales@best-ski-insurance.co.uk
www.best-ski-insurance.co.uk

**BUPA Travel Services**
**Tel** 0870 585 8585
btravint@bupa.com
www.bupa.co.uk/travel

**CGNU**
**Tel** 0800 888 112
support@norwich-union.co.uk
www.norwichunion.co.uk

**Direct Line Travel Insurance**
**Tel** 0845 246 8704
www.directline.com/travel

**Direct Travel Insurance**
**Tel** 01903 812345
info@direct-travel.co.uk
www.direct-travel.co.uk

**Douglas Cox Tyrie**
**Tel** 01708 385969

**Euclidian Insurance Services Ltd**
**Tel** 01784 484601
www.euclidian.co.uk

**Europ Assistance**
**Tel** 01444 442442
customerservices@europ-assistance.co.uk
www.europ-assistance.co.uk

**Matthew Gerard Travel Insurance Ltd**
**Tel** 01483 730900
sales@mgtis.easynet.co.uk

**P J Hayman & Company**
**Tel** 023 9241 9050
travel.insurance@pjhayman.com
www.pjhayman.com

**Preferential**
**Tel** 0870 600 7766
www.preferential.co.uk

**Primary Insurance Group**
**Tel** 0870 444 3434
customersupport@primary1.co.uk
www.primary1.co.uk

**Select Travel Insurance**
**Tel** 0870 737 0870
select@inter-group.co.uk
www.select-insurance.co.uk

**Skicoverdirect**
www.skicoverdirect.co.uk

**ski-insurance.co.uk**
**Tel** 0870 755 6101
info@ski-insurance.co.uk
www.ski-insurance.co.uk



**Skisure.com**
www.skisure-insurance.co.uk

**Snowcard Insurance Services Ltd**
**Tel** 01327 262805
enquiries@snowcard.co.uk
www.snowcard.co.uk

**Sportscover Direct Ltd**
**Tel** 0845 120 6400
contact@sportscover.co.uk
www.sportscover.co.uk

**Tag Insurance Services**
**Tel** 020 7621 2600
www.travel-general.co.uk

**Travel Insurance Direct**
**Tel** 01603 464123
info@insurance.uk.com
www.travelcover.co.uk

**WorldCover Direct**
**Tel** 0800 365 121
world.cover@gecapital.com
www.worldcover.com

**World Ski and Snowboard Association**
**Tel** 0870 757 2288
info@worldski.co.uk
www.worldski.co.uk

**Worldwide Travel Insurance Services Ltd**
**Tel** 01892 833338
sales@worldwideinsure.com
www.worldwideinsure.com

## NATIONAL TOURIST OFFICES

**Andorran Embassy**
**Tel** 020 8874 4806

**Argentine Embassy**
**Tel** 020 7318 1300
info@turismo.gov.ar
www.turismo.gov.ar

**Australian Tourist Commission**
**Tel** 09068 633235
www.australia.com

**Austrian National Tourist Office**
*Correspondence and phone calls only*
**Tel** 020 7629 0461
holiday@austria.info
www.austria.info/uk

**Canadian Tourism Commission**
**Tel** 0906 871 5000
visitcanada@dial.pipex.com
www.travelcanada.ca

**Chile – Consulate General**
**Tel** 020 7580 1023
cglonduk@congechileuk.demon.co.uk
www.echileuk.demon.co.uk

**Czech Tourist Authority**
**Tel** 09063 640641
www.visitczechia.cz

**Finnish Tourist Board**
**Tel** 020 7365 2512
finlandinfo.lon@mek.fi
www.finland-tourism.com

**French Government Tourist Office**
**Tel** 09068 244123
info@mdlf.co.uk
www.franceguide.com

**German National Tourist Office**
**Tel** 020 7317 0908
gntolon@d-z-t.com
www.germany-tourism.co.uk

**Italian State Tourist Office**
**Tel** 020 7399 3562
italy@italiantouristboard.co.uk
www.enit.it

**Japan National Tourist Organisation**
**Tel** 020 7734 9638
info@jnto.co.uk
www.seejapan.co.uk

**Norwegian Tourist Board**
**Tel** 0906 302 2003
www.visitnorway.com

**Romanian Tourist Office**
**Tel** 020 7224 3692
www.romaniatourism.com

**Scottish Tourist Board**
ski.visitscotland.com

**Slovenian Tourist Office**
**Tel** 0870 225 5305
info@slovenian-tourism.co.uk
www.slovenia-tourism.si

**Spanish Tourist Office**
**Tel** 020 7486 8077
info.londres@tourspain.es
www.tourspain.co.uk

**Swedish Travel and Tourism Council**
**Tel** 00800 3080 3080
info@swetourism.org.uk
www.visit-sweden.com

**Switzerland Tourism**
**Tel** 00800 100 200 30
info.uk@switzerland.com
www.MySwitzerland.com

**Tourism New Zealand**
**Tel** 09050 60 60 60
www.purenz.com

**Turkish Tourist Board**
**Tel** 020 7629 7771
info@gototurkey.co.uk
www.gototurkey.co.uk

**Visit USA Association**
**Tel** 09069 101020
www.visitusa.org.uk

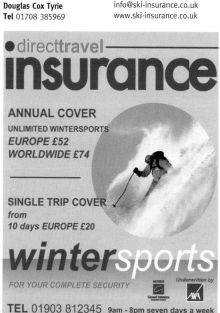

## RAILWAYS

**Deutsche Bahn**
**Tel** 0870 243 5363
sales@deutsche-bahn.co.uk
www.deutsche-bahn.co.uk

**Eurostar**
**Tel** 0870 518 6186
www.eurostar.com

**Rail Europe**
**Tel** 08705 848 848
reservations@raileurope.co.uk
www.raileurope.co.uk

**Swiss Federal Railways**
**Tel** 00800 100 200 30
(Switzerland Tourism)
info.uk@switzerland.com
www.rail.ch

## RETAILERS

### SOUTH-WEST ENGLAND

**Christchurch Ski Centre**
Matchams Lane, Hurn, Christchurch, Dorset
**Tel** 01202 499155
www.christchurch-skicentre.com

**Devon Ski Centre**
Oak Place, Newton Abbot, Devon
**Tel** 01626 351278
www.devonski.co.uk

**Kidski**
**Tel** 01202 631222
help@kidski.co.uk
www.kidski.co.uk

**Noahs Ark**
London Road, Chalford, Stroud, Gloucestershire
**Tel** 01453 884738
www.noahsark.co.uk

**Penrose Outdoors**
Town Quay, Truro, Cornwall
**Tel** 01872 272116
www.penroseoutdoors.co.uk

**Skate and Ski**
104 High Street, Staple Hill, Bristol
**Tel** 0117 970 1356

**Snow & Rock**
Units 1-3 Shield Retail Centre, Link Road, Filton, Bristol
**Tel** 0845 100 1017
www.snowandrock.com

**Team Ski**
37 High East Street, Dorchester, Dorset
**Tel** 01305 268035
www.teamski.co.uk

**Westsports**
Market House, Marlborough Rd, Old Town, Swindon
**Tel** 01793 532588
www.skishops.co.uk

### SOUTH-EAST ENGLAND

**Activ (Folkestone)**
145 Sandgate Road, Folkestone, Kent
**Tel** 01303 240110
www.activfolkestone.com

**Alpine Room**
71-73 Main Road, Danbury, Essex
**Tel** 01245 223563
www.alpineroom.co.uk

**Captain's Cabin**
93 High Street, Chatham, Kent
**Tel** 01634 819777
www.captainscabin.com



**Captain's Cabin**
14 St George's Walk, Croydon
**Tel** 020 8680 6968
www.captainscabin.com

**Captain's Cabin**
19 Wincheap, Canterbury, Kent
**Tel** 01227 457906
www.captainscabin.com

**John Pollock**
157 High Road, Loughton, Essex
**Tel** 020 8508 6626
www.johnpollock.co.uk

**John Pollock**
67 High Street, Barnet
**Tel** 020 8440 3994
www.johnpollock.co.uk

**Outdoor Life**
3 High Street, Old Town, Eastbourne, East Sussex
**Tel** 01323 725372

**Snow Boats**
8-10 The Street, Wrecclesham, Farnham, Surrey
**Tel** 01252 715169
www.snowboats.co.uk

**Snow & Rock**
188 Kensington High Street, London
**Tel** 0845 100 1011
www.snowandrock.com

**Snow & Rock**
4 Mercer Street, Covent Garden, London
**Tel** 0845 100 1018
www.snowandrock.com

**Snow & Rock**
150 Holborn, Corner of Grays Inn Road, London
**Tel** 0845 100 1013
www.snowandrock.com

**Snow & Rock**
99 Fordwater Road, Chertsey
**Tel** 0845 100 1016
www.snowandrock.com

**Snow & Rock**
The Boardwalk, Port Solent, Portsmouth, Hampshire
**Tel** 0845 100 1019
www.snowandrock.co.uk

**Snow Togs**
431 Millbrook Road, Southampton, Hampshire
**Tel** 023 8077 3925
www.skishops.co.uk

## MIDDLE ENGLAND

**Active Outdoor & Ski**
28 Castle Quay, Banbury, Oxfordshire
**Tel** 01295 273700
www.aosbanbury.com

**Beans**
86 Sheep Street, Bicester, Oxfordshire
**Tel** 01869 246451
www.beansonline.co.uk

**BestBuys**
Nene Court, 27-31 The Embankment, Wellingborough, Northamptonshire
**Tel** 01933 272699
www.best-buys.co.uk

**Force**
26 Bakers Lane, Lichfield, Staffordshire
**Tel** 01543 411249
www.skiforce.co.uk

**Force**
Guildhall Shopping Centre, Stafford
**Tel** 01785 225737
www.skiforce.co.uk

**Fox's**
1 London Road, Amersham
**Tel** 01494 431431
www.foxsoutdoor.co.uk

**Lockwoods Ski Shop**
125-129 Rugby Road, Leamington Spa, Warwickshire
**Tel** 01926 339388
www.lockwoods.com

**Mountain Fever**
25 Brunswick Street, Hanley, Stoke-on-Trent
**Tel** 01782 266137
www.mountainfever.co.uk

**Noahs Ark**
London Road, Chalford, Stroud, Gloucestershire
**Tel** 01453 884738
www.noahsark.co.uk

**Ski West**
Breadstone Business Park, Breadstone, Nr Berkeley, Glos
**Tel** 01453 519084
www.ski-west.co.uk

**Snow & Rock**
14 Priory Queensway, Birmingham
**Tel** 0845 100 1012
www.snowandrock.com

**Sporting Triangle**
18 West Street, Hereford
**Tel** 01432 271500
www.sportingtriangle.com

**Two Seasons**
39 Pelham Street, Nottingham
**Tel** 0115 950 1333
www.twoseasons.co.uk

**Two Seasons**
229-231 Wellingborough Road, Northampton, Northamptonshire
**Tel** 01604 627377
www.twoseasons.co.uk

**Two Seasons**
15 Pump Street, Worcester
**Tel** 01905 731144
www.twoseasons.co.uk

**Two Seasons**
64 Lower Precinct, Coventry
**Tel** 024 7663 0020
www.twoseasons.co.uk

**Two Seasons**
32-34 Mill Lane, Solihull
www.twoseasons.co.uk

## EASTERN ENGLAND

**Snow & Rock**
Hemel Ski Centre, St Albans Hill, Hemel Hempstead, Hertfordshire
**Tel** 0845 100 1014
www.snowandrock.com

**SnowFit**
2 Cucumber Lane, Brundall, Norwich
**Tel** 01603 716655
www.snowfit.co.uk

**Snowsun**
Suffolk Ski Centre, Bourne Hill, Wherstead, Ipswich, Suffolk
**Tel** 01473 602601
www.snowsun.com

**Top Gear**
3/5 Broadway, Leigh on Sea, Essex
**Tel** 01702 713165
www.skitopgear.co.uk

**Two Seasons**
34 Chesterton Road, Cambridge
**Tel** 01223 356207
www.twoseasons.co.uk

## NORTHERN ENGLAND

**BAC Outdoor Leisure**
Central Hall, Coronation Street, Elland, Halifax, West Yorkshire
**Tel** 01422 371146
www.bac-e.com

**Freetime**
1-2 Market Street, Carlisle, Cumbria
**Tel** 01228 598210
www.freetime1.co.uk

**Glide & Slide**
5/7 Station Road, Otley
**Tel** 01943 461136
www.glideslide.co.uk

**Mayhem Surf Snow Skate**
7 Jubbergate, York
**Tel** 01904 655062
www.mayhemboardstore.com

**Severn Sports / Boardworx**
80 Town Street, Armley, Leeds, West Yorkshire
**Tel** 0113 279 1618
www.severnsports.co.uk

**Snow & Rock**
Sheffield Ski Centre, Vale Road, Parkwood Springs, Sheffield
**Tel** 0845 100 1015
www.snowandrock.com

**Snow & Rock**
Princess Parkway, Princess Park, Didsbury, Manchester
**Tel** 0845 100 1020
www.snowandrock.com

## SCOTLAND

**Craigdon Mountain Sports**
61-65 High Street, Inverurie, Highland
**Tel** 01467 625855
www.craigdonmountainsports.com

**Craigdon Mountain Sports**
5 St Andrew's Street, Aberdeen
**Tel** 01224 624333
www.craigdonmountainsports.com

**Craigdon Mountain Sports**
25-29 Kinnoull Street, Perth
**Tel** 01738 831006
www.craigdonmountainsports.com

## NORTHERN IRELAND

**Macski**
140 Lisburn Road, Belfast
**Tel** 028 9066 5525
www.macski.com

## REPUBLIC OF IRELAND

**The Great Outdoors**
Chatham Street, Dublin 2, Ireland
**Tel** 00 353 1679 4293
www.greatoutdoors.ie

## SKI/BOARDING ORGANISATIONS

**British Association of Snowsport Instructors (BASI)**
**Tel** 01479 861717
basi@basi.org.uk
www.basi.org.uk

**British Ski and Snowboard Federation**
**Tel** 0131 445 7676
info@snowsportgb.com
www.bssf.co.uk

**British Ski Club for the Disabled**
BSCDWeb@hotmail.com
www.bscd.org.uk

**British Snowboard Association**
**Tel** 0131 445 2428
info@thebsa.org
www.thebsa.org

**English Ski Council**
**Tel** 0121 501 2314
admin@englishski.org
www.englishski.org

**Ski Club of Great Britain**
**Tel** 0845 458 0780
skiers@skiclub.co.uk
www.skiclub.co.uk

**Snowsport Scotland**
**Tel** 0131 445 4151
info@snowsportscotland.org
www.snsc.demon.co.uk

**Snowsport Wales**
**Tel** 029 2056 1904
admin.snowsportwales@virgin.net
www.snowsportwales.net

**The Uphill Ski Club**
*Ski organisation and ski school for people with disabilities*
**Tel** 01479 861272
info@uphillskiclub.co.uk
www.uphillskiclub.co.uk

**World Ski and Snowboard Association**
**Tel** 0870 757 2288
info@worldski.co.uk
www.worldski.co.uk

## SKI TRAVEL AGENTS

**Alpine Answers**
**Tel** 020 8871 4656
ski@alpineanswers.co.uk
www.alpineanswers.co.uk

**Avant-ski**
**Tel** 0191 285 8141
sales@avant-ski.com
www.avant-ski.com

**Iglu.com**
**Tel** 020 8542 6658
enquiries@iglu.com
www.iglu.com

**Independent Ski Links**
**Tel** 01964 533905
info@ski-links.com
www.ski-links.com

**Kwik Ski**
**Tel** 0870 499 3114
skireservations@kwikski.co.uk
www.kwik-ski.co.uk

**Let's Go Travel**
**Tel** 0870 241 2095

**Ski & Surf**
**Tel** 020 8958 2418
janm@skisurf.com
www.skisurf.com

**Skiers Travel**
**Tel** 0870 010 0032
sales@skiers-travel.co.uk
www.skiers-travel.co.uk

**Ski Expectations**
**Tel** 01799 531888
ski.expectations@virgin.net

**Ski Line**
**Tel** 020 8313 3999
angus@skiline.co.uk
www.skiline.co.uk

**Ski McNeill**
**Tel** 0870 600 1359
contact@skimcneill.com
www.skimcneill.com

**Skis and Tees**
**Tel** 0870 240 7416
enquiries@skisandtees.co.uk
www.skisandtees.co.uk

**Ski Solutions**
*A La Carte department: 020 7471 7777*
**Tel** 020 7471 7700
www.skisolutions.com

**Ski Tracer**
**Tel** 0870 420 5782
sales@skitracer.com
www.skitracer.com

**Ski Travel Centre**
**Tel** 0141 649 9696
snow@skitravelcentre.com
www.ski-travel-centre.co.uk

**Snow Finders**
**Tel** 01858 466888
sales@snowfinders.com
www.snowfinders.com

**Snow Line**
**Tel** 0870 333 0064
sales@snow-line.co.uk
www.snow-line.co.uk

# Resort index / directory

**This is an index to the resort chapters in the book; you'll find page references for about 400 resorts described elsewhere. But you'll also find brief descriptions here of another 700 resorts, most of them much smaller than those we've covered in full, but often still worth a short visit. We also list the companies offering package holidays to each resort. To get in touch with one of these tour operators, look them up in the list starting on page 664.**

## Key

🚡 *Lifts*
⛷ *Pistes*
☒ *UK tour operators*

**49 Degrees North** USA
Inland area with best snow in Washington State, including 120-acre bowl reserved for powder weekends.
*1195m; slopes 1195–1760m*
🚡 *5* ⛷ *780 acres*

**Abetone** Italy
Resort in the exposed Appennines, less than two hours from Florence and Pisa.
*1390m; slopes 1390–1900m*
🚡 *25* ⛷ *50km*
☒ *Alpine Tours*

**Abtenau** Austria
Sizeable village in Dachstein-West region near Salzburg, on large plain ideal for cross-country.
*710m; slopes 710–1260m*
🚡 *6* ⛷ *10km*

**Achenkirch** Austria
Unspoilt, low-altitude Tirolean village close to Niederau and Alpbach. Beautiful setting overlooking a lake.
*930m; slopes 930–1800m*
🚡 *7* ⛷ *25km*
☒ *Ramblers Holidays*

**Adelboden** 502
☒ *Interhome, Kuoni, Made to Measure Holidays, Swiss Travel Service*

**Les Aillons** France
Traditional village near Chambéry. Nicely sheltered slopes.
*1000m; slopes 1000–1900m*
🚡 *22* ⛷ *40km*

**Alagna** 406
Small resort on the western fringe of Monterosa Ski area.
☒ *Alpine Answers, Momentum Ski, Mountain Tracks, Ski FreshTracks, Ski Weekend*

**Alba** Italy
Picturesque Trentino village with a small, quiet area; access to the Sella Ronda at nearby Canazei.
*1515m; slopes 1515–2440m*
🚡 *5* ⛷ *10km*

**Albiez-Montrond** France
Authentic old French village in Maurienne valley with panoramic views. Own easy slopes and close to other ski areas.
*1500m; slopes 1500–2200m*
🚡 *12* ⛷ *40km*
☒ *Lagrange Holidays*

**Alleghe** Italy
Dolomite village near Cortina in a pretty lakeside setting close to numerous areas.
*980m*
🚡 *24* ⛷ *80km*

**Les Allues** 282
Rustic village on the road up to Méribel, close to the mid-station of the gondola up from Brides-les-Bains.

**Alpbach** 109
☒ *Crystal, Inghams, Interhome, Made to Measure Holidays*

**Alpe-d'Huez** 204
☒ *Airtours, Alpine Answers, Avant-ski, Chalet World, Chalets 'Unlimited', Club Med, Crystal, Directski.com, Erna Low, First Choice Ski, French Freedom Holidays, Independent Ski Links, Inghams, Interhome, La Source, Lagrange Holidays, Made to Measure Holidays, Mark Warner, Neilson, Panorama Holidays, Ski Arrangements, Ski Expectations, Ski France, Ski FreshTracks, Ski Independence, Ski Leisure Direction, Ski Life, Ski Line, Ski Miquel, Ski Supreme, Skitopia, Skiworld, Thomson, Tops Ski Chalets and Club Hotels*

**Alpe-du-Grand-Serre** France
Tiny resort near Alpe-d'Huez and Les Deux-Alpes. Good for bad-weather days.
*1400m; slopes 1400–2200m*
🚡 *20* ⛷ *55km*

**Alpendorf** 196
Outpost of St Johann im Pongau, at one end of an extensive three-valley lift network linking via Wagrain to Flachau – all part of the Salzburger Sportwelt area.

**Alpine Meadows** 520
☒ *Ski The American Dream*

**Alps** Korea
Korea's most northerly, snow-reliable resort, about five hours from Seoul. 🚡 5

**Alta** 559
☒ *Ski All America, Ski Independence, Ski The American Dream*

**Alta Badia** 415

**Altenmarkt** Austria
Unspoiled village, well placed just off the Salzburg-Villach autobahn for numerous resorts including snow-sure Obertauern and those in the Salzburger Sportwelt.
*855m*
☒ *Made to Measure Holidays, Sloping Off*

**Alto Campoo** Spain
Barren, desolate place with undistinguished slopes, but with magnificent wilderness views.
*1650m; slopes 1650–2170m* 🚡 *11*

**Alt St Johann** Switzerland
Old cross-country village with Alpine slopes connecting into Unterwasser area near Liechtenstein.
*900m; slopes 900–2260m*
🚡 *21* ⛷ *50km*

**Alyeska** USA
Alaskan area 60km/37 miles from Anchorage, with luxury hotel. 'Spectacular views – a very special place,' enthuses a 2004 visitor.
*75m; slopes 75–1200m*
🚡 *9* ⛷ *785 acres*
☒ *Frontier Ski, Inghams, Ski All America*

**Aminona** 445
Purpose-built resort on the eastern side of the Crans-Montana network.
☒ *Lagrange Holidays*

**Andalo** 427
Trentino village not far from Madonna.
☒ *Equity Ski, Rocketski, Sloping Off*

**Andermatt** 439
☒ *Made to Measure Holidays, Ski FreshTracks, Ski Weekend*

**Andorra la Vella** 90
☒ *Lagrange Holidays*

**Angel Fire** USA
Intermediate area near Taos, New Mexico. Height usually ensures good snow.
*2620m; slopes 2620–3255m*
🚡 *5* ⛷ *455 acres*

**Les Angles** France
Attractive resort with one of the best ski areas in the Pyrenees. Pretty, tree-lined, mostly easy skiing.
*1650m; slopes 1650–2400m*
🚡 *24* ⛷ *40km*
☒ *Lagrange Holidays, Pyrenees Ski Experience*

**Annaberg-Lungötz** Austria
Peaceful village in a pretty setting, sharing a sizeable area with Gosau. Close to Filzmoos.
*775m; slopes 775–1620m*
🚡 *33* ⛷ *65km*

**Anzère** Switzerland
Sympathetically designed modern resort on a sunny balcony near Crans-Montana.
*1500m; slopes 1500–2460m*
🚡 *13* ⛷ *40km*
☒ *Interhome, Lagrange Holidays*

**Aosta** Italy
Historic valley town with gondola up to the mountain resort of Pila; it's an 18-minute ride to the slopes. Aosta is a real working town with people in suits rather than skiwear. It has good-value accommodation, a lot more bars/restaurants than Pila, and a lovely traffic-free centre. Other resorts in the Aosta valley are within a day trip and covered by the lift pass.
*1800m; slopes 1550–2710m*
🚡 *13* ⛷ *70km*
☒ *Crystal*

**Apex** Canada
Small, friendly, rather isolated resort, well worth stopping off here for a night or two on a tour of western BC resorts. Modern, purpose-built slope-side base with some accommodation and a few bars and restaurants, including the atmospheric Gunbarrel Saloon. The Sheeprock Lodge is one of the nicest B&Bs we've stayed in – great rooms with big wooden beds (ask for Room 1), comfy sitting room with open fire and panoramic view of slopes, hot-tub, friendly owners. The slopes suit confident intermediates upwards best. There are some steep, narrow double-black-diamond runs in the trees, wonderful single-diamond Wildside glades, and great cruising blues, which adventurous intermediates will love but more timid ones might freeze on. There are also excellent beginner slopes and runs to progress to. There's a (unique as far as we know) 1km/0.5 mile ice-skating trail through the woods, floodlit at night.
*1575m; slopes 1575–2180m*
🚡 *4* ⛷ *1,112 acres*
☒ *AmeriCan Ski, Frontier Ski, Ski Safari*

**Aprica** Italy
Ugly, straggling village between Lake Como and the Brenta Dolomites, with bland slopes and limited facilities.
*1180m; slopes 1180–2310m*
*24 40km*
✉ *Thomson*

**Arabba** 415
✉ *Independent Ski Links, Inghams, Momentum Ski, Neilson, Ski Yogi*

**Aragnouet-Piau** France
Purpose-built mid-mountain satellite of St-Lary, best suited to families, beginners and early intermediates.
*1850m; slopes 1420–2500m*
*32 80km*

**Arapahoe Basin** USA
Small, exceptionally high day-skiing area near Keystone with excellent snowfall record and very long season. Good mix of open and wooded runs of every standard served by lifts, plus serious steeps reached by hiking.
*3285m; slopes 3285–3795m*
*6 490 acres*
✉ *Ski The American Dream*

**Arcalis** 90

**Les Arcs** 213
✉ *Airtours, Alpine Answers, Alpine Events, Avant-ski, Chalet World, Chalets 'Unlimited', Chez Jay Ski Chalets, Club Med, Crystal, Directski.com, Equity Ski, Erna Low, Esprit Ski, First Choice Ski, Independent Ski Links, Inghams, Interhome, Lagrange Holidays, Made to Measure Holidays, Neilson, Optimum Ski, Rocketski, Ski Activity, Ski Amis, Ski Arrangements, Ski Beat, Ski FreshTracks, Ski Independence, Ski Leisure Direction, Ski Life, Ski Line, Ski Olympic, Ski Supreme, Skiworld, Snow Monkey Chalets, Thomson, Total, Vanilla Ski*

**Ardent** 223
Quiet hamlet with quick access to Avoriaz and, more excitingly, Châtel's Linga sector.
✉ *Chalet Company, Family Ski Company*

**Åre** 650
✉ *Improve Your Skiing, Neilson*

**Arêches-Beaufort** France
Secluded little village 25km/16 miles from Albertville, with mostly intermediate terrain on two areas 3km/2 miles apart. The slopes of both Les Saisies and Les Contamines are less than 25km/15 miles away.
*1050m; slopes 1050–2300m*
*15 50km*
✉ *Lagrange Holidays*

**Argentière** 227
Unremarkable old village beneath a remarkable mountain, Chamonix's Grands Montets.
✉ *Alpine Answers, AmeriCan Ski, Bigfoot Travel, Board and Lodge, Chalets 'Unlimited', Collineige, Erna Low, Handmade Holidays, Independent Ski Links, Interhome, Lagrange Holidays, McNab Mountain Sports, Peak Retreats, Ski Arrangements, Ski FreshTracks, Ski Hillwood, Ski Independence, Ski Life, Ski Scott James, Ski Weekend, White Roc*

**Arinsal** 94
✉ *Airtours, Chalets 'Unlimited', Crystal, Directski.com, First Choice Ski, Inghams, Neilson, Panorama Holidays, Thomson*

**Arnoldstein/Dreiländereck** Austria
One of several little areas overlooking the town of Villach.
*680m; slopes 680–1455m*
*7 10km*

**Arolla** Switzerland
Tiny village in pretty riverside setting south of Sion. Main attraction is heli-skiing. Wonderful descents from 3800m/12,470ft. 'Good for a day,' says a 2004 reporter.
*2005m; slopes 2005–2890m*
*5 47km*

**Arosa** 441
✉ *Alpine Events, Interhome, Kuoni, Made to Measure Holidays, Momentum Ski, Powder Byrne, Ski Weekend, Swiss Travel Service, Switzerland Travel Centre, White Roc*

**Artesina** Italy
Purpose-built Piedmont resort south of Turin, lacking character and atmosphere. Part of Mondolé ski area with Prato Nevoso.
*1300m; slopes 1320–2100m*
*25 90km*

**Asiago** Italy
Sizeable resort close to Verona, but at low altitude and with limited vertical.
*1000m; slopes 1000–1380m 17*
✉ *Inntravel*

**Aspen/Snowmass** 523
✉ *Alpine Answers, AmeriCan Ski, American Ski Classics, Chalet World, Chalets 'Unlimited', Crystal, Erna Low, Independent Ski Links, Lotus Supertravel, Made to Measure Holidays, Momentum Ski, Ski Activity, Ski All America, Ski Expectations, Ski FreshTracks, Ski Independence, Ski Line, Ski Safari, Ski The American Dream, Skiworld, Trailfinders, United Vacations*

**Attitash** USA
One of the biggest ski areas in eastern US. Uncrowded slopes. Lodging in nearby North Conway, and other New Hampshire areas close by.
*slopes 180–715m*
*12 280 acres*
✉ *AmeriCan Ski*

**Auffach** 197
Unexceptional village with the longest, highest, sunniest runs in the Wildschönau area.

**Auris-en-Oisans** 204
Quiet hamlet with local ski area linked across the valley to Alpe-d'Huez.
✉ *Lagrange Holidays*

**Auron** France
Pleasant, family-oriented village (currently undergoing considerable development) with varied, sheltered, intermediate slopes; a stark contrast to nearby Isola 2000. Readers in 2003 commented on the abundance of mountain restaurants, the long queue at the base station in the morning and the friendliness of the resort staff.
*1600m; slopes 1165–2450m*
*26 130km*
✉ *Lagrange Holidays, Ski Life*

**Auronzo di Cadore** Italy
Sizeable village that's a cheaper base for visiting Cortina. Its own slopes are of negligible interest.
*865m; slopes 865–1585m*
*5 7km*

**Aussois** France
One of many rustic working villages near Modane in the Maurienne valley.
*1500m; slopes 1500–2750m*
*11 50km*
✉ *AmeriCan Ski, Peak Retreats*

**Autrans** France
Major cross-country village, close to Grenoble.
*1050m; slopes 1050–1710m*
*15 18km*
✉ *Lagrange Holidays*

**Avon** USA
Small town only a couple of miles from Beaver Creek. Inexpensive base from which to ski Beaver Creek, Vail and Breckenridge.
✉ *AmeriCan Ski, Ski Line*

**Avoriaz 1800** 223
✉ *Airtours, Chalets 'Unlimited', Club Med, Crystal, Directski.com, Erna Low, First Choice Ski, French Freedom Holidays, Independent Ski Links, Lagrange Holidays, Made to Measure Holidays, Neilson, Ski Arrangements, Ski Independence, Ski Leisure Direction, Ski Life, Ski Supreme, Thomson, White Roc*

**Axamer Lizum** 122
✉ *Crystal, Thomson*

**Axams** 122
Quiet village in Innsbruck area, below Axamer Lizum ski area.
✉ *Lagrange Holidays*

**Ax-les-Thermes** France
Sizeable spa village near Font-Romeu and Andorra.
*1400m; slopes 1400–2400m*
*17 75km*

**Bad Gastein** 111
✉ *Crystal, First Choice Ski, Made to Measure Holidays, Ski Line, Ski Miquel, Ski Wild*

**Badger Pass** USA
Base for 350 miles of superb backcountry touring in Yosemite National Park. Spectacular views.
*2195m; slopes 2195–2435m*
*5 90 acres*

**Bad Hofgastein** 111
Relaxed and spacious spa resort at the foot of the most attractive ski area in the Gastein Valley.
✉ *Crystal, First Choice Ski, Inghams, Made to Measure Holidays, Ski Line, Ski Wild*

**Bad Kleinkirchheim** 195
✉ *Alpine Tours, Crystal, Equity Ski, Rocketski, Sloping Off, Slovenija Pursuits*

**Banff** 596
✉ *Airtours, Alpine Answers, AmeriCan Ski, American Ski Classics, Canadian Powder Tours, Crystal, Equity Ski, First Choice Ski, Frontier Ski, Independent Ski Links, Inghams, Lotus Supertravel, Made to Measure Holidays, Neilson, Ski Activity, Ski All America, Ski FreshTracks, Ski Independence, Ski Line, Ski Safari, Ski The American Dream, Skiworld, Thomson, Trailfinders, United Vacations, Virgin Snow*

**Bansko** 638
✉ *Balkan Holidays, Neilson*

**Baqueira-Beret** 636
✉ *Ski Miquel*

**Barboleuse** 485
Quiet base from which to ski the Villars and Les Diablerets slopes.

**Bardonecchia** 432
✉ *Alpine Answers, Crystal, First Choice Ski, Neilson, Rocketski, Ski Arrangements, Thomson*

**Barèges** 372
✉ *Borderline, Lagrange Holidays*

**Les Barzettes** 445
Smaller base along the road from Crans-Montana, with a gondola up to the main section of slopes.

**Bear Mountain** USA
Southern California's main area, in the beautiful San Bernardino National Forest region. Full snowmaking.
*slopes 2170–2685m*
*12 195 acres*

**Bears Town** Korea
Modern resort with runs cut out of thick forest. Biggest resort near Seoul (only an hour's drive), so it can get very crowded. 8

**Beaulard** Italy
Little place just off the road between Sauze d'Oulx and Bardonecchia.
*1215m; slopes 1215–2120m*
*6 20km*

**Beaver Creek** 529
✉ *AmeriCan Ski, Crystal, Elegant Resorts, Made to Measure Holidays, Ski Activity, Ski All America, Ski Independence, Ski Line, Ski Safari, Ski The American Dream, Ski Wild, United Vacations, Virgin Snow*

**Beaver Mountain** USA
Small Utah area north of Salt Lake City, too far from Park City for a day trip.
*2195m; slopes 2195–2680m*
*3 525 acres*

**Beitostølen** Norway
Small family resort in southern Norway (east of Bergen), with lots of cross-country in the region.
*900m*
*9 25km*

**Belleayre Mountain** USA
State-owned resort near Albany, New York State. Cheap prices but old lifts and short runs.
*775m; slopes 775–1015m*
*7 170 acres*

**Belle-Plagne** 305
High-altitude satellite of La Plagne built in a pleasing neo-Savoyard style.

**Ben Lomond** Australia
Small intermediate/beginner area in Ben Lomond National Park, Tasmania, 260km/162 miles from Hobart.
*1450m; slopes 1460–1570m*
*6 14 ha*

**Berchtesgaden** Germany
Pleasant old town close to Salzburg, known for its Nordic skiing but with several little Alpine areas nearby.
*550m*
✉ *Moswin Tours*

**Bergün** Switzerland
Traditional, quiet, unspoiled, virtually traffic-free little family resort on the rail route between Davos and St Moritz. 5km/2.5 mile toboggan run.
*1375m; slopes 1400–2550m*
*5 25km*

**Berthoud Pass** 552
Powder heaven on the drive to Winter Park.

**Berwang** Austria
Unspoiled village nestling in a spacious valley, close to Lermoos.
*1335m; slopes 1335–1740m*
*12 40km*

**Bessans** France
Old cross-country village near Modane. Well placed for touring Maurienne valley resorts such as Val-Cenis.
*1710m; slopes 1740–2200m*
*4 5km*

**Besse** France
Charming old village built out of lava, with purpose-built slope-side satellite Super-Besse. Beautiful extinct-volcano scenery.
*1050m; slopes 1300–1850m*
*22 45km*
✉ *Lagrange Holidays*

**Bethel** USA
Pleasant, historic town very close to Sunday River, Maine. Attractive alternative to staying in the slope-side resort.

**Le Bettex** 274
Small base at the gondola mid-station above St-Gervais, with links to the Megève network.

**Bettmeralp** Switzerland
Central village of the sizeable Aletsch area near Brig, perched high above the Rhône valley, amid spectacular glacial scenery. Reached by cable-cars from the valley.
*1955m; slopes 1900–2900m*
*32 90km*

**Beuil-les-Launes** France
Alpes-Maritimes resort closest to Nice. Shares area with Valberg.
*1400m; slopes 1400–2100m*
*26 90km*

**Bezau** Austria
Virtually no slopes of its own, but the main village lies in the low Bregenzerwald region north-west of Lech.
*650m; slopes 1210–1650m 2*
✉ *Inntravel*

**Biberwier** Austria
Limited little village with a small area of its own. Best as a quiet base from which to access the Zugspitz area.
*1000m; slopes 1000–1790m*
*6 8km*

**Bichlbach** Austria
Smallest of the Zugspitz villages with very limited slopes of its own. Suitable as an unspoiled base for visiting the rest of the area.
*1070m; slopes 1070–1620m*
*3 7km*

**Bielmonte** Italy
Popular with day-trippers from Milan. Worthwhile on a bad-weather day.
*1200m; slopes 1200–1620m*
*13 20km*

**Big Mountain** USA
At least one of our reporters (who now makes an annual pilgrimage) rates this place, close to the Canadian border and even closer to Montana's Glacier National Park, as simply the best. Big is one thing that BM is not, with a modest base altitude, a middling vertical and a mere dozen lifts. But its 3,000 acres embrace a wide range of slopes that are not only impressively snowy but also blissfully devoid of people. There's easy cruising in dense forest around the base area, and steeper stuff higher up on 'gladed' slopes – mainly single diamond but with double-diamond runs dotted around. There is accommodation at the base, and more in the small town of Whitefish, a few miles away. Our principal reporter, a man, reckons Ladies' Night at the Great Northern bar is something not to be missed.
*1370m; slopes 1370–2135m*
*10 3,000 acres*
✉ *AmeriCan Ski, Inghams, Ski Activity, Ski All America, Ski Independence*

**Big Powderhorn** USA
Area with the most 'resort' facilities in south Lake Superior region – and the highest lift capacity too. The area suffers from winds.
*370m; slopes 370–560m*
*10 250 acres*

**Big Sky** 561
✉ *AmeriCan Ski, American Ski Classics, Ski All America, Ski Independence, Ski The American Dream*

**Big White** 602
✉ *AmeriCan Ski, Crystal, Frontier Ski, Independent Ski Links, Made to Measure Holidays, Ski Activity, Ski All America, Ski FreshTracks, Ski Independence, Ski Line, Ski Safari, Ski The American Dream*

**Bischofshofen** Austria
Working town and mountain resort near St Johann im Pongau, with very limited local runs and the main slopes starting nearby at Muhlbach.
*545m; slopes 545–1000m*
*1 2km*

**Bivio** Switzerland
Quiet village near St Moritz with easy slopes opened up by a few lifts.
*1775m; slopes 1780–2600m*
*4 40km*

**Bizau** Austria
One of two main areas in the low Bregenzerwald region north-west of Lech.
*680m; slopes 680–1700m*
*6 24km*

**Björkliden** 649

**Björnrike** 649

**Blackcomb** 621
Smaller and quieter than neighbouring Whistler, conveniently sited at the bottom of its own mountain.
✉ *Frontier Ski*

**Black Mountain** USA
New Hampshire area with lodging in nearby Jackson.
*4 143 acres*

**Blatten** Switzerland
Mountainside hamlet above Naters, beside the Rhône near Brig. Small but tall area in stunning glacial scenery, with larger Aletsch area nearby.
*1320m; slopes 1320–3100m*
*9 60km*

**Bled** 642
✉ *Balkan Holidays, Crystal, Slovenija Pursuits, Thomson*

**Blue Cow** 653

**Blue Mountain** Canada
Largest area in Ontario, with glorious views of Lake Huron. High-capacity lift system and 100% snowmaking.
*230m; slopes 230–450m*
*15 275 acres*

**Blue River** Canada
Base of world-famous Mike Wiegele heli-ski operation in Cariboo and Monashee mountains.

**Bluewood** USA
Particularly remote area even by American north-west standards. Worth a visit if you're in Walla Walla.
*1355m; slopes 1355–1725m*
*3 530 acres*

**Bogus Basin** USA
Sizeable area overlooking Idaho's attractive, interesting capital, Boise.
*1760m; slopes 1760–2310m*
*8 2,600 acres*

**Bohinj** 642
✉ *Balkan Holidays, Crystal, Slovenija Pursuits, Thomson*

**Bois-d'Amont** France
One of four resorts that make up Les Rousses area in Jura region.
*1050m; slopes 1120–1680m*
*40 40km*
✉ *Lagrange Holidays*

**Bolognola** Italy
Tiny area in Macerata region near the Adriatic Riviera.
*1070m; slopes 1070–1845m*
*7 5km*

**Bolton Valley** USA
Resort near Stowe with mostly intermediate slopes.
*465m; slopes 465–960m*
*6 155 acres*

**Le Bonhomme** France
One of several areas with snowmakers near Strasbourg.
*830m; slopes 830–1235m*
*9 12km*

**Bonneval-sur-Arc** France
Unspoiled, remote old village in the Haute Maurienne valley with many of its slopes at high altitude. The pass to neighbouring Val-d'Isère is closed in winter.
*1800m; slopes 1800–3000m*
*10 25km*

**Bons** 257
Rustic, unspoiled old hamlet linked to Les Deux-Alpes' skiing, conveniently placed down the valley for day trips to La Grave, Alpe-d'Huez and Serre-Chevalier.

**Boreal** USA
Closest area to north Lake Tahoe town, Truckee. Limited slopes, best for novices.
*2195m; slopes 2195–2375m*
*9 380 acres*

**Bormio** 383
✉ *Equity Ski, Interhome, Rocketski, Ski Arrangements, Sloping Off*

**Borovets** 638
✉ *Airtours, Balkan Holidays, Crystal, First Choice Ski, Inghams, Neilson, Ski Balkantours, Thomson*

**Bosco Chiesanuova** Italy
Weekend day-trippers' place near Verona. A long drive from any other resort.
*1105m; slopes 1105–1805m*
*18 20km*

**Les Bottieres** 335

**La Bourboule** France
Spa and cross-country village with the Alpine slopes of Le Mont-Dore nearby. Spectacular extinct-volcano scenery.
*850m; slopes 1050–1850m*
*41 80km*
✉ *Lagrange Holidays*

**Bourg-d'Oisans** France
Pleasant valley town on main Grenoble-Briançon road. Cheap base for visits to Alpe-d'Huez and Les Deux-Alpes.

**Bourg-St-Maurice** 213
French valley town, useful as a base for visiting nearby resorts and with a funicular to Les Arcs.
✉ *Erna Low, Interhome*

**Bovec** 642
✉ *Slovenija Pursuits*

**Boyne Highlands** USA
Area with impressive, high-capacity lift system for weekend Detroit crowds. Fierce winds off Lake Michigan a major drawback.
*225m; slopes 225–390m*
*10 240 acres*

**Boyne Mountain** USA
Resort popular with weekend Detroit crowds. Not as windy as sister resort Boyne Highlands.
*190m; slopes 190–340m*
*12 115 acres*

**Bramans** France
Old cross-country village near Modane. Well placed for touring numerous nearby resorts such as Val-Cenis and Valloire.
*1230m 1*

**Bramberg** Austria
Village near Pass Thurn (Kitzbühel area). Shares odd area with Neukirchen – the only valley lift is in Neukirchen.
*820m; slopes 820–900m*
*2 11km*

**Brand** Austria
Family resort, less popular now, perhaps because it lacks the charm to compensate for its small, low area.
*1050m; slopes 1050–1920m*
*13 50km*
✉ *Ski Wild*

**Les Brasses** France
Collective name for six traditional hamlets with some of the closest slopes to Geneva, but best known for cross-country.
*900m; slopes 900–1600m*
*17 50km*

**Braunwald** Switzerland
Sunny but limited area, a funicular ride above Linthal.
*1300m; slopes 1300–1910m 8*

**Breckenridge** 531
✉ *AmeriCan Ski, American Ski Classics, Avant-ski, Chalet World, Chalets 'Unlimited', Crystal, Erna Low, First Choice Ski, Independent Ski Links, Inghams, Made to Measure Holidays, Neilson, Ski Activity, Ski All America, Ski Expectations, Ski FreshTracks, Ski Independence, Ski Line, Ski Safari, Ski The American Dream, Ski Wild, Skiworld, Thomson, Trailfinders, United Vacations, Virgin Snow*

**Brentonico** Italy
Little resort just off Verona-Trento motorway.
*1160m; slopes 1160–1520m 16*

**La Bresse** France
Largest of ski areas near Nancy and Strasbourg. Snowmaking.
*900m; slopes 900–1350m*
*21 62km*
✉ *Lagrange Holidays*

**Bretton Woods** 581
✉ *AmeriCan Ski, Equity Ski*

**Briançon** 322
Part of the Grand Serre Chevalier region, but with own ski area.
✉ *Lagrange Holidays, Ski Leisure Direction*

**Brian Head** USA
Utah area south of Salt Lake City, too far from Park City for a day trip.
*2925m; slopes 2925–3445m*
*10 500 acres*

**Brides-les-Bains** 282
Quiet spa town in valley below Méribel, with a long gondola connection.
✉ *AmeriCan Ski, Avant-ski, Directski.com, Erna Low, First Choice Ski, Lagrange Holidays, Made to Measure Holidays, Peak Retreats, Ramblers Holidays, Ski Arrangements, Ski Leisure Direction, Ski Life, Ski Weekends, Snowcoach*

**Bridger Bowl** USA
Modest-sized day-trip resort (just a shop and fast-food restaurant at the base) – popular with residents of Bozeman, half an hour away, and an interesting excursion from Big Sky. Easy groomers at the bottom, but seriously steep ungroomed stuff at the top, especially for those who hike up to the famous Ridge. Good snow record.
*1855m; slopes 1855–2460m*
*6 1200 acres*

**Brighton** 579
✉ *AmeriCan Ski, Equity Ski, Ski The American Dream*

**Brixen** 172
Best equipped of Grossraum villages, with gondola access to the slopes, shared with Söll and Ellmau.

**Brodie Mountain** USA
Largest Massachusetts area. 100% snowmaking and mostly easy slopes.
*440m; slopes 440–820m*
*6 250 acres*

**Bromley** USA
New York City weekend retreat, reputedly the warmest place to ski in chilly Vermont.
*595m; slopes 595–1000m*
*9 300 acres*

**Bromont** Canada
Purpose-built resort an hour east of Montreal, with one of the best small areas in eastern Canada, popular for its night skiing.
*slopes 405–575m*
*6 135 acres*

**Bruck** Austria
Low beginners' resort, but could suit intermediates looking for a small, quiet base from which to visit nearby Zell am See.
*630m*

**Brundage Mountain** USA
Remote, uncrowded Idaho area with glorious views across the lake towards Hell's Canyon. Mostly intermediate slopes. Also has a snowcat operation.
*1760m; slopes 1760–2320m*
*5 1,300 acres*

**Bruneck** Italy
German name for Brunico.

**Brunico** Italy
Town with gondola link into the Plan de Corones/Kronplatz area.

**Bruson** 475
Relaxing respite from Verbier's crowds, on the other side of Le Châble. Well placed for car trips to Chamonix and Champéry.

**Burke Mountain** USA
Uncrowded, isolated family resort in Vermont with mostly intermediate slopes. Great views from the top.
*385m; slopes 385–995m*
*4 130 acres*

**Bürserberg** Austria
Undistinguished valley town near Brand.
*900m; slopes 1035–1850m*
*13 50km*

**Cairngorm** 652
✉ *Skisafe Travel*

**Caldirola** Italy
Genoese weekend day-tripper spot in a remote region off the motorway to Turin.
*1010m; slopes 1010–1460m*
*3 5km*

**Camigliatello** Italy
Tiny area on the foot of the Italian 'boot' near Cosenza. Weekend/day-trip spot.
*1270m; slopes 1270–1750m*
*4 6km*

**Campitello** 427
✉ *Crystal, Thomson*

**Campitello Matese** Italy
The only slopes near Naples. Surprisingly large area when snowcover is complete. Weekend crowds.
*1440m; slopes 1440–2100m*
*8 40km*

**Campo di Giove** Italy
Highest slopes in L'Aquila region east of Rome.
*1070m*
*6 23km*

**Campodolcino** Italy
Valley town with new funicular up to the fringe of Madesimo's slopes.
*1070m; slopes 1545–2880m*
*6 8km*

**Campo Felice** Italy
Easiest resort to reach from Rome, off Aquila motorway. One of the better lift systems in the vicinity.
*1410m; slopes 1520–2065m*
*14 40km*

**Campo Imperatore** Italy
One of the best of many little areas east of Rome in L'Aquila region.
*1980m*
*8 20km*

**Canazei** 427
✉ *Crystal, Equity Ski, First Choice Ski, Inghams, Rocketski, Thomson*

**Candanchu/Astún** 635

**Canillo** 98
Small, quiet town, with good sports facilities and newly developed lifts and slopes, linked to Soldeu.

**Canmore** Canada
Old frontier town on the way to Nakiska/Fortress, well placed for touring the region and an attractive alternative to staying in Banff.

**Cannon** 581
✉ *Equity Ski*

**The Canyons** 563
✉ *AmeriCan Ski, Ski All America, Ski Independence, Ski Safari, Ski The American Dream, United Vacations*

**Cardrona** 655

**Les Carroz-d'Arâches** 263
An attractive, spacious village on a sunny shelf on the road up to Flaine.
✉ *360 Sun and Ski, AmeriCan Ski, Erna Low, Lagrange Holidays, Peak Retreats, Ski Leisure Direction, Ski Life*

**Caspoggio** Italy
Attractive, unspoiled village north-east of Lake Como, with easy slopes (and more at nearby Chiesa).
*1100m; slopes 1100–2155m*
*8 22km*

**Castelrotto** Italy
Picturesque village west of Sella Ronda circuit with small sunny Alpine area and good cross-country trails.
*1060m*

**Castel S Angelo** Italy
Tiny area in Macerata region near Adriatic Riviera.
*805m*
*4 2km*

**Cauterets** 372
✉ *Lagrange Holidays*

**Cavalese** Italy
Unspoiled medieval town in Val di Fiemme with pretty slopes at Alpe Cermis.
*1000m; slopes 975–2265m*
*9 70km*
✉ *Alpine Tours, Thomson*

**The Cedars** Lebanon
The largest of Lebanon's ski areas, 130km/80 miles inland from Beirut. Good, open slopes with a surprisingly long season.
*1850m; slopes 2100–2700m 5*

**Ceillac** France
Tight cluster of rustic old buildings near Serre-Chevalier. Not far from the highest village in Europe, St-Veran.
*1600m; slopes 1600–2400m*

**Celerina** 469
Quiet, unpretentious village, with links up to St Moritz's Corviglia sector.
✉ *Made to Measure Holidays*

**Cerler** Spain
Very limited, purpose-built resort with a compact ski area similar to that of nearby Andorra's Arinsal.
*1500m; slopes 1500–2630m*
*16 45km*

**Le Cernix** France
Hamlet near Megève where Les Saisies' slopes link to those of Crest-Voland. Uncrowded retreat.
*1250m; slopes 1150–1950m*
*41 80km*

**Cerrato Lago** Italy
Very limited area near the coastal town of La Spezia.
*1270m; slopes 1270–1890m*
*5 3km*

**Cerro Bayo** Argentina
Limited area amid stunning scenery 10km/6 miles from La Angostura, and 90km/56 miles from San Carlos de Bariloche.
*slopes 1050–1780m*
*12 200ha*

**Cerro Castor** Argentina
The most southern ski runs in the world are on the Martial Glacier, Tierra del Fuego. Lodgings are in Ushuaia, the southernmost city in the world. Also plenty of cross-country skiing on the island.

**Cerro Catedral (Bariloche)** Argentina
The most developed ski and boarding resort in South America, to be found 19 km/12 miles from San Carlos de Bariloche. Lodgings available at the foot of the slopes.
*slopes 1040–2050m*
*28 600ha*
✉ *Elegant Resorts, Scott Dunn Latin America, Ski All America*

**Cervinia** 385
✉ *Alpine Answers, Alpine Events, Club Med, Crystal, Elegant Resorts, Erna Low, First Choice Ski, Independent Ski Links, Inghams, Interhome, Momentum Ski, Rocketski, Ski Arrangements, Ski Solutions, Ski Supreme, Ski Weekend, Thomson*

**Cesana Torinese** 292
Little Italian village linking the Sauze d'Oulx, Sestriere and Sansicario side of the Milky Way to the Clavière, Montgenèvre side.

**Le Châble** 475
Small village below Verbier, linked by gondola.

**Chacaltaya** Bolivia
Highest lift-served ski area in the world and the only ski area in Bolivia. Reached by four-wheel drive vehicle from La Paz 30km/19 miles away. Only open in summer (too cold in winter).
*5190m; slopes 5220–5420m*
*1 2km*
✉ *Scott Dunn Latin America*

**Chaillol** France
Cross-country base on the edge of the beautiful Ecrins National Park, near Gap. Small Alpine area, lots of snowmakers.
*1600m; slopes 1450–2000m 11*

**Chamois** Italy
A good choice when higher areas are affected by bad weather. Close to Valtournenche and Cervinia.
*1815m; slopes 1815–2270m*
*8 20km*

**Chamonix** 227
✉ *Airtours, Alpine Answers, Alpine Weekends, Avant-ski, Bigfoot Travel, Board and Lodge, Chalets 'Unlimited', Chamonix Lodge, Classic Ski Limited, Club Med, Club Pavilion, Collineige, Corporate Ski Company, Crystal, Erna Low, Esprit Ski, First Choice Ski, FlexiSki, Fraser Ralston, French Freedom Holidays, Handmade Holidays, Huski, Independent Ski Links, Inghams, Interhome, Lagrange Holidays, Made to Measure Holidays, Momentum Ski, Mountain Tracks, Neilson, Peak Retreats, Ski Arrangements, Ski Expectations, Ski France, Ski FreshTracks, Ski Independence, Ski Leisure Direction, Ski Life, Ski Line, Ski Solutions, Ski Supreme, Ski Weekend, Thomson, White Roc*

**Champagny-en-Vanoise** 305
Charming village with pretty, south-facing local slopes linking to the La Plagne network.
✉ *Barrelli Ski, Erna Low, Handmade Holidays, Independent Ski Links, Lagrange Holidays, Made to Measure Holidays*

**Champéry** 443
✉ *Alpine Answers, Alpine Events, Corporate Ski Company, Made to Measure Holidays, Piste Artiste Ltd, Ski Weekend, Switzerland Travel Centre, White Roc*

**Champex** Switzerland
Lakeside hamlet tucked away in the trees above Orsières. A nice quiet, unspoiled base from which to visit Verbier's area.
*1470m; slopes 1470–2220m*
*4 8km*

**Champfér** 469
Lakeside hamlet between St Moritz and Silvaplana with speedy access to the Corvatsch lifts.

**Champoluc** 406
Unspoiled, inexpensive village at one end of the Monterosa Ski area.
✉ *Alpine Answers, Chalets 'Unlimited', Crystal, Esprit Ski, Handmade Holidays, Momentum Ski, Ski 2*

**Champoussin** 443
Quiet mountainside village with convenient links to the rest of the Champéry slopes.

**Chamrousse** France
Functional family resort near Grenoble, with good, sheltered slopes.
*1650m; slopes 1400–2255m*
*26 77km*
✉ *Lagrange Holidays*

**Chandolin** Switzerland
Picturesque, unspoiled village in the Val d'Anniviers off the Valais, with high, easy open slopes (shared with St Luc) served almost entirely by drags. Valley pass also covers Zinal, Grimentz and Vercorin – 200km/124 miles in total.
*1935m; slopes 1660–3025m*
*16 75km*

**Chantemerle** 322
One of the main valley villages with direct access to Serre-Chevalier's slopes.

**Chapelco** Argentina
Small ski area with full infrastructure of services 19km/12 miles from sizeable town of San Martin de Los Andes. Accommodation in hotels 11km/7 miles from the slopes.
*slopes 1250–1980m*
*7 140ha*
✉ *Ski All America*

**La Chapelle-d'Abondance** 235
Unspoiled village 5km/3 miles down the valley from Châtel, with lift access to the Portes du Soleil network.
✉ *Ski La Cote*

**Charlotte Pass** 653

**Château d'Oex** Switzerland
Pleasant little valley town that is the main French-speaking component of the shared lift-pass area around Gstaad. Local slopes are pleasant and undemanding but low (La Braye, at the top, is at only 1650m/5,410ft), and not connected to any of the Gstaad sectors – though the local railway makes moving around to other resorts painless. This is where Alpine hot-air ballooning first took off, and it's still a local speciality.
*970m; slopes 890–3000m*
*67 250km*
✉ *Alpine Tours*

**Châtel** 235
✉ *Avant-ski, Chalets 'Unlimited', Connick Ski, First Choice Ski, Freedom Holidays, Haig Ski, Interhome, Lagrange Holidays, Peak Retreats, Ski Addiction, Ski Arrangements, Ski Independence, Ski Leisure Direction, Ski Line, Ski Rosie, Skialot, Snowfocus, Susie Ward Alpine Holidays, Tops Ski Chalets and Club Hotels*

**Le Chatelard** France
Small resort in remote Parc des Bauges between Lake Annecy and Chambéry.

**Cheonmasan** Korea
Purpose-built resort 30km/19 miles north-east of Seoul.
*7*

**Chiesa** Italy
Attractive beginners' resort with a fairly high plateau of easy runs above the resort.
*1000m; slopes 1700–2335m*
*16 50km*

**Chillán** Chile
Ski and spa resort 480km/300 miles south of Santiago. Base village has lodgings or you can stay at Las Trancas a few minutes' drive away.
*1650m; slopes 1600–2700m*
*9 35km*
⊠ *Elegant Resorts, Improve Your Skiing, Momentum Ski, Scott Dunn Latin America, Ski All America, Ski Safari*

**Le Chinaillon** **240**
Modern, chalet-style village at base of lifts above Le Grand-Bornand.

**Chiomonte** Italy
Tiny resort on the main road east of Bardonecchia and Sauze d'Oulx. A good half-day trip from either.
*745m; slopes 745–2210m*
*6 10km*

**Chsea** Algeria
Largest Algerian area, 135km/84 miles south-east of Alger in the Djur Djur mountains.
*1860m; slopes 1860–2510m 2*

**Churwalden** Switzerland
Hamlet on fringe of Lenzerheide-Valbella area.
*1230m; slopes 1230–2865m*
*35 155km*

**Claviere** **292**
Small Italian village linked to Montgenèvre (in France) and the rest of the Milky Way ski area.
⊠ *Crystal, Equity Ski, First Choice Ski, Rocketski*

**La Clusaz** **240**
⊠ *Aravis Alpine Retreat, Classic Ski Limited, Crystal, Frosty's Ski and Snowboard Holidays, Interhome, Lagrange Holidays, Last Resort, Made to Measure Holidays, Ski Activity, Ski Arrangements, Ski Leisure Direction, Ski Supreme, Ski Weekend, Snowlife*

**Les Coches** **305**
Small, purpose-built village, linked to the La Plagne ski area.
⊠ *Erna Low, Family Ski Company, Finlays, Independent Ski Links, Lagrange Holidays, Mountain Sun, Ski Independence, Ski Leisure Direction, Ski Life, Ski Line*

**Cogne** Italy
One of Aosta valley's larger villages. Small area worth a short visit from nearby Pila.
*1530m; slopes 1530–2245m*
*5 8km*
⊠ *Inntravel, Ramblers Holidays*

**Colfosco** **415**
Small village that makes up part of the Sella Ronda circuit.

**Colle di Tenda** Italy
Dour, modern resort that shares a good area with much nicer Limone. Not far from Nice.
*1400m; slopes 1120–2040m*
*33 80km*

**Colle Isarco** Italy
Brenner Pass area – and the bargain-shopping town of Vipiteno is nearby.
*1095m; slopes 1095–2720m*
*5 15km*

**Le Collet-d'Allevard** France
Ski area of sizeable summer spa Allevard-les-Bains in remote region east of Chambéry-Grenoble road.
*1450m; slopes 1450–2100m*
*13 35km*
⊠ *Lagrange Holidays*

**Collio** Italy
Tiny area of short runs in a remote spot between lakes Garda and d'Iseo.
*840m; slopes 840–1715m 14*

**Les Collons** **475**

**Combelouvière** **364**
Quiet hamlet tucked away in the trees at the foot of Valmorel's slopes.
⊠ *Lagrange Holidays*

**Combloux** **274**
Quiet, unspoiled alternative to linked Megève.
⊠ *Lagrange Holidays*

**Les Contamines** **246**
⊠ *Alpine Answers, Chalet Kiana, Chalets 'Unlimited', Classic Ski Limited, Interhome, Lagrange Holidays, Ski Arrangements, Ski Expectations, Ski Line, Skiworld, Total*

**Copper Mountain** **536**
⊠ *AmeriCan Ski, American Ski Classics, Crystal, Equity Ski, Erna Low, Ski All America, Ski Independence, Ski Safari, Ski The American Dream, Thomson, United Vacations*

**Le Corbier** **335**
⊠ *Equity Ski, Erna Low, Interhome, Lagrange Holidays, Rocketski, Ski Life*

**Coronet Peak** **658**
428m/1,400ft vertical. Closest area to Queenstown (20 minutes). Good mix of bowls, chutes, varied level pistes. Relies on large snowmaking facility for good snowcover. Spectacular views.

**Corrençon-en-Vercors** France
Charming, rustic village at foot of Villard-de-Lans ski area. Good cross-country, too.
*1160m; slopes 1160–2170m*
*25 130km*

**Cortina d'Ampezzo** **390**
⊠ *Alpine Answers, Alpine Events, Chalets 'Unlimited', Crystal, Elegant Resorts, Inghams, Momentum Ski, Ski Arrangements, Ski FreshTracks, Ski Solutions, Ski Weekend, Ski Yogi, White Roc*

**Corvara** **415**
The most animated Sella Ronda village, with lots of facilities and good lift links.
⊠ *Ski Yogi*

**Courchevel** **248**
⊠ *Airtours, Alpine Answers, Alpine Events, Alpine Weekends, Avant-ski, Bladon Lines, Chalet World, Chalets 'Unlimited', Corporate Ski Company, Crystal, Descent International, Elegant Resorts, Erna Low, Esprit Ski, Finlays, First Choice Ski, FlexiSki, Improve Your Skiing, Independent Ski Links, Inghams, Inspired to Ski, Jeffersons, Kaluma Ski, Lagrange Holidays, Le Ski, Lotus Supertravel, Made to Measure Holidays, Mark Warner, Momentum Ski, Neilson, Oxford Ski Company, Powder Byrne, Scott Dunn Ski, Silver Ski, Simply Ski, Ski Activity, Ski Amis, Ski Arrangements, Ski Deep, Ski Expectations, Ski France, Ski FreshTracks, Ski Independence, Ski Leisure Direction, Ski Life, Ski Line, Ski Link, Ski 'n' Action, Ski Olympic, Ski Solutions, Ski Supreme, Ski Weekend, Ski-Val, Skiworld, Thomson, Total, White Roc*

**Courmayeur** **395**
⊠ *Alpine Answers, Alpine Events, Alpine Weekends, Chalets 'Unlimited', Club Pavilion, Crystal, First Choice Ski, Independent Ski Links, Inghams, Interski, Mark Warner, Momentum Ski, Ski Arrangements, Ski Expectations, Ski Line, Ski Solutions, Ski Weekend, Ski Yogi, Thomson, White Roc*

**Cranmore** USA
Area in New Hampshire with attractive town/resort of North Conway. Easy skiing. Good for families.
*150m; slopes 150–515m*
*9 190 acres*

**Crans-Montana** **445**
⊠ *Alpine Answers, Alpine Events, Corporate Ski Company, Crystal, Erna Low, Independent Ski Links, Inghams, Interhome, Jeffersons, Kuoni, Lagrange Holidays, Made to Measure Holidays, Momentum Ski, Oxford Ski Company, Powder Byrne, Ski FreshTracks, Ski Line, Ski Weekend, Swiss Travel Service, Switzerland Travel Centre*

**Crested Butte** **557**
⊠ *AmeriCan Ski, American Ski Classics, Club Med, Ski Activity, Ski Independence, Ski Safari, Ski The American Dream, United Vacations*

**Crest-Voland** France
Attractive, unspoiled traditional village near Megève and Le Grand Bornand with wonderfully uncrowded intermediate slopes linked to Les Saisies.
*1150m; slopes 1230–1650m*
*17 45km*
⊠ *AmeriCan Ski, Peak Retreats*

**Crissolo** Italy
Small, remote day-tripper area, south-west of Turin. Part of the Monviso ski area.
*1320m; slopes 1745–2340m*
*4 20km*

**La Croix-Fry** **240**
Couple of hotels on the pass close to La Clusaz.

**Les Crosets** **443**
Isolated and limited mini-resort, in a prime position within the Portes du Soleil circuit, above Champéry.

**Crystal Mountain** USA
Area in glorious Mt Rainier National Park, near Seattle. Good, varied area given good snow/weather, but it's often wet.
*1340m; slopes 1340–2135m*
*10 2,300 acres*

**Cuchara Valley** USA
Quiet little family resort in southern Colorado, some way from any other ski area.
*2800m; slopes 2800–3285m*
*4 250 acres*

**Cutigliano** Italy
Sizeable village near Abetone in the Appennines. Less than 2 hours from Florence and Pisa.
*1125m; slopes 1125–1850m*
*9 13km*

**Cypress Mountain** Canada
Vancouver's most challenging area, 20 minutes from the city and with 40% for experts. Good snowfall record but rain is a problem.
*920m; slopes 910–1445m 5*

**Daemyeong Vivaldi Resort** Korea
One of the less ugly Korean resorts, 75km/47 miles from Seoul. 12

**La Daille** **354**
Ugly apartment complex at the entrance to Val-d'Isère.

**Daisen** Japan
Western Honshu's main area, four hours from Osaka.
*800m; slopes 740–1120m 8*

**Damüls** Austria
Scattered but attractive village in Bregenzerwald area close to the German and Swiss borders.
*1430m; slopes 1430–2010m*
*9 48km*

**Davos** **447**
⊠ *Alpine Answers, Alpine Events, Corporate Ski Company, FlexiSki, Independent Ski Links, Inghams, Interhome, Kuoni, Made to Measure Holidays, Momentum Ski, Ski FreshTracks, Ski Weekend, Swiss Travel Service, Switzerland Travel Centre, White Heat Skiing, White Roc*

**Deer Mountain** USA
South Dakota area close to 'Old West' town Deadwood and Mount Rushmore.
*1825m; slopes 1825–2085m*
*4 370 acres*

**Deer Valley** 565
⊠ *AmeriCan Ski, American Ski Classics, Made to Measure Holidays, Ski All America, Ski Independence, Ski Safari, Ski The American Dream, United Vacations*

**Les Deux-Alpes** 257
⊠ *Airtours, AmeriCan Ski, Avant-ski, Chalet World, Chalets 'Unlimited', Club Med, Crystal, Equity Ski, Erna Low, First Choice Ski, Independent Ski Links, Inghams, Interhome, Lagrange Holidays, Made to Measure Holidays, Mark Warner, Neilson, Panorama Holidays, Peak Retreats, Rocketski, Ski Arrangements, Ski Independence, Ski Leisure Direction, Ski Life, Ski Line, Ski Supreme, Skiworld, Thomson, Tops Ski Chalets and Club Hotels*

**Les Diablerets** Switzerland
Unspoiled but spread-out village towered over by the Diablerets massif, with two areas of local slopes, plus Glacier 3000. A high-speed quad followed by a slow chair lead up to the red runs of the Meilleret area and the link to Villars. A gondola in the centre of town takes you to Isenau, a mix of blues and reds served by drag-lifts. From Isenau there's a red run down to Col du Pillon and the cable-car to and from the glacier. You can also reach the glacier cable-cars by bus from town. On Glacier 3000, you'll find blue runs at over 3000m/9,840ft, stunning views and the long, red Combe d'Audon – a wonderful, usually quiet, run away from all the lifts with sheer cliffs rising up on both sides. The splendid Botta 3000 restaurant with stunning views at the top of the glacier is recommended for lunch. There's an evening toboggan run down from Les Mazots; there's also an ice rink and skate park.
*1150m; slopes 1150–3000m*
*46 125km*
⊠ *Crystal, Equity Ski, Interhome, Lagrange Holidays, Made to Measure Holidays, Momentum Ski, Rocketski, Sloping Off, Solo's, Swiss Travel Service, Thomson*

**Diamond Peak** 509
⊠ *Ski The American Dream*

**Dienten** Austria
Quiet village east of Saalbach at the heart of large, low-altitude Hochkönig area that spreads impressively over four mountains linking Maria Alm to Mühlbach.
*1070m; slopes 800–1825m*
*18 150km*

**Dinner Plain** Australia
Attractive resort best known for cross-country skiing. Shuttle to Mt Hotham for Alpine slopes. 4.5 hours from Melbourne.
*1520m; slopes 1490–1520m*

**Discovery Ski Area** USA
Pleasant area miles from anywhere except Butte, Montana, with largely intermediate slopes but double-black runs on the back of the mountain – and the chance of seriously good snow. Usually deserted. Fairmont Hot Springs (two huge thermal pools) nearby.
*2080m; slopes 2080–2485m*
*4 380 acres*

**Disentis** Switzerland
Unspoiled old village in a pretty setting on the Glacier Express rail route near Andermatt. Scenic area with long runs.
*1135m; slopes 1150–2920m*
*10 60km*
⊠ *Interhome*

**Dobbiaco** Italy
One of several little resorts near the Austrian border; a feasible day out from the Sella Ronda.
*1250m; slopes 1250–1610m*
*5 15km*
⊠ *Headwater Holidays, Ramblers Holidays, Waymark Holidays*

**Dodge Ridge** USA
Novice/leisurely intermediate area north of Yosemite. The pass from Reno is closed in winter, preventing crowds.
*2010m; slopes 2010–2500m*
*12 815 acres*

**Dolonne** 395
Quiet suburb of Courmayeur – the gondola link is no more, but the off-trail run home is still a classic.

**Dorfgastein** 111
Quieter, friendlier alternative to Bad Gastein and Bad Hofgastein, with its own intermediate ski area.

**Dundret** Sweden
Lapland area 100km/62 miles north of the Arctic Circle with floodlit slopes open through winter when the sun barely rises.
*slopes 475–825m*
*7 15km*

**Durango Mountain Resort** 557
⊠ *AmeriCan Ski, Ski Independence*

**Eaglecrest** USA
Close to famous Yukon gold rush town Skagway. Family resort famous for its ski school.
*365m; slopes 365–790m*
*3 640 acres*

**Eaux-Bonnes-Gourette** France
Most snow-sure resort in the French Pyrenees. Very popular with local families, so best avoided at weekends.
*1400m; slopes 1400–2400m*
*23 30km*

**Eben im Pongau** Austria
Part of Salzburger Sportwelt Amadé area that includes nearby St Johann, Wagrain, Flachau and Zauchensee. Village spoilt by the autobahn passing through it.
*855m; slopes 855–2185m*
*100 350km*

**Ehrwald** Austria
Friendly, relaxed, pretty village with several nicely varied areas, notably the Zugspitz glacier. Poor bus services, so a car is desirable.
*1000m; slopes 1000–3000m*
*11 45km*

**El Colorado/Farellones** Chile
One of Chile's best ski areas, 40km/25 miles east of Santiago, and connected to the Valle Nevado ski area. Crowded at weekends.
*slopes 2430–3335m*
*18 1000ha*

**Eldora Mountain** USA
Day-visitor resort with varied terrain (including plenty of steep stuff) close to Denver Boulder (45min by regular scheduled bus). All forest trails, but with some good glade areas. Crowded at weekends, and all the chairs are slow.
*2795m; slopes 2805–3230m*
*12 680 acres*

**Elk Meadows** USA
Area south of Salt Lake City, more than a day trip from Park City.
*2775m; slopes 2745–3170m*
*6 1,400 acres*

**Ellmau** 114
⊠ *Airtours, Crystal, Inghams, Interhome, Neilson, Ski Line, Ski Wild, Thomson*

**Encamp** 90

**Enego** Italy
Limited weekend day-trippers' area near Vicenza and Trento.
*1300m; slopes 1300–1445m*
*7 30km*

**Engelberg** 502
⊠ *Alpine Events, Corporate Ski Company, Crystal, Independent Ski Links, Inntravel, Interhome, Kuoni, Made to Measure Holidays, Momentum Ski, Ski Weekend, Swiss Travel Service, Waymark Holidays, White Roc*

**Entrèves** 395
Unremarkable cluster of hotels at the base of the lift up to Courmayeur's slopes.

**Escaldes** Andorra
Central valley town, effectively part of Andorra la Vella.

**Etna** Italy
Scenic, uncrowded, short-season area on the volcano's flank, 20 minutes from Nickolossi.
*1800m; slopes 1800–2350m*
*5km*

**Evolène** Switzerland
Charming rustic village with own little area in unspoiled, attractive setting south of Sion.
*1380m; slopes 1300–3330m*
*100 400km*

**Faak am See** Austria
Limited area, one of five overlooking town of Villach.
*560m*
*1 2km*

**Fai della Paganella** Italy
Trentino village near Madonna that shares its slopes with Andalo.

**Fairmont Hot Springs** Canada
Major luxury spa complex ideal for a relaxing holiday with some gentle skiing thrown in.
*2 60 acres*

**Faistenau** Austria
Cross-country area close to Salzburg and St Wolfgang. Limited Alpine slopes.
*785m; slopes 785–1000m*
*5 3km*

**Falcade** Italy
Trentino village south of the Sella Ronda with lifts up to slopes at San Pellegrino.
*1145m; slopes 1145–2170m*
*11 39km*
⊠ *Alpine Tours*

**Falera** 454
Small, rustic village, with improved access to big ski area shared by Flims and Laax.

**Le Falgoux** France
One of the most beautiful old villages in France, set in the very scenic Volcano National Park. Several ski areas nearby.
*930m; slopes 930–1350m*

**Falkertsee** Austria
Base area rather than a village, with bleak, open slopes in contrast to nearby Badkleinkirchheim.
*1690m; slopes 1690–2385m*
*5 15km*

**Falls Creek** 653

**La Feclaz** France
One of several little resorts in the remote Parc des Bauges.

**Fernie** 604
⊠ *Alpine Answers, AmeriCan Ski, Canadian Powder Tours, Crystal, Frontier Ski, Improve Your Skiing, Independent Ski Links, Inghams, Made to Measure Holidays, Ski Activity, Ski All America, Ski FreshTracks, Ski Independence, Ski Safari, Ski The American Dream, Skiworld*

**Fieberbrunn** Austria
Atmospheric and friendly Tirolean village, which sprawls along the valley road for 2km/1 mile. Its small but attractive area of wooded slopes is a bus-ride away and best suits beginners and leisurely intermediates. The nursery slopes are close to the village centre and graduation to long, gentle runs is easy. There are 35km/22 miles of good trails for cross-country skiers. Weekday queues are rare, but Fieberbrunn has a reputation for snow and can be invaded when other resorts are lacking. There are some decent mountain restaurants. Accommodation in the village is in hotels, and there is also accommodation at the lift station. Restaurants are mainly hotel-based and après-ski is liveliest at 4pm. Off the slopes, there's an adventure pool, skating, sleigh rides, cleared walks and a toboggan run, and train excursions are possible.
*800m; slopes 800–2020m*
*13 35km*
⊠ *Snowscape*

**Fiesch** Switzerland
Traditional Rhône valley resort close to Brig, with a lift up to Fiescheralp (2220m/7,280ft) at one end of the beautiful Aletsch area extending across the mountainside via Bettmeralp to Riederalp.
*1060m; slopes 1900–2900m*
*32 90km*

**Fiescheralp** Switzerland
Mountain outpost of Fiesch, down in the Rhône valley. At one end of the beautiful Aletsch area extending across the mountainside via Bettmeralp to Riederalp.
*2220m; slopes 1900–2900m*
*32 90km*

**Filzmoos** Austria
Charming, unspoiled, friendly village with leisurely slopes that are ideal for novices. Good snow record for its height. 'Nice resort; just not big enough,' says a 2004 reporter.
*1055m; slopes 1055–1645m*
*12 32km*
⊠ *Inghams*

**Finkenberg** 145
Between Mayrhofen and Hintertux, with a large area of mainly intermediate skiing.
⊠ *Crystal*

**Fiss** 196
Nicely compact, quiet, traditional village sharing an extensive, sunny area with bigger Serfaus.
⊠ *Alpine Tours, Interhome*

**Flachau** 196
Quiet, spacious village in a pretty setting at one end of an extensive three-valley lift network linking via Wagrain to Alpendorf. Flachauwinkl, up the valley, is at the centre of another similarly extensive lift system. All these resorts are covered by the Salzburger Sportwelt ski pass.
⊠ *Interhome*

**Flachauwinkl** Austria
Tiny ski station beside Tauern autobahn, at the centre of an extensive three-valley lift network linking Kleinarl to Zauchensee. Flachau, down the valley, is at one end of a similarly extensive lift system. All these resorts are covered by the Salzburger Sportwelt ski pass that our figures relate to.
*930m; slopes 800–2185m*
*59 200km*

**Flaine** 263
⊠ *Avant-ski, Classic Ski Limited, Club Med, Crystal, Erna Low, French Freedom Holidays, Independent Ski Links, Inghams, Lagrange Holidays, Made to Measure Holidays, Neilson, Ski Arrangements, Ski FreshTracks, Ski Independence, Ski Leisure Direction, Ski Life, Ski Supreme, Ski Weekend, Thomson*

**Flims** 454
⊠ *Alpine Answers, Alpine Events, Corporate Ski Company, Interhome, Kuoni, Made to Measure Holidays, Momentum Ski, Powder Byrne, Ski Weekend, Swiss Travel Service, Switzerland Travel Centre, White Roc*

**Flumet** France
Surprisingly large traditional village, the main place from which to ski the sizeable Val d'Arly ski area. Close to better-known Megève.
*1000m; slopes 1000–1600m*
*10 40km*
⊠ *AmeriCan Ski*

**Flumserberg** Switzerland
Collective name for the villages sharing a varied area an hour south-east of Zürich.
*1220m; slopes 1220–2220m*
*17*

**Folgaria** Italy
Largest of several resorts east of Trento. Old lift system.
*1165m; slopes 1185–2005m*
*38 70km*
⊠ *Alpine Tours*

**Folgarida** 404
Small, pleasant Dolomite village, with links to Madonna di Campiglio's extensive area. Life revolves around a handful of hotels close to the gondola.
⊠ *Equity Ski, Rocketski, Sloping Off*

**Foncine-le-Haut** France
Major cross-country village in the Jura Mountains with extensive trails.
⊠ *Lagrange Holidays*

**Fonni Gennaragentu** Italy
Sardinia's only 'ski area' – and it's tiny.
*1 5km*

**Font-Romeu** 372
⊠ *Headwater Holidays, Lagrange Holidays, Pyrenees Ski Experience, Solo's, Waymark Holidays*

**Foppolo** Italy
Relatively unattractive but user-friendly village, a short transfer from Bergamo.
*1510m; slopes 1610–2160m*
*9 47km*
⊠ *Equity Ski*

**Forca Canapine** Italy
Limited area near the Adriatic and Ascoli Piceno. Popular with weekend day-trippers.
*1450m; slopes 1450–1690m*
*11 20km*

**Formazza** Italy
Cross-country base with some downhill slopes.
*1280m; slopes 1275–1755m*
*8km*

**Formigal** 635

**Le Fornet** 354
Rustic, old hamlet 3km/2 miles further down the valley from Val-d'Isère.

**Forstau** Austria
Secluded hamlet above Radstadt–Schladming road. Very limited area with old lifts, but nice and quiet.
*930m; slopes 930–1885m*
*7 14km*

**Fortress Mountain** Canada
Primitive, wild and remote little mountain between Banff and Calgary, renowned for powder snow, dramatic scenery and uncrowded slopes. Training site for Canada's freestyle teams.
*2040m; slopes 2040–2370m*
*6 325 acres*
⊠ *Ski The American Dream*

**La Foux-d'Allos** France
Purpose-built resort that shares a good intermediate area with Pra-Loup.
*1800m; slopes 1800–2600m*
*52 167km*
⊠ *Lagrange Holidays*

**Frabosa Soprana** Italy
One of numerous little areas south of Turin, well placed for combining winter sports with Riviera sightseeing.
*850m; slopes 860–1740m*
*7 40km*

**Frisco** 531
Small town based on a Victorian settlement, down the valley from Breckenridge.
⊠ *AmeriCan Ski*

**Frontignano** Italy
Best lift system in the Macerata region, near the Adriatic Riviera.
*1340m; slopes 1340–2000m*
*8 10km*

**Fügen** Austria
Unspoiled Zillertal village with limited area best suited to beginners.
*560m; slopes 560–2400m*
*19 48km*

**Fulpmes** 122
⊠ *Crystal*

**Furano** Japan
Small Hokkaido resort, two hours from Sapporo. One of the few Japanese areas to get reasonable powder.
*235m; slopes 235–1065m 13*

**Fusch** Austria
Cheaper, quiet place to stay when visiting Zell am See. Across a golf course from Kaprun and Schuttdorf.
*805m*

**Fuschl** Austria
Attractive, unspoiled, lakeside village close to St Wolfgang and Salzburg, 30 minutes from its slopes. Best suited to part-time skiers who want to sightsee as well.
*670m*

**Gålå** Norway
Base for downhill and cross-country skiing, an hour's drive north of Lillehammer.
*930m; slopes 830–1150m*
*7 20km*
⊠ *Inntravel*

**Gallio** Italy
One of several low resorts near Vicenza and Trento. Popular with weekend day-trippers.
*1100m; slopes 1100–1550m*
*11 50km*

**Galtür** 126
Charming traditional village near Ischgl, in the news in 1998/99 due to a tragic avalanche disaster.
⊠ *Crystal, First Choice Ski, Inghams, Made to Measure Holidays*

**Gambarie d'Aspromonte** Italy
Italy's second most southerly ski area (after Mt Etna). On the 'toe' of the Italian 'boot' near Reggio di Calabria.
*1310m; slopes 1310–1650m 3*

**Gantschier** Austria
No slopes of its own but particularly well placed for visiting all the Montafon areas.
*700m*

**Gargellen** 150
Quiet, tiny and secluded village tucked up a side valley in the Montafon area, with a small but varied local area that is blissfully quiet.
⊠ *Interhome, Made to Measure Holidays*

**Garmisch-Partenkirchen** Germany
Twin classic old-fashioned winter sports resorts – unspoiled, traditional Partenkirchen is much the prettier. The ski areas are a bus-ride away, and offer limited challenge for experts and adventurous intermediates (though the long Kandahar black downhill course is excellent); there are good beginners' areas. The lift system is rather antiquated, although the 76-year-old Kreuzeck cable car was

replaced by a new lift in 2002/03. A visitor reports that piste maintenance and marking is poor. There are no bars or hotels near the slopes so you have to return to town for après-ski. There's plenty for non-skiers to do.
*720m; slopes 720–2830m*
*🚡 38 ⛷ 71km*
*✉ Moswin Tours*

**Gaschurn** 150
Attractive, unspoiled village with the largest of the pretty Montafon areas, well suited to intermediates.

**Gaustablikk** Norway
Small snow-sure Alpine area on Mt Gausta in southern Norway with plenty of cross-country.
⛷ 15km
*✉ Waymark Holidays*

**Geilo** 645
*✉ Crystal, Headwater Holidays, Inntravel, Neilson, Thomson*

**Gérardmer** France
Sizeable resort near Strasbourg with plenty of amenities. Night skiing, too.
*665m; slopes 750–1150m*
*🚡 20 ⛷ 40km*
*✉ Lagrange Holidays*

**Gerlitzen Alpe** Austria
A gondola ride above Villach and with good views. A worthwhile excursion from Badkleinkirchheim.
*500m; slopes 1003–1911m*
*🚡 14 ⛷ 20km*

**Gerlos** Austria
One of Austria's few inexpensive but fairly snow-sure resorts, now linked to Zell im Zillertal as well as Königsleiten to form a fair-sized intermediate area.
*1250m; slopes 1250–2300m*
*🚡 44 ⛷ 115km*
*✉ Interhome*

**Les Gets** 270
*✉ Alpine Answers, Avant-ski, Chalets 'Unlimited', Descent International, Independent Ski Links, Lagrange Holidays, Made to Measure Holidays, Peak Retreats, Ski Activity, Ski Expectations, Ski Famille, Ski Hillwood, Ski Independence, Ski Weekend, Skiworld, Total, Wood Advent Chalet*

**La Giettaz** France
Tiny rural village in steep-sided valley between La Clusaz amd Megève, about to be linked by lift and piste to the latter's Jaillet sector.
*1100m; slopes 1200–1930m*
*🚡 8 ⛷ 20km*

**Gitschtal/Weissbriach** Austria
One of many little areas near Hermagor in eastern Austria, close to Italian border.
*690m; slopes 690–1400m*
*🚡 4 ⛷ 5km*

**Glaris** Switzerland
Hamlet base station for the uncrowded Rinerhorn section of the Davos slopes.
*1455m; slopes 1455–2490m*
*🚡 5 ⛷ 30km*

**Glencoe** 652

**Glenshee** 652
*✉ Skisafe Travel*

**Going** 114
Small local ski area near Ellmau, linked to the huge Ski Welt area.
*✉ Solo's*

**Goldegg** Austria
Year-round resort famous for its lakeside castle. Limited slopes but Wagrain (Salzburger Sportwelt) and Grossarl (Gastein valley) are nearby.
*825m; slopes 825–1250m*
*🚡 2 ⛷ 2km*

**Golden** Canada
Small logging town, the place to stay when visiting Kicking Horse resort 15 minutes away. Also the launch pad for Purcell heli-skiing.

**Gore Mountain** USA
One of the better areas in New York State. Near Lake Placid, sufficiently far north to avoid worst weekend crowds. Intermediate terrain.
*455m; slopes 455–1095m*
*🚡 9 ⛷ 290 acres*

**Göriach** Austria
Hamlet with trail connecting into one of the longest, most snow-sure cross-country networks in Europe.
*1250m*

**Gortipohl** Austria
Traditional village in pretty Montafontal.
*920m; slopes 900–2395m*
*🚡 62 ⛷ 209km*

**Gosau** Austria
Straggling village with plenty of pretty, if low, runs. Snow-sure Obertauern and Schladming are within reach.
*765m; slopes 765–1800m*
*🚡 37 ⛷ 65km*

**Göstling** Austria
One of Austria's easternmost resorts, between Salzburg and Vienna. A traditional village in wooded setting.
*530m; slopes 530–1800m*
*🚡 12 ⛷ 19km*

**Götzens** Austria
Valley village base for Axamer Lizum slopes.
*870m 🚡 1*

**Grächen** Switzerland
Charming chalet-village reached by tricky access road off the approach to Zermatt. A small area of open slopes, mainly above the trees and of red-run difficulty, reached by two gondolas – one to Hannigalp (2115m/6,940ft), the main focus of activity with a very impressive children's nursery area. The village has almost a score of hotels, mostly 3-star; most of the accommodation is in chalets and apartments. The sports centre offers tennis and badminton, as well as a natural ice-rink.
*1615m; slopes 1615–2890m*
*🚡 13 ⛷ 50km*
*✉ Interhome*

**Le Grand-Bornand** 240
*✉ French Freedom Holidays, Inntravel, Lagrange Holidays*

**Grand Targhee** 567
Powder skiing paradise an hour from Jackson Hole.
*✉ AmeriCan Ski, Ski Safari*

**Grangesises** Italy
Small satellite of Sestriere, with lifts up to the main slopes.

**Grau Roig** 96
Mini-resort at foot of Pas de la Casa's only woodland runs, with one smart hotel and abundant day-tripper parking.

**La Grave** 272
*✉ Alpine Answers, AmeriCan Ski, Interhome, Lagrange Holidays, Peak Retreats, Ski Arrangements, Ski FreshTracks, Ski Weekend*

**Great Divide** USA
Area near Helena, Montana, best for experts. Mostly bowls; plus near-extreme Rawhide Gulch.
*1765m; slopes 1765–2195m*
*🚡 6 ⛷ 720 acres*

**Gresse-en-Vercors** France
Resort south of Grenoble. Sheltered slopes worth noting for bad-weather days.
*1250m; slopes 1600–1800m*
*🚡 16 ⛷ 18km*
*✉ Interhome, Lagrange Holidays*

**Gressoney-la-Trinité** 406
Smaller and higher of the two villages in the central valley of the Monterosa Ski area.
*✉ Alpine Answers, Crystal, Improve Your Skiing, Momentum Ski, Mountain Tracks, Ski Addiction*

**Gressoney-St-Jean** 406
Larger and lower of the two villages in the central valley of the Monterosa Ski area.
*✉ Alpine Answers*

**Grimentz** Switzerland
Located in the Val d'Anniviers, a side valley near the Valais town of Sierre, this an exceptionally cute, unspoiled mountainside village with high, varied runs including genuine reds and blacks, mostly on open slopes above the mid-mountain nursery area of Bendolla (2100m/6,890ft), which are mostly served by drag-lifts. The valley lift pass also covers St Luc/Chandolin, Vercorin and Zinal – 200km/125 miles of runs in total. Zinal is a short bus-ride up the valley, with a splendid itinerary run back to Grimentz. Good off-piste terrain, too. Grimentz has half a dozen small hotels, 2- and 3-star – the de Moiry is recommended by a 2004 reporter, who also describes the après-ski as 'very quiet'. There's a public pool and a natural ice-rink.
*1570m; slopes 1570–2900m*
*🚡 12 ⛷ 50km*

**Grindelwald** 456
*✉ Alpine Events, Corporate Ski Company, Crystal, Elegant Resorts, Independent Ski Links, Inghams, Interhome, Kuoni, Made to Measure Holidays, Momentum Ski, Powder Byrne, Ski FreshTracks, Solo's, Swiss Travel Service, Switzerland Travel Centre, Thomson, White Roc*

**Grossarl** 111
Secluded village linked to Dorfgastein in the Gastein valley.

**Grosskirchheim** Austria
Very limited area near Heiligenblut.
*1025m; slopes 1025–1400m*

**Grouse Mountain** Canada
The Vancouver area with the largest lift capacity. Superb city views from mostly easy slopes; night skiing.
*880m; slopes 880–1245m*
*🚡 11 ⛷ 120 acres*

**Grünau** Austria
Spacious riverside village in a lovely lake-filled part of eastern Austria. Nicely varied area, but very low.
*525m; slopes 600–1600m*
*🚡 14 ⛷ 40km*

**Gryon** 485
Village below Villars, with which it shares a ski area.

**Gstaad** 503
*✉ Alpine Answers, Alpine Events, Corporate Ski Company, Headwater Holidays, Interhome, Made to Measure Holidays, Momentum Ski, Ski Weekend, White Roc*

**Gunstock** USA
One of the New Hampshire resorts closest to Boston, popular with families. Primarily easy slopes. Gorgeous Lake Winnisquam views.
*275m; slopes 275–700m*
*🚡 8 ⛷ 220 acres*

**Guthega** 653

**Hafjell** Norway
Main ski area for Lillehammer.
*🚡 12 ⛷ 33km*
*✉ Crystal, Ramblers Holidays*

**Hakuba Happo One** Japan
European-style resort four hours from Tokyo. One of Japan's more challenging areas.
*750m; slopes 750–1830m 🚡 33*

**Harrachov** Czech Republic
Closest resort to Prague, with enough terrain to justify a day trip. No beginner area. A new quad replaced the old chair-lift in 2002/03.
*685m; slopes 650–1020m* 15

**Hasliberg** Switzerland
Four rustic hamlets on a sunny plateau overlooking Meiringen and Lake Brienz. Two of them are the bottom stations of a varied intermediate area.
*1055m; slopes 600–2435m*
16 *60km*

**Haus** 166
Village next to Schladming, with good local slopes connected to the rest of the network.

**Haystack** 581

**Heavenly** 510
✉ *AmeriCan Ski, American Ski Classics, Crystal, Equity Ski, First Choice Ski, Independent Ski Links, Lotus Supertravel, Neilson, Ski Activity, Ski All America, Ski Independence, Ski Line, Ski Safari, Ski The American Dream, Skiworld, Trailfinders, United Vacations*

**Hebalm** Austria
One of many small areas in Austria's easternmost ski region near Slovenian border. No major resorts in vicinity.
*1350m; slopes 1350–1400m*
6 *11km*

**Heiligenblut** Austria
Picturesque village in beautiful surroundings with mostly high terrain. Its remote position west of Bad Gastein ensures that it remains uncrowded.
*1300m; slopes 1300–2910m*
14 *55km*
✉ *Solo's*

**Hemlock Resort** Canada
Area 55 miles east of Vancouver towards Sun Peaks. Mostly intermediate terrain and with snowfall of 600 inches a year. Lodging is available at the base area.
*1000m; slopes 1000–1375m*
4 *350 acres*

**Hemsedal** 647
✉ *Crystal, Neilson, Thomson*

**Heremence** Switzerland
Quiet village in unspoiled attractive setting south of Sion. Verbier's slopes are accessed a few minutes' drive away at Les Masses.
*1250m*

**Hermagor** Austria
Main village base for the Nassfeld ski area in Carinthia.
*600m; slopes 610–2195m*
30 *100km*

**Hintersee** Austria
Easy slopes very close to Salzburg. Several long top-to-bottom runs and lifts means the size of the area is greatly reduced if the snowline is high.
*745m; slopes 750–1470m*
9 *40km*

**Hinterstoder** Austria
A very quiet valley village – neat but not overtly charming – spread along the road up the dead-end Stodertal in Upper Austria. The local Höss slopes are pleasantly wooded, less densely at the top, with splendid views. It's a small area, but has a worthwhile vertical of 1250m/4,100ft, and 450m/1,475ft above mid-mountain. A gondola from the main street goes up to the flat-bottomed bowl of Huttererböden (1400m/4,600ft), where there are several restaurants plus the modern 4-star Berghotel, very gentle but limited nursery slopes and lifts up to higher points. Most of the mountain is of easy red steepness. The run to the valley is a pleasant red with one or two tricky bits where it takes a quick plunge; it has effective snowmaking. Queues arise for the gondola and main chair on busy weekends. Further up the valley is the more limited Bärenalm area. The local pass also covers the Wurzeralm slopes near Spital am Pyrn. In the village there are only half a dozen hotels and guesthouses, of which the pick is the fairly simple Stoderhof.
*600m; slopes 600–1860m*
12 *35km*

**Hintertux/Tux valley** 117
✉ *Lagrange Holidays*

**Hippach** 145
Hamlet near a crowd-free lift into Mayrhofen's main area.

**Hochgurgl** 153
Quiet mountain-side hotel-village with a gondola connection to Obergurgl's slopes.
✉ *First Choice Ski, Inghams, Ski Expectations*

**Hochpillberg** Austria
Peaceful, virtually traffic-free hamlet with fabulous views towards Innsbruck and an antique chair-lift into varied terrain above Schwaz with good vertical of 1000m/3,280ft. Wonderfully safe for children; all accommodation within two minutes' walk of lift. Excellent restaurant at 1900m/6,230ft.
*1000m; slopes 1000–2030m*
6 *10km*

**Hochsölden** 170
Quieter mountain-side satellite above lively, sprawling Sölden, with links to the whole network.

**Hoch-Ybrig** Switzerland
Purpose-built complex only 64km/40 miles south-east of Zürich, with facilities for families.
*1050m; slopes 1050–2200m*
16 *50km*

**Hohuanshan** Taiwan
Limited ski area with short season in high, wild, inaccessible Miitaku mountains.
*3275m* 1

**Hollersbach** Austria
Pass Thurn hamlet near Mittersill. Uncrowded base from which to visit Kitzbühel if snowline is low – or Kaprun, Gerlos, Matrei and Uttendorf if high.
*805m; slopes 805–1000m*
2 *5km*

**Homewood** 509

**Hoodoo Ski Bowl** USA
Typical Oregon area with sizeable but short runs. Snow record isn't as good as its competitors near Portland. Two new quads installed in 2002/03.
*1420m; slopes 1420–1740m*
5 *800 acres*

**Hopfgarten** 172
Small chalet village with lift link into extensive Ski Welt area shared with Söll.
✉ *Contiki, First Choice Ski*

**Horseshoe Resort** Canada
Toronto region resort with high-capacity lift system and 100% snowmaking. The second mountain – The Heights – is open to members only.
*310m; slopes 310–405m*
7 *60 acres*

**Hospental** 439
Small village connected to Andermatt by road and rail and with local slopes of its own.

**Les Houches** 227
Varied, tree-lined area above spread-out village at the entrance to the Chamonix valley.
✉ *AmeriCan Ski, Avant-ski, Barrelli Ski, Bigfoot Travel, Chalets 'Unlimited', Erna Low, Handmade Holidays, Lagrange Holidays, Peak Retreats, Ski Expectations, Ski Life, Sloping Off*

**Hovden** Norway
Big, modern luxury lakeside hotel in wilderness midway between Oslo and Bergen. Cross-country venue with some Alpine slopes.
*820m; slopes 820–1175m*
5 *14km*

**La Hoya** Argentina
Small uncrowded resort 15km/9 miles from the small town of Esquel.
*slopes 1350–1950m* 4

**Huez** 204
Charming old hamlet on the road up to Alpe-d'Huez with lift into ski area.

**Hunter Mountain** USA
Popular New Yorkers' area so it gets very crowded at weekends.
*485m; slopes 485–975m*
14 *230 acres*

**Hüttschlag** Austria
Hamlet in a dead-end valley with lifts into the Gastein area at nearby Grossarl.
*1020m* 24 *80km*

**Hyundai Sungwoo Resort** Korea
Modern high-rise resort, 140km/87 miles from Seoul (a new expressway has reduced the journey time). Own English-language web site at www.hdsungwoo.co.kr. 9

**Idre Fjäll** Sweden
Collective name for four areas 490km/300 miles north-west of Stockholm.
*slopes 590–890m*
30 *28km*

**Igls** 122
✉ *Inghams, Lagrange Holidays, Made to Measure Holidays*

**Iizuna** Japan
Tiny area 2.5 hours from Tokyo. 6

**Incline Village** USA
Large village on northern edge of Lake Tahoe – it is a reasonable stop-off if you are touring.

**Indianhead** USA
South Lake Superior area with the most snowfall in the region. Winds are a problem.
*395m; slopes 395–585m*
12 *195 acres*

**Inneralpbach** 109
Small satellite of Alpbach, 3km/2 miles up the valley.

**Innerarosa** 441
The prettiest part of Arosa.

**Innichen** Italy
German name for San Candido.

**Innsbruck** 122
✉ *Corporate Ski Company, Made to Measure Holidays, Ramblers Holidays*

**Interlaken** 488
Large lakeside summer resort at the entrance to the valleys leading to Wengen, Grindelwald and Mürren.
✉ *Kuoni, Swiss Travel Service*

**Ischgl** 126
✉ *Alpine Answers, Alpine Events, Crystal, First Choice Ski, Inghams, Made to Measure Holidays, Momentum Ski, Ski Solutions, Ski Wild*

**Ishiuchi Maruyama-Gala-Yuzawa Kogen** Japan
Three resorts with a shared lift pass 90 minutes from Tokyo by bullet train and offering the largest ski area in the central Honshu region.
*255m; slopes 255–920m* 52

**Isola 2000** 373
✉ *Avant-ski, Club Pavilion, Crystal, Erna Low, Lagrange Holidays, Made to Measure Holidays, Ski Arrangements, Ski Life*

**Iso Syöte** Finland
The most southern downhill skiing area in Finland. Mostly easy slopes, and the main hotel is at the top of the mountain.
*430m; slopes 240–430m*
*🚡 11 ⛷ 21km*

**Itter** **172**
Next to Söll, skiing linked to Hopfgarten and Brixen, and to the whole of the Ski Welt region.
*✉ Directski.com*

**Jackson** USA
Classic New England village, and a major cross-country base. A lovely place from which to ski New Hampshire's Alpine areas.
*✉ Inntravel*

**Jackson Hole** **567**
*✉ Alpine Answers, AmeriCan Ski, American Ski Classics, Crystal, Inghams, Momentum Ski, Ski Activity, Ski All America, Ski FreshTracks, Ski Independence, Ski Line, Ski Safari, Ski The American Dream, Skiworld, Trailfinders, United Vacations, Virgin Snow*

**Jasná** Slovakia
Largest area in the Low Tatras mountains, linked to Chopok, which has an additional 11 lifts covering 11 km/7 miles.
*slopes 1240–2005m*
*🚡 13 ⛷ 21km*

**Jasper** **629**
*✉ AmeriCan Ski, Crystal, Frontier Ski, Inghams, Made to Measure Holidays, Ski Activity, Ski All America, Ski FreshTracks, Ski Independence, Ski Safari, Ski The American Dream*

**Jay Peak** **581**

**Jochberg** **132**
Straggling village, 8km/5 miles from Kitzbühel. Shares its varied, snow-sure ski area with Pass Thurn.

**La Joue-du-Loup** France
Slightly stylish little purpose-built ski-in/ ski-out family resort a few km north-west of Gap. Shares a fair-sized intermediate area with Superdévoluy.
*1500m; slopes 1500–2510m*
*🚡 32 ⛷ 100km*
*✉ Lagrange Holidays, Ski France*

**Jouvenceaux** **410**
Less boisterous base from which to ski Sauze d'Oulx's splendid cruising terrain.

**Jukkasjärvi** Sweden
Centuries-old cross-country resort with unique ice hotel rebuilt every December.

**June Mountain** USA
Small area a half-hour drive from Mammoth and in the same ownership. Empty slopes except on peak weekends.
*2300m; slopes 2300–3090m*
*🚡 8 ⛷ 500 acres*

**Juns** **117**
Small, spread out village between Lanersbach and Hintertux, with its own tiny beginners' area.

**Kals am Grossglockner** Austria
Village in a remote valley north of Lienz.
*1325m; slopes 1325–2305m*
*🚡 7 ⛷ 28km*

**Kaltenbach** Austria
One of the larger, quieter Zillertal areas, with plenty of high-altitude slopes, mostly above the tree line. 'Excellent' runs beneath the gondola,' says a 2004 reporter.
*560m; slopes 560–2300m*
*🚡 18 ⛷ 86km*

**Kananaskis** Canada
Small area near Calgary, nicely set in woods, with slopes at Nakiska and Fortress Mountain.
*slopes 1525–2465m*
*🚡 12 ⛷ 605 acres*
*✉ Frontier Ski*

**Kandersteg** Switzerland
Good cross-country base set amid beautiful scenery near Interlaken.
*1175m; slopes 1175–2000m*
*🚡 7 ⛷ 13km*
*✉ Headwater Holidays, Inghams, Inntravel, Kuoni, Swiss Travel Service, Waymark Holidays*

**Kanin** **642**

**Kappl** **126**
Small village down-valley from Ischgl and covered by the regional lift pass.

**Kaprun** **190**
Classic Austrian charmer of a village. Extensive sheltered slopes at nearby Zell am See.
*✉ Airtours, Crystal, Directski.com, Equity Ski, Esprit Ski, First Choice Ski, Inghams, Made to Measure Holidays, Neilson, Ski Line, Ski Wild, Thomson*

**Les Karellis** France
Resort with slopes that are more scenic, challenging and snow-sure than those of better-known Valloire, nearby.
*1600m; slopes 1600–2550m*
*🚡 19 ⛷ 60km*

**Kastelruth** Italy
German name for Castelrotto.
*✉ Inntravel*

**Kasurila** Finland
Siilinjarvi ski area popular with boarders. 🚡 5

**Katschberg** Austria
Cute hamlet on the road pass from Styria to Carinthia, now by-passed by Tauern motorway through Katschberg tunnel. Non-trivial area of intermediate slopes, linked to lower St Margarethen; lifts include fast chairs, one a six-pack.
*1140m; slopes 1075–2220m*
*🚡 16 ⛷ 60km*
*✉ Alpine Tours*

**Keystone** **538**
*✉ AmeriCan Ski, American Ski Classics, Crystal, Erna Low, Neilson, Ski Activity, Ski All America, Ski Independence, Ski Safari, Ski The American Dream, Trailfinders, United Vacations*

**Kicking Horse** **609**
*✉ AmeriCan Ski, Canadian Powder Tours, Crystal, Frontier Ski, Made to Measure Holidays, Ski All America, Ski Independence, Ski Safari, Ski The American Dream*

**Killington** **584**
*✉ American Ski Classics, Chalets 'Unlimited', Crystal, Equity Ski, Independent Ski Links, Inghams, Ski Activity, Ski All America, Ski Arrangements, Ski Independence, Ski Line, Ski Safari, Ski The American Dream, Solo's, Thomson, Trailfinders, United Vacations, Virgin Snow*

**Kimberley** **629**
*✉ AmeriCan Ski, Frontier Ski, Inghams, Made to Measure Holidays, Ski Activity, Ski All America, Ski Independence, Ski Safari, Ski The American Dream*

**Kirchberg** **132**
Lively little town close to Kitzbühel, with which it shares its slopes.
*✉ Directski.com, Interhome, Lagrange Holidays*

**Kirchdorf** **186**
Attractive village a bus-ride from St Johann in Tirol, with good local beginner slopes.
*✉ Snowcoach, Thomson*

**Kirkwood** **520**

**Kitzbühel** **132**
*✉ Airtours, Alpine Answers, Alpine Events, Avant-ski, Bladon Lines, Chalets 'Unlimited', Corporate Ski Company, Crystal, Directski.com, Elegant Resorts, First Choice Ski, Independent Ski Links, Inghams, Interhome, Lagrange Holidays, Made to Measure Holidays, Momentum Ski, Neilson, Panorama Holidays, Ski Arrangements, Ski FreshTracks, Ski Line, Ski Solutions, Ski Wild, Snowscape, Thomson*

**Kleinarl** Austria
Secluded traditional village up a pretty side valley from Wagrain, at one end of a three-valley lift network linking it via Flachauwinkl to Zauchensee – all part of the Salzburger Sportwelt ski pass area that our figures relate to.
*1015m; slopes 800–2185m*
*🚡 59 ⛷ 200km*

**Klippitztörl** Austria
One of many little areas in Austria's easternmost ski region near Slovenian border.
*1550m; slopes 1460–1820m*
*🚡 6 ⛷ 25km*

**Klosters** **447**
Affluent village sharing huge ski area with Davos.
*✉ Alpine Answers, Descent International, Elegant Resorts, FlexiSki, Inghams, Kuoni, Made to Measure Holidays, Momentum Ski, Powder Byrne, Ski FreshTracks, Ski Solutions, Ski Weekend, Swiss Travel Service, Switzerland Travel Centre, White Roc*

**Kobla** **642**

**Kolsass-Weer** Austria
Pair of Inn-side villages with low, inconvenient and limited slopes.
*555m; slopes 555–1010m*
*🚡 3 ⛷ 14km*

**Königsleiten** Austria
Quiet, high resort sharing fairly snow-sure area with Gerlos, now also linked to Zell im Zillertal to form a fair-sized area.
*1600m; slopes 1245–2300m*
*🚡 42 ⛷ 115km*

**Kopaonik** Serbia
Modern, sympathetically designed family resort in a pretty setting.
*1770m; slopes 1110–2015m*
*🚡 21 ⛷ 57km*
*✉ Balkan Holidays, Thomson*

**Koralpe** Austria
Largest and steepest of many gentle little areas in Austria's easternmost ski region near the Slovenian border.
*1550m; slopes 1550–2050m*
*🚡 10 ⛷ 25km*

**Kössen** Austria
Village near St Johann in Tirol with low, scattered and limited local slopes.
*600m; slopes 600–1700m*
*🚡 9 ⛷ 25km*

**Kötschach-Mauthen** Austria
One of many little areas near Hermagor in eastern Austria, close to the Italian border.
*710m; slopes 710–1300m*
*🚡 4 ⛷ 6km*

**Kranjska Gora** **642**
*✉ Balkan Holidays, Crystal, Inghams, Slovenija Pursuits, Solo's, Thomson*

**Krimml** Austria
Sunny area, high enough to have good snow usually. Shares regional pass with Wildkogel resorts (Neukirchen).
*1075m; slopes 1640–2040m*
*🚡 9 ⛷ 33km*

**Krispl-Gaissau** Austria
Easy slopes very close to Salzburg. Several long top-to-bottom lifts mean the size of the area is greatly reduced if the snowline is high.
*925m; slopes 750–1570m*
*🚡 11 ⛷ 40km*

**Kühtai** **122**
*✉ Crystal, Inghams*

**Kusatsu Kokusai** Japan
Attractive spa village with hot springs, three hours from Tokyo. 13

**Laax** 454
Old farming community with a lot of character and some new development nearby – linked to Flims.
✉ *Alpine Answers*

**Ladis** Austria
Smaller alternative to Serfaus and Fiss, with lifts that connect into the same varied ski area.
*1200m; slopes 1200–2540m*
*42 160km*
✉ *Alpine Tours*

**Le Laisinant** 354
Tiny hamlet a short bus-ride down the valley from Val-d'Isère.

**Lake Louise** 611
✉ *Alpine Answers, AmeriCan Ski, Crystal, Equity Ski, First Choice Ski, Frontier Ski, Independent Ski Links, Inghams, Lotus Supertravel, Made to Measure Holidays, Neilson, Ski Activity, Ski All America, Ski Independence, Ski Line, Ski Safari, Ski The American Dream, Skiworld, Solo's, Thomson, Trailfinders, United Vacations, Virgin Snow*

**Lake Tahoe** USA
Collection of 14 ski areas spectacularly set on California-Nevada border – Heavenly and Squaw Valley best known in Britain.
✉ *AmeriCan Ski, First Choice Ski, Independent Ski Links, Ski Activity, Skiworld, Thomson, United Vacations, Virgin Snow*

**Lamoura** France
One of four villages that makes up the Les Rousses Are in the Jura.
*1120m; slopes 1120–1680m*
*40 40km*

**Lanersbach** 117
Attractive village with charming little ski area of its own, plus Hintertux glacier nearby.

**Lans-en-Vercors** France
Village close to Villard-de-Lans and 30km/19 miles from Grenoble. Highest slopes in the region; few snowmakers.
*1020m; slopes 1400–1805m*
*16 24km*

**Lanslebourg** 373
One of the villages that makes up Val-Cenis.

**Lanslevillard** 373
One of the villages that makes up Val-Cenis.

**Lauterbrunnen** 460
Valley town in the Jungfrau region, with a funicular and rail connection up to Mürren.
✉ *Re-lax Holidays, Ski Miquel*

**Le Lavancher** 227
Quiet village between Chamonix and Argentière, with off-trail runs home for the insane.

**Lavarone** Italy
One of several areas east of Trento, good for a weekend day trip.
*1195m; slopes 1075–1555m*
*13 12km*

**Leadville** USA
Old mining town full of historic buildings. Own easy area (Ski Cooper) plus snowcat operation. Picturesque inexpensive base for visiting Copper Mountain, Vail and Beaver Creek.

**Lech** 138
✉ *Alpine Answers, Alpine Events, Avant-ski, Chalets 'Unlimited', Crystal, Elegant Resorts, Erna Low, FlexiSki, Independent Ski Links, Inghams, Jeffersons, Kaluma Ski, Lotus Supertravel, Made to Measure Holidays, Momentum Ski, Ski Expectations, Ski Solutions, Ski Weekend, Skiworld, Total, White Roc*

**The Lecht** 652
✉ *Skisafe Travel*

**Lélex** France
Family resort with pretty wooded slopes between Dijon and Geneva.
*900m; slopes 900–1680m*
*29 50km*

**Las Leñas** Argentina
European-style resort, 400km/250 miles south of Mendoza, with varied, beautiful terrain. Lodgings at the foot of the slopes.
*2240m; slopes 2240–3340m*
*11 230ha*
✉ *Scott Dunn Latin America, Ski All America*

**Lenk** Switzerland
Traditional village that shares a sizeable area of easy, pretty terrain with Adelboden.
*1070m; slopes 1070–2355m*
*55 166km*
✉ *Swiss Travel Service*

**Lenzerheide** 503
✉ *Interhome, Made to Measure Holidays*

**Leogang** 160
Quiet, spread-out village with over-the-mountain link to Saalbach-Hinterglemm.
✉ *Inntravel, Rocketski*

**Lermoos** Austria
Pleasant little village with its own small area of shady intermediate slopes on Grubigstein and a pass giving access to a variety of other areas in the locality, including the towering (and glacial) Zugspitze, on the border with Germany. Lots of cross-country trails along the flat valley.
*1005m; slopes 1005–2250m*
*9 30km*
✉ *Lagrange Holidays*

**Lessach** Austria
Hamlet with trail connecting into one of longest, most snow-sure cross-country networks in Europe. *1210m*

**Leukerbad** Switzerland
Major spa resort of Roman origin and recently revamped at vast expense. The super-neat towny result is very impressive, if you like that kind of thing. It is spectacularly set beneath towering cliffs, which are scaled by a cable-car up to high-altitude cross-country trails. The downhill slopes are on the opposite side of the valley, mainly above the tree line, served by drag-lifts and of red gradient, though there are a couple of blacks including a World Cup downhill course, which descends from the high, open slopes into the woods. There is also a slightly separate wooded sector served by a couple of chair-lifts. The spas have spawned a handful of very swanky 4-star hotels, but there are also over a dozen 3-stars, ranging from cute chalets to the plainly modern. As well as fabulous spa facilities, there are indoor and outdoor ice-rinks, tennis, squash and badminton courts and a golf driving range.
*1410m; slopes 1410–2700m*
*17 60km*

**Leutasch** Austria
Traditional cross-country village with limited slopes but a pleasant day trip from nearby Seefeld or Innsbruck.
*1130m; slopes 1130–1605m*
*3 6km*
✉ *Headwater Holidays, Inntravel*

**Levi** 643
✉ *Bladon Lines, Inghams*

**Leysin** Switzerland
This is a spread-out village, climbing up a wooded hillside. The lifts are to the east of the village and take you to a pretty mix of mainly red and blue runs. A gondola takes you up to La Berneuse, from which you head down to the two-stage Chaux de Mont chair, which takes you to the resort's highest point. There's a choice of black or red back down, both easily sun-damaged. On the lower half of the slope is a terrain-park. Itineraries from the top of Chaux de Mont provide Leysin's best options for experts, along with a heli-operation. From the bottom of Chaux de Mont it's easy to go to the other side of the resort, using a series of chairs and fairly short, mainly blue, runs in and out of trees. There are nursery slopes at village level. The revolving Kuklos restaurant at La Berneuse has stunning views. After hours, Leysin has a swimming pool and a tubing park.
*1300m; slopes 1300–2205m*
*19 60km*
✉ *Lagrange Holidays, Sloping Off, Solo's, Switzerland Travel Centre*

**Lienz** Austria
Pleasant town in pretty surroundings.
*675m; slopes 730–2290m*
*17 41km*

**Lillehammer** 645
✉ *Crystal, Directski.com*

**Limone** Italy
Pleasant old town not far from Turin, with a pretty area, but far from snow-sure.
*1010m; slopes 1030–2050m*
*25 80km*

**Lincoln** USA
Sprawling New Hampshire town from which to visit Loon mountain.
✉ *Crystal*

**Lindvallen-Högfjället** Sweden
Two of the mountains that make up the four unlinked ski areas of Sälen.
*800m; slopes 590–890m*
*46 85km*

**Le Lioran** France
Auvergne village near Aurillac with a purpose-built satellite above. Spectacular volcanic scenery.
*1160m; slopes 1160–1850m*
*24 60km*

**Livigno** 400
✉ *Airtours, Chalets 'Unlimited', Directski.com, Equity Ski, Independent Ski Links, Inghams, Interhome, Neilson, Panorama Holidays, Rocketski, Ski Arrangements*

**Lizzola** Italy
Small base development in remote region north of Bergamo. Several other little areas nearby.
*1250m; slopes 1250–2070m*
*9 30km*

**Llaima** Chile
Exotic area in central Chile, around and below a mildly active volcano.
*1500m* 5

**Loch Lomond** Canada
Steep, narrow, challenging slopes near Thunder Bay on the shores of Lake Superior. Candy Mountain is nearby.
*215m; slopes 215–440m*
*3 90 acres*

**Lofer** Austria
Quiet, traditional village in a pretty setting north of Saalbach with a small area of its own, and Waidring's relatively snow-sure Steinplatte nearby.
*640m; slopes 640–1745m*
*13 46km*
✉ *Ski Line, Ski Wild*

**Longchamp** 364
Dreary purpose-built resort with little to commend it over pretty Valmorel, with which it shares its ski area.

**Loon Mountain** 581
✉ *AmeriCan Ski, Equity Ski, Virgin Snow*

**Lost Trail** USA
Remote Montana area, open Thursday to Sunday and holidays. Intermediate slopes.
*2005m; slopes 2005–2370m*
*6 800 acres*

**Loveland** USA
The highest lift-served slopes in the northern hemisphere (if you discount Zermatt's summer skiing drags). On the Continental Divide – highway I70's Eisenhower Tunnel passes directly beneath the resort – and one of the best for snow (400 inches a year). Wide variety of slopes, though most of the serious stuff involves hikes. Good mix of open upper slopes and forest trails. A good day trip from Summit County resorts, especially Keystone. Lodgings also available 19km/12 miles east in Georgetown.
*3230m; slopes 3230–3870m*
*9 1,265 acres*

**Luchon** France
Sizeable village with plenty of amenities, with gondola (8 minutes) to its ski area and to purpose-built Superbagnères.
*630m; slopes 1440–2260m*
*16 35km*
✉ *Lagrange Holidays*

**Lurisia** Italy
Sizeable spa resort, a good base for visits to surrounding little ski areas and to Nice.
*750m; slopes 800–1800m*
*8 35km*

**Lutsen Mountains** USA
This area – in Minnesota – is the largest ski area between Vermont and Colorado and has panoramic views of Lake Superior. Four small linked hills with 95% snowmaking offer surprisingly good and extensive terrain. Moose Mountain has the biggest vertical (250m/820ft), with cruisers or bumps top to bottom and backcountry glade runs. Small slope-side village. Cross-country, snow-shoeing and snowmobiling nearby.
*80m; slopes 80–335m*
*9 1,000 acres*

**Luz-Ardiden** France
Spa village below its ski area. Cauterets and Barèges nearby.
*710m; slopes 1730–2450m*
*15 60km*

**Macugnaga** 432
✉ *Neilson*

**Madesimo** 433
✉ *Inghams, Ski Arrangements*

**Madonna di Campiglio** 404
✉ *Crystal, Equity Ski, Erna Low, First Choice Ski, Inghams, Interhome, Rocketski, Ski Arrangements, Ski Yogi, Solo's*

**Mad River Glen** 581

**La Magdelaine** Italy
Close to Cervinia, and good on bad-weather days.
*1645m; slopes 1645–1870m*
*4 4km*

**Maishofen** Austria
Cheaper place to stay when visiting equidistant Saalbach and Zell am See.
*765m*

**Malbun** Liechtenstein
Quaint user-friendly little family resort, 16km/10 miles from the capital, Vaduz. Limited slopes and short easy runs.
*1600m; slopes 1595–2100m*
*6 16km*

**Malcesine** Italy
Large summer resort on Lake Garda with a fair area of slopes, served by a revolving cable-car from the 2002/03 season.
*1430m; slopes 1430–1830m*
*8 12km*

**Malga Ciapela** Italy
Resort at the foot of the Marmolada glacier massif, with a link into the Sella Ronda. Cortina is nearby.
*1445m; slopes 1445–3270m*
*8 18km*

**Mallnitz** Austria
Village in a pretty valley close to Slovenia, with two varied areas providing a fine mix of wooded and open runs.
*1200m; slopes 1300–2650m*
*5 30km*

**Mammoth Mountain** 515
✉ *AmeriCan Ski, American Ski Classics, Crystal, Independent Ski Links, Made to Measure Holidays, Ski Activity, Ski All America, Ski Independence, Ski Line, Ski Safari, Ski The American Dream, United Vacations, Virgin Snow*

**Manigod** France
Small valley village over the Col de la Croix-Fry from La Clusaz.

**Marble Mountain** Canada
Area near the charming Newfoundland town Corner Brook and Gros Morne National Park. It has one of the east coast's highest snowfall records.
*85m; slopes 85–570m*
*5 126 acres*
✉ *Club Pavilion, Frontier Ski*

**Maria Alm** Austria
Charming unspoiled village east of Saalbach at one end of the varied Hochkönig area that spreads impressively over four linked mountains via Hintertal and Dienten to Mühlbach. A 2004 reporter warns of the 'nightmare' link between Hinterthal and Hintermoos.
*800m; slopes 800–2000m*
*36 150km*

**Mariapfarr** Austria
Village at the heart of one of the longest, most snow-reliable cross-country networks in Europe. Sizeable Mauterndorf-St Michael Alpine area and Obertauern area are nearby.
*1120m*
*5 30km*

**Mariazell** Austria
Traditional Styria village with an impressive basilica. Limited slopes.
*870m; slopes 870–1265m*
*5 11km*

**Maribor** 642

**Marilleva** 404
Small resort with direct links to Madonna di Campiglio's extensive intermediate slopes.
✉ *Erna Low, Interhome, Sloping Off*

**Masella** Spain
Pyrenean village linked with slopes of La Molina to form the Alp 2500 area.
*1600m; slopes 1600–2535m*
*20 100km*

**La Massana** 90

**Le Massif** 631
✉ *Frontier Ski, Ski All America, Ski Safari, Ski The American Dream*

**Matrei in Osttirol** Austria
Large market village south of Felbertauern tunnel. Mostly high slopes.
*1000m; slopes 1000–2400m*
*7 33km*

**Maurienne Valley** France
A great curving trench with over 20 winter resorts, ranging from pleasant old valley villages to convenience resorts purpose-built in the 1960s.

**Mauterndorf** Austria
Village near Obertauern with tremendous snow record.
*1120m; slopes 1075–2360m*
*21 60km*
✉ *Equity Ski, Sloping Off*

**Maverick Mountain** USA
Montana resort with plenty of terrain accessed by few lifts. Cowboy Winter Games venue – rodeo one day, ski races the next.
*2155m; slopes 2155–2800m*
*2 500 acres*

**Mayens de Riddes** 475
Tiny hamlet next to La Tzoumaz with its links up to Savoleyres and the Verbier network.
✉ *Interhome*

**Mayens-de-Sion** 475
Tranquil hamlet off the road up to Les Collons – part of the Verbier area.

**Mayrhofen** 145
✉ *Airtours, Alpine Events, Crystal, Equity Ski, First Choice Ski, Improve Your Skiing, Independent Ski Links, Inghams, Interhome, Made to Measure Holidays, Neilson, Rocketski, Ski Arrangements, Ski Line, Ski Wild, Snowcoach, Thomson*

**Méaudre** France
Small resort near Grenoble with good snowmaking to make up for its low altitude.
*1000m; slopes 1000–1600m*
*10 18km*

**Megève** 274
✉ *Alpine Answers, Alpine Events, AmeriCan Ski, Avant-ski, Chalets 'Unlimited', Classic Ski Limited, Corporate Ski Company, Erna Low, Interhome, Lagrange Holidays, Made to Measure Holidays, Momentum Ski, Peak Retreats, Simon Butler Skiing, Ski Arrangements, Ski Barrett-Boyce, Ski Expectations, Ski Independence, Ski Life, Ski Solutions, Ski Supreme, Ski Weekend, Stanford Skiing, White Roc*

**Meiringen** Switzerland
Varied terrain, a good outing from the nearby Jungfrau resorts or Interlaken. Particularly suitable for beginners. New high-speed gondola planned for 2003/04.
*600m; slopes 600–2435m*
*16 60km*
✉ *Kuoni*

**Les Menuires** 280
✉ *Club Med, Erna Low, Family Ski Company, First Choice Ski, French Freedom Holidays, Independent Ski Links, Interhome, Lagrange Holidays, Neilson, Ski Arrangements, Ski Independence, Ski Leisure Direction, Ski Life, Ski Olympic, Ski Supreme*

**Merano** Italy
Purpose-built base on a high plateau near Bolzano.
*2000m; slopes 2000–2240m*
*18 28km*

**Méribel** 282
✉ *Absolute Ski, Airtours, Alpine Action, Alpine Answers, Alpine Events, Avant-ski, Belvedere Chalets, Bladon Lines, Bonne Neige Ski Holidays, Chalet Group, Chalet World, Chalets 'Unlimited', Club Med, Club Pavilion, Cooltip Mountain Holidays, Corporate Ski Company, Crystal, Descent International, Directski.com, Elegant Resorts, Erna Low, First Choice Ski, French Freedom Holidays, Independent Ski Links, Inghams, Interhome, Kaluma Ski, Lagrange Holidays, Lotus Supertravel, Made to Measure Holidays, Mark Warner, Mark Warner, MasterSki, Meriski, Momentum Ski, Mountain Tracks, Neilson, Oxford Ski Company, Panorama Holidays, Purple Ski, Scott Dunn Ski, Silver Ski, Simply Ski, Ski Activity, Ski Amis, Ski Arrangements, Ski Basics, Ski Beat, Ski Blanc, Ski Bon, Ski Cuisine, Ski Expectations, Ski France, Ski FreshTracks, Ski Hame, Ski Independence, Ski Leisure Direction, Ski Life, Ski Line, Ski Olympic, Ski Solutions, Ski Supreme, Ski Weekend, Skiworld, Snowline, Thomson, Total, VIP, White Roc*

**Métabief-Mont-d'Or** France
Twin villages in the Jura region, not far from Geneva.
*900m; slopes 880–1460m*
*22 42km*

**Methven** 655
Nearest town/accommodation to Mt Hutt, and helicopter base for trips to Arrowsmith range – good for intermediates as well as advanced.

**Mijoux** France
Pretty wooded slopes between Dijon and Geneva. Lélex nearby.
*1000m; slopes 900–1680m*
*29 50km*
✉ *Lagrange Holidays*

**Mission Ridge** USA
Area in dry region that gets higher-quality snow than other Seattle resorts but less of it. Good intermediate slopes.
*1390m; slopes 1390–2065m*
*6 300 acres*

**Misurina** Italy
Tiny village near Cortina. A cheap alternative base.
*1755m; slopes 1755–1900m*
*4 13km*

**Mittersill** Austria
Valley-junction village near Pass Thurn. A good base from which to visit Kitzbühel if the snowline is low or Kaprun, Gerlos, Matrei and Uttendorf if the snowline is high.
*790m; slopes 1265–1895m*
*15 25km*

**Moena** Italy
Large village between Cavalese and Sella Ronda resorts, ideally located for touring the Dolomites area.
*1180m; slopes 1180–2515m*
*24 35km*

**La Molina** 635
✉ *Club Pavilion*

**Molltall Glacier** Austria
Little-known high slopes on the other side of the Tauern tunnel from Bad Gastein. Worthwhile excursion when the snowline is high.
*slopes 2570–3122m*
*4 11km*

**Molveno** Italy

**Monarch** USA
Wonderfully uncrowded area, a day trip from Crested Butte. Great powder. Good for all but experts.
*3290m; slopes 3290–3645m*
*5 670 acres*

**Monesi** Italy
Southernmost of the resorts south of Turin. Close to Monaco and Nice.
*1310m; slopes 1310–2180m*
*5 38km*

**Le Monêtier** 322
Quiet little village with a nice rustic feel and direct access to Serre-Chevalier's slopes.
✉ *Equity Ski, Rocketski*

**La Mongie** 372
✉ *Lagrange Holidays*

**Montafon** 150
✉ *Interhome, Made to Measure Holidays*

**Montalbert** 305
Traditional village with direct access to the La Plagne network.
✉ *Interhome, Ski Amis, Ski Arrangements*

**Mont Blanc** 631

**Montchavin** 305
Attractively transformed village on fringe of La Plagne ski area.
✉ *French Freedom Holidays, Mountain Sun, Snow Monkey Chalets*

**Mont-de-Lans** 257
Low village on the way up to Les Deux-Alpes, with lifts to the main resort.

**Le Mont-Dore** France
Attractive traditional small town, the largest resort in the beautiful volcanic Auvergne region near Clermont-Ferrand.
*1050m; slopes 1350–1850m*
*20 42km*
✉ *Lagrange Holidays*

**Monte Bondone** 427
Trento's local hill.
✉ *Solo's*

**Monte Campione** Italy
Tiny purpose-built resort, spread thinly over four mountainsides. 80% snowmaking helps to offset the low altitude.
*1100m; slopes 1200–2010m*
*16 80km*

**Monte Livata** Italy
Closest resort to Rome, popular with weekenders.
*1430m; slopes 1430–1750m*
*8 8km*

**Monte Piselli** Italy
Tiny area with the highest slopes of the many little resorts east of Rome.
*2100m; slopes 2100–2690m*
*3 5km*

**Monte Pora** Italy
Tiny resort near Lake d'Iseo and Bergamo. Several other little areas nearby.
*1350m; slopes 1350–1880m*
*11 30km*

**Monterosa Ski** 406
✉ *Alpine Answers, Crystal, Handmade Holidays, Momentum Ski, Mountain Tracks, Ski 2, Ski Addiction, Ski Arrangements, Ski Weekend*

**Mont Gabriel** Canada
Montreal area with runs on four sides of the mountain, though the south-facing sides rarely open. Two short but renowned double-black-diamond bump runs. 9

**Montgenèvre** 292
✉ *Airtours, Club Pavilion, Crystal, Equity Ski, Handmade Holidays, Independent Ski Links, Lagrange Holidays, Neilson, Rocketski, Ski Etoile, Ski France, Ski Life, Skitopia*

**Mont Glen** Canada
Least crowded Montreal area, so a good weekend choice.
*680m; slopes 680–1035m*
*4 110 acres*

**Mont Grand Fonds** Canada
Small area sufficiently far from Québec not to get overrun at weekends.
*400m; slopes 400–735m* 4

**Mont Habitant** Canada
Very limited area in the Montreal region but with a good base lodge. 3

**Mont Olympia** Canada
Small, two-mountain area near Montreal, one mostly novice terrain, the other best suited to experts. 6

**Mont Orford** Canada
Cold, windswept lone peak (no resort), worth a trip from nearby Montreal on a fine day.
*slopes 305–855m*
*8 180 acres*

**Mont Ste Anne** 631
✉ *Frontier Ski, Inghams, Ski Independence, Ski Safari, Ski The American Dream*

**Mont St Sauveur** 631

**Mont Sutton** Canada
Varied area with some of the best glade skiing in eastern Canada, including some for novices. Quaint Sutton village nearby.
*9 175 acres*

**Moonlight Basin** 561
Quiet area of slopes close to Big Sky, Montana.

**Morgins** 443
Resort on Portes du Soleil, indirectly linked to Champéry.
✉ *Ski Morgins Holidays, Ski Rosie*

**Morillon** 263
Valley village with a gondola link up to its purpose-built satellite and the Flaine network.
✉ *AmeriCan Ski, Erna Low, Lagrange Holidays, Peak Retreats, Ski Life*

**Morin Heights** Canada
Area in the Montreal region with 100% snowmaking. Attractive base lodge. 6

**Morzine** 296
✉ *Alpine Answers, Alpine Escapes, Alpine Events, Alpine Weekends, Avant-ski, Chalet Chocolat, Chalet Company, Chalet Gueret, Chalet Snowboard, Chalets 'Unlimited', Challenge Activ, Corporate Ski Company, Crystal, Equity Ski, Esprit Ski, First Choice Ski, Haig Ski, Independent Ski Links, Inghams, Lagrange Holidays, Made to Measure Holidays, Momentum Ski, Mountain Highs, Mountain Tracks, Ski Activity, Ski Arrangements, Ski Chamois, Ski Expectations, Ski Independence, Ski Life, Ski Line, Ski Morzine, Ski Weekend, Snowline, Thomson, Trail Alpine, White Roc*

**Les Mosses** Switzerland
Peaceful resort and area, best for a day trip from Villars or Les Diablerets. There's a terrain-park, a few chalet-style hotel-restaurants, shops and a rather fine church. Recent visitors recommend its quiet slopes and great views. There are only drag-lifts to access the mainly red and blue runs, though a chair is planned to Pic Chaussy. Lunch is mostly at valley level – the Bivouac in the Relais Alpin hotel is recommended by a 2004 reporter, or try the Buvette de l'Arsat or the self-service Drosera. Les Mosses prides itself on the number of activities on offer – such as ice-diving, an ice rink and an international dog-sled racing course.
*1500m; slopes 1500–2200m*
*13 60km*
✉ *Ramblers Holidays*

**Mottaret** 282
Purpose-built but reasonably attractive component of Méribel.
✉ *Airtours, First Choice Ski, Panorama Holidays, Ski Leisure Direction, Ski Line, Skiworld, Thomson*

**Mottarone** Italy
Closest slopes to Lake Maggiore. No village – just a base area.
*1200m; slopes 1200–1490m*
*25km*

**Les Moulins** Switzerland
Village down the road from Château d'Oex with its own low area of slopes, part of the big Gstaad lift-pass area.
*890m; slopes 890–3000m*
*67 250km*

**Mount Abram** USA
Small, pretty, tree-lined area in Maine, renowned for its immaculately groomed easy runs.
*295m; slopes 295–610m*
*5 170 acres*

**Mountain High** USA
Best snowfall record and highest lift capacity in Los Angeles vicinity – plus 95% snowmaking. Mostly intermediate cruising.
*2010m; slopes 2010–2500m*
*12 220 acres*

**Mount Ashland** USA
Arty town in Oregon renowned for Shakespeare. Mountain includes glaciated bowl rimmed with steeps. Best for experts.
*1935m; slopes 1935–2285m*
*4 200 acres*

**Mount Bachelor** USA
Extinct volcano in Oregon offering deserted runs on every side served by many fast chairs. Gets a lot of rain. You have to stay in Bend, 40km/25 miles away.
*1740m; slopes 1740–2765m*
*13 3,680 acres*
⊠ *AmeriCan Ski*

**Mount Baker** USA
Almost on the coast near Seattle, yet one of the top resorts for snow (averages 600 inches a year). Plenty of challenging slopes. Known for spectacular avalanches.
*1115m; slopes 1115–1540m*
*9 1,000 acres*

**Mount Baldy** Canada
Tiny area, but a worthwhile excursion from Big White. Gets ultra light snow – great glades/powder chutes.
*slopes 1705–2150m*
*2 150 acres*

**Mount Baldy** USA
Some of the longest and steepest runs in California. Near Los Angeles, but 20% snowmaking and antiquated lifts are major drawbacks.
*1980m; slopes 1980–2620m*
*4 400 acres*

**Mount Baw Baw** Australia
Small but entertaining intermediate area in attractive woodland, with great views. Closest area to Melbourne (150km/93 miles).
*1450m; slopes 1450–1560m*
*8 61 acres*

**Mount Buffalo** 653

**Mount Buller** 653

**Mount Dobson** New Zealand
Mostly intermediate slopes in a wide, treeless basin near Mt Cook, with good snow-cover. Accommodation in Fairlie, 40 minutes away.
*1610m; slopes 1610–2010m*
*3 990 acres*

**Mount Hood Meadows** USA
One of several sizeable areas amid magnificent Oregon scenery. Impressive snowfall record but snow tends to be wet, and weather damp.
*1375m; slopes 1375–2535m*
*12 2,150 acres*

**Mount Hood Ski Bowl** USA
Sizeable area set amid magnificent Oregon scenery. Weather can be damp.
*1095m; slopes 1095–1540m*
*9 960 acres*

**Mount Hotham** 653

**Mount Hutt** 655

**Mount Lemmon** USA
Southernmost area in North America, close to famous Old West town Tombstone, Arizona. Reasonable snowfall.
*2500m; slopes 2500–2790m*
*3 70 acres*

**Mount McKay** 653

**Mount Olympos** Greece
Ski mountaineering site with a chain of huts on both faces. Run by the army – permission needed.
*1800m*

**Mount Pilio** Greece
Pleasant slopes cut out of dense forest, only 15km/9 miles from the holiday resort of Portaria above town of Volos.
*1500m 3*

**Mount Rose** 509

**Mount Snow** 581

**Mount Spokane** USA
Little intermediate area outside Spokane (Washington State).
*1160m; slopes 1160–1795m*
*5 350 acres*

**Mount St Louis / Moonstone** Canada
Premier area in Toronto region, spread over three peaks. Very high-capacity lift system and 100% snowmaking.
*13 175*

**Mount Sunapee** USA
Area in New Hampshire closest to Boston; primarily intermediate terrain.
*375m; slopes 375–835m*
*10 230 acres*

**Mount Vermio** Greece
Oldest ski base in Greece. In central Macedonia 60km/37 miles from Thessaloniki. Barren but interesting slopes.
*slopes 1420–2000m 4*

**Mount Washington Resort** Canada
Scenic area on Vancouver Island with lodging in the base village. Impressive snowfall record but rain is a problem.
*1110m; slopes 1110–1590m*
*6 970 acres*
⊠ *Frontier Ski, Ski Safari*

**Mount Waterman** USA
Small Los Angeles area where children ski free. The lack of much snowmaking is a drawback.
*2135m; slopes 2135–2440m*
*3 210 acres*

**Mühlbach** Austria
Village east of Saalbach and west of Flachau, a short bus-ride from one end of the large but low Hochkönig area that spreads over four mountains via Dienten to Maria Alm.
*855m; slopes 800–1825m*
*23 80km*

**Mühltal** Austria
Small village halfway between Niederau and Auffach in the Wildschönau. No local skiing of its own.
*780m; slopes 830–1900m*
*29 42km*

**Muhr** Austria
Village by Katschberg tunnel well placed for visiting St Michael, Badkleinkirchheim, Flachau and Obertauern.
*1110m*

**Muju** Korea
Largest area in Korea and with a fair amount of lodging. Though it is the furthest resort from Seoul (some four hours south) it is still overcrowded. 13

**Mürren** 460
⊠ *Alpine Events, Inghams, Kuoni, Made to Measure Holidays, Ski FreshTracks, Ski Line, Ski Solutions, Swiss Travel Service, Switzerland Travel Centre*

**Mutters** Austria
Innsbruck satellite resort, temporarily closed.
*830m*

**Myoko Suginohara Kokusai** Japan
A series of small resorts two or three hours from Tokyo, which together make up an area of extensive slopes with longer, wider runs than normal for Japan. 15

**Naeba** Japan
Fashionable resort with lots of accommodation 2 hours north of Tokyo. Crowded slopes.
*900m; slopes 900–1800m 28*

**Nakiska** Canada
Small area of wooded runs between Banff and Calgary, with emphasis on downhill speed. Unreliable snow, but state-of-the-art snowmaking and pancake-flat grooming.
*1524m; slopes 1525–2215m*
*4 230 acres*
⊠ *Ski The American Dream*

**Nasserein** 178
Quiet suburb of St Anton, a short bus-ride from the lifts.

**Nassfeld** Austria
Fair-sized, scenic area – Carinthia's biggest – on the sunny side of the Alps, right on the Italian border. There is accommodation at Nassfeld itself (a mid-mountain lift base) and at Sonnleiten (the other main mid-mountain base), and more in the valley village of Tröpolach, at the bottom of the access gondola, or in the bigger village of Hermagor, 10km/6 miles to the east. The two-stage Millennium Express gondola takes you up directly to the centre of the slopes at Madritsche (1920m/6,300ft). There are nursery slopes here and at the gondola mid-station. Off to the right is a wide bowl served by two further gondolas beneath Trogkofel. Off to the left is the higher peak of Gartnerkofel (2195m/7,200ft). Two of the area's three six-packs are on the back of this peak. Most of the slopes are graded red, and the few blues are short. But each of the lifts between Madritsche and Trogkofel accesses a black piste or ski route as well as one or more red runs. There are two terrain-parks (including a novel twin-pipe), and a floodlit piste. There are very extensive cross-country trails and quite a range of other activities.
*1500m; slopes 610–2195m*
*30 100km*
⊠ *Equity Ski, Rocketski, Ski Line, Ski Wild, Sloping Off, Slovenija Pursuits*

**Nauders** Austria
Spacious, traditionally Tirolean village tucked away only 3km/2 miles from the Swiss border and almost on the Italian one. Its slopes start 2km/1 mile outside the village (free shuttle-bus) and are mainly high and sunny intermediate runs spread over three areas. There is lots of snowmaking. The area is not ideal for experts, though there is a lot of off-piste terrain. It's not ideal for complete beginners either – the village nursery slopes are some way out. There are five cross-country trails amounting to 40km/25 miles in all. Most of the hotels are comfortable 4-stars and many of the eating out possibilities are hotel-based. The après-ski scene has typically Tirolean jollity and there is quite a bit to do off the slopes, including tobogganing, curling, tennis, squash, bowling, and swimming.
*1400m; slopes 1400–2750m*
*30 111km*

**Nax** Switzerland
Quiet, sunny village in a balcony setting overlooking the Rhône valley. Own little area and only a short drive from Veysonnaz.
*1300m*

**Nendaz** 475
Enormous apartment development offering quiet alternative to Verbier.
⊠ *Interhome*

**Neukirchen** Austria
Quiet, pretty beginners' resort with a fairly snow-sure plateau at the top of its mountain.
*855m; slopes 855–2150m*
*14 35km*

**Neustift** 122
⊠ *Alpine Tours, Esprit Ski, Interhome, Made to Measure Holidays*

**Nevegal** Italy
Weekend place near Belluno, south of Cortina.
*1030m; slopes 1030–1650m*
*14 30km*

**Nevis Range** 652
⊠ *Skisafe Travel*

**Niederau** 197
Amorphous chalet-style village in the Wildschönau region.
✉ *Airtours, Directski.com, First Choice Ski, Inghams, Neilson, Panorama Holidays, Thomson*

**Niseko** Japan
Town on Hohhaido, three hours from Sopporo and with three ski areas close by. Good snow record and powder. 28

**Nockberge Innerkrems** Austria
Area just south of Katschberg tunnel.
*1500m; slopes 1500–2300m*
*10 33km*

**Nordic Valley** USA
Utah cross-country area close to Salt Lake City. Powder Mountain and Snowbasin are nearby Alpine areas.

**Nordseter** Norway
Cluster of hotels in deep forest north of Lillehammer. Some Alpine facilities but best for cross-country.
*850m; slopes 1000–1090m*
*2 2km*

**Norefjell** Norway
Norway's toughest run, a very steep 600m/1,970ft drop. 120km/75 miles north-west of Oslo.
*185m; slopes 185–1185m*
*10 23km*

**La Norma** France
Traffic-free, purpose-built resort near Modane and Val-Cenis, with mostly easy terrain.
*1350m; slopes 1350–2750m*
*18 65km*
✉ *AmeriCan Ski, Interhome, Lagrange Holidays, Peak Retreats, Ski Life*

**Norquay** 596

**North Conway** USA
Attractive factory-outlet-shopping town in New Hampshire close to Attitash and Cranmore ski areas.
✉ *AmeriCan Ski, Virgin Snow*

**Northstar-at-Tahoe** 521
✉ *AmeriCan Ski, Ski The American Dream, United Vacations*

**Nôtre-Dame-de-Bellecombe** 274
Pleasant village spoiled by the busy Albertville-Megève road. Inexpensive base from which to visit Megève, though it has fair slopes of its own.
✉ *AmeriCan Ski, Peak Retreats*

**Nova Levante** Italy
Village close to Bozen/Bolzano with lifts up to small network around Passo di Costalunga.
*1180m; slopes 1180–2200m*
*14 20km*

**Nozawa Onsen** Japan
Spa village with good hot springs 3 hours from Tokyo. The runs are cut out of heavy vegetation.
*500m; slopes 500–1650m* 24

**Nub's Nob** USA
One of the most sheltered Great Lakes ski areas (many suffer fierce winds). 100% snowmaking; weekend crowds from Detroit. Wooded slopes suitable for all abilities.
*275m; slopes 275–405m*
*8 245 acres*

**Oberau** 197
Pretty village, most central of those forming the Wildschönau region – but least convenient for the slopes.
✉ *Inghams, Neilson*

**Obereggen** Italy
Tiny resort close to Bozen/Bolzano with modest area of slopes also accessible from Predazzo in Val di Fiemme.
*1550m; slopes 1550–2200m*
*6 10km*

**Obergurgl** 153
✉ *Airtours, Alpine Events, Crystal, First Choice Ski, Independent Ski Links, Inghams, Made to Measure Holidays, Neilson, Ski Expectations, Ski FreshTracks, Ski Solutions, Thomson*

**Oberlech** 138
Car- and crowd-free family resort alternative to Lech. Snow-sure due to height, snow-pocket position and snow-guns.

**Oberndorf** 186
Quiet hamlet with beginners' area and a chair connecting it to St Johann's undemanding ski area.
✉ *Lagrange Holidays*

**Oberperfuss** 122

**Oberstdorf** Germany
Attractive winter-sports town near the Austrian border with three small areas. Famous ski-jumping hill. The Nordic World Ski Championships is due to be held here in 2005.
*815m; slopes 800–2220m*
*31 30km*
✉ *Moswin Tours*

**Obertauern** 158
✉ *First Choice Ski, Inghams, Made to Measure Holidays, Thomson*

**Ochapowace** Canada
Main area in Saskatchewan, east of Regina. It doesn't get a huge amount of snow but 75% snowmaking helps.
*4 100 acres*

**Oetz** Austria
Village at the entrance to the Oetz valley with an easy/intermediate ski area of its own and access to the Sölden, Kuhtai and Niederau areas.
*820m; slopes 820–2200m*
*10 25km*

**Ohau** New Zealand
Some of NZ's steepest slopes, with great views of Lake Ohau 9km/6 miles away (where you stay). 320km/200 miles south of Christchurch.
*1500m; slopes 1425–1825m*
*3 310 acres*

**Okemo** 581

**Oppdal** 645

**Orcières-Merlette** France
High, convenient family resort a few km north-east of Gap, Merlette being the ugly, purpose-built ski station above the village of Orcières (1450m/4,760ft). Snow-sure beginner area. Slopes with a good mix of difficulty spread over several mountain flanks, and currently being expanded – a process due to culminate in 2006/07 with the opening of a cable-car up to almost 3000m/9,840ft on Roche Brune. Most accommodation is in apartments, but there are a few simple hotels. There is an impressive Palais des Sports, with pools, bowling alley and ice-rink.
*1850m; slopes 1850–2725m*
*29 85km*
✉ *Lagrange Holidays*

**Ordino** 90
Valley village near La Massana, on the way up to Andorra's best snow at Arcalis.

**Orelle** France
Village in the Maurienne with access by gondola to Val-Thorens in the Trois Vallées.
✉ *AmeriCan Ski*

**Oropa** Italy
Little area just off the Aosta–Turin motorway. An easy change of scene from Courmayeur.
*1180m; slopes 1200–2390m*
*15km*

**Les Orres** France
Friendly modern resort with great views and varied intermediate terrain, but the snow is unreliable, and it's a long transfer from Lyon.
*1550m; slopes 1550–2720m*
*23 62km*
✉ *Handmade Holidays, Lagrange Holidays*

**Orsières** Switzerland
Traditional, sizeable winter resort near Martigny. Well-positioned base from which to visit Verbier and the Chamonix valley.
*900m*

**Ortisei** 415
Charming, lively, old market town in the Italian Dolomites with indirect links to the Sella Ronda.
✉ *Inghams*

**Oslo** Norway
Capital city with cross-country ski trails in its parks. Alpine slopes and lifts in Nordmarka region, just north of city boundaries.

**Otre il Colle** Italy
Smallest of many little resorts near Bergamo.
*1100m; slopes 1100–2000m*
*7 7km*

**Oukaimeden** Morocco
Slopes 75km/47 miles from Marrakech with a surprisingly long season.
*2600m; slopes 2600–3260m*
*8 15km*

**Ovindoli** Italy
One of the smallest areas in L'Aquila region east of Rome, but it has higher slopes than most and one of the better lift systems.
*1375m; slopes 1375–2220m*
*9 10km*

**Ovronnaz** Switzerland
Pretty village set on a sunny shelf above the Rhône valley, with a good pool complex. Limited area but Crans-Montana and Anzère are close.
*1350m; slopes 1350–2080m*
*10 25km*

**Owl's Head** Canada
Steep mountain rising out of a lake, in a remote spot bordering Vermont, away from weekend crowds.
*7 90 acres*

**Oz-en-Oisans** 204
Attractive old village with a higher satellite at the base of the lifts into Alpe-d'Huez.
✉ *Erna Low, Independent Ski Links, Lagrange Holidays, Ski Independence*

**Pajarito Mountain** USA
Los Alamos area laid out by nuclear scientists. Atomic slopes too – steep, ungroomed. Open Fridays, weekends and holidays. Fun day out from Taos.
*2685m; slopes 2685–3170m*
*6 220 acres*

**Pal** 94
Prettily wooded mountain, now linked with the slopes of Arinsal.
✉ *Panorama Holidays*

**Palandöken** Turkey
Varied skiing area, transformed by new lifts and two big hotels, overlooking the Anatolian city of Erzurum.
*slopes 2125–3125m* 7

**Pamporovo** 638
✉ *Balkan Holidays, Crystal, First Choice Ski, Inghams, Ski Balkantours, Thomson*

**Panarotta** Italy
Smallest of the resorts east of Trento. It is at a higher altitude than nearby Andalo, so it is worth a day out from there.
*1500m; slopes 1500–2000m*
*6 7km*

**Panorama** 616
✉ *AmeriCan Ski, Frontier Ski, Improve Your Skiing, Inghams, Made to Measure Holidays, Ski Activity, Ski All America, Ski Independence, Ski Safari, Ski The American Dream*

**Panticosa** Spain
Charming old Pyrenees spa village near Formigal with sheltered but limited slopes.
*1200m; slopes 1200–1900m*
*7 34km*

**Park City** 572
✉ *Alpine Answers, AmeriCan Ski, American Ski Classics, Crystal, Made to Measure Holidays, Momentum Ski, Ramblers Holidays, Ski Activity, Ski All America, Ski Independence, Ski Line, Ski Safari, Ski The American Dream, Thomson, Trailfinders, United Vacations*

**Parnassos** Greece
Biggest and best-organised area in Greece, 180km/112 miles from Athens and with surprisingly good slopes and lifts.
*slopes 1600–2300m*
*10 14km*

**Parpan** Switzerland
Pretty village linked to the large intermediate area of Lenzerheide.
*1510m; slopes 1230–2865m*
*35 155km*

**Partenen** 150
Traditional village in a pretty setting at the end of Montafontal. The slopes start at Gaschurn, and there are lots more in the vicinity.

**La Parva** Chile
One of Chile's best ski areas, linked with Valle Nevado and El Colorado ski areas. Only 50km/31 miles east of Santiago so it gets crowded at weekends.
*2660m; slopes 2660–3630m*
*14 38km*
✉ *Scott Dunn Latin America*

**Pas de la Casa** 96
✉ *Airtours, Chalets 'Unlimited', Crystal, Directski.com, First Choice Ski, Independent Ski Links, Inghams, Lagrange Holidays, Neilson, Panorama Holidays, Thomson*

**Passo di Costalunga** Italy
Dense network of short lifts either side of the road over a pass, close to Val di Fassa, with links up from Nova Levante.

**Passo Lanciano** Italy
Closest area to Adriatic. Weekend crowds from nearby Pescara when the snow is good.
*1305m; slopes 1305–2000m*
*13*

**Passo Rolle** Italy
Small group of lifts either side of the road over a high pass just north of San Martino di Castrozza.

**Passo San Pellegrino** Italy
Trentino area south of the Sella Ronda linked with Falcade.

**Passo Tonale** 427
✉ *Airtours, Alpine Tours, Crystal, Equity Ski, Inghams, Neilson, Rocketski, Sloping Off, Thomson*

**Pass Thurn** 132
Road-side lift base for Kitzbühel's most snow-sure, but unconnected, ski area.

**Pebble Creek** USA
Small area on Utah-Jackson Hole route. Blend of open and wooded slopes.
*1920m; slopes 1920–2530m*
*3 600 acres*

**Pec Pod Snezku** Czech Republic
Collection of hamlets spread along the valley road leading to the main lifts and the very limited ski area.
*770m; slopes 710–1190m*
*5 12km*

**Peisey** 213
Small village (often referred to as Peisey-Nancroix) linked to Les Arcs and the Paradiski area.

**Peisey-Vallandry** 213
Group of small villages linked to Les Arcs and the Paradiski area.
✉ *Erna Low, Esprit Ski, Independent Ski Links, MasterSki, Ski Beat, Ski Hiver, Ski Line, Ski Olympic, Snow Monkey Chalets*

**Pejo** 427
Trentino resort near Madonna.

**Perisher/Smiggins** 653

**Pescasseroli** Italy
One of numerous areas east of Rome in L'Aquila region.
*1250m; slopes 1250–1945m*
*6 25km*

**Pescocostanzo** Italy
One of numerous areas east of Rome in L'Aquila region.
*1395m; slopes 1395–1900m*
*4 25km*

**Pettneu** 178
Snow-sure specialist beginners' resort with an irregular bus link to nearby St Anton.

**Petzen** Austria
One of many little areas in Austria's easternmost ski region near the Slovenian border.
*600m; slopes 600–1700m*
*6 13km*

**Peyragudes-Peyresourde** France
Small Pyrenean resort with its ski area starting high above.
*1000m; slopes 1600–2400m*
*15 37km*
✉ *Lagrange Holidays, Ski Life*

**Pfunds** Austria
Picturesque valley village with no slopes but quick access to several resorts in Switzerland and Italy, as well as Austria.
*970m; slopes 970–2850m*
*28 110km*

**Phoenix Park** Korea
Golf complex with 12 trails in winter. Two hours (140km/87 miles) from Seoul.
*slopes 650–1050m 9*

**Piancavallo** Italy
Uninspiring yet curiously trendy purpose-built village, an easy drive from Venice.
*1270m; slopes 1270–1830m*
*17 45km*
✉ *Equity Ski, Sloping Off*

**Piani delle Betulle** Italy
One of several little areas near the east coast of Lake Como.
*730m; slopes 730–1850m*
*6 10km*

**Piani di Artavaggio** Italy
Small base complex rather than a village. One of several little areas near Lake Como.
*875m; slopes 875–1875m*
*7 15km*

**Piani di Bobbio** Italy
Largest of several tiny resorts above Lake Como.
*770m; slopes 770–1855m*
*10 20km*

**Piani di Erna** Italy
Small base development – no village. One of several little areas above Lake Como.
*600m; slopes 600–1635m*
*5 9km*

**Piau-Engaly** France
User-friendly St-Lary satellite in one of the best areas in the Pyrenees.
*1850m; slopes 1700–2500m*
*20 40km*
✉ *Lagrange Holidays*

**Piazzatorre** Italy
One of many little areas in the Bergamo region.
*870m; slopes 870–2000m*
*5 25km*

**Pichl** 166
In Dachstein-Tauern region, close to Schladming.

**Pico** 584
Low-key little family area (no resort) close to Killington in central Vermont.

**Piesendorf** Austria
Cheaper, quiet place to stay when visiting Zell am See. Tucked behind Kaprun near Niedernsill.
*780m*

**Pievepelago** Italy
Much the smallest and most limited of the Appennine ski resorts. Less than 2 hours from Florence and Pisa.
*1115m; slopes 1115–1410m*
*7 8km*

**Pila** 433
✉ *Crystal, Independent Ski Links, Interhome, Interski, Ski Supreme*

**Pinzolo** 427
Trentino resort near Madonna.
✉ *Alpine Tours*

**Pitztal** Austria
Long valley with good glacier area at its head, accessed by underground funicular.
*1250m; slopes 880–3440m*
*19 87km*

**Pla-d'Adet** France
Limited purpose-built complex at the foot of the St-Lary ski area (the original village is further down the mountain).
*1680m; slopes 1420–2450m*
*32 80km*
✉ *Lagrange Holidays*

**La Plagne** 305
✉ *Airtours, Alpine Answers, Avant-ski, Chalet World, Chalets 'Unlimited', Chez Jay Ski Chalets, Club Med, Crystal, Equity Ski, Erna Low, Esprit Ski, Finlays, First Choice Ski, French Freedom Holidays, Independent Ski Links, Inghams, Interhome, Lagrange Holidays, Made to Measure Holidays, Mark Warner, Neilson, Rocketski, Silver Ski, Ski Activity, Ski Amis, Ski Arrangements, Ski Beat, Ski Expectations, Ski France, Ski FreshTracks, Ski Independence, Ski Leisure Direction, Ski Life, Ski Line, Ski Olympic, Ski Supreme, Skiworld, Snow Monkey Chalets, Thomson*

**Plan-Peisey** 213
Small development above Peisey with cable-car link to Les Arcs and the Paradiski area. For package holidays see Peisey-Vallandry.

**Poiana Brasov** 641
✉ *Balkan Holidays, Inghams, Neilson, Ski Balkantours, Solo's*

**Pomerelle** USA
Small area in Idaho on the Utah–Sun Valley route.
*2430m; slopes 2430–2735m*
*3 300 acres*

**Pontechianale** Italy
Highest, largest area in a remote region south-west of Turin. Day-tripper place.
*1600m; slopes 1600–2760m*
*8 30km*

**Ponte di Legno** Italy
Attractive sheltered alternative to bleak, ugly neighbour Passo Tonale. Linked by piste and bus.
*1255m; slopes 1255–1920m*
*5 15km*

**Pontresina** 469
Small, sedate base linked to nearby St Moritz by road, with extensive cross-country trails.
✉ *Made to Measure Holidays*

**Port-Ainé** Spain
Small but high intermediate area in the Spanish Pyrenees near Andorra. Lifts include a six-pack; eponymous 3-star hotel at base.
*1975m; slopes 1650–2440m*
*8 44km*

**Porter Heights** New Zealand
Closest skiing to Christchurch (one hour). Open, sunny bowl offering mostly intermediate skiing – with back bowls for powder.
*1340m; slopes 1340–1950m*
*5 — 200 acres*

**Portes du Soleil** 313

**Portillo** Chile
Luxury hotel 150km/93 miles north-east of Santiago. Uncrowded snow-sure slopes used for training by US national ski team.
*2850m; slopes 2590–3350m*
*12 — 25km*
✉ *AmeriCan Ski, Crystal, Momentum Ski, Scott Dunn Latin America, Ski All America, Ski Safari*

**Powderhorn** USA
Area in west Colorado with plans (in 2002/03) to double its ski area, perched on world's highest flat-top mountain, Grand Mesa. Sensational views. Day trip from Aspen.
*2490m; slopes 2490–2975m*
*4 — 300 acres*

**Powder King** Canada
Remote resort in British Columbia, between Prince George and Dawson City. As its name suggests, it has great powder. Plenty of lodging.
*880m; slopes 880–1520m*
*3 — 160 acres*

**Powder Mountain** USA
Massive Utah area sprawled over six ridges, an hour and a quarter's drive from Salt Lake City. An ample 2,800 acres is lift served, a mix of mainly north-facing slopes with enough green, blue and black runs to satisfy all abilities. You access the rest by snowcat or snowmobile tow, buses and hiking. It is the abundance of intermediate free-ride terrain that makes it special: try the superb black powder runs plunging through trees beneath the Paradise Lift, and the Powder Country area which drains down to the access road. Away from the lifts, Lightning Ridge is great for black run free-riding. A couple of lifts run till 10pm and there's a terrain-park and half-pipe. Hidden Lake Lodge provides good food on the mountain. The spread-out base area is limited, with a couple of eateries, rental shops and one accommodation option. You can also stay in Ogden, 32km/20 miles away.
*2100m; slopes 2100–2740m*
*7 — 5,500 acres*

**Pozza di Fassa** Italy
Pretty Dolomite village with its own slopes, three other small areas close by, and access to the Sella Ronda at nearby Campitello.
*1340m; slopes 1340–2155m*
*6 — 20km*

**Pragelato** Italy
Inexpensive base, a short drive east of Sestriere. Its own area is worth a try for half a day.
*1535m; slopes 1535–2700m*
*6 — 50km*

**Prägraten am Grossvenediger** Austria
Traditional mountaineering/ski touring village in lovely setting south of Felbertauern tunnel. The Alpine ski slopes of Matrei are nearby.
*1310m; slopes 1310–1490m*
*2 — 30km*

**Prali** Italy
Tiny resort east of Sestriere – a worthwhile half-day trip.
*1450m; slopes 1450–2500m*
*7 — 25km*

**Pralognan-la-Vanoise** France
Unspoiled traditional village overlooked by spectacular peaks. Champagny (La Plagne) and Courchevel are close by.
*1410m; slopes 1410–2355m*
*14 — 30km*
✉ *Erna Low, Lagrange Holidays, Ski Independence*

**Pra-Loup** France
Convenient, purpose-built family resort with an extensive, varied intermediate area linked to La Foux-d'Allos.
*1500m; slopes 1500–2600m*
*32 — 83km*
✉ *Equity Ski, Lagrange Holidays, Rocketski, Ski Life*

**Prati di Tivo** Italy
Weekend day-trip place east of Rome and near the town of Teramo. A sizeable resort by southern Italy standards.
*1450m; slopes 1450–1800m*
*6 — 16km*

**Prato Nevoso** Italy
Purpose-built resort with rather bland slopes. Part of Mondolé ski area with Artesina.
*1500m; slopes 1500–1950m*
*25 — 90km*
✉ *Equity Ski, Rocketski*

**Prato Selva** Italy
Tiny base development (no village) east of Rome near Teramo. Weekend day-trip place.
*1370m; slopes 1370–1800m*
*4 — 10km*

**Le Praz** 248
The lowest and most attractive of the Courchevel resorts, with direct access to the slopes.
✉ *Ski Deep, Ski 'n' Action*

**Les Praz** 227
Quiet hamlet 4km/2 miles from Chamonix, with convenient lift link to the varied Flégère area.
✉ *High Mountain Holidays*

**Praz-de-Lys** France
Little-known snow-pocket area near Lake Geneva that can have good snow when nearby resorts (eg La Clusaz) do not.
*1500m; slopes 1200–2000m*
*23 — 60km*
✉ *Directski.com, Lagrange Holidays, Ski Life*

**Praz-sur-Arly** 274
Traditional village in a pretty, wooded setting just down the road from Megève.
✉ *Lagrange Holidays*

**Le Pré** 213
Charming, rustic hamlet with lifts up to Arc 2000 and excellent runs back down.

**Predazzo** Italy
Small, quiet place between Cavalese and the Sella Ronda resorts, with lift into modest area of slopes above Obereggen.
*1015m; slopes 995–2205m*
*8 — 17km*

**Premanon** France
One of four resorts that make up Les Rousses area in Jura region.
*1050m; slopes 1120–1680m*
*40*
✉ *Lagrange Holidays*

**La Presolana** Italy
Large summer resort near Bergamo. Several other little areas nearby.
*1250m; slopes 1250–1650m*
*6 — 15km*

**Pucón** Chile
Ski area on the side of the active Villarrica volcano in southern Chile, 800km/500 miles south of Santiago. Lodgings are at Pucón village, 30 minutes away from the slopes.
*1200m; slopes 1200–1800m 9*

**Puy-St-Vincent** 315
✉ *Equity Ski, Esprit Ski, Interhome, Lagrange Holidays, Snowbizz*

**Pyhä** 643

**Pyrenees, French** 372

**Pyrenees 2000** France
Tiny resort built in a pleasing manner. Shares a pretty area of short runs with Font-Romeu. Impressive snowmaking.
*2000m; slopes 1750–2250m*
*32 — 52km*

**Québec** 631
✉ *Crystal, Equity Ski, Inghams*

**Queenstown** 658

**Radium Hot Springs** Canada
Summer resort offering an alternative to the purpose-built slope-side resort of Panorama.
*slopes 975–2155m*
*8 — 300 acres*
✉ *AmeriCan Ski*

**Radstadt** Austria
Interesting, unspoiled medieval town near Schladming that has its own small area, with the Salzburger Sportwelt slopes accessed from nearby Zauchensee or Flachau.
*855m; slopes 855–2185m*
*100 — 350km*

**Rainbow** New Zealand
Northernmost ski area on South Island. Wide, treeless area, best for beginners and intermediates. Accommodation at St Arnaud.
*1440m; slopes 1440–1760m*
*5 — 865 acres*

**Ramsau am Dachstein** Austria
Charming village overlooked by the Dachstein glacier. Renowned for cross-country, it also has Alpine slopes locally, on the glacier and at Schladming. 'Spectacular cable car ride to Hunerkogel,' says a 2004 reporter.
*1200m; slopes 1100–2700m*
*18 — 30km*

**Ramundberget** 649

**Rauris** Austria
Old roadside village close to Kaprun and Zell am See, with a long, narrow area that has snowmakers on the lower slopes.
*950m; slopes 950–2200m*
*9 — 30km*
✉ *Crystal*

**Ravascletto** Italy
Resort in a pretty wooded setting near Austrian border, with most of its terrain high above on an open plateau.
*920m; slopes 920–1735m*
*12 — 40km*
✉ *Sloping Off*

**Reallon** France
Traditional-style village, with splendid views from above Lac de Serre-Ponçon.
*1560m; slopes 1560–2115m*
*6 — 20km*

**Red Lodge** USA
Picturesque Old West Montana town. Ideal for a combined trip with Big Sky or Jackson Hole.
*1800m; slopes 2155–2860m*
*8 — 1,600 acres*
✉ *AmeriCan Ski*

**Red Mountain** 630
✉ *AmeriCan Ski, Frontier Ski, Ski Safari*

**Red River** USA
New Mexico western town – complete with stetsons and saloons – with intermediate slopes above.
*2665m; slopes 2665–3155m*
*7 — 290 acres*

**Reichenfels** Austria
One of many small areas in Austria's easternmost ski region near the Slovenian border.
*810m; slopes 810–1400m*

**The Remarkables** 658
Three bleak basins with great views of 'remarkable' jagged alps, 45 minutes from Queenstown.

**Rencurel-les-Coulumes** France
One of seven little resorts just west of Grenoble. Unspoiled, inexpensive place to tour. Villard-de-Lans is the main resort.

**Reutte** Austria
500-year-old market town with many traditional hotels, and rail links to nearby Lermoos.
*855m; slopes 855–1900m*
*🚡 9 ⛷ 19km*

**Revelstoke** Canada
Town from which you can heli-ski in Monashees or cat-ski locally at a more reasonable cost than most places.
*460m*
*✉ Canadian Powder Tours, Powder Skiing in North America*

**Rhêmes-Notre-Dame** Italy
Unspoiled village in the beautiful Rhêmes valley, south of Aosta. Courmayeur and La Thuile within reach.
*🚡 2 ⛷ 5km*

**Riederalp** Switzerland
Pretty, vehicle-free village perched high above the Rhône valley amid the glorious scenery of the Aletsch area. Access by cable-car or gondola from the valley village of Mörel near Brig.
*1900m; slopes 1900–2900m*
*🚡 32 ⛷ 90km*

**Rigi-Kaltbad** Switzerland
Resort on a mountain rising out of Lake Lucerne, with superb all-round views, accessed by the world's first mountain railroad.
*1440m; slopes 1195–1795m*
*🚡 9 ⛷ 30km*

**Riihivuori** Finland
Small area with 'base' at the top of the mountain. 20km/12 miles south of the city of Jyväskylä. *🚡 5*

**Riksgränsen** 649

**Riscone** Italy
Dolomite village sharing a pretty area with San Vigilio. Good snowmaking. Short easy runs.
*1200m; slopes 1200–2275m*
*🚡 35 ⛷ 40km*

**Risoul** 317
*✉ Crystal, Erna Low, First Choice Ski, Handmade Holidays, Interhome, Lagrange Holidays, Made to Measure Holidays, Neilson, Ski Arrangements, Ski Independence, Ski Life, Skitopia, Thomson*

**Rivisondoli** Italy
Sizeable mountain retreat east of Rome, with one of the better lift systems in the vicinity.
*1350m; slopes 1350–2050m*
*🚡 7 ⛷ 16km*

**Roccaraso** Italy
Largest of the resorts east of Rome – at least when snow-cover is complete.
*1280m; slopes 1280–2200m*
*🚡 12 ⛷ 56km*

**Rohrmoos** 166
Situated below a small mountain in the Dachstein-Tauern region, next to Schladming.

**La Rosière** 320
*✉ Crystal, Erna Low, Esprit Ski, Interhome, Mountain Tracks, Ski Arrangements, Ski Olympic, Ski Supreme, Thomson, Vanilla Ski*

**Rossland** Canada
Remote little town 5km/3 miles from cult powder paradise Red Mountain.

**Rougemont** Switzerland
Cute rustic hamlet just over the French/German language border near Gstaad, with worthwhile local slopes and links to Gstaad's Eggli sector.
*991m; slopes 890–3000m*
*🚡 67 ⛷ 250km*

**Les Rousses** France
Group of four villages – Les Rousses, Premanon, Lamoura and Bois d'Amont – in the Jura mountains, 50km/31 miles from Geneva.
*1120m; slopes 1120–1680m*
*🚡 37 ⛷ 40km*
*✉ Lagrange Holidays*

**Ruka** 643
*✉ Inghams*

**Russbach** Austria
Secluded village tucked up a side valley and linked into the Gosau-Annaberg-Lungotz area. The slopes are spread over a wide area.
*815m; slopes 780–1620m*
*🚡 33 ⛷ 65km*

**Saalbach-Hinterglemm** 160
*✉ Airtours, Board and Lodge, Crystal, Directski.com, Equity Ski, First Choice Ski, Inghams, Interhome, Made to Measure Holidays, Neilson, Panorama Holidays, Rocketski, Thomson*

**Saalfelden** Austria
Town ideally placed for touring eastern Tirol. Extensive lift networks of Maria Alm and Saalbach are nearby.
*745m; slopes 745–1550m*
*🚡 3 ⛷ 3km*

**Saanen** Switzerland
Cheaper and more convenient alternative to staying in Gstaad – but much less going on.
*slopes 950–3000m*
*🚡 69 ⛷ 250km*

**Saanenmöser** Switzerland
Small village with rail/road links to Gstaad. Scenic and quiet local slopes, with good mountain restaurants (Horneggli and Kübelialp are 2004 recommendations).
*1270m; slopes 1270–1995m 🚡 14*

**Saas-Almagell** Switzerland
Compact village up the valley from Saas-Grund, with good cross-country trails and walks, and a limited Alpine area.
*1670m 🚡 6*

**Saas-Fee** 464
*✉ Alpine Events, Avant-ski, Crystal, Erna Low, Independent Ski Links, Inghams, Interhome, Kuoni, Made to Measure Holidays, Momentum Ski, Ski FreshTracks, Ski Independence, Ski Line, Ski Solutions, Sloping Off, Swiss Travel Service, Switzerland Travel Centre, Thomson*

**Saas-Grund** Switzerland
Sprawling valley village below Saas-Fee, with a separate, small but high Alpine area.
*1560m; slopes 1560–3100m*
*🚡 7 ⛷ 45km*

**Saddleback** USA
Small area between Maine's premier resorts. High slopes by local standards.
*695m; slopes 695–1255m*
*🚡 5 ⛷ 100 acres*

**Sahoro** Japan
Ugly, purpose-built complex on Hokkaido island. A limited area, but one of the most exotic package destinations.
*400m; slopes 400–1100m*
*🚡 9 ⛷ 15km*
*✉ Club Med*

**Les Saisies** France
Traditional-style cross-country venue in a pretty setting, surrounded by varied four-mountain Alpine slopes.
*1650m; slopes 1150–2000m*
*🚡 24 ⛷ 40km*
*✉ Classic Ski Limited, Erna Low, Inntravel, Lagrange Holidays, Peak Retreats, Ski Life*

**Sälen** 649

**Salt Lake City** USA
Underrated base from which to ski Utah. 30 minutes from Park City, Deer Valley, The Canyons, Snowbird, Alta, Snowbasin. Cheaper and livelier than the resorts.
*✉ AmeriCan Ski*

**Salzburg-Stadt** Austria
A single, long challenging run off the back of Salzburg's local mountain, accessed by a spectacular lift-ride from a suburb of Grodig.
*425m*

**Samedan** Switzerland
Valley town, just down the road from St Moritz.
*1720m; slopes 1740–2570m*
*🚡 3 ⛷ 7km*

**Samnaun** 126
Shares large ski area with Ischgl.

**Samoëns** 263
Beautiful rural valley village, a bus-ride from the lifts into Flaine's skiing.
*✉ AmeriCan Ski, Interhome, Lagrange Holidays, Peak Retreats, Ski Life*

**San Bernardino** Switzerland
Pretty resort south of the road tunnel, close to Madesimo.
*1625m; slopes 1600–2595m*
*🚡 8 ⛷ 35km*

**San Candido** Italy
Resort on the border with Austria on the road to Lienz.
*1175m; slopes 1175–1580m*
*🚡 4 ⛷ 15km*
*✉ Waymark Holidays*

**San Carlos de Bariloche** Argentina
Year-round resort, with five areas nearby.
*790m*
*✉ Scott Dunn Latin America*

**San Cassiano** 415
Pretty village linked to the Sella Ronda.
*✉ Mountain Sun*

**Sandia Peak** USA
The world's longest lift ride ascends from Albuquerque. Mostly gentle slopes; children ski free.
*slopes 2645–3165m*
*🚡 7 ⛷ 100 acres*

**San Grée di Viola** Italy
Easternmost of resorts south of Turin, surprisingly close to the Italian Riviera.
*1100m; slopes 1100–1800m*
*⛷ 30km*

**San Martin de los Andes** Argentina
Sizeable town with accommodation, 19 km/12 miles from the Chapelco ski area.
*✉ Scott Dunn Latin America*

**San Martino di Castrozza** 427
Trentino village south of Val di Fassa.
*✉ Solo's*

**San Pellegrino** Italy
Little ski area south of the Sella Ronda, with lifts each side of the pass road and links with the valley village of Falcade.

**Sansicario** 410
Small, stylish, modern resort, well placed in the Milky Way near to Sauze d'Oulx.
*✉ Rocketski*

**San Simone** Italy
Tiny development north of Bergamo, close to unappealing Foppolo area.
*2000m; slopes 1105–2300m*
*🚡 9 ⛷ 45km*

**Santa Caterina** Italy
Pretty, user-friendly village near Bormio, with a snow-sure novice and intermediate area.
*1740m; slopes 1740–2725m*
*🚡 8 ⛷ 25km*
*✉ Airtours, Equity Ski*

**Santa Cristina** 415
Quiet village on the periphery of the Sella Ronda.

**Santa Fe** USA
One of America's most attractive and interesting towns. Varied slopes – glades, bowls, cruiser pistes, desert views. Great excursion from Taos.
*3145m; slopes 3145–3645m*
*6 ⛷ 660 acres*

**Santa Maria Maggiore** Italy
Resort south of the Simplon Pass from the Rhône valley, and near Lake Maggiore.
*820m; slopes 820–1890m*
*5 ⛷ 10km*

**San Vigilio** Italy
Charming Dolomite village with a delightful, sizeable area well covered by snow-guns. German name is Kronplatz.
*1200m; slopes 1200–2275m*
*33 ⛷ 40km*
✉ *Equity Ski, Sloping Off*

**San Vito di Cadore** Italy
Sizeable, alternative place to stay to Cortina. Negligible local slopes, though.
*1010m; slopes 1010–1380m*
*9 ⛷ 12km*

**Sappada** Italy
Isolated resort close to the Austrian border below Lienz.
*1215m; slopes 1215–2050m*
*17 ⛷ 21km*

**Sappee** Finland
Resort within easy reach of Helsinki, popular with boarders and telemarkers. Lake views. 7

**Sarnano** Italy
Main resort in the Macerata region near Adriatic Riviera. Valley village with ski slopes accessed by lift.
*540m*
*9 ⛷ 11km*

**Le Sauze** France
Fine area near Barcelonnette, sadly remote from airports.
*1400m; slopes 1400–2440m*
*23 ⛷ 65km*

**Sauze d'Oulx** 410
✉ *Airtours, Avant-ski, Chalets 'Unlimited', Club Pavilion, Crystal, Equity Ski, First Choice Ski, Independent Ski Links, Inghams, Neilson, Panorama Holidays, Rocketski, Ski Arrangements, Thomson*

**Savognin** Switzerland
Pretty village with a good mid-sized area; a good base for the nearby resorts of St Moritz, Davos/Klosters and Flims.
*1200m; slopes 1200–2715m*
*17 ⛷ 80km*

**Scheffau** 172
Rustic beauty not far from Söll.
✉ *Crystal, Esprit Ski, Ski Line, Ski Wild, Thomson*

**Schia** Italy
Very limited area of short runs – the only ski area near Parma. No village.
*1245m; slopes 1245–1415m*
*7 ⛷ 15km*

**Schilpario** Italy
One of many little areas near Bergamo.
*1125m; slopes 1125–1635m*
*5 ⛷ 15km*

**Schladming** 166
✉ *Crystal, Equity Ski, Interhome, Made to Measure Holidays, Rocketski, Sloping Off*

**Schönried** Switzerland
A cheaper and quieter resort alternative to staying in Gstaad.
*1230m; slopes 890–3000m*
*67 ⛷ 250km*
✉ *Interhome*

**Schoppernau** Austria
A scattered farming community, one of two main areas in Bregenzerwald north-west of Lech.
*860m; slopes 860–2060m*
*8 ⛷ 37km*

**Schröcken** Austria
Bregenzerwald area village close to the German border.
*1260m; slopes 1260–2050m*
*14 ⛷ 60km*

**Schruns** 150
Pleasant little town at the heart of the Montafon region, south-west of Lech.
✉ *Interhome*

**Schüttdorf** 190
Ordinary dormitory satellite of Zell am See, with easy access to the shared ski area.

**Schwarzach im Pongau** Austria
Riverside village with rail links. There are limited slopes at Goldegg; Wagrain (Salzburger Sportwelt) and Grossarl (Gastein valley) are also nearby.
*600m*

**Schwaz** Austria
Valley town beside the Inn with a lift into varied terrain shared with the village of Pill and its mountain outpost, Hochpillberg.
*540m; slopes 540–2030m*
*6 ⛷ 10km*

**Schweitzer** USA
Excellent small family resort in the Rockies, near Spokane (Washington state), but long journey (from UK) a drawback. Low altitude but snow-sure.
*1215m; slopes 1215–1945m*
*6 ⛷ 2350 acres*
✉ *AmeriCan Ski*

**Scopello** Italy
Low area close to the Aosta valley, worth considering for a day trip in bad weather.
*slopes 690–1700m*
*6 ⛷ 35km*

**Scuol** Switzerland
Year-round spa resort close to Austria and Italy, with an impressive range of terrain.
*1250m; slopes 1250–2785m*
*15 ⛷ 80km*

**Searchmont Resort** Canada
Ontario area with modern lift system and 95% snowmaking. Fine Lake Superior views.
*275m; slopes 275–485m*
*4 ⛷ 65 acres*

**Sedrun** Switzerland
Charming, unspoiled old village on the Glacier Express rail route close to Andermatt, with fine terrain amid glorious scenery.
*1440m; slopes 1450–2350m*
*12 ⛷ 50km*

**Seefeld** 195
✉ *Crystal, Inghams, Interhome, Made to Measure Holidays, Thomson, Waymark Holidays*

**Le Seignus-d'Allos** France
Close to La Foux-d'Allos (which shares large area with Pra-Loup) and has own little area, too.
*1400m; slopes 1400–2425m*
*13 ⛷ 47km*

**Seis** Italy
German name for Siusi.

**Sella Nevea** Italy
Limited but developing resort in a beautiful setting on the Slovenian border.
*1140m; slopes 1190–1800m*
*11 ⛷ 8km*
✉ *Sloping Off*

**Selva/Sella Ronda** 415
✉ *Avant-ski, Bladon Lines, Chalets 'Unlimited', Crystal, Esprit Ski, First Choice Ski, Independent Ski Links, Inghams, Momentum Ski, Ski Arrangements, Ski Yogi, Thomson, Total*

**Selvino** Italy
Closest resort to Bergamo.
*960m; slopes 960–1400m*
*9 ⛷ 20km*

**Selwyn Snowfields** Australia
Popular with beginners and families. 6 hours from Sydney. Good lift system.
*1520m; slopes 1490–1615m*
*12 ⛷ 111 acres*

**Semmering** Austria
Long-established winter sports resort set in pretty scenery, 100km/62 miles from Vienna, towards Graz. Mostly intermediate terrain.
*1000m; slopes 1000–1340m*
*5 ⛷ 14km*
✉ *Slovenija Pursuits*

**Les Sept-Laux** France
Ugly, user-friendly family resort near Grenoble. Pretty slopes for all grades.
*1350m; slopes 1350–2400m*
*25 ⛷ 100km*
✉ *Lagrange Holidays*

**Serfaus** 196
✉ *Alpine Tours, Interhome, Made to Measure Holidays*

**Serrada** Italy
Very limited area near Trento.
*slopes 1250–1605m 5*
✉ *Alpine Tours, Equity Ski*

**Serre-Chevalier** 322
✉ *Airtours, Alpine Answers, Avant-ski, Bladon Lines, Chalet Chez Bear, Chalets 'Unlimited', Club Med, Crystal, Equity Ski, Erna Low, First Choice Ski, Handmade Holidays, Hannibals, Independent Ski Links, Inghams, Interhome, Lagrange Holidays, Made to Measure Holidays, Neilson, Panorama Holidays, Rocketski, Ski Arrangements, Ski Expectations, Ski France, Ski Independence, Ski Leisure Direction, Ski Life, Ski Miquel, Ski Supreme, Skitopia, Skiworld, Sloping Off, Thomson, Tops Ski Chalets and Club Hotels*

**Sesto** Italy
Dolomite village on the road to Cortina, surrounded by pretty little areas.
*1310m*
*31 ⛷ 50km*

**Sestola** Italy
Appennine village a short drive from Pisa and Florence with its pistes, some way above, almost completely equipped with snowmakers.
*900m; slopes 1280–1975m*
*23 ⛷ 50km*

**Sestriere** 423
✉ *Alpine Answers, Club Med, Crystal, Equity Ski, Independent Ski Links, Inghams, Interhome, Momentum Ski, Neilson, Rocketski, Ski Arrangements, Ski Weekend, Thomson*

**Sexten** Italy
German name for Sesto.

**Shames Mountain** Canada
Remote spot inland from coastal town of Prince Rupert and with impressive snowfall record. Deep powder.
*670m; slopes 670–1195m*
*3 ⛷ 183 acres*

**Shawnee Peak** USA
Small area near Bethel and Sunday River renowned for its night skiing. Spectacular views. Mostly groomed cruising.
*185m; slopes 185–580m*
*5 ⛷ 225 acres*

**Shemshak** Iran
Most popular of the three mountain resorts within easy reach of Tehran (60km/37 miles). 'Plenty of untracked lines and bumps; lifts get quite busy,' says a 2004 reporter.
*3600m; slopes 2550–3050m 7*

**Shiga Kogen** Japan
Largest area in Japan, the site of Nagano's 1998 Olympic skiing events and including 21 individual resorts.
*930m; slopes 1220–2300m*
*73 ⛷ 130km*

**Showdown** USA
Intermediate area in Montana cut out of forest north of Bozeman. 50km/30 miles to the nearest hotel.
*2065m; slopes 2065–2490m*
*4 · 640 acres*

**Sierra-at-Tahoe** 508
⊠ *Ski The American Dream*

**Sierra Nevada** 635
⊠ *Crystal, Independent Ski Links, Thomson*

**Sierra Summit** USA
Sierra Nevada area accessible only from the west. 100% snowmaking.
*2160m; slopes 2160–2645m*
*8 · 250 acres*

**Silbertal** 150
Low secluded village in the Montafon area, linked to Schruns. A good base for touring numerous areas.

**Sils Maria** 469
Pretty lakeside village, linked to the St Moritz Corvatsch slopes via a lift to Furtschellas.
⊠ *Interhome*

**Silvaplana** 469
Pretty lakeside village near St Moritz, a short drive from the lift connections.
⊠ *Interhome*

**Silver Creek** USA
Child-oriented resort close to Winter Park. Low snowfall record for Colorado.
*2490m; slopes 2490–2795m*
*5 · 250 acres*

**Silver Mountain** USA
Northern Idaho area near delightful resort town of Coeur d'Alene. Best for experts, but plenty for intermediates too.
*1215m; slopes 1215–1915m*
*6 · 1,500 acres*

**Silver Star** 630
⊠ *AmeriCan Ski, Crystal, Frontier Ski, Made to Measure Holidays, Ski Activity, Ski All America, Ski Independence, Ski Line, Ski Safari, Ski The American Dream*

**Silverthorne** USA
Factory outlet town on main road close to Keystone and Breckenridge. Good budget base for skiing those resorts plus Vail and Beaver Creek.
⊠ *AmeriCan Ski*

**Silverton** USA
Expert-only area in southern Colorado that used to be heli-ski country. Served by one lift. Avalanche transceiver, shovel and probe compulsory.
*3170m; slopes 3170–3750m 1*

**Sinaia** 641

**Sipapu** USA
Great little New Mexico area, with mostly tree-lined runs. Snow unreliable, but 70% snowmaking. Nice day out from Taos when conditions are good.
*slopes 2500–2765m*
*4 · 70 acres*

**Siusi** 415
Village west of the Sella Ronda circuit, since 2003 linked to the Alpe di Siusi area above Ortisei by a long, powerful gondola (as well as by road). Seis is the German version of its name.
⊠ *Equity Ski, Rocketski*

**Siviez** 475
A quieter and cheaper base for skiing Verbier's Four Valleys circuit.
⊠ *Interhome*

**Sixt-Fer-a-Cheval** 263
Traditional village near Samoëns, at foot of a new run down from the Flaine area. Own little area across the valley, too.
⊠ *AmeriCan Ski, Lagrange Holidays, Peak Retreats*

**Sjusjøen** Norway
Cluster of hotels in deep forest close to Lillehammer. Some Alpine facilities but better for cross-country.
*885m; slopes 1000–1090m*
*2 · 2km*
⊠ *Inntravel, Waymark Holidays*

**Ski Apache** USA
Apache-owned area south of Albuquerque noted for groomed steeps. Panoramic views. Nearest lodging in charming Ruidoso.
*2925m; slopes 2925–3505m*
*11 · 750 acres*

**Ski Cooper** USA
Small area close to historic Old West town of Leadville. Good ski/sightseeing day out from nearby Vail, Beaver Creek and Copper Mountain.
*slopes 3200–3565m 4*

**Ski Windham** USA
2 hours from New York City and second only to Hunter for weekend crowds. Decent slopes by eastern standards.
*485m; slopes 485–940m*
*7 · 230 acres*

**Smokovec** Slovakia
Spa town with small modern centre near Poprad, with three small areas known collectively as High Tatras. Funicular railway and snowmaking facilities.
*1480m; slopes 1000–1500m*
*6 · 4km*

**Smugglers' Notch** 588
⊠ *Ski Safari, Ski The American Dream*

**Snowbasin** 579
⊠ *AmeriCan Ski*

**Snowbird** 577
⊠ *AmeriCan Ski, Ski All America, Ski Independence, Ski The American Dream, United Vacations*

**Snowbowl (Arizona)** USA
One of America's oldest areas, near Flagstaff, Arizona, atop an extinct volcano and with stunning desert views. Good snowfall record.
*2805m; slopes 2805–3505m*
*5 · 135 acres*

**Snowbowl (Montana)** USA
Montana area renowned for powder, outside lively town of Missoula. Intermediate pistes plus 700 acres of extreme slopes. Grizzly Chute is the ultimate challenge.
*1520m; slopes 1520–2315m*
*4 · 1,400 acres*

**Snowmass** 540
⊠ *Alpine Answers, AmeriCan Ski, Ski All America, Ski Independence, Ski The American Dream, United Vacations*

**Snow Summit** USA
San Bernardino National Forest ski area near Palm Springs. Lovely lake views. 100% snowmaking. High-capacity lift system for weekend crowds.
*2135m; slopes 2135–2500m*
*12 · 230 acres*

**Snow Valley** USA
Area quite near Palm Springs. Fine desert views. High-capacity lift system copes with weekend crowds better than nearby Big Bear.
*2040m; slopes 2040–2390m*
*11 · 230 acres*

**Solda** Italy
The other side of the Stelvio Pass from Bormio. Very long airport transfers.
*1905m; slopes 1905–2625m*
*19 · 25km*

**Sölden** 170
⊠ *Made to Measure Holidays, Neilson, Thomson*

**Soldeu** 98
⊠ *Airtours, Chalets 'Unlimited', Club Pavilion, Crystal, Directski.com, First Choice Ski, Independent Ski Links, Inghams, Lagrange Holidays, Neilson, Panorama Holidays, Thomson*

**Solitude** 579
⊠ *AmeriCan Ski, Ski Independence, Ski The American Dream*

**Söll** 172
⊠ *Airtours, Crystal, Directski.com, First Choice Ski, Independent Ski Links, Inghams, Neilson, Panorama Holidays, Ski Hillwood, Ski Line, Ski Wild, Thomson*

**Sommand** France
Purpose-built base that shares area with Praz-de-Lys.
*1420m; slopes 1200–1800m*
*22 · 50km*

**Sorenberg** Switzerland
Popular weekend retreat between Berne and Lucerne, with a high proportion of steep, low runs.
*1165m; slopes 1165–2350m*
*18 · 50km*

**South Lake Tahoe** USA
Tacky base for skiing Heavenly, with cheap lodging, traffic and gambling.

**Spindleruv Mlyn** Czech Republic
Largest Giant Mountains region resort but with few facilities serving several little low areas.
*715m; slopes 750–1300m*
*23 · 25km*

**Spital am Pyhrn** Austria
Small village near Hinterstoder in Upper Austria, a bus-ride from its limited intermediate slopes at Wurzeralm. From the valley station a 3km/2 mile funicular goes up to a mid-mountain col with several restaurants and nursery slopes. Lifts and runs go off from here in several directions over pleasantly wooded intermediate terrain; the blues are tough, so transition from the nursery slopes is not easy. On the flat Teichlboden (1370m/4,500ft) beyond the col there are cross-country loops. The local lift pass also covers the slopes of Höss and Bärenalm at Hinterstoder, a short drive away.
*650m; slopes 810–1870m*
*8 · 14km*

**Spittal/Drau** Austria
Historic Carinthian town with a limited area starting a lift-ride above it. A good day trip from Bad Kleinkirchheim or from Slovenia.
*555m; slopes 1650–2140m*
*12 · 22km*

**Sportgastein** 111
Mountain village with some of the more interesting skiing in the Badgastein valley.

**Squaw Valley** 521
⊠ *AmeriCan Ski, American Ski Classics, Crystal, Lotus Supertravel, Made to Measure Holidays, Ski Activity, Ski All America, Ski Independence, Ski Safari, Ski The American Dream, United Vacations*

**Stafal** 406
Tiny, isolated village, with good access to the Monterosa Ski area.

**St Andrä im Lungau** Austria
Valley-junction village ideally placed for one of the longest, most snow-sure cross-country networks in Europe. Close to the Tauern pass and to St Michael.
*1045m*

**St Anton** 178
✉ *Airtours, Albus Travel, Alpine Answers, Alpine Events, Alpine Tours, Alpine Weekends, Avant-ski, Bladon Lines, Chalet World, Chalets 'Unlimited', Corporate Ski Company, Crystal, Elegant Resorts, Erna Low, Esprit Ski, First Choice Ski, FlexiSki, Improve Your Skiing, Independent Ski Links, Inghams, Kaluma Ski, Lotus Supertravel, Made to Measure Holidays, Mark Warner, Momentum Ski, Neilson, Simply Ski, Ski Activity, Ski Addiction, Ski Arrangements, Ski Expectations, Ski Line, Ski Solutions, Ski St Anton, Ski Wild, Ski-Val, Skiworld, Snowscape, St Anton Ski Company, Thomson, Total, White Roc*

**St Cergue** Switzerland
Limited resort less than an hour from Geneva, good for families with young children.
*1045m; slopes 1045–1700m*
*9 20km*

**St Christoph** 178
Small village on Arlberg pass above St Anton.
✉ *Alpine Answers, Elegant Resorts, FlexiSki, Inghams, Made to Measure Holidays, Powder Byrne, Slovenija Pursuits*

**St-Colomban-des-Villards** 335
Small resort in next side valley to La Toussuire.

**Steamboat** 542
✉ *Alpine Answers, American Ski Classics, Chalets 'Unlimited', Crystal, Independent Ski Links, Lotus Supertravel, Made to Measure Holidays, Ski Activity, Ski All America, Ski Independence, Ski Line, Ski Safari, Ski The American Dream, Skiworld, United Vacations*

**Ste-Foy-Tarentaise** 329
✉ *Alpine Weekends, Chalet Limited, Chalet Number One, Independent Ski Links, Mountain Tracks, Peak Leisure, Premiere Neige, Ski Arrangements, Ski Weekend, Weekends in Val d'Isère*

**Steinach** Austria
Pleasant village in picturesque surroundings, just off the autobahn near the Brenner Pass. An easy outing from Innsbruck.
*1050m; slopes 1050–2205m*
*6 15km*
✉ *Alpine Tours*

**Stevens Pass** USA
A day trip from Seattle, and accommodation 60km/37 miles away in Bavarian-style town Leavenworth. Low snowfall and no snowmakers. Mostly intermediate slopes.
*1235m; slopes 1235–1785m*
*14 1,125 acres*

**St-François-Longchamp** 364
Sunny, gentle slopes, with a couple of harder runs. Linked to Valmorel.
✉ *Lagrange Holidays, Peak Retreats, Ski Independence, Ski Leisure Direction, Ski Life*

**St Gallenkirch** 150
Smaller, less attractive village than Gaschurn, with which it shares a sizeable intermediate area in the Montafon valley.

**St-Gervais** 274
Small town sharing its ski area with Megève and Chamonix.
✉ *Interhome, Lagrange Holidays, Peak Retreats, Ski Express, Ski Life, Snowcoach*

**St Jakob in Defereggen** Austria
Unspoiled traditional village in a pretty, sunny valley close to Lienz and Heiligenblut, and with a good proportion of high-altitude slopes.
*1400m; slopes 1400–2520m*
*9 34km*

**St Jakob in Haus** Austria
Snowy village with its own slopes. Fieberbrunn, Waidring and St Johann are nearby.
*855m; slopes 855–1500m*
*8 16km*

**St-Jean-d'Arves** 335
Small traditional village south of the Maurienne valley that is now linked with the slopes of St-Sorlin-d'Arves, La Toussuire and Le Corbier, to form Les Sybelles.
✉ *AmeriCan Ski, Crystal, Lagrange Holidays, Peak Retreats, Ski France, Ski Leisure Direction, Ski Life, Thomson*

**St-Jean-de-Sixt** 240
Traditional hamlet, a cheap base for La Clusaz and Le Grand-Bornand (3km/2 miles to both).

**St-Jean-Montclar** France
Small village at the foot of thickly forested slopes. Good day out from nearby Pra-Loup.
*1300m; slopes 1300–2500m*
*18 50km*
✉ *Lagrange Holidays*

**St Johann im Pongau** 196
Bustling, lively town with its own small area. An extensive three-valley lift network starts 4km/2 miles away at Alpendorf, linking via Wagrain to Flachau – all part of the Salzburger Sportwelt ski pass area.

**St Johann in Tirol** 186
✉ *Crystal, Directski.com, Ski Line, Ski Wild, Snowscape, Thomson*

**St Lary Espiaube** 372

**St-Lary-Soulan** 372
✉ *Lagrange Holidays, Ski Life*

**St Leonhard in Pitztal** Austria
Village beneath a fine glacier in the Oetz area, accessed by underground funicular.
*1250m; slopes 1735–3440m*
*12 40km*

**St Luc** Switzerland
Quiet, unspoiled rustic village in the Val d'Anniviers on the south side of the Rhône valley, with plenty of high, easy slopes (shared with Chandolin) served almost entirely by drags. Most of the slopes are above the nursery area at Tignousa (2180m/7,150ft), reached by funicular – also the site of an astronomical observatory. Valley pass also covers Zinal, Grimentz and Vercorin – 200km/124 miles of runs in total.
*1650m; slopes 1660–3025m*
*16 75km*
✉ *Inntravel*

**St Margarethen** Austria
Valley village near Styria/Carinthia border, sharing slopes with higher Katschberg.
*1065m; slopes 1075–2210m*
*14 50km*

**St Martin bei Lofer** Austria
Traditional cross-country village in a lovely setting beneath the impressive Loferer Steinberge massif. Alpine slopes at Lofer.
*635m*

**St-Martin-de-Belleville** 333
✉ *Alpine Club, Chalets de St Martin, Handmade Holidays, Independent Ski Links, Kaluma Ski, Thomson*

**St Martin in Tennengebirge** Austria
Highest village in the Dachstein-West region near Salzburg. It has limited slopes of its own but nearby Annaberg has an interesting area.
*1000m; slopes 1000–1350m*
*5 4km*

**St-Maurice-sur-Moselle** France
One of several areas near Strasbourg. No snowmakers.
*550m; slopes 900–1250m*
*8 24km*

**St Michael im Lungau** Austria
Quiet, unspoiled village in the Tauern pass snowpocket with an uncrowded but disjointed intermediate area. Close to Obertauern and Wagrain.
*1075m; slopes 1075–2360m*
*26 60km*
✉ *Alpine Tours, Equity Ski, Rocketski*

**St Moritz** 469
✉ *Alpine Events, Alpine Weekends, Club Med, Corporate Ski Company, Elegant Resorts, FlexiSki, Independent Ski Links, Inghams, Interhome, Jeffersons, Kuoni, Made to Measure Holidays, Momentum Ski, Powder Byrne, Ski FreshTracks, Ski Line, Ski Solutions, Ski Weekend, Swiss Travel Service, Switzerland Travel Centre*

**St-Nicolas-de-Véroce** 274
Small hamlet with a handful of simple hotels on the northern fringes of the Megève network.

**St-Nizier-du-Moucherotte** France
Unspoiled, inexpensive resort just west of Grenoble with no lifts of its own. Villard-de-Lans is the main resort.

**Stoneham** 631
✉ *Frontier Ski, Inghams, Ski All America, Ski Safari, Ski The American Dream*

**Stoos** Switzerland
Small, unspoiled village an hour from Zürich. Overcrowded at weekends. Magnificent views of Lake Lucerne.
*1300m; slopes 570–1920m 7*

**Storlien** Sweden
Small family resort amid magnificent wilderness scenery, One hour from Trondheim, 30 minutes from Åre.
*600m; slopes 600–790m*
*7 15km*

**Stowe** 590
✉ *American Ski Classics, Chalets 'Unlimited', Crystal, Inghams, Ski All America, Ski Arrangements, Ski Independence, Ski Line, Ski Safari, Ski The American Dream, Trailfinders, United Vacations, Virgin Snow*

**St-Pierre-de-Chartreuse** France
Locals' weekend place near Grenoble. Unreliable snow.
*900m; slopes 900–1800m*
*14 35km*

**Stratton** 581

**Strobl** Austria
Close to St Wolfgang in a beautiful lakeside setting. There are slopes at nearby St Gilgen and Postalm.
*545m; slopes 545–1510m*
*9 12km*

**St-Sorlin-d'Arves** 335
✉ *AmeriCan Ski, Crystal, Lagrange Holidays, Peak Retreats, Ski France, Ski Life, Thomson*

**St Stephan** Switzerland
Unspoiled old farming village at the foot of the largest sector of slopes in the area around Gstaad.
*995m; slopes 950–2155m*
*69 250km*

**Stuben** 138
Small, unspoiled village linked to St Anton.
✉ *Alpine Answers*

**St Veit im Pongau** Austria
Spa resort with limited slopes at Goldegg; Wagrain (Salzburger Sportwelt) and Grossarl (Gastein valley) are nearby.
*765m*

**St-Veran** France
Said to be the highest 'real' village in Europe, and full of charm. Close to Serre-Chevalier and the Milky Way. Snow-reliable cross-country skiing.
*2040m; slopes 2040–2800m*
*15 30km*

**St Wolfgang** Austria
Charming lakeside resort near Salzburg, some way from any slopes, best for a relaxing winter holiday with one or two days on the slopes.
*540m; slopes 665–1350m*
🚡 *9* ⛷ *17km*
✉ *Crystal, Inghams, Thomson*

**Sugarbowl** 509

**Sugarbush** 581
✉ *Ski Arrangements*

**Sugarloaf** 581
✉ *Equity Ski*

**Summit at Snoqualmie** USA
Four areas – Summit East, Summit Central, Summit West and Alpental – with interlinked lifts. Damp weather and wet snow are major drawbacks.
*slopes 915–1645m*
🚡 *24* ⛷ *2,000 acres*

**Sun Alpina** Japan
Collective name for three ski areas four hours away from Tokyo. 🚡 20

**Sundance** USA
Robert Redford-owned, tastefully designed family resort set amid trees in snow-sure Utah. It's a small, narrow mountain but the vertical is respectable, the setting beneath Mt Timpanogos is spectacular and there is terrain to suit all abilities. The lower mountain is easy-intermediate, served by a quad chair, the upper part steeper: one triple chair serves purely black slopes, the other blue and black trails. Bearclaw's Cabin, at the top of it, is a small, basic restaurant with spectacular views. There are 17km/11 miles of cross-country trails, of varying difficulty, in a separate area just beyond the downhill slopes. There are beautifully furnished 'cottages' to rent, and grander chalets. The ski school started new targeted Performance Ski Lab clinics for 2003/04, including seminars and video analysis.
*1860m; slopes 1860–2515m*
🚡 *4* ⛷ *450 acres*
✉ *AmeriCan Ski, Ski All America, Ski Independence, Ski Safari, Ski The American Dream*

**Sunday River** 581
✉ *American Ski Classics, Crystal, Equity Ski, Ski Independence, Ski Safari, Ski The American Dream, Thomson, Virgin Snow*

**Sunlight Mountain Resort** USA
Quiet little area worth the easy trip from Vail to get away from its crowds for a day. Varied terrain. Good snowboard park. $300,000 of capital improvements in 2002/03.
*2405m; slopes 2405–3015m*
🚡 *4* ⛷ *460 acres*

**Sun Peaks** 619
✉ *AmeriCan Ski, Crystal, Frontier Ski, Made to Measure Holidays, Ski Activity, Ski All America, Ski FreshTracks, Ski Independence, Ski Line, Ski Safari, Ski The American Dream*

**Sunrise Park** USA
Arizona's largest area, operated by Apaches. Slopes are spread over three mountains; best for novices and leisurely intermediates.
*2805m; slopes 2805–3500m*
🚡 *12* ⛷ *800 acres*

**Sunshine Village** 580
One-hotel mountain station with Banff's second-largest ski area on its doorstep.
✉ *Ski The American Dream*

**Sun Valley** 580
✉ *AmeriCan Ski, Ski Activity, Ski All America, Ski Independence*

**Suomu** Finland
A lodge (no village) right on the Arctic Circle with a few slopes but mostly a ski-touring place.
*140m; slopes 140–410m* 🚡 *3*

**Superbagnères** France
Little more than a particularly French-dominated Club Med; best for a low-cost, low-effort family trip to the Pyrenees.
*1880m; slopes 1440–2260m*
🚡 *16* ⛷ *35km*
✉ *Lagrange Holidays*

**Super-Besse** France
Purpose-built resort amid spectacular extinct-volcano scenery. Shares area with Mont-Dore. Limited village.
*1350m; slopes 1300–1850m*
🚡 *22* ⛷ *45km*
✉ *Lagrange Holidays*

**Superdévoluy** France
Purpose-built but friendly family resort, consisting of a few huge apartment blocks, a few km north-west of Gap, with a sizeable intermediate area shared with La Joue-du-Loup.
*1500m; slopes 1500–2510m*
🚡 *29* ⛷ *100km*
✉ *Lagrange Holidays*

**Supermolina** Spain
Dreary, purpose-built satellite of Pyrenean resort of La Molina, with a reasonable sized area of its own and linked to the slopes of Masella to form an area called Alp 2500.
*1700m; slopes 1600–2535m*
🚡 *29* ⛷ *100km*

**Les Sybelles** 335

**Tahko** Finland
Largest resort in southern Finland. Plenty of intermediate slopes in an attractive, wooded, frozen-lake setting. 🚡 9

**Tahoe City** USA
Small lakeside accommodation base for visiting nearby Alpine Meadows and Squaw Valley.

**Talisman Mountain Resort** Canada
One of the best areas in the Toronto region, but with a relatively low lift capacity. 100% snowmaking.
*235m; slopes 235–420m* 🚡 *8*

**Tamsweg** Austria
Large cross-country village with rail links in snowy region close to Tauern Pass and St Michael.
*1025m*

**La Tania** 340
✉ *Airtours, Alpine Action, Avant-ski, Chalet World, Chalets 'Unlimited', Club Pavilion, Crystal, Erna Low, First Choice Ski, French Freedom Holidays, Independent Ski Links, Lagrange Holidays, Le Ski, Mountain Tracks, Neilson, Silver Ski, Ski Amis, Ski Arrangements, Ski Beat, Ski Deep, Ski France, Ski Hame, Ski Independence, Ski Leisure Direction, Ski Life, Ski Line, Ski Power, Ski Weekends, Snowline, Thomson*

**Taos** 580
✉ *AmeriCan Ski, American Ski Classics, Ski Activity, Ski Independence, Ski The American Dream*

**Tärnaby-Hemavan** Sweden
Twin resorts in north Sweden, with their own airport.
*slopes 465–1135m*
🚡 *13* ⛷ *44km*

**El Tarter** 98
Relatively quiet, convenient alternative to Soldeu, with which it shares its slopes.
✉ *Airtours, Club Pavilion, First Choice Ski, Panorama Holidays*

**Tarvisio** Italy
Interesting, animated old town bordering Austria and Slovenia. A major cross-country base with fairly limited Alpine slopes.
*750m; slopes 750–1860m*
🚡 *12* ⛷ *15km*

**Täsch** 493
The final base accessible by road on the way to car-free Zermatt – you take the train the rest of the way.
✉ *Interhome*

**Tauplitz** Austria
Traditional village at the foot of an interestingly varied area north of Schladming.
*900m; slopes 900–2000m*
🚡 *18* ⛷ *25km*

**Telluride** 544
✉ *Alpine Answers, AmeriCan Ski, American Ski Classics, Crystal, Ski All America, Ski Independence, Ski Safari, Ski The American Dream, Skiworld, United Vacations*

**Temù** Italy
Sheltered hamlet near Passo Tonale. Worth a visit in bad weather.
*1155m; slopes 1155–1955m*
🚡 *4* ⛷ *5km*

**Tengendai** Japan
Tiny area three hours by train and bus from Tokyo. One of Japan's best snow records, including occasional powder. 🚡 5

**Termignon** France
Traditional rustic village with good slopes of its own. A good base for touring Maurienne valley resorts such as Valloire and Val-Cenis.
*1300m; slopes 1300–2500m*
🚡 *6* ⛷ *35km*
✉ *Lagrange Holidays*

**Terminillo** Italy
Purpose-built resort 100km/62 miles from Rome with a worthwhile area when its lower runs have snow cover.
*1500m; slopes 1500–2210m*
🚡 *15* ⛷ *40km*

**Thollon-les-Mémises** France
Attractive base for a relaxed holiday. Own little area and close to Portes du Soleil.
*1000m; slopes 1600–2000m*
🚡 *19* ⛷ *50km*
✉ *Lagrange Holidays*

**Thredbo** 653

**La Thuile** 425
✉ *Avant-ski, Chalets 'Unlimited', Crystal, First Choice Ski, Independent Ski Links, Inghams, Interski, Neilson, Ski Arrangements, Thomson*

**Thyon 2000** 475
Extremely limited ski-from-the-door mid-mountain resort above Veysonnaz in the Verbier ski area.

**Tignes** 343
✉ *Airtours, Alpine Answers, Alpine Events, Avant-ski, Chalet World, Chalets 'Unlimited', Club Med, Corporate Ski Company, Crystal, Directski.com, Erna Low, Esprit Ski, First Choice Ski, Handmade Holidays, Improve Your Skiing, Independent Ski Links, Inghams, Inspired to Ski, Interhome, Lagrange Holidays, Made to Measure Holidays, Mark Warner, MasterSki, Neilson, Ski Activity, Ski Amis, Ski Arrangements, Ski Expectations, Ski France, Ski FreshTracks, Ski Independence, Ski Leisure Direction, Ski Life, Ski Line, Ski Olympic, Ski Solutions, Ski Supreme, Ski Weekend, Ski-Val, Skiworld, Snowstar Holidays, Thomson, Total*

**Timberline (Palmer Snowfield)** USA
East of Portland, Oregon, and the only lift-served summer skiing in the US: winter snow is maintained by spreading vast amounts of salt to harden it.
*slopes 1830–2600m*
🚡 *6* ⛷ *2,500 acres*

**Toblach** Italy
German name for Dobbiaco.

**Togari** Japan
One of several areas close to the 1998 Olympic site Nagano, 2.5 hours from Tokyo. 10

**Torgnon** Italy
Resort near Cervinia, good for bad-weather days.
*1500m; slopes 1500–1965m*
*4 6km*

**Torgon** Switzerland
Old village in a pretty wooded setting, with a connection to the Portes du Soleil. 'Appalling lifts,' says a recent reporter.
*1150m; slopes 975–2275m*
*219 650km*
⊠ *Interhome*

**Le Tour** 227
Charming, unspoiled hamlet at the head of the Chamonix valley.

**La Toussuire** 335
⊠ *Equity Ski, Interhome, Lagrange Holidays, Ski Life*

**Trafoi** Italy
Quiet, traditional (Austrian-style) village near Bormio, worth a day trip if snow is good at low levels.
*1570m; slopes 1570–2550m*
*6 10km*

**Treble Cone** 655

**Tremblant** 633
⊠ *Crystal, Elegant Resorts, Equity Ski, Erna Low, Frontier Ski, Inghams, Neilson, Ski All America, Ski Independence, Ski Safari, Ski The American Dream, Ski Wild, Thomson, Trailfinders, United Vacations, Virgin Snow*

**Trentino** 427

**Les Trois Vallées** 352

**Troodos** Cyprus
Ski area on Mt Olympus, a 70-minute drive from Nicosia. Pretty, wooded slopes and fine views.
*4 5km*

**Tröpolach** Austria
Small village at base of access gondola for Nassfeld ski area.
*610m; slopes 610–2195m*
*30 100km*

**Trysil** 645
⊠ *Neilson*

**Tschagguns** 150
Village with a varied little area of its own; part of the Montafon valley area.

**Tsugaike Kogen** Japan
Sizeable resort four hours from Tokyo, three hours from Osaka. Helicopter service to the top station.
*800m; slopes 800–1700m 28*

**Tulfes** 122

**Turoa** 655
On the south-western slopes of Mt Ruapeha, with NZ's biggest vertical. Mainly open, gentle runs, with steeper runs at the edges of the area. Plenty of scope for off-piste.

**Turracherhöhe** Austria
Tiny, unspoiled resort on a mountain shelf, with varied intermediate slopes above and below it. A good outing from Bad Kleinkirchheim.
*1765m; slopes 1400–2200m*
*11 30km*
⊠ *Alpine Tours*

**Tyax Mountain Lake Resort** Canada
Heli-skiing operation in the Chilcotin mountains – transfers from Whistler or Vancouver.

**Uludag** Turkey
Surprisingly suave, laid-back, well-equipped, purpose-built resort near Bursa, south of Istanbul. Popular with posers.
*1850m; slopes 1850–2320m*
*14 15km*

**Unken** Austria
Traditional village hidden in a side valley. Closest slopes to Salzburg.
*565m; slopes 1000–1500m*
*4 8km*

**Untergurgl** 153
Valley-floor alternative to staying in more expensive Hochgurgl or Obergurgl.

**Unternberg** Austria
Riverside village with trail connecting into one of the longest, most snow-sure cross-country networks in Europe. St Margarethen downill slopes close by.
*1030m*

**Unterwasser** Switzerland
Old but not especially attractive resort 90 minutes from Zürich. Fabulous lake and mountain views. The more challenging half of the area shared with Wildhaus.
*910m; slopes 900–2260m*
*21 50km*

**Uttendorf-Weiss-See** Austria
Astute alternative to crowded Kaprun when the snowline is high.
*805m; slopes 1485–2600m*
*9 20km*

**Vail** 546
⊠ *Alpine Answers, AmeriCan Ski, American Ski Classics, Avant-ski, Chalet World, Chalets 'Unlimited', Crystal, Elegant Resorts, Erna Low, Independent Ski Links, Inghams, Lotus Supertravel, Made to Measure Holidays, Momentum Ski, Neilson, Ski Activity, Ski All America, Ski Expectations, Ski FreshTracks, Ski Independence, Ski Line, Ski Safari, Ski The American Dream, Ski Wild, Skiworld, Thomson, Trailfinders, United Vacations, Virgin Snow*

**Valbella** Switzerland
Convenient but ordinary village sharing large intermediate Lenzerheide area.
*1540m; slopes 1470–2865m*
*35 155km*

**Valberg** France
Large Alpes-Maritimes resort (bigger than better-known Isola 2000) close to Nice.
*1650m; slopes 1430–2100m*
*26 90km*

**Val-Cenis** 373
⊠ *AmeriCan Ski, Erna Low, Lagrange Holidays, MGS Ski, Peak Retreats, Ski Leisure Direction, Snowcoach*

**Val di Fassa** 415

**Val d'Illiez** Switzerland
Peaceful, unspoiled village a few minutes below Champoussin. Open-air thermal baths. Good views of impressive Dents du Midi.
*950m*

**Val-d'Isère** 354
⊠ *Airtours, Alpine Answers, Alpine Events, Alpine Weekends, Avant-ski, Bladon Lines, Chalet Limited, Chalet World, Chalets 'Unlimited', Club Med, Corporate Ski Company, Crystal, Descent International, Directski.com, Elegant Resorts, Erna Low, Finlays, First Choice Ski, French Freedom Holidays, Handmade Holidays, Improve Your Skiing, Independent Ski Links, Inghams, Inspired to Ski, Interhome, Lagrange Holidays, Le Ski, Lotus Supertravel, Made to Measure Holidays, Mark Warner, Momentum Ski, Neilson, Oxford Ski Company, Panorama Holidays, Scott Dunn Ski, Silver Ski, Simply Ski, Ski Activity, Ski Amis, Ski Arrangements, Ski Beat, Ski Expectations, Ski France, Ski FreshTracks, Ski Independence, Ski Leisure Direction, Ski Life, Ski Line, Ski Olympic, Ski Solutions, Ski Supreme, Ski Weekend, Ski-Val, Skiworld, Snowline, Thomson, Total, Val d'Isère A La Carte, VIP, Weekends in Val d'Isère, White Roc, YSE*

**Val Ferret** Switzerland
Old climbing village near Martigny, with spectacular views. Own tiny area.
*1600m 4*

**Valfrejus** France
Small and unusual modern resort on a narrow, shady shelf in the Maurienne valley – built in the woods, with the slopes higher up above the tree line. The focus is Plateau d'Arrondaz, with steep, open slopes above, offering genuine bumpy blacks with excellent snow (snowmaking on the lower runs is urgently required, though). There's a natural terrain-park, and good off-piste is available above the main plateau. The nursery slopes are at mid-mountain and village levels. The Punta Bagna restaurant, at the top of the gondola, has superb views, and the Bergerie at the mid-station has table-service, though 'overpriced and not particularly good', says a 2004 reporter. There are two hotels, and restaurants include a pizzeria and a crêperie. Après-ski is limited – the Snow Club and the Bois Brûlé ('very rowdy', says a visitor) are the liveliest bars, and the Rhumerie was thought to have a 'good atmosphere'.
*1550m; slopes 1550–2735m*
*12 52km*
⊠ *AmeriCan Ski, Lagrange Holidays, Peak Retreats, Ski Life*

**Val Gardena** 415

**Vallandry** 213
Family-friendly satellite of Les Arcs with direct access to the Paradiski area. For package holidays see Peisey-Vallandry.
⊠ *Ski Independence*

**Valle Nevado** Chile
French designed resort 60km/37 miles east of Santiago. First detachable high-speed quad in Chile opened in 2001. 'The whole experience was surprisingly good,' says a 2004 reporter.
*slopes 2805–3670m 37km*
⊠ *Crystal, Elegant Resorts, Improve Your Skiing, Momentum Ski, Scott Dunn Latin America, Ski All America, Ski Safari*

**Valloire** 374
⊠ *AmeriCan Ski, Crystal, Erna Low, Lagrange Holidays, Peak Retreats, Ski France, Ski Leisure Direction, Ski Life, Snowcoach, Thomson*

**Valmeinier** 375
⊠ *Crystal, Erna Low, French Freedom Holidays, Lagrange Holidays, Ski Independence, Ski Leisure Direction, Ski Life, Snowcoach, Thomson*

**Valmorel** 364
⊠ *Airtours, Alpine Answers, Chalets 'Unlimited', Crystal, Erna Low, Independent Ski Links, Lagrange Holidays, Made to Measure Holidays, Neilson, Ski Arrangements, Ski Independence, Ski Leisure Direction, Ski Life, Ski Supreme, Thomson*

**Val Senales** Italy
Top-of-the-mountain hotel, the highest in the Alps, in the Dolomites near Merano.
*3250m; slopes 2005–3250m*
*10 24km*

**Val-Thorens** 366
⊠ *Airtours, Chalet World, Chalets 'Unlimited', Club Med, Crystal, Equity Ski, Erna Low, First Choice Ski, French Freedom Holidays, Independent Ski Links, Inghams, Interhome, Lagrange Holidays, Made to Measure Holidays, Neilson, Panorama Holidays, Rocketski, Silver Ski, Ski Activity, Ski Amis, Ski Arrangements, Ski Expectations, Ski France, Ski FreshTracks, Ski Independence, Ski Leisure Direction, Ski Life, Ski Line, Ski Supreme, Ski Tracer, Ski Weekend, Skiworld, Thomson, Total*

**Valtournenche** 385
Cheaper alternative to Cervinia, with genuine Italian atmosphere, and access to the extensive area.

**Vandans** 150
Sizeable working village well placed for visiting all the Montafon areas.

**Vars** 317
Large, convenient purpose-built resort linked to Risoul.
⊠ *Interhome, Lagrange Holidays, Ski Supreme, Tops Ski Chalets and Club Hotels*

**Vaujany** 204
Tiny, rustic village with lift accessing the heart of the Alpe-d'Huez ski area.
⊠ *AmeriCan Ski, Erna Low, Lagrange Holidays, Peak Retreats, Ski Independence, Ski Leisure Direction, Ski Life, Ski Peak*

**Vegas Resort** USA
Area formerly known as Lee Canyon, cut from forest only 50 minutes' drive from Las Vegas. Height and snowmaking gives fairly reliable snow. Night skiing.
*2590m; slopes 2590–2840m*
🚡 *3* ⛷ *200 acres*

**Vemdalen** 649
⊠ *Neilson*

**Vemdalsskalet** 649

**Venosc** France
Captivating tiny village of cobbled streets, ancient church and craft shops.

**Vent** Austria
High, remote Oztal village known mainly as a touring base, with just enough lift-served skiing to warrant a day trip from nearby Obergurgl.
*1900m; slopes 1900–2680m*
🚡 *4* ⛷ *15km*

**Ventron** France
One of several areas near Strasbourg. No snowmakers.
*630m; slopes 900–1110m*
🚡 *8* ⛷ *15km*

**Verbier** 475
⊠ *Alpine Answers, Alpine Events, Alpine Weekends, Avant-ski, Bladon Lines, Chalet World, Chalets 'Unlimited', Corporate Ski Company, Crystal, Descent International, Elegant Resorts, Erna Low, First Choice Ski, FlexiSki, Independent Ski Links, Inghams, Interhome, Jeffersons, Kaluma Ski, Lotus Supertravel, Made to Measure Holidays, Momentum Ski, Mountain Tracks, Peak Ski, Simply Ski, Ski Activity, Ski Expectations, Ski FreshTracks, Ski Independence, Ski Line, Ski Solutions, Ski Verbier, Ski Weekend, Ski with Julia, Skiworld, Swiss Travel Service, Thomson, Total, Vertical Reality at Verbier Ltd, White Roc*

**Vercorin** Switzerland
Cluster of picture-postcard chalets on a shelf overlooking the Valais, reached by roundabout road or cable-car from near Chalais. Mix of wooded and open intermediate slopes served by a gondola and drags. Valley pass also covers Zinal, Grimentz and St Luc/ Chandolin – 200km/124 miles of runs in total. The village has a natural ice rink.
*1330m; slopes 1330–2400m*
🚡 *9* ⛷ *35km*

**Verditz** Austria
One of several small, mostly mountain-top areas overlooking the town of Villach.
*675m; slopes 675–2165m*
🚡 *5* ⛷ *17km*
⊠ *Sloping Off*

**Vex** Switzerland
Major village in unspoiled, attractive setting south of Sion. Verbier slopes accessed nearby at Mayens-de-l'Ours.
*900m*

**Veysonnaz** 475
Little, old village within Verbier's Four Valleys network.

**Vic-sur-Mere** France
Charming village with fine architecture, beneath Super-Lioran ski area. Beautiful extinct-volcano scenery.
*680m; slopes 1250–1850m*
🚡 *24* ⛷ *60km*

**Viehhofen** Austria
Cheaper place to stay when visiting Saalbach. It is 3km/ 2 miles from the Schönleiten gondola, and there is a run back to the village from the Asitz section.
*860m*

**Vigo di Fassa** Italy
Best base for the Fassa valley, with Sella Ronda access via nearby Campitello.
*1430m; slopes 1465–2060m*
🚡 *8* ⛷ *25km*

**La Villa** 415
Quiet Sella Ronda village in pretty setting, surrounded by mostly very easy skiing.

**Villacher Alpe-Dobratsch** Austria
One of several small, mostly mountain-top areas overlooking the town of Villach.
*900m; slopes 980–2165m*
🚡 *8* ⛷ *15km*

**Villar-d'Arêne** France
Tiny area on main road between La Grave and Serre-Chevalier. Empty, immaculately groomed, short easy runs, plus a couple of hotels.
*1650m*

**Villard-de-Lans** France
Unspoiled, lively, traditional village west of Grenoble. Snow-sure, thanks to snowmaking.
*1050m; slopes 1160–2170m*
🚡 *29* ⛷ *130km*
⊠ *AmeriCan Ski, Lagrange Holidays*

**Villard-Reculas** 204
Rustic village on periphery of Alpe-d'Huez ski area, with few local amenities.

**Villaroger** 213
Rustic hamlet with direct links up to Arc 2000 and excellent runs back down.

**Villars** 485
⊠ *Alpine Events, Club Med, Corporate Ski Company, Crystal, Erna Low, Inghams, Interhome, Kuoni, Lagrange Holidays, Made to Measure Holidays, Momentum Ski, Ski Independence, Ski Line, Ski Weekend, Swiss Travel Service, Switzerland Travel Centre, Thomson*

**Vipiteno** Italy
Bargain-shopping town close to Brenner Pass.
*960m; slopes 960–2100m*
🚡 *12* ⛷ *25km*

**Virgen** Austria
Traditional village in a beautiful valley south of the Felbertauern tunnel. Slopes at Matrei.
*1200m*

**Vitosha** 638

**Vogel** 642

**Vorderlanersbach** 117
Small, satellite village of pretty Lanersbach, with access to Mayrhofen ski area.

**Voss** 645
⊠ *Crystal, Inghams*

**Vuokatti** Finland
Small mountain in a remarkable setting, surrounded on three sides by lots of little lakes. Good activity base. 🚡 8

**Wagrain** 196

**Waidring** Austria
Quiet valley village north of Kitzbühel, with nursery slopes on the doorstep and a powerful gondola (with big car parks) on the outskirts going up to Steinplatte – an area of mainly gentle open slopes which is also accessible from Germany. Impressive lift system with two six-packs and four quads, but still prone to weekend queues. Slopes face north, and there is extensive snowmaking.
*780m; slopes 1230–1860m*
🚡 *11* ⛷ *30km*
⊠ *Thomson*

**Waioru Nordic** New Zealand
Specialist cross-country base just over an hour from Queenstown. Spectacular views. Overnight huts.
*1600m*

**Wald im Pinzgau** Austria
Cross-country village surrounded by Alpine areas – Gerlos, Krimml and Neukirchen – and with Pass Thurn also nearby.
*885m*

**Wanaka** 655
Quiet, diffuse village in beautiful lakeside mountain setting, with two ski areas each half an hour away.

**Waterville Valley** 581
⊠ *AmeriCan Ski*

**Weinebene** Austria
One of many gentle little areas in Austria's easternmost ski region near the Slovenian border. No major resorts in the vicinity.
*1560m; slopes 1560–1835m*
🚡 *5* ⛷ *12km*

**Weissbach bei Lofer** Austria
Traditional resort between Lofer and Saalfelden. It has no slopes of its own, but it's well placed for touring the Tirol. Kitzbühel, Saalbach, St Johann and Zell am See are nearby.
*665m*

**Weissensee Naggeralm** Austria
Little area in eastern Austria and the location of Europe's largest frozen lake, which is used for all kinds of ice sports, including ice-golf.
*930m; slopes 930–1400m*
🚡 *5* ⛷ *7km*

**Weisspriach** Austria
Hamlet on snowy pass near Obertauern that shares its area with Mauterndorf and St Michael.
*1075m; slopes 1075–2360m*
🚡 *21* ⛷ *60km*

**Wengen** **488**
✉ *Alpine Events, Club Med, Crystal, Independent Ski Links, Inghams, Kuoni, Made to Measure Holidays, Re-lax Holidays, Ski FreshTracks, Ski Line, Ski Solutions, Swiss Travel Service, Switzerland Travel Centre, Thomson*

**Wentworth** Canada
Long-established Nova Scotia area with largest accessible acreage in the Maritime Provinces. Harsh climate ensures good snow-cover despite low altitude.
*55m; slopes 55–300m*
*6 150 acres*

**Werfen** Austria
Traditional village spoiled by the Tauern autobahn, which runs between it and the slopes. Good touring to the Dachstein West region.
*620m*

**Werfenweng** Austria
Hamlet with the advantage over the main village of Werfen of being away from the autobahn and close to the slopes. Best for novices.
*1000m; slopes 1000–1835m*
*11 40km*

**Westendorf** **188**
✉ *Inghams, Thomson*

**Whakapapa** **655**

**Whistler** **621**
✉ *Alpine Answers, AmeriCan Ski, American Ski Classics, Avant-ski, Chalet World, Chalets 'Unlimited', Crystal, Elegant Resorts, Equity Ski, Erna Low, Esprit Ski, First Choice Ski, Frontier Ski, Independent Ski Links, Inghams, Lotus Supertravel, Made to Measure Holidays, Momentum Ski, Neilson, Ski Activity, Ski All America, Ski Arrangements, Ski Expectations, Ski Hillwood, Ski Independence, Ski Line, Ski Miquel, Ski Safari, Ski The American Dream, Ski Wild, Skiworld, Solo's, Thomson, Total, Trailfinders, United Vacations, Virgin Snow*

**Whitecap Mountains Resort** USA
Largest, snowiest area in Wisconsin, close enough to Lake Superior and Minneapolis to ensure winds and weekend crowds.
*435m; slopes 435–555m*
*7 500 acres*

**Whiteface Mountain** USA
Varied area in New York State 15km/9 miles from attractive lakeside resort of Lake Placid. 93% snowmaking ensures good snowcover. Plenty to do off the slopes.
*365m; slopes 365–1345m*
*10 211 acres*

**White Pass Village** USA
Closest area to Mt St Helens. Remote and uncrowded with a good snowfall record. Mostly intermediate cruising.
*1370m; slopes 1370–1825m*
*6 635 acres*

**Whitewater** Canada
Renowned for powder (40% off-piste), food (fine day lodge) and weekend party atmosphere. Accommodation in the historic town of Nelson or a great day out from nearby Red Mountain.
*1640m; slopes 1640–2040m 3*
✉ *AmeriCan Ski*

**Wildcat Mountain** USA
New Hampshire area infamous for bad weather, but one of the best areas on a nice day. Lodging in nearby Jackson and North Conway.
*slopes 600–1250m*
*4 225 acres*

**Wildhaus** Switzerland
Undeveloped farming community in stunning scenery near Liechtenstein; popular with families and serious snowboarders.
*1100m; slopes 1100–2075m*
*9 50km*

**Wildschönau** **197**
✉ *Interhome*

**Wiler** Switzerland
Main village in secluded, picturesque dead-end Lötschental, north of Rhône valley, with small but tall slopes reached by cable-car.
*1420m; slopes 1420–2700m 6*

**Willamette Pass** USA
US speed skiing training base in national forest near beautiful Crater Lake, Oregon. Small but varied slopes popular with weekenders.
*1560m; slopes 1560–2035m*
*7 550 acres*

**Williams** USA
Tiny area above the main place to stay for the Grand Canyon.
*slopes 2010–2270m*
*2 50 acres*

**Windischgarsten** Austria
Large working village in Upper Austria with cross-country trails around and downhill slopes at nearby Hinterstoder and Spital am Pyrhn.
*600m*

**Winter Park** **552**
✉ *Alpine Answers, AmeriCan Ski, American Ski Classics, Chalets 'Unlimited', Crystal, Equity Ski, First Choice Ski, Independent Ski Links, Lotus Supertravel, Made to Measure Holidays, Neilson, Ski All America, Ski Independence, Ski Safari, Ski The American Dream, Skiworld, Thomson, United Vacations, Virgin Snow*

**Wolf Creek** USA
Remote area on a pass of the same name, with 'the most snow in Colorado' – 465 inches a year. One-third of the terrain is standard American trails through the trees; two-thirds is 'wilderness', served by a single lift. Great stop en route between Taos and Telluride. Stay in Pagosa Springs to the west, or South Fork to the east.
*3140m; slopes 3140–3630m*
*6 1,600 acres*
✉ *AmeriCan Ski*

**Xonrupt** France
Cross-country venue only 3km/2 miles from nearest Alpine slopes at Gérardmer.
*715m*
✉ *Lagrange Holidays*

**Yangji Resort** Korea
Modern resort an hour (60km/37 miles) south of Seoul, with runs cut out of dense forest. Gets very crowded. 7

**Ylläs** **643**
✉ *Bladon Lines, Inghams, Inntravel*

**Yong Pyong Resort** Korea
Also known as Dragon Valley. 200km/124 miles east of Seoul, with snowmaking on all its runs. English web site at www.yongpyong.co.kr.
*750m; slopes 750–1460m*
*16 20km*

**Zakopane** Poland
An interesting old town 100km/62 miles south of Kraków on the Slovakian border. Mostly intermediate slopes.
*830m; slopes 1000–1960m*
*20 10km*

**Zao** Japan
Big area with unpredictable weather, 4 hours from Tokyo by train. Known for 'chouoh' – pines frozen into weird shapes. Hot springs.
*780m; slopes 780–1660m 42*

**Zauchensee** Austria
Purpose-built resort isolated at the head of its valley, at one end of big three-valley lift network linking it via Flachauwinkl to Kleinarl – all part of the Salzburger Sportwelt ski pass area that our figures relate to.
*855m; slopes 800–2185m*
*59 200km*
✉ *Ski Hillwood, Sloping Off*

**Zell am See** **190**
✉ *Airtours, Alpine Events, Crystal, Directski.com, Equity Ski, First Choice Ski, Independent Ski Links, Inghams, Interhome, Lagrange Holidays, Made to Measure Holidays, Neilson, Panorama Holidays, PGL Teenski, Rocketski, Ski Line, Ski Wild, Thomson*

**Zell im Zillertal** Austria
Sprawling valley town with slopes on two nearby mountains. Now linked to higher Gerlos and Königsleiten to form a fair-sized area. 'Some of the best wide motorway skiing,' reports a 2004 visitor.
*580m; slopes 930–2410m*
*40 115km*

**Zermatt** **493**
✉ *Alpine Answers, Alpine Events, Avant-ski, Bladon Lines, Chalet World, Chalets 'Unlimited', Corporate Ski Company, Crystal, Descent International, Elegant Resorts, Erna Low, Independent Ski Links, Inghams, Interhome, Kuoni, Lagrange Holidays, Lotus Supertravel, Made to Measure Holidays, Momentum Ski, Powder Byrne, Scott Dunn Ski, Simply Ski, Ski Expectations, Ski FreshTracks, Ski Independence, Ski Line, Ski Solutions, Swiss Travel Service, Switzerland Travel Centre, Thomson, Total, White Roc*

**Zillertal** Austria
Valley of ten ski resorts, of which the most well known is Mayrhofen.
✉ *Rocketski, Sloping Off*

**Zinal** Switzerland
Pretty, rustic village with some modern development, near the head of the the Val d'Anniviers off the Valais. Cable-car up to a high area of open, steepish slopes – most runs are justifiably red or black. Excellent views. There are runs to the valley, including one excellent tough red off which an itinerary links to Grimentz, down the valley. The valley pass covers not only these two resorts but also St Luc/Chandolin across the valley, and Vercorin – 200km/124 miles of runs in total.
*1680m; slopes 1680–2895m*
*9 70km*
✉ *Interhome*

**Zug** **138**
Tiny village in scenic location with Lech's toughest skiing on its doorstep.

**Zürs** **138**
High, smart but soulless village on road to Lech, with which it shares extensive skiing.
✉ *Alpine Answers, Corporate Ski Company, Crystal, Elegant Resorts, Inghams, Kaluma Ski, Made to Measure Holidays, Powder Byrne*

**Zweisimmen** Switzerland
Limited but inexpensive base for slopes around Gstaad, with its own delightful little easy area too.
*965m; slopes 950–3000m*
*67 250km*

## MONEY BACK VOUCHER – PART 1

**To be sent to**
**SKI SOLUTIONS**, 84 Pembroke Road, London W8 6NX
along with your signed booking form

**Name**

**Address**

**E-mail address**

**Daytime phone number**

**Tour operator (if applicable)**

**Departure date** **Number in party**

I have bought a copy of Where to Ski and Snowboard 2005 and claim a refund of the £16.99 cover price. I understand this amount will be deducted from the cost of the holiday I am booking through Ski Solutions. Offer valid for bookings for 2004/05 and 2005/06 seasons holidays made before 30 April 2005.

**Signature** **Date**

## MONEY BACK VOUCHER – PART 2

WHERE *to* SKI AND SNOWBOARD 2005

**To be sent to**
**WHERE TO SKI AND SNOWBOARD,**
The Old Forge, Norton St Philip, Bath BA2 7LW

**Name**

**Address**

**E-mail address**

**Daytime phone number**

**Resort(s) to be visited**

**Departure date** **Number in party**

I have booked a ski holiday through Ski Solutions and claimed a refund of the £16.99 cover price of Where to Ski and Snowboard 2005.

**Signature** **Date**

Have you booked any other holiday through Ski Solutions in the last two seasons? ☐ **Yes** ☐ **No**